ADVANCE INTERNATIONAL ACCLAIM:

"The Dead Sea Scrolls contain copies of biblical manuscripts that are more than a thousand years older than those previously available. Yet these texts are never included in the standard editions of the Scrolls, and have remained virtually inaccessible to the general public. Here for the first time any reader can see at a glance how the readings from Qumran differ from other biblical texts."

> —John Collins, Professor of Hebrew Bible and Post-Biblical Judaism, The Divinity School at the University of Chicago

"The Dead Sea Scrolls Bible is just the kind of book that research scholars and students have been looking for: an exhaustive compendium of all the biblical manuscripts among the Dead Sea Scrolls. Assembled and annotated by three first-class and topnotch specialists, this volume will be of inestimable value to everyone involved in the study of the Dead Sea Scrolls. Congratulations are certainly in order."

> —David Noel Freedman, Editor-in-Chief, Anchor Bible Project

"Here, finally, are all the biblical manuscripts from the Judaean Desert caves translated and annotated, with explanatory introductions. It is a splendid complement to the translations of the non-biblical scrolls which HarperSanFrancisco published earlier. Here, as never before, the English reader can see personally just how fluid the Early Jewish or pre-Christian texts and canons of the First or Old Testament were, and how adaptable the biblical text was to ancient community concerns."

> —James Sanders, President, Ancient Biblical Manuscript Center

"This volume opens for the general reader the wealth of information for biblical studies to be culled from the Dead Sea Scrolls. It shows how Qumran manuscripts enable us to see the immense continuity of biblical tradition as well as the manner in which stabilization was accomplished by the Talmudic rabbis."

> —Lawrence H. Schiffman, Edelman Professor of Hebrew and Judaic Studies, New York University

"The biblical scrolls found in the Judean Desert are often mentioned and their great age frequently noted, but they are not included in English translations of the scrolls. Anyone wishing to know exactly what is in these ancient scrolls now has in this volume a comprehensive translation of the evidence together with introductions and notes."

> —James C. VanderKam, University of Notre Dame, author of *The Dead Sea Scrolls Today*

"For the first time all the biblical Qumran scrolls are now accessible in translation in this user-friendly book written by three prominent authorities in this field."

> —Professor Emanuel Tov, Editor-in-Chief, Qumran Publication Project

"The biblical scrolls and fragments discovered at Qumran are highly significant for our understanding of the early history of the Hebrew Bible. This translation of all the biblical materials among the Dead Sea Scrolls, along with lucid introductions and explanatory notes, is a welcome resource for all those interested in the Bible and its transmission."
—Carol Meyers, Professor of Biblical Studies and Archaeology, Duke University

"If you want to know what the Dead Sea Scrolls say about the text of the Bible and you want to read the 2000-year-old-texts themselves, this is the book to own."
—Hershel Shanks, Editor of *Biblical Archaeology Review* and author of *The Mystery and Meaning of the Dead Sea Scrolls*

"The biblical Dead Sea Scrolls have revolutionized our understanding of the Jewish scriptures, their origin, formation and role. Yet they remain largely ignored by the wider public that has devoured book after book on the non-biblical texts. Scholars, too, will find this volume invaluable. I have long wished for a resource such as this."
—Philip R. Davies, Professor of Biblical Studies, University of Sheffield

"[The editors] have completely succeeded in presenting the complex evidence in a very clear and accessible way. It should be used both by scholars and by the general public."
—Florentino García Martínez, author of *The Dead Sea Scrolls Translated* and of *The Dead Sea Scrolls Study Edition*

"*The Dead Sea Scrolls Bible* provides lay persons, pastors and students easy access to the biblical scrolls and clear comment on their significance to the Old Testament."
—Michael A. Knibb, Samuel Davidson Professor of Old Testament Studies, Department of Theology and Religious Studies, King's College, London

"The initiative to produce a translation into English of *The Dead Sea Scrolls Bible* is to be welcomed. This first translation will be most useful to students and readers of the Bible, and will surely stimulate the study of the transmission and interpretation of the biblical texts in Hebrew."
—Professor Arie van der Kooij, Leiden University, Editor of *Vetus Testamentum*

"This is an immensely useful work which makes the biblical Qumran material readily available in English for the first time for scholars and students. It deserves to be very widely used."
—John Barton, Professor of the Interpretation of Holy Scripture, University of Oxford

"The authors of *The Dead Sea Scrolls Bible* have done a great service. . . . Now laymen can judge for themselves whether the biblical manuscripts which predate Christian times differ radically from the received text found, for example, in the King James version. *The Dead Sea Scrolls Bible* is a magnificent piece of work."
—Frank Moore Cross, Hancock Professor Emeritus of Hebrew, Harvard University

THE
DEAD SEA SCROLLS
BIBLE

The Oldest Known Bible

Translated for the First Time

into English

MARTIN ABEGG, JR.,
PETER FLINT, AND
EUGENE ULRICH

HarperSanFrancisco
A Division of HarperCollinsPublishers

For our children:
Stephanie and Jennifer
Claire, Amy, Abigail, and Jason
Sabrina, Ivan, Meg, and Laura

FIRST EDITION

Library of Congress Cataloging-in-Publication Data
Bible. O.T. English. Abegg et al. 1999.
The Dead Sea scrolls Bible : the oldest known Bible translated for the first time into English [by] Martin Abegg, Jr., Peter Flint, and Eugene Ulrich.—1st ed.
p.   cm.
Includes bibliographical references.
ISBN 0–06–060063–2 (cloth)
ISBN 0–06–060064–0 (paper)
1. Bible. O.T. Hebrew—Versions—Dead Sea scrolls—Translations into English.
I. Abegg, Martin G.   II. Flint, Peter W.   III. Ulrich, Eugene Charles, 1938–.
IV. Title.
BS895.A24   1999
221.4'4—dc21   99–26866
99 00 01 02 03 RRD(H) 10 9 8 7 6 5 4 3 2

CONTENTS

INTRODUCTION

At the time of Jesus and rabbi Hillel—the origins of Christianity and rabbinic Judaism—there was, and there was not, a "Bible." This critical period, and the nature of the Bible in that period, have been freshly illuminated by the biblical Dead Sea Scrolls.

There was a Bible in the sense that there were certain sacred books widely recognized by Jews as foundational to their religion and supremely authoritative for religious practice. There was not, however, a Bible in the sense that the leaders of the general Jewish community had specifically considered, debated, and definitively decided the full range of *which* books were supremely and permanently authoritative and which ones—no matter how sublime, useful, or beloved —were not. The collection or collections of the Scriptures varied from group to group and from time to time. All Jews would have recognized "the Law" (the Torah) and most would have recognized "the Prophets" as belonging to that collection. Such a recognition is attested by references in the New Testament to the "Law and the Prophets" (Matt 7:12; Luke 16:16; and Rom 3:21). But the exact contents of "the Prophets" may not have been the same for all, and the status of other books beyond "the Law and the Prophets" was neither clear nor widely accepted. The notion of a wider collection of Scriptures that extended beyond the Law and Prophets is suggested by an intriguing passage in Luke 24, which says that "everything written about me [i.e., Jesus] in the Law of Moses, in the Prophets, and in the Psalms must be fulfilled" (vs. 44).

The Dead Sea Scrolls help us see the state of affairs more clearly from an on-the-spot perspective. "The Bible," or more accurately then, "the Scriptures," would have been a collection of numerous separate scrolls, each containing usually only one or two books. There is indeed persuasive evidence that certain books were considered "Scripture." But there is little evidence that people were seriously asking the question yet about the extent or the limits of the collection— the crucial question for a "Bible" or "canon"—which books are *in* and which books are *outside* this most sacred collection.

Thus, *The Dead Sea Scrolls Scriptures* may be a more historically accurate title for this volume. At any rate, it presents the remains of the books for which there is good evidence that Jews at that time viewed them as Sacred Scripture.

The "Bibles" Used Today

The word "Bible" has different meanings for different people and groups. The most obvious difference in content is between the Bible of Judaism (i.e., the Hebrew Bible or Old Testament) and that of Christianity, which contains both the Old and New Testaments. *The Dead Sea Scrolls Bible* does not include any New Testament books for one simple reason: by the time the vast majority of the scrolls had been copied (in 68 CE), the New Testament was only beginning to be written. Not surprisingly, then, there are no copies of New Testament books among the scrolls.

The list of books included in a Bible is termed a "canon." There are three main canons in the different Bibles used today (see Figure 1):

1. The Jewish Bible (or Tanak) contains twenty-four books in three sections: the Torah, the Prophets, and the Writings.

2. The Protestant Old Testament contains the same books as the Tanak, but in four sections and in a different order: the Pentateuch, the Historical Books, the Poetical Books, and the Prophets. In addition, the Protestant canon contains thirty-nine books, not twenty-four, because it counts separately several books that comprise single books in the Jewish Bible. For example, the one Book of the Twelve Minor Prophets in the Jewish canon becomes the twelve books of the Minor Prophets in the Protestant Bible.

3. The Roman Catholic Old Testament contains exactly the same four divisions and thirty-nine books as the Protestant Bible, but also includes further writings. Seven of these are entire books (Tobit, Judith, 1 and 2 Maccabees, Wisdom of Solomon, Ecclesiasticus, and Baruch [which includes the Letter of Jeremiah]); the others are sections added to Esther (the Additions to Esther) and to Daniel (the Prayer of Azariah, Song of the Three Young Men, Susanna, and Bel and the Dragon). For Catholics, these additional writings are part of the Bible and are thus known as the "deuterocanonical books" (that is, a second group of canonical books). However, Jews and most Protestants do not view these writings as Scripture, labeling them the "Apocrypha" (plural of "Apocryphon"), which means "hidden books."

Some scholars believe that these books are not in the Jewish and Protestant canons because they are later than most other biblical books (Daniel being an exception), while others point to their supposed secular or unorthodox content as the reason for exclusion. The real explanation, however, is more complicated and goes back to two ancient Bibles. Early Christians accepted the Greek Septuagint, which contains these additional books, as their Old Testament, while early Rabbis finalized the list of books for the Hebrew Bible in the second century CE. It is

Figure 1: Jewish, Protestant, and Roman Catholic Canons of the Old Testament

Jewish Tanak (24)	*Protestant OT (39)*	*Roman Catholic OT (46)*
Torah (5)	**Pentateuch (5)**	**Pentateuch (5)**
Genesis	Genesis	Genesis
Exodus	Exodus	Exodus
Leviticus	Leviticus	Leviticus
Numbers	Numbers	Numbers
Deuteronomy	Deuteronomy	Deuteronomy
Prophets (8)	**Historical Books (12)**	**Historical Books (16)**
Joshua	Joshua	Joshua
Judges	Judges	Judges
Samuel	Ruth	Ruth
Kings	1 & 2 Samuel	1 & 2 Samuel
Isaiah	1 & 2 Kings	1 & 2 Kings
Jeremiah	1 & 2 Chronicles	1 & 2 Chronicles
Ezekiel	Ezra	Ezra
Twelve Minor Prophets	Nehemiah	Nehemiah
Hosea	Esther	Tobit
Joel		Judith
Amos		Esther + Additions
Obadiah		1 & 2 Maccabees
Jonah		
Micah		**Poetry/Wisdom (7)**
Nahum		Job
Habakkuk	**Poetry/Wisdom (5)**	Psalms
Zephaniah	Job	Proverbs
Haggai	Psalms	Ecclesiastes
Zechariah	Proverbs	Song of Songs
Malachi	Ecclesiastes	Wisdom of Solomon
	Song of Songs	Ecclesiasticus
		Prophets (18)
		Isaiah
Writings (11)	**Prophets (17)**	Jeremiah
Psalms	Isaiah	Lamentations
Job	Jeremiah	Baruch + Letter of Jeremiah
Proverbs	Lamentations	Ezekiel
Ruth	Ezekiel	Daniel + Prayer of Azariah,
Song of Songs	Daniel	Song of the 3 Young
Ecclesiastes	Hosea	Men, Susanna, Bel and
Lamentations	Joel	the Dragon
Daniel	Amos	Hosea
Ezra–Nehemiah	Obadiah	Joel
Chronicles	Jonah	Amos
	Micah	Obadiah
	Nahum	Jonah
	Habakkuk	Micah
	Zephaniah	Nahum
	Haggai	Habakkuk
	Zechariah	Zephaniah
	Malachi	Haggai
		Zechariah
		Malachi

these two early collections (the shorter Hebrew one and the longer Greek one) that determine which books are included in the Bibles used by modern Jews, Protestants, and Catholics. Jews, followed by Protestants, regard the shorter collection as Scripture, whereas Catholics accept a larger canon that includes apocryphal/deuterocanonical writings found in the Septuagint.

Three Old Bibles

All modern Bibles are translations of older texts. The Scriptures used by most readers of this book (whether Jewish, Protestant, or Roman Catholic) are based on much older manuscripts that have been translated into English. The three most important of these older Bibles are known as the "Masoretic Text" (MT), the "Septuagint" (LXX), and the "Samaritan Pentateuch" (SP). Scholars believe that the books in these three texts are from pre-Christian times, but unfortunately no really early manuscripts were available before the discovery of the Dead Sea Scrolls. Translations were made from the oldest available manuscripts, most of them medieval, in the belief that these late documents were accurate copies of far more ancient texts.

The Masoretic Text

Almost all modern English translations of the Old Testament are based on a single manuscript, the Leningrad Codex, which was copied in 1008 CE and is our earliest complete copy of the Masoretic (or Rabbinic) Text of the Hebrew Bible. The Leningrad Codex is used by most biblical scholars in its published edition, *Biblia Hebraica Stuttgartensia* (or the earlier *Biblia Hebraica*).

Another important manuscript is the Aleppo Codex, which forms the basis of a new edition of the Hebrew Bible currently being produced at the Hebrew University in Jerusalem. This manuscript was copied in about 925 CE and is thus earlier than the Leningrad Codex; however, a substantial part has been lost, which means that for some books the Hebrew University project must rely on the Leningrad Codex and other Hebrew manuscripts.

Both the Leningrad Codex and the Aleppo Codex are part of what is known as the "Masoretic Text." This term is quite complicated, since it covers many manuscripts rather than a single one; "Masoretic *Group*" or "Masoretic *Family*" would thus be a more accurate name. Masoretic manuscripts—including the Leningrad Codex and the Aleppo Codex—contain the books of the Hebrew Bible in the threefold arrangement that was developed by the Rabbis and is found in modern Jewish Bibles: the Torah, the Prophets, and the Writings (though the specific order of books sometimes varies between manuscripts).

This form of the Old Testament text now found in the Masoretic Text grew and was finalized in three periods, or stages.

- The first stage originated among Babylonian Jews, the Pharisees, or "temple circles" and ended with the destruction of the Temple in 70 CE (or perhaps with the end of the Second Jewish Revolt in 135 CE).
- The second stage extended from the destruction of the Temple until the eighth century CE and was characterized by more and more textual consistency as rabbinic scholars sought to standardize the text of the Hebrew Bible.
- The third stage extended from the eighth century until the end of the Middle Ages and was characterized by almost complete textual uniformity. During this period, a group of Jewish scholars known as the Masoretes set out to produce a standard text of the Hebrew Bible—one that in their eyes would be true to the Scriptures revealed by God in ancient times. Since the ancient text consisted only of Hebrew consonants without any vowels (see Figure 2), many readings were open to diverse meanings (compare *dg* in English, which could be *dig, dog,* or *dug,* depending on which vowel is used). The Masoretes' solution was to add vowels, accents, and Masoretic notes (see Figure 3), which required fixed meanings for groups of consonants (for example, only *dig,* not *dog* or *dug*). As a result, the Masoretic Text became almost completely standardized during this time. It is this standardized form of the Hebrew Bible that is found in the Leningrad Codex and the Aleppo Codex, and upon which the Old Testaments of most English Bibles are based.

Because the Masoretic Text has become the Bible of Judaism and is the main text of the Old Testament used by scholars and Bible translators, its relationship to the biblical Dead Sea Scrolls is an important issue. In the translation presented in this book, all readings from the scrolls have therefore been carefully compared with the Masoretic Text, with any differences (or "variants") signaled by the use of italics.

The Septuagint

The Septuagint is the ancient Greek version of the Hebrew Scriptures or Old Testament, translated by a number of different Jewish scholars over the course of the third, second, and first centuries BCE. The oldest manuscripts of the Septuagint, which are very fragmentary, include John Rylands Papyrus 458 (second century BCE) and Papyrus Fouad 266 (about 100 BCE). Complete (or almost complete) manuscripts exist as well: Codex Sinaiticus (fourth century), Codex Vaticanus (fourth century), and Codex Alexandrinus (fifth century).

תהלים

אשרי האיש אשר לא הלך בעצת רשעים

ובדרך חטאים לא עמד ובמושב לצים לא ישב

כי אם בתורת יהוה חפצו ובתורתו יהגה יומם ולילה

והיה כעץ שתול על פלגי מים

אשר פריו יתן בעתו ועלהו לא יבול

וכל אשר יעשה יצליח

לא כן הרשעים

כי אם כמץ אשר תדפנו רוח

על כן לא יקמו רשעים במשפט וחטאים בעדת צדיקים

כי יודע יהוה דרך צדיקים ודרך רשעים תאבד

Figure 2: Psalm 1 in Its Ancient Format
The text contains no verse numbers, vowels, or other signs.

תהלים

1:1 אַשְׁרֵי הָאִישׁ אֲשֶׁר ׀ לֹא הָלַךְ בַּעֲצַת רְשָׁעִים

וּבְדֶרֶךְ חַטָּאִים לֹא עָמָד וּבְמוֹשַׁב לֵצִים לֹא יָשָׁב׃

2 כִּי אִם בְּתוֹרַת יְהוָה חֶפְצוֹ וּבְתוֹרָתוֹ יֶהְגֶּה יוֹמָם וָלָיְלָה׃

3 וְהָיָה כְּעֵץ שָׁתוּל עַל־פַּלְגֵי מָיִם

אֲשֶׁר פִּרְיוֹ ׀ יִתֵּן בְּעִתּוֹ וְעָלֵהוּ לֹא־יִבּוֹל

וְכֹל אֲשֶׁר־יַעֲשֶׂה יַצְלִיחַ׃

4 לֹא־כֵן הָרְשָׁעִים

כִּי אִם־כַּמֹּץ אֲשֶׁר־תִּדְּפֶנּוּ רוּחַ׃

5 עַל־כֵּן ׀ לֹא־יָקֻמוּ רְשָׁעִים בַּמִּשְׁפָּט וְחַטָּאִים בַּעֲדַת צַדִּיקִים׃

6 כִּי־יוֹדֵעַ יְהוָה דֶּרֶךְ צַדִּיקִים וְדֶרֶךְ רְשָׁעִים תֹּאבֵד׃

Figure 3: Psalm 1 in the Standardized Masoretic Format
Here is the same text with verse numbers and the Masoretic vowels, marks, and accents.

But why was a Greek translation of the Hebrew Scriptures necessary? Following the conquests of Alexander the Great in the late fourth century BCE, Greek was increasingly used in the Ancient Near East, including Palestine, and numerous Jews and other peoples emigrated to lands such as Egypt. Eventually, more and more Jews adopted Greek as their first language and became less and less fluent in Hebrew. For such Hellenized Jews to maintain and understand their religion, a translation of the Hebrew Scriptures into Greek became increasingly necessary.

The translation was begun in the third century BCE in Alexandria (Egypt), one of the centers of Hellenistic Judaism. According to a delightful legend in the *Letter of Aristeas,* seventy-two scholars, six from each of the twelve Israelite tribes, were brought from Jerusalem to translate the Pentateuch into Greek during the reign of Ptolemy Philadelphus (285–247 BCE). The precise number of scholars was rounded off to seventy, from which comes the term *Septuagint* (meaning "seventy" in Latin). Eventually, the "Septuagint" grew to embrace Greek translations of all the books of the Hebrew Bible, translations of some books excluded from the Hebrew Bible, and even a few sacred Jewish books originally composed in Greek.

The Septuagint is important for several reasons. First, almost all the books it contains were translated from an earlier Hebrew or Aramaic form (though a few books, such as 2 Maccabees, were originally composed in Greek). This means that the Septuagint gives readers a window on an ancient Hebrew form of the Old Testament that is earlier than the time of Jesus. Second, the Septuagint sometimes offers striking evidence of different ancient forms of biblical books (for example, Jeremiah is about 13 percent shorter in the Greek than in the Masoretic Text) as well as different ancient readings in specific passages. Third, because the Septuagint was the Bible of Hellenistic Judaism, it offers important insights into how Greek-speaking Jews used and understood Scripture. Fourth, since the Septuagint is quoted in the New Testament and was used by early Christian authors, it constitutes the Bible of the early church and helps to explain early Christian exegesis of Scripture. Finally, the Septuagint contains the books of the Old Testament in the fourfold arrangement that is found in modern Christian Bibles: Pentateuch, Historical Books, Poetical Books, and Prophets (though the specific order of books sometimes varies between Septuagint manuscripts). It is from the Septuagint that most modern Bibles have adopted this grouping and that Catholic Bibles have included the deuterocanonical books (or Apocrypha).

Because of the Septuagint's importance as an ancient translation, the list of variant readings in the footnotes of this book will often indicate whether or not the Septuagint agrees with readings found in the Dead Sea Scrolls, in the Masoretic Text, and in the Samaritan Pentateuch.

The Samaritan Pentateuch

The third ancient Bible is known as the Samaritan Pentateuch; as its name implies, it contains only the five Books of Moses. The Samaritan Pentateuch was finalized as a collection before the Christian era and has been used by the Samaritans, a small branch of Judaism, ever since. A small but active Samaritan community still exists, using this Bible and practicing its own customs and ceremonies.

The Discovery, Contents, and Origin of the Dead Sea Scrolls

This book provides only a brief overview of the discovery of the Dead Sea Scrolls and their contents, since detailed information is readily available elsewhere. The term "Dead Sea Scrolls" refers to ancient manuscripts discovered at sites in the Judean Desert in the vicinity of the Dead Sea. The most important and famous of these sites is Qumran, but scrolls were found at several other sites as well.

Discovery of the Scrolls

Between 1947 and 1956, eleven caves were discovered in the region of Khirbet Qumran, about a mile inland from the western shore of the Dead Sea and approximately fourteen miles east of Jerusalem. The eleven caves yielded various artifacts (especially pottery) and manuscripts written in Hebrew, Aramaic, and Greek, the three languages of the Bible. (The Hebrew Bible is written in Hebrew and Aramaic; the Septuagint and New Testament in Greek.)

In addition to the finds at Khirbet Qumran, several manuscripts were discovered at other locations in the vicinity of the Dead Sea, especially Wadi Murabbaʿât (1951–52), Naḥal Ḥever (1951–52 and 1960–61), and Masada (1963–65).

Description and Contents of the Scrolls

At Qumran, nearly 900 manuscripts were found in some twenty-five thousand pieces, with many no bigger than a postage stamp. A few scrolls are well preserved, such as the *Great Isaiah Scroll* from Cave 1 (1QIsa^a) and the *Great Psalms Scroll* from Cave 11 (11QPs^a). Unfortunately, however, most of the scrolls are very fragmentary. The earliest manuscripts date from about 250 BC, while the latest ones were copied shortly before the destruction of the Qumran site by the Romans in 68 CE. Approximately forty-five more manuscripts were discovered at the other sites: about fifteen at Wadi Murabba'ât, eighteen at Naḥal Ḥever, and twelve at Masada.

Scholars divide the Dead Sea Scrolls into two categories: the "biblical" manuscripts and the "nonbiblical" ones. Of course, this distinction is from our later viewpoint (and not necessarily that of the ancient copyists), but it is useful for purposes of organization and editing. The nonbiblical scrolls are already available in English translation: for example, *The Dead Sea Scrolls,* by Michael Wise, Martin Abegg, Jr., and Edward Cook (San Francisco: HarperSanFrancisco, 1996). But until now the biblical scrolls have never been translated into any modern language; *The Dead Sea Scrolls Bible* makes this material available in English for the first time.

Some 215 manuscripts from Qumran, plus twelve more from the other sites, are classified as biblical scrolls, since they contain material found in the canonical Hebrew Bible. Since these manuscripts contain the texts from which *The Dead Sea Scrolls Bible* has been translated, they will be discussed in greater detail later in this Introduction (see section headed "The Biblical Scrolls").

A few brief comments on the nonbiblical scrolls will be helpful at this point. There are approximately 670 of these scrolls, which can be divided into five groups: (1) rules and regulations (for example, the *Community Rule*); (2) poetic and wisdom texts (for example, the *Hodayot* or *Thanksgiving Psalms*); (3) reworked or rewritten Scripture (for example, the *Genesis Apocryphon*); (4) commentaries or *pesharim* (for example, the *Pesher on Habakkuk*); and (5) miscellaneous writings (for example, the *Copper Scroll*).

The nonbiblical scrolls can be very helpful for understanding Scripture at Qumran, since they often quote from or refer to biblical books and passages. These manuscripts also offer valuable insights into how Scripture was used and interpreted by the Essenes and other Jewish groups in the last few centuries BCE and up to the destruction of the Qumran community in 68 CE. Many of these documents are also of direct relevance to early Judaism and emerging Christianity, since they anticipate or confirm numerous ideas and teachings found in the New Testament and in later rabbinic writings (the Mishnah and Talmud).

Origin of the Scrolls

Most scholars agree that the group who lived at the Qumran site from about 150 BCE to 68 CE was a strict branch of the Essenes. Together with the Pharisees and Sadducees, the Essenes formed the three main divisions (or "denominations") of Judaism at the time of Jesus; they were previously known to us in works of the Hellenistic Jewish writers Josephus and Philo, and of Latin authors such as Pliny the Elder. It is also generally agreed that these Essenes deposited many scrolls in most of the Qumran caves. However, a smaller number of scholars disagree with these points. It has been suggested, for instance, that the members of the Qumran community were not Essenes at all but Sadducees, or that the site was in fact a military fortress or a winter resort.

These issues are of great importance for understanding the nonbiblical scrolls, since scholars distinguish between those manuscripts that were composed at Qumran and those that came to the Qumran "library" from elsewhere. Many scholars refer to the writings composed at Qumran as the "sectarian" scrolls, which is helpful for purposes of identification—but is also confusing. In modern Judaism and Christianity, a "sect" is usually an offshoot of a larger religion and is frequently viewed as eccentric or deviant with respect to beliefs. But both scholars and laypeople would do well to remember that during the entire Qumran period, the Pharisees and Sadducees were as much "sects" as the Essenes were! It was only from the second century CE onward that one type of Judaism—that of the Pharisees and their descendants, the Rabbis—became standard for the Jewish people as a whole.

These issues are of less importance with respect to the biblical scrolls. For one thing, all scholars agree that none of the biblical texts (such as Genesis or Isaiah) was actually composed at Qumran; on the contrary, they all originated before the Qumran period. It is also widely held that many or most of these manuscripts were brought to Qumran from outside and were thus copied elsewhere. This means that the value of most biblical scrolls lies not in establishing precisely where they were written or copied, but rather in studying the textual forms they contain.

Several distinctive biblical scrolls, however, *were* copied at Qumran, which raises some interesting issues. For example, it is likely that 4QSam^c was copied there, since it was copied by the same scribe who penned the main manuscript of the *Community Rule* (1QS). This offers helpful insights into scribal habits among the Qumran community. Another issue is whether or not such Qumran scribes modified the text they were copying in order to produce distinctive Qumranic readings of the biblical text. The evidence to date suggests that such alteration did not take place.

The Biblical Scrolls

The Dead Sea Scrolls include more than 225 "biblical" manuscripts, about 215 of which were found at Qumran. Unfortunately, with a few exceptions (such as 1QIsa^a and 11QPs^a), almost all these manuscripts are in fragmentary form. Parts of every book of the Jewish and Protestant Old Testament are included, with the exception of Esther and Nehemiah. In addition, some other books now included in Roman Catholic Bibles were found at Qumran: Tobit,

Ben Sira (also known as Sirach or Ecclesiasticus), and the Letter of Jeremiah (also known as Baruch 6). In terms of the Catholic canon, then, the total of biblical scrolls would be somewhat higher, at about 235 (about 222 from Qumran). It is also most likely that the Qumran community viewed the books of 1 Enoch and Jubilees as Scripture.

What was the "shape" of the Bible at Qumran? In other words, in what order did the books viewed as scripture at Qumran most likely occur? While most modern Bibles follow the order of the Christian Old Testament canon in four divisions (Pentateuch, Historical Books, Poetry, and Prophets), the ancient evidence from the scrolls suggests the following order: the Books of Moses, the Prophets, and the Psalms. A key passage that suggests this order can be found in the *Halakhic Letter* from Qumran (4QMMT): "And we have also written to you so that you may have discernment in the book of Moses and in the books of the Prophets and in Dav[id]." (It is interesting to note that Jesus uses almost the same terminology in Luke 24:44: ". . . that everything written about me in the Law of Moses, in the Prophets, and in the Psalms must be fulfilled.")

Which of these many biblical books are represented most among the Qumran scrolls? In other words, which writings were most popular for the Qumran community? The following list emerges: (1) the Psalms, with a total of thirty-seven manuscripts, (2) Deuteronomy (with thirty manuscripts), and (3) Isaiah (with twenty-one manuscripts). Although many scrolls have been lost, these statistics serve to indicate which books were most frequently used among the Qumran community. If we count the number of times an Old Testament passage is quoted or referred to in the New Testament, the same three books turn up most: the Psalms (cited about sixty-eight times), Isaiah (sixty-three times), and Deuteronomy (thirty-nine times).

How This Book Was Compiled

This book, containing the first translation of the biblical scrolls into any language, was compiled according to seven principles:

1. *Maintaining the Historical Order of Books*. The order of books in *The Dead Sea Scrolls Bible* corresponds to the ancient evidence as far as can be determined: the Books of Moses (including Jubilees), the Prophets (including 1 Enoch and Daniel), and the Psalms and remaining books (including Ben Sira, the Epistle of Jeremiah, and Tobit).

2. *Including Introductory Material*. The translation of each book is preceded by an introduction that includes a brief description of the relevant scrolls, the dates of at least some of these manuscripts, and the textual form or forms of the book in the scrolls.

3. *Depending on Large Manuscripts*. Among all the biblical scrolls, very large manuscripts are preserved for only two books: Isaiah and Psalms. Since a scroll of the entire book of Isaiah was found in a sealed jar in Cave 1 virtually intact, the translation of Isaiah presented here is of this complete manuscript (1QIsaᵃ). Similarly, another large, continuous scroll of the Psalms (11QPsᵃ) was found in Cave 11. The translation of Psalms 101 to 151, in a different order than that found in traditional Bibles, is mostly from this manuscript.

4. *Integrating Material from Several Manuscripts*. Unfortunately, for all the other biblical books, only fragments survive (some quite substantial, but most of them small). Thus for these books the translation is necessarily a patchwork of the remaining pieces from different scrolls. Since the text is constantly interrupted by the breaking off of the fragments, intervening text is inserted to provide context; this material is taken from our traditional Bible (based on the Masoretic Text). The preserved text is presented in regular type, with nonextant text supplied in square brackets. If only part of a verse or word is preserved in one scroll and another part can be found in a different scroll, the editors have combined the fragments to supply as much of the surviving text as possible.

   For example, in one scroll (4QGenᵇ), we have only the following words preserved for Genesis 1:1: "In the beginning Go[] made [   ]." If this were our only manuscript containing this verse, *The Dead Sea Scrolls Bible* would read: "In the beginning Go[d] made [the heavens and the earth]," with the supplied text in square brackets. Fortunately, however, another scroll (4QGenᵍ) also contains part of this verse—"In the beginn[   ] God [   ] the heavens and the earth"—a fragment that includes material missing from 4QGenᵇ. So when the preserved letters from the two scrolls are combined, the translation is as follows: "In the beginning God made the heavens and the earth."

5. *Signaling Variant Readings*. When the translation of a passage in the scrolls differs from the traditional biblical text (the Masoretic Text) or from any other Dead Sea Scroll, it is printed in *italics* to alert the reader. In order to emphasize the distinctive readings found in some scrolls, the editors have presented these variant readings in the main translation as far as possible (except for Isaiah and Psalms 101 to 151, where the translation is from a single large scroll, as explained above). Any alternative readings that are found in the scrolls, the Masoretic Text (MT), the Septuagint (LXX), or the Samaritan Pentateuch (SP) are listed in the footnotes. Thus the reader is able to compare all the different readings for a given word or passage on the same page.

   For example, near the end of Daniel 7:1 the traditional text says of

King Belshazzar, "then he wrote down the dream, he related the sum of the words," which is awkward. The only scroll that preserves this verse is 4QDan[b], which simply reads "then he wrote down the dream." Accordingly, *The Dead Sea Scrolls Bible* translation reads "then he wrote down *the dream*."[3] The corresponding footnote (which is indicated by the superscripted *3*) reads:

4QDan[b] and probably LXX. *the dream, he related the sum of the words* MT LXX[mss].

This shows that the translation is found in 4QDan[b] and most likely the original Septuagint, while the longer reading is found in the Masoretic Text and some Septuagint manuscripts.

6. *Highlighting Interesting or Important Readings. The Dead Sea Scrolls Bible* includes apocryphal books, new Psalms, previously unknown passages, and hundreds of individual readings that are significant or interesting for our understanding of Scripture. The translators highlight some of this new or interesting material with the use of italicized comments. One example is found before Isaiah 29:5:

■ *Several possibilities exist for the multitude referred to in Isaiah 29:5. Is the best reading "your strangers," mentioned in the Masoretic text, "the ungodly," referred to in the Septuagint, or "your enemies," as found in 1QIsa[a]? A solution is offered by the parallel phrase later in the verse "and the multitude of the ruthless ones," which suggests that the reading in 1QIsa[a] is the preferred one. "Your enemies" (or "Your foes") is found in several modern translations, including the Revised Standard Version, the New Revised Standard Version, and the New International Version.*

Although there are scores of such interesting readings, in order to produce *The Dead Sea Scrolls Bible* in one volume we were limited to highlighting only a selection of key readings in this way. But for the reader who seeks further examples, this book presents the rich variety of readings found in all the biblical scrolls in a complete fashion, whether in italicized form in the main text, or in the footnotes below.

7. *Emphasizing Accuracy over Style.* Since there are numerous aspects involved in the translation of a Bible, it usually takes a large team of translators more than a decade to produce one. In order to make *The Dead Sea Scrolls Bible* available in a reasonable amount of time, the main concern of the translators was to represent faithfully the text as found in the scrolls. We have not attempted to achieve overall stylistic consistency for the whole volume, since that would have required a far greater amount of time. Two points, however, should be emphasized. First, we have been consistent in translating the Divine Name by following the practice of the Revised Standard

Version and the New Revised Standard Version (i.e., the LORD for the Hebrew *YHWH,* and the LORD God for *YHWH elohim*). Second, inclusive language has been used to a considerable extent with respect to humans (but not for God). We realize all too well that more could be done in this regard, which we intend to carry out in a future edition of *The Dead Sea Scrolls Bible.*

HOW TO READ THIS BOOK

The various notes found in the main text and at the bottom of each page contain valuable information. Attention to a few details will greatly increase your appreciation of this book.

The Main Text

Numbers on the line within the text represent verse numbers.

Explanatory comments are printed in italics and set off by a square.

Square brackets surround areas lost in the scroll due to various types of damage.

■ *Verse 5 below witnesses to the reading* seventy-five *found in the Greek text of Exodus as well as at Acts 7:14 (see also Gen 46:27). The Masoretic Text and the Samaritan Pentateuch read* seventy. *The New International Version has chosen to note this as a marginal reading. To date, this is the only variant from Exodus reflected in any modern translation.*

[5] And all the souls that c]ame out of the loins of J[acob were] *seventy-five*[1] *souls*.[2] 6 And [Joseph] died, [and all his brethren, and all th]at [generation.] 7 And the children of Israel were fruitful, and incre[ased greatly, and multiplied, and became exceedingly mighty; and the land was filled with th]em. ▲

Readings from the scrolls that differ (variants) from the traditional Hebrew text (MT)—the text that forms the basis of our modern translations—are printed in italics.

The triangle indicates that there is a gap in the scroll evidence of more than two verses before the next line. These verses were likely in the scrolls originally, but fell prey to cave worms or the ravages of time.

Raised numbers following text variants in italics refer to footnoted information at the bottom of the page. In this case the reading *seventy-five* replaces the expected *seventy*. See the following discussion of the footnotes.

Footnotes

At the beginning of each new chapter a footnote corresponding to the chapter number will record the manuscripts that contain all or parts of the chapter. In the case of Exodus 1, a total of four manuscripts were found in the caves that contain this section. The existing verses follow each manuscript. The text of each chapter represents the combined manuscript evidence.

Each manuscript "name" begins with the number of the cave (in this case Cave 4) in which the manuscript was found. The site abbreviation follows:

Q = Qumran

A few manuscripts come from other areas:

Mur = Wadi Murabbaʿat
Ḥev = Naḥal Ḥever
Mas = Masada
Se = Wadi Seiyâl

Following the chapter information are the notes corresponding to the superlinear numbers in the main text.

Chapter 1. 4QExodᵇ: 1:1–6, 16–21; 4QpaleoGen-Exodˡ: 1:1–5; 4QGen-Exodᵃ: 1:3–17, 22; 2QExodᵃ: 1:11–14.

1. 4QExodᵇ 4QGen-Exodᵃ LXX. *seventy* MT SP.   **2.** 4QExodᵇ LXX. *souls and Joseph was in Egypt already* 4QpaleoGen-Exodˡ 4QGen-Exodᵃ MT SP.

Following the cave number and site is an abbreviation of the book title (in this case Exod = Exodus). Occasionally, there are two or more books in a scroll (Gen–Exod). If the scroll is written in ancient (paleo) Hebrew, this is indicated. If more than one manuscript of the book came from the site, a raised letter after the book name indicates which manuscript it is. In this case, "b" means the second manuscript of Exodus from Cave 4 at Qumran.

There are three ancient Bible versions referred to in the footnotes:

MT = Masoretic Text, the traditional Hebrew Bible

SP = the Samaritan Pentateuch, the edition of the Hebrew Bible used by the Samaritans

LXX = the Septuagint, the ancient Greek translation of the Hebrew Bible

See the introduction for more information concerning these versions.

Footnote 1 may be read as follows: The reading *seventy-five* (see discussion of the main text above) is found in two manuscripts from Qumran Cave 4: the first Genesis manuscript, which also contains Exodus, and the second Exodus manuscript. The Greek translation also reflects this reading. The traditional Hebrew text and the Samaritan Pentateuch read *seventy*.

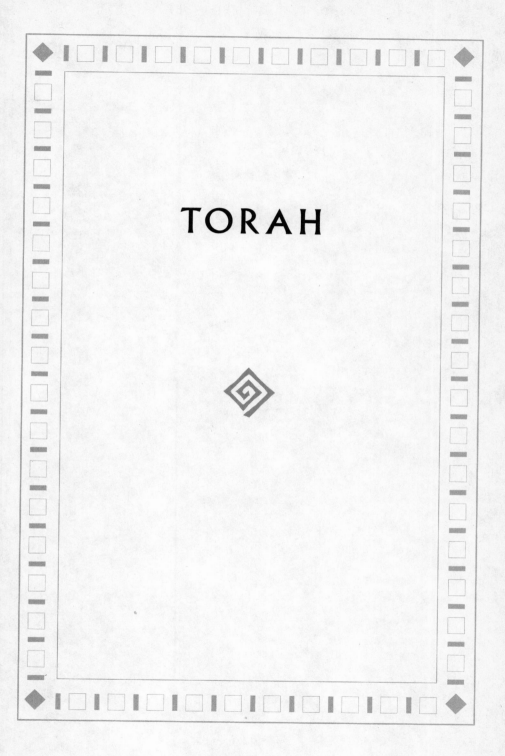

TORAH

GENESIS

Genesis—as the name has come to suggest, a book of beginnings and ge-
nealogical history—was very popular among the Qumranites. Both the
number of biblical manuscripts and the collection of scrolls involved with
retelling its compelling stories attest to this fact.

The remains of possibly twenty manuscripts were unearthed at Qumran itself:
one in Cave 1, one in Cave 2, perhaps as many as sixteen in Cave 4, one in Cave
6, and one in Cave 8.[a] In addition to these manuscripts from the caves to the
north of Wadi Qumran, remains of other Dead Sea Scrolls were also found—one
to the south at Masada and perhaps as many as three at Wadi Murabba'at.[b] There
is admittedly a certain degree of mystery surrounding this latter group. Due to
the secrecy of their Bedouin discoverers, there will forever be some doubt as to
their place of origin. In addition, it is very likely that at least two of the manuscripts are pieces of the same scroll, though they were obtained at different times
from the Bedouin.[c] Such are the intrigues of scroll research!

Although a scroll containing all the Books of Moses (Genesis through
Deuteronomy) may not have been a common item—it would necessarily have
been nearly five times as long as the *Great Isaiah Scroll*—at least two scrolls exist
that contain both Genesis and Exodus,[d] confirming an ancient order for these
two important books. Genesis is also attested in the ancient Hebrew script known
as paleo-Hebrew—4QpaleoGen-Exod[l] and 4QpaleoGen[m]—the latter being the
oldest scroll of Genesis, dating from the middle of the second century BCE.

Although the twenty-four manuscripts of Genesis are surpassed in number
only by Psalms, Isaiah, and Deuteronomy, they are all relatively fragmentary and

---

a. 1QGen, 2QGen, 4QGen-Exod[a], 4QGen[b]–4QGen[g], 4QGen[h1], 4QGen[h2], 4QGen[h-title],
4QGen[j], 4QGen[k], 4QpaleoGen-Exod[l], 4QpaleoGen[m], 4QGen[n], and pap4QGen (4Q483),
6QGen, 8QGen.   **b.** MasGen, MurGen 1, Mur (origin questionable), and Sdeir 1.
c. Mur (origin questionable) and Sdeir 1.   **d.** 4QGen-Exod[a] and 4QpaleoGen-Exod[l].

preserve only thirty-two chapters among their crumbs. They do, however, reveal a text of Genesis that is generally very close to the traditional Hebrew text. Only eleven manuscripts exhibit variants beyond the more common slight deviations in spelling. These few variants show no real pattern but are best classified as mixed, or "nonaligned." It is of special note that the two (or possibly three) manuscripts from Wadi Murabba'at, dated according to their script (which places their creation at the beginning of the second century CE), are identical to the traditional Hebrew text. Although the mechanics of the processes that led to the establishment of a "fixed text" are lost to us (see the Introduction), the evidence from the Dead Sea Scrolls suggests that the current character of the Hebrew Bible dates to the early second century CE. Indeed, this is one of the important contributions of the Dead Sea Scrolls: the Bible can now be seen in its final stages of development in the latter centuries BCE and even the first century CE. By the beginning of the second century CE, various historical factors had given rise to a final text form that has been passed down virtually unchanged to this day.

Retelling portions of Genesis was a popular business in the Qumran community. The *Genesis Apocryphon,* preserved to a length of twenty-three somewhat fragmentary columns, is an Aramaic work that rehearses the lives of Enoch, Lamech, Noah and his sons, and Abraham. The creation, the flood, and events in the life of Abraham were extremely popular with the writers of the Second Temple period. Theological issues found their beginnings in Genesis as well. Discussions concerning the pollution of humans and divine beings by sin were centered on the mysterious union of "the sons of God and the daughters of men" in Genesis 6:1–4, and messianic musings were founded on the blessings to the tribe of Judah in Genesis 49:10.

Although Genesis was not the source for legal rulings in the Qumran community (as were the next four books of the Torah), it does play a key role in a rather intriguing discussion concerning monogamy. The *Damascus Document* (CD) 4:19–5:1—in an obvious polemic against the polygamy of the Pharisees—argues on the basis of Genesis 1:27 ("male and female he created them") and Genesis 7:9 ("went into the ark two by two") that one wife was the biblical norm.

> ■ *Only four manuscripts among the more than eight hundred found in the caves at Qumran preserve the title of the scroll. These titles were written on the outside of the first column—so as to appear when it was rolled up*

(4Q249 and 4Q504)—or on a special "guard page" that covered the manuscript in the manner of a modern book cover (1QS). One of these is a manuscript of Genesis (4QGen^{h-title}). As the fragment containing the title has been separated from the rest of the scroll, it has not yet been determined if it is the sole remnant of an otherwise lost scroll, or whether it should be included with some existing fragments (the best candidate being 4QGen^k).

IN THE BEGINNING *(BERESHIT)*

1 1 In the beginning God created the heavens and the earth. [2 And] the earth [was] formless and void; and darkness was upon the fac[e of the dee]p: and the Spirit of God moved upon the face of the waters. 3 And God said, "Let there be light," [and there was light. 4 And] God saw that the light was good, and God separated the light [from the darkness.] 5 And God called the light *daytime,*[1] and the darkness he cal[led ni]ght. And there was evening [and there was morning,] one day.

6 And God said, "Let there be a firmament in the midst of the waters, and let it divide [the waters from the waters." 7 And] God [made] the firmament, and divided the waters which were under the firmam[ent from the waters] which were above the firmament. And it was so. 8 And God called the firmament heav[en. And there was evening and] there was morning, a second day.

▮ *Although no variants from the scrolls have yet worked their way into modern Bible translations of Genesis, footnotes 3 and 4 in verse 9 manifest prime candidates. The precursor to the Septuagint reading of "gathering" (miqveh) rather than the traditional Hebrew "place" (maqôm) is found in the Dead Sea Scroll classified as 4QGen^{h1}. In addition, the accomplishment of God's command (footnote 4), again found in the Greek, is evident in 4QGen^k. Although most of the variants from the scrolls are not necessarily "better," both of these readings may represent the original form of the text.*

Title. 4QGen^{h-title}.
Chapter 1. 4QGen^b: 1:1–28; 4QGen^g: 1:1–11, 13–22; 4QGen^{h1}: 1:8–10; 4QGen^k: 1:9, 14–16, 27–28; 4QGen^d: 1:18–27; 1QGen: 1:18–21; pap4QGen(?) (4Q483): 1:28.
 1. 4QGen^g. *day* MT SP LXX.

9 And God said, "Let the waters *underneath*[2] the heavens be gathered together in one *gathering,*[3] and let the dr[y land] appear." And it was so. [*And the waters under the heavens gathered to their gatherings*] *and the dr[y land] appeared.*[4] 10 And God called the dry land earth; and the gathering of the waters called he seas, and God saw that it was good. 11 And God said, "Let the earth put forth grass, herbs yielding seed, and fruit trees bearing fruit after their kind, with seed in them, on the earth." And it was so. 12 And the earth brought forth gra[ss,] herbs yie[lding seed after their kind, and] trees bearing fruit, with seed in them, after their kind. And God saw that it was good. 13 And [there was evening] and there was morning, a third day.

14 And God said, "Let there be lights in the firmament of heaven to separate the day fr[o]m the night; *and they were*[5] for signs, and for seasons, and for days and *for*[6] y[e]ars; 15 and let them be for lights in the firmament of heaven to give light upon the earth." And it was so. 16 And [God made] the two great lights, the greater light to [rule the day, and] the lesser [l]ight to rule the night; he made the stars also. 17 And [God] set [them in the firmament of] heaven to give light on the earth, 18 and to rule over the day and over the night, [and to divide] the light from the darkness, and God saw that it was good. 19 And there was evening and there was morning, a fourth day.

20 And God said, "Let the waters teem with swarms of living creatures, and let birds fly above the earth in the open firmament of heaven." 21 And God created the great sea monsters, and every living creature that moves, with which the waters swarmed, after their kind, and every [winged] bird after its kind. And God saw that it was good. 22 And God blessed them, saying, "Be fruitful, and multiply, [and fill] the waters in the seas, and *the birds shall*[7] multiply on the earth." 23 And there was evening [and there] was morning, a fifth day.

24 And God said, "Let the earth bring forth [living] creatures after [their kind,] cattle, and creeping things, [and beasts of the earth] after their kind." [And it was so.] 25 And [God] m[ade] the beasts of the [ea]rth after their kind, and the cattle [after their kind, and everything that creeps upon the ground after its kind. And Go]d [saw] that it was good.

[26 And God said, "Let us make humankind in our image, after our likeness, and let] them have dominion over the fish of the sea, and over the birds of the heavens, [and over the cattle, and over all the earth, and over every creeping thing

---

2. 4QGen^g. *under* MT SP.

3. 4QGen^h1 LXX. *place* 4QGen^b MT SP.

4. 4QGen^k LXX. Not in 4QGen^b MT SP.

5. 4QGen^g. *and let them be* 4QGen^b 4QGen^k MT SP.

6. 4QGen^k LXX. Not in MT SP.

7. 4QGen^g SP. *let the birds* 4QGen^b MT.

that creeps up]on the [ea]rth." 27 And God created humankind [in his own image, in the image of God created he them; male and fe]male he created them. 28 And [God] blessed [them; and God said to them, "Be fruitful, and multiply,] and replen[ish the earth, and subdue it; and have dominion over the fish of the sea, and over the birds of the heavens, and over every living thing that moves upon the earth."]▲

2 [1 And] the heavens [and the earth were finished, and all their hosts. 2 And on the seventh day God finished] his [work] which [he had made; and he rested on the seventh day from all his work which he had made. 3 And] Go[d] bless[ed the seventh day, and sanctified it; because in it he rested from al]l his work [which God had created and made.]▲

[6 But a mist used to rise up from the earth and water the whole face of the ground.] 7 And the L[ORD God] formed [man of the dust of the ground, and breathed into his nostrils the breath of life; and man became a living being.]▲

[14 And the name of] the third [river] is Tigris; it flows on the e[ast of Assyria. And the fourth river is the Euphrates.]

15 And the LORD God took the man [and put] him into the garden of Eden to cultivate [it and] to keep it. 16 And the LORD God commanded the man, [saying,] "Of every tree of the garden [you may] eat freely; 17 but of the tree of the knowledge of good and evil, you sh[all] not [eat from] it, for [in the day] that you eat from it you shall surely die."

18 And the LORD God sa[id,] "It is not good [that the man should be alone;] I will make him a partner for him." 19 And out of the gr[ound] the LORD God formed [every beast of the field, and every bird of the] s[ky; and brought them] to the man to [see what he would call them; and whatever the man called a living creature, that was its name.]▲

3 [1 Now the serpent was more] crafty [than any beast of the field which the LORD God had made. And he sai]d to the woman, ["Has God] really[8] [said, 'You shall not eat of any tree of] the garden?'" 2 And the woman said to the serpe[nt, "From the fruit of the trees of the garden we may eat. . . ."]▲

[11 And he said, "Who told you that] you were nak[ed? Have you eaten of the tree from which I commanded you not to eat?" 12 And the man said, "The woman] whom you gave to be with me, s[he gave me of the tree, and I ate." 13 And the LORD God said to the woman, "What is thi]s you have done?" And the wom[an] said, ["The serpent deceived me, and I ate." 14 And the LORD God said to the serpent, "Because] you ha[ve done] this, cursed are y[ou more than all

---

Chapter 2. 4QGen[k]: 2:1–3; 4QGen[g]: 2:6–7 (or 18–19); 4QGen[b]: 2:14–19; 4QGen[h2]: 2:17–18.

Chapter 3. 4QGen[k]: 3:1–2; 1QGen: 3:11–14.

8. Interrogative particle 4QGen[k]. Not in MT SP.

cattle, and more than every beast of the field; upon your belly shall you go, and dust shall you eat] all [the] day[s of your life."]▲

4[2 And a]gain [she] gave birth to his brother A[bel. And Abel was a keeper of flocks, but Cain wa]s a tiller of the ground. 3 And in [the course of t]ime C[ain] brought an offering to the LORD [from the fruit of the ground.] 4 And Abel also br[oug]ht of the fir[stlings of his flock and of their fat portions. And] the LORD looked with favor on Abel and his offering, 5 but on Ca[in and his offering he did not look with favor. And] Cain was very angry, and his face was downcast. 6 And [the LORD] said [to Cain, "Why are you angry, and why] is your face [do]wncast? 7 If you do well, will you not be ac[cepted? And] if [you do not well, si]n crou[ches at the door: and its] desire is [t]o have you, [but you must] rule [over it."]

[8 And Cain told Abe]l his brother. And when they were in the fie[ld, Cain] rose up [against Abel his brother, and killed] him. 9 And the LORD said to Cain, "Where is [your brother] Abel?" [And he said, "I do not know;] am [I] my brother's keeper?" [10 And he sai]d, "What [have you done? The voice of your brother's blood is cryin]g to me from the ground. [11 And now cursed are you from the ground, which has opened its mouth] to receive [your brother's blood from your hand. . . ."]▲

5[13 And] Kenan [lived eight hundred and forty years after he became the father of Mahalalel, and had other sons and daughters. 14 So all the days of Kenan were nine hundred and ten years, and he died.]▲

6[13 And God said to Noah, "The end of all flesh has come before me; for the earth is filled with violence becau]se of them; [and behold, I am about to destroy them with the earth. 14 Make for yourself an ark of gopher wood; make rooms in the ark, and coat it ins]ide and ou[t with pitch. 15 And this is how you shall make it: the length of the ark three hundred cubits, its breadth fifty cubits, and its] he[ight thirt]y [c]ubits. [16 You shall make a window for the ark, and finish it within a cubit of the top; and the door of the ark you shall set in the side; you shall make it with lower, se]cond, and thir[d decks. 17 And I myself am about to bring the flood of water upon this earth, to destroy all flesh in which is the breath of] life, from under [heaven; everything that is on the earth shall die. 18 But I will establish my covenant with you; and you shall go into the ark, y]ou and your sons, and your wife, [and your sons' wives with you. 19 And of every living thing of all flesh, you shall bring two of every kind into the ark to keep them alive] with you; [they shall be male and female. 20 Of the birds after their kind, and of the cattle after their kind, of every creeping thing of the ground

---

Chapter 4. 4QGen[b]: 4:2–11.

Chapter 5. 4QGen[b]: Gen 5:13 (or 14).

Chapter 6. 6QpaleoGen: 6:13–21.

after] *their*[9] [kin]d, two [of every sort shall come to you to keep them alive. 21 And as for you, you must take some of every kind of food that is to be eaten, and gather it to yourself; and it shall b]e [for food] for you, and for them." ▲

8 [20 And Noah built an altar to the LORD, and took of every clean beast and of every] clean [bird,] and [offered burnt offerings on the altar. 21 And the LORD smelled the pleasing aroma; and the LORD said in his heart, "I will never] again [curse the ground because of man, for the inclination of man's heart is evil from his youth; neither will I again destroy every living thing, as I have done."] ▲

17 [12 And he among you that is eight days old shall be circumcised, every] m[ale throughout your generations, he that is born in the house, or bought with money of any foreigner that is not of your offspring. 13 He that is born in your house, and he that is bought with your] mo[ney, must be circumcised. My covenant shall be in your flesh for an everlasting covenant. 14 And the uncircumcised male who is not circumcised in the flesh of his foreskin shall be cut off from his people. He has broken my covenant.]

[15 And God said to Abraham, "As for Sarai your wife,] you sh[all not call her name Sarai, but her name shall be Sarah. 16 And I will bless her, and I will surely give you a son of her. Indeed, I will bless her, and she shall be a mother of nations. Kings of] pe[oples shall come from her." 17 Then Abraham fell upon his face, and laughed, and said in his heart, "Shall a child be born to him that is a hundred years old? And shall Sarah, that is ninety years old, give birth?" 18 And] Abraham [said to God, "O that Ishmael might live before you!" 19 And God said, "No, but Sarah your wife shall bear you a son and you] shall cal[l his name Isaac. And I will establish my covenant with him as an everlasting covenant for his offspring after him."] ▲

18 [20 And the LORD said, "Because the cry of Sodom] and [Gomorrah is great, and because their sin is very grievous 21 I will go down now, and see whether] they have done as ba[dly as its outcry, which is come] to me. [And if not, I will know."]

[22 And the men turned from there and went toward Sodom. But Abraham was still standing] before the L[ORD. 23 And Abraham approached and said, "Will you destroy the righteous with the wicked? 24 Suppose there are fifty righteous with]in the [city. Will you destroy and not spare the place for the fifty righteous that are in it? 25 Far be it from you] *to do t*[*his thing,*[10] to slay the righteous with

---

9. 6QGen SP LXX. *its* MT.

Chapter 8. 4QGen-Exod[a]: 8:20–21(?).

Chapter 17. 8QGen: 17:12–19.

Chapter 18. 8QGen: 18:20–25.

10. 8QGen. *to do such a thing as this* MT SP LXX.

the wicked, so that the righteous should be treated as the wicked. Far be it from you.] Shall n[ot the Judge of all the earth] do [right?"]▲

19 [27 And Abraham arose early in the morning and went to the place wh]ere [he had stood] before [the LORD. 28 And he looked toward So]dom and Gomorrah, [and toward all the land of the Plain, and saw, and behold, the smoke of the land went up as the smoke of a furnace.]▲

22 [13 And Abraham lifted up his eyes, and looked, and behold, behind him a ram caught in the thicket by his horns. And Ab]raham [went] and t[ook the ram, and offered him up for a burnt offering instead of his son.]

> ■ *Since, according to the Bible itself, the name* Yahweh—*translated "*LORD*" in most modern editions of the Bible—was later revealed to Moses in the book of Exodus (3:13–15), students of the Pentateuch have long debated the use of* Yahweh *in the book of Genesis. A common solution suggests that an early author/editor indiscriminately used the term in his copying of the text.* 4QGen-Exod^a—*sure to fuel the debate afresh— "replaces" the term* Yahweh *in Genesis 22:14 with the more common Hebrew term for God. Thus the familiar* Jehovah Jireh *becomes* Elohim Jireh.

[14 And Abra]ham [called] the name of [that] pla[ce G]od[11] will provide. As it is s[aid to this day, On the mountain of the LORD it shall be provided.]

[15 And] the angel of the LORD called t[o Abraham a second time from heaven.]▲

23 [17 So Ephron's] field, [which was in Machpelah, before Mamre, the] field and the ca[ve which was in it, and all the trees that were in the field, that were within all the su]rrounding [boundaries of the field, were de]ed[ed] 18 to Abraham [for a possession in the presence of the children of Heth, before all that went in at the gate of his city. 19 And after this,] Ab[raham] buried [Sarah his wife in the cave of the field of Machpelah] before [Mam]re [(that is, Hebron) in the land of Canaan.]▲

24 [22 And when the came]ls [were done drinking, the man took a golden ring of half a shekel weight, and two bracelets for] her [hands of] ten [shekels weight of gold, 23 and said, "Whose daughter are you? Tell me, I pray you. Is there room in your father's house for us to lodge in?" 24 And she] s[ai]d to [him, "I am the daughter of Bethuel the son of Milcah, whom she had borne to Nahor."]▲

Chapter 19. 2QGen: 19:27–28.

Chapter 22. 1QGen: 22:13–15; 4QGen-Exod^a: 22:14.

   11. 4QGen-Exod^a. *the* LORD MT SP LXX.

Chapter 23. 1QGen: 23:17–19.

Chapter 24. 1QGen: 24:22–24.

26[21 And they] dug [another well, and they fought over that too. And he named it Sitnah. 22 And he moved from there, and dug *the*] *last*[12] [well] and [they] did not fight [over it. And he named it Rehoboth. And he said, "For now the LORD has made room for us, and we shall be fruitful in the land."]

23 And he went up from there to Beer-[sheba. 24 And the LORD appeared to him the same night, and said, "I am the God of Abra]ham your father. Fear not, [for I am with you, and will bless you, and multiply your seed for my servant Abraham's sake." 25 And he built an altar there, and called upon the na]me of the LORD, and pitched [his tent there. And there Isaac's servants dug a well.]

[26 Then Abimelech went to him from Gerar, and Ahuzzath] his [f]riend, and Phicol [the captain of his host. 27 And Isaac said to them, "Why have you come to me, since you hate me and have sent me away fro]m [y]ou?" 28 And they [said, "We saw plainly that the LORD was with you. And we said, 'Let there now be an oath between us, even between us and you, and let us make a covenant with you, . . .'"] ▲

27[38 And Esau said to his father, "Have you only one blessing, my father? Bless me, even me also, O my father." And Esau lifted up his voice, and] wept. 39 And Isaac [his father] answered [and said to him, "Behold, away from the richness of the earth shall be your dwelling, and away from the dew of heaven from above."] ▲

[42 And the words of Esau her elder son were] told to Rebe[kah. And she sent and called Jacob her younger son, and said to him,] "Behold, [your brother] Es[au is consoling himself concerning you, by plotting to kill you. 43 Now therefore, my son, obey my voice, and arise, flee to] Laban [my] brother [in Haran."] ▲

32[3 And Jacob sent] messengers before him to Esau his brother [to the land of Seir, the field of Edom. 4 And he] commanded [th]em, saying, ["Thus shall you say to my lord Esau: Thus says your servant Jacob, 'I have sojourned with Laban, and stayed until now: . . .'"] ▲

[29 And] Jacob [asked him,] and said, "Tell me, I pray you, [your] name." [And he said, "Why is it that you as]k about [my name?" And he blessed him there.] ▲

32 Therefore [the children of Israel] do not [e]a[t] the sinew of the hip which is upon the hollow of the thigh to this day, because he touched the socket [of Jacob's thigh in the sinew of the h]ip.

331 And Jacob lifted up his eyes, [and looked, and behold, Esau was coming, and with him four hundred men. And he divided the children to Leah, and to Rachel, and to the two maids.] ▲

Chapter 26. 4QpaleoGen^m: 26:21–28.

  12. 4QpaleoGen^m. *another* MT SP LXX.

Chapter 27. 4QGen-Exod^a: 27:38–39, 42–43.

Chapter 32. MurGen: 32:3–4 [H 4–5], 29 [H 30], 32 [H 33].

Chapter 33. MurGen: 33:1; Mur(?)Gen: 33:18–20.

[18 And Jacob came safely to the city of Shechem, which is in the land of Canaan, when he came from Paddan-aram, and camped] befo[re the city. 19 And he bought the plot of ground where] he had pitched [his tent from the children of Hamor, Shechem's father,] for one hundred p[ieces of money. 20 And he erected an altar there, and called it] El-Elohe-I[srael.]

34 [1 And Dinah the daughter of Leah, whom] she had borne to Jacob, [went out to see the daughters of the land. 2 And] Shechem [the son of Hamor the Hivite, the prince of the land, saw] h[e]r, a[nd took her, and violated her. 3 And] h[e was attracted to Dinah the daughter of Jacob, and he loved the girl and spoke from his heart to her. 4 And Shechem spoke to his father Hamor, saying, "Get this girl to be my wife."]

[5 Now when Jacob heard that he had defiled Dinah his daughter his sons were with his cattle in the field, so J]acob [kept quiet] until [they came. 6 And Hamor the fat]her [of] Shechem [went out]to Jacob to talk with him. 7 And the sons of Jacob came in from the field when they heard it and the men were grieved, and they were very angry because he had done an outrageous thing in Israel by lying with Jacob's daughter; a thing which ought not be done. ▲

[17 "But if you will not listen to us to be circum]cised, then we will take [our daughter and go."]

[18 And their words pleased Hamor and] Shechem, Hamor['s son.] 19 And [the young man] did not hesit[ate to do the thing, because he was delighted with Jacob's daughter. H]e was the most respected of all his father's household. [20 And Hamor and Shechem his son came to the gate of their city, and spoke with] the men of their [city,] saying, [21 "These men are friendly toward us, therefore let them live in the land, and trade in it; for,] b[ehold, the land is large enough for them. Let us take their daughters for our wives, and let us give them our daughters."]▲

[30 And Jacob said to Simeon and Levi, "You have brought trouble on me by making me odious to the inhabitants of the land, among the] Canaanites and the Perizzites. I being few in number, [they] will gather [themselves together against me] and attack me, and I shall be destroyed, I and my household." 31 And [they] s[aid,] "Should he treat our sister [as a harlot?"]

35 1 And God said to [Jacob, "Arise, go up to Bethel,] and live there; [and make an altar there to God who appeared t]o [you when you fled from Esau your brother."]▲

[4 And they gave to Jacob] a[ll the] foreign g[o]d[s which they had and the rings] which were in their ears, and [Ja]cob b[ur]ied [them under the o]a[k] which was at Shechem.

Chapter 34. Mur(?)Gen: 34:1–3; MurGen: 34:5–7, 30–31; 4QGen-Exodᵃ: 34:17–21.

Chapter 35. MurGen: 35:1; SdeirGen: 35:6–10, 24–29; MurGen: 35:4–7; 4QGen-Exodᵃ: 35:17–29.

5 And they journeyed, and [the] terror [of God fell upon the cities that were round about them so that they did not pursue the sons of Jacob. 6 So J]acob [came to Luz (that is, Bethel), which is in the land of Canaan,] he and all the people that [were with him. 7 And he built there an altar and called] the place El-bethel, because [God had revealed himself to him] there, [when he fled from his brother. 8 And Debo]rah, [Rebekah's nurse, died and she was buried under] the oak [below Bethel; so it was called Allon-bacuth.]

[9 And God appeared to Jacob again, when he came from Paddan-aram, and blessed him. 10 And God said to him, "Your name is Jacob, but] your [name shall no longer be called Jacob; Israel shall be your name." So he named him Israel.]▲

[17 And when her labor was difficult, the midwife] said [to her, "Do not be afraid, for you have another son." 18 And as her soul was departing—for she died—she na]med [him Ben-oni; but his father called him Benjamin. 19 So Rachel died and was buried on the way to Ephra]th (that is, Bethlehem). 20 And [Jacob] set up [a pillar over her grave; it is the pillar of Rachel's grave to this day. 21 And] Israel journeyed on and pitched his tent beyo[nd] the tower [of Eder. 22 And while Israel was living in that land, Reuben went and lay] with Bil[ha]h his father's concubine and Is[rael] heard about it. [Now the sons of Jacob were tw]elve: 23 the son[s of] Leah: Reuben, Jacob's firstborn, Sime[o]n,[13] [and Levi, and Judah, and Issachar, and Zebulun; 24 the sons of Rachel: Joseph] and Benjamin; 25 the[14] sons of Bilhah, Rachel's handmaid: Dan and Naphtali; 26 the[15] sons of Zilpah, [Leah's handmaid: Gad and Asher. These are the sons of Jacob wh]om she bore[16] to him [in] Pa[ddan]-aram.

27 And Jacob came to Isaac [his] father, to Mamre [of Kiriath-arba (that is, Hebron), wh]ere Abraham and Isaac sojourned. 28 And the days of Isaac were a hundred [and eighty] years. 29 And Isa[ac breathed his last and died and was gathered to his people, ol]d and full of days. And his sons Esa[u and Jacob] buried him.

36 1 Now these are [the generations of Esau (that is, Edom). 2 Esau took his wives] from the daughters of Canaan: Adah the daughter of Elon [the Hittite, and Oholibamah the daughter of Anah and granddaughter of Zibeon the Hivite, 3 and Basemath] Ishmael's daughter, sister of Nebaioth. [4 And Adah bore Eliphaz to Esau; and Basemath bore Reue]l]; [5 and] Oholibamah bore Jeush,[17]

---

13. 4QGen-Exod[a] LXX. *and Simeon* MT SP.

14. 4QGen-Exod[a]. *and the* MT SP LXX.

15. 4QGen-Exod[a]. *and the* MT SP LXX.

16. 4QGen-Exod[a]. *was born* SdeirGen MT. *were born* SP LXX.

Chapter 36. 4QGen-Exod[a]: 36:1–13, 19–27; SdeirGen: 36:1–2, 5–17; 2QGen: 36:6, 35–37; 4QGen[e]: 36:43.

17. 4QGen-Exod[a] MT qere SP LXX. *Jeish* MT ketib.

[and Jalam, and Korah: these are the sons of Esau who were born to him in] the land of Canaan.

6 And Esau took his wives and his sons and his daughters and all the members of his household, [and] his cattle, all his beasts, and all his possessions which he had gathered in the land of Canaan, and went into a land away from [his brother] Jacob. [7 For] their possessions [were] too great for them to live together and the land where [they] were living could not support them because of their livestock. [8 And Esau lived in the hill country of] Seir; Esau is Edom.

9 And these are the generations of Esau the father of the Edomites in the hill country of Seir. 10 These are the name[s of Esau's sons: Eliphaz] the son of Adah the wife of Esau, Reuel the son of Basemath the wife of [Esau.] 11 And the sons of Eliphaz were Teman, Omar, [Zepho, and Gatam, and Kenaz.] 12 And Timna was concubine to Eliphaz Esau's son, and she [bore] to [E]li[phaz] A[malek. These are the grandsons of Adah, Esau's wife. 13 And these are the sons of Reuel: Nahath, and Zera]h, Shamm[ah,] and Mizzah. The[se were the grandsons of Basemath, Esau's wife. 14 And] these were the s[ons of] Esau's wife [Oholibamah the daughter of Anah, the granddaughter of Zibeon;] and she bore [to Esau Jeush, and Jalam, and] Korah.

15 These are the chief[s of the sons of Esau: the sons of Eliphaz the firstborn of] Esau: chief Teman, chief [Omar, chief Zepho, chief Kenaz, 16 ch]ief Korah, chief Gatam, chi[ef Amalek: these are the chiefs of E]li[pha]z in the land of Edom; these are [the sons of Adah. 17 And these are the sons of Reuel, Esau's son: c]hi[ef] Nahath, chief [Zerah, chief Shammah, chief Mizzah; these are the chiefs that came of Reuel in the land of Edom; these are the sons of Basemath, Esau's wife. 18 And these are the sons of Oholibamah, Esau's wife: chief Jeush, chief Jalam, chief Korah: these are the chiefs born of Oholibamah the daughter of Anah, Esau's wife. 19 These are the sons of Esau] (that is, [Edom), and these are] their [chiefs.]

[20 These are the sons of Seir the Horite, the inhabitants of the land: Lotan and Shobal and Zibeon and Anah, 21 and Di]shon and E[zer and Dishan. These are the chiefs that came of the Horites, the children of Seir in the land of Edom. 22 And the children of Lotan were Ho]ri and H[eman. And Lotan's sister was Timna. 23 And these are the children of Shobal: Alvan and Manahath and Ebal, Shepho and Onam. 24 And] these are the children of Zibeon: Aiah [and Anah; this is Anah who found the hot springs in the wilderness as he fed] the donkeys [of Zibeon] his father. 25 And th[ese are the children of Anah: Dishon and Oholibamah the daughter of Anah. 26 And these are the children of Dishon: Hemdan] and Esh[ban and Ithran and Che]ran. 27 These are the chi[ldren of Ezer: Bilhan and Zaavan and Akan.]▲

[35 And Husham died, and Hadad the son of Bedad, who defeated Midian in the field of Moab, became king in his place. And the name of his city was] A[vith. 36 And Hadad died, and] Samlah of Mas[rekah became king in his place. 37 And Samlah died, and] Sha[ul of Rehoboth by the River became king in his place.]▲

[43 . . . chief Mag]diel, chief [Iram. These are the chiefs of Edom, according to their settlements in the land of their possession. This is] Esau, the father of the Edomites.

37 [1 And Jacob lived in] the land of his father's sojournings, in the land [of Canaan. 2 These are the generations of Jacob. Joseph, being seventeen yea]rs [old, w]a[s] feeding the f[lock] with his brothers; [and he grew up with the sons of Bilhah, and with the sons of Zilpah, his father's wives. And J]oseph [brought] a ba[d repor]t about them [to their father.]▲

5 And Jose[ph] had a dream, [and when he told it to his brothers, they hated him all the more. 6 And he said to them, "Plea]se [listen to this] dream [which I had."]▲

[22 And Reuben said to them, "Shed no blood; throw him into this pit that is] in the w[ilderness, but lay no hand upon him"—that he might rescue him from them, to restore him to his father] 23 And whe[n Joseph came to his brothers, they stripped Joseph of his coat—the coat of many colors that was] on him— 24 and they took him [and threw him into the pit. And the pit was empty; there was no water in it.]

[25 And they sat down to eat their meal.] And they lifted up their eyes [and looked, and behold, a caravan of Ishmaelites was coming from Gilead, with their camels bearing spi]ces and balm and my[rrh, on their way to carry them down to Egypt. 26 And Judah said to his brothers, "What profit is there] if we slay [our brother and conceal his blood? 27 Come, and let us sell him to the Ishmaelites, and not lay our hands on him;] for he is our brother, our fle[sh." And his brothers listened to him. 28 And when the Midianite merchants passed by, they pul]l[ed] and lifted Joseph out of [the pit and so]ld [him to the Ishmaelites for twenty pieces of silver. And they brought Jose]ph [to] Egy[pt.]

[29 And when Reu]ben [returned] to th[e pit, behold, Joseph was not in the pit; he tore his clothes. 30 And he returned to his brothers, and sai]d, "The bo[y is not there; and I, where shall I go?"]▲

39 [11 And about this time he we]nt to the house to do his work; and none of the men [of the house were there. 12 And she caught him by his garment,] saying, "Lie with me." And he left his garment in her hand and fled, and we[nt out. 13 And when she saw that he had lef]t his garment in her hand and run out, 14 she called to the men of her house, and spo[ke to them, saying, "See, he has brought in] a Hebrew to [u]s to take advantage of us. He came in to me to lie with me and I screamed. [15 And when he heard tha]t I screamed and called out, he left his garment by me and fled, and went out." [16 And she kept his garment with h]er until his master came home. 17 And she spoke with [these] words, [saying, "The He]brew [servant,] whom you have brought to us, came in to me to

---

Chapter 37. 4QGen^e: 37:1–2, 27–30; 4QGen-Exod^a: 37:5–6, 22–27.
Chapter 39. 4QGen-Exod^a: 39:11–23.

take advantage of me. 18 And when I screa[med and called out, he lef]t [his garment beside me] and ran out."

19 And when his master heard the words of [his] wife, [which she spoke to him, saying, "After] this [man]ner your servant did to me," his anger was great. 20 And J[oseph]'s master took [him, and put him into] the prison, the place where the king's prisoners were bound, and he was the[re in the prison. 21 But the Lo]RD [was] with Joseph, and showed kindness to him, and gave him favor in the sight of the keeper of the pri[son. 22 And the keeper of the prison char]ged Joseph with all the prisoners who were in the pris[on; and whatever they did there, he was responsible for it.] 23 The keeper of the prison paid no attention to anything [in his care, because the LORD was with him, and that which he d]id, the LORD made to prosper.

40 [1 And after these things, the] cu[pbearer of] the king of Egypt and the b[aker] offended their lord the king of Egypt. ▲

[12 And Joseph said to him,] "This [is its interpretation: the three branches are three days; 13 within three more days] Pharaoh [shall lif]t [up your head and restore you to your office; and you shall give Pharaoh's cup into his hand, after the former manner when you were his cupbearer."] ▲

[18 And Joseph answered and said, "This is its interpretation: the three baskets are th]ree [d]ays. [19 Within three more days Pharaoh shall lift up your head from off you, and shall han]g you on a tree and [the birds] shall e[at your flesh from off you."]

[20 And on the third day, which was] Pharaoh's *birth*[*da*]*y*,[18] he [made a feas]t for all [his] serva[nts and he lifted up the head of the chief cupbea]rer and the head [of] the chief ba[ke]r among his servants. 21 And he rest[ored the chief cupbearer to his cupbearing again;] and he gave the cup [into Pharaoh's hand;] 22 but [he hanged the] chief [baker as Joseph had interpreted to them. 23 Yet] the chief cupbearer [did not remember J]oseph, but forgot him.

41 [1 And at the end of two full years, Pharaoh had a drea]m: and behold, he stood by the river. 2 And behold, [there came up] out of the river [seven cows, sleek] and fat, and they fed among the ree[ds. 3 And beh]old, seven [other] cows [came up after them out of] the river, ugly and *th*[*in*,[19] and] stood by [the other cows upon the bank of the] river. 4 And the ug[ly] and gaunt cows ate up [the seven] sleek and fat [cow]s. So Pharaoh awoke. [5 And he slep]t and dreamed a second time: and behold, [seven] ears of grain came up upon one stalk, healthy

---

Chapter 40. 4QGen-Exodᵃ: 40:1; 4QGenᶜ: 40:12–13, 18–23; 4QGenᵉ: 40:18–23.

18. Masculine 4QGenᵉ. Feminine MT SP.

Chapter 41. 4QGenᶜ: 41:1–11; 4QGenᵉ: 41:1–8, 35–44; 4QGenʲ: 41:15–18, 23–27, 29–36, 38–43.

19. 4QGenᵉ SP. *gaunt* MT.

[and good. 6 And behold, seven ea]rs, *and*[20] blasted by the east wind, came up after them. 7 And [the ears, thi]n [*and*] *blasted by the east wind*,[21] swallowed up the seven healthy and full ears. And [Pharaoh] awoke, and behold, it was a dream. 8 And in the morning his spirit was troubled and he sent and called for all the magicians of Egypt, and all its wise men. And Pharaoh told them his dreams but there was none that could interpret them for Pharaoh.

9 Then spoke the chief cupbearer to Pharaoh, saying, "I do remember my sins this day: 10 Pharaoh was angry with his servants, and put me in jail in the house of the captain of the guard, me and the [chi]ef baker. 11 And we had a dream in one night, [I and he; we each dreamed according to the interpretation of his dream.]"▲

[15 And Pharaoh said to Joseph, "I have had a dream, and there is none that can interpret it, and I have been told of you, that when you hear a dream you can] interpret [it."]

■ *The scroll labeled 4QGen^j contains the precursor to the following reading found in both the Septuagint and the Samaritan Pentateuch texts. Because of the potentially arrogant interpretation of this particular version—it could be read as "Apart from me [Joseph], God will give no answer concerning the welfare of Pharaoh"—it is possible that a scribe in antiquity removed the second negative to protect the character of Joseph. 4QGen^j (with the Septuagint and the Samaritan Pentateuch) may, in fact, represent the original version.*

[16 And Joseph answered Pharaoh, saying, *"Apart from Go*]d, *the welfare of Phar*[*aoh*] *shall receive no answer."*[22] [17 And Pharaoh spoke to Joseph, "In my dream, behold, I stoo]d upon the brink of the river, 18 and beho[ld, there came up out of the river seven cows, fat] and sleek, and th[ey] f[ed among the reeds . . .]▲

[23 ". . . and behold, seven ears, w]ith[er]ed, th[in, and blasted by the east wind, came up after them. 24 And the] *sev*[*en*][23] thin [ea]rs [swall]ow[ed up] the [seven] good ears. [Now, I told it to the magicians, but there was none that could interpret it] for me."

25 And Joseph said t[o Pharaoh, "The dreams of Pharaoh are one and the same; what] God is about to d[o he has declared to Pharaoh. 26 The seven good cows] are [seven] years; [and the seven good ears are seven years: the drea]ms [are] one and the same. [27 And the seven lean and ugly cows that came up after them] ar[e seven year]s, [and also the seven empty ears blasted by the east wind; they

---

20. 4QGen^e. *thin and* 4QGen^c MT SP LXX.

21. 4QGen^c LXX. Not in MT SP.

22. 4QGen^j SP LXX. *It is not in me; God will give Pharaoh a suitable answer* MT.

23. 4QGen^j LXX. Not in MT SP.

shall be seven years of famine. 28 That is the thing which I spoke to Pharaoh; what God is about to do he has shown Pharaoh. 29 Behold, seven years of great abundance are coming throughout all the land of Egy]pt; 30 and [after them] came[24] [seven years of] famine; [and all the pl]enty [shall be forgotten] in the land of Egypt; [and the famine] shall destroy [the land. 31 And the pl]enty [shall not be known] in the land [because] of that famine [which follows; for it shall be ve]ry [severe.] 32 And the reason that the dream was repeated to Pharaoh [is because the thing is established] by God and [God] will shortly [bring it about. 33 Now therefore let Pharaoh look for] a man who is discerning and wise [and set him] over [the land of Egypt. 34 Let] Pharaoh [do this,] and let him appoint o[verseers over] the land, [and collect a fifth part of the produce of the land of E]g[y]pt in the s[eve]n years of a[bundance. 35 And let] them [gathe]r [all the food of] these coming good [years,] and store [the grai]n under [the authority of Pharaoh as food for the cities, and let them guard it. 36 And the food shall be] a reserve for the land against the se[ven years of famine, which shall be] in [the land of Egypt; that] the land might not be *destroyed*[25] by the famine."

[37 And the plan appeared good to Pharaoh,] and [to all his servants. 38 And] Pharaoh said to [his] s[ervants, "Can we find such a one as this,] a man [in wh]om is [the] spirit [of the gods?" 39 And] P[haraoh said to Joseph,] "S[in]ce God has shown [you all of this, there is none so discerning and *wiser*] than[26] you. 40 You shall be over [my house, and all my people] shall su[bmit to your word. Only in] the throne will I be greater than you." 41 And [Pharaoh] sa[id to Joseph, "See, I] have set [y]ou over all the land of Eg[ypt." 42 And Pharaoh took his signet ring from] his hand, and put it [upon Joseph's hand, and arrayed him in robes of fine linen, and put a gold] chain about [his] nec[k. 43 And he had him ride in] hi[s second chariot; and they cried before him,] "Bow the knee!" [And he set him over all the land of Egypt.] 44 And [Pharaoh] said [to Joseph, "I am Pharaoh, and without you shall no man lift up his hand] or [his foot in all the land of Egypt."] ▲

42 [15 . . . by this you shall be tested: by the life of Pharaoh, you shall not go forth from here unless your youngest brother] comes [here. 16 Send one of you to get your brother, and the rest of you shall remain confined that your words may be tested to see whether you are telling the truth. I]f not, by the life of Phar[aoh you are surely spies. 17 And he] put [the]m together i[n] j[ail for] three [d]ays.

18 And [Joseph] said [to them] on the [t]hird da[y,] "Do [thi]s and li[ve: for] I

---

24. 4QGen[j]. *shall come* MT SP LXX.

25. 4QGen[e]. *cut off* MT SP.

26. 4QGen[j]. *wise as* MT SP.

Chapter 42. 4QGen[j]: 42:15–22, 38; 4QGen[e]: 42:17–19.

f[ear G]od. [19 If] y[ou be honest men, let] *the*[27] [o]ne of your brothers be confined in [you]r [prison,] and the rest of you g[o, carry grain for the fami]ne of your households 20 and bri[ng] your [youngest] brother to me; so [your words] might be veri[fied, and] you shall not di[e]." And [they] did so. 21 And they said to [on]e another, "Cer[ta]inly we are being punish[ed] because of our brother. For [we] saw the distress of his s[oul,] when [he] pleaded [wi]th [us, but we would not listen;] therefo[re thi]s distress has co[me] upon us." 22 And *them Re[uben answered*[28] saying, "Did I not speak] to you, [say]ing, 'Do [not] s[in] against the b[oy'; and you would not listen? Now we must pay for the bloodshed."]▲

38 And he said, ["My son shall not go down with you; for his brother is dead, and he only is left. If] harm [should come to him] on the journey [you are taking, then will you bring down my gray hairs to Sheol with sorrow."]

43 [1 And the] famine was severe in the land. [2 And when they had eaten all the grain which they had brought out of Egy]pt, [their father] said [to them, "Go back, buy us a little more food."]▲

[5 But if you will not send him, we will not go down; for] the man [sai]d [to us, "You shall not see my face unless your brother is with you." 6 And Israel said,] "Why did you treat me so badly by t[elling the man yo]u [had another brot]her?" [7 And they said, "The man asked specifically] about us and about [our] family, [saying, 'Is yo]ur [father still] alive? Do [you have another brother?' And we answered his] qu[estions. How could we have known] that he would say, ['Bring your brother down?'" 8 And Judah said to Israel his father, "S]end [the boy with me and we will arise and go; that we may live and] not die, we and you and also our little ones. 9 I myself will be surety for him; *and*[29] [you may hold me] responsible [for him. If] I [do] n[ot return] him to you and set him before you, then let [me] bear the blame for[ever. 10 If] we [had not delay]ed, surely we could have returned twice by now."

[11 And] the[ir] father Israel [said to th]em, ["If it] must be so, do thi[s:] take some of [the choice fruits of the land in your vessels, and take them down to the man as a prese]nt, a little [balm, and a] litt[le honey, spices and myrrh, nuts, and almonds. 12 And take double the money in] your [hand;] and the money that was retur[ned in the mouth of your sacks return in your hand. Perhaps it was an oversight.] 13 And [take] your brother, [and arise, return to the man; 14 and may God Almighty grant you compassion before the] man, [that he may re]le[ase to you your other brother and Benjamin. And as for me, if I be bereaved,] I [am berea]ved."▲

---

27. 4QGen^j SP. Not in MT.

28. 4QGen^j. *Reuben answered them* MT SP LXX.

Chapter 43. 4QGen^j: 43:1–2, 5–8; 4QGen^e: 43:8–14.

29. 4QGen^e. Not in MT SP LXX.

45 [14 And he fell up]on [his brother] Benjamin's neck and wept; [and Be]n[jamin] wep[t upon his neck. 15 And he kissed all his brothers] and wept u[pon th]em, and afterwards his brothers talked wi[th him.]

16 And when the news [was heard in Pharaoh's ho]use, sa[y]ing, "Jo[seph's brothers have come," it] pleased Pharaoh and his servants. 17 And [Pha]raoh s[aid] t[o Joseph, "Say t]o your brothers, 'Do this: load up your b[ea]sts [and get up and] go [to the land of Canaan,] 18 and [tak]e your fat[her] and your households [and come t]o [me;] and I will [give you the best of the land of Egyp]t, and you shall eat [the fa]t [of the land. 19 Now yo]u [are commanded, do this: take] wag[ons from the land of Egyp]t [for] y[our litt]le [ones, and for your wives, and bring your father, and come. 20 Also do not concern yourself with your belongings; for the best of] all the la[nd of Egypt is yours.' "]

[21 And the children of Israel did so, and] Joseph [gave them wagons, according to the order of Pharaoh, and gave them provision for the trip.] 22 T[o each of them he gave changes of clothing; but to Benjamin he gave three hundred pieces of silver, and five changes of clothing. 23 And to his father he sent the following: ten donkeys loaded with the good things of Egypt, and ten female donkey]s loade[d with grain and bread and provision for his father on the journey.]▲

[26 And they told] him, [say]ing, ["Joseph is still alive, and he is ruler over all the land of Egypt." And he was numb, for he believed them] not. [27 And they told him all the words of Joseph which he had said to them; and when] he saw [the wagons which Joseph had sent to carry him, the spirit of their father Jacob revived.] 28 And [Israel] sai[d, "It is enough; Joseph my son is still alive: I will go and see him before I die."]▲

46 [7 . . . his sons, and his sons' sons with him, his daughters, and his sons' daughters, and he brought all his offspring with him] *to* Egypt.[30]

[8 And these are the names of the children of Israel who came] *to* [Egyp]t,[31] Jacob [and his sons: Reuben, Jacob's firstborn. 9 And the son]s of Reuben: Hanoch, [and Pallu, and Hezron, and Carmi. 10 And the sons of Simeon: Jem]uel, and Jamin, [and Ohad, and Jachin, and Zohar, and Shaul the son of a Canaanite woman.] 11 And the sons of Levi: [Gershon, Kohath, and Merari.]▲

47 [13 And there was no food in all the land, for the famine was very severe, so that the land of Egypt and the land of Canaan fainted because of the

---

Chapter 45. 4QGen^j: 45:14–22, 26–28; 4QGen-Exod^a: 45:23.

Chapter 46. MasGen(?): 46:7–11(?).

   30. Lacking directive particle MasGen. Directive particle MT SP.

   31. Lacking directive particle MasGen. Directive particle MT SP.

Chapter 47. 4QGen-Exod^a: 47:13–14.

fami]ne. 14 And [Joseph] gath[ered up all the money that was found in the land of Egypt and in the land of Canaan for the grain which they] bou[ght, and Joseph brought the money into Pharaoh's house.]▲

48 1 And a[fter] these [things] Joseph was told, "Behold, [your father is sick."] And he t[ook with] him [his two sons,] Manasseh and Ephrai[m. 2 And] Jacob [was told,] saying, ["Behold,] your [son] J[o]seph has come to you." And Israel [strengthened] himself and [sat up on the bed. 3 And Ja]cob [said] to [Joseph, "God] Almighty appeared t[o me at Luz in the lan]d of Canaan, and blessed [me, 4 and said] to me, 'Be[hold, I will] make you fruitful, [and multiply you, and I will make of you a company of peoples, and will give this] land [to your offspring after you as an everlasting possession.'] 5 And now [your] two son[s, who were born to you in] the land of Egypt [before] I came to you in Eg[ypt, are mine; Ephrai]m and Manasseh, even as R[euben and S]imeon are mine. 6 And your [children] which *others*[32] are born [to you] shall be yours; they shall be called by the name of th[eir] brothers in their inheritance. 7 And as for me, [when] I [ca]me from Paddan, [Rac]hel died, to my sorrow, in the land of Canaan on the way, when there was still *some distance*[33] to come to *Ephrath*[34] (that is,[35] Bethlehem)."

8 And Israel saw Joseph's sons and said, "Who are these?" 9 And Joseph *said,*[36] "They are my sons whom God has given me here." And he said, "Please bring them to me, and I will bless them." 10 Now the eyes of Israel were dim because of *old age*[37] so that he could not see. And he brought them close to him, and *he embraced them, and kissed them.*[38] 11 And Israel said to Joseph, ["I had not thought I would see your face again, and behold, God has let me see your children also."]▲

[15 And he blessed Joseph, and said, "The God] befo[re whom] my [fathe]rs Abraham [and Isaac did walk, the God who has fed me all my life to this day, 16 the ange]l who has redeemed me from [al]l evil, [bless the boys; and may they be called by my name, and the name of my fathers Abra]ham and Isaac; [and may they grow into a multitude in the midst of the earth."]

Chapter 48. 4QGen[f]: 48:1–11; 4QGen-Exod[a]: 48:2–4, 15–17, 18–22.

32. 4QGen[f]. *after them* MT SP.

33. 4QGen[f]. This unique and uncertain expression shows a slight variance as compared to MT and SP.

34. 4QGen[f]. *Ephrath. And I buried her there on the way to Ephrath* MT SP LXX.

35. Feminine 4QGen[f] MT qere SP. Masculine MT ketib.

36. 4QGen[f]. *said to his father* MT SP LXX.

37. 4QGen[f] SP. *age* MT.

38. 4QGen[f]. *he kissed them, and embraced them* MT SP LXX.

[17 And when Joseph saw that his father laid] his right [ha]nd [upon the h]ead of Ephraim, [it displeased him, and he took hold of his father's hand so as to remove it from Ephraim's head to Manasseh's head. 18 And Joseph said to his father, "Not so, my father, for this is the firstborn. Put] your [r]ight [hand upon his head." 19 And his father refused and said, "I know, my son, I know.] He shall [als]o beco[me a people, and he also shall be great, but his younger brother shall be greater than he, and his offspring shall become a multitude of nation]s." 20 And he blessed them t[hat] day, [saying, "By you Israel will bless, saying, 'May God make you like Ephraim and] Manasseh.'" And he [set] Ephraim before Manasseh. 21 And [Israel] s[aid to Joseph,] "Behold, [I am about to die, but] God [will be with] you, and br[i]ng you again to the la[nd of your fathers.] 22 And I [have given you one portion more than your brothers, which I took from the hand of] the Amor[ite with my sword and with my bow."]

49[1 And Jacob called to his sons, and said, "Gather yourselves together, that I may tell you that which will happen to] you [in the latter days. 2 Assemble yourselves and listen, you sons of Jacob; and listen to Israel] your father.

[3 "Reuben, yo]u [are my firstborn,] my might, [and the beginning of my strength, the preeminence of dignity, and the preeminence of power. 4 Turbulent as wate]r, [you shall] not [have the preeminence, because you went up to your] father's [b]ed, [then you defiled it; he went up to my couch.]

[5 "Simeon and Levi are brothers; their swords are weapons of violence. 6 Let my soul not come into their council; let my glory not be united with their] asse[mbly, for in their anger they killed men, and with pleasure they hamstrung oxen. 7 Let their anger be cursed, for it was fierce; and] their [wrat]h, [for it was cruel. I will scatter them in Jacob, and disperse them in Israel.]

[8 "Judah, your brothers shall praise you; your hand shall be on the nec]k of your enemies; [your father's sons shall bow down before you."]▲

50[26 So Joseph died, being a hundred and ten years old; and they embalmed him, and he was put in a coffin] in E[gypt.]

Chapter 49. 4QGen-Exodᵃ: Gen 49:1–5; 4QGenᵉ: 49:6–8.

Chapter 50. 4QpaleoGen-Exod¹: 50:26?

EXODUS

The second book of the Bible, Exodus, tells of the God who rescued Israel from Egypt, the giving of the Law, and the building of the Tabernacle. This history of Israel, with its main character—Moses the lawgiver—is no less compelling today than it was over two thousand years ago. What do the Dead Sea Scrolls have to say concerning this critical ancient document?

Outnumbered among the biblical manuscripts only by Genesis, Deuteronomy, Isaiah, Psalms, and 1 Enoch, the eighteen manuscripts of Exodus attest to the popularity of this book in the Qumran community. Seventeen of the manuscripts were discovered in four of the eleven caves in the vicinity of Wadi Qumran—one in Cave 1, three in Cave 2, twelve in Cave 4, and one in Cave 7—while one was found in a cave in the cliffs of Wadi Murabbaʻat that had been used as a hideout by rebels of the Bar Kokhba revolt (132–35 CE).[a] Taken together, these eighteen manuscripts attest to parts of each of the forty chapters in the book of Exodus.

Like the manuscripts of the book of Genesis, Exodus gives additional evidence that the five books known as the Torah were often copied together in the same scroll. Two scrolls preserve portions of Genesis,[b] one shows Exodus to have been followed by Leviticus,[c] while the remains of the scroll from Wadi Murabbaʻat include fragments of Genesis and Numbers in addition to Exodus. Thus the Torah appears to have been well established as a collection at least two centuries before the coming of Jesus.

In the main, the text of Exodus recorded in the Dead Sea Scrolls is that of the Masoretic Text. Indeed, even the scroll known as pap7QLXXExod—a Greek text from Cave 7—is more closely aligned to the Masoretic Text than it is to the

---

a. 1QExod, 2QExodᵃ, 2QExodᵇ, 2QExodᶜ, 4QGen-Exodᵃ, 4QExodᵇ–4QExodᵉ, 4QExod-Levᶠ, 4QExodᵍ, 4QExodʰ, 4QExodʲ, 4QExodᵏ, 4QpaleoGen-Exodˡ, and 4Qpaleo-Exodᵐ, pap7QLXXExod, MurExod.   b. 4QGen-Exodᵃ, 4QpaleoGen-Exodˡ.
c. 4QExod-Levᶠ.

Greek Septuagint. An examination of the following pages will show, however, that variants exist in fourteen of the eighteen manuscripts. Three of the four remaining scrolls—2QExod^c, 4QExod^h, 4QExod^k—amount to a grand total of only thirty words, hardly enough to establish the character of the text. The scroll labeled MurExod, however, is clearly unique. Although running for 144 words, it is identical in every detail to the traditional Hebrew Bible. The late date of this scroll—the early second century CE—gives evidence for an established Hebrew text by the end of the first century of the common era.

The scroll known as 4QpaleoExod^m is also a manuscript of great significance. Fragments of forty-three columns have survived, making it the most extensive manuscript found in Cave 4. In addition, it witnesses to an expanded textual tradition that formed the foundation of the Samaritan Pentateuch. A remnant of the Samaritan community, which figures prominently in the New Testament Gospels, uses a form of this Bible to this day. The harmonizations that are prevalent in this text will be highlighted in the translation that follows.

There is no doubt that Exodus was recognized as "God's word" among the members of the Qumran community. The book was quoted a dozen times in nonbiblical scrolls, introduced with such phrases as "for thus it is written" (1QS 5:15). In addition to such citations, Exodus was the frequent subject of a popular method of biblical interpretation found among the Dead Sea Scrolls. *A Commentary on Genesis and Exodus* (4Q422) is an example of this method, known among researchers as the "rewritten Bible." Although it has been suggested that such commentaries were created for popular use, the fragmentary nature of the remaining documents does not often reveal the exact point of the rewriting. However, the sheer number of scrolls that engage in this type of retelling clearly underscores the prominence of the genre, as well as the popularity of the book of Exodus, which was so often the subject of interpretation.

It should not be surprising that the book of Exodus was also a topic of legal discussion. Well-known passages concerning the law of damages (Exod 21:19, 28–29), first fruits (Exod 22:29), and proper sacrifice are rehearsed in *A Commentary on the Law of Moses* (4Q251). Exodus 22 through 35—along with portions of Leviticus, Numbers, and Deuteronomy—forms the foundation of the largest nonbiblical scroll, the *Temple Scroll,* a work that purports to be a new Torah for the Last Days in which God speaks to Israel—evidently through Moses—in the first person.

In keeping with the Last Days focus of the *Temple Scroll* (a focus that is clearly evident elsewhere the Dead Sea Scrolls), Exodus 15:17–18—"The place, O LORD, which you have made for your dwelling, the sanctuary, O LORD, which your hands have established"—is interpreted by 4Q174 (3:3) as a new temple prepared for the end times. This time of future glory was envisioned as the setting for the arrival of the inspired Interpreter of Scripture (4Q174 3:12) and the royal Messiah, the Branch of David (4Q174 3:12–13).

1

■ *4QpaleoGen-Exod^l—containing portions of twenty-two chapters—is one of the most complete manuscripts witnessing to the text of Exodus. Both 4QpaleoGen-Exod^l and 4QpaleoExod^m (see note at 6:25) are written in an ancient Hebrew script known as paleo-Hebrew. The fact that there are only eight biblical manuscripts written in this script, all of them representatives of the Torah (Gen–Deut) except 4Qpaleo-Job^c, suggests that this ancient script was reserved for especially important books.*

1 *These*[1] are the names of the sons of Is[rael, who came to Egy]pt with Jacob *their father;*[2] they came each one with his household. 2 R[e]uben, S[imeon, Levi, and Judah,] 3 *and*[3] Issachar, *and*[4] Zebulun, and Benja[min,] 4 Dan and Naphtali, [Ga]d and [Asher.]

■ *Verse 5 below witnesses to the reading* seventy-five *found in the Greek text of Exodus as well as at Acts 7:14 (see also Gen 46:27). The Masoretic Text and the Samaritan Pentateuch read* seventy. *The New International Version has chosen to note this as a marginal reading. To date, this is the only variant from Exodus reflected in any modern translation.*

[5 And all the souls that c]ame out of the loins of J[acob were] *seventy-five*[5] *souls.*[6] 6 And [Joseph] died, [and all his brethren, and all th]at [generation.] 7 And the children of Israel were fruitful, and incre[ased greatly, and multiplied, and be-came exceedingly mighty; and the land was filled with th]em.

Chapter 1. 4QExod^b: 1:1–6, 16–21; 4QpaleoGen-Exod^l: 1:1–5; 4QGen-Exod^a: 1:3–17, 22; 2QExod^a: 1:11–14.

  1. 4QpaleoGen-Exod^l. *And these* MT SP LXX.

  2. 4QExod^b LXX. Not in MT SP.

  3. 4QGen-Exod^a SP. Not in MT LXX.

  4. 4QGen-Exod^a SP. Not in MT LXX.

  5. 4QExod^b 4QGen-Exod^a LXX. *seventy* MT SP.

  6. 4QExod^b LXX. *souls and Joseph was in Egypt already* 4QpaleoGen-Exod^l 4QGen-Exod^a MT SP.

[8 Now there arose] a new [ki]ng over Egypt, who [did] not [know Joseph.
9 And he said to his people, "Behold, the people of the children of Israe]l are
more and mightier than we. 10 Come, let us deal wisely [with them, else they
multiply and when a war occurs,] they also [j]oin [themselves] to our enemies,
and fight against us, and go up out of t[he land." 11 Therefore they set taskmasters over them to afflic]t them with their burdens. And they built store-cities for
Pharaoh: [Pithom and Raamses. 12 But the more] they afflicted *them,*[7] the more
they[8] multiplied and the more *they increased greatly.*[9] And they were in dread [be-
cause of the chil]dren of Israel. 13 And the Egyptians made [the children of] Israel [serve with] rigor; 14 and *he*[10] made their lives bitter with hard service, in
mortar and in brick, [and in all manner of service in the field,] all their service, in
which they made them serve with rigor, [. . . ? . . .] *and Egypt was in dread because
of the children of Israe[l].*[11]

[15 And the king of Egypt spoke to the Hebrew midwives]—the name of the
one was Shiphrah, and the name of the other Puah—[16 and he said, "When]
you [act as a midwi]fe [to the Hebrew women, and see them upon the birth-]
stool, if it is a son, then you shall kill him; but if [it is a] daughter, [then *you shall
preserve*] *her.*"[12] [17 But the midwives feared God, and did not] do as the king of
E[gypt] commanded them, but saved [the males alive. 18 And the king of Egypt
called for the] *Hebrew*[13] [midwi]ves, and said to them, "Why have [y]ou don[e this
thing, and have saved the males alive?"] 19 And the midwives said to Pharaoh,
"Because [the Hebrew women are] not as the Egyp[tian] women; [for they are
lively,] and deliver [before] the midwife comes to them." 20 And God dealt
well with the mi[dwives, and the people multiplied, and became very mighty.
21 Then because the mi]d[wives feared Go]d, [he made households] for [them.
22 And Pharaoh charged all his people, saying, "Every son that is b]orn [you shall
cast into the river, and every daughter you shall save alive."]

2 [1 And there went a man of the hous]e of Levi and took as a wife a daughter
of Levi. [2 And the woman conceived, and bore a son, and when she saw that]
he [was a beautiful child,] she hid him for three months. 3 And when she could
no [long]er hide him, she to[ok an ark of bulrushes for him,] and daubed it with

---

7. 2QExod[a] LXX. *him* 4QGen-Exod[a] MT SP.

8. 2QExod[a] LXX. *he* 4QGen-Exod[a] MT LXX.

9. 2QExod[a] LXX. *he spread out* MT LXX 4QGen-Exod[a].

10. 4QGen-Exod[a]. *they* MT SP LXX.

11. 2QExod[a]. Not in MT SP LXX.

12. 4QExod[b] SP (variant spelling). *she shall live* MT. *preserve her* LXX.

13. 4QExod[b]. Not in MT SP LXX.

Chapter 2. 4QGen-Exod[a]: 2:1–5; 4QExod[b]: 2:2–18; 4QpaleoGen-Exod[l]: 2:10, 22–25.

slime and with pitch; and she put the child in it, *and said to her servant, "Go,"*[14] [and she] laid *it*[15] in the reeds by the river's brink. [4 And his sister stood afar off,] to know what would be done to him.

5 And the daughter of Pharaoh came down to bathe at the river; [and her maidens walked along by the ri]ver[side;] and she saw the ark among the reeds, and sent her handmaid [to fetch it. 6 And she opened it] and *saw*[16] the child; and b[ehold,] the baby [was crying. And] *the daughter of Pharaoh*[17] [had compassi]on on him, [and said,] "This [is one of the Hebrews' children."] 7 Then his sister said to Pharaoh's daughter, "Shall I go and call you [a nurse from the Hebrew women,] *and she shall nurse*[18] the child for you?" 8 And Pharaoh's daughter said to her, "Go." And the [maiden] went [and called the chi]l[d's mother. 9 And] Pharaoh's [daught]er [said] to her, "Take this child, [and nurse it for me, and I will give you your wages." And the woman took the child, and nursed it. 10 And the child grew, and she brought him to Pharaoh's daughter, and he became her son. And she called] his n[ame] Moses, [and said, "Because I drew him out of the wate]r."

[11 After] those *many*[19] [days, when Moses had grown up, he went out to his brethren and looked on their burdens, and he saw an Egyptian striking a He]brew, one of his brethren. 12 And he looked thi[s way and that,] and when he saw [that there was no one, he struck the Egyptian, and hid him in the sand.] 13 And he went out the second day, and *he looked, and behold,*[20] two men of the Hebrew[s] were fighting each other; [and he said to him that did the wrong, "Why do you strike] your fellow?" 14 And he said *to him,*[21] "Who made you a prince and *as*[22] judge over us? Are [you planning] to kill m[e as you killed] the Egyptian?" And Moses was *very*[23] afraid, and said, "Surely the [thing] is known."

[15 Now when Pharaoh heard] this [thing,] he sought to slay Moses. [But] Moses fled [from before Pharaoh, and went to the land of Midian and he sat down] by a well. 16 Now the priest of Mi[d]ian had seven daughters *who shepherded* [*the sheep,*[24] and they came and drew water, and filled] the troughs to water

---

14. 4QExod^b. Not in MT SP LXX.

15. 4QExod^b LXX. Not in MT SP.

16. 4QExod^b SP LXX. *saw him* MT.

17. 4QExod^b SP LXX. *she* MT.

18. 4QExod^b. *that she may nurse* MT SP.

19. 4QExod^b LXX. Not in MT SP.

20. 4QExod^b. *behold* MT SP. *he saw* LXX.

21. 4QExod^b. Not in MT SP LXX.

22. 4QExod^b SP. Not in MT.

23. 4QExod^b. Not in MT SP LXX.

24. 4QExod^b LXX. Not in MT SP.

their father's flock. 17 And [the shepherds] ca[me and drove them away; but Moses stood up and hel]ped them, and watered [their flock. 18 And when they returned t]o [Reuel their father, he said, "How is it that you are come so soon] tod[ay?"]▲

[22 And she bore a son, and he called] his [name] Gersh[o]m; [for he said, "I have been a sojourner in a foreign land."]

[23 Then in] the course of those many [d]ays, [the king of] Eg[ypt] di[ed and the children of Israel sighed] because of the bondage; and they cried, [and their cry came up] to [God because of the bondage. 24 And] God [heard] their groaning, [and Go]d [remembered his covenant with Abraham, with Isa]ac, and with Jacob. 25 And [God saw] the children of I[srael, and God took note of them.]

3 [1 Now Moses] was keeping the flock of J[ethro his father-in-law, the prie]st of Midian; [and he led the flock to the back of the wilderness, and] came [t]o [the mountain of God, to Horeb. 2 And the angel of the LORD appeared to him in a flam]e of fire out of the midst of a bush. And he lo[oked, and behold, the bush burned with fire, and the bush was not consumed.] 3 And Moses said, "I will turn aside now, and [see this great sight, why the bush is not consumed." 4 And when] the LORD [sa]w [that he turned aside to see, God called to him out of the midst of the bush, and said, "Moses, Moses." And he said, "Here am I."]▲

[8 "And I came down to deliver them out of the hand of the Egyptians, and to bring them up out of that land to] a good and large [land,] to a land flowing with milk and honey; to the pla[ce of the Ca]naanite, and the Hittite, *and the Perizzite, and the Amorite,*[25] and the Hivite, *and the Girgashite,*[26] and the Jebusite. 9 And now, behold, the cry of the children of Israel has come to me; moreover I have seen the oppression with which the Egyptians oppress them. 10 Come now therefore, and I will send you to Pharaoh, that you may bring forth my people, the children of Israel, out of Egypt." 11 And M[oses] said [t]o God, "Who am I, that I should go to Pharaoh, and that I should bring forth the children of Israel [out of Egypt?" 12 And he] said, "Certainly I will be with you; and this shall be the token to you, that I have sent you: when you have brought forth the people out of Egy[pt,] you shall serve God upon this mountain."

13 And Moses said to God, "Behold, when I go to the children of Israel and say *to*[27] them, 'The God of your father[s] has sent me to you,' they shall say to me, 'What is his name?' What shall I say to them?" 14 And God said to [Moses, "I] AM

Chapter 3. 4QpaleoGen-Exod^l: 3:1–4, 17–21; 4QGen-Exod^a: 3:8–16, 18–21; 4QExod^b: 3:13–21.

25. 4QGen-Exod^a. *and the Amorite, and the Perizzite* MT SP LXX.

26. 4QGen-Exod^a SP LXX. Not in MT.

27. Variant preposition (same translation: *to)* 4QExod^b. 4QGen-Exod^a MT SP.

THAT I AM." And he said, "Thus you shall say to the children of Israel, 'I AM has sent me to you.'" 15 And *God moreover*[28] said to Moses, *"That*[29] you shall say to the children of Israel, 'The LORD, the God of [your fathers,] the God of Abraham, *and*[30] the God of Isaac, and the God of Jacob, has sent me to you'; this is my name for[ever, and this is my memorial to all generations.] 16 Go, and gather the elders of *the children of*[31] [Israe]l together, [and say] to them, 'The LORD, the Go[d of your fathers,] the God of Abraham, *and the God of*[32] Is[aac, and *the God o]f*[33] Jacob, [has appeared to me,] saying, [I have sure]ly vi[sited you, and seen that which is done] to you in Egypt: 17 and I have said, [I will bring yo]u [up] out of the affliction of Egypt to [the land of the Canaanite, and the Hittite, and the Amorite,] *the Perizzite,*[34] *the Hivite,*[35] and the Jebus[ite,] to a land flowing with milk and honey.' 18 And they shall listen to [your voice; and you shall go, you] and the elders of *the children of*[36] Israel, to the ki[ng of Eg]ypt, and you shall say to him, 'The LORD, the God [of the Hebrews, has met with us;] and now let us go, we pray you, [three day]s' jo[urney] into the wilderness, [that] we may sacrifice to the LORD [our] G[od.' 19 And I] know [that the] king [of Egypt] will [not] allow you [to] go, *except*[37] by a mighty hand. 20 And I will put forth [my hand, and strike Egypt] with all my wonders [which I will d]o in their midst; and after that he will let you go. 21 And *thus*[38] [I will give this people favor in the sight of the] Egyp[tians; and when] you go, [you shall not go empty-handed."] ▲

4 [1 And Moses answered and said, "But behold, they will not believe me, nor listen to my voice; for] they will say, ['The LORD has no]t ap[peared to] you.'" [2 And the LORD said to him, "What is that in your hand?" And he said, "A rod." 3 And he said, "Th]row it *now*[39] on the ground." And he threw it [on the ground,

---

28. 4QExod[b]. *moreover God* 4QGen-Exod[a] MT SP.

29. 4QGen-Exod[a]. *Thus* 4QExod[b] MT SP LXX.

30. 4QGen-Exod[a] SP LXX. Not in 4QExod[b] MT.

31. 4QExod[b] SP LXX. Not in MT.

32. 4QExod[b] LXX. Not in MT. *and* SP.

33. 4QExod[b] LXX. Not in MT SP.

34. 4QExod[b]. *and the Perizzite* MT SP LXX.

35. 4QExod[b]. *and the Hivite* MT SP LXX.

36. 4QExod[b]. Not in MT SP LXX.

37. 4QExod[b] LXX. *and not* MT. *is it not* SP.

38. 4QExod[b]. Not in MT SP LXX.

Chapter 4. 4QExod[b]: 4:1–8; 4QGen-Exod[a]: 4:4–9, 26–31; MurExod: 4:28–31; 2QExod[b]: 4:31.

39. 4QExod[b]. Not in MT SP LXX.

and it became a serpent; and Moses fled from it. 4 And the LORD said to Moses,] "Put forth your hand, and *take hold of* [40] it by the tail"—and he put forth [his hand and took hold of it, and it became a rod in his hand—5 "that they may believe] that the LORD, the God [of their fathers, the God of Abraham, the God of Isaac, and the God of Jac]ob, has appeared to you."

6 And [the Lo]RD furthermore sai[d] *to*[41] him, "Put [your hand inside your cloak." And he put his hand inside his cloak; and when he took it out] *from his cloak,*[42] beh[old, his hand was lepro]us, as white as snow. 7 And he said, ["Put your hand inside your cloak again." And he put his hand ins]ide his cl[oak again; and when he took it out of] his [cloak, behold, it was once again as his other hand;] 8 *"So that*[43] [if they will no]t beli[eve you or listen to the message of the first sign, then they will believe the message of the latter sign. 9 Then if they will not be- lieve] even [these] t[wo signs, nor listen to your voice, then you shall take some water from the river, and pour it upon the dry land; and the water which you take out of the river shall become blood upon the dry land."]▲

[26 So he let] him [alon]e. Then she said, ["You are a bridegroom of blood, because of the circumcision."]

[27 And the LORD said to] Aaron, "Go into [the wil]derness [to meet Moses."] And he went, and met him in the mountain [of God, and kissed him.]

■ *The manuscript known as MurExod begins at Exodus 4:28. This scroll was found south of the Qumran site in Wadi Murabba'at, a hideout for a group of rebels dur- ing the unsuccessful uprising against Rome known as the Bar Kokhba revolt (132–35 CE). The text—dating to the early second century—is identical to the Masoretic Text. This fact gives some credence to the establishment of the traditional Hebrew Bible (at the so-called Council of Jamnia) at the end of the first century CE.*

[28 And Mose]s [told] Aaron all the words of the LORD w[ith which] he had sent him, and all the signs with which he had charged him. 29 And Moses and Aaron went and gathered together all the elders of the children of Israel; 30 and Aaron spoke all the words which the LORD had spoken to Moses, [and] did the signs in the sight of the people. 31 And th[e people] believed; and when [they] heard [tha]t the LORD had visited the children of Is[rae]l [and that he had seen their affliction,] then [they] bowed low [and] w[orshiped.]

5 [1 And afterwar]d Moses and Aaron came [and said to Pharaoh, "Thus says the LORD, the God of Israel: Let] my [peop]le [go,] that they may hold a feast [to

---

40. 4QExod[b]. *grasp* MT SP.

41. Variant preposition (same translation: *to*) 4QExod[b]. MT SP.

42. 4QGen-Exod[a] SP LXX. Not in MT.

43. 4QExod[b]. *And* MT SP LXX.

Chapter 5. 4QGen-Exod[a]: 5:1, 3–17; 4QExod[b]: 5:3–14; 2QExod[c]: 5:3–5; MurExod: 5:3.

me in the wilderness." 2 And Pharaoh said, "Who is the LORD, that I should listen
to his voice to let Israel go? I do not know the LORD, and furthermore, I will not
let Israel go." 3 And they said, "The God of the Hebrews has met with us;] let us
go, we pray you, [three days'] journey [into the wilderness, and sacrifi]ce to the
LORD our Go[d,] else [he fall upon us with pestilence, or] with the sword."
[4 And] the king of E[gypt said to them,] "Why do you, Moses and Aaron, *separate*[44] [the people from their labor? Get back to your work."] 5 And Pharaoh said,
"Behold, the people of the lan[d are n]ow many, [and you make them rest from
their work."] 6 And the same day Pharaoh commanded the taskmasters of the
people, [and] their officers, saying, [7 "You shall no longer giv]e the people straw
to make brick, as up until now: Let them go and [gather straw for themselves.]
8 And the number of the bricks, which they did make *as formerly,*[45] you shall require [of them;] you shall [not] reduce *anything from it,*[46] [for] they [are idle;]
therefore they are *the ones c[rying,]*[47] saying, 'Let us go *and*[48] sacrifice to our God.'
9 Let w[ork] be heavier upon the [men,] that they may *regard*[49] it; and [let them]
no[t] regard lying words."

10 And [the taskmasters of] the people went out, and their officers, and they
spoke[50] to the people, saying, ["Thus sa]ys Pharaoh: 'I will not give you straw.
[11 Go] yourselves, *and*[51] get straw for yourselves where you can find it; for none
of your work shall be diminished.'" 12 So [the people] were scattered abroad
[throughout all the land of] Egypt to gather stubble for straw. 13 And the
taskmasters [were] ur[gent, saying, "Fulfill your works, your] daily [tasks,] as
when there was straw g[iven to you."][52] [14 And the officers of the children of Israel,] w[ho]m Pharaoh's taskmasters [had set ove]r them, [were beaten, and demanded, "Why have you not fulfilled your task both yesterday and today, in
making brick] as be[fore?"]

[15 Then the officers of the children of Israel came] and cr[ied to Pharaoh,
saying, "Why do you treat your servants in this way? 16 There is no straw given
to your servants,] and [they] s[ay to us, 'Make] bricks'; [and behold, your servants
are beaten; but the fault is with your own people." 17 But he said, "You are] id[le,
you are idle; therefore you say, 'Let us go and sacrifice to the LORD.'"] ▲

---

44. 4QExod^b SP LXX. *draw away* MT.

45. 4QExod^b. *formerly* MT SP.

46. 4QExod^b. *from it* MT SP LXX.

47. 4QExod^b. *crying* MT SP.

48. 4QGen-Exod^a 4QExod^b LXX. Not in MT SP.

49. 4QExod^b SP LXX. *do* MT.

50. 4QExod^b SP. *said* MT LXX.

51. 4QExod^b. Not in MT SP LXX.

52. 4QGen-Exod^a SP LXX. Not in MT.

6[3 "And I appeared to Abraham, to Isaac, and to Jacob, as God Almighty; but by my name the LORD] I [was not known to] them. 4 And [I have also] e[stablished my covenant with them, to give them the land of Canaan, the land] in which they sojourned. 5 And moreover, I have heard the groaning of [the children of Israel, because the E]g[yptian]s [k]eep them in [bo]ndage; and I have remembered my covenant. 6 Therefore say to the children of Israel, 'I am the LORD, [and] I will bring you out from under the burdens of the Egyptians, and I will deliver you from their bondage, and I will redeem you with an [outstret]ched arm, and with great judgments. 7 And I will take you for my people, and I will be your God; and you shall know that I am the LORD your God, who delivers you from under [the] b[urdens of the] Egyptians. 8 And I will bring you to the land which I *swore*[53] to give to Abraham, to Isaac, [and] to [J]acob and I will give it to you for a possession; I am the LORD.'" 9 And Moses s[pok]e thus to the children of Israel; but they did not listen to Moses because of their discouragement and cruel bondage.

10 And the LORD spoke to Moses, sa[ying, 11 "Go in, speak t]o [Pharaoh king of Egypt, that he might let the children of Israe]l [go out of his land." 12 And Moses spoke before the LORD, saying, "Behold, the children of] Isra[el have not listened to me; how then shall Pharaoh hear me, for my speech is faltering?" 13 And] the LORD [spoke to Moses and to Aaron, and gave them a charge to the children of Israe]l and to [Pharaoh kin]g of Egy[pt, to bring the children of Israel out of the land of Egypt.]

[14 These are the heads of their fathers' households. The sons of Reuben the firstb]orn of Israel: [Hanoch, and Pallu, Hezron, and Carmi; these are the families of Reuben.] 15 And the sons of Sim[eo]n: Jemu[el, and Jamin, and Ohad, and Jachin, and Zohar, and Shaul the son of a Canaanite woman; th]ese are the families of Simeon. 16 And thes[e are the names of the sons of Levi according to their generations: Gershon, and Kohath,] and Merar[i;] and the length of Le[v]i's life [was a hundred thirty-]seven [years. 17 The sons of Gershon: Libni and Shimei,] according to [their] famili[es. 18 And the son]s of Kohath: [Amram, and Izhar, and Hebron, and Uzziel; and length of Kohath's life was a hundred thirty-three years. 19 And the sons of Merari: Mahli and Mushi. These are the families of the Levites according to th]eir [generations. 20 And Amram took Jochebed his father's sister for himself as a wife, and she bore him] Aaron and Moses. An[d the length of Amram's life was a hundred thirty-seven years. 21 And the sons of I]zhar: Korah, and Nepheg, and [Zichri.]

Chapter 6. 4QExod[h]: 6:3–6; 4QGen-Exod[a]: 6:4–21, 25; MurExod: 6:5–11; 4QpaleoExod[m]: 6:25–30.

53. 4QGen-Exod[a]. *swore with uplifted hand* MT SP LXX.

■ *4QpaleoExod^m, which begins at Exodus 6:25, is the most extensive witness to the book of Exodus. Besides being written in paleo-Hebrew, it is important because it introduces passages from Numbers and Deuteronomy. Before the discovery of the Dead Sea Scrolls, we had known this practice only from the later manuscripts of the Samaritan Pentateuch. 4QpaleoExod^m thus forms an early witness to the form of the Bible that was later adopted by the Samaritan community.*

[25 And Eleazar, Aaron's son, took one of the daughters of Pu]tiel as [a] wife; and she [bore him Ph]inehas. [These are the heads of the fathers' households of the Levites according to their families.]

26 It was the same Aaron and Moses to whom [the LORD said,] Bring the child[ren of] Israel out of the land of Egypt according to their [hosts.] 27 These are the ones who spoke to Pharaoh king of Egypt about bringing the children of [Israel] out from Egypt. It was the same Aaron and Moses.

28 Then on the day when [the LORD] spoke to Moses in the land of Egypt, 29 the LORD [spoke] to Moses, saying, "I am the LORD; speak to Pharaoh king of Egypt [all th]at I speak to you." 30 And Moses said before the LORD, ["Behold, my] speech is faltering; why would Pharaoh listen to me?"

7 1 And [the LORD] said to Moses, "See, I have made you as God to Pharaoh, and Aaron your brother shall be [your prophet.] 2 You shall speak all that I command you, and Aaron your brother shall speak to [Pharaoh that he might let] the children of Isr[ael go out of his land.] 3 And I will harden Pharaoh's heart, [and multiply] my [sig]ns [and] my wonders in the la[n]d of Egypt. 4 But [Pharaoh] will not listen [to you, and I will lay] my hand upon [Eg]ypt, and [bring for]th my hosts, [my people the children of Israel,] out of the land of Egypt by great judgment[s.] 5 And [the Egyptians] shall know [that I am the Lo]RD, when I stretch forth my hand upon Egy[pt,] and [bring out the children of] Israel from among them." 6 And Moses and Aaron did so; as the LORD commanded them, so they did. 7 And Moses was eigh[ty years old, and A]aron eighty-three years old, when they spoke to Pharaoh.

[8 And the LORD spoke t]o Moses and to Aaron, saying, 9 "When Pharaoh shall speak to you, [saying, 'Perform a miracle,'] then you shall say to Aaron, 'Take your rod, and cast it down before [Pharaoh, that it may bec]ome a serpent.' " [10 And] Moses and Aaron went in *before*[54] Pharaoh, and they did so, as [the LORD] had commanded, [and] Aaron [cast down] his rod before Pharaoh and before his servants, and it became a s[erpent. 11 Then] P[haraoh] also [called] for the wise

---

Chapter 7. 4QpaleoExod^m: 7:1–19; 2QExod^a: 7:1–4; 4QGen-Exod^a: 7:5–13, 15–20; 4QExod^c: 7:17–23.

54. 4QpaleoExod^m 4QGen-Exod^a SP LXX. *to* MT.

men and the sorcerers, and they also, the magicians of Egypt, did the same [with] their [secret arts.] 12 For everyone cast down his rod and [they became serpents. But Aaron's] rod [swallowed up] their rods. 13 And [Pharaoh's] he[art] was hardened [and he did] n[ot listen to them, a]s the LORD [had spoken.]

[14 And] the LORD *spoke*[55] to [Mo]ses, ["Pharaoh's heart is stubborn; he refuses to let the peo]ple [go.] 15 Go to Pharaoh in the morning *and as he himself*[56] [goes out to the water, and you shall stand by] the bank of the Nile [to meet him;] and the r[od] which was turned to a serpent you [shall take in your hand. 16 And you shall say] to him, 'The LORD, [the God of the Hebrews, has sent me] to you, saying, Let [my] p[eople go,] that they may se[rv]e me in the wilderness. [And behold, you have not listened until now.] 17 Thus [says] the LORD: By this you shall know that [I am] the LORD: [behold, I will strike] the water which is in the Nile [with the rod that is] i[n my hand,] and it shall be turned to blood.

> ■ *In an expansion of verse 18, 4QpaleoExod^m repeats the command of God from Exodus 7:16–18. This time it is Moses and his brother Aaron reporting the words to Pharaoh himself. This type of embellishment is characteristic of this manuscript and is also echoed in the Samaritan Pentateuch.*

[18 " 'And the fish that are] *in the mi[dst]*[57] the Nile shall die, [and the Nile shall stink; and] the Egyptians shall weary of drinking water from the Nile.' " [*And Moses and Aaron went to Pharaoh] and [s]aid to him, "The Lo[RD God of the Hebrews sent us to you, saying,] 'Let my people go that [they] may serve [me in the wilderness.' And behold, you have not listened until now.] Thus the LORD said: By [this you shall know that I am the LORD: behold I am] s[trikin]g [the water which is in the Nile] with the rod that [is in my hand and it shall be turned to blood] and [the f]ish that are in the mi[dst of the Nile shall die and the river shall stink and the] E[gy]ptians [shall weary] of dri[nking water from the Nile."*[58] 19 And] the LORD [sa]id [to Moses, "Say to Aaron,] 'Take your rod and stretch out [your hand] over the waters of Egypt, over [their rivers, over their streams,] over their pools, and over all [their] po[nds of water, that they may become blood; and there shall be blood throughout all the land of] Egypt, both in vessel[s] of wood and in [vessels of stone.' "]

[20 And Moses and Aaron did so, as the LORD commanded,] and he lifted [up the rod, and struck the waters that were in the Nile, in the sight of Pharaoh, and in the sight of his servants; and all the] waters that were in the Nile [were turned] to blood. 21 And [the fish that were in the Nile died, and the Nile became foul,

---

55. 4QpaleoExod^m SP. *said* MT LXX.

56. 4QpaleoExod^m. *as he himself* SP LXX. *as he* MT.

57. 4QpaleoExod^m. *in* MT SP LXX.

58. 4QpaleoExod^m SP. Not in 4QGen-Exod^a 4QExod^c MT LXX.

and the Egyptians could not drink water from] the Nile, and *blood*[59] was throughout all the land of Eg[ypt. 22 And the magicians of Egypt did the same with] their
[se]cret arts. [And Pharaoh's heart was hardened and he did not listen to them, as
the LORD had spo]k[en. 23 And Pharaoh turned and went into] his [hous]e and
did not take [even this to heart. 24 And all the Egyptians dug round about the
Nile for water to drink, for they could not drink of the water of the Nile.] ▲

8 [1 And the LORD spoke t]o Moses, "G[o to Pharaoh, and say to him, 'Thus
says the LORD: Let my people go, that they may serve me.' 2 And if you refuse
to let them go, behold,] I will strike a[ll your country with frogs; 3 and the Nile
shall swarm with frogs, which shall go up and come into your house, and into]
your [bedroom,] and on your bed, and into the house [of your servants, and on
your people, and into your ovens, and into your kneading-troughs.]

> ■ *In 4QpaleoExod^m—and possibly 4QExod^j—verse 4 is expanded, with Moses re-*
> *peating God's command (8:1–3) before Pharaoh. Verse 5 shows the same pattern as*
> *found in 4QExod^j. The Samaritan Pentateuch also shows these expansions.*

[4 "And the frogs shall come up both upon you, and upon your people,] and
upon all [your servants." *And Moses and Aaron entered before Pharaoh and spoke to*
him, "Thus says the LORD: Let my people go that they may serve me. If you refuse to let
them go, behold, I will strike all your country with frogs and the Nile will swarm with frogs.
And they shall enter your houses] and into [your bed]r[ooms *and upon your beds and in the*
houses of your servants and your people] and into [your] ov[ens *and your kneading bowls*
and upon you and all your servants the f]rogs [will come up."][60] 5 And the LORD s[ai]d
to Mos[es,] "Say to [Aaron, 'Stretch out your hand] with your rod [over the
rivers, over the streams, and ov]er the poo[ls, and make] frog[s] come up [on the
land of Egypt.'" *And Moses said to Aaron, "Stretch out your]* hand [*with your rod and*
make frogs come up on the land of Egypt."][61] 6 And Aaron stretched out his hand over
the waters of Egypt, and the frogs came up and covered the land of Egypt.] ▲

[9 And Moses said to Pharaoh, "Take the honor of telling me what time I shall
entreat for you and for your servants] and for your people, that [the frogs] might
be destroyed [from you and your houses, and remain only in the Nile." 10 And he
said, "Tomorrow." And he said, "May it be according to your word that you may
know that there is n]one like the LORD [our] G[od. 11 And the frogs shall depart

---

59. 4QExod^c. *the blood* MT SP LXX.

Chapter 8. 4QExod^c: 8:1–5 [H 7:26–29; 8:1]; 8:9–18, 22 [H 8:5–14, 12–14, 18]; 4QExod^j:
8:4–5 [H 7:29; 8:1]; 4QpaleoExod^m: 8:4–5, 16–26 [H 7:29; 8:1, 12–22]; 4QpaleoGen-Exod^l:
8:17–19; 23–24 [H 8:13–15, 19–21]; 4QGen-Exod^a: 8:24–26 [H 8:20–22].

60. 4QpaleoExod^m 4QExod^j(?) SP. Not in MT LXX.

61. 4QExod^j SP. Not in MT LXX.

from you, and from your houses, and from your servants, and from your people; they shall remain in the Nile only." 12 And Moses and Aaron went out fro]m Pharaoh, and Moses cried [to the LORD concerning the frogs which he had brought upon Pharaoh. 13 And the LORD did according to the word of Moses; and] the frogs [di]ed out of the [houses, out of the courts, and out of the fields. 14 And they gathered them together in heaps, and the land stank. 15 But when Pharao]h [saw] that there was relief, [he hardened his heart and did not listen to them, as] the Lo[RD had spok]en.

[16 And the LORD said to Moses, "Say t]o Aa[ron,] 'Stretch out *your hand* [*with*[62] your rod, and strike the du]st [of the earth, that it may be]come gnat[s throughout all the land of Egypt.'" 17 And they did so; and] Aaron [stretched out] his hand with his ro[d, and struck the dust of the earth, and there were] gnats [upon ma]n, and upon beast; [all the dust of the ear]th beca[me gnats throughout all the land of E]gypt. 18 And [the] magicians [tried to bring forth gnats with their secret arts, but] they could [not;] and there *were*[63] [gn]ats [upon man and] upon be[ast. 19 Then the magician]s [said] to Pharaoh, ["This is the] finger [of God." But Pharaoh's heart was hardened, and he did not listen t]o them, a[s the LORD had spoken.]

[20 And the LORD spoke to Moses,] *saying,*[64] ["Rise up early in the morning, and stand before Pharaoh, and when he c]omes forth [to the water say] to him, ['Thus says the LORD: Let] my people go, [that they may serve me. 21 Else, if you will not] let my people go, behold, I will send [swarms of fl]ies upon you, and upon [your servants, and upon your people, and into your houses;] and [the houses of the Egyptians] shall be full [of swarms of flies, and also the ground] where they are. 22 And [I will set apart in that day the land of Goshen, where my people dwell, that no swarms of flies shall be there; so that you may know that I, the LORD, am in the land. 23 And I will make a distinctio]n between my people and [your people. This sign shall happen tomorrow.'" *And Moses and Aaron entered before Pharaoh and said to him, "Thus*] sa[*ys the LORD: Let my people go that they might serve me, for if you do not let*] *my people* [*go,*] *behold, I* [*will send swarms of flies on you and on your servants and on your people and in your houses and*] *the houses of Egyp*[*t shall be fil*]*led* [*with swarms of flies and also the land where they are. And on*] *that* [*da*]*y* [*I will set apart the*] *land* [*of Goshen where my people dwell that there might not be any swarms*] *in order that you might know that I the Lo*[*RD am in the midst of the land. And I will distinguish between my people and your people; this sign*] *shall occur tomorrow."*[65] [24 And

---

62. 4QExod[c] SP LXX. Not in MT.

63. Masculine 4QpaleoExod[m]. Feminine MT SP.

64. 4QpaleoExod[m]. Not in MT SP LXX.

65. 4QpaleoExod[m] SP. Not in MT LXX.

the LORD did so; and there came] *very*[66] d[en]se swarms of flies into the house of Pharaoh, [and into his servants' houses. And in all the land of Egypt the lan]d [was ruined] because of the swarms of flies.

25 And [Pharaoh] cal[led for Moses and for Aaron, and said, "Go you, sacrifice] to your God in the land." [26 And] Moses said, ["It is] n[ot proper to do thi]s; [for we shall sacrifice] to the [L]ORD [our God that which is an abomination to the Egyptians. Shall we sacrifice that which is an abomination to the Egyptians in their presence?] Will they not stone u[s?"]▲

9

■ *In the latter half of verse 5, both 4QpaleoExod^m and the Samaritan Pentateuch present Moses and Aaron seeking freedom for the Israelites, repeating God's command (Exod 9:3–5a) in the presence of Pharaoh.*

[5 And the LORD appointed a set time, saying, "Tomorrow the LORD shall do this thing in the land." *And Moses and Aaron entered before Pharaoh and said to him, "Thus says the LORD God of the Hebrews: Let my people go that they might serve me, for if you refuse to let my people go and you still hold on to them, behold, the hand of the LORD will be on your livestock which is in the field, on the horses and the donkeys and the camel]s; on cattle and sheep, a very serious matter. And [the LORD] shall [distinguish between the livestock of Israel and] the livestock of Egypt and nothing shall die from all [that belongs to the children of Israel. Tomorrow the Lo]RD [shall do] this thing in the land."*[67] 6 And the LOR[D] did [that thing the next day, and al]l the cattle of the *Egyptians*[68] died; but not [one] of the cattle of the children of Israel [died. 7 And Phar]aoh [sent,] and behold, there was not even one of the cattle of *the children of*[69] Israel that had died. But [the heart of Pharaoh] was stubborn, [and he did not let] the people [go.]

[8 And the] L[ORD sp]oke [t]o Moses and to Aaron, *saying,*[70] "Take handfuls [of ashes from the furnace, and have Moses toss it] *in*[71] the air in the sight of Pharaoh.

---

66. 4QpaleoExod^m SP. Not in MT LXX.

Chapter 9. 4QpaleoExod^m: 9:5–16, 19–21, 35; 4QGen-Exod^a: 9:8(?); 4QExod^c: 9:10–12, 15–20, 22–25, 27–35; 4QpaleoGen-Exod^l: 9:25–29, 33–35; 2QExod^a: 9:27–29.

67. 4QpaleoExod^m SP. Not in MT LXX.

68. 4QpaleoExod^m LXX. *Egypt* MT SP.

69. 4QpaleoExod^m SP LXX. Not in MT.

70. 4QpaleoExod^m LXX. Not in MT SP.

71. 4QpaleoExod^m SP. *into* 4QGen-Exod^a MT.

9 And it shall become fine dust over *the land*[72] of Eg[ypt, and shall bec]ome [b]oils breaking out with sores [upon man and upon bea]st throughout all the land of Egy[pt." 10 And they took ashes from the furnace,] and stood befo[re Pharaoh;] and M[oses] sprinkled it [up toward heaven; and it became a boil breaking out with sores upon man and upon beas]t. 11 And [the magicians] could not [stand before Moses because of the boils; for the boils were] on the magicians, and on all the Eg[yptians. 12 And the LORD hardened the heart of Pharaoh, and he did not listen to them, as] the LORD [had spok]en [to Moses.]

[13 And the LORD said to Moses, "Rise up early in the morning and stand before Pharaoh and say to him, 'Thus says the L]ORD, the Go[d of the Hebrews: Let my people go, that they may serve me. 14 For this time I will s]end [all my plagues upon your heart, and upon your servants, and upon your people, that you may know that there is none like me in all the] earth. 15 F[or if by no]w I had put forth [my hand and struck you and your people with a plague, you would have been cut off from the earth.] 16 But [for this reason I have made you stand: to show] you [my] power, [and to dec]lare my name throughout [all the earth. 17 Yet you still exalt yourself against my people and will not let them go. 18 Behold, tomorro]w [about this time I will cause a very] heavy hail [to fall, such as has not been in Egypt since the day it was founded up until] now.

> ▨ *In the latter half of verse 19, 4QpaleoExod^m and the Samaritan Pentateuch show Moses and Aaron once more reciting God's lengthy command (Exod 9:13–19a) to Pharaoh.*

19 "'And now therefore bring in your [ca]ttle and all that [you have in the field, for eve]ry [man and beast that shall be found in the field and shall not be brought] home, the [hail] shall come do[wn up]on them [and] they [shall di]e.'" [*And Moses and Aaron entered before Pharaoh and said to him, "Thus says the LORD, the God of the Hebrews: Let my people go that they may serve me. For this time I will send all my plagues upon your heart, and upon your servants and your people that you may know that there is none like me in all the earth, For now I have sent forth my hand to strike you and your people with a plague and cut you off from the land. But, indeed, for this reason I have allowed you to stand, to show you my power and to declare my name throughout the earth. Yet still you exalt yourself against*] my [*peop*]le by not letting [*them*] go. Behold, [*tomorrow about this time*] I [*will cause very heavy hail to fall, such as has not been in*] Egypt *since the day* [*it was founded even until now. Now therefore send, gather your cattle and all tha*]t *you have in the field; every man* [*and beast that shall be found in the field and shall not be brought home,*] *the hail* [*shall come down*] *upon them,* [*and they shall die."*][73] 20 The one who feared [the word of the LORD among the servants of Pharaoh

---

72. 4QpaleoExod^m. *all the land* MT SP LXX.

73. 4QpaleoExod^m SP. Not in 4QExod^c MT LXX.

hurried his servants] and hi[s] cattle into [the houses. 21 And the one that did not regard the word of the LORD left his servants and h]is [cattle] in the f[ield.]

[22 And the LORD said to Moses, "Stretch forth your hand toward hea]ven that hail might [fall on all the land of Egypt, on man, and on beast, and on every herb of the field, throughout the land of Egypt." 23 And Moses stretched forth his rod toward heaven, and the LORD sent thunder and hail, and fire ran down] to the earth; and the L[OR]D brought hail [upon the land of Egypt. 24 So there was hail, and fire mingled with the hail, very severe,] such as [had not been in] all the land [of Egypt since it had become a nation. 25 And the hail struck throughout all the land of Egyp]t [all that was in the field, both man and beast;] and [the hai]l [struck] every [herb of the field] and [shattered every tree of the field. 26 Only in the land of Goshen, where the children of Israel were, wa]s [there no hail.]

27 And [Pharaoh sent, and called for Moses and Aaron, and said to them, "I have sinned this ti]me; the LO[R]D is righteous, and I and my people [are wi]c[ked. 28 Entreat the LORD, for there has been] enough [of] God's thunderings and hail *and fire;*[74] [and I will let you go and] you shall [stay no] longer." 29 And Moses said [to him,] "As soon as I have gone out of the city, I w[ill spre]ad out my hands to the LORD, the thunders shall cease, and there shall be no more hail; t[hat you may know that] the ear[th] is the [L]ORD's. [30 But as for y]ou and your servants, [I] know t[hat you will not yet] fear the *Lord* GOD."[75] 31 And the f[lax and the barley were ruined, for *the flax was in bl]oom and the ba[rley was in the ea]r.*[76] 32 But the w[heat] and the spelt w[ere] not [ruined, for they had not yet come up. 33 And Moses w]ent out [of the city from Pharaoh] and spread out his hands [t]o the L[ORD, and the thunder]s [and] hail cea[sed, and the rain was no longer poured on the earth. 34 And when Pharaoh saw that the rain] and the hail and the thunders [had ceased, he] si[nned once agai]n [and hardened his heart, he and his servants. 35 And] the heart of Pharaoh [was ha]rd[ened, and he did not let] the children of I[srael go,] as [the L]OR[D] had spo[ken by] Moses.

10 1 And [the LORD said to Moses,] "Go in to Ph[araaoh, for I have hardened his] he[art] and [the] heart of [his] ser[vants that I may show these my signs] amo[ng them,]

▪ *The indication in verse 2 that a recitation of God's mighty acts is to be passed down to future generations of Israelites elicits the following command in both 4Qpaleo-Exod^m and the Samaritan Pentateuch.*

---

74. 2QExod^a LXX. Not in MT SP.

75. 4QExod^c SP. *Lord God* MT. *LORD* LXX.

76. 4QExod^c. *the barley was in the ear and the flax was in bloom* MT SP LXX.

Chapter 10. 4QpaleoGen-Exod^l: 10:1–5; 4QpaleoExod^m: 10:1–12, 19–28; 4QExod^c: 10:1–5, 7–9, 12–19, 23–24.

[2 and that you may speak in the hearing of your son, and of] your son's son, [that which I have done] in Egy[pt, and] my signs [which I have performed among them, that] you [may kno]w that [I am the LORD. *And you shall say to Pharaoh, 'Thus says the LORD, the God of the Hebrews: How long will you refuse to humble yourself before me? Let my people go, that they may serve me. For, if you refuse to let my people go, behold, tomorrow I will bring locusts to your country, and they shall cover the face of the earth, so that one will not be able to see the earth. And they shall e]at [the remnant which escaped, which remains to you from the hail, and shall eat every tree which grows for you out of the field. And your houses shall be fill]ed, [and the houses of all your servants, and the houses of all the Egyptians; as neither your fathers nor your fathers' father]s [have seen, since the day that they were upon the earth unto this day.'"]*[77]

[3 And Mo]ses [and Aaron went to Pharaoh and sa]id to him, "Thus says the L[ORD, the G]od of [the Hebrews: How] long [will you refuse to humble yourself before me? Let] my people [go,] that [they may serve me.] 4 For if yo[u] refuse [to let my people] go, [behold, tomorrow will I bring lo]custs into [your] c[ountry. 5 And they shall cover the fa]ce [of the earth, so that one shall not be able to se]e the earth. And they shall eat [the] r[emnant which escaped, which remains to you from the hail, and shall eat] every *herb of the land, and all the* [*fruit of the*[78] tree which grows for you out of the field. 6 And your houses shall be filled,] and the houses of all your servants, and the ho[uses of all the Egyptians; as neither your fathers nor your fathers' fathers have seen, since the day that they were up]on the [ear]th to [this] d[ay." And he turned, and went out from Pharaoh.]

[7 And] Pharaoh['s servants said] to him, ["How long shall this man be a snare to us?] Let the me[n] go, [that they may serve] the LORD their God; [do you not know that Egypt is ruined?" 8 And] Mos[es] and Aaron [were broug]ht again to P[haraoh and he said to them, "Go, serve the LORD your God;] but who are the ones that shall go?" 9 And [Moses] s[ai]d, ["We will go with] our young and [with our old;] with [our] son[s] and with our daughters, with our flocks and with our herds [will we go; for we must hold a feast to the LORD." 10 And he said] to them, "The LORD will indeed be with yo[u, if I let you and your little ones go. Look out, for] your purpose is [ev]il. 11 It will not happen! [Go now, just the men, and serve the LORD, for that is what] you are asking." And [they were driven out from Pharaoh's presence.]

[12 And] the LOR[D s]aid to Mos[es, "Stretch out your hand over the lan]d of Egyp[t for the locusts, that they may come upon the land of Egypt, and ea]t [every plant of the land, even all that] the hail [has left."] 13 And M[ose]s [stretched forth his rod over the land of Egypt and the LORD brought an east wind upon the land all that day] and all night; when it w[as] morning, [the ea]st [wind]

---

77. 4QpaleoExod^m SP. Not in 4QpaleoGen-Exod^l 4QExod^c MT LXX.

78. 4QpaleoExod^m SP. Not in MT LXX.

brought [the locusts. 14 And the locusts went up over all the land of Egypt and settled] in all the borders of E[gypt; the situation was desperate;] there had [never] been such a swarm of locusts, [nor shall there ever be such again. 15 For they covered the face of the whole] earth so that the land was *destroyed;*[79] [and they ate every] herb of the l[and, and all the fruit of the trees which the hail had left. And] there remained [no] green thing, neither tree nor plant [of the fie]ld, through all the lan[d of Egypt. 16 Then Pharaoh hurriedly called for Moses and Aaron and he said, "I have sinned against the L]ORD your God and against [you.] 17 Now therefore *forgive,*[80] [I pray you, my sin just this once, and pray to the LORD your God that he may remove this death from me." 18 And he went out from Phar]aoh, and prayed t[o the LORD. 19 And the LORD] shifted [the wind to a strong west wind which took up the locusts and drove them into the Red Sea; there remained not one locust in all the] border of E[gypt. 20 But the LORD hardened Pharaoh's heart and he did not let the children of Is]rael [go.]

21 And the LORD *spoke*[81] to Moses, "Stret[ch out your hand toward heaven that there may be darkness over the land of Eg]ypt."[82] 22 And Moses stretched out [his] ha[nd toward heaven and there was a thick darkness in all the land of Eg]ypt for three days; [23 they could] not [see one another, n]o o[ne] rose [from his place] for three days; but all the children of [Israel had light in their dwellings. 24 And] Pharaoh [called] to Moses *and to Aaron,*[83] and said, "G[o, serve the LORD; just] leave [your flocks and] your [h]erds behind; [your little ones may] also go [with you." 25 And Moses said, "You must also allow us to have] sacrifices and [burnt offerings that w]e may sacrifice [to the LORD our God.] 26 Our [catt]le m[ust also go] with us; not [a hoo]f *is*[84] left behind. For [we must use some of them to serve the Lo]RD ou[r] God; and we know not [what we will] need to serve [the LORD until we get there."] 27 But the LORD hardened [Pharaoh's] heart, [and] he would not [let them go. 28 And Pharaoh said to him,] "Go away from [me, take care not to see my face again; for in the day you see my face you shall die."]

11 [3 And the LORD gave the people favor in the sight of the Egyptians and also the man Moses was very great *in the mids]t of*[85] [the] land [of Egypt, in the sight of Pharaoh's servants, and in the sight of the people.]

79. 4QExod^c LXX. *darkened* MT SP.

80. Plural 4QExod^c SP LXX. Singular MT.

81. 4QpaleoExod^m. *said* MT SP LXX.

82. 4QpaleoExod^m. *Egypt, even darkness which may be felt* MT SP LXX.

83. 4QpaleoExod^m SP LXX. Not in MT.

84. 4QpaleoExod^m LXX. *shall be* MT SP.

Chapter 11. 2QExod^a: 11:3–7; 4QpaleoGen-Exod^l: 11:4–10; 4QpaleoExod^m: 11:8–10; 4QExod^c: 11:9–10.

85. 2QExod^a. *in* MT.

4 And Moses [sai]d *to Phara[oh,*[86] "Thus says the LORD: About midnight I will go out into the midst of] Egypt 5 and all [the] firstborn [in the land of Egypt] shall die, [from the firstborn of Pharaoh that sits upon h]is [throne] to the first-born of the slave girl [who is behind the mill; and all the firstborn of cattle as well. 6 And there shall be] a great [cr]y throughout all [the] land [of Egypt, such as there has not been before, nor shall be any again.] 7 But against any of the children of Is[rael not even a dog will bark, against man or beast,] that you [may know] that [the LORD makes a distinction between the Egyptians and Israel. 8 And] all these your servants [shall come down to me and bow down before me, saying, 'Go,] you and all the people [who] follow you.' And after that [I will go out." And he went out from Pharaoh with great] anger.

9 And the LORD said to Mos[es, "Phar]aoh [will not listen to you] that my wonders may be multiplied in the land of Egypt." 10 And M[oses and Aaron did] all the[se] won[ders before Phara]oh; and the LORD hardened Phar[ao]h's heart, and he did not let the ch[ildre]n [of Israel go out of his land.]

12 1 And the Lo[RD] spoke to Moses and Aaron in the land of Egyp[t, saying,] 2 "This [month] shall be to you the beginning of months; it shall be the f[irs]t month of the year for you. [3 Speak to al]l the congrega[tion of] *the children of*[87] Isr[ael,] saying, 'In the tenth day of this [mont]h [every man] shall take [a lamb for himself, a lamb] *for [each] household, a l[amb according to the] f[ather]s' house-holds.*[88] 4 And if the household is too little [for a lamb, then he and his neighbor nex]t to his house [shall take] one according to the number of the persons; [ac-cording to what] each man [eats you shall make your count for the lamb.] 5 Your [lamb] shall be [without blemish, a ma]le a year old. [You shall take it] from the shee[p or from the goats, 6 and you shall ke]ep [it] until the fourteenth day of the [same] m[onth. And] the whole assembly of the congregation of [*the children of*][89] Israel shall kill *them*[90] at evening. 7 And [they] shall t[ake some of] the blood and put it on the two doorposts and on the lintel of the house[s in] which they shall eat i[t.] 8 And they shall eat the flesh in the same night, roasted with f[ire, and they shall eat it with unleavened bread] on [bitter herbs. 9 Do not] eat any of it

---

86. 2QExod[a]. Not in MT SP LXX.

Chapter 12. 4QpaleoGen-Exod[l]: 12:1–12, 42–46; 4QpaleoExod[m]: 12:1–2, 6–8, 13–15, 17–22, 31–32, 34–39; 4QExod[c]: 12:12–16, 31–48; 2QExod[b]: 12:26–27(?); 2QExod[a]: 12:32–41.

87. 4QpaleoGen-Exod[l] SP LXX. Not in MT.

88. 4QpaleoGen-Exod[l]. *according to their fathers' household, a lamb for each household* MT SP LXX.

89. 4QpaleoGen-Exod[l] SP LXX. Not in MT.

90. 4QpaleoExod[m]. *it* MT LXX SP.

raw or *cooked or boiled*[91] with w[ater, but roast it with fire, its head with] its [leg]s and with its inner parts. 10 And you shall not leave any of it [until the morning, but that which remains of it until the morning] you shall burn [with fire.] 11 And thus shall you eat it: with y[our] loins [girded, your sandals on your feet, and] your [staff in your hand;] and you shall eat it hurriedly; [it is the LORD's Passover. 12 For I will go through the land of Egypt] in that night and will strike all the firstborn [in the] land [of Egypt, both man and beast. And] I will execute [judgmen]ts [against all the] gods of Egy[pt;] I am the LORD. 13 And [the blood shall be a sign for you on the houses where you live.] And when I see the blood, I will pass over you, and n[o plague shall be upon you to destroy you, when I strike the land of] Egypt.

14 "'And [thi]s day shall be [a memorial for you and yo]u [shall] keep [it as a feast] to the LORD; throughout your generations you shall keep it as a feast by a lasting ordinance. 15 For seven days [shall you ea]t un[leavened bread.] But [on] the first [da]y [you shall put away leaven] from your houses, f[or whoev]er e[a]ts leavened bread [from the] firs[t day until the seventh day,] th[at person shall] be cut off [from Israel. 16 And on] the first [day there shall be a holy convocation, and again on the seventh day; no work shall be done on them, except that which every man must eat, that is all that you may do. 17 And you shall observe the feast of unleavened bread,] for [on this very day I brought your hosts out of the land of Egypt. Therefore you shall observe this day throughout your generations by an ordinance forever. 18 In the firs]t [month, on the fourteenth day of the month at evening, you shall eat unleavened bre]ad, until [the twenty-fi]rst [day of the month at evening. 19 No leaven] shall be found in your [houses for seven days,] for whoever [eats that which is leavened, that person shall be cut off from the congregation of Is]rael, whether he be a sojourner, or one that is born [in the land. 20 You shall eat nothing leavened; in all your habitations shall you eat] unleave[ned b]read.'"

[21 Then Moses called for all the elders of Israel and sai]d to [th]em, ["Go and select lambs according to your families and slaughter the Passover lamb. 22 And yo]u [shall take a bunch of hyssop and dip it in the blood that is in the basin, and strike the lintel and the two doorposts with the blood that is in the basin; and no one shall go out of the door of his house until the morning.] ▲

[26 "And when you]r [children shall say to you,] 'W[hat do you mean by this service?' 27 you shall say, 'It is the sacrifice of the Lo]RD['s Passover,] who p[assed over the houses of the children of Israel in Egypt, when he struck th]e Egyptians, [and delivered our houses.'" And the people bowed down and worshiped.] ▲

31 And h[e called for Mo]ses and Aar[on] at night, and said, ["Rise up, go out]

---

91. 4QpaleoGen-Exod[l]. *boiled at all* MT SP LXX.

from among [my] people, [both you and the children of Israel, and go, serve the
LORD, as] you [have s]aid. [32 Take] both your flocks and your herds, [as you have
said, and be gone.] And b[less me also."]

[33 And the Egyptian]s [were urging the] people to send them out of the land
hurriedly, for they said, ["We shall all be dead." 34 And the people took] their
dough before it was leavened, their kneading bowls bound up in their *garments*[92]
on their shoulders. 35 And the children of Israel [did according to the word of]
Moses; and they *asked*[93] for articles of si[lve]r [and arti]cles of [gold] and for
clothing. 36 And the LORD gave the people favor in the sight of [the Egyptians, so
that they let] them [have what they as]k[ed. And they] plun[dered] *the Egyptians*.[94]

[37 And] the children of Israel journeyed from Rameses to Succoth, about six
hundred thousand men on foot, besi[des child]ren. 38 And a mixed multitude
also went up with them; [along with] flocks and herds, livestock in great numbers. 39 And they b[aked] unleavened cakes of the dough which they brought out
of E[gyp]t, for it was not leavened, because *Egy[p]t drove them out*[95] and they could
[no]t [w]ait, nor had they prepared provi[sions] for themselves.

> ◼ *The Septuagint, the Samaritan Pentateuch, and apparently the Apostle Paul in
> Galatians 3:17 understood the 430 years of Exodus 12:40 to include the three gen-
> erations from Abraham to Jacob. The Masoretic Text and 4QExod*[c] *confine the period
> to the time in Egypt alone. The debate evident in these ancient texts continues to this
> day.*

[40 Now the time t]hat the children of Israel [dwel]t in *the land of E[gy]pt*[96] was
four hundred and thirty years. 41 Then at the end of [four hundred and] thirty
years, on the very [day,] all the h[ost]s of the LORD went out from the land of
E[gyp]t. [42 It is a] night [to be observed to the LORD for bringing them out from
the lan]d of Egypt; this night is for the LORD, to be ob[ser]ved by [al]l the children
of Israe[l throughout their generations.]

[43 And the LORD said to Moses and Aaro]n, This is the ordinance of the
Passover: no foreigner shall e[a]t of it, 44 but every [ma]n['s servant that has been
purchased with mo]n[ey,] after you have circumcised hi[m, then he shall eat of it.
45 A sojourner and a hired servant] shall not eat of it. 46 It shall be eaten in one
house; you shall not carry out [any of the flesh] outside of t[he house, nor shall

---

92. 4QExod[c]. *mantles* MT SP.

93. 4QExod[c]. *asked from Egypt* 2QExod[a] MT SP. *asked from the Egyptians* 4QpaleoExod[m]
LXX.

94. 4QpaleoExod[m] LXX. *Egypt* 4QExod[a] MT SP.

95. 2QExod[a] SP LXX. *they were driven from Egypt* MT.

96. 4QExod[c]. *in Egypt* MT. *in the land of Canaan and in the land of Egypt* SP. *in the land of
Egypt and in the land of Canaan* LXX.

you break a bone of it. 47 All the congregation of Isra]el shall celebrate it. [48 And] when a stranger resid[es] with *you*[97] a[nd celebrates the Passover to the LORD, let all his males be circumcised, and then let him come near and celebrate it; he shall be as a native in the land. And] no [uncircum]cised [person shall eat of it.]▲

13 [3 And Mo]ses [said] to the people, "Remember [this day, in which] you [ca]me out from *the land of*[98] Egypt; *for*[99] with a s[trong] hand [the LORD] b[rought] you out from this place; no [leavened bread] shall be eaten. [4 Today,] in the month Abi[b, you] are going out. [5 When the LOR]D *your God*[100] [brings] you to the lan[d of] the Canaanite, the Hittite, *the Hivite, the Amorite,*[101] and the Jebusite, *just as*[102] [he sw]ore to your fathers to give you, a land flowing with milk and h[oney, you shall] keep this service in [this] month. [6 Se]ven d[a]ys [you shall eat unleavened bread, and in the] seventh [day there shall be a feast to the LORD. 7 Unleavened bread shall be eaten for] seven [days; and no leavened bread shall be seen with you, neither shall there be leaven seen with you, in all your borders.]▲

[12 ". . . you shall set apart to the LORD the first offspring of the womb, and every first]born [of every beast; the males shall be the LORD's. 13 And every first-born of a donkey] you shall redeem with a lamb; [and if you will not redeem it, then you shall break its neck. And all the firstborn of man among your sons you shall redeem. 14 So, when your son asks you in time to come, saying, 'What is this?' You shall say to him, 'By the strength of hand the LORD brought us out from Egypt, from the house of bondage. 15 And when] Pharaoh refused to let us go, the LORD slew all [the firstborn in the land of Egypt, both the firstborn of man, and the firstborn of beast. Therefore] I sacrifice to the [Lo]RD every male that opens the womb [but every firstborn of my sons I redeem.' 16 And it shall serve as a sign upon your hand, and for] phylacteries between your eyes that by strength of hand [the LORD brought us forth out of Egypt." *Then M*]*oses and the children of Is-rael sang* [*this song to the LORD, and spoke, saying, "I will sing to the LORD, for he has tri-umphed gloriously: The*] *horse and his rider* [*he has thrown into the sea."*][103]

[17 When Pharaoh had let the people go, God did not lead them by the way of

---

97. Plural 4QExod[c] 4QDeut[j] SP LXX. Singular MT.

Chapter 13. 4QpaleoExod[m]: 13:3–7, 12–13; 4QExod[e]: 13:3–5; 4QExod[d]: 13:15–16; 4QExod[c]: 13:18–22.

98. 4QExod[e] SP LXX. Not in MT.

99. 4QExod[e]. *out of the house of bondage; for* MT SP LXX.

100. 4QExod[e] SP LXX. Not in MT.

101. 4QExod[e]. *the Amorite, the Hivite* MT. *the Amorite, the Perizzite, the Girgashite, the Hivite* SP. *the Hivite, the Girgashite, the Amorite, the Perizzite* LXX.

102. 4QExod[e]. *which* MT SP LXX.

103. 4QExod[d]. Follows 14:31 as 15:1 MT SP LXX.

the land of the Philistines, although that was near; for God said, "Lest the people repent when they see war, and return to Egypt." 18 So God led] the people [about,] by the way of the wilderness [by the Red Sea; and the children of Israel went out of the land of Egypt armed for battle. 19 And Mos]es [took the] bones of J[o]seph with him, for he had solemnly swo[rn the children of Israel, saying, "God will surely visit you;] and you shall carry my bones away with you." 20 And they set out [from Succoth and encamped in Etham, on the edge of the wilderness. 21 And the LORD went] before them [by da]y in a p[illa]r of cloud, to lead them on the wa[y, and by night in a pillar of fire, to give them light, that they might go by day] and by night. 22 The pillar of *cloud*[104] by day, and the pillar of *fire*[105] by night did not depart [from before the people.]

14 [1 And the LORD spoke to Moses, saying, 2 "Tell the children of] Israel to turn back and encamp befo[re] P[i]hahi[ro]th, between Migdol and [the sea, before Baal-zephon; you shall encamp opposite it by] the sea. 3 And P[harao]h will say *to*[106] the children of Israel, 'They are wandering aimlessly in the land; the wilderness [has shut] them [in.' 4 And I will harden Pharaoh's heart,] and he shall pursue [them, and I will be honored by Pharaoh and by all his host; and the Egypti]ans [shall know] that I [am the LORD."] And they did so.

5 And when the king [of Egypt] was told [that the people had fled, Pharaoh and his servants had a change of heart tow]ard the people, and [they said, "What is this w]e have done, th[at we have let Israel go from] serving [us?" 6 And he made ready his chariot, and took his people with him; 7 and he took six hundred of the best chariots,] and all [the] c[hariots of Egypt, and officers over all of them. 8 And] the Lo[RD hardened the heart of Pharaoh king of Egypt; and he pursued the child]ren of Israel, for the children of I[srael were going out boldly.] 9 And the Egypti[ans] pursued [them, al]l [the horses and chariots of Pharaoh, and his horsemen, and his army, and overtook them encamped] by the sea, [beside] Pi[hahiroth,] before B[aal-zephon.]

[10 And when Pharaoh drew near, the children of Israel lifted up their eyes, and behold, the *Egyptians were mar*]*chi*[*ng*[107] after them, and] they were [very] fearful. [And the children of Israel cried out to the LORD. 11 And they said to Moses, "Because there were no graves in Egypt, have you] ta[ken us away to di]e in the wilderness? W[hy have you treated us in this way to bring us out of Egypt? 12 Is this not the word that we spoke to you in Egypt, s]a[y]ing, ['Leave us alone, that

---

104. 4QExod^c SP. *the cloud* MT LXX.

105. 4QExod^c SP. *the fire* MT LXX.

Chapter 14. 4QExod^c: 14:1–13; 4QpaleoExod^m: 14:3–5, 8–9, 25–26; 4QpaleoGen-Exod^l: 14:15–24; 4QExod^g: 14:21–27.

106. 4QExod^c. *concerning* MT SP. *to his people* LXX.

107. 4QExod^c SP LXX. *Egypt was marching* MT.

we may serve the Egyptians'? For it was better for us to serve the Egyptians, than that we should die in the wilderness." 13 And Moses said to] the people, ["Fear not, stand firm, and see the salvation of the LORD which he will perform for you today; for the Egyptians whom you have seen today, you shall never ever see them again. The LORD will fight for you, and you shall hold your peace."]

15 And [the LORD] said [to] Moses, "Why do you cry [out to me? Tell the children of Israel to go forward.] 16 And you lift up your rod, and stretch out your hand over the sea, and d[ivide it, that the children of Is]rael [might go] into the sea on dry ground. 17 And I, b[ehold, I will harden the hearts of the Egyptians so that they go in] after them; and I will be honored over Pharaoh and over all his army, his chariots, and [his horsemen. 18 And the Egypt]ians [shall know] that I am the L[o]RD, when I am honored over P[haraoh,] over his chariots, and over [his horsemen."]

19 And the angel of [Go]d, who had been going in front of the [ca]mp of Is[rael, went around behind them;] and the pillar of [cloud] moved [from in front] of them, and stood [behi]nd [them. 20 And it came between the c]amp of Egyp[t and] the camp of Israe[l; and there was the cloud and the darkness, yet it gave light by night. And the one did not approach the other all that night.]

[21 And Moses stretched out his hand over the sea, and the L]ORD [drove] the sea [back with a strong] eas[t wi]nd [all that night, and turned the sea into dry land;] and the waters were divided. 22 And [the children of Israel] went [into the sea on dry ground; and the waters became a wa]ll [for them] on their ri[ght] and on their left. [23 And the Egyptians pursued, and went] into [the se]a [after them, all of Pha]raoh['s horses,] chariots, and horsemen. [24 Then at the morning watch] the LORD [looked down] on [the army of] the Eg[yptians through the pillar of] fire and of *cloud,*[108] [and confused the army of the Egyptians. 25 And he turned their] c[hariot wh]eels [so that they drove] with difficulty. And [the Egyptians] said, ["Let us] flee fro[m Israel, for the LORD fights for them against the Egyptians."]

26 And [the LORD said to Moses, "Stretch out your hand over the sea that the waters may return upon the Egy]ptians, [upon their chariots, and upon their horsemen." 27 And Moses stretched forth his hand over the sea, and the sea returned to normal i]n the morning; [and the Egyptians fled against it; and the LORD overthrew the Egyptians in the midst of the sea.]▲

15 [9 "The enemy said, 'I will pursue, I will overtake, I will divide the spoil; my desire shall be satisfied with them;] I will draw [my] sw[ord, m]y [hand shall destroy them.' 10 You blew with your wind, the sea covered them; they sank like lead in the mighty waters.]

---

108. 4QExod[g] uncertain.

Chapter 15. 4QExod[d]: 15:1; 4QExod[c]: 15:9–21; 4QpaleoExod[m]: 15:23–27.

[11 "Who is] like you, [O Lor]d, among the gods? W[ho is like you, glorious in holine]ss, [fearful in praises, doing wonders? 12 You stretched out your] right hand, the ear[th] swallowed them.

13 "You in your lovingkindness have led [the peopl]e [whom you have] redeem[ed. You have guided them in] your [strength] to [your holy habitation. 14 The people]s [have heard,] and they tremble; [angui]sh has taken hold of the inhabitants of P[hilistia. 15 Then were the] chi[efs of Edom dis]mayed, [the mighty men of] M[o]ab, tr[emblin]g takes hold upon them; [all the inhabit]ants of Canaan [are melted away.] 16 Terror and dread falls [upon] them; by the greatness of [your] arm [they are as still] as a stone; until your people pass over, O LORD. Until the people [who]m you have purchased pass over. 17 You will bring them in, and plant them in the mountain of [your] inheritance, [the place,] O LORD, [which you have made for yourself to dwell in.] The sanctuary, O LORD,[109] which your *hand has*[110] established. 18 The LORD shall reign *ever*[111] and ever."

19 When the horses of P[haraoh] went in [with] his chariots and with [his] h[orsemen into the sea, the LORD brought back] the waters of the sea upon them; but the children of Israel walked on dry land in the midst of the sea.

20 And Miriam [the prophetess, the sister of Aaron,] too[k a timbrel] in her hand, and all the women went out after her with timbrels and with dances. 21 And Miriam answered them, "Sing you to the L[ORD, for he has triumphed gloriously; the horse and his rider he has thrown into the sea."]

[22 Then Moses ordered Israel to set out from the Red Sea and they went into the wilderness of Shur. They went three days in the wilderness and found no water.] 23 And when they came to Marah, [they could not drink of the waters of Marah, for the]y [were bitter;] therefore [it] was called [Marah. 24 And the people murmured against Moses, sa]y[ing,] "What shall we drink?" [25 And he cried to the LORD, and the LORD showed him a tree, and] he cast it into the waters [and the waters were made sweet. There he made for them a statute and an ordinanc]e, and there he tested them. 26 And [he said, "If you will diligently listen to the voice of] the Lo[RD] your [God,] and [will do that which is right in] his eyes, [and will give ear to his commandments, and] keep [all] his statutes, [I will put none] of the d[isea]ses [up]on you whi[ch I have put upon the Egyptians; fo]r I am the LORD that h[ea]ls you."

27 And [they came to Elim, where were twelve springs of water and seventy palm trees; and they camped] there [by the] waters.

---

109. 4QExod^c SP. *Lord* MT.

110. 4QExod^c SP. *hands have* MT LXX.

111. 4QExod^c SP. *forever* MT.

16 1 And they set out from [Elim, and all the congregation of the children of I]s[rael came to the wi]lderness of Sin, which [is between Elim and Sinai, on the fifteenth day of the second month after their departure from the land of Egypt. 2 And] the w[hole congregation of the children of Israel] murmured [against Moses and against Aaron in the wilderness. 3 And the children of Israel said to them, "If] only we had died b[y the hand of the LORD in the land of Egypt, when we sat by the fleshpots, when we ate our] fill [of bread;] for [you have] brou[ght us forth into this wilderness to kill this whole assembly with hunger."]

[4 Then the LOR]D [said] to Moses, "Beho[ld, I will rain bread from heaven for you, and the people shall go out and gather a day's portion] every day, that I may test them, [whether they will walk in my law or not. 5 And on the sixth day, when] they [prep]are that which [they bring in, it shall be twice as much as they gather daily." 6 And Mo]ses and Aar[on said to all the children of Israel, "At evening you shall know that the LORD has brough]t yo[u out from the land of Egypt; 7 and in the morning you shall see the gl]ory [of the LORD, for he hears your complaints against the LORD; and what are we, that] you complain against us?" [8 And Moses said, "When the LORD gives you flesh to eat in the evening and your fill of bread] in the morn[ing because the LORD hears your complaints which you utter against him, then what are we? Your murmurings are not against us, but against the LORD."]▲

[12 "I have heard the complaints of the children of Israel; speak to them, saying, 'At evening you shall eat flesh and in the morning you shall be filled with bread; and] you [shall kn]ow that [I] am the LORD [your God.'"]

[13 Then at evening the quails came up and covered] the cam[p, and in the] morning there was [a layer of dew arou]nd the cam[p. 14 And when the layer of dew evaporated,] behold, on the [fa]ce of the wilderness *was a thin layer as a flake,*[112] [thin as the frost on the ground. 15 And when the children of] Israel [saw it,] they said one to another, "What is [it?" For they did not know what it was. And Moses said t]o them, "This is [the brea]d which [the LORD] has giv[en you to eat. 16 This is that which] the LORD [has commanded: Each of you] ga[ther from it according to your needs; you shall take an omer to a person according to the number of persons each of you has in his tent." 17 And the children of Israel did so, and they gathered some more, some less. 18 And when they measured it with an omer,] he that gathered m[uch] had [nothing o]ver, [and he that gathered little had no lack; every man gathered according to his need. 19 And] Moses said [to

---

Chapter 16. 4QpaleoExod^m: 16:1, 4–5, 7–8, 31–36; 4QpaleoGen-Exod^l: 16:2–7, 13–14, 18–20, 23–31, 33–36; 1QExod: 16:12–16.

112. 1QExod. *were small flakes* MT SP. *fine as coriander* LXX.

them, "Let no man leave any of it until the morning." 20 But they did not listen]
to Moses, [and some of them left a part of it until the morning, and it bred
worms and became foul. And Moses was angry with them.]▲

[23 And] he said to [them, "This is what the LORD has spoken: Tomorrow is a
solemn rest, a holy sabbath to the LORD. Bake th]at which you will b[ake, and boil
that which you want to boil, and all that is left over put aside] to be kept [until the
morning." 24 And they put it aside until the morning, as Moses had commanded;] and it did not become fo[ul, and there were no worms in it. 25 And
Moses said, "Eat it today, for today is] a sabbath [to the LORD; today you shall not
find it in the field. 26 Six days] you shall g[ath]er [it;] but on [the seventh] day,
[the sabbath, there shall be none."]

[27 Then on the] seventh [day, some of the people] went out [to gather, and
they found none. 28 And the LORD said to Moses, "How long will you refuse to
keep] my [commandments and] my laws? [29 See, the LORD has given you the
sabbath; therefore] he gives you [the bread for two days] on [the sixth] day. [Each
of you stay in his place; let no] one go out of [his] p[lace on the seventh day."
30 So the people rested on the sev]enth [day.]

31 And the house of Israel called [it manna, and it was white like coriander
seed, and the taste of it was like wafers made with hon]ey. 32 And Mos[es said,
"This is what the LORD has commanded: Let an omerful of it be kept throughout
your generations, that] they may see the bread which [I] fe[d yo]u in the
wildern[ess, when I brought you out of the land of] Egypt." 33 And Moses said
to Aaron, "T[ake] a po[t and put an] omer[fu]l of manna [in it,] and place it before the LORD to be kept [throughout your generations." 34 A]s [the LORD] commanded[113] Moses, so Aaron placed it before [the testimony, to be kept. 35 And the
children of Israel ate] the manna for forty years, u[ntil they came to an inhabited
land; they ate the manna] until they came to the borders of the land of C[anaa]n.
[36 Now an omer is a tenth part of an ephah.]

17 1 And all [the congregation of the children of] Israel [journeyed] *by stages
from the wilderness of* [S]in,[114] [according to the commandment of the
LORD, and encamped in Rephidi]m; and there was no [water] for the people to
dr[in]k. 2 So the people [contended] with Moses, and s[aid,] "Give us [water that
we may drink."] And Mos[es] said to them, ["Why do you contend wit]h me?
And[115] why do you test the LO[RD?" 3 And] the people thirsted there for water;
and [the people complained against] Moses, [and said,] "Why have you b[ro]ught

---

113. 4QpaleoExod^m SP. *commanded to* MT LXX.

Chapter 17. 4QpaleoExod^m: 17:1–16; 4QExod^c: 17:1–16; 4QpaleoGen-Exod^l: 17:1–3,
5–11.

114. 4QpaleoGen-Exod^l 4QExod^c. *from the wilderness of Sin by stages* MT SP LXX.

115. 4QExod^c 4QpaleoExod^m SP LXX. Not in MT.

us up from Egyp[t,] to kill us and [our children and our cattle with thirst?" 4 And] Moses [cried] to the LORD, [saying,] "What [shall I do with] this people? [They are almost ready to stone me."] 5 And the LORD *said*,[116] "Pass on before the [people and take with you some of the elders of Israel; and] your [r]od, with which you struck [the] river, [take] in your hand, and go. 6 Behold, [I will stand] before you there [upon the r]ock in Ho[reb; and you shall strike the rock, and] water [shall come out] of it, that the people may drink." And Moses [did so in the sight of the] elders of [Is]rael. 7 And he called the name of the place M[a]ssah and Me[ribah,] because of the c[onten]tion of the children of Is[rael, and because] they te[sted] the Lo[R]D, saying, "Is [the LORD] among us, *and if*[117] not?"

8 Then came Amalek, and fought [wi]th Israe[l in R]ephi]d[i]m. 9 And Moses s[a]id to Joshu[a,] "C[hoose some men for us,] and go out, fight with Amalek. Tomorrow I will stand on the to[p of the hil]l with [the rod of God in my hand." 10 So Joshua did a]s Moses had said to him, and fought with Amalek; and [Moses, Aaron, and Hur went up to the top of the] hill. [11 Then,] when Moses held up his hand, Israel prevailed; and when [he lowered] his hand, [A]malek [prevailed.] 12 But Moses' hands *were*[118] hea[vy,] so they took a stone and [pu]t it under him, and he sat on it; and Aaron [and Hur held up his hands,] one on one side, and [o]ne on the ot[her.] And his hands were steady until [the sun] set. [13 And] Joshua defeat[ed] *Amalek*[119] *and struck them*[120] with the edge of the sword.

[14 And] the L[OR]D said to Moses, "Write this for a memorial in a book, and reh[earse it in the hearing of J]oshua: I will utterly blot out the remembrance of Amalek from under heaven." 15 And [Moses] built [an altar, and] called its name, the LORD is my banner. 16 And he said, "A hand [up]on [the banner of the LORD;] the LORD will have [wa]r with Amalek *for all generations.*"[121]

18 [1 Now Jethro, the priest of Midian,] Moses' father-in-law, [heard] all tha[t Go]d [had done] for Moses [and for Israel his people; ho]w the LORD had brought [Is]rael out of Egypt. 2 And [Jethr]o, Moses' father-in-law, [took Moses'] w[ife] Zipporah, [afte]r he had sent her away, 3 and her two sons. The name of the one was Gersho[m, for] he said, "I [have be]en [a sojourner] in a foreign land"; [4 and the name of] the other was Eliezer, "for t[he Go]d of [my]

---

116. 4QExod^c. *said to Moses* 4QpaleoExod^m MT SP LXX.

117. 4QExod^c. *or* MT SP LXX.

118. 4QpaleoExod^m 4QExod^c SP LXX. *was* MT.

119. 4QpaleoExod^m. *Amalek and his people* 4QExod^c MT SP. *Amalek and all his people* LXX.

120. 4QpaleoExod^m SP. Not in 4QExod^c MT LXX.

121. 4QpaleoExod^m. *from generation to generation* MT LXX. *from all generations* SP.

Chapter 18. 4QpaleoExod^m: 18:1–27; 4QExod^c: 18:1–12; 4QpaleoGen-Exod^l: 18:17–24; 2QExod^b: 18:21–22.

father was my help, and delivered me from the sw[or]d [of Pharaoh." 5 And] Jethro, Moses' [father-in-law, came] with his sons and his wife to Moses in the wilderness where [he was cam]ped, at the mountain of God. [6 And] he said to Moses, "Behold,[122] Jethro, [your] father-in-law,[123] has come to [you,] and your wife and [her t]wo son[s] with her." 7 And Moses went out to meet [his] father[-in-law,] and bowed down [and] kissed him; [and] they asked ea[ch o]th[er] about their welfare, and he brought him[124] into the tent. [8 And Moses told his] father[-in-law] all that the LORD had [d]one to P[ha]raoh and to Egypt for Israel's sake, [all the hardshi]p that ha[d come upon them on the way, and how the LOR]D [had delivered them.] 9 And Jethro rejoiced for all the goodness which [the LORD] had d[one to Isra]el by delivering them out of the hand [of] Egypt.

[10 And] Jethro said, ["Bles]sed be the LORD who has delivered you [out of the hand of the Egyptian]s, and out of the hand of Pharaoh, [wh]o has delivered the people from under the hand of Egyp[t. 11 Now] I know th[at the LORD is greater than all] the gods, because of the incident wh[en they acted insolently] against them." 12 And Jet[hro, Moses' father-in-law,] took a burnt offering and sac[rifi]ces for [Go]d. And Aaron [ca]me, and [all the elders of Israel, to] eat b[read with] Moses' [father-in-]law before Go[d.]

[13 And it came about on the] following d[ay] that [Moses] sa[t to judg]e the people, and t[he people] stood [about Moses] from morning[125] [to the] evening. [14 And when] Moses' [father-in-law saw] all that [he did for the peo]ple, [he said, "What is this thing you] are doing for [the people? Why do you] sit alon[e and all the people stand about you from morning to evening?" 15 And] Moses [said] to [his] father-in-law, ["Because the people come to me to inquire of God. 16 When] they have a problem and[126] they [co]me to me, [I judge betwe]en a man and [his neighbor, and I make known the] statutes of God [and his laws." 17 And Moses' father-in-la]w [sa]i[d] to him, "What [you are doing is] not good. [18 You will surely wear yourself out,] both you and this people th[at is wit]h you. For [the thing is too hea]v[y for you; you are not able to perform it] by [your]self. 19 Now listen to me; I will give you counsel and God [be wi]t[h you. You represent the people before] God [and bring] the matters to God; [20 and you shall teach the]m the statutes and the laws, and sh[all show them] the way in which[127] they must walk and the work that they must do. 21 In addition, you shall

122. 4QpaleoExod^m SP LXX. I MT.

123. 4QExod^c LXX. your father-in-law, Jethro 4QpaleoExod^m MT SP.

124. 4QExod^c SP. they went MT LXX.

125. 4QpaleoExod^m LXX. the morning MT SP.

126. 4QpaleoExod^m LXX. Not in MT SP.

127. 4QpaleoExod^m 4QpaleoGen-Exod^l SP. Not in MT.

look o[ut] for able men from among all the people, those who fear *the* LORD;[128] men of truth, those who hate unjust g[ain; and appoint] *these*[129] over them, to be rulers of thousands, *and*[130] rulers of hundreds, *and*[131] rulers of f[ifties, and rulers of tens.] 22 And let them judge the people at all times and [they shall bring to you] every i[mportant ma]tter, [but every] minor [matter they themselves] shall jud[ge. So it shall] be easier for you and [they shall] b[ear the burden with you. 23 If you shall do] this [thi]ng, [and God so commands you, then] you [shall] be able to endure, and all this people shall also go *to*[132] [their] pla[ce in peace."]

> ▪ *Moses' response to Jethro's suggestion to ease the burden of leadership by establishing a "board of elders" is expanded in 4QpaleoExod^m by replacing Exodus 18:25 with the fuller details of Deuteronomy 1:9–18.*

[24 So Moses listened to the voi]ce [of his] father-in-law [and di]d all that he had sa[id. 25 *And Moses said to the people,*] "*I am* [no]*t able* [*to bear*] *you* [*al*]*one; the* LORD [*your God*] *has multiplied* [*you, and behold, you are*] *this day as the stars of* [*hea*]*ven for* [*mul*]*titude. The* LORD, [*the God of your*] *fathers,* [*made y*]*ou a thous*[*and time*]*s* [*as many*] *as you are, and* [*bles*]*sed yo*[*u, as*] *he has promised you.* [*H*]*ow* [*can*] *I* [*myself*] *alone* [*bear your heavy burden, and your*] *lo*[*ad,*] *your* [*burd*]*en and your strife?* [*Take you wis*]*e* [*me*]*n,* [*and understan*]*ding,* [*and known, according to*] *your* [*t*]*ribes, and I will ma*[*ke them hea*]*ds over y*[*ou. And you answered me, and*] *said,* [*'The thing*] *which you have spoken* [*is good for us to do.*'"] *And he took the heads of their tribes, wise and knowing men, and he appointed*] *them* [*as heads over them; leaders of thousands and leaders of hundreds and leaders of*] *fifties* [*and leaders of tens and officers according to*] *th*[*eir tr*]*ibes.* [*And*] *he commanded* [*the judges, saying, "Hear the causes*] *between* [*your*] *bro*[*thers, and judge righteously between*] *a man* [*and his brother, and the sojourner that is with him. You shall not respect persons in judgment; you shall hear the small and the great alike; you shall not be afraid of the face of man; for the judgment is God's. And the cause that is too hard for you, you shall bring to me, and I will hear it." And he charged them all the matters which they were to do.*[133] 26 And they judged the people at all times; the hard causes they brought to Moses, but every small matter] they [jud]ged themselves. [27 And Moses let his father-in-law depart;] and he *went*[134] into [his own land.]

---

128. 4QpaleoGen-Exod^l. *God* MT SP LXX.

129. 4QpaleoGen-Exod^l. Not in MT SP LXX.

130. 4QpaleoExod^m SP LXX. Not in MT.

131. 4QpaleoExod^m LXX. Not in 4QpaleoGen-Exod^l MT SP.

132. 4QpaleoExod^m SP. *upon* 4QpaleoGen-Exod^l MT.

133. 4QpaleoExod^m SP. *And Moses chose able men of all Israel and made them heads over the people; rulers of thousands, rulers of hundreds, rulers of fifties, and rulers of tens* MT LXX.

134. 4QpaleoExod^m. *went his way* MT SP.

19[1 In] the thir[d month after the children of Israel were gone forth from the land of Egypt, the same day, they came into the wilderness of Sinai.]▲

[7 And Moses came and called for the elders of the people, and set before them all] the[se words which the LORD commanded him. 8 And all the people answered together, and said,] "All [that the LORD has spoken we will do." And Moses reported the words of the people to the Lo]RD. [9 And the LORD said to Moses, "Behold, I am going to come to you in a thick] cloud, [that the people may hear when I speak with you, and may also believe you forev]er."

And Moses told [the words of the people to the LORD. *And the L]ORD sai[d] t[o Moses,*135 *"Behold, I am going to make a covenant. Before] all your people I will [do marvels, such as have not been produced in al]l the earth, nor in [any nation; and all the people] among [which yo]u [are shall see the work of the LORD, for it is an awesome thing that] I [am doing with you."*136 10 And the LORD said to Moses,] "Go to [the people and sanctify them today and tomorrow, and let them wash their garments, 11 and be ready for] the t[hird da]y; [for the third day the LORD will come down in the sight of all] the people upon Mount S[inai. 12 And you shall set bounds for the people round about,] saying, 'Be c[areful that you g]o [not] up on the mountain or tou[ch the edge of it. Anyone who touches the mountain] shall be surely put to death. [13 No] hand [shall touch] him, but [he shall] sur[ely be stoned, or shot through;] whe[ther it be beast or man,] he shall [not] live.' When [the trumpet sounds long, they shall come up to the mountain." 14 And Moses went down from the mountain to the people, and sanctified the peop]le; and they washed their garments. [15 And he said to the people, "Be ready for the third] day; do not go near [a woman."]

[16 Then on the third day, when it was mor]ning, th[ere were thunder and lightning, and a thick cloud upon the mountain, and the sound of a] ve[ry] loud trumpet, [and all the people who were in the camp trembled. 17 And Moses brought the people out of the camp] to meet [God; and they stood at the foot of the mountain.]▲

[23 And Moses said to the LORD, "The people cannot come u]p [to] Mo[unt] S[inai; for you commanded us, saying, 'Set bounds around] the mountain, and sanctify it.' " [24 And the LORD said to him, "Go down and come up again, you] and Aaron with you; but [do not let] the priests and the p[eople br]eak thro[ugh] to c[ome up to the LORD, lest he break forth upon the]m." 25 So Moses went down to the p[eople and told them.]

Chapter 19. 4QpaleoExod^m: 19:1, 7–17, 23–25; 2QExod^b: 19:9; 34:10; 1QExod: 19:24–25; 4QpaleoGen-Exod^l: 19:24–25.

135. 2QExod^b. *he said* MT SP LXX.

136. 2QExod^b. Follows 34:9 as 34:10 4QpaleoExod^m MT SP LXX.

20 1 And God spoke all these words, sa[y]ing, [2 "I am the Lord your God, who b]rought you out of the l[and of Egypt, out of the house of bondage.]▲

[5 "You shall not bow down yourself to them, nor serve them, for I the Lord] your [G]od [am a jealous] G[od, visiting the iniquity of the fathers upon the children, to the third and fourth generation of those who that hate me, 6 and showing] lovingkindness [to thousands, to those who love me and keep my commandments."]▲

[18 And all the people perceived the thunder and the lightning and the sound of the trumpet, and the mountain smoking; and when] the people [saw it, they trembled and stood at a distance.]

▮ *The abbreviated response of the Israelites to Moses' reading of the Ten Commandments in verse 19 below is filled out with a more detailed account from Deuteronomy 5:24–27 in both 4QpaleoExod^m and the Samaritan Pentateuch.*

[19 And they said to Moses, *"Beh]old, [the Lord] our [Go]d has shown us [his glory and his greatness, and w]e have heard [his voi]ce [out of the midst of the fire; we have seen this day that God speaks with man, and he lives. Now therefore why should we die? For th]is [great fire will consume us: if we hear the voice of the Lord] our [Go]d [any more, then we shall die. For who is there of all flesh that has heard the voice of the] li[ving God speaking out of the midst of the fire, as we have, and lived? Draw near, and hear all] that [the Lord our God shall say; and speak to us all t]hat [the Lord our God shall speak unto you; and we will hear it, and do it.*137 But let not God speak with us, lest we die."]▲

[25 "And if you make me an altar of stone, you shall not build it of hewn stones; for if you wield your tool upon it,] you pollute it. 26 And you shall not [go up by step]s to [my altar, that your nakedness might not be exposed on it."]

21 [1 Now these are the ordinances which you shall se]t before them. 2 I[f you bu]y a H[ebrew servant, six years he shall serve: and in the seventh he shall go out free for nothing. 3 If he comes in by himself, he shall go out by himself; if he is married, then his wife shall go out with him. 4 If his master gives him a wife and she bears him sons or daughters, the wife and her children shall be] her master's, [and h]e shall go out [by himself. 5 But if the servant shall plainly say, "I love my] mast[er,] my wife, and [my] child[ren; I will not go out a free man,"]

Chapter 20. 4QpaleoGen-Exod^l: 20:1–2; 1QExod: 20:1; 4QpaleoExod^m: 20:1, 18–19a; 1QExod: 20: 5–6, 25–26.

137. 4QpaleoExod^m SP. Not in MT LXX.

Chapter 21. 1QExod: 21:1–2, 4–5; 4QpaleoExod^m: 21:5–6, 13–14, 22–32; 2QExod^a: 21:18–20(?).

6 then his *master*[138] shall bring him t[o Go]d, and shall bring him [to the door, or to] the doorpost; and his [master] shall bor[e] his ear throu[gh] with [an awl; and he shall serve him forever.]▲

[13 And if it was not premeditated, but God allowed it, then I will appoint you a place] *where*[139] he may flee. [14 But if a man presumptuously attacks his neighbor, intending to slay him, you shall take him] from my altar [that he might die.]▲

[18 And if men contend, and one strikes the other with a stone or with his fist, and he does not die but remains in be]d, 19 if he recovers [and walks about outside with his staff, then the one who struck him shall be free, except to pay for the loss of his time, and shall see that he is fully] recovered.

20 And if [a man strikes his male or female slave with a rod, and he dies by his hand, he shall surely be punished. 21 But if he survives a day or two, he shall not be punished; for he is his money.]

[22 And if men fight together, and hurt a pregnant woman, so that the child is born, and yet no har]m [comes of the incident, he shall] certainly [be fined as the woman's husband demands of him; and he shall pay as the ju]dge[s determine. 23 But if any harm does come of it, then you shall give life for life, 24 eye for] eye, tooth [for tooth, hand for hand, foot for foot, 25 burn for] burn, woun[d for wound, blow for blow.]

[26 And if a man strikes the eye of his male or female slave, and destro]ys it, [he shall let him go] free [on account of his eye. 27 And if] he knocks out [the tooth of his male or female slave, he shall let him go] free [on account of his tooth.]

[28 And if an ox gores a man] or [a] w[oma]n [to death, the ox shall surely be stoned, and its flesh shall not be eaten; but the owner of the ox shall not be liable. 29 But if the ox was in the habit of goring in the past, and its owner] has been warned, [and yet he has not confined it, and it kills a man or a woman, the o]x shall be sto[ned and its owner shall also be put to death. 30 If a ransom is determined against him,] then he shall p[ay the redempti]on of his life according to a[ll that is determined against him. 31 Whether it gores a boy o]r a girl, [according to] t[his jud]gm[ent shall it be done to him. 32 If the ox gores a male or] a female slave, [he shall give their master thirty shekels of] s[ilver and the ox shall be stoned.]▲

22 [1 If] a man [steals] an o[x or a sheep, and slaughters it or sells it, he shall pay five oxen] for the o[x, and four sheep for a sheep.]

---

138. 4QpaleoExod[m]. *masters* MT SP.

139. 4QpaleoExod[m]. *to where* MT LXX.

Chapter 22. 2QExod[b]: 22:1–3, 26–30 [H 21:37; 22:1–2, 25–29]; 4QpaleoExod[m]: 22:4–5, 7–8, 12–14, 17–31 [H 22:3–4, 6–7, 11–13, 16–30]; 4QpaleoGen-Exod[l]: 22:24–25 [H 22: 23–24].

[2 If] the [thief is] found [breaking in and is struck so that he dies, there shall be no bloodguiltiness for him. 3 If the s]un [has risen] o[n him, there shall be bloodguiltiness for him. He shall make restitution; if he has nothing *to p]ay*,[140] [then he shall be sold for his theft. 4 If the theft be found in his hand ali]ve, [whether it be an ox, or donkey, or sheep, he shall pay *two for*] one.[141]

[5 If a man lets a field or vineyard to be grazed over, and then] lets [his b[east] loose, [and it grazes in another man's field, *he shall make compensation from his own field according to his produce, but if the*] *whole* [field is grazed over,[142] he shall make restitution from the best of his own field and from the best of his own vineyard.]

[6 If fire breaks out and catches in thorns, so that the shocks of grain, or the standing grain, or the field is consumed, he that kindled the fire shall surely make restitution.]

[7 If a man gives his neighbor money or stuff for safekeeping, and] it *is stolen*[143] from [the man's] ho[use, if the thief be found, he shall pay double. 8 If the thief] is [no]t fou[nd, then the master of the house shall be brought before God, to see whether or not he has laid] his [ha]nd on [his neighbor's goods.]▲

[12 But if it is stolen from him, he shall make restituti]on [to its owner. 13 If it be torn in pieces, let him bring it for evidence; he shall not] make restitution [for that which was torn.]

[14 And if a man borrows anything from his neighbor, and it is hurt, o]r dies, [its owner not being with it, he shall make full restitution. 15 If its owner is with it, he shall not make restitution; if it was a hired thing, it came for its hire.]

[16 And if] a m[an se]duces [a virgin who is not engaged, and lies] with her, [he shall surely pay a] do[wry for her to be his wife. 17 If her father utterly refuses] to give her [to him, he shall pay money equal to the dowry of] virgins.

[18 You shall not allow a sorceress to li]ve.

[19 Whoever lies with an animal] shall surely be put to de[ath.]

[20 He who sacrifices to any go]d, [except to the LORD only, shall be utterly destroyed.]

[21 And you shall not wrong or oppress a stranger, for you were strangers] in the land of Eg[ypt. 22 You shall not afflict any widow or orphan. 23 If you afflict them at all,] and they cry [o]ut [to me, I will surely hear their cry; 24 and my wrath shall burn, and I will kill] you with the sword; and [your] wiv[es] shall be widows [and your children orph]ans.

25 If you lend money to [my] pe[ople, t]o *poor*[144] among you, you shall not [act

---

140. 2QExod[b]. Not in MT SP LXX.

141. 4QpaleoExod[m] SP. *double* MT.

142. 4QpaleoExod[m] SP LXX. Not in MT.

143. *Niphal* 4QpaleoExod[m] SP. *Pual* MT.

144. 4QpaleoExod[m] SP. *the poor* MT LXX.

as a] c[reditor] to them; [you shall exact no] interest from them. 26 If [you t]ake your neighbor's garment as a pled[ge, you shall restore it] to him before [the sun] goes [down;] 27 for i[t][145] is [his only covering,] it[146] is the cloak for his body, in what [shall he sleep? And] when he cries to me, [I will hear; for] I am [gracio]us.

[28 You shall not revile against] Go[d, n]or [curse a] ruler of your people.

29 You shall not delay to offer [from your harvest and from the out]flow of your presses.

The firstborn [of your sons shall you give to me.] 30 Likewise you shall do with [your] o[xen, and with your sheep; seven] days [it shall be with its mother; on the ei]ghth [day] you shall give [it to me.]

[31 And you shall be holy men to me, therefore you shall not ea]t [any flesh that is torn by beasts in the field; you shall throw it to the dogs.] ▲

23 5 If [you see] the donkey of one who hates [you lying under his burden, you shall resist] abandoning him; [you] shall help release it with him.

6 You shall [not] pervert the ju[sti]ce [due to] your [po]or in his lawsuit. 7 Keep far away from a false matter; [and] do not kill [the inno]cent or righteous: for I will not acquit the guilty. 8 And yo[u shall take no] bribe, for a bribe blinds the eyes of[147] those who see clearly and perverts the words of [the righteous.]

[9 And] you[148] shall not oppress [a stranger,] for you know the heart of the stranger, [because you were strangers in the land of Egypt.]

10 And for six years you shall sow [your land, and shall gather in] its [yie]ld; 11 but on the seventh year you shall let it rest [and lie fallow, so that the poo]r of your people [may eat,] and what they leave the beast of the field shall eat. [In like manner you shall deal with your vineyard, and with] your [olive grove.]

12 Six days you shall do your work, [and on the seventh day you shall re]st, that [your ox and] your donkey may have rest; [and the son of your female slave and the stranger may be] r[efreshed. 13 And in all thin]gs [th]at I have [s]aid to [you take care; and] make [no] mention [of the name of other gods,] nor let [th]em be hea[rd out of your mouth.]

[14 Three times a year you shall keep a feast to me.] 15 The feast of unleavened bread [shall you keep; seven] days [you shall eat unleavened bread,] as I commanded you, [at the time appointed in the month Abib, for in it] you [ca]me out from Egypt. And no[ne shall appear before me empty-handed.]

---

145. Feminine 4QpaleoExod[m] SP MT qere. Masculine MT ketib.

146. Feminine 4QpaleoExod[m] SP MT qere. Masculine MT ketib.

Chapter 23. 4QpaleoGen-Exod[l]: 23:5–16; 4QpaleoExod[m]: 23:15–16, 29–31.

147. 4QpaleoGen-Exod[l] SP LXX. Not in MT.

148. Plural 4QpaleoGen-Exod[l] SP LXX. Singular MT.

[16 Also you shall observe the feast of harvest, the] f[irst frui]ts of your [la]bors [which you sow in the field; and the feast of ingathering, at the end of the year, when you gather in your labors out of the field.] ▲

[29 I will not drive] them [o]ut fro[m before you in one year, lest the land become desolate, and the beasts of the fiel]d [multiply against you.] 30 Little [by little I will drive them out from before you, until you have increased and possess the land. 31 And] I [will *establi*]sh[149] [your border from the Red Sea to the sea of the Philistines, and from the wilderness to the River Euphrates; for I will deliver the inhabitants of the land into] your hand, [and you shall drive them out before you.] ▲

24 [1 And he said to] M[oses, "Come up to the LORD, you and Aaron, Nadab, and Abihu, *Eleazar and*] Ithama[r[150] and seventy of the elders of Israel, and you shall worship at a distance. 2 And Moses] alone [shall come near to the LORD; but they shall not come near; nor shall the people go up with him."]

[3 And Moses came] and told [the people all the words of the LORD and all the ordinances; and all the people answered with] one [voice,] and [said, "All the words which the LORD has spoken will we do." 4 And Moses wrote down a]ll the wo[rds of the LORD, and rose up early in the morning and built an altar at the foot of the mountain, and twelve pillars, according to the twelve tribes of Israel. 5 And he sent young men of the children of Israel, who offered burnt offerings, and sacrificed peace offerings of oxen to the LORD. 6 And] Moses [took half of the blood and put it in basins, and half of the blood he sprinkled on the altar. 7 And he took the] book of the [covenant and read in the hearing of the people; and they said, "All that the LORD has spoken] *we will obey and* [*we will do.*"[151] 8 And Moses took the blood and sprinkled it on the people, and said, "Behold the blood of] the covenant, [which the LORD has made with you in accordance with all] these [words."]

9 Then [Moses, and Aaron, Nadab, and Abihu, *Eleazar and Ith*]amar[152] and [seventy of the elders of] Isra[el] went up. [10 And they saw the God of Israel; and under his feet there was something] like a [paved] wor[k of sapphire stone,] as pur[e as the sky itself. 11 And upon the nobles of the children of Israe]l [he did] not [stretch out his hand; and they beheld God, and they ate and drank.] ▲

---

149. 4QpaleoGen-Exod[l]. *set* SP MT.

Chapter 24. 4QpaleoExod[m]: 24:1–4, 6–11.

150. 4QpaleoExod[m] SP. Not in MT LXX.

151. 4QpaleoExod[m] SP. *we will do and we will obey* MT LXX.

152. 4QpaleoExod[m] SP. Not in MT LXX.

25 [7 . . . onyx stones, and stones to be s]et in the e[pho]d and in the b[reast-plate. 8 And let them make me a sanctuary, that I may dwell among them. 9 According to all that I show you, the patte]rn of the tabernacle, and t[he pattern of all its furniture, thus you shall make it.]

[10 And they shall make an ark of acacia wood, two and a half cubits shall be its length, and a cubit and a half its breadth, and a cubit and a half its height. 11 And you shall overlay it with pur]e [gold, you shall overlay it] within [and without, and you shall make] a molding of *gold*.[153] 12 And [you sh]all ca[st fo]ur ri[ngs of gold for it, and put them on its four feet; and two rings shall be on the one side of it, and two rings] on [the other] side [of it. 13 And you shall make poles of acac]ia wood, and over[la]y [th]em [with gold. 14 And you shall put the poles into the rings] on the sides [of the ark, to carry] the ark with them. 15 The p[oles] shall be left [in the ri]ngs of the ark; [they shall not be taken from it. 16 And you shall put into the ark the testimony which I shall give t]o [you.]

[17 And you shall make a mercy-seat of pure gold, two and a half its length, and a cubit and a half its breadth. 18 And you shall make] two cherubim [of gold; you shall make them of hammered work at the two ends of the mercy-seat. 19 And make one cherub] at the one [en]d, and one cherub [at the other end; you shall make the cherubi]m [of one piece with the mercy-seat] o[n its] two [ends. 20 And the cherubi]m [shall] spread out their wings [upward, covering the mercy-seat with their wings, with their faces facing *one a*]*nother*;[154] the faces of the cherubim shall be toward the [mercy-seat. 21 And you shall put the mercy-seat] on t[op of] the ark; [and in the ark you shall put the testimony that I shall give you. 22 And there I will meet with you, and I will speak] with you from above the [mercy-seat, from between the two cherubim which are upon the ark of the testimony, of all things] which I shall command you for the children of [Israel.]

[23 And you shall make a table of] acacia wood, two cubits shall be [its] le[ngth, and a cubit its breadth, and a cubit and a half its height. 24 And you shall overlay] it with pure gold, and ma[ke a molding of gold round about it. 25 And you shall make a rim] a handbreadth wide round about it; and make [a molding of gold round about the rim. 26 And you shall make four rings of] gold [for it,] and put the [rings in the four corners that are on its four feet. 27 The rings] shall be [clos]e to the rim [as holders for the poles to carry the table. 28 And you shall make the] poles of [acacia] wood [and overlay them with gold, that the table may be carried with them.] 29 And you shall ma[ke its] dis[he]s, [and its spoons, and

---

Chapter 25. 4QpaleoGen-Exod[l]: 25:7–20; 4QpaleoExod[m]: 25:11–12, 20–29, 31–34.

   153. 4QpaleoGen-Exod[l]. *gold round about* MT SP LXX.

   154. 4QpaleoExod[m] SP. *each other* 4QpaleoGen-Exod[l] MT.

its flagons, and its bowls, with *whi*]ch[155] [to pour drink offerings; you shall make them of pure gold. 30 And you shall set showbread upon the table before me always.]

[31 And you shall make a candlestick of pure gold. The candlestick and its base,] its shaft, [its cups, its knobs, and its flowers shall be of hammered work, of one piece. 32 And there shall be six branches] going ou[t of its sides; three branches of the candlestick out of the one side, and three branches of the] candlestick out of [the other] si[de. 33 Three cups made like almond-bloss]oms [on one branch, each with a knob and a flower; and three cups made like almond-blossoms in] the other [branc]h, [each with a knob and a flower; so for the six branches going out of the candlestick. 34 And on the candlest]ick there shall be fou[r cups made like almond-blossoms, each with its knobs and flowers.]▲

26[8 The length of each curtain shall be thirty cubits, and the width of each curtain four cubits; the el]even curtains [shall have the same measurements. 9 And you shall join] fiv[e curtains by themselves, and six curtains by the]mselves, and shall double over [the sixth curtain in the front of the tent.] 10 An[d you shall make *loop*]s *fifty*[156] on [the edge of the curtain that is outermost in the one set,] and fi[fty loops] upon the edge of the curta[in which is outermost in the second set.]

[11 And you shall make fifty] c[la]sps [of] bras[s,] and put the clasps [into the loo]ps, and join [the tent together, that it may be one. 12 And the overlapping part] that remains of the curtains of the tent] the half curtain [that remains, shall hang over the back of the tabernacle. 13 And the] cubit on [the one si]de and the [cubit on the other side,] of that which remains [in the length of the curtains of the tent, shall hang over the] s[ide]s of [the tabernacle on this side and on that side,] to [cover it. 14 And you shall make a covering for the tent of ra]ms' [skins dyed] r[ed, and a covering of fine skins above.]

[15 And you shall make the boards] for the tabernacle [of acacia wood, standing upright.]▲

[21 . . . and their forty sockets of silver; two] sockets u[nder one board and two sockets under another board. 22 And for the rear of] the taber[nacle westward you shall make six] boards. 23 And [you shall make] two [boards] for the rear [corners of the tabernacle. 24 And they shall be separate at the bott]om, and [completely] together [on the top at] the [first] ring, [thus it shall be the same for both of] them; they form the t[wo corners. 25 And there shall be eight] board[s,

---

155. Masculine 4QpaleoExod[m] SP. Feminine MT.

Chapter 26. 4QpaleoExod[m]: 26:8–15, 21–30; 30:10; 2QExod[a]: 26:11–13; 4QpaleoGen-Exod[l]: 26:29–37.

156. 4QpaleoExod[m] SP LXX. *fifty loops* MT.

and their sockets of silver,] sixteen [sockets; two sockets under one board, and two sockets under another board.]

[26 And you shall make] *bars of acacia wood,*[157] [five for the boards on the one side of the tabernacle, 27 and five ba]rs for the boards on the other side of the [tabernacle, and five bars for the boards on the side of the tabernacle, for the] rear westward. 28 And the [middle] ba[r in the center of the boards shall pass through from end to en]d. 29 And you shall o[verlay] the boards [with gold, *and thei*]r[158] [rings of] gold to hold [the bar]s; and you shall overlay th[e bars with gold. 30 And] you [shall erec]t the tab[ernacle according to] *commandment*[159] which has been shown you [on the mountain.]

[31 And you shall make a veil of blue, and purpl]e, and scarlet t[hreads, and] fine twined [line]n; it is to be the work of a s[killed craftsman with cherubim. 32 And you shall hang it upon four pillars of acacia over]laid with gold; [their] hook[s shall be of gold, upon fou]r [sockets of silver. 33 And you shall hang up the veil under the clasps, and shall] bring the [a]rk of the testimony *there,*[160] within [the veil; and] the vei[l shall separate for you between the holy place and] the [most hol]y. 34 And you shall put the mercy-s[eat on the ark of the testimony in the most] holy place.

> ■ *Both 4QpaleoExod^m and the Samaritan Pentateuch relocate the description of the altar of incense from Exodus 30:1–10 and place it between verses 35 and 36 of chapter 26.*

[35 And] you shall set the [table outsid]e the [v]eil, and the candlestick opposite [the table on the side of the tabernacle toward the sou]th; an[d you shall pu]t [the] table [on] the north side.

[*And you shall make an altar to burn incense; you shall make it of acacia wood; a cubit its length and a cubit its width, it shall be square; and two cubits its height; its horns of one piece with it. And you shall overlay it with pure gold, its top, and its sides round about, and its horns; and you shall make a border of gold round about it. And you shall make two golden rings for it under its border, on its two ribs; you shall make them on its two sides and they will be places for staves with which to carry it. And you shall make the staves of acacia wood, and overlay them with gold. And you shall place it before the veil which is over the ark of the testimony where I will meet with you. So Aaron shall burn sweet incense of sweet spices upon it morning by morning, whenever he trims the lamps he shall burn it. And when Aaron lights the lamps at twilight he shall burn incense continually before the LORD throughout the generations. You shall not offer strange incense upon it, and nor burnt offer*

---

157. 4QpaleoExod^m SP. *bars; acacia wood* MT.

158. 4QpaleoGen-Exod^l. *and make their* MT SP LXX

159. 4QpaleoGen-Exod^l LXX. *its commandment* MT SP.

160. 4QpaleoGen-Exod^l. *thither* MT SP.

ing or grain offering, and you shall pour no libation on it. And Aaro]n [shall make atonement] upon [its] hor[ns once a year from the blood of the sin offering of atonement; once a year he shall make atonement for it throughout] your generations; [it is most holy to the LORD.][161]

36 And you shall make a screen [for the door of the tent of blue, purple, and scarlet threads, and fine twist]ed [linen,] the work of the embroiderer. 37 And [you] shall m[ake f]i[v]e [pillars of acacia] for the scre[en, and overlay them with gold, their hooks shall be of go]ld; and you shall cast f[ive sockets of brass] for [them.]

27 1 And [you] shall m[ake the altar of acacia wood, five cubits long and five cubits wi]de; [the altar shall be] s[quare, and its height shall be three cubits. 2 And you shall make its horns on its] four corners; [its horns shall be of one piece with it; and you shall overlay it with bronze. 3 And you shall make its p]ots [to take away its ashes, and its shovels, and its basins, and its flesh-hooks, and its firepans; you shall make all its vessels of brass. 4 And you shall make a] grating [for it of a network of brass; and upon the net shall you make four bronze rings at its four corners. 5 And you shall put it under the ledge of the altar, that the net may extend halfway up the altar. 6 And you shall make poles for the altar, poles of acacia wood, and] overlay [th]em with bronze. 7 And its poles shall be pu[t through the rings, and the poles shall be on the two sides of the altar when] it [is carri]ed. 8 You shall make it hollow with planks, just as [he showed you on the mountain, so shall they make it.]

[9 And] you [shall ma]ke the court of the t[abernacl]e. On the south side [there shall be hangings for the court of fine twined linen a hundred cubits long for] one [side; 10 and] its [pillars shall be] twenty, and their [brass] sockets twenty; [the hooks of the pillars and their bands shall be of silver. 11 And likewise for the] north [side] in length [there shall be] hangings a hundred cubits long, [its] *pillars*[162] [twenty, and their brass sockets twenty;] the hooks of [the pillar]s and their fillets of silver. [12 And for the width of] the court on the [west] si[de shall be han]gings of fifty cubits; their [pillars] ten, [and their sockets ten *of bra*]*ss*.[163] [13 And the wid]th of the court on the east [si]de [shall be fifty cubits. 14 The hangings for the one side of the gate shall be fifteen cubits;] their [pillar]s three, and [their sockets three.] ▲

[17 All the] pil[lars of the court round about shall be banded with silver; their

---

161. 4QpaleoExod^m SP. Not in MT LXX.

Chapter 27. 4QpaleoExod^m: 27:1–3, 9–14, 18–19b; 4QpaleoGen-Exod^l: 27:1, 4(?), 6–14; 2QExod^b: 27:17–19.

162. 4QpaleoGen-Exod^l. *and they shall stand* MT ketib. *and its pillars* MT qere. *and their pillars* LXX SP.

163. 4QpaleoGen-Exod^l SP. Not in MT LXX.

hooks shall be of silver,] and [their] soc[kets of brass. 18 The length of the court shall be a hundred] cu[bits, and the width fifty throughout, and the height five cubits, of fine] t[wined] linen, [and their sockets of brass. 19 All the utensils of] th[e tabernacle used in all its] servic[e, and all its pegs, and all the pegs of the court shall be of brass.] *And you shall ma[ke clothing of blue and purple and scarlet material in which to serve in the holy place.]*[164] ▲

28 3 And you shall sp[eak to all who are skilled, whom I have endowed with ability, and they shall make] A[aron]'s garments [to sanctify him, that he may minister] to me [as a priest. 4 And these are the garments which they shall make: a breastplate, an ephod, a ro]be, and a coat [of checker work, a miter, and a sash, and they shall make holy garments for Aaron your b]r[ot]h[er, and h]is [sons,] that he may min[ister to] me as a pr[iest.] 5 And th[ey shall take] the gold, [and the blu]e, and th[e purple, and] the scarlet thr[eads, and the fine line]n.

6 An[d they shall make the e]ph[od of gold, of b]lu[e, and purple, and scarlet threads, and fine twined linen, the work of the skillful workman. 7 It s]hal[l have two shoulder-pieces joined *one to a*]*noth*[*er*[165] at its two ends, that it may be joined together. 8 And the skillfully woven band] which is upon it, [with which to gird it on, shall be like its work and of the same piece; of gold, of blue, purple, scarlet thread]s, and fine tw[ined] linen. [9 And you shall take two onyx stones and engrave on them the name]s [of the children of] I[srael, 10 six of their names on on]e [stone,] and the nam[es of the si]x [that remain on the other stone, in order of their birth. 11 As a jew]eler en[graves a signe]t, *he*[166] shall engrave [the two stones, according to the names of the children of Israel; you shall make them to be enclo]sed [in setti]ngs of g[old. 12 And you shall put the two stones upon the shoulder-piece]s [of the ephod, as stones of memorial for the children of Israel, and Aaron shall bear their names before the LORD on his two shoulders for a memorial.] ▲

[22 And you shall make on the breastplate chains, twiste]d corda[ge, of pure gold. 23 And you shall make on the breastplate two rings of gold, and shall put] the two [rings on the two ends of the breastplate. 24 And you shall put the two cords of gold i]n [the two rings at the ends of the breastplate. 25 And the other two ends of the two cords you shall put on the two settings, and put them in front of the shoulder-pieces of the ephod. 26 And you shall make two rings of gold and you shall put them on the two ends of the breastplate, on its edge, which is on the] inside [edge of the ephod.] 27 And [you] shall m[ake two rin]gs of g[old and

---

164. 4QpaleoExod[m] SP. Not in MT LXX.

Chapter 28. 4QpaleoExod[m]: 28:3–4, 8–12, 22–24, 26–28, 30–43; pap7QLXXExod: 28:4–7; 4QpaleoGen-Exod[l]: 28:33–35, 40–42.

165. pap7QLXXExod LXX. Not in MT SP.

166. 4QpaleoExod[m]. *you* MT SP LXX.

put them] on the bottom of [the two shoulder-pieces of the ephod,] in [the front of it, close to its] joining, [above the skillfully woven band of the ephod. 28 And they shall bind the] breastplate by [its] rings [to the] rings of the [ephod with a lace of blue, that it may be on the skillfully woven band of the ephod, and that] the breastp[late might] n[ot come loose from the ephod. 29 And Aaron shall bear the names of the children of Israel in the breastplate of judgment upon his heart, when he goes into the holy place, for a memorial before the LORD continually. 30 And you shall put in the breastplate of judgment the Ur]im and th[e Thummim, and they shall be over Aaron's heart when he goes in before the LORD; and Aaro]n [shall bear] the judgment of the children of [Israel on] his [hea]rt bef[ore the LORD continually.]

[31 And] you [shall make] the robe [of the ephod all of blue. 32 And it shall have an opening for the head in the] middle of it; [it shall have] a binding [of woven work] round [about] its opening, [like the opening of a coat of mail, that it might] not [be torn. 33 And] upon [its] h[em] you [shall make pomegranates of blue, purple, scarlet threads, round about its] hem, [and bells of gol]d between them all around: 34 a [golden] bell [and a pomegranate, a golden] bel[l and a pomegranate, all around the hem of the robe. 35 And it shall be on] A[aro]n to minister; and [its sound] shall be h[eard when he enters the holy place before the LORD, and when he comes out, so that he might not die.]

36 [And you shall make a plate of pure gold and engrave on it, like the engravings of a signet, Holy to the LORD. 37 And you shall put it on a lace of blue, and it shall be on the miter; it shall be on the front of the miter. 38 And it shall be upon Aaron's forehead, and Aaron shall bear the] ini[quity of the holy things which the children of Israel shall consecrate in all] their [h]oly [gifts;] and it s[hall be always upon his forehead, that they may be accepted before the LORD.]

[39 And] you [shall weav]e the tunic [of checkered wor]k of fine l[inen, and you shall make a miter of fine linen, and] you shall make [a sash, the] wor[k of the embroiderer.]

40 And for Aaron's sons [you shall make tunics, and y]ou [shall make] sashes for them, [and] you shall make [headdresse]s for them, [for glory and for beauty. 41 And] you[167] shall put them upon A[aron y]our [brother] and u[pon] his sons w[ith him, and shall anoint them, and] cons[ecrate them, and sanctify them, that they may minister to me as priests. 42 And you shall make the]m [linen] breeches [to cover their naked flesh; they shall reach from the loi]ns [even to the thighs. 43 And they shall be upon Aaron,] and upon [his sons when] they [e]nter the tent [of meeting, or when they approach the altar to] minister in the holy place, so that they do not bear iniquity [and die. It shall be a statute forever to him and to his offspring a]fter [him.]

---

167. Plural 4QpaleoExod[m]. Singular MT SP LXX.

29 1 And [this is the thing that you shall d]o to them to consecrate t[he]m to minister to me as priests: take [one young] bull [and] two [ram]s without blemish, 2 and unleavened bread, and [unleavened] cakes [mingled with oil,] and unleavened *wafers;*[168] you shall make [them] of fine wheat flour. [3 And you shall put them in o]ne [basket, and pre]sent [them] in the basket, with the bull [and the two rams. 4 And you shall bring Aaron and] his sons [to the door of the tent of meeting, and shall wash them with water.] 5 And you shall take [the garments, and put the tunic, the robe of the ephod, the ephod, and the breastplate on Aaron and gird him with the skillfully woven band of the ephod.]▲·

[20 Then shall you slaughter the ram, and take] some of its blood [and put it on the lobe of Aaron's right ear, and on the lobe of] his sons' [right ears, and on the thumb of their right hands, and on the big toe of] their right [fee]t, [and sprinkle the blood around on the altar.][169]

[22 Also] you shall take [the fat of] the ra[m] and [the fat tail, and the fat that c]overs the en[trails,] and *the*[170] ap[pendage of the liver, and the two kidney]s, [and the fa]t that is on [them, and the right thigh; for] it is [a ram of ordinatio]n, 23 and [one] loaf [of bread, and one cake of oiled bread, and] one [wafe]r fr[om the basket of unleavened bread that is before the LORD. 24 And] you shall put all of these on [the] h[ands of Aaron, and on the hands of] his sons, and sh[all wave] them for a wave offering be[fore the LORD. 25 And you shall take them] from their hands, and [offer them up in smoke on the altar on the burnt offering as a sweet savor before the LORD; it is an offering made by fire to the LORD.]▲

[31 And you shall take the ram of ordination and boil its flesh in a] holy [place. 32 And Aa]ron [and his sons shall eat the flesh of the ram and the] bread t[hat is] in the basket, at the door of the te[nt of meeting. 33 And they shall eat those things with which atonement was made, to] ordain [and to consecrate them, but no one else shall eat of them, because they are holy. 34 And if any of the flesh of the ordination, or of the bread, remain]s [until the morning, then you shall burn the remainder] with fire; it shall n[ot] be eaten, because it is holy.

[35 And thus shall you do to Aaron and to] his [so]ns, just [as] all that I have commanded y[ou; for s]even d[ays shall you or]dain them. 36 And [every day shall you offer the] bull as a s[in offering for atone]me[nt, and you shall cleanse] the altar, when [you] ma[ke atonement for it;] and you shall anoint i[t to consecrate

---

Chapter 29. 4QpaleoExod^m: 29:1–5, 20, 22–25, 31–41.

168. 4QpaleoExod^m SP. *wafers mixed with oil* MT LXX.

169. 4QpaleoExod^m SP omit 29:21. *And you shall take some of the blood that is on the altar, and some of the anointing oil, and sprinkle it on Aaron, and on his garments, and on his sons, and on the garments of his sons with him: and he shall be sanctified, and his garments, and his sons, and his sons' garments with him* MT LXX.

170. 4QpaleoExod^m. Not in MT SP.

it.] 37 For seven d[ays] you shall make atonement for the [altar and] consecrate it; [and] the altar [shall be most ho]ly; [whatever] touches the altar shall be holy.

[38 Now this is that which you shall offe]r on the alt[ar: two] one-year-old [lamb]s, [day by day continually.] 39 The on[e] lamb [you shall offer] in the mo[rning;] and [the other lamb you shall offer a]t twilight; [40 and with the one lamb a tenth of an ephah of fine flour mingled] with [the fourth part of a hi]n [of beaten] oil, [and the fourth part of a hin of wine for] a drink offering. [41 And the other] lamb [you shall offer at twiligh]t, [and shall do it] according to the grain offe[ring of the morning, and according to its drink offering, for a sweet savor, an offering made by fire] to the Lor[D.]▲

30[12 When you take a census of the children of Israel to register them, then shall each of them give a ransom for himself to the LORD, when you num]ber them; that there might be no] pla[gue among the]m [when you number them. 13 Each one who is registered shall give this:] hal[f a shekel after the shekel of] the sanctuary [(the shekel is twenty gerahs), half a shekel for an offering] to the LORD. [14 Everyone who is registered, from twenty years old and upward, shall give the offering of the L]ORD. 15 Th[e rich shall not give more, and the poor shall not give less, than] the [half] shekel, when [you give the offerin]g [of the LORD, to make atonement for you]r [souls.] 16 And [you shall ta]ke the [atonemen]t money [from the children of Israel, and shall appoint] it [for] the service of the te[nt of meeti]ng; [that it may be a] memorial [for the children of Israel] before the LORD, [to make atone]ment for [yourselves.]

17 And [the LORD spoke to Moses,] saying, 18 "You [shall also m]ake a laver of br[onze, and] its [base of bronze, for washing. And you shall put] it between the tent of meeting and the altar, [and you shall put water in it.]▲

[21 "So they shall wash] their [hand]s [and their feet, that they might not die; and it shall be a perpetual statute for them, for him and for] his [offsprin]g throughout [their] gen[erations."]

[22 Then the LORD spoke unto Moses, saying, 23 "Take for yourself the finest spices: of flowing myrrh five hundred shekels, and of swe]et [cinnamon] h[alf so much, two hundred and fifty, and of sweet cane two hundred and fifty, 24 and of cassia five] hundred, according to [the shekel of the sanctuary, and of olive oil a hin. 25 And you shall make of these a] holy [anointing oil,] a per[fume compounded according to the art of the perfumer; it shall be a holy anointing oil] *throughout [your] generations.*[171]▲

[29 "And you shall sanctify them, that they may be most ho]ly; [whatever touches them shall be holy. 30 And you shall anoint Aaron and his sons, and sa]nctify t[hem, that they may minister to me as priests. 31 And you shall speak to

---

Chapter 30. 4QpaleoExod^m: 30:12–18, 29–31, 34–38; 2QExod^a: 30:21(?), 23–25.

171. 2QExod^a. Not in MT SP LXX.

the children of Israel, saying, 'This shall be a] holy [anointing oil to me throughout your generations.' "]▲

[34 And the LORD said] to Mos[es, "Take sweet spices, stacte, and onycha, and
galbanum; sweet spices] with [pure] frankincense; [there shall be an equal part of
each. 35 And you shall make incense of it, a per]fume, the wo[rk of the perfumer,
salted, pure, and holy. 36 And you shall beat some of it very small, and] put some
[of it be]fore the testimo[ny in the tent of meeting, where I will meet with you;]
it shall be m[os]t holy to you. [37 And the incense which you shall make according to this composition,] you shall not make for [yourselves;] it shall be to you
holy [for the LORD. 38 Whoever shall make] any like it, to use it as a perfume,
shall be cut off from [his pe]ople."

31 [1 And] the Lo[R]D spo[ke t]o Moses, sa[ying, 2 "See, I have called by
name Bezalel the son of] U[ri, the son of Hur, of the tribe of J]u[dah:
3 and I have filled him with the Spirit of God, in wisdom,] in understanding, [in
knowledge, and in all manner of workmanship, 4 to devise skillful] designs, *to
work in*[172] [gold,] silver, and br[onze, 5 in cutting stones for setting, and in
car]ving wood, [to work] in all manner of workmanship. [6 And I, behold, I have
appointed with him Oholi]ab, the son of Ahis[amach,] of the tribe of [Da]n; [and
in the hearts of all that are skillful I have put wisdom, that they may make] all that
I have commanded [you:] 7 the [tent of meeting, and the ark of the testimony,
and the mercy-seat] that [is upon it, and] all the furnitu[re of the tent, 8 the table]
and [its vessels, and the pure candlestick with all its utensils, and the altar of incense. . . .]▲

[13 "And you,] speak to [the children of Israel, saying, 'You shall certainly
keep my sabbaths; for] *it is*[173] *a sign [for] you;*[174] everyone that profanes [it shall
surely be put to death; for whoever doe]s [any] w[ork on it, that soul shall be cut
off [from among the people. 15 For six] days [shall work] be d[one, but] on the
[seventh] day [is a sabbath of solemn rest, holy to the LORD; whoever does any
work on the sabbath day, he shall surely be put to death. 16 So the children of Israel shall keep the sab]bath *to the Lo[RD,*[175] observing the sabbath throughout
their generations, for a perpetual covenant. 17 It is a sign between me and the
childr]en of Isr[ael forever; for in six days the LORD made heaven and earth, and
on the seventh day he rested, and was refreshed.' "]▲

Chapter 31. 4QpaleoExod^m: 31:1–8, 13–15; 2QExod^b: 31:16–17.

   172. 4QpaleoExod^m meaning uncertain, scribal error?

   173. Feminine 4QpaleoExod^m MT qere SP. Masculine MT ketib.

   174. 4QpaleoExod^m a scribal error deleted the end of verse 13 and the beginning of 14: *it
is a sign between me and you throughout your generations; that you may know that I am the LORD
who sanctifies you. 14 You shall keep the sabbath, for it is holy for you* MT SP LXX.

   175. 2QExod^b. Not in MT SP LXX.

32 [2 And Aaron sai]d to them, ["Take off the golden rings which are in the ears of] your [wives,] your sons, [and your daughters, and bring them to me." 3 And all the people took off] the [golden] rings [which were in their ears and brought them to Aaron. 4 And] he took [it] from [them and fashioned it with a graving tool, and made it a molten calf; and they said, "This is your god, O Israel, who brought you up out of the land of Egypt." 5 And when Aaron saw this, he built an altar befo]re it; [and Aaron made proclamation and said, "Tomorrow shall be a feast to the LORD." 6 And] they rose up early on the next [day and offered burnt offerings, and brought peace offerings; and the people sat down to ea]t and to drink, and [rose up to play.]

[7 And the LORD spoke to Moses, sa]ying,[176] "Go down,[177] for [your people, whom you brought up out of the land of Egypt, have corrupted themselves: 8 they have quickly turned aside] from the way w[hich I commanded them; they have made themselves a molten calf,] and have [worshi]ped it, and have sacr[ificed to it, and said, 'This is your god, O Isra]el, who brought you up out of the la[nd of Egypt.']"]

■ *God's anger against Aaron for his part in the sin of the golden calf—not referred to in the prayer of Exodus 32:11—is imported from Deuteronomy 9:20 and appears in both 4QpaleoExod[m] and the Samaritan Pentateuch.*

[9 And the LORD said] to Moses, ["I have seen this people, and behold, they are a stiffnecked people; 10 now therefore let me alone, that my wrath may burn hot against them, and that I may consume them; and I will make of] y[ou] a great nation." [*And the LO]RD [was] very [angry with Aaron] to destroy him; and Moses prayed for A[aron.]*[178]

[11 And] Moses e[ntre]ated [the LORD his God, and sa]id, "O LORD, wh[y does your] wr[ath] burn hot against your people, whom [you] have broug[ht out of the land of Egypt with great power and] with a *mighty arm?*[179] 12 Wh[y should the Egyptians] sp[eak, saying, 'He brought them out with malice, intending to kil]l them in the mountain[s, and to consume them from the face of the earth'? Turn from] your [fierce wra]th, [and] change your mind about doing harm to your people. [13 Remember Abraham, Isaac, and Israel, your servants,] to whom you swore by yourself, [and said to them, 'I will multiply your seed as the st]ars of [the] heaven, and all [this] land [that I have spoken of I will give to your seed, and

---

Chapter 32. 4QpaleoExod[m]: 32:2–19, 25–30; 2QExod[a]: 32:32–34.

176. 4QpaleoExod[m] SP LXX. Not in MT.

177. 4QpaleoExod[m]. *Go down at once* MT SP. *Go down from here at once* LXX.

178. 4QpaleoExod[m] SP. Not in MT LXX.

179. 4QpaleoExod[m]. *mighty hand* MT. *outstretched arm* SP LXX.

they shall inherit] *it*[180] for eve[r.' " 14 And the LOR]D [changed his mind] a[bout the evil which he said he would do] to his people.

[15 And Moses turned, and went down from the mountain,] with the two [tablets of the testimony in his hand,] tablets that were wr[itten on both si]des; they [were written on the front and ba]ck. [16 And the tablets were the work of] Go[d, and the] writing was the writ[ing of Go]d, [engraved on the tablets.] 17 And when Joshu[a] heard the noise of the people [as they shout]ed, he s[a]i[d to Moses, "There is a noise of war in the camp." 18 And he said, "It is not the] sound of the cr[y of victo]ry, neither is it the so[und arising from defeat; but the sound of singing I hear." 19 Then as soon as he came nea]r the [camp, he saw the calf and the dancing; and Moses' anger burned, and he threw the tablets from his hands, and broke them at the foot of the mountain.]▲

[25 And when Moses saw] that [the people were] run[ning wild (for Aaron had let them run wild, to the derision of their enemies), 26 then Moses stood in the gate of the camp, and] said, "Whoever [is on LORD's side, let him come to me." And all the sons of] Levi [gathered together to him. 27 And he said to] them, "Thus [says the L]ORD, [the God of Israel:] Let every man put [his sword on his thigh,] *and*[181] go ba[ck and forth] from gat[e to gate throughout the camp,] and each of you kill [his brother, his companion, and his neighbor." 28 And] the sons of Levi [did] according to the wo[rd of Mo]ses; and abo[ut three thousand] of the people fell [on] that [da]y. 29 And [Mo]ses sa[id,] "Dedicate your[selves] today to the LORD, for [every man has been] against his son, and [his brother; so that he might grant on] you a blessing this day."

30 Then the next day, Moses said to the p[eople, "You have sinned] a great sin. And now I will go up to the L[ORD; perhaps I can make atonement for your sin." 31 And Moses returned to the LORD, and said, "This people have sinned a great sin and have made themselves gods of gold. 32 And now, if you will forgive their] si[n—and if not, please blot me out of your book which you have written." 33 And] the LORD [sai]d [to Moses, "Whoever has sinned against me, I will blot him out of my book. 34 And now go, lea]d t[he people to the place of which I have spoken to you. Behold, my angel shall go before you; nevertheless in the day when I punish, I will punish them for their sin."]▲

33 [12 And Moses said to the LORD, "See, you say to me, 'Bring up this people,' and you have not let me know whom you will send with me. Yet you have said, 'I know you by name, and you have al]so fou[nd favor in my sight.' 13 Now therefore, I pray you, if I have found favor in your sight, sh]ow me now [your ways, that I may know you, so that I may find favor in your sight. And con-

---

180. 4QpaleoExod^m SP LXX. Not in MT.

181. 4QpaleoExod^m SP LXX. Not in MT.

Chapter 33. 4QpaleoExod^m: 33:12–23.

sider] that [this] nat[ion] is your people." [14 And he said, "My presence shall go with you, and I will give you rest." 15 And he said] to him, "If [your presence go] n[ot with us, do not lead us up from here. 16 For how shall it be known that I have found favor in your sight, I and your people? Is it n]ot [in that you go with us,] so that we are set apart, [I] and your people, [from all the people that are on the face of the ea]rth?"

17 And the L[ORD sa]id [to Moses,] "I will also d[o] this th[ing] tha[t] you [have spoken; for you have found favor in my sight, and I know] you by name." 18 And he [s]aid, "Show me, [I pray you, your glory." 19 And he said, "I will make all] my goodness [pass before you, and will proclaim the name of the LORD] before [you; and] I will [be gracious to whom I will be gracious, and will show mercy on whom I will show mercy." 20 And] he said, ["You cannot see my face; for no one shall see me and live." 21 And the LORD said, "Behold, there is a place by me, and you shall stand on the] rock; 22 and [when my glory passes by, I will put you in a cleft of the rock and will cover] you [with] my [han]d until [I have passed by; 23 and I will take away my hand, and you shall see my back, but my face shall not] be seen."

34 [1 And the LORD said to Moses, "Cut] two [tablets of stone] like the first [one, and I will write on the tablets the wor]ds tha[t were on the *table*]*ts,*[182] which [you] b[roke. 2 And be ready by the morning, and come up] in the morning [to Mount Sinai, and present yourself there to me on the top of the mountain. 3 And no one] shall come up [with you; neither let anyone be seen throughout all the mountain; neither let the flocks nor herds feed in front of that mountain."]▲

[10 And he said, "Behold, I make a covenant. Before all your people I will perform marvels, such as have not been produced in all the earth, nor in any nation; and all the people among which you live shall see the work of the LORD;] for [it is] an awesome [thing that I will do with you.]

[11 "Observe that which I command] you today: [behold, I will drive out the Amorite from before you, and the Canaanite, *the Hittite,*] the *Girga[shite, the Perizzite, the Hivite,*[183] and the Jebusite. 12 Take care, lest you make a covenant] with [the inhabitants of the land where you are going, lest it be] a snare [among you. 13 But you shall break down their altars, and dash their pillars to pieces, and cut down] their Asherim; [for you shall worship no other god; for the LORD, whose name is Jealous, is a jealous God; 15 lest you make a covenant with the inhabitants

---

Chapter 34. 4QpaleoExod^m: 34:1–3, 10–13, 15–18, 20–24, 27–28; 2QExod^b: 34:10 (at 19:9).

182. 4QpaleoExod^m. *first tablets* MT SP LXX.

183. 4QpaleoExod^m SP. *the Hittite, the Perizzite, the Hivite* MT. *the Hittite, the Perizzite, the Hivite, the Girgashite* LXX.

of the land, and they play the harlot with their gods, and sacrific]e to [their] god[s, and someone invite you and you eat of his sacrifice; 16 and you take of their daughters for] your [so]ns,[184] and make [your] sons play the harlot [with their gods.]

17 "You shall ma[ke] no [molten gods] for [yourselves.]

[18 "You shall keep the feast of unleavened bread. For seven days you shall eat unleavened bread,] as I commanded you, [at the time appointed in the month Abib; for in the month Abib you came out from Egypt.]

[19 "All that open the womb are mine, and all your male cattle, the firstborn of the cow and sheep. 20 And the firstborn of a donkey you shall redeem with a lamb; and if you will not redeem it, then you shall break its neck. You shall redeem all the firstborn of your sons. And none shall appear before me] empty-handed.

[21 "Six days you shall work, but on the seventh day you shall] rest; even in plowing time an[d in harvest you shall rest. 22 And you shall observe the feast of weeks, the] first fruits of [the wheat] harve[st, and the feast of ingathering at the turn of the year. 23 Three] time[s in the year all your males shall appear before the LORD, the Lo]RD God of Isra[el. 24 For I will cast out nations before y]ou, and enlarge [your borders; no one shall covet your land, when you go up to appear before the LORD your God three times in the year."]▲

[27 And the LORD said to Moses, "Write these words:] for in [accordance with these words I have made a covenant with you and with Israel."] 28 And he was [there with the LORD forty days and forty nights; he neither ate brea]d, [nor drank water. And he wrote on the tablets the words of the covenant, the ten commandments.]▲

35 [1 And Mo]ses [assembled all the congregation of the children of Israel, and said to them, "These are the words which the L]ORD [has commanded you] to d[o."]▲

36 [9 The length] of each curtain was t[wenty]-eight [cubits, and the width of each curtain] four cubits; [all the curtains had the same measurements.]

[10 And] he joined [five curtains one to another, and the other five curtains he joined one to another.]▲

[21 Ten cubits was the length of each board, and a cu]bit and [a half the width of each board. 22 Each board had two tenons, joine]d one to [another; thus he did for all the] boa[rds of the tabernacle. 23 And he made the boards for the tabernacle:] twent[y boards for] the south side. [24 And he made forty sockets of

---

184. 4QpaleoExod[m]. *sons, and their daughters play the harlot with their gods* MT SP. *sons, and you give your daughters to their sons, and your daughters play the harlot with their gods* LXX.

Chapter 35. 4QpaleoExod[m]: 35:1.

Chapter 36. 4QExod[k]: 36:9–10; 4QpaleoExod[m]: 36:21–24; 4QpaleoGen-Exod[l]: 36:34–36.

silver under the twenty board]s: two socket[s under one board for its two tenons, and two sockets] under [another] b[oard for its two tenons.]▲

[34 And he overlaid the boards with gold, and made their] r[ings of gold to hold the bars, and overlaid the bars with gold.]

[35 And he made the veil of b]lue, and pur[ple, and scarlet threads, and fine twined linen; with cherubim, the work of the skillful workman, he made it. 36 And he made four pillar]s of acacia [for it, and overlaid them with gold, and their hooks were of gold. And he cast four sockets of silver for them.]▲

37 [9 And the cherubim spread out their wings above, covering the mercy-seat] with their wings, [with their faces turned toward one to another;] the face[s of the cherubim] were to[ward the mercy-seat.]

[10 And] he made th[e tabl]e [of acac]ia [wood:] two c[ubits its length, and a cubit] its width, and a cubit and a half its height. 11 And he over[laid it with pure gold, and] made a molding of gold round about it. 12 And he made a [border a handbreadth wide] round about it, and made [a gold]en [molding] r[ound about] its border. [13 And he cast four] rings of gold [for it, and put] the rings on the fo[ur corners that were] on[185] [its] four feet. 14 The r[ings] were [close to] the rim, [the holders] for the poles to carry [the tab]le. 15 And he made the p[oles of] acacia [wood] and overlaid [them with go]ld, to [carry the table. 16 And he made] the vessels [which were on the table of pure gold, its dishes, spoons, bowls, and its flagons, with which to pour out libations.]▲

38

■ *The manuscript 4QExod-Lev^f begins here at Exodus 38:18. It dates—with 4QSam^b—to the mid–third century* BCE. *These two scrolls are thought by experts in Hebrew writing to be the earliest scrolls found in the caves of Qumran.*

[18 And the screen for the gate of the court was the work of the embroiderer, of blue, purple, and scarlet threads, and fine twined linen. And twenty cubits was the length, and the breadth was five cubit]s, [corresponding to the hangings of the court. 19 And their four pillars and four sockets were bronze, th]eir [hooks silver, and the overlaying of their capitals and fillets silver. 20 And all the pegs of the tabernacle, and of the court round about, were of] bronze.

[21 These are the things recorded for the tabernacle, the tabernacle of the tes-timony, recorded by Moses, for the service of the Levites, by the] hand [of Ithamar, the son of Aaron the priest. 22 And Bezalel the son of Uri, the son of Hur, of the tribe of Judah, made all that the LORD commanded Moses.]▲

Chapter 37. 4QpaleoExod^m: 37:9–16.

185. 4QpaleoExod^m. *to* MT SP.

Chapter 38. 4QExod-Lev^f: 38:18–22.

39 [3 And they hammered out gold leaf, and cut it into threads to work it in the blue, purple, and scarlet threads, and in the fine linen, the work of the skillful workman. 4 They made shoulder-pieces for the ephod, joined together; at the two ends was it joined. 5 And the skillfully woven band that was on it, with which to gird it on, was of the same materials and like its work; of gold, of blue, and purple, and scarlet threads, and fine twined linen, as the LORD commanded Moses.]

[6 And they prepared the onyx stones, enclosed in settings of go]ld, [engraved with the engravings of a signet, according to the names of the children of Israel. 7 And he put] them[186] [on the shoulder-pieces of the ephod, to be stones of memorial for the children of Israel as the LORD commanded Mos]es.

[8 And he made the breastplate, the work of the skillful workman, like the work of the ephod: of gold, blue, purple, and scarlet threads, and fine twined linen. 9 It was square;] they [ma]de [the breastplate folded double: a span its length, and a span its breadth, folded double. 10 And they set four rows of] stone[s in it. A row of sardius, topaz, and carbuncle was the first row; 11 and the second row, an emerald,] a sapphire, [and a diamond; 12 and the third row, a jacinth, an agate, and an amethyst; 13 and the fourth row,] a beryl, [an onyx, and a jaspar; they were enclosed in settings of gold filigree. 14 And the] stones [were according to the names of the children of Israel, twelve, according to their names; like the engravings of a sig]net, [each according to the names of the twelve tribes.] 15 And they made [on the breastplate chains like cords, of twisted work of pu]re [gold. 16 And they made two settings of gold, and two gold rings, and put the two rings on the two ends of the breastplate. 17 And they put two] cords[187] [of gold in the two rings at the ends of the breastplate. 18 And the other] two [ends of the two cords they put on the two settings, and put them on the shoulder-pieces on the front of the ephod. 19 And they made two rings of gold, and put them] on [the] two [ends of the breastplate, on the inside edge next to the ephod. 20 And they made two rings of gold, and put them on the front of the lower part of the two shoulder-pieces of the ephod, by its] j[oining,] ab[ove the wov]en band of the ephod. 21 And [they bound the breastplate by its rings to the rings of] the ephod, j[ust] as the LOR[D] commanded Mos[es,[188] with a blue lace, that it might be on the woven band] on the inside[189] of the e[pho]d, and that the breast-

---

Chapter 39. 4QExod-Lev^f: 39:3–24.

186. Feminine 4QExod-Lev^f. Masculine MT SP.

187. 4QExod-Lev^f SP. *the two cords* MT.

188. 4QExod-Lev^f. Not in MT SP LXX.

189. 4QExod-Lev^f. Not in MT SP LXX.

plate might not come loose [from the ephod, as the LORD commanded Moses.] *And he made the Urim and [the Thummim just as the LORD commanded] Moses.*[190]

22 And he made *the*[191] ro[be of the ephod of woven work, all of blue. 23 And the opening of the robe] in its middle was as the opening of a coat of mail, [with a binding] r[ound] its opening [that it might not be torn. 24 And they made] p[omegranates of b]l[ue, a]nd p[urple, and scar]l[et threads, and twined linen on the hem of the robe.]▲

40 8 "And you shall set up the co[urt rou]nd [abo]ut and hang up the screen [of the gate of the court.] 9 And you shall take the anointing oil and anoint the tabernacle [and all that is in it, and shall consecrate] it and all its furniture; and it shall be holy. 10 And *anoint*[192] the altar of bu[rnt offering and all its vessels,] and consecrate the altar; and the a[ltar] shall be most hol[y. 11 And] you [shall] anoint [the laver] and its base, and consecrate it. 12 And *Aaron and his sons you shall bring*[193] to the door of the tent of me[eting,] and shall wash them with water. 13 And you shall put the holy garments on Aaron, and you shall anoint hi[m,] and consecrate him, that he may minister to me as a priest. 14 And [you shall brin]g [his sons] and put *the*[194] coa[ts] on them; 15 and you shall anoint them, as you anointed *their*[195] father, that they may minister [to me] as priest; [and] their anointing [shall] establish them for an everlasting priesthood throughout their generations."

16 Thus Mos[es] did, [according to all that] the LORD [commanded] *them.*[196] 17 Then in the first month in the second year *after they came out of Egyp[t,*[197] on] the first day of the month, the tabernacle was set up. 18 And he [erected] its sock-ets,[198] and set up [its] hooks [and][199] its boards, and *its bars were put in,*[200] and he erected its pillars. 19 And *the tent was put*[201] over the tabernacle and he put the covering of the tent above it, as the LORD commanded Moses. 20 And he took

---

190. 4QExod-Lev[f] SP. Not in MT LXX.

191. 4QExod-Lev[f] SP. Not in MT.

Chapter 40. 4QExod-Lev[f]: 40:8–27; 4QpaleoGen-Exod[l]: 40:15(?).

192. 4QExod-Lev[f]. *you shall anoint* MT SP LXX.

193. 4QExod-Lev[f]. *you shall bring Aaron and his sons* MT SP LXX.

194. 4QExod-Lev[f]. Not in MT SP.

195. Aramaic suffix? 4QExod-Lev[f].

196. 4QExod-Lev[f]. *him, so he did* MT SP LXX.

197. 4QExod-Lev[f] SP LXX. Not in MT.

198. 4QExod-Lev[f]. *Moses erected the tabernacle, and laid its sockets* MT SP LXX.

199. 4QExod-Lev[f]. Not in MT SP LXX.

200. 4QExod-Lev[f]. *put in its bars* MT SP.

201. 4QExod-Lev[f]. *he spread the tent* MT SP LXX.

the testimony and *it was put*[202] into[203] the ark, and [he set] the poles *in* the ark, and *the mercy seat was put*[204] *on*[205] the ark. 21 And he brought [the ark into the tabernacle,] and set up the vei[l] for the screen, and screened *the*[206] ark of the t[estimony, as] the LORD [commanded] Moses. 22 And *the table was put*[207] *into*[208] the t[ent of meeting, on] the *north* [*sid*]*e*[209] of the tabernacle, outside the veil. 23 And he set [the bread] i[n order] on it [before the LORD;] as the LORD commanded Moses. 24 And he put [the candlestick in the tent of] m[eeting, opposi]te the table, on the [south] side of the tabernacle. [25 And he lighted] the la[mps before the Lor]D; [a]s the LORD commanded Moses. [26 And] he p[ut the] gold[en altar] in the tent of meeting before the [veil, 27 and he burned incense] of sweet spices [o]n it *before him;*[210] as the L[ORD] commanded [Moses.] ▲

---

202. 4QExod-Lev[f]. *put it* MT SP.

203. 4QExod-Lev[f]. *on* MT SP LXX.

204. 4QExod-Lev[f]. *put the mercy seat* MT SP.

205. 4QExod-Lev[f]. *on top of* MT SP. LXX omits 20c.

206. Definite article on construct form 4QExod-Lev[f]. Not in MT SP.

207. 4QExod-Lev[f]. *he put the table* MT. *he set the table* SP.

208. 4QExod-Lev[f] LXX. *in* MT SP.

209. 4QExod-Lev[f]. *side to the north* MT SP.

210. 4QExod-Lev[f]. Not in MT SP LXX.

LEVITICUS

"**Y**ou shall be holy for I am holy" (Lev 11:45) is the keynote of the book of Leviticus. The title—taken from the Latin (Vulgate) and Greek (LXX) designation meaning "pertaining to the tribe of Levi"—indicates that it is a priestly book. It contains legislation that applies to the sons of Levi and, more particularly, the sons of the high priest Aaron, in order that they might instruct the people of Israel in holiness. As such, it is rather short on plot and long on legal discussions pertaining to ritual purity.

The sixteen manuscripts of Leviticus rank it as one of the most common of all the scrolls found at Qumran. Fourteen of the manuscripts were unearthed in five of the eleven caves in the vicinity of Wadi Qumran—one in Cave 1, one in Cave 2, nine in Cave 4, one in Cave 6, and two in Cave 11—while two were discovered in the ruins at Masada.[a] Only the text of chapter 12, of the twenty-seven chapters of Leviticus, did not survive the ravages of time in the caves above the Dead Sea.

Thirteen of the sixteen manuscripts exhibit some variation from the traditional Hebrew text. As is the norm, these variants are without a particular pattern and are as a group best described as "mixed" or "nonaligned." They are also minor and do not detract from the conclusion that our present book of Leviticus is an accurate reflection of a tradition that most certainly predates the Qumran community. Of the three manuscripts that show no variants, 6QpaleoLev contains parts of only fourteen words. MasLev[a] and MasLev[b], from Masada, are, however, more extensive in content and reflect the establishment of a text in the latter years of the first century that has been reproduced to the letter in the Masoretic manuscripts of the tenth and eleventh centuries. None of the variants

---

a. 1QpaleoLev, 2QpaleoLev, 4QExod-Lev[f], 4QLev-Num[a], 4QLev[b]–4QLev[e], 4QLev[g], 4QLXXLev[a], pap4QLXXLev[b], 6QpaleoLev, 11QpaleoLev[a], 11QLev[b], MasLev[a], MasLev[b].

found in the other thirteen manuscripts has as yet been accepted by modern Bible translators.

Astonishingly, every chapter of the book of Leviticus is referenced somewhere in the nonbiblical scrolls. Because only the book of Deuteronomy approaches this preeminence, it appears safe to conclude that Leviticus was the heart and soul of the priestly community at Qumran. The *Temple Scroll* by itself quotes or paraphrases portions of twenty-three chapters. Of the two dozen rulings of *A Sectarian Manifesto* (4QMMT), more than half are discussions based on legal issues concerning ritual purity from the text of Leviticus. The laws of the *Damascus Document* are also to a great extent rehearsals of various Levitical commands. The assorted collection of legal discussions recorded in *A Commentary on the Law of Moses* (4Q251) is also largely Levitical in origin. Indeed, the key to understanding the community's emphasis on purity is contained in Leviticus 15:31: "You must keep the people of Israel separate from their uncleanness, so that they might not die in their uncleanness by defiling my tabernacle which is in their midst."[b]

1 [1 And the LORD called to Moses, and spoke to him from the tent of meeting,] saying, 2 "Speak to the children of Israel, and say [to them, 'When any of you offers an offering to the LORD, you shall offer your offering of] animals, even from the herd and from [the] flock.

[3 " 'If his offering is a burnt offering] from the herd, he shall offer it a male without blemish; he shall offer it [at the door of the tent of meeting, that he may be accepted] before [the LORD. 4 And he shall lay] his [hand] upon the head of [the burnt offering; and it shall be accepted for him to make atonement for him. 5 And he shall slaughter the bull before the LORD; and Aaron's sons, the priests, shall off]er [the blood, and sprinkle the blood around on the altar t]hat [is at the door of the tent of meeting. 6 And he shall skin the burnt offering, and cut it into its pieces. 7 And the s]ons [of Aaron the priest shall put fire on the altar, and arrange the wood on the fire.]▲

> ■ *The text of 4QLXXLev^b found in the scrolls anticipates other Greek manuscripts of Leviticus by some four centuries. It is probable, on the basis of its age (100 BCE) and its text, that this is an accurate reflection of the very earliest Greek translations from the middle of the third century BCE.*

---

b. 4Q512 69 2, 11QTS 51:4b–10.

Chapter 1. 4QLev^c: 1:1–7; 4QLev^b: 1:11–17; pap4QLXXLev^b: 1:11; 4QExod-Lev^f: 1:13–15, 17.

11 " 'And [he shall] s[laughter] it [on the side] of the a[ltar northward bef]ore [the LORD: and Aa]ro[n's sons, the priest]s, [shall sprinkle] *the*[1] blood [around] on [the altar. 12 And he shall cut it into its pieces, with its head and its fat; and] the priest shall arrange them on [the wood that is on the fire which is on the altar.] [13 But the entrails and the leg]s he shall wash with water, and [the priest] shall offer [the whole, and burn it on the altar; it is a burnt offering, an offering made by fire, of a pl]easing odo[r] to the LORD.

■ *The manuscript of 4QExod-Lev[f]—which is extant only as far as Leviticus 2:1—is, along with 4QSam[b], the oldest of the manuscripts found in the caves of Qumran. Dating to the middle of the third century BCE, it is more than a millennium older than the earliest copy of Leviticus available prior to the discovery of the scrolls.*

[14 " 'And if] his offering to the LORD is a burnt offering [o]f birds, then he shall off[er his offering of turtledoves or of young pigeons. 15 And] the priest [shall brin]g it to the altar and wring off [its head, and burn it on the altar; and its blood shall be drained out on the side of the alta]r; 16 and he shall take away *its*[2] crop with its contents, [and throw it on the east side of the altar, in the place of] the ashes. 17 And he shall tear it by its wings, *and*[3] shall not sever it. [And the priest shall burn it on the altar, on the wo]od that is on [the fir]e; it is a *burnt offering,*[4] of a pleasing odor to the L[ORD.' "]

2 [1 " 'And] when [anyo]ne of[fers] *his*[5] [o]ffering of grain to the LORD, [his of-fering] shall be of fine flour; [and he shall pour oil on it, and put frankince]nse [on it; *it is*] a grain offering.[6] [2 And he shall bring it to Aaron's sons] the priests, and he shall take [from it his handful of the fine flour, and of its oil, with all its frank-incense; and the pries]t [shall burn it as its] memorial [on the altar, an offering made by fire, of a pleasing odor to the LORD. 3 And that which is left of the grain offering shall be Aaron's and] his [sons'; it is a thing most holy of the] offerings [of the LORD] made by fire.

[4 " 'And when you offer an of]fering of gra[in baked in the ove]n, [it shall be unleavened cake]s of fi[ne flour] mix[ed with oil, or unleavened wa]fers [anointed with oi]l. 5 And if your offering is grain [made on the grid]dle, [it shall

---

1. 4QLev[b]. *his* MT SP LXX.

2. Feminine 4QLev[b]. Masculine MT SP.

3. 4QLev[b] SP LXX. Not in MT.

4. 4QLev[b]. *burnt offering, an offering by fire* MT SP LXX.

Chapter 2. 4QLev[b]: 2:1–16; pap4QLXXLev[b]: 2:3–5, 7–8(?); 4QExod-Lev[f]: 2:1.

5. 4QExod-Lev[f]. Not in MT SP LXX.

6. 4QExod-Lev[f] SP LXX. Not in MT.

be of unleavened fine flour, mi]xed [with oil. 6 You shall break] it in p[ieces, and pour] oil on it; [it is a grain offering. 7 And if your offering is grain made in a pan,] it shall be made [of f]in[e flour with oil.] 8 And *he shall bring*[7] the grain offering t[hat is made of these things to the LORD; and it shall be presented to the priest, and he shall bring it] to the altar. 9 And the p[riest] shall take up [from the grain its memorial portion, and shall burn it on the altar, an offering made by fire, of] a pleasing odor to the LORD. 10 And that which is l[eft of the grain offering shall belong to Aaron and his sons; it is a thing most holy of the offerings to the LORD made by fire.]

11 "'*Every*[8] grain offering, which you shall offer to the [LORD, shall not be made with leaven; for you shall burn no leaven, nor any honey, as an offering made] by fire to the LORD. 12 [As an of]fe[ring of first fruits you shall offer them to the LORD, but they shall be offered for a] pleasing odor [on the altar.] 13 And you shall season ev[ery offering of your grain] with salt; [nor shall you allow the salt of the covenant of your God to be lacking] from your grain offerings; you shall offer salt with all [your of]ferings.

14 "'And *when*[9] you offer a grain offering of first fruits to the LORD, [you shall offer] for the grain of your fir[st fruits] g[rain in the ear] parched with fire, course grain of the fresh ear. [15 And] you [shall put] oil on it, and lay frankin[cense] on it; [it is a grain offering. 16 And] the priest [shall burn] its memorial portion, some of its course grain, and some of its oil, and all of its frankincense; [it is an offering made by fire to the LORD.'"]

3 [1 "'And if] his offering is a [sacrifi]ce *to the LORD*[10] of well-being, if [he offers] from the [herd, whether male or female, he shall offer it without blemish before the LORD. 2 And] he shall lay [his] hand [on the head of his offering and slaughter it at the door of the tent of meeting and Aaron's sons the priests shall sprinkle the blood a]ro[und on the altar.] 3 And he shall offer from the s[acrifice of well-being an offering made by fire to the LORD; the fat that covers the entrails, all the fat that is] on the entrails, 4 and the two [kidneys, the fat that is on th]em, which is by the loin[s, and the ap]pendage *from*[11] the liv[er, with the kidneys,] shall he taken [a]way. [5 And Aaron's sons shall burn it on the altar on the burnt offering, which is on the w]ood that is on the [fire; it is an offering made by fire, of a pleasing odor to the LORD.]

---

7. 4QLev[b] LXX. *you shall bring* MT SP.

8. 4QLev[b] LXX. *Each* MT SP.

9. 4QLev[b]. *if* MT SP.

Chapter 3. 4QLev[b]: 3:1, 8–14; pap4QLXXLev[b]: 3:4, 7, 9–14; 4QLev[e]: 3:2–8; 4QLev[c]: 3:16–17.

10. 4QLev[b] LXX. Not in MT SP.

11. pap4QLXXLev[b]. *on* MT SP LXX.

[6 " 'And if] his offering for *the*[12] sacrifice of well-bein[g to the LORD is from the f]lock, [male or female, he shall offer it without blemish. 7 If he offers a l]amb [for his offering,] then shall he offer it before the Lo[RD; 8 and he shall lay his hand on the head of his offering and slaughter it before the tent of meeting and] Aaron's sons [shall sprinkle its blood] around on the altar. 9 And he shall offer from the sacrifice of well-being [an offering made by fire to the LORD; its fat, the entire fat tail,] he shall remove it [close to] the backbone; and [the] fat that covers the [en]trails and [all the fat that is on the e]ntrai[ls,] 10 the [two] kidneys, the fat that is on them, which is b[y t]he l[oins, and the ap]pendage [on the liv]er, w[ith the kidneys, he shall take] it away. 11 And the priest shall *burn*[13] on the altar; it is the f[ood, *for a pleasing od*]*or*,[14] [of the offering made by fire to the LORD.]

12 " 'And if hi[s offer]ing [is a goat, then he shall offer it befo]re the LORD, 13 and he shall lay [his hand on its] head [and slaughter i]t bef[ore th]e te[nt of meeting; and the sons of Aaron shall sprinkle its blood] around o[n the alt]ar. 14 And he shall [offer from it his offering, even an offering made by fir]e to the [LORD; the fat that covers the entrails, and all the f]a[t that is on the entrails, 15 and the two kidneys, and the fat that is on them by the loins, and the ap-pendage of the liver, with the kidneys, he take shall away. 16 And] the priest [shall] burn them on the alta[r; it is the food of] the offering made by fire, [for a pleasing odor; all the fat is the LORD's.] 17 It shall be a perpetual [st]atute through-out your generations in all your [dwelling]s, [that you shall eat] neither [fat nor blood.' "]

4 [1 And the LORD spoke to] Moses, saying, 2 "Speak to the children of Israel, sa[ying, 'If anyone shall sin unintentionally,] in any of [the th]ings which the LORD has commanded not to be done, and shall d[o any one of them,] [3 if the ano]inted [priest] shall sin so as to bring guilt [on the people, then let] him offer for [h]is [sin,] which he has sin[ned, a young bul]l without ble[mish to the LORD for a sin offering.] 4 And he shall *lead in*[15] the bull to the door of the tent of meet-ing before [the LORD;] and he shall lay his hand o[n the head of th]e bull befo[*re the* LORD,][16] and slaughter the bull before the LORD. 5 And the anointed priest shall take [from the blood of the bull, and bring it to the tent of meeti]ng, 6 and the priest shall dip his finger in the blood, and sprinkle some of the blood seven

---

12. 4QLev^e SP. Not in MT LXX.

13. 4QLev^b SP LXX. *burn it* MT.

14. pap4QLXXLev^b LXX. Not in MT SP.

Chapter 4. 4QLev^c: 4:1–6, 12–14, 23–28; pap4QLXXLev^b: 4:3–4, 6–8, 10–11, 18–19, 26–28, 30; MasLev^a: 4:3–9; 11QpaleoLev^a: 4:24–26.

15. pap4QLXXLev^b. *bring* MasLev^a MT SP LXX.

16. pap4QLXXLev^b LXX. Not in MT SP.

[times *with his*] *finger*[17] [before the LO]RD, before the veil of the sanctuary. 7 And
the priest shall put some of the blood *of the b*[*ull*][18] on the horns of the altar of
sweet incense [before the LORD, which is] in t[he tent of meeting;] and all the
blood of the bull he shall pour out at the base of the altar of *offering,*[19] which is at
the door of [the t]ent [of m]eeting. 8 A[nd he shall take] from it [all the] f[at of
the b]ull of th[e sin offering;] the fat that covers the entrails, all the fat [that is on
the entrails, 9 the two kidneys, the fat tha]t is on them, which is by the loins, and
the appendage [on the liver, with the kidneys, shall he take away, 10 as it is taken
off from the ox of the sacrifice] of we[ll-being; and the prie]st [shall burn them]
on the a[ltar of burnt o]ffering. 11 And t[he skin of the bull,] all [its flesh, with its
head, and with its legs, its entrails, and its dung, 12 even the whole bull shall he
carry out of the camp to a clean place, where the ashes are poured out, and bur]n
it [on wood with fire; it shall be burned where the ashes are poured out.]

[13 "'And if the whole congregation of Israel sins unintentionally, and the
thing be hid from the ey]es of the assembly, and they have done any [of the things
which the LORD has commanded not to be done, and are guilty; 14 when] the sin
in which [they have sinned becomes kno]wn, [then the assembly shall offer a
young bull for a sin offering, and bring] *it*[20] [before the tent of meeting.]▲
[18 "'And he shall put some of the blood on the horns of the altar which is before the LORD, that is in the tent of meeting; and] all the [blood shall he pour out
at] the [base] of the a[ltar of burnt] offeri[ng, which is at the door] of the tent [of
meeting. 19 And] all the fa[t shall he take off from it, and burn it on the altar.]▲

■ *The manuscript known as 11QpaleoLev*[a] *begins in verse 4 and continues—seven*
columns and sixteen fragments later—to 27:19. One of the most complete manu-
scripts of the biblical scrolls, it is one of four Leviticus scrolls written in paleo-Hebrew
script. When the scroll was bought from its Bedouin discoverers in February of 1956,
its origin was unknown. Later that same year, the noted French archaeologist Roland
de Vaux found fragments of the scroll in what became known as Cave 11, determining
its place of origin with certainty.

[23 "'. . . if his sin, in which he has sinned, is made known to him, he shall
bring as] his offering *for that which he has sinned*[21] a goa[t, a male without blemish;
24 and he shall l]a[y his hand on the head of the goat, and] slaughter it in the
place [where they slaughter the burnt offering bef]ore the LORD; [it is a sin offer-

---

17. pap4QLXXLev[b] SP. Not in MT LXX.
18. pap4QLXXLev[b] LXX. Not in MasLev[a] MT SP.
19. pap4QLXXLev[b]. *burnt offering* MasLev[a] MT SP LXX.
20. Feminine 4QLev[c]. Masculine MT SP LXX.
21. Partially erased 4QLev[c]. Not in MT SP LXX.

ing.] 25 And the priest shall take some of [the blood of the sin offering with his finger and put it on the horns of the altar of] burnt offering; *and he shall pour out its blood*[22] [at the base of the altar of burnt offering. 26 And all its fat h]e shall burn on [the] altar, [as th]e fat [of the sacrifice of well-being;] ard [the priest] shall make atonement for [him for his sin, and it shall be forgiven] him.

[27 " 'And] if [anyone] of [the common people sin un]intentionally, in doing any of the *things*[23] the LORD has commanded not to be [do]ne, and be guilty, 28 or if [his] s[in,] which he has sinn[ed, is made] k[now]n to him, [then he shall bring for his offering] a female goat [without blemish,] for his [si]n which [he has sinned. 29 And he shall lay his hand upon the head of the sin offering, and kill the sin offering in the place of burnt offering. 30 And the priest shall take some of its blood] with his f[inger, and put it on th]e horn[s of the altar of burn]t of[fering; and all its blood shall he pour out at the base of the altar.' "]▲

5 [6 " '. . . and he shall bring his guilt offering to the LORD for his sin which he has sinned, a female from the flock, a lamb or a goat, for a sin offering; and the priest shall make atonement for him for] his sin [*which he sinned and*] it shall [*be forgiven to him.*][24]

[7 " 'And if he cannot afford a lamb, then he shall bring his penalty for that which he has sinned, two turtledoves, or two young pigeons, unto the LORD; one for a sin offering, and the other for a burnt offering. 8 And he shall bring them to the priest, who shall offer that which is for the sin offering first, and wring off its head from] its neck, bu[t shall not sever it, 9 and] he shall sprinkle some [of th]e blo[od of] the sin offe[ring o]n the side of the] alta[r; and the rest] of the blood [shall be drained out at] the base of t[he altar;] *for*[25] it is [a sin offerin]g. [10 And] he shall [perform the second] as a burnt [offering, according to the ordinance; and the priest] shall make [aton]ement [for him for] his [sin which he has sinned, and he shall be forgiven.]

[11 " 'But if he cannot afford two turtledoves or two young pigeons, then he shall bring as his offering for the sin that he has committed one-tenth of an ephah of choice flour for a sin offering; he shall not put oil on it or lay frankincense on it, for it is a sin offering. 12 And he shall bring it to the priest, and the priest shall take his handful of it a]s [its memorial, and burn it on the altar, on the offerings of the LOR]D [made by fire;] it is a sin offering. [13 And] the [priest shall make atonemen]t for him [for his sin that he has sinned in any of these things, and he shall be forgiven; and the rest shall be the priest's, as the grain offering.]▲

---

22. 11QpaleoLev[a]. *And its blood he shall pour out* 4QLev[c] MT SP LXX.

23. pap4QLXXLev[b]. *things which* MT SP LXX.

Chapter 5. pap4QLXXLev[b]: 5:6, 8–10, 16–19; 4QLev[c]: 5:12–13.

24. pap4QLXXLev[b] LXX SP. Not in MT.

25. pap4QLXXLev[b] LXX. Not in MT SP.

[16 " '. . . and he shall make restitution for that which he has sinned against the holy thing, and shall add to it a fifth part of it, and give it to the priest; and the priest shall make aton]e[ment for him with the ram] of the [guilt offering, and he shall be forgiven.]

[17 " 'And if] an[yone sins and does] any [of the things which the LORD has commanded not to be done; though he did not know it, yet he is guilty and shall bear his iniquity. 18 And he shall bring a ram without blemish from the flock, according to your estimation, for a guilt offering] t[o the priest; and] the pr[iest shall make atonement for] him [concerning h]is [sin] in which [he erred] unin[tentionally and] knew [it not,] and [he shall be] forg[iven. 19] For[26] [it is a guilt offering;] he [is certainly guil]ty [b]efor[e the LORD.' "]▲

6[1 And the LORD spoke] to [M]o[ses, saying, 2 "If anyone] sin[s and commits a trespass] against t[he LORD, and deals falsely with] his [neighbor concerning a deposit or a] ple[dge, or by robbery, or having defra]uded [his neighbor, 3 or having found that which was l]ost [and lied about it and s]worn to [the lie; in any of all] these things [that a man does, so] sinni[ng, 4 then it shall b]e, if he has sin[ned and is guil]ty, that he shall restore th[at which he took] by robbery, or the thing [which he has gotten by fraud, or the de]pos[it which was committed to him, or t]he lo[st thing which he found, 5 or an]y t[hing about which he has sworn falsely; he shall even restore it in full, and shall add the fifth part more to it: to him to whom it concerns he shall give it, in the day on which he is found guilty."]▲

7[19 " 'And the flesh that touches any unclean thing shall not be eaten; it shall be burned with fire. And as for other flesh,] every[one that] is clean shall eat it. [20 But the person that eats of the flesh of the sacrifice of well-being, th]at belongs to the LORD, having his uncleanness on him, that person shall be cut off from [his] people. [21 And when anyone touches any unclean thing, the uncleanness of] man, or an unclean animal, or any [unclean] abo[mination, and eat of the flesh of the sacrifice of well-being, which belongs to the LORD,] that soul shall be cut off from his people.' "

[22 " 'And the LORD spoke to Moses, saying, 23 "Speak to the childr]en of Israel, saying, [You shall eat] no fat, of o[x, or sheep, or goat. 24 And the fat of that which dies of itself, and the fat of that which is torn of anim]als, may be used for any other service; but you shall never ea[t any of it."]

■ *In the text of Leviticus 7:25, as found in 4QLev*[g]*, the unpronounceable name of God—Yahweh is a good guess—is written in ancient Hebrew characters (paleo-Hebrew), although the rest of the text is copied in the more familiar "square" letters.*

---

26. pap4QLXXLev[b] LXX. Not in MT SP.

Chapter 6. pap4QLXXLev[b]: 6:1–5 [MT 5:20–24].

Chapter 7. 4QLev[g]: Lev 7:19–26.

Early in scroll research this strange feature was thought to be a sign of nonbiblical material. However, now that the list of such biblical manuscripts totals at least nine, it seems clear that this judgment was incorrect. At the most, these scrolls may be evidence of a more popular edition of the Bible: their copyists may have tended to accommodate themselves to the spelling conventions that were current in the Second Temple period rather than the tradition of letter-by-letter accuracy.

[25 For whoever eats the fat of the animal,] from [which] *they*[27] shall make an *offering*[28] to the LORD [even the person that eats it shall be cut off from his people. 26 And you shall eat no blood, whether it is] of [bi]rd [or animal, in any of you]r d[wellings.' "]▲

8[12 And he poured some of the anointing oil] on Aa[ron's] he[ad, and anointed him, to sanctify him.] 13 And Moses brought [Aaron's sons, and clothed them] with tunics, and girded [them with sashes, and bound] head-dresse[s] on [th]em [as the LORD commanded Moses.]▲

[26 . . . and from the basket of unleavened bread, that was before the LORD, he took one unleavened cake, and] on[e cake of bread mixed with oil, and one wafer, and placed them on the fat, and on the right thigh. 27 And he put] all these o[n the hands of Aaron, and on the hands of his sons, and waved them for a wave offering before the LORD. 28 And] Moses [took] the[m from their hands, and burned them on the altar on the burnt offering: they were a consecration] for a pleas[ing] odor; [it was an offering made by fire to the LORD.]▲

■ *MasLev[b], a somewhat fragmentary manuscript of some five columns (Lev 8: 31–11:40), was found in a corner of the court that lies between Herod's northern palace and the large bathhouse to the south. Dating to the middle of the first century CE, it is the earliest exact representative of the Masoretic Text. Whereas other similarly sized manuscripts of this textual family reflect the relatively relaxed spelling conventions of the day, this scroll represents the Masoretic Text to the jot and tittle.*

[31 And Moses said to Aaron and to his sons, "Boil the flesh at the door of the tent of meeting and eat it there and the brea]d that is [in the basket of consecration, as I commanded, saying, 'Aaron and his sons shall e]at it.' [32 And that which remains of the flesh and of the bread shall you burn with fire. 33 And you shall n]ot [go out of the door of the tent of meeting for seven days, until the days of your consecration are fulfilled; for he shall consecrate you for seven days. 34 As has been done this day, so the LOR]D [has commanded to do, to make atonement for you."]▲

27. 4QLev[g]. *one shall make* MT SP LXX.

28. 4QLev[g]. *an offering by fire* MT SP LXX.

Chapter 8. 6QpaleoLev: 8:12–13; 4QLev[c]: 8:26–28; MasLev[b]: 8:31, 33–34.

9 [1 And on] the ei[ghth da]y, [Moses called Aaron and his sons, and the elders of Israel;] 2 and he said [to Aaron, "Take a calf for yourself from the] herd [for a s]in offe[ring] and a ram for a burnt offering, [without ble]mish, [and offer them before the LORD. 3 And to] the child[ren of Isra]el you shall speak, saying, ['Take] a male goat for [a sin offering; and a calf and a lam]b, both a ye[ar old, without ble]mish, [for a bur]nt offering; 4 and an ox and a r[am for an offering of well-being, to sacrifice before the] LORD; and [grain] mixed with oil; for today the LORD [shall appear to you.'" 5 And they brought that which Moses commanded] before the tent of meeting, and [all the congregation approached and stood before the LORD. 6 And Mos]es [said,] "This is the th[ing which the LORD commanded that you should do, and the glory of the LORD shall appear to you." 7 And Moses said to Aaron, "Approach the altar and offer] your [sin offering and your burnt offering, and make atonement] for [yourself and for] the people; and o[ffer] the [offering of] the people, and make atonement for them, [a]s [the Lor]D [commanded."]

8 So Aaron approached the al[ta]r, and slaughtered the calf of [the sin offering, whic]h was for himself. 9 And the sons of [Aaron] presented [the blood] to him; and he [dip]ped his finger [in the blood, and put it on the horn]s of the [a]ltar, and [poured out the blood at the base of the altar. 10 But the fat, the kidn]eys, [and the appendage from the liver of the sin offering] he burned [on the altar, as the LORD commanded Moses. 11 And the flesh and the skin he burned with fire outside the camp.]

[12 And he slaughtered the burnt offering; and] Aa[ron's sons brought him the blood, and he sprinkled it around on the altar. 13 And] they deli[vered the burnt offering] to him, [piece by piece, and the head, and he burned them on the altar. 14 And he washed the entrails and the legs, and burned them on the burnt offering on the altar.]

[15 And] he pre[sented the people's offering, and took the goat of the sin offering which was for the people, and slaughtered] it, [and offered it for sin, as the first.]▲

[22 And Aaron lifted up his hands toward the people and blessed them; and he came down from of]fering the si[n offering, the burnt offering, and the offering of well-being. 23 And Moses and Aaron went into the t]ent of meeting, and cam[e out, and blessed the] who[le] congre[gation;²⁹ and the glory of the LORD appeared to all] the people. 24 And there came forth fire from before the LORD, [and consumed] the burnt offering [and] the *fat of the offering of well-bein*[g³⁰ on the altar, and when all the people saw it, they shouted, and fell] on their faces.

Chapter 9. MasLevᵇ: 9:1–10, 12–13, 15, 22–24; 11QLevᵇ: 9:23–24.

  29. 11QLevᵇ. *the people* MT SP. *all the people* LXX.

  30. 11QLevᵇ. *fats* MT SP LXX.

10 ¹ And [Nadab and Abihu, the] *tw*[o³¹ sons of Aaron, e]ach took his censer, and put [fire] in th[em, and laid incense on it, and] offered [strange fire] before the LORD, [which *the LOR*]D³² [had not commanded] them. 2 And there came forth [fire from before the LORD and consumed them, and they died] be[fore the LORD. 3 Then Moses said to Aaron, "This is what the LORD spoke, saying, 'I will be sanctified through those who come near to me, and before all the people I will be glorified.' " And Aaron held his peace.]

[4 And Moses called Mishael and Elzaphan, the sons of U]zz[iel the uncle of Aa]ro[n, and said to them, "Come near; carry your brothers from before the sanctuary ou]t of the ca[mp." 5 So] they drew near, and [carried them in their tunics from the camp, as Moses had said. 6 And Moses said to Aaron] and to Eleazar and Itha[mar, his sons, "Do not dishevel your hair nor tear your clothes, that you might not die,] and that he might not be ang[ry] with all the congregation. [But let your brothers, the whole house of Israel, mourn the burning which the LORD has brought about. 7 And you shall] no[t go *out*]³³ the door of the tent of meeting, [lest you die; for the anointing oil of the LORD is on you." And they did according to the word of Moses.]

[8 And the LORD spoke to Aaron:] 9 "Do [n]ot drink any wine or strong dri[nk,] neither you nor your [sons with you, when you go into the tent of meeti]ng, that you might not die; it shall be a statute forever throughout your generations; 10 [and that you may make a distinction between the hol]y and the common, and between the unclean and [the cl]ean; [11 and that you might teach] the ch[ildren of] Israel all the statute[s which the LORD has spoken to them by] Moses."

[12 And Moses spoke to Aaron, and to Eleazar and] to Ithamar, his sons that [were left: "Take the grain that remains of the offerings of the Lo]RD [made by fire,] and eat it with[out leaven beside the altar; for it is most holy; 13 and] you [shall ea]t it in [a holy place, because it is your portion, and your sons' portion, of the offerings of the Lo]RD [made by fire;] for so [I am] comman[ded. 14 And the breast of the wave offering and the thigh of the heave offering you shall eat in a clean place, you, your sons, and your daughters with you; for they are given as your portion, and your sons' portion, from the sacrifices of well-being of the] children of [Israel. 15 The thigh of the heave offering and the breast of] the wave of[fering they shall bring] with [the offerings made by fire of the f]at, [to wave it for a wave offering before LORD; and it shall b]e yours, and your sons' [with you,] as a portion [forever, as the LORD has commanded."]

_____

Chapter 10. MasLevᵇ: 10:1, 9–20; 11QLevᵇ: 10:1–2; 11QpaleoLevᵃ: 10:4–7.

   31. 11QLevᵇ LXX. Not in MT SP.

   32. 11QLevᵇ LXX. Not in MT SP.

   33. 11QpaleoLevᵃ. *out from* MT SP LXX.

[16 And Moses diligently] soug[ht] the goat of the sin offering, [and behold, it had been burned, and he was angry] with Eleazar and with Ithamar, the sons of [Aaron that remai]ned, saying, 17 "Why have you not eaten the [si]n offering in the place of the [sanctuary, seeing] it is [mo]st holy, and he has given it to you to bear the iniqu[ity of the congregation, to make atonement for] them before the LORD? 18 Behold, its blood was not brought into the san[ctuary; you should certainly have ea]t[en it in the sanctuary, as] I [commanded."] 19 And Aaron spoke [to Moses: "Behold, this day have they] offe[red their sin offering and] their [burnt offering] before the LORD; when [things like the]se [have happened to me,] if I had eaten [the sin offering today, would it have been pleasing t]o the LOR[D?"] 20 And when [Moses heard that, it was pleasing to him.]

11 [1 And the LORD spoke t]o [Moses and to Aaron, saying to them, 2 "Speak to the children of Israel, saying,] 'These are the living things w[hich you may eat among all the animals that are] on the ear[th. 3 Whatever parts] the hoof, and is clef[tfooted and chews] the cud, among the animals, [that] you may [ea]t. 4 Nevertheless [these you shall not eat, of those that chew the cu]d, or of those that part the ho[of:] the [camel, because it chews the cud but] does not [part the ho]of, [it is] uncle[an to you. 5 And the rock badger, because i]t [chews the cud] but does not [part] the hoof, [it is unclean to you. 6 And the hare, because] it [ch]ews the cud but [does not part] the ho[of, it is unclean to you. 7 And] the swine, because [it] part[s the hoof, and is cleftfooted, but] does not chew the cud, it is unclean to you. [8 You shall not eat of their flesh, and] you shall [not] touch [their carcasses;] they are u[nclea]n to you.

[9 "'These may you eat, of all that are in the waters:] whate[ver has] fins and s[cales in the waters, in the seas, and in the rivers, yo]u may [e]at. 10 And all th[at] have not fin[s and scales in the seas, and in the rivers,] of all that move in the waters, and of all [the living creatures that are in the waters, they are an abomination] to [y]ou, 11 and they shall be an abomination [to yo]u; [you shall not eat] of their flesh, [and their carcasses you shall regard as an abomination.] 12 Whatever has no fins or scales in the waters [is an abomination to you.]

[13 "'And th]es[e] you shall regard as an abomination [among] the b[irds; they shall not be eaten, they are an abomination:] the [eagle, and the] vultu[re,] and the [osprey, 14 and the ki]t[e, and the falcon after its kind, 15 every] raven after its kind, 16 and [the ostrich, the night-hawk, the seagull, and the hawk after i]ts [kind,] 17 and the little o[wl, the cormorant, the great owl, 18 the horned owl,] the pelican, the [vulture, 19 the stork, the heron after its kind, the hoopoe,] and [the bat.]

Chapter 11. MasLev[b]: 11:1–21, 24–40; 1QpaleoLev: 11:10–11; 2QpaleoLev: 11:22–29; 11QpaleoLev[a]: 11:27–32.

[20 "'All winged insects that go on all fours are an abomination] to you. [21 Yet these may you eat of all winged insects that go on] all fou[rs, those which have legs above their feet, with which to leap on the ground. 22 These of them you may eat: the locust after] its k[ind, the bald locust after i·s kind, the cricket after its kind, and the grasshopper after] its k[ind. 23 But all other winged swarming things which have four feet are an abomination to you.]

[24 "'And] by these you shall become unclean, whoever touc[hes the carcass of them shall be unclean] until [the evening. 25 And whoever carries any part of the carcass of any of them] shall wash his clothes, [and be unclean until the eveni]ng. 26 Every anim[al which pa]rts the hoof and *cleaves* [*the foot*][34] and does no[t chew] the cud [is unclean to you; whoever] touches them shall be unclean. 27 And whatever goes on [its] *be*[*lly*][35] among all animals that go on] all fours, they are unclean to you; whoever touches their carcass shall be un[clean until the eveni]ng. 28 And he who carries [their] carc[ass shall was]h his clothes and be unclean until the evening; they are [unclean] to you.

29 "'And these are they which are unclean to you among the things [which] creep on the earth: the weasel, [the mo]use, the great lizard after its kind, 30 and the gecko, [the] land-crocodile, the lizard, the sand-lizard, and the chamele[on.] 31 These are they which are unclean to you among al[l] that creep; whoever touches them when they are dead shall be unclean until the evening. [32 And] what[ever] falls on [any of] them, when they are dead, it shall be unclean; whether it be any vessel of wood, or garme[nt, or skin,] or sack, whatever vessel with which [any wor]k is [done,] it must be p[u]t into water and it shall be unclean until the eveni[ng; then] shall it be clean. 33 And every earthen [vess]el in[to which] any of [th]em falls, whatever is in it shall be unclean, and you shall break it. 34 Any food which [may be ea]ten, [o]n [w]hich water [comes,] shall be unclean; and any liquid which may be drunk in every such vessel shall be unclean. 35 And everything on which any part of their carcass falls shall be unclean; whether oven or stove, it shall be broken in pieces; [they are unclea]n, and shall be un[clea]n to you. 36 Nevertheless a spring or a cistern collecting water shall be clean; [but that which touches their] carcass [shall be unclean. 37 And] if any part of their carcass falls on any seed for sowing, it is clean. [38 But if] water be put on the seed, and any part of their carcass fall on it, it is unclean [to you.]

39 "'And if any animal, of which you may eat, die, [he who touches its carcass] shall be unclean until the evening. 40 And he who eats of its carcass shall wash his clothes [and be unclean until the evening.] He also who carries its carcass shall wash his clothes and be unclean until [the evening.'"]▲

34. 2QpaleoLev LXX. *the foot does not cleave* MasLev[b] MT. *cleaves not the foot* SP.

35. 11QpaleoLev[a]. *paws* MT SP LXX.

13 [3 ". . . and the priest shall look at the mark on the skin of the body, and if the hair in the mark has turned white and the appearance of the mark is deeper than the skin of his flesh,] it is [a mark] of leprosy; and the [priest] shall look on him [and pronounce him unclean. 4 And if the bright spot is white on the skin of his body and] its appearance [is not deeper] than the skin, and [its] ha[ir has not turned white, then the priest shall shut up him who has the plague for seven days. 5 And] the priest [shall look at him] on the se[venth] day, [and behold, if in his eyes the mark has not changed and has not spread on the skin, then the prie]st [shall shut him up for se]ven m[ore] days. [6 And the priest shall look at him again the seventh day, and behold, if the mark has faded and] the mark has [no]t s[prea]d [on the skin, then the priest shall pronounce him clean; it is a scab, and he shall wash his clothes and be clean. 7 But if] the scab [sprea]ds [farther] on the ski[n, after he has shown himself to the priest for his cleansing, he shall show himself to the priest again. 8 And] the priest [shall lo]ok, and beho[ld, if the scab has spread on the skin, then the priest shall pronounce him unclean; it is leprosy.]

9 "When [the mar]k of leprosy [is on a man, then he shall be brought to the priest.]▲

[32 "And on the seventh day the] p[riest shall look at the mark, and behold, if the scale has not spread, and there is no yellow hair in it,] and [the] appearan[ce of the scale is not deeper than the skin, 33 then he shall be shaved, but the scale shall he not shave; and the priest shall shut up] him that has the sc[ale for seven more days.]▲

[39 ". . . then the priest shall look, and behold, if the bright spots on the skin of their body is a dull wh]ite, [it is a rash that has broken out in the skin; he is clean.]

[40 "And if a man's hair has fallen from his head, he is bald yet] he is [c]lean. [41 And if his hair has fallen out of the front part of his head, he is forehead-bald; yet he is clean. 42 But if there is] on *his*[36] bald head or the bald forehead a reddish-white mark, it is leprosy breaking out on his bald head o[r his bald forehead. 43 Then the priest shall look at him,] and behold, [if the swelling of the mark is reddish-white on his bald head or on his bald forehead, like the appearance of leprosy in the skin of the body.]▲

[58 "And the garment, either the warp or the w]oof, or what[ever thing of leather it be, which you shall wash, if the] mark [disappears from them,] then it shall be washed the second time, [and shall be clean.]

[59 "This is the law of the mark of leprosy on] a woolen or linen [ga]rment,

---

Chapter 13. 11QpaleoLev[a]: 13:3–9, 39–43; 4QLev-Num[a]: 13:32–33; 11QLev[b]: 13:58–59.

36. 11QpaleoLev[a] SP LXX. *the* MT.

[either in the warp or the woof, or anythi]ng of leather, *for its cleansing*[37] or [to pronounce it unclean."]

14 [16 ". . . and the priest shall dip his] righ[t finger in the oil that is in his left hand] and sprinkle some of the *oil*[38] seven ti[mes before the LORD. 17 And of the rest of the oil that is in his hand the pries]t [shall put] on the *tip*[39] of the [right] ear of the one that is to be clean[sed, and on the thumb of his right hand, and on the great toe of his righ]t [foot,] on the blood of the guilt offering. 18 And [the rest of the oil that is in the priest's hand he shall put on the head of the one that is to be cleansed, and the] priest [shall make atonement for him] befo[re the LORD. 19 And] the priest [shall off]er [the sin offering and make atonement for the one that is to be cleansed because of his uncleanness. And afterward he shall slaugh]ter the burnt off[ering; 20 and the priest shall offer the burnt offering and the grain offering on the altar. And] the prie[st shall make atonement] for him, [and he shall be clean.]

[21 "But if he is poor and cannot afford so much, then he shall take one male lamb for a guilt offering as a wa]ve offering to make at[onement for him, one-tenth part of an ephah of fine flour mixed with oil for a grain offering, a log of oil; 22 and two turtledoves or two] young pigeons, su[ch as h]e is able to afford; [and the one shall be a sin offering, and the other a burnt offering. 23 And on] the eig[hth da]y [he shall bring them] for [his] cleansing [to the priest, to the door of the tent of meeting, before the LORD; 24 and the priest shall take the lamb of the guilt offering, and the log of oil, and the priest shall wave them for a wave offering before the LORD.[40] 25 And he shall slaughter the lamb of the] guilt offering; and the priest shall take [some of the blo]od of the gu[ilt offering and put it on the tip of the right ear of the one that is to be cleansed, on the thumb of] his right hand, and on the great toe of his [right] foot. [26 And the priest shall pour some of the oil into the palm of his own le]ft [hand;] 27 and [the prie]st shall spri[nkle] with [his right] finger [so]me of the oil t[hat is in his left hand seven times be]fore the LORD. [28 And the priest shall put some of the oi]l that is in his hand o[n the tip of the righ]t [ear of the one that is to be cleansed,] on the thumb of his right hand, and on the great to[e of his right] fo[ot, on the place of the blood of the guilt offering. 29 And the] rest of the oil that is i[n the pr]iest's

---

37. 11QLev[b]. *to pronounce it clean* MT SP LXX.

Chapter 14. 11QpaleoLev[a]: 14:16–21, 52–57; 4QLev-Num[a]: 14:22–34, 40–54; 4QLev[d]: 14:27–29, 33–36.

38. 11QpaleoLev[a] SP. *oil with his finger* MT LXX.

39. Indecipherable scribal error 11QpaleoLev[a].

40. 4QLev-Num[a] may omit the entirety of verse 24. MT SP LXX all include it.

[hand] he shall put o[n the head of the one that is to be cleansed, to make atonement for him before the LORD. 30 And he shall offer one of the turtledove]s, or o[f the young pigeons, such as he is able to afford, 31 even such as he is able to afford, the one for a sin offering and] the o[ther for a burnt offering, with] the grain offering; and the p[riest] shall make atonement [for him that is to be cleansed before the LORD. 32 This is the law of him in whom is the plague of leprosy, w]ho is not able to afford [that which is necessary for his cleansing."]

[33 And the LORD spoke to Moses and to A]aron, saying, 34 "When you en[ter the land of Canaan, which I give to you for a possession, and I put the pla]gue of leprosy in a house in the lan[d of your possession, 35 then he who owns the house shall come and tell the priest, saying, There se]ems to me [to be a plague] in the house. 36 And [the priest] shall co[mma]nd [that they empty the house, before the priest goes in to see] the plague *of leprosy,*[41] so that [all that is in the house might] not [be made unclean; and afterward the priest shall go in to see the house.]▲

[40 ". . . then the priest shall command that they take out the stones in which the plague is and throw them into an unclean] place [outside the city. 41 And he shall have the inside of the house scraped thoroughly, and they shall dump the plaster that] they [scrape off] outside the city in an uncl[ean] place. [42 And they shall take other stones and put them in the place of] those stones, and *they*[42] shall take other plaster and plaster [the house.]

[43 "And if the plague returns and breaks out in the ho]use, after he has taken out the [sto]nes and after he has *plast[ered the house,*[43] 44 then the priest shall come in and lo]ok, and behold, if the plague has spread in the hou[se,] it [is a malignant disease in the house; it is unclean. 45 And] *they*[44] shall tear down the house, its *stone,*[45] and [its] timber, [and all the plaster of the house, and carry them outside the city to an unclean place.] 46 Moreover he who goes into the house wh[ile] it is [sh]ut [up shall be unclean until the evening. 47 And he who lies in the house shall wash] his clothes; and he who eats in the house shall w[ash his clothes.]

[48 "And if the priest comes, and looks, and behold,] the plague has not spread in the house, a[fter the house was plastered, then the priest shall pronounce the house clean, because] the plague [is] healed. 49 *He*[46] shall take [two birds] to *cleanse*[47] [the house, and cedar wood, a scarlet thread, and hys]sop, 50 and

---

41. 4QLev^d. Not in MT SP LXX.

42. 4QLev–Num^a SP LXX. *he* MT.

43. 4QLev–Num^a. *scraped the house and plastered* MT SP LXX.

44. 4QLev–Num^a SP LXX. *he* MT.

45. 4QLev–Num^a. *stones* MT SP LXX.

46. 4QLev–Num^a. *And he* MT LXX. *And they* SP.

47. 4QLev–Num^a. *to purify from uncleanness* MT SP LXX.

they[48] shall slaughter one of the birds [in an earthen vessel over running water, 51 and he shall take the cedar wood,] the hyssop, the scarlet thread, [and the living bird, and dip them in the blood of the sl]ain [bird,] and in the running water, and sprinkle *on*[49] [the house seven times. 52 And he shall cleanse the house with the blood of the bird,] the running water, the living bird, [the cedar wood, the hyssop, and the scarlet thread, 53 but he shall let] the living bird go free outside the city [in the open field. So he shall make atonement for the house; and it shall be clean."]

[54 This is the law] for every plague of leprosy and scale, 55 and [for the leprosy of a garment and a house, 56 and for a swelling, a scab, and bright spot; 57 to teach when they are unc]lean and when they are clea[n. This is the law of leprosy.]

15 [1 And the LORD spoke to Moses and to Aaron, saying, 2 "Speak to the children of Isra]el, and say to them, ['When any man has a discharge from his flesh, he is unclean because of his discharge. 3 And this sha]ll be his uncleanness in his discharge: [whether his flesh runs with his discharge or his flesh obstructs his discharge, it is his uncleanness] *in him all the days of the disc[harge of his flesh; even if his flesh obstructs his discharge, it is his uncleanness.*[50] 4 Every bed] on [which the one who has the discharge] lies [shall be unclean; and everything on which he sits shall be unclean. 5 And whoever touch]es his bed shall wash [his clothes, and bathe himself in water, and be unclean until the evening.]▲

[10 "'And whoever touches anything that was] under him shall be uncle[an until the evening, and the one who carries those things shall wash his clothes, and bathe himself in water, and be unclean until] the evening. 11 And whoev[er the one who has the discharge touches without having rinsed his hands in water shall wash his clothes, and bathe himself in water, and be unclean until the evening.]▲

[19 "'And if a woman has a discharge, and if her discharge in her flesh is blood, she shall b]e in her impurity [for seven days; and whoever touches her shall be unclean until the evening. 20 And everything that she lies on during her impurity shall] be unclean; and everything tha[t she sits on shall be unclean. 21 And whoever touches her bed shall wash his clothes, and bathe himself in wat]er, and be unclean until the evening. 22 And whoever tou[ches anything that she sits on shall wash his clot]h[es, and bathe himself] in wa[ter,] and be unclean until the evening. [23 And if it be on the bed, or on anything upon which she sits, when he touches] it, he shall be unclean until [the eveni]ng. 24 And [i]f [any man] l[ies

48. 4QLev-Num[a]. *he* MT SP LXX.

49. 4QLev-Num[a] SP LXX. *toward* MT.

Chapter 15. 11QpaleoLev[a]: 15:1–5; 4QLev-Num[a]: 15:10–11, 19–24; 4QLev[d]: 15:20–24.

50. 11QpaleoLev[a] SP LXX. Not in MT.

with her, and her impurity is on him, he shall be unclean for seven] day[s; and eve]ry [bed upon which he lies shall be unclean.'"]▲

16 [1 And the LORD spoke to Moses after the death of] the two sons of Aaron, [when they approached the LORD and died; 2 and the LORD said to Mos]es, "Speak to Aaron your brother, that [he is not to enter at any time into the holy place within the veil, bef]ore the mercy-seat which is on the a[rk, that he might not die,] for [I will appear in the cloud on the mercy-seat.] 3 Thus shall Aaron come into the holy pl[ace: with a young bull] for [a sin offering and a ram for a burnt offering.] 4 He shall put on the holy [linen tunic,] and he shall h[ave] the linen undergarments [next to his body, and shall be girded with the linen] sa[sh, and] shall wear [the lin]en miter; these are the holy garments. And he shall bath[e] his [flesh in water] and pu[t them on. 5 And] he shall take [from the congregation of the children of Isra]el two male goats [for a sin offering and one ram for a burnt offering.]

[6 "And Aaron shall present] the bull of the sin offering, which is for himself, and make atonem[ent for himself, and for his house.]▲

[15 "Then he shall slaughter the goat of the sin offering which is for the people, and bring its blood inside the veil, and do with his blood as he did with the blood of the bull, and sprinkle it on the mercy-seat and] befor[e the mercy-seat. 16 And he shall make atonement for the holy place, because of the uncleannesses of the children of Israel, and because of their transgressions, all their sins; and so he shall do for the tent of] meeting, [that dwells with them in the midst of their uncleannesses. 17 And there shall be no man in the tent of] meeting when [he goes in to make atonement in the holy place until] he comes out, to make atonement fo[r himself, for his household, and for all the assembly of Israel. 18 And he shall go out to] the altar that [is before the LORD and make atonement for it, and shall] ta[k]e some of the blood of the bu[ll, and the blood of the goat, and put it all around the horns of the altar. 19 And he shall sprink]le so[me of the blood] on it [with his finger seven times, and clea]nse it, [and dedicate it from the uncleannesses of the children of Is]rael.

20 "And when he has finished at[oning for] the ho[ly place, and the tent of meeting, and the] altar, he shall [present the live goat. 21 And Aaron shall lay] both of [his] hand[s o]n the head of the [live] go[at and confess over it] all the iniquities [of the children of Israel, and all their transgressions, all] their [sin]s; and he shall put them on the head of the [goat and shall send him away into the] wilderness [by means of a man that is designated. 22 And the goat shall bear on itself all] their iniquities t[o a solitary land; and he shall let the goat go in the wilderness.]

[23 "And Aaron shall come into the tent of meeting and shall put off the linen

Chapter 16. 11QpaleoLevᵃ: 16:1–6, 34; 4QLev-Numᵃ: 16:15–29.

garments] which he put on *and he shall g*[*o*[51] into the holy place, and shall] leave them there. [24 And he shall bathe his flesh in water in a holy place, put on his garments and come out, and offer his burnt offering] and the burnt offering of the [people, and make atonement for himself and for the] people. 25 And [he shall burn the fat of the sin offering on the altar. 26 And he who set]s the goat free [for Azazel shall wash his clothes and bathe his flesh in water, and afterward he shall come into the camp. 27 And] the bull of the sin offering and the go[at of the sin offering, whose blood was brought in to make atonement in the holy place, shall be carried out of the camp, and they shall burn] their skins in the fire, [along with their flesh and their dung. 28 And he who burns them shall wash his clothes and bathe his flesh in water, and afterw]ard he shall come into [the camp.]

[29 "And it shall be a statute forever to you, in the seventh month, on the tenth day of the month, you shall deny yourself and do n]o [work, the native or the stranger that resides among you;]▲

[34 "And this shall be an everlasting statute for you, to make atonement fo]r the children of Isra[el because of all their sins once every year." And he did] as the L[ORD] commanded [Moses.]

17 1 And the LORD spoke to [Moses, saying, 2 "Speak to] *Aaron*[52] and to all the children of Israel, and sa[y] to them: 'This is what [the Lo]R[D] has commanded, [sayi]ng, 3 "Any man from the house of Israel [*and the stranger who*] *resides in Israel*[53] who slaughters an ox, or [lamb, or goat, in the cam]p, or who slaughters it outside the camp, 4 and [has not brought it] to the door of the tent of meeti[ng *so as to sacrifice it as a burnt offering*] *or an offering of well-being to the LORD to be acceptable as* [*a pleasing odor, and has slaughtered it without and*] *does not bring it* [*to the door of the tent of me*]*eting*[54] to offer *it*[55] as an offering to LORD before the taber[nacle] of the LORD, [t]hat m[an] shall be guilty of bloodshed; he has shed blood and shall be cut off from am[ong] his people. 5 This is so [the children of] Israel will bring their sacrifices which they sacrifice i[n the] open field, that they may bring them to the L[ORD, t]o the door of the tent of meeting, to the priest, and sacrifice them for sac[rifices of well-being to the LORD. 6 And the priest shall sprinkle] the blood on the altar [of the LORD at the door of the tent of meeting, and burn the fat for a pleasing odor] to the [L]ORD. 7 And they shall no [longer] sacrifice [their sacrifices to the goat idols with which they play the harlot. This shall be a statute forever to them throughout their generations."']

---

51. 4QLev-Num[a]. *when he went* MT SP LXX.

Chapter 17. 11QpaleoLev[a]: 17:1–5; 4QLev[d]: 17:2–11.

52. 11QpaleoLev[a]. *Aaron and to his sons* MT SP LXX.

53. 4QLev[d]. Not in 11QpaleoLev[a] MT SP. *and the strangers who dwell among you* LXX.

54. 4QLev[d] SP LXX. Not in 11QpaleoLev[a] MT.

55. 4QLev[d] SP. Not in MT LXX.

[8 "And you shall say to them, 'Anyone of the house of Israel, or] of [the strangers that reside among them, who offers a burnt offering or sacrifice, 9 and] bri[ngs it] not [to the d]oor of the t[en]t of meeting [to sacrifice it to the LORD, that man shall be cut off from] his [people.]

10 " 'And anyone of the house of Israe[l, or of the strangers that reside among them, who eats any manner of blo]od, I will set my face against that person who [eats blood, and will cut him off from among his people. 11 For] the life of *all*[56] flesh is in *its*[57] blood, and I [have given it to you to make atonement for yourselves on the altar; for it is the blood that makes atonement by reason of the life.' "]▲

18 16 "You shall not uncover [the nakedness of] your [brot]her['s wife; it is your brother's] nakedness. [17 You shall not uncover the nakedness of a woman and her daughter,] you shall not take [her son's daughter, or her daughter's daughter,] to uncover [her] nakedness; [they are near relatives. It is wickedness. 18 And you shall not take a woman as a rival to her sister, to uncover] her nakedness, while the other is still a[live.]

[19 "And you shall not approach a woman to uncover her nakedness during her menstrual uncleanness. 20 And you shall] n[ot have sexual relations with your neighbor's wife, to defile yourself with her. 21 And you shall not give any of your offspring to offer them to Molech, nor shall you profane the name of your God:] I [am LORD.]▲

■ *As the scribe of 11QpaleoLev*[a] *began copying 18:27, his memory evidently completed the passage from the similar Leviticus 20:23–24. Realizing his mistake, he surrounded the passage with parentheses rather than erase it. The mistake evidently was not perpetuated—no other manuscripts are known to include it—but students of text criticism can point to other examples where this type of error (or "harmonization") is suspected to have occurred.*

[27 ". . . for] the men of the land who were befo[re you] have done [all] these [abomi]nations [(*and I have abhorred them and said to you, "Y]ou shall inherit their la[n]d,"*)[58] [but] the land [has become defil]ed; 28 so that the land might not vomit you out also, when you defile it, as it vo[mited out the nati]on that was before you. 29 For whoe[ver] shall do any of these abominations, [those person]s who do them shall be cu[t off] from among their people. 30 Therefore you shall ke[ep] my charge, that you might not practice any of these [abom]inable [cus-

---

56. 4QLev[d] LXX. *the* MT SP.

57. 4QLev[d] LXX. *the* MT SP.

Chapter 18. 4QLev-Num[a]: 18:16–21; 11QpaleoLev[a]: 18:27–30.

58. 11QpaleoLev[a] see Lev 20:23b–24a. Not in MT SP LXX.

toms,] which were practiced before you, [and] that you might [not] defile your-selves by them; *for*[59] I am the L[ORD you]r [God."]

19 [1 And] the LORD [spok]e to Moses, sayin[g, 2 "Speak to all the cong]rega-tion of the children of Israel and say [to them,] 'You shall be holy, for [I the LOR]D your God am ho[ly.] 3 Every one of you shall reverence his mother [and his father,] and [you shall keep] my sabbaths; [I am the L]ORD your God. 4 Do not turn [to idols nor make molten gods] for yourselves; I am the Lo[RD your God.]

5 "'And when you offer a sa[crifice] of well-being to the LORD, [you shall offer it] that [you may be accepted. 6 It shall be eaten the same day you offer it,] or on the next day; [and if anything remains until] the third [da]y, it shall be bu[rnt] with fire. 7 And if [it is eaten at all on the third day, it i]s [an abomination; it shall] n[ot be accepted. 8 But everyone who eats it] shall bear his iniquity, be-cause [he has profaned the holy thing of the LORD; and that person shall be cut off from his people.]▲

[30 "'You shall keep my sabbaths and reverence] my [sanc]tuary; [I am the LORD.]

[31 "'Do not turn to mediums] or the wizards; [do not seek them out, to be defiled by them; I am the LORD] your God.

[32 "'You shall rise up] before [the aged, and honor the old, and you shall fear] your God; I am the Lo[RD.]

[33 "'And if a stranger resides with you in your land, you shall not do] hi[m wrong. 34 The stranger that resides with you shall be to you] as the native among you, [and] you [shall love him as yourself; for you were sojourners in the land of Egypt; I am] the LORD your God.

[35 "'You shall do no unrighteousness in judgment, in measures of length, of weight, or] of quantity. 36 J[us]t weights,[60] [a just ephah, and a just hin, shall you have; I am the LOR]D your God who [brought you out of the land of Egypt. 37 And you shall observe all] my [statute]s, an[d all my ordinances, and do them; I am the LORD.'"]

20 [1 And the Lo]RD spoke to Moses, saying, 2 "And [you shall] say to the child[ren of Israel,] 'Anyone of the *house*[61] of [Israel, or] of the stranger who resides in Israel, who gives [any of his offspring] to Molech shall surely be put to death; the people of the la[n]d shall stone him with stones. 3 I will also set my face [against] that [man] and will cut him off from amo[ng his people,] be-

---

59. 11QpaleoLev[a] LXX. *Not in* MT SP.

Chapter 19. 11QpaleoLev[a]: 19:1–4; 4QLev-Num[a]: 19:3–8; 1QpaleoLev: 19:30–34; 4QLev[e]: Lev 19:34–37.

60. 4QLev[e]. *Just balances, just weights* MT SP LXX.

Chapter 20. 11QpaleoLev[a]: 20:1–6; 4QLev[e]: 20:1–3, 27; 1QpaleoLev: 20:20–24.

61. 11QpaleoLev[a] SP. *children* MT LXX.

cause he has given of his offspring to Molech, so as to de[file] my sanctuary and *profane*[62] [my] ho[ly] name. [4 And] if the people of the la[nd] ignore that man [when he gives of] his offspr[ing] to Molech and do not put [him] to death, [5 then] I [will set] my face against [that] ma[n and against] his family, and will cut off both him and [all that play the] harlot after him, to play the harlot wi[th Molech,] from [am]ong their people.

6 " 'And the person w[ho turns to medium]s and wizards, [to play the harlot after them, I will also set my face against that person and will cut him off from among his people.]▲

[20 " 'And if a man lies with his uncle's wife, he has uncovered his uncle's nakedness;] they shall bear [their s]i[n; they shall die childless. 21 And if a man takes] his [brot]her['s wife,] it is impurity; [he has uncovered his brother's] nakedness; [they shall be childless.]

[22 " 'Yo]u [shall keep] all my statutes and all [my] o[rdinances, and do them, so that] the land to which I [bring you to dwell in might not vomi]t you out. [23 And] you shall [not] walk in the customs of the na[tion which I am driving out before you; for they did] all the[se things, and therefore I abhorred them. 24 But I have said to you, "You shall inherit their] l[and, and I will give it to] you to poss[ess, a land flowing with milk and honey; I am the LORD your God, who] has [separated] y[ou from the peoples." ' "]▲

[27 " 'A man or a woman who is a] medium or a wiz[ard shall surely be put to death. They shall stone them with stones; their blood is upon them.' "]

21 1 And the LORD said [to Moses, "Speak to the priests, the sons of Aaron, and say to them, 'No one] shall defile himself [for the dead] among his people; [2 except for his relatives who are near to him, his mother and his father, and his son and his daughter] and [his] brother, [3 also] for [his virgin sister, who is near to him because she has had no husband; he may defile himself for her. 4 He shall] n[ot defile himself, as a husband among his people, to profane himself. 5 They shall not make bald spots upon their heads, or shave off the edges of their beard, nor make any gashes in their flesh. 6 They shall be holy to] their [Go]d and n[ot profane the name of their God, for] they present [the offerings of the LORD made by fire, the bread of] their [G]od; therefore they shall be [holy. 7 They shall not] marry [a wom]an that is a harlot, or defiled; neither shall they take a woman put away from her husband; for [they] are holy [to] their [G]od. 8 You shall sanctify them therefore; for they offer the bread of your God; they shall be holy to [you;] for [I] the LORD, who sanctify *them*,[63] am holy. 9 And the daughter of any

---

62. 11QpaleoLev[a] SP. *to profane* MT.

Chapter 21. 4QLev[c]: 21:1–4, 9–12, 21–24; 11QpaleoLev[a]: 21:6–12; 4QLev[b]: 21:17–20, 24; 1QpaleoLev: 21:24.

63. 11QpaleoLev[a] SP LXX. *you* (plural) MT.

priest, if she defiles herself through harlotry, she [de]files *the house of*[64] her father; she shall be burned with fire.

[10 "'And he who is] the high [pr]iest among his brothers, on [wh]ose he[ad] is poured [the anointing oil, and who is consecr]ated to wear the garments, shall not dishevel [his] h[air,] nor [tear his clothes;] 11 nor shall he appro[ach any] dead body, [nor] defile himself for [his] father [or for his mother;] 12 and [he shall not go out of the sa]nctua[ry, nor defile the sanctuary of his God; for the crown of the anointing oil of his God is on him; I am the LORD.'"] ▲

[17 "Speak to Aaron, saying, 'No one of your offspring throughout their generations who] has [a blemish shall approach to offer the bread of his God. 18 For no one who has a blemish shall approach: a blind] man, [or a lame, or he who is disfigured, or deformed, 19 or a man who has a broken foot or a broken hand,] 20 or [a hunchback, a dwarf, who has a blemish in his eye, or eczema, or scabs, or has crushed testicles. 21 No one of the offspring of Aaron the priest who] h[as a blem]ish [shall approach to offer the offerings of the LORD made by fire; he has a blemish; he shall not approach to offer the bread of his God. 22 He shall eat the bread of his God, both of the most hol]y and of the [holy, 23 only he shall not go in to the veil, nor approach the altar, because he has a blemish; that he might not profane my sanctuaries; for I am the LORD who sanctifies them. 24 So Moses spoke to Aaron and to his sons] and to [a]ll[65] Israel.'"

22 [1 And the LORD spoke to Moses, saying, 2 "Speak to Aaron] and to his sons, [that they be careful with the holy things of the children of Israel,] which [they dedicate] to me, [and that they might not profane my holy] n[ame;] I am the LORD. 3 Sa[y to them,] 'Anyone [of all your offspring throughout] your [generations] who [approaches to the holy things] which the children of I[srael] dedicate [to the LORD, while he is in his uncleanness, that person shall be cut off from b]efore me; I a[m the LORD. 4 No one of the offsprin]g [of Aa]ron [who is a leper, or] has a discharge, [shall eat] of the holy thing[s, until he is clean. And whoever touches anything that is un]clean by the dea[d, or] a man who h[as had a seminal emission, 5 or whoever touches any] *unclean*[66] [swa]rming thing by which he may become un[clean, or another person of wh]om he may [take] uncleanness, [whatever the] uncleanness [might be,] 6 *and*[67] the person [that to]uches [any such shall be unclean until the evening and shall not eat of the holy things un]less he [ba]the his flesh in w[ater. 7 And when the sun sets he shall be clean and afterward he may eat of the holy things, because they are his food. 8 That

---

64. 4QLev^e. Not in 11QpaleoLev^a MT SP. *the name of* LXX.

65. 4QLev^e. *all the children of* 1QpaleoLev MT SP LXX.

Chapter 22. 1QpaleoLev: 22:1–6; 4QLev^b: 22:2–33; 4QLev^e: 22:4–6, 11–18; 11QpaleoLev^a: 22:21–27.

66. 4QLev^e SP LXX. Not in 1QpaleoLev MT.

67. 1QpaleoLev. Not in MT SP LXX.

which has d]ied or was torn by animals he shall not eat, [becoming unclean by it;] I am the Lo[RD. 9 They shall keep] my [charg]e, so [that they might not bear] sin [for it] and die because of it for having p[rofan]ed it; I am the LORD who sanctifies them.

10 " '[N]o layperson [shall eat of the] holy gift; one who lives with a pr[iest or a hired servant shall not eat of the holy gift.] 11 But if a priest buys anyone, the one purchased with his money may eat of it; [and] *those who are born*[68] in his house, they shall eat of his food. 12 And [if a priest's daughter is married] to a layman, she shall not eat of the offering of the holy gift. [13 But] if a priest's daughter becomes a wido[w or is divorced, and] has [no child,] and r[etur]ns to her father's house as in her youth, she shall eat of her father's food; but no layman sha[ll eat any of it. 14 And if a man] eats of the holy gift unintentionally, then he shall add a fif[th] to it and shall give the holy gift to the priest. 15 And they shall not profane the hol[y gifts of the children of] Israel [whi]ch they offer to [the LORD,] 16 and so cause them to bear the punishment for guilt when they eat their holy gifts; [for I am] the LORD who sanctifies them.' "

17 And the LORD spoke to Moses, saying, 18 "Speak [to] Aaron and to his sons and to all the [chil]dren of [I]s[rae]l, [and] sa[y to them,] 'Anyone of the house of Israel or o[f] the aliens *who dwell*[69] in [I]srael, who presents [his offering, whether it be for any of their vows] *or*[70] their freewill offerings, which they present to the LORD for a burnt offering—19 that y[ou] may be acc[epted]—a male w[ithout blemi]sh, of the cattle [or the] sheep or the goats. 20 But whatever has a blemish, that shall you not offer: for it shall not be acceptable for *you*.[71]

21 " 'And whoever offers a sacrifice of peace offerings to the LORD to fulfill a vow, or *in the way of*[72] a freewill offering, from the herd or [the floc]k, it shall be perfect to be accepted; there shall be no blemish in it. 22 Anything blind, or broken, or maimed, or *having scabs or a rash or a discharge*[73] *or crushed [testic]les,*[74] you shall not offer *an offering made by fire*[75] to the LORD, nor make an offering by fire of them on the altar to the LORD. 23 Either a bull or a lamb that has anything too long or stunted, *you*[76] may offer it as a freewill offering; but for a vow it shall not

---

68. 4QLev[b] SP LXX. *he who is born* MT.

69. 4QLev[b] SP. Not in MT. *who dwell with them* LXX.

70. 4QLev[b] LXX. *and* MT SP.

71. Singular 4QLev[b]. Plural MT SP LXX.

72. 4QLev[b]. *for* MT. Not in SP.

73. 11QpaleoLev[a]. *having a discharge or rash or scabs* MT SP LXX.

74. 4QLev[b]. Not in 11QpaleoLev[a] MT SP LXX.

75. 4QLev[b]. *these* 11QpaleoLev[a] MT SP LXX.

76. Plural 4QLev[b] 11QpaleoLev[a] SP. Singular MT LXX.

be accepted. 24 Any animal which has its testicles bruised or crushed or torn or cut, you shall not offer *these*[77] to the LORD; you shall not do thus in your land. 25 Nor shall you receive any such animals from a foreigner [to offer as] food for your God; [because] *they [are corrup]t,*[78] they have a blemish, they shall not be accepted [for you.' ']

[26 And the LORD spoke to] Moses, saying, 27 "When a bull [or a sheep or a goa]t is born, it shall remain for seven days with [its mother, and from the eighth day on it shall be accepted as an offering by fire to the LORD. 28 And whether it be cow o]r ewe, [you shall not slaughter] both an animal and its young in [on]e day. [29 And when you sacrifice an offering of thanksgiving to the LORD, you shall sacrifice it so that you might be accepted. 30 It shall be eaten] on the same day; you shall leave none [of it until the morning: I am the LORD.]

[31 "Therefore shall you keep my commandments, and do] *them.*[79] 32 And [you shall] not [profane] my holy name; [but I will be sanctified among the children of Israel: I am the LORD who sanctifies you, 33 who brought] you [out] of the land of E[gypt, to be] y[our God: I am the LORD."]

23 1 And the L[ORD spoke to Mo]ses, [saying, 2 "Speak to the children of Israel, and say to them, 'The appointed feasts of the LORD, which] you shall proclaim as holy convocations, these are my appointed feasts: 3 for six days work shall be done; [but on the seventh day there is a sabbath of solemn rest,] a holy convocation. You shall not do any work: it is a sabbath to the LOR[D in all your dwellings.]

4 " 'These are the appointed feast[s of the LORD,] holy [convo]cations, which you shall pr[oclaim] the[m in their appointed season. 5 In the first month, on the fourteenth day] of the month at evening, [is the LORD's Passover. 6 And on the fifteenth day of the sam]e [month is] the feast of unleavened br[ead to the LORD; for seven day]s [you shall eat] unleavened bre[ad. 7 On] the f[i]rst day [you shall have] a holy convocation; [you] shall [not] work [at your occupation.] 8 But you shall offer an offering by fire to the Lo[RD for seven days. On the se]ve[nth day is a] holy [convocation;] you shall n[ot work at your] occu[pation.' "]

[9 And the LORD spoke to Moses, saying, 10 "Speak to the children of Israel, and say to them, 'When you enter the land which I am giving to you and reap its harvest, then] you shall bring t[he sheaf of the first fruits of your harvest to the priest. 11 And he shall wave the sheaf before the LORD, that] y[ou may be accepted;] on day aft[er the] sabbath the priest shall wave it. 12 And [on the day

---

77. 11QpaleoLev^a LXX. Not in MT SP.

78. 11QpaleoLev^a. *their corruption is in them* MT. *corrupted things are in them* SP LXX.

79. 4QLev^b SP LXX. *them: I am the LORD* MT.

Chapter 23. 4QLev^b: 23:1–8, 10–25, 40; 1QpaleoLev: 23:4–8; 11QpaleoLev^a: 23:22–29; 2QNum^d(?): 23:1–3(?) (or Num 18:8–9[?]).

when you wave the sheaf, you shall offer a male lamb] one year old [without blemish] as a burnt offering to the LORD. 13 And its grain offering shall be two-[tenths of an ephah of fine flour mixed with oil, an offering by fire to the LORD for a pleasing odor; and its drink offering shall be of] wine, a fourth of a h[in.] 14 And [you shall eat] no *bread,*[80] parched grain or f[resh ears until that very day, until you have brought the offering of your God.] It is a statute forev[er] throughout your generations in a[ll your dwellings.]

[15 " 'And you shall count for yourselves from the day after the sabbath, from the day that you brought the sheaf of] the [wave offering; there shall be seven complete sabbaths, 16 to the day after the seventh sabbath shall you count fifty days; and] you shall present [an offering of] new [grain] to [the LORD. 17 You shall bring from your dwelling places two loaves of bread as a wave offering, each made of two-tenths of an ephah; they shall be of fine] fl[our,] bak[ed] with leaven [as first fruits to the LORD. 18 And you shall present with the bread seven lambs a year old without blemish, one] young bul[l, and two rams; they shall be a burnt offering to the LORD, with the]ir [grain and their drink offerings,] an offering by fire of a pleasing odor to [the LORD. 19 And you shall offer one male goat as a sin offering, and two male lambs a] year [old] as a sacrifice of peace offerings. 20 And the [priest] shall wave [them with the bread of the first fruits for a wave offering before the LORD, with the two la]mbs. They shall be holy to the LOR[D for the priest. 21 And on the same day you shall make proclamation; you shall be a holy convocation. You shall] not [work at your o]ccupation. [It is a statute forever in all your dwellings throughout your generations.]

[22 " 'And when you reap the harvest of] your [lan]d, you shall not go to the very corners of [your field when you harvest, nor] shall you gather [the gleanings of] your [harves]t; [you shall leave th]em [for the poor and the alien. I] am [the Lo]RD your God.' "

23 And the LORD spoke to Moses, saying, 24 "Speak to the children of Israel, saying, 'In the seventh month, on the first day of the month, shall be a solemn rest for you, a holy convocation commemorated with the blowing of trumpets. 25 You shall not work at your occupation and you shall present an offering by fire to the LORD.' "

26 And the LORD spoke to Moses, saying, 27 "Now, on the tenth day of this seventh month is the day of atonement: it shall be a holy convocation for you. And you shall humble yourselves and yo[u] shall present an offering by fire to the LORD. 28 And you shall do no work during that entire day; for it [is] a da[y of atonement,] to make atonement for you bef[ore] the Lo[RD] your God. 29 For anyone that [does not humble himself during that entire day shall be cut off from his people.]▲

---

80. 4QLev[b]. *bread or* MT SP LXX.

[40 "And] y[ou shall ta]ke [for yourselves on the first day the fruit of goodly trees, branches of palm trees, and boughs of thick trees, and willows of the brook; and] you [shall re]joice be[fore the LORD your God seven days."] ▲

24 [2 "Command] the children of Israel, [that they bring you pure oil of beaten olives for the light, to keep a lamp burning continually. 3 Outside the veil of testimony] in the tent [of meeting, Aaron shall keep it in order from eveni]ng to [morning before the LORD continually; it shall be a statute forever throughout] your [genera]tions. 4 [He shall keep] the lamps [in order] o[n the pure gold lampstand] before [the LORD continually.]

[5 "And you shall take fine flour, and ba]ke t[welve cakes] from it; [two-te]nths of an ephah shall be [in each cake. 6 And you shall set them in two] rows, s[ix on a row, on the pu]re [table] before the LORD. [7 And you shall put pure frankincense on each row, that i]t [may b]e [a memorial portion] for the bread, [even an offering by fire to the LORD. 8 Sabba]th [day] by sabbath day [he shall set it in order before the LORD continually; it is on the behalf of the children of] Israel, [an everlasting covenant.] 9 And it shall b[e for Aaron and his sons, and] they [shall] eat it in a holy place; for it is most holy to him of the offerings of the LORD by fire, a perpetual statute."

10 And the son of an Israelite woman, whose father was an Egyptian, went out among the children of Israel; and the son of the Israelite woman and *the Israelite man*[81] fought together in the camp. 11 And the son of the Israelite woman blasphemed the Name and cursed; and they brought him to Moses. And his mother's name was Shelomith, the daughter of Dibri, of the tribe of Dan. 12 And they put *him*[82] in custody that it might be made clear to them by the command of the LORD.

13 And the LORD spoke to Moses, saying, [14 "Bring forth] the one who has cursed outside [the camp and let all that heard him lay their hands] on his head, and let a[ll the congregation] stone [him. 15 And you shall speak to the children of Israel, saying, 'Whoever curses his God shall bear his sin.] 16 And he who blasphemes the name of the LORD, he shall surely [be] put to death; [all the congregation shall certainly stone him. The native as well as the alien, when he blasphemes the name of the LORD, shall be put to death. 17 And he who] kills [any] man [shall sure]ly [be put to de]ath. [18 And he who kills an animal shall make it good, life for life. 19 And if a man who causes] a disfigurement in his neighbor; as he has done, [so shall it be done to him: 20 fracture for fracture, eye for eye, tooth for tooth; as] he has caused a disfigurement in a man, [so shall it be inflicted on him.

Chapter 24. 4QLev[b]: 24:2–23; 11QpaleoLev[a]: 24:9–14; 4QLev-Num[a]: 24:11–12.

81. 4QLev[b] 11QpaleoLev[a] LXX. *a man, the Israelite* MT. *an Israelite man* SP.

82. Independent pronoun 11QpaleoLev[a]. Suffix pronoun MT SP.

21 And he who kills an animal shall make it good;] and he who kills a man shall be p[ut to death. 22 You shall have one law, as it is for the alien, so also for the native; for I am the LORD your God.' "] 23 And Moses spoke [to the children of Israel; and they brought the one that had cursed outside the camp, and stoned him with stones. And the children of] Is[rael did as the LORD commanded Moses.]▲

25 [28 "But if there is not sufficient means to get it back for himself, then that which he has sold] shall remain in the ha[nd of the one who has bo]ught [it] until the ye[ar of jubilee;] and in the jubi[lee] it shall be rele[ased, and he shall ret]urn to [his] prop[erty.]

29 "And if a man sells a dwelling house in a walled city, then he may redeem it within a whole year after it is sold; for a full year shall he have the right of redemption. 30 And if it is not redeemed within the space of a full year, then the house that is in the city *having a wall*[83] shall pass permanently to the one who bought it, throughout his generations; it shall not be released in the jubilee. 31 But the houses of the villages which have no wall around them, *they*[84] shall be reckoned with the fields of the country; they may be redeemed; *they*[85] shall be released in the jubilee. 32 Nevertheless the cities of the Levites, the houses of the cities of their possession, the Levites may redeem forever. 33 And that which may be redeemed from the Levites, it shall be released—the sale of a house in a city of his possession—in the jubilee, for the houses of the Levitical cities are their possession among the children of Israel. 34 But the open field around their cities may not be sold, for *it*[86] is their permanent possession.

35 "And if your brother becomes poor and he becomes dependent on you, then you shall support him; he shall live with you as a stranger and a sojourner. 36 Do not take interest or profit from him, but fear your God; let your brother live with you.▲

[45 "And also from the children of the sojourners who resid]e among you, from t[hem you may make acquisition, and from their families that are among you, who have been born in your land; and they shall be your possessio]n. 46 And you may *bequeath*[87] t[hem to your children after you, to inherit as property. You may treat them as permanent slaves; but as for your brothers, the children of I]srael, [you shall not rule severely over] one another.

[47 "And if an alien or a sojourner among you becomes wealthy and your brother who is wit]h him [becomes poor] and sells himself to the alien or so-

Chapter 25. 11QpaleoLevᵃ: 25:28–36; 4QLevᵇ: 25:28–29, 45–49, 51–52.

83. 11QpaleoLevᵃ. *which has a wall* MT SP LXX.

84. 11QpaleoLevᵃ SP LXX. *it* MT.

85. 11QpaleoLevᵃ. *and they* MT SP LXX.

86. Feminine 11QpaleoLevᵃ SP. Masculine MT.

87. 4QLevᵇ LXX. *possess yourselves of* MT SP.

journer among you, [or to a branch of the alien's family, 48 after he is sold he retains the right of redemption. One of his brothers may redee]m him, 49 or his uncle, or [his] uncle's son, [may redeem him, or any of his blood relatives may redeem him; or if he becomes wealthy, he may redeem himself. 50 And he shall compute with purchaser from the year that he sold himself to him until the year of jubilee; and the price of his sale shall be accounted to the number of years; according to the time of a hired servant he shall be with him. 51 If there are still many years, according to them he shall refund part of] the price of his redemption [from the money that he was bought for. 52 And if there remain but few years to the year of jubilee, then he shall calculate according to his years and refu]nd part of the price of [his] red[emption."] ▲

26 [2 "You shall keep my sabbaths and] reverence [m]y [sanctuary:] I a[m the Lord.]

[3 "If] you walk [in my statutes] and [keep my] comm[andments, and do them, 4 then I will give rains] *in your land*[88] in the[ir] season [and the land shall yield its increase a]nd the *fru[it]*[89] trees [of the field shall yield their fruit. 5 And your] threshing [shall last to the] vint[age, and the vintage shall last to the s]owing time; an[d] you shall [ea]t [your bread to the full, and d]well [in your land safely. 6 And I will give p]eace in t[he land,] and [you shall lie down, and none shall] make you afraid; a[nd] I will [re]move [dangerous animals from the land, a]nd no sword shall [go] through [your land. 7 And yo]u [shall chase] your enemies [a]nd [they shall] f[all before you by the sword. 8 And] five of you shall [cha]se a hu[ndred, and a hundred of you sh]all [chase] ten thousand; and [your enemies] shall fall b[efore you by the sword.] 9 And I will look upon you with favor [and make you fruitful and multiply you, and I will establish m]y covenant with you. [10 And you shall eat old grain long stored, and yo]u [shall clear out the old] because of the new. [11 And I will make my dwelling among you,] and my soul shall not abhor you. 12 *And I will b[e*[90] your God,] and you shall be my peopl[e. 13 I am the Lord your God who b]rought you forth out of the land of Egy[pt, so that you should not be their slaves, and] I have broken the *yoke of [your bars*[91] and made you walk] upright.

[14 "But] if [you will not listen to me and will not do all] *my*[92] commandments, 15 b[ut if you reject my statutes, and if your soul] abhor[s] my

---

Chapter 26. 4QLXXLev[a]: 26:2–16; 11QpaleoLev[a]: 26:17–26; 4QLev-Num[a]: 26:26–33.

88. 4QLXXLev[a]. Not in MT SP LXX.

89. 4QLXXLev[a]. Not in MT SP LXX.

90. 4QLXXLev[a]. *I will walk among you and I will be* MT SP LXX.

91. 4QLXXLev[a]. *bars of your yoke* MT SP LXX.

92. 4QLXXLev[a]. *these* MT SP. *these my* LXX.

[ordina]nces, [so that you will not observe all] my commandments, b[ut break my covenant,] 16 I also will do [this to you: I will appoint terror over you, even] consumption and [fever that shall consume the eyes] and [cause] the so[ul to pine away; and you shall sow] your [seed in vain, for your enemies shall eat it. 17 And I will set my face against you, and you shall be defeated before your enemies; they that hate you shall rule over you, and you shall flee when] no one pursues [you. 18 And i]f [in spite of] these things you do [not] lis[ten to me, then I will p]unish [you] seven times [more] for your sins. 19 And I will break the pride of your power; and I will make your sky as iron, and your earth as brass. 20 And your strength shall be spent in vain, for your land shall not yield its produce, and the trees of the land shall not yield their fruit.

21 "And if you walk contrary to me and will not listen to me, I will plague you sevenfold according to your sins. 22 And I will *send*[93] the animal of the field among you, which shall rob you of your children and destroy your cattle and make you few in number; and your roads shall become deserted.

23 "And if by these things you will not turn back to me, but will walk contrary to me, 24 then *I will*[94] walk against you *in ho[st]ile wrath;*[95] and I myself will strike you sevenfold for your sins. 25 And I will bring a sword on you that shall execute the vengeance of the covenant; and when you are gathered together in your cities I will sen[d] the pes[tilence] among you, and you shall be delivered into the hand of the enemy. 26 When I break your staff [of brea]d, [ten women shall bake your bread in one oven, and they shall deliver your bread again by weight, and you shall eat and no]t be satisfied.

[27 "And if you, in spite of all this, will not listen to me, but walk contrary to me, 28 then I will walk] contrary [t]o you in wrath; [and I also will punish you sevenfold for your sins. 29 And you shall eat the fle]sh of your sons and the flesh [of your daughters you shall eat. 30 And I will destroy your high places and cut down] your incense altars, and appoint [your dead bodies on the bodies of your idols; and] my [so]ul [shall abhor] you. 31 And I will make your cities [a waste, and will make your sanctuaries desolate, and I will not smell] the savor of your sweet odors. 32 And I will make [the land desolate and your enemies that dwell in it shall be astonished] at it. 33 And I will scatter you among the nations, [and I will draw out the sword after you; and your land shall become de]solate, and your cities shall be a waste." ▲

27 [5 "And if it is from five to twenty years old, then your valuation for the male shall be twenty shekels, and for the female ten shekel]s. 6 And if it is

---

93. *Piel* 11QpaleoLev^a SP. *Hiphil* MT.

94. 11QpaleoLev^a. *I will indeed* MT. *I will also* SP.

95. 11QpaleoLev^a LXX(?). *with hostility* MT SP.

Chapter 27. 4QLev-Num^a: 27:5–22; 11QpaleoLev^a: 27:11–19; 1QpaleoLev: 27:30–31(?).

from a [month old to five years old, then your valuation for the male shall be five shekels of silver, and for the female your valuation shall be three shekels of silver. 7 And if it is from sixty] years [old and upward, if it is for a male, then your valuation shall be fifteen shekels, and for the female ten] shekels. [8 But if he is poorer than your valuation, then he shall be brought before the priest and the priest shall value him; according to the ability] of the one that vo[wed shall] the priest [value] him.

[9 "And if it is an animal,] from [which they] prese[nt] an of[fering to] the Lord, all t[hat one gives of such to the Lord shall be] holy. 10 He shall [no]t substitute for it, [or] change it, [a good for a bad, or a bad for a good; and if] he shall change an animal [for animal, then both it and its substitute shall be holy. 11 And if] it is any unclean animal, of which [they do not present an offering to the Lord,] then he shall present the animal before the priest, 12 and the priest shall [val]ue it, whether it be good or bad; as you, the priest, value it, so shall it be. 13 But if he wants to redeem *it*,[96] then he shall add one-fifth of it to your valuation.

14 "And when a person consecrates his house as holy to the Lord, then the priest shall estimate it, whether it be good or bad; as the priest shall estimate it, so shall it stand. 15 And if he who consecrates it wants to redeem his house, then he shall add one-fifth of the money of your valuation to it, and it shall be his.

16 "And if a person consecrates to the Lord part of the field of his possession, then your valuation shall be according to its sowing: the sowing of a homer of barley shall be valued at fifty shekels of silver. 17 And if he consecrates his field from the year of jubilee, according to your valuation it shall stand. 18 But if he consecrates his field after the jubilee, then the priest shall calculate the value for him according to the years that remain to the year of jubilee; and a reduction shall be made from your valuation. 19 And if [he who] consecrates it wants to redeem the field, then he shall add one-fifth of the money [of your valuation to it, and it shall revert to him. 20 And if he does not redeem the field, or i]f he has sold [the field to another man, it shall] no longer [be rede]em[able.] 21 But [the field, when it is released in the jubilee, shall be holy to the Lord, as a devoted field; it shall become the priest's property. 22 And if he consecrates] a field [he has] bou[ght to the Lord, which is not a field of his possession.]▲

30 "And all the tithe of the land, whether of the seed of the land, or of the fruit of the tree, is the Lord's; it is holy to the Lord. 31 And if a man wants to redeem any of his tithe, he shall add one-fifth to it."▲

---

96. Masculine 11QpaleoLev^a SP. Feminine MT.

NUMBERS

This book begins with the Israelites in the Sinai desert, covers their forty years of wandering, and ends with the people poised to cross the river Jordan into the Promised Land. Our English heading comes from the Greek title *Arithmoi,* perhaps chosen because Numbers opens with a census. However, the Hebrew title *Bemidbar,* which means "In the Desert," seems more appropriate to the main theme of the book.

A total of eleven Numbers scrolls have been found in the Judean Desert. Eight of these were discovered at Qumran: one in Cave 1,[a] four in Cave 2,[b] and three in Cave 4.[c] Three more were found at sites further to the south: two at Naḥal Ḥever[d] and one at Wadi Murabba'ât.[e] While none of these scrolls is complete, of the thirty-two chapters of Numbers only chapters 6 and 14 are not represented in at least one of them.

Three of the Numbers manuscripts deserve special mention. The first is 4QLev-Num[a], which originally also contained the book of Leviticus. Scrolls containing more than one book of the Pentateuch must have been very long indeed and are rare at Qumran, the only other two cases being 4QGen-Exod[a] and 4QExod-Lev[f]. The second unusual scroll is 1QpaleoLev, which, as its abbreviated title shows, was written in the old paleo-Hebrew script. Although listed as a Leviticus scroll, 1QpaleoLev preserves at least two passages from Numbers (1:48–50 and 36:7–8?) somewhere between Leviticus 23 and 27.

The third special Numbers scroll is 4QNum[b], which is by far the best preserved and contains material from chapters 11 to 36. This manuscript may be described as an early Jewish "Living Bible," since it features many interpolations of other material and expansions of the biblical text. Several of these interpolations or expansions are large, consisting mainly of speeches. The book of Deutero-

---

a. 1QpaleoLev.   **b.** 2QNum[a], 2QNum[b], 2QNum[c], and 2QNum[d](?).   **c.** 4QLev-Num[a], 4QNum[b], and 4QLXXNum.   **d.** 5/6Ḥev/Num[a] and XḤev/SeNum[b].   **e.** MurNum.

nomy in our Bibles contains several speeches not found in the Masoretic Text of Numbers—but which were uttered during the events also recounted in Numbers. So where these speeches are not included in the traditional book of Numbers, 4QNum[b] imports them from Deuteronomy into the appropriate place in the narrative. These speeches include Moses' plea that he be allowed to enter Canaan (Deut 3:24–28, which is interpolated into Num 20:13b), God's prohibition to Moses to fight Moab (interpolated from Deut 2:9 into Num 21:12a), the prohibition to fight Ammon (from Deut 2:18–19 into Num 21:13a), God's command to fight the Amorites (from Deut 2:24–25 into Num 21:21a), and Moses' exhortation to Joshua to be courageous (from Deut 3:21–22 into Num 27:23b).

Many of the longer readings included in 4QNum[b] are not found in the Masoretic Text and the Septuagint but are often preserved in the Samaritan Pentateuch. To a lesser extent, 4QNum[b] also contains readings present in the Greek Bible but not in the Masoretic Text or Samaritan Pentateuch. This important scroll was copied about 30 BCE, which was a critical time in the history of the transmission of the biblical text. Within a few decades, rabbinical circles began actively striving to establish a standardized form for the books of the Hebrew Bible, which many scholars term the "proto-Masoretic text."[f] This effort included the elimination or suppression of textual forms that deviated from the proto-Masoretic text. Since 4QNum[b] is one example of these "different" textual forms, it gives us a precious window on one textual tradition that differs markedly from the Hebrew Bible and English translations that are used today. One final feature of this fascinating scroll is that it contains words written in red ink, which is most unusual among the scrolls. It appears that the function of this red writing was to introduce passages for liturgical reading (see the note on Num 20:22–23).

1

■ *The first two scrolls listed in the footnotes are both unusual. 4QLev-Num[a] originally contained at least the books of Leviticus and Numbers; such scrolls containing more*

---

f. See the Introduction to *The Dead Sea Scrolls Bible.*
Chapter 1. 4QLev-Num[a]: 1:1–5, 21–22, 36–40; 1QpaleoLev: 1:48–50.

than one book of the Pentateuch are very rare. 1QpaleoLev, written in the old paleo-
Hebrew script, is listed as a Leviticus scroll but preserves at least two passages from
Numbers (1:48–50 and 36:7–8?) somewhere between Leviticus 23 and 27.

[1 And the LORD spoke to Moses in the wilderness of Sinai, in the tent of
meeting, on the first day of the second month, in the second year] after they had
come out of the land [of Egypt, saying, 2 "Take a census of all the congregation
of the Israelites, by their families, by their fathers' houses,] according to the number of the names, ev[ery male, each one individually; 3 from twenty years old and
upward, all who are able to go out to war in Israel, you and Aaron shall number]
them by [their] armie[s. 4 And a man of every tribe shall be with you; each one] is
[head of his fathers' house.] 5 And the[se are the names of the men that shall stand
with you. Of Reuben: Elizur son of Shedeur.]" ▲

[21 The numbered men, of the tribe of Reuben, were] fort[y-six thousand
five hundred. 22 Of the descendants of Simeon, their generations, by their families, by their fathers' houses, their numbered men,] according to the numb[er of
the names, individually, every male from twenty years old and upward, all who
were able to go out to war. . . .] ▲

[36 Of the descendants of Benjamin, their generations, by their families, by
their fathers' houses, according to the number of the names, from twenty years
old and upward, all who] were able to go out to war; 37 [their] nu[mbered men,
of the tribe of Benjamin, were thirty-five thousand four hundred.] 38 Of the *son*[1]
of Dan, their generations, by [their] fam[ilies, by their fathers' houses, according
to the number of the names, from twenty years old and upward, all who were
able to go out to] war; 39 their numbered men, of [the tribe of Dan, were
sixty-two thousand seven hundred.] 40 Of the descendants of A[sher, their gen-
era]t[ions, by their families, by their fathers' houses, according to the number
of the names, from twenty years old and upward, all who were able to go out to
war. . . .] ▲

48 [For the LORD] s[poke to Moses, saying, 49 "Only the tribe of Levi] you
shall [not] number, [n]or [shall you take their census among the Israelites; 50 but
appoin]t [the Levites over the tabernacle of the testimony, and over all its furniture, and over all that belongs to it; they shall carry the tabernacle and all its furniture; and they shall take care of it, and shall encamp around the tabernacle.] ▲

2 18 "On the west side [shall be the standard of the camp of Ephraim by th]eir
[companies;] and the leader [of the descendants of Ephraim shall be Elishama
son of Ammihud. 19 And his army, even their numbered men, are forty thousand

---

1. **4QLev-Num**[a]. *descendents* MT SP LXX.
Chapter 2. 4QLev-Num[a]: 2:18–20, 31–32.

five hundred. 20 And n]ex[t to him shall be the tribe of Manasseh; and the leader of the descendants of Manasseh shall be Gamaliel son of Pedahzur.]" ▲

[31 "All the numbered men of the camp of Dan are a hundred and fifty-seven thousand six] hundred. [They] sh[all set out] last [by their standards." 32 These are the numbered men of the Israelites by their fathers' houses; all who were numbered of the camps] by [their] companies [were six hundred and three thousand five hundred and fifty.] ▲

3

■ *One of the Numbers scrolls, 4QLXXNum, was written in Greek, with the preserved text starting at Numbers 3:40. The presence of Greek manuscripts at Qumran (others include pap7QLXXExod, 4QLXXLevᵃ, pap4QLXXLevᵇ, and 4QLXXDeut) reminds us that during the Hellenistic and Roman periods many Jews—including those at Qumran—knew Greek as well as Hebrew and Aramaic.*

[3 These are the names of the sons of Aaron, the] an[ointed priests, wh]om *they*² [ord]ained t[o minister in the priest's of]fice. [4 But Nadab and Abihu died before the LORD, when they offered illicit fire before the LORD,] in the wilderness of Sinai. They had no children, [so] Eleazar [and Ithamar ministered in the priest's office in the lifetime of Aaron their father].

5 [Then] the LORD [sp]oke to Moses, say[ing, 6 "Bring the tribe of Levi near, and set them before] Aaron the priest, so that they may minister to him. 7 And they shall perform the duties for him, and for the whole [congregation before the tent of meeting, doing] service at the tabernacle. 8 And [they] shall take ca[re of] all the furniture of the te[nt of meeting, and the duties of the Israelites, as they do servic]e at the tabernacle. 9 And you shall give the Levites [to Aaron and] t[o his sons; they are wholly given to him from among the Israelites. 10 So] you shall appoint Aaron and his sons, and they shall attend to [their priesthood; but any layman who comes near shall be put to death]."

11 [And] the LORD [spo]ke to Moses, sa[y]ing, [12 "Now see, I have taken the Levites from among the Israelites instead of every firstborn that opens the womb] *among*³ the Israelites.⁴ So the L[evites] shall be mine, [13 for all the firstborn are mine; on the day that I slew all the firstborn in the land of Egypt I consecrated

---

Chapter 3. 4QLev-Numᵃ: 3:3–19, 51; 2QNumᵃ: 3:38–41, 51; 4QLXXNum: 3:39(?), 40–43, 50–51(?).

2. 4QLev-Numᵃ LXX. *he* MT LXXᵐˢˢ.

3. 4QLev-Numᵃ MTᵐˢˢ. *from* MT.

4. 4QLev-Numᵃ MT. *the Israelites; their ransom shall be among the Israelites* SP LXX.

for my own al]l the firstborn in Israel, both human a[nd animal; they shall be mine. I am the LORD]."

14 [Then the LORD spoke to Moses in the wilderness of Sinai,] saying, 15 "Number the de[scendants of Levi by their fathers' houses and by their families; every male from a month old and upward you shall number." 16 So] Moses [num]bered them acco[rding to the word of the LORD, as he was commanded].

17 [These then were the sons of Levi by their names: Gershon and Kohath and Merari. 18 And th]ese are the names of the so[ns of Gershon by their families: Libni and Shimei. 19 And the sons of Kohath by their families: Amram and Izhar, Hebron and Uzzi]el.▲

[38 And those who were to encamp before the tabernacle eastward, before the tent of meeting toward the sunrise, were Moses and Aaron and his sons, having charge of the] ri[tes of the sanctuary, whatever had to be done for the Israelites]; but the [layman coming near was to be put to death. 39 All the numbered men of the Levites,] who[m Moses and Aaron numbered at the commandment of the LORD,] by [their] fa[milies, all the males from a month old and upward, were twenty-]two [thousand.]

40 Then [the LORD] s[aid to Moses,] "Number [all the firstborn males] of the Israelites fro[m a month old and upward, and ma]ke a list [of their names. 41 And] you shall [ta]ke the Levite[s for me—]I [am the LORD—instead of all] the fir[st-born among the Israelites; and the catt]le [of] t[he Levites instead of all the fi]rst-born [among the cattle of the Isra]el[ites.]" 42 So [Moses] nu[mbered, as the LORD had com]mande[d him, all the firstborn among t]he Isra[el]ites. [43 And all the first]bor[n m]ales [according to the number of names, fr]om a mo[nth old and upward, for their numbered men were twenty-two thousand two hundred and seventy-three.]▲

[49 So Moses took the redemption money from those who were above the number redeemed by the Levites; 50 from the firstborn of the Israelites he took the money, one thousand three hundred and sixty-fi]ve shek[els, reckoned by the shekel of the sanctuary; 51 and Moses gave the redemption m]one[y to Aaron and] to his sons, [according to the word of the LORD, as the L]ORD [had commanded] Moses.

4 1 Then the LORD spoke to Moses [and t]o Aaron, saying, 2 "Take a census of the sons of Kohath from among the sons of Levi, by their families and their fathers' houses, 3 from thirty [yea]rs old and on up to f[if]ty years old, all who can enter in the service, to [d]o the work in the tent of meeting.

4 "[Thi]s is the service o[f the sons of Kohath] in the tent of m[eeting: concerning the m]ost [ho]ly things. 5 When [the camp] sets out, [Aaron and] his

---

Chapter 4. 4QLev-Numᵃ: 4:1–12, 40–49; 4QLXXNum: 4:1(?), 5–9, 11–16; 2QNumᵃ: 4:1–3.

[sons] shall g[o in, and] t[he]y shall take [down] the veil of the [screen,] and cov[er] the ark of the testimony with it, 6 an[d they shall put a covering of s]eal[s]k[in on i]t, and shall spre[ad a cloth of pure blue] over it, [and shall put in *the p*]oles.⁵ 7 And over the table of the bread [of the pres]ence [they] shall spr[ead] a blu[e cl]oth, [and put] the p[l]at[es on i]t, a[nd the dishes], and the bowls and [the c]ups for drink offerings *with them;*⁶ [the continu]al bre[ad] sha[ll] also [be] on it. [8 Then they shall spread ov]er them a cloth [of scarlet,] and cover it [with a] co[vering of] seal[sk]in, and shall put in *the poles.*⁷

9 "An[d they shall take a cloth of bl]ue, and [cover] the lampstand for [th]e light, [with its lamps,] its [snuffers,] its trays, and all [its oil] vessels, with [which it is supplied; 10 and they shall put it and all its utensils in a covering of] seal[ski]n, and shall put it on the carrying fr[ame. 11 And over the golden altar they shall spread] *clo[th]s [of b]lue,*⁸ and cover i[t with a coverin]g of s[ea]lskin, and shall [put in it]s poles; 12 and they shall take all the ut[ensils of serv]ice, with which they mi[ni]ster in [t]he s[anctuary,] and put them in a cloth of b[lue,] and cover [them with a covering of] se[alsk]in, [and put them] o[n] the carrying frame. [13 Then they shall take away the ashes from the alt]ar, a[nd spread a pur]ple clo[th over it; 14 and they shall put on it all its vessels, with which they serve in connection with it: the firepans, the forks, the shovels,] and the ba[sins, all the utensils of the al]tar; [and they shall spread over it a co]vering [of seal]s[kin, and p]ut [in its poles].

15 "[And when Aaron and] h[i]s sons [have finished covering the sanctuary, and a]ll [the furniture of the sanctuary, as th]e ca[mp sets out, after that the sons of Kohath shall come to carry it; but they must not touch the sanctuary, lest they die. These are the things of the tent of meeting that the sons of Kohath are to carry. 16 And the responsibili]ty [of] E[leazar son of Aaron the priest shall be the oi]l for t[he light, the frag]rant [incense, the continual grain offering, and the anointing oil, with the oversight of the entire tabernacle, and of all that is in it,] in t[he sanctuary, and its furniture.]" ▲

[40 And] their numbered men, by [the]ir fa[milies, by their fathers' houses, were two thousand six hundred and thirty. 41 These are the numbered men of] the families of the sons of Gershon, all who served [in the te]nt of m[eeting, whom Moses and Aaron numbered according to the commandment of] the LORD. 42 And the numbered men of the families of the sons of Merari, by their fa[milies, by their fathers' houses, 43 from thirty yea]r[s old] up to fi[ft]y years old, every[one who could ent]er the service, [for work in the tent of meeting— 44 even] their [nu]mbered men by their families [were] three t[housan]d two

---

5. 4QLXXNum LXX (synonymous term). *its poles* MT SP.

6. 4QLXXNum. Not in MT SP LXX.

7. 4QLXXNum LXX (synonymous term). *its poles* MT SP.

8. 4QLXXNum. *a cloth of blue* MT SP LXX.

hundred. 45 T[hese are the numbered men of the families of the sons of Merari, whom Moses and A]aron [numbered] accor[ding to the commandment of the Lord] by Moses.

46 A[ll the numbered m]en [of the Levites] wh[om Moses and Aaron an]d [the] le[aders of Isra]el [numbered,] by [their] families [and by] their fathers' [houses, 47 from thirty] years [old] up [to fifty years old, everyone who could enter] t[o do the work of service and the work of bearing bu]rdens in the tent of meeting, 48 even [their numbered men were eight thousand five hundred and eighty. 49 According to the commandm]ent of the Lord [through Moses they] were appointed, [each one by his serving or carrying; thus were they numbered] by him, a[s the Lord commanded Moses].

5 [1 Then the Lord spoke to Moses, s]ay[ing,] 2 "Command [the Israelites to send away from t]he camp every lep[er, and everyone who has a discharge, and whoever is unclean through contact with a corpse;] 3 both male *and*[9] [female you shall send away, o]utside the camp you shall se[nd them, so that they might not defile th]eir [camp] where [I dwell in their midst." 4 And the Israelites did so, and sent them outside the c]amp; as the Lord spo[ke to Moses, so the Israelites did].

5 [Then the Lord spok]e [to Moses, saying, 6 "Speak to the Israelites: 'When a ma]n or woman [commits any of the sins that people commit by breaking faith with the Lord, and] *that*[10] [person is guilty,] 7 then [they] shall c[onfess their sin which they have committed; and he shall make restitution for his guilt in f]ull, [adding to it a f]i[fth part of it, and giving it to the one whom he has wronged. 8 But if the man has no] kinsman [to whom] restitution may be made [for the wrong, the restitution for wrong which is made must go to the Lord for the priest, in addition to the ram of the atoneme]nt, by which [atonement is made for him. 9 And every offering pertaining to all the holy things of the Israelites, which they present to the priest,] shall b[e his]. ▲

7 [84 This was the dedication offering for the altar, on the day when it was anointed, from the leaders of Israel: twelve silver plates, ▲ 88 and all the oxen for the sacrifice of peace offerings, twenty-]fo[ur] bulls, [the rams sixty, the male goats sixty, the male lambs a] year [old,] sixty. [This was the dedication of the altar, after it was anointed]. ▲

8 [7 "And thus you shall do to them,] to cleanse them: sprinkle the water of pu-rification on them, [let them shave their whole body with a razor, and let

---

Chapter 5. 4QLev-Num[a]: 5:1–9.

9. 4QLev-Num[a] MT[mss] SP[mss]. Not in MT SP.

10. Feminine 4QLev-Num[a] MT *qere* SP. Masculine MT *ketib*.

Chapter 7. 2QNum[c]: 7:88.

Chapter 8. 4QLev-Num[a]: 8:7–12, 21–22.

them wash their clothes, and so cleanse themselves. 8 Then let them take] a young bull and its grain offering of fine flour mixed wi[th oil, and you shall take another young bull for a sin offering. 9 And you shall present the Levites] before the tent of meeting, and assemble [the whole congregatio]n of the Israelites. 10 When you present the Levites before the LORD,] the [I]sraelites [shall lay the]ir hands on the Levites; [11 and Aaron shall offer the Levites before the LORD as a wave offering from the Israe]l[ites], that it may be theirs to do the service of the L[ORD].

12 "[Now the Levites shall lay their hands upon the heads of the bulls, then offer the one for a si]n offering and the ot[her for a burnt offering to the LORD, to make atonement for the Levites]." ▲

[21 And the Levites purified themselves from sin, and washed their clothes; and Aaron offered them as a wave offering before the LORD, and Aaron made atonement for] them [to cleanse them. 22 And after that the Levites went in to do their service in the tent of meeting before Aaron and] before his sons. [As the LORD had commanded Moses concerning the Levites, so they did to them]. ▲

9 [3 "On the fourteenth day of] this [mon]th, *on the day* [. . . ,[11] you shall keep it at its appointed time; according to all its statu]t[es and accord]ing to a[ll] its [ordina]nces [you shall keep i]t."

4 So Moses [spoke] t[o the Israelites, that they should keep the Passover. 5 And th]ey [kept] the Passover in the first month, [on the fourteenth day of the month, at twilight, in the wilderness of S]inai. According to all that the LORD commanded Moses, [so the Israelites did].

[6 Now there were certain people who were uncl]ean through touching a dead body, so that they could not keep [the Passover on that day; and they came before Moses and Aaro]n on that day. 7 And [those] people said [to him, "We are unclean through touching a dead body; why are we kept back from] o[f]fering the LORD's offering [at its appointed time among the Israelites?" 8 Then Moses said to them, "Wait, that I may hear] what the LORD will command concerning you." [9 And the LORD spoke to Moses, saying, 10 "Spea]k to the Israelites, sa[y]ing, '[If any of your people or of] your descendants [are unclean because of a dead body, or are on a distant journey,] he shall still keep the Passover to the Lo[RD].' " ▲

[19 Even when the cloud lingered over the tabernacl]e many days, then [the Israelites] ke[pt the charge of the LORD, and did not set out. 20 Sometimes the cloud remained a fe]w [d]ays [over the tabernacle, and according to the command of the LORD they remained in camp; then according to the command of the LORD they set out]. ▲

Chapter 9. 4QLev-Num[a]: 9:3–10, 19–20.

11. Remainder of variant uncertain 4QLev-Num[a]. *at twilight* MT SP LXX.

10 [13 And they set out for the first time accor]ding to the command of the Lor[d by Moses].

[14 The standard of the camp of the people of Judah set out first by their companies; and over] its [army was] Nahshon son of Amminadab. 15 A[nd over the army of the tribe of the people of Issachar was Nethanel son of Zuar. 16 And over the army of the tr]ibe of the people of Zebulun was Eliab son of Helon.

17 Then th[e tabernacle] was taken down, [and the sons of Gershon and the sons of Merari, who carried] the tabernacle, set out. 18 Next the standard of the camp of Reuben set out by [their] compani[es; and over its army was Elizur son of Shedeur. 19 And over the arm]y of the tribe of the people of Simeo[n was She]lumiel son of Zur[ishaddai. 20 And over the army of the tribe of the people of Gad was Eliasaph son of Deuel].

21 Then] the Kohathites set out, carrying the holy things; [and the tabernacle was set up before their arrival. 22 And the standard of the cam]p of the people of Ephraim set out by their companies, and over [its army was Elishama son of Ammihud. 23 And over the army of the tribe of the people of Manas]seh [was Gama]l[ie]l [son of Pedahzur].▲

11 [4 Now the rabble among them had an intense craving; and] the Israelites also [wept again, and said, "If we only had meat to eat! 5 We remember the fish we used to eat in Egypt for nothing,] the cucumber[s, the melons, the leeks, the onions, and the garlic];"▲

[16 So the Lord said to Moses, "Gather for me seventy men of the elders of Israel, whom you know to be the elders of the people and officers over them; and bring them to the tent of meeting, and let them take their place ther]e [with you. 17 And I will come down and talk with you there; and I will take some of the spirit that is on you and put it on] them; [and they shall bear the burden of the people with you, so that you might not bear it all by yourself. 18 And say to the people: 'Conse]crate yourselves for tomorrow, [and you shall eat meat; for you have wailed in the hearing of the Lord, saying, "If only we had meat to eat! For it was well with us in] Egy[p]t." [Therefore the Lord will give you meat, and you shall eat. 19 You shall not eat only one day, or two days, or f]ive days, or ten days, [or twenty days, 20 but for a whole month, until it comes] out of your nostrils [and becomes loathsome to you—because you have rejected the Lord who is among you, and have wailed before hi]m, saying, ["Why did we come out of Egypt]?"'"

21 [But Moses said, "The people] among [whom] I [am number six hundred thousand on foot; and you say, 'I will give them meat, so that they may eat for a

---

Chapter 10. 4QLev-Numᵃ: 10:13–23.

Chapter 11. 4QLev-Numᵃ: 11:4–5, 16–22; 4QNumᵇ: 11:31–35.

whole month.' 22 Are there sufficient flocks and herds to be slaughtered for them?] Or [are there] enough [fish in the sea to be caught for them?]"▲

▨ *The ancient sources have very few variant readings for Numbers 11. For verse 32 4QNum^b tells us "And all the people rose up that day," whereas the Masoretic Text, the Samaritan Pentateuch, and the Septuagint read "And the people rose up that day." While such small differences do not greatly impact our understanding of the text, they serve to emphasize various aspects (in this case, that all the Israelites partook of God's provision by gathering the quails he had provided). See also the comment on Numbers 16:8.*

[31 Then a wind went out from the Lord and brought quails from the sea, and let them fall beside the camp, about a day's journey on this side, and a day's journey on the other side, round about] the camp, [and about two cubit]s [deep] on the surface of [the gr]ound. 32 And *all*[12] the people went out all th[at day, and all the night] and all *the* [*day,*] *the next,*[13] and gathered the quails; the one who gathered least gathered [ten homers; and they spread them out] for themselves all around the camp. 33 While the meat was still bet[ween their teeth, before it was chewed, the anger of] the Lord burned [against the people, and the Lor]d [struck the] people with a very great plague. 34 So [the name of th]at [place was called] Kib[roth–hattaavah, because there they buried the people who had been greedy].

35 [From Kibroth–hattaava]h the people *journeyed;*[14] and [they] s[tayed at Hazeroth].

12 1 Then [Miriam and Aaron] spo[ke] against Moses [because of the Cushite woman whom he had marrie]d; for [he had married] a Cush[ite] woman. [2 And] they said, "H[as the Lord indeed spoken only through Moses? Has] he [not] spoken through us also?" And the Lor[d] heard it. [3 Now the man Moses was ve]ry [humble, more so than all the people wh]o were on the face of the earth.

▨ *Several readings in 4QNum^b are in agreement with the Greek Septuagint, in opposition to the Masoretic Text and the Samaritan Pentateuch. One of these is found in 12:6, where the subject the* Lord *is specified in 4QNum^b and the Septuagint. In contrast, the Masoretic Text and the Samaritan Pentateuch simply have the pronoun* he, *which draws less attention to the speaker.*

4 And [the Lord spoke suddenly to Moses, to Aaron, and to] M[iria]m, "Come out, you three, to the tent of m[eeting." So the three of them came out.

---

12. 4QNum^b. Not in MT SP LXX.

13. 4QNum^b SP LXX. *the next day* MT.

14. Singular 4QNum^b (also LXX). *journeyed* (plural) *to Hazeroth* MT SP LXX.

Chapter 12. 4QNum^b: 12:1–6, 8–11; 4QLev-Num^a: 12:3–11.

5 And the Lo]rd [came down] in a pillar of cloud, and stood [at the d]oor of the tent, and c[alled Aaro]n and Miriam; and they [both] came forward. [6 And] *the Lord*[15] said *to them,*[16] ["Hear now] my words: if there is a prophet among you, I the Lord will make myself known t]o hi[m] i[n a vision; I will speak with him [in a drea]m. [7 Not so with my servant] Moses; he is faithful in all my house. 8 With him [I] speak mouth t[o mouth,] *even openly,*[17] and not [in dark sayings; and he beholds the form of the Lord. Why] then were you not afraid to speak [against m]y [servant,] against Moses?" 9 And the anger [of the Lord] burned [against them, and he departed].

10 [When the cloud moved away from over the tent,] behold, Miriam had become leprous, as white as snow. And Aaron turned toward [Miriam, and behold, she was leprous. 11 Then Aaron said to Moses, "Please,] my [lo]rd, do not l[ay] the punishment [o]n [us because we have acted foolishly and because we have sinned]." ▲

13 [4 These were their names: . . . . 7 from the tribe of] Issachar, Igal son of Jos[eph; . . . ,] 10 from the tribe of Zebulun, Gaddi[el son of] Sodi; 11 from [the tri]be of [Joseph, namely, of the tribe of Manasseh, Gaddi son of Susi; 12 from the tribe of Dan,] Ammiel son of Gemalli; 13 from the tr[ibe of Asher,] Sethur son of Mic[hael; 14 from the tribe of Naphtali, Nahbi son of Vophsi; 15 from the tribe of Gad, Geu]el son of *Micha.*[18]

■ *The exact form of proper names was often problematic in ancient texts. (Compare the English names* Claire, Clare, Clara.) *For instance, Numbers 13:15 mentions the father of an Israelite as* Micha *in 4QNum[b],* Maki *in the Masoretic Text,* Miki *in the Samaritan Pentateuch, and* Makchi *in the Septuagint. These differences show that the spoken forms of a language change over time and distance, and suggest that many Israelite traditions were handed down orally for a considerable time before they were committed to writing.*

16 These [are the names of] the men whom [Moses sent to spy out the land. And M]oses renamed Hoshea son of Nu[n as Joshua.] 17 Then Mo[ses] sent them [to spy out the land of Canaan, and said to them,] "Go up there into the Negev, and g[o up into] the hill country, 18 and see [what the land is like, and whether the people who dwell] in it are strong [or if] t[he]*y are weak,*[19] whether [they are] fe[w or many; 19 and how the land is [in wh]ich they li[ve,] whether [it is] good

---

15. 4QNum[b] LXX[ms]. *he* MT SP LXX.

16. 4QNum[b] LXX. Not in MT SP.

17. 4QLev-Num[a]. *openly* 4QNum[b] MT[mss] SP LXX. *even appearance* MT.

Chapter 13. 4QNum[b]: 13:7, 10–13, 15–24; 4QLev-Num[a]: 13:21.

18. 4QNum[b]. *Maki* MT. *Miki* SP. *Makchi* LXX.

19. 4QNum[b]. *or weak* MT SP LXX.

[or bad; and how are the cities in whi[ch] they live, whether li[ke camps] *or whether*[20] with fo[rtifica]t[ions; 20 and how the land is, whether it is fertile o]r *it is*[21] poor, whether there [is wood] in it [or not.] And be bold, and bring back [some of the fruit of the] land." Now the time was the season of the *first ripe*[22] [grapes].

> ■ *4QNum*[b] *contains some readings that agree with the Samaritan Pentateuch rather than with the Masoretic Text or the Septuagint. For instance, in Numbers 13:21 the Masoretic Text and the Septuagint relate that the people "went up and spied out the land." But 4QNum*[b] *and the Samaritan Pentateuch have an additional verb, telling us that the people "went up, and entered, and spied out the land." This evidence shows that 4QNum*[b] *and the Samaritan Pentateuch preserve a very ancient form of the biblical text—one that sometimes differs from our Bibles.*

21 So they went up, *and entered,*[23] and spied out [the land from the wilder]ness of Zin to Rehob, near the entrance of H[amath. 22 And they went up through the Negev,] and came to Hebron; and Ahaiman, [Sheshai, and] *Tol*[*mai,*[24] the] des[cendants of Anak,] were *over there.*[25] [Now Hebron] was built [seven years] before Zoan in Egypt. 23 And [they] ca[me to the Valley of Eshcol, and cut down from there] a branch with one cluster of grapes *on it,*[26] [and they carried it on a pole between two of them; they also brought some pomegranates and figs.] 24 That [place] was *called*[27] the valley of Eshcol, because of the [cluster which the Israelites cut down from there]. ▲

15 [41 "I am the LORD your God, who brought you out of the land of Egypt, to be your God: I am the LORD your] God."

16 1 Now K[orah] son of I[zha]r, son of Kohath [son of Levi, along with Dathan and] *Abirom*[28] the sons of [Eliab, and On son of] Peleth *son*[29] [of Reu]ben, took action 2 and rose up befo[re] Mos[es, with some me]n [of] the

---

20. 4QNum[b]. *whether* MT. *or* SP LXX.

21. 4QNum[b]. Not in MT SP LXX.

22. Feminine 4QNum[b] SP. Masculine MT.

23. 4QNum[b] SP. Not in MT LXX.

24. 4QNum[b]. *Talmai* MT SP. *Thelamin* LXX.

25. 4QNum[b]. *there* MT SP LXX.

26. 4QNum[b] LXX. Not in MT SP.

27. Plural *(they called that place)* 4QNum[b] SP LXX. Singular *(he called that place)* MT.

Chapter 15. 4QNum[b]: 15:41.

Chapter 16. 4QNum[b]: 16:1–11, 14–16, 47–50 [MT 17:12–15].

28. 4QNum[b]. *Abiram* MT SP. *Abiron* LXX.

29. 4QNum[b] MT[ms] SP LXX. *sons* MT.

Israelites, [two hundre]d and fif[ty] lea[ders of the congregation,] chosen from the a[ssembly,] and[30] men of renown. 3 And [they] assem[bled together against] Moses [and agai]nst Aaron, and said [to them, "You] have gone too far! For all the congregation are holy, every one of them, and [the LORD is] among th[em; why then do you exalt yourselves above the assembly of the LORD]?"

> ■ *Whether an action takes place in the past, present, or future affects our understanding of the text. In Numbers 16:5, 4QNum[b] and the Septuagint tell us that the LORD "has brought whomever is holy near to himself; the one whom he has chosen," whereas both the Masoretic Text and the Samaritan Pentateuch depict these actions as taking place in the present or future. The past actions in 4QNum[b] and the Septuagint have a finality or decisiveness that is not present in the other texts.*

4 [When Moses heard it,] he fell on his face; 5 and he spoke to Korah and to [all his company, saying, "In the morning the LORD will show who is his, *and*] he has brought [whomever is ho]ly near[31] to himself; the one whom he has c[hosen[32] he will bring near to himself. 6 Do this: take cense]rs [for yourselves,] Korah, and all his company; 7 and tomorrow put [fire in them, and put incense on them before the LORD; and the man wh]om [the LORD] chooses [shall be the holy one. You have gone too far, sons of Levi]."

> ■ *With the presence of a few additional words, 4QNum[b] sometimes contains a more inclusive text. For example, in Numbers 16:8, 4QNum[b] tells us that Moses speaks "to Korah and all of his company," who had rebelled against him. But the Masoretic Text, the Samaritan Pentateuch, and the Septuagint limit the blame—at least in this case—by addressing Moses' words only "to Korah."*

8 [Then Moses said to Korah *and*] all of his company,[33] "Now listen, [you sons of Levi! 9 Is it too small a thing for you that the God of Israel has separated you from] the congregation of Is[ra]el, to bring [you near to himself in order to perform the service of the tabernacle of the LORD, and to stand before the congregation] to minister to them; 10 and that he has brought you near, as well as [all your brothers the sons of Levi with you? Now are you seeking the priesthood also? 11 Therefore you and all] your company have g[athered together against the LORD. But as for Aaron, who is he that you grumble so against him]?" ▲

[12 Then Moses sent a summons to Dathan and Abiram sons of Eliab; but they said, "We will not come! . . . 14 Indeed you have not brought us into a land flow-

---

30. 4QNum[b] LXX. Not in MT SP.

31. 4QNum[b] LXX. *and he shall bring whoever is holy near* SP. *and who is holy, and he will bring him near* MT.

32. 4QNum[b] LXX. *shall choose* MT SP.

33. 4QNum[b]. Not in MT SP LXX.

ing with milk and honey, nor given us an inheritance of fields and vineyards. Would you put out the] eyes of [these men? We will not come up]."

15 [Then Moses became very angry, and said to the LORD, "Do not accept] their [offerin]g; [I have] no[t taken one donkey from them, and I have not harmed one of them." 16 And Moses said to K]orah, "As for yo[u and all your company, be present tomorrow before the LORD, you and they and Aaron."]▲

[46 ³⁴Then Moses said to Aaron, "Take your censer, ... 47 So Aaron took it as Moses had said, and] ran into the midst of the assembly; [and behold, the plague had begun among the people, but he put on the incense, and made atone-ment for the people.] 48 And he sto[o]d between the dead [and the living; and the plague was checked. 49 Now those who] died by the plague were fou[rteen thousand seven hundred, besides those who died in the affair of Korah. 50 Then] Aaron [returne]d t[o Moses at the door of the tent of meeting, for the plague had been checked].

17 [1 Then the LORD spoke to Moses, sayin]g, 2 "Speak to the Is[raelit]es, [and get from them staffs, one for each ancestral house, from all the lead-ers] according to their ancestral houses—[twelve staffs. Write every man's name on his rod]."

18

■ *Occasionally two passages from different parts of the Hebrew Bible are similar or even identical—which makes them difficult to identify when they are preserved on small fragments of the Dead Sea Scrolls. One example is Numbers 18:8–9, which is very similar to Leviticus 22:1–3, 23:1–3, or 23:26–28! In such a case the relevant Numbers manuscript is listed with a question mark (2QNumᵈ?), in recognition that it may be a Leviticus manuscript instead.*

8 Then [the LORD] spo[ke to Aaron: "Now behold. I have given you charge of my offerings, even all the] hol[y gifts of the Israelites; I have given them to you as a priestly portion, and to your sons, as a perpetual due. 9 This shall be] for [you from the most holy things, reserved from the fire: every offering of theirs, even every grain offering of theirs and every sin offering of theirs and every guilt offer-ing of theirs, which they render to me, shall be most holy for you and for your sons]."▲

[25 Then the LORD spoke to Moses, sayi]ng, 26 "You shall speak to the Levites, and say [to them, 'When you take from the Is]rael[ites] the tithe which I have given you fro[m them for your inheritance, then you shall offer up from it] *a*

---

34. Hebrew 17:11. English 16:46.
Chapter 17. 4QNumᵇ: 17:1–2 [MT 17:16–17].
Chapter 18. 2QNumᵈ(?): 18:8–9 (or Lev 23:1–3[?]); 4QNumᵇ: 18:25–32.

tithe offering from the tithe.[35] 27 And [your offering] shall be reckoned to y[ou as though it were the grain of the threshing floor, and as the] fullness of the wine press. 28 So [you] also shall present [an o]ffering [to the LORD from all your tithes, which you receive f]rom the Israelites; and you shall give some of it [as the L]OR[D's offering to Aaron the priest. 29 Out of all your gifts] you shall present every offering due to the LORD, from all the best of them, [their] sacred part [from them].'

30 "[Therefore you shall say to them,] 'When you offer the best of it, then the rest shall be reckoned to *you*[36] *as your offering,*[37] as the pr[oduce of the threshing floor, and as the produce] *from*[38] the wine press. 31 And you shall eat *them*[39] in every place, you and you[r] *households;*[40] [for it is your reward] in return for your service in the tent of meeting. 32 And you shall bear no sin because of it, [when you have offered some of the best] from it; and you shall not profane the holy gifts of the Israelites, lest you die.' "

19 1 Now the LORD spoke to *them*[41] and to Aaron, saying, 2 "T[h]is is the statute of [the law which] the LORD [has commanded,] saying, 'Tell the Israelites to bring you an [unblemished red] heifer, in [which] is no defect, and on which no yoke has been laid. 3 And *you*[42] shall give it to Elea[zar the priest, and they shall bring] it outside the camp, and *they*[43] shall slaughter it b[ef]ore him. 4 Then El[eazar the priest] shall take [some of its blood] with his finger, and sprinkle some of its blood toward the *door*[44] of the tent [of meeting seven times. 5 Then he shall burn] the heifer in his sight; its skin, a[nd its flesh, and its blood, together with its dung, he shall burn. 6 And the priest shall take cedarwood and hyssop] and scarl[et ma]terial, [and cast them in the midst of the burning heifer].' " ▲

20 [7 Then the LORD spoke] to Moses, saying, 8 "Take the rod, [and assemble the congregation, you and Aaron your brother, and command the rock

---

35. 4QNum^b. *an offering to the LORD, a tithe from the tithe* MT SP LXX.

36. 4QNum^b. *the Levites* MT SP LXX.

37. 4QNum^b. Not in MT SP LXX.

38. 4QNum^b LXX. *of* MT SP.

39. 4QNum^b LXX^mss. *it* MT SP LXX.

40. 4QNum^b MT^mss SP LXX. *household* MT.

Chapter 19. 4QNum^b: 19:1–6; 5/6HevNum^a: 19:2–4.

41. 4QNum^b. *to Moses* MT.

42. Singular 4QNum^b LXX. Plural MT SP.

43. 4QNum^bLXX. *he* MT SP.

44. 4QNum^b. *front* MT SP LXX.

Chapter 20. 5/6 HevNum^a: 20:7–8; 4QNum^b: 20:12–13, 16–17, 19–29.

before their eyes to yield its water. So you shall bring water out of the rock for them; so you shall provide drink for the congregation and their cattle].▲

> ▓ *4QNum^b and the Samaritan Pentateuch follow Numbers 20:13a with a passage that is not found in modern Bible translations, which accord with the Masoretic Text and the Septuagint. After Moses has sinned in the desert by striking the rock twice in anger (verse 11), God informs him that neither he nor Aaron will enter the Promised Land (verse 12). The additional passage contains Moses' response—his plea that he be allowed to cross the Jordan—and the Lord's concession that he be permitted to view the land from the top of Mount Pisgah. The speech has been taken from Deuteronomy 3:24–25, 26b–27, and probably Deuteronomy 3:28 and 2:2–6. (See the introduction to Numbers.)*

[12 But the LORD said to Moses and Aaron, "Because you did not believe in me, to show my holiness in the eyes of the Israelites, therefore you shall not bring this assembly into the land that I have given t]h[em." 13 These are the waters of Meribah, where the] people of [Israel quarreled with the LORD, and by which he showed his holiness. *And Moses sa]id, ["O LORD God, you have] begun t[o show your servant] your [greatnes]s and [your strong hand; for what god is there] in heaven or o[n earth who can act in comparison with you]r [works,] and in comparison with your mighty acts? [Please let me cross over and see] the good [land that is beyond] the Jordan, [that good] hill country, [and Lebanon." But the LORD] said [to Moses,] "Enough; [speak] no [more to me of this matter! Go up to the] t[op of Pisgah, and lift up] your [eye]s to the west [and to the north and to the south and to the east, and see it with your eyes, for you shall not cross over this Jordan].*"[45]▲

[14 Moses sent messengers from Kadesh to the King of Edom, "Thus says your brother Israel: 'You know the adversity that has befallen us; 15 how our ancestors went down to Egypt, and we lived in Egypt a long time, and the Egyptians mistreated us and our ancestors. 16 But when we cried to the LORD, he heard our voice, and sent an angel and brought us out of Egyp]t; [and here we are in Kadesh, a city on the edge of your territory. 17 Please let us pass through your land;] we will [no]t go [through any field or vineyard, nor drink water from any well. We will go along the king's highway, and not turn to the r]ight hand [o]r [to] the le[ft, until we have crossed your border.'" But Edom said to him, "You shall not pass through us, or I will come out with the sword against you]."

[19 So the Israelites said] to [him, "We will stay on the highway; and if we drink any of your water, whether I or my cattle, then will I pay] its p[rice. It is] only [a small matter, just let me pass through on foot." 20 But he said, "You shall not pass through us, o]r I will come out [again]st y[ou] with a s[wo]rd."[46] [Then

---

45. 4QNum^b SP. Not in MT LXX.

46. 4QNum^b. Not in MT SP LXX.

Edom came out against them with many soldiers, and with a stron]g [force.] 21 Thus Edom refused to gi[ve Israel passage through his territory; so Israel turned away from him].

> ■ *In column 12 of 4QNum^b, one and a half lines of red writing are partially preserved. Such writing sometimes extends both beyond one verse (20:22–23) and beyond one line (lines 21–22), and a second line that begins in red sometimes finishes in black (line 22). Red ink is found elsewhere in 4QNum^b in the first half of 21:21, and in 22:21; 23:13, 27; 31:25, 37–38, 48; 32:25; 33:1. But why was red writing used? It seems that its likely function was to introduce pericopes (that is, short passages) for liturgical reading. Red ink is also found in one of the Psalms scrolls, 2QPs, where it has a liturgical function by drawing the reader's or reciter's attention to the first four verses of Psalm 103. Other Dead Sea Scrolls with red writing are 4Q270 and 4Q481d. Red ink is also found in writings from Egypt (especially the New Empire), Greece, and Rome, and is referred to in the Talmud. In Codex Sinaiticus, red writing is used for the titles of the Psalms and for some notes associated with the Church Father Eusebius.*

22 [Then they journeyed from Kadesh, and the Israelites, the whole congregation, came to] Mount [Hor.] 23 And the LORD spoke to Mos[es and Aaron at Mount Hor, on the border of the land of Edom, saying,] 24 "Aaron [will] be gathered to his *people;*[47] for [he shall] not enter into the [land that I have given to the Israelites, becau]se you rebelled against my command at the waters of Meribah. 25 Take Aar[on] and [his son] El[eazar and bring them up to Mount Hor; 26 and] *you [shall str]ip*[48] Aaron of his garments, and put [them upon his son Eleazar. But Aaron will be gathered to his people, and will di]e [there]."

27 [So] Moses [did] as the Lo[RD] com[manded; and they went up to Mount Hor in the sight of the whole congregation. 28 Then] Moses stripped Aaron [of his garments, and put them upon his son Eleazar; and Aaron died] there [on] the top of the m[ountain. Then] Moses and Eleazar came down [from the mountain. 29 And when all the congregation saw that Aaron was dead, [a]ll [the house of Israel wep]t for Aaron thirty days.

21 [1 When the Canaanite, the king of Arad, who dwelt in the Nagev, heard that I]srael [was coming by the] ro[ad of Atharim, he fought against Israel and took some of them captive. 2 So Israe]l [made a vow to the LORD, and said, "If you will indeed deliver this people into my hand, then I will totally destroy their cities]." ▲

---

47. 4QNum^b SP LXX. *peoples* MT.

48. 4QNum^b SP. *Strip!* MT LXX.

Chapter 21. 4QNum^b: 21:1–2, 12a–13a, 20–21a.

■ *For Numbers 21, 4QNum^b and the Samaritan Pentateuch differ markedly from the Masoretic Text and the Septuagint by inserting three speeches that also appear in the book of Deuteronomy. (1) In verse 12a God's prohibition to Moses to fight Moab is imported from Deuteronomy 2:9. (2) In verse 13a the prohibition to fight Ammon is taken from Deuteronomy 2:18–19. (3) In verse 21a God's command to fight the Amorites is imported from Deuteronomy 2:24–25. (See the Introduction to Numbers.)*

12 [*And the* LORD] *sai*[*d to Moses, "Do not harass Moab nor engage them in battle, for*] *I will not give an*[*y of its land to you as a possession, since I have given Ar to the descendants of Lot for a possession."*]⁴⁹ *From there they set out, and camped*] in the Valley of Zer[ed. 13 *And the* LORD *spoke to Moses, saying, "Today you are going to cross at Ar, the*] *border of M*[*oab; and when you approach the Ammonites, do not harass them or engage them,*] *for* [*I will not give you any of the territory of the Ammonites as a possession, since I have given it to the descendants of Lot as a possession."*]⁵⁰ From there they set out, and camped on the other side of the Arnon, which is in the wilderness that extends from the boundary of the Amorites; for the Arnon is the boundary of Moab, between Moab and the Amorites]. ▲

[18 . . . And from the wilderness they continued to Mattanah, . . . 20 and from Bamoth to the valley that is in the region of] Moab, [at the] t[op of Pisgah that overlooks the desert].

21 Then [*the* LORD] *spoke* [*to Moses: "Arise, be on your way, and cross the valley of the Arnon. See, I have given into your hand*] *Sih*[*on the Amorite, king of Heshbon, and his land; start taking possession, and engage in b*]*attle.* [*Today I will begin to put the dread and fear of you upon the peoples that are under the whole heaven, who will hear the news of you and will tremble and be in anguish because of you."*]⁵¹ Then Israel sent messengers to Sihon king of the Amorites, saying, "22 Let me pass through your land . . ."] ▲

22

■ *Although 4QNum^b often agrees with the Samaritan Pentateuch against the Masoretic Text and the Septuagint, in several instances it shares with the Septuagint readings that are not in the Masoretic Text or the Samaritan Pentateuch. Two examples are in verse 11: Balak's statement "and they [that is, the Israelites] are dwelling next to me" (compare verse 5), and his hope that he will be able to drive them out "of the land" (compare verse 6). In both cases the longer reading repeats information found*

---

49. 4QNum^b SP. Not in MT LXX.
50. 4QNum^b SP. Not in MT LXX.
51. 4QNum^b SP. Not in MT LXX.

Chapter 22. 4QNum^b: 22:5–21, 31–34, 37–38, 41; 4QLev-Num^a: 22:5–6, 22–24.

earlier in the chapter. Such agreements between 4QNum^b and the Septuagint remind us that it is no easy task to decide which is the most ancient form of the biblical text.

5 [Then Moab s]ent m[essengers to Balaam son of Beor at Pethor, which is near] the River Euphrates, in the land of the descendants of [his] p[eople, to sum]mon him, sayin[g, "See, a people has come out from Egypt; they cover the face of] the earth, and they have settled [next to me. 6 So please come now and curse this people for me; for th]ey ar[e too mighty] for me. Perhaps I shall be able to defeat [them and drive them from the land; for I know that the one whom you bless is] blessed, and the one whom you curse [is cursed]."

[7 So the elders of Moab and the elders of Midian departed with the fees for divination in their hand; and they] came [t]o [Ba]laa[m, and repeated to him] the words of Balak. 8 And he said [to them, "Stay he]re [to]ni[ght, and] I [will bring back word to] y[ou, just as] the LORD speaks to me." So the leaders of Mo[a]b stayed with [Ba]laam.

9 Then [Go]d came to B[alaam and said] to him,[52] "Who are these men [wi]th you?" 10 And Balaam said to God, "Balak son of Z[ippor, king of Moab, has sent word] to me, *saying,*[53] 11 'See, this people *has come out*[54] of Egypt and they cover the face of the earth, *and they are dwelling* [next to me.[55] Now, come] cur[se] them [for me;] perhaps I shall be able [to] fight against them and drive them out [*of the lan*]*d.'* "[56] 12 And [God] said [to Balaam, *"Do*] *not* [*go*[57] wit]h *the men,*[58] *and*[59] *do not* [*curs*]*e*[60] the people; for they are blessed." 13 So [Balaam rose] up [in the mor]ning, and s[aid to the leaders of Bala]k, "Go back t[o] your *lord,*[61] for the LORD has refused to let me to g[o with you]." 14 [So] the leaders of M[o]a[b rose and went t]o Balak, and said *to him,*[62] "Balaam refuses to come with us."

■ *While variant readings in 4QNum^b often agree with the Samaritan Pentateuch, sometimes with the Septuagint, and more rarely with the Masoretic Text, some are unique to the scroll. Two examples are found in verse 16, where only 4QNum^b re-*

---

52. 4QNum^b LXX. Not in MT SP.

53. 4QNum^b LXX. Not in MT SP.

54. 4QNum^b SP LXX. *who has come out* MT.

55. 4QNum^b LXX. Not in MT SP.

56. 4QNum^b LXX. Not in MT SP.

57. 4QNum^b. *You shall not go* MT SP LXX.

58. 4QNum^b. *them* MT SP LXX.

59. 4QNum^b MT^mss SP LXX. Not in MT.

60. 4QNum^b. *You shall not curse* MT SP LXX.

61. 4QNum^b LXX. *land* MT SP.

62. 4QNum^b LXX. Not in MT SP LXX^ms.

minds us that Zippor was "king of Moab" (compare verse 10), and in verse 19, where we are told, "And the princes of Moab stayed with Balaam" (compare verse 8). As was the case in verse 11, both of these longer readings repeat information found earlier in the chapter.

15 Then [Balak] aga[in sent leade]rs, more numerous [and more distinguish]ed than the first. 16 And they came to Balaam [and] said to him, ["Thus says Balak son of Zippor, *ki*]*ng* [*of Moab,*[63] 'Please let n]o[thing hind]er you from coming to me; 17 for I will surely do you great honor, and wh[atever you say to me I will d]o *for you;*[64] [so please] co[me, cur]se [this] p[eople for me.'" 18 But Balaam answered and said [to the servants of Balak, "Even if] Balak [would give m]e [his house] ful[l of] silver and gold, [I can]no[t go be]yond the word of the Lord [my] Go[d, to do less or mo]r[e *in my hear*]*t.*[65] [19 Now therefore,] please [also wait here this] night, [so that I may know wha]t [the Lord will speak to me in addition." *And the*] princes [*of Moab stayed with Balaam*].[66]

20 [And] God [came] to [Balaam at night, and said to him, "If the men] have come to call you, [get up and go wit]h them; but only [the word that I speak to] you shall you do."

[21 So Balaam rose in the morning, and saddled his donkey and went with] the leaders of Moab. [22 But] G[od's anger was inflamed] because [he] went; [and the angel of the Lord took his stand in the road as an adversary against him. Now he was riding on his donkey, and] his [two] servants were with him. 23 Then the do[nkey] saw [the angel of the Lord standing in the road, with his sword drawn in his hand. So] the donkey [turned off] from the road, and went [into the field; and Balaam struck the donkey, to turn her back onto the road. 24 Then the angel of the Lord stood in a narrow pa]th between the vineyard[s, with a wall on this side and a wall on that side]. ▲

[31 Then the Lord opened the eyes of Balaam, and he saw the angel of the Lord standing in the ro]ad, with [his] sword [drawn in his hand; and he bowed his head, and fell *be*]*fore him.*[67] [32 And] the angel of the Lord [said to] him, "Why have you struck your donkey [these three times? Behold,] I [have come out as an adversary] *against you,*[68] because your way is *evil*[69] before me. 33 But the

---

63. 4QNum[b]. Not in MT SP LXX.

64. 4QNum[b] LXX. Not in MT SP.

65. 4QNum[b] LXX. Not in MT SP.

66. 4QNum[b]. Not in MT SP LXX.

67. 4QNum[b]. *on his face* MT SP LXX.

68. 4QNum[b]. Not in MT SP LXX.

69. 4QNum[b]. *perverse* MT LXX. *he has made your way evil* SP.

donkey saw me, and turned away *from*[70] before me these [three] ti[me]s; if she had not turned aside *from before* [*me,*][71] by now I would certainly have killed you, and let her live."

34 Then Balaam said to the angel of the LORD, "I have sinned, for I did not know that you were standing in the way against me. Now therefore, if it is displeasing to [you, I will go back again]." ▲

[37 Then Balak said to Balaam, "Did I not urgently send word to you to call you? Why did you not come to me? Am I] really [unable to honor you?" 38 So Balaam said to Balak, "Look, I have come to you now, but am I] ab[le to say just anything? The word that God puts in my mouth, that is what I must say]." ▲

[41 And it came to pa]ss in the mo[rning that Balak took Balaam, and brought him up to Bamoth-Baal; and from there he saw a part of] the people.

23 1 Then [Balaam said to Balak, "Build seven altars for me here, and prepare seve]n bulls and seven [rams for me here." 2 And Balak did as Balaam had said; and] B[ala]k and Balaam [offered] on each altar a b[ull and a] ram. [3 Then Balaam said to Balak, "Stand by your burn]t offering, and I *myself*[72] will go; perhaps *God*[73] will come [to meet me, and whatever he shows me] I [will tell] to [you." *And*] *Balak went and stood by his offering and Balaam called to God and went off to a barren height.*[74]

4 [And] *the* ang[el of][75] God met Ba]laam; and Balaam s[ai]d to him, ["I have prepared the seven altars, and I have offered up a bull and a ram on each altar." 5 Then the LORD put a word in Balaam's mouth and said, "Return to Balak, and you shall speak in this way." 6 So he returned to him, and behold, he was standing be]side [his burnt offering, he and all the leaders of Moab]. ▲

[13 Then Balak said to Balaam, "Please come with me to another place, from where you may see them; you shall see only] a part of t[hem, and shall not see them all; then curse them for me from there." 14 So he took him to the field of Zophim, to the top of] Pisgah, [and built seven altars, and offered a bull and a ram on each altar. 15 And he said to Ba]lak, "S[tand here beside your burnt offering while I meet the LORD over there]." ▲

[18 Then Balaam uttered his oracle and said, ". . . 21 God has not observed misfortune in Jacob; n]or has he seen [trouble in Israel. The LORD his God is with

---

70. 4QNum[b] SP LXX. Not in MT.

71. 4QNum[b]. *because of me* MT SP. Not in LXX. *from me* LXX[mss].

Chapter 23. 4QNum[b]: 23:1–4, 6, 13–15, 21–22, 27–30.

72. 4QNum[b] LXX[mss]. Not in MT SP LXX.

73. 4QNum[b] SP LXX. *the LORD* MT.

74. 4QNum[b]. *And Balak went to a barren height* MT SP. *And Balak stood by his offering and Balaam called to God and went to a barren height* LXX.

75. 4QNum[b] SP. Not in MT LXX.

them, and the shout of a king is among them. 22 God, who brings them out of Egyp]t, [is like the horns of the wild ox for them]." ▲

[27 Then Balak said to Balaam, "Come now, I will take you to another place; perhaps it will] please *God*[76] [that you may curse them for me from there." 28 So Balak took Balaam to the top of] Peor that overlooks the desert. [29 And Balaam said to Balak, "Build here seven] altars for me, and prepare seven bulls [and seven rams] for me here." [30 So Balak did as Balaam had said,] and offered a bull and a ram on every altar.

24 1 Now when Balaam saw [that it pleased the LORD to bless Israel,] he did not go, as at other times, to look for *the*[77] om[ens, but set] his face [toward] the wilderness. 2 And B[alaa]m lifted up [his eyes and saw Israel encamping tribe by tribe. Then] the Spirit of God [came on him,] 3 and he uttered his oracle and said:

"[The] oracle [of Balaam son of Beor, and the oracle of the man whose eye is opened; 4 the oracle of the one who hears the words of God, who sees the vision of the Almighty, who falls] down, yet has [his] e[yes] uncovered. [5 How fair are] your [tents, O Jacob, your encampments, O Israel! 6 Like valley]s [that stretch out, like gardens be]side a riv[er, *like tents that the LORD*] has set up,[78] like ce[dar trees beside the waters. 7 Water will flow from] his [bucket]s, and his seed [will be] by [many waters; and] his king [will be higher than Agag,] and [his kingdom] will [be exalted. 8 God, who brings him out of Egypt, is like] the horns of the wild ox for him; [he will devour the nations who are his adversaries, and will break their] bones [in pieces, and run them through with his arrows.] 9 He *is ugly;*[79] he *stretches out*[80] like a l[ion, and like a lioness; who dares rouse him? Blessed is everyone who blesses you, and cursed is everyone who curses you]."

10 [Then Ba]lak['s anger burned] against Bal[aam, and he clapped his hands together. And Balak said to Balaam, "I called you to curse my enemies, but see, instead you have blessed them these three times]." ▲

25 [4 Then the LORD said to Mos]es, "Take [all the leaders of the people, and im]pale t[hem before the LORD in the sun, so that the fierce anger of the LOR]D [may turn away from Israel." 5 So] Moses [sai]d to [the judges of Israel, "Each one of you must slay his men] who have yoked themselves [to Baal of Peor]."

---

76. 4QNum[b]. *the God* MT SP LXX.

Chapter 24. 4QNum[b]: 24:1–10.

77. 4QNum[b] SP LXX. Not in MT.

78. 4QNum[b] SP LXX. *like aloes that the LORD has planted* MT.

79. 4QNum[b] (scribal error caused by transposition of letters!). *crouched* MT.

80. 4QNum[b] SP[ms]. *lies down* MT SP.

Chapter 25. 4QNum[b]: 25:4–8, 16–18.

6 [Then behold,] one of the [Israelit]es [came and brought into his family a Midianite woman,] in the sight of [Moses and in the sight of the whole congregation of the Israelites, while they were weeping at the entrance of the tent of meeting. 7 And when Phinehas son of Eleazar, son of Aaron the priest, saw it, he rose up from the midst of the congregation] and took [a spear in his hand; 8 then he went after the Israelite man into the tent, and pierced both of them through, the man of Israel and the woman, through her belly. So the plague was checked among the children of Israel].▲

[16 Then the LORD spoke to Moses, saying, "Speak to the I]srae[lites, saying,[81] 17 'Harass] the Midianites, [and defeat them; 18 for they have harassed you] with their tricks, with which [they have deceived] you [in the affair of Peor, and in the affair of Cozbi daughter of the princ]e [of Midian,] their sister who was killed [on the day of the plague because of Peor].' "

26 [1 And it came about after the plague,] that the LORD spoke to [Moses and to Eleazar son of Aaron the priest, saying, 2 "Take] a census of all the congregation of the [Israel]ites, [from twenty years old and upward, by their fathers' houses, all] in Israel who are able to go out to war." [3 And Moses and Eleazar the priest spoke with them in the plain]s of Moab by [the Jordan at Jericho, saying, 4 "Take a census of the people, from twenty years old and upward, as the LOR]D [commanded] Moses."

[Now the Israelites who came out of the land of Egypt were: 5 Re]uben, the firstborn of Israel,] the descendants of [Reuben: of Hanoch, the clan of the Hanochites; of Pallu,] the clan of the Palluites; [6 of Hezron, the clan of the Hezronites; of Ca]rmi, [the] clan of [the Carmites. 7 These are the clan]s of the Reubenites; and [those who were numbered of them] were [forty-three thousand] seven [hu]n[dre]d [and thirty].

8 [And the descendants of Pallu:] Eliab. [9 And the descendants of Eliab: Nemuel, Dathan, and Abirom. These are the same Dathan and Abi]rom,[82] [who were chosen from the congregation, w]ho [rebelled against Moses and] against Aaron [in the company of Korah, when] they [rebell]ed against the L[ORD, 10 and the earth opened its mouth, and] *the* e[*arth*[83] swallowed] them [up along with Korah, when] that company [die]d, [when the fire devoured two hundred and fifty men *who offered incen*]*se;*[84] and [they] became [a warning].

---

81. 4QNum[b] LXX. Not in MT SP.

Chapter 26. 4QNum[b]: 26:1–5, 7–10, 12, 14–34, 62–65; 4QLev-Num[a]: 26:5–7.

82. 4QNum[b]. *Abiram* MT SP. *Abiron* LXX.

83. 4QNum[b] SP. Not in MT LXX.

84. 4QNum[b]. Not in MT SP LXX.

[12 The descendants of Simeon according to their clans: of Nemuel, the] cl[an of the Nemuelites; of Jamin, the clan of the Jaminites; of Jachi]n, [the cl]an [of the Jachinites; 13 of Zerah, the clan of the Zerahites; of Shaul, the clan of the Shaulites].

14 These are the clans of the Sim[eonites: twenty-two thousand two hundred].

15 And[85] the descendants of Gad by their clans: [of Zephon, the clan of the Zephonites; of Haggi, the clan of the Haggites; of Shuni,] the clan of the Sh[unit]es; 16 of Ozni, the clan of the O[znites; of Eri, the clan of the Erites; 17 of Ar]od, [the clan of the Arodites;] of [Ari]el,[86] the clan of the Arielit[es.[87] 18 These are the clans of the sons of Gad according to those who were numb]ered of them: [forty thousand five hundred].

19 The sons of J[udah: E]r [and Onan; and Er and Onan died in the land of Canaan. 20 And] the descendants of J[udah by their clans were: of Shelah, the clan of the Shelanites; of Perez, the clan of the Perezites; of Zerah, the c]lan of the Zerahites. 21 And [the descendants of Perez were: of Hezron, the clan of the Hezronites; of Hamul, the clan of the Ham]uelites.[88] 22 These [are the clans of Judah according to those that were numbered of them: seventy-three thousand five hundred].

23 [The] descendants [of Issachar by their clans: of Tola, the clan of the Tolaites; of Puvah, the clan of the Puvi]tes;[89] 24 of Jashub, the c[lan of the Jashubites; of Shimron, the clan of the Shimronites. 25 These are the clans of Issachar according to those that were numbered] of them: [sixty-four thousand three hundred].

26 [The descendants of Zebulun by] their [cla]ns: [of Sered, the clan of the Seredites; of Elon, the clan of the Elonites; of Jahleel, the clan of the Jahlee]lites. 27 These [are the clans of the Zebulunites according to those that were numbered of them: sixty thousand five hundred].

28 The descendants of [J]oseph according to [their] cl[ans: Manasseh and Ephraim. 29 The descendants of Manasseh: of Machi]r, the clan of the Machirites, and Mac[hir was the father of Gilead; of Gilead, the clan of the Gileadites. 30 These are the] descenda[nts of Gilead:] of Ahiezer,[90] the clan of [the

85. 4QNum[b]. Not in MT SP LXX.

86. 4QNum[b] LXX. Areli MT. Aruli SP.

87. 4QNum[b] LXX. Arelites MT. Arulites SP.

88. 4QNum[b] SP LXX. Hamulites MT SP[ms].

89. 4QNum[b] SP LXX. Punites MT.

90. 4QNum[b] LXX. Iezer MT SP[mss]. Ahiezer SP LXX[mss].

Ahiezerites; of Helek, the clan of the Helekites; 31 and of A]sriel, the clan of the Asrielites; and of Shechem, [the clan of the Shechemites; 32 and of Shemida, the clan of the Shemida]ites; *and of Hopher,*[91] the clan of the *Hopherites.*[92] 33 Now Zelophehad [son of Hopher had no sons, but daughter]s; and *these are the names*[93] of the daughters of Zelophehad: [Mahlah, and Noah, Hoglah, Milcah, and Tirzah.] 34 These are the clans of Manasseh; *of*[94] those who were numbered of them there were [fifty]-[two thousand seven hundred]. ▲

[57 These are those who were numbered from the Levites by their families: . . . 62 And those numbered of them were twenty-three thousand, every male from a month old and upward; for they were not numbered among the Israelites, because there was no inheritance given them among the Israelites].

63 [These are those numbered by Moses and Eleazar the priest, who numbered the Israelites in the plains of Moab by the Jordan at Jericho. 64 But among these there was not one of those numbered by Moses and Aaron the priest, who had numbered the Israelites in the] wilderness [of Si]n[ai. 65 F]or [the L]ORD had said [of them, "They will surely die in the wilderness." There was not lef]t anyone of them, [ex]cept Caleb s[on of] Jephunneh, and Joshua [son of Nun].

27 [1 Then the daughter]s of Zelophehad son of *Hopher,*[95] son of Gilead, son of Machir, son of Manasseh, [from the clans of Manasseh son of Joseph, drew near. And these are the names of] his [daugh]ters: Mahlah, *and*[96] Noah, Ho[g]lah,[97] [and Milca]h, and *Torzah.*[98] [2 And they stood before Mos]es and before E[leazar the pri]est, [and] be[fore the leaders and all the] congregation, at the entrance [of the tent of meeting, saying, 3 "Our father died in the] wilderness, and h[e was not amon]g the company [of those who gath]ered [themselves toge]ther against the Lo[RD in the company of Korah, but he died in his own sin; and] he [ha]d[99] no [son]s. 4 Why should [the name of our father] be taken away [from] his family, beca[use he had no son? Give to us a possession] among the relatives of our [father]."

---

91. 4QNum[b] LXX. a*nd of Hepher* MT SP. *of Hopher* LXX[mss].

92. 4QNum[b] LXX. *Hepherites* MT SP.

93. 4QNum[b] LXX. *the name* MT SP.

94. 4QNum[b] MT[ms] SP LXX. *and* MT.

Chapter 27. 4QNum[b]: 27:1–5, 7–8, 10, 18–19, 21–23[b]; XHev/SeNum[b]: 27:2–13.

95. 4QNum[b] LXX. *Hepher* MT SP.

96. 4QNum[b] MT[mss] SP LXX. Not in MT.

97. 4QNum[b] MT[mss] SP. *and Hoglah* MT LXX.

98. 4QNum[b]. *Tirzah* MT SP LXX.

99. Singular verb (though it should agree with *sons* in the Hebrew expression) 4QNum[b] SP[mss]. Plural MT SP LXX.

5 So [Moses] brought their [ca]se be[fore the LORD. 6 And] the LORD [spo]ke to [Mo]s[es, saying, 7 "The daughters of Zelophehad spea]k [correctly;] you must indeed give [them possession of an inheritance among] their [fat]her['s relatives;] and you shall transfer the inheri[tance of their father to them].

8 "[And] you shall speak [t]o the Israelites, saying, ['If] a m[an] dies, [and] has no [son,] then you shall cause his inheritance [to pass] t[o] his daughter. [9 And if] he has no daughter, then you shall give [his inheritance] to his brothers. 10 And if he has no brothers, then you shall [gi]ve his inheritance to his father's brothers. 11 And if [his] fat[her] has no brothers, [then you shall give his inheritance to his kinsman] that is nearest [to him of his clan, and he shall possess it. It shall be] for the [Israeli]tes [a statute and ordinance, a]s the Lo[RD] commanded Moses.' "

[12 Then the LORD said to Moses, "Go up] to this mountain of Abarim, and see the land which I have given to the people of [Israel. 13 And when] you [have s]een it, you also will be gathered to your people, [as your brother Aaron was gathered]." ▲

18 [So] the LORD [said to Moses, "Take Joshua son of Nun, a man in whom is the spirit, and lay] your [hand on him; 19 have him stand before Eleazar the priest and before all the congre]gation, [and commission him in their sight. 20 You shall give him some of your authority, so that all the congregation of the Israelites may obey. 21 But he shall stand before Eleazar the priest, who shall inquire for him by the decision of the Urim before the LORD; at his word they shall go out, and at his word they shall come in, both he and all] the Isra[el]ites with him, the entire congregation *wi*]*th him."*[100]

■ *Numbers 27:12–23 informs us that Joshua has been chosen by God to succeed Moses. In the Masoretic Text and the Septuagint, the passage ends with Moses laying hands on Joshua. 4QNum*[b]*, however, then inserts a passage taken from Deuteronomy 3:21–22, in order to emphasize Joshua's need to have courage: "for the LORD your God, he is the one who fights for you."*

22 So [Moses did as the LORD commanded him. He took] Joshua *son of Nun,*[101] and had him stand before Eleazar t[he priest and before all the congregation; 23 and he lai]d his hands on him, and commissioned him as the LORD had directed through Moses. [*And Mose*]s [*said*] *to him, "Your eyes have seen what the LORD your God has done to* [*these*] *two k*[*ings; so shall the LORD do to all the kingdoms into which you are going. You shall not fear them; for the LORD your God, he is the one who fights for you*]*."*[102]

100. 4QNum[b]. Not in MT SP LXX.

101. 4QNum[b]. Not in MT SP LXX.

102. 4QNum[b] SP. Not in MT LXX.

28 [11 Then at the beginnings of your months you shall offer] a burnt off[ering to the LORD: two young bulls and] one [ram, seven] male la[mbs a year old without blemish;] 12 also three-[tenths of an ephah of fine flour as a grain offering, mixed with oil,] for each bull; [and two-tenths of fine flour as a grain offering, mixed with oil, for the one ram; 13 and a tenth of fine flour mixed with oil as a grain offering for every lamb. This is for a burnt offering of a pleasing aroma, an offering by fire] to the LORD. [14 And] their drink offerings [shall] be half a hin of wine [for a bull, a third of a hin for a ram,] and a quarter of a hin of wine[103] for [e]ach[104] lamb. [This is the burnt offering of each month throughout the months of] the year. 15 Also o[ne] male goat [for a sin of]fering [to the LORD; it shall be offered in addition to the regular burnt offering] and [its] drink offering. 16 Then in the fi[rst] month, [on the fourteenth day of the month, shall be the LORD's Passover].

17 And on the fifteenth [day of this month is a feast; for seven days unleavened bread shall be eaten]. ▲

[27 But you shall present a burnt offering, a pleasing aroma to the LORD: two young bulls, one ram, seven male lambs a year old; 28 also their grain offering of fine flour mixed with oil, three-tenths for each bull, two-tenths for] the o[ne ram, 29 a tenth for each of the seven lambs; 30 with one male goat] to make atonement fo[r you. 31 In addition to the regular burnt offering and its grain offering, you shall offer them and their] drink offering. [They shall be for you without blemish].

29 [9 "The grain offering shall be of fine flour mixed with oil, three-tenths of an ephah for the bull, two-tenths for the one ram, 10 a tenth for] ea[ch lamb of the seven lambs; 11 one male goat for a sin offering, besides the sin offering of atonement, and the continual burnt offering and] their[105] grain offering, [and their drink offerings].

12 "[Then on the fifteenth day of the seventh month you shall have a] holy [convocation; you shall do no laborious work, and you shall celebrate a festival to the LORD for seven days. 13 And you shall] offer [a burnt offering, an offering by fire, of a pleasing aroma to the LORD: thirteen young bulls, two rams, fourteen male lambs a year old; they shall be without blemish. 14 Their grain offering shall be of fine flour mixed with oil, three-tenths of an ephah for each of the thirteen bulls, two-tenths for each of the two rams, and one-tenth for each of the four-

---

Chapter 28. XHev/SeNum[b]: 28:11–12; 4QNum[b]: 28:13–17, 28, 30–31.

   103. 4QNum[b]. *for the lamb, wine* MT. *for each lamb, wine* SP LXX.

   104. 4QNum[b] SP LXX. Not in MT.

Chapter 29. 4QNum[b]: 29:10–13, 16–18, 26–30, 40 [MT 30:1].

   105. 4QNum[b] MT[mss]. *its* MT SP LXX.

teen lambs; 16 also] o[ne male goa]t [for a sin offering, besides the regular burnt offering, its grain offering, and its drink offering].

17 "[Then on the second day:] tw[elve] young bulls, [two rams, fourteen male lambs a year old without blemish, 18 with their grain offering and their drink offerings for the bulls,] for [the rams, and for the lambs, by their number according to the ordinance].▲

26 "[Then on the fifth day: nine bulls, t]wo [ra]ms, [fourteen male] lam[bs a year old without blemish, 27 with their grain offering and their drink offerings for the bulls,] for the ra[m]s, and for the lam[bs, by their number according to the ordinance; 28 also one male goat for a sin offering *to make atonement f*]or *you,*[106] besides the regu[lar] burnt of[fering, and its grain offering, and its drink offering].

29 [Then on the sixth day: eight bulls, two rams,] four[teen male lambs] a year [ol]d [without blemish, 30 with their grain offering and their drink offerings for the bulls, for the rams, and for the lamb]s, by their number [according to the ordinance].▲

[40 And Moses spoke to the Israelites in accordance with] all that the LORD had commanded Moses.

30 [1 Then Moses spoke to the heads of the tribes of the Israelites, saying,] "This is the word that the Lo[RD] has commanded. [2 When a man makes a vow to the LORD, or swears an o]ath to bind [himself] by a pl[edge, he shall not break his word; he shall act in accordance with all that proceeds] out of his mouth.

[3 "When a woman makes a vow to the LORD, or binds herself by a pledge, while (still living) in her father's house, in her youth, 4 and her father hears of her vow or her pledge by which she has bound herself, and her father says nothing to her; then all her vows shall stand, and every pledge by which she has bound herself; *he shall estab*]*lish it.*[107] 5 But i[f her father forbids her at the time that he hears about it, none of her vows, nor of he]r [pledges by which] she has [bo]und herself, [shall stand; and the LORD will forgive her, because her father opposed] her.

6 A[nd if] she is married to a husband, [while under her vows or any thoughtless utterance of] her lips [by which she has bound] herself, 7 and her husband hears of it *and says nothing to her* [*on the day that he hears it;*[108] then her vows shall

---

106. 4QNum[b]. Not in MT SP LXX.

Chapter 30. 4QNum[b]: 30:1–2, 4–8, 14–16 [MT 30:2–3, 5–9, 15–17]; 4QLev-Num[a]: 30:2(?), 6(?) (8? 12?) [MT 30:3(?), 7(?) (9? 13?)].

107. 4QNum[b]. *(every pledge) shall stand* MT. *(all her pledges) shall stand* SP. *(every pledge) shall remain over her* LXX.

108. 4QNum[b] LXX. *on the day that he hears it and says nothing to her* MT SP.

stand, and] her pledg[es] by which she has bound herself shall stand. 8 But i[f her husband forbids her on the day that he hears of it, then he shall nullify] *all*[109] her vows *and her pledges,*[110] [and the thoughtless utterance of her lips with which she has bound herself; and the LORD will forgive her]. ▲

14 ["But if her husband indeed says nothing to her from day to day, then he validates all her vows or all her pledges that are upon her; he has validated the]m, [because he said nothing to her at the time that he heard of them. 15 But if he makes them null and void after] he has heard of [them, then he shall bear her guilt]."

16 [These are the statutes which the LORD commanded Moses, as between a ma]n [and his wife, and as between a father and his daughter, while in her youth, still in her father's house].

31 [1 The LORD said to Moses, 2 "Execute] vengeance for the Isr[ael]ites [on the Midianites; afterward you will be gathered to your people]."

3 [So Moses spoke to the *childr*]*en of Israel,*[111] saying, ["Arm men from among you for the war, that they may go against Midian to execute the LORD's vengeance] on Midian. 4 From [each] tribe a thousand, [throughout all the tribes of Israel, you shall send to the war. 5 So there were provid]ed out of the thousands of Isr[ael, a thousand from each tribe, twelve thousand arm]ed for war." 6 And [Moses sent them, a thousand from each tribe, to the war, them and Phinehas] son of Eleazar the pr[iest, to the war, with the vessels of the sanctuary and the trumpets for sounding the alarm in his hand]. ▲

[21 Then Eleazar the priest said to the men of war who had gone to battle, "This is the statute of the law which the LORD] has commanded [Moses: 22 only the gold, the silver, the bronze, the iron, the tin, and] the [lead, 23 everything that can withstand fire, you shall pass through the fire, and it shall be clean. Nevertheless it shall also be purified with the water for impurity; and whatever cannot withstand fire you shall pass through the wate]r *for impurity.*[112] [24 And you shall wash your clothes on the seventh day, and you shall be clean; and afterward you may come] into the ca[mp]."

25 [Then the LORD spoke to Mo]ses, [saying,] . . . ▲

[30 "But from the Israelites' half you shall take one out of every fifty, of the persons, of the ox]en, [and] *of t*[*he flo*]*cks, of the donkeys*[113]—o[f all the animals—

---

109. 4QNum[b] LXX. Not in MT SP.

110. 4QNum[b] LXX. Not in MT SP.

Chapter 31. 4QNum[b]: 31:2–6, 21b–25, 30–33, 35–36, 38, 43–44, 46–54.

111. 4QNum[b]. *people* MT SP LXX.

112. 4QNum[b]. Not in MT SP LXX. *and it shall be clean* LXX[mss].

113. 4QNum[b] LXX. *of the donkeys, of the flocks* MT SP.

and give them to the Levites who have charg]e [of the taberna]cle of the LORD."
[31 And Moses and Eleazar the priest did as the LORD had commanded] Moses.

32 Now the booty [remaining from] the spoil [that the men of war took was six hundred and sevent]y-five thousand [sheep,] 33 a[nd seventy-]tw[o thousand cattle, 34 sixty-one thousand donkeys, 35 and of pe]ople, of the women who [had not known a man by sleeping with him, thirty-two thousand persons in all].

36 [And the half-sh]are, the portion of those who had gone out to w[ar, was in number three hundred and thirty-seven thousand five] hundred [sheep and goats, 37 and the LORD's tribute of sheep and goats was six hundred and seventy-five. 38 And the cattle were thirty-]six [thousand, of which the LORD's tribute was seventy-two].▲

[42 As for the Israelites' half, which Moses separated from that of the fighting men— 43 now the congregation's half was three hundred and thirty-seven thousand five hundred shee]p and goats, 44 [and] thirty-six tho[usand cattle, 45 thirty thousand five hundred donkeys, 46 and sixteen] thousand [persons.] 47 And [from the Israelites' half Moses] took [one out of every fifty, both of persons and of animals, and gave them to the Levites who had charge of the tabernacle of the LORD, as the LORD had commanded Moses].

48 [Then] all[114] the officers who were over the thousands of the army, the commanders [of thousands and the commanders of hundreds, *who came from the service of*] *the war*,[115] [approached Mo]ses, 49 and said to [Mos]es, "Your servants have made [a count of the men of war who are under our command and not] one of us is [mi]ssing. 50 And we have b[rought the LORD's offe]r[ing, what each man found, articles of gold, armlets and bracelets, signet r]ings, *and*[116] earrings, and pendants, *and he made aton*[ement[117] for us before the LORD]."

51 [Then Moses and Eleazar the priest received] the gold from them, all the wro[ught] articles. 52 And al[l the gold of the offering that they offered to the LORD,] from [the commanders of thousands and from the commanders of hundreds,] was [sixt]een thousand *and*[118] seven hundred and fifty shekels. 53 (For the men of war had taken booty, every man for himself.) 54 So Moses and Eleazar [the priest] received [the gold of the commanders of thousands] and of hundreds, and brought it into the tent of meeting as a memo[rial for the Israelites before the LORD].

---

114. 4QNum[b] LXX. Not in MT SP.
115. 4QNum[b]. Not in MT SP LXX.
116. 4QNum[b] LXX. Not in MT SP.
117. 4QNum[b]. *to make atonement* MT SP LXX.
118. 4QNum[b] MT[mss] SP LXX. Not in MT.

32 1 [Now] the descendants of Reuben and the descendants of [Gad] had [a very great num]ber [of cattle; and when they saw the land of Jazer and] the land of Gilead, behold, [the place was suitable for cattle. 2 So the descendants of Gad and the descendants of Reuben came and spoke to Moses, to Eleazar the priest, and to the leaders of the congregation, saying:▲

3 "Ataroth, Dibon, Jazer, Nimrah, Heshbon, Elealeh, Sebam, Nebo, and Beon— 4 the land that the LORD conquered before the congregation of Israel—is a] land [for cattle; and your servants have cattle." 5 And] they said, "I[f we have found favor in your sight, let this land be given to your servants for a possession; do not] make [us] cross [the Jordan]."

[6 But Moses said to the descendants of Gad and to the descendants of Reuben, "Shall your brothers go to war while you yourselves sit here? 7 And why do you discourage] the heart of the Isr[ael]ites from going over into the land which the LORD has given them? 8 This is what your ancestors did, when] I [sen]t them from Kadesh-barnea to see [the land. 9 For when they went up to the Valley of Eshcol and saw] the land, they discouraged the hearts of the Israelites from going into the land [that the LORD had given them. 10 And the LOR]D['s anger burned] on that day, and he swore, saying, 11 'Surely none of the people who came up out of Egypt, [from twenty years old and upward, shall see the] land that I swore to give to Abraham, to Isaac, and to Jacob, because they have not completely [followed me 12 —none except Caleb son of Jephunneh the Kenizzite and Joshua son of Nun, for they have unreservedly] followed the LORD.' 13 So the LORD's anger burned against Israel, [and he made] them [wander] in the wild[erness for forty years, until all the generation that had done evil in the si]ght of the LORD [was gone].

14 "Now behold, you have risen up in [your] an[cestors'] place, [a brood of sinful people, to increase still more the fierce anger of the LOR]D against Israel! 15 For if you turn away from following him, [he will again abandon them in the wilderness; and you will destroy all this people]."

16 [And they approached] h[im and] said, ["We will build sheep]folds [here for our flocks, and towns for our little ones; 17 but we ourselves take up arms, ready to go before] the Israelites, until [we have brought them to their place. Meanwhile our little ones will stay in the fortified towns because of the inh]abitants of [the land. 18 We will not return to our homes until every one of the Israelites has received his inheritance. 19 For we will not have an inheritance with] them [on the other side of the Jordan and beyond, because our inheritance has come to us on this side of the Jordan to the east]."

[20 So Moses said to them, "If you do this, if you arm yourselves before the

---

Chapter 32. 4QNum^b: 32:1, 4–5, 7–10, 13–17, 19, 21–30, 35, 37–39, 41; 4QLev-Num^a: 32:8–15, 23–42.

LORD for battle, 21 and every armed man of you crosses the Jordan before the
LORD, until he has driven out his ene]mi[es before him 22 and the land is subdued
before the LORD, then after that you may return and be free of obligation to the
LORD and to Israel, and] t[his l]and [will be your possession before the LORD.
23 But if] y[ou do no]t d[o so, behold, yo]u [have sinned] against the L[o]RD; and
be sure [yo]ur s[in will] find [you] out. [24 Build citie]s for your little ones, and
folds for your *flocks,*[119] and do what you have pro[mised].''

25 [*And the descen*]*dants of Reuben and the descendants of Gad*[120] [*and the half-tri*]*be
of Manasseh*[121] [spoke to] Moses, saying, ''Your servant[s] will do as my lord commands. [26 Our little ones, ou]r [wives,] *and*[122] our *flocks,*[123] and all [our] c[attle
will rem]a[in there in the cities of] Gilead; 27 but your servants will cross over,
every man who is armed for war, to do battle before [the LORD], just as [my lord
orders].''

28 [So] Moses [gave command concerning them to Eleazar] the priest, to
Joshua son of Nun, and [to the heads of the fathers' houses of the tribes of the Israelites. 29 And Moses] said [to them, ''If] the descendents of Gad and the descendents of R[euben, every man who is a]rmed for [battle before the LORD,] will
cross [the Jordan with you and the land will be subdued before] you, then you
shall give them the land of Gilead for a possession. [30 But if they] will [not]
c[ross over with you armed *for battle before the LORD, but carry over their little ones
and*] the[ir] *wives* [*and their flocks before you to the land of Canaan,*[124] they shall have
possessions among yo]u in the land of Canaan.''

31 Then the descendants of Gad a[nd the descendants of Reuben] answered,
[saying, ''As the LORD has spoken to your servants, so will we do. 32 We] will
cross over armed before the LORD into the la[nd of Canaan, but the possession of
our inheritance shall remain with us on this side of the Jordan].''

33 [So Mose]s [gave to them]—to the descendants of Gad and to the descendants of Reuben and to the half-tribe of Man[asseh son of Joseph—the kingdom
of Sihon king of the Amorites and the kin]gdom of Og king of Bashan, the land
and its towns [with their territories, the towns of the surrounding land. 34 And
the descendants of Gad built] Di[bo]n, Ataroth, Aroer, 35 Atroth-shophan, [and]
Ja[zer, Jogbehah, 36 and Beth-nimrah, and] Beth-haran as [forti]fied cities, and
folds for sheep. 37 And the descendants of Reuben built Heshbo[n, Elealeh,

---

119. 4QLev-Num[a] MT[mss] SP. variant form (error?) MT.

120. 4QNum[b]. *And the descendents of Gad and the descendents of Reuben* MT SP LXX.

121. 4QNum[b] SP. Not in MT LXX.

122. 4QNum[b]. Not in MT.

123. 4QNum[b] MT[ms] SP. *flock* MT. Not in LXX.

124. 4QNum[b] LXX. Not in 4QLev-Num[a] MT SP.

Kiriathaim, 38 Nebo, and Baal-m]eon—their names being changed—and Sibmah; and they gave [other names to the towns that they built].

39 [And the descendants of Machir son of] Manasseh [*son of Jose*]*ph*[125] [went] to Gilead and captured [it, and dispossessed the Amorites who were in it. 40 And Moses gave Gilead to Machir son of Manasseh, and he lived in it.] 41 And Jair [the] son [of Manasseh went and captured their villages, and named them Havvoth-j]air. [42 And Nobah went and captured] Kenath and [its] v[illages, and called it Nobah after his own name].

33 [1 These are the journeys of the Isra]el[ites, when [they went out of the land of Egypt by their divisions under the leadership of Moses and Aaron. 2 Moses wrote down their starting-places according to] their [st]ages by the command of [the LORD, and these are their stages according to their starting-places].

3 A[nd they set out from Rameses in the first month, on the fifte]e[nth] day of [the first] mo[nth; on the day after the Passover the children of Israel went out boldly in the sight of all the Egyptians,] 4 while the Egyptians [were burying all their firstborn, whom the LORD had struck down among them. The LORD executed judgments even against their gods].

5 [So the Israelites set out from Rameses, and encamped at] Succoth. 6 And [they] set out [from Succoth, and encam]ped in Eth[am, which is on the edge of the wilderness. 7 And they set out from Etham, and turned back to Pi-hahiroth, which] fac[es Baal-zepho]n; and they encamped be[fore Migdol. 8 And they set out from before Hahiroth, and passed through the midst of the sea into the wilderness; and] they went [three day]s' journey in the wil[derness of Etham, and encamped at Marah. 9 Then they set out from Marah and came to Elim; and at Elim there were t]w[elve springs of water, and seventy palm trees; and they encamped there]. ▲

22 [Then they set out] from Ris[sah, and encamped at Kehelathah. 23 And they set out from Kehela]thah [and encamped at Mount Shepher. 24 And they set out from Mount Shepher and encamped at Haradah.] 25 And they set out from Harad[ah and] encamped [at Makheloth. 26 And they set out from Makheloth and encamped at Tahath. 27 And they set out from Tahath and encamped at Terah.] 28 And they set out from Terah [and encamped at Mithkah. 29 And they set out from Mithkah and encamped at Hashmonah. 30 And they set out from Hashmonah and encamped at Moseroth.] 31 And they set out from [Mo]seroth and encam[ped at Bene-jaakan. 32 And they set out from Bene-jaakan and encamped at Hor-haggidgad. 33 And they set out from Hor-haggidgad] and en-

---

125. 4QNum[b]. Not in 4QLev-Num[a] MT SP LXX.

Chapter 33. 4QNum[b]: 33:1–4, 23, 25, 28, 31, 45, 47–48, 50–52; 4QLev-Num[a]: 33:5–9, 22–34, 52–54; 2QNum[b]: 33:47–53.

camped at Jotbathah. 34 Then they set out [from Jotbathah and encamped at Abronah]. ▲

[45 Then they set out from Iyim and encamped at D]i[bon-gad. 46 And they set out from Dibon-gad and camped at Almon-diblathaim. 47 And they set out from Almon-diblathaim] and encamp[ed in the moun]tains of Aba[rim, before Nebo. 48 And they set out from the mountains of Abarim and encamped in the plain]s of M[oab by the Jordan at Jericho. 49 Then they encamped by] the Jordan from Be[th]-je[shimoth, as far as Abel-shittim in the plains of Moab].

50 [Then the LORD spoke to Moses in the plains of Moab by the Jordan at Je]richo, sa[ying, 51 "Sp]eak to the Israelites, and s[ay to them, 'When you cross over the Jordan] into [the] land [of Canaan, 52 then] you [shall drive out] *the in-habitants*[126] of the lan[d from before you, and destroy all] their [figured stones, and] dest[roy all] their mo[lten] images, and [demolish] all their high places. [53 And you shall take possession of the land and settle in i]t; for I have g[iven] the [land] to you to [possess it. 54 And you shall apportion the land by lot according to] your [clan]s; tó a large one you shall [give a la]rge inherita[nce, and to a small one you shall give a small inheritance. Wherever the l]ot [falls] to [anyone, that shall be his; you shall inherit according to the tribes of your fathers].' " ▲

34

[1 The LORD spoke to Moses, saying: 2 "Command the Israelites, and say to them, 'When you enter the land of Canaan . . . 3 Your southern sector shall extend from the wilderness of Zin along the side of Edom, and your south-ern border shall extend from the end of the Salt Sea on the east; 4 and your boun]dary [shall turn] south [of the ascent of Akrabbim, and cross to Zin, and its outer limit shall be south of Kadesh-barnea; then it shall go on to] Hazar-addar [and cross to Azmon; 5 and the boundary shall turn from Azmon to the Brook of Egypt, and its termination shall be] at [the s]ea.

6 " 'And [for the western] boun[dary, you shall have the Great Sea and its coast; this shall be your western boundary].

7 " '[And this shall be your] no[rthern] boundary: [from the Great Sea you shall trace your line to Mount Hor; 8 from Mount Hor you shall trace it] to the entrance of H[amath, and the] outer [limit of the boundary shall b]e [at Zedad; 9 then the boundary shall proceed to Ziphron, and its end shall be at Hazar]-enan; this [shall be your northern boundary].

" '[10 And you shall trace] your e[astern] boun[dary from Hazar-enan to Shepham;]' " ▲

[16 The LORD spoke to Moses, saying: ". . . 18 You shall take one leader of every tribe to divide the land for inheritance. 19 And these are the name]s of the

---

126. 2QNum[b]. *all the inhabitants* MT SP LXX.
Chapter 34. 4QNum[b]: 34:4–9, 19–21, 23; MurNum: 34:10.

m[en: Of the tribe of Judah, Caleb son of Jephunne]h. 20 And of the tribe [of the descendants of Simeon, Shemuel son of Ammihud. 21 Of the tribe of Benjamin, Elidad son of Chislon. 22 And of the tribe of the descendants of Dan a leader, Bukki son of Jogli. 23 Of the descendants of Joseph: of the tribe of the descendants of Manasseh a lead]er, Han[niel son of Ephod]." ▲

35 3 "And the to[wns] shall be [theirs to live in, and] their [pasture la]nds [shall be for their cattle, for their livestock, and for all] their animals. 4 An[d the pasture lands of the towns], whi[ch you shall give] to the Levites, shall reach from the wa[ll of the town outward a thousand cubits all around.] 5 And you shall measure [outside the town for the] east [sid]e [two] thousand cubits, [and for the south side two thousand cubits, and for] the *side to the west*[127] [two thousand cubits, and for the north side two tho]usa[nd cubits, with the town in the middle. This shall belong to them as pasture lands of] their [tow]ns. ▲

[10 "Speak to the Israelites, and say to them: 'When you cross the Jordon into the land of Canaan, 11 you shall select cities for yourselves as cities of refuge for you, so that the manslayer] who [has killed any person without intent may flee there. 12 And the cities shall be for you a refuge from the avenger, so that the manslayer may not die until he stands] before the congrega[tion for trial. 13 And the cities that you designate shall be your six cities of refuge.] 14 You shall designate [three cit]ies [beyond the Jordan, and you shall designate three cities in the land of Canaan; they are to be cities of refuge. 15 For] the Is[rael]ites [and for the stranger and for the sojourner among them, these six cities shall be for refuge, so that anyone who kills a person without intent may flee there]." ▲

[18 "Or if he struck him with a weapon of wood in the hand, by which he can cause death, and that person dies,] he shall [*surely*] *be put to death; the one who s[truck him is a murderer,*[128] the murderer shall surely be put to death. 19 The avenger of blood is the one who shall put the murderer to death; when he meets him,] he shall put h[im] to death. [20 Likewise, if he pushes him from hatred, or hur]ls [something at him *so that he*] d[ie]s, *lying in wait,*[129] 21 [or in] enmity strikes him down with [his] hand, [so that he die]s, [then the one who struck him] shall surely be put to death. [He is a murderer,] *the murderer shall surely be put to death;*[130] the avenger of blood [*hims*]*elf*[131] shall put the mur[derer] to death when he meets him.

22 "[But if] he pushes him [suddenly without en]mity, or hurls [anything at

---

Chapter 35. 4QNum^b: 35:3–5, 11–12, 14–15, 18–25, 27–28, 33–34; 4QLev-Num^a: 35:4–5.

127. 4QNum^b SP LXX. *west side* MT.

128. 4QNum^b. *he is a murderer* MT SP LXX.

129. 4QNum^b. *lying in wait, so that he dies* MT SP LXX.

130. 4QNum^b LXX. Not in MT SP.

131. 4QNum^b. Not in MT SP LXX.

him wit]hout lying in wait, 23 or *with a weapon of*[132] stone, [by which a person may die, and without] seeing him drops it on him so that [he] dies, th[ough he was not his enemy] and sought [him no harm, 24 then the congregation shall judge between the sl]ayer and the avenger of [blood in accordance with] these [ordinances]. 25 Then [the congregation] shall deliver [the manslayer from the hand of the avenger of blood, and the congregation shall restore him to his city of refuge, to which he had fled; and he shall live in it until the death of the high priest who was anointed with the holy oil].

[26 "But if the manslayer shall at any time go beyond the bounds of his city of refuge to which he fled, 27 and] the aveng[er of blood fi]nds [*him*[133] outside the bounds of his city of refuge, and the avenger of blood slays the man]slayer, he shall not be guilty of b[lood, 28 because the manslayer should have remained in hi]s [ci]t[y of refuge until the death of the high priest; but after the death of the hig]h [priest] the [manslayer] shall return [to the land of his possession]." ▲

[33 "So you shall not pollute the land in which you live; for blood pollutes the land, and] no ex[piation can be made for the lan]d [for the blood that is shed in it, except by the blood of the one who shed it. 34 And you shall not defile the] land which y[ou inhabit, in the midst of which I dwell; for I, the LORD, dwell in the m]idst of the Israelites."

36 [1 Then the heads of the fathers' houses of the clans of the descendan]ts of Gilead son of Machir, [son of Manasseh, of the clans of the descendants of Joseph, came forward and spoke before Moses *and before Ele*]*azar the priest*[134] and before the [leaders, the heads of the fathers' houses of the Israelites. 2 And they said,] "The LORD [comm]anded [my lord] to give [the land for an inheritance by lot to the Israelites; and my lord was commanded by the LORD to give the inheritance of Zelophehad our brother to his daughters. 3 But if they are married to any of the sons of the other Israelite tribes, their inheritance will be taken from the inheritance of our fathers and will be added to the inheritance of the tribe to which they belong; so it will be taken away from our allotted inheritance. 4 And when the jubilee of the Israelites comes, then their inheritance will be added to the] inherita[nce of the tribe to which they belong; so their inheritance will be taken from the inheritance of the tribe of our fathers." *And they spoke before Moses and before*] *Eleazar the* [*priest and before the leaders, the heads of the fathers' houses of the Israelites; and they said, "The LORD commanded my lord, and Joshua son of*] *Nun and Ca*[*leb son of Jephunneh, to give the land as an inheritance*]."[135]

---

132. 4QNum[b]. *with any* MT SP LXX.

133. Evidently a variant word order (verb/subject/object) 4QNum[b]. Verb/object/subject MT SP.

Chapter 36. 4QNum[b]: 36:1–2a, 4a–7; MurNum: 36:7–11; 1QpaleoLev: 36:7–8(?).

134. 4QNum[b] LXX. Not in MT SP.

135. 4QNum[b]. Not in MT SP LXX.

5 [Then Moses commanded the Israelites according to the word of] the LORD, saying, ["The tribe of the descendants of Joseph speaks] cor[rectly. 6 This is the thing which the LORD commands concerning the daughters of Zelophehad, saying, 'Let them] sure[ly[136] marry whomever seems good] to them; [but they must be married with the family of the tribe of their father.] 7 Thus no i[nheritance of the Israelites shall be transferred from tribe to] tr[ibe; for each of the] Israel[ites shall retain the inheritance of the tribe of his] ancestors. 8 And every da[ughter who possesses an inheritance in any of the tribe]s [of the I]srael[ites shall] be wife to one from [the] cla[n of her father's tribe,] so that [every Israelite] may possess [the inheritance of] his ancestors. 9 Thus no inheritance shall be transferred f[rom one tribe to another tribe; for the tribes of the] [Israel]ites shall [each] hold on [to] his own [inher]itance.' "

[10 Just as the LORD commanded Mose]s, so [the] daughters [of Zelophehad did; 11 for Mah]l[ah,] Tir[zah, and Hoglah, and Milcah, and Noah, the daughters of Zelophehad, were married to sons of their father's brothers].

---

136. 4QNum[b]. Not in MT SP LXX.

DEUTERONOMY

The hero of this book is Moses, whose life and speeches are chronicled from the time the Israelites left Mount Sinai (or Mount Horeb) to the death and burial of Israel's great leader. Since Deuteronomy also includes the authoritative Law given by God through Moses to Israel, and is the only book of the Pentateuch that explicitly identifies itself as a record of Moses' laws (Deut 1:5; 4:8, etc.), it is not difficult to see why this book was one of the most popular at Qumran. In fact, Deuteronomy is second only to the Psalms in terms of the number of scrolls that were found in the Judean Desert.

Of the thirty-three Deuteronomy scrolls, thirty were discovered at Qumran (two in Cave 1,[a] three in Cave 2,[b] twenty-two in Cave 4,[c] and one each in Caves 5, 6, and 11),[d] and three more were found at sites farther to the south (one at Masada, one at Nahal Hever, and one at Murabba'at).[e] Although none of these scrolls is complete, at least part of every chapter of the book is represented between them.

The list given is quite unusual for several reasons. First, it indicates that one Greek copy of Deuteronomy (4QLXXDeut) was used or stored at Qumran, which means that at least some of the Qumran community spoke Greek as well as Hebrew and Aramaic. Second, two of these manuscripts (4QpaleoDeut[r] and 4QpaleoDeut[s]) were written in the ancient paleo-Hebrew script rather than the square script used for the vast majority of the Dead Sea Scrolls. Third, one scroll (pap6QDeut) was written on papyrus, which is much more fragile than the leather on which most other scrolls were written. Finally, the somewhat

---

a. 1QDeut[a] and 1QDeut[b].   **b.** 2QDeut[a], 2QDeut[b], and 2QDeut[c].   **c.** 4QDeut[a], 4QDeut[b], 4QDeut[c], 4QDeut[d], 4QDeut[e], 4QDeut[f], 4QDeut[g], 4QDeut[h], 4QDeut[i], 4QDeut[j], 4QDeut[k1], 4QDeut[k2], 4QDeut[k3], 4QDeut[l], 4QDeut[m], 4QDeut[n], 4QDeut[o], 4QDeut[p], 4QDeut[q], 4Qpaleo-Deut[r], 4QpaleoDeut[s], and 4QLXXDeut.   **d.** 5QDeut, pap6QDeut(?), and 11QDeut.
e. MasDeut, XHev/SeDeut, and MurDeut.

confusing symbols 4QDeut^{k1}, 4QDeut^{k2}, and 4QDeut^{k3} serve to remind us just how difficult it is to categorize fragments of ancient writing, to piece them together, and to identify the scroll to which each belongs. When earlier editors first identified these fragments as belonging to the book of Deuteronomy, they believed them all to be part of a single scroll, which they termed "4QDeut^k." But when it was later discovered that the fragments actually belonged to three different scrolls, it was too late to assign the next symbols, "l" and "m," to the two new fragments, since these symbols had already been allocated to these scrolls. For this reason, the symbol "k" is now shared by three different manuscripts of Deuteronomy!

What distinctive or interesting readings are found in the Deuteronomy scrolls? As we read through the following translation of those scrolls, it becomes clear that the text of the traditional Hebrew Bible—the Masoretic Text—is confirmed or supported in most cases. But on several occasions readings from some scrolls clearly support other ancient textual traditions: for example, in Deuteronomy 32, 4QDeut^q most often agrees with the Septuagint, not the Masoretic Text or the Samaritan Pentateuch.

On other occasions a scroll has a reading not found elsewhere: for example, 4QDeut^c stresses that the Israelites are going over "the Jordan" to occupy the land in Deuteronomy 4:14, whereas the Masoretic Text, the Samaritan Pentateuch, and the Septuagint do not mention this river. Sometimes material that is found in other biblical manuscripts is completely omitted: for example, in Deuteronomy 3:20, 4QDeut^m and the Septuagint say "until the LORD *your God* gives rest to your countrymen . . . ," while 4QDeut^d, the Masoretic Text, and the Samaritan Pentateuch merely read "until the LORD gives rest to your countrymen. . . ." The longer reading brings the person of God into sharper focus. An unusual and unexpected passage occurs in 4QDeut^j, where Deuteronomy 11:21 is directly followed by material from Exodus 12:43–46. Some readings are rather controversial: for example, in Deuteronomy 8:6, the Masoretic Text, the Samaritan Pentateuch, and the Septuagint tell us to keep God's commandments and to *fear* him. This reading is also found in 4QDeut^j—but another scroll (4QDeut^n) says instead that we are to *love* him!

Why was Deuteronomy so popular at Qumran? One reason is its emphasis on God's "covenant" with Israel, a term that is found twenty-six times in this book (see, for example, Deut 4:13; 9:9; 29:1). Several references to the Community of the New (or Renewed) Covenant in their writings show that the Qumran community saw themselves in covenant with God. Examples include the *Damascus Document* (CD 2:2; 19:14, 33), the *Community Rule* (1QS 1:16, 18, 20; 8:21), and the *Habakkuk Pesher* (1QpHab 2:3).

A second reason for Deuteronomy's importance among the scrolls is the prominent place it gives to the Law and its interpretation. This was also a subject of great significance at Qumran; note, for example, the legal rulings in the document abbreviated 4QMMT. It is not surprising, therefore, that Deuteronomy would play an important part in the religious life and legal rulings of the Qumran community.

1 [1 These are the words which Moses spoke t]o all Israel [acr]oss [the Jo]rdan in the wilderness, in the Arabah opposite [Suph, between Paran, Tophel, Laban, Hazeroth, and Di-zahab. 2 (It is eleven days' journey from Horeb by the way of Mount] Seir to Kadesh-barnea.) 3 Then in the fo[rtieth year, in the ele]venth month, on the first day of the month, [Moses spoke to the Israelites, according to all tha]t the LORD had commanded h[im] concerning them, 4 after he had defeated Sihon the king of the Amorites, who lived [in Heshbon], and Og [the king of Bashan, who li]ved in Ashtaroth, at Edrei. 5 Beyond the Jordan, in the land of Moab, Moses began to explain [this] law, [saying]:

[6 The LORD our God spoke] to us in Horeb, as follows: "You have stayed long enough at this mountain; 7 turn and take your journey and go to the hill country [of the Amorites and to all their neighbors in the Arabah, in the hill country and in the lo]wland, *in*[1] the Negev and by the sea, the land of the Canaanites, and Lebanon, as far as the great river, the river [Euphrates. 8 S]*ee,*[2] I have set [the land] bef[ore you; go in and occupy] the land which the LORD swore to your ancestors, to Abraham, to Isaac, and to Jacob, [to give to them and to their descendants after th]em."

9 And I spoke [to you at th]at [time], saying, "I am not able to bear you by myself alone; 10 the LORD your God has multiplied you, [and see, you are this day like the stars of heaven in multitude. 11 The LORD, the God of] your [an]cestors, made you a thousand times as many as you are, and has blessed you, as [he promised] you! [12 How can I alone bear your load and your burden and you]r

---

Chapter 1. 4QDeut[h]: 1:1–17, 22–23, 29–39, 41, 43–46; 11QDeut: 1:4–5; 2QDeut[a]: 1:7–9; 4QpaleoDeut[r]: 1:8(?), 45(?); 1QDeut[b]: 1:9–13; 1QDeut[a]: 1:22–25.

1. 4QDeut[h] SP. *and in* MT LXX.

2. Plural 2QDeut[a] SP LXX. Singular MT.

[strife?] 13 Choose wise and understanding and experienced men, according to your tribes, and [I will pu]t them [in authority over you]."

[14 Then you answered me, and said, "The thing which] you have spoken [is good for us] to do." 15 So I took the heads of your tribes, wis[e and experienced] men, [and made them heads over you, commanders of thousands], commanders of hundreds, commanders of fifties, commanders of tens, and officers, according to y[our] tribes. [16 And I charged your judges at that time, as follows: "Hear the cases between your countrymen, and jud]ge righteously between one person and another, and the resident alien as well. 17 You shall not show partiali[ty in judgment; you shall hear the small and the great alike; you shall not be afraid of anyone; for the judgment] is [God's]. Any case that is too hard for you, you shall bring to me, a[nd I will hear it]." ▲

[22 And] all of you [came] to me and said, "Let us send me[n before us, so that they may search the land for us and bring back to us a report of the way by wh]ich [we should go up], and the cities which we will encounter." [23 And the thing pleased me and I took] twelve of your m[en, one man for every tribe. 24 Then they turned and went up into the hill country, and came to the valley of Eshco]l, [and sp]ied out *the land*.³ 25 And th[ey took some of the fruit of the land in their hands and brought it down to us, and brought us back word again, and said, "It is a good land which the LORD our God is giving to us]."

[29 Then I said to you, "Do not dread or] be afraid [of them. 30 The LORD your God who goes before you—he will fight for you, according to all that he did for you in Egypt before your eyes, 31 and in the wilderness] where [you] saw [how the LORD your God carried you, as a man bears his son, in all the way that you went, until you came to this place]. 32 Yet in [this] thi[ng you did not believe the LORD your God, 33 who went before you in the way, to seek out a place for you to pitch your tents, in fire] by night, to *show* [you⁴ the way you should go, and in the cloud by day]."

[34 Then the LORD heard the voice of your words, and was angry, and swore as follows: 35 "Surely not] one of [these] people [of this evil generation will se]e [the good land which I swore to give to your ancestors, 36 except Caleb son of Jephunneh—he shall see it]; and to him I shall give [the land that he has walked on, and to his children, because he has followed the LORD completely." 37 Moreover, the LORD was angry with me because of you, saying], "You [also] shall [no]t enter *to there;*⁵ 38 Joshua [son of Nun, who stands before you—he shall enter there; encourage him, for he shall cause Israel to inherit it." 39 Moreover, your little ones, who you said would be a prey, and your children, who] this day do not

---

3. 1QDeutᵃ. *it* MT SP LXX.

4. Pronoun independent 4QDeutʰ. Pronoun suffixed MT SP.

5. 4QDeutʰ SP MTᵐˢˢ. *there* MT.

know[6] of good [or evil—they shall enter there, and to them will I give it, and they shall occupy it. 40 But as for you, turn around and set out for the wilderness in the direction of the Red Sea].

41 Then you answered [and said to me, "We have sinned against the LORD! We will go up and fight, according to all that the LORD our God commanded us." And each of your men strapped on his weapons of war, and thought it easy to go up into the hill country. 42 Then the LORD said to me, "Say to them, 'Do not go up and do not fight, for I am not in your midst; otherwise you will be defeated by your enemies.'" 43 So I spoke to you, but you would not listen; you rebelled against the commandment of the LORD, and were presumptuous, and went up] into the hill country. 44 Then [the Amorites that lived in that hill country came out against you, and chased you like bees, and beat you down] in Seir, even to the[7] Hormah. 45 And [you returned and wept before the LORD; but the LORD did not listen to you]r [voice], nor gave ear to you. 46 So you stayed in Kadesh for [many] days, [according to the days that you spent there].

2 [1 Then we turned, and journeyed to the wilderness on the way to the] Red [Sea], as the LORD spoke to me; and we circled Mount Seir for [many] day[s].

◾ *According to 4QDeut[h], in chapter 2:3 God speaks to Moses and says, "You [singular] have circled this mountain long enough . . . ," which focuses firmly on Moses as the recipient of God's command. In contrast, the Masoretic Text, the Samaritan Pentateuch, and the Septuagint read, "You [plural] . . . ," which emphasizes that the words that follow are being given by God to the Israelites as a people and that Moses is receiving the words as their representative as well as their leader. However, in view of the frequent use of the second-person plural elsewhere in this chapter, this particular reading in 4QDeut[h] seems less appropriate than that found in the other witnesses.*

[2 Then the LOR]D [spoke] to me as follows: 3 "You[8] have circled this mountain long enough; now turn north. 4 And [command the people, saying, 'You are to pass through the border of your brothers the children of Esau who dwell] in Seir. They *will be afraid* o[f yo]u, but be very careful. 5 Do not provoke [them; for I will not give you any of their land—no, not so much as for the sole of a foot to tread on, because I have given Mount Seir to Esau as a possession]. 6 You shall p[urchase] food [from them with money, so that you may eat; and you shall also buy water from them with money, so that you may drink. 7 For the LORD your God has blessed you in all the work of your hands; he has known your wander-

---

6. Singular 4QDeut[h] LXX. Plural MT SP.

7. 4QDeut[h]. Not in MT SP LXX.

Chapter 2. 4QDeut[h]: 2:1–6, 28–30; 4QDeut[o]: 2:8; 4QDeut[d]: 2:24–36.

8. Singular 4QDeut[h]. Plural MT SP LXX.

ings through this vast wilderness. These forty years the LORD your God has been with you, and you have lacked nothing].'"

[8 So we passed by our brothers the descendants of Esau who dwell in Seir, away from the Arabah, away from Elath and from Ezion-geber. And we turned and] passed by the way of the wilderness [of Moab]. ▲

[24 "Arise, be on your way, and cross the valley of the Arnon. See, I have given into your hand Sihon the Amorite, king of Heshbon, and his land; start taking possession, and] contend with him in bat[tle. 25 Today I will begin to put the dread and fear of you upon the nations that are under the whole] heaven; they will hear t[he news of you, and will tremble and be in anguish because of you]."

[26 And I sent messengers from] the wilderness of Kedemoth to Sihon king of Heshbon [with words of peace, saying, 27 "Let me pass through your land]; I will go [only a]long by the highway; I will turn neither to the right hand nor to the left. 28 You shall sell me f[ood for mone]y, that I may eat, and [give me] water for money, [that] I may drink. Only let me pass through on foot, 29 just as [the descendents of Esau who dwell] in S[e]ir, and the Moabites who dwell in Ar, did for me—[until I cross over] the Jordan into the land whi[ch the LORD our God is giving to us." 30 But] Siho[n ki]n[g of Heshbon] would [not] let us pass by him; for [the Lo]RD [your God hardened his spirit, and made his heart obstinate], so that he might deliver him [into] your hand, as he is [to]day.

[31 Then the LORD] said [to me, "Behold, I have begun to deliver up Sihon and] his land [to you]; start taking possession, so that you may i[nherit] his [la]nd."

[32 Then Sihon came out against us, he and all his people, to do battle at Jahaz. 33 And] the LORD our God [delive]red him [up before] us; [and we defeated him, and his sons, and all his people. 34 And we took all h]is [cities] at th[at]⁹ time, [and utterly destroyed eve]ry [inhabited city, together with the women and the little ones—we left no survivors. 35 Only] the cattle [we took as plunder for ourselves, together with the spoil of the ci]ties [which we had taken. 36 From Aroer—which is on the edge of the valley of the Arnon—and from the ci]ty that is in the valley, even as far as Gilead, there was [no]t [a city too high for us; the LORD our God delivered up them all before us]. ▲

3 [14 Jair the son of Manasseh took all the region of Argob, to the border of the Geshurites and the Maacathites, and called them—that is, Bashan—after his own name, Hav]voth [Jair, as it is t]o th[is] d[ay. 15 And I gave Gilead to Machir. 16 And to the Reubenites and to the Gadit]es I [gave the territory] from Gilead to¹⁰ the val[ley of the Arnon—the middle of the valley and its border—as far as the rive]r [Jabbok], which is the boundary of Ammonites; 17 the Arabah also,

---

9. Feminine 4QDeutʰ MT *qere* SP. Masculine MT *ketib.*

Chapter 3. 4QDeutᵈ: 3:14–29; 4QDeutᵐ: 3:18–22; 4QDeutᵉ: 3:24; 4QDeutᶜ: 3:25–26.

10. 4QDeutᵈ MTᵐˢˢ SPᵐˢˢ LXX. *even to* MT SP.

and the [Jordan and its banks, from] Chinnereth as far as [the sea of the Arabah], the Salt [Sea], under the slopes of Pisgah [on the e]ast.

> ■ *In Deuteronomy 3:20 "until the* LORD *your God gives rest" is found in 4QDeut*ᵐ *and the Septuagint, while 4QDeut*ᵈ*, the Masoretic Text, and the Samaritan Penta-teuch have "until the* LORD *gives rest." The longer reading, which is repeated later in the verse, serves to remind us who the Lord is. This is one more instance of agreement between a particular scroll and the Septuagint for a particular reading. The same longer text is found only in 4QDeut*ᵐ *at Deuteronomy 5:5 and in 4QDeut*ᶜ *at Deutero-nomy 7:4.*

18 And I commanded you [at that tim]e, "The LORD your God has given you this land to occupy; [you shall cross over] armed [before] your [country]men the Israelites, all the men of valor. 19 But your wives, *your*[11] little ones, and your cattle (I know [that] you have much [ca]ttle) shall remain in your cities which I have given you 20 until the LORD *your God*[12] gives rest to your countrymen, as he has to you, and they also occupy the land which the LORD your God is giving them across the Jo[rdan]. Then each of you shall return to his possession which I have given you."

21 And I commanded Joshua at *that*[13] time, "Your eyes have seen all that the L[ORD] your [G]od has done to these two kings; so will the LORD do to all the kingdoms *which*[14] you [are about to cross]. 22 *And*[15] *you*[16] shall not fear them; for the LORD your God himself fights for you."

23 And I pleaded wi[th the LORD at th]at [time], 24 "O LORD God, you have begun to show [your servant your greatness and] your mighty hand—for what god is there in heaven or on e[ar]th [who can perform such works and mighty acts like yours? 25 Please let me] go over, and see the good land that is acro[ss the Jordan]—that [fine hill country]—and Lebanon."

26 But the LORD was angry with me for your sakes, and did not listen [to me; and] the Lor[D said to me, "Eno]ugh! Speak no longer to me of [this] mat[ter. 27 Go] up *on*[17] the top of Pisgah, [and lif]t up your eyes westward, and north-ward, and southward, and eastward, an[d look with] your [ey]es; for you shall not cross over this Jordan. 28 But com[mission] Joshua, and encourage him, [and

---

11. 4QDeutᵈ MTᵐˢ. *and your* 4QDeutᵐ MT LXX. *your little ones and your wives* SP.

12. 4QDeutᵐ LXX. Not in 4QDeutᵈ MT SP.

13. Feminine 4QDeutᵐ MT *qere* SP. Masculine MT *ketib.*

14. 4QDeutᵐ. *into which* MT SP.

15. 4QDeutᵐ. Not in 4QDeutᵈ MT SP LXX.

16. Singular 4QDeutᵈ MTᵐˢˢ SP. Plural 4QDeutᵐ MT SPᵐˢˢ LXX.

17. 4QDeutᵈ LXX. Not in MT. *to* SP.

strengthen him; for] he will cross over at the head of this people, and he will *cause* them to inherit [the lan]d [that you will see." 29 So we remained] in the valley opposite Beth-peor.

4 [1 And now, O Israel, listen] to th[e statutes and] to the ordinances [which I am teaching you to do, so that you may live, and go in and take possession of the land which the LORD, the God of your fathers, is giving to you]. ▲

> ■ *In 4:14 the traditional reading as found in the Masoretic Text, the Samaritan Penta-teuch, and the Septuagint speaks of the land that the Israelites are "crossing over to possess." But 4QDeut^c has a longer reading: "crossing over the Jordan to possess." (The same longer reading is found at 11:8 in 4QDeut^{k1} and the Septuagint.) This small piece of additional information serves to make the text clearer by supplying the object of the verb; it is interesting to note that the New International Version trans-lates "crossing the Jordan to possess," which must have been a paraphrase for clearer sense, since the NIV translators completed their work in the early 1980s, when they could not have had access to 4QDeut^c.*

[13 And he declared to you his covenant which he commanded you to d]o, even the te[n commandments; and he wrote them on two tablet]s of stone. [14 Then the LORD] comma[nded] me [at that time to teach you] statutes and or-dinances, that you might observe t[hem in the land] wh[ere you are crossing over the] Jordan[18] [to possess].

[15 For your own sake, be very careful, for] you saw [no] for[m] at all [on the day that the LORD spoke to you in Horeb from the midst of the fire— 16 lest you corru]pt [yourselv]es, and make [for yourselves a graven image in the form of any figure, the likeness of male or female, 17 the likeness of any] animal that [is on the earth, the likeness of any winged bird that flies in the sky, 18 the likeness of any-thing that creeps on the ground, the likeness of any fish that is in the waters under the earth]. ▲

[24 For the LORD your God] is [a devouring fire], a jeal[ous] God. [25 When you have had children and children's children, and yo]u [have been long] in the land, and corrupt yourselves, and [ma]ke a graven image [in the form of any-thing, and do what is evil in the sight of the L]ORD your God, so as to provoke him to anger, 26 I call [heaven and earth] to witness against you [this day, that you shall] soon [utterly perish] from the land that you are crossing o[ver the Jordan to possess. You shall not prolong your days o]n [it, but shall] be ut[terly] destroyed. ▲

[30 When you are in distress and all these things have come upon you, in later days you shall return to the LORD] your [Go]d [and listen to his voice, 31 for the

---

Chapter 4. 4QDeut^d: 4:1; 4QDeut^c: 4:13–17, 31–32; 4QDeut^f: 4:24–26; 4QDeut^o: 4:30–34; 4QDeut^h: 4:31–34; 4QDeut^m: 4:32–33; 1QDeut^a: 4:47–49.

18. 4QDeut^c. Not in MT SP LXX.

LORD your God is a merciful God; he will not fail you], nor [destroy you, nor forg]et t[he covenant of your ancestors] which he swore [to them].

[32 For ask now of the days that] are past, which were before you, since [the day] that [God] created [humans on the earth], and from the one end of heaven to [the othe]r: Has there been anything as [great as this] thing, or has anything been heard like it? 33 Did [ever a people] hear [the voice of God speaking from the midst of the fire as] y[ou][19] have heard, and live? 34 Or [has any god tried to go and ta]k[e for himself a nation from the midst of another nation by trials], by signs and wonder[s, by war, by a mig]hty [hand] and an [outstretched] arm, [or by great terro]r[s, as the LORD your God did for you in Egypt before your eyes]? ▲

[47 And they took possession of his land and the land of Og king of Bashan, the two kings of the Amorites], who were acro[ss the Jordan to the east; 48 from Aroer, which is on the edge of the valley of the Arnon, as far as Mount Sion (that is, Hermon), 49 and all the Arabah across the Jordan to the east, as far as the sea of] the Arabah, under [the slopes of Pisgah].

5 1 Then Moses summoned all Israel, and said to them, *"Hear,* O Israel, the statutes and the ordinances which I am speaking in year hearing *this day,*[20] so that you may learn them, and be sure to carry them out. 2 The LORD our God made a covenant with us in Horeb. 3 The LORD did not make this covenant with our ancestors, but with us, yes with us who are here today, all of us alive *today.*[21] 4 The LORD spoke with you face to face on the mountain from the midst of the fire. 5 *But*[22] as for me, I was standing between the LORD and you at that time to declare to you the *words*[23] of the LORD *your God;*[24] for you were afraid because of the fire and did not go up to the mountain. And he said:

6 "I am the LORD your God who brought you from the land of Egypt, from the house of bondage.

7 "You shall have no other gods before me.

8 "You shall not make for yourself a graven image, *or*[25] any likeness of anything that is in heaven above, or that is in the earth beneath, or that is in the water under the earth. 9 You shall not bow down to them, nor serve them—for I, the

---

19. Plural 4QDeut[m]. Singular 4QDeut[c] MT SP LXX.

Chapter 5. 4QDeut[n]: 5:1–33; 4QDeut[j]: 5:1–11, 13–15, 21–33; 4QDeut[o]: 5:1–5, 8–9; 4QDeut[k1]: 5:28–32.

20. 4QDeut[j] LXX. today 4QDeut[n] 4QDeut[o] MT SP.

21. 4QDeut[n] LXX. Not in MT SP.

22. 4QDeut[n] SP LXX. Not in MT.

23. 4QDeut[n] SP LXX. *word* MT.

24. 4QDeut[n]. Not in 4QDeut[j] MT SP LXX.

25. 4QDeut[n] SP LXX. Not in MT.

LORD your God, am a jealous God, visiting the iniquity of the parents on the children, to[26] the third and fourth generation of those who reject me, 10 showing[27] steadfast love to thousands of those who love me and keep my[28] commandments.

11 "You shall not take the name of the LORD your God in vain, for the LORD will not hold guiltless the one who takes his name in vain.

> *Our manuscripts present a shorter and a longer version of Deuteronomy 5:15. In the shorter, traditional version, which appears in the Masoretic Text, the Samaritan Pentateuch, and the Septuagint, the Lord has commanded the Israelites ("you") to perform the sabbath day (though the Septuagint reads keep). But the longer version, which is found only in 4QDeut[n], enjoins the Israelites to keep and to hallow the sabbath day and then provides two reasons for this observance as found in the Exodus version (Exod 20:11) of the fourth commandment: the Lord rested and blessed the sabbath day (see the text of verse 15, below). Another very early manuscript known as the Nash Papyrus has both reasons, but in the reverse order.*

12 Observe the sabbath day, to keep it holy, as the LORD your God commanded you. 13 Six days you shall labor, and do all your work, 14 but the seventh day is a sabbath to the LORD your God. On it[29] you shall not do any work, *you, your son, your daughter, your male servant, nor your female servant, your ox, nor your ass, nor your cattle, your stranger[30]* who is within your gates, so that your male servant and your female servant may rest as well as you. 15 You shall remember that you were a servant in the land of Egypt, and the LORD your God brought you out from there with a mighty hand and an outstretched arm. Therefore the LORD your God commanded you to keep[31] the sabbath day *to hallow it. For in six days the LORD made heaven and earth, the sea, and all that is in them and rested the seventh day; so the LORD blessed the sabbath day and hallowed it.*[32]

16 Honor your father and your mother, just as the LORD your God commanded you, so that your days may be long and that it may go well with you in the land which the LORD your God is giving to you.

17 You shall not commit murder.

18 *You* shall not commit adultery.

---

26. 4QDeut[n] SP LXX. *and to* MT.

27. 4QDeut[n]. *and showing* MT SP LXX.

28. 4QDeut[n] MT *qere* SP LXX. *his* MT *ketib.*

29. 4QDeut[n] SP LXX. Not in MT.

30. 4QDeut[n] LXX. *you, nor your son, nor your daughter, nor your male servant, nor your female servant, nor your ox nor your ass, nor any of your cattle, nor your stranger* 4QDeut[j] MT. *you, nor your son, nor your daughter, your male servant, nor your female servant, your ox nor your ass, nor any of your cattle, nor your stranger* SP.

31. 4QDeut[n] LXX. *to perform* MT SP.

32. 4QDeut[n]. Not in MT SP. *and to hallow it* LXX.

19 *You*[33] shall not steal.

20 *You*[34] shall not bear false witness against your neighbor.

21 *You*[35] shall not covet your neighbor's wife; *you*[36] shall not *covet*[37] your neighbor's house, his field, *his male servant, his female servant, his ox, his ass,*[38] or anything that belongs to your neighbor.

22 These are the words which the LORD spoke to all your assembly on the mountain from the midst of the fire, *darkness, cloud, and thick darkness,*[39] with a g[rea]t voice; and he added no more. Then he wrote them on two tablets of stone and gave them to me.

23 Then, [when] you [he]ard the voice from the midst of the darkness, while the mountain was burning with fire, you came near to me, all the heads of your tribes and your elders. 24 And you s[ai]d, "See, the LORD our God has shown us his glory and his greatness, and we have hea[r]d his voice from the midst of the fire; we have seen *in*[40] this day that *the LORD*[41] speaks with [huma]ns, and they live. 25 So now, why should we die? For this great fire will consume us; if *we [con]tinue*[42] to hear the voice of the LORD our God, then we shall die. 26 For who is there of all living beings who has heard the voice of the *living*[43] God speaking from the midst of the fire—as we have—and has lived? 27 Go near, and hear all that the LORD our God *speaks*[44] to *you,*[45] and tell us all that the LORD our God speaks to you; and [we] will hear it, and carry it out."

28 And the LORD heard your words, when you spoke t[o me.] Then the L[ORD] said [to me], "I have [he]ard [the words of this people, which] they have spoken to you; they have done well in all [that they have spoken. 29 If only there were] s[uch a heart] in them, that they would fear m[e and] keep [*my*]

---

33. 4QDeut[n] SP LXX. *And you* MT.

34. 4QDeut[n] SP LXX. *And you* MT.

35. 4QDeut[n] SP LXX. *And you* MT.

36. 4QDeut[n] SP LXX. *And you* MT.

37. 4QDeut[n] SP LXX. *desire* MT.

38. 4QDeut[n]. *or his male servant, or his female servant, his ox, or his ass* MT SP (*his male servant,* etc.) LXX (. . . *or his ox,* etc.).

39. 4QDeut[n] 4QDeut[j](?) SP. *the cloud and the thick darkness* MT. *darkness, thick darkness, whirlwind* LXX.

40. 4QDeut[n] LXX. Not in MT SP.

41. 4QDeut[n]. *God* MT SP LXX.

42. *Hiphil* 4QDeut[j]. *Qal* 4QDeut[n] MT SP.

43. Singular 4QDeut[n]. Plural MT SP.

44. 4QDeut[n]. *says* MT SP.

45. 4QDeut[j] LXX. Not in 4QDeut[n] MT SP.

commandments[46] [alwa]ys, so that it might go well with them and with their children forever!

[30 "Go, say to them], 'Return to your tents.' 31 But as for you, stay here with me, and I will speak [to you] all [the com]mandment, *the*[47] [st]atutes and the ordinances, which you shall teach them, [so that they may carry them out] in the land [whi]ch I [g]ive them to possess."

32 You shall take care, [therefore, to do a]s the LORD [your G]od [has] c[ommanded] you; you shall not turn aside [to the] r[igh]t hand [or to the left]. 33 You shall walk [in a]ll the wa[y] that [the LORD] your God [has commanded you so that you may live, and so that it may] go well with [you], and so that [you] may pr[olong your days] in the land which [you shall po]ss[ess].

6 1 Now this [is the commandment, the statutes, and the ordinances] w[hich the LORD] your [God comm]anded [me] to [teach you, so that you might do them in the land which you are crossing over] to pos[sess; 2 so that you might fear the LORD your God, to keep] all [his] st[atutes and his commandments, which I command you—you, and your son], and your son's son, [all the days of your life; and so that your days may be prolonged. 3 Hear therefore, O I]srael, [and take care to carry it out, so that it may go well with you, and so that you may increase mightily—just as the LORD, the God of your ancestors, has promised you, in a land flowing with milk and honey].

[4 Hear, O Israel, the LORD] our [God], the LORD is o[ne; 5 and you shall love the L]ORD [your God with all your heart, and with all your soul, and with all your might]. 6 And [these] word[s, wh]ich [I command you this day], shall be [on your heart. 7 You shall teach them diligently to your children, and shall speak of them when you sit in your house, and when you walk along the road, and when] you [lie] down, [and when you rise up. 8 And you shall bind them as a sign on your hand], and they shall be for frontlets [between your eyes. 9 And you shall write them on the doorposts of] your house [and on your gates].

[10 Then when the LORD] your [G]od [brings you] into [the land which he swore to your ancestors, to Abraham, to Isaac], and to Jacob, [to give you—a land with gr]e[at and fine cities which you did not build, 11 houses full of all good things which] you did not fi[ll, hewn cisterns which you did not dig, vineyards and olive trees which you did not plant—then when you eat and are satisfied, 12 be careful not to forget the LORD, who brought you out of the land of Egypt, out of the house of slavery.] ▲

---

46. 4QDeut[k1] MT[ms] SP LXX. *all my commandments* MT. MT also has the definite article.

47. 4QDeut[j] MT[mss] SP. *and the* MT LXX.

Chapter 6. 4QDeut[j]: 6:1–3; 4QDeut[n]: 6:1; 4QDeut[p]: 6:4–11.

7 [1 When the LORD your God brings you into the land that you are about to enter and possess, and drives away many nations before you—the Hittites, the Girgashites, the Amorites, the Canaanites, the Perizzites, the Hivites, and the Jebusites, seven nations mightier and stronger than you— 2 and when the LORD your God delivers them up before you, and you defeat them, then] you must [total]ly destroy t[hem. You shall make no treaty with them, nor show mercy to them. 3 You shall not intermarry with them]; you shall not give your daughters to [their] sons, [nor shall you take their daughters for] your sons. 4 Fo[r they will turn your sons away from following] me so that *he*[48] may serve [other] god[s; thus the anger of the LORD *your*] God[49] [will be kindled against you, and he will destroy you quickly]. 5 But th[is is how you must deal with them: you shall break down their altars, dash their pillars into pieces, cut down their Asherim, and burn their graven images with fire. 6 For you are a holy people to the LORD] your God; the LORD [your] God [has chosen you to be a people for his own possession, above all] the people[s that are on the face of] the earth. [7 The LORD did not set his love on you or choose] you [because you were more in number than any people—for you were the fewest of all peoples]. ▲

■ *For Deuteronomy 7:15, one of the scrolls has been corrected in an interesting way. The original reading in 5QDeut is very much like that found in the Masoretic Text and the Samaritan Pentateuch: ". . . none of the evil diseases of Egypt, which you know." However, 5QDeut has then been corrected with two additional Hebrew words, written above the line containing "which you know," to produce "which you have seen and which you know." This longer reading, which is also found in the Septuagint, makes the evil diseases of Egypt more vivid to the listeners by recalling that they have personally witnessed them. An important question for scholars is whether the corrector here is merely fixing an error, is attempting to make his text more vivid, or is deliberately altering the original reading to make it conform more closely with another text (in this case, one mirroring the Septuagint).*

[12 And if you listen to these ordinances, and take care to carry them out, the LORD your God] will kee[p with y]ou [the covenant and steadfast love which he swor]e to your ancestors. 13 And he will love you, bless you, and multiply you; he will also ble[ss the offspring of your body and the fruit of your ground], your [grai]n and your new wine and your oil, the increase of your [ca]t[tle] and the youn[g of your flock in the] land w[hich he sw]ore to your ancestors to give you.

Chapter 7. 4QpaleoDeut[r]: 7:2–7, (19[?] or 29:2–4[?]), 16–25; 4QDeut[c]: 7:3–4; 4QDeut[e]: 7:12–16, 21–26; 5QDeut: 7:15–24; 4QDeut[m]: 7:18–22; 4QDeut[f]: 7:22–25.

48. 4QpaleoDeut[r] MT[mss] SP LXX. *they* MT.

49. 4QDeut[c]. Not in MT SP LXX.

14 You will be blessed above all people[s]; there will [no]t be male or female barren among you or among your cattle. 15 And the LORD will take away from you all [sickness]; none of the evil d[iseases of Eg]ypt, *which you have seen and*[50] which you know, will he infli[ct] on you, but will lay them on all of those that hate you. 16 And you shall destroy all [the peoples that the L]ORD your God [shall] d[eliver to you]. Your eye [shall not pity] them, and you shall not serve [their gods—for that will be a snare to you].

17 If [you] say in your h[ear]t, "These [nations are] mo[re] than I; how can I dispossess them?" 18 you shall not be afraid of them. Remember [w]ell [what] the LORD your God did to Pharaoh, and to all [Egypt— 19 the] great [trial]s *today*[51] which your eyes saw, *the*[52] s[ig]ns and wonders, [the] mighty hand and [out]stretched arm, by which the [LORD your God] brought you out. [So shall] the LORD your God [do] to all the peoples of whom you are afraid. 20 More[over,] the LORD your God will sen[d the hornet] among them, until [those] who are left [and have] hidden [themselves] perish [befo]re you. 21 You shall not be afraid of them, for the LORD [your] God [is] in your midst, a gre[at and awes]ome God. 22 And the LORD your God will cast out those nations b[efo]re you [littl]e by little; you may not be able *to*[53] put an end to them at once, lest the wild animals multiply against you. 23 But the L[o]RD your God [will] deliver them up *into your hand,*[54] and will throw them into a great panic until they are destroyed. 24 And he will deliver their kings into your hand, [and] you shall [w]ipe out their names from under heaven. No one shall be able to stand *before*[55] you, until you have destroyed them. 25 The graven images [of their gods you shall bur]n with fire; *you*[56] shall not covet the silver [or the gol]d that is on them, nor take [it for yourself, lest you be ensnared by them; for] that is [an abomina]tion to the LORD your God. 26 And [you shall] not [bring an abomination into your house, or you will be set apart for destruction like it]. You shall [utterl]y detest it, and you shall utterly abhor it, [for it is set apart for destruction].

8 [1 All the commandments which I command] you today you must diligently [observe, so that you may live, and multiply, and go in and possess] the l[a]nd

---

50. 5QDeut[corr] LXX. Not in MT SP.

51. 5QDeut. Not in MT SP LXX.

52. 4QpaleoDeut[r] 5QDeut MT[mss] SP LXX. *and the* MT LXX[mss].

53. Preposition introduces infinitive 4QDeut[m]. No preposition before infinitive 4QDeut[e] 5QDeut 4QpaleoDeut[r] MT SP.

54. 4QDeut[e] LXX. *before you* 4QpaleoDeut[r] MT SP.

55. 4QpaleoDeut[r] 4QDeut[f] MT[ms] SP. *against* MT LXX.

56. Plural 4QpaleoDeut[r]. Singular 4QDeut[e] MT SP LXX.

Chapter 8. 4QDeut[c]: 8:1–7, 10–11, 15–16; 4QDeut[c]: 8:1–5; 4QDeut[f]: 8:2–14; 5QDeut: 8:5–20; 4QDeut[j]: 8:5–10; 4QDeut[n]: 8:5–10; 1QDeut[b]: 8:8–9; 1QDeut[a]: 8:18–19.

which the L[ORD] swore [to your ancestors. 2 And you shall remember the entire way which] the LORD your God has led you these forty years [in the wilderness, in order to humble you], to[57] prove you, and[58] to know what was in your heart, whether or not you would keep his commandments. 3 And he [humbled you], and let you be hungry, and fed you with manna—which you had not known, neither had your ancestors known—so that he might make you realize that people do not live by bread alone, but people live by everything that pr[oceeds from the mouth of the] LORD. 4 Your *clothing*[59] did not grow old on you, nor [did your] feet [swell], these forty years. 5 So you shall know in your heart that as a man disciplines his son, so[60] the LORD your God disciplines you.

◼ *Most other versions of chapter 8:6 agree with the Masoretic Text by stating that we should keep God's commandments by* fearing *him. But one scroll, 4QDeut[n], speaks of keeping God's commandments by* loving *him. This raises an interesting question: Just how far apart are fearing and loving God?*

6 And you shall keep the commandments of the LORD your God, by walking in *all*[61] his ways and by *loving*[62] him. 7 For the LORD your God is bringing you into a good *and spacious*[63] land—a land of brooks of water, of fountains and springs, flowing out in valleys and hills; 8 a land of wheat and barley, vines, *fig*[64] trees and pomegranates; a land of olive oil and honey; 9 a land where you shall eat bread without scarcity, *and*[65] in which you shall not lack anything; a land whose stones are iron, and from whose hills you may dig copper.

10 And when you have eaten and are satisfied, you shall bless the LORD your God for the good land which he has given you. [11 Be careful lest you] forget the LORD your God by not keeping his commandments, [his ordinances, and his statutes, which I] co[mmand you this day]. 12 Otherwise, when you have eaten and are full, and have built [fine] house[s], and have lived *in them,*[66] 13 *when*[67] your herds and your flocks multiply, and your silver and your gold is multiplied, [and

---

57. No preposition before infinitive 4QDeut[c]. Preposition introduces infinitive MT SP.

58. 4QDeut[c] LXX. Not in MT SP.

59. 4QDeut[c]. Alternate form of word 4QDeut[e] MT SP.

60. 4QDeut[j] LXX. Not in 4QDeut[n] MT SP.

61. 4QDeut[j]. Not in 4QDeut[n] MT SP LXX.

62. 4QDeut[n]. *to fear* 4QDeut[f] MT SP LXX.

63. 4QDeut[f] 4QDeut[j] 4QDeut[n] SP LXX. Not in MT.

64. 4QDeut[n] SP LXX. *and fig* 4QDeut[f] 4QDeut[j] MT.

65. 4QDeut[f] 4QDeut[n] LXX. Not in 4QDeut[j] MT SP.

66. 5QDeut[corr] LXX. Not in 5QDeut MT SP.

67. 5QDeut SP[mss]. *and when* MT SP LXX.

all that you have is multiplied, 14 then your heart will become proud, and you will forget the LORD] your [God] who brought you from the land [of Egypt], from the house of bondage. 15 H[e led you through the great and terrible wilderness, in which there were fiery snakes and scorpions, and thirsty ground] wh[ere there was n]o water; he brought [water] for you [from the rock of] flint; [16 he fed you in the wilderness with] manna [which your ancestors did not know, so that he might humble you, and so that he might prove you], to do you good in the end. [17 And] you may say in your heart, ["My power and the might of my hand have obtained for me this wealth." 18 But you shall remember the LORD your God], for it is he who gives y[ou power to obtain] wealth, [so that] he may establish [his covenant which he swore to your ancestors, *to Abraham, to Isaac, and to Jacob,*[68] as it is] this [day].

> ■ *As was mentioned in the introduction to Deuteronomy, this book lays great emphasis on God's "covenant." In 8:18 the traditional Masoretic Text refers only to the fathers (or ancestors) with whom God established the covenant. However, 5QDeut is much more vivid, spelling out just who these ancestors were: Abraham, Isaac, and Jacob. Here the Qumran scroll agrees with the Samaritan Pentateuch and the Septuagint.*

19 And [if you forge]t [the L]ORD [your God, and walk] after [other gods, and serve them, and worship them], I call [*the heavens*] *and* [*the earth*][69] as witnesses [against you] to[day], that you will [sur]ely per[ish. 20 Like the nations which the LORD is destroying before you, so you will perish—because you would not listen to the voice of the LORD] your [God].

9[1 Hear, O Israel, you are to pass over the Jordan this day, to go in to dispossess nations greater and mightier than your]self, cities great [and] fortified [up to heaven. 2 The people are great and tall, the sons of the Anakim, whom you know, and of whom you have heard it said, "Who can stand before the so]ns of Anak?" [3 But be assured today that the LORD your God is the one who crosses over before you like a devouring fire. He will defeat them and subdue them before you, so that you may drive them out and destroy them quickly, just as the LORD has promised you].

[4 Do not say in your heart when the LORD your God has driven them out before you, "Because of my righteousness the LORD has brought me in to possess this land"—no, it is because of the wickedness of th]ese [nations that the LORD is driving them out before you. 5 It is not because of your righteousness, or because of the upr]ightness of your heart, [that you are entering to possess their land—but

---

68. 5QDeut SP LXX. Not in MT.

69. 5QDeut^corr LXX. Not in 5QDeut MT SP.

Chapter 9. 5QDeut: 9:1–2; XHev/SeDeut: 9:4–6, 21–23; 4QDeut^f: 9:6–7; 1QDeut^b: 9:10; 4QDeut^c: 9:11–12, 17–19, 29; 1QDeut^a: 9:27–28.

because of the wickedness of these] nations [the LORD your God is driving them out before] you, and so that [he may establish the word which the LORD swore to] your ancestors, [to Abraham, to Isaac, and to Jacob. 6 Know, therefore, that the LORD your God is not giving you] this [goo]d [land to possess] because of your righteousness; [for you are a stubborn people].

[7 Remem]ber, [do not forget how you provoked the L]ORD [your] G[od to wrath in the wilderness; from the day that you went from the land of Egypt until you came t]o⁷⁰ [this place, you have been rebellious against the LORD].▲

[10 And the LORD gave to me the two tablets of stone written] with the finger of God; [and on them was written in accordance with all the words which the LORD spoke with you on the mountain from the midst of the fire on the day of the assembly].

[11 Then at the end of forty days and forty nights the LORD gave] to me [the two tablets of stone, the tablets of the covenant. 12 Then the LOR]D [said] to me, "[Arise, go down quickly from here, for your people] whom [you have brought from Egyp]t [have corrupted themselves]. They have [quickly] turned aside [from the way which I commanded them—they have made themselves a molten image." 13 In addition, the LORD spoke to me as fol]lows: "I have seen [this people, and yes—they are a stubborn people. 14 Let me alone, so that I may destroy them] and blot out [their name from under heaven; then I will make of you a nation mightier and greater than they]."▲

[17 Then I took hold of the two tablets, and thre]w them from [my] t[wo hands and smashed them before your eyes. 18 And I fell down before the LOR]D, as at the first, [for forty days and forty nights. I neither ate bread] no[r] drank [water because of all your sin which you had committed by doi]ng what was evil in the sight of [the LORD, so provoking him to anger. 19 For I was afraid of the anger and hot displeasure with] which the LOR[D] was angry enough [with you so as to destroy you. But the LORD listened to me that time also. 20 The LORD was so angry with Aaron that he was ready to destroy him, but at the same time I also interceded on behalf of Aaron. 21 Then I took your sin—the calf which you had made—and burned it with fire and crushed it, grinding it very small until it was as fine as dust]; and I [threw its dust into the brook that descended from the mountain].

[22 And at Taberah], at Mass[ah, and at Kibroth-hattaavah, you provoked] the LORD [to wrath. 23 And when the LORD sent you out from Kadesh-barnea, saying], "Go u[p and occupy the land which I have given you," then you rebelled against t]he [commandment of the LORD your God, and you did not believe him or listen to his voice].▲

[27 "Remember your servants, Abraham, Isaac, and Ja]cob; [do not look at the

---

70. 4QDeutᶜ. *up to* MT SP LXX.

stubbornness of this people, or at their wickedness, or at their sin. 28 Otherwise the land from whic]h *he*[71] brought u[s] out [will say, 'Because the LORD was not able to bring them into the land which he promised them and because he hated them, he has brought them out to slay them in the wilderness.' 29 Yet they are your people and your inheritance which you brought out by your great power and by your outstret]ched [arm].''

10

■ *According to MurDeut, the only Deuteronomy scroll from Murabba'at (see the general Introduction)—as well as the Masoretic Text, the Samaritan Pentateuch, and the Septuagint—Moses is reminded in Deuteronomy 10:2 of "words that were on the first tablets which he broke." But 4QDeut[c] emphasizes his transgression more strongly by stressing that these were the very words "of the LORD" himself.*

[1 At that time the LORD said to me, "Hew for yourself two tablets of sto]ne, *the*[72] firs[t ones, and come up to me on the mountain, and make] yourself an ark of wood. 2 And I will write on the tablets the words *of the LORD*[73] [th]at [were on the first tablets which you broke, and you shall put them in the a]rk.''

3 So I made an ark [of acacia wood, and hewed two tablets of stone like the first ones, and went up on the mountain with the two tablets in my hand. 4 Then he wrote on the tablets the same words as before—the ten commandments that the LORD had spoken to you on the mountain out of the fire on the day of the assembly—and the LORD gave them to me. 5 And I turned and came down from the mountain and put the tablets into the ar]k [which] I had [m]ade; [and there they are, just as the LORD commanded me].

[6 Then] the children of Israel jour[neyed from Beeroth Bene-jaakan to Moserah. There Aaron died, and] there he was buried; and [Eleazar his son] m[inistered in the priest's office in his place. 7 From there they journeyed to Gudgodah, and] from Gudgodah [to Jotbathah, a land of brooks of water]. 8 At [that time the LORD set apart the tri]be [of Levi to bear the ark of the covenant of the LORD], *and*[74] to st[and before the LORD to minister to him and to pronounce blessings in his name, to this day. 9 Therefore Levi has no portion n]or inheritance [with his countrymen; the LORD is his inheritance, in accordance with what the LORD your God spoke to him].

---

71. 1QDeut[a]. *you* MT SP LXX.

Chapter 10. 4QDeut[c]: 10:1–2, 5–8; MurDeut: 10:1–3; 4QpaleoDeut[r]: 10:6(?) (or 28:23[?] or 32:22[?]), 11–12; 2QDeut[c]: 10:8–12; 4QDeut[l]: 10:12, 14–15.

72. 4QDeut[c]. *like the* MT SP LXX.

73. 4QDeut[c]. Not in MurDeut MT SP LXX.

74. 2QDeut[c] MT[mss]. Not in MT SP LXX.

[10 And I stayed] on the mountain, [like the first time, for forty days and forty nights; and the LORD listened to me] *that*[75] [time also], an[*d*[76] the LORD would not destroy you]. 11 Then the L[ORD] said [to me, "Arise, take your journey before the people, and they will go in and possess the land which I] s[wor]e to their ancestors [to give to them]."

12 And now, I[srael, what does the Lo]RD [your God require of you, but to fear the LORD] your [God], to walk in all [his ways, and to love him, and to serve the LORD your God] with all your h[ea]rt and with all [your soul, 13 and to observe the commandments of the LORD your God and his decrees that I am commanding you today, for your own good]?

[14 See, to the LORD your God belong heaven and the heaven of heavens], the earth, and all [that is in them. 15 Only the LORD had a delight in your ancestors to love] them, [and he chose their descendants after them, even you above all peoples, just as it is this day]. ▲

11 [1 You shall love the LORD your God, therefore, and keep his requirements, his decrees, his ordinances, and his commandments always. 2 And know] today that I am not speaking with your children w[ho have not known and who have not seen the chastisement of] the LORD your God, his greatness, [his mighty hand and his outstretched arm, 3 and] his signs and his works, which [he did in the midst of Egypt to Pharaoh the k]ing of Egyp[t and to all his land; 4 and what he did to the army of Egypt, to their horses and to the]ir [chariots]; how he ma[de the water of the] Red Se[a] over[flow them as th]ey pur[sued after you], and how [the LORD] has des[troyed them to thi]s da[y; 5 and what he did to you in the wilderness, until you arrived at this place; 6 and what he did to Dathan and Abiram, the sons of Eliab son of Reuben; how the earth opened its mouth and swallowed them up, and their households, and] their tents, and [eve]ry [living thing that] followed them, *from*[77] the midst of all [Israel. 7 But your eyes have seen all] the *great*[78] works of the LORD that [he did].

[8 Therefore you shall keep] every commandment *and the statute[s]*[79] *and the ordinances*[80] [which I command you this day], so that you may be strong *and*

---

75. Feminine 2QDeut[c] MT *qere*. Masculine MT *ketib* SP.

76. 2QDeut[c] MT[mss] SP LXX. Not in MT.

Chapter 11. MurDeut: 11:2–3; 4QDeut[c]: 11:3, 9–13, 18; 4QLXXDeut: 11:4; 4QDeut[k1]: 11:6–13; 4QDeut[j]: 11:6–10, 12–13, 21(?); 1QDeut[a]: 11:27–30; 4QpaleoDeut[r]: 11:28, 30–32; 1QDeut[b]: 11:30–31.

77. 4QDeut[j]. *in* 4QDeut[k1] MT SP.

78. Plural 4QDeut[j] 4QDeut[k1] LXX. Singular MT SP.

79. 4QDeut[k1]. Not in MT SP LXX.

80. 4QDeut[j] 4QDeut[k1]. Not in MT SP LXX.

multiply,[81] and go in and possess the land [which you] are crossing over *the Jordan*[82] to possess, 9 and so that you may prolong [your] da[ys in the land] which the LORD swore to your ancestors to give to them and to their descendants, a l[and] flowing with milk and honey. 10 For the land which *you*[83] are *about*[84] [to possess], *it*[85] is not as the land of Egypt from where [you came], where you s[owed your seed] and watered it with your *feet,*[86] like a garden of herbs; 11 but the land which you [are crossing] to possess is a land of hills and valleys [that drinks water] from the rain of heaven, 12 [a land] which the LORD your God cares for. The eyes of the LORD your God are always [upon it, from the beginning of] *a year*[87] even to the end of the year.

13 So if you shall list[en] diligently t[o my commandments which I command you] today, [to love the LORD your God, and to serve him with all your heart and with all your soul, . . .]▲

[18 Therefore you shall fix] these [m]y [words] up[on your heart and in your soul, and you shall bind them as a sign on your hand, and they shall b]e as frontlets between yo[ur] eyes.▲ [. . . 21 so that your days may be multiplied, and the days of your children, in the land which] the LORD [swore to your ancestors to give them, like the days of the heavens above the earth]. *And [the LORD] s[aid to Moses and Aaron, This is the ordinance of the Passover]; n[o] fore[igner shall eat of it; but every man's servant who is bought for money, when you have circumcised him], then he shall e[at of it].*[88]▲

▮ *From Deuteronomy 11:21 onward, 4QDeut*[j] *seems to contain an unusual text, although the scroll is quite fragmentary at this point. The remaining words and reconstruction show that verse 21 was followed by Exodus 12:43–46 at the bottom of one column, continuing on to the top of the next column, and ending with Exodus 12:51. This longer text is not found in the Masoretic Text, the Samaritan Pentateuch, or the Septuagint.*

[26 See, I am setting before you today a blessing and a curse: 27 the blessing, if you shall listen to the commandments of the LORD your God which] I [command you this day; 28 and the curse, if you will not listen] to the commandments of the L[ORD your God, but turn aside from the w]ay which I [command you] today, by

---

81. 4QDeut[kl] LXX. Not in MT SP.

82. 4QDeut[kl] LXX. Not in MT SP.

83. Plural 4QDeut[kl] SP LXX. Singular 4QDeut[j] (corrected from plural) MT LXX[mss].

84. Plural 4QDeut[kl] SP LXX. Singular MT LXX[mss].

85. Feminine 4QDeut[kl] 4QDeut[c] SP. Masculine MT.

86. 4QDeut[kl] SP LXX 4QDeut[c]. *foot* 4QDeut[c] (corrected from plural) MT.

87. 4QDeut[kl] MT[mss]. *the year* MT SP.

88. 4QDeut[j] (probable reading; cf. Exod 12:43–44). Not in MT SP LXX.

g[oing after other gods which you have not known. 29 And when the LORD your God brings you into the land where you are going to possess it, you shall place the blessing on Mount] Gerizim and [the curse on Mount Ebal. 30 Are they] not [beyond the Jordan, som]e [distance to the west, in the land of the Canaanites who dwell in the] Arabah, opposite Gilgal [besi]de [the oaks of Moreh? 31 For you are to cross the Jordan to go i]n to possess [the lan]d which the LORD [your God is giving to you, and you shall possess it and dwe]ll in it. [32 And] you [shall] be [sure] to carry out all the s[tatutes and the ordinances which I] am setting before you today.

12 1 And[89] the[se are the statutes and the ordinances which you shall be careful] to carry out [in the] land which the L[ORD, the God of your ancestors], has given [you to possess—all the days that you live on the earth. 2 You shall surely destroy all the places where the nations that you dispossess have served their gods: on the high mountains, and on] the hills, and under every [green tree. 3 And you shall break down their altars, and dash] their pillars [to pieces, and b]u[rn their] Asheri[m with fire; you shall hew down the graven images of their gods]; you [shall oblite]rate their name from tha[t] place. [4 You shall not act like this toward the LORD your God. 5 But you are to seek the] place which the LORD [your] Go[d ch]ooses [from all your tribes to put his name there for his dwelling, and there you shall go], ▲

[11 Then to the place which the LORD you]r [God chooses to cause his name] to [dwell, you shall bring there all that I command you: your burnt offerings], and your sacrifices, [your tithes, and the heave offering of your hand, and all] your [choice vows] which you vow [to the LORD. 12 And you shall rejoice before the LORD your God: you, your sons, your daughters, your menservants, your female servants, and the Levite who is within your gates, since he has no portion or inheritance with you]. ▲

[18 Instead you shall eat them before the LORD your God in the place which the LORD your God shall choose: you, your son], your [daug]hter, [your male servant, your female servant, and the Levite who is within] your gates; [and you shall rejoice before the LORD] your [God] in all [that you put your hand to. 19 For your own sake, be very careful] not to forsake [the Levite as long as you live in *the* la]nd.[90] ▲

[22 Just as] the gazelle and [the deer are eaten, so you shall eat of them; the unclean and the clean person may eat from them alike . . . 25 You shall not eat it, so that it may go well with you and with] your [childre]n after you, [since you will

---

Chapter 12. 4QpaleoDeut[r]: 12:1–5, 11–12, 22; 4QDeut[c]: 12:18–19, 26, 31; MurDeut: 12:25–26; 1QDeut[a]: 12:32 [MT 13:1].

89. 4QpaleoDeut[r] LXX. Not in MT SP LXX[mss].

90. 4QDeut[c] LXX. *your land* MT SP LXX[mss].

be doing what is right in the eyes of the Lord]. 26 Take [only yo]ur [holy things] which you have [and] your [vows], and g[o to the place which the Lord shall choose].▲

[31 You shall not act like this toward the Lord your God. For they have performed for their gods every abominable act which the Lord] hates; [for they even burn their sons and their daughters in the fire to their gods. 32 Whatever I command you, you must be careful] to carry out; [you shall not add to it, nor take away from it].

13

▮ *In Deuteronomy 13:4 various texts differ as to what people must do (and in what order) to follow God. The probable reading in 1QDeut^a speaks of serving him, listening to his voice, clinging to him, fearing him, and keeping his commandments. But in 4QDeut^c, the Masoretic Text, and the Samaritan Pentateuch the order is different: we are told to fear God, keep his commandments, obey his voice, serve him, and cling to him. The Septuagint contains much the same text as the latter three but omits the command to serve God. These readings are significant for exegesis and interpretation, since they offer both a definition of what it means to follow God and a sequence in which the specified actions should be undertaken.*

[1 If there arises in your midst a prophet or a dreamer of dreams, and he gives you a sign or a won]der, 2 and if the si[gn or the wonder] takes place, [concerning which he spoke to you; and if he says, "Let us go after other gods—which you have not known—and let us serve them," 3 yo]u[91] [shall not li]sten t[o the words of] that prophet [or to that dreamer of dreams. For the Lord your God is testing you, to k]now whether you [love the Lord your God with all your heart and with all your soul]. 4 You shall walk [after the Lord] your God, and *you shall ser[ve him, and listen to his voice], and cling t[o him, and fear him, and kee]p [his commandments]*.[92] 5 And that prophet or dreamer of [dreams shall be put to death, because he has spoken rebellion against the Lord your God who brought you from the land of E]gypt and [redeemed you] from the hou[se of bondage, by drawing you aside from the way in which the Lord your God commanded you to walk. So you are to purge the evil from your midst].

Chapter 13. 1QDeut^a: 13:1–5, 12–13 [MT 13:2–6, 13–14]; 4QDeut^c: 13:4, 6, 10–11, 15 [MT 13:5, 7, 11–12, 16]; 11QDeut: 13:6–10 [MT 13:7–11]; 4QpaleoDeut^r: 13:18 [MT 13:19].

91. Plural 1QDeut^a LXX. Singular MT SP.

92. 1QDeut^a (probable reading). *fear him, and keep his commandments, and obey his voice, and you shall serve him, and cling to him* 4QDeut^c MT SP. LXX omits *and you shall serve him*.

[6 If your neighbor—whether *the son of*] *your father* [or[93] the son of] your [mother] *or your son,*[94] or the wi[fe you cherish, or your friend] who is closest to you—[entices you] secretly, [sayin]g, "Let us g[o and serve other gods"—ones which you have not known, neither you nor] your [an]cestors, 7 from the gods of [the peoples who are around you, near you or far off from] you, from the *ends*[95] of the earth to [the other end of the earth— 8 you shall not consent to him or listen to him]. Your [eye shall not pity] him; nor shall you spare h[im[96] or shield him, 9 but you must certainly put him to death. Your hand shall be fi]rst [upon him] to put him to death, and [afterward] the hands [of all the people. 10 You shall stone him to death with stones, because he has sought to dr]aw you aw[ay from the LORD your God who brought you out of the land of E]gypt, out of the h[ouse of bondage. 11 Then all Israel will hear and be afraid, and] will no longer [do evil such as this is in your midst].

12 If you hear it said concerning one of your cities which [the LORD your God is giving you to dwell in, 13 "Wicked men have gone out from your midst and have led the inhabitants of] their city [astray] by saying, ['Let us go and serve other gods, which you have not known,'"] 14 then you shall make inquiries, search out and investigate thoroughly. If the charge is established that such an abhorrent thing has been done among you, 15 you must certainly punish the inhabitants of that city with the edge of the sword, destroying it completely, everything in it and its livestock, [with the edge of the sword. . . . 18 when] you list[en to the voice of the LORD your God, by keeping all] his [com]mandments wh[ich I command you this day, to do what is right *and*] *good*[97] [in the eyes of the LORD your God].

14 [1 You are the children of the LORD your God. You shall not cut yourselves, nor shave your forehead for the dead. 2 For you are a holy people to the LORD your God, and the LORD has chosen you to be] a people for his own possession [above all peoples who are on the face of the earth. 3 You shall not eat any abominable thing. 4 Thes]e are the beasts [which you may eat: the ox, the sheep, and the goat]. ▲

[19 And all winged creeping things ar]e [unclean] to you; *you shall not eat* [of *them.*[98] 20 Of all clean birds you may eat. 21 You shall not eat of] anything that

---

93. 4QDeut[c] SP LXX. Not in MT.

94. 4QDeut[c]. *or your son or your daughter* MT SP LXX.

95. 11QDeut. *end* MT SP LXX.

96. 11QDeut LXX. Not in MT SP.

97. 4QpaleoDeut[r] SP LXX. Not in MT LXX[ms].

Chapter 14. 4QpaleoDeut[r]: 14:1–4, 19–22, 26–29; 1QDeut[a]: 14:21, 24–25.

98. Singular 4QpaleoDeut[r]. *they shall not be eaten* MT. *you* [plural] *shall not eat of them* SP LXX.

dies by itself. [You may give it] to the stranger [who is within your gates, so that he may eat it, or you may sell it to a foreigner]; for [yo]u a[re] a holy people [to the LORD your God. You shall not boil a kid i]n its mother's milk.

[22 You shall indeed tithe all the increase of your seed, which comes from] the fields year [by year. 23 In the presence of the LORD your God, at the place he will choose as a dwelling for his name, you shall eat the tithe of your grain, your wine, and your oil, as well as the firstborn of your herd and flock, so that you may learn to fear the LORD your God always. 24 But if the road is too long for you, so that you are not abl]e to[99] carry the tithe—since [the place] is too distant [from you, where the LORD your God chooses to set his name when the LOR]D your God [blesses you— 25 then you shall exchange it for money, bind up the money in your hand, and go to the place which] the LORD your God [cho]oses. [26 And you shall spend the money for whatever your heart desires: for oxen, or for sheep, or for wine, or for strong drink, or for whatever yo]ur [heart desires]. Then you shall eat there b[efore the LORD your God, and you shall rejoice, you and your household. 27 And as for the Le]vite who is within [your] ga[tes—you shall not neglect him, fo]r [he] has n[o portion or inheritance with you].

[28 At the end of every three year]s you shall bring [the full tithe of your increase in the same year, and lay it up with]in your gates. 29 And [the Levite, because he has no portion or inheritance with you, and the foreigner, the orphan and the widow who are within your gates] shall co[me, and eat and be satisfied, so that the LORD your God may bless you in all the work of your hands which you undertake].

15

■ *Deuteronomy 15:2 prohibits the exacting of debts at the end of every seven years. In the Masoretic Text and the Samaritan Pentateuch we are told that debt repayment is not to be required of one's neighbor or brother, whereas the Septuagint exempts only one's neighbor from debts. But 4QDeut^c specifies no party from whom debts cannot be exacted, which seems to make the prohibition applicable to everyone who owes debt (and is thus more wide-ranging). Comparison of these different rulings shows that legal differences arose early on as to exactly who was exempted from paying debts at the end of the seventh year.*

[1 At the end of every seven years you shall] grant a remission of debts. 2 And this is the m[anner of the remission]: every creditor [shall release] wh[at] [he has

---

99. Preposition 1QDeut^a. Not in MT SP.

Chapter 15. MurDeut: 15:2; 4QDeut^c: 15:1–4, 15–19; 4QpaleoDeut^r: 15:5–6, 8–10; 1QDeut^b: 15:14–15.

lent to his neighbor]; he shall [no]t *exact it*[100] because [the LORD's] remission has been proclaimed. [3 You may exact it of a foreigner, but whatever of] yours is with [your] b[rother your hand shall remit. 4 However, there shall be no p]oor [among you], for [the LORD will surely] bless [you in the land which the LORD] your God is giving [you for an inheritance to possess, 5 if only you listen fully to the voice of the L]ORD [your] Go[d, by being careful to carry out this entire commandment] which I command you [this day. 6 For the LORD your God will bless you, just a]s he promised you; [you] will lend [to many nations but not borrow, yo]u [will rule over] ma[ny natio]ns but [they shall not rule] over [you].

[7 If there is among you anyone in need—a member of your community in any of your towns within the land which the LORD your God is giving you—do not be hard-hearted or tight-fisted toward your poor neighbor. 8 Rather] you shall [indeed] open your hand to him, and [shall indeed] lend [him sufficient for his need, whatever he requires]. 9 Be care[ful] lest there be a [wicked] th[ought in your heart which says], "The seventh year, the year of remis[sion, is at hand," and your eye is hostile toward your ne]edy [neighbor], and you [giv]e nothing to [him]. Then he may cry out [to the LORD against you, and it will be accounted as a sin to you. 10 You shall indeed giv]e to him, and [your] he[art] shall not be g[rieved when you give to him; because of this the LORD your God will bless you in all your work, and in everything you put your hand to]. ▲

[14 . . . you shall supply him liberally from your flock, from your threshing-floor, and from your winepress; just as the L]ORD[101] your G[od has blessed] you shall give to him. 15 A[nd you shall remember that you were a slave in the land of Egypt, and the LORD your God redeemed you; therefore] I command you *to d[o*[102] this] thi[ng today. 16 And if he says to you, "I will not leave you," becau]se he lov[es you and your house and because he fares well with you, 17 then you shall take an awl and thrust it] through his earlobe [into the door, and he shall be your servant forever. And you shall also do the same to your female servant]. 18 This will [not] seem hard [to you when you let him go free from you, for he has served you for six years, t]wice [as much as] the hire of a hired hand; [and the LORD your God will bless you] in all that you do.

[19 All the firstborn males that are born of] your herd [and of your flock you shall consecrate to the LORD your God; you shall do no work with the firstborn of your herd, nor shear the firstborn of your flock]. ▲

---

100. 4QDeut[c]. *exact it of his neighbor and his brother* MT SP. *exact it of his neighbor* LXX.

101. 1QDeut[b]. *LORD* MT SP.

102. 1QDeut[b] LXX. Not in MT SP.

16

[1 Observe the month of Abib and keep the Passover for the LORD your God, because in the month of Abib the LORD your God brought you out of Egypt by night. 2 And you shall sacrifice the Passover to the LORD your God, from the flock and] the herd, [in the place which the LORD chooses to make his name dwell there. 3 You shall ea]t [no] le[avened bread] with it; [for seven days you shall eat unleavened bread with it, the bread of affliction, since you came out of the land of Egypt in haste—so that you may remember the day when you came out of the land of Egypt all the days of your life. 4 And] no [leaven] shall be seen with you [in all your borders for seven days; nor shall any of the meat which you sacrifice on the evening of the first day remain all night until the mo]rning.

> ■ *In a section concerned with the celebration of Passover, the Masoretic Text, the Samaritan Pentateuch, and the Septuagint allow the eating of unleavened bread for six days, followed by a solemn assembly on the seventh day (Deut 16:8). However, 4QDeut^c specifies that unleavened bread may also be eaten on the seventh (see verse 3), possibly before the solemn assembly.*

[5 You are not allowed to offer the Passover sacrifice within any of your towns that the LORD your God is giving you, 6 but rather at the place which the LORD] your [Go]d [chooses] to make his name to dwell there. [There you shall sacrifice the Passover at evening, at the setting of the sun, at the time when you came out] o[f Egypt]. 7 Then you shall cook and eat [it in the place which] the LORD your God [chooses; and you shall return in the morning and go to your tents. 8 *For s*]*even*[103] *days unleavened bread you shall eat,*[104] [and on the seventh day there shall be a solemn assembly to the Lor]D your Go[d]; you shall not do *any*[105] [work] *on it.*[106]

9 You shall count off seven weeks [for yourself; from the time you begin to put the sickle to the standing grain you shall begin] to count seven weeks. 10 And you shall celebrate [the feast of weeks to the LORD your God with a gi]*ft*[107] of *freewill offerings*[108] from your hand, which you shall give [in ac]cordance with how [the LORD your God blesses you; 11 and] you [shall rejoice] before the LORD your God—[yo]u, *your*[109] son, [your daughter, your male servant, your female servant, the] Levite who is within your gates, [the foreigner, the orphan, and the widow

---

Chapter 16. 4QDeut^c: 16:2–3, 6–11, 21–22; 1QDeut^a: 16:4, 6–7.

103. 4QDeut^c. *Six* MT SP LXX.

104. Pronoun is plural 4QDeut^c. *you* [singular] *shall eat unleavened bread* MT SP LXX.

105. 4QDeut^c SP LXX. Not in MT.

106. 4QDeut^c LXX. Not in MT SP.

107. 4QDeut^c. *sufficiency* MT SP LXX.

108. 4QDeut^c. *a freewill offering* MT SP LXX.

109. 4QDeut^c. *and your* MT SP LXX.

who are] in your midst, in [the place which the LORD] your God [chooses] to [make his name dwell there. 12 Remember that you were a slave in Egypt, and carefully observe these statutes]. ▲

21 You shall not plant for yourself [an Asherah of any kind of tree beside the altar of the LORD your God which] you shall make for yourself. 22 Neit[her shall you set up for yourself a pillar, which the LORD your God hates].

17 1 You shall not sacrifice to the Lo[RD your God an ox or a sheep on which there is a blemish or an]y defect, for [that is] an abomi[nation to the LORD your God].

2 If there is found in [your] midst—[within any of your gates which the LORD your God gives you—a man or woman who does what is evil in the sight of the LORD your God by transgressing] his covenant, 3 and has go[ne and served other gods and worshiped them, or the sun or] the moon o[r any of the host of heaven, which I have not commanded; 4 and if this is reported to you and you have heard of it], then you shall investigate this tho[roughly. And if it is really true, and if the matter is certain that such abomination has been committed] in Israel, 5 then [you] shall b[ring out that man or that] woman wh[o has done] this [evi]l [thing] to [your gates—that same man or woman—and you shall stone them to death with stones. 6 On the testimony of two witnesses, or of three witnesses, the one who is to die shall be put to death; but on the testimony of one witness he shall not be put to death. 7 The hands of the witnesses shall be] the firs[t against him to put him to death, and afterward the hands of all the people. So you must purge the evil from] your [mid]st. ▲

[12 And as for the man who acts presumptuously by not listening to the priest who stands to minister there before the LORD your God, or to the judge, that same] ma[n shall die. You must purge the evil from Israel. 13 And all the people shall hear and be afraid, and no longer act presumptuously].

[14 When you come to the land which the LORD your God] is giving you and you possess [it and dwell in it, and say, "I will set a king over me, like all the nations that are ar]ound [me," 15 you must] inde[ed m]ake [king] ov[er you the one whom the LORD your God chooses. You shall make] king [over you one from among your countrymen]—you may not put [over you a foreigner, who is] not your countryman. [16 Even so], he shall [not] multiply [horses] for himself, [nor cause the people to return to Egypt, with the purpose of multiplying horses; for the LORD] has said to you, ["You shall] never again [return] that [way." 17 Nor shall he multiply wives for himself] lest [his heart] tur[n away; nor shall he] g[rea]tly [mult]iply for himself [silver and gold].

18 And when [he sits on the throne of his kingdom, he shall write for himself a

---

Chapter 17. 4QDeut^c: 17:1–5, 7, 15–20; 4QpaleoDeut^r: 17:5–6(?); 2QDeut^b: 17:12–15; 1QDeut^b: 17:16; 4QDeut^f: 17:17–18.

cop]y of [this] law [in] a book, in the pre[sence of the Levitical priests. 19 And it shall remain with him and he shall read] *it*[110] [al]l the days of his life, so that he may l[earn to fear the LORD his God by ke]eping all the words of this [law] and [these statutes, and by carrying them out], 20 so that [his] he[art] may not be exalted [above his countrymen, and so that he may turn not aside from the commandment to the right hand or to the left. Then] he will prolong his days [in his kingdom, both he and his children, in the midst of Israel].

18 [1 The Levitical priests, indeed all the tribe of Levi], shall h[ave] no [portion or inheritance with Israel, but shall eat the offerings of the LORD made by] fire [that are his portion]. ▲

[6 And if a Levite moves from any of your towns anywhere in Israel], wh[ere] he is living, [and comes with all the desire of his soul to the place which the LORD chooses, 7 then he shall minister] in the name of the LORD [his] Go[d, as do all his countrymen the Levites who stand there before the LORD]. 8 They shall [have equal portions to] eat, besides what comes of the sale [of his family estate].

[9 When you come into the land which the LORD] your God is giving you, you sh[all not learn to imitate the abominations of those nations. 10 No one shall be found among you who makes] his son or [his daughter pass through] the fire, [one who practices] d[ivination or soothsaying, or interprets omens, or is a sorcerer, 11 or one who casts spells, or who consults ghosts or spirits, or who consults the dead]. ▲

[17 Then the LORD replied to me, "They are right in what they have said. 18 I will raise for them a prophet like you from among their countrymen; I will put my words in] his mouth, and he will speak to them [all that I command him. 19 And whoever does not listen to my words which] he will speak in my name, I [will hold] that person [accountable. 20 But the prophet who presumes to speak in my name a word that] I have not commanded him to speak, [or who] speaks [in the name of other go]ds—[that prophet will die." 21 You may say in your] he[art, "How shall we recognize the wo]rd which [the LORD has] not s[poken?" 22 When a prophet speaks in the name of the LORD, but the thing does not come about or co]me [true], that is the mes[sage which the LORD has not spoken. The prophet has spoken it presumptuously; you shall not be afraid of him].

19 [1 When the LORD your God has destroyed the nations whose land the LORD your God is giving you, and you have driven them out and settled in their towns and in their houses, 2 you shall set apart three cities for yourself in the

---

110. Feminine 4QDeut[c] SP. Masculine MT.

Chapter 18. 4QDeut[c]: 18:1; 4QDeut[f]: 18:6–10, 18–22.

Chapter 19. 4QpaleoDeut[r]: 19:2–3; 4QDeut[k2]: 19:8–16; 4QDeut[f]: 19:17–21; 4QDeut[h]: 19:21.

midst of your land, whic]h the L[OR]D [your] G[od is giving to you to possess. 3 You shall prepare the] way, and divide the bor[ders of your land which the LORD] your [G]od [causes you to inherit] into three parts, so that [any manslayer] c[an flee there]. ▲

[8 And] if [the LORD your God] enlar[ges your border, as he swore to your ancestors, and gives you] all the land which he prom[ised to give to your ancestors— 9 provided you keep this entire commandment by carrying it out, as I command] you[111] today, by lov[ing the LORD your God and by walking always in his ways—then you can add thr]ee cities [more for yourself], in addition to [these] three. [10 Do this so that innocent blood might not be shed in the midst of your land which the LORD your God is giving to you for an inheritance, and so that] bloodguilt will [not] be on you. [11 But if anyone hates his neighbor and lies in wait for him, and rises up against him and strikes him so that he dies, and then flees to one] from[112] these cities, [12 the elders of his city shall send and take him from there, and deliver him into the hand of the avenger of blood so that he may die]. 13 Your eye [shall not pit]y him, bu[t you shall purge the guilt of innocent blood from Israel, so that it may go well with you].

[14 You shall not remove your neighbor's boundary marker, which former generati]ons [have set], in your inheritance w[hich you will hold in the land that the LORD your God is giving to you to possess].

[15 A single witness shall not come forward against a person] with respect to any iniquity or a[ny sin, in connection with any offense that he may have committed; a charge shall be sustained on the evidence of two witnesses, or on the evidence of three witnesses].

16 If [a malicious witness comes forward against anyone to accuse him of wrongdoing, 17 then both parties who have the dispute shall appear before the LORD, before the priests and the judg]es who [are in office at that time. 18 Then the judges are to conduct a thorough investigation; and] indeed, if [the witness] proves to be a false witness [and has testified] falsely against [his] bro[ther, 19 then you shall do to him just as he had intended to do to] his [broth]er. So you must purge the evil from your midst. 20 Then the re[st will hear of this and be afraid, and will never] again [com]mit such an evil [thing] in your mid[st. 21 Your[113] eyes shall] show no [pity]: his[114] life [for life, eye fo]r eye, tooth for tooth, [hand for hand], foot for foot.

---

111. Plural 4QDeut^k2. Singular MT SP LXX.

112. 4QDeut^k2. *of* MT SP.

113. 4QDeut^f. *And your.*

114. 4QDeut^h. Not in MT SP LXX.

20[1 When you go out to w]ar against [your] e[nemies, and you see horses and] chariots *and*[115] a people [more] numerous [than you, you shall not be afraid of them—for the LORD your God, who brought you up from the lan]d of Egypt, is with you. 2 And [when you draw near to battle, the priest shall approach and speak to the people, 3 and say t]o [them], "Hear, [O Israel, you are drawing near today to make war against your enemies. Do not lose heart or be afraid or panic or be in dread of them, 4 for it is the LORD your God who goes with you, to fig]ht for you against [your] enemie[s, to give you victory]."

> ■ *Deuteronomy 20 lays down regulations for going to war. As we might expect, some verses (5, 9) refer to the role of the army officers. In verse 8 the Masoretic Text, the Samaritan Pentateuch, and the Septuagint again call these leaders* officers, *but 4QDeut*[k2] *instead refers to them as* judges. *The Qumran scroll may have also used this term instead of* officers *in verses 5 and 9, but unfortunately the key words are not preserved. It is also interesting to note that both words are found in 4QDeut*[b] *and the Septuagint at Deuteronomy 31:28, whereas the Masoretic Text and the Samaritan Pentateuch use only the term* officers.

[5 Then the officers shall speak to the people, sayi]ng, "Has anyone [built a new house and not yet dedicated it? Let him go and return to his house, lest he die in the bat]tle and someone else [dedicates it. 6 And has anyone] plan[ted a vineyard and not yet used its fruit? Let him go and retur]n to [his] ho[use, lest he die in the battle and someone else use its fruit. 7 And is anyone] en[gaged to a wom]an, and [has] not [yet married her? Let him go and return to his house, lest he die in the battle and someone else marries her." 8 And] the *judges*[116] [shall] speak [further] to the p[eople and say, "Is anyone fearful and faint-hearted? Let him go and return to his house, lest] his neighbor's heart [melts] like his own heart." 9 And [when the officers have finished speaking to the people they shall appoint arm]y [commanders] at [the he]ad of the people.

10 When you approach [a city] to [fight] against it, offer terms of peace [to it]. 11 And if it accepts your terms of peace [and ope]ns its gates to you, then all the people who are foun[d in it shall become] forced labor for you and shall serve you. 12 But if the city will not make peace wit[h you], but makes [war against you, then you shall besiege it; 13 and when] the LORD your Go[d] delivers it [into your hand], you shall kill e[very male from there with the] e[dge of the sword. 14 But] you shall take as plunder f[or yourself the women, the children, and the cattle, and all that is in the city, all] its [sp]oil; [and you shall eat the spoil of your

---

Chapter 20. 4QDeut[f]: 20:1–6; 4QDeut[k2]: 20:6–19; 4QDeut[i]: 20:9–13.

115. 4QDeut[f] SP LXX. Not in MT.

116. 4QDeut[k2]. *officers* MT SP LXX.

enemies which the LORD your God gives you. 15 This is what you are to do] to all [the cities which are very far off from you, which are not the cities of the nations nearby].

[16 But of the cities of these nations that the LORD your God is giving to yo]u as an in[heritance you shall leave alive nothing that breathes. 17 For you shall utterly destroy them—the Hittites and the Amorites, the Canaanites and the] Perizzites, *and*[117] the Hi[vites, and the Jebusites—just as the LORD your God has commanded you, 18 so that they may not teach you both to practice] all [their] abominati[ons which they do for their gods and to sin against the LORD your God. 19 When you besiege] a city for a [long] tim[e, making war against it in order to take it, you shall not destroy its trees by wielding an ax against them; for you may] eat [from them], but [you shall not cut them down. For are the trees of the field people, that they should be besieged by you? 20 However, you may destroy and cut down trees that you know do not produce fruit, and use them for building siegeworks against the town that is making war with you, until it falls].

21 4 . . . and the elder[s] of th[at][118] c[ity] shall bring the heifer down [to] a valley [with running water, which has been neither plowed] no[r] sown, and they shall break [the he]ifer's neck there in [the valley. 5 Then] t[he priests, the sons of Levi, shall com]e near; [for] the LORD [your] Go[d has ch]osen [them] to minister to him a[nd to pronounce bless]ings in the name [of the LORD, and in accord]ance [with their word shall all cases of dispute and ass]ault [be settled]. 6 And all the eld[ers of tha]t [city] who are nearest to the slain man [shall wash their hands over the heifer whose neck was broken in the valley, 7 and they shall answer and say], "Our [han]ds *have not shed*[119] [this] b[lood, neither have our eyes seen it]. 8 O LORD, [forgive yo]ur [people] Israel, [wh]om you have r[ede]emed, and do not allow [innocent] blood [to remain in the midst of your people Israel." And] the bloodguilt [shall be forgi]ven them. 9 So you shall purge *the blood of the* [inno]cent[120] fr[om your midst, when you do what is right in the sight of the LORD].

10 When you go out to w[ar against your enemies, and the LORD your God delivers them into your hands and you carry them away captive, 11 if you see among the] captives [a beautiful] wom[an, and have a desire for her and wish to take her as a wife for yourself, 12 you shall bring her home to your house. Then

---

117. 4QDeut[k2] MT[mss] SP LXX. Not in MT.

Chapter 21. 4QDeut[f]: 21:4–12; 1QDeut[b]: 21:8–9; 4QpaleoDeut[r]: 21:8–9(?) (or 30:7–8[?]); 4QDeut[k2]: 21:16(?); 4QDeut[i]: 21:23.

118. Feminine 4QDeut[f] MT *qere* SP. Masculine MT *ketib*.

119. 4QDeut[f] MT *qere* SP. *has not shed* MT *ketib* LXX.

120. 4QDeut[f]. *the innocent blood* 1QDeut[b] MT SP LXX.

she shall] shave [her head, trim her nails, 13 discard her captive's garb, and live in your house a full month, mourning for her father and mother. Then you may go in to her and be her husband, and she shall be your wife].▲

[15 If a man has two wives, one of them loved and the other unloved, and if both the loved one and the one he does not love bear him sons, the firstborn being the son of the unloved wife, 16 then on the day when] he wills [his property to his sons, he cannot make the son of the beloved wife the firstborn in preference to the unloved wife's son, who is the actual firstborn].▲

[22 When someone is convicted of a capital offense and is executed, and you hang him on a tree, 23 his body shall not remain all night on the tree, but you shall indeed bury him that same day. For anyone who is hanged is under God's curse; you must not defile your land which the LORD yo]ur [God] is giving [to] you [as an inheritance].

22[1 You shall not watch your neighbor's ox or his sheep straying off and ignore them]; you shall certainly take them back [to your neighbor. 2 And if your neighbor is not near you, or if you do not know him, then you shall bring it home to your house and it shall rem]ain [with you until your neighbor looks for it; then you shall return it to him. 3 And you shall d]o [the same with his donkey], you shall do the same [with hi]s [garment, and you shall do the same with every lost item of your neighbor's, which he loses] and you find—you m[a]y not ignore it. [4 You shall not see your neighbor's donkey or] his [ox] fallen down on the road, and ignore th[em]; you shall certainly help [him] lift [them up].

5 A woman sh[all] not wear [a man's clothing], nor shall a man pu[t on] a woman's *garment;*[121] for whoever does [these things is] an abomination to the LORD your God.

[6 If] a bird's nest [happens to be] before you on the road, whether in any tree or on [the ground, with fledglings or] eggs, and the mother is sittin[g o]n the fledglings or [on the eggs], you shall not take the mother [wi]th [the fledglings. 7 You shall certainly let the mother go, but you may take the fledglings for] yourself, [so that it may go well with you and you may prolong your days].

[8 When you build a new house, then you shall make a parapet around your roof, so that] you may [not] bring [bloodguilt on your house if anyone falls from it].

[9 You shall not sow your vineyard with two kinds of seed, or the wh]ol[e yield will have to be forfeited, both the seed which you have sown and the yield of the vineyard].▲

[12 You shall make yourself tassels on the four corners of your cloak] with [which you] cover [yourself].

[13 If any man takes a wife and goes in to her, and then spurns her, 14 and

---

Chapter 22. 4QDeut[i]: 22:1–9; 4QpaleoDeut[r]: 22:3–6; 4QDeut[f]: 22:12–19.

121. One form of word 4QDeut[i]. Alternate form 4QpaleoDeut[r] MT SP.

charges sha]meful things [against he]r and gi[ves her a bad name, saying], "I married [th]is [woman], but when I lay with [her I found no evidence of h]er virgi[nity," 15 then the] girl's [father] and mother [shall bring] a[nd submit the evidence of the girl's virginity] to the elder[s of the city at the gate. 16 Then the girl's father shall say to the elders, "I gave my daughter] to [this man as] a wife, [but he spurns her, 17 and now he has charged her with shameful things], saying, '[I found no evidence of] your daughter's [virginity.' But here is the proof of my daughter's virginity." Then they shall spread out the cloth] before the elder[s of the ci]ty. 18 And [the elders of that city] shall take [the man and punish him. 19 They shall fine him a hundred shekels of si]lver [and give these to the father of the girl, because he has given a bad name to a virgin of Israel. She shall remain his wife; he may not divorce her as long as he lives]. ▲

23 [5 Yet the LORD your God would not listen to Balaam, but the LORD your God turned] the curse into a blessing [for you] becaus[e the LORD your God loved you. 6 You shall not promote their welfare n]or their prosperity [as long as you live].

[7 You shall not despise an Edomite, since he is your countryman; you shall] not [despise an Egyptian, since you were a foreigner residing in his land]. ▲

[10 If one of you becomes unclean because of a nocturnal emission, he is to go outside the camp and must not come within the camp. 11 But when evening arrives he shall bathe himself in water; and when] the sun [sets] he can come back wi[thin the camp].

[12 You shall also have a place outside the camp] where you can go to relieve yourself; 13 and [you shall have] a spade [among your tools, and when you sit down] outside[122] you shall dig with it a[nd rest]ore[123] and cover [your excrement. 14 For the LORD] your [God] walks in the midst of your camp, to sa[ve you and to deliver your enemies before you; this is why your camp shall b]e holy, so that he may not s[ee anything indecent among you and turn away from you].

15 You shall [not] ha[nd ba]ck [to his master] a s[lave who has run away from his master to you. 16 He can live with you, in your midst, in any place that he chooses in any one of your towns, wherever he likes—you shall not oppress him].

17 No[ne of the daughters of Israel] shall be [a cult prostitute, nor shall any of the sons of Israel be a cult prostitute. 18 You shall not bring the] wages of a prostitute [or the wages of a male prostitute into the house of the LORD yo]ur [God to pay any vow; for] both of these [are an abomination to the LORD your God].

[19 You shall not charge interest to your countryman—whether interest on

---

Chapter 23. 4QDeut^i: 23:5–7, 11–15, 21–25 [MT 23:6–8, 12–16, 22–26]; 4QpaleoDeut^r: 23:6, 11–14 [MT 23:7, 12–15]; 4QDeut^g: 23:17–19 [MT 23:18–20]; 4QDeut^f: 23:20–25 [MT 23:21–26]; 4QDeut^k2: 23:21–25 [MT 23:22–26]; 4QDeut^a: 23:25 [MT 23:26].

122. With directive particle 4QpaleoDeut^r SP. No directive particle 4QDeut^i MT.

123. 4QpaleoDeut^r LXX. turn MT SP.

money, interest on food, or interest on anything that] may accrue interest.
[20 You may charge interest to a foreigner, but you shall not charge interest to
your countryman], so that the LORD [your God] may bless you [in all that you put
your hand to in the land which you are entering] to possess.

[21 When you make a vow to the LORD your God, you shall not] be slow in
paying it, for [the LORD your God will] surely [hold you responsible] and there
would be [sin in you]. 22 But if you refrain [from] vowing there shall be no s[in]
in you. [23 You shall be ca]reful to perform what goes forth from your lips, just as
you have vowed [to the LORD your God as a freewill offeri]ng what [you] have
promised with your own mouth.

24 When you go into your neighbor's vineyard, [you may eat] your [f]ill [of
grapes for yourself], but you shall not pu[t] any in your basket. 25 When you go
into your neighbor's [standing grain], then [you may] pl[uck the ears with your
hands, but you shall] n[ot] put [a sickle] to your neighbor's standing grain.

24

▇ *Among other matters, Deuteronomy 24 deals with divorce. In verse 2, one scroll—
4QDeutᵃ—and the Septuagint assume that the wife has actually departed from the
husband's house after he has sent her away (verse 1); this is reflected in the translation
below. However, another scroll—4QDeutᵏ²—along with the Masoretic Text and the
Samaritan Pentateuch, specifies in verse 2 that she may become another man's wife
only after she has physically departed. The second stipulation, more specific, prevents a
situation where the rejected wife may be living in two homes at once.*

[1 If a man takes a wife and marries her, but she fin]ds [no] favor in his eyes because he has found something objectionable about her, [then he shall write her a
bill of divorce and put it in her hand and] send her from his house. 2 *She*[124] may
then go and be [another] man's [wife. 3 And if the latter husband *who took her*] *to
be his wife*[125] [dislikes her] and writes her a bill of divorce and puts it in her hand
and sends her from his house, [or if the latter husband] who took her to be his
wife [dies], 4 her former husband, [who had sent her away], cannot take her again
to be his wife after she has been defiled. For [tha]t is [an abomination] before the
LORD; you shall not bring sin upon the land which the LORD your God is giving
you [as an inheritance].

5 When a man takes a new wife, he shall not go out with the army, nor shall he

---

Chapter 24. 4QDeutᵃ: 24:1–8; 4QDeutᵏ²: 24:1–3; 4QDeutⁱ: 24:1; 4QDeutᶠ: 24:2–7;
1QDeutᵇ: 24:10–16; 4QDeutᵍ: 24:16–22.

124. 4QDeutᵃ LXX. *And when she has departed from his house, she* 4QDeutᵏ² MT SP.

125. 4QDeutᵏ². Not in 4QDeutᵃ MT SP LXX.

be *charged*[126] an[y duty]; for one year he shall be free at home and be happy with the wife he has marr[ied].

6 N[o one shall tak]e [a mi]ll or an upper millstone [as a pledge]; for he would be taking a man's life in pledge.

7 If a man is found kidn[apping any of his countrymen from the] Israel[ites, and mi]streats him or sells him, then [that] thi[ef] shall die. [So you shall purge the evil from your midst].

8 Guard [against an outbreak of] leprosy by taking care to observe and a[ct according to all that the Levitical priests teach you; just as] I [commanded] th[em, so you shall take care to do. 9 Remember what the LORD your God did to Miriam along the road as you came out of Egypt].

[10 When you make your neighbor a] lo[an of any kind, you shall not go into his house to take his pledge. 11 You shall stand outside, and the man to whom you are lending] shall bring [the pledge] out t[o you. 12 And if he is a poor man, you shall not go to sleep with his pledge in your possession; 13 you shall certainly restore to him] the pledge when the sun goes down, [so that he may sleep in his garment and bless you. And it will be regarded as a righteous act by you before the LORD your God].

14 You shall not take advantage of a hired servant who is poor and needy, [whether he is one] of [your] country[men, or of your foreigners who reside in your land in your towns. 15 You shall pay him his wages each day, before] the sun [goes down] on it, for he is poor and [sets his heart o]n [it. Otherwise he may cry to the LORD against you, and it would become s]in [in you].

16 Parent[s] shall not *be put to death*[127] [for their children, nor shall children be put to death for their par]ents; each [shall be put to death] for [his own] sin.

[17 You shall not pervert the justice that is due to resident aliens or to orphans, nor shall you take a] widow's [clothi]ng [as a pledge]. 18 Remember that [you] w[ere] a slave [in Egypt, and the LORD your God redeemed you from there; therefo]re I command you to do this thing.

[19 When you reap your harvest in your field, and have forgotten] a sheaf in the field, you shall not go again to retrieve it. It shall be left for the foreigner, the orphan [and the widow, so that the LORD] your God [may bless you] in all the work of your hands. 20 When you beat [your] o[live tree, you shall not go over the boughs again]; this shall be [for the foreigner, the orph]an and the widow. 21 When you gather the grapes of your vineyard, [you shall] not [glean what is left over]. This is [for the foreigner, the orphan and the widow]. 22 And you shall remember that you were a slave in the land of Eg[ypt; therefore I command you to do this thing].

---

126. 4QDeut[a] MT[mss] LXX. *charged with* MT SP.
127. Singular 1QDeut[b]. Plural MT SP LXX.

25 1 If there is a di[spute between people and they go to court, and the judges decide between them, they shall vindicate the righteous and co]nd[emn] the guilty. [2 And if the guilty party deserves to be flogged, the judge shall make him lie down and be beaten in his presence] with the num[ber] of strokes in proportion to his offense. [3 He may give him forty lashes but no more, so that he does not beat him with many stripes more than these and] your neighbor [is degra]ded in [yo]ur e[yes].

[4 You shall not muzzle the ox when it treads out the grain].

[5 If brothers dwell together and] one of them [di]es [leaving no son, the wife of the deceased shall not be married outside the family to a stranger; her husband's brother shall go in to her and take her for himself] as a wife, and perform the duty of a husband's brother [to her. 6 And the firstborn th]at she bears [shall assume the name of his deceased brother, so that his name may not be blotted out of Israe]l.

7 But if [the man] has no des[ire] to take [his brother's wife, then his brother's wife shall go up to the elders at the gate and say, "My husband's brother refuses] to [raise up for his brother a name in] Israel; [he will] no[t perform the duty of a husband's brother to me." 8 Then the elders of his city shall call him and speak to him; and if he persists and sa]ys, ["I] do not wa[nt to tak]e her," 9 then [his brother's wife] shall co[me to him in the presence of the elders and pull his shoe from his foot], and spit in [his] f[ace, and she shall declare, "This is what is done to the man who does not build up his brother's house. 10 Throughout Israel his line will be known as 'The house of him whose sandal was pulled off].'" ▲

[13 You shall not have in your bag two kinds of] weights, [large and small. 14 You shall not have in your house two kinds of measures, la]rge a[nd small. 15 You] shall have only [an accurate and hone]st [weight, you shall have only an accurate and honest measure, so that your days] may be long [in the land which the LORD your God is giving you. 16 For] all who do such things, a[ll who act dishonestly, are an abomination to the LORD] your [G]o[d].

[17 Remember] wh[at Amalek did to you] along the road when you came out of E[gypt— 18 h]ow he met [you on the] road and struck down all [who lagged behind] at your rear, when you were faint [and we]ary; he did not [fear God]. 19 Therefore, [when the LORD your God has given you rest from all your surroundi]ng ene[mies], in the land [which the LORD your God is giving you for an inheritance to possess, you shall blot out the remembrance of Amale]k from under heav[en; you must not forget].

26 [1 And when you come int]o [the land which the LORD] your [God] is giving [you for an inheritance, and possess it and dwell in it, 2 you shall

---

Chapter 25. 4QDeut^g: 25:1–5, 14–19; 4QDeut^f: 25:3–9; 1QDeut^b: 25:13–18; 4QDeut^{k2}: 25:19.

Chapter 26. 4QDeut^{k2}: 26:1–5, 18–19(?); 4QDeut^g: 26:1–5; 4QpaleoDeut^s: 26:14–15; 4QDeut^f: 26:18–19; 4QDeut^c: 26:19; pap6QDeut(?): 26:19(?).

take some of the first fruits of all the produ]ce of the ground w[hich you bring in from your land that the Lo]rd your G[o]d [is giving you, and you shall put it] in a basket, and go to [the place which the LORD your God chooses as a dwelling for his name]. 3 Then you shall go to the priest [who is officiating] at [that] time and say to him, "I profess [this da]y *before*[128] the LORD [your] God [that I have come to the land wh]ich the LORD [s]wore to our ancestors to give [us." 4 Then] the priest shall take the [basket from your hands and set it down before the altar of the L]ORD your God. 5 And [you] shall answer [and sa]y be[fore the LORD your God, "My father was a wandering Aramean, and he went down into Egypt and] resided there, few in number. [And there he became a great, mighty, and populous nation]." ▲

[14 I have not eaten from it while in mourning, nor have I removed any of it while unclean, nor offered any of it for the] dead. I have listened to the voice of the L[ORD my God; I have acted in accordance with all that you commanded me. 15 Look down from] your holy [dwelling] place, from heav[en, and bless your people Israel and the ground which you have given] us, just as [you] swore [to our ancestors, a land flowing with milk and honey]. ▲

■ *Deuteronomy 26 closes with God's promise that the Israelites are to be a holy people to the Lord their God. Whereas the Masoretic Text, the Samaritan Pentateuch, and the Septuagint end by saying that God has spoken this, the translation below adopts the reading of 4QDeut^c and some Septuagint manuscripts; here the promise is made more personal by stating that it was specifically spoken to the Israelite people who were present ("to you").*

[18 And the LORD has promised today that you are his people, his treasured possession, as he promised yo]u, and that you are to keep [all his commandments]. 19 And he shall set you h[igh above all the nations tha]t he has made, [*for fame and*] *for praise*[129] and for ho[nor; and for you to be a holy people to the LOR]D your God, just as [he] has sp[oken] *to you.*[130]

27 1 Then M[oses and the elders of Israel] commanded the people: K[eep al]l *this commandment*[131] [which I command you this day. 2 And on the day when you cro]ss th[e Jordan to the land] which the Lo[RD your God is giving you, you shall set up large stones for yourself and coat them with plaster. 3 Then you shall write on them all the words of this law, when you have crossed over, so that] you may go [into the land which the LORD your God is giving you—a land flowing with] milk and hon[ey—just as the LORD, the God of your ancestors, has

---

128. 4QDeut^k2. *to* MT SP LXX.

129. 4QDeut^c LXX. *for praise and for fame* MT. *for praise, for fame* SP.

130. 4QDeut^c LXX^mss. Not in MT SP LXX.

Chapter 27. 4QDeut^c: 27:1–2, 24–26; 4QDeut^f: 27:1–10; 4QDeut^k2: 27:1(?).

131. 4QDeut^c. *the commandment* MT SP. *these commandments* LXX.

promised you. 4 And] when you have crossed [the Jordan, you shall set up these stones about which] I command you to[day, in Mount Ebal, and you shall coat the]m with plaster. [5 And] there you shall build an altar [to the LORD your God, an altar of stones on which you shall use no] iron tool. 6 [You shall build the alta]r of the LORD your God [from unhewn] stones, and you shall offer on [it burnt offerings to the LORD your God. 7 You shall sacrifice peace offerings, and ea]t there, and [you] shall rejoice [before the Lo]RD your G[od]. 8 Then you shall write very clearly on the sto[nes all the words of this law].

[9 Then Mo]ses and the Levitical [priests spoke] to [all Is]rael: "[Be silent, O Israel, and listen! Today you have become the people of the LORD your G]o[d. 10 Therefore you shall obey the] voice [of the LORD your God and carry out his commandments and his statutes that I am commanding you this day]." ▲

24 C[ursed is the one who strikes down his neighbor in secret. And all the people shall say, "Amen." 25 Cursed is the one who takes a bribe [to slay an innocent person. And all the people shall say, "Amen." 26 Cu]rsed is the one wh[o does not uphold the words of th]is [law] by [carry]ing [them out. And] a[ll the peo]ple [shall] *say,*[132] "Amen."

28 [1 And] if you listen carefully to the voice of the LORD your God so as *to carry out*[133] [all his commandments which] I command you today, the LORD your God will set you [on high above all the nations of the eart]h. 2 All these blessings will come upon you and o[verta]ke you, [if you listen to the voice of the LORD] your [Go]d. 3 You will be blessed in the city, and you will be blessed [in the countryside. 4 The frui]t of your womb [will be blessed], and the fruit of your ground, the fruit of your livestock, the increase of your cattle, [and the young of your flock]. 5 Your basket and your kneading-bowl will be blessed. 6 You will be blessed when you come in, [and you will be blessed when] you [go o]ut.

7 The LORD will cause your enemies who rise [up] against you [to be defeated before you]; they [will] come out against you [one way], but [will flee before you] seven w[ays. 8 The LORD will command] the blessi[ng upo]n you [in your barns and in all that you put your hand to; and he will bless you in the land which the LORD your God is giving to you. 9 The LORD will establish you as a holy people for him]self [just as he has sworn to you, if you keep the commandments of the LORD] your [G]od [and walk in his ways. 10 And all the peoples of the earth will see that] you [are c]alled [by the name of the LORD, and they will be afraid of you. 11 And the LORD will make you abound in prosperity, in the fruit of your body],

---

132. Plural 4QDeut^c SP LXX. Singular MT.

Chapter 28. 4QDeut^c: 28:1–14, 20, 22–25, 29–30, 48–50, 61; 4QpaleoDeut^r: 28:15–18, 20, 23(?) (or 10:6[?] or 32:22[?]); 4QDeut^o: 28:15–18, 33–36, 47–52, 58–62; 4QDeut^g: 28:21–25, 27–29; 1QDeut^b: 28:44–48; 4QDeut^l: 28:67–68.

133. 4QDeut^c. *being careful to carry out* MT SP LXX.

in the fruit of your g[round, and] in the fruit of [your] c[attle[134] in the land which the
Lord swore to your ancestors to give you].

[12 The Lord will open for you his rich storehouse, the heavens, to give rain
for your land in its season and to bless all the work of your h]nds. You will lend
to] many [nations], and you [will not borrow. 13 The Lord will make you the
head, and not the tail, and you shall only be] at the top, and not [at the bottom—
if you listen to the commandments of the Lord your God which] I [comma]nd
you tod[ay, by carefully observing them. 14 And do not turn aside from any of the
words which I am commanding you this day, either to the right or to the left, by
going after other gods to serve them].

■ *Deuteronomy 26:19— "You will be cursed when you go in, and you will be cursed
when you go out"—is completely absent from 4QpaleoDeut*[r] *and some Septuagint
manuscripts but is present in the Masoretic Text, the Samaritan Pentateuch, the Septuagint, and modern Bibles. The longer text forms a counterpart to verse 6 earlier in
the chapter: "You will be blessed when you come in, and you will be blessed when you
go out."*

[15 But] if *you*[135] do not listen to the voice of the Lord [your] G[od, by carefully observing all his commandments and his statute]s [wh]ich I command you
today, [all] these curses [will come upon you] and overtake you. 16 You will be
cursed in the cit[y, and you will be cursed in the field]. 17 Your basket [will
be cursed and also] your [kn]ea[ding-bo]wl. 18 The fruit of [your] womb will be
[c]ursed, [as well as the fruit of] your ground, the increase of [your] cattle, and
the young of your flock.[136]

20 The Lo[r]d will send [upon you cursing, confus]ion, and re[buke] in all
[that you] put [your] ha[nd to do, un]til [you] are des[troyed and until you perish
quickly, because of the evil of your deeds in that you have forsaken me. 21 The
Lord will make a plague cling to you until it consumes you from the land which
you are about to] possess. [22 The Lord will inflict you] with consumption, with
f[ever, with inflammation, with fiery heat, with drought, with bli]ght, and with
mildew; [*they*] *will pursue you*[137] until [you perish. 23 Then the sky that is over
your head will be bronze, and the earth] that is beneath you will be iron. [24 The
Lord] will change [the rain of your land into powder and dust]; it will co[me
down from] heaven upon you until you are destroyed.

---

134. 4QDeut[c] LXX[mss] (probable reading). *in the fruit of your cattle, and in the fruit of your
ground* MT SP LXX[mss].

135. Plural 4QpaleoDeut[r] LXX[mss]. Singular MT SP LXX.

136. Omits vs 19 4QpaleoDeut[r] LXX[mss]. *You will be cursed when you go in, and you will be
cursed when you go out* MT SP LXX.

137. 4QDeut[c] SP. *and they shall pursue you* 4QDeut[g] MT LXX.

[25 The LORD will cause you to be defeated before your enemies; you shall go out] on[e w]ay [against them, and shall flee seven ways before them; and you shall be tossed to and fro among all the kingdoms of the earth. 26 Your corpses shall be food for all the birds of the air and the animals of the earth, and there shall be no one to frighten them away. 27 The LORD will inflict you with the boil]s [of Egypt, and with ulcers, and with scurvy, and with the itch, from which you cannot be healed. 28 The LORD will inflict you with madness, and with blindness], and with confusion [of heart; 29 and you shall grope about] at noon, a[s blind people grope in darkness], and you shall not prosper in your ways; [and you shall only be] oppressed and robbed [continually, and there shall be no one to save you].

[30 You shall become engaged to a woman, and another man shall li]e with her; [you shall build] a ho[use, and you shall not dwell in it; you shall plant a vineyard, but not enjoy its fruit].▲

33 A nation which [you do not know shall] consume [the fruit of your ground and all your labors; and you shall be only oppressed and crushed co]ntinua[lly; 34 so that you shall be driven mad by the sight of what you see. 35 The L]ORD [will] inflict y[ou in the knees, and in the legs, with grievous boils from which] you [can]not [be healed, from the sole of your foot to the crown of your head].

[36 The LOR]D [will bring] you, [and your king whom you set over you, to a nation that you have] not [known, neither you nor your ancestors; and there you shall serve oth]er [gods, of] w[ood and stone].▲

[43 The foreigner living among you shall rise above you higher and higher, but you shall sink lower and lower. 44 He shall lend to you, and you shall not lend to him; he shall b]e the he[ad, and you shall be the tail].

[45 And all these curses shall come upon you and pursue you and overtake you until you are destroyed, because you did not listen to the] voice of the LORD your God, [by keeping his commandments and his statutes which he commanded you; 46 and they shall be on you as a sign and for a portent, and on your descendants forev]er. 47 Because [you did] not [serve the L]ORD your God [with joyfulness and gladness of heart for the abundance of all things, 48 therefore you shall serve] your enemies which [the L]o[R]D shall se[nd] against you, in hunger and thirst, in nakedness [and lack of all things; and he shall put a yoke of iron on] your neck until [he] has destroyed [you].

[49 The LORD will bring a nation against you from far away], from the end of the earth, as [the eagle flies; a nation whose language you do not understand; 50 a nation of grim] countenance [who shall not respect the old or show favor to the young. 51 And it shall consume the fruit of your] livesto[ck and the fruit of your ground, until you are destroyed, leaving you neither grain, new wine, or oil, the increase of your cattle, or the yo]ung of [your] flock, [until they have made you perish. 52 And they shall besiege you in all your towns, until your high and fortified walls in which you trusted come down] throughout all [your land; and they shall besiege you in all your towns throughout all your land, which the LORD your God has given you]. ▲

[58 If] you are not care[ful to do all the words of this law that are written in this book, so that you may fear] this [glorious and awesome n?me, the LORD your God, 59 then the LORD will make your plagues overwhelming, and the plagues of your seed, even great] and lasting [plagues, and serious and chronic sicknesses. 60 And he will bring on you again all the diseases of Egypt which you were afraid of; and they shall cling to you. 61 Also every sickness and] every plague which [is] not [written in the book of this law, these the LORD will bring on you, until you are destroyed. 62 And you shall be left few in number, whereas] you were [like the stars of heaven for multitude; because you did not listen to the voice of the LORD your God]. ▲

[67 In the morning you shall say, "If only it were evening!" and at evening you shall say, "If only it were morning!" because of the dread of your heart which you shall fear and the sight of] your [eye]s w[hich you shall see. 68 And the LORD will bring you into Egypt again with ships, by a route wh]ich [I] pro[mised you, "You shall never see it again"; and there you shall sell yourselves to your enemies as male and female slaves, but no one shall buy you].

29 [1 These are the terms of the covenant the LORD commanded Moses to make with the Israelites in the land of Moab, in addition to the covenant he had made with them at Horeb. 2 Moses summoned all Israel and said to them: You have seen all that the LORD did before your eyes in the land of Egypt, to Pharaoh, to all his servants and all his land; 3 the great trials which your eyes saw, the signs, and] those [grea]t [wonders]. 4 But [the LORD has no]t [given you a heart to know, and eyes to see, and ears to hear], to this day. 5 And I have [le]d [you forty years in the wilderness; your clothes have not grown old] on you, and your sandals have not worn off [your feet. 6 You have not eaten bread, nor have you drunk wine or strong drink, so t]hat you may know that I am the LORD [your God]. ▲

[9 Therefore carefully observe the terms of this covenant, in order that you may succeed in everything that you do. 10 You] are standing [this day, all of you, before the LORD your God—your leaders, your tribes, your elders, and your officers, all the men of Isra]el, 11 *your children, and* [*your*] *w*[*ives*,138 and your foreigner who is in the midst of your camps, from the hewer of your wood to the drawer of your water—12 so that you may enter into the covenant of the LORD your G]od, [and into his oath which the LORD your God makes with you this day; 13 so that

---

Chapter 29. 4QpaleoDeut^r: 29:3–5(?) [MT 29:2–4(?) or 7:19(?)]; 4QDeut^l: 29:3–6 [MT 29:2–5]; 1QDeut^b: 29:10–21 [MT 29:9–20]; 4QDeut^c: 29:18–20 [MT 29:17–19]; 4QDeut^o: 29:23–26 [MT 29:22–25]; 4QDeut^b: 29:25–28 [MT 29:24–27].

138. 1QDeut^b SP. *your children, your wives* MT. *your wives and your children* LXX.

he may establish you this day to himself for a people, and that he may be your God, as he spoke to you, and as he swore to your ancestors, to Abraham, to Isaac, and to Ja]cob. 14 Nor is it with you [only] that I make [this covenant and this oath, 15 but with] those who [are here] *standing with us*[139] this day before the LORD our God, and [also with those who are not here with us this day. 16 For you know] how we lived in the land of Egypt, and how [we came through the midst of the nations through which you passed; 17 and] you have s[ee]n [thei]r [abominations], and their idols of wood and stone, of silver and gold, [which were among them. 18 Beware lest there be among you a man or woman], or a family o[r tribe, wh]ose heart turns away this day from the LORD our God [to go and serv]e [the gods of those nations; lest there be among you a root that be]ars poisonous and bitter fruit.

19 And when he hears the words of [this curse, he blesses himself in his heart, saying], "I shall have [peace], though I walk [in the stubborn]ness of my heart," this will [destroy the moist along with the dry]. 20 The LORD [will not] be willing [to pardon him, but rather the anger of the LORD and] his [jealou]sy [will burn] against that man, and all [the curses that are written in this book] shall *cling*[140] on him, [and the LORD will blot out his name from under heaven. 21 And the LORD will] set him apart [for calamity out of all the tribes of Israel, according to all the curses of the covenant that are written in this book of the law].

[22 The next generation, your children who rise up after you, as well as the foreigner who comes from a distant land, will see the devastation of that land and the calamities with which the LORD has afflicted it— 23 all its soil brimstone and salt, and a burnt-out waste, unsown, and growing nothing, where no vegetation can grow like the overthrow of Sodom and Gomorrah, Admah and Zeboiim, which the LORD overthrew in his anger and] in his wrath— 24 indeed a[ll the nations] shall say, ["Why has the LORD done thus to this land? What does the heat of this great anger mean]?"

25 They shall conclude, "Because they forsook [the covenant of the LORD, the God of] their ancestors, [which he made with them when he brought them] out of the land of Egypt, [26 and wen]t [and served other gods, and worshiped them, gods they did not know, and which] he had not allotted to them. [27 Therefore the anger of the LORD burned against this land, to bring on it every curse that is written in this book. 28 The LORD rooted them out of] their [la]nd [in anger and in wrath and in great indignation, and cast them into another land, as it is this day]." ▲

---

139. 1QDeut[b] has an apparent scribal error.

140. Singular 4QDeut[c]. *lie* singular MT. *lie* plural SP. Plural LXX.

30

■ *Deuteronomy 30:9 speaks of the prosperity that God will bestow on his obedient people. Whereas the Masoretic Text refers to "the fruit of your cattle," and "the fruit of your ground," the order is reversed in 4QDeut^b, the Samaritan Pentateuch, and the Septuagint. The second sequence seems to lay greater emphasis on agriculture than on animal husbandry.*

[3 . . . then the LORD your God will restore you from captivity, and have compassion on you, and will return and gather you from all the peo]ples, [from] where [the LORD your God has scattered you. 4 If any of your outcasts are in the uttermost parts of heaven, from there the LORD your God will gather you, and from the]re he will fetch you; 5 and the [LORD your God] will bring you [into the land which your ancestors possessed, and you shall take possession of it; and he will do you good, and multiply you more than your ancestors. 6 And the LORD your God will circumcise] your heart, and the heart [of your descendants, so that you will love the LORD your God with all your heart and with all your soul, so that you may live. 7 And the LORD] your [God will put] all these curses [on your enemies, and on those who hate you and who persecuted you. 8 Then you shall again obey the voice of the LORD, and carry out] all his commandments which I [command you this day. 9 And the LORD your God will make you abundantly] prosperous [in all the work of your hands, in the fruit of your body, *and in the fruit of your ground, and in the fruit of*] your livestock.[141] For [the LORD] will again [rejoice over you for good, a]s he rejoiced [over your ancestors; 10 if you obey the voice of the LORD your God, by keeping] his commandments [and] his statutes which are *written*[142] [in this book of the law; if you] turn to the LORD your God with all [your] heart, [and with all your soul].

[11 For this commandment which I] command you today [is not too hard for you, neither] is *it*[143] far away *from you.*[144] [12 It is] not in hea[ven, that you should say, "Who shall go up for us to heaven and bring it to us, and make us hear it, that we may do it?" 13 Neither] is *it*[145] beyond the sea, that you should say, "Who shall cross over [the sea for us and bring it to us, and make us hear it, that we may do

---

Chapter 30. 4QDeut^b: 30:3–14; 4QpaleoDeut^r: 30:7–8(?) (or 21:8–9[?]); 4QDeut^k3: 30:16–18; 1QDeut^b: 30:19–20.

141. 4QDeut^b SP LXX. *and in the fruit of your cattle, and in the fruit of your ground* MT.

142. Plural 4QDeut^b. Singular MT SP.

143. Feminine 4QDeut^b SP. Masculine MT.

144. 4QDeut^b LXX. Not in MT SP.

145. Feminine 4QDeut^b SP. Masculine MT.

it?" 14 But the wor]d [is] very [near to you, in yo]ur [mouth] and in your heart *and in your hand,*[146] that you may car[ry it out].

■ *In the Masoretic Text and the Samaritan Pentateuch, Deuteronomy 30:14 describes the word of God as being in the mouth and heart of the Israelites. By including "and in your hand," 4QDeut^b and the Septuagint further emphasize that God's word is in the Israelites' possession and is to be carried out.*

[15 See, I have set before you today life and prosperity, death and adversity, 16 in that I command you this day to love the LORD your God, to walk in his ways, and to keep his commandments and his statutes and his ordinances, so that you may live and multiply, and so that the LORD your God may bless you in the land which] yo[u are about to possess].

[17 But if] your heart [turns away] and you will not lis[ten, but are drawn away to worship] other gods [and serve them, 18 I declare to you] today that [you shall] surely [perish; you shall not prolong your] days i[n the land, which you are crossing the Jordan to enter and possess. 19 I call heaven and earth to witness against you this day, that I have set before you life and death, blessing and curse]; there[fore choose life, so that you may live, you and your descendants, 20 loving the LORD your God, obeying his voice], and clinging to him. For [he is your life, and the length of your days, so that you may dwell in the land which the LORD swore] to give to [your ancestors, to Abraham], to Isaac, and to Jacob.

31 1 And Moses *finished speaking all*[147] [these] w[ords to all Israel. 2 And he said to them, "I am a hundred and twenty years old] today; I can no longer go out and [come in; and the LORD has said to me, 'You shall not cross over the Jordan.' 3 The LORD your God, he will] cross over before you; he will destroy [these nations before you, and you shall dispossess them; and Joshua shall cross over before you], as the LORD has spoken. 4 And [the LORD] will do [to them as he did to Sihon and to Og, the kings of the Amorites, and to their land, when he destroyed them]. 5 And the LORD will deliver them up before *you,*[148] [and you shall do to them in accordance with every commandment that I have commanded you. 6 Be strong and of good courage, do not be afraid or terrified because of them; for the] LORD [your] G[od, it is he who goes with you; he will not fail you, nor forsake you]."

---

146. 4QDeut^b LXX. Not in MT SP.

Chapter 31. 1QDeut^b: 31:1–10, 12–13; 4QDeut^h: 31:9–11; 4QDeut^b: 31:9–17, 24–30; 4QDeut^l: 31:12; 4QDeut^c: 31:16–19; 4QpaleoDeut^r: 31:29.

147. 1QDeut^b MT^mss LXX. *went and spoke* MT SP (cf. Deut 32:45).

148. Plural 1QDeut^b LXX. Singular MT SP.

[7 Then Moses summoned Joshua, and said to him in the sight of all Israel, "Be strong and of good courage, for you shall go with this people into the land] which [the LORD] has s[worn to their ancestors to give them; and you shall cause them to inherit it. 8 And the LORD, it is he who goes before you; he will] be with you, [he will not fail you, nor forsake you; do not be afraid or be discouraged]."

▪ *The Masoretic Text and the Samaritan Pentateuch describe God's law in Deuteronomy 31:9 as simply written down; they do not specify how this writing was done—whether inscribed on tablets, clay, or papyrus. But 4QDeut^h and the Septuagint are more specific, stating that the writing was done "in a book," perhaps reflecting the growing emphasis on books of the Law after the Jews returned from the Babylonian exile.*

[9 Then Moses wrote] this [law] in [a book,¹⁴⁹ and delivered it to the priests], the sons of Levi, who carried [the ark of the covenant of the LORD, and to all the elders of Israel. 10 And] Moses [commanded] th[em, saying, "At the end of every seven years, in the] set time of the year of [remission, during the feast of tabernacles, 11 when] all Israel [comes] t[o appear before the LORD your God in the place which] he shall choose, *you*¹⁵⁰ shall read [this law before all Israe]l [in their hearing. 12 Assemble the people, the me]n and the w[omen] and the children, and your foreigner [who is within your gates, so that they may hear, and may learn, and may fear] the LORD *their*¹⁵¹ [God], and be care[ful] to carry out all the words of [this] l[aw; 13 and so that their children, who have not known it, may hear and learn to fear the L]ORD your God [as long as you live in the land which you are crossing the Jordan to possess]."

14 Then [the LORD said to Moses, "Behold, your days are approaching when you must die; call Joshua, and present yourselves in the tent of meeting so that I may commission him." So Moses and Joshua went and presented themselves in the tent of meeting].

[15 Then the LORD appeared in the tent in a pillar of cloud, and the pillar of cl]oud [stood] *at*¹⁵² the door of the te[nt. 16 And the LORD said to Moses, "Behold, you shall sleep with your ancestors]; and this people will rise up, and prostitute themselves with the strange gods of the l[an]d, [where they go] to be among them, and *will forsake*¹⁵³ me, and *break*¹⁵⁴ my [covena]nt [which I have made with

---

149. 4QDeut^h LXX. Not in MT SP.

150. Plural 4QDeut^b LXX. Singular MT. *he shall read* SP.

151. 4QDeut^l MT^mss SP LXX^mss. *your* MT LXX.

152. 4QDeut^b. *over* MT SP LXX.

153. Plural 4QDeut^c SP LXX. Singular MT.

154. Plural 4QDeut^c SP LXX. Singular MT.

them. 17 Then my anger shall burn] against them in that day, and I will forsake you,[155] and I will hide my face [from them, and they shall be] devoured, and many evils and troubles shall c[ome on them]; so that *they will say*[156] [in] that [da]y, 'Have not these disasters come on us be[cause] *the* LORD [*my*] G[od[157] is not] a[mong us?' 18 And] I [will surely hide] my [face *from* hi[m[158] in] that [day] for all the evil which [they have] d[one, in that they have turned to other gods].

[19 "Now theref]ore write [*the wor*]*ds of*[159] [this] song for yourselves, [and teach it to the children of Israe]l; put *it*[160] in their mouths, so t[hat this song] may be [a witness] for me [against the Israelites]." ▲

[24 And when] Moses [had finished] writing the words of this law in a book, until they were finished, 25 Moses commanded [the Levites who carried the ark of] the covenant of the LORD, saying, 26 "Take *this*[161] book of the law and put it alongside [the ark of the covenant of the LORD] your [God], so that it may be there as a witness against you. 27 For I know your rebellion, and your [stub]born-ness; [behold, while I am still alive wit]h you this day, you have been rebellious against the LORD; so how much more after my death? 28 As[semble before me all the elders of] your tribes, [*and your elders*] *and your judges*[162] and your officers, so that I may speak these [words] i[n their ears], and call [hea]ven and earth [to wit-ness against them]. 29 For I know that after [my] de[ath] you will [utterly] cor-rupt yourselves, [and turn aside from] t[he w]ay which I have commanded [yo]u; and [disaster] will b[efall you in the da]ys [to come]; because you will do [e]vil in [the sig]ht of the LORD, provoking him to anger [through the work of your hands]."

[30 Then Moses spoke in the ears of all the assembl]y of Israe[l] the words of this song, u[ntil they were finished].

32 [1 Give ear, O heavens], and I will speak; and let the earth hear [the] wo[rds of my mouth. 2 May my te]ach[ing] drop as the rain]; my speech

---

155. 4QDeut[c]. *them* MT SP LXX.

156. 4QDeut[c] SP LXX. *he will say* MT.

157. 4QDeut[c] LXX. *my God* 4QDeut[corr] ("my God" written above the line, probably in the same hand) MT SP.

158. 4QDeut[c]. *from them* SP LXX. Not in MT.

159. 4QDeut[c] LXX. Not in MT SP.

160. Masculine 4QDeut[c]. Feminine MT SP.

161. Feminine 4QDeut[b]. Masculine MT SP.

162. 4QDeut[b] LXX. Not in MT SP.

Chapter 32. 4QDeut[b]: 32:1–3; 4QDeut[c]: 32:3; 4QpaleoDeut[r]: 32:6–8, 10–11, 13–14, 22(?) (or 28:23[?] or 10:6[?]), 33–35; 4QDeut[j]: 32:7–8; 4QDeut[q]: 32:9–10(?), 37–43; 4QDeut[k1]: 32:17–18, 22–23, 25–27; 1QDeut[b]: 32:17–29.

[condense like the de]w, [like gentle rain] on te[nder grass, and like showers on new growth. 3 For I will proclaim the name of the LORD]; ascrib[e] greatness to [our God].▲

▮ *In the famous poem found in Deuteronomy 32, verse 8 tells us that God set the bounds of the peoples according to a certain number. Following the Masoretic Text and the Samaritan Pentateuch, most modern Bibles describe this as the number of the "children of Israel." 4QDeutᵍ, however, specifies it as the number of the "children of God," apparently denoting the divine beings who would serve as protectors for various nations. See also vs. 43.*

[6 Is this how you repay the LORD, O foolish and unwise people?] Is [he] not [your father who bought you? He has made you and established you. 7 Remember the days of old], consider [the years of many generations; ask your father, and he will show you]; your elders, a[nd they will tell you]. 8 When [the Most High] gave [to the nations] their inherit[ance, when] he separated [humankind, he set the bounds of the peoples according to the number of] the children of *God*.¹⁶³ [9 For the LORD's portion is his people; Jacob is the lot of] his [inher]itance.

[10 He found him in a desert land, and in a howling wildernes]s [waste]; he shielded [him, he cared for him, he guarded him as the apple] of his eye. 11 As an eagle [that stirs up her nest, that hovers over her young, that spreads her wings, he took them and carried them on his pinions. 12 The LORD alone guided him; no foreign god was with him. 13 He made him ride on the high places of the] earth, [and he ate the increase of the field; and he made him suck honey from the ro]ck, and oil [from the flinty rock; 14 curds from the herd, and milk from the] flock, w[ith f]at of l[a]mbs, and ram[s, herds of Bashan and goats, wi]th the finest of the whea[t—and from the blood of the grape you drank wine].▲

[17 They sacrificed to] demons, [which were not God, to gods they did not know, to new gods that] had come in re[cently, which] your ancestors] had not feared. 18 Of the Rock that bore you, you were unmindful, and you] for[got the God who gave you birth. 19 And the LORD saw it, and rejected them, because of the provocati]on of his sons and his daughters. [20 And he said, "I will hide my face from them, I will see what their end shall be; for they are a very perverse generation, childr]en in whom there is no faithfulness. [21 They have moved me to jealousy with what is no] God; [they have provoked me to anger with their idols; and I will move them to jealousy with those that are not a people; I will provoke them to anger with a fooli]sh [nation. 22 For a fi]re is kindled by my anger, [and burns to the lowest Sheol, and devours the earth with] its [incre]ase, and sets on fire [the foundations of the mountains].

---

163. 4QDeutᵍ LXX. *Israel* MT SP.

[23 "I will heap disasters on them; I will spend] my arrows [on them. 24 They shall be wasted with hunger, and devo]ured with burning heat [and bitter destruction; and I will send against them the fangs off wild beasts, wi]th the ve[nom of things crawling in the dust. 25 Outside the sword shall bereave, and in the cha]mbers [terror; it shall destroy both young man and virgin, the] nursing child and the man [with] gray hairs. 26 I said, ['I will scatter them afar, I will] make [the remembrance of them] cease from [humankind'; 27 but] I feared [the provo]cation of the enemy, for [their adversaries might misunderstand and say, 'Our hand is exalted, and] the *Lord*[164] [has] not [done all this].' "

[28 For they are a nation void of sense, and there is no understanding in them. 29 If only they were wise, they would] under[stand this, they would consider their end]!▲

33 Their wine [is the poison of serpents], and [the cruel] ve[nom of asps].

[34 Is not this laid up in store with me, sealed up among my treasures? 35 Vengeance] is mine, [and recompense, for the time when their foot shall slip; for the day of their calamity is at hand, and what is about to come on them comes swiftly].

[36 Indeed the LORD will vindicate his people and have compassion on his servants, when he sees their strength is gone and there is no one left, neither bond nor free. 37 And] *the LORD*[165] [will s]ay, ["Where are their gods], *the*[166] r[oc]k [in] *which*[167] [they took refuge; 38 who ate the] *fa*[*t*]*s*[168] of [their] sacrifice[s, and drank the] wine [of their drink offerings? Let them rise up and] help you, [let them be your protection]."

■ *Deuteronomy 32:43 is an unusual verse in view of its contents. As the list of variant readings shows, 4QDeut^q—supported by the Septuagint—differs markedly from the Masoretic Text and the Samaritan Pentateuch. For example, in the Qumran scroll it is "the heavens" which rejoice, not the nations; and God will avenge the blood of "his* sons," *not "his* servants." *Moreover, the mention of gods "bowing down to God" and "recompensing those who hate him" is absent from the Masoretic Text and the Samaritan Pentateuch. This verse provides a striking example of the very different readings that sometimes appear in the Dead Sea Scrolls.*

[39 See now] that I, ev[en I, am he, and there is no god with me; I kill and] I [make alive; I wound and I heal; and there is no one who] can del[iver from my

164. 1QDeut[b]. *LORD* MT SP.

165. 4QDeut[q] LXX. Not in MT SP.

166. 4QDeut[q]. Not in MT SP.

167. 4QDeut[q] LXX. Not in MT SP.

168. Plural 4QDeut[q]. Singular MT SP LXX.

hand. 40 For I] lift up my [han]d to [heaven, and say, "As] I [live forever, 41 i]f I whet [my] g[litterin]g swo[rd, and my] hand [takes hold] of judgment, I will render venge[ance] to my enemies, [and] will recompense [those who hat]e me. [42 I will make] my arrows [drunk] with blood, [and my sword shall de]vour flesh— [with the blood of the slain and] the captives, *and*[169] from the head of the lo[ng-haired le]aders of the enemy. 43 Rejoice, O *heavens, together with him;*[170] *and bow down to him all you gods,*[171] for he will avenge the blood of *his sons,*[172] and will render vengeance to his enemies, *and will recompense those who hate him,*[173] and *will* atone[174] *for the land of his people."*[175] ▲

33 [1 And this is the] blessing, [with] whi[ch] Moses [the man of God ble]ssed [the Israelites before his death. 2 And he said]:

[The LORD] came from Sinai, [and rose from Seir upon them; he shone forth from Mount Paran, and came] from the ten thousand[s of holy ones; at his right hand was a fiery law for them. 3 Indeed, he loves his people; all his holy ones are in your hand; and they] marched [at your feet; everyone received direction from him. 4 Moses charged us with a law, an inheritance for the assembly of Jacob]. 5 And he was [king in Jeshurun, when the leaders of the people were gathered, all the tribes of Israel together].

6 Let Reu[ben] live, [and not die out; nor let his numbers be few. 7 And this is the blessing of Judah: and he said, "Listen, O L]ORD, *to*[176] the voice [of Judah, and bring him in to his people. With his hands he contends for himself]; and you shall be *for him*[177] [a help against his enemies." 8 And of Levi he said: "Your Thummim and your Urim are with your godly one, whom you proved at Massah, with whom you contended at the waters of Meribah; 9 who said of his father and of his mother, 'I have not seen him'; neither did he recognize his brothers or acknowledge his own children. For they have observed your word and have kept your covenant. 10 They shall teach Jacob your ordinances, and Israel your law. They shall put incense before you, and whole burnt offering on your altar.

---

169. 4QDeut^q SP^ms LXX^mss. Not in MT SP LXX.

170. 4QDeut^q LXX. *O nations, with his people* MT SP.

171. 4QDeut^q LXX (*. . . you sons of God*). Not in MT SP.

172. 4QDeut^q LXX. *his servants* MT SP.

173. 4QDeut^q LXX. Not in MT SP.

174. Imperfect verb 4QDeut^q. Perfect consecutive verb MT SP.

175. 4QDeut^q SP LXX. *his land, for his people* MT.

Chapter 33. 4QDeut^l: 33:1–2; 4QpaleoDeut^r: 33:2–8, 29; 4QDeut^h: 33:8–22; 1QDeut^b: 33:12–19, 21–24; MasDeut: 33:17–21.

176. 4QpaleoDeut^r. Not in MT SP.

177. 4QpaleoDeut^r. Not in MT SP LXX.

11 Bless, O Lord, his substance, and accept the work of his hands; crush the loins of those who rise up against him, and of those who hate him so that they do not rise again."

12 Of Benjamin he said: "The beloved of the Lord shall dwell in safety by him. He covers him all the day long, and he dwells between his shoulders." 13 And of Joseph he said: "Blessed by the Lord be his land, for the precious things of heaven, for the dew, and for the deep that lies beneath, 14 and for the precious things of the fruits of the sun, and for the precious things of the growth of the months, 15 and for the finest produce of the ancient mountains, and for the precious things of the everlasting hills, 16 and for the precious things of the earth and its fullness, and the favor of him who dwelt in the burning bush. Let the blessing come on the head of Joseph, and on the crown of the head of him who was separate from his brothers. 17 The firstborn of his herd—majesty is his! His horns are the horns of the wild ox. With them he shall push the peoples, all of them, to the ends of the earth. And they are the ten thousands of Ephraim, and they are the thousands of Manasseh."

18 And of Zebulun he said: "Rejoice, Zebulun, in your going out; and, Issachar, in your tents. 19 They shall call the peoples to their mountain; there they shall offer sacrifices of righteousness. For they shall suck the abundance of the seas, and the hidden treasures of the sand." 20 And of Gad he said: "Blessed is he who enlarges Gad; he lives like a lion, and tears the arm and the crown of the head. 21 He chose the best part for himself, for there a commander's portion was reserved; when he came to the heads of the people, he executed the righteousness of the Lord and his ordinances with Israel." 22 And of Dan he said: "Dan is a lion's whelp that leaps out from Bashan." 23 And of Naphtali he said: "O Naphtali, satisfied with favor, and full with the blessing of the Lord, possess the west and the south." 24 And of Asher he said: "Blessed be Asher with children; let him be acceptable to his brothers, and let him dip his foot in oil]." ▲

[29 Happy are you, O Israel; who is like you, a people saved by the Lord, the shield of your help, and the sword of] your [tr]iumph! [Your[178] enemies] shall subm[it themselves to you; and you shall tread on their high places].

34 [1 And Moses went up from the plains of Moab to Mount Nebo, to the top of Pisgah, which is opposit]e Jerich[o. And the Lord showed him all the land: Gilead as far as Dan, 2 and all Naphtali, and the land of Ephraim and Manasseh, and all the land of Judah, to the western sea, 3 and the Negev, and the plain of the valley of Jericho the city of palm trees, to Zoar. 4 And the Lord said to him, "This is the land which I swore to Abraham, to Isaac, and to Jacob, saying,

---

178. 4QpaleoDeut^r. *And your* MT SP LXX.

Chapter 34. 4QpaleoDeut^r: 34:1; MasDeut: 34:2–6; 4QDeut^l: 34:4–6, 8(?).

'I will give it to your descendants']; I have allowed you to se[e it with your eyes, but you shall not cross over there]."

> ▨ *In Deuteronomy 34:6 we read that Moses was buried in a valley in the land of Moab. According to the Masoretic Text and the Samaritan Pentateuch, it was he who buried Moses, which emphasizes God's role in Moses' being laid to rest. But 4QDeut^l, some manuscripts of the Samaritan Pentateuch, and the Septuagint offer a very different picture by stating that they—the Israelites themselves—buried their great leader.*

[5 So] Moses [the servant of the LORD died there in the land of Moab, according to the word of the LORD. 6 And] *they*[179] buried him [in the valley in the land of Moab opposite Beth-peor; but no one knows of his burial place to this day. 7 Moses was a hundred and twenty years old when he died, yet his sight was unimpaired and his strength was not gone. 8 And the Isra]el[ites wept] for [Moses in the plains of Moab for thirty days; then the days of weeping in the mourning for Moses were ended]. ▲

---

179. 4QDeut^l SP^mss LXX. *he* MasDeut MT SP.

JUBILEES

The book of Jubilees is a fascinating ancient Jewish work that is very unfamiliar to most modern readers. Containing an account of things revealed to Moses during his forty days on Mount Sinai (Exod 24:18), Jubilees presents an overview of the history of humankind and of God's chosen people until Moses' time, and is revealed to him by an angel. This book, which is usually categorized as "rewritten Bible," may be divided into seven sections:

- An Introduction (chap. 1), in which God describes the apostasy of his people and their future restoration.
- A Primeval History (chaps. 2–4), dealing with the creation and Adam.
- Stories about Noah (chaps. 5–10).
- Stories about Abraham (chaps. 11–23:8).
- Thoughts on Abraham's death (chaps. 23:9–32).
- Stories about Jacob and his family (chaps. 24–45).
- Stories about Moses (chaps. 46–50).

The author follows the general outline of Genesis and the early part of Exodus, but in the process of retelling the biblical narratives, he at times omits, condenses, expands, supplements, or alters the biblical accounts. For example, the long account of the plagues in Exodus 7–10 receives only a few verses in Jubilees (48:4–11), and Reuben's apparent incest (Gen 35:22) is extensively explained in Jubilees 33:2–20.

Before the discovery of the Dead Sea Scrolls, Jubilees was known to scholars in Greek, Syriac, Latin, and Ethiopic translations, and was part of the most ancient canon of the Ethiopic church. The discovery of a large number of Jubilees manuscripts at Qumran was surprising to many, and has aroused considerable interest. Approximately fifteen Jubilees scrolls were found in five caves (two each in Caves

1 and 2,[a] one in Cave 3,[b] nine in Cave 4,[c] and one in Cave 11[d]). The actual total of these manuscripts is not certain, and may be as low as thirteen or as high as sixteen.[e] Whatever the precise number, all of them were written in Hebrew, and one on papyrus.

Is the form of Jubilees found in the Scrolls similar to the one that is preserved in the Ethiopic version?[f] On comparing the Judaean Desert fragments with the Ethiopic text, we may conclude that the Hebrew fragments demonstrate that the ancient translators of Jubilees took great care to render a mostly literal version, although not in every case.

To judge from both the large number of copies and other works related to it that were yielded by the caves,[g] Jubilees was extensively used at Qumran. As an influential pre-Qumranic writing, composed in the first third of the second century BCE, the book is frequently compared by scholars to 1 Enoch. It has been suggested that Qumran scribes and readers gradually lost interest in compositions attributed to Enoch, and that Jubilees became increasingly important to the Qumran community during their later history.

Jubilees is especially significant in view of its relationship to several of the sectarian texts from Qumran. Prominent themes include the 364-day calendar, its division of the course of history into 94-year jubilee periods, and its practice of dating covenants to the third month (especially the fifteenth day), which may have inspired the practice at Qumran of renewing the covenant annually on the Festival of Weeks.

Several factors lead to the conclusion that Jubilees was viewed and used as Scripture by the Qumran community. First, a work called 4QText with a Citation of Jubilees (4Q228) seems to denote Jubilees by its Hebrew title "The Divisions of the Times,"[h] and later introduces the first word of the title by a citation formula: "For thus it is written in the Divisions [of the Times]."[i] Second, Jubilees

---

a. 1QJub[a], 1QJub[b], 2QJub[a], 2QJub[b].　**b.** 3QJub.　**c.** 4QTanḥuma frgs.19–21, 4QJub[a], pap4QJub[b](?), 4QJub[c], 4QJub[d], 4QJub[e], 4QJub[f], 4QJub[g], pap4QJub[h].　**d.** 11QJub.
e. 1QJub[a] and 1QJub[b] may belong to the same scroll, the Cave 3 fragments may represent more than one manuscript, and the precise identification of pap4QJub[b](?) is uncertain.
f. The Ethiopic is the most complete translation.　**g.** For example, 4QPseudo-Jubilees[a, b, c] (4Q225–27) and 4QText with a Citation of Jubilees (4Q228).　**h.** Frg. 1 i 1.　**i.** Frg. 1 i 9.

claims to be divine revelation in that its contents are given by an angel of God[j] and have been inscribed on heavenly tablets.[k] Third, the fact that Jubilees is represented by such a large number of manuscripts shows that it was extensively used at Qumran, which points to its popularity and most likely its authoritative status. Jubilees is found in about fifteen scrolls; of all the biblical books at Qumran, only the Psalms, Deuteronomy, Isaiah, Exodus, and Genesis (in descending order) are represented by more manuscripts. Fourth, Jubilees is quoted in some of the nonbiblical scrolls, which indicates its authoritative status to the authors of such texts. For example, the *Damascus Document* (CD) 16:2–4 cites Jubilees as the source of information concerning the times when Israel would be blind to the law of Moses, while CD 10:7–10 may well be based on Jubilees 23:11, which refers to people's loss of knowledge in their old age.

---

j. Jub 1:26-29; 2:1.   **k.** Jub 3:10, 31.

PROPHETS

JOSHUA

Only two scrolls of the book of Joshua were recovered in the Judean Desert, but one of them makes quite an impact, and several other previously unknown parabiblical works related to Joshua that were found among the scrolls have enriched our knowledge of the ancient world.

4QJosh[a] is the oldest witness to the text of Joshua in any language, dating roughly to 100 BCE, and it provides a dramatic example of the light that the scrolls shed on the Bible. It takes us back to an earlier stage in the development of the biblical text and thus helps solve a problem that has long puzzled readers.

In the traditional narrative, Joshua leads the people across the Jordan, fights the battle for Jericho, mounts another victory over the city Ai, and then eventually goes twenty miles north to Shechem to build an altar on Mount Ebal, opposite Mount Gerizim, where the Samaritans much later were to center their religion. He then immediately marches back down south, abandoning the newly built altar and leaving it exposed in enemy territory.

On a single fragment, 4QJosh[a] contains the end of the altar-building episode, followed by the beginning of chapter 5. This means that Joshua would have constructed the first altar in the Promised Land immediately after crossing the Jordan and before beginning any battles of conquest. This is, of course, what would be expected—that in thanksgiving for the fulfillment of the promise of the land, and in order to sanctify the land to the Lord, Joshua would have immediately erected an altar there at Gilgal. Gilgal continued to be known as an important place for worship,[a] whereas Mount Ebal is never referred to again as a worship site for Israel.

Two further pieces of evidence clinch the significance of this scroll's sequence of events. First, the historian Josephus, retelling the biblical story in the first century CE, also appears to have had a biblical text like 4QJosh[a]. He describes

---

a. Cf. 1 Sam 10:8; 11:14–15.

Joshua's building of an altar immediately after crossing the Jordan,[b] while not mentioning either the journey to Mount Ebal or an altar at the point where the Masoretic Text places it.[c] Though he does eventually describe an altar at Shechem, it is not until noticeably later in the narrative,[d] and certainly the tradition of Joshua's covenant ceremony at Shechem after the conquest would have been widely known.[e]

Second, both the Samaritan Pentateuch and the Old Latin version have the reading "on Mount Gerizim" in the text at Deuteronomy 27:4, a passage in which Moses commands the building of this altar. What this undoubtedly shows is that "on Mount Ebal" in the Masoretic and Greek tradition is a later Jewish polemical change from the unacceptable Samaritan claim that the first altar was built "on Mount Gerizim." Thus there was a three-stage history in the development of this command-fulfillment passage. First, the altar was simply to be built at an unspecified place—wherever the people crossed the Jordan. Second, northerners, perhaps the Samaritans, specified the site of the first altar as "on Mount Gerizim." Finally, Jewish scribes discounted that claim by changing "Mount Gerizim" anomalously to the otherwise insignificant "Mount Ebal."

This does not mean that the text of 4QJosh[a] is always superior. For example, at 7:14 it drops out almost a whole line, skipping from one phrase to the next occurrence of that similar phrase, thus losing the intervening text.

The text of Joshua was already known to have existed in two successive variant literary editions. As in the case of Jeremiah, the Greek text is an earlier, shorter edition of the book that was later developed into a fuller edition appearing in the Masoretic Text. 4QJosh[a] now presents yet an earlier version of the text—one that is shorter in spots. For example, at 8:3–14 the space available on the original scroll suggests that verses 12–13 were not yet in the text. The Greek text presents a somewhat longer text than 4QJosh[a], and the Masoretic Text is still longer. The individual textual variants displayed by both 4QJosh[a] and the second scroll, 4QJosh[b], move back and forth, agreeing sometimes with the Greek text, sometimes with the Masoretic Text, and at other points showing their own distinctive wording.

---

b. *Jewish Antiquities* 5.16–20.   **c.** *Jewish Antiquities* 5.45–49.   **d.** *Jewish Antiquities* 5.68–69.
e. Cf. Josh 24:1.

2 "... 11 [When we heard it, our hearts melted,] n[o] courage remained in any
one [because of you. For it is the LORD your God who is God in the heavens
above and on earth below." 12 *And she sai*]d, "*Swear*[1] [to me by the LORD, since I
have been loyal to you, that you also will be loyal to my family . . .]."▲

3

■ *The scribe of 4Q Josh[b] here provides an example of intentional correction away from
what we know as the traditional text toward what he thought was a better version.
The scribe had finished verse 15 with "at the time of the harvest" and had begun
verse 16. Subsequently, he inserted the word "wheat" above the line, thus modifying
the line that appears in the Masoretic Text. The Greek text reflects the revision.*

15 [When those who carried the ark reached the Jordan, and the feet of the
priests] who carried the ark dipped in [the edge of the wat]er[—now the Jordan
overflows all its banks] *at*[2] the time of the *wheat*[3] harvest—16 the waters which
came down from [upstream] stood still [and rose up in one heap, a] long [way
off], *at Adam,*[4] the city that is beside Za[rethan. The water which flowed down to
the sea of the Arabah], the Salt [S]ea, was entirely cut of[f, and the people crossed
opposite Jericho. 17 The priests who carried the ark of the cove]nant of the LORD
[stood] on [dry ground in the middle of the Jordan], . . . *Josh*[ua][5]. . . .▲

4

■ *Just as this earlier version agrees with the Greek text in not having "from here"
(added by the Masoretic Text in verse 3), so too the space available in the missing part
of the fragment suggests that it agrees with the Septuagint in not having other small
additions made in the Masoretic Text: "twelve men" in verse 2, and in verse 3 "saying" and "from the place where the priests' feet are standing."*

1 [When the whole nation had] fin[ished crossing the Jordan, the LORD said]
to Josh[ua, 2 "From the people select one from each tribe 3 and give them this

---

Chapter 2. 4QJosh[b]: 2:11–12.

  1. 4QJosh[b]. *"And now, swear* MT LXX.

Chapter 3. 4QJosh[b]: 3:15–17.

  2. 4QJosh[b]. *throughout* MT. *about* LXX.

  3. 4QJosh[b] (with *wheat* written in above the line) LXX. MT lacks *wheat*.

  4. The text of 4QJosh[b] is disturbed at this point, as possibly also MT.

  5. 4QJosh[b] adds *Joshua* above the next line, at which the fragment breaks off; *Joshua* is not
in MT LXX. It could fit as *until* Joshua *and the whole nation finished crossing.*

Chapter 4. 4QJosh[b]: 4:1–3. 4QJosh[a]: 4 [MT 8]: 34–45.

command: Pick up] for yourselves [twelve stones] *from the middle of the* [*Jordan,*[6] and carry them over wi]th you, and set t[hem down in the place where you camp tonight]." ▲

34 [After this he read all the words of the law, the blessing and the curse, just as it is written in the book of] the [l]aw. 35 There was not a word of *all*[7] Moses commanded [Jo]shua[8] which Joshua did not read before all [. . .] *the Jorda[n,*[9] and] the women and children, and the stra[ngers] living among them.

> ■ *The passage above, which occurs at the end of chapter 8 in the Masoretic Text but after 9:2 in the Greek text, appears in 4QJosh^a before the beginning of chapter 5. It flows into the following passage, the different sequence in the Masoretic Text requiring a different introductory sentence. The scroll apparently displays the original order, with the Masoretic and Greek texts secondarily rearranged (see the introduction to Joshua).*

5 X *After they had removed* [*their feet from the Jordan, . . .*] *the book of the law. After that, the ark-bearers*[10] [. . . . 5:2 At t]hat [time] the LORD said to Josh[ua, "Ma]k[e yourself flint knives, and again circumcise the children of *Israel*."[11] 3 So Jo]shua [made flint] kn[ives] for [himself, and circumcised the children of Israel at the hill of the foreskins. 4 And this is the reason why Joshua had them circumcised: a]ll [the people who had come out of Egypt, all the males of military age, had died in the desert along the way, after leaving] E[g]ypt. 5 F[or all the people who had come out had been circumcised, but those born in the desert on the way, after leav]ing E[gypt, had not been circumcised. 6 For the Israelites journeyed forty years in the desert, until the whole nation, that is, the m]en of mili[tary age, who had come out of Egypt, died, because they did not obey the LORD—those to whom the LORD swore that *they would n*]*ot see*[12] [the land which the LORD had sworn to their ancestors that he would give us, a land flowing with milk and honey. 7 So th]eir [sons, whom he] r[aised up in their place, Joshua circumcised; they had been uncircumcised, because they had not circumcised them along the way.]

---

6. 4QJosh^b LXX. *from here, from the middle of the Jordan* MT. MT may be a conflation of two traditions: *twelve stones from here* and *twelve stones from the middle of the Jordan.*

7. 4QJosh^a. *all that* MT LXX.

8. 4QJosh^a LXX. Not in MT.

9. 4QJosh^a has space for about two words before *the Jordan.* Not in MT LXX.

Chapter 5. 4QJosh^a: 5:X, 2–7.

10. 4QJosh^a. MT LXX lack this verse and have the secondary traditional wording of 5:1 in its place.

11. 4QJosh^a LXX. *Israel a second time* MT. The length of the line suggests that 4QJosh^a agrees with LXX against MT in not adding *a second time.*

12. 4QJosh^a LXX. *he would not let them see* MT.

6 5 [When a long blast is sounded on the ram's horn, when you hear the sound of the trumpet, all the people will give a] loud [shout]. Then [the city] wa[ll] will colla[pse], and the peo[ple] will *advance,*[13] [ea]ch one [strai]ght ahead. 6 [So] Joshua son of Nun [called] the [priests and said] t[o them], "Take up [the ark of the covenant], and have seven priests car[ry seven ra]ms' [horns] ahead of [the ark of the LORD." 7 Then] *Joshua*[14] [said] to the people, ["Go forward, march around the city, and let the armed guard march ahead of the ark of the LORD." 8 After] J[oshua had spok]en [to the people, the seven priests carrying the seve]n [rams'] hor[ns advanced before the LORD, blowing the trumpet]s, and the ark of the [co]venant of the L[OR]D went [after them. 9 The armed guard went ahead of the priests who were blowing] the tru[m]pets, and the rea[r gua]rd went [after the ark, while they sounded the trumpets. 10 Jo]shua [commanded the people] as foll[ows: Do not shout, do not let your voices be heard, do not let a word come out of your mouth,] until the t[ime I tell you, Shout! Then you shall shout]. ▲

7 12 ["So the Israelites cannot stand before their enemies; they turn their backs t]o [their] enemi[es], *not their faces,*[15] because they have been condemned to destruction. *Now*[16] I will no longer be [with you, un]less you destroy whatever you have that has been devoted to destruction. 13 Get up, sanctify the people, and say, [Sanctify yourselves] for tomorrow. For thus says the LORD, the God of Israel: There is a devoted thing in *your*[17] midst, [Israel]. You will [not] be able to [stan]d before *your*[18] enemies, until you remove the devoted thing from among you. 14 In the morning, [you shall come forward] by tribe[s. The]n the tribe the LORD selects *shall come forward*[19] [by house]holds. [Then the household which the LORD selects] shall come forward individually. 15 Then the one *among them*[20] who is selected shall be destroyed [by fire, he and all that he has, because he vi]olated the [co]venant of the LORD, *because*[21] he committed [a disgrace in Israel]."

Chapter 6. 4QJosh[a]: 6:5–10.

13. Singular 4QJosh[a] LXX. Plural MT.

14. 4QJosh[a]. *he* MT LXX.

Chapter 7. 4QJosh[a]: 7:12–17.

15. 4QJosh[a]. Not in MT LXX.

16. 4QJosh[a]. Not in MT LXX.

17. Plural 4QJosh[a] LXX. Singular MT.

18. Plural 4QJosh[a] LXX. Singular MT.

19. 4QJosh[a]. MT LXX have an additional stage by clans, which 4QJosh[a] skips. Following *shall come forward,* MT LXX correctly have *by clans. Then the clan which the LORD selects shall come forward (by households).*

20. 4QJosh[a]. *with the devoted thing* MT LXX[mss]. Not in LXX.

21. 4QJosh[a]. *and because* MT LXX.

16 [Early in the morning, Joshua had Israel come forward by tr]ibes; and he selected [the tribe of Judah. 17 He had the clans of Judah] come forward, [and he
selected the] cla[n of the Zerahites. He had the clan of] the Ze[rahites come forward individually, and Zabdi was selected].▲

8 3 [So] Joshua and the whole army [rose up and marched on Ai. Joshua chose
thirty thousand men], valiant warriors, and he sen[t] them out [at night,
4 giving them these orders: Listen closely. You are going to set an ambush] against
the city from be[hind. Do not go too far from it, and all of you be on the alert.]
5 I and all [the troops with me will approach the city. Then, when they come
out against us like] be[fore, we will run away from them. 6 They will come out
a]fter us un[til we have drawn them away from the city, for they will think, They
are running away from us like before. While we are running from them, 7 you
rise up from the ambush and take possession of] the ci[ty. 8 . . . set the cit]y on
fi[re. . . .]

9 [. . .] they [wen]t [. . .] 10 [. . . *the*] elders[22] [. . .] 11 [. . .] and *returned*
[. . .[23] in front of] the [city. . . . 14[24] So,] when [the king of Ai] saw it,
[. . . r]ushe[d . . . to m]eet *them*[25] [. . .].[26] ▲

> ■ *4QJosh*ᵃ*—to judge from the relative positions of the extant words in 8:8–14—had*
> *a shorter text even than the Greek, which itself is shorter than the Masoretic Text. At*
> *the bottom of the fragment a later scribe, using much larger letters, added some words*
> *from verse 18: "[Extend the javelin in] your hand toward Ai."*

10 3 [Then Adoni-]zedek king of [Jerusalem sent a message to Hoham king
of Hebron, Piram king of Jarmuth, Japhia] king of Lachish, and De[bir]
ki[n]g of Eglon: 4 Come up to me and h[elp me defeat Gibeon, because] it has
made peace with [Jo]shua and *Israel*.[27] 5 So [the five kings of the Amorites—the
king of Jerusalem, the king of Hebron, the ki]n[g of Jarmuth, the ki]n[g of]
Lach[ish, and the king of Eglon—with all their armies,] joined forces and
march[ed on Gibeon, encamped there, and waged war against it].▲

8 [The Lor]d [said t]o [Joshua, "Do not fear them,] for I have delivered

---

Chapter 8. 4QJoshᵃ: 8:3–11, 14, 18(?). For 8:34–35, see above, at the end of chapter 4.

22. 4QJoshᵃ LXX. *the elders of Israel* MT.

23. 4QJoshᵃ. *went up and approached and arrived* MT LXX.

24. 4QJoshᵃ lacks space for vss 12–13. See the Joshua introduction.

25. 4QJoshᵃ LXX. *to meet Israel* MT.

26. 4QJoshᵃ. In the following line, a later scribe added: [. . . *in*] *your hand toward Ai.* This
wording reflects that of vs 18 in MT: *Then the Lord said to Joshua, Extend the javelin in your
hand toward Ai.*

Chapter 10. 4QJoshᵃ: 10:3–5, 8–11.

27. 4QJoshᵃ. *the Israelites* MT LXX.

[them] into your hands. [Not one of them will be able to stand] before you."
9 [Joshua] came [on them suddenly, *having*] mar[*ched*][28] the whole night [from
Gilgal. 10 The L]ORD [threw them into a panic] befor[e] Israel, who [inflicted a
crushing defeat on them at Gibeon and pursued them on the road up to Beth-
horon, and attacked them all the way to Azekah and] Makkedah. 11 Then, [as]
they [were fl]eeing [from Israel, while they were going down from Beth-horon],
the LORD cast *stone*[*s*][29] from the sk[y] on them [all the way to Azekah, and they
died. More of them died] from the hailstones than the [Israelites] killed [with the
sword].▲

17 1 [This was the lot for the tribe of Manasseh—he was the first]born of
Jose[ph. Because Machir, firstborn of Manasseh and father of Gilead, was
a warrior], he was assigned [G]ilead [and Bashan. 2 Then portions were assigned
to the rest of the descendants of Manasseh according to their clans: to the descendants of Ab]iezer, H[elek, Asriel, Shechem, Hepher, and Shemida]. These were
the [male] children of M[anasseh son of Joseph by their clans. 3 But Zelophehad,
son of Hepher, son of Gilead], son of [Machir, son of Manasseh, had no sons,
only daughters. These are the name]s of his daughters: M[ahlah and Noah,
Hoglah, Milcah, and Tirzah. 4 They presented themselves to Eleazar] the priest
and to Jo[shua son of Nun and to the leaders, saying, "The LORD himself commanded Moses to give us an in]heritance [a]mong [our brothers." So, according
to the word of the LORD, he gave them an inheritance among their father's brothers.]▲

11 [Within Issachar and Asher, Manasseh had Beth-shean and its towns,] the
in[hab]itants of E[*n*]-*Dor*[30] and [its] t[owns, Ibleam and its towns, the inhabitants
of *Do*]*r* and its towns, the inhabitant[s of Taa]nach [and its towns, and the inhabitants of Megiddo] and [its] towns—th[r]ee heights. 12 [But the Manassites could
not drive out the inhabitants of tho]se cities, and the Canaa[nites] were determined to [live in that region. 13 La]ter, when the Israelites grew stronger, they
subjected the Cana[anites to forced labor but did not completely] drive them out.
14 [The Jo]seph[ites spoke] to J[o]shua, saying, "W[h]y have you given [us an
in]heritan[ce of only one lot and one district]? We are a numerous people, which
the LORD *has thus blessed.*"[31] 15 [J]oshua [answered them, "If you are a numerous
people, g]o up [to the] forest [and clear land for yourselves there in the land of
the] Pe[rizzites and Rephaim, insofar as] the hill [country of] E[phraim is too
small] for you."▲

---

28. 4QJosh[a]. MT uses a different but synonymous verb for *having marched*.

29. 4QJosh[a]. *huge stones* MT.

Chapter 17. 4QJosh[b]: 17:1–4, 11–15.

30. 4QJosh[b]. In MT, *En-Dor* follows *Dor*.

31. 4QJosh[b]. *has blessed this much* MT.

JUDGES

The book of Judges is well known today—if not by name, certainly by its famous characters: Gideon and his fleece, Jephthah's unfortunate daughter, and Samson and Delilah. The Qumran community was, however, evidently more interested in the weightier matters of law and the poetic praise of the Psalms than in the narratives of the "historical books." The sparse pattern begun in Joshua (only two scrolls) continues to Chronicles (one scroll!).

Only three manuscripts of the book of Judges survived at Qumran, but they confirm the patterns of the early biblical text provided by other biblical manuscripts. 4QJudgᵃ reveals that this earlier text is shorter than all other extant Hebrew and Greek witnesses, because it does not yet include a theological passage (Judg 6:7–10) inserted into the later versions.

4QJudgᵇ may also have had a shorter text (see 21:18), although the evidence for the possibly missing text is no longer preserved on the fragments but is instead deduced from the reconstruction of the space available on the original manuscript.

6 2 [The power of Midian was strong over Israel. Because of Midian, the Israelites made themselves the hiding places that are] in the [moun]tains, [the] caves and [the strongholds. 3 Whenever Israel had sown its crops, the Midianites would come up, or the Amalekites] or other people from the *east*.[1] 4 They encamped again[st] them and destroyed [the land's produce as far as Gaza. They left no]thing living in Israel: *sheep, ox,*[2] or do[nke]y. 5 Indeed, they [and their livestock would come up, with their tents *and camels*.[3] They entered,] numbering [like

---

Chapter 6. 4QJudgᵃ: 6:2–6 directly followed by 11–13; 1QJudg: 6:20–22.

1. 4QJudgᵃ. MT LXX add *and they marched against them*.

2. 4QJudgᵃ. *not a sheep or ox* MT.

3. The spacing of the fragment suggests that 4QJudgᵃ (with LXXᴸ) probably included *and camels*, whereas MT, LXXᴬ, and LXXᴮ do not.

lo]custs—*they*[4] [were innumerable. They en]tered the la[nd to destroy it. 6 So Israel was brought very low because of Midian, and] the Is[rael]ites cried [to the LORD.

> ▓ *The Masoretic Text and all other traditions insert a theological paragraph here (Judg 6:7–10) reciting the Deuteronomistic pattern: Israel cried to the Lord, the Lord sent a prophet, and the prophet charged the people with disobedience. 4QJudg*[a] *retains the original, unembellished narrative.*

11 [Then the messenger of the LORD came and sat under the oak in Ophrah] which belonged to Joash the *Abiezrite,*[5] while Gi[deon his son was beating out wheat in the winepress, to hide it from the Midianites]. 12 The messenger of the LORD [appeared] to him and said [to him, "The LORD is with you, valiant warrior]." 13 Gideon [said to him], "With your permission, sir, if *God*[6] is [with us, why has all this happened to us? Where are all his wondrous works] *which*[7] our ancestors recounted to us, sayi[ng, 'Did not the LORD bring us up from Egypt?' But now the LORD has cast us off and delivered us into the power of Midian]." ▲

20 [The messenger of God said to him, "Take the meat and the unleavened cakes, lay them on this rock, and pour] out [the broth]." And he did so. 21 Then [the messenger of the LORD,] ext[ending the tip of the staff in his hand, touched the meat and the unleavened cakes], and flames rose [from the rock and consumed the meat and unleavened cakes. Then the messenger of the LORD vanished from his sight. 22 When] Gideon [sa]w that [he was the messenger of the LORD, Gideon said, "Oh no, LORD God! I have seen the messenger of the LORD face t]o [face]." ▲

8 1 [The men of Eph]raim [said to him], "Wh[y did you treat us this way, not calling us when you went] to [fi]g[ht with Midian]?" ▲

9 1 [Abimelech son of Jerubbaal went to Shechem, to his mother's brothers, speaking with them and with the whole] cl[an of his maternal grandfather's] fa[mily, saying, 2 "Please ask in the h]earing of [all] the people of She[chem: 'What is better for you, that all seventy sons of Jerubbaa]l [rule over you] or that [one r]ule [over you? Remember that I am your flesh and blood.'" 3 So] his mother's [brothers said these things] *about*[8] him in [the hearing of all the people of

---

4. 4QJudg[a]. *they and their camels* MT.

5. *h'by 'zry* 4QJudg[a] LXX[A] LXX[L]. *'by h 'zry* MT LXX[B].

6. 4QJudg[a]. *the* LORD MT LXX.

7. 4QJudg[a] uses the shortened form of this word. MT uses the full form.

Chapter 8. 1QJudg: 8:1(?).

Chapter 9. 1QJudg: 9:1–6, 28–31, 40–43, 48–49.

8. 1QJudg. MT uses a different word for *about.*

Shechem. And they were inclined to follow] Abimelech, because [they] thought, ["He is our kinsman]."

4 [So they gave him seventy silver pieces out of the temple of Baal-berith, with which Abimelech hired] worthless [and reckless me]n [to follow him]. 5 Then [he] we[nt to his father's house at Ophrah and executed his brothers, the sons of Jerubbaal, seventy people, on one stone. But Jotha]m, the [youngest] son of Jerubba[al, was spared because he hid himself. 6 Then everyone from Shechem assembled together, along with everyone from Beth-millo, and they went and made] Abi[me]le[ch king by the oak of the pillar in Shechem].▲

28 [Gaal son of Ebed said, "Who is Abimelech and who are we of Shechem that we should serve him? Did not the son of Jerubbaal and Zebul his officer serve the men of Hamor the father of Sheche]m? So w[hy should we serve him? 29 If only this people were under me! I would depose Abimelech." Then] they⁹ [said] to A[bimelech], "[In]crea[se your army and come out]!"

30 [When Zebul the ruler of the city heard what Gaal son of Ebed had said, he became] extremely¹⁰ [angry]. 31 He sent messengers to A[bimelech in secret, saying, "Listen, Gaal son of Ebed and his relatives are en]tering Shechem, and they indeed¹¹ are pressuring against¹² the [city against you]."▲

40 Abimelech [pursued] them,¹³ [while they fled from him, and many fell slain all the] way to the entrance of the g[ate] of the [city.¹⁴ 41 Abimelech remained at Arumah, while Zebul drove out] Gaal [and his relatives, ridding Shechem of them].

42 The next da[y, the people went out into the] fields, and someone¹⁵ informed [Abimelech. 43 So he took] his army, divided it into [th]r[ee co]mpanies, [and waited in ambush in the fields. He was watching, and when the people came out] o[f] the city, [he rose up against them and attacked them].▲

48 [. . . He said to the troops wh]o were with him, "What xx [. . . ¹⁶ me do, quickly do the same!" 49 So each of the troops also cut a branch and, fo]llow[ing Abimelech, they piled them against the stronghold and set the stronghold on fire

---

9. 1QJudg. he MT. I LXX.

10. 1QJudg. Not in MT.

11. 1QJudg. watch out, they MT.

12. 1QJudg. Not in MT.

13. 1QJudg. him MT LXX.

14. 1QJudg. the gate MT LXXᴮ. the city LXXᴬ.

15. 1QJudg LXX. they MT.

16. 1QJudg has two letters before the fragment breaks off, but they differ from MT, which reads you have seen.

over those inside. So all the people in the tower of Shechem also died, about a thousand men and women].

19 5 [Then, on the fourth day, they got up early in the morning, and he prepared to go. But the gi]rl['s father said] to his son-ir-law, ["Strengthen yourself with a bit to eat and then go." 6 So the two of] them [sat down] toge[ther and ate] and drank. And [the girl's father said to the man, "Decide to stay the night and e]njoy yourself." 7 When the [man] prepared [to go, his father-in-law pressed him. So he stayed the night there again].

21 12 [They found among the inhabitants of Jabesh-gilead four hundred young women who had not had sexual relations with a man, and they brought them to the camp at Shiloh, which is in the l]and of [Ca]naan.

13 [The whole assembly sent word to the Benjaminites at the rock of Rimmon and] declared [peace] with them. [14 So Benjamin returned at that time, and they gave them the women whom they had spared from the women of Jabesh-gilead, but even so there were not enough for them. 15 The people felt compassion for Benja]min, because the L[ORD] had made [a breach in the tribes of Israel. 16 So the elders of the congregation said, "How shall we get wives for those who are left, seeing the women of Benjamin have been killed?"] 17 And they said, ["There must be an inheritance for the survivors of Benjamin, so that a tribe may not be not blotted out from Israel. 18 But we may not give them wives from among our own daughters]."

■ *The Masoretic Text gives a reason: the Israelites had sworn, "Anyone who gives a wife to Benjamin is cursed." Spatial requirements in the reconstruction of 4QJudgᵇ indicate either that the scroll did not yet contain this reason, which may be a subsequent embellishment (see also Judg 6:7–10 above), or that an equivalent amount of text was lost and/or perhaps written in the margin.*

19 [Then they said, "Listen, there is a feast of the L]ORD [every year] in [Shiloh," which is north of Bethel, e]a[s]t of [the highway that goes] up [from Be]th[el to Shechem, and south of Lebonah. 20 So they instructed the Benjaminites, "Go and lie in wait in the vineya]rd[s, 21 and watch to] se[e if the women of Shiloh] c[ome out to take part in the dances. Then come out of the vineyards, and each of you seize a wife from the women of Shiloh and go to the lan]d [of Benjam]i[n. 22 T]hen, [when their] fathers [or brothers] come [to complain to us, we will say to them, 'Be generous with us about them, because none of us] too[k a wi[fe in] ba[tt]l[e. And, bec]ause [you did not give them to them, you are innocent]."

Chapter 19. 4QJudgᵇ: 19:5–7.
Chapter 21. 4QJudgᵇ: 21:12–25.

23 [The Benjaminites did so. As many as there wer]e [forcibly carried off *wives*][17] *from*[18] the dancing [women. Then they went and returned to their inheritance, and] they [rebui]lt the [cit]ies [and] l[ived in th]em. 24 So [the Israelites] left [there at that time, each one to] his [tribe] and to [his] famil[y]. [They] al[l went back to their inheritance. 25 In] that [period], there was n[o ki]ng [in] Isra[el. Every]one [did whatever seemed right in his own eyes].

---

17. Some MT manuscripts add *for themselves*, but most agree with 4QJudg[b], which apparently does not have space for the word.

18. 4QJudg[b] uses the shortened form of this word. MT uses the full form.

SAMUEL

The book of Samuel—1 Samuel and 2 Samuel were treated as a single book in antiquity—offers some of the most dramatic learnings from the biblical Dead Sea Scrolls. The extensively preserved 4QSam^a has been known since 1953, one year after its discovery, to differ widely and frequently from the traditional Masoretic Text.

There were four manuscripts of Samuel found at Qumran: one in Cave 1 and three in Cave 4. These Samuel manuscripts, while containing some errors, also preserve a large number of original or superior readings that help correct errors in the traditional Masoretic Text. For proper perspective, it should be pointed out that the textual form of 4QSam^b is much closer than the Masoretic Text to the text from which the Septuagint was translated. Similarly 4QSam^a, while showing many agreements with the Septuagint in contrast to the Masoretic Text, is the type of Samuel manuscript that the author of Chronicles used in composing that book.

The variants recorded in the following pages improve our knowledge of the text of Samuel beyond the traditional Masoretic Text. Some of these variants involve individual words or phrases. Intermittently, there are whole sentences either left out of the Masoretic Text by mistake or added by the scrolls as supplementary material. Arguably the single most dramatic passage among the newly discovered biblical scrolls occurs in 4QSam^a at the beginning of 1 Samuel 11. An entire paragraph, missing from all our Bibles for two thousand years, has now been restored in the New Revised Standard Version. Its existence had already been footnoted in the New American Bible in 1970. This paragraph graphically describes the atrocities of King Nahash of the Ammonites. 4QSam^a is the oldest extant witness to this text. The historian Josephus, writing in the second half of the first century CE, recounts the same details at the same point in his account of the history of the Jewish people, *Jewish Antiquities*. This demonstrates that the story was also in the Greek Bible that he was using. Thus our two most ancient witnesses attest to the existence of this passage in the biblical manuscripts of antiquity.

These manuscripts have also helped to realign scholars' assessments of the value of the ancient Septuagint translation. Traditionally, when the Septuagint differed from the Masoretic Text (which had been considered *the* Hebrew original), the Septuagint was routinely thought to be a "free" translation (or even a paraphrase, or just plain wrong). The Hebrew manuscripts of Samuel found at Qumran, however, very often agree with the Septuagint when it differs from the Masoretic Text. This demonstrates that the Septuagint was translated from a Hebrew text form similar to that of the Qumran manuscripts. The problem in assessing the Septuagint, as with so many historical documents, had been with scholars' vision and criteria, not with the data. The Septuagint, of course, just like the Masoretic Text, the Dead Sea Scrolls, and every other ancient manuscript tradition, does have its share of errors. But the important lesson here is that the Septuagint is not a free or false rendering, but rather a generally faithful translation of its Hebrew source.

1QSam (1Q7) has only eight fragments remaining. It is interesting to note that as the scroll lay rolled, a fragment roughly the size of a quarter was preserved at the same position on each of eight successive layers of leather.

4QSam^b is the oldest of the manuscripts, dating roughly to 250 BCE. One large fragment, containing nineteen continuous lines, is preserved, along with seven small fragments.

4QSam^c, dating roughly to 100–75 BCE, contains one small fragment from 1 Samuel 25:30–32 and numerous fragments that can be pieced together to form a generous amount of two consecutive columns containing 2 Samuel 14–15. The same idiosyncratic scribe who copied it also copied two other manuscripts, the main scroll of the *Rule of the Community* (1QS) and a collection of scriptural quotations entitled the *Testimonia* (4Q175). The same scribe is also responsible for a correction in the *Great Isaiah Scroll* (1QIsa^a). Of the sixty-seven partial lines preserved of 4QSam^c, there are twenty-one errors or corrections—roughly one for every three lines. It is likely that this scribe was entrusted with such an important task because he was a high-ranking community leader rather than because of his scribal skills.

4QSam^a dates from the middle of the first century BCE. It is one of the most extensively preserved and important biblical manuscripts. Hundreds of fragments are preserved, spanning from the first chapter of 1 Samuel to the final chapter of 2 Samuel.

1 SAMUEL

1 11 [Hannah made this vow: "LORD of hosts, if you truly look on the misery of your servant and remember me, and do not forget your servant but give your servant a so]n, then I will give him to [. . .[1] and] no razor *shall cross*[2] [his head." 12 As she continued praying before the LORD, E]li watched her mouth. 13 *She*[3] was speaking [in her heart; though her lips moved, her voice was not heard. So Eli] th[ought she was drunk]. ▲

> *The following passage already shows a number of the typical variants between 4QSamᵃ, the Masoretic Text, and the Septuagint. There are three indications that 4QSamᵃ, often in agreement with Septuagint, has a longer text than the Masoretic Text. 4QSamᵃ preserves extra details, such as explicitly referring to Samuel as a Nazirite. It also correctly preserves "a three-year-old bull," in contrast to the Masoretic Text's "three bulls." Finally, 4QSamᵃ displays a different theological motif, with Elkanah praying that the LORD establish what Hannah has vowed, whereas the Masoretic Text elevates it to establishing the LORD's word.*

22 [But Hannah did not go up, and] she [to]ld her husband, ["Not] *until*[4] [the child is weaned. Then I will bring him to appear] befo[re] the LORD and to stay *before*[5] [. . . . And] I will [*dedicate*] *him as a Nazirite forever, all the days of*[6] [. . . . " 23 Elkanah her husband said to her,] "Do what seems good to you. Wait until [you have weaned him. May the LOR]D [*establish*] *the words of your mouth.*"[7] So the woman waited [and nursed her son until she weaned] him.

Chapter 1. 4QSamᵃ: 1:11–13, 22–28.

1. 4QSamᵃ spacing indicates a text more like the longer LXX than the short MT. *the LORD all the days of his life* MT. *your presence as a gift until the day of his death. He shall not drink wine or strong drink* LXX.

2. 4QSamᵃ. *shall go over* MT LXX.

3. 4QSamᵃ LXX. *As for Hannah, she* MT.

4. 4QSamᵃ and MT use different wording.

5. 4QSamᵃ. *there* MT LXX.

6. 4QSamᵃ. Not in MT LXX.

7. 4QSamᵃ LXX. *his word* MT.

24 Whe[n she had weaned him], she took *him*[8] *to Shiloh,*[9] along with *a three-year-old* [*bull, the calf of a*] *cow, bread,*[10] [. . . to the house of] the Lo[r]d in Shiloh. *The child*[11] [. . .] *the sacrifice, as* [. . .] 25 *he slaughtered*[12] [. . . . 26 . . .] "My lord! [As you live, my lord, I am the woman who stood beside you here, praying to] the Lord. [27 I prayed for this child, and the Lord granted me my request which I asked of him. 28 Therefore I in turn have given him to the Lo]rd. As long as [he lives he is dedicated to the Lord." *So she left*] *him there and she worshiped*[13] [the Lord there].

2 1 [Hannah prayed: My heart exults in the Lord.] My strength is exalted in [the Lor]d. [My mouth speaks boldly against my enemies, because I rejoice in your salvation. 2 *In*]*deed,*[14] there is no one h[o]ly like the Lo[rd. There is none righteous like our God. There is none holy besides] you. There is no rock like our God. 3 [Stop talking so very proudly. Let no in]solence [come out of] your mouth. For [the Lord] is a God of know[ledge and by him actions are weighed. 4 The bows of mighty m]en *shatter,*[15] but those who stumbled put o[n strength. 5 Those who were well-fed hire themselves out for bread, but those who were hungry hunger no more. The bar]ren woman bears [seven, but the woman with many children languishes. 6 The Lord kills and brings to life.] He sends down [to Sheol and raises up. 7 The Lord makes poor and rich. He brings low and exalts. 8 He raises the poor from the dust and lifts up the needy from the ash-heap. He makes them sit with] prince[s and inherit a seat of honor. For the pillars of the earth are the Lord's, and] on them [he has set the w]orl[d. 9 He guards] the *path*[16] of [his faithful ones, but the wicked are silenced in darkness]. *He grants the re*[*quest of the one who prays*]. *He blesses the y*[*ears of the righteous.*[17] For no one prevails by

---

8. 4QSam[a] uses a separate word for *him*, while MT uses a suffix.

9. 4QSam[a]. *with her* MT. *with her to Shiloh* LXX.

10. 4QSam[a] LXX. *three bulls, one ephah of flour* MT.

11. 4QSam[a]. *And the child* MT LXX.

12. 4QSam[a] had a much longer text, probably agreeing with the LXX rather than the truncated MT; the few words preserved indicate that 4QSam[a] could read with LXX. *And the child was a child. 25 They slaughtered the bull and brought the child to Eli* MT. *And the child was with them. When they brought him into the presence of the Lord, his father slaughtered the sacrifice, as he did annually for the Lord. Then he brought the child, 25 and he slaughtered the calf. And Hannah his mother brought him to Eli* LXX.

13. 4QSam[a]. *So he worshiped* MT LXX[mss]. Not in LXX.

Chapter 2. 4QSam[a]: 2:1–6, 8–10, 16, 13–14, 17–36.

14. 4QSam[a] LXX. Not in MT.

15. 4QSam[a]. *are shattering* MT.

16. 4QSam[a]. *feet* MT.

17. 4QSam[a] LXX. Not in MT.

strength.] 10 *The* LORD *will shatter his* en[em]ies.[18] *Who is* [holy?[19] . . .] *when he re-pays* [. . .] *Who*[20] [. . .] *And he thundered*[21] [. . .] *his anointed* [. . .]." ▲

■ *The narrative sequence and details in 2:13–17 are quite at variance in 4QSam*[a] *and the Masoretic Text, and the Septuagint is generally but not consistently closer to the Masoretic Text than to 4QSam*[a].

16 If *the man answered* [and] *s*[aid] *to the priest's servant,*[22] "*Let the priest burn*[23] [the fat] first. Then take *everything*[24] you wish," then he would say, "No, you shall give it to me now, *or*[25] [I will *take*] *the ram by force to give him the meat.*"[26] 13 *And taking*[27] a three-pronged fork in his hand, 14 he would thrust it into *the boiler or pot*[28] and *take*[29] everything the fork brought up. *If* [. . .] *good alone* [. . .] *daily.*[30] 17 The si[n of the servants] was very great [in the sight of the L]ORD, because *they*[31] treated the LORD's offering with contempt.

18 Samuel [minister]ed [before the L]ORD. The boy wore a linen ephod, 19 [and] every year [his mother] made [him a little robe and br]ought it to him when [she] came [up with her husband] to offer the [year]ly sacri[fice]. 20 El[i] used to bless E[lkanah and his wife], *saying,*[32] "May the L[ORD] *repay you with*[33] children by this woman [in place of the one she prayed for] and dedicat[ed to the Lo]rd." *Then the man returned to*[34] his home.

---

18. 4QSam[a] LXX. *The* LORD, *his enemies will be shattered* MT.

19. 4QSam[a]. Not in MT. *The Lord is holy* LXX.

20. 4QSam[a]. Not in MT.

21. 4QSam[a]. *He will thunder* MT.

22. 4QSam[a]. *the man said to him* MT. *the man who was making the sacrifice said* LXX.

23. 4QSam[a]. *Certainly they will burn* MT. *Let him burn* LXX.

24. 4QSam[a] LXX. *anything* MT.

25. 4QSam[a]. *if not* MT LXX.

26. 4QSam[a]. *take it by force* MT LXX.

27. 4QSam[a]. This and the following sentence come earlier in MT. 4QSam[a] supplies the verb *take* but does not contain the beginning of the MT sentence. *When anyone offered a sacrifice, the priest's servant came while the meat was boiling, with a three-pronged fork in his hand* MT LXX.

28. 4QSam[a]. *the pan or kettle or caldron or pot* MT. *caldron or kettle or pot* LXX.

29. 4QSam[a]. *the priest took for himself* MT LXX.

30. 4QSam[a]. Not in MT. 4QSam[a] does not contain vss 14b and 15 of MT.

31. 4QSam[a] LXX. *the men* MT.

32. 4QSam[a]. *and said* MT.

33. 4QSam[a]. *give you* MT.

34. 4QSam[a] LXX. *they would return to* MT.

21 *And the L[ORD] visited*[35] Hannah, and *she bore more children,*[36] t[hr]ee sons and two daughters. Meanwhile [the boy Samuel] grew up *there*[37] in the presence of the L[ORD].

■ *The variant forms of the narrative in verse 22 add different details. 4QSam[a] gives Eli's age (cf. Masoretic Text 1 Sam 4:15), whereas the Masoretic Text specifies the sexual sin of the priests.*

22 Now Eli, who was very old, *ninety[-eight] years old,*[38] *heard what*[39] his sons *were doing*[40] to *the Israelites.*[41] 23 So [he said to them, "Why] do you d[o these things]? F[or] even I[42] [hear of your evil] dea[lings from *all the LORD's people.*[43] 24 *No, my sons, the repo]rt which I h[ear is not good. Do not act so. For the report wh]ich I hear God's people cir[culating is no]t goo[d].*[44] 25 If one person sins *gravely*[45] against another, *he will appeal to the Lo[r]D.*[46] [But if someone sins against the LORD, who will intercede for him?" But they did not follow *the]* advice,[47] because [the LORD's will was to put them to death. 26 But the boy Samuel increased in stature and favor wi]th [the LORD] and with [people.]

27 [A man of God came to Eli and] *said,*[48] "Thus says the LORD, [*I did*[49] indeed reveal myself to your father's house, when they were in Egy]pt, *slaves*[50] of [Pharaoh]'s house. 28 [I chose *your father's house*[51] out of all the tr]ibes of Israel to

---

35. 4QSam[a] LXX. *When the* LORD *visited* MT.

36. 4QSam[a] LXX. *she conceived and gave birth to* MT.

37. 4QSam[a]. Not in MT LXX.

38. 4QSam[a]. Not in MT LXX.

39. 4QSam[a] LXX. *would hear all that* MT.

40. 4QSam[a]. *would do* MT.

41. 4QSam[a] LXX. *all of Israel, and how they lay with the women who served at the entrance to the tent of meeting* MT.

42. 4QSam[a] uses the shorter form of the word *I,* while MT uses the longer form.

43. [4QSam[a]] LXX. *all this people* MT.

44. 4QSam[a] LXX. The spacing of this manuscript and the repetition of *which I hear* suggest that this text is from LXX. *No, my sons, the report which I hear the* LORD's *people circulating is not good* MT.

45. 4QSam[a] LXX. Not in MT.

46. 4QSam[a]. *God will mediate* MT.

47. 4QSam[a]. *the advice of their father* MT LXX. This is probably a simple error of omission in 4QSam[a].

48. 4QSam[a] LXX. *said to him* MT.

49. [4QSam[a]] LXX. *Did I not . . . ?* MT.

50. 4QSam[a]. Not in MT.

51. [4QSam[a]] LXX. *him* MT.

be my priest, [to go up to my altar to burn incense and] to wear the eph[o]d.[52] I gave to [your father]'s house [all the fire offerings of the children of Israel]. 29 Why do *you look down on*[53] my sacrifice and my offering, [which I commanded for my dwelling, and honor your sons over me, to] fatten *yourself*[54] on the best of *all the offerings*[55] of [Israel *in my presence.*][56]

30 ["Therefore thus says the LORD, the God of Israe]l: I *said,*[57] [your] h[ouse and your father's house would continue in my presence forever. But now the LORD says, Far be it from me! For those who honor me I will honor, but those who despise me will be cursed. 31 Watch, the time] is co[m]ing when I will cut off [your strength and the strength of your father's *house,*[58] 32 and] you will [ne]ver [again] have an old man in *my*[59] house. 33 [Anyone of yours I do not cut off from] my altar, it will be only to punish *his*[60] eyes and to grieve his spirit. All the descendants of your house *will fall by the human sword.*[61] 34 And [what happens to your two sons, Ho]phni and Phineha[s, will be the sign to you—on a single day both of them will die].

■ *For the biblical redactor's linkage of this prophetic denunciation with a subsequent military defeat, see 1 Sam 4:11 below.*

35 "I [will rai]se up [for myself a faithful priest, who will ac]t [in accordance with my heart and my mind]. I will build for [him a secure house, and he will continue in the presence of my anointed forever. 36 Then who]ever is left [in your house will come and bow down to him for a piece of silver and a loaf of brea]d, *saying,*[62] ['Appoint me to one of the priests' offices so that I may have a bit of bread to eat].'"

3 1 [The child Samuel ministered to the LORD under Eli.] The word of the LO[RD was rare in those days. Visions were infrequent. 2 At] that time, El[i, who had weak eyes and could not s]ee, [was sleeping in his place. 3 Before the]

---

52. 4QSamª LXX. *ephod in my presence* MT LXX[mss].

53. 4QSamª LXX (singular). *you* (plural) *tread down* MT.

54. 4QSamª. *yourselves* MT.

55. 4QSamª. *every offering* MT LXX.

56. [4QSamª] LXX. *for my people* MT.

57. 4QSamª. *clearly said* MT LXX.

58. [4QSamª] LXX. MT is disturbed, adding two variant phrases.

59. 4QSamª LXX. *your* MT.

60. 4QSamª LXX. *your* MT.

61. 4QSamª LXX. *will die as mortals* MT.

62. 4QSamª LXX. *and say* MT.

Chapter 3. 4QSamª: 3:1–4, 18–20.

lamp of [God had gone out, when Samuel was sleeping in the temple of the Lord,[63] 4 the Lor]d [called,] *Sam[uel."* [64] He responded, "Here I am."] ▲

18 [So Samuel told him] everythi[n]g, [hiding nothing from him. Then he said, "He is the Lord.] Let him do [what seems good to him." 19 As Samuel] grew, [the Lord was with him and let none of his words fall] to the ground. 20 [All Israel from Dan to Beersheba] knew [that Samuel was confirmed] as [a prophet] of [the Lord]. ▲

4 9 ["Be strong! Be] men, Philistines! [Or you will be slaves to the Hebrews, as they were to you. B]e men and fig[ht!" 10 And the Philistines did fight. Israel was defeated, and] everyone [f]led to his tent. [The slaughter] w[as very great. Israel lost thi]r[ty th]ousand foot soldiers. [11 The ark of God was taken, and the two sons of Eli, Hophni and Phinehas, died.] 12 A ma[n of Benjamin ran from the battle lines and came to Shiloh the same day, with] his [clothes] torn [and with dust on his head]. ▲

5 8 [So they sent for and assembled all the lords of the Philistines and said, "What shall we do] with the ark [of the God of Israel?" They answered, "*Let*] *them bring*[65] [the ark of the G]od of Is[rael around to Gath." So they brought the ark of the God of] Israel *to G[ath*.[66] 9 But then, wh[en] they [b]rought it *to Gath,*[67] [the hand of the L]ord went [against the city, throwing it into a very] great [panic. He afflicted] the people of the city, both small and [great, with an outbreak of] tumors. 10 [So they sent] *the ark of the God of Israel*[68] to [E]kro[n].

[Then, when the ark of God came to Ekron, the Ekron]ites [cried out], s[ay]ing, *"Why have yo[u]*[69] brought around [the ark of the God of Israel to us—to kill] us and our [peo]ple?" 11 So [they] sent [for and gathered to]gether [all the lords of the Philistines and said, "Send away the ark of] the God of I[sra]e[l], and let [it return to its own place, so that it does not kill us and our people." For there was p]*anic of the Lor[d* . . .][70] throughout [the city. The hand of God was very heavy th]ere. 12 For the [peopl]e who [did] not [die were stricken with the tumors, and the cry of the cit]y [went up to] h[eave]n.

---

63. 4QSamᵃ. Lord *where the ark of God was* MT LXX. 4QSamᵃ does not have space for this clause.

64. 4QSamᵃ. *to Samuel* MT. *"Samuel, Samuel"* LXX.

Chapter 4. 4QSamᵃ: 4:9–12.

Chapter 5. 4QSamᵃ: 5:8–12.

65. 4QSamᵃ and MT LXX use different forms.

66. 4QSamᵃ LXX. Not in MT.

67. 4QSamᵃ. Not in MT LXX.

68. 4QSamᵃ. *the ark of God* MT LXX.

69. 4QSamᵃ LXX. *They have* MT.

70. 4QSamᵃ. *deadly panic* MT LXX.

6 1 [The ark of the Lord was in the territory of the Philistines s]even months. 2 Then the Philistine[s cal]led [for the priests, the diviners,] *and the magicians,*[71] saying, "What should we do [with the ark of the Lord? Tell us how to] send it *to*[72] its place." 3 They answered, ["I]f [you send back the ark of] the *covenant of the Lord,*[73] God of Israel, do not send [it back empty. You must] return him a sin [of]fering. Then [you] will be healed, [and you] *will make atonement for [yourselves. Will his hand not leave you?"]*[74]

4 [Then they asked, "What] is the sin offering [wh]ich we are to ret[ur]n to [him?" They answered, *"Five] golden tumors,*[75] [according to the number of the Philistine lords]. For there was one plague on [all of you and on your lords. 5 Therefore make images of the tumor]s and images of *the*[76] mice [that destroy the land, and you will give glory to the God of Israel. Per]haps he will lift [his hand from you and your gods and your land. 6 So why would you harden your] hear[ts, as the Egyptians and Pharaoh hardened their hearts]? Was it not only after he had made foo[ls of them, that they let the people go, and they went on their way? 7 Now then, get and prepare on]e [new cart] and two [milk cows which have never been yoked. Tie the cow]s to the [ca]r[t. But take their calves home, separate from them."] ▲

12 [The cows went straight in the direction of Beth-shemesh. They went along the highway, lowing as they went, and did not turn aside, either to the ri]ght [or to the left, while the lords of the Philistines followed them to the] Beth-she[mesh borde]r. 13 [The people of Beth-shemesh were reaping their wheat harvest in the valley, when they lifted] their [ey]es [and saw the ark, and they rejoiced at the sight].▲

16 [The five lords of the Philistines saw this,] then re[turned to Ekron that day. 17 These are the golden tumors which] the Philist[ines returned as a sin offering to the Lord: one for Ashdod, one for Gaza, on]e [for Ashkelon, one] for Ga[th, on]e [for Ekron. 18 The golden] mi[ce were numbered according to all the Phili]st[i]ne [cities belonging to the five lords]—the forti[fied] cities [and their country villages. The large stone] on [whi]ch they [se]t [the ark of the Lord is a witness to this day in the field of Joshua the Beth-shemeshite]. ▲

20 [The people of Beth-shemesh said, "Who is able to stand in the presence

---

Chapter 6. 4QSam^a: 6:1–7, 12–13, 16–18, 20–21.

71. 4QSam^a. Not in MT. *and the enchanters* LXX.

72. 4QSam^a and MT use different words.

73. 4QSam^a LXX. Not in MT.

74. 4QSam^a. *will know why his hand was not removed from you* MT.

75. 4QSam^a LXX. MT adds *and five golden mice.*

76. 4QSam^a. *your* MT LXX.

of] *this holy* LORD?[77] Where [should the ark go from here?" 21 Then they sent messengers] to the inhabitants of Ki[riath-je]arim, sayi[ng, "The Philistines have brought back the ark of the LORD. Come down and take] it back with you."

7 1 [So] the people of Kiria[th-jearim came and took the ark of the LORD. They brought it t]o [the house of Abina]dab, *whi[ch is*[78] on the hill, and consecrated Eleazar his son to keep the ark of the LORD]. ▲

8 9 [Now listen to them. Only warn them strongly and instruct them] in the customs of [the ki]ng wh[o will rule over them. 10 So Samuel reported everything the LORD had said to the] people who had a[sked] him for a king. 11 [And] he said, "These [are the customs of the ki]n[g who will rule over you: He will take your sons and use them for his benefit, some to serve with] his [chariots], to be [his] horsemen, [and to run in front of his chariots. 12 Others he will assign to be captains of thousands and of fifties. He will assign some to plo]w [his] gr[ound and reap his harvest, others to make his weapons of war and the equipment for his chariots. 13 And he will take your daughters, to be perfumers and cooks and bakers.] 14 He will ta[ke your fields, your vineyards, your olive orchards]—the best of them—[and give them to his] attendant[s. 15 He will take a tenth of your seed and of your vineyard harvest, and give it to his officers and attendants. 16 He will take] your manservants and your *maidservants*[79] [and the best of your young men and your donkeys], and use them for his own work. 17 [He will take a tenth of] your flocks. [And you yourselves will be his servants. 18 When] that [day comes, you will cry for help be]cause of your kin[g], who[m you chose for yourself, but in] *those* [*days,*[80] the LORD will not answer you." 19 But the people refused to listen to Samuel's advice. They said, "No. There] must be a king [over us. 20 Then we too will be like all the other nations, and our king will be a judge for us and lead us and fi]g[ht our] b[attles]." ▲

9 6 [The servant said to Saul, "Look, there is a man of Go]d [in this city. The man is held in high esteem—everything he says is certain to happen. Now, let us *g*]o.[81] Perhap[s he will tell us which way we should go." 7 Then S]aul [*said*],[82] "Bu[t if we go, what shall we bring the man? For the bread in our sacks is gone, and there is no gift to b]ring to the m[an of God. What do we have?"] ▲

---

77. 4QSam[a] LXX. *the* LORD, *this holy God* MT.

Chapter 7. 4QSam[a]: 7:1.

78. 4QSam[a]. Not in MT.

Chapter 8. 4QSam[a]: 8:9–12, 14, 16–20.

79. 4QSam[a] and MT use different words for *maidservant*.

80. 4QSam[a] LXX. *on that day* MT.

Chapter 9. 4QSam[a]: 9:6–7, 11–12, 16–24.

81. 4QSam[a] LXX. *go there* MT.

82. 4QSam[a]. *said to his servant* MT. *said to his servant with him* LXX.

11 [As] they [went up the road to the city, they met young women going out to draw water] and sai[d to them, "Is the seer here?" 12 They answered them, "He is.] Loo[k, he is ahead of you. Now hurry. He just arrived in the city, because the people have a sacrifice today at the high place]." ▲

16 [About this time tomorrow, I will send you a man from the land of Benjamin. You will anoint him prince over my people Israel, and he will save] my people from the power of [the Philis]tines. For I have looked on [my people, because their cry has come to me].

17 [When Samuel saw] Sau[l, the LORD s]aid to him, This is the m[an I spoke to you about. This man will rule over my people. 18 Then Saul drew near t]o[83] [Samuel *inside the ci*]ty,[84] and sai[d, "Please tell me where the seer's house is." 19 Samuel answered Saul, "I am *h*]*e*.[85] Go [on ahead of me to the high place. For you will eat with me today. In the morning I will send you off and will inform] you [about everything you have on your mind. 20 As] for the donk[eys which you lost three days ago, do not worry about them, because they have been found. And for whom is every desirable thing in Israel? Is it not for you and for everyone in your father's house?" 21 Saul answered, "Am not I a Benjamite,] the smal[lest of the tribes of Israel? And is not my family the least of all the families of the tribe of Benjamin? Why then do] you [speak] t[o me this] way?"

22 [But Samuel took Saul and his servant and led them into the hall, and had them sit at the h]ead of those [who were invited, about thirty people. 23 Then Samuel said to the cook, "Bring the portion] whi[ch] I [ga]ve [you, the one I told you to set aside." 24 So the cook took the leg and *what was o*]*n it*[86] and [plac]ed [it in front of Saul . . .]. ▲

10 3 ["Then you will continue on from there. When you reach the oak of Tabor, three men] going up to [God at Bethel will meet you there, one carrying three kids, another carrying] three loaves of [bread, and another carrying a skin of wine. 4 They will greet you and give you two] loaves of bread [*for a wa*]*ve offering,*[87] which you should accept [from them].

5 ["After that you will come to the Hill of God, where there is a Philistine garrison.] Then, [as you reach the city, you will meet a band of pro]phets coming [down from the high place, with] a harp, [tam]bourine, [flute, and lyre playing in front of] them, [and they will be prophesying]. 6 Then the spi[rit of the LORD] will come on you in power, [and you will prophesy with them], and [you] will

---

83. 4QSam[a] and MT have different words.

84. 4QSam[a] LXX. *at the gate* MT.

85. 4QSam[a] LXX. *the seer* MT.

86. 4QSam[a] has an unusual form.

Chapter 10. 4QSam[a]: 10:3–12, 14, 16, 18, 25–27.

87. 4QSam[a]; cf. LXX. Not in MT.

become [a new man. 7 When these signs have been fulfilled for you, then do whatever your] hands find [to do; for God is with you].

8 ["Then go down to Gilgal ahead of me. Now listen, I will come d]own to you to [of]fer [burnt offerings and to sacrifice peace offerings. But you must wait seven days until I come to you] and tel[l you what to do." 9 So, when he had turned around to leave Samuel,] God[88] [changed his heart, and all those signs were fulfilled that day].

10 [When they reached the hill,] a band of [prophets did in] fact [meet him, and the spirit of God came on him in power, and he prophesied along with them. 11 Then, when everyone who had known] him previously [saw this, that he was actually prophesying with the prophets, the people asked each] other, "What [has happened to the son of Kish? Is Saul also among the prophets?" 12 And someone who lived there answered, "And who is] their father?" There[fore, "Is Saul also among the prophets?" became a saying].

13 [When he had finished prophesying, he went to the high place.] 14 Now [Saul's] uncle asked [him and his servant, "Where did you go?" He answered, "To look for the donkeys. When we realized that they were] not to be found, we went [to Samuel." 15 Saul's uncle said, "Tell me what Samuel said to you." 16 So] Saul [said] to [his uncle, "He informed us that the donkeys had been found." But he did not tell him wh]at [Samuel] had said [concerning the kingship].

17 [Now Samuel called the people together to the LORD at Mizpah. 18 He said to] all [the Israelit]es, ["Thus says the LORD, the God of Israel, I myself brought Israel out of Egypt. I delivered you from the power of the Egyptians and from the power of all the kingdoms that oppressed you."] ▲

25 [Then Samuel explained to the people the or]dinances of [the kingship and wrote them in a book, and deposited it in the LORD's presence. Then Samuel dismissed all the peo]ple; each *went*[89] to [his] *pla[ce.*[90] 26 S]aul [al]so [went to his house in Gibeah]. The valiant *men*[91] [wh]ose hearts the Lo[RD][92] had touched [went] *with Saul.*[93] 27 But certain worthless men s[aid, "How will this man save us?" And] they despise[d] him and brought him no *gift.*[94]

■ *The following passage in 4QSam*[a] *is one of the single most dramatic discoveries among the biblical scrolls. 4QSam*[a] *has an entire three-and-a-half-line paragraph*

---

88. 4QSam[a] LXX precede *God* with an article, which is not in MT.

89. 4QSam[a] LXX. Not in MT.

90. 4QSam[a] LXX. *house* MT.

91. 4QSam[a] LXX. Not in MT.

92. 4QSam[a] LXX. *God* MT.

93. 4QSam[a] LXX. MT has *with him* earlier in the sentence.

94. 4QSam[a] LXX. MT adds *But he kept silent* (= error for *after about a month* in 11:1).

missing from the Masoretic Text, the Septuagint, and all other biblical manuscripts. The first-century historian Josephus, however, documents that the passage was in the ancient form of the Bible that he used. The New Revised Standard Version of the Bible has incorporated the passage into its translation.

11 [Na]hash king of the [A]mmonites oppressed the Gadites and the Reubenites viciously. He put out the right [ey]e of a[ll] of them and brought fe[ar and trembling] on [Is]rael. Not one of the Israelites in the region be[yond the Jordan] remained [whose] right eye Naha[sh king of] the Ammonites did n[ot pu]t out, except seven thousand men [who escaped from] the Ammonites and went to [Ja]besh-gilead.[95] 1 Then *after about a month,*[96] Nahash the Ammonite went up and besieged Jabesh-[gilead]. So all the people of Jabesh said to Nahash, ["Make a covenant] with [us, and we will serve you." 2 But] Nahash [the Ammonite said t]o [th]em, "I will ma[ke it with you on this condition: that I gouge out the right eye of every one of you and so disgrace all Israel]." ▲

7 [He took a yoke of] ox[en and cut them in pieces and sent them throughout the territory of Israel by messengers, saying, "Whoever does not march out behind] Saul and be[hind Samuel, so shall it be done to his oxen." The dread of the LORD fell on the people, and they came out as] on[e] man.

8 [When he mustered them at Bezek, the Israelites numbered three hundred thousand and the men of Judah] *seventy thousand.*[97] 9 [They said to the messengers who came, "Tell this to the people of Jabesh-gilead: 'Tomorrow,]* the LORD's* del[iverance[98] . . .] *to you, they will open the*[99] [. . . .'"] 10 So] the men [of Jabesh] sai[d, "Tomorrow we will come out to you, and you may do with us whatever seems good to you]."

11 [The next day Saul divided the people into three companies, and they invaded the camp during the morning watch and slaughtered the Ammonites until the heat of the day. Those who survived] were scattered, so that no [two of them] were lef[t together. 12 Then the people said to Samuel, "Who is it that] sai[d, 'Shall Saul reign over us?' Bring the men, that we may put them to death."] ▲

12 7 [So now, stand there so that I can argue the case with you, in the presence of the LORD, concerning all the LORD's righteous acts which he did

---

Chapter 11. 4QSam^a: 11:X–2, 7–12.

   95. 4QSam^a; cf. Josephus. Not in MT LXX.

   96. 4QSam^a LXX. Not in MT (= *But he kept silent* in MT 10:27).

   97. 4QSam^a LXX. *thirty thousand* MT.

   98. 4QSam^a. *you will have deliverance* MT LXX.

   99. 4QSam^a has an entire line that is not in MT LXX.

Chapter 12. 4QSam^a: 12:7–8, 14–19.

for you and for] your [an]cestors. 8 Wh[en Jacob was in Egypt and] your[100] [ancestor]s [cried out] to the Lo[rd, then the Lord sent Moses and Aaron, who brought your ancestors out of Egypt and settled them in this place.] ▲

14 [If you revere the Lord and serve him, listen to his voice and do not rebel against the commandment of the Lord, if both you and the king who reigns over you follow] the Lo[rd your God, very well. 15 But if you do not listen to the voice of the Lord and you rebel against the commandment of the L]ord, then [the hand of the Lord] will [be against you, as it was against your ancestors].

16 [Now therefore stand there and watch this great] thing [which the Lord will do before your eyes. 17 Is it not wheat harvest today? I will call to the Lord to send thunder and rain, and you will know and realize that your wickedness is great, which you have done in the sight of the Lord, in asking for] a king [for yourselves].

18 So Sa[muel] called [to the Lord, and the Lord sent thunder and rain that day. Then] all [the peo]ple gr[eatly] fear[ed the Lord and Samuel. 19 So all the people said to Samuel, "Pra]y [for your servants to the Lord your God so that we do not die, because we have added to all our sins this evil of asking for a king for ourselves."] ▲

14 24 [The Israelites were in distress that day, because S]au[l had put the army under oath, saying, "Cursed be anyone who eats any food until it is] evening and [I] have av[enged myself on my enemies." So no one tasted food. 25 The whole army entered the forest,] and there wa[s honey on the ground. 26 When the army entered the forest, the honey was dripping down; yet no one put his hand to his mouth, because the troops feared the oath.]

[27 But Jonathan had not heard when his father put the army under oath. So he stretched out the staff in his hand, dipped the end in the honeycomb, and put his hand to his mouth, and his eyes lit up. 28 Then one of the people spoke up, saying, "Your father strictly charged the army with an oath, 'Cursed be anyone] who [eats food today.' " So the troops were weak.]

29 [Then] Jonathan said, "My father has caused trou[ble] for the country. [See how my eyes lit up because I tasted] a little of *this honey.*[101] 30 How [much better it would have been if the troops had eaten freely today of the spoil] they got [from their enemies. But as it is,] *the slaughter*[102] [among the Philistine]s *has not been great.*"[103]

---

100. The spacing in 4QSam[a] points to a longer text than that of MT and could accommodate the text of LXX, which reads, *When Jacob and his sons were in Egypt and Egypt abased them, and your ancestors cried out. . . .*

Chapter 14. 4QSam[a]: 14:24–25, 28–34, 47–51.

101. 4QSam[a] LXX. MT uses an unusual construction.

102. 4QSam[a]. MT does not contain the article.

103. 4QSam[a] uses the masculine form of the verb, though *slaughter* is a feminine noun; this lack of agreement is not uncommon. MT uses the feminine form of the verb.

31 [They struck down the Philistines that da]y [from Michmash to Aijalon. But the troops were very faint, 32 and] the troops [set] on[104] [the spoil. Taking sheep, oxen, and calves, they slaughtered them] on the ground and [the troops] at[e them with the blood. 33 Then they told Saul, "Look, the troops are sinning against the LORD] by eating [with the blood." So he said, "You have been faithless. Roll a large stone to me now."] 34 Then Saul s[ai]d, "Go out among the troops and te[ll them, 'Everyone, bring his ox and his sheep to me and slaughter them here and eat. Do not sin against the LORD by eating with the blood.' " Everyone brought his ox with him that night and slaughtered them there.]▲

47 [Now that Saul had assumed rule] over Isra[el, he fought in every direction against] all his enemies—against Moa[b, the Ammonites, Edom,] the king[105] of Zobah, and the Philistines. Wherever he tur[ned, he punished them. 48 He fought valiantly, conquering] the Amalekites and delivering Israel from the power of those who [des]poiled them.

49 Now Saul's sons we[re] Jonathan, [Ishvi, and] Malchishua, and [his two daughters were] Merab, [the firstborn, and] Michal, the younger. 50 S[aul's wife was Ahinoam daughter of Ahimaaz]. The captain of the[106] army [was Abner] son of Ner, [Saul's uncle. 51 Kish, Saul's father, and Ner, Abner's father, were] sons of Abi[e]l.▲

15 25 ["Now, please pardon my sin and return with me, so that I may wor-ship the L]ORD." 26 [But Samuel answered Saul, "I will not return with you. Because you have rejected the word of] the LORD, [the LORD has rejected you as king over Israel." 27 As Samuel turned to go,] Saul[107] grabbed [the hem of his robe, and it tore. 28 Then Samuel said to him, "The LORD has torn the ki]ngdom of Israe[l away from you today and has given it to one of your neigh-bors, someone better than you. 29 Moreover, the Glory of Israel does not] change his mind[108] [or r]epen[t], fo[r] h[e is not a human being, that he should repent." 30 Then he replied, "I have sinned. Yet, I beg you, honor me now, in fro]nt of the elders of [my] peo[ple and Isra]el—retu[rn[109] with me, so that I may worship the LORD your God." 31 So] Sam[uel] return[ed with Saul, and] he[110] [worsh]iped the LORD. 32 [Then] Sam[uel] said, ["Bring Aga]g kin[g of the Amalekites here to me." And Agag came to him cheerfully, for he thought, "The threat of death is surely over."] ▲

---

104. 4QSam[a]. MT uses a different word.

105. 4QSam[a] LXX. *kings* MT.

106. 4QSam[a] LXX. *his* MT LXX[mss].

Chapter 15. 4QSam[a]: 15:25–32.

107. 4QSam[a] LXX. *he* MT.

108. 4QSam[a] LXX. *lie* MT.

109. 4QSam[a]. *and return* MT LXX.

110. 4QSam[a] LXX. *Saul* MT.

■ *A different manuscript, 4QSam^b, has an extensive fragment here. Like 4QSam^a, it differs noticeably from the Masoretic Text, often with preferable readings and often in agreement with the Septuagint.*

16 1 [The LORD said to Samuel, "How long will you grieve over Saul, seeing that I have rejected him as king over Israel? Fill your horn with oil, and go. I am sending] you [to Jesse the Bethlehemite, because I have selected a king for myself from his sons." 2 But Samuel said, "How can I go? If Saul hears, he will kill me." The LORD replied,] *"Ta[ke*[111] *a hei]fer* [with you and say, 'I have come to sacrifice to the LORD.' 3 Invite Jesse to the sacrifice, and then I will show you what to do. You are to anoint for me the one] I indicate to you."

4 [So Samuel did what the LORD said. When he arrived at Bethlehem, the elders of the city came trembling to meet him and said,] *"Seer,*[112] [do you come in peace?"] 5 And he said, ["Yes, in peace. I have come to sacrifice to the LORD. Consecrate yourselves and come with me to the sacrifice." He also consecrated Jesse and his sons and invited them to the sacrifice.]

6 When they entered, he saw [Eliab and thought, "Surely the LORD's anointed is in his presence." 7 But the LORD said to Samuel, "Do not regard his appearance or] his [tall] frame, because I have rejected him. Fo[r the LORD does not see as humans see. Humans see the outward appearance, but the LORD sees the heart."]

8 [Then] Jesse [called] Abinadab [and had him present himself to Samuel. But he said, "The LORD has not chosen this one either." 9 Next Jesse had Shammah present himself. But he said,] "The LORD [has not chosen this one either]." 10 Je[sse had seven of his sons present themselves to Samuel. But Samuel said to Jesse, "The LORD has not chosen these." 11 Then Samuel said to] Jesse, ["Are all your sons here?" He replied, "There is still the youngest, but he is tending the sheep." Samuel told Jesse, "Send for him. We will not sit down until he comes."] ▲

■ *The next passage illustrates how ancient narratives sometimes grew at the hand of narrators or scribes. 4QSam^a gives the height of Goliath as "four cubits" (equaling about six feet), and this is what the original Septuagint, followed by the historian Josephus, also records. Later Septuagint manuscripts read "five cubits," and the Masoretic Text, followed by yet later Septuagint manuscripts, reads "six cubits" (equaling about nine feet).*

17 3 [The Philistines were positioned on a mountain on one side, and Israel was positioned on a mountain on the other, with a valley between th]em. 4 [Then] a cha[mpion named Goliath, who was from Gath, ca]me out [of the

---

Chapter 16. 4QSam^b: 16:1–11.

111. 4QSam^b and MT use different forms.

112. 4QSam^b LXX. Not in MT.

Chapter 17. 4QSam^a: 17:3–6.

Philistine camp. His height was *f]our*[113] [cu]bits and a span. 5 [He had a bronze helmet on his head and wore bronze scale-armor—and] the armor weighed [five thousand shekels. 6 He had bronze greaves on his legs, and a bronze javelin was slung between] his [shoulder]s.▲

18 17 [Saul said to David, "Here is my elder daughter Merab. I will give her to you as a wife. Simply be a valiant warrior on my behalf and fi]ght [the LORD's] battl[es." But Saul was thinking, "I will not touch him. Instead let the power of the Philistines go against him." 18 David answered S]aul, ["Who am I, and what is my life or my father's family in Israel, that I should be son-in-law to the king?"] ▲

19 10 [Saul tried to pin David to the wall with his spear, but he slipped away] from [Saul as he drove the spear into the wall. David fled and escaped that night. 11 Saul sent messengers to David's house, to watch him, and to] kill him [in the morning. But Michal, David's wife, told him, "If you do not save your life tonight, tomorrow you will be killed." 12 So Michal let Davi]d [down] through the window, [and he slipped away, fled, and escaped].

13 [Then Michal took an idol, laid it on the bed, put braided goats' hair at its head, and covered it] with clothes. 14 [When Saul sent messengers to take David, she said, "He is sick." 15 Then Saul sent the messengers to see David,] saying, "Bring [him to me in the bed so that I may kill him." 16 When the messengers came in, there was the idol in the bed with the braided goats' hair at] its [hea]d. 17 So [Saul] said [to Michal, "Why did you deceive me like this and send away my enemy so that he could escape?" Michal answered Saul, "He said to me, 'Let me go. Why should I kill you?'"] ▲

20 26 [Nevertheless Saul did not say anything that day, thinking, "Something has happened to him. He is not clean,] *because he has not been cleansed."*[114] 27 Th[en on the next da]y, the [seco]nd of [the mo]nth, [David]'s place was empty. [So Saul asked Jonathan his son, "Why has the son of Jesse not come] *to the table*[115] [either yesterday] or today?" 28 Jonathan answered Saul *and* [*said,*[116] "David earnestly asked my permission to go to Bethlehem. 29 He said, 'Allow me to go, please, because] *our family has* [*a sacrifice*][117] in the city, and as for *me, my brothers have ordered me*[118] to be there. Now, if I have found [favor with you, please

---

113. 4QSam[a] LXX. *five* LXX[mss]. *six* MT LXX[mss].

Chapter 18. 1QSam: 18:17–18.

Chapter 19. 4QSam[b]: 19:10–17.

Chapter 20. 4QSam[b]: 20:26–42.

114. 4QSam[b] LXX. *because he is not clean* MT.

115. 4QSam[b] LXX. *to the meal* MT using a different word for *to*.

116. 4QSam[b] LXX. Not in MT.

117. 4QSam[b] LXX. *our family sacrifices* MT.

118. 4QSam[b]. *my brother, he has ordered me* MT.

let me get away and see my brothers.' That is why he has not come to the table of] the king."

30 Then Saul exploded in *hot*[119] anger at Jonathan, and he said to him, "You son of a *rebellious slave girl!*[120] [Do I not know that you are allied with the son of Jesse, to your own shame and to the shame of your mother's nakedness?] 31 For as long as the son of Jesse lives on earth, *your kingdom will not be established.*[121] So no[w, send for him and bring him to me, for he must die." 32 But Jonathan answered Saul] his father, and *said,*[122] "Why should he be put to death? What has he done?" 33 Then Saul hurled his spear at him to kil[l him. So Jonathan knew that his father was determined to put David to death.] 34 Jonathan *shot up from*[123] the ta[b]le in hot anger and ate no food that second day of the month, [because he was upset about David because his father had disgraced him].

35 [In the morning,] Jonathan [went out] to the field for his meeting with David and brought a small boy with him. 36 He said to *the*[124] boy, "Run [and find the arrows I shoot." As the lad ran, he shot an arrow beyond him,] *toward the city.*[125] 37 The boy reached the spot where the *arrow*[126] Jonathan shot lay; then [Jonathan call]ed [out to the boy and said, "Isn't the arrow beyond you?" 38 Then Jonathan called out] to the *lad,*[127] "Be quick, hurry, do not linger." Jonathan's boy picked up [the arrow and returned to his master. 39 But the boy was not aware of anything—only Jonathan and David understood] the matter. 40 Jonathan gave his weapons *to*[128] the boy and [sai]d [to him, "Go and carry them to the city."]

41 [As soon as the boy had gone, David got up from his place on the south side of the stone and prostrated himself, with his face] to the ground, bowing three times. They kissed one [another and wept together, but David more. 42 Jonathan said to David, "Go in peace. For] *both*[129] of us [have sworn], in the name of the LORD, saying, 'The LORD will be between me and you [and between my descen-

---

119. 4QSam[b] LXX. Not in MT.

120. 4QSam[b]. *perverse rebellious woman* MT.

121. 4QSam[b]. *neither you nor your kingdom will be established* MT.

122. 4QSam[b] LXX[ms]. *said to him* MT LXX[ms].

123. 4QSam[b] LXX. *got up from* MT (using a different word for *from*).

124. 4QSam[b] LXX. *his* MT.

125. 4QSam[b]. Not in MT LXX.

126. 4QSam[b]. *arrows* MT.

127. 4QSam[b]. *boy* MT.

128. 4QSam[b] and MT use different words.

129. 4QSam[b]. *we both* MT.

dants and your descendants forever.' "] Then *David*[130] got up and left, and
Jonathan went back to the *city*.[131]

21 1 Then David went to Nob, to [Ahimelech the priest. Ahimelech came
trembling to meet David and said to him, "Why are you alone?] Why is
no one *with*[132] you?" 2 David said to *the priest,*[133] "The king charged me with
some business [and said to me, 'Do not let anyone know anything about the matter on which I am sending you and with which I have charged you.'] So I *arranged
to meet*[134] the young men at a certain plac[e. 3 Now then, what do you have on
hand? Give me five loaves of bread or whatever you can find."] 4 The priest answer[ed] [David] and said, "There is no ordinary bread *on ha*[*nd,*[135] but there is
consecrated bread. If the young men have kept themselves] from women, *they
may eat i*[*t*."[136] 5 David answered] the priest and sa[id to him, "Yes, women have
been kept from us as previously whenever I set out.] *All*[137] the young men [a]re
holy for [even an ordinary] jou[rney. So today how much more will they be so!"
6 So the priest gave him consecrated bread, because the only bread there was the
bread of the Pres]ence, *which had been taken from*[138] before the Lo[RD and replaced
by hot bread on] the [day it was taken out.]

7 [Now one of Saul's servants was there that day, detained before the LORD; his
name was Doeg the Edomite, the head of the shepherds] who [worked for Saul. 8
David said to Ahimelech, "Do you have a spear or sword on hand? For I did not
bring my sword or my weapons with] me, because [the king's business] required
[haste." 9 The priest said, "The sword of Goliath the Philistine, whom you slew
in the Elah valley, is here, wrapped in a cloth] *behind an ephod.*[139] [If you want to
take that, take it. There is none except that here." David replied, "There is none
like that. Give it to me."] ▲

23 9 [David learned that] Saul was plotting [evil] against him, [and he said to
Abiathar the priest, "Bring the ephod here." 10 Then David said, "O

---

130. 4QSam[b] LXX. *he* MT.

131. 4QSam[b] and MT use different forms.

Chapter 21. 4QSam[b]: 21:1–9.

132. 4QSam[b] and MT use different words.

133. 4QSam[b]. *Ahimelech the priest* MT.

134. 4QSam[b] LXX. MT is corrupt here.

135. Literally, *under your hand* 4QSam[b]. *at under your hand* MT.

136. 4QSam[b] LXX[mss]. Not in MT.

137. 4QSam[b] LXX. *The vessels of* MT.

138. Singular (correctly) 4QSam[b]. Plural (incorrectly) MT.

139. 4QSam[b]. *behind the ephod* MT (with a different form for *behind*). Not in LXX.

Chapter 23. 4QSam[b]: 23:9–17.

LORD, God of Israel,] your servant [has certainly hea]rd that Saul means [to come to Keilah to destroy the city on my account. 11 *Will the citizens of Keilah surrender me into his hand?*[140] Will Saul come down, as your servant has heard? O LORD,] God of Israel, *tell*[141] [your] serva[nt." The LORD answered, "He will come down." 12 Then David said, "Will the men of Keilah surrender me and my men into the hand of Sa]ul?" The LORD answered, "Th[ey] wi[ll." 13 Then David and his men, numbering about six hundred, got up and left Keilah, and went wherever they could. Sau]l [was told that David had es]caped from [Ke]ilah; [so he did not go on].

14 [David lived in the wilderness in the strongholds and stayed in the hill country in the Ziph wilderness. Saul hunted for him every da]y, but *the Lo[RD]*[142] did not deliver him [into his hand. 15 David saw that Saul had come out to s]eek his life [while David was in the Ziph wilderness at Horesh. 16 Jonathan, Sau]l[['s son, got up and w]ent to [David at Horesh and encouraged him in *the LOR*]D.[143] 17 He said to him, "Do n[ot be afraid. For Saul my father will not find you. You will be king over Israel, and I will be second to you. Saul my father also knows this."]▲

24 3 [Coming to the sheepfolds on the wa]y, [where th]ere [was a cave, Saul went in to relieve himself, but David and] his [m]en [were sitting] in the rear of [the cave. 4 David's men said to him, "Here is the day of w]hich [the LORD] said [to you, 'I will indeed deliver your enemy into your hand, and you may treat him as you like.'" So David got up and secretly cut off an edge of Saul's robe.] ▲

8 [Then David also got up and went out of the cave,] and he called [out to Saul, "My lord the king!" When Saul looked behind him, David bowed with his face to] the earth [and prostrated himself].▲

13 ["As the o]ld[144] pro[verb s]ays, ['Out of the wicked comes wickedness.' So my hand shall not be against you. 14 After] whom [*have*] you [*the ki*]ng[145] of [Israel come out? Whom do you pursue? After a dead dog] or[146] af[ter a single fl]ea. 15 [May the LORD be our judge and decide between us. May he take notice and argue] my [case] and deliver me [from your hand]."

---

140. MT. 4QSam^b apparently does not have space for the long, repetitive text as in MT (see vs 12).

141. 4QSam^a. *please tell* MT.

142. 4QSam^a LXX. *God* MT.

143. 4QSam^a LXX. *God* MT.

Chapter 24. 4QSam^a: 24:3–4, 8, 13–22.

144. Plural 4QSam^a. Singular (as expected) MT.

145. 4QSam^a LXX. *has the king* MT.

146. 4QSam^a LXX. Not in MT.

16 [Then, when David finished saying these things to] Sa[u]l, [Saul said, "Is
that your voice, my son David?" Wee]ping [out loud, 17 Saul] said to [David,
"You are more righteous than I. For you have treated me] w[ell, though] I have
done you harm. 18 [You have shown just now how] you [have done g]ood t[o
me] in that when [the LORD] delivered me [into your hand, you did not kill me.
19 When a m]an [finds] his [ene]my, [does he l]et him go [safely] on his way?
[May the LORD reward you with good for what yo]u [have *done*[147] toda]y. 20 Now
[indeed, I know that you will certainly be king and that the kingdom of Israel
will be placed] in your hand. 21 [So now, swear to me by the LORD that you will
not cut off] my descendants [af]ter me and th[us eliminate my name from my father's family." 22 So David swore to Saul. Then Saul we]nt [home, but David and
his men went up to the stronghold.] ▲

25

3 [The man's name was Nabal, and his wife's name was Abigail. The
woman was intelligent and beautiful, but the man was stubborn and an-
tagonistic in] business. *The man*[148] was a Caleb[ite. 4 When] David [heard] in the
desert that [Nabal was shearing his sheep, 5 David] sent ten ser[vants. And]
Dav[i]d [s]aid *to*[149] the servant[s, "Go up to Carmel, visit Nabal. Greet him] in my
name 6 [and say,] 'Live [long! P]eace [to you and to your house and to all that is
yours. 7 I] have [jus]t heard [that you are shearing. Your shepherds have lately
been with us, and we did not mistreat them, and] they [missed nothing all the
time they were in Carmel. 8 Ask your servants and they will tell you. So let my
servants find favor] in your sight; fo[r we come on a festive day. Please give whatever is on hand to the servants and to your son David.' "]

9 [When David's young men] arrived, [they said all these things to Nabal in
David's name and then waited. 10 Nabal answered David's servants,] "Who is
Da[vid? Who is the son of Jesse? There are many servants these days who *break
aw*]*ay*[150] [from their masters. 11 So should I take] my [br]ead [and water and my
meat, which I have slaughtered for] my [shear]ers, to give [it to men from I don't
know] where?" 12 [So David's servants returned on their journey and went back.
When they arrived,] they repeated [every word to him]. ▲

20 [Then as Abigail rode on her donkey, descending under the cover of the
mountain, there were David and his men descend]ing toward [her, and she met
them. 21 Now David had said, "All] for nothing [have I guarded everything this
man had in the wilderness, so that] no[t one thing of all his belongings was missing. Yet he returns me evil for good."] ▲

---

147. 4QSam[a] LXX. *done for me* MT.

Chapter 25. 4QSam[a]: 25:3–12, 20–21, 25–26, 39–40; 4QSam[c]: 25:30–31.

148. 4QSam[a] LXX. *he* MT.

149. 4QSam[a] and MT use different words.

150. 4QSam[a] and MT spell the verb differently.

25 ["Please, my lord, pay no attention to this worthless man, Nabal. He is just like his name. His name is Folly, and fo]lly is with him. But I, [your maidservant, I did not see my lord's servants whom you sent. 26 So now, my lord, as the LOR]D [lives] and as [your] soul lives, [seeing that the LORD has held you back from shedding blood, and from avenging yourself with your own hands, so now let] your [en]emies and those [who seek harm for my lord be as Nabal]." ▲

■ *4QSamᶜ exhibits the rare method of writing four dots in place of the four letters* YHWH *for the divine name.*

30 ["Then, when • • • • has fulfilled for] my lord all [the good] he has promised [you and has appointed you prince over Israel,] 31 you [will no]t have this *vengeance*[151] and [distress for] my [lord, having shed blood without cause or having taken vengeance] himself. When • • • •[152] has prospered [my] lord, [then remember your maidservant."] ▲

39 [When David heard that Nabal was dead, he said, "Blessed be the LORD, who has taken up my] cause [for the insult I received from Nabal and has kept his servant from evildoing. Nabal's evildoing the LORD has brought back on his own head." Then David sent a message to Abigail to make her his wife. 40 When] David's [servant]s [came to Abigail at Carmel, they said to her, "David has sent us to you,] to [make you his wife]." ▲

26 10 [But David said, "As the LORD lives, the LORD will strike him. Either his day will come to die or he will fall in ba]ttle [and be swept away. 11 The LORD forbid that I extend my hand against the LORD's anointed. But now take] *his spear*[153] [at his head and the jug of water, and let's go." 12 So David took the spear and] the jug of wa[ter from Saul's head, and they stole away. No one saw it or knew about it or even woke up]—for [they were all asleep, because a deep sleep had fallen on them from the LORD].▲

21 [Then Saul said, "I have done wrong. Come back, my son David. I will no longer do you harm, because my life was precious to you today. Look at me—I have been a fool.] I have been te[rribly] wrong." 22 [David answered,] "Here is [the king's] sp[ear.[154] Have one of the young men come over and get it. 23 The LORD will return to ea]ch [his] righ[teousness and faithfulness. Although the LORD delivered you into my hand today, I would not] exte[nd my] ha[nd against the LORD's anointed. 24 See here, as your life was precious to me today, so may my life be precious t]o [the LORD, and may he deliver me from all distress]." ▲

---

151. 4QSamᶜ. *stumbling* MT. *abomination* LXX.

152. 4QSamᶜ. *the* LORD MT.

Chapter 26. 4QSamᵃ: 26:10–12, 21–24.

153. 4QSamᵃ. *the spear* MT LXX.

154. 4QSamᵃ LXX. *the spear, O king* MT.

27⁸ [David and his men went out and raided the Geshurites, the Girzites, and the Amalekites. Those peoples lived in land from ancient times, as far as Shur and] Egypt. 9 [When David attacked a region, he allowed neither man nor woman to live. But he took away sheep,] cattle, don[keys, camels, and clothes, and then returned to Achish. 10 Then] Achish asked, *"Against [whom*[155] did you make a raid today?"* David replied, "Against the South of Judah"] or *"To the South of Jera[hmee]l"*[156] or *"Against*[157] the South of [the Kenites." 11 David allowed neither man nor woman to live, to bring them] to Gath, thi[n]king, "Otherwise [they] might repo[rt about us, saying, 'David did thus and so.'" That was what he did] the whole time he lived [in the country of the Philistines. 12 Achish trusted David,] thinking, ["He has made himself ut]terly [abhorrent to his people, to Israel. So he will be my servant always."]

28¹ [At that time,] the Philist[in]es mustered [their forces for war, to fight against Israel.] Achish [said] to Da[vi]d, "Be as[sured that you must go out with us in the camp, you and your men, *to b]attle at Jezreel."*[158] 2 [David s]aid [to Achish, "Very well, you will see what your servant can do."] Ach[ish said] *to*[159] [David], "Good, [I will make you my] bo[dyguard for life."] ▲

22 ["So now, please, you too listen to your maidservant, and let me put a little bread in front of you. Then eat, so that you have strength] for [your] j[ourney." 23 But he refused and said, "I will not eat." But his servants, along with the woman, urged him. So he gave in to their urging,] got up *from*[160] [the gr]ound, and [sat on the bed. 24 The woman had a fatted calf in the house. So hurrying, she slaughtered it. She] took flour [and] kneaded it and [baked unleavened bread. 25 Then she brought it to Saul and his servants, and they ate. Then they got up and w]ent away t[hat] night.[161] ▲

30²⁷ [It is for tho]se [in Bethel and] for those [in Ramoth Negev and for those in Jattir 28 and for those in Aroer and for those in Siphmoth and for those] in [E]shtemoa 29 and for th[ose in Racal and for those in the cities of the Jerahmeelites and for those in the citie]s of the *Kenezites*[162] 30 and for th[ose in

---

Chapter 27. 4QSam^a: 27:8–12.

   155. 4QSam^a LXX. 4QSam^a LXX. MT errs.

   156. 4QSam^a. *Against the South of the Jerahmeelites* MT. *Against the South of Jesmega* LXX.

   157. 4QSam^a LXX. *To* MT.

Chapter 28. 4QSam^a: 28:1–2, 22–25.

   158. 4QSam^a. Not in MT LXX.

   159. 4QSam^a and MT use different forms.

   160. 4QSam^a and MT use different forms.

   161. 4QSam^a. *on that night* MT.

Chapter 30. 4QSam^a: 30:27–31.

   162. 4QSam^a LXX. *Kenites* MT.

Hormah and for those in Bor-ashan and for those in Athach 31 and for those] in Hebro[n and for all the places where David himself and his men were accustomed to roam]. ▲

31 2 [The Philistines] over[took Saul and his sons and killed J]onathan and [Abinadab and Malchi-shua, Saul's sons. 3 The battle went heavily] *against*[163] Saul. [Then the archers fou]n[d him and he was badly wounded by them. 4 So] S[au]l [said] *to*[164] [his armor-bearer, "Draw your sword and thrust me through, or th]e[se uncircumcised will come and thrust me through and abuse me." But his armor-bearer would not—he was too frightened. So Saul took his own sword and fell on it.] ▲

2 SAMUEL

■ *The books traditionally labeled 1 Samuel and 2 Samuel were originally considered a single book. 2 Samuel followed 1 Samuel on the same scroll, 4QSam*[a]*.*

2 5 [David sent messengers to the people of Jabesh-gilead and said to] them, "May you be blessed [by the LORD, because you have performed thi]s [act of faithfulness] *toward*[1] yo[ur] lord [Saul and buried him. 6 Now may the L]ORD [show steadfast love and faithfulness] *to*[2] you. [And I too will return to you] the same [faithfulness] which [you have shown in this matter. 7 So now be firmly re-solved and b]e valian[t, because your lord Saul is dead, and the house of Judah has anointed me *ov*]*er them as* [*king*."[3] 8 But Abner son of Ner,] the commander of *the*[4] army wh[ich had been Saul's, took Ishbosheth son of Saul and brought hi]m [over] to Mahana[im. 9 He made him king over Gilead, the Ashurites, Jezreel, Eph]raim, [Benjamin, and all Israel. 10 Ishbosheth son of Saul was forty years old when he began to reign over Israel, and he reigned two years. Nevertheless the house of Judah followed David. 11 David was king in Hebron over the house of Judah for seven years and six mo]nt[h]s. 12 But [Abner son of Ner and those who

---

Chapter 31. 4QSam[a]: 31:2–4.

    163. 4QSam[a] and MT use different words.

    164. 4QSam[a] and MT use different words.

Chapter 2. 4QSam[a]: 2:5–16, 25–27, 29–32.

    1. 4QSam[a] LXX. *with* MT.

    2. 4QSam[a] and MT use different words.

    3. 4QSam[a] LXX. *as king over them* MT.

    4. 4QSam[a]. Not in MT.

followed Ishbosheth son of Saul] marched out [from Mahanaim to Gi]beon. 13
So Joab so[n of] Zeru[iah and David's followers marched out and came to]gethe[r
with them] at the pool of Gibeon. [They held up there, one band on one side of
the pool and the other on the other side of] the p[o]ol. 14 [Then] A[bner sa]id
[to Joab, "Let the young men come forward and compete] befo[re us." J]oab
repl[ied], "Let [them] come for[ward." 15 Then they came forward and were
counted as they passed: twe]lve *for the Benjamini[te]s of Ish[bosheth*[5] son of Saul, and
twelve of] David['s followers]. 16 But each [one] g[r]abbed [his opponent by the
head and thrust his sword in his opponent's side, and they fell together]. So that
pla[ce] was nam[e]d [Helkath-hazzurim, which is in Gibeon]. ▲

25 [The Benjaminites rallied behind] A[bne]r [and, as a si]ngle [force, stood at
the top of a hill]. 26 Then A[bner] called [to Joab and said, "Must the sword devour forever? Do] you not see that [it will be bitter in the end? How long will it
be before you tell] your troops to stop pursu[ing their kinsmen?" 27 Joab replied,
"As God lives, if] you had [not s]poken, [the troops would not have given up
pursuing their kinsmen un]til m[orning." 28 Then Joab sounded the trumpet and
his troops stopped. They did not pursue Israel any further, and they ended the
fighting.]

29 [Abner and his men marched all that night through the Arabah, crossed the
Jordan, and marched through all Bithron and arrived at Maha]naim. 30 After
Joa[b gave up the pursuit of Abner, he assembled all his troops, and nineteen men,
besides Asahel, were missing from] David's followers. 31 [But David's followers
had defeated] Benjamin, and of [Abner's] men [three hundred sixty died. 32
They carried Asahel away] and buried him in [his father's] tomb, [wh]ich was in
[Bethlehem. Joab and] his men [marched all night], and day broke [on] them at
Hebron.

3 1 Afterward, there [was a long war between the house of] Saul and the house
of David. While David continued [to gain strength, the house of Saul] steadily
[weakened].

2 Sons were born to David in Hebron. [His firstborn was A]mnon [by A]hi-
noam of Jezreel; 3 his [s]econd was *Dal[ujah]*[6] by *Abigail the [Carmelite;*[7] the] third,
Absa[lom] son of Maacah daugh[ter of] King Talmai of Geshur; 4 the four[th,
Adonijah son of Ha]ggith; the fi[fth], Shephatiah *by*[8] A[bi]tal; 5 and the sixth,
Ithream, by [David's wife Eglah—th]e[se were born] to David [in Heb]ron.

---

5. 4QSam[a] LXX. *for Benjamin and for Ishbosheth* MT.

Chapter 3. 4QSam[a]: 3:1–8, 23–39.

6. 4QSam[a] LXX. *Chileab* MT.

7. 4QSam[a] LXX. *Abigail the wife of Nabal the Carmelite* (masculine) MT.

8. 4QSam[a] LXX. *son of* MT.

6 [T]hrough[o]ut [the] war between the house of Sa[ul and the house of David, Abner was acquiring power for himself] in the house of Saul.

7 Now Saul had a concubine, *Rizpah*[9] [daughter of Aiah, and *Mephibosheth son of*] *Saul*[10] said to Ab[ne]r, "Wh[y have you] gone in to [my father's] con[cubine?" 8 But Abner was furious at what Mephibosheth said,] and he said *to him,*[11] ["Am I a dog's head from Judah? To this day I have shown loyalty to the house of Saul your father, to his kinspeople, and to his friends, and I have not surrendered you into the hand of David, and yet today you accuse me over this woman?"] ▲

23 [When Joab and his whole army arrived, he was informed that Abner] son of Ner [had come] to *David,*[12] and David had let him go, and he had gone away [in peace. 24 So Joab approached the king and said, "What] were you doing? Abner came to you! Why [did you let him go? Now he has gotten away. 25 You do realize] that [A]*bner*[13] [came] to deceive you [and to gather information on your comings and goings, to gather information on] everything you do?

26 Joab left David and sen[t] mes[sengers] after Abner, [and] th[ey brought him back from the cistern of Si]rah. David, however, knew [nothing] of it. 27 When [Abne]r ret[urn]ed to [*Heb*]ron,[14] [Joab] took hi[m] aside [within the] gate to speak [t]o him privately, [and th]ere [he stabbed him] *in*[15] the stomach. So [he] died [for shedding the blood of] Asahel, his brother.

28 When [David] hear[d about this afterward, he sa]id, "I and [my] king[dom] are *forever innocent before the* Lord. 29 [*May*] the blood of [*Abner son of Ner f*]*all*[16] o[n] Joa[b]'s [he]ad and *on*[17] a[ll] *Joab's*[18] house. May [Joab's] hou[se never] be without [someone with a discharge] or a leper or a man who h[olds the] spindle or who falls by the sword or who [la]cks food." 30 For Joa[b and Abashai his brother murder]ed Abner [f]or having kil[led Asahe]l their brother [in battle] at Gi[beon.]

31 [David said t]o Joab [and to all the people who were with him], "T[ear] yo[ur cl]othes, [put on sackclo]th, and lament over [Abner." King David] fol-

---

9. 4QSam[a] LXX. *named Rizpah* MT.

10. 4QSam[a] LXX. *he* MT. 4QSam[a] LXX have wrongly inserted *Mephibosheth* in place of the correct name *Ishbosheth*.

11. 4QSam[a] LXX. Not in MT.

12. 4QSam[a] LXX. *the king* MT.

13. 4QSam[a]. *Abner son of Ner* MT LXX.

14. 4QSam[a] and MT use different forms.

15. 4QSam[a]. Implicit in MT.

16. 4QSam[a] LXX. *forever innocent before the* Lord *of the blood of Abner son of Ner.* 29 *May it fall* MT.

17. 4QSam[a] LXX. *to* MT.

18. 4QSam[a] (*yw'b*). *his father's* (*'byw*) MT.

lowed behi[nd the bie]r, 32 [and] when they buried Abner [at Hebron], the king wept [out] loud [at A]bner['s grave]. Indeed, everyone wept. 33 [The king sang this lament] *over*[19] Abner:

> [Should] Abner die the dea[th of a scoun]drel?
> 34 [Your hands were not] b[ound] *in fetters.*[20]
> *Your feet were not p[u]t into shack[le]s.*[21]
> As *a f[ool*[22] before the ruthless, you fell].

[And] *all*[23] continued to wee[p] over him. 35 All the people [c]ame to [per-suade David to take some food while] it was still day, but Dav[id sw]ore, "So may [God] d[o to me and more, if] before the sun rises [I taste brea]d or any[thing whatever." 36 The people took note of it and it seemed good] to them, [just as everything] the [king d]id [*seemed*[24] to the people].

37 And [that day, all the people and] all [Israel knew that the king had not or-dered the] death [of] Abner [son of Ner. 38 The king said to his servants, "Do] you [no]t know that this [very da]y a prince, a great man, has fallen [in Israel? 39 Today I was mild, though I am anointed] king, [while th]ese [m]en, the sons of Ze[ruiah, were more severe than I. May the LORD repay the wicked according to their wickedness."]

4

▨ *There is confusion in the textual tradition of 2 Samuel 4 concerning two individuals: Ishbosheth, son of King Saul, and Mephibosheth, the lame son of Jonathan and grandson of Saul. In 4:1–2, 4QSam[a] transmits the incorrect name (instead of Ishbosheth); the Masoretic Text perhaps never had a name in verses 1–3 or had Mephibosheth and removed it without replacing the correct name. For both names, the latter part would originally have been -baal. The element -baal, however, was objectionable because it was the name of a Canaanite god, and it was replaced with -bosheth (meaning "shame"), probably in the Second Temple period.*

---

19. 4QSam[a] LXX. *to* MT.

20. 4QSam[a]. Not in MT LXX.

21. 4QSam[a] and MT have different forms and word order.

22. 4QSam[a] LXX. *one who falls* MT.

23. 4QSam[a]. *all the people* MT LXX. The absence of *the people* in 4QSam[a] is probably due to an error.

24. 4QSam[a] LXX. *seemed good* MT. Though the other words are not preserved, the Hebrew word order and extant letters make it clear that the word *good* is not on this manuscript.

Chapter 4. 4QSam[a]: 4:1–4, 9–12

1 [When] *Mephibo[sheth son of Saul]*[25] hear[d that] A[b]ner [had died] in He-bron, [he lost] his courage, [and all the Israelites were anxious]. 2 *Mephibosheth son of Saul*[26] had[27] [two captains of raiding band]s, [o]ne na[med Baanah, and the other Rechab], sons of Rimmon the Be[e]rothite, Benja[min]ites—[since Beeroth] also [was considered to be]long to Benjami[n]. 3 (The Beero[th]ites fle[d] to Gittai[m and have been sojourners] there [until] this day.)

■ *In the parenthetical verse 4, Mephibosheth is the correct name.*

4 Now Jonathan [son of Saul] had [a son whose feet were lame. He was five year]s [old when the] re[port of Saul and Jonathan ar]rived [from Jezreel], and [his nurse] picked him up [and fled. But in her haste to flee, he fell and became lame. His name was Mephibosheth.]▲

9 [David answered Rechab and] his [bro]ther [Baanah], the sons of [Rimmon the Beerothite, saying to them, "As the LORD lives, who has saved my life] in every dang[er], 10 when someone told me, ['See, Saul is dead,'—thinking he brought good news—I] seized him and killed him in Zikla[g—this was the re-ward I gave him for his good news. 11 How much more, when wicke]d [men] have kil[led a righ]teous [man in] his own h[ou]se [on his bed! Now do you think I will not require] his blood [from you and] wipe you of[f the earth?" 12 David gave orders to the you]ng men, [and they killed them, cut] off their hands and [feet, and hung them up beside the p]ool in Heb[ron. Then] *he*[28] took [the hea]d of *Mephibosheth*[29] and [buried it in the grave of Ab]ner at He[bron].

5 1 [Then all the tribe]s of Is[rael came to David] at Hebron, *saying,*[30] ["Look, we are your flesh and blood. 2 Pr]evi[ou]sly, when [S]aul wa[s king over us, you were the one who led] I[srae]l [out and brought it back, and the LORD said to you, 'You will shepherd my people Israel, and you will be a ruler over Israel.' " 3 Thus all the elders of Israel came to the king at Hebron. King David made a covenant with them] in Hebro[n before the LORD, and they anointed David king over *Israel*].[31]

---

25. 4QSamᵃ LXX. *the son of Saul* MT.

26. 4QSamᵃ LXX. *the son of Saul* MT. 4QSamᵃ transmits the incorrect name (instead of *Ishbosheth*); MT perhaps never had a name in vss 1–3 or had *Mephibosheth* and removed it without replacing the correct name.

27. 4QSamᵃ and MT use different constructions to indicate possession.

28. 4QSamᵃ. *they* MT LXX.

29. 4QSamᵃ LXX. *Ishbosheth* MT (correctly).

Chapter 5. 4QSamᵃ: 5:1–3, 6–16 [omitted 5:4–5].

30. 4QSamᵃ LXXᴹᴺ. *and said, saying* MT. *and said to him* LXXᴮᴬ.

31. 4QSamᵃ OL MT–1Chr. *Israel. 4 David was thirty years old when he began to reign, and he reigned forty years. 5 In Hebron, he reigned over Judah seven years and six months, and in Jerusalem he reigned over all Israel and Judah thirty-three years.* MT LXX.

■ *4QSam^a, followed by the Old Latin and 1 Chronicles (and probably Josephus), moves directly from 5:3 to 5:6. The Masoretic Text, followed by the Aramaic and Syriac, adds a chronological note about David's age and the length of his reigns in Hebron and Jerusalem.*

6 [The king] and his men [marched to Jerusalem against the Jebusites, the inhabitants of the region, who told David, "You will never get in here,] for³² [the blind and the lame] *will incite*³³ [. . . "; thinking,] "David [cannot get in her]e." 7 Nevertheless David captured the stronghold of Zion, which became [the city of David]. 8 That day, Da[vid had said], "Who[ever has a mind to de]feat [the Jebu]sites, *let him seize*³⁴ the water conduit and strike *the bl[ind and]* the [lam]e³⁵ whom David hates." [That is w]hy they say, "The [bl]ind and the lame cannot [come into the house]."

9 David [occu]pied [the] stronghold and nam[ed] it the city of David. *He built a city*³⁶ [all around from] the Millo inward. 10 [All the while] Dav[id] became [greater and great]er, for the LORD *of ho[s]ts*³⁷ [was with him].

11 So King Hi[ram] of Tyre sent [messengers t]o David, with [cedar] lo[gs, woodworkers,] and *maso[n]s,*³⁸ [and th]ey built [David] a hou[se. 12 David recognized that the LORD had established him as king] over Isra[el and that he had exalted his kingdom for the sake of his people Israel. 13 Da]vid [took] more con[cub]ines [and wives from Jerusalem, after he arrived from Hebron, and] m[o]re [son]s and daughters [were born] to David. 14 [These are the names of those who were born to him in Jerusalem: Shammua,] Shobab, [Nathan,] Solo[mon, 15 Ibhar, Elishua, Nepheg, Japhia, 16 E]lishama, [Eliada, and Eliphelet].▲

6 2 [So David made preparations and went with all the people with] him *to Baalah—that is, Kir[yath-jearim] of Judah*³⁹—to bring u[p from it the ark of G]o[d], which is [called by *the name of the LORD*],⁴⁰ enthron[ed on] the cherub[im. 3 They placed the ark of God] *on*⁴¹ a [new] ca[rt and brought it] out of the house of A[binadab, which was on a hill. Uzzah and Ahio, the sons of Abinadab, drov]e

---

32. 4QSam^a. *but* MT.

33. 4QSam^a. *turn you away* MT LXX.

34. 4QSam^a LXX. *will seize* MT.

35. 4QSam^a LXX^MN. *the lame and the blind* MT LXX^BAL.

36. 4QSam^a LXX. *David built* MT.

37. 4QSam^a LXX. LORD *the God of hosts* MT.

38. 4QSam^a. *stone-masons* MT.

Chapter 6. 4QSam^a: 6:2–9, 12–18.

39. 4QSam^a MT–1Chr. *from the citizens of Judah* (uncertain) MT.

40. [4QSam^a] LXX. *the name the name of the LORD of hosts* MT.

41. 4QSam^a and MT use different words for *on.*

[*the*] *cart* 4 [*with*⁴² the ark of God. Ahio walked in front of the a]rk, 5 [while David and all] *the Is[rae]l[i]tes*⁴³ p[layed] be[fore the LORD with *all their might, and*] *with songs*⁴⁴ [and lyre]s, [harps], tambourines, [castan]ets, [and cymbals].

6 [When th]ey [came] to the thre[shing-floor of] *Noran,*⁴⁵ Uzzah touched *his* [*ha*]*nd*⁴⁶ to the ark of [G]o[d, grabbing it because the] oxen [had stumbled]. 7 Then the anger of the LORD flamed out against U[zzah, and] Go[d] struck him there [*for touching his hand*] to [*the*] *ark,*⁴⁷ and he died [there] *be[fore G]o[d.*⁴⁸ 8 Then] Da[vid] was angry, [because the LOR]D [had burst] out against Uzzah— [that] plac[e is named Pere]z-Uzzah [to this day]. 9 David was afraid of [the LORD that day], *saying,*⁴⁹ ["How can the a]rk of the Lo[RD come to me]?" ▲

12 [It was reported to King David that the LORD had blessed the house of Obed-edom and everything that was his because of the ark of God. So David went and brought the ark of God from the house of Obed-edom up to the city of David, with a ce]lebration. 13 And [when the bearers of the ark of the LORD had gone six steps, he sacrificed] *sev[en]* *bul[l]s and seve[n rams.*⁵⁰ 14 Then David danced before the LORD with all his might (Dav]id was wearing a linen ephod). 15 So Da[vid and all the house of Israel brought up the ark of the LORD with cheers and with] trumpet [blas]ts. 16 (Now, as [the ark of the LORD entered the city of David, Michal daughter of Saul looked out the window and saw King David leaping and dancing before the LORD, and she despised him in her heart].)

17 [Th]ey brought in [the ark of the LORD and set it in its place, in the middle of the tent Da]vid [had pitched for it]. Then David offered bu[rnt offerings and peace offerings before the LORD. 18 When David had finished offering the burnt offering and the peace offerings, he blessed] the [people in the name of the LORD of hosts]. ▲

7 6 [For I did not dwell in a house from the day I brought the Israelites up from Egyp]t [until now. Rather I have been moving about in tent and tabernacle. 7 In all] my [tr]avels [among the entire people of Israel, did I bring up such a thing

---

42. 4QSamª. *the new cart and brought it out of the house of Abinadab, which was on a hill with* MT (an accidental repetition of previous text).

43. 4QSamª LXX. *house of Israel* MT.

44. 4QSamª LXX MT–1Chr 13:8. *all fir trees* MT.

45. 4QSamª LXX. *Nacon* MT.

46. 4QSamª LXX MT–1Chr. Not in MT.

47. 4QSamª. *for his error* MT.

48. 4QSamª. *by the ark of God* MT.

49. 4QSamª. *and he said* MT.

50. 4QSamª MT+LXX–1Chr 15:26. *an ox and a fatling* MT LXX.

Chapter 7. 4QSamª: 7:6–7, 22–29.

to any of the leaders of Israe]l, [whom I had charged to shepherd my people Israel, saying "Why did you not build me a house of cedar?"] ▲

22 ["Therefore you are great, Lord GOD. There is no one like you, and no god
other than you, in all that we have] h[eard. 23 And who is like your people, like
Israel? It is a singular nation on earth, whom] Go[d moved to redeem as a people,
and to make a name for himself and to d]o [great things and marvelous things for
you and for your land], in the pre[sence of your people, whom you redeemed out
of Egypt, from the nations and] *tents*.[51] 24 Thus [you established your people Israel to be] your [people forever, and you, the LORD, became their] God.

25 "And [now, Lord GOD], the promise [you have made concerning your servant and his house, hold it up forever and do as you have said. 26 Let your name
be exalted forever, with people saying, 'The LORD of host]s [is Go]d [over Israel.'
May the house of your servant David be established in your presence. 27 Because
you, the LORD of] hosts, the God of I[srael, have revealed this to your servant,
saying, 'I will build you a house,'] your servant [foun]d it in his heart to p[ray this
prayer to you. 28 And now, Lord GOD, you a]re God, and your words [will come
true, and you have promised this good thing to your servant. 29 So] now may you
be [pl]eased to bless [the house of your servant, so that it may continue forever
before you. For you, Lord GOD, have spoken, and with] your blessing [the house
of your servant will be blessed forever]." ▲

8 2 [Then he defeated Moab, and making] them [lie down on the ground, he
measured them off with a cord. He measured two lines of those to be put to
death and one full line of those to be spare]d. So [the Moabites] be[came[52] vassals
to David. 3 David also defeated Hadadezer] son of Rehob, [king of Zobah, when
he went to restore his monument at the Euphrates. 4 Da]vid [took] *a thousand*[53]
[horsemen and twenty thousand footmen. David also hamstrung all the chariot
horses, after setting aside enough for a hundred chariots. 5 When the Arameans
of Damascus came to aid King Hadadezer of Zobah, David killed twenty-two]
thousand [Arameans. 6 Then David put garrisons among the Arameans of Damascus, and the Arameans became] *vassals*[54] [to Dav]id. [The LORD gave victory
to David wherever he went.]

7 David [too]k [the gold shields from the servants of Hadadezer and brought
them to Jerusa]l[em], (*which,* [*later on, were*] *also* [*taken by Shoshak king of Egypt,*

---

51. 4QSamᵃ LXX. *its gods* MT.

Chapter 8. 4QSamᵃ: 8:2–8.

52. Masculine 4QSamᵃ. Feminine MT.

53. 4QSamᵃ. *took from him a thousand seven hundred* MT.

54. 4QSamᵃ. *as vassals* MT.

when] he [w]ent up to Je[rusalem] *in the time of Rehoboam son of Sol[omon).* [55] 8 From Betah and Berothai,] Hadadezer['s cities], King David took *a gr[eat] quantity* [56] of bronze. ▲

10

4 [Hanun took David's servants and shaved off half of their beards and cu]t off [half their] cl[othes at their buttocks, then sent them away. 5 When David was told *about]* the men, [57] he [sent messengers to meet them—for the men were] great[ly embarrassed. The king said,] "S[ta]y [in Jeri]cho [until your beards] have grown; [then return]."

6 [When the Ammonites saw that they and David had become enemies, *Hanun and the Ammonites sent]* a thousand silver talents [to hire] chariots and horsemen [*from Aram-naharaim, Aram-maa]cah,* [*and Zobah. They hired thir]ty-[two] thousand chari[ots, the king of Maacah, and the me]n of Tob.* [*When they came and encamped near Medeba,]* the Ammon[ites] mustered from [their cities. . . .*[58] 7 When David heard about this, he se]n[t] Joa[b and the entire army, the warriors]. ▲

18 [As the Syrians fled before Israel, David killed seven hundred Syrian chari-oteers and forty thousand horsemen. He also] wounded [Shobach, the captain of their army], so that he died [there. 19 When all the kings who served Hadadezer saw that they were routed before Isra]el, they made peace [with Israel and served them. So the Syrians were afraid to help the children of Ammon any longer].

11

■ *4QSam*[a] *adds the detail that Uriah was Joab's armor-bearer, which the Masoretic Text lacks. Josephus includes this detail, suggesting that an ancient form of the Sep-tuagint had it, though it was excised from later Septuagint manuscripts to conform with the Masoretic Text.*

2 [Then, in the evening, David got up from his couch and t]ook a walk [on the roof of the palace. From the roof he saw a woman bathing,] and the woman [was very beautiful. 3 So David sent messengers and inquired about the woman. One said, "Isn't sh]e Bathsheba [daughter of] El[iam, the wife of Uriah the Hittite,] *the armor-[b]earer of Joab?"* [59]

---

55. 4QSam[a] LXX. Not in MT.

56. 4QSam[a] and MT use different forms.

Chapter 10. 4QSam[a]: 10:4–7, 18–19.

57. 4QSam[a] LXX. Not in MT.

58. 4QSam[a] MT+LXX–1Chr 19:6–7. *the Ammonites sent and hired twenty thousand foot sol-diers from the Arameans of Beth-rehob and Zobah, the king of Maacah with a thousand men, and twelve thousand men from the men of Tob* MT.

Chapter 11. 4QSam[a]: 11:2–12, 16–20.

59. 4QSam[a] Josephus. Not in MT.

4 [Then David sent] messengers [to bring her], and she came to [him]—just *purified*[60]—[and he lay with her]. Then she [returned to] her house. 5 But [the woman] concei[ved, and she se]nt a message to inform Davi[d, saying], "I am with child." 6 So [D]avid [sent to Joab, saying, "Se]nd me [Uriah the Hittite," and] Joab [se]n[t Uriah t]o [David. 7 When Ur]iah [had come] to [him, David] asked [him how Joab was doing and how the troops fa]r[ed and how the war was going]. 8 Then David [said] t[o Uriah, "Go to your house and wash your feet." When] Uriah [left the palace, a banquet from the king was sent after him. 9 But Uriah slept at the door of the palace with all the servants of his lord, and did not go down to his house. 10 When they re]ported [to David, "Uriah did not go to his house," David said to Uriah,] "Have [you] not [come from a journey? Why did you not go home?" 11 Uriah replied] to David, "The ark, [Israel, and Judah are living in tents. My lord Joab] and my lord's troops [are encamped in the open field. Can I then go into my house, to eat and drink] and to lie with [my wife? As you live, as your soul lives, I will not do such a thing."] 12 David [sa]id to [Uriah, "Remain here today also. Then tomorrow I will let you go." So Uriah remained in Jerusalem that day and the next.] ▲

16 Then, as [Joab] held the sie[ge on the city, he assigned Uriah to the place where he knew] there were [skill]ed [war]riors. 17 [The] m[en of the city] came out [and fought against Joab. Some of the army, Dav]id['s troops, fell]—and U[riah the Hittite] died as well. 18 [When Joab sent word to David, reporting to him] everything about the battle, 19 [he instructed the messenger, "When you have finished reporting] to [the ki]n[g all about the battle, 20 if the king becomes angry and says to you, 'Why did you go so close to the ci]ty [to fight? Did you not realize that they would shoot from the wall? . . . .' "] ▲

12 4 ["A traveler came to the rich man, but he did not want to take some-thing from his own flock or herd to prepare for the wayfarer who had come to him. Instead he took the poor man's lamb and prepared it for the man] who had co[me to him." 5 David was furious at the man and said to Nathan, "As the LORD lives,] the man [who has done this shall die]!" ▲

8 ["I gave you] your [master's house]—and [your master's wives into your arms—and I gave you the house of Israel and of Juda]h. And if [that had been too] li[ttle, I would have given you in addition such and such things. 9 Why have you despised the word of the L]ORD, to d[o what is evil in his sight? Uriah the Hittite you struck down with the sword. You took] his [wi]fe as [your own, and you killed him using the sword of the Ammonites]." ▲

13 [David said to Nathan, "I have sinned against the LORD." Nathan said to David, "The LORD also has forgiven your sin]—you will [no]t d[ie]. 14 However,

---

60. 4QSam[a]. *purified from her uncleanness* MT LXX.
Chapter 12. 4QSam[a]: 12:4–5, 8–9, 13–19.

[because you have] despised the *word*[61] of the LORD by [this] a[ct, the child that has been born] to you will surely die." 15 Then [Nathan] returned to his house. *God*[62] struck the [child which the *whic*]h[63] of Uriah [had borne] to *David.*[64] 16 So [David] *pray[ed] to*[65] God on behalf of the child. [David fast]ed [and went in and] *lay in sackcloth*[66] on the ground. 17 The [elders] of his house ca[me up] *to*[67] him, to get him to [rise up fr]om the gr[ound, but he would not, nor would] he *eat*[68] food with them. 18 Then [on the] seven[th d]ay, [the child died. David's servants were afraid to t]ell him that the chi[ld was de]ad, [thinking, "Look, while the child was still alive, we spoke to him, and he would not listen to us.] How can we tell him [that the child is] de[ad! He may do something bad!" 19 But seeing his servants whispering together, David] realized [that] the child was dead, [and David asked his servants, "Is the child dead?" They answered, "He is dead."] ▲

30 [He took the crown of their king from his head—it weighed as much as a gold talent and contained precious stones. Then it was set on David's head. He carried a very great amount of] spoi[l out of the city. 31 He also led out the people who were in it and put them to work with saws, iron har]ro[ws, and iron axes, or put them to work making bricks. This is what he did in all the A]mmo[nite cities. Then David and the whole army returned to Jerusalem.]

13 1 [Then, later on, Absalom son of David had a beautiful sister, named Ta]mar, [and Amnon son of David lo]v[ed] her. 2 [Amnon was so tormented over his sister Tamar that he became ill.] For she was a virgin, [and it seemed to Amnon difficult to do anything to her. 3 But Amnon had a friend, named *J*]onathan[69] son of Shimeah, [David's brother, and *Jonathan* was a very shrewd man. 4 He said to him, "Why,] pri[n]ce, [are you] so dejected [day after day? Will you not tell me?" Amnon told him, "I am in love with Tamar,] my brother Absalom's [si]ster." 5 [*Jonathan* said to him, "Lie down on your bed and pretend to be si]ck. When your [fa]ther [co]m[es] to see you, [say to him, 'Allow my sister Tamar to come and give me food to eat,] prepa[ring the food in my presence, so that I may watch and eat it as she serves me.' " 6 So Amnon lay down] and pre[tended to be sick. When the king came to see him, Amnon said to the

---

61. 4QSam[a]. *enemies* MT LXX.

62. 4QSam[a] LXX[L]. *The* LORD MT LXX.

63. 4QSam[a]. *wife* MT LXX. The two words are identical except for the last letter.

64. 4QSam[a]. *David, and it was deathly ill* MT LXX.

65. Literally, *sought from* 4QSam[a]. *sought* MT.

66. 4QSam[a] LXX[L]. *and spent the night sleeping* MT LXX[A].

67. 4QSam[a] and MT use different words for *to*.

68. 4QSam[a] (*brh*). *create* MT (*br'*).

Chapter 13. 4QSam[a]: 13:1–6, 13–16, 18–34, 36–39.

69. 4QSam[a] LXX[L]. *Jonadab* MT LXX[B].

king, "Allow my sister] Tamar [to come and make me a couple of cakes in my presence, so that I may eat it as she serves me]." ▲

13 ["I, where will I carry my shame? As for you, you will be like any of the rogues in Israel. So] now, [please, speak to] the king. [He will not withhold me from you." 14 But he would not listen to her advice, and being stro]nger than she, [he overpowered her and] lay with her.

15 [Then Amnon felt a burning hatred toward her]—the hat[red he fel]t [toward her was greater] than the pas[sion he had felt for her—and Amnon said to her, "Get up!] And[70] [get out!"] 16 She said [to him, "No! For se]nding [me away is a worse wrong than than the other you did to me." But he would not listen to her, 17 and he called the servant who attended him and said, "Get this woman away from me! And lock the door behind her!"]

18 [She was wearing a gorgeous robe—the sort of robe which the king's virgin daughters wore. When his servant put her out and bolted the door] behind [her, 19 Tamar threw ashes on her head and ripped the gorgeous robe she was wearing,] and put[ting her hands on her head, she left, crying out as she went].

20 [Absalom her brother asked her,] "Has [your brother Amnon been with you? For now, my sister, keep quiet. He is your brother. Don't keep thinking about this thing." So Tamar lived in her brother Absalom's house, desolate. 21 When King David] heard about [all these things, he was furious. *But he would not inflict pain on his son Amnon's spirit, because he lo]ved him, since [he was his] firstborn.*[71] 22 [Absalom did not say anything to Amnon, either good or bad, but A]bsalom [hated Amnon, because he had raped his sister Tamar].

■ *4QSam^a, followed by the Septuagint, preserves the note about David's failure to punish Amnon and the reason for it. The Masoretic Text seems to have lost it when the scribe's eye skipped from the negative that begins the skipped line to the negative that begins verse 22.*

23 [Two years later, Absalo]m [had sheep-shearers in Baal-hazo]r, which [is near Ephraim, and Ab]salom [invited] al[l the king's sons]. 24 Absa[l]om approached the king and said, ["Listen, your servant has sheep-shearers.] Let [the k]ing and his servants go to[72] his[73] servant." 25 The king said [to Absalom, "No, my son, we should not] all go, [or] we will be a burden to you." And though he *pressed*[74] him, he w[ould] not [go, but he blessed him. 26 Then Absalom said, "If

---

70. 4QSam^a. Not in MT.

71. 4QSam^a LXX. Not in MT.

72. 4QSam^a LXX^L. *with* MT LXX^B.

73. 4QSam^a. *your* MT.

74. 4QSam^a *(pzr). broke through* MT *(prz).*

not, let] my brother Amnon g[o]."⁷⁵ The ki[ng re]sponded, ["Why should he go with you?" 27 But Absalom *pressed*⁷⁶ him until he sent] Amnon and [all] the king's sons [with him. *Absalom prepared a roy]al [feast].*⁷⁷

28 Absalom [gave orders to] his servants, saying, ["Watch now, when Amnon's spirits are high with wine, when] I [te]ll you, 'Strike Amnon,' *kill hi[m.*⁷⁸ Do not be afraid. Is it not I giving you orders? Be coura]geous and strong. 29 [A]bsa[lom's servants] did [to Amnon as Absalom had commanded. All the ki]n[g's sons rose, and each one, mounting] his [mu]le, fled.

30 [While they were on the way, a report reached David, saying that A]bsalo[m had struck down all the king's sons and that not one of them was alive]. 31 The [king] stood up [and tore his clothes, and then lay on the ground, and all his servants stood by with] *his*⁷⁹ clothes [torn. 32 Jonathan son of Shimeah, David's brother,] answered [and said, "My lord must not believe that they have killed all] the young men, *all*⁸⁰ the ki[ng]'s sons. [Amnon alone is dead. For at Absalom's command,] this *has been*⁸¹ [planned from the day] he [raped his sister Tamar. 33 So now my lord the king must not take the] th[ing to heart, to think that all the king's sons are dead. Amnon alone is dead." 34 Meanwhile Absalom fled.]

The young man [keeping the watch ra]is[ed his eyes and looked, and there was a large crowd approaching on the road behind him by the side of the mountain]. ▲

36 [Then, as soon as he had fi]nished s[peaking, in came the king's sons, weeping out loud. The king and all] his servants [also] wept bitt[erly].

37 [Absalom, fleeing, went to] Talm[ai son of Ammihur, the ki]ng of Geshur *in the la[nd of Maacah.*⁸² David mourned for his son every] day. 38 [But Absalom] fled and went to Gesh[ur and lived there three years. 39 Then *the spiri]t of the king*⁸³ [longed] for [Ab]salom. For [he had been comforted concerning Amnon's death].

14 1 [When Joa]b son of Zeru[iah realized that the ki]n[g's mind was on Ab-salom, 2 Joab sent to Tekoa and brought a wise] woman [from th]ere, [and

---

75. 4QSamᵃ. *go with us* MT.

76. MT has *broke through* here as well.

77. 4QSamᵃ reconstructed from LXX. Not in MT.

78. 4QSamᵃ and MT have different verb forms.

79. 4QSamᵃ. Not in MT.

80. 4QSamᵃ. Not in MT.

81. Masculine 4QSamᵃ. Feminine MT.

82. 4QSamᵃ LXX. Not in MT.

83. 4QSamᵃ LXXᴸ. *David the king* MT LXXᴮ.

Chapter 14. 4QSamᵃ: 14:1–3, 18–19; 4QSamᶜ: 14:7–33.

he said to her, "Pretend to be in mourning. Put on mourning clothes] and do not anoint [yourself with oil, but look like someone who has been mourning for the dead a long time. 3 Then approa]ch the kin[g and say this to him." And Joab put the words in her mouth.]▲

■ *While 4QSam^a continues, at this point a separate manuscript, 4QSam^c, begins. It contains a gratifying amount of connected text, continuing through 15:15.*

7 ["Now you see, the whole clan has risen up against your maidservant. They say, 'Hand over the one who struck down his brother, so that we can put him to death for the life of the brother he killed'—and so destroy the heir also. They will put out *the only coal*] I have [*remai*]*ning*[84] and leave my husband neither [name nor remnant on the face of the earth]."

8 The [ki]ng [said] to the wo[m]an, "Go home [*in peace*,[85] and I will issue an order for you]."

9 [Then the woman of Tekoa said to] the [ki]ng, "My lord, [the king,] let [the guilt be] on me [and on my father's house, and let the king and *the throne of his kingdom*[86] be gu]iltless."

10 The ki[ng] said, ["If anyone says anything to you, bring him to me, and he will not] bother you [again]."

11 Then she sai[d, "Please, let the king invoke • • • • your God, so that the avenger of blood does not continue to destroy] o[r my son] be destroyed."

■ *4QSam^c exhibits the rare method of using four dots in place of the four letters* YHWH *for the divine name.*

[He] said, ["As • • • • lives, not one ha]ir [of your son will fall to the ground]."

12 [Then the woman said, "Allow] your [m]aidse[rv]ant [to say one more wo]rd [to my] lor[d the king]."

["Speak," he said.]

13 ["Why," asked the woman, "have you planned just such a thi]ng against the [peo]ple of G[o]d? [For in speaking this word the king convicts himself, because the king does not bring home his banished one. 14 Indeed we must surely] die [and are like water spilled on the ground which cannot be recovered. God does not take away] life, [but devises a plan so that the one who has gone astray does not remain estranged from him. 15 So now, I have come to say this to *my*] lord[87] [because the people have made me afraid. Your handmaid thought, 'I will speak t]o the king [now, and perhaps the king will grant the request of his servant. 16

---

84. 4QSam^c LXX^L. *my only coal that remains* MT LXX^B.

85. [4QSam^c] LXX. Not in MT.

86. [4QSam^c] LXX. *his throne* MT.

87. 4QSam^c. *to the king my lord* MT.

For the king will decide to deliver] his servant [from the power of the one *who wants*[88] to eliminate both me and my son from the inheritance of God.'" 17 Then the woman concl]uded, "Oh, let the [word of my lord the king be a comfort. For as an angel of God, so is] my [l]ord [the king to judge good and bad. May • • • • your God be with you."]

18 [The king *responded to*] *the* woman [*of Tekoa and said*],[89] "Do not [hide from me anything that I a]sk you."

[The woman] answered, "L[et my lord the king sp]eak."

19 [The kin]g [asked, "Has Joab been involved wi]th you in all this?"

[The woman *said to the king,*[90] "As your soul lives, my lord the ki]ng, *it is* [91] not to the right or to the left [from anything my lord the king has said. For your servant Joab,] he inst[ructed me, and] h[e] put [all these words] in the mouth of your handmaid. 20 Your servant J[oab has do]ne [this to show the] mat[ter in a different light. My lord is wise, like the wisdom of an angel of Go]d, [to kno]w *what is*[92] on earth."

21 [The king] s[aid to Joab, "All right, I will do it.] So go *and*[93] bring back the young man A[b]salom."

22 [Joa]b [fell to the ground on his face, prostrating himself and blessing the king. Joab said,] "Today your servant knows that I [have] f[ound] favor [in your sight, my lord the king, in that the king has granted] the request of *your*[94] servant."

23 *So Joab and* we[nt[95] to Ge]sh[ur and brought Absalom to Jerusalem. 24 Then the] king [said], "Let him go to his own house. He will n[o]t s[ee] my face." [So Absalom went to his own house and] did not see the king['s face].

25 *Moreover, Absalom*[96]—[in all Israel no one was so much praised as he for his fine appearance]. From the sole of his foot to the *crown*[97] of [his] head, [he was without flaw. 26 When he cut the hair of his head]—he used to cu[t] it at the end of every year; [when it became too heavy for him,] he cu[t it—he used to weigh it, and it weighed] 200 shekels on the roy[al] standard. 27 [Absalom had three sons and] one [daughter, whose na]me was Tamar, *and*[98] she was [a beautiful woman].

---

88. [4QSam[c]] LXX. Not in MT.

89. 4QSam[c] and apparently 4QSam[a]. *responded and said to the woman* MT.

90. 4QSam[c]. *answered and said* MT and apparently 4QSam[a].

91. 4QSam[c]. *no one can turn away* MT.

92. 4QSam[c]. *all that is* MT.

93. 4QSam[c]. Not in MT.

94. 4QSam[c] MT[qere] MT[mss] LXX[ms]. *his* MT[ketib] LXX.

95. 4QSam[a] appears to err. *So Joab got up and went* MT.

96. 4QSam[c]. *And as Absalom* MT LXX.

97. 4QSam[c] misspells this word.

98. 4QSam[c]. Not in MT.

28 [Absalom lived two full ye]ar[s in Jeru]salem [without seeing] the king's face. 29 [So A]bsalom [sent for Jo]ab, [to] se[nd him t]o the king, but he would not [come to him. Then he se]nt a second time *to him,*[99] and again he wou[ld] n[ot co]me. 30 So he said to [his] servants, ["Look, Joab's field is nex]t to [mine]. He has barley there. [Go and s]et it on fire." So [Absalo]m['s servants] se[t the field on fi]re. [*So] Joab's [s]ervants [came] to him with [their] cl[othes] torn [and said],* "Absalom's [servant]s [have set the f]ield on fire.*[100]

> ▨ *The Masoretic Text lost the entire last sentence, which is preserved in 4QSamᶜ and the Septuagint, as well as the Old Latin. A scribe's eye simply skipped from one "on fire" to another.*

31 [Then J]oab got up [and went to Absalom at his hou]se and demanded of him, "Why did your servants set [my field on fire]?"

32 Absalom answered Joab: "Look, I sent to you, [saying, 'Come here,' so that I may] send you to [the k]ing, to say, 'Why have I come from Ge[shur? It would have been better for me if I were still there.'] Now, *let me s[e]e*[101] the king's face. If I am guilty of anything, [let him put me to death]."

33 [So Joab went t]o the king [and told] him. Then he called for Absalom, and he came [to the king and] *bowed down,*[102] [and the king kissed Absalom].

15

> ▨ *The scribe of 4QSamᶜ at first skipped a full line of text at 15:1 but noticed the error and inserted the missing text above the line.*

1 *Afterward Absalom used to fur[nish*[103] himself with a chariot and horses, with fifty men to ru]n in front of him. 2 Absalom used to get up early [and stand] beside *the road.*[104] Then, wh[en a]nyone [had a law]suit which should c[o]me to the king *for*[105] a decision, Absal[om] would call *to*[106] him [and s]ay, "What city are you from?" *The man would answer and say,*[107] "Your [servant is] from o[n]e of the tribes

---

99. 4QSamᶜ. Not in MT.

100. 4QSamᶜ LXX. Not in MT.

101. 4QSamᶜ adds an untranslatable particle to this phrase, which is not in MT.

102. 4QSamᶜ. *bowed down to him with his face to the ground before the king* MT.

Chapter 15. 4QSamᵃ: 15:1–6, 27–31; 4QSamᶜ: 15:1–15.

103. 4QSamᶜ LXXᴸ. *Afterwards, Absalom furnished* MT. 4QSamᶜ and MT use different forms and word order in this phrase.

104. 4QSamᵃ. *the road to the gate* MT.

105. Implicit in 4QSamᶜ. 4QSamᵃ and MT use different prepositions.

106. 4QSamᵃ and MT use different forms.

107. 4QSamᶜ and 4QSamᵃ. *he said* MT.

of Israel." 3 Then Absalom would say to him, ["Look, your claims are good] and right, [but there is no o]ne from the king [to hear] you." 4 [Absalom] would say [further, "Oh,] if only they would appoint [me a judge in the land! Then every-one] who *had*[108] a suit or [cause] could co[me to] me, [and I would do him jus-tice!" 5 When anyo]ne [came near] to d[o obeisance to him, he exte]nded [his hand, took hold of him, and kissed him. 6 Absa]l[om used to act] t[his] way to-ward all [the Israelites who came to the king for judgment, and] Absalom [sto]le [the allegiance of the people of Israel].

7 [After *four*[109] years, Absalom said to the king, "Allow me to] g[o to fulfill a vow which I made to • • • • in Hebron. 8 For your servant made a vow while] I [live]d at Geshur in Syria, [saying, 'If] • • • [• does indeed bring me back to Jerusalem, then I will serve •] • • • .' " 9 So [the king] said to him, ["Go in peace]."

[Thus] he went [to Hebron. 10 But Absalom sent *messengers*] *from Jerusalem*[110] throughout all the tr[ibes of Israel, saying, "As soon as you hear] the trumpet [bl]ast, [say, 'Absalom is king in Hebron!' " 11 (Two hundred men went with Ab-salom] from Jerusalem. [They had been invi]ted [and went innocently, not know-ing any of this.) 12 While he was offering sacrifices, *he sen*]t [*and invit*]ed[111] Ah[i]thophel [the] Gi[lonite, David's counselor, from his hometown, Giloh. The con]spiracy gr[ew strong, as the people with Absalom increased constantly].

13 Then a [messenger] came [to David, saying, "The hearts of the Israelites have gone with Absalom."]

14 Then [David] said [to all his servants with him at Jerusalem, "Come! We must flee]! Let us [escape from Absalom. Leave quickly, or he will soon overtake us] and bring ruin [on us and strike the city with the edge of the sword]."

15 [The] king[',s servants said] t[o the king, "Your servants are ready to do whatever my lord the king decides]." ▲

27 [The kin]g [said also to Zadok the priest, "Don't you see? Return to the city while it is safe, you and your two sons with you, Ahimaaz your son, and J]onathan son of A[biathar. 28 Listen, I will wait at the fords of the wilderness, until word] comes from [you with intelligence for me." 29 So Zadok and Abi-athar carried the ark of God back] to [Jeru]salem, [and they stayed there].

30 [Meanwhile David went up on the ascent of the Mount of Olives. He wept as he w]ent, [barefoot and with his head covered. All the people with him, every one of them, covered their heads. They ascended, weeping as they went.]

---

108. Implicit in 4QSam^c. Explicit in MT.

109. 4QSam^c and 4QSam^a presumably had *four,* just as the LXX^L, the Syriac, and Josephus have. *forty* MT LXX^B.

110. 4QSam^c. *secret messengers* MT.

111. 4QSam^c. *Absalom sent for* MT.

31 [Someone reported] *to*[112] Davi[d, "Ahithophel is among the conspirators with Absalom]."

[David said, "LORD, turn Ahithophel's counsel into foolishness."] ▲

16 1 [When David was] jus[t past the top of the ascent, there was Ziba the servant of Mephibosheth. He met him, with a pair of] sad[dled don]keys, [bearing two hundred loaves of bread, a hundred clusters of raisins, a hundred pieces of summer fruit, and a ski]n of wine. 2 [The king said to Ziba, "What do you intend to do with them?" Ziba answered, "The do]nk[eys are for the king's household to ride on, the bread and summer fruit for the young men to eat, and the wine for those who are faint in the wilderness to drink]." ▲

10 [The king said, "What do I have to do with you, sons of Zeruiah? If he is cursing because the LORD told him, 'Curse David,' then] who [shall say, 'Why have you done this?'" 11 David said to Abishai and all his servants, "Loo]k! My son, m[y own offspring, seeks my life. How much more would this Benjamite! Leave him alone. Let him] curse, for [the LORD] has direc[ted him. 12 Perhaps the LORD will look on my difficulty, so that the LORD will recompense me with good for his cursing of me] today."

13 So [David and his men continu]ed [along the road, while Shimei w]e[nt along on the mountainside opposite him, cur]s[ing as he went, throwing dust and stones at him]. ▲

17 [Absalom said to Hushai, "Is this your loyalty to your friend? W]hy [did you] no[t go with your friend]?"

18 [Hushai answered Absalom, "Rather, I serve the one whom the LOR]D, this people, [and all the Israelites have chosen, and with him I will remain]." ▲

21 [Ahithophel said to Absalom, "Go in to your father's concubines, whom he left to take care of the pala]ce. Then al[l Israel] will hear [that you are abhorred by your father. Then the resolve of everyone with you will be strengthened."]

22 [So they spread a tent] for Absal[om on the roof, and Absalom went in to his father's concubines] in the sight of all I[srael]. ▲

17 23 [When Ahithophel saw that his counsel had not been followed,] he saddled [his donkey and returned to his hometown. He set his house in order. Then he hanged himself and died. He was bu]ri[ed] in the to[mb of his father]. ▲

18 2 [David sent out the army, one-third under Joab's command, one-third under the command of Abishai son of Zeruiah, Joab's brother, and one-

---

112. Explicit in 4QSam^c. Implicit in MT.

Chapter 16. 4QSam^a: 16:1–2, 10–13, 17–18, 21–22.

Chapter 17. 4QSam^a: 17:23.

Chapter 18. 4QSam^a: 18:2–7, 9–11.

third under the command of Ittai] the Gittite. [And the king said to the army, "I, myself, shall go out with you, too."]

3 [But] the army [said], "You will [no]t go out. [For if we must retreat, they will not care about us. Not if half of us were to die would *they c*]*are*[113] *about*[114] us. [You are worth ten thousand of us. So at present, it is better that] you be [ready to help] us [from the city]."

4 [The king said to them, "Whatever seems best to you, I will do." So the] ki[ng stood beside the gate, while the entire army marched out by hundreds and by thousands].

5 [The king gave orders t]o Joab, [Abishai, and Ittai, saying, "Deal gently, for my sake, with the young man Absalom." And ever]y[one] *heard*[115] [the king give all the captains orders concerning Absalom].

6 [Thus the army marched out into the] field [a]g[ains]t [Israel], to do [batt]le [in the Ephraim forest. 7 The army of I]srael [was defeated] b[y David's troops. There was a tremendous slaughter there that day, of twenty thousand men.]▲

9 [Absalom happened on some of David's troops. As] *he*[116] [rode his mule, the mule went under the thick branches of a large oak, and his head got caught in the] oak, and he *hung*[117] [between the sky and the ground, while the mule under him continued on].

10 *A man*[118] [sa]w it, and reporting it [to Joab, said, "I saw Absalom hanging in an oak]!"

11 Joab [sai]d to the man [reporting to him, "You saw it? Why didn't you strike him to the ground right there? I] would have [paid you ten silver coins and a belt."]▲

19 6 ["You love those who hate you] and ha[te those who love you! Today you have declared that leaders and troops mean nothing to you!] No[w I see that] if Absa[lom had lived and all of us had die]d [today], the[n it would have seemed] righ[t to you. 7 So, get up, go out,] and sp[eak words of] comfort [to your] troo[ps now. For I sw]e[ar by the LORD], if [you do] no[t go out, not] one m[an will stay with you to]night, and that would be wor[se for you] than al[l the distress] th[at has come to you from your youth until now." 8 So the ki]n[g got up and sat in the] gate. Ev[eryone heard the report that the king was there, sitting in the gate. So everyone came to the king.]

---

113. Singular 4QSam[a]. Plural MT.

114. 4QSam[a] and MT use different words.

115. 4QSam[a] and MT use different forms.

116. 4QSam[a] LXX[L]. *Absalom* MT LXX[B].

117. 4QSam[a]. *was stuck* MT.

118. 4QSam[a]. *A certain man* MT.

Chapter 19. 4QSam[a]: 19:6–15, 26–27.

Now Israel had fled, ea[ch to his own home. 9 Everyone throughout all the tribes of Israel was arguing, sayin]g, *"King Dav[id]*[119] s[aved us from the power of our enemies—he delivered us from the power of the Philistines! But now he has had to flee] the la[nd, from Absalom. 10 But Absalom, whom we anointed over us, is dead in battle. So now why do you not say anything about] bring[ing back the king]?"

11 [King David sent a message] to Zadok [and Abiathar] the prie[sts, "Talk to the elders of Judah and ask, 'Why are you the la]st [to bring the king back to his palace, when the talk of all Israel has reached the king]?' " ▲

13 ["S]ay [to Amas]a, ['Are you not my flesh and blood? Thus may God do to me and mo]re if you are not the [comm]ander [of the army from now on, instead of Joab.' " 14 He united the hearts of the people of Judah,] and *they sent*[120] [word to the king, "Return with all your servants." 15 The king returned. He arrived at the Jor]da[n, and Judah came to Gilgal to go out to meet the king, to bring the king across the Jordan]. ▲

26 [He answered, "My lord the king, my servant tricked me. For your servant told him, 'Saddle the] donk[ey for me, so that I may ride it and go with the king'—for your servant is lame. 27 But he slandered your serv]ant to [my lord the king. Still my lord the king is like the angel of God. So do what seems right] to [yo]u. ▲

206 [David said to Abishai, "Now Sheba son of Bichri will do us more harm than Absalom. Take your lord's servants and pursue him or he will find] fortifi[ed cities and escape from us]." 7 Joa[b]'s [m]en [followed him, along with the Cherethites, the Pelethites, and all the warriors]. They march[ed] out of Jer[usalem to pursue Sheba son of Bichri].

8 When they were at the [great stone in *Gib]eon*,[121] it dropped out. 9 Joab said [to Amasa, "Are you well,] my [bro]ther?" And Joab took [Amasa] by the beard with his right hand to [ki]ss [him. 10 Amas]a [did] no[t notice the dagger in] Joab['s hand,] and he stabbed him with it in the abdo[men] and [his bowels spilled onto the ground. Without a second blow, he died. Then Joab and Abishai] his brother pursued She[b]a son of [Bichri].

11 [One of Joab's young men stood by him and said,] "Who[ever] is for Joab and whoever is for Da[vid, follow Joab." 12 Meanwhile Amasa lay wa]llowing [in his blood in the middle of the road. When the ma]n [saw] that all the [troops]

---

119. 4QSam[a]. *the king* MT.

120. Singular verb 4QSam[a]. Plural verb MT (same meaning).

Chapter 20. 4QSam[a]: 20:9–14, 22–25; 1QSam: 20:6–10.

121. 1QSam. MT adds *Amasa came to meet them. Joab was wearing his military attire, with a dagger in the sheath fastened on a belt tied at his waist. As he went forward.* The sense of the passage is disturbed by the absence of this text; it is probably an accidental omission.

stop[ped, he carried Ama]sa of[f the r]oa[d into the field and threw a garment over him, becau]se he recognized that everyone [who reached him came to a stop. 13 When he was removed from the road, all the troops] follow[e]d Joab [in pursuit of Sheba son of Bichri. 14 He marched through all the tribes of Israel to Abel Be]th-maa[cah and the whole region of the Berites, and they gathered together and followed him].▲

22 [. . . So he blew the trumpet, and they dispersed from the city, and everyone returned home, while Joab returned to Jerusale]m t[o the king. 23 Now Joab commanded the entire army of Israel. Benaiah son of Jehoiada was in charge of the Cherethites and] Pelethites. 24 [Adoram was in charge of conscripted labor. Jehoshaphat son of Ahilud was the recorder, 25 and Sheva was scribe. Zadok and Abiathar were] priests, [26 and also Ira the Jairite was David's priest].

21 1 [During Da]vid[']s reign, there was a famine lasting] thr[ee consecutive years. When Davi]d [inquired] o[f the LORD, the LORD answered, "It is because of the bloodguilt of Saul and his hou]se, [because he put the Gibeonites to death."]

[2 So the king called the Gibeonites and negotiated with them. Now the Gibeonites were not part of the Israelites, but a remnant of the Amorites. Though the Israelites had sworn to spare them, Saul tried to wipe them out in his zeal for the people of Israel and Judah.]

[3 David asked the Gibeonites, "What should I do for you? How can I make expiation, so that you will bless the heritage of the LORD?"]

4 [The Gibeonites told him, "This is no matter of silver or gold between us and Saul and his house. But it is not for us] to put [anyone] to d[eath in Israel]."

[So he said, "Whatever you ask, will I do on your behalf]."

5 [They said to the king,] "The man w[ho consumed us and who plotted against us, that we should be destroyed from our place within the borders of Israel]— 6 have [seven of his sons] delivered to [us. We will execute them before the LORD in Gibeah of Saul, the chosen of the LORD."]

[The king answered, "I will deliver them."]▲

15 [The Philistines again waged war with Israel. David and] the troops with him [went down and did battle with the Philistines. David became weary. 16 Ishbibenob, a] descendant [of the giants, whose spear] weighed [three hundred bronze shekels, w]as [. . .] *angry*[122] and intended [to kill David]. 17 But Abishai son of Ze[ruiah came] to his [aid, struck] the [Phi]li[stine] and killed him. Then David's [m]en *sw[ore*,[123] "You will never ag[ain] go to battle with us, so that [you do] not [put out the lamp of I]srael." 18 After [this there was another battle] *of*

Chapter 21. 4QSamᵃ: 21:1–2, 4–6, 15–17; 1QSam: 21:16–18.

122. 4QSamᵃ. *armed with a new sword* MT.

123. 1QSam MTᵐˢˢ LXX. *swore to him* MT.

mighty men[124] with the Philistin[es, in which *Si]bbecai*[125] the Hushathite [killed Saph], a descendant of [the giants]. ▲

■ *2 Samuel 22 presents a full version of Psalm 18. There are textual variants between the Psalm as it occurs in the Masoretic Text, and this chapter as it occurs in the Masoretic Text. There are also textual variants between the two Greek texts of the Septuagint as well as between the Greek and their Hebrew originals. The Psalm's text as witnessed by 4QSam^a adds yet another valuable source for comparison.*

22 30 [For by you] I can [ru]sh [a battalion; by my God, I can take a wall. 31 As for God, his way is perfect: the word of the LORD is test]ed; he is a shield [to all who take refuge in him. 32 For who is God, except the LORD? Who is a rock, except our God? 33 Go]d is *girding me with str[ength;*[126] and his path remains perfect. 34 He makes my feet like hinds' feet, and] sets me [on] my high places. 35 He teaches my hands to fi[g]ht, so that [my arms] can be[nd a bow of bronze. 36 You have also given me the shield of] your salvation; and your *help*[127] has made me great. 37 You have en[la]rged my *steps;*[128] [my feet have] no[t . . .[129] 38 I have pursued my enemies and] destroyed them; I did not turn back until they were finished off. 39 *I have run [them through,*[130] so that they cannot arise. They fell under my feet.] 40 You have *equipped me*[131] with strength for battle, *and*[132] you have [su]bdued un[der me] those who rose up against me. 41 [You have made my enemies turn their backs to me, *that]*[133] I might annihilate [those who hate me. 42 They looked, but there was no]ne to save; to the LORD, but [he did not answer them. 43 Then I ground them as fine as the dust *on]* the surface of a path;*[134] [like the m]ire of the stree[t]s, *I trampled them.*[135] 44 You have delive[red me from strife with my people; you have kept me as the head of] the nations: a people whom I

---

124. 1QSam. *at Gob* MT.

125. 1QSam apparently adds an extraneous word.

Chapter 22. 4QSam^a: 22:30–51.

126. 4QSam^a LXX^L MT+LXX-Ps. *strengthens me* MT LXX^B.

127. 4QSam^a. *answering me* MT^L LXX^B. *gentleness* MT^mss LXX^L.

128. 4QSam^a. *steps under me* MT.

129. 4QSam^a had both one negative clause in the text and a second written above the line.

130. 4QSam^a LXX^L MT+LXX-Ps. *And I have consumed them and run them through* MT LXX^A.

131. 4QSam^a MT^mss MT-Ps. MT^L misspells.

132. 4QSam^a. Not in MT.

133. 4QSam^a. *and that* MT.

134. 4QSam^a. *of the earth* MT.

135. 4QSam^a MT-Ps. *I crushed them, I trampled them* MT.

have not known [will] serve me. 45 *Just*[136] he[aring from me, they obey me. 46 Foreigners *come cringing to me;*] *they are not shackeled in chains.*[137] 47 The LORD lives. Bl[essed be my Rock. May God be exalted, the Rock of my salvation, 48 the God] who *executes*[138] vengeance for me, and who *tramples*[139] peoples under [me, 49 who brings me out from my enemies. Yes, you exalt me over those who rise up against me;] you *protect*[140] me from the viol[en]t. 50 There[fo]re I give thanks to you, [LORD; among the nations, I sing praises to your name.] 51 He gives [great] *deliverance*[141] to his king, and shows lovingkindness to his anoi[nted], to Da[vid and to his posterity forevermore].

23

■ *2 Samuel 23:1–7 is called David's Last Words. The latter part of verse 7 appears in the Great Psalms Scroll (11QPsª) at the top of column 27, just before the listing of David's Compositions, and the remainder of 23:1–7 surely had been written in the lost bottom part of the preceding column of that scroll.*

1 Now these are the las[t] words of David, [the oracle of David son of Jesse, the oracle of] the man *God*[142] lifted up, the anointed of [the Go]d of J[acob, the sweet Psalmist of Israel: 2 The spirit of the LORD] spoke in me, and his word was on [my] tongue. 3 [The God of Israel spoke, the Rock of Israel said to me: The one who rules over] people [righteo]usly, who rules [in the fear of God, 4 will be like the light of the morning, when the sun rises, a morning without clouds, with the splendor of the r]ain [on the grass of the land. 5 For is not my house like this with God? For he has established an everlasting covenant with me, ordered] in all things, and [secure: it is all my salvation, and all my desire. Will he not make it grow?] 6 But the ungodly [will be, all of them, like thorns to be pushed aside, because they cannot be grasped with the hand; 7 anyone touching them must use an iron bar] or the shaft of a s[p]e[a]r. They are consumed with fire; they are burned where they grow. ▲

9 [And next to him] among [the three migh]ty men [was Elea]zar *the son of*

---

136. 4QSamª MT+LXX-Ps. *Foreigners come cringing to me. Just* MT LXXᴮᴬ.

137. 4QSamª. *wither; they are girt from their strongholds* MT LXXᴮᴬ. *come cringing to me; foreigners wither; they come out from their strongholds* LXXᵐˢˢ MT+LXX-Ps.

138. 4QSamª and MT use different forms.

139. 4QSamª LXXᴸ. *brings down* MT.

140. 4QSamª LXXᴸ. *rescue* MT LXXᴮ MT+LXX-Ps.

141. 4QSamª LXXᴸ. *deliverances* MT LXXᴮ MT+LXX-Ps.

Chapter 23. 4QSamª: 23:1–6; 1QSam: 23:9–12; 11QPsª: 23:7.

142. 4QSamª LXX. MT uses an alternate word for *God* or misspells.

[A]*hohi*.[143] He was with David [when] they [taunted the Philistines who were gathered there] for battle and the Israelite tr[oo]ps had withdrawn. 10 He rose up and attacked the Philistines until his hand grew ti[re]d and was stuck to his sword. The LORD brou[ght] about a great victory that day, and the troops returned after him only to take spoil. 11 Next to him was Shammah [son of A]gee the Hararite. The Philist[in]es had banded together at Lehi where there was a plot of ground full of lentil[s, and the troops fled fro]m them. 12 But he [took his stand in the mid]dle of [the p]l[ot, defending it] and striking down [the Phi]lis[tines, while the LORD brought about a great victory]. ▲

24 16 [When the angel stretched out his hand toward Jerusalem to destroy it, the LORD relented from the calamity, and said to the angel destroying the people, "That is enough. Now stay your hand." The angel of the L]ORD *was stand-ing*[144] b[y the threshing-floor of Arau]nah the [Jeb]usite. [*David*] *rai*[*sed his eyes and saw the angel of the* LORD *standing bet*]*ween earth and* [*heav*]*en;* [*his*] *drawn sword was in his hand* [*stretched out toward Jerusalem. David and the elders, cover*]*ed* [*in sackclo*]*th,* [*fell down on*] *their* [*face*]*s.*[145] 17 David sai[d] to the LOR[D, *"Was it not I who ordered the census of the people? Look,*[146] *I have sinned, and*] *I have done gre*[*a*]*t evil.*[147] But [these sheep, what have they done? Set your hand against me and against my father's house." 18 Gad came to David] that [day] and *said,*[148] "Go up, [set up an altar to the LORD on the threshing-floor of Araunah the Jebusite." 19 So David went up, as Gad had said, a]s the LORD had commanded. 20 Now [Araunah] loo[ked down . . . *covered*] *in sackcloth, as Araunah was threshing wheat.*[149] [He went out . . . *cov*]*ered in sackcloth,*[150] and came [. . .]. ▲

143. 1QSam. *son of Dodi son of Ahohi* MT.

Chapter 24. 4QSamª: 24:16–20.

144. 4QSamª LXX^L MT+LXX-Chr. *was* MT LXX^B.

145. 4QSamª 1 Chr 21:16. Not in MT LXX.

146. 4QSamª 1 Chr 21:17. *when he saw the angel striking down the people, and he said, "Look* MT.

147. 4QSamª LXX^L 1 Chr 21:17. *I have acted perversely* MT LXX^B.

148. 4QSamª. *said to him* MT.

149. 4QSamª. Not in MT LXX (cf. 1 Chr 21:20).

150. 4QSamª. Not in MT LXX.

KINGS

Only three manuscripts of the book of Kings—the work that we now designate 1 and 2 Kings—were found in the various Judean Desert caves: one each on leather in Cave 4 and Cave 5, and a papyrus manuscript in Cave 6. The last presents a typical snapshot of the Qumran scrolls. About ninety-four fragments that presumably belonged to this manuscript were found, but only seventeen can be identified and placed, since the majority of the fragments preserve only a few letters each. Many have not even one complete or nearly complete word, while others with only "these" or "all" or "he made" or "[J]udah" could have come from multiple loci within the book.

Despite the limited scope of text on most fragments, however, there are enough indications of text significantly divergent from the traditional Masoretic Text to suggest that the text of Kings was pluriform in antiquity, just as the text of Samuel has been demonstrated to be.

In addition to numerous small variants, sometimes in agreement with the Greek text, there are more significant variants as well, with the Qumran manuscripts at times preserving the superior variant and the Masoretic Text at other times doing so. Just as 4QSam^a recovers bits of text thought to be lost, so too 4QKgs preserves a passage (1 Kings 8:16) lost from the Masoretic Text when a scribe's eye skipped from one phrase to a similar phrase below.

Moreover, an additional clue near the end of 1 Kings 7 (see note at 7:25–27) suggests that Kings may have had an expanded text on which the author of Chronicles based his composition. Though the evidence is slight, it tends to confirm that the ancient text of Samuel-Kings that the Jewish author of Chronicles used was not the Masoretic Text but one similar to those documented at Qumran.

1 KINGS

1 16 [Bathsheba bowed and prostrated herself before the king.] The [k]ing *said,*[1] "What [concerns you?" 17 She said to him, "My lord, you swore by the LORD your God to your maidservant, 'Solomon your son will] reign aft[er] me; he is the [one who will sit on my throne].' " ▲

27 ["Has this come about by order of my lord the king, and yet you have not informed your] ser[vants who is to sit on the throne of my lord the king after him?" 28 Then King David answered, "Call Bathsheba to me."] She came into [the king's presence and stood before him].

29 [Then the king swore, "As the LORD lives, who has saved my life from every] difficulty, 30 just [as I swore to you by the LORD the God of Israel— 'Solomon your son will reign after me,] he will sit on [my] thro[ne in my stead'— today I will accomplish that!" 31 Then Bathsheba bowed, face to the ground, prostrating herself] before the king, and said, "Let [my lord King David live forever]."

32 King David sai[d, "Call Zadok the priest, Nathan the prophet, and Benaiah son of Jehoiada." When they arrived in the king's presence,] 33 the king said to them, "Take [the servants of your lord with you, have Solomon my son ride on] my [mule], and lead him down to G[ihon. 34 Zadok the priest and Nathan the prophet are to anoint him there as king over Israel. Then] blow the trumpet and proclaim, 'Long li[ve king Solomon.' 35 Then come back up following him, and he will come and sit on my throne. For] he will rule in my stead; he is the one I have decreed to [be prince over Israel and over Judah]."

36 [Benaiah the son of Jehoiada answered] the king and said, "Amen! [May the LORD, the God of my lord the king, declare this. 37 As the LORD has been with my lord the king,] so may he be [with Solomon. May he make his throne even greater than the throne of my lord King David]." ▲

3 12 [. . . See, I have given you such a wise and understanding mind that there] has be[en no] one [like you before you, and no one like you will arise after you. 13 I have also given you what you have not requested, both] riches [and honor, so that all your days no other king will compare to you]. ▲

7 20 [There were capitals on top of both pillars, above] the rounded projection wh[ich was next to the network, and there were two hundred pomegranates in rows surrounding the two capitals].

Chapter 1. 5QKgs: 1Kgs 1:16–17, 27–37.

1. 5QKgs MT LXX. *said to her* MT^mss MT^C LXX^L.

Chapter 3. pap6QKgs: 1Kgs 3:12–13.

Chapter 7. 4QKgs: 1Kgs 7:20–21, 25–27, 29–42, 51.

21 [He set up] the pillar[s at the portico of the temple. Setting up the right pillar, he named it Jachin. Setting up the left pillar, he named it Boaz].▲

25 [It stood on twelve oxen, three facing north, three facing west, three facing south, and] three fa[c]ing [east. The sea was set above them, with all their hindquarters inward. 26 It was a handbreadth thick, and its brim was fash]ioned [like] the brim of a cup, [like] a lily blossom. [It held two thousand baths. 27 He made] ten bronze [stands], four [cubits long, four wide, and three high].▲

■ *The fragment with 7:25–27 above offers an additional important clue about the pluriform text of Kings in antiquity. The fragment contains the left ends of the original lines of text but extends farther left to reveal the beginning of a line in the next column (which should contain the final verses of 1 Kings 7). Only the single word for* chambers *(with the last letter missing) has been preserved from the passage, which describes Solomon's construction of the Temple and its vessels. In the Masoretic Text of Kings (1 Kings 7:48–51) that word does not appear, but it does in the related passage in Chronicles (1 Chron 28:12–18). Just as 4QSam^a does at several points, 4QKgs here shows that it had an expanded wording on which the author of Chronicles based his text. Though the evidence is slight, it tends to confirm that the text of Samuel-Kings that the Jewish author of Chronicles used was not the Masoretic Text but one similar to those documented at Qumran.*

29 [On the panels between the cross-bars were lions, oxen, and cherubim, and on the cross-bars as well. Above and below the lions and oxen were wr]eaths of [hanging] w[ork].

30 [Each stand had f]ou[r bronze wheels with bronze axles. Its four sides] ha[d] supports [under]neath a basin. [The supports were cast, with a wreath at their side. 31 Its opening was inside a capital, which extended up]ward [one cubit. Its opening was round, the way a pedestal is made, measuring a cubit and a half. At its opening, there were engravings. Their panels were square, not] roun[d. 32 The four wheels were underneath the panels, and the axles of the wheels were attached to the base. Each wheel was a] cubit and a half [high. 33 The wheels were made like a chariot wheel.] Their [axles, rims,] spokes, and hu[bs were all cast metal].

34 [There were four supports at the four corners of each stand;] the [s]upports were [of one piece] with the stand. 35 At [the top of the stand was a round band half a cubit high. And at the top of the stand,] the [s]tays and panels were of one piece [with it. 36 On the surfaces of the stays and panels, he engraved cherubim,] lions, and palm trees, *on the open space*[2] of ea[ch, with wreaths all around. 37 He

---

2. 4QKgs and MT use different words for *on*, neither of which is normally used in this sense.

made the ten bases this way:] all of th[em were cast alike], with *one size and one shape*.[3]

38 [And he made ten bronze basins,] each basin holding for[ty baths. Each basin measured four cubits. There was a basin on each of the ten] stands. 39 He placed [five of the stands on the right side of the temple and five on the] left side. [The sea he placed on the right side of the temple—that is, when facing east, toward the south. 40 Hiram also made] the *pot*[*s*,[4] shovels, and bowls].

[Thus Hiram finished all the work which] he had undertaken for [King Solomon in the house of the LORD: 41 the two pillars, the bowl-shaped capitals which were on the top of the two pillars,] and the [two] network[s to cover the two bowl-shaped capitals on the top of the pillars]; 42 also the [four hundred] pom[egranates for the two networks—two rows of pomegranates for each network—to cover the two bowl-shaped capitals on the pillars].▲

51 [Thus all the work that King Solomon had undertaken in the house of the LORD was completed. And Solomon brought in the things which David his father had dedicated—the silver, the gold, and the vessels—and put them in the treasuries of the] house of [the LORD].

8 1 [Then Solomon assembled the elders of Israel, all the hea]ds of tribes, the lea[ders of the ancestral houses of the Israelites, to King Solomon in Jerusalem, in order to bring up the ark of] the covenant of the LORD from the city of D[avid, which is Zion].

2 [All the people of Israel assembled to King Solomon] at the time of the feast, [in the month of Ethani]m, se[*venth*] *month*.[5] 3 [All the elders of Israel came, the priests took up the ark, 4 and] they [brou]ght up the ark of the LORD. The ten[t of meeting and all the holy vessels that were in the tent—the pr]iests and the Levites [brought these up as well].

5 King Solomon and [all the congregation of Israel which had assembled to him gathered before the ark, sac]rificing [so many] sheep and oxen that they could not be counted or [numbered. 6 The priests brought in the ark of the covenant of] the LORD to its place, *to*[6] the inner sanctuary of the temple, to the most holy [place, under the wings of the cherubim. 7 For the cherubi]m *spread*[7] their wings over the place of the ark and covered [the ark and its poles. 8 The poles were so long that] the ends of the poles [were seen] from the holy place [in front of the inner sanctuary, though they could not be seen outside. They are still

---

3. 4QKgs MT[mss] LXX. *one size, one shape* MT.

4. 4QKgs LXX. *basins* MT.

Chapter 8. 4QKgs: 1Kgs 8:1–9, 16–18.

5. 4QKgs. *the seventh month* MT.

6. 4QKgs. MT uses a different word for *to*.

7. 4QKgs and MT use different plural forms of *spread*.

there today. 9 There was nothing in the ark except] *the two tablets of stone*[8] [which Moses put there at Horeb, when the LORD made a covenant with the Israelites, when they came out of the land of Egypt].▲

16 [" 'From the day I brought my people Israel out from Egypt, I have not chosen a city from among the tribes of Israel to build a house for my name to be there, *nor did I choose anyone*] to be a leader over [my] people [*Israel, but I chose Jerusalem for my name to be there,*[9] and I chose David*] to be over my people, *over*[10] [Israel.' 17 Now David my father had it in mind to build a house for the name of the LORD, the God of I]srael. 18 But [the LORD] said [to David my father, 'Because you had a mind to build a house for my name, you did well; for it was your intention].' "▲

12 28 [After the king took counsel, he made two calves of gold. Then he said to them, "It is too much for you to travel to Jerusalem. Behold your gods,] I[srael, who brought you up from the land of Egypt]."

29 [He set up one in Bethel, and the o]ther he placed [in Dan. 30 This th]ing [became a sin, because the] people [journeyed even as f]ar as Dan [to worship before the one there. 31 He set up shrines for the hi]gh places and a[ppointed priests from among all the people, except from the Levites].▲

22 29 [But] the king of I[srael and Jehoshaphat king of Judah] march[ed to Ramoth-gilead. 30 The king of Isra]el [said] to Jehoshaphat [*king of Judah,*[11] "I will disguise myself and go into the battle, but you wear] your [robes]." So the king of [Israel disguised] himself [and went into battle. 31 Meanwhile *the*] kin[*g of Syria gave orders*[12] to his thirty-two] chariot [captains, saying, "Fight no one, either small or great, except the] ki[ng of Israel]."▲

---

8. 4QKgs adds an extra *the* to this phrase.

9. 4QKgs [2 Chron 6:5b–6a]. MT of Kings omits, having skipped from the first occurrence of *my name to be there* to the second. LXX omits the first clause but retains the second, having skipped from *nor did I choose* to *but I chose.* MT of Chronicles retains the entire reading intact. This reconstruction is strongly indicated by the repetition of *over my people,* the manuscript spacing, the partial parallel in LXX, and the full parallel in 2 Chron.

10. 4QKgs. Not in MT LXX.

Chapter 12. pap6QKgs: 1Kgs 12:28–31.

Chapter 22. pap6QKgs: 1Kgs 22:29–31.

11. Spacing in pap6QKgs indicates a text longer than that of MT. LXX adds *king of Judah* here, which would fit perfectly in pap6QKgs. Not in MT.

12. pap6QKgs with usual verb-followed-by-subject pattern. Order reversed MT LXX.

2 KINGS

5 26 [Then he said to him, "Did I not go with you in spirit, when the man stepped down from his chariot to mee]t you? [Is this the time to receive money, garments, olive orchards and vineyards, sheep] and oxen, [and menservant]s and mai[dservants]?" ▲

6 32 [Elisha was sitting in his house, and the elders were sitting with him, when the king sent a man ahead of him. But before the messenger arrived, he said to the elders,] "Do [you] se[e how this son of a murderer has sent to take off my head? Listen,] when [the messenger] comes, [shut the door and keep the door shut to him. Is not the sound of his master's feet] behind [him]?" ▲

7 8 [When the lepers reached the edge of the camp, they went into on]e [tent] and ate and [dr]ank. Then [they] carried [away silver and gold and clothing, and went off and hid it. When they came back, they entered] another [te]nt, and carri[ed] loot away from it as well, then wen[t and hid it].

9 [Then they said one to another, "What we are doing is not right. T]oday [is a da]y of good [news, but we keep it to ourselves. If we delay until the morning light, we will be punished. Come on,] let us go and [tell the ki]ng['s household]."

10 [So they came and called the gatekeepers of the city and told] them thi[s: "We went in]to [the camp of the Syrians and,] you see, [there was no one there, not a human voice, but the horses and donkeys were tied and the tents remained] just a[s they had been]." ▲

20 [And so it happened to him. The people trampled him at the gate, and he died, *just as the man of Go*]d [*had said*].[13]

■ *At the end of verse 20, pap6QKgs—in agreement with two Vulgate manuscripts— repeats the prophetic link in 7:17, cross-referencing the death of the king's captain with the prophecy in 7:2. There Elisha, "the man of God," had predicted that food would suddenly become plentiful, but the captain—because he had doubted Elisha's word—would not eat any of it.*

8 1 [Elisha said to the woman whose son he had restored to life, "Make prepara]tio]ns [and] leave, you [and your household, and sojourn wherever you can. For the LORD has called for a fam]ine which will come *against*[14] the land for

---

Chapter 5. pap6QKgs: 2Kgs 5:26.

Chapter 6. pap6QKgs: 2Kgs 6:32.

Chapter 7. pap6QKgs: 2Kgs 7:8–10, 20.

   13. pap6QKgs Vulg[2mss]. Not in MT LXX Vulg.

Chapter 8. pap6QKgs: 2Kgs 8:1–5.

   14. pap6Kgs LXX. *to* MT.

se[ven years." 2 So the woman made preparations *and left, following the instructions of the man of G]o[d], living in*[15] [the land of the Philistines] se[ven] yea[rs].

3 [*The woman*[16] returned from the land of the Philistines, and *she came to the city,*] to the king, concerning her house and [*land.*[17] 4 Meanwhile the king was talking with Gehazi, the servant of *E]l[i]sha,*[18] saying, "Please tell me [all the great things Elisha has done." 5 Just as he was tell]ing [the] king [that he had restored to life one who was dead . . .].▲

9 1 [Elisha the prophet summoned one of the prophetic group and said to him, "Gird up your loins, take this vial of] oil [in your hand, and go to Ramoth-gilead. 2 When you arrive there, find Jehu son of Jehoshaphat son of] Nimshi. Then go i[n, have him leave his associates, and take him to a private room]."▲

10 21 Jehu [se]nt word [throughout Israel, and all the worshipers of Baal came, so that there was no one left who] did n[ot] come. [. . .]▲

---

15. pap6Kgs. *following the instructions of the man of God, and left with her household, sojourning in* MT LXX.

16. pap6Kgs. *Seven years later, the woman* MT LXX. At this point, the text of pap6Kgs is shorter than that of MT and the versions. Thus *Seven years later* was probably not included in that manuscript.

17. pap6Kgs. *she went out to plead to the king for her house and land* MT LXX. Traces of *to the city* remain on the leather.

18. pap6Kgs LXX[ms]. *the man of God* MT LXX[ms]. *Elisha, the man of God* LXX.

Chapter 9. pap6QKgs: 2Kgs 9:1–2.

Chapter 10. pap6QKgs: 2Kgs 10:21.

ISAIAH

For both Jews and Christians, the Isaiah scrolls found in the Judean Desert are of great interest, in view of their contents and because the *Great Isaiah Scroll* (1QIsaᵃ) is perhaps the best known of all the Dead Sea Scrolls. This, the only manuscript preserving a biblical book virtually in its entirety, was found wrapped in protective linen inside a pottery jar and is among the seven scrolls that were first discovered (and published soon afterward). The circumstances surrounding this scroll's discovery by the Bedouin in 1947, its transportation to the United States by the Metropolitan Samuel (head of the Syrian Orthodox Church), its clandestine purchase by the Israeli scholar Yigael Yadin, and its return to Israel in 1954 form a gripping tale.

The book of Isaiah was one of the three most popular books at Qumran, with twenty-one manuscripts recovered. The only books represented in greater number are the Psalms (with thirty-seven scrolls) and Deuteronomy (with thirty). At Qumran, two Isaiah scrolls were found in Cave 1, eighteen in Cave 4, and one in Cave 5; one additional manuscript was discovered further south at Wadi Murabba'at. While only 1QIsaᵃ survives completely, a few other scrolls are quite substantial,[a] and together the fragmentary Isaiah scrolls preserve generous portions of the book. These manuscripts were copied over the course of nearly two centuries, ranging from about 125 BCE (1QIsaᵃ) to about 60 CE (4QIsaᶜ).

Though large-scale variant editions are preserved for some other books (for example, Jeremiah and 1 Samuel), for Isaiah the scrolls and the other ancient witnesses preserve apparently only one edition of this book, with no consistent patterns of variants or rearrangements. Nevertheless, these scrolls (most notably 1QIsaᵃ) contain hundreds of highly instructive variants from the traditional form of the Hebrew text—variants that teach us much about the late stages of the his-

---

a. 1QIsaᵇ, 4QIsaᵇ, and 4QIsaᶜ.

tory of the book's composition and provide many improved readings. These variant readings fall into four categories.

First, some variant readings are major in that they involve one or more verses present in some texts but absent from others. A contrasting pair of examples can be seen in chapter 2. On the one hand, the second half of verse 9 and all of verse 10 are not in 1QIsa[a]; these were most likely a later addition to the text of Isaiah by some unknown scribe, though made early enough to be recorded in 4QIsa[a], 4QIsa[b], the Masoretic Text, and the Septuagint. On the other hand, verse 22 was not yet in the Hebrew text translated by the Septuagint but was inserted later into 1QIsa[a] and the traditional Masoretic Text. Numerous similar examples are scattered among the Isaiah scrolls and will be noted in the translation. The existence of such variants provides a privileged window—one that was unavailable before the scrolls—on the gradual growth process of the biblical text in general.

A second category of variant readings involves hundreds of differences—often insignificant for purposes of understanding or interpretation—in spelling, the forms of names, the use of the plural versus the singular, and changes in word order, to name a few. While these are quite minor variants, when taken together they provide rich evidence for the use of Hebrew, different spelling systems, and scribal conventions during the late Second Temple period.

A third category includes a wide spectrum of variants, usually a single word or two, ranging between the large-scale compositional variants described in the first category and the mostly insignificant alternative spellings in the second. One example is found at 1:15, which in 4QIsa[f] and the Masoretic Text concludes with "your hands are filled with blood," while 1QIsa[a] completes the parallelism by adding "your fingers with iniquity." Another example is at 2:20, where the idols of silver and of gold are described in the Masoretic Text as "which they have made for themselves to worship," but in 1QIsa[a] as "which their fingers have made to worship."

The final category involves errors made by the Qumran scribes or found in the text that they were copying.[b] These are often difficult to identify as real errors,

---

b. It is often impossible to tell for sure whether an error was committed by the scribe or was already in the text he was copying.

since a reading that to some scholars is "incorrect" may represent for others an alternative reading or a different textual tradition. But even with all necessary caution, we sometimes find that certain scribes were careless or wrote down variants that are better explained in terms of errors than viable alternative textual forms. One example is found in Isaiah 16:8–9, where 1QIsaᵃ reads:

> 8 For the fields of Heshbon and the vineyards of Sibmah languish. 9 I will water you with my tears, Heshbon and Elealeh, for the battle cry has fallen upon your summer fruits and upon your harvest.

The Masoretic Text, however, has a much longer passage (which is also found in the Septuagint, but with some variations):

> 8 For the fields of Heshbon and the vineyards of Sibmah languish. *The leaders of the nations have broken down its choice branches, which reached as far as Jazer and extended into the wilderness; its shoots were spread and wide, even crossing the sea. 9 Therefore I will weep with the crying of Jazer for the vine of Sibmah.* I will water you with my tears, Heshbon and Elealeh, for the battle cry has fallen upon your summer fruits and upon your harvest.

In this example, the eye of the scribe must have skipped from *Sibmah* (which follows *languish* in the Hebrew) in verse 8 to *Sibmah* in verse 9, resulting in the omission of the intervening text. But was this omission made by the scribe who copied 1QIsaᵃ or by an earlier scribe whose text the Qumran scribe was now copying? Since there are several more such lengthy examples (as well as many smaller ones) in 1QIsaᵃ, the most likely conclusion is that our scribe was somewhat careless and was responsible for many or most of the errors in this large scroll.

Because Isaiah is a lengthy book virtually preserved in its entirety in IQIsaᵃ, and since there are so many Isaiah scrolls, for the translation of this book and accompanying variants a somewhat different approach has been taken here than with other books in *The Dead Sea Scrolls Bible*. The translation that follows is consistently from 1QIsaᵃ, with the readings from the other scrolls shown in the footnotes. Some of the insignificant variants (usually involving spelling) are not noted. Moreover, in this translation the Septuagint is sometimes, but not always, collated for variant readings. The main reason for this is that Isaiah is mainly

poetry,c and the Septuagint contains a rather free Greek translation of the unvo-
calized Hebrew poetry; it is thus often difficult to tell exactly which Hebrew
form is being translated. However, most of the more significant Septuagint variants are recorded.

Isaiah was one of the most influential and most quoted books among the Dead
Sea Scrolls, providing evidence of its influence on authors both of general Jewish
works imported to Qumran and of works that were specifically composed by the
Qumran covenanters. Five commentaries, or *pesharim,* on Isaiah were found in
Cave 4 and another in Cave 3. Using a system of quoting a base text and com-
menting on it, these commentaries underscore the authoritative and scriptural
status of the book of Isaiah at Qumran.

With its emphasis on prophecy and the end times, it is not surprising that the
book of Isaiah was so popular at Qumran, just as it was among New Testament
authors. In fact, the Qumran ascetics and all four Evangelists quoted Isaiah 40:3
for purposes of self-identity, in support of the respective missions of both the
desert community and John the Baptist. The Hebrew form of the verse is quoted
in the *Community Rule:*

> . . . [T]hey shall separate from the session of perverse men to go to the
> wilderness, there to prepare the way of truth, as it is written:
>
> In the wilderness prepare the way of the LORD,
> make straight in the desert a highway for our God.
>
> (1QS 8:13–14)

The New Testament authors, however, quote this verse from the Septuagint,
which had lost the exact sense of the parallelism:

> This is the one of whom the prophet Isaiah spoke when he said:
>
> The voice of one proclaiming in the wilderness:
> "Prepare the way of the LORD,
> make straight his paths."
>
> (Matt 3:3; see Mark 1:3, Luke 3:4, John 1:23)

---

c. However, text was subsequently written down in prose format in the scrolls as well as in the
Hebrew text used by the Septuagint translator(s).

The Qumran covenanters show that they were fulfilling Isaiah's prophecy by separating from the Jerusalem Jews and going out to the wilderness to prepare the way of the LORD through study of the Torah. In contrast, the Gospel passages see Isaiah 40:3 as describing John the Baptist in the wilderness calling his audience to prepare for the arrival of Jesus. In these two different, self-defining uses of the same scriptural passage, the Qumran covenanters view the Isaiah passage as fulfilled in themselves, while the Evangelists present it as about to be fulfilled in John's witness to Jesus the Messiah.

1 1 The vision of Isaiah son of Amoz, which he saw concerning Judah and Jerusalem in the days of Uzziah, Jotham, Ahaz, and *Yehizqiyah,*[1] kings of Judah. 2 Hear, heavens, and listen, earth; for the LORD has spoken. Children have I nourished and raise[d], but they have rebelled against me. 3 The ox knows its owner, and the ass its masters' manger; *Israel*[2] does not know, *and*[3] my people does not un[dersta]nd. 4 Ah, sinful nation, people laden with iniquity, seed of evildoers, corrupt children! They have abandoned the Lo[RD], they have despised the Holy One of Israel. They are estranged, gone backward.

5 Why would you sti[ll] be beaten, that you continue to rebel? The whole head is sick, and the whole heart weak. 6 From sole of foot to head there is no healthy spot, but bruises and sores and bleeding wounds; they have not been pressed out nor bound up nor softened with oil. 7 Your country is desolate, your cities burned with fire; your land—right in front of you foreigners are devouring it. *They have brought devastation upon it,*[4] as overthrown by for[eign]ers. 8 And the daughter of Zion *is left*[5] like a hut in a vineyard *and*[6] like a shelter in a cucumber field, like a besieged city. 9 If the LORD of hosts had not left us a few survivors, we would have become like Sodom, we would have been like Gomorrah.

10 Hear the [word] of the LORD, rulers of Sodom, *and*[7] listen to the instruction of our God, people of Gomorrah! 11 What is the multitude of your sacrifices to me? says the LORD. I have had enough burnt offerings of rams and fat of fed beasts. I do not delight in the blood of bulls or lambs or goats. 12 That you enter

---

Chapter 1. 1QIsa[a]: all; 4QIsa[a]: 1:1–3; 4QIsa[b]: 1:1–6; 4QIsa[f]: 1:10–16, 18–31; 4QIsa[j]: 1:1–6.

1. *Yehizqiyah* (with *Ye-* prefixed above *Hizqiyah* as a correction) 1QIsa[a]. *Yehizqiyahu* MT.

2. 1QIsa[a] MT. *but* Israel 4QIsa[j].

3. 1QIsa[a]. Not in 4QIsa[j] MT.

4. 1QIsa[a]. *Devastated,* MurIsa MT LXX.

5. 1QIsa[a] and MT use different forms.

6. 1QIsa[a]. Not in MT.

7. 1QIsa[a]. Not in 4QIsa[f] MT.

to see my face[8]—who has required this of you, to[9] trample my courts? 13 Do not continue to[10] bring meaningless offerings! Incense is an abomination unto me. New moon and sabbath, the calling of assemblies—I cannot bear iniquity with her[11] solemnity. 14 Your new moons and your feasts I detest. They have become a burden to me that I am weary of carrying. 15 When you spread out your hands, I will turn my eyes away from you. Even multiply[12] prayers, I will not listen. Your hands are filled with blood, *your fingers with iniquity*.[13]

16 Wash *and*[14] make yourselves clean; *and*[15] remove the evil of your actions from my sight. Cease to do evil, 17 learn to do good. Seek justice, guide the injured, get justice for the orphan, defend the widow. 18 Come n[ow], and let us reason together, says the LORD. Though your sins be like *scarlet,*[16] they shall be as white as snow; though they be *red*[17] like crimson, they shall be like wool. 19 If you are willing and obey, you shall eat the good of the land. 20 *But*[18] if you refuse and rebel, you shall be devoured *by*[19] the sword; for the mouth of the LORD has spoken.

21 Alas, she has become a harlot, the faithful c[i]ty! She was filled with justice; righteousness dwelled [within her, but now] murderers. 22 Your silver *has turned*[20] to dross, your wine mixed with water. 23 Your rulers are r[ebels and friends of] thieves. *They all love*[21] bribes and *chase*[22] after rewards. They do not seek just[ice] for the orphan, [nor does the cause of] the widow reach them.

24 Therefore says the Lord, the LORD of hosts, [the Mighty One of Israel], *Ah,*[23] I will take vengeance on *his*[24] adversaries and avenge myself on *his*[25] ene-

---

8. Or, *for my face to appear.*

9. Explicit in 1QIsa[a]. Implicit in MT.

10. Explicit in 1QIsa[a]. Implicit in MurIsa MT.

11. 1QIsa[a]. Not in MT.

12. 1QIsa[a]. *you will multiply* MT.

13. 1QIsa[a]. Not in 4QIsa[f] MT.

14. 1QIsa[a]. Not in 4QIsa[f] MT.

15. 1QIsa[a]. Not in MT.

16. Singular 1QIsa[a] MT[mss] LXX. Plural MT.

17. It is not clear whether *ydwmw* in 1QIsa[a] meant *be red* or *be like*.

18. 1QIsa[a] MT. Not in 4QIsa[f].

19. Explicit in 1QIsa[a]. Implicit in MT.

20. Plural 1QIsa[a]. Singular MT.

21. Plural 1QIsa[a]. Singular MT.

22. Plural 1QIsa[a]. Singular MT.

23. 1QIsa[a] (*hwh*; see *hw hw* Amos 5:16). Variant spelling *[hwy]* MT.

24. 1QIsa[a]. *my* 4QIsa[f] MT.

25. 1QIsa[a]. *my* MT.

mies. 25 *He*[26] will turn my hand against you, and I will [refine . . .][27] your dross and will take aw[ay] all your alloy. 26 I will restore your judges as at first [and your counselors] as at the beginning. Afterward *they will call*[28] you the City of Righteousness, Faithful Town. 27 Zion will be redeemed with justice, and *her repentant ones*[29] with righteousness. 28 But rebels and sinners will both be crushed, and those who abandon the LORD will perish. 29 For they will be ashamed of the terebinths that you desired, and you will blush for the gardens that you chose. 30 For you will be like a terebinth whose leaves are withering and like a garden that has *no water.*[30] 31 *Your strong one*[31] will become as tow, and *your*[32] work a spark; they will both burn together, with none to quench them.

2 1 The word that *Isaiah*[33] son of Amoz saw concerning Judah and Jerusalem. 2 It shall come to pass in the latter days that the mountain of the LORD's house *shall be*[34] established above *mountains*[35] and *be*[36] exalted above the hills, and all nations shall flow *over*[37] it. 3 Many peoples shall go and say, "Come, let us go up *to*[38] the house of the God of Jacob, so *they*[39] may teach us his ways, so we may walk in his paths." For out of Zion goes forth instruction, and the word of the LORD from Jerusalem. 4 He will judge between the nations and *give judgment*[40] for many peoples; they will beat their swords into plowshares and their spears into pruninghooks; *and*[41] nation will not lift up sword against nation, nor will they learn war anymore. 5 House of Jacob, come, let us walk in the light of the LORD. 6 Indeed

---

26. 1QIsa^a. *I* 4QIsa^f MT.

27. 1QIsa^a has a lacuna where MT has *as lye*, which some consider an error for *in a furnace*.

28. 1QIsa^a and MT use different forms.

29. 1QIsa^a MT. *her repentant ones and her repentant ones* 4QIsa^f.

30. 1QIsa^a. *water not* 4QIsa^f MT.

31. Literally, *the your* [plural] *strong one* 1QIsa^a. Traditionally, *the strong one* 4QIsa^f MT (but possibly *your treasure*).

32. 1QIsa^a. *his* MT.

Chapter 2. 1QIsa^a: all; 4QIsa^a: 2:7–10; 4QIsa^b: 2:3–16; 4QIsa^e: 2:1–4; 4QIsa^f: 2:1–3.

33. 1QIsa^a *(Yesha'yah).* Variant spelling *(Yesha'yahu)* MT.

34. Explicit in 1QIsa^a 4QIsa^f MT. Implicit in 4QIsa^e.

35. 1QIsa^a. *the mountains* 4QIsa^e MT.

36. 1QIsa^a MT. *it shall be* 4QIsa^e.

37. 1QIsa^a LXX (cf. Mic 4:1). *to* 4QIsa^e 4QIsa^f MT.

38. 1QIsa^a. *to the mountain of the LORD, to* 4QIsa^e MT.

39. 1QIsa^a (= LXX Mic 4:2). *he* 4QIsa^e(?) MT LXX (= MT Mic 4:2).

40. The scribe of 1QIsa^a wrote the first two letters of this word at the end of the line, stopped, and wrote the whole word at the beginning of the next line; see also 49:11. He also next wrote *between*, crossed it out, and wrote *for* above the line.

41. 1QIsa^a. Not in MT.

you have abandoned your people, the house of Jacob, because they are filled (with practices) from the east[42] and are soothsayers like the Philistines; they shake hands with the children of foreigners. 7 Their land is full of silver and gold, and there is no limit to their treasures. Their land is full of horses, and there is no end to their chariots. 8 Their land is full of idols; they worship the work of their own hands, that which their own fingers have made. 9 But humanity will be humbled and a mortal brought low.[43]

> ▪ *The second half of verse 9 and all of verse 10 were a late addition to the text by a scribe. It was not yet in 1QIsaᵃ, though it was early enough to be in 4QIsaᵃ, 4QIsaᵇ, the Masoretic Text, and the Hebrew text from which the Septuagint was translated. See also verse 22 below.*

11 And[44] the haughty looks of humankind *will be brought low,*[45] and human pride *will be abased;*[46] the LORD alone will be exalted on that day. 12 Indeed the LORD of hosts will have his day: against all that is proud and haughty *and lifted up,*[47] and it will be brought low; 13 against all the cedars of Lebanon, tall and lofty, and against all the oaks of Bashan; 14 against all the [hig]h mountains and against all the lofty hills; 15 against every tall tower and against every fortified [wall]; 16 against all the Tarshish ships and against all the stately vessels. 17 The haughtiness of humanity will be humbled, and human pride will be brought low; the LORD alone will be exalted on that day. 18 The idols will totally *vanish.*[48] 19 People will go into caves in the rocks and into holes in the earth, before the [terror of the Lo]RD and before the glory of his majesty, when he rises to terrify the earth. 20 [On t]hat [day] humans will throw away to the moles and bats their idols of silver and their idols of gold, which *their* [fin]gers [have made][49] to worship. 21 They will go into the crevices [in the rocks and into the cr]acks in the cliffs, before the terror of the LORD and before the glory of his majesty, when he rises to terrify the earth. 22 Have no more to do with mortals, who have but a breath in their nostrils, for what are they worth?[50]

---

42. Literally, *they are filled from the east* 1QIsaᵃ MT.

43. 1QIsaᵃ. 4QIsaᵃ 4QIsaᵇ MT LXX add *And you will not forgive them.* (*And do not forgive them* MT) 10 *Enter into the rock, and hide in the dust before the terror of the* LORD *and before the glory of his majesty* [LXX further adds *when he rises to terrify the earth;* see 2:19, 21].

44. 1QIsaᵃ. Not in 4QIsaᵇ MT.

45. 1QIsaᵃ. *are low* MT.

46. 1QIsaᵃ and 4QIsaᵇ MT use different forms.

47. 1QIsaᵃ. *and upon all that is lifted up* 4QIsaᵇ MT.

48. Plural 1QIsaᵃ. Singular MT.

49. 1QIsaᵃ. *they have made for themselves* MT.

50. Vs 22 is not in LXX, though it is in 1QIsaᵃ MT.

■ *Verse 22 was a late addition to the text. It was not yet in the Hebrew text from which the Septuagint was translated, though it was early enough to be in 1QIsa^a and the Masoretic Text. See also 2:9b–10 above.*

3 1 Indeed, the Lord, the LORD of hosts, is removing from Jerusalem and from Judah support and staff, the entire supply of food, and the entire supply of water; 2 soldier and warrior, judge and prophet, diviner and elder, 3 captain of fifty, and dignitary and counselor, expert artificer and skillful enchanter.

4 I will make young boys their rulers, and infants will govern them. 5 The people will be oppressed, everyone by another, and everyone by his neighbor. The young will be disrespectful of the old, and the base of the honorable.

6 One person will take hold of another in his own house and say, "You have clothing; be our ruler, and let this ruin be under your command." 7 *But*[51] in that day he will lift up his voice, saying, "I will not be a healer. In my house there is neither food nor *clothing.*[52] You will not make me ruler of the people."

8 For Jerusalem is ruined, and Judah is *fallen;*[53] because their speech and their actions are *against*[54] the LORD, provoking his glorious eyes. 9 The *expressions*[55] on their faces bear witness against them. They announce their sin like Sodom, *and*[56] they do not hide it. Woe to them! For they have worked evil on themselves. 10 Say *to*[57] the righteous that it will be well. For they will eat the fruit of their actions. 11 Woe to the wicked! It will be ill. For the recompense of his *hand*[58] *will be repaid*[59] to him.

12 As for my people, children are their oppressors, and women rule over them. My people, your leaders mislead and confuse the *courses*[60] of your paths. 13 The LORD rises to argue a case, stands up to judge the peoples. 14 The LORD will enter into judgment against the elders of *his*[61] people and his princes: You have consumed the vineyard. The spoil of the poor is in your houses. 15 What do you

---

Chapter 3. 1QIsa^a: all; 4QIsa^b: 14–22.

51. 1QIsa^a. Not in MT.

52. 1QIsa^a and MT use different spellings.

53. Feminine 1QIsa^a. Masculine MT.

54. 1QIsa^a. *to* MT.

55. 1QIsa^a. *expression* MT.

56. 1QIsa^a. Not in MT.

57. 1QIsa^a. Not in MT.

58. 1QIsa^a. *hands* MT.

59. 1QIsa^a. *will be done* MT.

60. 1QIsa^a. *course* MT.

61. 1QIsa^a MT. Not in 4QIsa^b.

mean by crushing my people and grinding the face of the poor? *says my Lord, the* LORD *of hosts.*[62]

16 The LORD said, Because the daughters of Zion are haughty and walk with outstretched necks and roving eyes, mincing along as they go and tinkling with *their*[63] feet, 17 the LORD[64] will afflict the scalps of the daughters of Zion with scabs, and *my Lord*[65] will lay bare their secret parts. 18 In that day *my Lord*[66] will take away the beauty of their anklets and headbands, crescents, 19 *and*[67] pendants, and bracelets, veils 20 *and*[68] turbans, armlets and *sashes,*[69] perfume boxes, amulets, 21 *and*[70] signet rings and nose rings, 22 *and*[71] festal robes, *mantles,*[72] purses, 23 mirrors, fine linen, headdresses and veils. 24 Then, instead of *perfume*[73] *there will be*[74] stench; instead of a sash, a rope; instead of well set hair, baldness; instead of a fine robe, sackcloth; instead of beauty, *shame.*[75] 25 Your men will fall by the sword and *your forces*[76] in battle. 26 Her gates will lament and mourn, and she will be cleaned out and sit upon the ground.

4 1 Seven women will *take hold*[77] of one man on that day, saying, "We will eat our own bread and wear our own *clothes.*[78] Only let us be called by your name. Take away our disgrace."

2 On that day the branch of the LORD will be beautiful and glorious, and the

---

62. 1QIsa^a MT. Not in LXX. 1QIsa^a initially skipped *my Lord,* then wrote it above the line.

63. Feminine 1QIsa^a. Masculine (incorrectly) MT.

64. The original scribe of 1QIsa^a corrected from *my Lord* to *the* LORD. *my Lord* MT. *God* LXX.

65. 1QIsa^a. *the* LORD MT.

66. The original scribe of 1QIsa^a corrected from *the* LORD (= LXX) to *my Lord* (= MT).

67. 1QIsa^a. Not in MT.

68. 1QIsa^a. Not in MT.

69. 1QIsa^a lacks the expected definite article as in 4QIsa^b and MT.

70. 1QIsa^a. Not in MT.

71. 1QIsa^a. Not in MT.

72. 1QIsa^a. *mantles and cloaks* 4QIsa^b MT.

73. 1QIsa^a unnecessarily adds the definite article.

74. Plural 1QIsa^a. Singular MT. Following *stench,* MT contains an additional form of the verb *to be* that is not in 1QIsa^a.

75. 1QIsa^a. Not in MT.

76. Plural 1QIsa^a. Singular collective MT.

Chapter 4. 1QIsa^a: all; 4QIsa^a: 5–6.

77. Singular 1QIsa^a. Plural MT LXX.

78. 1QIsa^a and MT use different spellings.

fruit of the land will be the pride and boast of the escaped remnant of Israel *and Judah*.[79] 3 Then, whoever is left in Zion and whoever remains in Jerusalem will be called holy, everyone in Jerusalem inscribed for life, 4 when my Lord has washed away the filth of the daughters of Zion and cleansed the blood of Jerusalem from within it by the spirit of judgment and by the spirit of *storm*.[80] 5 The LORD *will create*[81] over the whole site of Mount Zion and over its assembly a cloud *by day* 6 *from the heat*,[82] and a refuge and hiding place from storm and rain.

5 1 *I will sing*[83] for my beloved my love-song about his vineyard. My beloved had a vineyard on a very fertile hill. 2 He dug it out, cleared it of stones, and planted it with choice vines. He built a watchtower within it and also hewed out a winepress in it. Then he waited for it to produce grapes, but it produced wild grapes. 3 Now, *inhabitants*[84] of Jerusalem and people of Judah, *judge*[85] between me and my vineyard. 4 What more could have been done *in*[86] my vineyard than what I have done for it? Why, when I expected it to produce grapes, did it *raise*[87] wild grapes? 5 *Now*[88] *I will tell*[89] you what I intend to do to my vineyard. *I will take away*[90] its hedge, and it *will be*[91] *devoured*.[92] I will break down its wall, and it *will be*[93] trampled down. 6 I will make it a waste. It will not be pruned or hoed, and briers and thorns will spring up. I will command the clouds to drop no rain upon it.

7 Now, the vineyard of the LORD of hosts is the house of Israel, and the people

---

79. 1QIsa[a]. Not in MT.

80. 1QIsa[a]. *burning* MT LXX.

81. 1QIsa[a] and MT use different forms.

82. 1QIsa[a]. *by day and smoke, and the brilliance of a flaming fire by night. Over the glorious whole there will be a canopy and 6 shelter, a shade by day from the heat* 4QIsa[a] MT. Apparently the eye of the scribe of 1QIsa[a] (or a predecessor) skipped from *by day* in vs 5 to *by day* in vs 6.

Chapter 5. 1QIsa[a]: all; 4QIsa[a]: 5:1; 4QIsa[b]: 5:15–28; 4QIsa[f]: 5:13–14, 25; pap4QIsa[p]: 5:28–30.

83. 1QIsa[a]. *Let me sing* MT.

84. Plural 1QIsa[a]. Singular collective MT.

85. 1QIsa[a] misspells the word.

86. 1QIsa[a]. *for* MT.

87. 1QIsa[a]. *produce* MT.

88. 1QIsa[a] misspells *Now*.

89. 1QIsa[a] and MT use different forms.

90. 1QIsa[a]. *Take away* (imperative) MT.

91. 1QIsa[a] and MT use different forms.

92. 1QIsa[a]. *for devouring* MT.

93. 1QIsa[a] and MT use different forms.

of Judah are his *delightful*[94] plant. He expected justice, but there was *bloodshed;*[95] righteousness, but there was an outcry. 8 Woe to those who join house *to*[96] house, who add field to field, till there is no more room, and *you place yourselves alone*[97] in the midst of the land! 9 In my hearing, the LORD of hosts declared, Surely many houses will be desolate, large and beautiful houses without inhabitant. 10 For ten acres of vineyard will yield only *one*[98] bath, and a [homer of] see[d will yie]ld only an ephah. 11 W[oe to those who rise early in the] morning to pursue strong drink, *holding on*[99] in the darkness while wine inflames them. 12 They have banquets with [lyre and harp, timbrel and flu]te, [and] wine, but they *pay no attention*[100] to the *deeds*[101] of the LORD, nor [do they consider] the work of [his hands].

13 [Therefore] my people are [exil]ed without knowledge. *My*[102] nobles die of hunger, and their multitude is [parched with thirst. 14 Therefore] Sheol has increased its appetite and opened its mouth without limit. Splendor and multitude, the uproarious and jubil[ant] descend into it. 15 *People*[103] are bowed down, humans are humbled, the eyes of the haughty are lowered. 16 But the LORD of hosts *is lifted up*[104] in justice; the holy God proves himself holy in righteousness. 17 Then the lambs will feed as in their pasture, and the fatlings and the aliens will eat among the waste places.

18 Woe to those who pull iniquity with ropes of falsehood, sin with a cart rope, 19 who say, "Let him hurry, let him *expedite*[105] his work, so that we can see it. Let the plan of the Holy One of Israel *happen,*[106] so that we can *recognize*[107] it." 20 Woe to those who call evil good and good evil, who put darkness for light and light for darkness, who put bitter for sweet and sweet for bitter! 21 Woe to those who are wise in their own eyes and discerning in their own sight! 22 Woe to those who are mighty at drinking wine and powerful at mixing strong drinks,

---

94. Singular 1QIsa[a]. Plural MT.

95. 1QIsa[a] begins *bloodshed* with a prefix, which is not in MT.

96. 1QIsa[a] does not contain the word *to*. MT does.

97. 1QIsa[a]. *you are made to live alone* MT.

98. Masculine 1QIsa[a]. Feminine MT.

99. 1QIsa[a]. *lingering* MT.

100. 1QIsa[a] and MT use different forms.

101. Feminine singular or plural 1QIsa[a]. Masculine singular MT.

102. 1QIsa[a]. *Its* MT.

103. 1QIsa[a]. *And people* MT.

104. 1QIsa[a] MT and 4QIsa[b] use different forms.

105. 1QIsa[a] and 4QIsa[b] MT use different forms.

106. 1QIsa[a], 4QIsa[b], and MT use different forms.

107. 1QIsa[a] and MT use different forms.

23 who acquit the guilty for a bribe and remove the innocent status of the righteous from him!

24 Therefore as the tongue of fire devours the stubble and as *fire*[108] sinks down in the *flames,*[109] just so their root will become rotten and their blossom will go up like dust, because they have rejected the law of the LORD of hosts and despised the word of the Holy One of Israel. 25 *Therefore*[110] the anger of the LORD[111] was kindled against his people, and he stretched out his *hands*[112] against them and afflicted them. The mountains tremble, and their corpses are like refuse in the middle of the streets. For all this his anger has not turned away, his *hands are*[113] stretched out still.

26 He will send up a signal to the nations far away and will whistle for them from the end of the earth. And, indeed, they come speedily and swiftly. 27 *No one*[114] is *weary*[115] or stumbles. *And*[116] no one slumbers or sleeps. The belts around their waists *will not come undone,*[117] nor will their sandal-thongs break. 28 Their arrows are sharpened and all their bows bent. Their horses' hooves are like flint and their chariots like a whirlwind. 29 *With a roar like a lion, they roar. And like young lions, they growl,*[118] lay hold of the prey, and carry it off, and there is no one to rescue it. 30 *They will roar*[119] over it on that day like the roaring of the sea. If one *looks*[120] to the land, there is darkness and distress. The light grows dark in the clouds.

6 1 In the year that king *Uzziah*[121] died I *saw*[122] my Lord sitting on *his*[123] throne, high and exalted, and the skirts of his robe filled the temple. 2 Seraphs stood

---

108. 1QIsa^a. *dry grass* 4QIsa^b MT.

109. 1QIsa^a. *flame* MT.

110. 1QIsa^a MT. *Upon* 4QIsa^b (in error).

111. 1QIsa^a MT. LORD *of hosts* 4QIsa^b.

112. 1QIsa^a. *hand* MT.

113. 1QIsa^a. *hand is* MT.

114. 1QIsa^a. *No one among them* MT.

115. 1QIsa^a and 4QIsa^b MT use different forms of this word.

116. 1QIsa^a. Not in MT.

117. Feminine 1QIsa^a. Masculine MT.

118. 1QIsa^a. *Their roaring is like a lion; they roar like young lions. They growl* MT.

119. 1QIsa^a. *And they will roar* MT.

120. 1QIsa^a MT. *will look* pap4QIsa^p.

Chapter 6. 1QIsa^a: all; 4QIsa^a: 6:4–8; 4QIsa^f: 6:3–8, 10–13.

121. *Uzziyah* 1QIsa^a. *Uzziyahu* MT.

122. 1QIsa^a does not contain an extra *and* contained in MT.

123. 1QIsa^a. *a* MT.

above him, each with *six wings*.[124] With two they covered their face, with two they covered their feet, and with two they flew. 3 *They called*[125] to each *other*:[126] "Holy, *holy*[127] is the Lord of hosts: the whole earth is full of his glory." 4 The foundations of the thresholds shook when they called, and the house *was full*[128] of smoke. 5 Then I said, "Woe is me! for I am lost; because I am a man of *unclean*[129] lips, and I live among a people of unclean lips. [In]deed my eyes have seen the King, the Lord of hosts."

6 Then one of the seraphs flew to me, holding a live coal in his hand, which he had taken fr[o]m the [altar] with tongs. 7 He [touched my mouth and] said, "Now this has touched *your*[130] lips; your iniquity is removed, and your *sins*[131] forgiven." 8 And I heard the voice of my Lord saying, "Whom will I send, and who will go for us?" Then I said, "Here am I; send me."

9 So he said, "Go, and say to this people: Hear indeed, but do *not*[132] understand; *see*[133] indeed, but do *not*[134] comprehend. 10 Make the heart of this people *fat,*[135] dull their ears, and blind their eyes; so they do not see with their eyes, or *hear*[136] with their ears, *with*[137] their heart understand, or turn back and be healed."

11 Then I said, "How long, Lord?"[138] And he answered, "Until cities lie waste, without inhabitant, and houses without occupant, and the land becomes utterly desolate, 12 and the Lord banishes the inhabitants, and *desolate places*[139] are multiplied in the midst of the land. 13 Even if a tenth remain in it, it too will in turn be burnt, like a terebinth or oak, the stump of which, *felled,*[140] remains." *The*[141] holy seed is its stump.

---

124. 1QIsa^a. MT repeats *six wings*.

125. Plural 1QIsa^a. Singular MT.

126. 1QIsa^a. MT adds *and said*.

127. 1QIsa^a. MT adds a third *holy*.

128. 1QIsa^a. *was filled* MT.

129. 1QIsa^a misspells the word but spells it correctly a few words later.

130. 1QIsa^a MT *the* 4QIsa^f.

131. 1QIsa^a. *sin* MT.

132. 1QIsa^a misspells the word.

133. 1QIsa^a. *and see* MT.

134. 1QIsa^a misspells the word.

135. 1QIsa^a apparently omitted the final letter of this word.

136. Plural 1QIsa^a. Singular 4QIsa^f MT.

137. 1QIsa^a. *or* MT *or with* 4QIsa^f MT^mss.

138. 1QIsa^a. *Lord* MT.

139. 1QIsa^a. *the desolate places* MT.

140. 1QIsa^a. *when felled* MT.

141. 1QIsa^a. Not in MT.

7 1 In the days of Ahaz son of Jotham, son of Uzziah, king of Judah, Rezin king of Aram and Pekah son of Remaliah, king of Israel, went up to attack Jerusalem, but *they were unsuccessful.*[142] 2 When it was reported to the house of David that Aram had allied itself with Ephraim, *the heart of his people*[143] trembled, as the trees of *the*[144] forest tremble in *the*[145] wind.

3 Then the LORD said to Isaiah, Go meet Ahaz, you and Shear-jashub your son, at the end of the conduit of the upper pool, on the highway to the fuller's field. 4 Say to him, "Take care, be calm, *and*[146] do not be afraid. Do not lose heart over these two smoldering stumps of torches, *because of*[147] the fierce anger of Rezin and Aram and the son of Remaliah, 5 because Aram, Ephraim, and the son of Remaliah have plotted against you, saying, 6 'Let us go up against Judah and terrify it. Let us conquer it for ourselves and install the son of Tabeel as king in it.' 7 Thus says my Lord, the LORD: It will not stand. It will not happen. 8 For the head of Aram is *Damascus,*[148] and the head of Damascus is Rezin—within sixty-[fiv]e years Ephraim will be shattered, no longer a people— 9 the head of Ephraim is Samaria, and the head of [Samaria is] Remaliah's [son]; if you will not believe, surely you will not be established."

10 [The LORD again] spoke to Ahaz, 11 "Ask for a sign from the LORD your God, [one as deep as Sh]eol or as high as heaven above." 12 But Ahaz said, "I will not ask. [I will] not [test] the LORD." 13 So he answered, "Listen, house of David! Is it not enough that you [weary] people; must you weary my God also? 14 Therefore *the LORD*[149] *himself*[150] will give y[ou a sign. Loo]k, the young woman has conceived and is bearing a son, and *his name will be*[151] Immanuel. 15 He will eat cur[ds and honey] by the time he knows to refuse evil and choose good. 16 For before the child knows to refuse evil and choose good, the land whose two kings you dread will be deserted. 17 *And*[152] the LORD will bring on you, your people, and your father's house days that have not come since the day that Ephraim separated from Judah—the king of Assyria."

Chapter 7. 1QIsaᵃ: all; 1QIsaᵇ: 7:22–25; 4QIsaᶜ: 7:17–20; 4QIsaᶠ: 7:16–18, 23–25; 4QIsaˡ: 7:14–15.

142. 1QIsaᵃ. *he was unsuccessful* MT.

143. 1QIsaᵃ. *his heart and the heart of the people* MT.

144. 1QIsaᵃ. Not in MT.

145. 1QIsaᵃ. Not in MT.

146. 1QIsaᵃ. Not in MT.

147. 1QIsaᵃ. Not in MT.

148. 1QIsaᵃ and MT spell Damascus differently.

149. 1QIsaᵃ. *my Lord* MT.

150. 1QIsaᵃ misspells the word.

151. 1QIsaᵃ. *she will name him* MT.

152. 1QIsaᵃ. Not in MT.

18 On that day, the LORD will whistle for the fly that is at the end of the rivers
of Egypt and for the bee that is in the land of Assyria. 19 They will all come and
settle in the steep ravines and in the clefts of the rocks and on all thorn bushes and
in all pastures. 20 On that day the LORD will shave with a razor hired from the region beyond the River—with the king of Assyria—the head and the hair of the
feet, and it will cut off the beard as well. 21 On that day, a man will keep alive a
young heifer and two sheep. 22 And from the abundance of milk which they produce he will eat curds. Indeed, *the one*[153] left within the land will eat curds and
honey. 23 On that day, every place where there once were a thousand vines
worth a thousand shekels of silver *will be*[154] grown over with briers and thorn
bushes. 24 With *bows*[155] and arrows, people will go out, because the entire land
will be briers and thorns. 25 As for all the hills that used to be cultivated with a
hoe, you will not go near for fear of *iron*[156] briers and thorns, but they *will be*[157]
rangeland for cattle and sheep to trample.

8 1 The LORD said to me, Take a large tablet and write on it in ordinary script,
"For Maher-shalal-hash-baz," 2 and *call*[158] faithful witnesses, Uriah the priest
and Zechariah son of Jeberechiah, to testify for me.

3 I went in to the *prophet,*[159] and she conceived and bore a son. Then the LORD
said *to me,*[160] Name him Maher-shalal-hash-baz. 4 For before the child can *call*[161]
his father or his mother,[162] the wealth of *Damascus*[163] and the spoil of Samaria will be
carried off by the king of Assyria.

5 The LORD spoke to me yet again, saying, 6 Because this people has refused
the waters of Shiloah that flow gently and rejoice in Rezin and [Remaliah's] son
7 now then, the LORD God[164] will indeed bring up against them the waters of the
River, [strong and many[165]—the kin]g of Assyria and all his glory—and it will rise

---

153. 1QIsaᵃ wrote *everyone* (=MT), then deleted it.

154. 1QIsaᵃ has the verb once. MT has it twice.

155. 1QIsaᵃ. *bow* 1QIsaᵇ MT.

156. 1QIsaᵃ. Not in MT.

157. 1QIsaᵃ and MT use different forms.

Chapter 8. 1QIsaᵃ: all; 1QIsaᵇ: 8:1; 4QIsaᵉ: 8:2–14; 4QIsaᶠ: 8:1, 4–11; 4QIsaˡ: 8:11–14.

158. 1QIsaᵃ. *I will call* MT.

159. Masculine 1QIsaᵃ. Feminine MT.

160. 1QIsaᵃ MT. Not in 4QIsaᵉ.

161. 1QIsaᵃ and MT use different forms.

162. 1QIsaᵃ. *"My father" or "My mother"* MT.

163. 1QIsaᵃ and MT spell Damascus differently.

164. 1QIsaᵃ. *Lord* MT.

165. *many and strong* 4QIsaᶠ. *strong and many* MT.

[above all its channels and overflow all] its banks. 8 It will sweep into Judah; it will overflow and pass through. It will reach up to the neck, and its outstretched wings will fill the breadth of your land. *Immanuel!*[166]

9 Band together, nations, but be shattered. Listen, all distant countries, *gird yourselves but be shattered.*[167] 10 Take counsel together, but it will be brought to nothing. Speak a word, but it will not stand. For *Immanuel!*[168] 11 For the LORD spoke to me with *great power,*[169] *instructed*[170] me not to walk in the way of this people, saying, 12 Do not call a conspiracy everything that this people calls a conspiracy. Do revere or be in awe of what they revere. 13 The LORD of hosts—consider him holy, revere him, be in awe of him. 14 *He will be*[171] a sanctuary but also a stone of stumbling and a rock of offense to both the houses of Israel, a trap and a snare to the inhabitants of Jerusalem. 15 Many among them will stumble and fall, be broken, snared, and captured.

16 Bind up the testimony, *and*[172] seal the instruction among my disciples. 17 I will wait for the LORD, who is hiding his face from the house of Jacob, and I will hope for him. 18 Here I am, with the children the LORD has given me as *a sign and a wonder*[173] in Israel from the LORD of hosts, who dwells in Mount Zion.

19 When they say to you, "Consult the ghosts and familiar spirits which chirp and mutter. Should not a people consult their *god,*[174] or the dead for the sake of *the*[175] living, 20 for instruction and testimony?"—surely there will be no dawn for one who speaks like this. 21 They will go through it, *while*[176] severely distressed and hungry. When he is hungry, he *will become angry*[177] and curse by his king and by his *god,*[178] and look up. 22 Then he will look to *the*[179] land, and there will be distress and darkness, the gloom of anguish. Then they will be driven into darkness.

---

166. Written as one word 1QIsaᵃ 4QIsaᵉ 4QIsaᶠ. Two words (=*God is with us*) MT.

167. 1QIsaᵃ. MT adds a second *gird yourselves but be shattered.*

168. Written as one word 1QIsaᵃ 4QIsaᵉ. Two words (=*God is with us*) MT.

169. 1QIsaᵃ. *the great power* MT.

170. 1QIsaᵃ. *and instructed* MT.

171. 1QIsaᵃ and 4QIsaˡ MT use different constructions for *He will be.*

172. 1QIsaᵃ. Not in MT.

173. 1QIsaᵃ. *signs and wonders* MT.

174. 1QIsaᵃ. *gods* MT.

175. 1QIsaᵃ. Not in MT.

176. 1QIsaᵃ. Not in MT.

177. 1QIsaᵃ and MT use different forms.

178. 1QIsaᵃ. *gods* MT.

179. 1QIsaᵃ. Not in MT.

9 1 For one who was in anguish there will be no gloom.[180] In the former time he treated the land of Zebulun and the[181] land of Naphtali with contempt, but in the latter time he will make it glorious, by the way of the sea, beyond the Jordan, Galilee of the nations.

2 The people who walked in darkness have seen a great light. On those who lived in the land of deep shadows, light has shined. 3 You have expanded the nation, you have increased its joy. They rejoice in your presence, as with the joy at harvest, as people cheer when they divide spoil. 4 For the yoke of their burden and the pole on their shoulder, the rod of their oppressors, and[182] *you have broken,*[183] as in the day of *Midiam.*[184] 5 For every boot tramping in the tumult and the garments rolled in blood will be burned as fuel for fire.

6 For a child is born to us, a son is given to us. The government will be on his shoulders. He *is called*[185] Wonderful Counselor, Mighty God, Everlasting Father, *the*[186] Prince of Peace. 7 His government will expand, and peace will be endless for the throne of David and his kingdom, to establish *it*[187] and to sustain *it*[188] with justice and righteousness from now on and forevermore. The zeal of the LORD of hosts will do this.

8 The LORD[189] sent a word against Jacob, and it fell upon Israel. 9 All the people *were evil*[190]—Ephraim and the inhabitants of Samaria, who said in arrogance and pride of heart, 10 "The bricks have fallen, but we will build with hewn stone. The sycamores have been cut down, but we will substitute cedars." 11 The L[ORD] raised the adversaries of Rezin against him and spurred his enemies on— 12 Aram from the east and the Philis[tines from the w]est—and they devoured Israel with an open mouth. *And*[191] for all *this,*[192] his anger is not turned away, his *hands*[193] are stretched out still.

Chapter 9. 1QIsa^a: all; 4QIsa^b: 9:11–12; 4QIsa^c: 9:3–13; 4QIsa^e: 9:18–21.

180. 1QIsa^a and MT exhibit slight differences in the ambiguous Hebrew.

181. 1QIsa^a. Not in MT.

182. 1QIsa^a. Not in MT.

183. 1QIsa^a MT. *I have broken* 4QIsa^c.

184. 1QIsa^a. *Midian* MT.

185. 1QIsa^a. *will be called* 4QIsa^c MT.

186. 1QIsa^a. Not in MT.

187. Masculine (referring to *throne*) 1QIsa^a. Feminine (referring to *kingdom*) MT.

188. Masculine (referring to *throne*) 1QIsa^a. Feminine (referring to *kingdom*) MT.

189. 1QIsa^a. *Lord* MT.

190. 1QIsa^a. *knew* MT.

191. 1QIsa^a. Not in MT.

192. 1QIsa^a misspells the word.

193. 1QIsa^a. *hand* MT.

13 The people did not turn *to*[194] him who afflicted them, nor did they seek the LORD of hosts. 14 So the LORD will cut off from Israel head and tail, palm branch and reed, *in*[195] one day. 15 The elder and dignitary is the head, and the prophet who teaches lies is the tail. 16 Those who guide this people mislead, and those who are guided by them are confused. 17 For that reason my Lord does not *spare*[196] their young men or have compassion on their orphans and widows. For everyone is godless and an evildoer, and every mouth speaks profanity. For all this, his anger is not turned away, his *hands*[197] are stretched out still.

18 For evil consumed like a fire. It devoured the briers and thorns. It kindled in the thickets of the forest, and they rolled upward in a column of smoke. 19 *From*[198] the wrath of the LORD of hosts *the*[199] land *was burned up,*[200] and the people *were*[201] like the fuel for a fire—no one spared his neighbor. 20 On the right hand, they snatched but remained hungry. *On*[202] the left, they ate but were not satisfied. Everyone *ate*[203] the flesh of his own arm. 21 Manasseh *devoured*[204] Ephraim, and Ephraim Manasseh, and together they went against Judah. *And*[205] for all this, his anger is not turned away, his *hands*[206] are stretched out still.

10 1 Woe to *ones enacting*[207] iniquitous decrees and writing oppressive documents, 2 to turn aside the needy from justice and to rob the poor of my people of their right, so that widows may be their spoil, so that they may make orphans their booty! 3 What will you do in the day of punishment, when the calamity comes from far away? To whom will you run for help, where will you leave your wealth, 4 to keep from sinking down under *those in fetters*[208] and falling

---

194. 1QIsaᵃ. *toward* MT.

195. 1QIsaᵃ. Not in MT.

196. 1QIsaᵃ. *rejoice over* MT.

197. 1QIsaᵃ. *hand* MT.

198. 1QIsaᵃ. *By* MT.

199. 1QIsaᵃ. Not in MT.

200. 1QIsaᵃ misspells the word.

201. Plural 1QIsaᵃ. Singular MT.

202. 1QIsaᵃ contains an extraneous *and* before *on*. 4QIsaᵉ MT do not.

203. Implicit in 1QIsaᵃ. Explicit in MT.

204. Explicit in 1QIsaᵃ. Implicit in MT.

205. 1QIsaᵃ. Not in 4QIsaᵉ MT.

206. 1QIsaᵃ. *hand* MT.

Chapter 10. 1QIsaᵃ: all; 1QIsaᵇ: 10:16–19; 4QIsaᶜ: 10:23–33; 4QIsaᵉ: 10:1–10.

207. 1QIsaᵃ. *the ones enacting* MT.

208. 1QIsaᵃ. *prisoners* MT LXX.

under the slain? *And*[209] for all this his anger is not turned away, his *hands*[210] are stretched out still.

5 Woe to Assyria, the rod of my anger! The staff in their hands is my punishing wrath. 6 Against an ungodly nation I will send him, and against the people of my fury I will command him to take spoil and to seize booty and to *trample them down*[211] like the mire of the streets. 7 This is not what he intends nor is he aware of this; rather he intends to destroy and to cut off many nations. 8 For he says, "Are not my commanders all kings? 9 Was not Calno just like Carchemish? Was not [Ha]math just like Arpad? Was not Samaria just like *Damascus?*[212] 10 Because my power has found the kingdoms of the *worthless gods,*[213] whose images were greater than those of Jerusalem and of Samaria, 11 will I not do to Jerusalem and her idols as I have done to Samaria and her worthless gods?"

12 *For*[214] my Lord has finished all his work on Mount Zion and on Jerusalem; I will punish the product of the arrogant heart of the king of Assyria and his haughty boasting. 13 For he *says,*[215] "I have done this with my own strength and understanding—[fo]r I am intelligent. I have moved the boundaries of nations and pl[u]ndered their treasuries. [Like a bull,] I have brought down those [who sit on thrones]. 14 My hand has found the wealth of the peoples like a nest. Just as they gather [abandoned] eggs, I myself have gathered [the entire wor]ld, and none moved a wing or opened a mouth to chirp." 15 Does the ax vaunt itself over the one who chops with it, or the saw think itself better than the one who *uses*[216] it? As if a rod raised *the*[217] person who lifted it, or a staff lifted one that is not wood!

16 Therefore my Lord, the LORD of hosts, will send leanness to those who are fat, and under their weight will kindle a flame, burning like fire. 17 The light of Israel will become a fire and his holy one a flame, and it will burn and consume its thorns and thistles in a single day. 18 He will destroy the bounty of its forest and farm land, both soul and body, and it will be like a sick person wasting away. 19 So few trees will remain of its forest that a child could record them.

20 From that day, what remains of Israel and those of the house of Jacob who

---

209. 1QIsa[a]. Not in MT.

210. 1QIsa[a]. *hand* MT LXX.

211. 1QIsa[a] and 4QIsa[e] MT use different forms. *them* is implicit in 1QIsa[a], explicit in 4QIsa[e] MT.

212. 1QIsa[a] and MT spell Damascus differently.

213. 1QIsa[a]. *worthless god* MT.

214. 1QIsa[a]. *When* MT.

215. 1QIsa[a]. *said* MT.

216. MT. 1QIsa[a] seems to divide into two words what is one word in MT, yielding *from his mouth.*

217. 1QIsa[a]. *and the* MT.

have escaped will never again rely on the one who beat them, but will sincerely rely on[218] the LORD, the Holy One of Israel. 21 Only a remnant will return, a remnant of Jacob, to the mighty God. 22 For though your people, Israel, were like the sand of the sea, only a remnant of them will return. Destruction is decreed, overwhelming victory. 23 For my Lord, the LORD of hosts will execute the decreed annihilation, throughout the land.

24 Therefore thus says my Lord, the LORD of hosts: My people living in Zion, do not be afraid of the Assyrian, *of the rod that strikes you*[219] or the staff lifted up against you, in the fashion of Egypt. 25 For very soon, my indignation will cease. Then my anger will be directed to his destruction. 26 The LORD of hosts *will brandish*[220] a whip against it, as in the slaughter of Midian at the rock of Horeb. His rod will be against the sea, and he will lift it up, as he did against Egypt. 27 On *that*[221] day, his burden will be removed from your shoulder and his [y]oke from your neck, and the yoke will be broken because of fatness.

28 He has come *on*[222] Aiath. He has passed through Migron. At Michmash he *stored*[223] his baggage. 29 *He has crossed*[224] *by*[225] the pass. He has lodged at Geba. Ramah trembles. Gibeah of Saul has fled. 30 Cry aloud, daughter of Gallim! Listen, Laish! Answer her, Anathoth! 31 *Marmenah*[226] retreated. The inhabitants of Gebim fled for safety. 32 This very day he will halt at Nob. He will *shake*[227] his *fists*[228] at the mount of the *daughter*[229] of Zion, the hill of Jerusalem. 33 See, the Lord, the LORD of hosts, will lop off treetops with terror, and the tall trees will be hewn down, and the lofty will be brought low. 34 He will cut down the thick[et]s of the forest with an ax, and Lebanon in its majesty will fall.

11 1 A shoot will come forth from the stump of Jesse, and a branch from his roots will bear fruit. 2 The spirit of the LORD will rest upon him, the spirit of wisdom and understanding, the spirit of counsel and mig[h]t, the spirit of

---

218. 1QIsaª and MT use different words for *on*.

219. 1QIsaª. *who strikes you with a rod* MT.

220. 1QIsaª and MT use different forms.

221. 1QIsaª MT. Not in 4QIsaᶜ.

222. 1QIsaª MT. *to* 4QIsaᶜ.

223. 1QIsaª and MT use different forms.

224. 1QIsaª. *They have crossed* MT.

225. 1QIsaª. Not in MT.

226. 1QIsaª. *Madmenah* MT.

227. 1QIsaª and MT use different forms.

228. 1QIsaª. *fist* MT.

229. 1QIsaª 4QIsaᶜ MTᑫᵉʳᵉ LXX. *house* MT.

Chapter 11. 1QIsaª: all; 4QIsaª: 11:11–15; 4QIsaᵇ: 11:7–9; 4QIsaᶜ: 11:4–11, 15–16; 4QIsaᵉ: 11:14–15.

knowledge and the fear of the LORD. 3 His delight will be in the fear of the LORD. He will not judge by appearances, nor decide by what he hears, 4 but with righteousness he will obtain justice for the poor and decide with equity for the meek of *the*[230] land. He will strike *the*[231] land with the rod of his mouth, and with the breath of his lips *the wicked will be killed.*[232] 5 Righteousness will be the belt around his waist and *faithfulness*[233] the belt around his loins.

6 The wolf will live with the lamb, and the leopard *will lie down*[234] with the kid, and the calf and the young lion *will graze*[235] together, and a little child will herd them. 7 *The cow and the bear will graze together, and their young will lie down,*[236] and the lion will eat straw like the ox. 8 A baby *will play*[237] on the viper's hole, and the toddler will put his hand on the *dens*[238] of *adders.*[239] 9 They will not hurt or destroy *on my*[240] holy mountain. For the earth *will be full*[241] of the knowledge of the LORD,[242] as the waters cover the sea.

10 On that day, the root of Jesse, which stands as a signal for the peoples—the nations will seek him, and his dwelling *will be*[243] honored. 11 On that day, my Lord will extend his hand a second time to recover the remnant of his people that are left, from Assyria, Egypt, Pathros, Nubia, Elam, Shinar, Hamath, and the coastlands. 12 He will raise a signal for the nations and assemble the banished of Israel and gather the dispersed of Judah from *the corners*[244] of the earth. 13 Ephraim's envy will cease, and Judah's hostility will end. Ephraim will not envy Judah, and Judah will not be hostile toward Ephraim. 14 They *will swoop down*[245] on the back of the Philistines in the *west together, and*[246] they will plunder

---

230. Explicit in 1QIsa[a]. Implicit in MT.

231. 1QIsa[a]. Not in MT.

232. 1QIsa[a]. *he will kill the wicked* MT.

233. 1QIsa[a] (no definite article). MT (definite article).

234. Singular 1QIsa[a] MT. Plural 4QIsa[c].

235. 1QIsa[a]. *and the fatling* MT.

236. 1QIsa[a]. *The cow and the bear will graze—together their young will lie down* MT.

237. 1QIsa[a] and MT use different forms.

238. 1QIsa[a]. *den* 4QIsa[c] MT.

239. 1QIsa[a] 4QIsa[c]. *an adder* MT.

240. 1QIsa[a]. *on all my* MT.

241. Feminine 1QIsa[a]. Masculine 4QIsa[c] MT.

242. 1QIsa[a] MT. *to know the glory of the* LORD 4QIsa[c].

243. 1QIsa[a] and MT use different constructions for this clause.

244. 1QIsa[a]. *the four corners* MT.

245. 1QIsa[a] and MT use different forms.

246. 1QIsa[a]. *west; together* MT.

the peoples of the east, extending their hand against Edom and Moab. And the Ammonites will obey them. 15 The LORD will utterly destroy the tongue of the Egyptian sea, and with *a*[247] scorching wind he will wave his *hands*[248] over the River and split it into seven streams, so that people can march over in sandals. 16 There will be a highway for the remnant of his people who remain from Assyria, just as there was for Israel on the day that it came up out of the land of Egypt.

12 1 On that day you will say, I [give thanks] to you, LORD. You had been angry with me, *but*[249] your anger *turned*[250] and you comforted me. 2 God, God[251] is truly my salvation. I will trust and not be afraid, because the LORD is my strength and *song; he*[252] has become my salvation. 3 With joy you will draw water from the wells of salvation.

4 On that day *you*[253] will say, *I give thanks*[254] to the LORD, call on his name, declare his deeds among the peoples, celebrate that his name is exalted. 5 Sing *to*[255] the LORD, because he has done excellent things. This should be *known*[256] through all the earth. 6 Shout and cheer, inhabitant of Zion, because great in your presence is the Holy One of Israel.

13 1 The oracle of Babylon which Isaiah the son of Amoz saw. 2 Raise a signal on a windswept mountain, shout to them, wave your hand, *for him to enter*[257] the gates of the nobles. 3 I have commanded my holy ones; I have called my warriors to carry out my wrath, my proudly [b]oasting ones. 4 The roar of a mob on the mountains, like a large army! The noise of kingdoms, nations gathering together! The LORD of hosts is mustering an army for battle, 5 coming from a far country, from the end of the heavens, the LORD and the instruments of his

---

247. 1QIsaᵃ. *his* MT.

248. 1QIsaᵃ. *hand* MT.

Chapter 12. 1QIsaᵃ: all; 1QIsaᵇ: 12:3–6; 4QIsaᵃ: 12:4–6; 4QIsaᵇ: 12:2; 4QIsaᶜ: 12:1.

249. 1QIsaᵃ. Not in MT.

250. 1QIsaᵃ and MT use different forms.

251. 1QIsaᵃ. Not in MT.

252. 1QIsaᵃ. *song, and he* 4QIsaᵉ MT. Both 1QIsaᵃ and MT display minor difficulties in their texts.

253. Singular 1QIsaᵃ 4QIsaᵉ. Plural MT.

254. 1QIsaᵃ. *Give thanks* MT.

255. 1QIsaᵃ. Not in MT.

256. 4QIsaᵃ. 1QIsaᵃ and MT each have troubled forms of this word.

Chapter 13. 1QIsaᵃ: all; 1QIsaᵇ: 13:1–8, 16–19; 4QIsaᵃ: 13:1–16; 4QIsaᵇ: 13:3–18; 4QIsaᶜ: 13:1–4.

257. 1QIsaᵃ. *for them to enter* 4QIsaᵉ. *and let them enter* MT.

wrath, to destroy the whole earth. 6 Wail, because the day of the LORD is near, like destruction from the Almighty it comes. 7 Therefore all *hands*[258] will be weak, and all human courage will fail. 8 They will be terrified. Seized by pangs and throes, they will writhe like a woman in childbirth. They will look at one another in astonishment, *and*[259] their faces will be afire.

9 Indeed, the day of the LORD is coming, *cruel,*[260] with wrath and fierce anger, to make *earth*[261] desolate and to destroy *sinners*[262] from it. 10 Indeed the stars of the heavens and their constellations will not *shine*[263] their light—when it rises, the sun will be dark, and the moon will not glow. 11 I will punish the world for its evil, and the wicked for their sins. I will end the pride of the insolent and lay low the haughtiness of the tyrants. 12 I will make people scarcer than fine gold, mortals than the pure gold of Ophir. 13 Therefore I will shake the heavens, and the earth will be *dislodged*[264] by the wrath of the LORD of hosts, on the day of his rage. 14 Like a hunted gazelle and like unherded sheep, all *will*[265] seek their own people and flee to their own land. 15 Everyone who is found will be [thrust throu]gh, and everyone who is captured will fall by the sword. 16 Their infants will be dashed to pieces before their eyes, *and*[266] their houses will be plundered, and their wives [tak]en.[267] 17 Indeed, I am stirring up the Medes against them, people [w]ho *have no regard*[268] for silver and no pleasure in gold. 18 Their bows will destroy the youth, and *on infants they will have no pity,*[269] *and*[270] their eyes will have no compassion on children. 19 Babylon, the glory of kingdoms, the beauty and pride of the Chaldeans, will be like Sodom and Gomorrah when God over[thr]ew them. 20 It will never again be inhabited; it will not be lived in from generation to generation. Arabs will not pitch tents there; shepherds will not make their flocks lie down there. 21 Rather wild creatures will lie down there, and their houses will be full of jackals. Ostriches will live there, and wild goats

---

258. 1QIsaᵃ has the Aramaic plural; 1QIsaᵇ 4QIsaᵃ MT have the Hebrew plural.

259. 1QIsaᵃ. Not in 4QIsaᵃ 4QIsaᵇ MT.

260. 1QIsaᵃ misspells the word.

261. 1QIsaᵃ. *the earth* MT.

262. 1QIsaᵃ LXX. *its sinners* 4QIsaᵃ 4QIsaᵇ MT.

263. 1QIsaᵃ. *beam* MT.

264. 1QIsaᵃ MT. Misspelled in 4QIsaᵃ.

265. Plural 1QIsaᵃ. Singular MT.

266. 1QIsaᵃ. Not in 4QIsaᵃ MT.

267. 1QIsaᵃ MTqere. *raped* 4QIsaᵃ MT. See Deut 28:30.

268. Singular 1QIsaᵃ. Plural MT.

269. 1QIsaᵃ. *they will not pity infants* MT.

270. 1QIsaᵃ MTmss. Not in MT.

will dance there. 22 Wolves will howl in their towers and jackals in *their luxurious palaces*.[271] *Its*[272] time is drawing near, and its days will not be drawn out *any further*.[273]

14 1 For the LORD will have compassion on Jacob, and will yet choose Israel, and set them in their own land; and the sojourner will join himself with them, and they will cleave to the house of Jacob. 2 And *many*[274] peoples will take them and bring them *to their land and their place*,[275] and the house of Israel will possess them in the land of the LORD as servants and as handmaids. They will take captive those whose captives they were, *and will be rulers*[276] over their oppressors.

> ■ *The last section of Isaiah 14:4 begins with "How the oppressor has ceased!" but then goes on to make little sense in the traditional Masoretic Text: "How the golden city has ceased!" The reading in 1QIsaᵃ is "How (his) assault has ceased!" which makes far better sense and is partially supported by the Septuagint, which has "(How his) attacker has ceased!"*

3 And then, on the day the LORD will give you rest from your sorrow, from your trouble, and from the hard service with which *they made you serve*,[277] 4 you will take up this parable against the king of Babylon, saying:

How the oppressor has ceased! How (*his*) *assault*[278] has ceased! 5 The LORD has broken the staff of the wicked, the scepter of the rulers 6 who smote the peoples in anger with unending blows, who ruled the nations in anger, with a persecution that no one could restrain. 7 The whole earth is at rest and is quiet; they break forth into singing. 8 Indeed, the fir trees rejoice at you, and the cedars of *Lebanon*,[279] saying, "Since you have been laid low, *and*[280] no hewer has come up *against us*."[281] 9 Sheol from below is excited over you to meet you at your arrival. It *stirs up*[282] the dead for you, even all the chief ones of the earth; it *has raised*

---

271. 1QIsaᵃ and MT display minor variants.

272. 1QIsaᵃ. *And its* MT.

273. 1QIsaᵃ. Not in MT.

Chapter 14. 1QIsaᵃ: all; 4QIsaᵉ: 14: 1–13, 20–24; 4QIsaᶜ: 14:1–5, 13 (?); 4QIsaᵒ: 14:28–32.

274. 1QIsaᵃ. Not in MT LXX.

275. 1QIsaᵃ. *to their place* MT LXX.

276. 1QIsaᵃ (participle). *and will rule* (perfect) 4QIsaᶜ LXX MT.

277. Apparent meaning 1QIsaᵃ 4QIsaᵉ. *you were made to serve* MT (LXX similar).

278. 1QIsaᵃ (cf. *the attacker* LXX). *the golden city* MT.

279. Literally, *the Lebanon* 1QIsaᵃ. *Lebanon* MT.

280. 1QIsaᵃ. Not in MT LXX.

281. 4QIsaᵉ. *against them* 1QIsaᵃ MT LXX.

282. Feminine 1QIsaᵃ (matching the earlier verb *is excited*). Masculine MT.

up[283] all the kings of the nations from their thrones. 10 They will *all*[284] answer and say to you, "Have you also become as weak as we are? Have you become like us?" 11 Your pomp *and the noise*[285] of your harps have been brought down to Sheol; the worm has spread under you, *and your covering is a worm.*[286]

12 How you are fallen *from the heaven,*[287] O day-star, son of the morning! How you have been cut down to the ground—you who laid low *the nation!*[288] 13 You said in your heart, "I will ascend into heaven, I will exalt my throne above the stars of God; *I will sit*[289] upon the mount of gathering in the furthest parts of the north. 14 I will ascend above the heights of the clouds, I will make myself like the Most High." 15 Yet you will be brought down to Sheol, to the uttermost parts of the Pit. 16 They who see you will gaze at you; they will think about you, saying, "Is this the man, *the one who*[290] made the earth tremble, *the one who*[291] shook kingdoms, 17 who made the world like a wilderness (and) *overthrew its cities,*[292] who did not release his prisoners to their homes?" 18 All the kings of the *nations*[293] sleep in glory, each in his own house. 19 But you have been cast away from your grace like a reprehensible branch, clothed with the slain who have been pierced through with the sword, who go down *to the Pit,*[294] just like a dead body trodden underfoot. 20 You will not be *under*[295] with them in burial, because you have destroyed your land and have slain your people; *the seed of evildoers will never be remembered*[296] again. 21 Prepare slaughter for his children because of their ancestors' iniquity, so that they will not rise up and possess the earth, and cover the surface of the world with cities.

22 I will rise up against them, says the LORD of hosts, and cut off from Babylon name and *remnant, and offspring (and) posterity,*[297] says the LORD. 23 I will also *make*

---

283. Feminine 1QIsa[a]. Masculine MT.

284. 1QIsa[a] MT LXX. Not in 4QIsa[e].

285. 1QIsa[a]. *the noise* MT LXX.

286. 1QIsa[a] LXX. *and a worm covers you* MT.

287. 1QIsa[a]. *from heaven* MT.

288. 1QIsa[a]. *the nations* 4QIsa[e] MT LXX.

289. 1QIsa[a] LXX. *and I will sit* MT.

290. 1QIsa[a] (LXX similar). *who* (implied) MT.

291. 1QIsa[a]. *who* (implied) MT.

292. 1QIsa[a]. *and overthrew its cities* MT. *and overthrew cities* LXX.

293. 1QIsa[a] LXX. *nations, every one of them* MT.

294. 1QIsa[a]* LXX *(to Hades). to the stones of the Pit* 1QIsa[a(corr)] MT.

295. 1QIsa[a] (error?). *joined* MT.

296. Singular noun and plural verb 1QIsa[a]. Singular noun and singular verb MT. *May you not remember forevermore the evil seed* LXX.

297. 1QIsa[a]. *and offspring and posterity* MT. *and posterity* LXX.

(it)[298] a possession for *the hedgehog*,[299] *pools*[300] of water; and I will *sweep* (it)[301] with the broom of destruction, says the LORD of hosts. 24 The LORD of hosts has sworn: Surely as I have thought, *so will she be;*[302] and as I have purposed, so it will stand. 25 I will defeat the Assyrian in my land, and tread him underfoot on my mountains. Then his yoke will depart *from you,*[303] and his burden *from your shoulder.*[304] 26 This is the plan that has been imposed on the whole earth, and this is the hand that is stretched out upon all the nations. 27 For the LORD of hosts has planned this, so who will cancel it? His hands are stretched out, so who will turn it back?

28 This oracle happened in the year that king Ahaz died. 29 Do not rejoice, all you Philistines, that the rod which struck you has been broken; for an adder will come forth from the serpent's, and its issue will be a fiery flying serpent. 30 The firstborn of the poor will feed, and the needy will lie down in safety; and I will kill your root with famine, *and I will slay*[305] your remnant. 31 Wail, O gate; cry, O city. You have melted away, all you Philistines; for smoke is coming out of the north, and there is *none who metes out payment*[306] among its kinsmen.[307]

32 What then will *they*[308] say to the *kings*[309] of the nation? That the LORD has founded Zion, and *in it*[310] the afflicted of his people take refuge.

15 1 The oracle concerning Moab: Yes, in a night Ar of Moab has been laid waste and brought to nothing; yes, in a night *the city*[311] of Moab has been laid *waste and brought to nothing.*[312] 2 They have gone up to Bayith and Dibon, to the high places to weep; Moab wails over Nebo, and over Medeba. There is bald-

---

298. 1QIsaᵃ (implied). *make it* MT LXX.

299. This word seems incorrectly spelled in 1QIsaᵃ.

300. 1QIsaᵃ. *and pools* MT.

301. 1QIsaᵃ (implied). *sweep it* MT.

302. I.e., Babylon 1QIsaᵃ LXX. *so has she been* MT.

303. 1QIsaᵃ. *from them* MT LXX.

304. 1QIsaᵃ. *from their shoulder* MT. *from the shoulders* LXX.

305. 1QIsaᵃ. *and he will slay your remnant* MT LXX.

306. 1QIsaᵃ (error?). *no straggler* 4QIsaº MT.

307. Possible meaning 1QIsaᵃ 4QIsaº. *in its ranks* MT.

308. 1QIsaᵃ LXX. *one* MT.

309. 1QIsaᵃ LXX. *messengers* MT.

310. 1QIsaᵃ (masculine). *in her* MT.

Chapter 15. 1QIsaᵃ: all; 4QIsaº: 15:1-2; 1QIsaᵇ: 15:3-9.

311. Or, *'Ir* 1QIsaᵃ. *the wall* (or *Kir*) 4QIsaº MT LXX.

312. 1QIsaᵃ. *waste; it is brought to nothing* MT.

ness *on all its head,*[313] *and*[314] every beard is cut off. 3 In *its*[315] streets they dress themselves with sackcloth; on its housetops and in its open squares everyone is wailing *and melting*[316] into tears. 4 Heshbon and Elealeh are crying out, their voice is heard as far as Jahaz; this is why the armed men of Moab cry aloud, each man's *soul trembles*[317] within him.

5 My heart cries out for Moab; her nobles are fleeing to Zoar, to Eglath-shelishiyah. For they go up with weeping by the ascent of Luhith; for they raise up a cry of destruction in the road of Horonaim. 6 For the waters of Nimrim will be deserted; the grass has withered away, the tender grass is gone, and nothing green remains. 7 Therefore they will carry away over the *Brook of the Arabs*[318] the wealth they have amassed and what they have accumulated. 8 For the cry has traveled around the borders of Moab, whose wail has reached Eglaim, whose wail has reached Beer-elim. 9 For the waters of *Dibon* are full of blood; indeed, I will bring still more upon *Dibon,*[319] like a lion upon the Moabites who escape, *upon*[320] those who remain in the land.

16 1 Send the lambs for the ruler of the land from *Selah*[321] to the wilderness, to Mount Zion's daughter. 2 For the daughters of Moab will be like wandering birds, like a scattered nest, at the fords of the (river) Arnon. 3 Give counsel and execute justice; make your shade like the night in the middle of the day; hide outcasts and do not betray fugitives. 4 Let my outcasts dwell with you. As for Moab, be a hiding-place to him from the destroyer's presence.

For the extortioner has been brought to nothing, destruction ceases, the oppressor *is eliminated*[322] from the land. 5 Then a throne will be established in mercy, and one will sit upon it in truth, in the tent of David, judging, seeking justice, and being quick to do what is right.

▮ *In verses 8–9, after "languish" and before "I will water you," the Masoretic Text has "The leaders of the nations have broken down its choice branches, which reached as far*

---

313. 1QIsaᵃ. *on all its head* MT. *on every head* LXX.

314. 1QIsaᵃ. Not in MT LXX.

315. Feminine, as with *its housetops* and *its open squares* later in the vs 1QIsaᵃ LXX. Masculine MT.

316. 1QIsaᵃ. *melting* MT.

317. The ending of the verb indicates the noun is masculine 1QIsaᵃ. Feminine MT.

318. 1QIsaᵃ (possible meaning; cf. LXX). *Brook of the Willows* MT.

319. 1QIsaᵃ (2x). *Dimon . . . Dimon* MT LXX.

320. 1QIsaᵃ LXX. *and upon* MT.

Chapter 16. 1QIsaᵃ: all; 1QIsaᵇ: 16:1–2, 7–12; 4QIsaᵒ: 16:7–8 (?).

321. 1QIsaᵃ LXX. *Sela* MT. *not the rock* LXX.

322. 1QIsaᵃ LXX. *are eliminated* MT.

*as Jazer and extended into the wilderness; its shoots were spread and wide, even cross-
ing the sea. 9 Therefore I will weep with the crying of Jazer for the vine of Sibmah."
The eye of the scribe of 1QIsaᵃ must have skipped from* Sibmah *(which follows* languish *in the Hebrew) in verse 8 to* Sibmah *in verse 9, resulting in the omission of
the intervening text. Examples such as this lead to the conclusion that this scribe was
somewhat careless (see the earlier introduction to Isaiah). The longer text is also found
in the Septuagint, but with some variations.*

6 We have heard of the pride of Moab, *how he became very proud;*[323] (we have
heard) of his arrogance, his pride, and his anger—*indeed, of his boastings.*[324]
7 Therefore *let not Moab wail,*[325] (but) let everyone wail for Moab! You will
mourn for the raisin-cakes of Kir-hareseth, being utterly devastated. 8 For the
fields of Heshbon and the vineyards of Sibmah languish.[326] 9 I will water you
with my tears, Heshbon and Elealeh, for the battle cry has fallen upon your summer fruits and upon your harvest. 10 Gladness has been taken away, as well as joy
from the fruitful field; in the vineyards *people will sing no songs*[327] *and*[328] there will
be no joyful noise. No treader will tread out wine in the presses; I have made the
vintage cry out to end. 11 Therefore my heart sounds like a harp for Moab, and
my innermost being for Kir-heres.

12 *When*[329] Moab presents himself—when he *comes*[330] upon the high place and
comes to its sanctuary to pray—he will not prevail.

13 This is the word that the LORD spoke concerning Moab in times past.
14 But now the LORD has spoken again: Within three years, just like the years of a
hired laborer, Moab's glory will be disgraced together with all its great multitude;
and the remnant will be very small *and*[331] of no account.

17 1 The oracle concerning *Dramascus:* See, *Dramascus*[332] is eliminated from
being a city but will be a heap of ruins. 2 The cities of *Oraru*[333] are

---

323. 1QIsaᵃ MTᵐˢˢ (cf. Jer 48:29). *how very proud he was* MT.

324. 1QIsaᵃ. *but his boasts mean nothing* MT LXX.

325. 1QIsaᵃ (cf. LXX). *let Moab wail* MT.

326. 1QIsaᵃ. MT and LXX have a longer text for vss 8–9 (see the comment above).

327. 1QIsaᵃ. *no songs are sung* MT.

328. 1QIsaᵃ. Not in MT.

329. 1QIsaᵃ. *And when* MT LXX.

330. 1QIsaᵃ. *tires himself* MT LXX.

331. 1QIsaᵃ LXX. Not in MT.

Chapter 17. 1QIsaᵃ: all; 4QIsaᵇ: 17:8–14; 4QIsaᵃ: 17:9–14.

332. 1QIsaᵃ (2x). *Damascus . . . Damascus* MT LXX.

333. Possible form; different vowels could be used 1QIsaᵃ. *Aroer* MT. *forever* LXX.

deserted; they will be places for flocks, which will lie down with no one to make them afraid. 3 Fortresses will come to an end in Ephraim, and the kingdom in *Dramascus*.[334] As for the remnant of Syria, *it will be*[335] like the glory of the children of Israel, says the LORD of hosts.

4 On that day the glory of Jacob will be diminished, and the health of his body will be reduced. 5 It will be like when harvesters gather standing grain, and their arms reap the ears of corn; indeed, it will be like when people glean corn in the valley of Rephaim. 6 Yet gleanings will be left in them, just like the shaking of an olive tree, with two or three berries on the top of the highest bough and four or five on *the branches of*[336] a fruitful tree, says the LORD, the God of Israel.

7 On that day people will look to their Maker, and their eyes will concentrate on the Holy One of Israel. 8 They will not look *upon*[337] the altars, *their works;*[338] *they will not*[339] concentrate on what their fingers have made, (*whether*)[340] the Asherim or the sun-images. 9 On that day their strong cities will be *like the deserted places*[341] of the Hivites and the Amorites, which were deserted before the Israelites; it will all be desolation.

10 For you have forgotten the God of your salvation, and have not remembered the rock of your strength; this is why you plant attractive plants but dress them with foreign slips. 11 At the time when you plant you hedge it in, and in the morning you make your seed blossom—but the harvest flees away at the time of grief and tragic sorrow.

12 Ah yes, the cries of many peoples who cry out like the roaring of the seas; and the tumult of nations who rush along like the rushing of mighty waters! 13 The nations will be in tumult like the rushing of many waters, but he will rebuke them; and they will flee far away and will be chased like mountain-chaff before the wind, and like the whirling dust before a storm. 14 At dusk—look, there is terror! And before morning comes *and*[342] they are no more. This is the portion of those who despoil us, and the lot of those who rob us.

18 1 Ah, the land of the rustling of wings, beyond the rivers of Ethiopia, 2 which sends out ambassadors by sea in vessels of papyrus upon the wa-

---

334. 1QIsaᵃ. *Damascus* MT LXX.

335. 1QIsaᵃ. *they will be* MT.

336. 1QIsaᵃ. *its branches* MT.

337. 1QIsaᵃ. *to* MT.

338. 1QIsaᵃ. *the work of their hands* MT LXX.

339. 1QIsaᵃ (cf. LXX). *and they will not* MT.

340. Meaning supplied 1QIsaᵃ LXX. *whether* (literally, *and*) 4QIsaᵇ MT.

341. 1QIsaᵃ (cf. LXX). *like the deserted place* MT.

342. 1QIsaᵃ 4QIsaᵇ LXX. Not in MT.

Chapter 18. 1QIsaᵃ: all; 4QIsaᵇ: 18:1, 5–7.

ters, saying, Go, swift messengers, to a tall and handsome nation, to a people that were frightening from their very beginning, a nation that metes out and tramples, whose land is divided by the rivers!

3 All you inhabitants of the world, and dwellers on the earth: when a signal is lifted up on the mountains, then watch; and when the trumpet is sounded, then listen! 4 For this is what the LORD has told me: I will be still, and I will watch in my dwelling-place, like clear heat in sunshine and like a cloud of dew *in the heat*[343] of harvest. 5 For before the harvest, when the budding is over and the blossoms become ripening grapes, he will cut off the sprigs with pruning-hooks, and take away and cut down the spreading branches. 6 *And*[344] they will be left together for the ravenous *mountain*[345] birds and for the *wild animals;*[346] the ravenous birds will feast all summer long on them, and *all the wild animals*[347] will feast all the winter on them.

7 At that time a present will be brought to the LORD of hosts *from a tall and handsome people,*[348] from a people that were frightening from their very beginning, a nation that metes out and tramples, whose land is divided by the rivers, to the place of the name of *the LORD,*[349] to Mount Zion.

19 1 The oracle concerning Egypt: See, the LORD is riding on a swift cloud and coming to Egypt. The idols of Egypt will tremble at his presence; and the heart of the Egyptians will melt within them. 2 And I will stir up Egyptians against Egyptians; everyone will fight against his brother, and everyone against his neighbor, *and city*[350] against city, and kingdom against kingdom. 3 The spirit of the Egyptians will fail within them, and I will confound their plans. They will consult *idols*[351] and the spirits of the dead, the mediums and the spiritists. 4 I will deliver the Egyptians into the hand of a hard master; a fierce king will rule over them, says the LORD GOD of hosts.

5 The waters of *the Nile*[352] will dry up, and the riverbed will become parched

---

343. 1QIsaᵃ MT. *on the day* MTᵐˢˢ LXX.

344. 1QIsaᵃ LXX. Not in MT.

345. Literally, *of mountains* 4QIsaᵇ MT. *of the mountains* 4QIsaᵇ.

346. Literally, *beasts of field* 1QIsaᵃ LXX. Literally, *beast of the field* 4QIsaᵇ⁽ᶜᵒʳʳ⁾ MT.

347. Literally, *all beasts of (the) field* 1QIsaᵃ. *every beast of the field* MT LXX.

348. 1QIsaᵃ LXX. *a tall and handsome people* 4QIsaᵇ MT.

349. 1QIsaᵃ. *the LORD of hosts* 4QIsaᵇ MT LXX.

Chapter 19. 1QIsaᵃ: all; 4QIsaᵇ: 19:1–25; 1QIsaᵇ: 19:7–17, 25; 4QIsaᵃ: 19:24–25.

350. 1QIsaᵃ. *city* MT LXX.

351. 1QIsaᵃ. *the idols* MT. *their idols* LXX.

352. Or, *the sea.*

and dry. 6 And *the canals*[353] will become foul; *and*[354] the streams of Egypt will dwindle and dry up, *reeds and rushes, and they will wither away.*[355] 7 The reeds *along the Nile,*[356] on the brink of the Nile, and all the sown fields of the Nile, will dry up *and*[357] be driven away, *and there will be nothing in it.*[358] 8 Those who fish will mourn, and all who cast hooks into the Nile will lament, and those who spread nets upon the waters will pine away. 9 *Those*[359] who work with combed flax and the weavers of white cloth will be in despair. 10 *Its*[360] weavers will be broken in pieces, and all who work for wages will be sick at heart.

11 The princes of Zoan are utterly foolish; the advice of Pharaoh's wisest counselors has become stupid. How can you say to Pharaoh, I am one of the wise men, a disciple of ancient kings? 12 Where are your wise men now? Please let them tell you and make known what *the* Lord[361] has planned against Egypt. 13 The princes of Zoan have become fools, the princes of Memphis are deluded; those who are the cornerstones of her peoples led Egypt astray. 14 The Lord *has mixed*[362] in its midst a spirit of confusion; and they have led Egypt astray in everything it does, like a drunkard staggers around in his own vomit. 15 And there will be no work for Egypt which its head or tail, palm branch or rush, *can do.*[363]

16 *On that day the Egyptians*[364] will be like women; *they will tremble and be afraid*[365] at the uplifted hand of the Lord of hosts *when he brandishes his hand against her.*[366] 17 The land of Judah will become a terror to the Egyptians; everyone to whom Judah is mentioned will be afraid, because of the plan that the *hand of the* Lord *of hosts*[367] is planning against them. 18 On that day there will be five cities in

---

353. 1QIsaᵃ LXX. *canals* MT.

354. 1QIsaᵃ LXX. Not in MT.

355. 1QIsaᵃ. *reeds and rushes will wither away* 4QIsaᵇ MT.

356. 1QIsaᵃ MT. Not in LXX.

357. 1QIsaᵃ. Not in 4QIsaᵇ MT.

358. 1QIsaᵃ. *and will be no more* 4QIsaᵇ MT.

359. 1QIsaᵃ 4QIsaᵇ. *And those* MT (cf. LXX).

360. I.e., Egypt's.

361. 1QIsaᵃ*. *the* Lord *of hosts* 1QIsaᵃ⁽ᶜᵒʳʳ⁾ (with *of hosts* added above the line) MT LXX.

362. 1QIsaᵃ MT LXX. *has poured* 4QIsaᵇ.

363. 1QIsaᵃ MT LXX. *can do on that day* 4QIsaᵇ.

364. 1QIsaᵃ MT LXX. *The Egyptians* 4QIsaᵇ.

365. 1QIsaᵃ. *he will tremble and be afraid* 4QIsaᵇ MT.

366. Possible translation 1QIsaᵃ (with *her* as feminine). *which he is brandishing against it* (masculine) MT. *which he is brandishing against them* LXX.

367. 4QIsaᵇ. Lord *of hosts* 1QIsaᵃ MT LXX.

the land of Egypt that speak the language of Canaan and swear allegiance to the LORD of hosts. One of these will be called the *City of the Sun*.[368]

> ▌ *The ending of 19:18 is rather complex but fascinating. The original reading seems to be that of 1QIsa^a, which also occurs in 4QIsa^a, a few Masoretic manuscripts, and several translations such as the Latin Vulgate: "City of the Sun," most likely Heliopolis in Egypt (cf. Jer 43:13). The Masoretic Text, however, reads "City of Destruction." Since the words* sun *and* destruction *are very similar in Hebrew, involving a difference of only one letter, it is possible that one of the two readings is simply an error. But there is a more likely explanation: that* destruction *is a deliberate word play on* sun *for the purpose of denigrating Heliopolis, which was one of Egypt's most important cities and was associated with sun worship.*

19 On that day will there be an altar to *the* LORD[369] in the heart of the land of Egypt, and a pillar to the LORD at its border. 20 It will be a sign and a witness to the LORD of hosts in the land of Egypt; for when they cry to the LORD because of their oppressors he *will send*[370] them a savior *and he will go down*[371] and will rescue them. 21 So the LORD will make himself known to Egypt, and the Egyptians will acknowledge the LORD on that day. They will even worship with sacrifices and burnt offerings; they will make vows to the LORD and will carry them out. 22 The LORD will strike Egypt, striking but healing. Then they will return to the LORD, and he will respond to them and will heal them.

23 On that day will there be a highway from Egypt to Assyria. The Assyrians will come to Egypt and the Egyptians to Assyria, and *they*[372] will worship with the Assyrians. 24 On that day Israel will be the third, along with Egypt and Assyria, a blessing in the midst of the earth, 25 whom the LORD of hosts has blessed, saying, Blessed be Egypt my people, and Assyria the work of my hands, and Israel my heritage.

20 1 In the year that the supreme commander, who was sent by Sargon the king of Assyria, came to Ashdod and attacked Ashdod and took it— 2 at that time the LORD spoke through Isaiah the son of Amoz: Go and loosen the sackcloth from your hips, and take *your sandals*[373] off your feet. And he did so, walking around naked and barefoot.

---

368. 1QIsa^a 4QIsa^b MT^mss. *City of Destruction* (possible meaning) MT. *Polis-Asedek* (i.e., *City of Righteousness*) LXX.

369. 1QIsa^a MT LXX. *the* LORD *of hosts* 4QIsa^b (cf. vss 18, 20).

370. *waw* + perfect 1QIsa^a. *waw* + imperfect 4QIsa^b MT. *and he will send* LXX.

371. 1QIsa^a. *and he will defend* MT LXX.

372. 1QIsa^a. *the Egyptians* 4QIsa^b MT LXX.

Chapter 20. 1QIsa^a: all; 4QIsa^a: 20:1–6; 4QIsa^b: 20:1–4; 1QIsa^b: 20:1; 4QIsa^f: 20:4–6.

373. 1QIsa^a LXX. *your sandal* MT.

3 Then the LORD said, Just as my servant Isaiah has walked around naked and barefoot for three years as a sign and a portent against Egypt and Ethiopia, 4 so the king of Assyria will lead away the Egyptians as captives and the Ethiopians as exiles, both young and old—naked and barefoot, even with their buttocks bared, to the shame of Egypt. 5 And they will be afraid and put to shame because of Ethiopia their *hope*[374] and Egypt their boast. 6 At that time the inhabitants of this coastland will say, "See, this is what has happened to those we relied on and *on whom we rely*[375] for help and deliverance from the king of Assyria! How then can we ourselves escape?"

21 1 The oracle concerning *the pasture*[376] by the sea: As whirlwinds in the Negev sweep on, it comes from the desert, from a *distant*[377] land. 2 A dire vision has been shown to me; the traitor betrays, and the destroyer destroys. Go up, Elam, lay siege, Media! I am bringing to an end all the groaning she has caused. 3 Therefore my loins are racked with pain; pangs have seized me like the pangs of a woman in labor. I am so staggered that I cannot hear, I am so bewildered I cannot see *as I reel.* 4 *And as for my mind,*[378] horror has appalled me; the twilight of my desire has been turned into trembling for me. 5 They set the tables, *they prepare the rugs,*[379] they eat, they drink! Rise up, you commanders, oil the shields!

6 For this is what the LORD said to me: Go, post a lookout, *and*[380] let him announce what he sees. 7 When he sees chariots, *each man with a pair of horses,*[381] *riders* on donkeys or *riders*[382] on camels, let him listen diligently, very diligently. 8 The *lookout*[383] shouted, O LORD, I stand continually upon the watchtower in the daytime, and am stationed at my post throughout the night. 9 Look, there comes a troop of riders, horsemen in pairs. Then he answered and said, Fallen,

---

374. 1QIsaᵃ uses a different, similar Hebrew word than MT.

375. Possible meaning 1QIsaᵃ. *to whom we fled* MT LXX.

Chapter 21. 1QIsaᵃ: all; 4QIsaᵃ: 21:1–16; 4QIsaᵇ: 21:11–14.

376. 1QIsaᵃ (error?) For the reading, compare Isa 5:17; or *plague;* cf. 1 Kings 8:37; Jer 14:12. *the wilderness* MT LXX.

377. 1QIsaᵃ*. *terrible.* 1QIsaᵃ⁽ᶜᵒʳʳ⁾ MT LXX.

378. 1QIsaᵃ 4QIsaᵃ. [vs 4] *My mind reels* MT LXX.

379. 1QIsaᵃ MT. Not in LXX.

380. 1QIsaᵃ LXX. Not in MT.

381. 1QIsaᵃ 4QIsaᵃ. *each with a pair of horses* MT LXX.

382. *riders . . . riders* 1QIsaᵃ LXX. While the consonants of MT can have the same meaning, that text most likely reads *chariots* as occurs earlier in the verse.

383. 1QIsaᵃ Syriac. *A lion* MT. *Uriah* LXX.

fallen is Babylon, and *they have shattered all the images of her gods*[384] to the ground. 10 O my threshed one and child of *my stone wall,*[385] I am telling you what I have heard from the LORD of hosts, the God of Israel.

11 The oracle concerning *Dumah.*[386] Someone is calling to me from Seir: Watchman, what (is left) of the night? Watchman, what (is left) of the night? 12 The watchman says, Morning is coming but also the night. If you would inquire, then inquire; come back again.

13 The oracle concerning Arabia. You will lodge in the scrub in Arabia, you caravans of Dedanites. 14 Bring water for the thirsty, O inhabitants of the land of Tema, meet the fugitive *with bread.*[387] 15 For *he has fled*[388] from the swords, from the drawn sword, and from the bent bow, and from the heat of battle.

16 This is what *the LORD*[389] says to me: Within *three years,*[390] according to the years of a hired worker, *the pomp*[391] of Kedar will come to an end. 17 The surviving numbers of the bowmen, the warriors of the sons of Kedar, will be few; for the LORD, the God of Israel, has spoken.

22 1 The oracle concerning the Valley of Vision: What troubles you now, that you have all gone up to the housetops, 2 you that were full of noise, tumultuous city, joyful town? Your slain have not been killed with the sword, nor are they dead in battle. 3 All your rulers have fled together; *she is captured*[392] without any bow. All of you who were found were captured, although they fled (while the enemy was) still far away. 4 Therefore I said, Look away from me, *and*[393] let me weep bitterly. Do not try to console me over the destruction of *my beloved people.*[394]

5 For the LORD GOD of hosts has a day of tumult and trampling and confusion

---

384. 1QIsaᵃ (cf. LXX: *all the images of her gods are shattered*). *all the images of her gods he has shattered* MT.

385. 1QIsaᵃ. *my threshing-floor* MT.

386. 1QIsaᵃ MT. *Edom* MTᵐˢˢ LXX.

387. 1QIsaᵃ LXX. *with his bread* 4QIsaᵇ MT. *and with [his] bread* 4QIsaᵃ.

388. 1QIsaᵃ. *they have fled* MT.

389. 1QIsaᵃ. *the Lord* 4QIsaᵃ MT.

390. 1QIsaᵃ. *a year* MT LXX.

391. 1QIsaᵃ LXX. *all the pomp* MT.

Chapter 22. 1QIsaᵃ: all; 4QIsaᶜ: 22:10–14, 23; 1QIsaᵇ: 22:11–18, 24–25; 4QIsaᵃ: 22:13–25; 4QIsaᶠ: 22:14–22, 25; 4QIsaᵇ: 22:24–25.

392. Apparent meaning 1QIsaᵃ. *they were captured* MT (cf. LXX).

393. 1QIsaᵃ. Not in MT LXX.

394. Literally, *the daughter of my people.*

in the Valley of Vision, a battering down of *his holiness on*[395] the mountains. 6 Elam bore the quiver with charioteers and cavalry, and Kir uncovered the shield. 7 And it *comes to pass*[396] that your choicest valleys were full of chariots, and the cavalry took their positions at the gate. 8 He has taken away the defense of Judah. On that day you looked to the weapons of the House of the Forest, 9 and you saw that the breaches in the city of David were many, and you stored up the waters of the lower pool. 10 Then you counted the houses of Jerusalem, and broke down the houses in order to fortify the wall. 11 You also made a reservoir between the *walls*[397] for the waters of the old pool. But you did not *look upon*[398] the One who made it, or have regard for the One who planned it long ago.

12 And in that day the LORD GOD of hosts, called (you) to weeping and mourning, to baldness and putting on sackcloth; 13 but see, there is joy and revelry, slaughtering of cattle and killing of sheep, eating flesh *and drinking*[399] wine: Let us eat and drink, for tomorrow we will die! 14 But the LORD of hosts has revealed himself in my hearing: Surely *for you*[400] this iniquity will not be forgiven you until you die, says the LORD GOD of hosts.

15 This is what the LORD GOD of hosts[401] says: Come, go to this steward, to Shebna who is in charge of the household, and say, 16 What are you doing here, and *who are your relatives here*[402] that you have cut out a tomb here for yourself, cutting your tomb on the height and chiseling a resting-place for yourself in the rock? 17 Beware, the LORD is about to hurl you away violently, my strong fellow. *And*[403] he *is about to seize*[404] you firmly, 18 whirl you round and round, and toss you like a ball into a large country. *There* you will die, *and there*[405] your splendid chariots will lie—you disgrace to your master's house! 19 I will depose you from your office, and *you are pulled down*[406] from your position.

---

395. 1QIsa^a. *walls, and a cry for help to* MT.

396. 1QIsa^a. *came to pass* MT.

397. Feminine 1QIsa^a. *two walls* MT (masculine) LXX.

398. 1QIsa^a. *look to* MT LXX.

399. 1QIsa^a MT. *and they drink* 1QIsa^c.

400. 1QIsa^a. Not in 4QIsa^c MT LXX.

401. 1QIsa^a MT. LORD *of hosts* MT^mss LXX.

402. Literally, *whom do you have here.*

403. 1QIsa^a 4QIsa^a 4QIsa^b LXX. Not in MT.

404. 1QIsa^a MT (participle). *will seize* (imperfect) 4QIsa^a 4QIsa^b.

405. 4QIsa^f. Literally, *to there* (or *thither*) 1QIsa^a 1QIsa^b 4QIsa^a MT LXX.

406. Literally, *he has pulled you down* 1QIsa^a. Literally, *he will pull you down* 4QIsa^f MT LXX^ms. Not in LXX.

20 On that day I will summon my servant Eliakim son of *Hilkiah,*[407] 21 and will clothe him with *your robes*[408] and fasten your girdle on him. I will entrust your authority into his hand, and he will be a father to the inhabitants of Jerusalem and to the house of Judah. 22 I will place on his shoulder the key to the house of David; he will open and no one will shut it, he will shut and no one will open it. 23 And I will fasten him like a peg in a firm place, and he will become a throne of honor to his father's house. 24 So they will hang on him all the glory of his father's house: its offspring and issue—every lesser vessel, from the cups to all the flagons.

25 On that day, says *the* LORD[409] of hosts, the peg that was fastened in a firm place will give way; it will be cut down and will fall, and the load that was on it will be cut off. The LORD has spoken.

23

1 The oracle concerning Tyre:

The oracle to Tyre is particularly interesting in the light of the Dead Sea Scrolls and the Septuagint. Study of the translation presented below and of the various alternative readings in the footnotes shows that while many readings are common to all the texts that are referred to, some readings are special to certain scrolls, to the Septuagint, and to the Masoretic Text, while others are shared by two or more of these sources but not by others. Several articles and at least one book have been written on the oracle to Tyre in the light of the Isaiah scrolls, the Septuagint, and other witnesses.

Wail, you ships of Tarshish, for Tyre is destroyed and left without house or harbor. From the land of *Cyprus*[410] it was reported *to them.* 2 *Be silent,*[411] O you inhabitants of the coast, *you merchants of Sidon, whose messengers crossed over*[412] the sea 3 and were on many waters. Her revenue was the grain of Shihor, the harvest of the Nile, and she became the marketplace of nations.

4 Be ashamed, O Sidon, for the sea *has spoken,*[413] the stronghold of the sea: I have neither labored nor given birth, I have neither reared young men nor

---

407. Literally, *Hilkiyah* 1QIsaᵃ 4QIsaᶠ. Literally, *Hilkiyahu* 4QIsaᵃ MT.

408. 1QIsaᵃ. *your robe* MT LXX.

409. 1QIsaᵃ 4QIsaᵃ MT LXX. *the Lord* GOD 4QIsaᶠ.

Chapter 23. 1QIsaᵃ: all; 4QIsaᵃ: 23:1–12; 1QIsaᵇ: 23:1–4; 4QIsaᶜ: 23:8–18.

410. Literally, *Kittim.*

411. 1QIsaᵃ MT. [vs 2] *To whom are they like?* 4QIsaᵃ (apparently) LXX. The fact that 4QIsaᵃ writes the two Hebrew words together (with no break) suggests that the scribe of 4QIsaᵃ may have understood the text as evidenced in the LXX translation.

412. 1QIsaᵃ 4QIsaᵃ LXX. *you whom the merchants of Sidon, passing over* (singular) *the sea, have replenished* MT.

413. 1QIsaᵃ (with *the sea* feminine). *he has spoken* (masculine) 1QIsaᵇ 4QIsaᵃ MT.

brought up young women. 5 When the report comes to Egypt, they will be in anguish at the report concerning Tyre. 6 *O you crossing over*[414] to Tarshish; wail, you inhabitants of the coast! 7 Is this your happy city whose origin is from days of old, *and*[415] whose feet carried her to settle far away? 8 Who has planned this against Tyre, the bestower of crowns, *whose merchants were princes,*[416] whose traders were the honored of the earth? 9 The LORD of hosts has planned it, to defile *all the pride of glory,*[417] to shame all the honored of the earth. 10 *Cultivate*[418] your own land like the Nile, O daughter of Tarshish, for there is no longer a harbor. 11 He has stretched out his hand over the sea, *he has made*[419] the kingdoms tremble; the LORD has given orders concerning Canaan to destroy her fortresses. 12 He said, You will *rejoice no longer,*[420] O crushed virgin daughter of Sidon; get up, cross over to Cyprus—even there you will find no rest.

13 Look at the land of the Chaldeans, this is the people; it was not Assyria. They made Tyre (a place) for *desert creatures;*[421] they erected *her siege towers,*[422] they stripped her palaces, they made her a ruin. 14 Wail, you ships of Tarshish, for *your*[423] stronghold is destroyed. 15 And it will happen at that time *to Tyre as in the song of the prostitute:*[424] 16 Take up a harp, walk about the city, you forgotten prostitute! Make sweet melody, sing many songs, so that you will be remembered.

17 At the end of seventy years the LORD will deal with Tyre. Then she will return to her trade, and will prostitute herself with *the kingdoms*[425] of the world upon the face of the earth. 18 Yet her merchandise and her earnings will be set apart for the LORD; they will not be stored or hoarded *but her merchandise will become abundant food and choice attire for those who dwell in the presence of the LORD.*[426]

---

414. 1QIsa^a. *Cross over* (imperfect) MT LXX.

415. 1QIsa^a. Not in MT.

416. 1QIsa^a(corr) (with original scribe inserting *merchants* above the words who *were princes*).

417. 1QIsa^a LXX. *the pride of all glory* MT.

418. Or, *Worship* 1QIsa^a LXX. *Pass through* 4QIsa^c MT.

419. 1QIsa^a 4QIsa^a MT LXX. *to make* 4QIsa^c.

420. 1QIsa^a MT LXX. either *not take refuge to rejoice* or *not rejoice with strength* 4QIsa^c.

421. Or, *demons.*

422. 1QIsa^a. *his siege towers* MT.

423. Singular 1QIsa^a. Plural MT.

424. 1QIsa^a (scribal error, skipping from *Tyre* to the same word later in the verse). *that Tyre will be forgotten for seventy years, the span of a king's life; but at the end of seventy years* [and 4QIsa^c] *it will happen to Tyre as in the song of the prostitute* 4QIsa^c MT LXX (with small variations).

425. 1QIsa^a. *all the kingdoms* MT LXX.

426. 1QIsa^a MT. *but (will be) for those who dwell in the presence of the LORD. And her merchandise will become abundant food and choice attire* 4QIsa^c.

24 1 See, *the* Lord[427] is about to lay waste the *land*[428] and devastate it; he will turn it upside down and scatter abroad its inhabitants. 2 And as it will be with the people, so with the priest; as with the slave, so with his master; as with the maid, so with her mistress; as with the buyer, so with the seller; as with the lender, so with the borrower; as with the creditor, so with his debtor. 3 The earth will be totally emptied and completely laid waste; for the Lord has spoken this word.

4 The earth dries up and withers, the world languishes and fades away; heaven *fades away*[429] together with the earth. 5 The earth also lies polluted under its inhabitants, because they have transgressed the *laws,*[430] violated the statutes, and broken the everlasting covenant. 6 Therefore a curse *consumes,*[431] and those dwelling in it are held guilty; therefore the inhabitants of *earth*[432] are burned up, and few people are left. 7 The new wine dries up, the vine, *the oil*[433] decays, all the merrymakers groan. 8 The gaiety of timbrels ceases, the noise of merrymakers ends, the mirth of the harp is silent. 9 No longer do they drink wine with singing, *and*[434] strong drink is bitter to those who drink it. 10 The chaotic city is broken down; every house is shut up so that no one can enter. 11 There is an outcry for wine in the streets; all gaiety turns to gloom, the gladness of the land is banished. 12 *Desolation*[435] is left in the city, its *gate*[436] is battered to ruins. 13 For so it will be on the earth and among the peoples, as when an olive tree is beaten, or as at the gleaning when the grape harvest is ended.

14 They lift up their voices, *they shout*[437] for joy; *they cry out*[438] from *the west*[439] over the majesty of the Lord. 15 Therefore *in the east*[440] glorify the Lord, in the

---

Chapter 24. 1QIsa^a: all; 4QIsa^c: 24:1–15, 19–23; 4QIsa^f: 24:1-3, 22 (?); 4QIsa^b: 24:2, 4; 1QIsa^b: 24:18–23.

427. 1QIsa^a MT. *the Lord* 4QIsa^c.

428. 1QIsa^a. *earth* 4QIsa^c MT (with words that are different in form but similar in meaning).

429. 1QIsa^a 4QIsa^c. Plural MT (cf. LXX).

430. 1QIsa^a MT. *law* 4QIsa^c LXX.

431. 1QIsa^a. *consumes the earth* 4QIsa^c MT LXX.

432. 1QIsa^a MT. *the earth* 4QIsa^c LXX.

433. 4QIsa^c. Not in 1QIsa^a MT LXX.

434. 1QIsa^a. Not in 4QIsa^c MT LXX.

435. 1QIsa^a MT LXX. *And desolation* 4QIsa^c LXX^ms.

436. Masculine 1QIsa^a MT. Feminine 4QIsa^c.

437. 1QIsa^a MT. *and they shout* 4QIsa^c.

438. 1QIsa^a MT. *and they cry out* 4QIsa^c.

439. Literally, *the sea* 1QIsa^a MT (cf. LXX). *the day* 4QIsa^c.

440. 1QIsa^a MT. *in the east, in Aram* 4QIsa^c.

coastlands of the sea glorify the name of the LORD, the God of Israel. 16 From the ends of the earth we hear songs of praise: Glory to the Righteous One. But I say, I am pining away, I am pining away. Woe is me! For the treacherous deal treacherously—the treacherous deal very treacherously! 17 Terror, and the pit, and the snare are upon you, O inhabitant of the earth! 18 Then whoever flees at the sound of the terror will fall into the pit, and whoever climbs out of the pit will be caught in the snare. For the windows above are opened, and the foundations of the earth shake. 19 The earth is utterly broken, the earth is torn asunder, the earth is violently shaken. 20 *The earth*[441] staggers like a drunkard, it sways to and fro *and like a hut.*[442] Its transgression lies heavy upon it, and *it falls*[443]—never to rise again.

21 On that day the LORD will punish the host of the high ones *in heaven,*[444] and the kings of the earth upon the earth. 22 *They*[445] will be gathered together *in a dungeon;*[446] they will be shut up in prison, and after many days will be punished. 23 Then the moon will be abashed and the sun will be ashamed; for the LORD of hosts will reign on Mount Zion and in Jerusalem, and before his elders there will be glory.

25 1 O LORD, you are my God! I will exalt you and praise your name, for you have done marvelous things, plans formed long in faithfulness and truth. 2 For you have made the city a heap of rubble, the fortified city a ruin, the *foreigners' palace*[447] a city no more—it will never be built. 3 Therefore strong peoples will glorify you, cities of ruthless nations will fear you. 4 For you have been a refuge to the poor, a refuge to the needy in their distress, a shelter from the storm and a shade from the heat. For the breath of the ruthless is like a storm against a wall, 5 like heat in a dry place. You subdue the uproar of foreigners like heat with the shade of clouds; the song of the ruthless will be stilled.

6 On this mountain the LORD of hosts will make for all peoples a feast of rich food, a feast of aged wine, of choice meats filled with marrow, of refined and aged wines. 7 And on this mountain he will destroy the shroud that covers all peoples, the sheet that is spread over all nations; 8 *he has swallowed up*[448] death forever. Then the LORD GOD will wipe away the tears from all faces, and he will re-

---

441. 1QIsa^a. *Earth* MT LXX.

442. 1QIsa^a. *like a hut* MT.

443. Masculine (referring to *the earth*) 1QIsa^a. Feminine MT.

444. Literally, *on high.*

445. 1QIsa^a. *And they* 4QIsa^c MT LXX.

446. 1QIsa^a LXX. *like prisoners in a dungeon* 4QIsa^c MT.

Chapter 25. 1QIsa^a: all; 1QIsa^b: 25:1–8; 4QIsa^c: 25:1–2, 8–12.

447. 1QIsa^a MT. *palace of arrogant people* MT^mss LXX.

448. 1QIsa^a MT. *and he will swallow up* MT^mss (cf. Syriac, Theodotian, and 1 Cor 15:54).

move the disgrace of his people from all the earth—for the LORD has spoken. 9 *And you will say*[449] on that day: See, *the* LORD[450]—this is our God; we have waited for him so that he might save us. This is the LORD for whom we have waited; let us be glad *and we will rejoice*[451] in his salvation! 10 For the hand of the LORD will rest on this mountain.

The Moabites will be trodden down in their place, just as straw is trodden down *in the water of*[452] a manure pit. 11 They will spread forth his hands in the midst of it, as swimmers spread out their hands to swim, but the LORD will lay low their pride together with the cleverness of their hands. 12 He brings down the high fortifications of your walls and lays them low; *he will cast them*[453] to the ground, even to the very dust.

26 1 On that day *one will sing that song*[454] in the land of Judah: We have a strong city; God makes victory *its walls and ramparts*.[455] 2 Open *your gates,*[456] so that the righteous nation that keeps faith may enter in. 3 You will keep in perfect peace the one whose mind is fixed on you, because *he is in you*.[457] 4 Trust in the LORD[458] forever, for in the LORD GOD we have an everlasting rock. 5 For *he has made drunk*[459] those who dwell on high; as for the lofty city, *he lays it low*[460] to the ground and casts it to the dust. 6 *The feet of the oppressed trample*[461]— the footsteps of the needy.

7 The way of *righteousness*[462] is level; *O Upright One,*[463] you *bring to safety*[464] the

---

449. 1QIsa[a]. *And he will say* 4QIsa[c] MT. *And they will say* LXX.

450. 1QIsa[a]. Not in MT LXX.

451. 1QIsa[a]. *and let us rejoice* MT.

452. 1QIsa[a] MT. *in* MT[qere].

453. Imperfect 1QIsa[a]. *he casts them* (perfect) 4QIsa[c] MT (a wording that is more consistent with the preceding verbs).

Chapter 26. 1QIsa[a]: all; 4QIsa[c]: 26:1–9; 4QIsa[b]: 26:1–5, 7–19; 1QIsa[b]: 26:1–5.

454. 1QIsa[a]. *this song will be sung* 1QIsa[b] 4QIsa[c] MT. *they will sing that song* LXX.

455. Literally, *walls and ramparts* 1QIsa[a] MT LXX (singular). *its walls and its ramparts* 4QIsa[c].

456. 1QIsa[a]. *the gates* MT LXX.

457. 1QIsa[a] 1QIsa[b] LXX. *he trusts in you* 4QIsa[c] MT.

458. 1QIsa[a] MT. *the* LORD *God* (literally, *Yah the Lord*) 4QIsa[b]. *the Lord, the Lord* LXX.

459. Meaning unclear (possibly different Hebrew spelling for the form found in MT) 1QIsa[a]. *he has brought low* 1QIsa[b] 4QIsa[b] 4QIsa[c] MT. *he has humbled and brought down* LXX.

460. 1QIsa[a] LXX. *he lays it low; he lays it low* MT.

461. 1QIsa[a] (*oppressed* singular). *The foot tramples it, the feet of the oppressed* MT.

462. 1QIsa[a] 4QIsa[b] MT. *they go straight ahead* 4QIsa[c]. Not in LXX.

463. 1QIsa[a] 4QIsa[c] MT. Not in LXX.

464. 1QIsa[a]. *make level* MT LXX (*prepare*).

path of *justice*.[465] 8 Yes, LORD, *we wait*[466] in the path of your judgments; your name and *your law*[467] are *our soul's*[468] desire. 9 My soul yearns for you in the night; my spirit within me diligently seeks you; for when your judgments are on the earth, the inhabitants of the world learn righteousness. 10 Although favor is shown to the wicked, they do not learn righteousness; even in the land of uprightness they act perversely and do not see the majesty of the LORD. 11 O LORD, your hand is lifted up, but they do not see it. *And*[469] let them see your zeal for *your people*[470] and be put to shame; yes, let the fire reserved for your adversaries consume them. 12 LORD, you will *decide*[471] peace for us, for all that we have accomplished you have done for us. 13 O LORD our God, other lords besides you have had dominion over us, but through you alone we acknowledge your name. 14 The dead will not live, *and the departed spirits*[472] will not rise. You punished and destroyed them, and *imprisoned*[473] all memory of them. 15 But you have enlarged the nation, O LORD, you have enlarged the nation. You are glorified; you have enlarged all the borders of the land.

16 O LORD, in distress *they*[474] sought you; they were distressed, they *poured out their magical prayer*[475] when *your chastenings were*[476] upon them. 17 Like a woman with child who writhes in pain and cries out in her pangs as she approaches her time, so have we been before you, O LORD. 18 We have been with child, we have been in pain, but we gave birth only to wind. We have not won *your deliverance*[477] for the earth, nor have inhabitants of the world been born. 19 But your dead will live, their dead bodies will rise. The dwellers in the dust *will awake and shout for joy!*[478] For your dew is like the dew of the dawn, and the earth will give birth to the dead.

---

465. 1QIsa^a 4QIsa^c. *the righteous* MT LXX (plural).

466. 1QIsa^a LXX. *we wait for you* MT.

467. 1QIsa^a. *mention of you* 4QIsa^c MT (cf. LXX).

468. 1QIsa^a MT. *my soul's* 4QIsa^b.

469. 1QIsa^a. Not in MT.

470. Literally, *the people* 1QIsa^a. Literally, *people* MT.

471. 1QIsa^a. *prepare* MT. *give!* LXX.

472. 1QIsa^a LXX. *the departed spirits* MT.

473. 1QIsa^a. *wiped out* MT.

474. 1QIsa^a MT. *we* MT^mss LXX^mss. *I remembered you* LXX.

475. 1QIsa^a. *a magical prayer* 4QIsa^b MT.

476. 1QIsa^a. *your chastening was* MT LXX.

477. 1QIsa^a LXX. *deliverance* MT.

478. 1QIsa^a. *Awake and shout for joy* [imperative], *you . . .* MT. *(Those in the dust) will rejoice, for . . .* LXX.

20 Come, my people, enter your chambers and shut your doors behind you. *Hide yourselves*[479] for a little moment until the wrath is past. 21 *For*[480] the LORD is coming from his place to punish the inhabitants of the earth for their sins; the earth will disclose the blood shed on it, and will no longer conceal its slain.

27 1 On that day the LORD will punish with his cruel and great and strong sword Leviathan the *gliding*[481] serpent, Leviathan the coiling serpent, and he will kill the dragon that is in the sea.

2 On that day: A *diminishing*[482] vineyard, sing about it! 3 I the LORD am its keeper; every moment I water it. I guard it night and day so that no one can harm it. 4 I have no anger. If only there were briers *and thorns*[483] confronting me in battle! I would march against them, *and*[484] I would set them all on fire. 5 Or else let it rely on my protection; let it make peace with me, let it make peace with me.

6 In days to come Jacob will take root, *and*[485] Israel will blossom and put forth shoots, and fill the whole world with fruit. 7 Has (the LORD) struck them down as he struck down those who struck them? Or have they been slain as *their slayers*[486] were slain? 8 By banishment, by exile you contended with them; he removed them in the day of the east wind with his fierce blast. 9 Therefore by this the guilt of Jacob will be forgiven, and this will be the full fruit of the removal of his sin: when he makes all the altar stones like pulverized chalkstones, no Asherim or incense-altars will remain standing. 10 For the fortified city is desolate, a habitation abandoned and forsaken like the desert; there the calves graze, there they lie down and strip its branches bare. 11 When its boughs are dry, they are broken off; women *make a fire*[487] of them. For this is a people without understanding; so he who made them will not have compassion upon them, and he that formed them will show them no favor.

12 And on that day the LORD will thresh *from the river*[488] Euphrates to the Wadi of Egypt, and you will be gathered one by one, O people of Israel. 13 And on that day a great trumpet will be sounded, and those who were perishing in the

---

479. 1QIsa^a. *Hide yourself* MT.

480. 1QIsa^a. *For see,* MT LXX.

Chapter 27. 1QIsa^a: all; 4QIsa^f: 27:1, 5–6, 8–12.

481. Participle 1QIsa^a (cf. LXX). Adjective MT.

482. Apparent meaning 1QIsa^a. *pleasant* MT LXX. *fermenting* (possible wording) MT^mss.

483. 1QIsa^a. *thorns* MT.

484. 1QIsa^a. Not in MT.

485. 1QIsa^a LXX. Not in MT.

486. Active participle + suffix 1QIsa^a. Passive participle + suffix 1QIsa^a.

487. 1QIsa^a*. *come and make a fire* MT (cf. LXX).

488. Masculine 1QIsa^a. Feminine MT.

land of Assyria and those who were driven out to the land of Egypt will come and *bow down to*[489] the LORD in the holy mountain at Jerusalem.

28 1 Woe to the proud garland of the drunkards of Ephraim, and to the fading flower of its glorious beauty, which is on the head of the bloated valley of those overcome with wine! 2 See, *the* LORD[490] has one who is powerful and strong. Like a hailstorm, a destroying tempest, like a storm of mighty overflowing waters *and*[491] he will bring it forcefully to the ground. 3 The proud garland of the drunkards of Ephraim will be trampled underfoot. 4 And the fading flower of its glorious beauty, which is on the head of the bloated valley, will be like a first-ripe fig before the summer; when someone sees it, he swallows it as soon as it is in his hand.

5 In that day the LORD of hosts will be a glorious crown and a beautiful diadem for the remnant of his people, 6 and a spirit of justice to the one who sits in judgment, and strength to those who turn back the battle *at the gate.*[492]

7 *These*[493] reel with wine and stagger with strong drink. The priest and the prophet reel with strong drink, they are swallowed up with wine and stagger with strong drink; they err in vision and stumble in judgment. 8 For all the tables are covered with vomit and filth, so that no place is clean.

9 To whom will he teach knowledge, and to whom will he interpret the message? Those who are weaned from milk, and taken from the breast? 10 For it is precept upon precept, precept upon precept, line upon line, line upon line, here a little, there a little.

11 But by men of strange lips and with another tongue will he speak to this people, 12 to whom he said, This is the rest, give rest to him that is *weary,*[494] and this is the refreshing; yet they would not listen. 13 Therefore the word of the LORD will be to them precept upon precept, precept upon precept, line upon line, line upon line, here a little, there a little—so that they may go, and fall backward, and be broken, and be snared, and be taken.

14 Therefore *hear*[495] the word of the LORD, you scoffers, who rule this people that is in Jerusalem. 15 Because you have said, We have made a covenant with death, and we are in agreement with Sheol; when the overflowing scourge *exam-*

---

489. The form of this word is unclear in 1QIsa[a].

Chapter 28. 1QIsa[a]: all; 4QIsa[c]: 28:6–14; 4QIsa[f]: 28:6–9, 16–17, 18 (?), 22, 24(?); 1QIsa[b]: 28:15–20; 4QIsa[k]: 28:26–29.

490. 1QIsa[a]. *the Lord* MT.

491. 1QIsa[a]. Not in MT.

492. 1QIsa[a]. *to the gate* (directive *he*) MT.

493. 1QIsa[a]. *These also* MT.

494. 1QIsa[a] and MT use different but related words.

495. Singular 1QIsa[a]. Plural 4QIsa[c] MT LXX.

ines,[496] it will not come to us; for we have made lies our refuge, and under falsehood we have hid ourselves. 16 Therefore thus says *the* LORD,[497] Behold, I *am laying*[498] in Zion a foundation stone, a tried stone, a precious cornerstone of sure foundation; whoever believes will not be in panic. 17 And I will make justice the line, and righteousness the plummet; and the hail will sweep away the refuge of lies, and the waters will overflow the hiding-place. 18 And your covenant with death will be annulled, and your agreement with Sheol will not stand; when the overflowing scourge passes through, then you will be trodden down by it. 19 As often as it passes through, it will take you; for morning by morning it will pass through, by day and by night—*sheer terror*[499] to understand the message. 20 For the bed is too short *for people to stretch themselves*[500] on it, and the covering *to wrap themselves*[501] in it. 21 For the LORD will rise up *on*[502] Mount Perazim; he will be angry *in*[503] the valley of Gibeon, so that he may do his work, his strange work, and bring to pass his act, his strange act. 22 *But as for you,*[504] do not be scoffers, lest *your bonds*[505] be made strong; for I have heard a decree of destruction from *the* LORD[506] of hosts, upon the whole earth.

23 Give ear, and hear my voice; listen, and hear my speech. 24 Does he who plows to sow plow continually? Does he continually open and harrow his ground? 25 When he has leveled its surface, does he not cast abroad the caraway, and scatter the cumin, and put in the wheat in rows, and the barley in the designated place, and the spelt as *its borders?*[507] 26 For his God instructs him aright, and teaches him.

27 For caraway is not threshed with a sharp threshing instrument, neither is a cartwheel rolled over the cumin; but the caraway is beaten out with a staff, and the cumin with a rod. 28 *It*[508] *is ground,*[509] but one does not always thresh it;

---

496. 1QIsa^a (error?). *passes through* MT LXX.

497. 1QIsa^a* LXX. *the* LORD GOD 1QIsa^a(corr) MT.

498. Different forms of the same verb are used in 1QIsa^a and MT.

499. 1QIsa^a. *and it will be sheer terror* MT.

500. 1QIsa^a. *to stretch oneself* MT.

501. 1QIsa^a. *too narrow to wrap oneself* MT.

502. 1QIsa^a. *as (on)* MT.

503. 1QIsa^a LXX. *as (in)* MT.

504. 1QIsa^a LXX. *So now* MT.

505. Masculine 1QIsa^a. Feminine MT.

506. 1QIsa^a LXX. *the* LORD GOD MT.

507. 1QIsa^a LXX. *its border* MT.

508. 1QIsa^a MT. *And it* 4QIsa^k.

509. 1QIsa^a. *is ground for bread* 4QIsa^k MT.

although *his cart*[510] and his horses may scatter it, he does not grind it. 29 This also *comes*[511] from the LORD of hosts, who is *distinguished*[512] in counsel, *and*[513] excellent in wisdom.

29 1 Ah, *Aruel, Aruel*,[514] the city where David encamped! *Add*[515] year to year, let the feasts come round; 2 then I will distress *Aruel,* and there will be mourning and lamentation, and she will be to me as *Aruel*.[516] 3 And I will encamp against you all around, and will lay siege against you with towers, and I will raise siegeworks against you. 4 And you will be brought down, and will speak from the ground, and your speech will be low from the dust; your voice will be like that of a ghost from the ground, and your speech will whisper from the dust.

> ■ *Several possibilities exist for the multitude referred to in Isaiah 29:5. Is the best reading "your strangers," mentioned in the Masoretic Text, "the ungodly," referred to in the Septuagint, or "your enemies," as found in 1QIsaᵃ? A solution is offered by the parallel phrase later in the verse—"and the multitude of the ruthless ones"—which suggests that the reading in 1QIsaᵃ is the preferred one. "Your enemies" (or "Your foes") is found in several modern translations, including the Revised Standard Version, the New Revised Standard Version, and the New International Version.*

5 But the multitude of *your enemies*[517] will be like fine dust, and the multitude of the ruthless ones like chaff that blows away. Suddenly, in an instant 6 you will be punished by the LORD of hosts with thunder, with an earthquake and great noise, with whirlwind and tempest, and the flame of a devouring fire. 7 And the multitude of all the nations that fight against *Aruel*,[518] even all that fight against her and her *fortification*[519] and distress her, will be like a dream, a vision of the night. 8 And it will be as when a hungry man dreams, and see—he eats but awakes and is empty; or it will be like when a thirsty man dreams, and see—he

---

510. 1QIsaᵃ*. *the wheel of his cart* 1QIsaᵃ⁽ᶜᵒʳʳ⁾ MT LXX.

511. Feminine verb 1QIsaᵃ MT. Masculine verb 4QIsaᵏ.

512. Possible meaning 1QIsaᵃ. *wonderful* MT.

513. 1QIsaᵃ. Not in MT.

Chapter 29. 1QIsaᵃ: all; 4QIsaᵏ: 29:1–9; 1QIsaᵇ: 29:1–8; 4QIsaᶠ: 28:1, 8 (?).

514. 1QIsaᵃ. *Ariel, Ariel* MT LXX.

515. Possibly feminine singular imperative 1QIsaᵃ 4QIsaᵏ. Masculine plural imperative MT.

516. 1QIsaᵃ. *Ariel, . . .Ariel* MT LXX.

517. 1QIsaᵃ. *your strangers* MT. *the ungodly* LXX.

518. 1QIsaᵃ. *Ariel* MT LXX.

519. 1QIsaᵃ. *mountain stronghold* MT. *Jerusalem* LXX (but different word order).

drinks but wakes up faint, and is still thirsty. So will the multitude of all the nations be that fight against Mount Zion.

9 Tarry and wonder, take your pleasure and be blind; they *are drunken,*[520] but not *from wine;*[521] they stagger, but (*not*) *with strong drink.*[522] 10 For the LORD has poured out upon you the spirit of deep sleep, and has closed your eyes, you prophets; and he has covered your heads, you seers. 11 And this whole vision has become to you like the words of a book that is sealed, which people deliver to one who is learned, saying, "Read this, I pray you"; but *he says,*[523] "I cannot, for it is sealed." 12 Then *they deliver the book*[524] to one who is not learned, saying, "Read this, I pray you"; but *he says,*[525] "I am not learned."

13 And the LORD said, Inasmuch as this people draw near to honor me with their mouth and with their lips, but have removed their hearts far from me, and *fear of me*[526] has been *like a human commandment*[527] that has been taught them; 14 therefore, see, *as for me*[528] I am about to do a marvelous work among this people, even a marvelous work and a wonder; and the wisdom of their wise men will perish, and the *insights*[529] of their prudent men will be hidden.

15 Woe to those who hide deep their counsel from the LORD, and whose works *have been*[530] in the dark, and who say, "Who sees us?" and "Who *has known*[531] us?" 16 *He has overturned things from you.*[532] Will it be thought of like *the potter's heat,*[533] so that the thing made should say of the one who made it, "He did not make me"; or the thing formed say of the *ones*[534] who formed it, "He has no understanding"?

17 Is it not yet a very little while, and Lebanon will be turned into a fruitful

---

520. Participle 1QIsa^a. *have become drunk* (perfect) MT.

521. 1QIsa^a LXX. (*from*) *wine* MT (no preposition).

522. 1QIsa^a (with *not* understood). *not* (*with*) *strong drink* MT.

523. 1QIsa^a. *he will say* MT LXX.

524. 1QIsa^a. *the book will be delivered* MT LXX.

525. 1QIsa^a. *he will say* MT LXX.

526. 1QIsa^a. *their fear of me* MT.

527. 1QIsa^a. *a human commandment* MT.

528. 1QIsa^a LXX. Not in MT.

529. 1QIsa^a. *insight* MT (although plural is also possible) LXX.

530. 1QIsa^a. *are* (or, *will be*) MT LXX.

531. 1QIsa^a. *knows* MT LXX.

532. Apparent meaning 1QIsa^a. *You turn things upside down!* MT.

533. Apparent meaning 1QIsa^a. *the potter's clay* MT LXX.

534. 1QIsa^a (error?). *one* MT LXX.

field, and the fruitful field will be regarded as a forest? 18 And on that day the deaf will hear the words of the book, and the eyes of the blind will see out of *gloom*[535] and darkness. 19 The meek also will increase their joy in the LORD, and the poor among men will rejoice in the Holy One of Israel. 20 For the terrible one is brought to naught, and the scoffer ceases, and all who watch for iniquity are cut off, 21 those who make a man an offender in his cause, and lay a snare for him who reproves in the gate, and turn aside the just with meaningless arguments.

22 Therefore thus says the LORD, who redeemed Abraham, concerning the house of Jacob: Jacob will not now be ashamed, neither will his face now grow pale. 23 But when he sees his children, the work of my hands, in the midst of him, they will sanctify my name; yes, they will sanctify the Holy One of Jacob, and will stand in awe of the God of Israel. 24 Moreover, those who err in spirit will come to understanding, and those who complain will receive instruction.

30 1 Woe to the rebellious children, says the LORD, who take counsel, but not of me; and who make a league, but not of my spirit, so that they may add sin to sin; 2 who set out to go down into Egypt, and have not asked my counsel; to strengthen themselves in the strength of Pharaoh, and to take refuge in the shadow of Egypt! 3 Therefore the strength of Pharaoh will be your shame, and the refuge in the shadow of Egypt will be your *longing*.[536] 4 For their princes *is*[537] at Zoan, and their ambassadors have come to Hanes. 5 *Destruction is odious*[538] to a people that cannot profit them, that are not *a help*[539] nor profit, but a shame and also a reproach.

6 The oracle concerning the beasts of the South. Through the land of trouble *and dryness*[540] and anguish, *where there is no water,*[541] the lioness and the lion, the viper and fiery flying serpent, which *carries*[542] their riches upon the shoulders of young asses, and their treasures upon the humps of camels, to a people that will not profit them. 7 For Egypt helps in vain and to no purpose; therefore I have called her "Rahab who sits still."

8 Now go, *write it*[543] before them on a tablet, and inscribe it in a book, so that

---

535. Masculine noun 1QIsa[a]. Feminine noun MT.

Chapter 30. 1QIsa[a]: all; 4QIsa[c]: 30:8–17; 1QIsa[b]: 30:10–14, 21–26; 4QIsa[r]: 30:23.

536. 1QIsa[a]. *humiliation* MT LXX.

537. 1QIsa[a] (error?). *are* MT LXX.

538. 1QIsa[a]. *They were all ashamed* MT.

539. Feminine 1QIsa[a]. Masculine MT.

540. 1QIsa[a] (cf. Isa 41:18). Not in MT LXX.

541. 1QIsa[a]. *from whence (come)* MT LXX.

542. 1QIsa[a]. *carry* MT LXX.

543. 1QIsa[a] MT. *write* 4QIsa[c] LXX.

it may be for times to come forever and ever. 9 For it is a rebellious people, lying children, children who will not hear the law of the LORD, 10 who say to the seers, "Do not see," and to the prophets, "Do not prophesy right things to us; speak to us smooth things, prophesy deceits, 11 *get out*[544] of the way, turn aside from the path, cause the Holy One of Israel to cease before us." 12 Therefore, thus says the Holy One of Israel: Because you despise this word, and trust in oppression and *you rejoice,*[545] and rely on it, 13 therefore this iniquity will be to you like a breach ready to fall, swelling out in a high wall, *whose crash comes suddenly, in an instant.*[546] 14 And he will break it like a potter's vessel is broken, breaking it in pieces *without sparing,*[547] so that there will not be found among its pieces a shard with which to take fire from a hearth, or to scoop up water from a cistern.

15 For thus said the LORD,[548] the Holy One of Israel: In returning and rest you will be saved; in quietness and in confidence will be your strength. But you were unwilling; 16 but you said, "No, for we will flee upon horses." Therefore you will flee; and, "We will ride upon the swift"; therefore those who pursue you will be swift. 17 One thousand will flee *before*[549] one; at the threat of five you will flee, until you are left like a beacon upon the top of *a mountain,*[550] and like an ensign on a hill.

18 And therefore the LORD will wait, so that he may be gracious to you; and therefore he will be exalted, so that he may have mercy upon you. For the LORD is a God of justice; blessed are all those who wait for him.

19 For the people will dwell in Zion *and in Jerusalem;*[551] *you*[552] will weep no more, *the LORD*[553] will surely be gracious to you at the sound of your cry; when he hears, he will answer you. 20 And although the LORD gives you the bread of adversity and *the water of affliction,*[554] yet *your teachers will not hide themselves*[555] anymore, but your eyes will see your teachers. 21 And your ears will hear a word

---

544. Imperfect 1QIsaᵃ. Imperative 4QIsaᶜ MT LXX.

545. Apparent meaning 1QIsaᵃ. *and perverseness* MT.

546. 1QIsaᵃ MT (cf. LXX). [*which is*] *suddenly for breaking open, and its crash comes* (meaning unclear) 1QIsaᵇ.

547. Literally, *they do not take pity* 1QIsaᵃ. Literally, *he does not take pity* MT.

548. 1QIsaᵃ* LXX. *the LORD GOD* 1QIsaᵃ⁽ᶜᵒʳʳ⁾ MT.

549. 1QIsaᵃ. *at the threat of* MT LXX.

550. 1QIsaᵃ. *the mountain* MT.

551. 1QIsaᵃ. *at Jerusalem* MT.

552. Plural 1QIsaᵃ. Singular MT.

553. 1QIsaᵃ. *he* MT LXX.

554. The normal form of this phrase occurs in 1QIsaᵃ rather than in MT.

555. 1QIsaᵃ. *your teacher will not hide himself* MT.

behind you, saying, "This is the way, walk in it"; when you turn to the right hand and when you turn to the left. 22 And you will defile your graven images overlaid with silver, and your molten images *plated*[556] with gold: you will cast them away like an unclean thing; you will say to them, "Away with you!"

23 And he will give the rain for your seed, with which you will sow the ground, and bread of the increase of the ground; *it will be*[557] abundant and plenteous. On that day your cattle will feed in large pastures; 24 the oxen likewise and the young asses that till the ground will eat *leavened*[558] fodder, which *one winnows*[559] with shovels and forks. 25 And there will be upon every lofty mountain, and upon every high hill, brooks and *canals*[560] of water, in the day of the great slaughter, when the towers fall. 26 Moreover, the light of the moon will be like the light of the sun, and the light of the sun will be sevenfold, *like the light of seven days,*[561] on the day when the LORD binds up the hurt of his people, and heals the wound he has inflicted.

27 See, the name of the LORD comes from afar, burning with his anger, and in thick rising smoke. His lips are full of indignation, and his tongue is like a devouring fire, 28 and his breath is like an overflowing stream; *and it reaches*[562] even to the neck, *to winnow*[563] the nations with the sieve of destruction; and a bridle that causes people to err will be in the mouths of the peoples.

29 You will have a song as in the night when *people keep a holy feast,*[564] and gladness of heart as when one goes with a pipe to come to the LORD's mountain, to the Rock of Israel. 30 And the LORD will *make heard, make heard*[565] his glorious voice, and will show the descending blow of his arm, with the indignation of his anger, and the flame of a devouring fire, with a blast, a tempest, and hailstones. 31 For through the voice of the LORD the Assyrians will be dismayed, with his rod he will smite them. 32 And every stroke of the staff of *his foundation,*[566] which the LORD will lay upon them, will be with the sound of timbrels and harps, and in battles with the brandishing of his arm he will fight *with her.*[567] 33 For *an open-*

---

556. Plural 1QIsaᵃ. Singular MT.

557. 1QIsaᵃ LXX. *and it will be* MT.

558. Apparent meaning 1QIsaᵃ. *salted* or *choice* MT. *prepared* LXX.

559. Imperfect 1QIsaᵃ. Participle MT.

560. 1QIsaᵃ. *streams* MT.

561. 1QIsaᵃ MT. Not in LXX.

562. 1QIsaᵃ. *it reaches* MT LXX.

563. Apparent meaning 1QIsaᵃ. *to sift* MT.

564. 1QIsaᵃ. *one keeps a holy feast* MT.

565. 1QIsaᵃ. *make heard* MT LXX.

566. 1QIsaᵃ. *of (the) foundation* MT. *punishment* MTᵐˢˢ.

567. 1QIsaᵃ MT. *with them* MTᵐˢˢ.

ing[568] place has been prepared of old; yes, *it was for the king; it will be made ready,*[569] he has made it deep and large, *and*[570] its pile is fire and much wood. The breath of the LORD, like a stream of brimstone, kindles it.

31 1 Woe to those who go down *to*[571] Egypt for help, and rely on horses, and trust in *the chariot*[572] because they are many, and in horsemen because they are very strong—but do not look *to*[573] the Holy One of Israel nor seek the LORD! 2 Yet he is also wise and will bring disaster, and will not recall his words, but will arise against the house of the evildoers, and against the help of those who work iniquity. 3 Now the Egyptians are humans, not God; and their horses are flesh, not spirit; when the LORD stretches out his hand, both he who helps will stumble, and he who is helped will fall; *they*[574] all will be consumed together.

4 For thus says the LORD to me: Just as the lion or the young lion growling over his *objects of prey,*[575] if a multitude of shepherds is called forth against him, will not be dismayed at their voice, nor daunted at their noise, so the LORD of hosts will come down to fight upon Mount Zion and upon its hill. 5 Like birds hovering, so the LORD of hosts will protect Jerusalem; he will protect and deliver it, *and*[576] he will pass over and *bring it to safety.*[577]

6 Turn back *to him whom, to him whom*[578] you have deeply betrayed, O children of Israel. 7 For on that day everyone will cast away his idols of silver, and his idols of gold, which your own hands have sinfully made for you.

8 And the Assyrians will fall by a sword not of man; and a sword not of men will devour them; and they will flee *not before*[579] the sword, and their young men will be put to forced labor. 9 And their rock will pass away by reason of terror, and their princes will be dismayed at the banner, says the LORD, whose fire is in Zion and whose furnace is in Jerusalem.

---

568. Meaning unclear 1QIsa^a. *his burning place* (possible wording) MT.

569. 1QIsa^a. *it is made ready for the king* MT.

570. 1QIsa^a. Not in MT.

Chapter 31. 1QIsa^a: all.

571. With preposition 1QIsa^a LXX. Preposition understood MT.

572. 1QIsa^a. *a chariot* MT. *chariots* LXX.

573. 1QIsa^a. *upon* MT.

574. 1QIsa^a. *and they* MT LXX.

575. 1QIsa^a. *prey* (singular) MT LXX.

576. 1QIsa^a (cf. LXX). Not in MT.

577. 1QIsa^a. *rescue it* MT.

578. 1QIsa^a. *to him whom* MT.

579. Apparent meaning 1QIsa^a LXX. *from* MT.

32 1 Behold, a king will reign in righteousness, and princes will rule in justice. 2 And each will be like a refuge from the wind and a shelter *from*[580]
the storm, like streams of water in a dry place, *in*[581] the shade of a great rock in a
weary land. 3 And the eyes of those who see will not be dim, and the ears of
those who hear will listen. 4 And the heart of the rash will understand knowledge, and the tongues of stammerers will be ready to speak plainly. 5 *People will
no longer call a fool*[582] noble, nor a villain said to be honorable. 6 For a fool speaks
nonsense, and his heart *plans*[583] iniquity, in order to practice profaneness and to
speak error against the LORD, to leave the craving of the hungry unsatisfied, and
to deprive the thirsty of drink. 7 And the villainies of a villain are evil; *and*[584] he
devises evil plans to ruin *the poor*[585] with lying words, even when the *needy ones
speak*[586] what is right. 8 But the noble person devises noble things, and by noble
deeds he stands.

9 Rise up, you women who are at ease, and hear my voice; you careless daughters, give ear to my speech. 10 For days beyond a year you will be troubled, you
careless women; for the vintage will fail, the ingathering will *not*[587] come.
11 Tremble, you women who are at ease; be troubled, you careless ones; strip
yourselves and make yourselves bare, and put on sackcloth *and beat your breasts*[588]
around *your loins.*[589] 12 Beat your breasts for the pleasant fields, for the fruitful
vine, 13 for the soil of my people growing up in thorns *and*[590] briers; yes, for all
the joyous houses in the jubilant city. 14 For the palace will be forsaken, the populous city will be deserted; the hill and the watchtower will become dens forever,
a delight of wild asses, a pasture *for*[591] flocks; 15 until a spirit is poured upon us
from on high, and the wilderness becomes a fruitful field, and the fruitful field is
considered a forest. 16 Then justice will dwell in the wilderness, and righteousness will abide in the fruitful field. 17 The effect of righteousness *will be for*

Chapter 32. 1QIsa^a: all.

> **580.** Possible reading 1QIsa^a. *of* MT.
>
> **581.** 1QIsa^a. *like* MT.
>
> **582.** 1QIsa^a LXX. *A fool will be no longer called* MT.
>
> **583.** 1QIsa^a LXX. *works* MT.
>
> **584.** 1QIsa^a LXX. Not in MT.
>
> **585.** 1QIsa^a and MT use two different but similar words.
>
> **586.** 1QIsa^a. *needy one speaks* MT.
>
> **587.** 1QIsa^a. Literally, *without* MT.
>
> **588.** 1QIsa^a (error?). Not in MT LXX.
>
> **589.** Literally, *the loins* 1QIsa^a LXX. Literally, *loins* MT.
>
> **590.** 1QIsa^a LXX. Not in MT.
>
> **591.** 1QIsa^a. *of* MT (cf. LXX).

peace,[592] and the result of righteousness will be quietness and confidence forever. 18 And my people will abide in a peaceful habitation, in secure dwellings, and in quiet resting places. 19 But it will hail when the forest comes down, and *the wood*[593] will be completely laid low. 20 Happy will be you who sow beside every stream, *and*[594] who let out freely the ox and the donkey.

> ▪ *In Isaiah 32:19 the Masoretic Text tells us that "the city" will be completely laid low, but 1QIsaᵃ specifies "the wood" (or "the thicket"). While these may simply be two alternative and equally valid readings, the two Hebrew words involved are very similar: h'yr ("city") versus hy'r ("wood"). The parallel term "the forest," found earlier in the verse, suggests that 1QIsaᵃ in fact preserves the better reading—"the wood." "The city," as found in the Masoretic Text, seems to be the inferior reading, which most likely arose through an early scribal misreading of the more common h'yr for hy'r.*

33 1 Woe to you, O destroyer, who yourself have not been destroyed; woe to you, O traitor, *with whom*[595] no one has dealt treacherously! When you have *sunk down in*[596] destroying, you will be destroyed; and when you have *finished*[597] dealing treacherously, you will be dealt with treacherously.

2 O LORD, be gracious to us; we long for you. *And*[598] be our arm every morning, *our salvation*[599] in the time of trouble. 3 At the sound of tumult peoples fled; at *your silence*[600] nations scattered. 4 And your spoil is gathered like the caterpillar gathers; *like*[601] locusts leap men *have leapt*[602] upon it. 5 The LORD is exalted, for he dwells on high; he has filled Zion with justice and righteousness. 6 *There will be*[603] stability in your times, abundance *and salvation,*[604] wisdom and knowledge; the fear of the LORD is your treasure.

---

592. 1QIsaᵃ. *will be peace* MT LXX.

593. 1QIsaᵃ. *the city* MT.

594. 1QIsaᵃ. Not in MT LXX.

Chapter 33. 1QIsaᵃ: all; 4QIsaᶜ: 33:2–8, 16–23; 4QIsaᵃ: 33:16–17 (?).

595. Literally, *with you* 1QIsaᵃ. Literally, *with him* MT.

596. Possible meaning 1QIsaᵃ. *stopped* MT.

597. 1QIsaᵃ. *ceased* (similar but different verb) MT.

598. 1QIsaᵃ. Not in MT LXX.

599. 1QIsaᵃ has a very unusual form of this word in comparison to MT and other passages in the Hebrew Bible.

600. 1QIsaᵃ. *the rising up of yourself* MT. *from fear of you* LXX.

601. Not in 1QIsaᵃ (meaning supplied).

602. 1QIsaᵃ. *leap* MT.

603. 1QIsaᵃ. *And there will be* MT.

604. 1QIsaᵃ. *of salvation* MT.

7 Look, their brave men *cry out*[605] in the streets; the envoys of peace weep bitterly. 8 The highways lie deserted, travelers have left the road; (the enemy) has broken the covenant, has despised *witnesses*[606] and has regard for no one. 9 The land mourns and languishes; Lebanon is ashamed and withers, Sharon is like a desert, *Bashan*[607] and Carmel shake off their leaves.

10 Now will I arise, *the* Lord *has said,*[608] now will I lift myself up; now I will be exalted. 11 You conceive *chaff,*[609] you bring forth stubble; your breath is a fire that will devour you. 12 And the peoples will be like the burnings of lime, like thorns cut down, that are burned in the fire.

13 *Those who are far away have heard*[610] what I have done; and *those that are near have acknowledged*[611] my might. 14 The sinners in Zion are afraid, trembling has seized the godless: Who among us can live with the devouring fire? Who among us can live with everlasting burnings? 15 The one who walks righteously *and he has spoken*[612] uprightly; the one who despises the gain of oppression, who waves *his hand*[613] from taking a bribe, who blocks *his ears*[614] from hearing of bloodshed, and who shuts his eyes from looking on evil— 16 such a person will dwell on high; his place of defense will be the fortresses of rocks, his bread will be given him, his waters will be sure.

17 Your eyes will see the king in his beauty; they will behold a land that reaches afar. 18 Your heart will muse on the terror: Where is that one who counted? Where is the one who weighed the tribute? Where is the one who counted the towers? 19 *You*[615] will not see the fierce people, a people of a deep speech that you cannot comprehend, of a strange tongue that you cannot understand.

20 Look on Zion, the city of *our appointed festivals!*[616] Your eyes will see Jerusalem, a peaceful habitation, a tent that will not be removed; its stakes will never be pulled up, nor any of its cords be broken. 21 But there the Lord in

---

605. 1QIsaᵃ and MT use different but similar Hebrew words.

606. 1QIsaᵃ. *the cities* MT.

607. 1QIsaᵃ. *and Bashan* MT.

608. 1QIsaᵃ. *says the* Lord MT LXX.

609. Feminine 1QIsaᵃ. Masculine MT.

610. 1QIsaᵃ. *You who are far away, hear* MT.

611. 1QIsaᵃ. *you that are near, acknowledge* MT.

612. 1QIsaᵃ. *and who speaks* MT LXX.

613. 1QIsaᵃ. *his hands* MT LXX.

614. 1QIsaᵃ LXX. *his ear* MT.

615. Plural 1QIsaᵃ. Singular MT.

616. 1QIsaᵃ. *our appointed festival* MT.

majesty will be for us a place of broad *rivers*[617] and streams, where no galley with oars can go, nor any stately ship can pass. 22 For the LORD is our judge, *and*[618] the LORD is our lawgiver, *and*[619] the LORD is our king, *and*[620] he will save us.

23 Your rigging hangs loose; it cannot hold *indeed*[621] the base of the mast, nor *keep*[622] the sail spread out. Then prey and abundant spoil will be divided; even the lame will carry off plunder. 24 And no inhabitant will say, "I am sick"; the people who live there will be forgiven their iniquity.

34 1 Come near, nations, to hear; and pay attention, peoples. Let the earth hear and everything in it, the world and all that it brings forth. 2 For the LORD is angry against all the nations and furious at all their host. He has doomed them *and*[623] has determined *that they be slaughtered.*[624] 3 Their slain and their corpses will be cast down, and their stench will rise up. *The*[625] mountains will be soaked with their blood. 4 *The valleys will be split, all the host of the heavens will fall,*[626] and the heavens will be rolled up like a scroll. All their host will wither, *like a leaf withering*[627] off the vine or like withering off the fig tree. 5 Indeed my sword will *be seen*[628] in the heavens. Watch, it will come down upon Edom, upon the people I have doomed for judgment. 6 The LORD has a sword filled with blood, gorged with fat, with the blood of lambs and goats, with the fat of rams' kidneys. Indeed the LORD has a sacrifice in Bozrah, and a great slaughter in the land of Edom. 7 The wild oxen will fall with them and the young bulls with the mighty steers. Their land will be drunk with blood and their soil saturated with fat.

■ *From the end of verse 9 through the end of verse 10 the punctuation of 1QIsaᵃ shows that the series of clauses was intentionally divided in a way different from that chosen in the Masoretic Text.*

8 Indeed the LORD has a day of vengeance, a year of recompense for the cause of Zion. 9 Its streams will be turned into pitch, and its soil into sulfur, and its land

---

617. Feminine 1QIsaᵃ. Masculine MT.

618. 1QIsaᵃ. Not in MT LXX.

619. 1QIsaᵃ. Not in MT LXX.

620. 1QIsaᵃ. Not in MT LXX.

621. 1QIsaᵃ. *firmly* MT.

622. Singular 1QIsaᵃ. Plural MT.

Chapter 34. 1QIsaᵃ: all.

623. 1QIsaᵃ. Not in MT.

624. 1QIsaᵃ. *them for slaughter* MT.

625. 1QIsaᵃ. Not in MT.

626. 1QIsaᵃ. *All the host of the heavens will rot away* MT.

627. 1QIsaᵃ. *as when a leaf withers* MT.

628. 1QIsaᵃ. *drink its fill* MT.

will become *pitch*. 10 *It will burn night and day and will never be extinguished. Its smoke will go up from generation to generation, and it will lie waste forever and ever. No one will pass through it.*[629] 11 The pelican and the porcupine will possess it, and the owl and the raven will dwell in it. Over it he will stretch *a line, and chaos,*[630] *and plumb lines of emptiness, and its nobles.* 12 *They*[631] will call it No Kingdom There, and all its princes will be *nothing.*[632] 13 Thorns will grow in its palaces, nettles and thistles in its fortresses. It will be a habitation of jackals, an abode for ostriches. 14 Desert cats will meet *hyenas,*[633] and goat-demons will call to each other. There too, *liliths will settle, and they will find themselves*[634] a place of rest. 15 The *owl*[635] will make its nest there, and lay, and hatch, and gather under her shade; indeed, *indeed,*[636] buzzards will gather there, every one with its mate.

16 Study and read from the book of the LORD: *and not one*[637] will be missing, *each its mate.*[638] For it is *his*[639] mouth that has commanded, and *it*[640] is his spirit that has gathered *them.*[641] 17 It is he who has cast the lot for them, and his *hands*[642] divided it for *them*[643] with *the line forever.*[644]

---

629. 1QIsa[a]. *burning pitch. 10 Night or day it will not be extinguished. Forever its smoke will go up; from generation to generation it will lie waste. Forever and ever no one will pass through it* MT. LXX divides differently and does not have the final sentence.

630. 1QIsa[a]. *a line of chaos* MT.

631. 1QIsa[a]. *plumb lines of emptiness are its 12 nobles. They* MT. *satyrs will dwell in it. 12 Her nobles* LXX.

632. 1QIsa[a(corr)] (with original scribe first writing *as nothing* but then marking *as* to be deleted).

633. 1QIsa[a] has an unusual spelling of this word.

634. 1QIsa[a]. *the lilith will settle, and it will find itself* MT.

635. 1QIsa[a] and MT have different spellings of this word; it occurs only this once in the Bible, and the identity of the animal it designates is disputed.

636. 1QIsa[a]. Not in MT.

637. 1QIsa[a]. *not one of them* MT.

638. 1QIsa[a]. *none of them lacks a mate* MT.

639. 1QIsa[a]. *my* MT.

640. Feminine (correctly) 1QIsa[a]. Masculine MT.

641. Masculine 1QIsa[a]. Feminine MT.

642. 1QIsa[a]. *hand* MT.

643. 1QIsa[a(corr)] (with original scribe first writing the masculine form [= MT] but then changing it to the feminine).

644. 1QIsa[a]. *the line. Forever they will possess it; from generation to generation will they dwell in it.*¶ 35:1 *The wilderness and the dry land will rejoice, the desert will celebrate and blossom like the crocus. 2 It will blossom luxuriantly and rejoice greatly with joy and song. The glory of Lebanon will be given to it, the splendor of Carmel and Sharon. They will see the glory of the LORD, the splendor of our God* MT (LXX).

■ *1QIsaᵃ ends chapter 34 with "forever" in Isaiah 34:17 and then continues with the beginning of Isaiah 35:3. A later hand has inserted the passage containing the last few words of 34:17 and 35:1–2, which the Masoretic Text and the Septuagint also contain. It is possible that the passage had been in the text from which the scribe of 1QIsaᵃ was copying and he simply omitted it by mistake. But 35:1–2 makes sense by itself and appears more likely to have been a late supplement that was inserted into the originally shorter text of 1QIsaᵃ on the basis of a growing variant text. The Masoretic Text also sets it off as a separate paragraph explicitly through the use of paragraph markers. The last words of Isaiah 34:17 can be understood as referring to the wild animals that will inhabit the ruined land just described in Isaiah 34 or to the redeemed exiles of Isaiah 35 who will inherit Zion.*

35 3 Strengthen the weak hands, support the stumbling knees. 4 Say to those who are disheartened, "Be strong, do not fear; see, your God will *bring*[645] vengeance, he will *bring*[646] divine recompense to save you." 5 Then the eyes of the blind will be opened, and the ears of the deaf will unclose. 6 Then the lame will leap like a deer, and the tongue of the mute will sing. Yes, water will burst out in the wilderness, and streams *will run*[647] through the desert. 7 The scorching desert will become a pool, and the thirsting ground fountains of water; in the habitation of jackals, *a grassy resting place with*[648] reeds and rushes. 8 A highway will be *there,*[649] and *they will call it*[650] The Holy *Way.*[651] The unclean will not pass over it; *it and for whomever is traveling,*[652] even fools, will not go astray. 9 There will be no lion or violent beast there; it will *not*[653] come up on it, *and*[654] *it will not be found*[655] there. But the redeemed will walk, 10 and the ransomed of the LORD will return and enter Zion with singing. Everlasting joy will be upon their heads. They will *attain*[656] joy and happiness, and sorrow and mourning will flee away.

Chapter 35. 1QIsaᵃ: 35:3–10; 4QIsaᵇ: 35:9–10.

645. 1QIsaᵃ. *come with* MT.

646. 1QIsaᵃ. *come with* MT.

647. 1QIsaᵃ. Not in MT LXX.

648. 1QIsaᵃ. *is her resting place; the grass (will become)* MT.

649. 1QIsaᵃ, unlike MT, repeats *there.*

650. 1QIsaᵃ. *it will be called* MT.

651. MT, unlike 1QIsaᵃ, repeats *Way.*

652. 1QIsaᵃ. *but it will be for them; travelers* MT. Both Hebrew texts appear troubled here.

653. 1QIsaᵃ, unlike MT, has two negatives.

654. 1QIsaᵃ. Not in MT.

655. Masculine 1QIsaᵃ. Feminine MT.

656. The scribe of 1QIsaᵃ added *in it* (i.e., Zion), but marked that it should be deleted.

36 1 In the fourteenth year of King *Hezekiah*,[657] Sennacherib king of Assyria came up against all the fortified cities of Judah and took them. 2 The king of *Assyria*[658] sent the Rabshakeh from Lachish to *Jerusalem*[659] to King Hezekiah with a *very*[660] large army. He stood by the conduit of the upper pool on the highway of Fuller's Field. 3 Eliakim son of Hilkiah, who was over the household, Shebna the scribe, and Joah son of Asaph the recorder came out to him. 4 The Rabshakeh said to them, "Say to Hezekiah *king of Judah*,[661] 'Thus says the great king, the king of Assyria: What is this source of confidence that you *yourself*[662] are trusting *in*?[663] 5 Do you think that words alone equate to counsel and strength for battle? Now in whom do you trust, that you have rebelled against me? 6 Indeed, you are depending on Egypt, that broken reed of a staff, which pierces the palm of anyone who leans on it: so is Pharaoh king of Egypt to all who trust in him.'

■ *1QIsaᵃ and the Masoretic Text both contain the last two-thirds of verse 7, though the Septuagint does not. The Septuagint is probably original, while the other traditions have inserted a typically Deuteronomistic theological commonplace.*

7 "But if *you*[664] say to me, 'We trust *in*[665] the LORD our God'—is he not the one whose high places and altars Hezekiah removed, after which he said to Judah and Jerusalem, 'You will worship before this altar *in Jerusalem*?'[666]— 8 come now, *make a wager*[667] with my lord, the king of Assyria. I will give you two thousand horses, if you are able to supply riders for them. 9 How can you reject one captain *from*[668] among the least of my master's servants, and entrust *yourselves*[669] to

---

Chapter 36. 1QIsaᵃ: all; 4QIsaᵇ: 36:1–2.

   657. 1QIsaᵃ usually uses the shorter form *Hizqiyah* throughout these chapters, whereas 4QIsaᵇ and MT use the longer *Hizqiyahu.*

   658. The scribe inadvertently omitted the final letter, although he had spelled it correctly in the previous verse.

   659. 1QIsaᵃ and MT use variant spellings.

   660. 1QIsaᵃ. Not in MT LXX.

   661. The scribe wrote *king of Judah* but marked that it should be deleted. Not in MT LXX.

   662. 1QIsaᵃ. Not in MT LXX.

   663. 1QIsaᵃ. Not in MT LXX.

   664. Plural 1QIsaᵃ LXX. Singular MT.

   665. 1QIsaᵃ and MT use two different words for *in.*

   666. The scribe wrote *in Jerusalem* but marked that it should be deleted. Not in MT.

   667. Plural verb 1QIsaᵃ LXX. Singular MT.

   668. 1QIsaᵃ. Not in MT.

   669. 1QIsaᵃ. *yourself* MT.

Egypt for chariots and horsemen? 10 Now do you think that it is without the
LORD that I have come up against this land to destroy it? It was the LORD who said
to me, 'Go up to this land to[670] destroy it.' " 11 Then Eliakim and Shebna and
Joah said to him,[671] "Please speak with[672] your servants in Aramaic since we understand it. But do not speak this message so that the men sitting on[673] the wall can hear."

> ■ 1QIsaᵃ reads "Speak with your servants," while the Masoretic Text has "Speak to
> your servants." But 1QIsaᵃ also writes "with us" in the margin. It is possible that an
> early form of the text simply read "with us" and was changed to mirror more diplo-
> matic language. The scroll conflates the two readings.

12 But the Rabshakeh said, "Was it to you and against your lord[674] that my lord
sent me to speak this message? Was it not rather against the men sitting on the
wall, who will have to eat their own dung and drink their own urine with you?"
13 Then the[675] Rabshakeh stood and called out with a loud voice in Judean. He
said, "Listen to the words of the great king, the king of Assyria. 14 Thus says the
king of Assyria,[676] 'Do not let Hezekiah deceive you, for he will not be able to deliver you. 15 Do not let Hezekiah compel you to trust in the LORD, thinking, The
LORD will surely deliver us, and[677] this city will not be given into the power of the
king of Assyria.' 16 Do not listen to Hezekiah, for thus says the king of Assyria:
'Make your peace with me, and come out to me; then everyone will eat from his
vine and everyone from his fig tree, and everyone will drink from the water of his
own cistern 17 until I come and take you to a land like your own land, to[678] a land
of grain and wine, a land of bread and vineyards. 18 Beware lest Hezekiah per-
suade you by saying, The LORD will deliver us. Has any of the gods of the nations
saved his land from the power of the king of Assyria? 19 Where are the gods of
Hamath and Arpad? Where are the gods of Sepharvaim? Have they saved Samaria
from my power? 20 Which among all the gods of those countries has delivered
their country from my power, so that the LORD might deliver Jerusalem from my
power?' " 21 But they did not speak or answer at all, for the king's command was:
"Do not respond to him." 22 Then Eliakim the son of Hilkiah, who was over

---

670. 1QIsaᵃ. and MT.

671. 1QIsaᵃ. MT has to the Rabshakeh at a later point.

672. 1QIsaᵃ. to MT.

673. 1QIsaᵃ. to us in Judean so that the people on MT.

674. Was it to you [plural] and against your [plural] lord 1QIsaᵃ. Was it to your [singular] lord
and to you [singular] MT.

675. 1QIsaᵃ. Not in MT.

676. 1QIsaᵃ. Not in MT LXX.

677. 1QIsaᵃ. Not in MT.

678. 1QIsaᵃ. Not in MT.

the household, Shebna the scribe, and Joah son of Asaph the recorder, came to Hezekiah with their clothes torn and reported the words of the Rabshakeh to him.

37 1 When *Hezekiah the king*[679] heard this, he rent his clothes, covered himself with sackcloth, and went into the house of the LORD. 2 He sent Eliakim, who was over the household, and Shebna the scribe, and the elders of the priests, covered with sackcloth, to the prophet Isaiah, the son of Amoz. 3 They said to him, "Thus says Hezekiah: This day is a day of trouble, and of rebuke, and of disgrace; for children are at the point of birth, but there is no strength to bring them forth. 4 Perhaps the LORD your God will hear the words of the Rabshakeh, whom the king of Assyria his master has sent to scorn the living God, and will rebuke the words which the LORD your God has heard: therefore lift up a prayer for the remnant that is left *in this city*."[680] 5 *So the servants of King Hezekiah came to Isaiah. 6 And Isaiah said to them,*[681] *"Thus you will say to your master, 'Thus says the LORD: Do not be afraid of the words that you have heard, those with which the servants of the king of Assyria have blasphemed me. 7 Behold, I will put a spirit in him,*[682] *and he will hear a rumor, and he will return to*[683] *his own land; I will make him fall by the sword in his own land.' "*[684]

> ■ *1QIsa*ᵃ *adds "in this city," writing it and the next three verses smaller and as a clear afterthought. The text originally went from verse 4 to verse 8. The intervening verses 5–7 appear to be a secondarily inserted prophecy pointing toward the manner of Sennacherib's death in 37:36–38.*

8 So the Rabshakeh returned and found the king of Assyria fighting Libnah; for he had heard that he had left Lachish. 9 He heard a report *about*[685] Tirhakah king of Ethiopia, "He is coming out to fight you." When he heard this, *he returned*[686] and sent messengers to Hezekiah, saying, 10 *"Say*[687] this to Hezekiah

---

Chapter 37. 1QIsaᵃ: all; 1QIsaᵇ: 37:8–12; 4QIsaᵇ: 37:29–32.

679. 1QIsaᵃ. *the king Hezekiah* MT LXX. In addition, 1QIsaᵃ usually uses the shorter forms *Hizqiyah* and *Yesha'yah* throughout these chapters, whereas 4QIsaᵇ and MT use the longer *Hizkiyahu* and *Yesha'yahu*.

680. 1QIsaᵃ. Not in MT LXX.

681. 1QIsaᵃ and MT have different forms.

682. 1QIsaᵃ. *in him a spirit* MT LXX.

683. 1QIsaᵃ and MT have different forms for *to*.

684. 1QIsaᵃ⁽ᶜᵒʳʳ⁾ (with original scribe adding these verses secondarily) MT LXX.

685. 1QIsaᵃ misspells this preposition.

686. 1QIsaᵃ LXX (cf. 2 Kings 19:9 MT). Not in MT.

687. 1QIsaᵃ and MT have different forms.

king of Judah, 'Do not let your God in whom you trust *deceive you*[688] by saying,
Jerusalem will not be delivered into the power of the king of Assyria. 11 Indeed,
you have heard what the kings of Assyria have done to all lands, absolutely anni-
hilating them. Will you be rescued? 12 Have the gods of the nations rescued
them, those nations which my fathers destroyed, Gozan, Haran, Rezeph, and the
people of Eden who were in Telassar? 13 Where is the king of Hamath, the king
of Arpad, the king of Lair *and*[689] of Sepharyaim *and*[690] of Na, Ivvah, *and
Samaria?'*"[691]

14 Hezekiah received the letters from the messengers and read *them*.[692] Then
Hezekiah went up to the house of the LORD and spread *it*[693] out before the LORD.
15 Hezekiah prayed to the LORD, saying, 16 "LORD of hosts, God of Israel, enthroned above the cherubim, you alone are God of all the kingdoms of the earth;
you made heaven and earth. 17 Incline your ear, LORD, and listen. Open your
eyes, LORD, and see. Listen to every word of Sennacherib, which he sent to mock
the living God. 18 Truly, LORD, the kings of Assyria have devastated all the
lands,[694] 19 and *they have cast*[695] their gods into the fire—for they were not gods
but the *works*[696] of human hands, wood and stone; thus they have destroyed them.
20 Now, LORD our God, *I will save us*[697] from his power, so that all the kingdoms
of the earth may know that you *alone, LORD, are God.*"[698]

21 Then Isaiah son of Amoz sent *to*[699] Hezekiah, saying, "Thus says the LORD,
the God of Israel *to whom you prayed*[700] about *Sennacherib*[701] king of Assyria; 22 this
is the word which the LORD spoke concerning him: The virgin daughter of Zion
has despised you and mocked you. The daughter of Jerusalem has shaken *her*[702]
head at you. 23 Whom have you mocked and blasphemed? Against whom have

---

688. 1QIsa^a and MT have different forms.

689. 1QIsa^a. Not in MT.

690. 1QIsa^a. Not in MT.

691. 1QIsa^a. Not in MT LXX.

692. 1QIsa^a. *it* MT.

693. Feminine 1QIsa^a. Masculine MT.

694. 1QIsa^a. *lands and their land* MT^L. *nations and their land* MT^mss.

695. 1QIsa^a and MT use different verb forms.

696. 1QIsa^a. *work* MT.

697. 1QIsa^a. *save us* MT.

698. 1QIsa^a. *alone are LORD* MT.

699. 1QIsa^a and MT use different words for *to*.

700. 1QIsa^a. *because you prayed to me* MT.

701. 1QIsa^a and MT spell *Sennacherib* differently.

702. 1QIsa^a. Implied in MT.

you raised your voice and arrogantly lifted up your eyes? Against the Holy One of Israel. 24 By your servants you have reviled my Lord and said, 'With my many chariots I myself have climbed the highest mountains, to the farthest parts of Lebanon where I cut it[703] down, its tallest cedars and its choicest cypresses. I entered its highest point, its most fertile forest. 25 I myself *cried out*[704] and drank *foreign*[705] waters, and with the sole of my foot I dried up all the rivers of Egypt.' 26 Did you not hear how in the distant past I decided to do it, in ancient times *planned*[706] it? Now I have made it happen that *fortified cities should become devastated, besieged heaps.*[707] 27 Their inhabitants *had little*[708] power. They were dismayed and *ashamed.*[709] They were wild plants, *grassy*[710] sprouts, grass on the roofs, *scorched by the east wind.*[711] 28 But I know your *rising up*[712] and sitting down, your going out and coming in, and your *raging*[713] against me. 29 *I have heard of your arrogance,*[714] so I will put my hook in your nose and my bit on your *lips,*[715] and I will turn you back on the way *on which is destruction.*[716]

30 "This will be the sign for you: *Eat*[717] this year what grows of itself and in the second year *what springs from that.*[718] In the third year sow seed, reap, *plant*[719] vineyards, and *eat*[720] their fruit. 31 The escapees of the house of Judah will *gather*[721] and *those who are found*[722] will take root below ground and bear fruit

---

703. 1QIsa^a. Not in MT.

704. 1QIsa^a. *dug wells* MT.

705. 1QIsa^a. Not in MT.

706. 1QIsa^a. *and planned* MT.

707. 1QIsa^a. *you should make fortified cities crash into ruined heaps* MT.

708. 1QIsa^a and MT use different forms.

709. 1QIsa^a and MT have different forms.

710. 1QIsa^a. *and grassy* MT.

711. 1QIsa^a. *and a field before the standing grain* MT.

712. 1QIsa^a. Not in MT.

713. 1QIsa^a and MT use different forms.

714. 1QIsa^a. *Because I have heard of your raging against me and your arrogance* MT.

715. 1QIsa^a. *lip* MT.

716. 1QIsa^a (literally, but probably a simple misspelling of the word as in MT). *on which you came* MT.

717. 1QIsa^a and MT use different forms.

718. 1QIsa^a misspells the word.

719. 1QIsa^a and 4QIsa^b MT use different forms.

720. 1QIsa^a and 4QIsa^b MT use different forms.

721. 1QIsa^a. *be increased* MT.

722. 1QIsa^a. *the remainder* MT.

above.[723] 32 For a remnant will go forth out of *Zion*[724] and escapees from *Jerusalem.*[725] The zeal of the LORD of hosts will perform this.

33 "Therefore thus says the LORD concerning the king of Assyria: He will not enter this city, *nor build up a siege-mound against it, nor shoot an arrow there, nor oppose it with a shield.*[726] 34 By the way he came, he will return. He will not enter this city, says the LORD. 35 I will defend this city to save it, for my own sake and for my servant David's sake."

36 Then the angel of the LORD went out, and struck 185,000 in the camp of the Assyrians. When morning came, there they were, all of them dead bodies. 37 So Sennacherib king of Assyria broke camp, left, and returned, and remained at Nineveh. 38 As he was worshiping *in*[727] the temple of Nisroch his god, his sons Adrammelech and Sharezer struck him down with the sword, and they escaped to the land of Ararat. And his son Esar-haddon reigned in his place.

38

1 In those days Hezekiah became deathly ill. Isaiah the prophet the son of Amoz came to him and said to him, "Thus says the LORD: *Set*[728] your house in order, because you are going to die, you will not live."

2 Then Hezekiah turned his face to the wall, and prayed to the LORD, 3 and said, "Remember, LORD, how I have conducted myself before you faithfully and wholeheartedly and have done what is good in your eyes." And Hezekiah wept bitterly.

4 Then the word of the LORD came to Isaiah, 5 "Go, tell Hezekiah, 'Thus says the LORD, the God of David your father: I have heard your prayer, *and*[729] I have seen your tears. See now, I will add fifteen years to your life. 6 Moreover I will rescue you and this city from the power of the king of Assyria. I will defend this city *for my sake and my servant David's sake.*'[730] 7 This will be the sign to you from the LORD, that the LORD does this thing which he has spoken: 8 See now, I will make the shadow on the steps of the *upper*[731] dial of Ahaz, marking *the*[732] setting

---

723. 1QIsa[a] and 4QIsa[b] MT use different forms.

724. 1QIsa[a]. *Jerusalem* 4QIsa[b] MT LXX.

725. 1QIsa[a]. *Mount Zion* 4QIsa[b] MT LXX.

726. 1QIsa[a]. *nor shoot an arrow there, nor oppose it with a shield, nor build up a siege-mound against it* MT.

727. 1QIsa[a]. Implicit in MT.

Chapter 38. 1QIsa[a]: all; 1QIsa[b]: 38:12–22.

728. 1QIsa[a] and MT use different forms.

729. 1QIsa[a]. Not in MT.

730. 1QIsa[a]. Not in MT LXX.

731. 1QIsa[a]. Not in MT.

732. 1QIsa[a]. Implicit in MT.

sun, return backward ten steps." Then the sun returned ten steps on the dial, steps on which it had descended.

9 A writing of Hezekiah king of Judah, after he had been sick and recovered from his illness:

10 I said, At the height of my life I must go. I must visit the gates of Sheol— *bitter are*[733] my years. 11 I said, I will not see *the* L ORD[734] in the land of *the*[735] living. *And*[736] I, among the inhabitants of the grave, will no longer look upon humans. 12 My dwelling is pulled up and *vanishes*[737] from me like a shepherd's tent. Like a weaver, I *make an accounting of*[738] my life. My threads are cut from the loom. Day and night you bring me to the finish. 13 *I am laid bare*[739] until morning. Just like a lion, he breaks all my bones. Day and night you bring me to the finish. 14 Like a swallow or a crane I chirp, I moan like a dove. My eyes look feebly on high. My Lord, *I am in distress;*[740] *so*[741] be my security. 15 What can I say, *I tell myself, since he has done this to me?*[742] I will walk slowly all my years because of the bitterness of my soul. 16 My Lord is against them *yet they live,*[743] and all of *them*[744] *who live have his spirit.*[745] Now you have restored my health and let me live. 17 Indeed, for my own good it was *exceedingly bitter*[746] for me. You yourself loved my life, delivering it from the pit of *its confinement.*[747] Yes, you have tossed all my sins behind your back. 18 For Sheol cannot glorify you, death *cannot*[748] praise you, *and*[749] those who descend into the grave cannot hope for your loyalty. 19 The living, it is the living who will praise you, as I do this day. Parents will make your faithful God

---

733. 1QIsa[a]. *the rest of* MT.

734. *Yah* 1QIsa[a]. *Yah Yah* MT.

735. Implicit in 1QIsa[a]. Explicit in MT.

736. 1QIsa[a]. Not in MT.

737. 1QIsa[a]. *is stripped* MT. A number of words in 38:12–17 are obscure in both 1QIsa[a] and MT.

738. 1QIsa[a]. *roll up* MT.

739. Both 1QIsa[a] and MT are obscure.

740. IQIsa[a] MT. *I have desire* 1QIsa[b].

741. 1QIsa[a]. Not in 1QIsa[b] MT.

742. 1QIsa[a]. *he has spoken to me, and it is he who has done it* MT.

743. 1QIsa[a] and 1QIsa[b] MT have different forms.

744. Masculine 1QIsa[a]. Feminine 1QIsa[b] MT.

745. 1QIsa[a]. *have the life of my spirit* MT.

746. 1QIsa[a]. *bitter, bitter* 1QIsa[b] MT.

747. 1QIsa[a]. *annihilation* MT.

748. 1QIsa[a]. Implied in MT.

749. 1QIsa[a]. Not in 1QIsa[b] MT.

known to their children. 20 O LORD, save me! *The living, the living will praise you, as I do this day. Parents will make your loyalty known to their children. O LORD, save me!*[750] *And we will make music with stringed instruments all the days of our lives in the house of the LORD.*[751]

21 Isaiah said, "Have them take[752] *a cake of figs and apply it to the boil so that he may recover."* 22 Hezekiah said, *"What will be the sign for me to go up to the house of the LORD?"*[753]

> ■ *The original scribe stopped after the opening words of verse 20; then a second scribe inserted additional text: a repetition of verse 19 and the beginning of 20, plus the rest of 20. Yet a third scribe added the two odd sentences in 21–22, which occur in 2 Kings 20, after verse 39. The resulting text (without the repetition) agrees with the text transmitted by the Masoretic Text and the Septuagint.*

39 1 At that time Merodach-baladan son of Baladan, king of Babylon, sent letters and a gift to Hezekiah, *when*[754] he heard that he had been sick but *he lived.*[755] 2 Hezekiah was delighted that they came and showed them *all of his*[756] treasure-houses: the silver, gold, spices, precious oil, all his armor, and everything that was in his storehouses. There was nothing in his palace or his entire *kingdom*[757] that Hezekiah failed to show them. 3 Then the prophet Isaiah came to King Hezekiah and said to him, "What did these men say, and where did they come from to visit you?" Hezekiah said, "From a far country—they came to visit me from Babylon." 4 Then he said, "What did they see in your palace?" Hezekiah answered, "They saw everything in my palace. There is nothing in my storehouses that I did not show them." 5 Then Isaiah said to Hezekiah, "Listen to the word of the LORD of hosts: 6 The time will indeed come when everything that is in your palace and that your ancestors have stored up till now *will be carried*[758] to Babylon. *They will come in, and*[759] nothing will be left, says the LORD.

---

750. A second scribe inserted into 1QIsaᵃ a repetition of vs 19 and the beginning of vs 20, with different spelling and a word missing.

751. The same second scribe continued with the rest of vs 20 (= MT). Not originally in 1QIsaᵃ.

752. MT. Not in 1QIsaᵃ.

753. Not in the original 1QIsaᵃ but added by yet a later, third scribe. In MT LXX.

Chapter 39. 1QIsaᵃ: all; 1QIsaᵇ: 39:1–8; 4QIsaᵇ: 39:1–8.

754. 1QIsa MT. *for* 4QIsaᵇ.

755. 1QIsaᵃ. *had recovered* MT.

756. 1QIsaᵃ. *the* MT.

757. 1QIsaᵃ. *realm* MT.

758. Plural 1QIsaᵃ. Singular MT.

759. 1QIsaᵃ. Not in MT.

7 Some of your own sons who will have come from *your loins,*[760] whom you will have begotten, they will take away *to be*[761] eunuchs in the palace of the king of Babylon." 8 Then Hezekiah said to Isaiah, "The word of the LORD which you have spoken is good," since he thought, "There will be peace and stability in my lifetime."

40 1 Comfort, comfort my people! says your God. 2 Speak tenderly to *Jerusalem,*[762] and declare to her that her hard service *is completed,*[763] that her punishment is accepted. Indeed she has received from the LORD's hand double for all her sins.

3 A voice cries out, "In the wilderness prepare the way of the LORD, *and*[764] in the desert make a smooth highway for our God. 4 Let every valley be raised and every mountain and hill be lowered. Let the uneven spots be leveled and the rough places made a plain. 5 The glory of the LORD will be revealed, and all flesh together will see it. The mouth of the LORD has spoken."

6 A voice says, "Proclaim!" So *I*[765] said, "What am I to proclaim?" "All flesh is grass, and all its beauty is like the flowers of the field. 7 The grass withers, the flowers fade, *when the breath of • • • • blows on it."* (*Surely the people are the grass.*) 8 *The* grass[766] *withers, the flowers fade, but the word of our God,*[767] but the word of our God[768] stands forever.

> ■ *The original scribe either wrote an early, short form of Isaiah 40:7–8 or skipped some original text; the early, short form is more likely, since it makes sense by itself and the Septuagint has the identical short form. In either case a later scribe filled in the longer form, repeating "but the word of our God," which the original scribe had already written. That later scribe is the same one who copied the* Rule of the Community *(1QS) from Cave 1, and he used four dots as a substitute for the divine name* YHWH.

9 Climb up a high mountain, messenger to Zion! Raise your voice powerfully, messenger to Jerusalem! Raise it; do not be afraid! Say to the cities of Judah, "Here is your God!" 10 Look, the Lord GOD comes with power, and his arm

---

760. 1QIsa[a]. *you* MT.

761. 1QIsa[a] and MT use different forms.

Chapter 40. 1QIsa[a]: all; 1QIsa[b]: 40:2–3; 4QIsa[b]: 40:1–4, 22–26; 5QIsa: 40:16, 18–19.

762. 1QIsa[a] regularly uses a different spelling than 4QIsa[b] MT.

763. Masculine 1QIsa[a]. Feminine MT.

764. 1QIsa[a]. Not in 1QIsa[b] 4QIsa[b] MT.

765. 1QIsa[a] LXX. *he* MT.

766. The secondary scribe of 1QIsa[a] misspells *grass.*

767. Not originally in 1QIsa[a] LXX. In MT.

768. 1QIsa[a] has *the word of our God* (= MT) but marks *the word of* for deletion.

rules for him. Look, his payment is with him, and his reward before him. 11 Like a shepherd he pastures his flock; he gathers the lambs in his arms, carries them near his heart, and gently leads the nursing sheep.

12 Who has measured *the waters of the sea*[769] in his palm? marked out the heavens with *his compass*[770] and measured out the dust of the earth in a measuring bowl? weighed the mountains in scales and the hills in a balance? 13 Who has directed the spirit of the LORD, or as his counselor has taught *him?*[771] 14 With whom did he consult, to instruct him and guide him in the ways of justice? *or taught him knowledge or showed him the ways of wisdom? 15 Look, the nations are like a drop from a bucket and are considered but dust on the balance. Look, he even*[772] *lifts up the islands like powder. 16 Lebanon is not sufficient fuel, nor are its beasts a sufficient burnt offering.*[773] 17 All the nations are as nothing to him, and*[774] he considers them *as*[775] nothingness and chaos.

▨ *Verses 14b–16 and the first two words of verse 20 were not written by the original scribe but were added by a later scribe in the space curiously left blank by the original scribe.*

18 To whom will you *compare me—God?*[776] or what likeness will you compare to *me?*[777] 19 The idol?—a craftsman *made the image,*[778] and a smith with gold *and*[779] hammered it out and cast silver chains; 20 *the poor person an offering,*[780] wood that will not *rot,*[781] and *chooses*[782] a skillful artisan *and*[783] *seeks*[784] to set up an image that will not topple.

---

769. 1QIsaᵃ *(my ym). the waters* MT *(mym).*

770. 1QIsaᵃ. *a compass* MT.

771. Refers to *spirit* in 1QIsaᵃ. To *the* LORD in MT.

772. 1QIsaᵃ. Not in MT.

773. 1QIsaᵃ⁽ᶜᵒʳʳ⁾ (wording added later) MT LXX.

774. 1QIsaᵃ. Not in MT.

775. 1QIsaᵃ. *as from* MT.

776. 1QIsaᵃ. *compare God* MT.

777. 1QIsaᵃ. *him* MT.

778. 1QIsaᵃ. *casts* MT.

779. 1QIsaᵃ. Not in MT.

780. 1QIsaᵃ⁽ᶜᵒʳʳ⁾ (wording added later) MT; the Hebrew is uncertain.

781. 1QIsaᵃ probably misspells the word.

782. 1QIsaᵃ. In MT, *chooses (a wood)* goes with the preceding clause.

783. 1QIsaᵃ. Not in MT.

784. 1QIsaᵃ probably misspells the word, which in MT goes with the preceding clause: *seeks (a skillful artisan).*

21 Have you not known? Have you not heard? Have you not been told from the beginning? Have you not understood from the foundations of *the*[785] earth? 22 He is the one who dwells above the disk of the earth, whose inhabitants are like grasshoppers. He is the one who stretches the skies like a curtain and spreads them out like a tent to dwell in, 23 who brings princes to nothing, who makes the judges of the earth like a void. 24 Scarcely are they planted, scarcely are they sown, scarcely *have*[786] their stalk taken root in the earth, *and*[787] then he *blows*[788] on them and they wither, and the whirlwind carries them away like stubble.

25 *To*[789] whom will *you*[790] compare me that I should be similar? says the Holy One. 26 Raise your eyes heavenward and see: Who has created these? He who draws out their host by number, who calls them all by name, by his great might and *his*[791] powerful strength, *and*[792] not one is missing. 27 Why do you say, Jacob, and claim, Israel, "My way is ignored by the LORD, and my case is passed over by my God?" 28 Do you not know? Have you not heard? The LORD is the eternal God, the Creator of the ends of the earth. He does not faint, he does not grow weary, *and*[793] his understanding is unfathomable. 29 *The*[794] one who gives might to the faint will make power abound in those without strength. 30 Even youths faint and grow weary and young men collapse, 31 but those who wait for the LORD will renew their strength. *Then*[795] they will ascend with wings like eagles. They will run and not grow weary. They will march and not faint.

41 1 Be silent before me, coastlands, and let the peoples renew their strength. Let them come near then speak together; let us approach for a ruling. 2 Who has roused victory from the east *and*[796] summoned it to his path *and*[797] delivers nations before him and *brings down*[798] kings, *and*[799] makes their swords like

---

785. Implicit in 1QIsa[a]. Explicit in MT.

786. 1QIsa[a]. *has* 4QIsa[b] MT LXX.

787. 1QIsa[a]. Not in 4QIsa[b] MT.

788. 1QIsa[a] misspells the word.

789. 1QIsa[a]. *And to* 4QIsa[b] MT.

790. Plural 1QIsa[a] MT. Singular 4QIsa[b].

791. 1QIsa[a]. Not in MT.

792. 1QIsa[a]. Not in MT.

793. 1QIsa[a]. Not in MT.

794. Explicit in 1QIsa[a]. Implicit in MT.

795. 1QIsa[a]. Not in MT.

Chapter 41. 1QIsa[a]: all; 1QIsa[b]: 41:3–23; 4QIsa[b]: 41:8–11; 5QIsa: 41:25?

796. 1QIsa[a]. Not in MT.

797. 1QIsa[a]. Not in MT.

798. 1QIsa[a] and MT use different forms.

799. 1QIsa[a]. Not in MT.

dust, their bows like *wind-driven*[800] chaff? 3 *And*[801] he pursues them *and*[802] travels on safely, by a way that his feet had not *known*.[803] 4 Who has acted and done it, calling the generations from the beginning? I, the LORD, the first and with the last, I am he.

5 The coastlands have seen and are afraid. The ends of the earth, *together,*[804] they have drawn near and *come*.[805] 6 They all help their neighbor. *They*[806] say to each other, "Take heart." 7 The carpenter encourages the smith, and the one who smoothes with the *hammer*[807] encourages the one who strikes the anvil. *He says*[808] of the soldering, "It is good," and reinforces it with nails, so that it cannot loosen.

8 But you, Israel my servant, Jacob whom I have chosen, seed of Abraham my friend, 9 you whom I encouraged at the ends of the earth and called from its corners and said to you, "You are my servant. I have chosen you, and I have not rejected you." 10 Do not fear, for I am with you. Do not be anxious, for I am your God. I strengthen you. I indeed help you. I indeed hold you up with my vindicating right hand. 11 *Look!*[809] All who are incensed at you will be disgraced and put to shame. Those who contend with you *will all die*.[810] 12 *Those who quarrel with you will be nothing,*[811] and non-existent those who fight you. 13 For I am the LORD your God, who strengthens your right hand, who says to you, "Do not be afraid. I will help you." 14 Do not fear, you worm Jacob *and*[812] people of Israel. I will help *you,*[813] says the LORD and *your*[814] Redeemer, the Holy One of Israel.

15 See, I will make *you*[815] into a new, sharp, multi-edged thresher. You will thresh and crush mountains and turn the hills to chaff. 16 You will winnow them,

---

800. 1QIsa^a and MT use different forms.

801. 1QIsa^a. Not in MT.

802. 1QIsa^a. Not in MT.

803. 1QIsa^a. *come* MT.

804. 1QIsa^a. *tremble* MT.

805. 1QIsa^a and MT use different forms.

806. 1QIsa^a. *And they* MT.

807. 1QIsa^a and MT have two different spellings.

808. 1QIsa^a. *saying* MT.

809. 1QIsa^{a(corr)} (word added by a later scribe). MT LXX.

810. 1QIsa^a. *will become nothing and be ashamed* 1QIsa^b. *will become nothing and die* MT.

811. 1QIsa^a. *You will seek but not find those who quarrel with you* MT.

812. 1QIsa^a. Not in MT.

813. Masculine 1QIsa^a. Feminine MT.

814. Masculine 1QIsa^a. Feminine MT.

815. Masculine 1QIsa^a. Feminine MT.

and the wind will carry them away, and the whirlwind will scatter them. You will rejoice in the LORD, *and*[816] you will glory in the Holy One of Israel.

17 The poor, *the needy, those seeking*[817] water when there is none, whose tongues are parched with thirst—I, the LORD, will answer them. I, the God of Israel, will not abandon them. 18 I will open up rivers on the bare heights and *fountains*[818] in the midst of the valleys. I will make *the*[819] wilderness a pool of water and the dry land springs of water. 19 In the wilderness, I will put the cedar, the acacia, the myrtle, and the olive; in the desert, I will set the cypress, the *yew,*[820] and the elm together; 20 so that together they may see and recognize, *consider*[821] and comprehend, that the hand of the LORD has done this, and the Holy One of Israel created it.

21 Present your case, says the LORD. Submit your arguments, says the King of Jacob. 22 Let them approach and tell us *what will happen.*[822] The former things, what were they? Tell us, so that we may consider *them and know.* Or[823] the latter things or the things to come, let us hear. 23 Report on what is to come in the future, so that we may know that you are gods. Yes, do good or do evil, so that we together may *hear*[824] and see it. 24 Indeed, *you and your work are nothing,*[825] and whoever chooses you is an abomination. 25 *You are*[826] stirring one up from the north, and *they are*[827] coming from the rising of the sun. *And*[828] he is called by *his*[829] name. *Rulers will come like mire*[830] and like the potter, *and*[831] he will trample the clay. 26 Who has declared it from the beginning, that we may know? *beforehand,*[832] that we may say, *"It is right"?*[833] Indeed, no one declared it, no one made a

---

816. 1QIsa^a. Not in MT.

817. 1QIsa^a. *and the needy seeking* MT.

818. Masculine 1QIsa^a. Feminine MT.

819. Explicit in 1QIsa^a. Implicit in MT.

820. 1QIsa^a and MT have different spellings of this obscure tree.

821. The 1QIsa^a scribe first wrote *perceive,* then wrote *consider* (= MT) above the line.

822. 1QIsa^a and MT use different forms.

823. 1QIsa^a *them. And we may know* MT.

824. 1QIsa^a. *stare at one another* MT.

825. 1QIsa^a. *you are nothing, and your work does not exist* MT.

826. 1QIsa^a. *I am* MT.

827. 1QIsa^a. *one is* MT.

828. 1QIsa^a. Not in MT.

829. 1QIsa^a. *my* MT.

830. 1QIsa^a. *He will come, rulers like mire* MT.

831. 1QIsa^a. Not in MT.

832. 1QIsa^a. *and beforehand* MT.

833. 1QIsa^a. *He is right* MT.

proclamation, no one heard your words. 27 First, for Zion, *there is slumber.*[834] To Jerusalem, I will send a messenger. 28 When I look, no one is there among them, no one gives counsel or responds when I inquire of them. 29 Indeed, none of them exists, *and*[835] their works are nothing. Their molten images are formless wind.

42 1 Here is my servant, whom I support, my chosen, in whom my soul delights. I have placed my spirit on him *so that*[836] he may deliver *his*[837] justice to the nations. 2 He will not cry out or raise his voice or make it heard in the street. 3 A crushed reed he will not break, and a faintly burning wick he will not *quench.*[838] He will truly bring forth justice. 4 *And*[839] he will not grow faint or be crushed until he has established justice on earth; and the coastlands will *inherit*[840] his law.

5 Thus says *the God, and God*[841] who created the heavens and stretched them out, who spread out the earth and its produce, who gives breath to the people upon it, and spirit to those who walk on it: 6 *I*[842] have called you in righteousness and have taken hold of your hand. I have preserved you and established you as *a covenant to the people,*[843] as a light to the nations, 7 to open blind eyes, to lead *those bound*[844] out of the dungeon *and*[845] those sitting in darkness out of the prison.

8 I the LORD am the one, *and*[846] I will not give my name or my glory to another nor my praise to idols. 9 See, the former things have come about, and I am announcing *the*[847] new things. Before they unfold I am making you aware of them.

10 Sing to the LORD a new song *and*[848] his praise from the end of the earth, you

---

834. 1QIsa[a]. *look, there they are* MT.

835. 1QIsa[a]. Not in MT.

Chapter 42. 1QIsa[a]: all; 4QIsa[b]: 42:2–7, 9–12; 4QIsa[g]: 42:14–25; 4QIsa[h]: 42:4–11.

836. 1QIsa[a]. Not in MT.

837. 1QIsa[a]. Not in MT.

838. Or perhaps *be quenched* 1QIsa[a]. *quench it* MT.

839. 1QIsa[a]. Not in 4QIsa[b] MT.

840. 1QIsa[a.] *wait for* 4QIsa[h] MT.

841. 1QIsa[a]. *the God the LORD* MT.

842. 1QIsa[a]. *I the LORD* 4QIsa[h] MT. *I the LORD God* LXX. Though not originally in 1QIsa[a], *the LORD* may possibly have been written above the line.

843. 1QIsa[a] MT LXX. *an everlasting covenant* 4QIsa[h].

844. 1QIsa[a]. *prisoners* 4QIsa[h] MT.

845. 1QIsa[a]. Not in 4QIsa[h] MT.

846. 1QIsa[a]. Not in 4QIsa[h] MT.

847. 1QIsa[a]. Not in 4QIsa[b] 4QIsa[h] MT.

848. 1QIsa[a]. Not in 4QIsa[h] MT.

who travel the sea and everything in it, coastlands and their inhabitants. 11 Let the desert *cry out,*[849] *its cities and the*[850] villages that Kedar inhabits, *and*[851] let the inhabitants of Sela sing for joy. Let them *shout aloud*[852] from the tops of the mountains. 12 Let them give glory to the LORD and declare his praise in the coastlands.

13 The LORD goes forth like a warrior. He fires up his furor like a man of war. *Showing his anger, he shouts aloud.*[853] He prevails against his enemies. 14 *Certainly*[854] I have kept silent for a long time. I have kept still and restrained myself. Now I will cry out like a woman giving birth; I will gasp and pant together. 15 I will devastate mountains and hills and dry up all their vegetation. I will make the rivers islands and dry up the ponds. 16 I will help the blind walk by a way *that*[855] they do not know. In paths they do not know I will lead them. I will make the *dark places*[856] before them light and rough places level. I will do these things and I will not abandon them. 17 Those who trust in idols will be turned back *and*[857] utterly *shamed,*[858] who say to images, "You are our gods."

18 Listen, you who are deaf; look, you who are blind, and see. 19 Who is blind but my servant or deaf like my messenger whom I send? Who is blind like the one allied with me and blind like the LORD's servant? 20 *You have seen*[859] many things, but you do not observe. His ears are *open,*[860] but he does not hear.

21 The LORD had desired, for the sake of his vindication, *that*[861] he should increase his torah and glorify *it.*[862] 22 Instead, this is a people despoiled and plundered. All of them are trapped in holes and hidden in *prisons.*[863] They have become prey whom no one rescues, *a spoil*[864] and no one says, "Restore."

---

849. Singular 1QIsa[a] 4QIsa[h] LXX. Plural MT.

850. 1QIsa[a]. *and its cities, the* MT.

851. 1QIsa[a]. Not in MT.

852. 1QIsa[a]. *cry joyfully* MT.

853. 1QIsa[a]. *He makes a war cry and shouts his anger aloud* MT.

854. 1QIsa[a]. Not in MT.

855. 1QIsa[a]. Not in MT.

856. 1QIsa[a] misspells the word. *dark place* MT.

857. 1QIsa[a]. Not in MT.

858. 1QIsa[a] and MT use different forms.

859. 1QIsa[a] MT. *To see* MT[qere].

860. 1QIsa[a]. *to open* MT.

861. Explicit in 1QIsa[a]. Implicit in MT.

862. Explicit in 1QIsa[a]. Implicit in MT.

863. Plural 1QIsa[a] MT LXX. Singular 4QIsa[g].

864. 1QIsa[a] and MT use different syntax here.

23 Who is among you *that*[865] will hear this? *Indeed*[866] let him pay attention and listen for the time to come. 24 Who gave Jacob over to be despoiled and Israel to plunderers? Was it not the LORD, against whom we have sinned, and in whose ways they were not willing *to*[867] walk and whose instruction they would not obey? 25 So he poured upon him *the heat of his anger*[868] and the *fierceness*[869] of war. It set hi[m] on fire all around, but he did not recognize it. It burned him, but he did not think about it.

43 1 But now thus says the LORD who created you, Jacob, and who formed you, Israel: Do not fear, for I have redeemed you. I have called you by name; you are mine. 2 When you pass through the waters, I will be with you, and through the rivers, they will not overwhelm you. When you walk through the fire, you will not be scorched, nor will the flame burn you.

3 *I*[870] am the LORD your God, the Holy One of Israel, your *Redeemer.*[871] *And*[872] I give *Egypt for your ransom,*[873] Cush and *the people of Seba*[874] in exchange for you. 4 Because you are precious in my sight and honored, and I love you, I give people in your stead and nations in exchange for your life. 5 Do not fear, for I am with you. I will bring your children from the east and gather you from the west. 6 I will say to the north, "Give up!" and to the south, "Do not hold back!" *Bring*[875] my sons from afar and my daughters from the *ends*[876] of the earth, 7 everyone who is called by my name, whom I created for my glory, whom I formed, whom I made. 8 *Bring forth*[877] the blind who have eyes and the deaf who have ears.

9 Let all the nations be gathered together, and let the peoples be assembled.

---

865. 1QIsa^a. Not in 4QIsa^g MT.

866. 1QIsa^a. Not in MT.

867. Explicit in 1QIsa^a. Implicit in MT.

868. 1QIsa^a. *the heat, his anger* 4QIsa^g MT.

869. 1QIsa^a spells the word differently than MT.

Chapter 43. 1QIsa^a: all; 1QIsa^b: 43:1–13, 23-27; 4QIsa^b: 43:12–15; 4QIsa^g: 43:1–4, 16–24.

870. 1QIsa^a. *For I* 1QIsa^b 4QIsa^g MT LXX.

871. 1QIsa^a. *Savior* MT LXX.

872. 1QIsa^a. Not in MT.

873. 1QIsa^a. *for your ransom Egypt* MT.

874. 1QIsa^a. *Seba* 1QIsa^b 4QIsa^g MT.

875. Masculine plural 1QIsa^a. Feminine singular MT.

876. 1QIsa^a and MT use different forms.

877. Plural 1QIsa^a. *I will bring forth* 1QIsa^b. *He has brought forth* MT.

Who is among them *that*[878] could *declare*[879] this or *announce*[880] the former things? Let them produce their witnesses so they can be vindicated. Let them *proclaim*[881] so people will say, "It is true."

10 You are my witnesses, says the LORD, and my servant whom I have chosen, so that you might know and trust me and understand that I am the one; before me no God was formed nor will there be after me. 11 I, I am the LORD, and besides me there is no savior. 12 I declared, I saved, I made it known. There was no strange god among you. You are my witnesses, says the LORD: I am God. 13 From this day forth, I am the one, and no one can deliver out of my hand. I work, and who can undo it?

14 Thus says the LORD, your Redeemer, the Holy One of Israel: For your sake I will send *to Babylon,*[882] and I will break down all the bars, and the Chaldeans' ringing cry will become lamentation. 15 I am the LORD, your Holy One, the Creator of Israel, your King. 16 Thus says the LORD, who makes a way in the sea and a path through the mighty waters, 17 who brings forth chariot and horse *and*[883] army and warrior together. They lie down, they cannot rise. They are extinguished, quenched like a wick.

18 *Do not remember*[884] the former things, nor consider the things of old. 19 I am about to do a new thing, *and*[885] it is now springing up. Do you not recognize it? I am making a road in the wilderness and *paths*[886] in the desert. 20 Wild animals, jackals and ostriches, will honor me, because I *am putting*[887] water in the wilderness and rivers in the desert, for *my people, my chosen,*[888] to drink, 21 the people which I formed for myself, *and*[889] that they might *speak*[890] my praise.

22 *And*[891] yet you have not invoked me, Jacob; indeed you are weary of me, Is-

---

878. 1QIsa[a]. Not in MT.

879. Plural 1QIsa[a]. Singular MT.

880. 1QIsa[a]. *announce to us* MT.

881. 1QIsa[a]. *hear* MT.

882. 1QIsa[a], 4QIsa[b], and MT each spell the word differently.

883. 1QIsa[a]. Not in MT.

884. Singular 1QIsa[a]. Plural MT.

885. 1QIsa[a]. Not in MT.

886. 1QIsa[a]. *streams* MT.

887. 1QIsa[a]. *have put* MT.

888. 1QIsa[a]. *my chosen people* MT.

889. 1QIsa[a]. Not in 4QIsa[g] MT.

890. 1QIsa[a]. *recount* 4QIsa[g] MT.

891. 1QIsa[a] MT. Not in MT[mss].

rael. 23 You have not brought me sheep for *a burnt offering,*[892] nor have you honored me *with*[893] your sacrifices. *You have not made meal offerings for me.*[894] I have not wearied you about frankincense. 24 *You*[895] have not bought me sweet cane with silver, nor satisfied me with the fat of your sacrifices. Instead, you have burdened me with your sins; you have wearied me with your iniquities.

25 I, I am the one who blots out your *transgression*[896] for my own sake, and I will *remember your sins no longer.*[897] 26 Recall it for me. Let us argue together. Present your case, so that you may be vindicated. 27 Your first ancestor sinned, and your interpreters have transgressed against me. 28 Therefore I profaned the holy princes; I devoted Jacob to destruction, and Israel to reviling.

44 1 But now hear, Jacob my servant and Israel whom I have chosen: 2 Thus says the LORD who made you, and formed you from the womb, *who will help*[898] you: Do not fear, Jacob my servant and Jeshurun whom I have chosen. 3 For I will pour water upon thirsty ground and streams on parched land. *Just so*[899] will I pour my spirit upon your descendants and my blessing upon your posterity. 4 *They*[900] *will spring up*[901] *like*[902] that which grows in the green grass, like willows by watercourses. 5 One will say, "I am the LORD's," and another will go by the name of Jacob, and another will have inscribed on his hand, "the LORD's," and adopt the name of Israel.

6 Thus says the LORD, the King of Israel and its Redeemer, the LORD of hosts *is his name:*[903] I am the first and I am the last, and apart from me there is no God. 7 Who is like me? Let him proclaim and announce it and set it in order for *himself,*[904] *making them*[905] an ancient people. And the future *let him say; what*[906] is to

---

892. 1QIsaª. *your burnt offerings* MT. *your burnt offering* LXX.

893. Explicit in 1QIsaª. Implicit in MT.

894. 1QIsaª. *I have not burdened you with meal offerings* 4QIsaᵍ MT. Not in LXX.

895. 1QIsaª 1QIsaᵇ MT. *And you* 4QIsaᵍ.

896. 1QIsaª. *transgressions* MT.

897. 1QIsaª. *not remember your sins* MT.

Chapter 44. 1QIsaª: all; 1QIsaᵇ: 44:21–28; 4QIsaᵇ: 44:19–28; 4QIsaᶜ: 44:3–7.

898. 1QIsaª. *he will help* MT.

899. 1QIsaª. Not in MT.

900. 1QIsaª. *And they* MT.

901. 1QIsaª and MT use different forms.

902. 1QIsaª. *among* MT.

903. 1QIsaª. Not in MT.

904. 1QIsaª. *me* MT

905. 1QIsaª. MT uncertain (*from my making?*).

906. 1QIsaª. *and what* 4QIsaᶜ MT.

come let them declare to them.

8 Do not be in awe. Do not be *afraid*.[907] Have I not declared to you of old? I announced it. You are my witnesses. Is there a god besides me? I know that there is no other rock. 9 *Now,*[908] all *forming of*[909] images is nothing, and the things they value will not profit. Their own witnesses do not see; *they*[910] do not know. So they will be put to shame.

10 Who would fashion a god or cast an image that is useless? 11 Certainly, all associated with it will be put to shame. The artisans, they are only human. Let them all gather together *and*[911] stand up. *Then*[912] let them be in awe. They will be put to shame together. 12 The ironworker prepares a tool with the coals and hammer, *and*[913] fashions it, working by the strength of his arm. Yes, if he were hungry, he would have no strength. If he were to drink no water, he would become faint.

13 The woodworker stretches *it*[914] out with a line; he traces its shape with a stylus. He *fashions*[915] it with planes and shapes it with a compass. He makes it like a human figure, with human beauty, to dwell in a shrine.

14 He cuts down cedars and takes a holm tree [or an o]ak. He secures for himself trees from the forest. He plants a fir tree, and the rain makes it grow. 15 *He divides it up*[916] for humans to burn. He takes part of it and warms himself. He kindles a fire and bakes bread. *Or perhaps*[917] he constructs a god and worships it; he makes it an idol and bows down to it. 16 Half of it he burns in the fire, *and*[918] *over*[919] that half *is meat so he may eat. He sits by its coals, warms himself,*[920] and says, "Ah, I am warm *in front of*[921] the fire." 17 The remainder of it he makes into a *god*.

---

907. 1QIsa[a]. MT misspells.

908. 1QIsa[a]. Not in MT.

909. 1QIsa[a]. *those who form* MT.

910. 1QIsa[a]. *and they* MT.

911. 1QIsa[a]. Not in MT.

912. 1QIsa[a]. Not in MT.

913. 1QIsa[a]. Not in MT.

914. 1QIsa[a]. Not in MT.

915. 1QIsa[a] and MT use different forms.

916. 1QIsa[a]. *It is* MT.

917. 1QIsa[a]. *Also* MT.

918. 1QIsa[a]. Not in MT.

919. 1QIsa[a(corr)] (wording added above the line).

920. 1QIsa[a]. *eats meat he roasted as a roast and is sated. He also warms himself* MT.

921. 1QIsa[a]. *I see* MT.

To blocks of wood he[922] bows down to it and worships, prays to it and says, "Deliver me, for you are my god."

18 They do not know. They do not understand. For their eyes are smeared, they cannot see; and their minds, they cannot think. 19 No one gives it any thought; there is no knowledge or understanding to think *to think,*[923] "Half of it I burned in the fire. I also baked food on its coals. *And*[924] I roasted meat and ate it. *And*[925] the rest of it I will make into *abominations?*[926] Will I bow down to *blocks*[927] of wood?" 20 He tends ashes. A deceived mind has turned him from the way. *It cannot his life,*[928] nor does he say, *"There is a lie in my right hand."*[929] 21 Remember these things, Jacob, *Israel,*[930] for you are my servant. I have formed you; you are a servant to me. *Israel,*[931] *you must not mislead me.*[932]

22 I have blotted out your transgression like a cloud and your sins like mist. Return to me; for I have redeemed you. 23 Shout, heavens, for the LORD has done it. Shout aloud, depths of *the*[933] earth. Burst out with singing, mountains, forest, and every tree in it. For the LORD has redeemed Jacob and will glorify himself in Israel. 24 Thus says the LORD, your Redeemer and the one who formed you in the womb: I am the LORD who made everything, who alone stretched out the heavens, who spread out the earth unassisted; 25 who frustrates the omens of the idle talkers and makes diviners mad, who turns the sages back and renders their knowledge *foolish;*[934] 26 who confirms the word of his servant and brings to fruition the counsel of his messengers; who says of Jerusalem, "It will be inhabited," and of the cities of Judah, "They will be rebuilt, and I will raise up their ruins"; 27 who says to the deep, "Be dry; I will dry up your rivers"; 28 who says of Cyrus, "He is my shepherd and will carry out everything I desire,"

---

922. *Blocks* is misspelled, or an error (for *to his Baals?*) in 1QIsa[a] (see vs 19). *god, for his idol.* *He* MT.

923. Repeated in 1QIsa[a]. Not in MT.

924. 1QIsa[a]. Not in MT.

925. 1QIsa[a] MT. Not in 4QIsa[b].

926. 1QIsa[a]. *an abomination* 4QIsa[b] MT.

927. 1QIsa[a]. *a block* MT.

928. 1QIsa[a] (word missing?). *It does not save his life* 4QIsa[b] MT.

929. 1QIsa[a]. *"Is there not a lie in my right hand?"* 4QIsa[b] MT.

930. 1QIsa[a]. *and Israel* 4QIsa[b] MT.

931. 1QIsa[a] MT. *and Israel* 4QIsa[b].

932. 1QIsa[a]. *you will not be forgotten by me.* 4QIsa[b] MT.

933. 1QIsa[a]. Not in MT.

934. 1QIsa[a] 1QIsa[b] 4QIsa[b] LXX. *wise* MT.

saying of Jerusalem, "It will be rebuilt," and of *my*[935] temple, "Your foundation will be laid again."

45 1 Thus says the LORD to his anointed, Cyrus, whose right hand I have strengthened to subdue nations before him, as I expose the loins of kings, to open the *doors*[936] before him and gates they cannot keep shut: 2 I myself will go before you, and *he*[937] will make *the mountains*[938] level. I will shatter bronze doors, cut through iron bars. 3 I will give you concealed treasures and secret riches hidden away, so that you will know that I, the LORD, who call you by name, am the God of Israel. 4 For Jacob my servant's sake, *Israel*[939] my chosen, *I have called you, and he has established you with a name,*[940] though you did not know me. 5 I am the LORD, and *there is none else besides me; and there are no gods.*[941] I will help you, though you did not know me, 6 so that they may know from east to west that there is none besides me. I am the LORD, and there is none else.

7 I form light and create darkness; I make *goodness*[942] and create evil. I am the LORD, who does all these things. 8 *Shout out, skies above and clouds, and let righteousness stream down.*[943] *The one who says to the earth, "Let salvation blossom, and let righteousness sprout forth."*[944]

9 Woe to the one who contends with his *makers,*[945] being just a potsherd among the potsherds of *the*[946] earth. *Woe to the one who says*[947] [to] the one who [f]orms him, "What are you doing?" or "Your work has no *human*[948] hands?" 10 Woe to *the*[949] one who says to a father, "What are you begetting?" or to a woman, ["What are you] bearing?"

---

935. 1QIsa^a. *the* 1QIsa^b MT.

Chapter 45. 1QIsa^a: all; 1QIsa^b: 45:1–3; 4QIsa^b: 45:20–25; 4QIsa^c: 45:1–4, 6–8.

936. Plural 1QIsa^a. Dual MT.

937. 1QIsa^a. *I* MT.

938. 1QIsa^a 1QIsa^b LXX. *the rises* MT.

939. 1QIsa^a. *and Israel* MT.

940. 1QIsa^a. *I have called you by your name, given you a title* MT.

941. 1QIsa^a. *there is none else; besides me there are no gods* MT.

942. 1QIsa^a. *well-being* MT.

943. 1QIsa^a. *Sprinkle, skies above, and let the clouds stream down righteousness* MT.

944. 1QIsa^a. *Let the earth open up, let them bear the fruit of salvation, and let righteousness sprout forth together. I the LORD have created it* 4QIsa^c(?) MT.

945. 1QIsa^a. *maker* MT.

946. Explicit in 1QIsa^a. Implicit in MT.

947. 1QIsa^a. *Will clay say* MT.

948. 1QIsa^a. Not in MT.

949. Explicit in 1QIsa^a. Implicit in MT.

11 Thus says the LORD, *the creator of the signs: Question me concerning my children, and concerning the work*[950] [of my hands co]mmand me? 12 I myself made the earth and humanity I created upon it. My own hand stretched out the skies; I commanded all [their host]. 13 I have aroused him with righteousness, and I will make all his paths smooth. It is he who will rebuild [my city] and free my [ex]iles, not for price nor reward, says the LORD of hosts.

14 [Thus says] the LORD: The wealth of Egypt, and the merchandise of Cush, *the*[951] Sabeans, men of *height,*[952] will come over to you, and they will be yours. They will walk [behind you]; in chains they will come over. They will bow down to you; they will pray to you, "Surely God is in you; and there is no other [Go]d [at all]." 15 Truly you are a hidden God, O God of Israel, the Savior. 16 They will be shamed, indeed, disgraced, all of them to[gether]; the makers of idols *will walk*[953] in confusion. 17 But Israel will be saved by the LORD with everlasting salvation. You will not be shamed or disgraced ever again.

18 For thus says the LORD who created the heavens—he is God *and*[954] the one who fashioned the earth and made it; *and*[955] he is the one who established it; not *for*[956] chaos did he create it, but to be inhabited he formed it—I am the LORD and there is no other. 19 I have not spoken in secret, at a place in a land of darkness; I did not say to the descendants of Jacob, "Seek me in chaos"; I, the LORD, spea[k] righteousness, declaring what is right. 20 Assemble and enter; draw near *and come,*[957] escapees from the nations. Those who carry their wooden idols know nothing, nor do those who pray to a god that cannot save. 21 Explain, present a case, even let them take counsel together. Who announced this long ago, declared it of old? Was it not I, the LORD? There is no other god besides me; a just God and Savior, *and*[958] there is none besides me. 22 Turn to me and be saved, all the ends of the earth; for I am God, and there is no other. 23 By myself I have sworn, from my mouth righteousness has gone forth, a word that will not come back: that to me every knee will bow, *and*[959] every tongue will swear. 24 "Only in

---

950. 1QIsaᵃ. *the Holy One of Israel and its creator: (About) the things to come question me; concerning my children and the work* MT. In 1QIsaᵃ, after LORD a later scribe added *the Holy One of Israel* above the line.

951. 1QIsaᵃ. *and the* MT.

952. Plural 1QIsaᵃ. Singular MT.

953. 1QIsaᵃ and MT use different forms.

954. 1QIsaᵃ. Not in MT.

955. 1QIsaᵃ. Not in MT.

956. Explicit in 1QIsaᵃ. Implicit in MT.

957. 1QIsaᵃ. *together* MT.

958. 1QIsaᵃ. Not in MT.

959. 1QIsaᵃ. Not in 4QIsaᵇ MT.

the LORD," *one will say*[960] of me, "are victories and might; to him *will come*[961] all who were incensed against him and they will be shamed. 25 In the LORD all the descendants of Israel will have victory and glory."

46 1 Bel bows down, Nebo stoops. Their images are on beasts, *on*[962] cattle. Your loads are *more burdensome than their reports.*[963] 2 They stoop, they bow down together, *and*[964] they are not able to rescue the burden, but themselves *go*[965] into captivity.

3 *Listen*[966] to me, house of Jacob, and all the remnant of the house of Israel, carried from birth, *and*[967] borne from the womb: 4 *Even*[968] till old age I am he, and even till I have grown gray I will carry you. It is I who have made, and I who will bear, and I who will carry and save. 5 To whom will you liken me, and *consider me equal,*[969] or compare me, that *I*[970] may seem similar? 6 Those who pour gold *into*[971] a purse and weigh silver in a balance hire a goldsmith, that he may *make*[972] a god; *and*[973] they prostrate themselves and even worship it. 7 *And*[974] they lift *it*[975] onto their shoulder and carry it and set it in its place. It stands there and *does not move*[976] from its place. Indeed, one may *cry out to*[977] it, but it cannot answer nor deliver anyone from distress.

8 Remember this, and remain firm; recall it to mind, you sinners. 9 Remem-

---

960. 1QIsa[a] and MT use different forms.

961. Plural 1QIsa[a] MT[mss] LXX. Singular MT.

Chapter 46. 1QIsa[a]: all; 1QIsa[b]: 46:3–13; 4QIsa[b]: 46:1–3; 4QIsa[c]: 46:8–13; 4QIsa[d]: 46:10–13.

962. 1QIsa[a]. *and on* MT.

963. 1QIsa[a]. *burdensome, the load upon a weary (beast)* 4QIsa[b](?) MT.

964. 1QIsa[a]. Not in MT.

965. Plural 1QIsa[a]. Singular 4QIsa[b] MT.

966. Singular 1QIsa[a]. Plural MT.

967. 1QIsa[a]. Not in 1QIsa[b] MT.

968. 1QIsa[a]. *and even* MT.

969. Singular verb + object? 1QIsa[a]. *consider equal* (plural; no object) MT.

970. 1QIsa[a]. *we* MT.

971. 1QIsa[a]. *out of* MT.

972. 1QIsa[a]. *make it* MT.

973. 1QIsa[a]. Not in MT.

974. 1QIsa[a]. Not in MT.

975. 1QIsa[a] and MT have different forms of the object here and with the next two verbs.

976. 1QIsa[a]. *one does not remove it* MT.

977. 1QIsa[a] and MT have different forms of both the verb and the preposition.

ber the former things of old; for I am God, and there is no other. I am God, and there is none like me, 10 declaring from the beginning *things to follow,*[978] and from ancient times things that have not yet happened, saying, My counsel will stand, and whatever I desire *he*[979] will do; 11 calling a bird of prey from the east, and from a distant country a man *with his*[980] purpose. Indeed, I have spoken, I will certainly bring it to pass; I planned *it,*[981] I will certainly do it. 12 Listen to me, you bold-hearted, who are far from triumph: 13 my triumph *is brought near, and*[982] it is not far off, and my deliverance, *and*[983] it will not tarry. *I*[984] will give deliverance in Zion, *and*[985] to Israel my glory.

47 1 Come down and sit in the dust, virgin daughter of Babylon. Sit *on*[986] the ground without a throne, daughter of the Chaldeans; for no more *will they call*[987] you delicate and attractive. 2 Take the millstones and grind meal. Remove your veil, strip off your *robes,*[988] uncover your leg, pass through the rivers. 3 Your nakedness *will be*[989] uncovered, and your shame will also be seen. I will exact vindication, and no mortal will I spare. 4 Our Redeemer—the LORD of hosts is his name, the Holy One of Israel. 5 Sit *silent,*[990] and enter into the darkness, daughter of the Chaldeans; for no more *will they call*[991] you mistress of kingdoms. 6 I was angry with my people, *and*[992] I profaned my heritage and gave them into your power. *You*[993] showed them no mercy; upon the elderly *you laid*[994] your yoke very

---

978. 1QIsa^a. *the latter things* 4QIsa^c. *the future* MT.

979. 1QIsa^a. *I* 4QIsa^c MT.

980. 1QIsa^a 4QIsa^c MT^ketib. *of my* MT^qere LXX.

981. Explicit in 1QIsa^a. Implicit in 4QIsa^c MT.

982. 1QIsa^a. *I have brought near* 4QIsa^c MT.

983. 1QIsa^a. Not in 1QIsa^b MT.

984. 1QIsa^a. *And I* 4QIsa^c MT.

985. 1QIsa^a. Not in 1QIsa^b 4QIsa^c 4QIsa^d MT.

Chapter 47. 1QIsa^a: all; 1QIsa^b: 47:1–14; 4QIsa^d: 47:1–6, 8–9.

986. 1QIsa^a and MT use different prepositions.

987. 1QIsa^a and MT use alternate forms.

988. 1QIsa^a. *skirt* MT.

989. 1QIsa^a. *let it be* MT.

990. 1QIsa^a and MT use alternate forms.

991. 1QIsa^a and MT use alternate forms.

992. 1QIsa^a. Not in MT.

993. 1QIsa^a and MT use alternate forms.

994. 1QIsa^a and MT use alternate forms.

heavily. 7 You said, "Always shall I be mistress forever." *You did not take*[995] these things into *your*[996] thinking nor were *you mindful*[997] of their *consequences.*[998]

8 Now hear this, voluptuous one, sitting securely enthroned, who says in her heart: "I am the one, and there will be none besides me; I will not live as a widow, nor will I *see*[999] the loss of children." 9 Both these things will come upon you suddenly on a single day: childlessness and widowhood. They will come upon you in full, despite the multitude of your incantations and your very power-ful spells. 10 You trusted in your *knowledge.*[1000] *You*[1001] said, "No one sees me"— but your wisdom and your knowledge have misled you. You said in your *heart,*[1002] "I am the one, and there will be none besides me"— 11 but evil will *come*[1003] upon you *and*[1004] you will not know how to charm it away; disaster will befall you of which you will not be able *to*[1005] rid yourself, and devastation will come upon you suddenly, *and*[1006] you will have no foreknowledge of it.

12 *But*[1007] stand up now with your spells and with the multitude of your incan-tations, with which *you have toiled*[1008] from your *youth until today*[1009] 13 *according to*[1010] your multiple schemes. Let them stand up now and save you, those who *con-jure*[1011] the heavens *and*[1012] gaze at the stars, predicting at the new moons what *is about to happen to them.*[1013] 14 See, they are like stubble that the fire burns. They *did*[1014] not deliver themselves from the power of the flame. This is no coal for

---

995. 1QIsa[a] and MT use alternate forms.

996. 1QIsa[a] and MT use alternate forms.

997. 1QIsa[a] and MT use alternate forms.

998. 1QIsa[a] and MT use alternate forms.

999. 1QIsa[a]. *know* 4QIsa[d] MT LXX.

1000. 1QIsa[a]. *evil* MT.

1001. 1QIsa[a] and MT use alternate forms.

1002. 1QIsa[a] and MT use alternate forms.

1003. Feminine (correctly) 1QIsa[a]. Masculine (incorrectly) MT.

1004. 1QIsa[a]. Not in MT.

1005. Explicit in 1QIsa[a]. Implicit in MT.

1006. 1QIsa[a]. Not in MT.

1007. 1QIsa[a]. Not in MT.

1008. 1QIsa[a] and MT use alternate forms.

1009. 1QIsa[a]. *youth. Perhaps you can gain some profit; perhaps you may inspire fear* MT.

1010. 1QIsa[a]. *You are wearied by* MT.

1011. 1QIsa[a]. *divide* MT.

1012. 1QIsa[a]. Not in MT.

1013. 1QIsa[a]. *(things) are about to happen to you* MT.

1014. 1QIsa[a]. *can* MT.

warming oneself, no hearthfire to sit before. 15 So will those be to you, those with whom *you have toiled,*[1015] those with whom you have trafficked from your youth. They each wander on their far-off way; there is none to save you.

48 1 Hear this, house of Jacob, who are called by the name of Israel and have come forth from the *loins*[1016] of Judah, who swear by the name of the LORD and invoke the God of Israel, but not in truth, nor in righteousness— 2 for they call themselves after the holy city, and rely upon the God of Israel; the LORD of hosts is his name: 3 I announced the former things long ago; *it*[1017] went forth out of my mouth, and I disclosed them. Suddenly I acted, and they came to pass.

> ▪ *In verse 4 the text from which the scribe copied apparently read "Because I knew that. . . ." But either that original copy or the scribe knew another tradition, recorded in the Masoretic Text, and so placed dots above and below three of the letters to yield "my knowledge" instead of "I knew."*

4 Because of my knowledge that you are stubborn, that your neck is an iron sinew, and your forehead brass, 5 I had declared it to you long ago; before it happened I had announced it to you, lest you should say, "My idol did them; *my*[1018] carved or metal idol commanded them." 6 You had heard it. Observe all this; and yourselves, will you not declare it? From now on, I make new things known to you, hidden things *which*[1019] you have not known. 7 They are created now, not long ago. Before today *you*[1020] had not heard them, lest you should say, "Look, I knew *them.*"[1021] 8 *And*[1022] neither had *you*[1023] heard, nor did you know, nor *was your ear uncovered*[1024] long ago. Indeed, I knew *that*[1025] you would act very deceitfully, and *they would call*[1026] you a rebel from the womb. 9 For my name's sake I

1015. 1QIsaᵃ and MT use alternate forms.

Chapter 48. 1QIsaᵃ: all; 1QIsaᵇ: 48:17–22; 4QIsaᵇ: 48:6–8; 4QIsaᶜ: 48:10–15, 17–19; 4QIsaᵈ: 48:8–22.

1016. Misspelled in both 1QIsaᵃ and MT.

1017. 1QIsaᵃ. *they* MT.

1018. 1QIsaᵃ. *and my* MT.

1019. Feminine (correctly) 1QIsaᵃ. Masculine (incorrectly) MT.

1020. 1QIsaᵃ and MT use different forms.

1021. Masculine 1QIsaᵃ. Feminine MT.

1022. 1QIsaᵃ. Not in MT.

1023. 1QIsaᵃ and MT use different forms.

1024. Or, *did you uncover your ear* 1QIsaᵃ. *did your ear uncover (it)* MTᴸ. *had your ear been uncovered* MTᶜ.

1025. 1QIsaᵃ. Not in MT.

1026. 1QIsaᵃ. *calling* 4QIsaᵈ MT.

delay my anger, and for my *beginning*[1027] I restrain it for you, so that I need not cut you off.

10 Look, I have refined you, but not with silver; I have *purified*[1028] you in the furnace of affliction. 11 For my own sake, for my own sake, I do it; indeed, how can *I be profaned?*[1029] And my glory I will not give to another.

■ *There are many minor variants between the scrolls and the Masoretic Text in the following passage. Many are probably inadvertent changes or misreadings, but the meaning is sometimes noticeably affected.*

12 Listen to *these things,*[1030] Jacob, and Israel whom I have called: I am he; I am the first, I am *also*[1031] the last. 13 Moreover, my *hands laid*[1032] the foundation of the earth, *and*[1033] my right hand spread out the heavens. I call to them, *and*[1034] they stand up at once. 14 *Let all of them assemble and listen.*[1035] Who is there among them that *could declare*[1036] these things? The LORD loves *me, and he will accomplish my purpose*[1037] against Babylon, *its*[1038] army the Chaldeans. 15 I myself have spoken; indeed, I have *called and*[1039] I have brought him, and *his path will be successful.*[1040] 16 Draw near to me, *and*[1041] hear this: from the beginning I have not spoken in secret; *at*[1042] the time it came to be, I was there. And now the LORD God has sent me and his spirit.

17 Thus says the LORD, your Redeemer, the Holy One of Israel: I am the LORD your God, who teaches you to profit, *who leads you*[1043] on the way by

---

1027. Or, *profanation* 1QIsaᵃ. *praise* 4QIsaᵈ MT.

1028. 1QIsaᵃ. MT uses an alternate verb that can also mean *chosen*.

1029. 1QIsaᵃ 4QIsaᶜ. *it be profaned* MT (or, *I wait* 1QIsaᵃ 4QIsaᶜ. *it wait* MT).

1030. 1QIsaᵃ. *me* MT.

1031. 1QIsaᵃ MT and 4QIsaᵈ use alternate forms.

1032. 1QIsaᵃ. *hand laid* MT.

1033. 1QIsaᵃ MT. Not in 4QIsaᵈ.

1034. 1QIsaᵃ. Not in MT.

1035. 1QIsaᵃ LXX. *Assemble, all of you, and listen!* 4QIsaᵈ MT.

1036. 1QIsaᵃ. *has declared* 4QIsaᵈ MT.

1037. 1QIsaᵃ (misspelling *accomplish*). *him. He will accomplish his purpose* 4QIsaᵈ MT.

1038. 1QIsaᵃ. *and its* MT.

1039. 1QIsaᵃ. *called him* MT.

1040. Feminine 1QIsaᵃ. Masculine 4QIsaᵈ MT (either = 1QIsaᵃ or *he will make his path successful*). *I will make his path successful* LXX.

1041. 1QIsaᵃ. Not in MT.

1042. 1QIsaᵃ. *from* MT.

1043. 1QIsaᵃ misspells this form.

which[1044] you should go. 18 *But*[1045] would that you had paid attention *to*[1046] my commandments! Then your peace *would be*[1047] like a river, and your vindication like the waves of the sea. 19 Your descendants would be like the sand, and *your offspring*[1048] like the grains of sand. Their name would not be cut off or destroyed from before me.

20 Go forth from Babylon; flee from the Chaldeans! With a festive shout declare, and announce *this*[1049] to the *ends*[1050] of the earth: "The LORD has redeemed his servant Jacob." 21 They did not thirst when he led *him*[1051] through the desolate places. He made water *flow*[1052] from a rock for them; he split a rock, and water flowed forth.

22 *And*[1053] there is no peace, says the LORD, for the wicked.

49 1 Listen to me, O coastlands; *pay*[1054] attention, peoples from afar. The LORD has called me from the womb; while yet inside my mother my name he pronounced. 2 He made my mouth like a sharp sword; in the shadow of his *hands*[1055] he hid me. He made me *like*[1056] a polished arrow; in his *quivers*[1057] he concealed me. 3 He said to me, "You are my servant, Israel, in whom I will glorify myself."

4 *I*[1058] said, "For nothing have I labored. I have exhausted my strength on *worthlessness*[1059] and *on*[1060] emptiness. Yet my cause is with the LORD, and my reward is with my God."

1044. 1QIsaᵃ. Not in 4QIsaᶜ 4QIsaᵈ MT.

1045. 1QIsaᵃ 1QIsaᵇ 4QIsaᶜ. Not in MT.

1046. 1QIsaᵃ and MT use different prepositions.

1047. 1QIsaᵃ and MT use different forms.

1048. 1QIsaᵃ. *the offspring of your loins* MT.

1049. 1QIsaᵃ. *this. Send it forth* 4QIsaᵈ MT.

1050. 1QIsaᵃ. *end* 4QIsaᵈ MT.

1051. 1QIsaᵃ. *them* 4QIsaᵈ MT.

1052. 1QIsaᵃ uses, in contrast to 1QIsaᵇ 4QIsaᵈ MT, the synonym for *flow* which all have in the next clause.

1053. 1QIsaᵃ. Not in MT.

Chapter 49. 1QIsaᵃ: all; 1QIsaᵇ: 49:1–15; 4QIsaᵇ: 49:21–23; 4QIsaᶜ: 49:22; 4QIsaᵈ: 49:1–15.

1054. 1QIsaᵃ. *and pay* MT.

1055. 1QIsaᵃ. *hand* MT.

1056. 1QIsaᵃ. Not in 4QIsaᵈ MT.

1057. 1QIsaᵃ. *quiver* 1QIsaᵇ 4QIsaᵈ MT.

1058. 1QIsaᵃ. *But I* 4QIsaᵈ MT.

1059. 1QIsaᵃ misspells this form.

1060. Explicit in 1QIsaᵃ. Implicit in MT.

5 And now says the LORD—who formed *you*[1061] from the womb as his servant, to bring Jacob back to him again, that Israel might be gathered to *him;*[1062] I have gained honor in the sight of the LORD, and my God has been my *help*[1063]— 6 he says, "It is too small a thing that you should be my servant, to raise up the tribes of *Israel*[1064] and bring back the preserved of *Jacob.*[1065] I will also give you as a light to the nations, to be my salvation to the *ends*[1066] of the earth."

7 Thus says *my Lord,*[1067] the LORD *your Redeemer, Israel,*[1068] and his Holy One, to one *despised,*[1069] to *ones abhorred*[1070] as a nation, to a servant of rulers—kings *see and rise, and princes*[1071] will bow down, because of the LORD who is faithful, the Holy One of Israel, *the one*[1072] who chose you— 8 thus says the LORD: In a time of favor I *will answer*[1073] you, and in a day of salvation I *will help*[1074] you. I have protected you, and given you as a covenant of the people, to reestablish the land, to redistribute the inheritances that have been devastated; 9 saying to prisoners, "Come out!" *and*[1075] to those who are in darkness, "Go free!" They will feed upon *all the mountains,*[1076] and their pasture will be on all the heights. 10 They will not hunger or thirst, nor will the scorching desert or sun harm them; for one who has compassion on them will lead them and guide them along springs of water. 11 I will turn all my mountains into a road, and my highways will be elevated. 12 See, they will come from afar: these from the north and from the west, and others from the land of *Syene.*[1077]

13 Sing out, heavens, and rejoice, earth! *Break out, mountains*[1078] into song! The

---

1061. 1QIsa\a. *me* MT.

1062. 1QIsa\a MT\qere. 4QIsa\d MT\L misspell this form.

1063. 1QIsa\a. *strength* MT.

1064. 1QIsa\a. *Jacob* MT.

1065. 1QIsa\a. *Israel* MT.

1066. 1QIsa\a. *end* MT.

1067. 1QIsa\a. Not in MT.

1068. 1QIsa\a. *the Redeemer of Israel* MT.

1069. 1QIsa\a and MT use different forms.

1070. 1QIsa\a. *one abhorred* MT.

1071. 1QIsa\a. *will see, and princes will rise, and they* MT.

1072. 1QIsa\a. *and the one* MT.

1073. 1QIsa\a. *have answered* MT.

1074. 1QIsa\a. *have helped* MT.

1075. 1QIsa\a. Not in MT.

1076. 1QIsa\a. *the ways* MT.

1077. 1QIsa\a. *Sinim* MT.

1078. 1QIsa\a. *Let the mountains break out* MT.

LORD *is comforting*[1079] his people and will have compassion upon his oppressed ones.

■ *In the second clause of verse 14 the scribe of 1QIsaᵃ first wrote "my Lord" (in agreement with the Masoretic Text), then wrote "my God" above it, at least as an alternative reading but probably as the preferred reading.*

14 But Zion had said, "The LORD has abandoned me; *my God*[1080] has forgotten me." 15 Can a woman forget her infant, lack compassion for the child of her womb? Even these may forget; I, however, I will not forget you. 16 Look, I have inscribed you upon the palms of my hands, *and*[1081] your walls are constantly before me. 17 Your *builders*[1082] are working faster than your destroyers, and those who devastated you will depart from you. 18 *Look up*[1083] all around and see: they have all gathered to come to you. As I live, says the LORD, you will be clothed with all of them like ornaments and adorn yourself with them like a bride. 19 Indeed, your ruins, your desolate places, your destroyed land—indeed now you will be too cramped for inhabitants, and those who would swallow you up will be far distant. 20 You will yet hear the children of your bereavement say, "This place is too cramped for me. Make space for me where I may settle." 21 Then you will say to yourself, "Who has begotten these for me—though I was bereaved and barren, *and*[1084] an exile and cast away—*who*[1085] has raised these? Behold, I was left in solitude; these, from where did they come?"

22 *For*[1086] thus says *the LORD:*[1087] Watch, I will lift up my hand to the nations and raise my signal to *the*[1088] peoples. They will bring your sons in their arms, and your daughters will be carried on their shoulders. 23 *Ho,*[1089] kings will be your foster fathers and their princesses those nursing for you. They will bow to you with their faces to the earth and lick the dust of your feet. Then you will know that I am the LORD. Those who wait for me will not be shamed. 24 Can *they seize*

1079. 1QIsaᵃ. *has comforted* MT.

1080. 1QIsaᵃ⁽ᶜᵒʳʳ⁾ (with *my God* written above *my Lord*). *my Lord* MT.

1081. 1QIsaᵃ. Not in MT.

1082. 1QIsaᵃ Aquila Vulg. *sons* MT.

1083. 1QIsaᵃ misspells this form.

1084. 1QIsaᵃ. Not in MT.

1085. 1QIsaᵃ. *and who* MT.

1086. 1QIsaᵃ. Not in MT.

1087. 1QIsaᵃ. *my Lord the* LORD MT.

1088. Explicit in 1QIsaᵃ. Implicit in MT.

1089. 1QIsaᵃ (*whwy;* see 55:1). *It will happen that* (= *whyw*) MT.

prey[1090] from a warrior, *or*[1091] the captives of a *tyrant*[1092] be rescued? 25 Thus says the LORD: Even the *prey*[1093] of the warrior will be *seized,*[1094] and the *captives*[1095] of the tyrant will be rescued. I myself will oppose *those who oppose you,*[1096] and I myself will save your children. 26 Those who maltreat you *I will make eat*[1097] their own flesh; and they will be drunk with their own blood as with sweet wine. Then all flesh will know that I am the LORD, your Savior, and your Redeemer, the Mighty One of Jacob.

50 1 Thus says the LORD: Where is your mother's divorce decree, by which I sent her away? Or to which of my creditors have I sold you? Look, because of your sins you were sold, and because of your transgressions your mother was sent away. 2 Why, when I came, was there no one there? When I called, was there no answer? Was my hand too limited to redeem? *Have*[1098] I no strength to rescue? Look, with my rebuke I dry up the sea, transform the rivers into a wilderness. Their fish stink for lack of water and die of thirst. 3 I spread darkness over the heavens and make sackcloth their covering.

4 My Lord the LORD has given me a learned tongue to know how to sustain the weary with words. *And*[1099] he stirs morning after morning, *and*[1100] he stirs my ear to listen like those being instructed. 5 My Lord *God*[1101] has opened my ear, and I did not rebel; I have not shrunk back. 6 I gave my back to those who beat me and my cheeks to those who *pulled out the beard.*[1102] My face I did not *turn aside*[1103] from insults and spitting. 7 My Lord the LORD will help me, so I will not be shamed. So I have made my face like flint, and I know that I will not be put to shame. 8 He who justifies me is near. Who will dispute with me? Let us stand up together. Who has a case against me? Let him approach me. 9 See, my Lord the

---

1090. 1QIsaᵃ. *prey be seized* MT.

1091. 1QIsaᵃ. MT adds an extra particle.

1092. 1QIsaᵃ. *righteous one* MT.

1093. 1QIsaᵃ. *captives* MT.

1094. 1QIsaᵃ spells the word differently than MT.

1095. Or, *returnees* 1QIsaᵃ. *prey* MT.

1096. 1QIsaᵃ. *your opponent* MT.

1097. 1QIsaᵃ misspells this word so that it appears to say *I will eat.*

Chapter 50. 1QIsaᵃ: all; 1QIsaᵇ: 50:7–11.

1098. 1QIsaᵃ. *Or have* MT.

1099. 1QIsaᵃ. Not in MT.

1100. 1QIsaᵃ. Not in MT.

1101. 1QIsaᵃ. *the LORD* MT.

1102. MT. 1QIsaᵃ has a different word or errs.

1103. 1QIsaᵃ. *hide* MT.

LORD will help me. Who is it that will condemn me? See, they will all wear out like a garment; the moth will eat them. 10 Who among you *revere*[1104] the LORD, obeying the voice of his servant? Who *walk*[1105] *in darkness*[1106] and have no light? Let him trust in the name of the LORD, and rely upon his God. 11 But, all *those*[1107] who light a fire, who surround yourselves with torches, walk by the light of your fire, and by the torches that you have set ablaze. You will have this from my hand: you will lie down in the place of torment.

51 1 Listen to me, you who pursue righteousness, who seek the LORD. Look to the rock from which you were hewn, to the quarry from which you were dug. 2 Look to Abraham your father, and to Sarah who bore you. For when he was only one person I called him. I *made him fruitful*[1108] and made him many. 3 For the LORD will comfort Zion, comfort all her waste places. He will make her wilderness like Eden, and her desert like the garden of the LORD. Joy and gladness will be *found*[1109] in her, thanksgiving and the sound of music. *Sorrow and mourning will flee away.*[1110]

4 Pay attention to me, my people! Listen to me, my nation! For a law will go forth from me, and my justice will be a light for the peoples. I will quickly bring 5 my victory near; my salvation will go forth. *His arm*[1111] will *judge*[1112] the peoples, the coastlands will wait for *him,*[1113] and in *his*[1114] arm they will hope. 6 Raise your eyes *to*[1115] the heavens, and look to the earth beneath, *and see who created these.*[1116]

Its inhabitants will die like a gnat, but my salvation will be forever, and my victory will not fail.

7 Listen to me, you who know righteousness, people who have my law in

---

1104. Plural 1QIsaᵃ. Singular MT.

1105. Plural 1QIsaᵃ. Singular MT.

1106. 1QIsaᵃ and MT have different forms.

1107. 1QIsaᵃ. *you* MT.

Chapter 51. 1QIsaᵃ: all; 1QIsaᵇ: 51:1–10; 4QIsaᵇ: 51:1–2, 14–16; 4QIsaᶜ: 51:8–16.

1108. 1QIsaᵃ. *blessed him* MT.

1109. Plural 1QIsaᵃ. Singular MT.

1110. 1QIsaᵃ. Not in MT; see 51:11.

1111. 1QIsaᵃ. *My arms* MT.

1112. Plural in both 1QIsaᵃ and MT.

1113. 1QIsaᵃ. *me* MT.

1114. 1QIsaᵃ. *my* MT.

1115. Implicit in 1QIsaᵃ. Explicit in MT.

1116. 1QIsaᵃ. *for the heavens will disappear like smoke, and the earth will wear out like a garment* 1QIsaᵇ MT LXX.

their hearts. Do not fear the insults of mortals, nor be dismayed at their *hateful words*.[1117] 8 For the moth will eat them up like a garment, and the worm will eat them like wool; but my victory will be forever, and my salvation to all generations.

9 Awake, awake, be clothed with strength, arm of the LORD! Awake, as in the days of old, ancient times. Was it not you who *broke*[1118] *Rehob*[1119] to pieces, who pierced the sea monster? 10 Was it not you who dried up Sea, the waters of the great deep, who made *in*[1120] the depths of the sea a path for the redeemed to pass over? 11 The *dispersed*[1121] of the LORD will return, and enter Zion with singing. Everlasting joy *will be*[1122] upon their heads. They will *attain*[1123] joy and gladness, *and*[1124] sorrow and mourning will *flee away*.[1125]

12 I, I am he who comforts you. Who are you, that you are afraid of humans who will die, and of mortals *made*[1126] like grass? 13 that you forgot the LORD who made you, who stretched out the heavens and established the earth, and you continue to fear every day the fury of the oppressor *since he is ready to destroy? Where is the fury of the oppressor?*[1127] 14 *Distress*[1128] will quickly be freed. He will not die for the Pit, nor will he lack food.

15 I am the LORD your God, stirring up the sea, so that its waves roar—the LORD of Hosts is his name. 16 *I*[1129] have put my words in your mouth, and with the shadow of my hand have covered you, to plant the heavens and to establish the earth, to say to Zion, "You are my people."

17 Awake, awake, stand up, Jerusalem, who drank at the hand of the LORD the cup of his anger. To the bottom of the cup of staggering you drank and drained it. 18 There is no one to guide *you*[1130] out of all the children she bore, none to

---

1117. 1QIsa[a] perhaps misspells the word.

1118. 1QIsa[a] 4QIsa[c]. *hewed* MT.

1119. 1QIsa[a] 4QIsa[c](?) spell the word differently than MT.

1120. 1QIsa[a]. Not in MT.

1121. 1QIsa[a(corr)] (with original scribe first writing *redeemed* and then replacing it with *dispersed*). *redeemed* MT.

1122. Implicit in 1QIsa[a] MT LXX. Explicit in 4QIsa[c].

1123. 1QIsa[a] and 4QIsa[c] MT use different forms.

1124. 1QIsa[a] 4QIsa[c] MT[mss]. Not in MT LXX.

1125. Singular 1QIsa[a]. Plural MT.

1126. 1QIsa[a] and MT have different forms.

1127. The scribe of 1QIsa[a] apparently skipped from *oppressor* to *oppressor* but luckily was able to write the omitted words at the top of the new column.

1128. 1QIsa[a]. *The one stooped over* MT.

1129. 1QIsa[a] LXX. *And I* 4QIsa[b] MT.

1130. 1QIsa[a]. *her* MT.

take her by the hand out of all the children she raised. 19 These two things have come upon you—who will empathize with you? ruin and destruction, famine and the sword. Who will comfort you? 20 Your sons have fainted. They lie at the end of every street, like an antelope in a trap, filled with the anger of the LORD, the rebuke of your God.

21 Therefore listen to this, afflicted one, *drunken*[1131] one, but not with wine: 22 Thus says your Lord, the LORD your God, who pleads the cause of his people: See, I have taken out of your hand the cup of staggering. The deep cup of my anger you will never again drink. 23 I will put it into the hand of those who afflicted *and oppressed you,*[1132] who said to you, "Bow down, so that we may step over," so that you had to make your back like the ground, like the street, for them to step over.

52 1 Awake, awake, put on *strength,*[1133] O Zion; put on your beautiful garments, O Jerusalem, the holy city; for the uncircumcised and the unclean will not enter *you.*[1134] 2 Shake yourself from the dust; *and*[1135] arise, *and*[1136] sit on your throne, O Jerusalem; loose the bonds from your neck, O captive daughter of Zion.

3 For thus says the LORD: You were sold for nothing; and you will be redeemed without money. 4 For thus says *the LORD:*[1137] My people went down long ago into Egypt to sojourn there; the Assyrian, too, has oppressed them without cause. 5 Now therefore, *what*[1138] am I doing here, says the LORD, seeing that my people are taken away without cause? Those who rule over them *are deluded,*[1139] says the LORD, and continually, all the day long, my name is blasphemed. 6 Therefore my people will know my name; *in that day*[1140] they will know that it is I who speaks; here am I.

> ■ *In the moving poetry presented in 52:7–12, several differences are evident between 1QIsa^a and the Masoretic Text. For example, the Masoretic Text ends verse 8 with "the return of the LORD to Zion," whereas 1QIsa^a goes on to read "with compassion," thus reminding the reader that although God is a mighty king (cf. vs 7), he now*

1131. 1QIsa^a. *and drunken* MT.

1132. 1QIsa^a. Not in MT.

Chapter 52. 1QIsa^a: all; 4QIsa^b: 52:2, 7; 4QIsa^d: 52:4–7; 1QIsa^b: 52:7–15; 4QIsa^c: 52:10–15.

1133. 1QIsa^a. *your strength* MT LXX.

1134. 1QIsa^a. *you again* MT LXX.

1135. 1QIsa^a LXX. Not in 4QIsa^b MT.

1136. 1QIsa^a. Not in MT LXX.

1137. 1QIsa^a LXX. *the LORD GOD* MT.

1138. 1QIsa^a LXX. Literally, *who* MT.

1139. Meaning unclear 1QIsa^a. *wail* MT LXX.

1140. 1QIsa^a LXX. *therefore in that day* MT.

comes in mercy. Another difference is found at the end of verse 12, where only 1QIsa^a
ends with "He is called the God of all the earth," thus encouraging the exiles to leave
Babylon with confidence, since God's presence and power are universal, as was men-
tioned earlier in verse 10.

7 How *beautiful*[1141] upon the mountains are the feet of the one *who brings news*
of peace,[1142] *who announces good things, who announces salvation,*[1143] who says to Zion,
"Your God reigns!" 8 Listen, your watchmen lift up *their voices,*[1144] together they
sing for joy; for in plain sight they will see the return of the LORD to Zion *with*
compassion.[1145] 9 Break forth together *into singing,*[1146] you ruins of Jerusalem; for
the LORD has comforted his people, *and*[1147] he has redeemed Jerusalem. 10 The
LORD has bared his holy arm in the eyes of all the nations; and all the ends of *the*
earth[1148] will see the salvation of our God.

11 Depart, depart, go out from there, touch no unclean thing; go out from the
midst of her. Purify yourselves, you who carry the vessels of the LORD. 12 For
you will not go out in haste, nor will you go in flight; for the LORD will go before
you, and the God of Israel will be your rear guard. *He is called the God of all the*
earth.[1149]

■ *The fourth Servant Song is found in Isaiah 52:13–53:12, and is quoted more fre-*
quently in the New Testament than any other Old Testament passage. As the transla-
tion indicates, 1QIsa^a and the other scrolls preserving text from this Servant Song
contain mostly small differences in comparison to the received text on which modern
translations are based, but vs 11 is rather striking, with its emphasis on "lighT"
(which is not found in the Masoretic Text). While it is possible that vs 3 reads: ". . . no
majesty that we should look at ourselves, and no attractiveness that we should desire
ourselves," the Hebrew in 1QIsa^a is more likely a different form from that found in
the Masoretic Text and has the same meaning (". . . look at him, . . . desire him").

1141. Literally, *they are beautiful* 1QIsa^a MT LXX^mss. Literally, *it is beautiful* 4QIsa^b.

1142. 1QIsa^a. *who brings good news* MT LXX.

1143. 1QIsa^a. *who announces peace, who brings news of good things, who announces salvation* MT
(cf. LXX).

1144. Literally, *their voice* 1QIsa^a. Literally, *the voice* MT.

1145. 1QIsa^a (cf. LXX). Not in MT.

1146. Literally, *sing for joy* (singular), although the form of this word in 1QIsa^a could also
mean *rattle*. Literally, *sing for joy* (plural) MT.

1147. 1QIsa^a LXX. Not in MT.

1148. 1QIsa^a LXX. *earth* MT.

1149. 1QIsa^a. Not in MT LXX.

13 See, my servant will prosper, *and*[1150] he will be exalted and lifted up, and will be very high. 14 Just as many were astonished *at you*[1151]—so was *he marred*[1152] in his appearance, more than any human, and his form beyond that of the sons of *humans*[1153]— 15 so will he *startle*[1154] many nations. Kings will shut their mouths at him; for what had not been told them they will see; and what they had not heard they will understand.

53 1 Who has believed our message? And to *whom*[1155] has the arm of the LORD been revealed? 2 For he grew up before him like a tender plant, and like a root out of a dry ground; he had no form *and he had no majesty*[1156] that we should *look at him,*[1157] and had no attractiveness that we should *desire* him.[1158] 3 He was despised and rejected by others, *and*[1159] a man of sorrows, and *familiar*[1160] with suffering; and like one from whom people hide their faces *and*[1161] *we despised him,*[1162] and we did not value him.

4 Surely he has borne our sufferings, and carried our sorrows; yet we considered him stricken, *and*[1163] struck down by God, and afflicted. 5 But he was wounded for our transgressions, *and*[1164] he was crushed for our iniquities, *and*[1165] the punishment that made us whole was upon him, and by his bruises we are healed. 6 All we like sheep have gone astray; we have turned, each of us, to his own way; and the LORD has laid on him the iniquity of us all.

7 He was oppressed and he was afflicted, yet he did not open his mouth; like a

---

1150. 1QIsa^a L. Not in 1QIsa^b 4QIsa^c MT. LXX omits *(and) he will be exalted*.

1151. 1QIsa^a MT LXX. *at him* MT^{mss}.

1152. Possibly, *my marring* 1QIsa^a. Literally, *marring of* MT.

1153. Literally, *the human* 1QIsa^a (cf. *the humans* LXX). Literally, *human* MT.

1154. Or, *sprinkle*.

Chapter 53. 1QIsa^a: all; 1QIsa^b: 53:1–12; 4QIsa^c: 53:1–3, 6–8; 4QIsa^d: 53:8–12; 4QIsa^b: 53:11–12.

1155. 1QIsa^a. *on whom* (possible meaning) MT.

1156. 1QIsa^a. *and no majesty* MT LXX.

1157. 1QIsa^a MT LXX. 1QIsa^a could also read *look at ourselves*.

1158. 1QIsa^a MT LXX. 1QIsa^a could also read *desire him*.

1159. 1QIsa^a. Not in MT LXX.

1160. Active *(knowing)* 1QIsa^a LXX. 1QIsa^b is ambiguous. Passive (known to) MT.

1161. 1QIsa^a 1QIsa^b. Not in MT LXX.

1162. 1QIsa^a. *he was despised* MT LXX.

1163. 1QIsa^a (cf. LXX). Not in MT.

1164. 1QIsa^a LXX. Not in MT.

1165. 1QIsa^a 1QIsa^b. Not in MT LXX.

lamb that is led to the slaughter, *as*[1166] a sheep that before its shearers is silent, so he *did not open*[1167] his mouth. 8 From detention *and*[1168] judgment *he was taken away*[1169]—and who can even think about his *descendants?*[1170] For he was cut off from the land of the living, *he was stricken*[1171] for the transgression of my people. 9 Then *they made*[1172] his grave with the wicked, and with *rich people*[1173] his *tomb*[1174]—although he had done no violence, nor was any deceit in his mouth.

10 Yet the LORD was willing to crush him, *and he made him suffer.*[1175] Although you make his soul an offering for sin, *and*[1176] he will see his offspring, *and*[1177] he will prolong his days, and the will of the LORD will triumph in his hand. 11 *Out of the suffering of his soul he will see light,*[1178] *and*[1179] find satisfaction. *And*[1180] through his knowledge *his servant,*[1181] the righteous one, will make many righteous, and he will bear their iniquities. 12 Therefore will I allot him a portion with the great, and he will divide the spoils with the strong; because he poured out his life to death, and was numbered with the transgressors; yet he bore *the sins*[1182] of many, and made intercession for *their transgressions.*[1183]

54 1 Sing, O woman barren *and*[1184] who never bore a child; burst into song, and shout for joy, *and*[1185] you who were never in labor! For the children of the desolate woman will be more than the children of her that is married, says the

---

1166. 1QIsa^a. *and as* MT LXX.

1167. 1QIsa^a. *does not open* MT.

1168. 1QIsa^a MT. Not in 1QIsa^b.

1169. 1QIsa^a MT LXX. *they took (him) away* 1QIsa^b.

1170. Or, *future.*

1171. 1QIsa^a. *an affliction* MT.

1172. 1QIsa^a. *he made* 4QIsa^d MT. *I will give* LXX.

1173. 1QIsa^a*. *a rich man* 1QIsa^{a(corr)} MT.

1174. 1QIsa^a. *in his deaths* MT. *in his death* LXX.

1175. 1QIsa^a. *he made (him) suffer* 4QIsa^d MT. *with a blow* LXX.

1176. 1QIsa^a. Not in MT LXX.

1177. 1QIsa^a 4QIsa^d. Not in 1QIsa^b MT.

1178. 1QIsa^a 1QIsa^b 4QIsa^d LXX. *He will see some of the suffering of his soul* MT.

1179. 1QIsa^a 4QIsa^d (questionable). Not in MT.

1180. 1QIsa^a. Not in 4QIsa^d MT.

1181. 1QIsa^a. *my servant* 4QIsa^d MT.

1182. 1QIsa^a 1QIsa^b 4QIsa^d LXX. *the sin* MT.

1183. 1QIsa^a 1QIsa^b 4QIsa^d LXX. *the transgressors* MT.

Chapter 54. 1QIsa^a: all; 4QIsa^d: 54:1–11; 1QIsa^b: 54:1–6; 4QIsa^c: 54:3–5, 7–17; 4QIsa^q: 54:10–13.

1184. 1QIsa^a 4QIsa^d. Not in 1QIsa^b MT LXX.

1185. 1QIsa^a. Not in 4QIsa^d MT LXX.

LORD. 2 Enlarge the place of your tent, and let the curtains of your dwellings be stretched wide; and[1186] do not hold back, lengthen your cords, and strengthen your stakes. 3 For you will spread out to the right hand and to the left, and your descendants[1187] will possess[1188] the nations and will populate the deserted towns.

4 Do not be afraid; for you will not be ashamed; and do not fear shame, for you will not be humiliated. For you will forget the disgrace of your youth, and the reproach of your widowhood you will remember no more. 5 For your maker is your husband; the LORD of hosts is his name, and the Holy One of Israel is your Redeemer; he is called the God of the whole earth. 6 For the LORD has called you back like a wife deserted and grieved in spirit, like the wife of a man's youth when she is cast off, says the LORD your God.[1189] 7 For a brief moment I abandoned you; but with great compassion I will gather you. 8 In a surge of anger I hid my face from you for a moment, but with my[1190] everlasting lovingkindness I will have compassion on you, says the LORD your Redeemer.

9 For this is to me like the waters of Noah: when I swore that the waters of Noah would never again go over the earth, so have I sworn that I will not be angry with you again[1191] and will not rebuke you. 10 For the mountains may collapse and the hills reel,[1192] but my steadfast love will not depart from you, neither will my covenant of peace totter, says the LORD who has compassion on you.

11 O afflicted (city), passed back and forth[1193] and not comforted, behold, I am about to set your stones in antimony and lay your foundations with sapphires. 12 And I will make your battlements of rubies, and your gates of jewels, and all your walls of precious stones. 13 And all your children will be taught by the LORD; and great will be your children's prosperity. 14 In righteousness you will be established; you will be far from tyranny, for you will not be afraid, and far from terror, for it will not come near you. 15 See, if anyone does attack you, it will not be from me; whoever will attack[1194] you, they will fall[1195] because of you. 16 See, it is I who have created the blacksmith who fans coals in the fire, and produces a weapon for his purpose. It is I[1196] who have created the ravager to wreak havoc.

1186. 1QIsa^a. Not in MT LXX.

1187. Literally, seed.

1188. Plural 1QIsa^a. Singular MT.

1189. 1QIsa^a. your God MT LXX.

1190. 1QIsa^a 4QIsa^c. Not in MT LXX.

1191. 1QIsa^a LXX. Not in MT.

1192. One form of this word (hithpolel) 1QIsa^a. Another form of this word (qal) MT.

1193. Apparent meaning 1QIsa^a. storm-tossed 4QIsa^d MT. unsteady LXX.

1194. 1QIsa^a. attacks MT.

1195. 1QIsa^a 4QIsa^c. he will fall MT. they will flee LXX.

1196. 1QIsa^a. And it is I MT LXX.

17 No weapon that is forged against you will be *effective*.[1197] This is the heritage of the Lord's servants, and their righteousness from me, says the Lord.

55 1 Ho, everyone who is thirsty, come to the waters; and you that have no money, *come, buy*[1198] wine and milk without money and at no cost. 2 Why spend your money on what is not bread, and your labor on what *does not satisfy?*[1199] Listen carefully to me, and eat what is good, and let your soul delight itself in rich food. 3 Incline your ear, and come to me; *and*[1200] listen, so that you may live; and *I will make*[1201] with you an everlasting covenant, my faithful, sure love for David. 4 See, I have made him a witness to the peoples, a leader and commander of the peoples. 5 See, you will call a nation that you do not know, and *a nation that does not know*[1202] you *will run*[1203] to you, because of the Lord your God, *even*[1204] the Holy One of Israel, for he has glorified you.

6 Seek the Lord while *he*[1205] may be found, call upon him while he is near. 7 Let the wicked forsake his way, and the unrighteous person his thoughts; let him return to the Lord, and he will have mercy upon him, and to our God, for he will freely pardon. 8 For my thoughts are not your thoughts, nor are your ways my ways, declares the Lord. 9 For *as*[1206] the heavens are higher than the earth, so are my ways higher than your ways, and my thoughts than your thoughts.

10 For as the rain and snow come down from heaven, and do not return there without watering the earth and making it bring forth and sprout, yielding seed for the sower and bread for *eating,*[1207] 11 so will my word be that goes out of my mouth; it will not return to me empty, but it will accomplish what I desire, and achieve the purpose for which I sent it.

1197. 1QIsaᵃ. *effective, and you will refute every tongue that rises against you in judgment* 4QIsaᶜ MT LXX (with minor variations).

Chapter 55. 1QIsaᵃ: all; 4QIsaᶜ: 55:1–7; 1QIsaᵇ: 55:2–13.

1198. 1QIsaᵃ (with scribe skipping from the first *come, buy* to the second *come, buy,* resulting in the omission of the words in between). *come, buy and eat! Come, buy* 4QIsaᶜ MT LXX (with some variations).

1199. Literally, *is not satisfaction* 1QIsaᵃ. Literally, *is not for satisfaction* MT LXX.

1200. 1QIsaᵃ. Not in MT LXX.

1201. 1QIsaᵃ. *let me make* 1QIsaᵇ 4QIsaᶜ MT (cohortative).

1202. Singular 1QIsaᵃ. *a nation* [collective] *that do not know* 1QIsaᵇ MT. *nations that do not know* LXX.

1203. Singular 1QIsaᵃ. Plural MT LXX.

1204. 1QIsa* 1QIsaᵇ. *and (because) of* 1QIsaᵃ⁽ᶜᵒʳʳ⁾ MT.

1205. 1QIsaᵃ 1QIsaᵇ MT LXX. Implied 4QIsaᶜ.

1206. 1QIsaᵃ LXX. Not in MT (implied?).

1207. 1QIsaᵃ (infinitive). *the eater* MT (participle).

12 For you will go out in joy, and *come back*[1208] with peace; the mountains and the hills will burst into song before you, and all the trees of the fields will clap their hands. 13 Instead of thorn bushes pine trees will grow, *and*[1209] instead of briers myrtles will grow; and *they*[1210] will be for the LORD's *sign and for an everlasting renown*[1211] that will not be cut down.

56 1 *For*[1212] thus says the LORD: Maintain justice, and do what is right, for soon my salvation will come, and soon my deliverance will be revealed. 2 Blessed is the one who does this, and the person that holds it fast, who observes the sabbath without profaning *it*,[1213] and restrains *his hands*[1214] from doing any evil.

3 *Let*[1215] no foreigner who has joined himself to the LORD say, "The LORD will surely exclude me from his people"; and let no eunuch say, "I am just a dry tree." 4 For thus says the LORD: To the eunuchs who observe my sabbaths, and who choose the things that please me and hold fast my covenant: 5 to them I will give in my house and within my walls a monument and a name better than sons and daughters. I will give *them*[1216] an everlasting name that will not be cut off.

6 Also the foreigners who join themselves to *the* LORD,[1217] to be his servants, *and to bless the LORD'S name and observing*[1218] the sabbath without profaning it, and who hold fast my covenant: 7 these I will bring to my holy mountain, and make them joyful in my house of prayer. Their burnt offerings and their sacrifices *will rise up to be accepted*[1219] on my altar; for my house will be called a house of prayer for all peoples. 8 Thus says the Lord GOD, who gathers the outcasts of Israel: I will gather still others to them besides *those already gathered.*[1220]

1208. 1QIsa[a]. *be led back* MT (cf. LXX), passive.

1209. 1QIsa[a] MT[mss]. Not in MT LXX.

1210. 1QIsa[a]. *it* MT LXX.

1211. 1QIsa[a]. *renown, for an everlasting sign* MT LXX.

Chapter 56. 1QIsa[a]: all; 1QIsa[b]: 56:1–12; 4QIsa[i]: 56:7–8.

1212. 1QIsa[a]. Not in 1QIsa[b] MT LXX.

1213. Feminine (referring to *the sabbath*). Masculine 1QIsa[b] MT.

1214. 1QIsa[a] LXX. *his hand* 1QIsa[b] MT.

1215. 1QIsa[a] LXX. *And let* 1QIsa[b] MT.

1216. 1QIsa[a] LXX. *him* 1QIsa[b] MT.

1217. 1QIsa[a]. *the* LORD, *to minister to him, to love the name of the* LORD 1QIsa[b] MT LXX.

1218. 1QIsa[a]. *all who observe* 1QIsa[b] MT LXX.

1219. 1QIsa[a]. *will be accepted* 1QIsa[b] 4QIsa[i] MT LXX.

1220. Literally, *their gathered ones.*

9 *All you wild animals,*[1221] come and devour—*even*[1222] *all you wild animals.*[1223]
10 *His watchmen*[1224] are blind, they are all without knowledge; they are all mute
dogs, they cannot bark; they dream, lie down, love to sleep. 11 The dogs have a
voracious appetite, they can never have enough. And as for them, they are *the*[1225]
shepherds who lack understanding; they have all turned to their own way, each
one to his gain, each and every one. 12[1226] Come, they say, *let us*[1227] fetch wine,
and let us fill ourselves with strong drink! And tomorrow will be like *today,*[1228] or
even much better.

57 1 *And*[1229] the righteous person *perishes,*[1230] but no one takes it to heart; *devout people*[1231] are taken away, while none understands that the righteous
are taken away from calamity. 2 *And*[1232] he enters into peace, *and*[1233] they will rest
on *his couches,*[1234] each one walking in *her uprightness.*[1235]

3 But as for you—come here, you children of a sorceress, you offspring of
adulterers and *prostitutes!*[1236] 4 Whom are you mocking? *And*[1237] against whom do
you make a wide mouth and stick out your tongue? Are you not children of
transgression, the offspring of lies, 5 you who burn with lust among the oaks,
under every spreading tree, who slaughter your children in the ravines, under the
clefts of the rocks? 6 Among the smooth stones of the ravines is your portion.
There they go as[1238] your lot; to them you have poured out drink offerings, you

---

1221. 1QIsa^a LXX. *Every wild animal* 1QIsa^b MT.

1222. 1QIsa^a. Not in 1QIsa^b MT LXX.

1223. 1QIsa^a LXX. *Every wild animal* 1QIsa^b MT.

1224. I.e., Israel's watchmen 1QIsa^a MT^qere. *His watchman* MT. *See, they all* LXX.

1225. 1QIsa^a. Not in 1QIsa^b MT LXX.

1226. Vs 12 1QIsa^a 1QIsa^b MT. Not in LXX.

1227. 1QIsa^a MT^ms. *I will* 1QIsa^b. *let me* MT.

1228. Literally, *this the day* 1QIsa^a. Literally, *this day* 1QIsa^b (no room for *the*) MT.

Chapter 57. 1QIsa^a: all; 1QIsa^b: 57:1–4, 17–21; 4QIsa^i: 57:5–8; 4QIsa^d: 57:9–21.

1229. 1QIsa^a. Not in 1QIsa^b MT.

1230. 1QIsa^a (participle). *has perished* 1QIsa^b MT LXX.

1231. Literally, *people of the mercy* 1QIsa^a. Literally, *people of mercy* MT. *Just men* LXX.

1232. 1QIsa^a. Not in MT LXX.

1233. 1QIsa^a. Not in MT.

1234. 1QIsa^a. *their couches* 1QIsa^b MT.

1235. Apparent meaning 1QIsa^a 1QIsa^b. *his uprightness* MT.

1236. LXX (cf. Syriac). 1QIsa^a and MT read *she has practiced prostitution,* which is textually problematic.

1237. 1QIsa^a LXX. Not in 1QIsa^b (no room for *And*) MT.

1238. 1QIsa^a. *They, yes they, are* 4QIsa^i MT. *This is* LXX.

have brought grain offerings. Am I to be appeased for these things? 7 You have made your bed on a high and lofty mountain, and there you went up to offer sacrifice. 8 Behind the doors and the doorposts you have set up your pagan sign; for in deserting me you have uncovered your bed, you have climbed up into it and have opened it wide, and *you*[1239] have made a pact for yourself with them; you have loved their bed, you have looked on their penis. 9 You went to *Molech*[1240] with olive oil and increased your perfumes; you sent your ambassadors far away, you sent them down to Sheol itself! 10 You grew weary with your many *wanderings,*[1241] but you would not say, "It is useless." You found new strength for your desire, and so you felt no regret.

11 Whom did you dread *and you feared me,*[1242] that you lied and you did not remember me *and*[1243] did not lay to heart *these things?*[1244] Have I not kept silent for a long time, and so that you do not fear me? 12 I will denounce *your righteousness*[1245] and your works, for *your contingents*[1246] (of idols) will not benefit you. 13 When you cry out, let your contingents deliver you! The wind will carry them all off, *and*[1247] a mere breath will take them all away. But *whoever*[1248] takes refuge in me will possess the land, and inherit my holy mountain.

14 And *one has said,*[1249] "Build up, build up *the road,*[1250] prepare the highway! Remove every obstacle from my people's way." 15 For thus says the high and lofty One who inhabits eternity, whose name is Holy: *he will dwell*[1251] in the height and in the holy place,[1252] and also with the one who is of a contrite and humble spirit, to revive the spirit of the humble, and to revive the heart of the contrite. 16 For I will not accuse forever, nor will I always be angry; for then the spirit would grow faint before me—the souls that I have created. 17 At his wicked covetousness I

1239. Apparently plural 1QIsa[a]. Singular MT.

1240. Or, *the king.*

1241. 1QIsa[a] LXX. *wandering* (singular) MT.

1242. 1QIsa[a]. *and fear* 4QIsa[d] MT LXX.

1243. 1QIsa[a] 4QIsa[d] LXX. Not in MT.

1244. 1QIsa[a]. Not in 4QIsa[d] MT. *me* LXX.

1245. 1QIsa[a] MT. *your justice* 4QIsa[d].

1246. 1QIsa[a]. *they* 4QIsa[d] MT LXX.

1247. 1QIsa[a] LXX. Not in MT.

1248. Literally, *the one* (with article) 4QIsa[d] MT. Literally, *the one* (without article) 1QIsa[a].

1249. 1QIsa[a]. *one will say* or *I will say* MT. *they will say* LXX.

1250. 1QIsa[a] (cf. LXX). Not in 4QIsa[d] MT.

1251. 1QIsa[a] 4QIsa[d]. *I dwell* MT.

1252. 1QIsa[a]. *(inhabit) the high and holy* [place] 4QIsa[d] MT.

was angry and I struck him, *and*[1253] I hid my face and was angry—but he kept turning back in *his willful ways.*[1254] 18 I have seen *his ways,*[1255] but I will heal *him,*[1256] and restore *to him*[1257] *comfort*[1258] to him and to *those who mourn for him,*[1259] *when*[1260] I create the fruit of the lips, (saying), 19 *Peace*[1261] to the one who is far away and near, says the LORD, and I will heal him. 20 But the wicked are *tossed like the sea;*[1262] for it is not able *to*[1263] keep still, and its waters toss up mire and mud. 21 *But*[1264] there is no peace, says my God, for the wicked.

58 1 Shout aloud, do not hold back! Lift up your voice like a trumpet! Declare to my people their *rebellions,*[1265] and to the house of Jacob their sins. 2 *They*[1266] seek me *day after day,*[1267] and are eager to know my ways, as if they were a nation that practices righteousness and has not forsaken the justice of their God. They ask me for just decisions; they are eager to draw near to God. 3 Why have we fasted (they say), but you do not see? Why have we humbled *ourselves,*[1268] but you take no notice? Look, on your fast day you serve your own interest and oppress all your workers. 4 Look, you fast only for quarreling, and *for*[1269] fighting, and for hitting with wicked fists. You cannot fast as you do today and have your voice heard on high. 5 Is this the kind of fast that I have chosen, only a day for a person to humble himself? Is it only for bowing down one's head like a bulrush,

---

1253. 1QIsaᵃ 4QIsaᵈ LXX. Not in 1QIsaᵇ MT.

1254. Literally, *the way of his heart.*

1255. 1QIsaᵃ MT LXX. *his way* 4QIsaᵈ.

1256. 1QIsaᵃ. *him, and I will guide him* MT. *him, and I will exhort him* LXX.

1257. 1QIsaᵃ (error?). Not in 1QIsaᵇ MT LXX.

1258. 1QIsaᵃ and 1QIsaᵇ MT use two different but related words.

1259. Literally, *his mourners.*

1260. 1QIsaᵃ. Not in 1QIsaᵇ 4QIsaᵈ MT.

1261. 1QIsaᵃ. *Peace, peace* 1QIsaᵇ MT LXX.

1262. 1QIsaᵃ LXX. *like the tossing sea* 4QIsaᵈ MT.

1263. 1QIsaᵃ. Implied in 4QIsaᵈ MT.

1264. 1QIsaᵃ. Not in MT LXX.

Chapter 58. 1QIsaᵃ: all; 1QIsaᵇ: 58:1–14; 4QIsaᵈ: 58:1–3, 5–7; 4QIsaⁿ: 58:13–14.

1265. 1QIsaᵃ LXX. *rebellion* 1QIsaᵇ MT.

1266. 1QIsaᵃ 1QIsaᵇ 4QIsaᵈ LXX. *And they* MT.

1267. Literally, *day and day* 1QIsaᵃ. Literally, *day, day* 1QIsaᵇ 4QIsaᵈ MT.

1268. 1QIsaᵃ 1QIsaᵇ LXX. *ourself* MT.

1269. 1QIsaᵃ 1QIsaᵇ. Not in MT LXX.

for lying[1270] on sackcloth and ashes? Is this what *you*[1271] call a fast, *an*[1272] acceptable day to the LORD?

6 Is not this *the*[1273] fast *that*[1274] I choose: to loose the bonds of injustice, *and*[1275] to untie the cords of the yoke, *and*[1276] to let the oppressed go free, and to break every yoke? 7 Is it not to share your bread with the hungry, and to bring the homeless poor into your house; when you see the naked, to cover him *with clothing,*[1277] and not to *raise yourself up*[1278] from your own flesh and blood? 8 Then your light will break forth like the dawn, and your healing will spring up quickly; and your vindication will go before you, *and*[1279] the glory of the LORD will be your rear guard. 9 Then you will call, and the LORD will answer; you will cry for help, and he will say, Here I am.

If you do away with the yoke among you, *and*[1280] with the pointing finger, and with evil talk, 10 if you spend yourself for the hungry and satisfy the needs of the afflicted soul, then your light will rise in darkness, and your gloom will be like the noonday. 11 And the LORD will guide you always, and satisfy your soul in *parched places,*[1281] and *they will*[1282] strengthen your bones; and you will be like a watered garden, like a spring of water, whose waters never fail. 12 And your people will rebuild the ancient ruins; you will raise up the age-old foundations,[1283] and *people will call you*[1284] Repairer of the Breach, Restorer of Streets to Live In.

13 If you keep your feet from trampling the sabbath, *from*[1285] pursuing your own interests on my holy day, if you call the sabbath a delight *and*[1286] the LORD's

---

1270. 1QIsaᵃ 1QIsaᵇ. *and for lying* MT LXX.

1271. Plural 1QIsaᵃ 4QIsaᵈ LXX. Singular 1QIsaᵇ MT.

1272. 1QIsaᵃ 1QIsaᵇ. *and an* MT.

1273. 1QIsaᵃ. Not in 1QIsaᵇ MT LXX.

1274. 1QIsaᵃ. Not in 1QIsaᵇ MT LXX.

1275. 1QIsaᵃ. Not in 1QIsaᵇ MT LXX.

1276. 1QIsaᵃ MT. Not in 1QIsaᵇ 4QIsaᵈ LXX.

1277. 1QIsaᵃ. Not in 1QIsaᵇ MT LXX.

1278. 1QIsaᵃ. *hide yourself* 1QIsaᵇ MT. *disregard* LXX.

1279. 1QIsaᵃ 1QIsaᵇ LXX. Not in MT.

1280. 1QIsaᵃ LXX. Not in 1QIsaᵇ MT.

1281. This word seems to be incorrectly spelled in 1QIsaᵃ.

1282. 1QIsaᵃ 1QIsaᵇ. *he will* MT. *(and your bones) will be strengthened* LXX.

1283. Literally, *the foundations of many generations.*

1284. 1QIsaᵃ. *you will be called* 1QIsaᵇ MT LXX.

1285. 1QIsaᵃ 4QIsaⁿ. Not in 1QIsaᵇ MT.

1286. 1QIsaᵃ 1QIsaᵇ 4QIsaⁿ. Not in MT LXX.

holy day honorable; and if you honor it by not going *your own ways*[1287] *and*[1288] seeking your own pleasure or speaking idle words— 14 then you will take delight in the LORD, *and he*[1289] will make you ride upon the heights of the earth; *and he*[1290] will feed you with the heritage of your ancestor Jacob—yes, the mouth of the LORD has spoken.

59 1 See, the LORD's hand is not too short to save, nor *his ears*[1291] too dull to hear. 2 Instead, your iniquities have been barriers between you and your God, and your sins have concealed his face from you so that he does not hear. 3 For your hands are defiled with blood, and your fingers with iniquity; *your tongue*[1292] mutters wickedness. 4 No one sues fairly, and no one pleads his case honestly; *they have relied*[1293] on empty arguments and speak lies; *they conceive*[1294] trouble and *give birth to*[1295] iniquity. 5 *They hatch*[1296] adders' *eggs*[1297] and *weave*[1298] a spider's web; whoever eats their eggs dies, and a crushed (egg) hatches out *futility.*[1299] 6 Their webs cannot become clothing, they cannot *cover*[1300] themselves with what they make. Their deeds are deeds of iniquity, and acts of violence are in their hands. 7 Their feet rush into evil, and they make haste to shed innocent blood. Their thoughts are thoughts of iniquity; ruin, destruction, *and violence*[1301] are in their highways. 8 The way of peace they do not know, and there is no justice in their paths. They have made their roads crooked; no one who walks in them knows peace.

9 Therefore justice is far from us, and righteousness does not reach us. We wait

---

1287. 1QIsa[a] 4QIsa[n] MT. *your own way* 1QIsa[b].

1288. 1QIsa[a]. Not in 1QIsa[b] MT.

1289. 1QIsa[a] 1QIsa[b] 4QIsa[n] LXX. *and I* MT.

1290. 1QIsa[a] LXX. *and I* 1QIsa[b] 4QIsa[n] MT.

Chapter 59. 1QIsa[a]: all; 1QIsa[b]: 59:1–8, 20–21; 4QIsa[c]: 59:15–16.

1291. 1QIsa[a]. *his ear* 1QIsa[b] MT LXX.

1292. 1QIsa[a]. *your lips have spoken lies, your tongue* 1QIsa[b] MT. *your lips have spoken lies, and your tongue* LXX.

1293. 1QIsa[a] 1QIsa[b] (perfect). *they rely* MT (infinitive absolute).

1294. Perfect 1QIsa[a]. Infinitive absolute 1QIsa[b] MT.

1295. Perfect 1QIsa[a] 1QIsa[b]. Infinitive absolute MT.

1296. Imperfect 1QIsa[a]. *They have hatched* (perfect) 1QIsa[b] MT. Aorist LXX.

1297. 1QIsa[a] LXX. *an adder's eggs* 1QIsa[b] MT.

1298. 1QIsa[a] has an unusual form of the word found in 1QIsa[b] and MT.

1299. Or, *a viper* (masculine) 1QIsa[a]. *a viper* 1QIsa[b] MT (feminine) LXX.

1300. One form of this word *(piel)* 1QIsa[a]. Another form of this word *(hithpael)* 1QIsa[b] MT.

1301. 1QIsa[a]. Not in MT LXX.

for light, but see—there is darkness; (we wait) for brightness, but we walk in *dark-ness*.[1302] 10 *Let us grope*[1303] along the wall like the blind, let us grope like those who have no eyes; we stumble at midday as in the twilight, among *vigorous*[1304] people we are like the dead. 11 We all growl like bears, *we*[1305] moan mournfully like doves; we look for justice, but there is none; *and*[1306] for deliverance, but it is far from us. 12 For our transgressions before you are many, and our sins *testify*[1307] against us; for our transgressions are with us, and as for our iniquities, we ac-knowledge them: 13 *they have rebelled,*[1308] and denying the LORD, and turning away from following our God, *and they have spoken*[1309] oppression and revolt, *and uttering*[1310] lying words from the heart. 14 *I will drive back justice,*[1311] and righteous-ness stands at a distance; for truth has fallen in the public squares, and uprightness cannot enter. 15 Truth is absent, and whoever avoids evil is plundered.

And the LORD saw this, and it displeased him that there was no justice. 16 He saw that there was no one, and was appalled that there was no one to intervene; so his own arm brought him victory, and *his righteous acts*[1312] upheld him. 17 He put on righteousness like a breastplate, and a helmet of salvation on *his heads;*[1313] he put on garments of vengeance for clothing, and wrapped himself in fury like a mantle. 18 According to their actions, so he will repay—wrath to his enemies, retribution to his foes; to the coastlands he will render requital. 19 So will they fear the name of the LORD from the west, and *his glories*[1314] from the rising of the sun; for he will come as a pent-up stream that the breath of the LORD drives along.

20 And a Redeemer will come to Zion, to those in Jacob who turn from transgression, says the LORD. 21 And as for me, this is my covenant *with them,*[1315]

1302. Singular 1QIsaᵃ LXX. *deep darkness* (plural) MT.

1303. 1QIsaᵃ. *We grope* MT. *They grope* LXX.

1304. The meaning of this word is uncertain.

1305. 1QIsaᵃ. *and we* MT.

1306. 1QIsaᵃ. Not in MT LXX.

1307. 1QIsaᵃ (cf. LXX). *testifies* (singular) MT.

1308. 1QIsaᵃ. *rebellion* (infinitive absolute) MT. *we have sinned* LXX.

1309. 1QIsaᵃ. *speaking* MT. *we have spoken* LXX.

1310. 1QIsaᵃ. *conceiving and uttering* MT. *we have conceived and thought about* LXX.

1311. 1QIsaᵃ (apparent meaning). *Justice is driven back* MT. *We withdrew justice* LXX.

1312. 1QIsaᵃ. *his righteousness* MT LXX (same Hebrew word as 1QIsaᵃ, but singular).

1313. 1QIsaᵃ. *his head* MT LXX.

1314. 1QIsaᵃ. *his glory* MT. *(his) glorious name* LXX.

1315. 1QIsaᵃ MTᵐˢˢ LXX. *them* (object) 1QIsaᵇ MT (error).

says the LORD: *and*[1316] my spirit that is upon you, and my words that I have put in your mouth, will not depart from your mouth, or from the mouths of your children, or from the mouths of your children's *children,*[1317] from now on and forever.

60 1 Arise, shine; for your light has come, *the glory*[1318] of the LORD has risen upon you. 2 For see, darkness will cover the earth and thick darkness the peoples, but the LORD will arise upon you, and his glory will appear over you. 3 Nations will come to your light, and kings *before*[1319] your dawn.

4 Lift up your eyes and look around: they all assemble, they come to you; your sons will come from far away, and your daughters will be carried on *the hip.*[1320] 5 Then you will look and be radiant; your heart *will swell with joy,*[1321] because the wealth of the seas will be brought to you, the riches of the nations will come to you. 6 A multitude of camels will cover you, the young camels of Midian and *Ephu;*[1322] all those from *Shebu*[1323] will come. They will bear gold and frankincense, and proclaim the praise of the LORD. 7 All Kedar's flocks will be gathered to you, the rams of Nebaioth will serve you; *and*[1324] they will come up with acceptance *upon*[1325] on my altar, and I will glorify my glorious house.

8 Who are these that fly like clouds, and like doves to their *dovecotes?*[1326] 9 For the coastlands will wait for me, the ships of Tarshish in the lead, to bring *my*[1327] children from far away, their silver and gold with them, for the name of the LORD your God, and for the Holy One of Israel, because he has glorified you. 10 Foreigners will rebuild your walls, and their kings will serve you. Though in my wrath I struck you down, in my favor I have shown you mercy. 11 Your gates will always stand open, day or night, *and*[1328] they will not be shut, so that nations will bring you their wealth, with their kings led in procession. 12 For the nation or

---

1316. 1QIsaᵃ. Not in 1QIsaᵇ MT LXX.

1317. 1QIsaᵃ. *children, says the* LORD 1QIsaᵇ MT LXX.

Chapter 60. 1QIsaᵃ: all; 1QIsaᵇ: 60:1–22; 4QIsaᵐ: 60:20–22.

1318. 1QIsaᵃ. *and the glory* 1QIsaᵇ MT LXX.

1319. 1QIsaᵃ. *to the brightness of* MT.

1320. Or, *the side.*

1321. 1QIsaᵃ. *will throb and swell with joy* 1QIsaᵇ MT. *you will be amazed in your heart* LXX.

1322. 1QIsaᵃ. *Ephah* 1QIsaᵇ MT.

1323. 1QIsaᵃ. *Sheba* 1QIsaᵇ MT.

1324. 1QIsaᵃ LXX. Not in 1QIsaᵇ MT.

1325. 1QIsaᵃ LXX. Not in 1QIsaᵇ MT.

1326. Literally, *windows* (of dovecotes).

1327. 1QIsaᵃ. *your* 1QIsaᵇ MT LXX.

1328. 1QIsaᵃ. Not in 1QIsaᵇ MT LXX.

kingdom that will not serve you will perish; those nations will be utterly ruined. 13 *He has given you*[1329] the glory of *Lebanon, and it will come*[1330] to you, the cypress, *and the plane,*[1331] and the pine, to adorn the place of my sanctuary; and I will glorify the place where my feet rest. 14 *All*[1332] the descendants of those who oppressed you will come bowing low before you, and all who despised you will bow down at your feet; they will call you the City of the LORD, Zion of the Holy One of Israel. 15 Although you have been forsaken and hated, with no one traveling through, I will make you the everlasting pride, the joy of all generations. 16 You will suck the milk of nations, you will suck the breasts of kings; then you will know that I, the LORD, am your Savior and your Redeemer, the Mighty One of Jacob.

> ▪ *As is evident in this translation, 1QIsa^b usually agrees with the Masoretic Text for the text of Isaiah. In 60:19–20, however, this scroll contains a much shorter text than that found in 1QIsa^a MT LXX. In this case the scribe of 1QIsa^b, who was usually careful in his work, appears to have made a major error. His eye inadvertently skipped* from for the LORD will be your everlasting light *in verse 19 to the identical phrase in verse 20, resulting in the omission of the words in between. Such a "skipping over" is technically known as a* paralepsis *(from the Greek, an oversight or a sideways look).*

17 Instead of bronze I will bring gold, and instead of iron I will bring silver; instead of wood, bronze, and instead of stones, iron. I will appoint Peace as your sentry and Righteousness as your taskmaster. 18 *And*[1333] violence will no longer be heard in your land, nor devastation or destruction within your borders; you will call your walls Salvation, and your gates Praise. 19 The sun will no longer be your light by day, nor for brightness will the moon shine on you *by night;*[1334] for the LORD will be your everlasting light, and your God will be your glory. 20 Your sun *will not*[1335] set, or your moon withdraw itself; for the LORD will be your everlasting light, and your days of mourning will end. 21 Then your people will all be righteous; they will possess the land forever. They are *the shoot*[1336] that *the LORD*

1329. 1QIsa^a. Not in 1QIsa^b MT LXX.

1330. 1QIsa^a. *Lebanon will come* 1QIsa^b MT LXX.

1331. 1QIsa^a (name of tree unclear, has unusual spelling). *the plane* 1QIsa^b MT.

1332. 1QIsa^a. Not in 1QIsa^b MT LXX.

1333. 1QIsa^a LXX. Not in 1QIsa^b MT.

1334. 1QIsa^a LXX. Not in 1QIsa^b MT.

1335. 1QIsa^a LXX. *will no longer* MT.

1336. 1QIsa^a 4QIsa^m. Not in 1QIsa^b. *guarding* LXX.

planted,[1337] *the works of his hands,*[1338] so that I might be glorified. 22 The least of them will become a thousand, and the smallest one a mighty nation. I am the Lord; in its time I will do this quickly.

61 1 The spirit of *the* Lord[1339] is upon me, because the Lord has anointed me; he has sent me to bring good news to the oppressed, *and*[1340] to bind up the brokenhearted, to proclaim freedom for the captives, and *release from darkness*[1341] for the prisoners; 2 to proclaim the year of the Lord's favor, *the day*[1342] of vengeance of our God; to comfort all who mourn; 3 to provide for those who mourn in Zion—to bestow on them a garland instead of ashes, the oil of gladness instead of mourning, a mantle of praise instead of a disheartened spirit. And *people will call them*[1343] oaks of righteousness, the planting of the Lord, in order to display his splendor. 4 They will rebuild the ancient ruins, they will restore the places formerly devastated; they will repair the ruined cities, *they will erect again*[1344] the places devastated for many generations. 5 Strangers will stand and feed your flocks, foreigners will work your land and dress your vines; 6 but you will be called priests of the Lord, *and*[1345] you will be named ministers of our God. You will feed on the wealth of the nations, and in their riches you will glory. 7 Instead of your shame (you will receive) double, and instead of dishonor they will rejoice in *your lot;*[1346] therefore *you*[1347] will inherit *a double portion in their land,*[1348] everlasting joy will be *yours.*[1349]

8 For I the Lord love justice, *and*[1350] I hate robbery and iniquity; I will faithfully *give (you) your reward*[1351] and make an everlasting covenant *with you.*[1352]

1337. Literally, *of the plantings of the* Lord 1QIsa[a]. *of his plantings* 1QIsa[b]. *of his planting* MT. *of my planting* MT[qere]. *the planting* LXX.

1338. 1QIsa[a] LXX. *the work of his hands* 1QIsa[b] MT.

Chapter 61. 1QIsa[a]: all; 4QIsa[b]: 61:1–3; 1QIsa[b]: 61:1–2; 4QIsa[m]: 61:1–3, 6.

1339. 1QIsa[a] 1QIsa[b] LXX. *the Lord God* 4QIsa[m] MT.

1340. 1QIsa[a]. Not in MT LXX.

1341. Or, *opening of the eyes.*

1342. 1QIsa[a] LXX[ms]. *and the day* 4QIsa[b] MT LXX.

1343. 1QIsa[a]. *they will be called* MT LXX.

1344. 1QIsa[a]. Not in MT LXX.

1345. 1QIsa[a]. Not in MT LXX.

1346. 1QIsa[a]. *their lot* MT.

1347. 1QIsa[a]. *they* MT.

1348. 1QIsa[a]. *in their land a double portion* MT (word order).

1349. 1QIsa[a]. *theirs* MT LXX.

1350. 1QIsa[a] LXX. Not in MT.

1351. 1QIsa[a]. *give (them) their reward* MT LXX.

1352. 1QIsa[a]. *with them* MT LXX.

9 *Your*[1353] descendants will be known among the nations, and *your*[1354] offspring among the peoples; all who see them will acknowledge them, that they are a people whom the LORD has blessed. 10 I shall greatly rejoice in the LORD, my soul will delight in my God; for he has clothed me with garments of salvation, he has arrayed me in a robe of righteousness, as a bridegroom, *as a priest*[1355] with a garland, and as a bride adorns herself with her jewels. 11 For as the soil brings forth its shoots, and as a garden makes what is sown in it spring up, so the LORD God[1356] will make righteousness and praise spring up before all the nations (62:1) *for Zion's sake.*[1357]

62 1 *And*[1358] I will not *keep silent,*[1359] and for Jerusalem's sake I will not remain quiet, until her vindication shines out like the dawn, and her salvation like a *burning torch.*[1360] 2 The nations will see your vindication, and all the kings your glory; and *people will call you*[1361] by a new name that the mouth of the LORD will bestow. 3 You will be a crown of splendor in the LORD's hand, and a royal diadem in the hand of your God. 4 *And*[1362] you will no longer be called Deserted, and your land will no longer be called Desolate; but *people will call you*[1363] *My Delight Is in Her,*[1364] and your land *Married;*[1365] for the LORD takes delight in you, and your land will be married. 5 For *just as*[1366] a young man marries a maiden, so will your sons marry you, and just as a bridegroom rejoices over his bride, so will your God rejoice over you.

6 Upon your walls, O Jerusalem, I have posted watchmen; all day and all night they will *not*[1367] be silent. You who acknowledge the LORD, take no rest, 7 and

---

1353. 1QIsa*ᵃ*. *Their* MT LXX.

1354. 1QIsa*ᵃ*. *their* MT LXX.

1355. 1QIsa*ᵃ*. *decks himself* MT LXX.

1356. 1QIsa*ᵃ* (YHWH *elohim*). *the Lord God (adonay* YHWH) MT. *the Lord (Kurios)* LXX.

1357. Ends chapter 61 1QIsa*ᵃ*. Begins chapter 62 MT.

Chapter 62. 1QIsa*ᵃ*: all; 1QIsa*ᵇ*: 62:2–12.

1358. 1QIsa*ᵃ*. Not in MT LXX.

1359. 1QIsa*ᵃ* and MT use different Hebrew verbs.

1360. Feminine 1QIsa*ᵃ*. Masculine MT.

1361. 1QIsa*ᵃ*. *you will be called* 1QIsa*ᵇ* MT. *he will call you* LXX.

1362. 1QIsa*ᵃ* LXX. Not in MT.

1363. 1QIsa*ᵃ*. *you will be called* MT. *it* [i.e., the land] *will be called* LXX.

1364. Hebrew *Hephzibah.*

1365. Hebrew *Beulah.*

1366. 1QIsa*ᵃ* LXX. Not in 1QIsa*ᵇ* MT.

1367. 1QIsa*ᵃ* 1QIsa*ᵇ*. *never* MT LXX.

give *him*[1368] no rest until he *prepares and establishes*[1369] Jerusalem and makes it an object of praise throughout the earth. 8 The LORD has sworn by his right hand and by his mighty arm: *I will never again give your grain*[1370] as food for your enemies, *foreigners*[1371] will not drink the wine for which you have toiled; 9 but *surely*[1372] those who harvest it will eat it and praise the *name of*[1373] LORD, and those who gather it will drink it in the courts of my sanctuary, *says your God.*[1374]

10 *Pass through*[1375] the gates, prepare the way for the people! Build up, build up the highway! Clear it of *stumbling-stones,*[1376] *speak among the peoples.*[1377] 11 *Behold the LORD! Proclaim*[1378] to *the ends*[1379] of the earth; say to daughter Zion, "See, your salvation is coming! See, his reward is with him, and *his recompenses are*[1380] before him." 12 People will call them "The Holy People," "The Redeemed of the LORD"; and *they will call you*[1381] "Sought After," "The City Not Deserted."

63 1 Who is this coming from Edom, from Bozrah with his garments stained crimson? Who is this robed in such splendor, marching in his great strength? It is I, announcing vindication, mighty to save.

2 Why are your robes red, and your garments like theirs who tread the *winepress?*[1382]

3 I have trodden the winepress alone, and from *my people*[1383] no one was *with*

1368. 1QIsa[a] MT. *you* (plural) 1QIsa[b] LXX.

1369. 1QIsa[a]. *establishes* 1QIsa[b] (no space for the longer text) MT LXX.

1370. 1QIsa[a] 1QIsa[b]. *I will never give your grain again* MT (word order).

1371. 1QIsa[a]. *and foreigners* MT LXX.

1372. 1QIsa[a]. Not in MT.

1373. 1QIsa[a]. Not in 1QIsa[b] (insufficient space) MT LXX.

1374. 1QIsa[a]. Not in 1QIsa[b] MT LXX.

1375. 1QIsa[a] LXX. *Pass through, pass through* 1QIsa[b] MT.

1376. 1QIsa[a] (for *stumbling-stones;* cf. Isa 8:14). *of stones* 1QIsa[b] (probable reading) MT LXX.

1377. 1QIsa[a]. *raise a banner over the peoples* 1QIsa[b] MT LXX.

1378. 1QIsa[a]. *See, the Lord has proclaimed* 1QIsa[b] MT LXX.

1379. 1QIsa[a]. *the end* 1QIsa[b] MT LXX.

1380. 1QIsa[a]. *his recompense is* 1QIsa[b] MT. *(his) work* LXX.

1381. 1QIsa[a]. *you will be called* 1QIsa[b] MT LXX.

Chapter 63. 1QIsa[a]: all; 1QIsa[b]: 63:1–19.

1382. The Hebrew word in 1QIsa[a] (*gd*) could technically be *coriander* or *clothing;* it is, however, an alternative or incorrect spelling for *winepress* (*gt*) as found in MT.

1383. 1QIsa[a]. *the peoples* 1QIsa[b] MT LXX.

me,[1384] and *I have stained*[1385] all my clothing. 4 For the day of vengeance was in my heart, and the year for my redeeming work had come. 5 I looked, but there was no helper, I was appalled that there was no one *to take hold of me;*[1386] so my own arm brought me victory, and my wrath supported me. 6 I trampled down peoples in my anger; in my wrath I made them drunk, and I poured out their lifeblood on the ground.

7 I will recount the gracious deeds of the LORD, the praiseworthy acts of the LORD, in accordance with all the LORD has done for us, and the great goodness to the house of Israel that he has shown them according to his mercy, according to the abundance of his steadfast love. 8 For he said, Surely they are my people, children who will not act falsely, and so he became their savior. 9 In all their distress *he was not distressed,*[1387] but the angel of his presence that saved them; *in his acts of love*[1388] and in his *pity*[1389] he redeemed them; he *carried them and lifted them up*[1390] all the days of old.

10 Yet they rebelled and grieved his holy spirit; so he changed and became their enemy, *and*[1391] he himself fought against them. 11 Then they remembered the days of old, of Moses his servant. Where is the one who *brought up*[1392] out of the sea *the*[1393] shepherds of his flock? Where is the one who set his holy spirit among them, 12 *and*[1394] who made his *glorious*[1395] arm march at Moses' right hand, who divided the waters before them *to win*[1396] an everlasting name, 13 who led them through the depths? Like a horse in the open desert they did not stumble; 14 like cattle that go down into the plain, the spirit of the LORD gave them rest. *For*[1397] you led your people, to win for yourself a glorious name.

1384. 1QIsaᵃ. *with me; I trod them in my anger and trampled them in my wrath; their juice* [i.e., their blood] *spattered on my garments* 1QIsaᵇ MT (cf. LXX).

1385. The form of this word is appropriate in 1QIsaᵃ 1QIsaᵇ but problematic in MT.

1386. 1QIsaᵃ. *to support me* 1QIsaᵇ MT.

1387. 1QIsaᵃ MT LXX. *he was distressed* MTqere.

1388. 1QIsaᵃ. *in his love* MT. *because of his love for them* LXX.

1389. Plural 1QIsaᵃ. Singular MT.

1390. 1QIsaᵃ. *lifted them up and carried them* 1QIsaᵇ MT.

1391. 1QIsaᵃ LXX. Not in MT.

1392. 1QIsaᵃ LXX. *brought them up* MT.

1393. Object marker 1QIsaᵃ. Preposition *with* MT.

1394. 1QIsaᵃ. Not in MT LXX.

1395. Literally, *of his glories* 1QIsaᵃ. Literally, *of his glory* MT.

1396. 1QIsaᵃ. *to win for himself* MT LXX.

1397. 1QIsaᵃ. *This is how* MT LXX.

15 Look down from heaven, and see from your holy and glorious dwelling. Where are your zeal and your might? The yearning of your heart and your compassion? They are withheld from me. 16 But you are our father, *and*[1398] Abraham does not know us and Israel *has not acknowledged*[1399] us; *you are he,*[1400] O LORD, our father, our Redeemer from long ago is your name. 17 Why, *O LORD, do you make us stray*[1401] from your ways and harden our hearts, so that we do not fear you? Come back for the sake of your servants, for the sake of the tribes that are your heritage. 18 Your holy people *took possession*[1402] of it for a little while, but now our enemies have trampled down your sanctuary. 19 For a long time we have been like those whom you do not rule, like those who are not called by your name.

64 1 O that you would tear open the heavens *and*[1403] come down, so that the mountains would quake at your presence— 2 as when fire kindles brushwood and the fire causes water to boil—*to your adversaries to make known your name, to your adversaries before you,*[1404] so that the nations might quake at your presence! 3 When you did awesome deeds that we *looked for,*[1405] you came down, the mountains quaked before you. 4 *Since*[1406] ancient times no one has heard, *and*[1407] no ear has perceived, *and*[1408] no eye has seen any God besides you, who acts on behalf of those who wait for him. 5 You meet those who gladly do right, those who remember you in your ways. See, you were angry, and we sinned against them for a long time, but we will be saved. 6 All of us have become like one who is unclean; *all,*[1409] all our righteous acts are like a polluted cloth. And we all shrivel up like a leaf, and like the wind our *iniquities*[1410] sweep us away. 7 There is no one

---

1398. 1QIsaª. *but* or *although* MT LXX.

1399. 1QIsaª LXX (aorist). *does not acknowledge* MT.

1400. 1QIsaª. *you* 1QIsaᵇ MT LXX.

1401. 1QIsaª. *do you make us stray, O LORD* MT LXX.

1402. Singular 1QIsaª. Plural MT. *(so that) we may take possession* LXX.

Chapter 64. 1QIsaª: all; 1QIsaᵇ: 64:1, 6–8 [Heb 63:19, 64:5–7]; 4QIsaᵇ: 64:5–11 [Heb 64:4–10].

1403. 1QIsaª. Not in MT.

1404. 1QIsaª (cf. LXX). *to make your name known to your adversaries* MT.

1405. 1QIsaª. *did not look for* MT.

1406. 1QIsaª LXX. *And since* MT.

1407. 1QIsaª. Not in MT.

1408. 1QIsaª LXX. Not in MT.

1409. 1QIsaª 4QIsaᵇ LXX. *and all* MT.

1410. Feminine 1QIsaª. Masculine MT.

who calls on your name or strives to take hold of you; for you have hidden your face from us, and *have given us*[1411] into the hand of our iniquity.

8 *But as for you,*[1412] O LORD, you are our Father; *and*[1413] we are *clay,*[1414] and you are our potter; we are all the work of *your hands.*[1415] 9 Do not be angry beyond measure, O LORD, and do not remember our iniquity *for a long time.*[1416] Please look now, we are all your people. 10 Your holy cities have become a wilderness; Zion has become *like*[1417] a wilderness, Jerusalem a desolation. 11 *Our holy temple and our splendor,* where our ancestors praised you, *have become*[1418] a conflagration of fire, and *all our dearest places have become*[1419] ruins. 12 After all this, can you hold yourself back, O LORD? Will you keep silent, and punish us so severely?

65 1 I let myself be sought out by those who did not *ask me,*[1420] be found by those who did not seek me. I said, "Here I am, here I am," to a nation that did not call on my name. 2 I held out my hands all day long to a *disobedient*[1421] people, who walk in a way that is not good, pursuing their own inclinations; 3 a people who continually provoke me to my face, *they*[1422] keep sacrificing in gardens and *waving their hands*[1423] on *stone altars;*[1424] 4 who sit inside tombs, and spend the night in secret places; who eat swine's flesh, with the *broth*[1425] of detestable things *in*[1426] their pots; 5 who say, "Keep to yourself; do not *touch*[1427] me, *I am*[1428]

1411. Possible meaning 1QIsaᵃ. *have melted us* MT. *have delivered us* LXX.

1412. 1QIsaᵃ. *But now* MT LXX.

1413. 1QIsaᵃ LXX. Not in MT.

1414. 1QIsaᵃ LXX. *the clay* 1QIsaᵇ MT.

1415. 1QIsaᵃ LXX. *your hand* MT.

1416. 1QIsaᵃ LXX. *forever* MT.

1417. 1QIsaᵃ LXX. Not in 1QIsaᵇ MT.

1418. 1QIsaᵃ. *Our holy and glorious temple . . . has become* MT LXX.

1419. 1QIsaᵃ. *all our dearest places has become* MT (error?). *our every dearest place has become* MTᵐˢˢ. *all the glorious places have collapsed* LXX.

Chapter 65. 1QIsaᵃ: all; 4QIsaᵇ: 65:1; 1QIsaᵇ: 65:17–25.

1420. 1QIsaᵃ LXX. *ask* MT.

1421. 1QIsaᵃ. *an obstinate* MT.

1422. 1QIsaᵃ LXX. Not in MT.

1423. 1QIsaᵃ. *offering incense* MT LXX.

1424. 1QIsaᵃ. *brick altars* MT LXX.

1425. 1QIsaᵃ MTqᵉʳᵉ LXX. *violence* (or, *bits*) MT.

1426. 1QIsaᵃ. Not in MT LXX.

1427. 1QIsaᵃ. *come near* MT LXX.

1428. 1QIsaᵃ. *for I am* MT LXX.

too holy for you." Such people are smoke in my nostrils, a fire that keeps burning all day long. 6 See, it stands written before me: I will not keep silent, but I will repay; I will indeed repay *into*[1429] their laps 7 both your iniquities and your ancestors' iniquities together, says the LORD; because they offered incense on the mountains and insulted me on *hills,*[1430] I will measure *into*[1431] their laps full payment for their previous actions.

8 Thus says the LORD: As when wine is found in the cluster, and people *have said,*[1432] "Do not destroy it, for there is a gift in it," so I will do for my servants' sake, by not destroying them all. 9 I will bring forth descendants from Jacob, and from Judah *they will inherit*[1433] my mountains; my chosen people will inherit it, and my servants will settle there. 10 Sharon will become a pasture for flocks, and the Valley of Achor *for the resting of herds,*[1434] for my people who have sought me. 11 But as for you who forsake the LORD, who forget my holy mountain, who spread a table for Fortune and *fill*[1435] *drink offerings*[1436] for Destiny; 12 I will destine you for the sword, and all of you will bend down for the slaughter. For I called, but you did not answer; I spoke, but you did not listen—but you did evil in my sight, and chose what I took no pleasure in.

13 Therefore thus says the LORD:[1437] See, my servants will eat, but you will go hungry; my servants will drink, but you will go thirsty; my servants will rejoice, but you will be put to shame; 14 my servants will sing *in gladness*[1438] of heart, but you will *lament*[1439] from anguish of heart, and will wail from brokenness of spirit. 15 You will leave your name for my chosen ones to use as a curse, and the Lord GOD will put you to death *permanently.*[1440] 16 *Then whoever takes an oath*[1441] by the God of faithfulness, and whoever takes an oath in the land, will swear by the God of faithfulness; for the former troubles are forgotten and are hidden from my eyes.

1429. 1QIsaᵃ. *upon* MT LXX.

1430. 1QIsaᵃ. *the hills* MT LXX.

1431. 1QIsaᵃ MTqere. *upon* MT LXX.

1432. 1QIsaᵃ. *say* MT LXX.

1433. Literally, *he will inherit* (imperfect) 1QIsaᵃ LXX. Literally, *one who will inherit* (participle) MT.

1434. 1QIsaᵃ LXX. *for herds to lie down* MT.

1435. 1QIsaᵃ. *who fill* MT.

1436. 1QIsaᵃ. *cups of mixed wine* or *mixing vessels* MT LXX.

1437. 1QIsaᵃ* LXX. LORD GOD 1QIsaᵃ(corr) MT.

1438. 1QIsaᵃ LXX. *out of gladness* MT.

1439. 1QIsaᵃ. *cry out* MT LXX.

1440. 1QIsaᵃ. *but to his servants he will give a different name.* MT LXX.

1441. 1QIsaᵃ. *Then whoever invokes a blessing in the land will bless* MT LXX.

17 For see, I am about to create new heavens and a new earth; the former things will not be remembered, nor will they come to mind. 18 But *be glad*[1442] and *rejoice*[1443] forever in what I am creating; for I am about to create Jerusalem as a joy, and its people as a delight. 19 I will rejoice over Jerusalem, and take delight in my people; no longer will the sound of weeping be heard in it, or the cry of distress. 20 *And*[1444] there will no longer be in it *a young boy*[1445] who lives but a few days, or an old person who does not live out his days; for one who dies at a hundred years will be considered a mere youth, and one who falls short of a hundred will be considered accursed. 21 They will build houses and dwell in them; they will plant vineyards and eat their fruit. 22 They will not build for others to inhabit; they will not plant for others to eat; for like the days of *a tree*[1446] so will be the days of my people, and my chosen ones will long enjoy the work of their hands. 23 They will not toil in vain or bear children doomed for calamity; for they will be offspring *blessed*[1447] by the LORD—and their descendants with them. 24 Before they call I will answer; while they are yet speaking I will hear. 25 The wolf and the lamb will feed together, and the lion will eat straw like the ox; but as for the serpent—its food will be dust! They will not harm or destroy on my entire holy mountain, says the LORD.

66 1 Thus says the LORD: Heaven is my throne, and the earth is my footstool. Where is the house that you would build for me, and where will my resting-place be? 2 All these things my hand has made, and so all these things came into being, says the LORD. But this is the one whom I will look upon: the one who is humble and contrite in spirit, and *who*[1448] trembles *at*[1449] my word.

3 Whoever slaughters an ox is *like*[1450] one who kills a human being; whoever sacrifices a lamb is like one who breaks a dog's neck; whoever makes a grain offering is like one who offers pig's blood; whoever makes a memorial offering of frankincense is like one who blesses an idol. These have chosen their own ways, and they take delight in their abominations; 4 so I also will choose harsh treatment for them, and will bring upon them what they dread. For when I called, *no*

1442. Singular 1QIsaᵃ. Plural MT.

1443. Singular 1QIsaᵃ. Plural 1QIsaᵇ MT.

1444. 1QIsaᵃ LXX. Not in 1QIsaᵇ MT.

1445. 1QIsaᵃ. *an infant* 1QIsaᵇ MT (cf. 49:15).

1446. 1QIsaᵃ. *the tree* 1QIsaᵇ MT LXX.

1447. Singular 1QIsaᵃ LXX. Plural 1QIsaᵇ MT.

Chapter 66. 1QIsaᵃ: all; 1QIsaᵇ: all; 4QIsaᶜ: 66:20–24; 4QIsaᵇ: 66:24.

1448. 1QIsaᵃ. Not in 1QIsaᵇ MT.

1449. 1QIsaᵃ, 1QIsaᵇ, MT all use different Hebrew prepositions.

1450. 1QIsaᵃ LXX. Not in 1QIsaᵇ MT.

one[1451] answered, when I spoke, they did not listen; but they did what is evil in my sight, and chose what displeases me. 5 Hear the word of the LORD, you who tremble at *his words:*[1452] Your own brothers who hate you and exclude you because of my name have said, "Let the LORD be glorified, *he will see*[1453] your joy"— but it is they who will be put to shame.

6 Listen, an uproar *in*[1454] the city! A noise from the temple! It is the sound of the LORD, dealing retribution to his enemies! 7 Before she went into labor she gave birth; before her pangs came upon her *she delivered*[1455] a son. 8 Who has ever heard of such a thing? *And*[1456] who ever *sees*[1457] such things? Can a country be born in one day, or can a nation be a child in one moment? Yet no sooner Zion was in labor then she delivered her children. 9 Am I to open the womb and not deliver? says the LORD. And when I bring to delivery, *am I to close*[1458] the womb? asks your God.

10 Rejoice with Jerusalem, and be happy for her, all you who love her; rejoice with her in gladness, all you who mourn over her— 11 so that you may nurse and be satisfied at her comforting breasts, and so that you may drink deeply with delight from her glorious bosom.

12 *Thus*[1459] says the LORD: I shall extend prosperity to her like a river, and the wealth of nations like a flooding stream; and you will nurse and *you*[1460] will be carried on her hip, and bounced on her knees. 13 Like a child whom his mother comforts, so I will comfort you; and you will be comforted in Jerusalem. 14 And when you see this, your heart will rejoice and your bodies will flourish like grass; and the hand of the LORD will be made known beside his servants, but his indignation against his enemies. 15 For see, the LORD will come with fire, and *his chariot*[1461] like the whirlwind, to pay back his anger, *yes his anger,*[1462] in fury, and *his rebukes*[1463] in flames of fire. 16 For with fire and with his sword the LORD will

---

1451. 1QIsaᵃ. *and no one* MT LXX.

1452. 1QIsaᵃ. *his word* MT LXX.

1453. 1QIsaᵃ. *so that we may see* MT. *so that* [*the name of the* LORD] *may be seen* LXX.

1454. 1QIsaᵃ. *from* MT LXX.

1455. 1QIsaᵃ. Literally, *and she delivered* 1QIsaᵇ MT LXX.

1456. 1QIsaᵃ LXX. Not in 1QIsaᵇ MT.

1457. 1QIsaᵃ. *has seen* 1QIsaᵇ MT LXX.

1458. *waw* + imperfect 1QIsaᵃ. *waw* + perfect 1QIsaᵇ MT.

1459. 1QIsaᵃ. *For thus* MT LXX.

1460. Apparently feminine plural 1QIsaᵃ. Masculine plural MT.

1461. 1QIsaᵃ. *his chariots* MT LXX.

1462. 1QIsaᵃ. Not in 1QIsaᵇ MT LXX.

1463. Apparently plural 1QIsaᵃ. *his rebuke* 1QIsaᵇ MT.

proceed to judgment[1464] on all *humanity,*[1465] and those slain by the LORD will be many.

17 Those who sanctify and purify themselves to go into the gardens, following the one at the center of those who eat the flesh of pigs, *detestable things*[1466] and rats—*together,*[1467] *says*[1468] the LORD. 18 But as for me, I know their deeds and their thoughts; *come*[1469] and gather all nations and tongues, and they will come and see my glory. 19 I will set up *signs*[1470] among them, and from them I will send survivors to the nations, to Tarshish, *Put,*[1471] and *Lud*[1472]—which draw the bow—to Tubal and *Javan,*[1473] to the distant coastlands that have not heard of my fame or seen my glory. Then they will proclaim my glory among the nations. 20 They will *bring all, all*[1474] your kindred from all the nations, *to*[1475] my holy mountain Jerusalem as an offering to the LORD—on horses, in chariots, in wagons, and on mules, *yes and on mules,*[1476] and on camels, says the LORD—just as the Israelites bring a grain offering to the house of the LORD in a clean vessel. 21 And I shall also select some of them *for myself*[1477] as priests and as Levites, says the LORD. 22 For just as the new heavens and the new earth that I am about to make will endure before me, says the LORD, so will your descendants and your name endure. 23 From new moon to new moon, and from sabbath *to sabbath,*[1478] all *humanity*[1479] will come to worship before me, says the LORD.

24 And they will go out and look upon the dead bodies of the people who rebelled against me; for their worm will not die, nor will their fire be quenched, and they will be an object of revulsion to all *humanity.*[1480]

1464. 1QIsaᵃ. *settle his claim* 1QIsaᵇ MT.

1465. Literally, *the humanity* 1QIsaᵃ. *humanity* MT.

1466. Or (possibly), *vermin*.

1467. 1QIsaᵃ. *they will come to an end together* 1QIsaᵇ MT LXX.

1468. 1QIsaᵃ. *declares* MT.

1469. IQIsaᵃ (imperative, or *they have come*). *I am about to come* MT LXX.

1470. IQIsaᵃ LXX. *a sign* 1QIsaᵇ MT.

1471. I.e., Lybia.

1472. I.e., Lydia.

1473. I.e., Greece.

1474. 1QIsaᵃ (with the first *all* written above the line). *bring all* 1QIsaᵇ MT. *bring* LXX.

1475. 1QIsaᵃ LXX. *upon* MT.

1476. 1QIsaᵃ (error). Not in 1QIsaᵇ MT LXX.

1477. 1QIsaᵃ LXX. Not in 1QIsaᵇ LXX.

1478. Literally, *to her sabbath* 1QIsaᵃ 4QIsaᶜ. *to his sabbath* MT.

1479. Literally, *the humanity* 1QIsaᵃ. Literally, *humanity* 4QIsaᵇ MT LXX.

1480. Literally, *the humanity* 1QIsaᵃ. Literally, *humanity* 4QIsaᵇ MT LXX.

JEREMIAH

The prophet Jeremiah preached during the closing years of the kingdom of Judah, and witnessed the destruction of Jerusalem and the Temple by the Babylonians in 587 BCE. After many Jews were exiled to Babylon, he chose to stay in Jerusalem in order to help those who had remained to begin again. But a few years later this prophet was forced to flee to Egypt in exile and soon thereafter was heard of no more.

Six Jeremiah scrolls were found at Qumran: one in Cave 2[a] and five in Cave 4.[b] Although these manuscripts between them preserve much of the book's fifty-two chapters, they are all so badly damaged and fragmentary that not even a trace of twenty-one chapters is preserved.[c] These Jeremiah manuscripts were copied over a period of approximately two hundred years, ranging from about 200 BCE (4QJer[a]) to the latter part of the first century BCE (4QJer[c]).

Two important scrolls are 4QJer[b] and 4QJer[d], which reflect a Hebrew text that is very different than the Masoretic form of Jeremiah from which modern Bibles have been translated. It is also interesting to note that the biblical text in these two manuscripts is very similar to the Hebrew text from which the Septuagint (LXX) was translated. This is true not only in small details but also in major aspects where the Septuagint differs from the Masoretic Text. Most notably, 4QJer[b] and 4QJer[d] (before they were damaged) and the Septuagint present a version of Jeremiah that is about 13 percent shorter than the longer version found in modern Bibles! One example of this shorter text is in Jeremiah 10:3–11, which is a satire on idols. While the Masoretic Text has all nine verses, the Greek Bible and 4QJer[b] lack verses 6–8 and 10, which extol the greatness of God.[d]

---

a. 2QJer.   **b.** 4QJer[a], 4QJer[b], 4QJer[c], 4QJer[d], and 4QJer[e].   **c.** Chapters 1–3, 5–6, 16, 23–24, 28–29, 34–41, 45, and 51–52.   **d.** Although some text has to be reconstructed here for 4QJer[b], enough remains to show that it never contained the three verses for this section.

Another fascinating scroll is 4QJer[a], one of the oldest of all the Dead Sea Scrolls (copied, as we noted, about 200 BCE or even earlier). This manuscript contains a large number of corrections; in fact, no other Qumran text has as many corrections in proportion to the length of the document. The most noticeable example is in column 3, which contains additions made by a second scribe after the original scribe had written Jeremiah 7:28 to 9:2 but had omitted a long section (7:30 to 8:3). The second scribe's attempt to insert so much missing text has resulted in a most unusual format: he squeezed Jeremiah 7:30–31 into the gap between 7:29 and 8:4, then filled in 7:32 to 8:3a sideways along the left margin and wrote 8:3b upside down at the bottom of the page!

Besides the six Jeremiah scrolls, several other Qumran scrolls mention Jeremiah or have some relationship to his book. One of these is the Epistle of Jeremiah,[e] written in Greek and found in Catholic and Orthodox Christian Bibles as part of the Apocrypha (Baruch 6); a translation of papEPJer gr follows the book of Jeremiah in *The Dead Sea Scrolls Bible*. The theme of the Epistle of Jeremiah, supposedly written by Jeremiah himself, is condemnation of idolatry; the preserved text in the Qumran scroll is from verses 43–44. Another interesting text is 4QApocryphon of Jeremiah A (4Q383), where we find the phrase "And I, Jeremiah,"[f] which claims the prophet to be the speaker.

A final text worthy of mention is 4QApocryphon of Jeremiah C (4Q385b). This fragment, which contains two columns, draws on Jeremiah 40 to 44, although 1:4–6 recalls the fall of Jerusalem as found in Jeremiah 52:12–13. It is also interesting to note that the name *Nebuzaradan* in 4Q38b and 4QJer[d] (43:6) is spelled the same, and slightly different to the form in the Masoretic Text.[g] The first column seems to be concerned chiefly with Jeremiah's relations with the deportees to Babylon, whereas the second is clearly about his relations with the Jews in Egypt. The first column includes the following lines:

2 [. . . and] Jeremiah the prophet [went] from before the Lord.
3 [to go with the] exiles who were led captive from the land of Jerusalem and came [to]
4 [. . .] king of Babylon, when Nebuzaradan, the Chief Cook, struck

---

e. papEpJer gr (7Q2), which is written on papyrus.   f. 4Q383 frg. 1, line 2.   g. The MT reads *Nebuzara'dan*.

5 [. . .] and he took the utensils of the House of God, the priests

6 [. . .] and the Israelites and brought them to Babylon. And Jeremiah the
prophet went

7 the river and he commanded them what they should do in the land of
[their] exile

8 [. . . to listen to] the voice of Jeremiah concerning the words which God
had commanded him

9 [. . . so that] they should keep the covenant of the God of their ancestors in
the land

10 [of their captivity . . . and should not d]o as they had done, they themselves
and their kings and their priests

11 [and their princes] . . . [they de]file[d the na]me of God . . .

It appears that Jeremiah is here being portrayed here in terms similar to Moses.
For the Qumran community who passed down these texts, both Moses'
prophetic status and Jeremiah's Mosaic status seem to have been of particular interest.

4

■ *Chapters 1:1 to 4:4 were originally among the Jeremiah scrolls, but are unfortunately
now lost. The first preserved passage from Jeremiah is in 4QJer*, beginning at 4:5; the
prophet goes on to predict the invasion and destruction of the kingdom of Judah.*

5 [Announce in Judah and proclaim in Jerusalem, and say, "Sound the trumpet
in the land!" Cry aloud and say, "Gather together, and let us go to] the fortified
[cities]!"▲

13 See, [he goes up] like the clo[uds, and his chariots are like the whirlwind;
his horses are swifter than eagles]. Woe to us—for [we are ruin]ed! 14 [O
Jerusalem], wash [your] heart of wickedness, [so that you may be saved. How
long] will [your wicked th]oughts [dwell] within you? 15 [For a voice is declaring
from Dan, and proclaiming disaster] from Mount Ephraim: 16 "T[ell it to the nations, now! Proclaim over Jerusalem]: 'Besiegers are com[ing from a distant land,
and raising their war cry against the cities of Judah']."▲

Chapter 4. 4QJer^c: 4:5, 13–16.

7 1 [The word that came to Jeremiah from the Lord, sayi]ng: 2 Stand [at the gate of the Lord's house, and proclaim there this message, and say: Hear the word of the Lord, all you people of Judah who enter through these gates to worship the Lord.]▲

15 [And I will thrust you out of my sight, just as I have thrust out all your brothers, all the offspring of E]phraim.

16 [So as for you, do not pray for this people, nor lift up any plea or prayer for them; do not interce]de with me. For [I will] not [listen to you. 17 Do you not see what they are doing in the cities of Judah and in the st]ree[ts of Jerusalem? 18 The children gather wood, the fathers light the fire, *and the women knead dough* . . . ;[1] and they pour out dr]ink offer[ings] to [other] go[ds in order to provoke me to anger. 19 But am I the one they are provoking? asks the Lord. Is it not themselves], to [their own shame]?▲

27 [And you shall speak all these words to them, but they will not listen to you; and you shall call to them, but they will not answer you. 28 And you shall say to them: "This is] the nati[on that did not obey the voice of the Lord their God, and did not accept discipline; truth has perished, and] is cut off from [their mou]th. 29 [Cut off your hair, and cast it away, and take up a lamenta]tion [on the bare heights]; for [the Lord] has rejected [and forsaken the generation of his wrath]."

30 [For the children of Judah have done what is evil in my sight, sa]ys the Lord; they have set their abominations in [the house whi]ch [is called by my name, to defile it. 31 And] they ha[ve built] the high places of Topheth, which is in the valley [of the son of Hinnom, to burn their sons and] their da[ughters] in the fire—which I did not command, [no]r did it enter my mind. 32 [Therefore, beho]ld, the days are coming, says the Lord, when it will no lon[ger] be called [Topheth, or the Valley of the son of Hinnom, but the Valley of Slaughter: for they will bury the dead in Topheth until there is no more room left. 33 Then the corpses of this people will be food for the birds of the air], and for the animals of the ea[r]th; and no o[ne will frigh]ten them away. 34 Then I will bring to an end from the cities of Judah, and from [the streets of Jerusalem, the sound of joy and the sound of gladness, the voice of the bridegroom and the voice of the bride; for the land will become a waste].

8 1 [At that time, says the Lord], *they will bring out*[2] the bones of the kings of Judah, and the bones of its princes, and [the bones of the priests, and the

---

Chapter 7. 4QJer[a]: 7:1–2, 15–19, 28–34.

1. Spacing shows that 4QJer[a] most likely had a shorter text here. *and the women knead dough to make cakes for the Queen of Heaven* MT LXX.

Chapter 8. 4QJer[a]: 8:1–12, 18–19, 23; 4QJer[c]: 8:1–3, 21–23.

2. 4QJer[a] MT[qere] LXX. *and they will bring out* MT.

bones of the prophets, and the bones of the inhabitants of Jerusalem from] their [graves]. 2 Then they will spread them before the sun [*and all star*]s,[3] which they have loved and which they have served, and after which [they have followed], and which [they have consulted, and which they have wor]shiped. *And they*[4] will not [be gathered up nor buried, but will be like] dung upon the surface of the ground. 3 [And] death [will be preferred to li]fe by all the remnant [that remains] of this evil family, that remains [in all the pla]ces where [I have] *scattered them*,[5] [says the L]ORD of hosts.

4 [Then you shall say to them, Thus says the LORD: When men fall down, do they not get up again? *When someone goes astray*,[6] 5 why then] has this people of [Jerusalem] turn[ed away in perpetual backsliding? They cling to deceit, they refuse to return]. 6 I have paid heed and heard, [but they do not speak honestly; no one repents of his wickedness, saying, "What have I done?" Every one pursues] his own course like a horse [charging headlong into battle. 7 Even the stork in the heavens knows her appointed seasons, and the dove, the swallow and] the crane *will observe*[7] the [time of their coming—but my people do not understand the ordinance of the LORD.

8 How can you say, "We are wise, and the law of the LORD is with us"? But Se]e, the false pen of the scribes has handled it falsely. 9 [The wise men are put to shame, they are dismayed and taken. See, they have rejected the word of the LORD; w]hat kind of wisdom [is in] them? 10 [Therefore I will give their wives to others, and their fields to new owners. For] every one from the least to the greatest is greedy for gain; [from prophet to priest every one deals falsely. 11 And they have treated th]e [wound of] my people's [daughter] care[lessly, saying, "Peace, peace," when there is no peace. 12 Were they ashamed when] *they had committed*[8] [abominati]on? Yet they were [not] at all [ashamed, nor could they blush. Therefore they will fall among those who fall; at the time of their visitation they will be cast down, says the LORD]. ▲

18 [My joy is gone, grief is upon] me, [my heart is faint within me. 19 See, the sound of the cry of my people's daughter from a land that is very far off: "Is] not [the L]ORD in [Zion? It not her King in her?" Why have they provoked me to anger with their graven images, and with foreign idols? 20 The harvest is past, the

---

3. 4QJer^c (probable reading). *and the moon and all the host of heaven* 4QJer^a MT LXX.

4. 4QJer^c MT^{mss}. *And they* MT LXX.

5. 4QJer^c (probable meaning). *driven them* MT LXX.

6. 4QJer^a (shorter text, reconstructed). *When someone goes astray, does he not return?* MT LXX.

7. 4QJer^a. *have observed* MT LXX.

8. 4QJer^a originally omitted *they had committed* but then added it above the line. This reading agrees with MT LXX.

summer is ended, and we are not saved. 21 For the hurt of my people's daughter I am hurt; I mourn], dismay has taken hold of me. 22 Is there no balm [in Gilead? Is there no physician there]? Why then has the health of [my people]'s daughter not recovered?

9 1 O that [my head] were a spri[ng of water, and] my eyes a fountain [of tears, so that I might weep day and night for the slain of my people's daughter]! 2 O that I had [in the desert a travelers' lodging-place, so that I might leave my people and go away from them! For they are all adulterers, a crowd of treacherous people. 3 And they bend their tongues like bows, and have grown strong in the land for falsehood—but not for truth. For they proceed from evil to evil, and they do not acknowledge me, *says the L]ORD of hosts.*[9] 4 Let every one [beware of his neighbor, and put no trust in any brother; for every] brother act[s deceitfully, and every neighbor goes around as a slanderer. 5 And every one deceives his neighbor, and does] not [speak the tru]th. [They have taught their tongues to speak lies; they weary themselves with committing iniquity]. 6 Your dwelli[ng is in the midst of deceit; in their deceit they refuse to acknowledge me, says the LORD.

7 Therefore, thus says the LORD of hosts: See, I will refine and test them; for what else can I do, because of the daughter of my people]? 8 Their to[ngue is a *dea]dly*[10] [arrow]; it speaks deceit. With his mouth [one speaks peaceably to his neighbor, but in his heart he sets a trap for him. 9 Should] I not punish them [for] these things? asks the LORD. [Should I not avenge myself] on a nation such as this? 10 I will take up weeping and wailing *for mountains,*[11] and a la[mentation] for the pastures of the wilderness. [For they are laid waste so that no one passes through, nor] is the lowing of cattle heard; both the birds of the air and the anima[ls have fled and are gone. 11 I will make Jerusalem a heap of ruins], a dwelling-place of jackals; and I will make the towns of Judah a desolation, with[out inhabitant].

12 Which [person] is wise enough *to understand*[12] this? And [to] whom has the mo[uth of the Lo]RD spoken [to declare it? Why is] the la[nd rui]ned (and) laid waste like a desert, so that no one passes through? 13 [And the Lo]RD [says]: Because they have forsaken [my la]w [which] I s[et] before them, and have not obeyed my voi[ce], nor walk[ed] according to it, 14 but have followed the stub[bornness of their own hearts, and (have followed) the Baals], just as [their an]cestors taught them. 15 Therefore, thus says [the L]OR[D of hosts, the God of

---

Chapter 9. 4QJer^c: 9:0–6 [Heb 8:23–9:5]; 4QJer^a: 9:2–3, 8–16 [Heb 9:1–2, 7–15]; 4QJer^b: 9:23–26 [Heb 9:22–25].

9. 4QJer^c. *says the LORD* MT. Not in LXX.

10. 4QJer^a MT LXX. *deadly* MT^{qere}.

11. 4QJer^a. *for the mountains* MT LXX.

12. 4QJer^a (corrected text). *to understand* 4QJer^a (uncorrected text) MT.

Israe]l: See, I am feeding them, [this very people, with wormwood], and I am gi[ving them poisonous water to drink. 16 I will also scatter them among nations whi]ch [neither they nor their ancestors have kno]wn; [and I will send the s]word [after them, until I have destroyed them].▲

23 [Thus says the LORD: Do not let the wise person boast in] his wisd[om], nor let [the strong man boa]st [in his might, do not the rich glory in his riches; 24 but let the one who boasts boast in this: that he understands and knows me, that I am the LORD who exercises lovingkindness, justi]ce, and righteousness in the earth— for [in these things I delight, says the LORD.

25 See, the days are coming, says the LORD, when I will punish all those who are circumcised only in their foreskin: 26 Egypt, Judah, Edom, the Ammonites, Moab, and all those] with shaven temples who liv[e in the desert. For all these nations are uncircumcised, and all the house of Israel is uncircumcised in heart].

10 1 [Hear the word that the LORD speaks to you, O house of Israel. 2 Thus says the LORD: Do not learn] the way of the nations, [and do not be dismayed at the signs of heaven; for the nations are dismayed at them. 3 For the customs of the peoples are false; for *they*[13] are a tree cut down from the forest, the work of a craftsman's hands with an ax]. 4 They deck it [with silver and with go]ld; [they fasten it] with hammer [and nails so that it cannot move].▲

9 [Hammered silver is brought from Tarshish and gold from Uphaz; *they are all the products of skilled workers and the hands of the goldsmith*], *with blue and purple* [*for their clothing.*[14] 10 *But the LORD is the true God; he is the living God and*] *the everlasting King; at* [*his a*]*nger* [*the earth quakes, and the nations cannot endure his wrath*].[15]

11 [T]his is what you shall say to them: [The gods who did not make the heavens and the earth] will perish from the earth [and from under the heavens. 12 It is he who made the earth by his power, who established the world by his wisdom, and by his understanding st]retched out the heavens. 13 *When* [*he*] *utters his voi*[*ce,*[16] there is a tumult of waters in the heavens], and he makes clouds rise [from the en]ds of the earth. He makes lightnings for the rain, [and] brings forth the wind [from his storehouses. 14 Every one is senseless and without knowledge;

Chapter 10. 4QJer^b: 10:2, 4, 9, 11, 13, 15, 18–19, 21; 4QJer^a: 10:9–14, 23; 4QJer^c: 10:12–13.

13. Literally, *it*.

14. The latter part of vs 9 (following *Uphaz*) is arranged differently in the ancient sources. The reading reflected in our translation is found in 4QJer^b LXX. In contrast, 4QJer^a MT reads: *the work of the craftsman and of the hands of the goldsmith, with blue and purple for their clothing; they are all the product of skilled workers.*

15. 4QJer^a MT. Not in 4QJer^a LXX.

16. 4QJer^a MT. Not in 4QJer^c LXX.

every goldsmith is put to shame by his idols. For his images are false, and there is n]o breath in [them. 15 They are worthless, a work of delusion]; at the moment of their punishment [they will perish. 16 He who is the portion of Jacob is not like these, for he is the one who formed all things, and Israel is the tribe of his inheritance; the LORD of hosts is his name].

17 [Pick up your bundle from the ground, you who live under siege! 18 For thus says the LORD: See, I am going to hu]rl out *the inhabitant*[17] of [the land at this time, and I will bring distress on them, so that they will be captured. 19 Woe to me because of my injury! My wound is severe, but I said, "Truly this is my punishment, and I must bear it." 20 My tent is destroyed, and all my ropes are broken: my children have gone from] me [and are no more; there is no one to spread my tent again, and to set up my curtains. 21 For the shepherds are senseless, and do not] inquire [of the LORD; therefore they have not prospered, and their entire flock is scattered. 22 Listen—a noise! Hear it coming, a great commotion from the land of the north to make the cities of Judah a desolation, a haunt of jackals].

23 [I know, O LORD, that a person's way is not in himself, that a person], as he walks, cannot direct [his steps]. ▲

11 [1 The word that came to Jeremiah from the Lord: 2 Hear the words of this covenant, and speak to the people of Judah and the inhabitants of Jerusalem. 3 You shall say to them, Thus says the LORD, the God of Israel: Cursed be anyone who does not hear] the words of [this] covenant, 4 [which I commanded your ancestors at the time I brought th]em out of the land of Egypt, from the [ir]on-smelting furnace, say[ing: Listen to my voice, and] you [do] everything that I command you. So you will be my people, and [I will be your] God, 5 so that I may establish the oath which I swore [to your ancestors, to give th]em a land flowing with mil[k and honey, just as it is] tod[ay]. Then I answer[ed and said, "Amen, LORD!" 6 Then the L]ORD [said] to m[e: Proclaim all these words in the towns of Judah and in the streets of Jerusalem: Hear the words of this covenant and carry them out]. ▲

18 [It was the LORD who made it known to me, and I knew; then you showed me their (evil) deeds. 19 But I was like a gentle lamb led to the slaughter]; and I did not [realize that it was against me they had devised schemes, saying, "Let us destroy the tree with its fruit, and let us cut him off from the land of the living, so that his name may no] longer be remembered." 20 [But, O LORD of hosts, you who judge righteously and test] the heart and the mind, let me [see your vengeance upon them—for to you have I revealed my cause]. ▲

---

17. 4QJer[b]. *the inhabitants* MT LXX.
Chapter 11. 4QJer[a]: 11:3–6, 19–20.

12 3 [But you, O Lord, know me; you see me, and test my attitude toward you. P]ull them out like [sheep for the slaughter, and set them apart for the day of slaughter. 4 How long will the la]nd [mourn], and the grass of every fie[ld wither? Because of the wickedness of those who live there, the animals and the birds are swept away], because people said, [*"The Lo*]RD[18] will not see [what happens to us!" 5 If you have raced with footrunners and they have tired you out, how can you co]mpete with horses? [And if you fall down] on [safe ter]rain, [how will you manage in the thickets of the Jordan? 6 For even] your k[insmen] and your father's household—even th[ey have betrayed you; yes, they have raised a loud cry against you. Do not trust th]em, though they may say [nice things] to y[ou].

7 [I have forsaken my house, I have abandoned my heritage; I have given my] heart's be[loved into the hands of her enemies]. ▲

13 [They have sown wheat but have reaped thorns; they have tired themselves out but profit nothing. So] be ashamed of [your har]vests [because of the LORD's fierce anger].

14 [Thus] says the LORD with respect to a[ll my evil] neighbors [who seize the inheritance which I have given] my people Israe[l to inherit: See, I am] about to pluck them up [from off their land, and I will pluck up the house of Judah] from [among them. 15 And after] I have [pl]ucked [th]em up, [I will again have compassion on them, and I will bring each of them back to his own inheritance and to his own country. 16 And then], if they really l[earn the ways of my people, to swear by my name: "As the LORD lives"—just as they taught] my peo[ple] to swear by [Baal—then they will be established in the midst of my people. 17 But if they will not listen], then I will completely uproot that [nati]on and destroy it, says the LORD.

13 1 Thus the LORD said to [me]: "Go and buy yourself a linen loincloth, and [put it around your waist, but do not] dip it [in water]." 2 So I bought a loincloth according to the word of the LORD, and put it around my waist. 3 Then [the word of the LORD came to me] a second time, saying, 4 "Take the loincloth that you bought and are wearing around your waist, and [get up and go] to the Euphrates, [and hide it] there in a crevice in the rocks." 5 So I went, and hid it by the Euphrates, as the LORD *commanded.*[19] 6 Then after many days the LOR[D sai]d to me, "Get up and go [to the Euphrates, and take from there the] loinc[loth th]at I commanded you to hide [there." 7 Then I went to the Euphrates, and dug, and

---

Chapter 12. 4QJerᵃ: 12:3–7, 13–17.

18. 4QJerᵃ. *God* LXX. Not in MT.

Chapter 13. 4QJerᵃ: 13:1–7, 22(?), 27; 2QJer: 13:22(?).

19. 4QJerᵃ*. *commanded me* 4QJerᵃ⁽ᶜᵒʳʳ⁾ MT LXX.

took the loincloth from the place wh]ere [I had hidden it. But now the loincloth was ruined and good for nothing].▲

22 [And if] you s[ay in your heart, "Why have these things happened to me?"—it is because of the greatness of your iniquity that your skirts have been removed and *your*] bo[dy[20] has been vi]olated.▲

27 [I have seen your abominations, your adulteries, and your neighings, your shameless prostitutions on the hills in the countryside. Woe to you, O Jerusalem]! H[ow long] will you remain [u]nclean?

14[2 Judah mourns and her gates languish; they lament on the ground, and Jerusalem's cry has ascended. 3 Her nobles send their servants for water; they come to the cisterns, but find no water and return with their vessels empty. They are ashamed and dismayed and cover their heads, 4 because the ground is cracked. Because there is no rain] in the land, the farme[rs are dismayed [and cover their heads. 5 Even the doe in the field] de[serts her newborn fawn because there is no] grass. 6 The wild asses stand on the barren heights and *are bald*[21] for air like jackals; their eyes fail [because there is no vegetation].

7 [Although our iniquities testify] against us, O LORD, do something for your name's sake. For [our ap]ostasies are many—[we have sinned] against [you].▲

15[1 [Then the LORD said to me: Even though Moses and Samuel were to stand before me, yet my heart would not go out to this people. Send them away] from my presence, and le[t them go! 2 And when they ask you, "Where shall we go?" then you are to tell them: Thus says the LORD: Th]ose destined for death shall go [to death; those destined for the sword, to the sword; those destined for famine, to famine; and those destined for captivity, to captivity].▲

17[7 [Blessed is the person who trusts in the LORD and whose trust is the LORD. 8 For he shall be like a tree planted by the waters, sending out its roots by the stream. It is not afraid when heat comes, and its leaves will stay green; in the year of drought it is not anxious, and it does not cease to be]ar fruit.

9 The hea[rt is more dev]ious [than all else; it is perverse—who can understand it? 10 I the LORD search the heart and examine the mind, to reward ea]ch according to his ways, according to the fruit of his deeds. 11 Like the par[tridge] that hatches eggs it did not lay, [so is the person who amasses wealth by unjust means. In midlife it wi]ll leave him, and at his end he will prove to be a fool. 12 [A glorious thro]ne, [set on high from the be]ginning, is the pl[ace of our

---

20. Literally, *heels.*

Chapter 14. 4QJer[a]: 14:4–7.

21. 4QJer[a] (spelling error). *pant* MT. *have drunk* in LXX.

Chapter 15. 4QJer[a]: 15:1–2.

Chapter 17. 4QJer[a]: 17:8–26.

sanctuary. 13 O hope of Israel! O LORD]! All who forsake you will be put to shame; *and my faithless ones*[22] [will be writ]ten in the dust, [because they have forsaken the fountain of] living [water], the LORD.

14 Heal me, O LORD, and I shall *heal;*[23] save me, and [I shall be save]d—[for] *you are my praise.*[24] 15 See how they say to me, "Where is [the word of the LORD? Let it come] now!" 16 But as for me, *I have not run away*[25] from being a shepherd *in your service,*[26]nor have I desi[red] the fat[al day. Yo]u know what passed from [my] lips; it was *your mouth.*[27] 17 Do not become a ter[ror] to me; you are my refuge in the day of [disaster]. 18 Let my persecutors be [put to sh]ame, but let [me not] be put to shame; let them be terrified, [but let m]e no[t] be terrified. [B]ring on them the day of ev[il], and *you will destro[y*[28] them] with twofold destruction!

19 Thus said the LORD [to] me: Go, and [stand *at*] *the public gate,*[29] through which the *king of Judah enters*[30] and through which [he goes out]; (stand also) at all [the gates of] Jerusalem. 20 Then sa[y] to them: Hear [the word of the Lo]RD, you kings of Judah, and all Judah, and all the inhabitants of Jer[usalem], who en[ter through] these [gates]. 21 Thus sa[ys the L]ORD: Take car[e of] *yourself*[31] by not *bearing*[32] a burden on the sabbath day or bringi[ng it through the gates of] Jerusalem. 22 And do not ca]rry [a burden] out of your houses or do any work on the [sa]bbath day, but keep [the sabbath day] holy, [as] I command[ed] your ancestors. 23 Yet they did not listen [or] pay attention; they stiffened their necks and wo[uld not listen or receive instruction].

24 But if you listen properly to me, says the [L]ORD, and bring in no burden through the gat[es of this city on the sabbath day, but keep] the sabbath day [holy] by not doing [any wo]rk on it, 25 then there shall enter through the gat[es of this city kings and princes who sit upon the thro]ne of David, riding in chariots [and] on horses, [they and their princes, the people of Judah and the inhabitants of

---

22. 4QJer[a] MT[qere] MT[mss]. *those who depart from me* (probable meaning) MT.

23. 4QJer[a]. *be healed* MT LXX. (It is possible, however, that 4QJer[a] simply has a rare spelling of the Hebrew word found in MT.)

24. The scribe of 4QJer[a] first wrote *my praise,* and then inserted *you are* above the line.

25. The scribe of 4QJer[a] first wrote *I have run away,* and then inserted *not* above the line.

26. Literally, *after you.*

27. 4QJer[a]★. *in your presence* 4QJer[a(corr)] MT LXX.

28. 4QJer[a]★. *destroy!* (imperative) 4QJer[a(corr)] MT LXX.

29. Literally, *[in] the gate of the children of the people.* Here 4QJer[a] agrees with MT in reading *people,* not with MT[qere], which reads *the people.*

30. 4QJer[a]. *the kings of Judah enter* MT LXX.

31. 4QJer[a]★. *yourselves* (literally, *your lives*) 4QJer[a(corr)] MT LXX.

32. Singular 4QJer[a]★. Plural 4QJer[a(corr)] MT LXX.

Jerusalem; and this city will be inhabited forever. 26 And people will come] from the towns of J[ud]ah [and the places around about Jerusalem, from the land of Benjamin, from the Shepelah, from the hill country, and from the Negev, bringing burnt offerings and sacrifices, grain offerings and frankincense, and bringing thank offerings to the house of the LORD].▲

18 [13 Therefore thus says the LORD: Ask now among the nations: Who has heard anything like this? The virgin Israel has done a most appalling thing. 14 Does the snow of Lebanon leave the rocky slopes of Sirion? Do the mountain waters, the cold flowing streams, cease to flow? 15 Yet my people have forgotten me, they burn incense to worthless idols; they have stumbled in their ways, in the an]cient pat[hs], so as to walk in bypaths, not on a highway, 16 making [their land a horror, an object of perpetual scorn. All who pas]s by it will be appalled and will shake their heads. 17 Like a wind from the east, [I will scatter them before the enemy. I will s]how them [my back, not my face], on the day of their disaster.

18 [Then] they sa[id], "Come, let us devise plo[ts] against Jeremiah; [for instruction will not perish from the priest, nor counsel from the wise], nor the word from the prophet. Come, let us attack him with our tongues and [take] no [notice of any of his words."

19 Take notice of] m[e, O LORD, and] listen to what my accusers are saying! 20 Should [evil] be a recompense f[or good? Yet they have dug a pit for *me*].[33] Remem[ber] how I [stood] before [you] to speak we[ll] on [their] behalf, to turn [your wrath away from them. 21 So give their children over to famine]; hand [them over to the pow]er of the sword. May th[eir w]ives become [childless and widows; may their men be struck with death, and their young men slain b]y the sword in battle. 22 May [a cry be hea]rd [from their houses, when you suddenly bring invaders upon them! For they have dug] a pit to [capture me], and [have laid] snares [for my feet. 23 Yet you know, O LORD, all their deadly designs against me; do not] forgiv[e] their [iniquity or blot out their sin from your sight. Let them be overthrown before you; deal with] them [in the time of your anger].

19 1 [Thus said the LORD: Go and] bu[y a potter's earthenware jar. Take along some of the elders of the people and some of the senior priests],▲

[7 And I will ruin the plans of Judah and Jerusalem in this place, and will make them fall by the sword before their enemies, and at the hands of those who seek their life. I will give their dead bodies as food to the birds of the air and to the wild animals of the earth. 8 I will also make this city a horror and an object of scorn]; every one that passes [by it will be appalled and will scoff because of all its

---

Chapter 18. 4QJer[a]: 18:15–23.

33. LXX adds *and they have hidden their punishment for me,* but spacing shows that 4QJer[a] contained the shorter text found in MT.

Chapter 19. 4QJer[a]: 19:1; 4QJer[c]: 19:8–9.

disasters. 9 And] *they will eat*[34] the flesh of [their sons and the flesh of their daughters, and they will eat one another's flesh in the siege and in the distress with which their enemies and those who seek their life afflict them].▲

20[1 When the priest Pashhur son of Immer, who was chief officer in the house of the LORD, heard Jeremiah prophesying these things, 2 Pashhur had th]e [prophet Jeremiah beaten, and put him in the] stocks [that were in the] upper [Benjamin Gate] which was by the house of [the LORD. 3 Then on the next d]ay, when Pashhur released [Jeremiah from the stoc]ks, Jeremiah said to him, "The LORD [has not nam]ed you [Pashhur], but *Terror-all-[around.*[35] 4 For thus say]s the LORD: See, I am making you *a terror*[36] [to yourself and to all] your [fr]iends; and they will fall by the sword of th[eir] enemies [while your eyes loo]k on. And I will giv[e ov]er all Judah [into the hand of the king of Babylon, and] he will carry them away as exiles *(to) Babylon*[37] or will put them [to the sword. 5 I will also give over all the we]alth of [this] city, [all its produce, all its valuables— yes, all the treasures of the kings of Judah I will give into the hand of their enemies. And they will plunder them and take them away, and carry them off to Babylon. 6 And you, Pashhur, and all who live in your house will go into exile. You will go off to Babylon, and there you will die, and there you will be buried—you, and all your friends to whom you have prophesied falsely]!"

7 O LORD, you have deceived me, [and I was deceived; you have overpowered me, and you have prevailed. I have become a laughingstock] all day long, every one [mocks me. 8 For whenever I speak, I cry out]; I proclaim, ["Violence] and destruction!" [So for me the word of the LORD has become a reproach and derision] all da[y long. 9 But if I say, "I will not mention him or speak any more in his name," then in my heart there is something like a burning fire shut up in my bones. I am weary of holding it in; indeed, I cannot].▲

13 [Sing] to [the LORD, praise the LORD! For he has delivered the life of the needy from the hands of evildoers. 14 Cursed be the da]y when I was bor[n! The day when my mother bore me—may it not be blessed]! 15 Cursed be the man [who brought the n]ews to [my fa]ther, sayi[ng, "A baby boy is born to you," making him very glad. 16 May t]hat man [be] like the tow[ns that the LORD overthrew without pity. May he hear wailing in the morning and a battle cry at no]on, 17 becau[se he did not kill me in the womb, so my mother would have been my grave and her womb always enlarged]. 18 W[hy did I ever come out of the womb to see trouble and sorrow, so that my days have been spent in shame]?

---

34. 4QJer[c] LXX. *I will make them eat* MT.

Chapter 20. 4QJer[c]: 20:2–5, 7–9, 13–15; 4QJer[a]: 20:14–18.

35. Hebrew, *Magor-[missabib]*.

36. 4QJer[c]. Literally, *as for a terror* MT. *for captivity* LXX.

37. 4QJer[c] (with *to* understood). *to Babylon* MT (with directive *he*). Not in LXX.

21 1 [The word which came to Jeremiah from the LORD when king Zedekiah sent to him Pa]shhur [son of Malkijah, and the priest Zephaniah son of Maaseiah, saying]:▲

7 [Then afterward, declares the LORD, I will hand over King Zedekiah of Judah, and] his [servants], and [the people in this city—those who survive *the pestilence*] *and*[38] *the sword*[39]—into the hands of [King Nebuchadrezzar of Babylon, into the hands of their enemies, and into the hands of] those that seek their lives. [He will strike them down with the edge of the swo]rd; [he will] not [spare them n]or have pity nor [have compassion].

8 [And to] this peop[le] you are to say, Th[us says the LORD: See], *I myself*[40] am setting [before you the way of life and] the way of death. 9 Whoever stays [in] this cit[y will die by the sword, by famine and by plague]; but whoever goes out [and sur]renders to the Chaldeans who [are besieging you will live and will have his life as a prize of war. 10 For I have set] my face [against this city for harm and not for good, says the LORD. It will be given into the hands of the king of Babylon, and he will burn it with fire].▲

22 3 [Thus says the LORD: Act with justice and righteousness, and deliver the one who has been robbed from the hand of] the oppressor. [And do no wrong or violence to the alien, the orphan and the widow, nor shed innocent blood in this place. 4 For if] you truly obey [this wo]rd, [then kings who sit on Dav]id's [throne will enter through the gates of this house], riding in chariots, *on horse*[s[41]—the king himself], *and his ser*[*vants*[42] and his people. 5 But if you will not obey these] words, [I swear by myself], declares the LORD, that [this house] will become a ruin. 6 [For thus says the LORD] concerning the house of the king of Ju[d]ah: You are like Gilead to me, like the summit of Lebanon, yet most as-sured[ly I will make you like a desert, like towns that are uninhabited. 7 And I will set apart des]troyers [against you], each one with his weapons; they will cut down [your] choicest [cedars and throw them into the fire].

8 [And many nations will pass by th]is [city], and they will say *onto*[43] one [an]other, "Why [has the LORD dealt in such a way with thi]s [great city?" 9 Then] they will answer, "Be[cause they forsook the covenant of the L]ORD their God, and worship[ed other gods and served them." 10 Do] not [weep for him

---

Chapter 21. 4QJer[a]: 21:1(?); 4QJer[c]: 21:7–10.

38. 4QJer[c] MT[mss]. Not in MT.

39. 4QJer[c]. *the pestilence and the sword and famine* MT. *death and famine and the sword* LXX.

40. 4QJer[c(corr)] LXX (cf. Deut 30:15). *I* 4QJer[c]★ MT.

Chapter 22. 4QJer[a]: 22:3(?) (or 13:22[?]), 3–16; 4QJer[c]: 22:4–6, 10–28, 28–30?

41. 4QJer[a]. *and on horses* MT LXX.

42. 4QJer[c] MT[qere]. *and his servant* MT. *and their servants* LXX.

43. 4QJer[a] (*'l*). *to* (*'l*) MT.

who is dead, n]or mourn for him; rather, wee[p bitterly] for him who goes away; for he will never return nor see [his native land] again.

11 For thus says the Lo[RD concer]ning Shallum so[n] of Josiah king of Judah, [who suc]ceeded his father Josiah who w[ent away from this place: He will n]ever [return] there; 12 but in the place where *he has*⁴⁴ led him [cap]tive, the[re he will die, and] he will neve[r] see this land [a]gain.

13 Woe to him who buil[ds] his [house] by unrighteousness, and [his upper roo]ms [by injus]tice; who makes [his neighbors] work for nothing, and does not pay them their wages; 14 who [says, "I will b]uild [my]self a spacious house with larg[e] upper rooms," *cutting*⁴⁵ out its wi[ndows, paneling it with cedar and painting it with vermilion. 15 Does] it make you a ki[ng because y]ou com[pete] in cedar? Did not your father e[at and drink, and do what is ju]st and ri[ght? Then things went well with him. 16 He defended] the cause of [the poor] and needy; then all went well. Is that not what is means [to know me? declares] the LORD. 17 [But your eyes and heart are set only on your own dishonest gain, and on shedding] *innocent*⁴⁶ [blood, and] on practicing oppression and vio[lence. 18 Therefore thus says the LORD concerning Jehoiakim the s]on of Josia[h, king of Judah: They will not mourn for him, saying, "Alas, my brother!" or "Alas, my sister]!" They will not mourn [for him: "Alas, master!" or "Alas, his majesty!" 19 He will be buried with a donkey's burial]—dragged off and th[rown outside] the gates of Jeru[salem].

20 Go up *in Lebanon*⁴⁷ [and cry out, and lift up your voice in Bashan; cry out from Abarim; for] all your *sup[porters]*⁴⁸ have been *poured out.*⁴⁹ 21 [I spoke to you in your prosperity, but you said, "I will not listen]!" This has been your practice from [your] youth, [that you have not obeyed my voice. 22 The wind will sweep away all your shepherds, and] your [lo]vers [will go] into captivity; th[en you will surely be ashamed and disgraced because of all your wickedness. 23 O inhabitant of] Lebanon, you who *make your nest*⁵⁰ in the cedars, ho[w you will groan when pangs come upon you, pain like that] of a woman in labor!

24 As I live, says the LORD, even [if Coniah son of Jehoiakim ki]ng of Judah were a [si]gnet-ring upon [my rig]ht hand, [even from there I would pull you off 25 and give you into the hands of those who are seek]ing your life, into [the hands of those wh]ose [presence] y[ou dread, into the hands of] King [Neb-

---

44. 4QJerᵃ★. *they have* 4QJerᵃ⁽ᶜᵒʳʳ⁾ MT. *I have* LXX.

45. 4QJerᶜ LXX *(separating). and he cuts* 4QJerᵃ MT.

46. 4QJerᶜ★. Literally, *the innocent* 4QJerᶜ⁽ᶜᵒʳʳ⁾ MT LXX.

47. 4QJerᶜ. Literally, *the Lebanon* MT. *to Lebanon* LXX.

48. Or, *lovers.*

49. 4QJerᶜ. *crushed* MT LXX.

50. 4QJerᶜ MT LXX. *are nested* (passive) MTqᵉʳᵉ.

uchadrezzar] of Babylon, and into the hands of the Chaldeans. 26 [Then I will hurl you and your mother who] bore you into another country, whe[re neither of you was born—and there you both will die]. 27 But as for the land [to] which they long [to return], they will not return [there].

28 Is [this man Coniah] a despised, broken jar? [Is he a vessel which no one wants? Why are he and his offspring hurled out and cast away into the land that they do n]ot k[now? 29 O land, land, land, hear the word of the LORD! 30 Thus says the LORD]: Write do[wn this man as childless, a man who will not prosper in his days; for none of his descendants will succeed in sitting on the throne of David, and ruling again in Judah].

25 7 [Yet you did not listen to me, says the LORD, so that you provoked me to anger] with the work of [your h]ands to [yo]ur own detriment.

8 Therefore thus say[s the LORD of hosts: Because you have not listened to my words, 9 I am going to send for all the peoples of the north, says the LORD, including King Nebuchadrezzar of Babylon, my servant, and I will bring them against this land and its inhabitants and against all these surrounding nations. I will utterly destroy them, and make them an object of horror and of scorn, and an everlasting disgrace].▲

15 [For thus the LORD, the God of Israel, said to me: Take this cup of the w]ine of wra[th from my hand, and make all the natio]ns to whom I [send y]ou [drink it]. 16 When they drink they will stagger and go ou[t of their minds because of the sword] that I am sending among them. 17 So I took the [cup from the LORD's hand, and made all the nations to whom the LORD had sent me drink it: 18 Jerusalem and the towns of Judah, . . . 24 and all the kings of Arabia, and all the kings of the mixed peoples who l]ive in the des[ert]; 25 and [all the kings of Zimri, all the kings of Elam], and all the kings of [Media; 26 all the kings of the north, both far and] nea[r, one after another, and all the kingdoms of the wo]rld [that are on the face of the earth. *And the king of Sheshach will drink*] *after them.*[51]▲

26 10 [And when the officials of] Judah [heard these things, they came up from] the king's [hou]se to the hou[se of the LORD and took their places in the entrance of the New Gate of the LORD's house. 11 Then] the priests [and the prophets sai]d [to the officials and to all the people, "This] man deserves [the death sentence because he has prophesied against this city—just as you have hea]rd [with yo]ur [ears]!"

12 Then [Jeremiah] spoke [to all the officials and all] the people: "[The LOR]D sent me [to prophesy against this house and against] this [city all the thi]ngs [that you have heard. 13 So now amend your ways] and your actions, [and o]bey [the

---

Chapter 25. 4QJer^c: 25:7–8, 15–17, 24–26.

51. This is one of several passages found in 4QJer^c and MT, but not included in LXX.
Chapter 26. 4QJer^a: 26:10(?); 4QJer^c: 26:10–13.

LORD your God. Then the LORD will change his mind about the disaster he has pronounced against you]." ▲

27 1 [In the beginning of the reign of Jehoiakim son of Josiah, king of Judah, this word came to Jeremiah from the LORD, as foll]ows. 2 Thus the LORD said to me: Ma[ke for yourself (a yoke of) bonds and bars], and put them on *your ne[ck]*.[52] 3 Then send word to the king of [Edom, the k]ing of Moab, the king of the Ammoni[tes], the k[ing of Tyre, and the k]ing of Si[don by the hand of the messengers who have come to Jerusalem to King Zedekiah of Judah]. ▲

[12 I spoke to King Zedekiah of Judah in the same manner: Bring your necks under the yoke of the king of Babylon, and serve him and his people—and live! 13 Why should you die, both you and your people, by the sword, by famine, and by plague, just as] the Lo[RD has spok]en [concerning the nation *that will not serve the king of Babylon?* 14 *So do not listen*[53] to the words of] the proph[ets who say t]o [you, "You shall not serve the king of Babylon," for] they are prophesy[ing a lie to you. 15 For I have not sent them, declares the LORD, but they are prophesying falsely] in [my] name, [with the result that I will drive you out and you will perish—both you and the prophets who are prophesying to you]. ▲

30 [4 Now these are the words which the LORD spoke concerning Israel and Judah: 5 Thus says the LORD: We have heard a cry of panic, of terror and no peace. 6 Ask now, and see if] a man [can give birth. Why do I see every man with his hands o]n his loins [like a woman in labor? And why have] all face[s tur]ned pale? 7 Alas! for that day is so great there will be none like it; it will be [the time of] Jacob's [distress], but [he will be rescued] from it. 8 [On that day, says the LORD of hosts, I will break his yoke of]f your neck and [I will burst] your bonds, [and foreigners will no longer make a slave of him. 9 But they will serve the LORD their God and Dav]id their king, [whom I will raise up for them]. ▲

17 [But I will restore health to you and I will heal you of your wounds, declares the LORD], because they have called you an outcast: "[It is Zion—no one cares for her]!"

18 Thus says the LORD: See, I am going to res[tore the fortunes of Ja]cob's [tents] and I will have compassion on his dwellings; the city *will be rebuilt*[54] on her

---

Chapter 27. 4QJer^c: 27:1–3, 13–15.

52. 4QJer^c spells *your neck* differently from MT, most likely in error since it preserves the alternative spelling in Jer 30:8.

53. 4QJer^c must have contained a few words less than MT at the end of vs 13 or at the beginning of vs 14. Since this portion of the scroll is no longer extant, it is not possible to identify the missing text.

Chapter 30. 4QJer^c: 30:6–9, 17–24.

54. Masculine verb 4QJer^c (treating *the city* as masc.). Feminine verb MT (treating *the city* as fem.).

ruins, and the palace will be set on its proper place. 19 From them shall come thanksgiving and the sound of merrymak[ers]. I will make them many, [and] they will not be decreased; [I] will also honor [them], and they will n[ot] be disdained. 20 Their children, too, will be as before, and *their communities*[55] [will be established] before me; [and] I will pun[ish all who oppress] them. 21 *Their nobility will be*[56] from their own, and their ruler [will arise] from their midst. [I will bring him n]ear [and he will approach] me; for who would otherwise commit himself [to approach me? says the LOR]D.

22 *So you will be my people, and I will be your* [God.[57] 23 Look, the storm of the LORD! Wrath goes forth—a swee]ping [tempest; it will burst down] on the he[ads of the wicked. 24 The fierce anger of the LORD will not turn back] until he has performed [and accomplished the intents of his heart. In the latter day]s you will understand this.

31 1 [At that time, says the LORD, I will be the Go]d of all [Israel's famil]ies, [and they will be my people. 2 Thus says the LORD]: The people who survived the swo[rd found favor in the wilderness *as they went*.[58] 3 The LORD appeared to me long ago, saying]: I have loved you with an everlasting l[ove, s]o [I have drawn you with steadfast love]. 4 I will bui[ld you up] again, [and you will be re]built, O virgin [Isr]ael! Once again [you will take up your tambourines and go forth] to the dance[s of] the merrymak[ers. 5 Once again you will plant vineyards on the hills of Samaria]; the planters will [pl]ant and will enjoy the[ir fruit. 6 For there will be a day when watchmen will cry out on the hil]ls of Ephraim: Get up, and let us go up [to Zion, to the LORD our God.

7 For thus says the LORD: Sing aloud with gladness] for Jacob, [and raise a sh]out among the foremost of the nations; procl[aim, praise, and] say, "The [L]ORD *has saved*[59] your people, the remnant of Israel!" 8 Se[e, I am going to bring th]em from the land of the north and *I have gathered them*[60] from the farthest parts of the earth, among [them] the blind and the lame, the woman with child and the woman in labor; together a great company, they will return here. 9 Th[ey] will come with weeping, [and I will lead them ba]ck [with supplicatio]ns; [I will make] them wa[lk] *by*[61] stream[s of wa]ter, on a level path *and in which*[62] they will

---

55. 4QJer^c LXX (translating the same plural form as *their testimonies*). *their community* MT.

56. 4QJer^c (with *will be* plural; LXX similar). *Their prince will be* MT (with *will be* singular).

57. Vs 22 is another example of a passage found in 4QJer^c MT, but not in LXX.

Chapter 31. 4QJer^c: 31:1–9, 11–14, 19–23, 25–26.

58. 4QJer^c (probable reading). *namely Israel, when they went to find rest* MT.

59. 4QJer^c MT^mss LXX. *O LORD, save* MT.

60. 4QJer^c. *and I will gather them* MT LXX.

61. 4QJer^c LXX. *towards* MT.

62. 4QJer^c LXX. *in which* MT.

not stumble, for I have become Israel's fathe[r and Ephraim] i[s my firstbo]rn. [10 Hear the word of the LORD, you nations, and declare it in the distant coastlands: "He who scattered Israel will gather him, and will watch over him as a shepherd watches over his flock." 11 For the LORD has ransomed Jac]ob [and has redeemed him from the hand of those too strong for him. 12 Then they will come and sing aloud on Zion's heights], and they will be radiant *over*[63] the bounty of the LORD, [over the grain, the wine and the oil, and over the young of the flocks] and the herds; their life will become like a [watered] garden, and they will never languish [ag]ain. 13 Then maidens [will rejoice] in the dance, [y]oung men [and old ones as well; I will turn] *your mournings*[64] [into joy, I will com]fort them, and give them joy instead of sorrow. 14 [And I will satiate the desire of the] pries[ts] with fatness, and [my] people will be satisfied [with] my goodness, declares the LORD.

[15 Thus says the LORD: A voice is heard in Ramah, mourning and bitter weeping, Rachel weeping for her children, refusing to be comforted for her children—because they are no more. 16 Thus says the LORD: Restrain your voice from weeping and your eyes from tears; for there is a reward for your work, declares the LORD. They will return again from the land of the enemy, 17 and there is hope for your future, says the LORD; your children will come back to their own country. 18 I have surely heard Ephraim pleading: "You disciplined me, and I endured the discipline; I was like an untrained calf. Bring me back so that I may be restored—for you are the LORD my God]. 19 [For after] I turned back, [I repented; and after I was discovered, I struck my thigh. I was ashamed and also humiliated] because I bor[e the disgrace of my youth. 20 Is Ephraim my dear son, the child I delight in]? For al[though I speak against him, I still remember him vividly. Therefore my heart yearns for him; I will indeed have mercy upon him, says the LORD].

21 Set up roadsi[gns for yourself, [make yourself guideposts; fo]cus [your mind on the highway, the road by which] you wen[t]. Return, O virg[in Israel, return to th]ese [your cities]. 22 How long will you waver to and fro, you faithless daughter? F[or the LORD has created a ne]w thing on earth—a wom[an will sur]round a man. 23 [Thus says the LORD of *ho*]*sts*, [*the God of Israel:*[65] Once again they will speak this word in the land of Judah and in its towns when I restore their fortunes: May the LORD bless you, O dwelling of righteousness, O holy mountain! 24 And Judah and all its towns will live there together, farmers and those who move about with their flocks. 25 For I will satisfy the weary one, and ev]ery soul [who is faint I will replenish. 26 At this I awoke and looked—and my sleep had been pleasant to me]. ▲

---

63. 4QJer^c LXX. *to* MT.

64. 4QJer^c. *their mourning* MT LXX.

65. 4QJer^c MT. Not in LXX.

32 24 [See, the siege-ramps have reached the city in order to take it; and because of the sword, famine, and plague, the city has been given into the hands of the Chaldeans who are attacking it]. And what [you spoke has happened, as you now can see. 25 Yet you, O LORD God, have said to me, "Buy] for yourself [the field with money, and find witnesses—although the city has been given into the hands of the Chaldeans]."▲

33 [15 In those days and at that time I will cause a righteous Branch to spring up for David; and he will execute justice and righteousness in the land. 16 In those days Judah will be saved and Jerusalem will live in safety. And this is the name by which it will be called]: "The LORD is [our right]eousness." 17 [For thus says the LORD: David shall never fail to have] a man sitting upon the throne of the hou[se of Israel; 18 nor will the Levitical priests fail to have a man] in my presence to offer burnt offerings, to burn [meal offerings and to make sacrifices continually].

19 Then the word of the LORD came to Jeremiah, [*saying:* 20 *Thus says the* LORD: *If you can break my covenant with the day and*][66] my covenant with [the] night, so that [day and night would not occur at their appointed time, 21 then my covenant with my servant David—and my covenant with my ministers the Levitical priests—can also be broken, so that he would not have a son to reign on his throne].▲

42 7 Now at the en[d of ten days the word of the LORD came to Jeremiah. 8 So he sum]moned Johanan son of Ka[reah and all the commanders of the forces that were with him, and all the people from the least to the greatest, 9 and *their god,* [s]aid,[67] ["Thus says the LORD, the God of Israel, to whom you sent me to present] your *peti*[*tions*][68] be]fore him: 10 If [you will only remain in this land, then I will build you up and not tear you down; I will plant y]ou and not up[root you, for I am sorry over the calamity that I have inflicted on you. 11 Do not be afraid of the king of Babylon, whom y]ou now fe[ar; do not be afraid of him, declares the LORD, for I am with you to save you and deliver you from his hands. 12 I will show you mercy, and he will have mercy on you and restore you to your native soil. 13 But if you keep saying, 'We will not stay in this land,' thereby disobeying the voice of the LORD your God, 14 and saying, 'No, but]

Chapter 32. 2QJer: 32:24–25(?).

Chapter 33. 4QJer^c: 33:(?), 16–20.

    66. This portion of 4QJer^c is no longer preserved. The size of the gap, however, is too short to accommodate the text found in MT (which is given above). 4QJer^c either contained a shorter text at this point, or had one or two words written above the line.

Chapter 42. 2QJer: 42:7–11, 14.

    67. 2QJer (possible error). *and he said to them* MT LXX.

    68. 2QJer. *petition* MT.

we will rather g[o to the land of Egy]pt—[where we shall not see war or hear the sound of the trumpet or be hung]ry [for bread]—and [we will stay the]re, . . .'" ▲

43 [1 And when Jeremiah finished speaking to all the people all the words of the LORD their God—all these words with which the LORD their God had sent him to them, 2 Azariah son of Hoshaiah and Johanan son of Kareah and all the other arrogant men said to Jeremiah, "You are lying! The LORD our God has not sent you to say, 'You are not to enter Egypt to settle the]re'; 3 no, Ba[ruch][69] is incit[ing you against u]s t[o deliver us into the hands of the Chaldeans, so that they may kill us or take] us [into exile] in Ba[bylon." 4 So] Johanan[70] [and all] the commanders of the for[ces] and all [the people] diso[beyed the LORD's command to stay in the land of Judah. 5 Instead Jo]hanan[71] [and all the com]manders of the for[ces to]ok all the remnant of [Judah who had returned *from all the nations whe*]*re* [*they had been driven away*][72] 6 —the men, the wome[n], the children, the [king]'s daughters, [and every person whom] *Nebuzaradan*[73] had le[ft] with Gedaliah *son of Ahikam,*[74] including the prophet Jeremiah [and Baruch son of Neriah. 7 And they entered the la]nd of Egypt, for they disobeyed the voice of the LORD; [and] they arrived *(at) Tahpanhes.*[75]

8 [Then the word of the LORD came to Jeremiah] in Tahpanhes: 9 Take some large stones in your hands, and bury them [*in the clay in the brick pavement of Pharaoh's palace*] *which is at the entrance of Tahpanhes,*[76] in the sight of the men of Judah, 10 [and say to them, Thus says the LORD of hosts, the God of Israel: See, I am going to se]nd and tak[e my servant Ki]ng *Nebuchad*[*nezzar*[77] of Babylon, and will set his throne right over th]ese [stones] that I have buried, [and] he will spread [his royal canopy over them. 11 He will come and attack the land of Egypt, giving those] who are destined for death over to death, and tho[se destined for captivity to captivity, and those destined for the sword to the sword]. ▲

Chapter 43. 4QJer^d: 43:2–10; 2QJer: 43:8–11.

69. 4QJer^d. *Baruch son of Neriah* MT.

70. 4QJer^d LXX. *Johanan son of Kareah* MT.

71. 4QJer^d LXX. *Johanan son of Kareah* MT.

72. 4QJer^d. *from all the nations where they had been driven away, in order to settle in the land of Judah* MT. *in order to settle in the land* LXX.

73. 4QJer^d LXX. *Nebuzaradan the captain of the guard* MT.

74. 4QJer^d LXX. *son of Ahikam son of Shaphan* MT.

75. 4QJer^d (*at* understood). *at Tahpanhes* MT LXX.

76. 4QJer^d (probable reading). *in the clay in the brick pavement which is at the entrance of Pharaoh's palace in Tahpanhes* MT. *in the doorway at the entrance of Pharaoh's house at Tahpanhes in view of the men of Judah* LXX.

77. 2QJer. *Nebuchadrezzar* MT.

44 1 [The word that came to Jeremiah for all the Jew]s [living in the land of Egypt, living at Migdol, at Tahpanhes, and at Memph]is, and in the land of Path[ros: 2 Thus says the LORD of hosts, the God of Israel: You yourselves have see]n all the calami[ty that I have brought on Jerusalem and on all the towns of Judah. Look], tod[ay they are *in ruins*],[78] 3 beca[use of their wickedness which they committed so as to provoke me to anger by continuing to burn incense, to ser]ve other gods whom they had not known—[neither they, nor you, nor your ancestors].▲

[11 Therefore, thus says the LORD of hosts, the God of Israel: See, I am determined to bring disaster on you and to bring all Judah to an end. 12 Then I will take the remnant of Judah who are determined to enter the land of Egypt to settle there; and they will all perish in the land of Egypt. They will fall and perish by the sword and by famine; from the least to the greatest they will die by the sword and by fa]mine; [and they will become an object of cursing and horror, of condemnation and ridicule. 13 And I will] punish [those who live in the land of Egypt, just as I have punished Jerusalem—by the swo]rd, by fam[ine, and by pestilence— 14 so that none of the remnant of] Ju[dah who have come to settle in the land of Egypt will escape or survive to return to the land of Judah, where they long to return and live; for none will return except a few fugitives].▲

46 27 [But as for you, have no fear, my servant Jacob, and do not be dismayed, O Israel! For] see, I am going to save you from fa[r away, and your offspring from the land of their] captivity. [Jacob will return and have peace and securi]ty, and no one will make him afraid. 28 As for y[ou, have no fear, my servant Jacob, says the LORD, for I am with you. For] I will pu[t a comple]te end [to all the nations where I have driven you—yet I will not put a complete end to you! But I will discipline] you in just mea[sure, and will not let you go entirely unpunished].

47 1 The wo[rd of the LORD that] came [to the prophet Jeremiah concerning the Philistines, before Pharaoh attacked Ga]za.

2 Thus say[s the LORD: See, waters are rising from the north and will become an overflowing torrent; they will overflow] the land [and everything in it, the city and those who li]ve [in it. The people will cry out, and every inhabitant of the land will wail]. 3 At the sound of the gal[loping h]oofs of his stallions, at the clat[ter of his chariots, at the rumble of his wheels, fathers will not turn back] for their child[ren] due to the limpness of their hands, 4 because of the day [that is

---

Chapter 44. 2QJer: 44:1–3, 12–14.

78. 2QJer. *in ruins and no one lives in them* MT (LXX similar).

Chapter 46. 2QJer: 46:27–28.

Chapter 47. 2QJer: 47:1–7.

coming to destroy all] the Philistines, *and I will cut off*[79] from Tyre and Si[don every ally that is left. For the LORD is going to destroy the Philistines], the remnant of Caphtor's coastlands.[80] 5 [Baldness has co]me [upon Gaza, Ashkelon is silenced. O remnant of their valley]—how long will you *scratch yourselves?*[81] 6 Ah, sw[ord of the LORD! How long until you are quiet? Put thyself into your scabbard], rest and be still! 7 But how can it r[est when the LORD has given it a charge against Ashkelon and against the seacoast]—*to there*[82] he has as[signed it]!

48 [1 Concerning Moab. Thus says the LORD of hosts, the God of Israel: Woe to Nebo, how it has been destroyed! Kiriathaim has been put to shame, it has been captured; the fortress has been disgraced and shattered. 2 The renown of Moab is no more; in Heshbon they have plotted evil against her: Come, let us cut her off from being a nation! You too, you madmen, will be silenced]; the sword [will pursue you]. 3 The sound of [an outcry from Horonaim: Devastation and great destruction! 4 Moab is destroyed]—her little ones have soun[ded out a cry. 5 For by the ascent of Luhith they go up weeping bitterly; for at the descent of Horonaim they have heard the anguished cry of destruction. 6 Flee! Save your lives! Become like a juniper in the desert]! 7 [Surely, since you have trusted in your achievements and in your treasures], you [too will be taken captive, and Chemosh will go off into exile, together with his priests and his princes]. ▲

25 [Moab's hor]n has been cut o[ff and] his ar[m br]oken, declar[es the L]ORD. 26 *Ma[ke her] drunk,*[83] for *she has become arrogant*[84] [toward the LORD]; so Moab will [wal]low in his vomit, and will also become a laughingstock. 27 For wa[s n]ot Israel [a laughingstock to you], although *he*[85] was not fou[nd] among [*your*] *thieves?*[86] Yet whenev[er you spoke of him] *you*[87] shook your head! 28 Le[ave] *your* cit[ies]*[88] and live on the rocks, you *inhabitant*[89] of Moab, and b[e*[90] like the dove

---

79. 2QJer LXX. *to cut off* MT.

80. 2QJer. *Caphtor's coastland* MT. *the coastlands* LXX.

81. 2QJer. *cut yourselves* MT. *cut (yourselves) down* LXX.

82. 2QJer. *there* MT.

Chapter 48. 2QJer: 48:2–4(?), 7, 25–39, 41–42(?), 43–45.

83. 2QJer. *make him drunk* MT LXX.

84. 2QJer. *he has magnified himself* MT (and LXX, from the context).

85. 2QJer MT^qere MT^mss. *she* MT.

86. 2QJer. *thieves* MT. *your thefts* LXX.

87. Feminine 2QJer. Masculine MT.

88. 2QJer. *the cities* MT LXX. (Masculine plural) MT LXX.

89. Feminine singular 2QJer. *inhabitants* (masculine plural) MT LXX.

90. Singular 2QJer. Plural MT. *They have become* LXX.

that n]ests beyo[nd] the mouth of a cave. 29 *Now listen to*[91] the pride of Moab—
he is v[ery pr]oud—of *his pride,* [*his*] *vanity,*[92] his arrogance, [and the haughti]ness
of his heart. 30 I my[self kn]ow [his fury], declares the Lo[RD—but it is futile, his
idle boasts] *she has not thus carried out.*[93] 31 Therefore I will wail for Mo[ab, yes], I
will cr[y out] for all Moab; I will mourn [for the men of *Kir*]-*hareseth.*[94] 32 More
than the weeping for Jaz[er] I will weep for you, O vi[*ne*][95] of Sibmah! [Your
bran]ches [stretched across the sea], reaching [as far as the sea of Jaz]er. *And*[96] [the
destroyer has descended] on your summer fru[its] and on [your grape harvest.
33 So gladness and joy have been taken away from the fruitful fiel]ds and from the
land of Moab. [I have stopped] the flow of wine from [the presses; no one treads
them with shouts of joy—the shouting is not the shout o]f joy.

34 From the outcry at Heshbon [as far as Elealeh and as far as Jahaz they have
raised their voice, from Zoar as far as Horonai]m and as far as Eglath-shelishiyah;
for [even the waters of Nimrim will become desolate. 35 And in Moab, says the
LORD, I will put an end to those who offer sacrifice on] the high place, and [to
those who burn incense to their go]ds. 36 [Therefore my heart wails for Moab
like flutes, and my heart w]ails like flute[s for the people of Kir]-heres; f[or the
riches they acquired are gone. 37 For every head] is bald and eve[ry be]ard is cu[t
off; there are gashes on all the hands and] sackcloth [on the loins]. 38 On all the
ho[usetops of] Moab [and in her streets there is lamentation everywhere; for I
have broken Moab] like a vessel th[at] no one w[ants, declares the LORD. 39 How
shattered he is! How they wail! How Moab] *have turned their*[97] back [in shame! So
Moab has become a laughingstock and an object of horror to all those around
him].

40 [For thus says the LORD: See, he will swoop down like an eagle and will
spread out his wings against Moab]. 41 [Kerioth will be captured and the strongholds will be seized. So the hearts of Moab's war]riors [on that day will be like the
heart of a woman in labor. 42 And Moab will be destroyed from being a nation,
because he has become arrogant] toward the LORD. 43 [Terror and pit and trap are
upon yo]u, [O inhabitants of Moab, says the LORD. 44 *Then the one who flees at the*

---

91. 2QJer. *We have heard of* MT. *I have heard of* LXX.

92. 2QJer *his loftiness, his pride* MT.

93. 2QJer. *have achieved nothing* MT. *he has not thus carried out* LXX.

94. 2QJer (cf. Isa 16:7). *Kir-heres* MT.

95. 2QJer LXX. *the vine* MT.

96. 2QJer. Not in MT LXX.

97. 2QJer. *has turned his* MT. *has turned her* (LXX, from context).

sound of the terror[98] will fall into the pit, and the one who cl]imbs [out of the pit will be caught in the trap. For I shall bring upon her, upon Moab, the year of their punishment, declares the L]ORD. 45 [In the shadow of Heshbon the fugitives stand without strength; for a fire has gone forth from Heshbon, and a flame] from *the town of*[99] [Sihon. It has devoured Moab's forehead, and the scalps of the riotous people].▲

49 [7 Concerning Edom. Thus says the LORD of hosts:▲ 10 [But as for me, I have stripped Esau bare; I have uncovered his hiding places, so that he will] n[ot be able to conceal himself. His offspring are destroyed along with his relative and his neighbors; and he is no more].▲

50 4 [In those days] and at that time, says the LORD, [the children of Israel will come, both they and the children of Judah together. They will go on their way weeping as they seek] the LORD their God. 5 [They will ask the way to Zion with their faces turned toward it, (saying), "Come, let us join ourselves] to the LORD in an everlasting covenant that will n[ot be forgotten]."

6 [My people have become lost sheep; their shepherds have led them astray]; *they have turned back*[100] from on the mountains. [They have gone from mountain t]o hi[ll, and have forgotten their own resting place].▲

---

98. 2QJer (reconstructed longer text; cf. Isa 24:18). *The one who flees from the terror* MT LXX.

99. 2QJer. *the midst of* MT. *the house of* MT[mss].

Chapter 49. 2QJer: 49:10(?).

Chapter 50. 4QJer[e]: 50:4–6.

100. 4QJer[e] MT. *they have turned them away* MT[qere] LXX.

EZEKIEL

The setting of the prophecies of Ezekiel is the Babylonian exile in the sixth century BCE. The book answers a key question that must have occurred to Jews of that disturbing time: "Has God abandoned us?" From the intriguing otherworldly description of God's glory coming to earth by the River Chebar in Babylon to the plan of the gigantic end-of-time temple, the book sets the stage for the answer in the last verse: "The LORD is there."

Small fragments from six manuscripts of Ezekiel were found at Qumran and another atop Masada. All of them and the traditional Masoretic Text fairly uniformly attest the same textual tradition. Only seven minor variants are clearly preserved, though reconstruction according to spatial requirements indicates that in two places (5:13 and 23:16) the scrolls may have had a shorter text than the Masoretic Text.

One manuscript, 4QEzek^b, may not have been a copy of the complete book of Ezekiel but perhaps contained only the prophet's inaugural vision or a few episodes. Another manuscript, 4QEzek^c, survives in only one fragment measuring about a half-inch in diameter. It contains only three complete words and a couple of letters from six other words. Nonetheless, the fragments that do remain range over the course of the entire book, from chapter 1 to chapter 41, and show that the inherited text of Ezekiel was very carefully copied from antiquity.

The relatively small number of manuscripts does not prepare the reader for the importance that Ezekiel exerted among the members of the Dead Sea community. Ezekiel's emphasis on the High Priest Zadok and his descendants is evident in the community's self-designation: "Sons of Zadok." The description of the end-time temple is also embellished in several copies of a text entitled the *New Jerusalem* and forms a key component of the largest of the nonbiblical Dead Sea manuscripts: the *Temple Scroll*.

1 8 [They had human hands under their wings. On their f]ou[r sides, the four of them had faces and wings. 9 Their wings touched each other. Each went straight forward without t]urning as [they] w[ent].

10 [This was the appearance of their faces: they had the face of a man; all f]our [had the face of a lion on the right side]; all [four] *of them*[1] [had] the face of an o[x on the left side]; and [all] fo[ur] had the face [of an eagle. 11 Such were their faces. Th]eir [wings] spread [out upwa]r[d; each had two] touching *another*[2] and tw[o covering its body]. 12 Each we[nt straight forward. Wherever the spi]rit [was going, they went, without turning as they went]. 13 The likeness of the living beings, [their] ap[pearance, was like burning coals of fire], like the light of torches. The fire [went] back [and forth among] the living beings. The fire was bright, and [lightning] flashed from the fire. [14 The living beings ran back and forth like bolts of lightning].

15 [Looking at the living beings, I saw one wheel on the ground beside each of the four living beings. 16 This was the appearance of the wheels and their construction: They shone like chryso]lite, [all four looked alike, and] their [form and construc]tion [were as if there were a wheel within a wheel. 17 When they moved, they went in any of the f]ou[r directions without turning as they went. 18 As for their rims, they were high and awesome, and the rims of all four were full of eyes all around. 19 And when the living beings moved, the wheels went beside them; and when the living beings rose from the ground, the wheels rose. 20 Wherever the spirit went, they went. The wheels rose with th]em, because the spirit of the living beings [was in the wheels. 21 When those went, these went;] when those stood still, these stood still; when [those rose from the ground], the wheels [ro]se with them; [because the spirit of the living beings was in] the wheels.

22 Over the hea[ds of the living beings] *their appearance*[3] was like the sky, like the [glis]tening of ice. It was awesome, stretched [out] over [their heads]. 23 Under the firmament [their wings were stretched out straight], each toward the other. Each had t[wo wings] co[vering their bodies] on [each] side. 24 [When they went, I he]ard [the sound of their wings, like the roar of the great waters, like the voice of the Almighty, a noise of tumult like that of an army camp. When they stood still, they let down their wings]. ▲

4 3 [Take an iron pan, set it up like an iron wall between you and the city, and face it. It will be besieged]—you shall lay siege against it. [This shall be a sign

---

Chapter 1. 4QEzek[b]: 1:10–13, 16–17, 18–24; 11QEzek: 1:8–10.

  1. Masculine 4QEzek[b]. Feminine MT.

  2. Implicit 4QEzek[b]. Explicit MT.

  3. 4QEzek[b]. *the appearance* MT.

Chapter 4. 1QEzek: 4:16–17; 11QEzek: 4:3–6, 9–10.

to the house of Israel. 4 Lie down on your lef]t [side], and plac[e the sin of the house of Israel on it. You shall bear their sin all the days you lie on that side. 5 For] I [myself have ass]igned to [you the years of their iniquity as a corresponding number of days, three hundred ninety days. Thus you shall bear the iniquity of the house of Israel. 6 Then, when you have finished that, you shall lie down again, on your right side, and bear the sin of the house of Judah. For forty days, each day for a] year, I have assigned this to [you].▲

9 [You, take wheat and barley, beans and lentils, millet and spelt. Put them into a vessel and make yourself some bre]ad. [You will eat it during the three hundred ninety days that you are lying on your side. 10 The food] th[at] you eat by [weight will be twenty shekels a day. You must eat it regularly].▲

16 [Then he said to me: Look, Mortal, I will cut off the supply of food in Jerusalem, and they will eat br]ead by w[eight with anxiety and drink water by measure in dismay, 17 because bread and water will be scarce. They will be appalled with one anoth]er and waste away in their sin.

5 1 [And you, Mortal, take a sharp sword, use it as a barber's razor, and pass it over your head and] over [your beard. Then] ac[quire a balance] for [yourself and divide the hair].▲

11 [Therefore, as I live, says the Lord GOD, surely, because you have defiled my sanctuary with all your detestable things and all your abominations], so I myself [will decimate you. My eye will not spare. I will have no pity. 12 A third of you will die from pestilence or be consumed by famine] in your area; a [third will fall by the sword around you; and a third I will scatter to every wind, following] them [with drawn sword]. 13 Thus my anger will be spent [and my wrath toward them *subside and I will be appeased.*[4] When I have spent] my [wra]th on them, [they will know that I, the LORD, have spoken in my passion].▲

▨ *In the passage above, the Greek text is shorter than the Masoretic Text. Though the full text is not preserved in 11QEzek, indications of space suggest that it too may have been shorter than the Masoretic Text (see the introduction to Ezekiel).*

15 So it shall be a reproach and a [taunt, a warn]ing and a h[orror, to the surrounding nations, when I execute judgments on you in anger and in w]rath, with [w]rathful rebuke[s]. I, the LORD, have s[poken. 16 When I shoot the deadly arrows of famine, arrows of de]struction, whi[ch I sh]oo[t] to destr[oy you, I will intensify the famine until I cut off your food supply]. 17 I [will se]nd [famine and wild beasts] ag[ainst you, and they shall make you childless . . .].▲

Chapter 5. 1QEzek: 5:1; 11QEzek: 5:11–17.

4. 11QEzek, like LXX, may have had a shorter text than MT.

7 9 [My] ey[e shall not] spare. [I will not have pity. I will repay you according to your ways, while your abominations are present to you. Then you shall know that it is I], the LORD, who strikes.

10 [The day is here! See, it has come! Your doom has burst forth, the rod has budded, arrogance has blossomed. 11 Violence has grown up] into a rod of wickedness. None of [them shall remain, none of their multitude, none of their wealth, none of their preeminence. 12 The time has come, the day has arrived. Let not the buyer] rejoi[ce, nor the seller mourn. For wrath is on the whole multitude].▲

10 6 [Then, when he commanded the man clothed in linen, "Take fire from between] the whirling wheels, [from between the cherubim," he went in and stood beside a wheel. 7 One of the cheru]b[im extended his] hand [to the fire between the cherubim and too]k some and put it into [the hands of the one clothed in linen, who took it and went out. 8 The cherubim seemed to have something li]ke *human hands*[5] [under their wings].

9 [Then I looked, and there were four wheels beside] the cherubim, [one] wheel [beside each cherub]. The wheel[s shone] like [chrysolite. 10 As for their appearance,] all [fo]ur [looked alike], as if [a wheel were within a wheel. 11 When they moved,] they went [in] any of the [fo]ur [directions] without turning as [they] wen[t. Wherever the lead wheel faced, the others went without tu]rning as they went. 12 [Their whole body, their backs, hands, and wings and the four wheels] were [full] of eyes [all around—the wheels belonging to the four of them].

13 I heard [the wheels called "the whirling wheels." 14 Each one had] fo[ur faces: the first was the face of a cherub, the second the face of a man], the third [the face of a lion, and the fourth the face of an eagle.]

15 [The cherubim rose up. These were the] living beings wh[ich I saw by the Chebar River. 16 When the cherubim moved, the wheels moved besi]de [them, and when the cherubim spread their wings to rise up from the ground, the wheels did not leave their side. 17 When] these stood still, those stood still; and when these rose, those rose with them; [for the spirit of the living beings was in them. 18 Then the glo]ry of the LORD [crossed] over the threshold of the temple and hovered over the cherubim. 19 [Then the cherubim spread] their [wings] and rose up from the ground, as I watched. When they departed, the wheels [went beside them. They stopped at the door of] the east [gate of the house of the L]ORD, while the glory of the G[o]d of Israel [hovered] ab[ove them.]

Chapter 7. 11QEzek: 7:9, 11–12.

Chapter 10. 4QEzek[a]: 10:6–22; 11QEzek: 10:11.

  5. 4QEzek[a] LXX. *a human hand* MT.

20 [These were the living beings] I [s]aw under the God of Israel by the Cheba[r] River; [so I knew that they were cherubim]. 21 Each [of the four] had [four face]s, ea[ch] had four wings, [and under their wings was something like a human hand. 22 As for the form of] their faces, they were the faces whi[ch I saw by the Chebar River. Each o]ne moved straight ahead.

11 1 [Then the spirit lifted me up and brought me to] the east [gate of the LORD's house], which faces east[ward. At the door of the gate, there were twenty-five men. I saw] among them Jaaza[niah son of Azzur and Pelatiah son of Benaiah, leaders of the people. 2 And he said to me, "Mortal, these are the men who p]lot evil and giv[e wicked counsel in this city, 3 who say, 'This is no time to build] houses. This city is the p[ot, and we are the meat.' 4 So prophesy against them; prophesy, Mortal]!"

5 Then the spirit of the L[ORD] fell on me [and said to me, "Say, Thus says the LORD: This is what you say, house of] Israel, [and I know] what goes through [your mind. 6 You have multiplied the slain in] this [city]. You have filled [its] st[reets with them. 7 Therefore thus says the Lord GOD: The slain whom] you have laid inside it, [they are the meat, and this city is the pot. But you will be forced out of it]. 8 You have feared the sword; [so I will bring the sword on you, says the Lord GOD. 9 I will force you out of] the city, [deliver you into the hands of strangers, and execute judgments against you]. 10 You [will] fall [by the sword. I will judge you] a[t Israel's borders. Then you will know that I am the LORD. 11 This c]ity [will not be your pot. You will not be the meat inside it. I will judge you at Israel's borders]." ▲

16 31 [When you built your] shr[ines at the head of every street and made your high places in every square, you were not like a prosti]tute, because you scorned [payment. 32 You adulteress wife, receiving strangers instead of her husband! 33 Men] al[ways give gifts to prostitutes, but you—you give gifts to all your lovers, bribing them to come to you from every direction for your lechery]. ▲

23 14 [She went still further in her harlotries when she saw men portrayed on the wall, i]mages of [Chaldeans portrayed with vermilion, 15 girded with belts on their loins, with flowing turbans on their heads, all of them looking like chariot officers, images of Babylonians] whose [n]ative [land was Chaldea. 16 . . .⁶ 17 . . . until] she turned [from them] in disgust. 18 [When she carried on her harlotry openly and exhibited her nakedness, I turned from her in disgust, just] as [I had turned from her sister]. ▲

Chapter 11. 4QEzek^a: 11:1–11.

Chapter 16. 3QEzek: 16:31, 33.

Chapter 23. 4QEzek^a: 23:14–18, 44–47.

   6. 4QEzek^a lacks space for all of 23:16–17.

■ *If the complete lines of 4QEzek^a are filled out as they would have originally appeared, it becomes clear that the scroll did not have enough space for all of verses 16 and 17. It is possible that verse 16 is missing because a scribe's eye skipped down one line too many.*

44 They have gone in to her. As [men] g[o in to a prostitute, so they went in to Oholah and Oholibah, the lewd women]. 45 But as righteous men, they will convict th[e]m, [sentencing them as adulteresses and women who shed] blood, because th[ey] are adulteresses and blood is on their hands. 46 For thus says [the Lord GOD]: Bring up an assembly against [th]em and g[ive them over to terror and spoil. 47 The assembly] shall stone [them with stones] and cut [them] down [with their swords. They shall kill their sons and their daughters and burn down their houses].▲

24 2 [Mortal, record this date, this] ver[y date: the king of Babylon laid siege to Jerusalem on this date. 3 And tell a parable to the] rebellious [house]. Sa[y to them, "Thus says the Lord GOD: Put on the soup pot; put it on, and pou]r wat[er] into it 4 [. . .]."▲

35 11 [Therefore, as I live, says the Lord GOD, I will treat you in accordance with your anger and your jealousy which you showed] in your hatred of them. I will make myself [kno]wn among them [wh]en I judge you. 12 You will know [that] I, the LORD, [have heard] all [the contemptible thing]s you [have spoken against the mountain]s of Israe[l, saying, "They have been laid waste]. They have been given to us to de[vour]."

13 And y[ou have boasted] against me with [your] mou[th. Y]ou have multip[lied] your words [agai]nst me. [I] have heard it. 14 [This is what] the Lord [GOD says: While] the whole ear[th] rejoices, I [will make you de]solate. 15 As you rejoiced over the [inhe]ritance of the hou[se of I]sra[el] beca[use] it [was deso]late, so will I treat you. [You] will be de[solate], Mount Sei[r and all E]dom, all of it. They [will kn]ow that I am the LORD.

36 1 [Now you, Mortal, prophesy t]o [the mountains of I]srael and [say], Moun[tains of] Is[rael, hear the word of the LORD. 2 This is what] the Lord GOD [s]ays: Because [the enemy] has s[aid against you, "Aha!" and, "The] ancie[nt height]s [have beco]me our [pos]sess[ion]," 3 therefore [prophesy and say, This is what the Lord] GOD [says: Because they have made you de]so[late and crushed you on every side, so that you became] a po[ssession to the rest of the nations and the object of gossip and slander among the people, 4 therefore, mountains of Israel, hear the word of the Lord GOD: This is what the Lord GOD says to the mountains and to the hills, to the ravines] and to the [valleys, to the desolate

---

Chapter 24. 4QEzek^c: 24:2–3.

Chapter 35. MasEzek: 35:11–15.

Chapter 36. MasEzek: 36:1–11, 13–14, 17–35.

wastes and to the forsaken cities], which [have been prey and objects of derision for the rest of the sur]rounding [nations]; 5 therefore this is what [the Lord GOD] s[ays: In my burning] zea[l] I [s]peak [against the rest of the nations and against all Edom, which appropriated my] la[nd as their own possession, with wholehearted glee and ut]ter [contempt, to plu]nder [it. 6 Therefo]re [prophesy concerning the land of Israel and say to the mountain]s and to the hill[s, to the ravines and to the valleys, This is what the Lord GOD says: Listen now, I sp]eak in [my] jea[lousy and in] my [wrath, because you have endured the ridicule of the nations. 7 Therefore] this [is what] the Lord GOD s[a]ys: [I swear that the nations wh]ich [sur]rou[nd you, they too will endure ridicule.]

8 [But yo]u, mountains of Is[rael, you will sprout branches and yield fruit for my people] Israel. [For they will soon come home, 9 because I am certainly for you, and I will turn to you. You will be] plowed [and sown. 10 I will multiply your people, the whole house of Israel, all of it, and] the [cities will be inhabit]ed [and the ruins rebuilt]. 11 I will multiply [people and animals for you, and they will increase and be fruitful. I will settle you as before and will prosper you more than ever. Then you will know that I am the LORD].

12 [I will bring people, my people Israel, to walk on you, and they will possess you, and you will be their inheritance. Never again will you bereave them of children. 13 This is what the Lord GOD says: Because they s]ay [to you, "You de- vour your people and bereave your nation of children," 14 therefo]re, [you will no longer devour] peop[le and no longer bereave your nation of children, says the Lord GOD. 15 I will no longer make you hear derision from the nations, and you will no longer endure the ridicule of the nations or make your nation stumble, says the Lord GOD].

16 [Again the word of the LORD came to me: 17 Mortal, when] the people of Isra[el] were living i[n] their own [la]nd, they de[fil]ed [i]t with their conduct and their [deed]s. Their con[duct] in my presence [was] like the [un]clea[nness of contact with a corpse. 18 [So] I poured out my w[ra]th on th[em] for the blood [wh]ich they poured out o[n the land], for they [de]filed it with [their] id[ols]. 19 And [I scattered them among the nations, and they were dispersed through the countri]e[s. According to] their [con]duct [and according to] their deeds [I judged them. 20 When they came] t[o the nations, wh]erever they went, [th]ey pro[faned] my [hol]y [name], in that people [sai]d of them, "These are the people of the LORD; yet they had to leave [his] la[nd]." 21 But I had concern [for] my holy name, which the house of Israe[l] had profaned among the nations, *wherever*[7] they [we]nt.

22 Therefore say to the h[ou]se of I[sra]el, [This is what the L]ord [GOD] says: [It is not] for [yo]ur s[ake, hou]se of Is[rael], that I am about to act, [but] for my

---

7. MasEzek and MT have variant forms of *wherever*.

[holy name], which you have profaned among the nations, wher[ever] you went. 23 [I will sanctify my] great [name], which [has been profaned among the nations, wh]ich [you have profaned among] them, and [the nations] will kn[ow that] I am the LORD, [say]s [the Lord G]OD, [when I prove my holiness among you in their sight].

24 For I will take [you from among the na]tions [and gather you out of all the countrie]s and [will bring you into] your own l[a]n[d. 25 I will sprinkle] clean [wa]ter [on you], and you will be cl[ean]. I will cl[eanse y]ou from all [your] filthiness [and all] your [idols]. 26 I [will give] you a new heart, and [I will] put a [new] spirit wi[thin you]. I will remove the heart of stone from yo[ur] flesh, [and I will give] you a heart [of flesh. 27 I will] put [my spirit] within you and cau[se] you to walk [in] my [statutes and] carefully k[eep] my [ordinances]. 28 You will [dwell] in the la[nd that I gave to yo]ur [ancestors]. You will be my peo[ple, and I will be your G]od. 29 [I] will save you from [all your uncleanness. I will call fo]r the grain and will multiply [it] and [bring] no [famine on you. 30 And] I [will mul]ti[ply the fruit] of [the] trees and the produce of the [field, so] that yo[u] no [longer] endure the re[proach of] fa[mi]ne among the nation[s].

31 [Then you will remember] yo[ur evil] w[a]ys [and your] a[ctions] th[at were not good], and you will loathe your[selves for your sins and abominable deeds]. 32 It is not for your sake that I [do this, says the Lord GOD, let it be known to you. Be ashamed and confou]n[ded] for your way[s, hou]se of [Israel. 33 This is what the Lord GOD says: In the day that] I [cleanse] you from [all your sins, I will settle the cities and rebuild] the [ruins, 34 and the desolate land will be plowed], though it had [been a desolation in the sight of all who passed by. 35 They will say, "T]his de[solate land has become like the garden of Eden. The cities which were devastated, desolate, and in ruins are fortified and inhabited]." ▲

37 1 [The hand of the LORD] wa[s on me], and he brough[t me out in the spirit of the LORD, and set me in the middle of] the va[lley, and it was] fu[ll of bones. 2 He brought me a]ll ar[ound] them. [There were very many on the floor of the valley, and they were very] dry. 3 [He said] to [me, "Mortal, can t]hese [bones live]?" And I answered, "L[ord GOD, you know.]"

4 [Then he said to] me, "Prophesy ov[er these bones, and sa]y [t]o them, D[ry] bones, [hear the word of the LORD. 5 This is what] the Lord GOD [s]ays to [thes]e bones: Li[sten. I will] make breath [enter y]ou, and you will l[ive. 6 I] will put tendons [on] you, and [I] will form flesh [o]n you [and cover you with] skin, [and] I [will pu]t breath in you, [and] you [will live. Then you will know that I am] the LORD."

Chapter 37. MasEzek: 37:1–16, 28.

7 So I prophesied [a]s I was commanded. [As I prophesied, there was] a nois[e and a ra]ttling. [*The*] *bones*[8] came together, each bone to [its] bo[ne. 8 As I watched], indeed sinews and flesh fo[rmed] on them, [and skin] covered [them] over, but there was no breath in them. 9 [Then he sai]d t[o me, "Prophesy to the wind; pro]phesy, Mortal, and say [to the wind, This is what the Lo]rd [GOD s]ays: Com[e] from the four winds, breath, and breathe on [the]se slain, so they may [come to] li[fe]." 10 So I prophesied as he commanded me, and breath entered them, and [they came to life] and st[oo]d up on their feet—a huge army.

11 Then he sai[d t]o me, Mort[al], these bones [ar]e the whole house of Is[rae]l. Listen, they [s]ay, "[Our bones] are dried up, [and our h]o[pe is gone]. We [are completely cut off]." 12 Therefore prophesy and say [to them, This is what] the Lord GOD *says says:*[9] [Listen. I] will open [your graves and br]ing you up out of your graves, my people, and I will bring you [into the land of Isra]el. 13 You will know [that I am the L]ORD when [I] have opened your [gr]aves and brought [y]ou up [out of your] gr[aves], my [people]. 14 I will put my spirit in you, and you will live, [and I will settle] you in your own land. Then y[ou] will know [that] I, [the LORD, have said it and done it, says the LORD.]

15 [The word of the LORD came to me again, saying, 16 Mo]rtal, take [a stick and write on it, "For Judah and for] the Israel[it]es, [his] compan[ions." Then take another stick and write on it, "For Joseph, the] stick of [Ephraim, and the whole house of Israel, his companions]." ▲

28 [Then the nations will know that I the LORD sanctify Israel when my sanctuary is among them] for al[l time].

38 1 [The word of the LORD] came [to me, saying, 2 Mortal, look toward] Gog of [the land of Magog, the chief prince of Meshech, and Tubal. Prophesy against him] 3 and s[ay: This is what the Lord GOD says: Listen. I am opposed to you, Gog, chief prince of Meshech, and Tubal. 4 I will turn you around, put hooks into your jaws], and b[ring you out with your whole army, with horses and horsemen in] f[ull armor, a great company with buckler and shield, all of them wielding swords; 5 Persia, Ethiopia, and Put with them, all of them with shield and helmet; 6 Gomer with all its troops; Beth-togarmah from the far north with all its troops—many nations are with you]. 7 Get ready. Prepare yourself, [you and all your companies assembled around you]. Be [a guard] for them. 8 [After a long period you will be summoned. In the latter] years [you will invade a land that has been restored from war, whose inhabitants have been

---

8. MasEzek. *And bones* MT. MasEzek has *The* but apparently lacks *And,* whereas MT lacks *The.*

9. MasEzek, unlike MT, contains a scribal error, repeating the word *says.*

Chapter 38. MasEzek: 38:1–4, 7–8.

gathered from many] nation[s to the mountains of Israel which had long been devastated, whose people have been brought out from the nations and who are all living in safety]. ▲

41 3 He stepped [into the] inner room and [measur]ed [the jambs of the entrance, two cubits, the height of the entrance, six cubits, and the width of] the entrance, seven cu[bits. 4 Then he measured the length of the room, twenty cubits, and the width, twenty] cubits, be[fore the nave, and he said to me, "This is the most holy place." 5 Then he measured the wall of] the temple, [six] cu[bits, and the width of every side room a]rou[nd the] temple, [four cubits]. 6 Now, [the side rooms were on three levels, one atop the other, with thirty on each level. The side rooms extended to a structure which served as a support all around the temple and were fastened to it, rather than to the temple wall]. ▲

Chapter 41. 4QEzek^a: 41:3–6.

THE BOOK OF THE TWELVE MINOR PROPHETS

The scrolls of the twelve Minor Prophets are of special importance because they allow a very early window not only into the text of the individual books but also into what is perhaps of equal interest: the order of the books as a unit.

Of a total of ten manuscripts, eight were found in the caves at Qumran: seven in Cave 4 and one in Cave 5.[a] These manuscripts range in age from 150 BCE (4QXII[a] and perhaps 4QXII[b]) to 25 BCE (4QXII[g]). The two remaining scrolls were found in caves that were utilized as hideouts by Jewish rebels during the Bar Kokhba revolt, an unsuccessful uprising against Rome (132–135 CE). These scrolls are thus likely to be later productions: 50 BCE to 50 CE (8ḤevXII gr) and 75 CE to 100 CE (MurXII). Letters signed by the leader of the revolt, Bar Kokhba himself, were found in both of these caves.

Do the Dead Sea manuscripts evidence the tradition of printing these twelve small books together? This question can now be answered in the affirmative, according to the text of seven of the Dead Sea Scrolls. The remaining three are so fragmentary that they contain parts of but one book each.[b]

Do the scrolls witness to the order that is found in the Greek Septuagint or to that preserved in the Masoretic Text? All of the scrolls but one appear to follow the traditional Hebrew order. This is the same order that is followed by every major English translation available today. Of particular interest among these scrolls is 8ḤevXII gr, which—despite being a Greek scroll—displays the order of

---

a. 4QXII[a]–4QXII[g], 5QAmos.   **b.** 4QXII[d], 4QXII[f], 5QAmos.

the Hebrew text of books 2–6 (Joel, Amos, Obadiah, Jonah, Micah), rather than that of the Greek tradition (Amos, Micah, Joel, Obadiah, Jonah). The one odd scroll, 4QXII^a (the oldest of all the manuscripts), suggests a third order in which Jonah follows Malachi. Jonah is certainly not in the first half of the twelve, as in the Greek and Hebrew traditions, but likely last in the collection.

The text of the books evidenced in the scrolls is, in the main, that of the Masoretic Text. Indeed, even the Greek manuscript found in Naḥal Ḥever exhibits the Greek tradition as systematically corrected by comparison with the Hebrew. However, the number of variants indicated in the translations that follow suggest that the best description for the text is "slightly mixed"—not entirely that of the traditional form of the Hebrew Bible, but showing some agreement with the Septuagint as well as some independence from both the Hebrew and the Greek traditions. The nine Hebrew texts among the Dead Sea Scrolls also evidence—in varying degrees—a slightly fuller approach to spelling (analogous to the British *colour* as opposed to the American *color*) than that of the traditional Hebrew Bible.

As was the case among the early Christians, the Minor Prophets were quite popular at Qumran. The sectarians at Qumran often understood the prophecies found in these twelve books to be speaking to their contemporary situation. A particular type of interpretation known as *pesher*—not known before the discovery of the Dead Sea Scrolls—was incorporated in the commentaries found at Qumran. *Pesher* is a prophetic commentary in which the interpretation—in the eyes of the community—shares the same authority as the original prophecy. The word is used frequently in the book of Daniel to introduce the "authoritative" interpretation of dreams (Dan 2:16). Of the fifteen known *pesharim,* six were written on the books of the Minor Prophets: two on Hosea, and one each on Micah, Nahum, Habakkuk, and Zephaniah.

HOSEA

In addition to the two *pesharim* and the three biblical manuscripts containing portions of the book of Hosea,[a] the prophet Hosea's words can be found in several quotations in the Dead Sea Scrolls.

Hosea 2:15 and 18 are cited in the text of *Barki Nafshi* in general reference to God's goodness to Israel. The remainder of the citations are characteristic of *pesher* interpretation, in which warnings spoken by Hosea to historical Israel in the period before the exile of the northern tribes at the hands of Assyria (722 BCE) are interpreted to address the situation of the Qumran sectarians in the first or second century BCE. Hosea 3:4, and its description of Israel as "without king or prince" before the coming of the future Davidic king, is understood by the *Damascus Document* (CD) 20:16 as prophesying the chaotic period following the death of the Teacher of Righteousness. Corresponding to this, "like a rebellious cow" (Hosea 4:16) is quoted in CD 1:13–14 in reference to the Jews who rejected the ways of the Qumran community during this same time period. Hosea 5:10 and its characterization of the "boundary shifters" refers to this same rebellious group (CD 8:3 with 19:15–16) who manipulated the law—a likely description of the Pharisees. Finally, the "horn" and "trumpet" of Hosea 5:8 are cryptically interpreted by 4Q177 to be the first and second books of the Law, which were rejected by the apostate in the Last Days.

In light of the *pesher*-like treatment of these quotations, it is curious that the surviving portions of the *pesharim* (4Q166–67) appear to refer primarily to pre-exilic Israel.

---

a. 4QXII[c], 4QXII[d], 4QXII[g].

1 [6 And she conceived again, and gave birth to a daughter. And the LORD said to him, "Name her Lo-ruhamah, for I will no longer have mercy upon the house of] Israel, that [I should in any way pardon them. 7 But I will have mercy upon the house of Judah, and will save them] by the LORD th[eir] God, [and will not save them by bow, or by sword, or by battle, by horses,] or by horsemen."

8 Now when she had w[eaned Lo-ruhamah, she conceived, and gave birth to a son. 9 And the LORD said, "Na]me him Lo-ammi; f[or you are not my people, and I am not your God."]

[10 Yet] the number of the children of [Israel shall b]e [as the sand of the sea, which cannot be measured] or numbered; and then in [the place where it was said to them,] "You [are not my people,"] he shall say¹ t[o them, "You are the sons of the living God."] 11 And [the] c[hildren of Judah] and the children of Israe[l] shall be gathered [together, and they shall appoint themselves one head, and shall go u]p from the land; for [great shall be the d]ay [of Jezreel.]

2 [1 Say you to your brethren,] Ammi; and to [your] sister[s, Ruhamah.] 2 C[onten]d² [with your mother, contend;] for she is not [my] w[ife, and I am not her husband; and let her put away] her harlotry from betwee[n . . . ,³ and he]r [adult]er[y from between her breasts;] 3 else I strip [her naked, and expose her as on the day that she was born, and make] her as a wilderness, [and make her like a dry land, and slay her with thirst.]▲

[11 I will also cause all] her [mirth to cease, her feasts, her new moons, her sab-baths, and all her appointed feasts. 12 And I will lay waste her vines and] her [fi]g trees, of which [she has said, "These are my wages that] my lovers [have giv]en me." [And I will make them a forest, and the wild] animal[s⁴ of the field shall eat] them. [13 And I will punish] her for the days of the Baal[s, to which she burned incense, and decked herself with] her [earrin]g and her jewelry, and [went after her lovers, and forgot me, says the LORD.]

14 Therefore, behold, I will allu[re her, and bring her into the wilderness, and speak tenderly to her. 15 And I will give to her] her [vineyar]ds from there, and [the] valley [of Achor for a door of hope; and she shall respond there as in the days of her youth, and as in the day when she came up from the land of Egypt. 16 And it shall be on that day, says the L]ORD, you shall c[all me Ishi, and shall no longer

---

Chapter 1. 4QXII^d: 1:6–11 [H 1:6–9; 2:1–2]; 4QXII^g: 1:10–11 [H 2:1–2].

    1. 4QXII^d. it shall be said MT LXX.

Chapter 2. 4QXII^d: 2:1–3 [H 2:3–5]; 4QXII^g: 2:2–3 [H 2:4–5], 13–17(?) [15–19(?)], 20–23 [H 22–25]; 4QXII^c: 2:11–13 [2:13–15].

    2. Singular 4QXII^g. Plural MT LXX.

    3. 4QXII^d. her face MT LXX.

    4. Misspelled 4QXII^g.

call me Baali. 17 For I will remove the names of] the Baals [from her mouth, and they shall be mentioned by their name no longer.]▲

20 I [will even take] you [as for my wife in faithfulness; and you shall know the LORD. 21 And in that day, I will answer, says the] LORD, [I will answer the heavens, and they shall answer the earth; 22 and the earth shall answer the grain,] and t[he ne]w wine, [and the oil; and they shall answer Jezreel. 23 And I will sow her for myself in the land;] and I will have mercy [upon her that had not obtained mercy; and I will say to them that were not my people, "You are my people"; and they] shall sa[y, "You are my God."]

3 1 And [the LORD said to me, "Go again, love a woman who has a lover and is an adulteress, even as the LORD loves] t[he] c[hildren of Israel, though they turn unto other gods, and love raisin cakes." 2 So I bought her for myself for fif]tee[n pieces of silver and a homer of barle]y [and a] lethech [of barley; 3 and I said to her,] "You shall [remain with me ma]ny [days; you shall not play the harlot, and you shall not have a man, so will I also be toward you." 4 For the children of Israel] shall remain [for] many [d]ays [without king or prince, and without sacrifice or pillar, and without e]phod [or te]raphim. 5 Afterward [the children of Israel shall] return, [and seek the LORD] their [God] and David [their] king, [and shall come with fear unto the LORD and to his goodness in the latter d]ays.

4 [1 Hear the word of the L]ORD, O children of Israel; for [the LORD has a case against the inhabitants of the land, because there is no truth or goodness, and no knowled]ge of God in the la[n]d. 2 S[wearing, lying, murder, stealing, and adultery have spread abroad and bloodshed follows bloodshed. 3 Therefore the land shall mourn and all] those [who dwel]l⁵ in it [shall languish;] with [the] an[imals of the field and the birds of the air; even the fish of the sea shall be taken away.]

[4 Yet let no one contend, and let no] one [reprove,] for your people [are like those that contend with the priest. 5 And you shall stumble by day, and the prophet also shall stumble with you by night, and I will destroy your mother. 6 My people are destroyed for] lack of knowledge; because [you have rejected knowledge, I will also reject you, that you shall be no priest to me. Because you have forgotten the law of your God, I also will forget your children.]

7 The more they were multiplied, they sinned [against me; I will change their glory into shame. 8 They feed on the sin of my people and set their heart on their iniquity. 9 And it shall be, like people, like pri]est; and I will punish [them for their ways, and will repay them their deeds. 10 And they shall eat, and not have

---

Chapter 3. 4QXII^g: 3:1–5; 4QXII^c: 3:2–4.

Chapter 4. 4QXII^c: 4:1–19; 4QXII^g: 4:1, 11, 13–14.

  5. 4QXII^c LXX. *everyone who dwells* MT.

enough;] they shall play the harlot, [and shall not increase; because they have stopped giving he]ed [to the LORD.]

11 Whoredom, [wine, and new wine take away the understanding. 12 My people ask counsel of a piece of wood, and their divining staff informs them; for the spirit of whoredom has led them astray, and they have played the harlot, departing from their G]o[d. 13 They sacrifice upon the t]ops of the [mountains, and burn incense upon the hills, under oak and po]plar and terebinth, [because their shadow is good. Therefore yo]ur [daughters play the harlot] and [your] brides [commit adultery.] 14 I will [no]t punish [your daughters when they play the harlot, nor your brides when they commit adultery; for the men themselves go apart with harlots, and they sacrifice with the prostitutes; and the people that do not understand shall be overthrown.]

[15 Though you, Israel, play the harlot, do not let] Jud[ah become] guilty. [Do not go to Gilga]l, [do] not⁶ [go up to Beth-aven, and do not swear, "As the LORD lives!" 16 For] Israel [has behaved stubbor]nly, [like a stubborn heifer; can the LORD feed them] as a lamb [in a broad pasture?]

[17 Ephraim is joined to idols; let him alone. 18 Their drink is gone, they play the harlot continually; her rulers dearly love sh]ame. 19 [The wind] has wrapped [her up in its wings; and they shall be put to shame because of their sacrifices.]

5 [1 Hear this, O priests, and listen, O hous]e of Israe[l, and give ear, O house of the king; for the judgment pertains to you; for you have been a snare at Mizpah, and a net spread upon Tabor.]▲

6 [3 And let us know, let us follow on to know] the LORD; [his going forth is sure] as the morning; [and he will come to us as the rain, as the latter rain that waters] the earth.▲

[8 Gilead is a city of evildoers; it is trac]ked [with blood. 9 And as bands of robbers wait for a man, so the company of priests] murder [on the way to] Sh[echem; indeed they have committed wickedness. 10 In the house of Israel I have seen a horrible thing:] there whoredom [is found in Ephraim; Israel is defiled.]

[11 Also, O Judah, there is a harvest appointed for you, when] I [bring ba]ck [the] f[ortunes of my people.]

7 [1 When I would heal] I[srael, then the iniquity of Ephraim is uncovered, and the wickedness of Samaria; for they commit falsehood, and the thief enters in, and the band of robbers ravages outside.]▲

[12 When they go, I will spread my net over them;] I will bring [them] do[wn

---

6. 4QXII^c. *and do not* MT LXX.

Chapter 5. 4QXII^c: 5:1.

Chapter 6. 4QXII^g: 6:3, 8–11.

Chapter 7. 4QXII^g: 7:1, 12–16; 4QXII^c: 7:12–13.

as the birds of the sky; I will chastise them, according to the] report [of their con-gregation. 13 Woe] to them! [For they have wandered from me. Destruction to th]em! for they have trespassed against me. And [I would redee]m them yet they [have spoken lies against me.]

[14 And they have not cried t]o me with their heart, but they howl upon their beds; [they assemble themselves for grain and new wine; they rebel against me.] 15 Although I have trained and strengthened their arms, yet [they plot evil against me. 16 They return, but not upward; they are] like *the*[7] deceitful bow; [their princes] shall fall by the swo[rd because of the rage of their tongue. This is their derision in the land of Egypt.]

8 [1 Set the trumpet t]o [your lips. As an eagle he comes against the house of the Lord, because they have transgressed my covenant, and rebelled against my law.]▲

9 [1 Do not rejoice, O Israel, for joy, like the peoples; for you have played the harlot, departing from your God. You have loved a prostitute's wages on every] grain [floo]r. 2 Threshing [floor and the winepress shall not feed them, and the new wine shall fail them. 3 They shall not remain in] the Lord['s land;] but [Ephraim] shall re[turn to Egypt and they shall eat unclean food in Assyria.]

[4 They shall not pour out drink offerings] to the L[or]d, [and their sacrifices shall not be pleasing to him. Their bread shall be as the bread of mourners; all that eat of it shall be defiled; for their bread shall be for their own appetites; it shall not come into the house of the Lord.]▲

[9 They have deeply corru]pted [themselves] as in the days of [Gibeah; he will remember their iniquity, he will punish their sins.]

[10 I found Israe]l [like grapes in the wilderness. I saw your fathers] as the first fruit on the f[ig tree in its first season; but they came to Baal-peor, and conse-crated themselves to the shameful thing,] and became [abominable like that which they loved. 11 As for] Ephraim, [their glory] shall fly [away like a bird: there shall be no birth, and none with child, and no conception. 12 Though they bring up their children, yet will] I [bereave] them, [so that not a man shall be left.] For indeed, [woe to them when I depart from them! 13 Ephraim, as I have seen, is like Tyre, planted in a pleasant meadow;] but Ephraim shall bring out [his chil-dren to the slayer. 14 Give them, O Lord—what will you give? Give them a mis-carrying womb and] dry [breasts.]

[15 All their wickedness is in Gilgal; for there I hated them; because of the wickedness of th]eir doings [I will drive them out of my house; I will love them no more; all their princes are rebels.]

---

7. 4QXII[g]. *a* MT LXX.

Chapter 8. 4QXII[g]: 8:1.

Chapter 9. 4QXII[g]: 9:1–4, 9–17.

[16 Ephraim is struck down, their root is dried up, they shall bear no fruit: yes, though they bring forth, yet will I slay the belo]ved ones of [their] womb. 17 My God [will cast] them [away, because they did not listen to him; and they shall be wanderers among the nation]s.

10 [1 Israel is a luxuriant vine that puts forth his fruit; according to the abunda]nce of [his] fruit [he has multiplied his altars; according to the goodness of their land they have improved their pillars. 2 Their heart is divided; now] they will be found guilty; he will strike down [their] al[tars, he will destroy their pillars.]

[3 Surely now they will say, "We have no king, for] we do not [f]ear th[e L]ORD; and the king, [what can he do for us?" 4 They speak mere words, with empty oaths they make covenants; therefore judgment springs up as poison weeds] in the furrows [of the field. 5 The inhabitants of Samaria shall be in terror of the calves of Beth-aven; for its people shall mourn over it, and its priests] shall cry over [it, over its glory, becau]se it is departed fr[om it. 6 It also shall be carried off to Assyria as a present to the great king; E]phraim shall receive [shame, and Is]rael [shall be ashamed] of [his own] co[unsel.]

[7 As for Samaria, her king is cut off, as foam upon the water. 8 Also the] high places [of Aven, the sin of Israel, shall be] destroyed; [the thorn and the thistle shall come up on their altars; and they shall say to the mountains,] "Cover u[s"; and to the hills, "Fall on us."]

[9 O] Israe[l,] you have sinned [from the days of Gibeah. There they stood; will not the battle against the children of iniquity overtake them in Gibeah? 10 In my desire, I will chastise them, and the] peoples [shall be gathered against them,] when they are b[ound for their double guilt.]

[11 And Ephraim is a trained heifer that loves to tread out the grain, but] I have spared [her] fair [neck; I will set a rider on Ephraim; Judah shall plow; Jacob shall harrow for himself. 12 S]ow for yourselves righteous[ness, reap according to kindness; break up your fallow ground; for it is time to seek the LORD, until he] comes *and they rain*[8] righteousness upon you.

[13 You have plowed wickedness, you have reaped iniquity; you have eaten the fruit of lies; for you trusted in your way,] in the multitude of [your] mighty men. [14 Therefore a tumult shall arise among your people, and all your fortresses shall be destroyed, as Shalman destroyed Beth-arbe]l [in the day of battle, when the mothers were dashed in pieces with their children.]▲

11 [2 The more the prophets called them, the more they went from them; they sacrificed to the Baalim, and the]y [burned incense to graven images.]

Chapter 10. 4QXII[g]: 10:1–14.

　8. 4QXII[g]. *and he rains* MT. *harvest* LXX.

Chapter 11. 4QXII[g]: 11:2–5, 6–12 [H 6–11; 12:1].

3 Yet [I taught Ephraim to walk, I took them on my arms; but they did not know that] I [healed] them. 4 With co[rds of a man I drew them, with] band[s of love; and I became to them as those that lift up the yoke] from their jaws; [and I reached out and fed them.]

[5 They shall not return into the land of Egypt; but the Assyrian shall be] the[ir king,] because [they] r[efused to return to me. 6 And the sword shall fall upon their cities, and shall consume] their [bar]s, [and devour them, because of their own counsels. 7 And my people are bent on turning from me. Though they call to him that is on high, none at all will exalt him.]

8 How [shall I give you up, Ephraim? How shall I cast you off, Israel? How shall I make you as Admah? How shall I set you as Zeboiim?] *He has turned back upon my heart;*[9] [my compassions are kindled] together. [9 I will not execute the fierceness of my anger; I will not return] to destroy Ephraim; for [I am] G[od, and not man—the Holy One in the midst of you—and I will not come in wrath.]

[10 A]fter *him,*[10] the LORD, *he*[11] shall walk, *and*[12] [he will roar] like a li[on; for he will roar, and the children shall come trembling from the west. 11 They shall come trembling] as *birds*[13] out of Egypt, [and as a dove out of the land of Assyria; and I will settle them in their houses, says] the LORD.

[12 Ephraim has] su[rrounded me with falsehood, and the house of Israel with deceit; but Judah still walks] with God, [and is faithful with the Holy One.]

12 [1 Ephraim feeds on wind, and follows after the east wind all day long; he multiplies lies and violence; and they make a] covenant [with Assyria, and oil is carried to Egypt.]

[2 The LORD also has a dispute with Judah, and] will punish [Jacob according to] his [ways;] *and*[14] according to [his] de[eds will he repay him. 3 In the womb he took his brother by the heel; and] in [his] manh[ood he strove] with G[od. 4 He] strove with [the angel and prevailed; he wept and sought his favor; he found him at Beth-el, and there he spoke with us, 5 even the LORD, the God of hosts; the LORD is his name. 6 Therefore] return [to] y[our] God, [keep] k[indness and justice, and wait for your God continually.]

[7 A merchant, in whose hand are f]alse [scales, he] lo[ves] to oppress. [8 And Ephraim said, "Surely I am become rich, I have found wealth for myself; in all] my [lab]ors [they] shall find [in me no iniquity that would be sin." 9 But I am the

---

9. 4QXII⁸. *My heart is turned over within me* MT. *My heart is turned over* LXX.

10. 4QXII⁸. Not in MT LXX.

11. 4QXII⁸. *they* MT LXX.

12. 4QXII⁸. Not in MT LXX.

13. 4QXII⁸. *a bird* MT LXX.

Chapter 12. 4QXII⁸: 12:1–10 [H 2–11], 11–14 [12–15].

14. 4QXII⁸ LXX. Not in MT.

LORD your God since the land of Egypt; I will yet again make you to dwell in tents, as in the days *that I] brought you up for the appointed feast.*[15]

[10 I have also spoken to the prophets, and I have multiplied visions; and by the prophets I have spoken parables. 11 In Gilead there is iniquity; they shall come to nothing. In Gilgal they sacrifice bullocks; their] alta[rs are] also [as stone heaps on the furrows of the field. 12 And Jacob fled into the field of Aram,] and [Israel] served [for a wife, and for a wife he kept sheep. 13 And by a prophet the LORD brought Israel up out of] Egy[pt, and by a prophet was he preserved. 14 Ephraim has provoked to anger most bitterly; therefore his bloodshed shall be] left [on him, and his reproach shall his Lord return to him.]

13 [1 When Ephraim spoke, there was trembling; he exalted himself in Is]rael; [but when he became guilty in Baal he died. 2 And now they sin more and more, and have made themselves molten images of their silver, even idols according to their own understanding, all of them the work of the craftsmen. They say of them, "Let the men that sacrifice kiss the calves." 3 Therefore they shall be like the morning cloud,] and like [the dew that goes away early, like the chaff that is driven with the whirlwind out of the threshing-floor, and like the smoke out of the chimney.]

[4 Yet I am the LORD yo]ur [God] *who fortifies heaven [and creates the earth, whose hands made the whole host of heaven, but I did not show them to you to go after them, but] I brought you up*[16] [from the land of Egypt; and you were not to know any god but me, and besides me there is no savior. 5 I knew you in the wilderness, in the] land of great drought. [6 When I fed them, so were they satisfied; they were filled, and their heart was exalted; therefore have they forgotten me. 7 So I have become like a lion to them;] as a leopard [I will wat]ch by the way; 8 I will meet them as [a bear that is robbed of her cubs, and will tear open the covering of their heart; and I will devour them there as a lioness; as a] wild [animal] would tear them.

[9 It is your destruction, O Israel, that you are against me, against your help. 10 Where now is your king, that he may save you in all your cities? And your judges, of] whom [you said, Give me a king and princes? 11 I have given you a king in my anger,] and I have t[aken him away in my wrath.]

[12 The iniquity of Ephraim is bound up;] his [sin is laid up in store.] 13 The s[orrows of a childbirth shall come upon him; he is an unwise son, for at the time of birth he should not delay at the mouth of the womb.]

[14 I will ransom them from the power of Sheol; I will redeem them from death; O death, where are thy plagues? O Sheol, where is thy destruction? Repentance shall be hidden from my eyes.]

---

15. 4QXII[g]. *of the appointed feast* MT LXX.

Chapter 13. 4QXII[g]: 13:1, 6–8(?), 11–13; 4QXII[c]: 13:3–10, 15–16 [H 13:15–14:1].

16. 4QXII[g] LXX. Not in MT.

[15 Though he flourishes among the reeds, an east wind shall come, the wind of the LORD coming up from the wilderness;] and [his] spr[ing] shall become dry, [and his fountain shall be dried up. It shall plunder the treasury of every precious vessel. 16 Samaria shall bear her guilt, for she has rebelled] against her God; [they shall fall] by the swo[rd; their infants shall be dashed in pieces, and their pregnant women shall be ripped open.]

14 2 Take with you words, and re[turn to the LORD. Say to him, "Take away all iniquity, and accept that which is good, and will offer the fr]uit of our lips. 3 Assyria shall not [save us; we will not ride upon horses; we will no longer say to the work of ou]r [hands, 'You are our gods.'] For in you the orphan finds mercy."

[4 I will heal their apostasy, I will love them freely; for my anger has turned away from them. 5 I will be as the dew to I]srael; he shall blossom as the lily; *cast*[17] forth [his] ro[ots as Lebanon.]▲

[8 O Ephraim, what have I to do with idols? I myself have answered and watched him. I am like a] l[uxuriant cypre]ss; [from me comes your fruit. 9 Who is wise, that he may understand these things? Prudent,] that he may know them? For [the ways of the LORD are right, and the just shall walk in them; but transgresso]rs [shall stumble in them.]

Chapter 14. 4QXII^c: 14:2–5 [H 14:3–6]; 4QXII^g: 14:8–9 [H 14:9–10].

   17. 4QXII^g. *and cast* MT LXX.

JOEL

Three of the ten Minor Prophets manuscripts in the Dead Sea Scrolls contain sections of the book of Joel.[18] Although the book of Acts quotes a rather extensive portion of chapter 2 (2:28–32 in Acts 2:17–21) in perhaps the clearest *pesher*-type quotation in the New Testament—in which the outpouring of God's Spirit that the early church experienced was in fact prophesied by Joel—the caves divulged neither commentaries on Joel nor documents that capitalized on language expressive of the central topic of the prophet's declaration: the coming of the day of the Lord. It seems odd that, though the concept of the day of God's coming in great power permeates the scrolls (see the *War Scroll*), the expression "day of the Lord" is never found in the nonbiblical manuscripts.

The only surviving quote of Joel found elsewhere in the Qumran manuscripts is in 4Q266—one of the Cave 4 copies of the *Damascus Document*—applying the exhortation to return to God, originally addressed to sinful Israel (Joel 2:12–13), to the disobedient community member who has been told the punishment due his sin.

1 [10 The field is laid waste,] the land [m]ourns; f[or the grain is destroyed, the new wine is dried up, the oil fails. 11 Be dismayed, O farmers, wail, O vinedres]sers, [for the wh]eat and for the barl[ey; for the harvest of the field is ruined. 12 The vine has withe]red, [and the fig tree has faile]d; the pomegranate, [the palm also, and the apple tree, all] the trees of the field have wit[hered;] for j[o]y has withered a[way from the sons of men.]

[13 Gird yourselves with sackcloth, and lament, O priest]s; wa[i]l, [O] ministers of the alta[r;] come, l[ie all night in sackcloth, O ministers of my God, for] the grain offering and the d[rink offering are with]held from the house of your

---

18. 4QXII^c, 4QXII^g, MurXII.

Chapter 1. 4QXII^c: 1:10–20; 4QXII^g: 1:12–14.

G[o]d. [14 Sanctify a] fast, *and*[19] call a solemn [assembly;] gather the old men and all the inhabi[tant]s of the la[nd to the house of the LORD your God, and cry to the LORD. 15 Alas] for the day! For the day [of the LORD] is at hand, [and as destruction from the Almighty it shall come. 16 Is not the food cut off before our eyes, joy] and gladness [from the house of our God?] 17 The *heifers*[20] *decay*[21] in [their] s[talls; the storehouses are desolate, the barns are broken down; for the grain is dried up. 18 How] the animals [groan!] *The*[22] herds of cattle wander aimlessly because [they have] n[o pasture; the flocks of sheep are also made desolate. 19 O LORD, to you I cry;] for the fire has devoured the pastures of *the*[23] wilderne[ss, and the flame has burned all the trees of the field. 20 Even the wild animals pant for you;] for the water brooks are dried up, and the fire [has devoured the pastures of the wilderness.]

2 1 Blow the trumpet in Zi[on, and sound an alarm on my holy mountain. Let all the inhabitants of the land tremble, for the day of the LORD is coming, it is near at hand; 2 a day of darkness and gloom, a day of clouds and thick darkness, as the dawn spreads upo]n the [mountains; a great and strong people; there has never been anything like it, nor shall there] be again [after it,] t[o the years of many generations. 3 A fire devours before them, and] behind the[m a flam]e [burns. The land is] as the garden of E[den before them, and behind them a desolate wilderness. Inde]ed, [there is no] escape for [them. 4 Their appearance is like the appearance of horses; and as war-horses, so do they run. 5 Like the nois]e [of chariots] they leap on the tops of the mountains, [like the sound of a flame of fire that devours the stubble, like a] mighty [people] ar[rayed] *for*[24] b[at]tle. 6 Before them [the peoples] are in anguish; [all faces have become pale. 7 They] run [like mi]ghty men; [they] climb [the wall] like so[ldi]ers; [and they march every one on his own course, and they do not break] their ranks. 8 And [they do not push on]e *and*[25] anoth[er; they march every one in his own path; and] they burst through the w[eapons, and they do not break ranks. 9 Th]ey rush [on the cit]y; they run upon the wall; [they climb up into the houses;] they enter [in at the wi]ndows like a thief. 10 The earth [quakes] before th[em; the heavens] tremble; [the sun and the moon are darkened, and the stars withdraw] their shining. 11 And the LORD utters his voice befor[e] his army; for [his camp is very] great; [for he is

---

19. 4QXII[c]. Not in MT LXX.

20. 4QXII[c] LXX. *seed* MT.

21. 4QXII[c]. *shrivel* MT. *leap* LXX.

22. 4QXII[c]. Not in MT LXX.

23. 4QXII[c]. Not in MT.

Chapter 2. 4QXII[c]: 2:1, 8–23; 4QXII[g]: 2:2–13; MurXII: 2:20, 26–32 [H 2:26–27; 3:1–5].

24. 4QXII[g] LXX. Not in MT.

25. 4QXII[g]. Not in MT LXX.

strong that obeys his word; for the da]y of the Lord [is great] and very terrible;
[and] who can *bear*[26] it? 12 Yet even now, [says the Lord, turn to me with all]
your [heart,] with fas[ting, with weeping,] and with mourning; 13 and rend your
hearts and not y[our] *goats,*[27] [and turn] to the Lord [your] God; [for he is gracious and merciful, slow to] anger and abundant in lovingkindness, and relents of
e[vi]l. [14 Who knows whether he will not turn and repent, and leave a blessing
behind him, even a grain offering and a drink offering] to the Lord your God?
[15 Blow the trumpet in Zion, sanctify a fast, call a solemn assembly;] 16 gather
the people, sanctify the assembly, [assemble the old men, gather the children, and
the nursing infants; let the bridegroom come out of his chamber, and the bride]
out of her canopy. [17 Let the priests, the ministers of the Lord, weep] between
the porch [and the altar, and let them say, Spare your people, O Lord, and] do
[not] appoint your heritage to repro[ach, that the] natio[ns should rule over
th]em. [Why should they say among the peoples, "Where is their God?"]

[18 Then the Lord was jealous] for his land, and had pi[ty on] his people.
19 And [the Lo]rd [answered] and [said to his people: Behold, I will send you
grain, and new wine, and oil,] *and you shall eat*[28] and you shall be satisfied [with
them; and] I will no [longer make y]ou [a reproach among the nations; 20 but I
will remove] the northern army [far from you, and will drive it in]to [a barren
and] desolate [land,] its front into the [eastern sea, and its rear into the western
sea; and] its [stenc]h [shall come up,] and [its] foul s[mell] shall come up. Surely he
has [done] great things.

[21 Fear n]ot, [O land, be glad and rejoice; for the Lord has done great things.
22 Fear not, you animals of the field;] for [the pastures of the wilderness] have become gre[en, for the tree bears its fruit, the fig tree and the vine have yielded in
full. 23 Be glad then, O children of Zion, and rejoice in the Lord your Go]d; [for
he has given you the former rain for your vindication, and he showered you with
rain, the former rain and the latter rain as before.] ▲

[26 And you shall eat in plenty and be satisfied, and shall praise the name of the
Lord yo]ur [God, who has dealt wondrously with you; and my people shall]
never [be put to shame.] 27 And you shall know that [I am] in the m[idst of Israel,
and that I am the Lord your God, and there is no]ne el[se;] and [my] people shall
never be put to shame.

[28 Then afterward, I will] pour out my Spirit upon [all flesh; and your sons
and your daughters shall prophesy, your old men shall dre]am [dreams,] your
[you]ng men [shall see visions.] 29 And also up[on the male servants and the female servants in] those [day]s will I pour out [my] Spirit. [30 And] I will show

---

26. 4QXII[c]. *endure* MT LXX.
27. 4QXII[c]. *garments* MT LXX.
28. 4QXII[c]. Not in MT LXX.

wonder[s in the heavens and in the earth: blood, and fi]re, and pillars of s[moke. 31 The sun shall be turned] into darkness, and the moon [into blood, before] the great and ter[rible day of] the LORD [comes. 32 Then whoever] shall call on the name [of the LORD shall be saved; for in Mount Zi]on and in Jerusale[m there shall b]e those that escape, as the LO[RD] has said, [and among the remnan]t those w[hom the LOR]D cal[ls.]

3 1 For behold, in *that*[29] days, and in [tha]t time, [when I shall] bring back the captivity of Judah and Jerusalem, 2 I will [gat]her all the [nation]s, [and I will] bring them down into the valley of Jehoshaphat; and I will execute judgment [upon] them there for my people and my inheritance, Israel, whom they have scattered among the nations. And they have [di]vided [my] lan[d,] 3 and have cast lots *upon*[30] my people, and have given a boy for a harlot, and sold a girl for wine, that th[ey may drink.] 4 So, what are you to me, O Tyre and Sidon, and all the *region*[31] of Philistia? Will you render me a recompense? And if [y]ou recompense me, swiftly and speedily will I return your recompense [upon] your [own head.] 5 For you have taken my silver and [my] gold, and have carried my precious treasures into your *temple,*[32] 6 and have sold the children of [J]uda[h] and the [chi]ldren of [Je]rusalem to the Greeks, that you may remove them far from [their own bord]er. [7 Behold, I will] rouse them from the place where you have sold them, and I will return [your recompense upon yo]ur [own head;] 8 and I will sell your sons and your daughters into the hand of the children of [Juda]h, and they shall sell them[33] to the Sabeans, to a nation far away; for the LO[R]D [*of hos*]ts[34] has spoken.

9 P[roclai]m this among [the nat]ions; prepare a war; stir up the mighty men; [let] all the soldiers [draw near, let them come up.] 10 Beat your plowshares into sw[o]rds, and your pruning hooks [into spears;] let [the w]eak say, I am strong. 11 H[as]ten and [co]me, all you nations round about, [and gather yourselves together. Bring] down your mighty ones, O LORD. 12 Let the nations rouse themselves, and come up to the valley of Jehoshaphat; for there I will sit to judge all the nations round about. 13 Put in the sickle; for [the harve]st is r[ip]e. Come, tread; for the winepress is full, [the] vats overflow; [fo]r [their wickedness is] great.

Chapter 3. MurXII: 3:1–16 [H 4:1–16]; 4QXII[g]: 3:4–9, 11–14, 17, 19–20 [H 4:4–9, 11–14, 17, 19–20]; 4QXII[c]: 3:6–21 [H 4:6–21].

29. MurXII. *those* MT LXX.

30. MurXII. *for* MT.

31. 4QXII[g]. regions MT. *Galilee* LXX.

32. MurXII. *temples* MT LXX.

33. 4QXII[c] may have omitted 6b to 8a (from *sold* to *sell*) due to a scribal error.

34. 4QXII[c]. Not in MT LXX.

[14 Multitudes, multitudes in the] valley of decision! For the d[a]y [of the LORD] is near [in the valley of decision. 15 The sun and the moon] are darkened, and the st[a]rs withd[raw] their shining. 16 And the Lo[RD will roar from Zion, and utter his voice from Jerusalem;] and the heavens and the earth shall shake. But the LORD [is a refuge for his people, and a stronghold for the children of Israel. 17 So yo]u [shall kno]w [that I am] the LORD your God, *who dwells*[35] [in Zion my holy mountain; then shall Jerusalem be holy, and strangers shall not pa]ss through [her any more.]

[18 Then in that day,] the m[ountains] shall drip [sweet wine, and the h]ills shall flow with m[ilk, and all the brooks of Judah shall flow with waters;] and a fountain [shall come forth] from the hou[se of the LORD, and shall water] *all*[36] the valley of Shitt[im. 19 Egypt shall be a desolation, and Edom shall be] *a wilderness,*[37] a desolate wilderness, because of the violence done to the children of Judah, because [they have] s[hed innocent blood in their land. 20 But Judah] shall be inhabited [forever, and Jerusalem from generation to generation. 21 And] I [will avenge] their blood that [I have] no[t avenged; for the LORD dwells in Zion.]

---

35. 4QXII[c] LXX. *dwelling* MT.

36. 4QXII[c]. Not in MT LXX.

37. 4QXII[c]. Not in MT LXX.

AMOS

Four of the ten Minor Prophets scrolls contain text from the book of Amos.[38] Elsewhere in the scrolls, a recast quotation of Amos 5:26–27 provides for the historical genesis of the Qumran sect in the land of Damascus (see the *Damascus Document* [CD] 7:14–15). The expression "tents of Damascus" ("beyond Damascus," in the traditional text of the Hebrew Bible) is then interpreted in light of Amos 9:11—"I will re-erect the fallen tent of David"—as a reference to the neglected books of the Law which were reestablished in Damascus. Another reference to this passage—perhaps more sensitive to the context—appears in Acts 7:43, notably replacing Damascus with Babylon. In light of this, it is possible that the Qumran community understood Damascus as a figure for the Babylonian exile when they spoke of the new covenant made in the "land of Damascus" (*Damascus Document* [CD] 8:21 and 19:34).

Amos 9:11 turns up again in 4Q174 3:12. On this occasion, the "fallen tent of David" is the messianic Branch of David who was expected to appear in the Last Days to deliver Israel. Finally, Amos 8:11 is also employed in true *pesher* fashion in the *Prophetic Apocryphon* (4Q387 2 8–9) and becomes a thirsting for the "words of the Lord" brought about in the Last Days by the apostate priesthood.

1 [2 And he s]aid, the L[ORD will roar from Zion, and utter] his voice [from Jerusalem; and the] pastures [of the shepherds shall] m[o]urn, [and the to]p of C[ar]mel [shall wither.]

[3 Thus] says the LORD: [For three transgressions of Damascus, and for] four, [I will] not [revoke its punishment; because they have threshed] *the pregnant women*

---

38. 4QXII^c, 4QXII^g, MurXII, 5QAmos.

Chapter 1. 5QAmos: 1:2–5; 4QXII^g: 1:3–8, 9–15; MurXII: 1:5–15.

of[39] Gilead [with threshing tools of iro]n. 4 So [I] will sen[d a fire into the house of Hazael, and it shall consume the palac]es of Ben-hadad. [5 And] I [will] break the gate b[ar of Damascus, and cut off the inhabitan]t from the valley of Aven, and the one that holds the scepter from Be[th-eden;] an[d the people of Syria shall go into exile to Kir, says the LOR]D.

6 Thus says [the LORD: For three transgressions of Gaza,] and f[or four, I will not revoke their punishment]; because they carried into exile [the] w[hole people to deliver them up] to Ed[om. 7 So] I [will] send a fire [on the wall of] Gaza, [and it shall co]nsume [its palaces. 8 And I will cut off the inhabitant from Ashdod, and him that holds the scepter from A]shkelon; and [I will turn my hand against Ekron; and the remnant of the Philistines shall perish,] said the Lord Go[D.]

9 Thus says the L[O]R[D: For three transgressions of Tyre, and for four, I will not revoke its punishment;] because they delivered up [the whole people to Edom, and remembered not the covenant of] bro[therho]od. [10 So I will] send [a fire] on the wall of Tyre, [and it shall consume its palaces.]

11 Thus says the LORD: [For three transgressions of Edom, and for fou]r, I will not revoke its punishment; [because he pursued his brother] with the s[word, and cast off all pity, and] his anger [tore] continually, [and] he kept his wrath [forever. 12 So I will send a fire upon Teman, and it shall consu]me the p[alaces of] Bozrah.

13 Thus says the LORD: For thre[e transg]ressions of the children of Ammo[n, and for four, I will not revoke its punishment;] because they have ripped open the pregnant women of G[ilea]d, that they may e[nlarge their border. 14 So I will kindle a fire] on the wall of Rabbah, and it shall co[nsume its palaces, with shouting in the day of] the[40] battle, [with a tempest] in the day of the whirlw[ind;] 15 and their king shall g[o] into e[xile,] he an[d his princes together, says the LORD.]

2 1 Thus sa[ys the LORD: Fo]r three [transgressions of Moab, and for four, I will not revoke its punishment; because he burned the bones of the king of Edom to lime.]▲

[7 . . . they that trample the head of the poor into the dust of the earth, and turn aside the way of the meek; and a man] and [his] father [go to the same girl to profane my holy name. 8 And they lay themselves down upon clothes] taken in pledge [beside every altar; and in the house of] their [God they drink the wine of those who have been fined.]

[9 Yet I destroyed the Amorite before them, whose height was like the height of the cedar]s, [and he was strong as the oaks; yet I destroyed his fruit above, and

---

39. 5QAmos LXX. Not in MT.

40. 4QXII[g]. Not in MT LXX.

Chapter 2. 4QXII[g]: 2:1, 7–9, 15–16; MurXII: 2:1; 4QXII[c]: 2:11–16.

his roots beneath. 10 Also I brought you up out of the land of Egypt, and led you forty years in the wilderness, to possess the land of the Amorite. 11 And I raised up some of your sons as prophets, and some of your young men as Nazirites. Is this not even so, O children of] Israe[l? says the LORD.]

[12 But you gave the Nazirites wine to drink, and commanded the prophets,] s[ay]ing, ["Do not prophesy."]

13 *And behold,*[41] I [will weigh you down in your place, as a cart is weighed down when it is full of shea]ves. 14 And [flight] shall perish [from the swift; and the strong shall no]t strengthen himself; neither shall the mighty save [him]self. [15 The one who grasps the bow shall not stand; and he that is swift of foot] shall [not] escape; [nor shall he that r]ides [the horse de]liver himself; 16 and he that *finds heart*[42] among the mighty shall flee away naked in [that day, declar]es [the LORD.]

3 1 H[ear thi]s [word] t[hat the LORD has sp]oken against you, O children of Is-rael, against the whole family which [I brought up out of the land of Egypt, saying, 2 You only have I known] of all the families of the eart[h; therefore I will punish] you for all your i[niquitie]s.

[3 Shall two walk together, except they have made an appointment? 4 Will] a lion [roa]r in the forest, [when] he has [n]o [prey? Will] a young lion [cry] out from his [d]en, [if he has caught nothing? 5 Will a bird fall in a snare upon the earth, where there is no bait in it? Shall] a snare [spring u]p from the ground, when [it] has taken [nothing] at all? [6 Shall the trumpet be b]lown [in a city, and the people not be afraid? Shall disaster befall a city, unless the LORD has done it?] 7 Surely [the Lord GOD will do] no[thing unless he reveals his secret to his servants the prophets. 8 The lion has roared; who will not fear? The Lord GOD has sp]oken; who can but [prophesy?]

[9 Proclaim to the palaces in Ashdod, and in the palaces in the land of Egypt, and say, "Assemble yourselves upon the mounta]ins of [Samari]a, and see what great tumults [are in it, and what oppressions are in its midst." 10 For they do not know how to do right,] declares [the Lord GOD, those who store up violen]ce and robbery in their palaces. [11 Therefore thus says the LORD: An adversary shall surround the land] and str[ip] your strength from you; [and] your [palac]es [shall be plundered.]

[12 Thu]s [says the LORD: As the shepherd rescues out of the mouth of the lion two] leg[s or a piece of an ear, so shall the child]ren of Israel who li[ve in Samaria be rescued, with the corner of a couch and with the cover of a bed.]

13 H[ear, and testify against the house of Jacob, declar]es the Lo[rd] GOD, the

---

41. 4QXII[c]. *Behold* MT. *Because of this, behold* LXX.

42. 4QXII[c] LXX. *is courageous* MT.

Chapter 3. 4QXII[c]: 3:1–15; 4QXII[g]: 3:1–2.

G[od of hosts. 14 For on the day that I punish the transgressions of Israel, I will also punish the altars of Bethel; and the horns of the altar shall be cut off] and f[all to the ground. 15 And I will strike the] winter [house with the summer house;] and [the houses of ivory shall] p[erish, and the great houses shall come to an end, says the LORD.]

4 [1 Hea]r this word, O cow[s of Bashan, who are in the mountain of Samaria, who oppress the poor, who crus]h the needy, [who say to th]eir [husbands,] *Bring*[43] that we might dri[nk. 2 The Lord GOD has sworn by] his [holin]ess, Behol[d, the days are coming upon you, when they shall take you away with hooks, and the last] of you with fish-*beaters*.[44] [3 And you shall go out through the breaches, everyone straight ahead; and you shall cast yourselves into Harmon, says the LORD. 4 Come to Bethel, and transgress; to Gilgal, and multiply transgression; and bring your] s[acrifi]c[es every morning, and your tithes every three days; 5 and offer a sacrifice of thanksgiving of that which is leavened,] and p[roclaim] freewill offeri[ngs and make them known. For so you love to do, O you children of Israel, says the Lord GOD.]

[6 And] I [also have given you cleanness of teeth in all your cities, and lack of bread in all] your [pl]aces; yet [you have not] returned to [me, says the LORD.]

[7 And I also have withheld the rain from you, when there were yet] three m[onths to the harvest; and I sent rain upon one city, and I did not send rain upon another city:] I did not rain upon [one] fie[ld, and the field on which it did not rain withered.] 8 So two or three [cities] staggered [to another city to get a drink of water, and were not satisfied;] yet y[ou] have not returned to me, [declares the LORD.]

[9 I struck you with blight and mildew; your many gardens,] your [vin]eyards, [fig trees, and olive trees the locust has devoured, yet have you not returned to me, says the LORD.]▲

5 [1 He]ar [this word which I take up for a lamentation over you, O house of Israel. 2 The virgin of Israel] is fallen, [she shall no longer rise; she is cast down upon her land, there is none to raise her up.]▲

[9 It is he that brings sudden] destruction upon [the stron]g, and de[struction comes upon the fortress.]

[10 They hate him that reproves in the gate, and they abhor him that speaks uprightly. 11 Therefore, because you trample upon the poor and take levies of grain] from him, [you have] b[uilt] houses of hewn stone, [but you shall not dwell in them; you have planted pleasant vineyards, but you shall not drink] their

---

Chapter 4. 4QXII[c]: 4:1–2; 4QXII[g]: 4:4–9.

43. Plural 4QXII[c] LXX. Singular MT.

44. 4QXII[c](?). *hooks* MT LXX.

Chapter 5. 4QXII[g]: 5:1–2, 9–18.

[win]e. 12 For I know [that your transgressions are many, and your sins are mighty—you that afflict the just,] take a bribe, [and turn aside the] n[eedy in the gate. 13 Therefore the prudent shall keep silence in such a time, for] it is [an evil time.]

14 Seek g[oo]d and n[ot evil, that you may live; and so the LORD, the God of hosts, will be with you,] as you have said. 15 *We hated*[45] evil and [loved good, and established justice in the gate; it may be that] the LORD, the God of hosts, will be gracious to *us,*[46] the rem[nant of Joseph.]

16 Therefore thus says the LOR[D], the God of hos[ts, the Lord: There shall be wailing in all the squares; and] they shall say [in all the streets,] "Al[as!] Alas!" [And] they [shall cal]l the farmer to [mourning, and such as are skilled in lamentation to wailing. 17 And in all vineyards there shall be] wailing; for [I will pass] through the midst of you, says [the LORD.]

[18 Woe to you that desire the day of the LORD! What is the] day [of the LORD to yo]u? [It is darkness, and not light.]▲

6 [1 Woe to those who are at ease in Zion, and to those who are secure on the mountain of Samaria, the notable men of the foremost of the nati]ons, and [the house of Israel] comes [to them! 2 Cross over to Calneh, and see; and from there go to] Hamath the great; then [go down to Gath of the Philistines. Are they better than] these [ki]n[gdoms?] Or is their territory great[er than your territory? 3 You put off the evil day,] and you bring on [a reign of violence.]

[4 Alas for those who lie upon beds of ivory and recline upo]n [their] couche[s, and eat the lambs from the flock, and the calves from the midst of the stall; 5 who sing idle songs to the sound of the harp, who like David compose for themselves on instruments of music; 6 who] drink [wine in b]ow[ls, and anoint themselves with the finest oils, but are not grieved over the ruin of Joseph. 7 Therefore shall they now go into exile at the head of the exiles; and the banquet of those who recline shall pass away.]

8 The Lor[d Go]D has sworn by himself, [says the LORD, the God of hosts]: I [a]bhor [the] p[rid]e of Jacob, [and] I hate [his palaces;] therefore will I deliver up the c[ity and all that is in it.]

[9 Then if there remain ten me]n in one house, [they] shall die. [10 And when a man's uncle, one who cremates him, shall take him up to carry his bones out of the] house, and shall say to one that [is in the innermost parts of the house, "Is there anyone still with you?" And he shall say, "No one"; then he shall say, "Hush, for we] must not me[ntion the name of the Lor]D."

[11 For behold, the LORD commands, and the] great [house shall be smashed

---

45. 4QXII^g LXX. *Hate!* MT.

46. 4QXII^g. Not in MT LXX.

Chapter 6. 4QXII^g: 6:1–14; MurXII: 6:1(?); 4QXII^c: 6:13–14.

to] pieces, and the [little] h[ouse to bits. 12 Do] horses [run upon the] rock? Does one plow [there with oxen? For you have turned] justice [into poison,] and the fruit of righteousness into wormw[ood; 13 you that re]joi[ce in Lo-]debar, who s[ay, "Have we] not by [our own] streng[th taken Karnaim for ourselves?" 14 For behold, I am going to raise up against you] a nation, [O house of Israel,] declares the LORD, [the God of host]s; and they shall afflict [you from the entrance of Hamath to the brook of the Arabah.]

7 1 Thus the Lo[rd GOD] showed me, [and behold, he was forming locusts at the time the latter grow]th [began to come up;] and b[ehold, it was the latter growth after] the king[´s mowings.] 2 And when [they had] f[inished eating the grass of the land, then I said, "O Lord GOD, forgive, I beg you; how can] Jacob [stand?] For he is small." [3 The LORD relented concerning thi]s; "It shall not be," said the LORD.

4 Thus the Lord G[OD] showed me, [and behold, the Lord GO]D [was calling for judgment by fire;] and it devoured [the great deep and was eating up the land. 5 Then said I, "O Lord GOD, cea]se, I beg you; [how can Jacob stand? For he is small." 6 The LORD relented concerning this.] "T[hi]s too shall not be," [said the Lord GOD.]

[7 Thus he showed me, and behold, the LORD was st]and[ing] be[side a wa]ll built with a plumb line, and a plumb line was in his [han]d. 8 And [the *Lo*]*rd* *GOD*[47] s[aid to me], ["Amos,] what [do you see?"] And I said, "A plumb line." Then the LORD said, "Behold, I *have set*[48] a plumb line in the midst [of my] people [I]srael; [I will never] again pa[ss] them b[y;] 9 and the high places of Isaac shall be desolate, and the sanctuaries of I[srael shall be laid was]te; and [I] will rise [against the] house [of Jerobo]am with the sword."

[10 Then] Am[aziah the pr]iest of Bethel sent to Jeroboam king of Israel, s[ay]ing, "Amos [has conspired against you in the mi]dst of the house of Israel; the land is not able to b[ear all] his [wor]ds. 11 For th[us] Amos says, 'Jeroboam shall die by the sword [and] Israel [must] go into exile out of his land.' " [12 Also] Amaziah [said] to Amos, "O seer, go, flee away [int]o [the land of J]uda[h, and] t[here] eat [bre]ad, [and] prophesy there; 13 but never again proph[esy] at Bethel, [for it is the king´s sa]nctuary [and it is] a royal [hou]se."

14 Then Amos answered and said to Amaziah, "I [am] n[o prophet,] nor am I a prophet[´s] s[on;] but [I am a] he[rdsman, and a dresser of] sycamore trees; 15 and the LORD took me from following the flock, and the Lo[RD] *said,*[49] 'Go, prophesy

---

Chapter 7. 4QXII[c]: 7:1–16; 4QXII[g]: 7:1, 7–12, 16–17; MurXII: 7:3–17.

47. 4QXII[g]. *LORD* MT LXX.

48. 4QXII[c] LXX. *am setting* 4QXII[g] MT.

49. 4QXII[g]. *said to me* MT LXX.

upon⁵⁰ my people Israel.' 16 Now therefore hear [the] wor[d of the Lᴏʀᴅ. You say,] 'Do not prophesy against Israel, and do not p[rea]ch *any longer*⁵¹ [against the house of Isaac.' 17 Therefore thus says] the *Lord Gᴏᴅ*:⁵² 'Your wife shall become a prostitute in the city, and your sons and [your] daughters [shall fall by the sword,] and your land shall be divided by measuring line; [and you yourself shall die i]n [an unclean] l[and, and Israel shall surely] go into exile away from its land.' "

8 [1 This is what the Lord Go]ᴅ [showed me,] and behold, there was a basket of summer fruit. 2 And he sa[id, "Amos, what do you see?" And I said, "A basket of summer fruit." Then the Lᴏʀᴅ] said to me, "The end has come [upon my people Israel; I will no longer pardon them. 3 And the] s[ong]s of the temple [shall become wailings in] th[at da]y," [declares the Lord Gᴏᴅ. "The dead bod]ies [shall be many,] cast out in every place. Hush!"

[4 Hear this, you who] trample the ne[edy, and bring an end to] the poor of the land, 5 saying, "W[hen will the new moon be over, that] we may *be satisfied*,⁵³ [and the sabbath, that we may set] out the wheat; making [the ephah] small [and the shekel great, and dealing deceitfully with fals]e [balances;] 6 that we may buy [the] p[oor] for silver, [and the needy for a pair of shoes, and sell the refuse of the wheat?"]▲

[7 . . . the L]ᴏʀ[ᴅ] has swo[rn by the pride of Jacob, "Surely I will never forget any of their deeds."]▲

[11 Behold, the days are coming, says] the Lord Gᴏᴅ, that [I] will se[nd a fam]ine in the land, not a f[ami]ne of bread, nor a thirst for water, but of hearing [the] word[s of the Lᴏʀ]ᴅ. 12 And they [shall wand]er from sea to sea, and from the north even to the east; they shall run to and fro seeking [the wo]rd of the [L]ᴏʀᴅ, but they shall not find it.

13 In that day the beautiful virgins and the young men shall faint for thirst. 14 Those who swear by the sin of Samaria, and say, "As your god lives, O [Da]n," and, "As the way of Beer-sheba lives"; they shall fall, and never rise up again.

9 1 I sa[w] the Lord standing beside the al[ta]r, and he said, Strike the c[apit]als so that the thresholds may shake, and shatter them on the heads of all of them; and I will slay the last of them with the sword. [No]t one of them shall run away, [and] not one of them shall escape.

2 Though they dig into Sheol, there shall my hand take them; and though they

---

50. MurXII. *to* MT.

51. MurXII. Not in MT LXX.

52. 4QXIIᵍ. *Lord* MT LXX.

Chapter 8. 4QXIIᵍ: 8:1–5, 11–14; MurXII: 8:3–7, 11–14.

53. Meaning uncertain 4QXIIᵍ. *sell grain* MT LXX.

Chapter 9. MurXII: 9:1–15; 4QXIIᵍ: 9:1, 5–6, 14–15.

climb up to heaven, from there will I bring them down. 3 And though they hi[d]e themselves on the top of Carmel, I will search and take them from there; and tho[ugh] they be hid from my sight in the bottom of the sea, there will I command the serpent, and it shall bite them. 4 And though they go into captivity before [their enemies,] from there will I command the sword, and it shall slay them; and I will set [my] e[y]e[s] upon them for evil and not for good.

5 For the Lord GOD of hosts, he who touches the land [and it mel]ts, [and] *everyone who dwells*[54] that dwell in it shall mourn; and a[ll of] it shall rise up like the Nile, and shall sink again, like the Nile of Egypt; 6 it is he who builds his chambers [in the hea]vens, and has f[oun]ded his vault upon the [ea]rth; he who calls for the waters of the [sea, and po]urs them out upon the face of the earth; the LO[R]D is his name.

7 Are you n[ot] as the children of the Ethiopian[s to me, O children of Israel? sa]ys the LORD. Have not [I brought up] Isr[ae]l [out of the land of Egypt, and the Philistines from] Caphtor, [and the Arameans from Kir? 8 Behold, the eyes of the Lord GOD are upon the sin]ful [kingdom, and I will destroy it from the face of the earth;] except [that I will] n[ot] utterly de[stroy the house of Jacob, says the LORD.]

[9 For behold,] I am commanding, [and I will sift the house of Israel among all the nations, as grain is sif]ted in a [si]eve, [yet no kernel shall fall upon the earth. 10 All the sinner]s of my [peo]ple [shall die by the sword,] those who say, ["The evil shall not overtake or meet us."]

[11 In tha]t [day] will I raise up [the booth of David that is fallen, and close up their breaches; and] I will [rai]se up his [ru]ins, [and I will build it as in the days of old; 12 that] they [may poss]ess the remnant of Edom [and all the nations who are called by my name,] declares the LORD that does this.

[13 Behold, days are coming, says the LORD, when the plowm]an [shall over-take] the reaper, and the treader of grape[s the one who sows the seed; and the mountains shall drop] sw[eet wine, and all the] hil[ls] shall [melt. 14 And I will re-store the fortunes of my people Is]rael, [and they shall rebuild the] r[uined] cit[ie]s [and inhab]it; and they shall pl[ant] vineyard[s and] drink their [wi]ne; they shall also make gardens and eat [their] f[ruit. 15 And] I [will plant them] upon their land, and [they shall] never ag[ain be plucked up] out of [their] lan[d wh]ich I have given them, says the LORD your God.

---

54. MurXII. *all who dwell* MT LXX.

OBADIAH

The twenty-one-verse postexilic vision of Obadiah concerning Edom—Israel's cousin and foe from across the Dead Sea to the southeast—is found in two of the ten Minor Prophets manuscripts (4QXII^g, MurXII). Although Edom is mentioned in the scrolls (see the *War Scroll* 1:1 and 4Q434 7b 3), no use of Obadiah is found in the surviving nonbiblical manuscripts. Obadiah is, however, credited with a psalm whose fragmentary first line is found in *A Collection of Royal Psalms* (4Q380 1 ii 8–9).

1 *In*[55] the vision of Obad[iah. Thus] says [the Lord GOD concerning Edom:] We have [hea]rd [a report] from the LOR[D,] and an envoy [is sent] among the nations: ["Arise and let us ris]e up [against] her in battle." [2 Be]hold, [I have] ma[de] you small among the nations; you are [greatly] despised. [3 The pride of] your [hea]rt has deceived you, you who dwell in the clefts of the rock, [whose] habita[tion] is high; who says in his heart, "Who shall bring me down to the ground?" 4 Though you mount on high as the eagle, and though *you set your nest*[56] a[mon]g the stars, [I will] bring you down from there, declares the LORD.

5 If thieves came to you, if [robbers by] night—how you have been destroyed!—would they not steal only till they had enough? If gr[ape gatherer]s [came] to you, would they not leave some gleanings? 6 How Esau has been plundered, how are [his] hidden treasure[s] sought out! 7 All your allies have driven you to your border, your confederates have deceived and overpowered you; those [who eat] your bread lay a snare under you; the[re is no] understanding in him. 8 Shall I not in that day, declares the LORD, destroy the wise men from [Ed]om, and understandi[ng from] the mountain of Esau? 9 And your mighty men, O Teman, shall be dismayed, in [ord]er that [every]one may be cut off from the mountain of Esau by slaughter. 10 Because of the violence done to your brother

---

Obadiah. MurXII: 1–21; 4QXII^g: 1–5, 8–12, 14–15.

55. 4QXII^g. Not in MT LXX.

56. 4QXII^g (original scribe altered his text) LXX. *your nest be set* 4QXII^g MT MurXII.

Jacob, shame shall co[ver you, and] you [shall be cu]t off for[e]ver. 11 In the day that you stood aside, in the day that strangers carried away [his wealth,] and foreigners entered his *gate*[57] [and] cast lots upon Jerusalem, [yo]u too were as one [of] them. 12 But do not look on the day of your brother, on the day of [his] misfor[tune, and] do not rejoice over the children of Judah on the day of their destruction; [do] not speak [proudly] in the [da]y of distress. 13 *And*[58] do not enter the gate of my people on the day of their calamity; indeed, [do no]t [look on] his [afflic]tion in the day of his calamity, and lay hands [on his we]alth on [the day of] his calamity. 14 And do [not] stand in the crossroads to cut down his fugi[ti]ves; and do not betray his survivors on the day of distress.

15 For the day of the Lo[RD] draws near on all the nations; as you have done, it shall be done to you; your *dealings have returned*[59] upon your own head. 16 For just as you have drunk upon my holy mountain, so [shall] all the nations drink continually; indeed, they shall drink, and swallow down, and shall be as though they had not been. 17 But [on] Mount Zion there shall be those that escape, and it shall be holy; and the house of [Ja]cob shall possess *those who possess them.*[60] 18 And the [hou]se of Jacob shall be a fire, and the house of Joseph a flame, and the house of Esau will be as stubble, and they shall burn among them, and de[vou]r them; and there shall be no survivor of the house of Esau; for the LORD has spoken. 19 And those of the Negev [shall possess] the mount of Esau, and they of the lowland the Philistines; [and] they [shall posses]s [the country of] Ephraim, and the country of Samaria; [and] B[en]jamin shall possess Gile[ad. 20 And the exiles of] this host [of] the children of [I]srael, who are among the Canaan[it]es, as far as [Zarephath, and the exile]s of Jerusalem who are in Sepharad shall possess the c[ities of the Negev. 21 And] deliverers [shall ascend] Mount Zion to judge the mountain of [Es]au; and the kingdom [shall] b[e the L]ORD['s].

---

57. MurXII MT ketib. *gates* MT qere LXX.
58. Erased MurXII. Not in MT LXX.
59. 4QXII[g]. *dealing shall return* MT LXX.
60. MurXII LXX. *their possessions* MT.

JONAH

The famous account of Jonah and the giant fish is found in five of the ten Minor Prophets manuscripts.[61] Neither the book nor the prophet attracted any attention among the nonbiblical scrolls that survived the two-thousand-year storage in the caves. One wonders what the Qumran community members might have thought of God's forgiving Nineveh, the capital of Assyria, one of Israel's greatest enemies.

1 1 And the word of the LORD came to Jonah the son of Amittai, saying, [2 "Arise, go to Nine]veh, that great city, [and c]ry against it; for their wickedness has come up before me." [3 But] Jon[ah ros]e [up to flee] *Tarshish*[62] from the presence of the LORD; and he went down to Joppa, and found a ship [going to Tarshish,] paid its fare, [and went down into it] to [g]o with them *Tarshish*[63] from the presence of the [L]ORD.

4 But the Lo[RD s]ent out a gr[ea]t wind up[on the] sea, and there was a mighty storm on the sea, so that the ship was about to break up. [5 Then] the [sa]ilors [were af]raid, and cried every man to his god; and they cast forth the wares that were in the ship into [the sea,] to lig[hten it] for them. But Jonah had gone [down] into the hold of the s[hip;] and had lain down, and was fast asleep. 6 So the shipmaster came to him, and said to him, "What are you doing sleeping? Get up, [call] to your god. [Per]haps the god will take notice of us that we might not perish."

7 And they said [to] o[ne] anoth[er,] "Come, and let us cast lots, that we may know on whose acco[unt] this evil [has come upon us."] So they cast lots, and the l[o]t fell on Jonah. 8 Then they said to him, "Tell us, we pray you, on whose ac-

---

61. 4QXII^a, 4QXII^f, 4QXII^g, MurXII, 8HevXII gr.

Chapter 1. MurXII: 1:1–17 [H 1:1–16; 2:1]; 4QXII^g: 1:1–9; 4QXII^a: 1:1–5, 7–10, 15–17 [H 15–16; 2:1]; 4QXII^f: 1:6–8, 10–16; 8HevXII gr: 1:14–17 [H 14–16; 2:1].

62. 4QXII^a. *to Tarshish* MT.

63. 4QXII^g. *to Tarshish* MurXII MT.

count this evil has come on us. And[64] what is your occupation? And where do you come from? W[hat] is your country? And of what people are you?" 9 And he said to them, "I am a Hebrew, *the Lo[r]d the God of heaven, and I fear he who*[65] has made the sea and the dr[y] land." 10 Then were the men exceedingly afraid, and said to him, "What is this you have done?" [For] the men knew that he was flee-ing from the presence of the [Lo]rd, because he had told them.

11 Then [they] s[aid] to him, "What shall we do to you, that the sea may calm down for us?" For the sea grew more and more tempestuous. 12 And he said to them, "Pick me up, and throw me into [the] sea; then the sea shall calm down for you, for I know that it is because of me that [thi]s gr[eat] storm is [up]on you." 13 Nevertheless the me[n] rowed hard [to] get back to the land, but they could not, for the sea grew more and more tempestuous against them.

> The Greek manuscript known as 8HevXII gr—so named because it was found in Cave 8 at Nahal Hever and contains the twelve Minor Prophets, written in Greek—begins in Jonah 1:14, the first half of the manuscript having fallen prey to the ele-ments. It is of critical importance in the history of the Septuagint; and because it was systematically revised to reflect the Masoretic Text, it is a significant witness to the He-brew tradition as well. Its origin was reported in 1952 by the Bedouin to be Wâdi Seiyâl some twenty-five miles to the south of Qumran. However, scraps of the manu-script found in the so-called Cave of Horrors in 1961 by archaeologists clearly place its origin at Nahal Hever, five miles to the north of the original claim. The Bedouin were evidently determined to keep the cave of origin—and source of additional in-come—to themselves. An additional curiosity is the fact that the personal name of God—Yahweh—is not translated into Greek but is represented by the four Hebrew letters YHWH, written in the ancient Hebrew script known as paleo-Hebrew.

14 So they cried to the Lord, and said, "We beseech you, O Lord, let us not perish for this man's life, and do not make us responsible for innocent blood; for you, O Lord, have done as it pleased you." 15 So they picked up Jonah, and threw him into the sea; and the sea ceased from its raging. 16 Then the men feared the Lord exceedingly, and they offered a sacrifice to the Lord, and made vows.

17 And the Lord prepared a [gr]eat fish to swallow up Jonah, and he was in the belly of the fish for three days and three nights.

2 1 Then Jonah prayed to the Lord his [G]od from the fish's belly. 2 And he s[aid,] "I called to the L[o]rd *in*[66] my affliction, [and he] answered me; [out of

---

64. 4QXII[g] LXX. Not in 4QXII[f] MurXII MT.

65. 4QXII[a]. *and I fear the Lord, the God of heaven, who* MT LXX.

Chapter 2. MurXII: 2:1–10 [H 2:2–11]; 8HevXII gr: 2:1–7 [H 2:2–8]; 4QXII[a]: 2:6 [H 2:7]; 4QXII[g]: 2:2–10 [H 2:3–11].

66. 8HevXII gr LXX. *because of* MT.

the be]lly of Sheol [I] cried, you [he]ard my voice. 3 For you cast me into the deep, into the heart of [the seas, and the] flo[o]d was round about me; all your waves and your billows passed over me. 4 And I said, 'I have been cast out of your sight; how will I look again toward your holy temple?' 5 The waters *closed*[67] over me; the deep encircled me; the weeds were wrapped around my head. 6 I went down to the roots of the mountains; the [earth with] its [b]ars closed upon me for[e]ver; yet you have brought *the life of my soul*[68] up from the pit, O LORD my [God.] 7 When my life [fa]d[ed] within me, [I] remembered the LORD; [and my] pra[y]er came in to you, i[nto] your [holy] t[emple.] 8 They that regard [vai]n idol[s] forsake their faithfulness. 9 But I [will sac]r[ifice] to you with the voice of t[hanksgiving;] I will pay that which I have vowed. [Salvat]ion is from the LORD." [10 And] the LORD [sp]oke to [the fis]h, and it vomited [J]onah out [up]on the dry land.

3 1 And the word [of the LORD] came [to Jonah the sec]ond time, saying, 2 "Ar[is]e, go to Nineveh, that great city, [a]nd cal[l] out [t]o it [the] message *as this*[69] that I am going to tell you." 3 So [J]onah arose, and went to N[i]neveh, according to the word of the LORD. Now N[i]neveh was an exceeding great city, a three days' journey. 4 And Jonah began to go into the city, one day's walk, and he cried out and said, "Yet forty days, and Nineveh shall be [overthro]wn." 5 And the people of Nineveh belie[v]ed God; and they called a fast, and everyone, both great and [s]mall, put on sackcloth.

6 And the word [reached] the king of Nineveh, and he arose from his throne, and laid aside his robe, and covered himself with sackcloth, [and sat] in ashes. 7 And he had a proclamation made in Nineveh: "By the decree of the king and [his] noble[s,] Let neither m[a]n nor animal, herd nor f[lo]ck, taste anything; let them not feed or [dri]nk [water;] 8 but let both man and animal be covered with sackcloth, an[d] let them cry [mi]ght[ily] *over*[70] God, and let *him*[71] tu[rn] each from his evil way, and from the violence that is in their hands. 9 Who knows? God [may] tu[rn and] c[han]ge his mind, and turn away from his fierce anger, so that we do not perish."

10 And God saw the[ir] deeds, that they turned from their evil way; and *God*[72] changed his mind concerning the evil which he s[ai]d he would do to them; and he did not do it.

---

67. Singular 4QXII[g]. Plural MurXII MT.

68. 4QXII[g]. *my life* MT LXX.

Chapter 3. MurXII: 3:1–10; 4QXII[g]: 3:1–3; 8HevXII gr: 3:2–5, 7–10; 4QXII[a]: 3:2.

69. 4QXII[a] LXX. Not in MT.

70. MurXII. *to* 8HevXII gr MT LXX.

71. 8HevXII gr. *them* MT LXX.

72. Lacks article 8HevXII gr. Article present MT LXX.

4 1 But it displeased Jonah greatly, and he was angry. 2 And he p[r]ayed to the LORD, and said, "I pray, O LORD, was this not what I said while I was still in [my own] country? [There]fore I fled to Tarshish at first; for I knew that you are a gracious God, and merciful, [slo]w [to ange]r, and abundant in lovingkindness, and one who relents concerning evil. 3 Therefore now, O LORD, take, I pray, my l[ife] from me; for it is better for me to die than to live." 4 And the Lo[R]D said, ["Is] it good for you to be angry?" 5 Then Jonah [we]nt out of the city, and sat on the east side of the city, and there he made a booth for himself, and sat under it in the shade, until he might see what would become of the city.

6 And the *Lord* GOD[73] appointed a plant, and made it to come up over Jonah, that it might shade his head, to deliver him from his discomfort. And [Jonah] was [v]ery glad about the plant. 7 But God appointed [a worm,] *as*[74] the morning rose *on the next day,*[75] and it attacked the plant, so that it withered. 8 And when the [sun] rose, [God] appointed a sultry east wind; [and the su]n beat down on the h[ead of Jonah, so that he became f]aint and p[leaded] with his so[ul] to [d]ie, and said, "It is better for me to die than to live."

9 And [Go]d s[ai]d [t]o Jo[nah, "Are] you right to be a[ngry] over the plant?" And he said, "It is right that I am angry, even [to death." 10 And] the LORD [sai]d, "You have had concern for the plant, [for w]hich you have not labored or made grow; [which] came up [in a nig]ht, and perished in a night. 11 And should not I have conce[rn] for Nineveh, that [great] c[ity,] in which are more than one hundred and twenty thousand persons who do not kn[ow] their right hand from their left hand; and also many animals?"

Chapter 4. MurXII: 4:1–11; 8HevXII gr: 4:1–2, 5; 4QXII^g: 4:5–11.

73. 4QXII^g. *LORD God* MurXII MT.

74. 4QXII^g. *when* MT.

75. 4QXII^g. *on the morrow* MurXII MT.

MICAH

Micah is found in three of the Minor Prophets manuscripts[76] as well as in a fragmentary *pesher*.[77] This commentary interprets portions of chapter 1—which addresses the judgment of Samaria (Israel) and Jerusalem (Judah) at the end of the eighth century BCE—as fulfilled in the time of the Teacher of Righteousness, enumerating the judgments due his enemies.

Quotations from Micah in nonbiblical texts are relatively numerous. The false prophets of the eighth century BCE who commanded Micah to keep silent (Micah 2:6a) become, in good *pesher* style, the Pharisees of the late Second Temple period—in particular, the leadership, who evidently sought to silence the Teacher (*Damascus Document* [CD] 4:20). Micah 2:10–11 and its command to "rise and go, for this is not a place of rest," is interpreted by 4Q177 as evidence of God's desire that the sect remove itself from Jerusalem and go into exile. Micah 4:13 and its prediction of Jerusalem's—the daughter of Zion's—glory in the Last Days is incorporated into the blessing of the messianic Prince or Leader of Israel in *Priestly Blessings for the Last Days* (1QSb 5:26). Micah 7:11 is understood by the *Damascus Document* (CD) 4:12 to be fulfilled at the end of the then-present wicked age, when "the wall is built, the boundary removed [*or* extended]."

As has been evidenced in earlier discussion, quotations from these Minor Prophets are normally employed to illuminate the events of God's program—that which is termed *pesher* interpretation. Rarely, as is the case with the quotation of Micah 7:2 in the *Damascus Document* (CD) 16:15, is a prophetic text used to determine a legal issue. In this instance, the issue is what might be offered or vowed to God. If the item is necessary for subsistence and therefore liable to be reneged—setting one up to be "hunted with a net"—it should not be vowed.

---

76. 4QXII^g, MurXII, 8HevXII gr.
77. 1Q14.

1 1 The w[or]d of the LORD th[at] came to [Mi]cah of Morasheth in the days of Jotham, Ahaz, and [Hezeki]ah, *king*[78] of Judah, which he saw [concerning] Sa[mari]a and Jerusalem.

2 Hea[r,] you p[eoples,] all of you; *and*[79] lis[t]en, O e[art]h, and all that is in it; and [let] the Lord GOD [be] a witnes[s] against you, the Lord from his holy temple. 3 For behold, the LORD is coming out of [his] pl[ace, and] will come down and tread upon [the high places of the] earth. 4 And the mountains shall melt u[nde]r him, and the v[alle]ys shall be s[p]lit, like wax [ne]ar the [fir]e, like water that is poured down [a st]eep place. 5 All this for the transgression of [Ja]cob, and for the *sin*[80] of the house of Israel. What is the transgression of Jacob? Is it not Samaria? And what are the high places of [Ju]dah? Are they not Jerusalem? 6 Therefore I will make Samaria as a heap of the field, *and*[81] places for planting [vineyar]ds; and I will pour her stones into the valley, and I will uncover her foundations. 7 And all her graven images shall be beat[en] to pieces, and all her wages shall be burned with fire, and all her idols I will lay waste; for as the wages of a prostitute has she gathered them, and as the wag[es of a prostitute shall they re]turn.

8 For this I will lament and wail; I will go barefoot and naked; I will m[ake a lament] like the jackals, and mourning like the [os]triches. 9 For [her wounds] are incurable; [for it has com]e even to J[udah;] it has reached to the gate of my people, even to Jerusalem.

[10 Tell it not] in Gath, [do not wee]p [at all;] at [Beth-lea]phrah *roll yourself*[82] in the dust. 11 Pass on your way, inhabitan[t of Shaphir, in nakedness and] shame; the [inh]abitant of Zaanan has not come forth; [the wailin]g of B[e]th-ezel, he shall take from you [his] s[tay. 12 For the] i[nhabitant of] Maroth waits anxiously for good, because evil has come down from the LORD to the gate [of Jerusalem.] 13 Harness the chari[ot to the swift stee]d, O inhabitant of Lac[hish; i]t was [the be]ginning of sin to the [daught]er of Zion; for the transgressions of Israel were found in you. [14 There]fore you shall give parting gifts to Moresheth-gath; the houses of Achzib [shall be a deception] to the [kin]gs of Is[rael.] 15 I will again bring a conqueror to you, O inhabitant of Mareshah; the glory of I[srael shall enter] A[dullam.] 16 Make yourself bald and cut off your hair for the children of your delight; make yourself as [ba]ld [as the eagle; for they have gone from you into exile.]

Chapter 1. MurXII: 1:1–16; 8HevXII gr: 1:1–8; 4QXII[g]: 1:7, 12–15.

78. 8HevXII gr. *kings* MT LXX.

79. MurXII LXX. Not in MT 8HevXII gr.

80. 8HevXII gr LXX. *sins* MT.

81. 8HevXII gr LXX. Not in MT.

82. MurXII MT qere. *I rolled myself* MT ketib.

2 1 Woe to them that devise iniquity and wo[rk evil] upon their beds! When [the morning] comes, they practice it, because it is in their power. 2 And they covet f[ields, and sei]ze them; and houses, and take them away; [and they oppress] a man and [his house, even a m]an and his inheritance. [3 There]fore thus says [the LORD: Be]h[old,] against [this] family [I] am devising e[vil,] from [which you cannot] remove *their*[83] necks, nor shall you walk haughtily; for it i[s] an evil time. [4 In] that [day] shall *they*[84] ta[ke up a taunt song] against you, [and lam]ent with bitter lamentation; s[a]y, "We are [ut]terly ruined; [he changes the portion of my] people; how he removes it [from me! To the apostat]e he divid[es] our fields." 5 Therefore [you] shall have none that shall ca[st] the line by lot in the as[sembly of the L]ORD.

6 "Do not p[reach," thus th]ey preach. [Th]ey shall not preach of these thi[ngs;] reproaches shall [no]t be turned back. [7 Shall it be said,] "O house of Jacob, 'Is the patience of Spirit of the LORD short? A[re th]ese his doings?' Do not [my words] do good to him that *walked*[85] uprightly?" 8 But latel[y] my people *rise*[86] up as an enemy; [you] strip [the clo]ak from off the garment [from unsuspecting] passersby, [*they*] r[etu]rned[87] from war. 9 The women [of my people] you drive out from their p[leasan]t houses; fr[om] their young children [you take away] my glory forever. 10 Aris[e and] go, for this is no [resting-plac]e; be[cause of unclean]ness that destroys, even with a grievous destruction. 11 *A man does not go*[88] about speaking empty [and base]less li[es,] saying, "I will preach to you of wine and of [stro]ng drink"; he shall be [thi]s people's [prea]cher.

[12 I will] surely assemble all of you, O Ja[cob;] I will surely gat[her the re]mnant of I[srael;] I will put them together as the s[hee]p [of Bozrah, as a flock] in the midst [of] their pasture; they shall be noisy wi[th people.] 13 The breaker [is g]one up before them; [they have broken forth] and passed on to the gate, and have gone out of [it; and] their [king has passed on] before them, [and the LORD at their head.]

3 1 And I s[aid,] Hear now, O head[s of J]acob, and ru[lers of the house of Isra]el: [Is it not for you] to [kno]w justice? [2 You who h]ate good and l[ove evil, who te]a[r their] skin [from themselves,] and their flesh from their [bon]es;

Chapter 2. MurXII: 2:1–13; 4QXII^g: 2:3–4; 8ḤevXII gr: 2:7–8.

83. 4QXII^g. *your* MT LXX.

84. 4QXII^g. *he* MT LXX.

85. MurXII LXX. *walks* 8ḤevXII gr MT.

86. 8ḤevXII gr. *rises* MT LXX.

87. 8ḤevXII gr. *who return* MT. *the conflict [of]* LXX.

88. MurXII LXX. *If a man was going* MT.

Chapter 3. MurXII: 3:1–12; 8ḤevXII gr: 3:5–6; 4QXII^g: 3:12.

3 who also have eaten the fle[sh of my people, and flayed their skin from them, and] have broken their bones, and chopped them in pieces, as for [the] pot, and [as meat in] a cauldron.

[4 Th]en shall they cry to the LORD, but he will not answer them; [indeed he will] hide his face from [th]em at [tha]t time, in accordance with their evil deeds.

5 Thus say[s the] L[OR]D [concerning] the prophet[s] who le[ad] my people [astray;] who when t[hey] have something to eat, [cry *to hi*]*m*,[89] ["Peace";] and against the one who does not [fil]l their mouths, [they prepare a] h[oly] w[ar.] 6 T[heref]ore it shall be night for you, without vision; and it shall be dar[k] for [y]ou, without divining; and the sun shall go down [on] the prophets, and the day shall become dark over them. 7 And the [seers] shall be put to sh[ame, and the di]viners [confounded;] indeed [they] shall all cover their lips, for there is no answer from Go[d. 8 B]ut [as for me,] I am [fil]led with power by the Spirit of the LORD, and with judgment and might, to declare to J[acob his transgression, and] to Israel his sin.

[9 Hear] thi[s no]w, O heads of the house of Jacob and rule[rs] of the house of Israel, who ab[hor justi]ce, and perv[ert al]l that is straight. [10 They build up Zi]on with [bloo]dshed, and Jerus[alem with injustic]e. 11 Her heads jud[ge] for a bribe, [and her priests teach for a f]ee, and [her] prophets d[i]vine [for money; yet they] l[ean] upon the LORD, [saying, "Is not the Lo]RD in [our] midst? [No] evil [shall] c[ome] upon [us."] 12 Therefore for [your sake Zion will be plowed as a field, and Jerusalem] shall become [heaps of ruin]s, and the [Temp]le Mount as the high places of a fo[rest.]

4 1 But in the latter [da]ys [the mountain of the LORD's house shall be established on the top of the mountains,] and it shall be exalted [above the] hills; and [peoples] shall f[low to it. 2 And many nations shall go and say,] "Come and let us go up to [the mountain of the LORD, and to the house of the God of Jacob; and he will teach us of his ways,] and we will walk [in his path]s." [For out of Zion shall go forth the law, and the word of the LORD] from Jerusalem. 3 And he will judge betw[een] many [peoples, and will decide concerning strong nations,] no matter how far away. And [they shall] beat [thei]r sword[s] into plowshares and [t]heir spea[rs into pruning-]hooks; natio[n] shall not *lift up*[90] sword against nation, nor shall they learn war anymore. [4 But] they [shall sit] every man under his vine and under his [f]ig tree; [an]d none shall m[ake them afraid,] fo[r] the mouth of the Lo[RD o]f h[o]sts has spoken.

5 For all the peo[ples] wa[lk each one in the name of its gods,] but we will wa[lk] in the name of the LORD o[u]r God for[ever and ever.]

---

89. 8HevXII gr LXX. Not in MT.

Chapter 4. MurXII: 4:1–13; 4QXII[g]: 4:1–2; 8HevXII gr: 4:3–10.

90. Singular 8H̦evXII gr LXX. Plural MT.

6 In that [day,] declares the LORD, I will assem[ble the lame, and I will gather the outcast, even] the one whom [I] have afflicted; 7 and I will make the lame a r[emna]nt, [and the outcast] a strong nation; and the LORD will reign over them on Mount Zi[on from now and ev]en forever.

[8 And yo]u, O tower of the flock, [the hi]ll of the daughter [of Zion, to you it shall come, even] the [for]mer dominion [shall come,] the kingdom of the daughter [of Jerus]alem.

[9 Now why do you cry out aloud?] Is there no king among you, has your counselor per[ished, that pan]gs [have taken hold of you] as a woma[n in child-birth?] 10 Writhe [and cry out, O da]ughter of Zion, like a woman in child-bir[th; for now shall you go forth out of the city and dwell in the] field, [and you shall go] to Babylon; there y[ou shall be rescued; there will the LORD redeem you from the hand of] your [enem]ies.

[11 And now many nations] are assembled [against you, who say, "Let her be defiled, and let] our [ey]e [gaze upon Zion."] 12 But t[hey do not know the thoughts of the LORD, nor do] they understand his counsel; for he has gathered them as sheaves to the threshing-floor. 13 Arise and thr[esh, O daughter of Zion; for] I will make [your horn] iron, and I will make your hoofs bra[ss; and you shall crush man]y peoples, and [I will devote their gain] to [the LORD,] and their wealth to [the Lord of the whole earth.]

5 [1 Now muster yourselves in troops, O daughter of troops: he has laid a siege again]st [us; they shall strike the judge of Israel on the cheek with] a rod.

2 But you, [O Bethlehe]m [of E]phrathah, too li[t]tle to [b]e among the th[ousands of J]udah, out of you *one shall not come forth*[91] to be rul[e]r in I[srael; and] whose goings forth are from of o[l]d, from ev[erlasting.] 3 Therefore he will gi[ve them up, until the time that she who is to give bir]th has brought forth; then [the rest of] his [brethren] shall return to th[e children of Israel.] 4 And he shall [st]and and shall sh[e]pherd in the s[tr]ength of the L[ORD,] *and*[92] in the majesty of the name of the LORD [his] God; and they shall abide; for now *they*[93] will be[come] great to the ends of the earth. 5 And [this] sh[all be our peace.]

When the Assyrian comes [int]o [ou]r [land,] and when he treads in [our] pala[ces, then] shall we raise against him seven sh[epherds, and] eight leaders of men. [6 And] they [shall shepherd] the land of Assyria with the s[word, and the] land of Nimrod in [its] entrance[s; and he shall deliver us from] the Assyrian, when he comes into [our land and when] he treads within [our] border.

Chapter 5. MurXII: 5:1–2, 6–15 [H 4:14; 5:1, 5–14]; 8ḤevXII gr: 5:2–7 [H 5:1–6]; 4QXII[f]: 5:2–3 [H 5:1–2].

91. 4QXII[f]. *one shall come forth for me* 8ḤevXII gr MT LXX.

92. 8ḤevXII gr LXX. Not in MT.

93. 8ḤevXII gr. *he* MT LXX.

7 And the remnant of Jacob shall be [in the midst of many peoples] as dew [from] the Lor[d,] as s[hower]s upon the grass that [wait for] no [man,] nor wait for [humank]ind. 8 And [the rem]nant [of] Jacob [shall be among the nation]s, in the midst of many peoples, *with*[94] a li[on] among the animals of the for[est, as a young lion among the flocks of sheep; who, i]f he passes through, [tramples d]own and tears in pieces, and there is no one to deliv[er. 9 Your hand will prevail over] your [adversar]ies, [and all your enemies will be cut off.]

[10 Then on] that [day,] declares [the Lord, I will cut off your horses from your midst, and will] destroy your chariots. 11 And I will cut off the cities of [your] l[and,] and w[ill throw down all] your [stronghold]s. 12 And I w[ill cut off sorcer]y from your hand; and [you] shall have [n]o more soothsayers. [13 And I will cut off] your [gra]ven images and your sacred pillar[s from] your midst; and you shall no [longer] w[or]s[hip the wor]k of your hands. 14 And I will uproot [your] Ash[e]r[im] from the midst of you; and I will [destroy your cities.] 15 And I will execute [veng]eance in anger and wrath upon the nations which have not ob[eyed.]

6 1 Hear [now w]ha[t the L]ord says: Arise, plead the case before the mount[ains,] and let [the hills] h[ear your voice.] 2 Hear, O mountains, the Lord's case, [and you enduring foundations of the earth. For] the Lord has [a ca]se against his [peo]ple, and he will contend with Israel.

[3 "O my people, what have I done to you? And ho]w have I wearied you? [Testif]y against me. 4 For I brought you up out of [the land of Egypt, and] redeemed you [from the hous]e of bondage; and I sent before you Mos[es, Aaron,] and Miriam. 5 O my people, remember now what Balak king of M[oa]b counseled, and what Balaam the son of Beor [answered hi]m; [remember from] Shittim to Gilgal, [t]hat you may know the righteous acts of the [L]ord."

[6 How shall I come b]efore the Lord? Shall I bow myself before God on high? Shall I com[e before] him with burnt offer[ings, with cal]ves a y[ear] old? 7 Will the Lord be p[leased with thousands of rams, or with ten thous]ands of [rive]rs of oil? Shall I gi[ve my firstborn for my transgression, the fruit of my body for own sin?] ▲

[11 Shall I justi]fy [wicked scales, and a bag of deceitful weights? 12 For] its [rich men] are full [of violence, and its inhabitants have spoken lies, and their tongue is deceitful in] their [mouth.] 13 Therefore I also [have begun to strike you making you desolate because of your sins. 14 Yo]u shall eat, but not [be satisfied; and your hunger shall be in your midst; and you shall put away, but shall not sa]ve[; and that which you save I will give up to the sw]ord. [15 You shall sow but shall not reap; you shall tread the olives, but shall not anoi]nt [yourself] with oil;

---

94. MurXII. *as* MT LXX.

Chapter 6. MurXII: 6:1–7, 11–16.

[and the vintage, but shall not drink the wine. 16 For the statutes of Omri and all the w]orks of the house of [Ahab are observed, and you walk in their counsels, that I may make you a desolation, and] its [in]habitants [a hissing; and you shall bear the reproach of my people.]

7[1 Woe is] me! For I have become [as at the gathering of summer fruits, as at the gleanings of the vintage. There is no cluster to] eat; [my soul] desires the first-ripe fig. 2 The godly man [has perished] from the [earth, and] there is none [upright among men;] they all [lie in wait] for bloodshed; they hunt [each oth]er with a net. 3 Concerning evil, both hands do it diligently; the prince [and the judg]e a[sk] for a reward; and the great man utters the desire of his soul; thus they weave [it] together. [4 The best of] them is as a brier; the most [up]ri[ght] a thorn hedge; the d[a]y of your watchmen, your [judgm]ent, has come; [now] their confusion [shall come about.] 5 Do not trust in a neighbor; *and*[95] do not [put confid]ence in a [fr]iend; guard your mouth from her that lie[s in] your [boso]m. 6 For the son dishonors [the father, the daug]hter rises up against her mother, the daughter-in-law against her mother-in-law; a man's enemies are the members of his own household. [7 But as for me,] I will l[oo]k to the LORD; I will wa[it for] the God of my salvation; [my] G[od] will hear me.

[8 Rejoi]ce [not] against me, O my enemy; wh[en] I [fall, I shall] arise; [when] I sit [in darknes]s, [the LORD will be a ligh]t to me. 9 I wi[ll bear the indignatio]n of the LORD, [because I have sinned ag]ainst him, until he pleads my case and execu[tes judgment for me; he will br]ing me forth to the light, [and I shall behold] his [right]eousness. 10 Then [my] enemy shall [se]e [it, and shame shall cover her who] says to me, ["Where is the LOR]D your God?" [My ey]e[s shall] look [upon her; now] she shall be trodden down [as the mire of the] streets.

11 A day for building your [walls!] In [that] day [shall] the decree [be far r]emoved. 12 On[96] [that] d[ay] shall they come to you from Assyria [and the cities of Egypt, and from Egypt even to the Euphra]tes, and from sea to sea, and from mountain to mountain. 13 Yet shall [the land] be [desolate because of those who dwell in it, for the fruit of] their deeds.

[14 Shepherd your people with your rod, the flock of your inher]ita[nce] which dwells alone in the forest in the midst [of a fruitful land; let them feed in Bashan and Gilead, as in the days of o]ld. 15 As in the days of your coming forth out of the land [of Egypt I will show] them marvelous things. 16 The nation]s [shall see] and be ashamed of all their might; [they shall lay their hand upon their mouth; their ears] shall be deaf. [17 They shall] lick the dust [like a serpent, like crawling things of the earth; they shall come trembling out of their fortresses;

Chapter 7. MurXII: 7:1–20; 4QXII^g: 7:2–3; 20.

95. MurXII LXX. Not in MT.

96. MurXII. Not in MT LXX.

they] shall come i[n fear of the LORD] our God, and shall be afraid [because of]
you.

18 Who [is a God like to you who forgives iniquity and passes over the transgression of the remnant of] his inheritance? [He do]es not [maint]ain [his anger
forever, because he delights in lovingkindness. 19 He will again have compassion
upon us;] he will tread [our] iniqui[ties] under foot; [and you will cast all their
sins into the depths of the sea. 20 You will give] truth to Jacob, lovingkindness to
Ab[raham, which you have sworn to our fathers from the days of old.]

NAHUM

Nahum's late-seventh-century-BCE oracle against Nineveh is found in three of the ten Minor Prophets manuscripts and is the subject of one of the most important and extensive of the *pesher* texts found in the caves at Qumran (4Q169).[97] In that *pesher,* the prophecy's original setting—the imminent fall of Nineveh, capital of the waning superpower Assyria—is ignored and the prophet's words of judgment are turned against a group called "Seekers of Smooth Things" or "Flattery-Seekers." As is evident from the context, this designation is clearly meant to represent the Pharisees.

In addition to this large-scale *pesher,* Nahum 2:11 undergoes similar treatment in 4Q177, along with a collection of other biblical quotes referring to the vindication of the righteous and the judgment of the company of darkness in the Last Days.

Nahum 1:2, "On his enemies God takes vengeance; against his foes he bears a grudge," is cited in the *Damascus Document* (CD) 9:5 in conjunction with Leviticus 19:18, "Take no vengeance and bear no grudge against your kinfolk," to demonstrate that vengeance taken on a fellow sectarian is not proper. To deal with a fellow in such a way would be to regard kinfolk as the enemy.

1 [1 The oracl]e of Nineveh. The book of the vision of Nahum [the Elkoshite.] [2 A jealous and aven]ging [God is] the LORD; the LORD is avenging [and is ful]l of wrath; the LORD takes vengeance on [his] advers[aries,] and he reserves wrath [for his] enemi[es. 3 The LORD is] slow to [an]ger, and great in power, and will by no means [c]lear the guilty; the LORD [has his way] in the w[hirl]wind [and in the storm, and the clouds are the du]st of his feet. 4 He rebukes the sea, and makes it dry, and dries up all the rivers; [Bashan and Car]mel languish, and

---

97. 4QXII^g, MurXII, 8HevXII gr.

Chapter 1. MurXII: 1:1–15 [H 1:1–14; 2:1]; 4QXII^g: 1:7–9; 8HevXII gr: 1:13–14.

the flower of Leban[o]n withers. 5 *The*[98] mountains quake because of him, and the hil[ls melt]; and the earth is upheaved [before him, the world,] and all that dwell in it.

6 W[ho] can stand before [his] indignation? [And] who [can] abide in the fierceness [of his anger? His wrath] is poured out like fire, [and] the rocks [are br]oken apart [by] him. 7 The [L]ORD is good, [a stronghold in the day of trouble; and] he knows them that take refuge in [him.] 8 But with an overrunning fl[oo]d [he will m]ake a full e[nd of] its place, [and will pursu]e [his] e[nem]ies into darkness. 9 What do you devise against the [Lo]RD? [H]e will make a full end; afflic[tion] shall not rise up the s[econd tim]e. [10 For like] tangled thorns, and drunken as with [their] drink, they are [utterly] consumed as dry s[tubble. 11 There is one gone out from you] that devises ev[il] against the Lo[RD], that counsels wickedness.

12 Thus s[ays the L]OR[D: "Though they be in ful]l [strength and likewise many], even [s]o shall they be cut down [and p]ass away. Though I have aff[licted] you, I will afflict you [no longer. 13 And now will I break his yoke] from off [you,] and I will t[ear apar]t your bonds."

14 And [the LORD] has com[manded concerning you:] "Your [name] shall not co[n]tinue any longer; [o]ut of the house of your gods will I cut off the graven image [and the molten image; I will ma]k[e your grave, for you are] worthless."

[15 Behold,] upon the mountains the fe[et of the one who brings good tidings, who proclaims peace!] Keep your feasts, [O Judah, perform yo]ur [vow]s; for [the wicked one shall] n[o longer pass through you;] he is utte[rly cut] off.

2 [1 The one who dashes in pieces has come up against you; keep the fortress, watch the way,] make your loins strong, fortify [your power mightily. 2 For the LORD restores the majesty of Jacob, as the ma]jesty of Is[rael;] for [the destroyers have destroyed them, and devastated their vine branches.]

[3 The shield of] his mighty men is made red; the [valiant] men [are dressed in scarlet; the chariots flash with steel in the day] of his preparat[ion, and the cypr]ess spears [are brandished. 4 The chariots race wildly through the streets;] they r[ush to and f]ro through the squares; their appearan[ce like torche]s, [th]ey [run like the lightning.] 5 He remembers his nobles; they stumble in their march; *and*[99] they make haste to its wall, and [t]he mantelet is prepared. [6 The gate]s of the rivers are opened, and the pal[a]ce is swept away. 7 And it is decreed: she is ex-

---

98. MurXII LXX. Not in MT.

Chapter 2. MurXII: 2:1–13 [H 2:2–14]; 8HevXII gr: 2:4–9, 12–13 [H 2:5–10, 13–14]; 4QXII*ᵍ*: 2:8–10 [H 2:9–11].

99. 8HevXII gr LXX. Not in MT.

iled, she is carried away; and her slave women mo[an] a[s with the voi]ce of doves, beating upon [their breasts.] 8 But Nineveh has been through *her*[100] days *a po[ol*[101] *of*] water; yet they fl[ee away.] "Stand, sta[nd," they cry; but none lo]oks back. 9 "Plunder the silver, plunder the gold; [fo]r there is no end of t[reasur]e, [wea]lth from eve[ry precious article."]

[10 She is empt]y, and desolate, and waste; and the h[eart] melts, and [the knees] kn[ock together, and all the loins sha]ke, [and al]l their [faces] have become p[ale. 11 Where is the d]en [of the lions, and the feeding-place of the young lions,] where the lion, the l[ion]ess, and [the lion's] cubs have gone, [and none disturbing them?] 12 The lion has to[r]n enough for his whelps, and strangled for his lionesses, and filled his caves with p[rey,] and his *den*[102] with torn flesh.

13 Behold, I am against you, declares the LORD of hosts, and I will burn her chariots in smoke, and the s[wor]d shall devour your young lion[s]; and [I] will cut off your prey from the earth, and the v[oi]ce of your messengers shall no longer be heard.

3 1 W[o]e to the bloody cit[y! Comp]letely full of [l]ies and plu[nde]r; the p[rey] never departs. [2 The noise of the] whip, and the [noi]se of the rattling of wheel, and prancing horses, [and bound]ing chariots, [3 the horseman] mounting, and the f[lashing] sword, and the glittering spear, and a multitude of slain, and a great h[eap of corpses,] and there is no e[n]d of the bodies; they stumble over their bodies;— 4 because of the many prostitutions of the harlot, alluring, a mistress of wit[chcra]fts, who s[ells natio]ns by her prostitutions, and familie[s through] her sorceries. 5 Behold, I a[m agai]nst you, declares the L[ORD of host]s, and I will uncover [your] skirt[s ove]r [your fac]e; and I will show the nations your nakedness, and the kingdo[ms your sh]ame. 6 And [I will throw] filth [on you,] and make you vile, and will make you a [spectacle. 7 Then all that look upon] you [shall] fl[ee from you,] and say, ["Nineve]h is laid waste; who will bemoan [her?" Wh]ere shall I seek c[omforters] for you?

8 Are you better than [N]o-amo[n, that was] situated by the Nile, [that had the waters round about her, *whose*] *wall was a rampart of the sea?*[103] 9 Ethiopia and Egy[pt] were her strength, [and there was no end;] Put and Lubim were your helpers.

---

100. 4QXII[g] LXX. Not in MT.

101. 8HevXII gr. *like a pool* MT LXX.

102. 8HevXII gr LXX. *dens* MT.

Chapter 3. MurXII: 3:1–19; 4QXII[g]: 3:1–3, 17; 8HevXII gr: 3:3, 6–17.

103. MurXII. *[whose] strength is the sea, wate[r her wall]* 8HevXII gr. *whose rampart was the sea, and whose wall was of the sea* MT. *whose dominion is the sea, and whose wall is water* LXX.

10 Yet was she carried away to exi[le; she went into ca]ptivi[ty;] her young children also [were dashed in pi]eces at the head of every street; [and they] cast [lots] for her honorable men, and all h[e]r g[reat me]n were bound in [ch]ains. 11 *You*[104] also will become drunk; you shall be [hidden;] you [also] shall seek [a stronghold from the enemy. 12 Al]l your fortresses [are like fig trees with the] first-r[ipe] figs; [i]f [they] be shaken, [they] fall [into the] mout[h of the eat]er. 13 Behold, [your people] in your midst [are women;] the gates of [your] la[nd are set wi]de op[en] *to*[105] your enemies; fire [has devoured] your gat[e bars.]

14 Draw yourself water for the siege; [strengthen your fortresses; go] into the cla[y, and tread the mortar;] take hold of the brick mold. 15 There [shall the fire devour you;] the swo[rd] shall [cu]t you off; [it shall de]vour you like the locust. Multiply yourself as the locu[st; multiply yourself] as the swarming locust. [16 You] have multi[plied your merchants] *as*[106] the stars of heaven; [the locust ravages, a]nd fl[ees] away. [17 Your guards are as the] swarming locusts, [and your] marshal[s as the] swarms of [grassh]oppers, which en[camp in the hedges on the cold day, but when the su]n arises [they flee away] and [their] pl[ace where they are] is not known.

[18 Your shepherds are asleep, O king of Assyria; your nobles are at rest; your] people [are scat]tered [upon the mountains, and there is none to gather them. 19 There is no relief for] your [hurt; your] wound is seve[re; all that hear the report about you clap their hands over you;] for upon wh[om] has not [your wickedness] pas[sed continually?]

---

104. 8HevXII gr. *You yourself* MT LXX.

105. MurXII. *for* MT.

106. 8HevXII gr. *more than* MT LXX.

HABAKKUK

Habakkuk, the subject of one of the most extensive *pesher* texts *(A Commentary on Habakkuk),* also exists in three of the ten Minor Prophets manuscripts.[107]

A Commentary (or *Pesher) on Habakkuk* exploits the original setting of the prophecy set in the early sixth century BCE and the disturbing message of the coming of the Chaldeans—God's agents of judgment on sinful Judah—to interpret the events of five hundred years later. The Chaldeans become the "Kittim," or Romans, and the unjust of Judah are none other than the foes of the Qumran community, the Pharisees. Oddly, apart from this extensive *pesher,* there are no citations or allusions to Habakkuk among the scrolls.

1 [3 Why do you make me see] iniquity and loo[k upon] trouble? Destruction and violence are before me; [and there is] strife, [and] contention [rises up. 4 Therefore the l]aw [is ignored, and] justice ne[ver prevai]ls; for the wicked [sur]round the ri[ghteous; therefore justice goes forth] perverted.

5 Look [at] the nations, and [obser]ve, and be amazed! W[ond]er! For I am wor[king] a work [in] your [day]s [which you will] n[ot believe though you] were [told.] 6 For behold, I am raising up the Chaldeans, that bitter [and impetuous nation, that m]arc[h] throu[gh] the brea[dth of the earth,] to possess dwelling-places that are not theirs. 7 Th[ey] are terrible and d[read]ful; their judg[m]ent [and their dignity proceed] fr[om th]emselves. 8 Their horses also are swifter than leopards, and are more fierce than wo[lves in the eve]ning; and their horsemen press proudly on, their [hors]emen come from af[ar;] they fly as an eagle that hastens to devour. 9 All of them come for violence; they set their faces forward; and they gather captives as the sand. 10 And th[e]y scoff at kings, and princes are a derision [to them; th]ey laugh at every stronghold; for they heap up rubble, and

---

107. 4QXII[g], MurXII, 8HevXII gr.
Chapter 1. MurXII: 1:3–13, 15; 8HevXII gr: 1:5–11, 14–17.

tak[e it. 11 Then] shall they sweep by as a wind, and [shall] pass over, and be g[uilty, even they wh]ose [mig]ht [is their g]od.

[12 Are y]ou [not] from everlasting, [O LORD] my God, my Holy One? [We shall not] die. O L[ORD, you have ordained him for] j[udgmen]t; [and you, O Rock, have] esta[blished him] for correction. [13 Your] eyes [are too pure to] b[ehold evil, and you cannot look on perverseness. Why do you look on those that deal treacherously, and are si]le[nt when the wicked swallows up the man that is more righteous than he? 14 Have you made men as the fish o]f the se[a, as the creeping things, that hav]e [no] ruler [over them?]

15 He brings up [al]l of the[m with a hook,] and[108] he catches [them in] his [n]et and gath[ers them in] his seine; therefore he re[joices] and is glad. 16 Therefore he sacrifices [to] his ne[t], and burns incense to [hi]s se[ine;] be[cause] by them [his] *bread*[109] is large, [and] his f[o]od plentiful. 17 Shall he theref[ore emp]ty his *sword,*[110] and keep o[n slaying] the nations continually?

2 [1 I] will stand [upon] my [watch,] and se[t myself upon the towe]r, and will keep watch to se[e what he will say t]o me, and what [I] shall answer [concerning my reproof.] 2 And [the LORD] answered me, [and said,] Write the vision, and make it plain [on tablet]s, [that he may run] that reads [it. 3 For the vision is ye]t [for the ap]pointed time, and it hastens [toward the end, and] shall not fail. Though [it] tar[ries, wait for i]t; because it will su[rely] come; [it will not delay.] 4 Beh[old] the proud one, his soul is not right [within him; but the rig]hteous shall liv[e] by his faith. [5 Yea, moreover, wine betrays] a haughty man, so that [he does] not [stay at home. He enlarges his] desir[e] as Sheol, [and he is as dea]th; *he cannot*[111] be satisfied, [but gathers to him]self all nations, and collec[ts to him]self all pe[opl]es.

6 Shall not all these tak[e] up a taunt against him, and a moc[ki]ng riddle against him, an[d sa]y, "Woe to him that increases that which is not his!" *For* [*ho*]*w long?*[112] *A*[*nd loa*]*ds himself down with thick mud!*[113] 7 Shall your creditors not rise up sud[denl]y, and those who cause you to tremble awake? Then you shall be as booty [for] them. 8 Because *you*[114] have plu[n]dered many nations, *and*[115] all the remnant of the peoples [shall] plunder you, [because of men's blood and the violence done to the land, to the city, and to all that dwell in it.]

---

108. 8ḤevXII gr LXX. Not in MT.

109. 8ḤevXII gr. *portion* MT LXX.

110. 8ḤevXII gr. *net* MT LXX.

Chapter 2. 8ḤevXII gr: 2:1–8, 13–20; MurXII: 2:2–3, 5–11, 18–20; 4QXII^g: 2:4(?).

111. 8ḤevXII gr LXX. *and cannot* MT.

112. 8ḤevXII gr omits.

113. 8ḤevXII gr. *And makes himself rich with loans* MT. *And heavily loads his yoke* LXX.

114. 8ḤevXII gr. *you yourself* MT LXX.

115. 8ḤevXII gr. Not in MT LXX.

[9 "Woe to him that gets an evil gain for his house, that he may set his nest on high, that he may be delivered from the hand of] evil!" 10 You have devised [shame to your house by cutting off many peoples, and have sinned against yourself. 11 For the very stone] shall c[ry ou]t of the wall, [and the beam out of the timber shall answer it.]

[12 "Woe to him that builds a town with blood, and establishes a city by iniquity!" 13 Is it not indeed from the LORD of ho]s[ts that the peoples labor fo]r [fire, and the nations weary themselves for] nothing? [14 For the earth] shall be [filled with the knowledge of the glory of] the LORD, as [the waters cover the] sea.

[15 "Woe] t[o you that giv]e [your] neig[hbor drink, to you that] ad[d your venom, and make him drunken also, tha]t [you may] lo[ok on] th[ei]r [nakedn]ess!" [16 You are] filled [with shame rather] than glory. [Dr]ink, you also, and [be as one uncircumcised;] the c[up of] the LORD['s right hand] shall come round to you, and foul [shame shall come upon] y[ou]r glory. 17 For the violence [done to Lebanon] shall [cover] you, and the destruction [of the animals terrified] *you,*[116] because of m[en]'s blood and violence done to the land, to the city, [a]nd to all that dwell in [i]t.

18 What good is the idol when [its maker has carved] it; the image, [even] the *lying [ap]pearance?*[117] For the [m]aker trusts in its form, that he might [m]ake dumb idols. [19 "Wo]e to him that says to the wood, 'Awake!' To the dumb stone, 'A[rise!' "] Shall] this tea[ch? Behold,] it is overlaid with gol[d and silv]er, and there is no breath at all in the midst of it.

20 But the LORD is in [h]is holy temple; let all the earth keep silence before him.

3 1 A prayer of Habakkuk the prophet, set to [Shigio]noth.
2 O LORD, I have heard the report about you and am afraid. O LORD, revive [your] wor[k] in the midst of the years; in the midst of the years m[ake it know]n; in wrath rem[em]ber [me]rcy. 3 God [co]mes from Teman, and the Holy One from Mount Paran. Sel[ah.] His glory [cove]red the heavens, and the earth was full of his praise. 4 And his brightness was as the light; [he had] ra[y]s [coming forth] from [his] hand; [and there was where] his power [was hid]den. 5 Before him went the pestilence, and fiery bolts went forth at [his] feet. [6 He s]tood, and measured the ear[th; he beheld, and made the nations tremble;] and the eternal mountains were shattered; the everlasting hills did bow; [his] goings were as of old. 7 I saw the te[nts] of Cushan i[n] affliction; [the curtain]s of the land of Midian did tremble. 8 Was the LORD displeased with the ri[v]ers? [Was] your anger against the rivers, or your wrath against the sea, that you rode upon your horses,

---

116. 8HevXII gr LXX. *them* MT.

117. 8HevXII gr LXX. *a teacher of falsehood* MT.

Chapter 3. MurXII: 3:1–19; 8HevXII gr: 3:9–15.

upon your chariots of salvation? 9 *You [indeed] awa[ke]ned your bow;*[118] staffs are ready for command. Selah. *He*[119] split the earth with rivers. 10 The mountains saw you, and were afraid; *the clouds poured out water;*[120] the deep uttered its voice and lifted up its hands on high. 11 The sun [and moo]n stood still in their habitation, at the light of your arrows as they went, at the shining of your glittering spear. [12 You] marched though the land in [indignati]on; [you] th[re]shed the nations [in anger.] 13 You went forth for the salvation of your people, [for the sa]lvation of your anointed; [you wounded] the head of the house [of the wi]cked, laying bare the foundation even to the neck. Selah. [14 You] pierced with his own staves the head of his *warrior;*[121] they storm in to scatter *us;*[122] their rejoicing was as to [de]vour the poor secretly. 15 You tread [the sea with your horses,] the heap of mighty [water]s.

[16 I] heard, [and] my body [tre]mbled, my lips quivered at [the voice; rottenness] ent[ers into] my [bones,] and I trem[ble] in [my] place; [be]cause I must wait quietly for [the day of trouble, for the coming up] of the people [that inva]des us.

[17 For though the] fig tr[ee shall] not [flourish, nor shall fruit be in the] vine[s, the labor of the olive shall] fail, [and the fiel]ds shall yield no food; the flock shall be cut off from [the fold, and there shall be no] herd in the stall[s: 18 Yet I will rejoice in the LORD; I will exu]lt in the G[o]d of my salvation. 19 The LORD, the L[ord,] is my strength; and he makes [my] f[eet like hinds' feet, and will make me to walk upon my high places.]

For the ch[oirmas]ter, on my strin[ged instrument]s.

---

118. 8HevXII gr. *Your bow was made bare* MT. *You indeed bent your bow* LXX.

119. 8HevXII gr LXX. *You* MurXII MT.

120. MurXII. *the tempest of waters passed by* 8HevXII gr MT. *(you) scatter the moving water* LXX.

121. MurXII MT ketib. *unfortified ones* 8HevXII gr. *warriors* MT qere LXX.

122. 8HevXII gr. *me* MT. *it* LXX.

ZEPHANIAH

The four short chapters of Zephaniah are well attested in the scrolls, preserved in five of the ten Minor Prophets manuscripts.[123] There is also an extremely fragmentary *pesher,* which was found in Cave 1 (1Q15).

Zephaniah is also appealed to in two instances among the nonbiblical scrolls. 1QS 5:11 quotes Zephaniah 1:6, "They have not sought him or inquired of his statutes"—a charge originally made against idolatrous Judah near the end of the seventh century BCE—characterizing those who did not enter the covenant of the Qumran community. *Lives of the Patriarchs* (4Q464 3 i 9) cites Zephaniah 3:9, "For I will give purified lips to the people"—a passage that in its original setting referred to the conversion of the Gentile nations in the Last Days. Although the rabbinic commentary *Midrash Tanhuma* §28 (edited by S. Buber) captures this intent—"purified lips" becoming the Hebrew language—it is rather unlikely that the Qumran community would have included the Gentile nations in their interpretation of the passage. All that can be said of the rather difficult fragment is that the scroll also understood "purified lips" to be referring to Hebrew and that speaking Hebrew may have been seen as part of the promise to Abraham.

1 1 The wo[rd of the Lo]RD which came [to Zephaniah the son of Cushi, the son of Gedaliah, the son of Amarah, the son of Hezekiah, in the days of Josia]h the son of A[mon,] king of Judah.

2 I will utterly consume [all things] from off the [f]ace of the g[round, says the LORD. 3 I will consume ma]n an[d animal; I will consume the birds] of the he[avens, and the fish of the sea, and the stumbling blocks with the wicked; and I will cut off man from the fac]e of the earth, s[ay]s the L[ORD. 4 And I will stretch out] my hand upon Ju[dah, and upon al]l [the] inhabitants of Jer[usalem; a]n[d] I

---

123. 4QXII^b, 4QXII^c, 4QXII^g, MurXII, 8HevXII gr.

Chapter 1. 8HevXII gr: 1:1–6, 13–18; 4QXII^b: 1:1–2; MurXII: 1:1, 11–18.

will c[u]t [off the] re[mnant of] Baal from t[his] place, the name of th[e idola-tro]us priests [with the p]riests; 5 t[hos]e[124] who wor[ship] the [host of] he[av]en [u]p[on the housetops;] a[n]d [those who worship, that swear to the LORD and swear] by [Milcom; 6 and those who are turned back from] following [the LORD; and those who have not sought the LORD, nor inquired after him.]▲

[11 Wail, you inhabitants of the] Mortar; for all the people of Canaan are si-lenced; [all they who weigh out silver are cut off. 12 Then at that time] I will search Jerusalem with lamps; [and I will punish the men who are settled on their dregs,] that say in their heart, "The LORD will not do good, neither [will he do evil." 13 And their wealth shall become a spoil, and their houses] a desolation; and they shall build h[ouses,] but [shall] not inhabit; an[d] they shall [plant] vineyard[s, but shall not drink] their wine.

14 The great [day of the LORD] is near; it is near and is c[oming] quickly, [even the voice of the day of the L]ORD; [the mighty man cries there] bitterly. [15 Th]at d[a]y is [a da]y of wrath, [a d]ay [of trouble and di]stress, a day of wasteness [and desolation, a d]ay of darkness and gloominess, [a day of clouds an]d thick dark-ness, 16 a day of the trumpet [and] alarm, against t[h]e f[ortified cit]ies, [and against] the h[i]gh [battlement]s.

17 And I [will bring] d[istress] upon men, that they shall walk like [blind men, because they have] si[n]ne[d against the L]ORD; a[n]d [thei]r [blood shall be poured out] as [dust, a]n[d] their flesh as dung. 18 Neither their silver nor t[heir] gold [shall be able to deliver them i]n [the day of the] LORD's wr[at]h; but the whole land shall be d[evo]ured by the fire of his jealousy: f[or he will make an end, yea, a terrible end,] of all them that dwell in the la[nd.]

2 1 Gather yourselves together, yes, gather together, O nation of no [shame; 2 before the decree takes effect,] the [d]ay passes as the chaff, [before] the fierce anger of the LORD comes upon you, before the day of the L[ORD]'s anger comes [upon you. 3 See]k the LORD, all you [me]ek *of earth,*[125] who have [ke]pt his ordinances; seek righ[teousne]ss, seek meekness; it may be you will be hidden in the day of the L[o]RD's anger. 4 For Gaza shall [be] forsaken, [and A]shkelon a desolation; [th]ey shall drive out Ashd[od at noon]day, and Ekron shall [be rooted up.]

5 Woe to the inhabitants of the seacoast, the nat[ion] of the Cherethites! The word of the LORD is against you, [O Canaan, the land of the Philistines;] I will destroy you, so that there shall be no inhabitant. 6 And the seacoast shall be [pas-ture]s, cave[s for shepherds and folds for] fl[ocks.] 7 And the coast shall be for the remnant of the house of Judah; they shall pasture on it; in the houses of

---

124. 8HevXII gr. *and those* MT LXX.

Chapter 2. MurXII: 2:1–15; 8HevXII gr: 2:9–10; 4QXII[b]: 2:13–15; 4QXII[c]: 2:15.

125. MurXII LXX. *of the earth* MT.

A[shkelon] shall they lie down [in the evening;] for the Lo[r]d their God will visit them, and bring back [their for]t[u]ne.

[8 I have heard the taunt of Moab,] and the revilings of the children of Ammon, with which they have taunted my people, [and boas]ted against [their te]rri[tory.] 9 T[herefore as I live, says] the Lord of [host]s, the Go[d of Isra]el, S[urely] M[oab shall be as Sodom, and the children of Ammon as Gomorrah, a land taken] over by nettles and saltpits, [and a] perpetual desolation; [the remn]an[t of m]y people [shall plunder them,] and [th]e remain[der of my nation] shall inherit them. 10 This they shall have for their p[ride,] because [they have] reproach[ed and magnified themselves] against the people of the Lo[rd of hosts. 11 The Lord will be terrible] to them; [for he will starve all the gods of the earth; and men shall] worshi[p him, everyone from his place, even all the islands of] the nati[on]s.

[12 You Ethiopians] also, [you shall be slain by my sword.]

[13 And he will stretch out his hand against the north and] destroy [A]ssyria, and [will] make [Nineveh a desolation, and dry like the wilderness. 14 And] herds [shall lie dow]n in the midst of her, a[ll] the animals of the nation[s: both the pelican and the hedgehog] shall lo[dge] in its capitals; [their voice shall sing] in the windows; desolation shall be in the thresholds: fo[r] he has laid bare the cedarwork. 15 Is th[is the] exu[ltan]t [city that lived securely,] that said in her heart, "I am, and there is n[on]e besides me?" [How she has become] a desolation, a res[ting pla]ce [for animals!] Everyone that passes by her shall hiss, and wave his hand.

3 [1 Woe to] her [who is rebelli]ous and polluted! The oppressing city! [2 She] did not ob[ey] any voice; she did n[ot receive] correction; she did not trust in the Lord; she did not draw near to her God.

3 Her princes in [her] m[idst] are roaring [lio]ns; [her judges are] evening wolves; they leave nothing until the morning. 4 Her prophet[s] are reckless, trea[cherous] p[erso]ns; [her] priests [have profaned the sanctuary;] they have done violence to the law. 5 The Lo[r]d in [her midst] is righteous; he will [no]t do [iniquity; every morning he b]rings his [justic]e to light, he does not fail; [but the] unjust [knows no shame.]

[6 I have cut off nations; their battlements are desolate; I have made their streets waste, so that no]n[e passes by; their cities are destr]o[yed, so that ther]e i[s no] ma[n, so that there is no inhabi]tant. [7 I] said, ["Surely you will fear me; rec]eive correction; [so h]er *spring*[126] [shall not be cut off, according to] al[l] t[hat I

Chapter 3. MurXII: 3:1–6, 8–20; 4QXII^c: 3:1–2; 4QXII^g: 3:3–5; 8ḤevXII gr: 3:6–7; 4QXII^b: 3:19–20.

126. 8ḤevXII gr. *dwelling* MT. *eyes* LXX.

have appointed concerning he]r"; but [they] r[ose early and corrupted] all [their] do[ings.]

[8 Therefore wait for me, says the LORD, until the day that I rise up] to the prey; for my determination is to gather the nations, [that I may assemble the kingdoms, to pour upon th]em my indignation, even all my fierce anger; for [all the earth shall be devoured] with the fire of my zeal.

[9 For then will I change the speech] of[127] the peoples to a pure speech, that they may all call [upon the name of the LORD, to serve him with] one [con]sent. 10 From beyond the rivers of Ethiopia my suppliants, even my scattered one, shall bring [my offering.]

[11 In that day] you shall not be put to shame fo[r a]ll your doings by which you have transgressed against me; for then [I will remove from the midst of you] your [proudl]y [exulting ones,] and you shall no longer be haughty in my holy mountain. [12 But I will leave in your midst an afflic]ted and poor [people] and they shall take refuge in the name of the LORD. [13 The remn]ant of [I]srael [shall] no[t do iniquity, nor speak li]es; neither shall a deceitful tongue be found in their mouth; [for] they [shall feed and lie d]own, and none shall make them afraid.

14 Sing, O daughter of Zion; shout, O Israel; be glad and rejoice with all the heart, O daughter of [Jerusa]lem. [15 The L]ORD [has taken away] your judgments; he has cast out your *enemies;*[128] the King of Israel, even the LORD, is in your midst; [you shall not fea]r evil any longer. 16 In [tha]t [day] it shall be said to Jerusalem, Fear not; [O Zion,] do [no]t let your hands be slack. 17 The LORD your God is [in] your midst, a mighty one who will save; he will rejoice over you with joy; he will rest in [his love; he will exult over] you with singing. [18 I] will gather them that sorrow for the solemn assembly, who [were] of you; to whom the burden upon her was a reproach. 19 Behold, at t[ha]t time I will deal with all them that afflict you; and [I] will save that which is lame, and gather that which was driven away; and I will make them a praise and a name, whose shame has been in all the earth. 20 At that time I will bring you in, and at that time I will gather you; for I will make [y]ou a name and a praise among all the peoples of the earth, when I bring back your captivity before your eyes, says the LORD.

---

127. MurXII. *(belonging) to* MT LXX.

128. MurXII LXX. *enemy* MT.

HAGGAI

The diminutive but powerful book of the postexilic prophet Haggai is preserved in only three of the ten Minor Prophets manuscripts.[129] The pointed
challenge to rebuild the Temple destroyed by the Babylonians is not cited in any
of the nonbiblical writings, nor is the name Haggai mentioned in the scrolls.

1 1 In the [secon]d ye[ar] of Darius the kin[g, in] the [si]xth month, on the
first d[a]y [of the mo]nth, c[ame] the word of the [L]o[RD] by the prophet
Hag[gai to] Zerubbabel [the son of Shea]ltiel, gove[rnor of J]udah, [and] to
[Joshua] the son of Jehoza[dak, the] high priest, saying, [2 Thus] says the LORD of
hosts, s[ay]ing, "This [people] s[ays,] 'The time has [not] c[ome to rebuild the
house of the LORD.' " 3 Then c]ame [the word of] the LORD by the prophet Haggai, s[ay]ing, [4 "Is it a time for you yourselves to dwell in your] paneled [houses]
while this house lies waste?" 5 Now therefore thus sa[ys] the LORD of hos[ts:
"Con]sider your ways. 6 You have sown much, [and b]r[ing in] little; [you] e[at,
but you have not enough; you] drink, [but you are no]t fille[d with d]rink; you
clothe yourselves, but no one is warm; [and] he that earns wages [earns wages to
put it into] a bag with h[ol]es."

7 Thus [s]ays the LORD of host[s:] "Consi[der your ways. 8 Go up to the
mountain,] and bring wood, and build the house; and I will [take pleasure] in it,
and I will [be glorified," says the LORD. 9 "You looked] for much, and lo, it came
to lit[tle; and when] you [brou]ght [it home, I blew it away. Why? dec]lares the
LORD of hosts, be[cause of] my [hous]e which [lies waste while each o]ne [runs]
to his own h[ous]e. 10 Therefore for your sake [the heavens] withhold [the dew,
and the earth withholds] its [frui]t. 11 And I [cal]led for a drought [upon the land,
and upon the mountains, and upon the grain, and upon the new wine, and up]on
[the oil, and upon that which the ground brings forth, and upon men, and upon
cattle, and upon all the labor of the hands."]

---

129. 4QXII^b, 4QXII^e, MurXII.
Chapter 1. MurXII: 1:1–15; 4QXII^b: 1:1–2.

12 Then Z[erubbabel] the son of Shea[ltiel, and Joshua the son of Jehozadak,] the high [pr]iest, [with] all the r[emnant of the people,] obey[ed the voice of the Lord] their God, [and] the words of [the prophet] Hag[gai, as the Lo]rd their [Go]d [had sen]t him; and [the people] did fear [before the Lor]d. 13 Then [s]poke Hag[gai, the messenger of the Lord, to the people with the Lor]d's [messag]e, say[ing], "I am [with you, decla]res the Lord." [14 And] the Lord stirred up the spirit of Zerubbab[el the son of Shealti]el, governor [of Judah, and] the spirit of Joshua the son of Jeh[ozadak, the high priest,] and [the spirit of al]l the remnant of the people; [and they came and did work on the hou]se of the Lo[rd] of ho[st]s, their [God, 15 in the] four and [twentie]th [day of the month, in the sixth month, in the] second year of D[ari]us the [ki]ng.

2 1 In [the seventh month,] on the tw[ent]y-first day of the month, the w[ord] of the Lord c[ame] *to*[130] Haggai the prophet, saying, 2 "Speak now to Zerubbabel the son of S[hea]l[tie]l, gove[rnor] of Judah, [and to Joshua the son of] Jehozadak, the high priest, and to the remnant of the people, s[ay]ing, [3 'Who] is left among you that saw t[his] house [in] its former [glor]y? And how do you [see] it [n]o[w? Is it not] in your e[y]es as n[othi]ng? [4 Yet] now [be strong,] O Zerubbab[el,' says the Lord;] 'and be strong, O [Jo]shua, son [of Jehozadak, the high priest; and] be strong, [al]l [you] people [of the land,' says the Lord, 'and work:] for I a[m] with you,' [says the Lor]d of hosts, [5 'according to the word that I covenanted with you when] you came out [of Egypt, and my Spirit is abiding among you; do not fea]r.'"

[6 For thus says the Lord of hosts, "Once more, in a litt]le while, [and I will shake the heavens, and the earth, and the sea, and the dry land; 7 and I will shake all nation]s; [and the treasure of all nations shall come; and I will fill this hous]e [with glory," says the Lord of hosts. 8 "The silver is] mine, [and the gold is mine," says the Lord of hosts. 9 "The latter glory of this house shall be greater than the former," says the Lord of hosts; "and in this place will I give peace," says the Lord of hosts.]

[10 In the twenty-fourth day of the] ninth [month,] in [the second year of Darius, the word of the Lor]d [came] to Haggai the [prophet, saying, 11 Thus says the Lord of hosts, "Ask now the priests concerning the law, saying, 12 'If one carries holy meat in the fold of his garment, and with the fold touches bread,] or [stew, or wine, or oil, or any food, shall it become holy?'" And the priests answered] and sai[d,] "N[o." 13 Then said Haggai, "If one that is unclean by contact with a dead body touches] any of these, shall it be u[nclean?" And the priests answered and said, "It shall be unclean."] 14 Then Hagg[ai] answered and s[aid, "So is this people, and so is this nation before me,]" declares the Lord; "and

---

Chapter 2. MurXII: 2:1–8, 10, 12–23; 4QXII^b: 2:2–4; 4QXII^e: 2:18–19, 20–21.

130. MurXII. *by* MT LXX.

s[o is every work of their hands; and that which they offer] there is unclean. [15 And now, I pray you, consider from] this [day] on, b[efore a stone was laid upon a stone] in the temple of the Lord, [16 from the time when one came to a heap of] twenty [measures,] and there were [ten; when one came to the wine vat to draw out] fifty measures, [there were but twenty. 17 I struck you] with b[lig]ht and mil[dew and hail in all the work of your hands; yet yo]u [did not turn] t[o me," says the Lord. 18 "Consider, I pray you, from] this day [on, from the twenty-fourth day of the ninth month, since the day that the foundation of the Lord's temple was laid, consider it. 19 Is the seed yet in the b]arn? [Do the vine, the fig tree, the pomegranate, and the olive tree still] yield [nothing?] From th[is day will I bless you."]

20 And the word of the Lor[d came the] s[econd time to Haggai] on the twe[nty-]fourth day of the month, sa[y]ing, [21 "Speak to Zerubbabel,] governor of Judah, saying, 'I [will shake the heavens] and the earth; 22 and [I] will ov[erthrow the throne of kingdoms; and I will destroy the stre]ngth of the k[ing]do[m]s [of the nations; and I will overthrow the chariots, and those that ride in them;] and [the] ho[rses and their riders] shall come down, [every one by the sword of his brother. 23 In] th[at day,' says the Lord of hosts, 'I will take you, O Zerubbabel, my servant, the son of Shealtiel,'] decl[ares the Lord,] 'and [will make you as a signet; for I have chosen you,'] declares the Lord of hos[ts."]

ZECHARIAH

The postexilic prophet Zechariah is attested in five of the ten Minor Prophets scrolls[131] and, though not the subject of any preserved commentaries, was cited frequently among the nonbiblical manuscripts from Qumran.

An Aramaic Text on the Persian Period (4Q562 2 1) refers to Zechariah 2:8, "One who touches you is as one who touches the apple of his eye," evidently in reference to the time of return from Babylon and God's promise to judge those who would plunder Israel.

In true *pesher* fashion, the community saw a reference to their own sufferings in the "seven eyes" of Zechariah 3:9. This passage was interpreted to be the "seven-fold" refining of Psalm 12:6 (4Q177). Likewise, *A Commentary on Consoling Passages in Scripture* (4Q176 15 3–4) quotes Zechariah 13:9, "I will bring one-third in the fire, and refine them . . . ," in a context that tempers the suffering prophesied by Zechariah with words of comfort.

The messianic hope that characterized the Qumran community was likely the setting of the "two anointed sons" of Zechariah 4:14, perhaps cited in reference to the blessing on Judah (Gen 49:8–12) in one of the *Commentaries on Genesis* (4Q254 4 2). Qumran doctrine found an acknowledgment of the priestly (anointed of Aaron) and royal (anointed of Israel) messiahs in such passages. This very hope forms the setting of the reference to Zechariah 13:7—"If you strike down the shepherd, the flock will scatter"—in the *Damascus Document* (CD) 19:7–9. The interpretation appears to refer to the martyrdom of the community's leader in the Last Days. The "poor of the flock" (a reference to Zech 11:7) escape the subsequent punishment when the unrighteous are delivered up for judgment at the coming of the messiahs of Aaron and Israel.

---

131. 4QXIIᵃ, 4QXIIᶜ, 4QXIIᵍ, MurXII, 8ḤevXII gr.

1 1 In the eighth month, in the [second] year of [Darius,] the word of the LORD [came] to Zechariah the so[n of Berechiah, the so]n of Iddo, [the prophet,] saying: 2 The LORD was [very] angry [wi]th [your fathers. 3 Therefore say t]o them, Thus says the Lo[RD of h]osts: [Return to me, dec]lares the LORD of host[s, and] I will [return] to you, says the L[ORD of h]osts. 4 Do not b[e] li[ke] your [fa-ther]s, to whom the former [prophe]ts cried, saying, ["Thus says] the LORD of hosts, Re[turn now from your evil ways, and from your] evil [doings";] but they did not hear, nor liste[n to me, says the LORD. 5 Your fathers, where are they?] And the prophets, do they live forever? [6 But my words and my statutes, which I commanded my servants] the prophets, did [they not] ove[rtake your fathers? And they turned and said, "Like as the LORD of hos]t[s thought] *to* [*do*],[132] according to [our] ways, [and according to our doings, so has he dealt with us."] ▲

[9 Then I said, "O my lord, what are these?" And] the ange[l who talked with me said to me, "I will show you what these are." 10 And the man that stood among the myrtle trees answered] and sai[d, "These are those whom the LORD has sent to patrol the earth." 11 And they answered the angel of the LORD that stood among the myrtle trees, and said, "We have patrolled the earth, and behold, all the earth is at rest." 12 Then the angel of the LORD answered and said, "O LORD of hosts, how long will you not have mercy on Jerusalem and on the] c[ities of Judah, against which you have been indignant these sev]e[nty years?" 13 And the LORD answered] the [angel that talked with me with] goo[d words, even com-fortable wor]ds. [14 So the angel that talked with me said] to [me, "Cry o]ut, s[aying, Thus says the LORD of] hosts: [I am jealous for Jerusalem and for] Zi[on with a great jealousy."] ▲

[19 And I said unto the angel that talked with me, "What ar]e thes[e?" And he answered me, "These are the horns] which have scat[tered Judah, Israel, and] Jeru[salem." 20 And the LORD showed me fou]r [craftsmen. 21 Then said I, "What are they coming t]o [do?" And he spoke, saying, "These are the horn]s [which scattered Judah so that no man lifted up his head; but these have come to terrify them, to cast down the horns of the nations, which lifted up their horn against the land of Judah to scatter it."]

2 [3 And behold, the angel] that ta[lked with me went forth, and] ano[ther angel went out to meet him, 4 and said to him, "Run, speak] to [that young man, saying, Jerusalem shall] be in[habited without wall]s, [because of the mul-titu]de [of men and cattle in it. 5 For I, says the LORD, will be a wall of fire

---

Chapter 1. MurXII: 1:1–4; 8ḤevXII gr: 1:1–4, 12–14, 19–21 [H 2:2–4]; 4QXIIᵉ: 1:4–6, 9, 13–14.

132. 4QXIIᵉ LXX. *to do to us* MT.

Chapter 2. 8ḤevXII gr: 2:3–5, 7–8, 12–13 [H 2:7–9, 11–12, 16–17]; 4QXIIᵉ: 2:6–10 [H 2:10–14].

r]ou[nd] about [her, and I will be the glory in her midst."]

[6 Ho there, flee from the land of the north, says the LORD; for I have spread you abroad as the four] winds of the heavens, [says the LORD. 7 Ho] Zion, [escape, you that d]well [with the] d[au]ghter of Babylon. [8 For thu]s say[s the Lo]RD of hosts: After [gl]ory has he s[e]nt [me to the nations which] plundered you; [for he that touches you] touches the apple of his eye. [9 For behold, I will shake my hand ove]r them, and they shall be [a spoil to those that served them;] and you shall know th[at the LORD of hosts has sent me. 10 Sing] and rejoice, [O daughter of Zion; for lo, I come, and I will dwell in your midst, says the LORD. 11 And many nations shall join themselves to the LORD in that day, and shall be my people; and I will dwell in the midst of you, and you shall know that the LORD of hosts has sent me to you. 12 And the LORD shall inherit Judah as his portion in the holy land, and] shall [yet choo]se [Jerusalem.]

[13 Be silent, all] flesh, b[efore the LORD; for] he is [aroused from his holy habitation.]

3 1 Then [he show]ed [me Joshua the high priest standing before the angel of the LORD, and] S[atan standing at] hi[s right hand to be his adversary. 2 A]nd the Lo[RD] said [to Satan, "The LORD r]ebu[ke you, O Satan; yea, the LORD that has chosen Jerusalem rebuke you;] is not [this a brand plucked out of the fire?" 3 Now Joshua was clothed with filthy garments, and was standing before the a]ng[el. 4 And he answered a]nd spoke t[o] those that stoo[d before hi]m, saying, "T[ake the filthy garments from off] him." An[d to him he said, "Behold,] I have [caused your iniquity to] pass from you, [and I will clothe] you with ric[h apparel." 5 And I said, "Let them set] a c[lea]n miter upon his head." So [they] set a [clean] mi[ter] upon his h[ead], a[nd clothed him] with garments; [and the a]ngel of the Lo[RD was standing by.]

6 And [the a]ngel of the L[ORD] protest[ed to Joshua, saying,] 7 "Thus says the LORD of h[osts: If] you will walk in my ways, [and if] you will keep my [char]ge, then you also [shall judge] my house, and shall also k[e]ep [my] cou[rts,] and I [will give] you [a place of] a[c]c[ess among these that stand by.] 8 Hear [now, O Joshua the high priest, you and your fellows that sit before you; for they are men that are] a sign; [for behold, I will bring forth my servant the Branch. 9 For behold, the stone that I have set before] Joshua; [upon one] stone [are seven eyes; behold, I will engr]ave [an engraving, says the LORD of hosts,] and I will *draw out*[133] *all*[134] [the iniquity of that land in o]ne [day.] 10 In t[hat] day, [says the LORD of] host[s,] you shall invite [every man his neighbor under the vine and] under the fig tree."

Chapter 3. 8HevXII gr: 3:1–2, 4–7; 4QXII^c: 3:2–10.

133. 4QXII^c. *remove* MT LXX.

134. 4QXII^c LXX. Not in MT.

4 1 And [the angel that talked with me] came again, [and awakened me, as] a man that [is awakened out of his sleep. 2 And] he said to me, "W[hat do you see?" And I said, "I have seen, and behol]d, a candlestick [all of gold, with its bo]wl upon the top [of it, and its seven lamps on it; there are seven pipes to each of the lamps, which are on] its top; [3 and two olive trees by it, one upon the right side of the bowl, and the other at its left side." 4 And I answered] and spoke [to the angel that talked with me, saying, "What are these, my lord?"] ▲

5 [8 And he said, "This is Wickedness": and he threw her down into the midst of the ephah; and he cast the weight of lead upon] its opening. [9 Then I lifted] up my eyes [and loo]ked, and behold, [there came forth two women, and the wind was in their wings; now they had w]ings like the wings of a s[tork; and they lifted up the ephah between earth and heaven. 10 Then] I said to the an[gel that talked with me, "Where are these bearing the ephah?" 11 And he said t]o me, "To build her [a house in the land of Shinar: and when it is prepared, she shall be set there in] her [own plac]e."

6 [1 And again I lifted up my eyes and looked, and behold, four chariots came out from between two mountains; and the mountains were mountains of bra]ss.[135] 2 With [the first] ch[ariot were red horses; and with the second chariot black horses;] 3 and with [the third] chari[ot white horses; and with the fourth chariot] strong [dappled horses. 4 Then I answered and said to the angel that talked with me, "What are these, my lord?"] 5 And the angel answered and sai[d to me, "These are the four winds of heaven, which go forth from standing before the] Lord of all the ear[th."] ▲

8 [2 Thus s]ays the Lo[RD of hosts: I am jealous for Zion with great jealousy, and I am jealous for her with great wrath.] 3 Thus sa[ys the LORD: I will re-turn to Zion and will dwell in the midst of Jerusalem: and Jerusalem shall be called the City of Truth; and the mountain of the LORD of hosts, the] Holy [Mountain. 4 Thus says the LORD of hosts: Old men and old women will dwell again in the streets of Jerusalem, every man with his] staff [in his hand because of his great age. 5 And the streets of the city shall be full of boys and girls playing in its streets. 6 Thus says the LORD of hosts: If it seems impossible in the eyes of the remnant of this people in tho]se [days,] should [it] also [be impossible] i[n my eyes? says the LORD of hosts. 7 Thus says the LORD of hosts: Behold, I will save] my people fr[om the east country, and from the west country;] ▲

[19 Thus says the LORD of hosts: The fast of the fourth month, and the fast of

---

Chapter 4. 4QXII^e: 4:1–4.

Chapter 5. 4QXII^e: 5:8–11.

Chapter 6. 4QXII^e: 6:1–5.

135. 4QXII^e. *bronze* MT.

Chapter 8. 4QXII^e: 8:2–4, 6–7; 8HevXII gr: 8:19–21, 23.

the fifth, and the fast of the seventh, and the f]as[t of the tenth, shall be to the h]ouse o[f Judah joy and gladness,] and [cheerful feasts; therefore] l[ove] t[ruth and] peace. [20 Thus says the LORD]D of hos[ts: Then] peoples shall [co]me, and [the inhabitants of] ma[ny] cities; [21 and] the inha[bitants of one city] shall [go t]o another, [saying, "Let] us [go] sp[eedily to entreat the favor of the LORD, and to seek the LORD of hosts: I will go also."] ▲

[23 Thus says the LORD of hosts: In] tho[se day]s te[n men of all] the [languages of the nati]ons shall [take hold of a Jew, grasping the skirt, saying,] "We will [g]o with yo[u, for] we have [h]eard that God is with [you."]

9 1 The oracle of the word of the LORD is against [the land of Hadrach,] and Damascus shall be [its] resting-pla[ce]. For the ey[e] of [m]an and of all the t[ribes of] Israel is toward the LORD; 2 and Hamath, also, [which borders i]t; Tyre and Sid[on, because] they are very wise. [3 And] Tyre [bui]lt [herself] a strong[hold,] and heaped up si[lver as] the dust, and fine gold [as the mire] of the streets. 4 Behold, the *Lo[RD]*[136] will [dispose]ss her, and [he will] h[url her] wealt[h into] the sea; and she [shall be] de[voured] with fire.

5 A[n]d[137] [Ashkelon shall] s[ee it, and fear; Gaza also, and shall writhe in an-guish; and Ekron, for her expectation shall be put to shame; and the king shall perish from Gaza, and Ashkelon shall not be inhabited.] ▲

10 [11 And he will pass through the sea of affliction, and will strike the waves in the sea, and all the depths of the Nile shall dry up; and the pride of] Ass[y]ria [shall be brought down, and the] s[cepter of Egypt shall depart. 12 And I will strengthen them in the LORD; and they shall *prai*]se[138] in his name, says the LORD.

11 [1 Open your doors, O Lebanon, that the fire may devour] your [ce]dars. 2 Wail, [O cypress, for the cedar has fallen, because the glorious trees have been destroyed: wail, O you oa]k[s of] Bash[an, for the strong forest has come down.] ▲

12 [1 The oracle of the word of the LORD concerning Israel. Thus says the LORD,] who stretches [out the heavens, and lays the foundation of the earth, and forms the spirit of man within him: 2 Behold, I will] make [Jerusalem a cup of reeling to all the peoples round about, and upon] Judah [also shall it be in the siege against Jerusalem. 3 Then on that day I will make Jerusalem a heavy

---

Chapter 9. 8HevXII gr: 9:1–5.

   136. 8HevXII gr. *Lord* MT.

   137. 8HevXII gr. Not in MT LXX.

Chapter 10. 4QXII^g: 10:11–12.

   138. 4QXII^g LXX. *walk up and down* MT.

Chapter 11. 4QXII^g: 11:1–2.

Chapter 12. 4QXII^g: 12:1–3; 4QXII^c: 12:7–12.

stone for all the peoples; all that burden themselves with it shall be severely injured; and all the nations of the earth shall be gathered together against it.] ▲

[7 The LORD also shall save the tents of Judah first, that the glory of the house
of David and the glory of the inhabitan]t of Jerusalem [be not magnified] above
Judah. [8 In that day shall the LORD defend the inhabitant of] Jerusalem: and he
[that is feeble among them at that day] shall be [as David; and the house of David
shall be as God, as the angel of the LORD before them. 9 And] then on that day [I
will seek to destroy all the nations that come against Jerusalem.]

[10 And I will pour upon] the house of David, [and upon the inhabitant of
Jerusalem, the spirit of grace and of supplication; and they shall look to me
whom] they [have pier]ced; and they shall mourn [for him, as one mourns for his
only son, and shall be in bitterness for him, as one that is in bitterness for his firstborn. 11 In that day shall there be a great mourning in Jerusalem, as the mourning of Hadadrimmon] in the valley of Megiddon. [12 And the land shall mourn,
every family apart; the family of the hou]se of David by itself, [and their wives by
themselves; the family of the house of Nathan by itself, and their wives by themselves;] ▲

■ *The manuscript known as 4QXII^a begins here with Zechariah 14:18. It is significant for three reasons. First, it is the oldest of all the Minor Prophets manuscripts, dating from the middle of the second century BCE. Second, it is one of the few Hebrew
biblical manuscripts from Qumran written with cursive script rather than the more for-
mal "square" script. Third, and perhaps most important, the fact that the fragments of
the manuscript include Jonah along with Zechariah and Malachi suggests that this
book was placed in the final third rather than in the first half of the collection. The
shape and size of the fragments make it likely that it was the last book of the Twelve,
following Malachi. This order is not followed in any other manuscript of the Minor
Prophets.*

14 [18 And if the family of Egypt does not go up and ente]r, then o[n them
shall] not [come the plague with which the LORD will strike the nations]
that do not g[o up to keep the feast of tabernacles.] ▲

Chapter 14. 4QXII^a: 14:18.

MALACHI

O nly two of the ten manuscripts of the Minor Prophets contain the text of Malachi.[139] This deterioration of the ends (and beginnings) of scrolls is a pattern seen frequently in the remains of the Qumran library. Although no *pesher* texts survive, a number of quotations reflect the manner in which the book was used by the Qumran community.

The exhortation of Malachi 1 to cease the presentation of worthless offerings to God is reaffirmed to the community in the *Damascus Document* (CD) 6:5. Better to "lock the door" than to "light up my altar in vain" (Mal 1:10). In an ironic twist, it was the Temple—and not the offering—that had become the central problem. The altar had been defiled because the officiating priests had refused to enter into the covenant of the Qumran community.

Malachi 3:16 and 18 were cited in the *Damascus Document* 20:19–22 in order to press the point that it was those who kept God's covenant—the Qumran community—who were the righteous ones recorded in God's book of remembrance.

A small fragment of *Portions of Sectarian Law* (4Q265 4 1–2) quotes Malachi 2:10—"Why are we faithless to one another, profaning the covenant of our ancestors"—evidently as part of an argument that denied young boys and females entrance to the Passover feast. Unfortunately, the fragmentary condition of the text does not preserve the logic behind this ruling, which is nowhere present in the biblical record.

2 [10 Have we not all one father?] Has not [one God created us? Why do we deal treacherously each against] his [brother,] profaning the covenant [of our fathers? 11 Judah has dealt treacherously, and an abomination is committed in

---

Chapter 2. 4QXII[a]: 2:10–17.

I]srael and in Jerusalem; [for Judah has profaned the holiness of the LORD which he loves, and has married] the *house*[140] of a foreign god. [12 The LORD will cut off the man that do]es this—*one who witnesses or answers*[141]—from the tent[s of] Jacob, [and the one who offers an offering to the Lo]RD of hosts.

13 And this again [yo]u do: you cover [the alt]ar of the LORD [with tears,] *and*[142] with weeping, and with sighing *because of troubles, does he still regard* [*the offering and accept*[143] it with favor from] your [han]d? 14 Yet you say, "Why?" Because [the LORD has been witness between you and the wi]fe of your *youth,*[144] though she is your companion, [and the wife of your covenant. 15 But not one has done so who has] a remnant [of the Spirit. And what did] this one seek? A [godly] seed. [Therefore take heed] to your spirit, and [let none deal tr]eacherously against the wife of [his youth.] 16 *For if you hate and divorce,*[145] [says the LORD,] the God of Israel, *they cover my* [*garmen*]*t*[146] with violence, says the LORD of hosts: therefore take heed to your spirit, [that] you do [no]t deal treacherously.

17 *And*[147] you have wearied [Go]*d*[148] with your words. Yet you say, "How have we wearied him?" [In that] you [say,] *"All those who do*[149] evil is good in the si[ght of the LORD, and he] delights [in them"];] or "Where is the Go[d of] justice?"

3 1 *Therefore,*[150] b[ehold, I] send [my] mes[senger, and he shall prepare] the way before me: and *they*[151] will suddenly come to [his] te[mple, the Lor]d, whom you seek and the messenger of the co[venant, whom y]ou desire; behold, he *himself*[152] comes, says the LORD of ho[sts. 2 But] who can *endure them; they come?*[153] And who shall stand [when] he appears? For he is like a refiner's fire, and like

---

140. 4QXII^a. *daughter* MT LXX.

141. 4QXII^a. *one who wakes or answers* MT. *until he be even cast down* LXX.

142. 4QXII^a LXX. Not in MT.

143. 4QXII^a. *because he no longer regards the offering and accepts* MT. *because of troubles; is it worthy to regard the offering and accept* LXX.

144. 4QXII^a. *youth, against whom you have dealt treacherously* MT LXX.

145. 4QXII^a LXX. *For I hate divorce* MT.

146. 4QXII^a. *and the one who covers his garment* MT. *and it (violence) shall cover your thoughts* LXX.

147. 4QXII^a. Not in MT LXX.

148. 4QXII^a LXX. *the LORD* MT.

149. 4QXII^a. *Everyone who does* MT LXX.

Chapter 3. 4QXII^a: 3:1–18; 4QXII^c: 3:6–7.

150. 4QXII^a. Not in MT.

151. 4QXII^a. *he* MT LXX.

152. 4QXII^a. Not in MT LXX.

153. 4QXII^a. *abide the day of his coming* MT LXX.

fuller's soap; 3 and he will sit as a refiner and p[urif]ier of silver, and he will purify the sons of Levi, and refine them as gold and silver; and [they shall] offer to the LORD offerings in righteousness. 4 Then shall the offeri[ng of] Judah and Jerusalem be pleasant to the LORD, as in the days of old, and as in fo[rm]er years.

[5 And I will come near to you for judgment; and I will be a swift witness against the sorcerers, and against the adulterers, and against the false swearers, and against those that oppress the hireling in his wages, the] wi[dow, and the orphan, and those who turn aside the sojourner from his right, and do not fear me, says the L]ORD Go[d.][154]

[6 For I, the LORD, change not; therefore you, O sons of] Jacob, [are] n[ot consu]med. [7 From the days of your fathers you have turned aside from my ordinances, and] you have [no]t kept them. Return to me, [and I will return to you, says the LORD of hosts.] But you[155] say, "Ho[w shall we return?"]

[8 Will a man rob God? Yet you] rob m[e. But you say, "How have we robbed you?" In tithes and offerings.] 9 *You are looking on appearances;*[156] [for you rob me, even this whole nation.] 10 Bring *every tithe*[157] into the [store]hou[se, that there may be food] in my *houses,*[158] and prove me now in this, says [the LORD of hosts, if] I will [not] open for you the windows of he[aven, and pour out] *the*[159] blessing [for you,] until it overflows. 11 And [I] will r[ebuke the devourer for your sakes, and he shall not destroy] the fruits of your ground; neither [shall your vine cast its fruit before its time in the field,] says the LORD of hosts. 12 And [all nations] shall call y[ou] happy; [for] you shall be a delightful la[nd, says the LORD of hosts.]

13 Your words [have been arrogant] against me, sa[ys the LORD. Yet you say, "Wha]t have we spoken against you?" [14 You have] said, ["It is vain to serve God;] and what profit is it that we have kept [his] charg[e and that we have walked mournfully before the LORD of hos]ts? 15 And now [we call the proud happy; indeed, those who work wickedness are built up;] *and*[160] indeed, they tempt [God, and escape."]

[16 Then those who feared the LORD spoke one] to[161] another; and the LORD listened, and [heard, and a book of remembrance was written before him, for

---

154. 4QXII[c]. *of hosts* 4QXII[a] MT.

155. Singular 4QXII[a]. Plural MT LXX.

156. 4QXII[a]. *You are cursed with the curse* MT. *And you certainly turn your attention away* LXX.

157. 4QXII[a]. *the whole tithe* MT LXX.

158. 4QXII[a]. *house* MT LXX.

159. 4QXII[a]. *a* MT. *my* LXX.

160. 4QXII[a]. Not in MT.

161. 4QXII[a]. *with* MT.

those who feared] the LORD, and that thought upon his name. 17 *So that*[162] they shall be [mine, says the LORD of hosts,] even my own possession, [in the day] that I make; and [I] will spare [them, as a man spares] his own son that serves hi[m. 18 Then you will again distinguish between the righteous and the wicked, between the one who se]rves [God and the one who serves him not.]

4 [1 For behold, the day is coming;] it burns [as a furnace; and all the proud, and all that work wickedness shall be stubble; and] the day that is coming [shall burn th]em [up,] sa[ys the LORD of hosts,] so that it shall leave them [neither] root nor branch. [2 But] to you that fear my name [shall] the sun of righteousness [arise] with healing in its wings; [and you shall go forth,] and skip about as *a calf*[163] of the stall. 3 And you shall *counsel*[164] the wicked; [for they shall be] ashes under the soles of your feet in the day that I [make, says the LOR]D of hosts.

4 Remember the law of Moses my [se]rvant, [which I commanded him in] Horeb for all I[sra]el, even statutes and [judgments.]

[5 Behold, I will send] you Elijah the prop[het] before [the great and] terrible [day of the LORD comes. 6 And he shall turn the heart of the] fathers [to the children, and the heart of the children to their fathers; else I come] and strike [the earth with a curse.]

---

162. 4QXII[a]. *And* MT LXX.

Chapter 4. 4QXII[a]: 4:1–4 [H 3:19–24].

163. 4QXII[a]. *calves* MT LXX.

164. 4QXIIa. *tread down* MT LXX.

1 ENOCH

Of all the "nonbiblical" books found in the caves adjacent to the Dead Sea, the one that offers the most promise of having been considered authoritative to the Jewish community at Qumran is 1 Enoch. That some have considered this writing to be God's word is without question. It was quoted by the writer of the New Testament book Jude (vss 14–15, see 1 Enoch 1:9) and has been held in high regard by Ethiopian Christians.

This book, as known before the discovery of the Dead Sea Scrolls, may be divided into five sections:

- The Book of the Watchers (chs. 1–36) containing an introduction and a narrative describing the fallen angels and their intercourse with human women (Gen 6:1–4).
- The Book of the Similitudes (chs. 37–71) describing the final judgment of the righteous and the wicked and a character called the "son of man."
- The Book of Astronomical Writings (chs. 72–82) detailing a solar calendar of 364 days.
- The Book of Dreams (chs. 83–90) describing the future of the world and Israel.
- The Epistle of Enoch (chs. 91–107) concludes with a return to the theme of the reward of the righteous and wicked.

The Qumran mansucripts exhibit a more focused interest on the offspring of the angels and humans, which became a unit in its own right: The Book of Giants. The scrolls also reveal a much lengthier form of the Book of Astronomical Writings. On the other hand, the Book of Similitudes does not appear to have been included in manuscripts of the Qumran community.

The mysterious nature of this book begins with Enoch himself. The son of Jared and the sixth generation from Adam, the Bible reports that Enoch "walked with God; then was no more, for God took him away" (Gen 5:24). The New Testament interprets: "Enoch was taken (to heaven) by faith, so that he would not see death" (Heb 11:5). The account of this strange incident created great interest in Enoch in antiquity and gave rise to the notion that he would be knowledgeable concerning the details of God's program for Israel, having learned them first-hand. The writer of 1 Enoch capitalized on this interest and gave the biblical hero credit for a work that ranges from angels, the universe, and calendar issues to the future of Israel. Scholars refer to the type of literature characterized by 1 Enoch as pseudepigraphical—an author assuming the identity of some ancient notable perhaps in an attempt to attract curious readers.

The caves at Qumran have produced twenty manuscripts of Enoch—as many as the book of Genesis—all of them in Aramaic. Although the early history of the book is still unknown (written in about 400 BCE?), the debate about the original language—Greek, Hebrew, Aramaic?—seems now to have been answered in favor of the latter.

Another mystery that the scrolls have only clouded concerns the origin of the important and frequent (88x) New Testament title for Jesus: Son of Man (e.g., Matt 12:32). I Enoch 37–71 also features a messianic character of this name. As noted, this section has not been found among the scroll fragments, giving rise to the speculation that the New Testament influenced the final form 1 Enoch rather than the reverse.

Because the text is available elsewhere, and because of the admittedly speculative nature of including it even in a Dead Sea Scroll Bible, we have chosen not to reproduce the text here.[a]

---

a. E. Isaac, "1 (Ethiopic Apocalypse of) Enoch," in J. H. Charlesworth ed., *The Old Testament Pseudepigrapha* (vol. 2; Garden City: Doubleday & Company, 1985) 5–89 and F. García Martínez, *The Dead Sea Scrolls Translated: The Qumran Texts in English* (Leiden/New York: E. J. Brill, 1994) 246–62.

DANIEL

For a group of Jewish men living in the desert, waiting for the end of the world, believing that almost everyone else was among the "sons of darkness," the book of Daniel would have been welcome reading. Its tales of a godly man and his friends resisting persecution, refusing to compromise, and triumphing over wickedness and idolatry must have brought encouragement to the Qumran covenanters.

For modern readers and scholars, the Daniel scrolls and other related manuscripts are interesting for three reasons. First, of all the biblical books found at Qumran, these copies of Daniel are closest in date to when the book itself was written. Second, they provide our earliest evidence for the contents and form of Daniel. Finally, some related scrolls contain new stories surrounding Daniel that have only now come to light in the Dead Sea Scrolls.

Eight Daniel manuscripts were found at Qumran: two in Cave 1,[a] five in Cave 4,[b] and one in Cave 6.[c] Unfortunately, none is complete due to the ravages of time, but between them they preserve a substantial amount of the book of Daniel. All eight scrolls were copied in the space of 175 years, ranging from 125 BCE[d] to 50 CE.[e] Since Daniel was compiled later than any other book in the Hebrew Bible (about 165 BCE), these scrolls show that it was becoming popular and widely used at Qumran only forty years after being written.

What forms of this book are found in the scrolls? This is an important question, since Jewish and Protestant Bibles contain Daniel in twelve chapters, whereas Roman Catholic and Orthodox Bibles have a longer version that includes the Prayer of Azariah, the Song of the Three Young Men, Susanna, and Bel and the Dragon. Seven of the Daniel scrolls contained the book in the shorter

---

a. 1QDan[a] and 1QDan[b].   **b.** 4QDan[a], 4QDan[b], 4QDan[c], 4QDan[d], and 4QDan[e].   **c.** This scroll is classified as "pap6QDan" because it was written on papyrus.   **d.** 4QDan[a].
e. 4QDan[c].

form found in Jewish and Protestant Bibles—not the longer form known from Roman Catholic and Orthodox Bibles. But one scroll (4QDan^e) preserves only material from Daniel's Prayer in chapter 9, which suggests that it probably contained this prayer alone. It is also interesting to note that every chapter of Daniel is represented in the eight manuscripts, except for chapter 12. Yet this does not mean that the book lacked the final chapter at Qumran, since one of the nonbiblical scrolls, known as the *Florilegium* (4Q174), quotes Daniel 12:10 as written in the "book of Daniel the prophet."

Another question in the case of Daniel concerns the bilingual nature of the book, which in the Hebrew Bible opens in Hebrew, switches to Aramaic at chapter 2:4b, and then reverts again to Hebrew at 8:1. The four scrolls that preserve material from two or all three of these sections make the very same transitions from Hebrew to Aramaic and back again.^f While the precise reasons for having Hebrew and Aramaic sections in the same book are complex, the scrolls show us that Daniel existed in this form very early on and thus was most likely compiled in Hebrew and Aramaic. This is not really surprising in the case of such a late book—one that was written at a time when Aramaic was widely spoken by Jews in Palestine.

Do the scrolls offer clues to the position of the book of Daniel in the canon of the Hebrew Bible or Old Testament, which was not complete but still being formed during the Qumran period? This is an important issue, since Daniel is found in different sections of the Jewish canon (among the Writings) and the Septuagint Christian canon (among the Prophets)—see the general Introduction for further details. We have already mentioned the quotation of Daniel 12:10 in the *Florilegium,* which says that the verse is written in the "book of Daniel *the Prophet.*" This indicates that at Qumran Daniel was classified among the Prophets rather than the Writings, which is highly significant for our understanding of prophecy and the existence of different ancient Jewish collections of Scripture.

To say that the Daniel scrolls contain a book like the one found in the Hebrew Bible does not mean that they contain exactly the same text. On the contrary, readings for individual words or groups of words frequently differ. Such variants will be of great interest to many readers, especially those desiring to find out how the scrolls affect our understanding of certain key verses of Scripture. Many of

---

f. 1QDan^a, 4QDan^a, 4QDan^b, and 4QDan^d.

these readings are minor, with little or no effect on the meaning or interpretation of the book—but some are more significant. For instance, near the end of Daniel 7:1, the awkward phrase "he related the sum of the words" is completely absent from 4QDan[b], the only scroll that preserves this verse. The importance of this reading is underscored by the New Revised Standard Version, which simply has "then he wrote down the dream," in line with 4QDan[b] and not with the Hebrew Bible. A second example is seen in Daniel 10:16, where the Hebrew Bible reads "one in the likeness of the sons of men," but pap6QDan most likely agrees with the Septuagint's "something in the likeness of a human hand." In this case, the editors of the New International Version decided to retain the reading of the Masoretic Text (as do other English translations) but considered the variant reading important enough to merit an extensive footnote.

Was the book of Daniel quoted or referred to in other writings at Qumran? Since Daniel was not written until about 165 BCE, it would be surprising to find it used in this way—yet this is precisely the case. 11QMelchizedek, for example, refers to the "Anointed of the Spirit, of whom Daniel spoke" (Dan 9:25–26). The quotation of Daniel 12:10 as from the "book of Daniel the Prophet" in the *Florilegium,* referred to above, is significant for three reasons:

- It proves that by about 25 BCE Daniel was already being quoted as Scripture.
- It shows that the author(s) of the *Florilegium* knew Daniel as a complete book. They were not simply using traditions about Daniel that may have been circulating before the book was written.
- It suggests that at Qumran Daniel was included among the Prophets and not among the Writings (see above).

Several other manuscripts—all written in Aramaic—also mention Daniel or events associated with his book. These are the *Prayer of Nabonidus,*[g] two pseudo-Daniel documents,[h] the *Daniel Apocryphon* (or *Son of God* text),[i] 4QDaniel Susanna(?),[j] 4QFour Kingdoms,[k] and pap4QApocalypse.[l] With their tales of

---

g. 4Q242.   **h.** Consisting of 4Q243–244 and 4Q245.   **i.** 4Q246.   **j.** 4Q551. This text is very fragmentary and is probably not part of the Susanna portion of the Additions to Daniel found in the Septuagint and in Catholic and Orthodox Bibles (see the introduction to Daniel). **k.** 4Q552–53.   **l.** 4Q489.

courage in the face of persecution and their vision of the end of the world, these nonbiblical scrolls offer fascinating insights into Jewish thinking concerning inspired sayings, the course of history, and the end times during a period of Greek and Roman rule that was of great significance for both Judaism and Christianity.

The existence at Qumran of both biblical and nonbiblical scrolls involving Daniel shows that many traditions and writings associated with him were circulating in Palestine from the second century BCE well into the first century CE. Some of these (that is, the eight biblical Daniel scrolls) were selected by early Jewish leaders as Scripture and now appear in modern Bibles, while others (the nonbiblical scrolls) were not included. It is not difficult to understand why this late book had achieved such prominence in so short a time if we consider its contents and the outlook of the Qumran community. An apocalyptic community such as they were, waiting in the desert for the end of the age, would have found such a book very appealing and significant. With its focus on the end of history, the triumph of good over evil, God's coming kingdom, and the vindication of those who remain righteous and faithful, Daniel was no doubt essential reading for many of the Qumran covenanters.

1 [8 But Daniel resolved that he would not defile himself with the king's food and wine, so he asked the chief official to allow him not to defile himself. 9 God mercifully favored Daniel over the chief official. 10 The chief official said to Daniel, "I am too afraid of my lord the king who allotted your food and drink. Why should he see you in a less healthy condition than the other youths of your age? You would jeopardize] my he[ad] with the king!"

11 So Daniel asked [the guard whom the chief] official [had appointed] over Daniel, Hananiah, [Mishael, and Azariah: 12 "Please test] your servants for ten days. Let [us] be given [vegetables to eat and water] to drink. 13 Then let our appearance [and the appearance of the young men who eat] from the king's food be observed by you, and according to what you see [deal with your servants." 14 And he listened to] them as to this plan and tested them for [ten] days. 15 [At the end of ten days it was observed that they ap]peared healthier and better nour[ished than all the other youths who had been eating from the] kin[g's food]. 16 So the guard [continued to remove] their fo[od and the wi]ne they were to drink [and

---

Chapter 1. 1QDanª: 1:10–17; 4QDanª: 1:16–20.

gave] them *vegetables*.[1] 17 [As for these four young men], God [gave] them knowledge [and pro]ficiency [in every aspect of writing and wisdom, and Daniel especially had insight into all kinds of visions and dreams].

18 At the [e]nd of [the time when the king had specified that they be presented. The chief offic]ial [brought them] into Neb[uchadnezzar's] presence. 19 [And when the king spoke with them, among them all none was found equal to Daniel, Hananiah], *and*[2] M[i]shael, and A[zariah; therefore they were stationed in the] king's [court]. 20 In every matter of *wi*[*sdo*]*m and*[3] under[standing concerning which the king asked of them, he found them ten tim]es better than all the magicians [and enchanters in] his whole kingdom.

[21 And Daniel remained there until the first year of King Cyrus].

2[1 In the second year of the reign of Nebuchadnezzar, Nebuchadnezzar had such a dream that his spirit was troubled and his sleep fled from him. 2 So the king ordered the magicians, the enchanters, the sorcerers, and] *the Chaldeans*[4] [to be summoned] in order to tell [the king his dreams. When they came in and stood before] the king, 3 the [king] said to them, "[I had such a dream that my spirit is anxious] to understand the dream." 4 Then [the Chaldeans] said [to the king in Aramaic], "O king, li[ve] forever! [Tell your servants the dream], and we will reveal its meaning."

5 The king answered the Chaldeans, "[The decision from me] is public: if you do not te[ll me both the dream and its interpretation], you shall be torn [limb from limb], and your houses [shall be destroyed. 6 But if you do tell me the dream and its interpretation, you shall receive from me g]ifts and [presents and great honor. Now tell me the dream and its interpretation." 7 They answered a second time, "Let the king first tell his servants the dream, and we will give its interpretation." 8 The king answered, "I know with certainty that you are playing for time, because you see that the decision from me is public 9 that if you do not tell me the dream, there is but one verdict for you. You have conspired to speak ly]ing [and wor]ds [before me until the times change]. Therefore [tell me the dream, so I may know that you can give me its interpretation." 10 The Chaldeans answered the king, "There is not a person on earth] who [can reveal] the mat[ter for the king! No great and powerful king has ever requested such] a thing [of any magician or enchanter or Chaldean. 11 The thing] that the ki[ng requests is too difficult, and no one can reveal it to the king except] the go[ds, whose dwelling is not with mortals]." ▲

---

1. 1QDan[a] and MT use similar but not identical words for *vegetables*.

2. 1QDan[a] LXX. Not in MT.

3. Literally, *wisdom, understanding* 4QDan[a]. Literally, *wisdom of understanding* MT.

Chapter 2. 1QDan[a]: 2:2–6; 4QDan[a]: 2:9–11, 19–49.

4. Literally, *Chaldeans* 1QDan[a]. Literally, *to the Chaldeans* MT.

[17 Then Daniel went home and informed his companions, Hananiah, Mishael, and Azariah, 18 in order to implore mercy of the God of heaven concerning this mystery, so that Daniel and his companions might not perish along with the rest of the wise men of Babylon. 19 Then the mystery was revealed to Daniel in a vision during the night, and Daniel blessed] the God of heaven. 20 Daniel sa[id]: "Blessed be the name of *the great God*[5] [from a]ge to age, for wisdom and power a[re] his. 21 It is he who removes the changes in [ti]mes and seasons, causes [k]ings and establishes kings; he gives wisdom to the wise and knowledge to those who have und[er]standing. 22 It is he who reveals deep and mysterious things; *and he knows*[6] what is in the darkness, and the light dwel[ls with him]. 23 To you, *to the God*[7] of my ancestors, [I] give thanks and praise, because [you] have given [me] wisdom and pow[er, and] have now revea[led to me] what we asked of you, for [you have made known to us] the mat[ter for the king]."

24 So *Daniel* [*went*][8] to [Ario]ch, [whom the] king [had appointed to destroy the wise men of Babylon, and said] to him, "[Do not] destroy [the wise men of Babylon]; bring m[e in before the ki]ng, [and] I will give the king *its*[9] [interpretation]." 25 Then Arioch qui[ckly brought Daniel] before the king and [said] to him, "I have fo[und] among the exiles from *the Jews*[10] a man [who] can help [the king] know [the interpretation]."

26 The king said to Daniel, whose name was Belteshazzar, "Are you [able to tell me] the dream [that] I saw and its interpretation?" 27 Daniel answered [the] king, "[No] wise men, enchanters, magicians, or diviners can explain to the king the mystery which the ki[ng is asking], 28 bu[t there is a God in heaven who reveals] mysteries, *and he is disclosing*[11] to King Nebuchadnezzar what is to come at the end of days. *O k[ing, may you live forever,*[12] your dream] as you lay in bed was as follows:

29 "To you, O king, as you lay in bed came thoughts of what wo[uld happen in the future], and the one who reveals mysteries disclosed to you what will happen. 30 To me, not because of any wisdom that I have *exceptionally*[13] [more than any others alive], has this mystery been revealed, but so that the interpretation

---

5. 4QDan[a] LXX. *God* MT.

6. 4QDan[a] LXX. *he knows* MT.

7. 4QDan[a]. *O God* MT LXX.

8. 4QDan[a] had a shorter reading here, but only one letter is preserved. *Therefore Daniel went* MT.

9. 4QDan[a]. *the* MT LXX.

10. 4QDan[a]. *Judah* MT LXX.

11. 4QDan[a]. *and he has disclosed* MT LXX.

12. 4QDan[a] LXX. Not in MT.

13. 4QDan[a]. Not in MT LXX.

may be known to the king and so that [you may understand] the thoughts of your mind. 31 As you looked, O king, there was a gre[at] statue! That statue was huge, *its appearance*[14] surpassing, standing be[f]ore you, and its appearance was terrifying. 32 As for that statue, its head was of pure gold, its chest and arms of silver, its waist and thighs of bronze, 33 its legs of iron, its feet partly of iron and *partly*[15] clay. 34 As you continued looking, [a stone was c]ut out [by no human hand and it struck the image on its feet of iron] and clay and broke them in pieces. 35 The[n the iron, the clay, the bronze, the silver, and the gold all together were broken in pieces] and became like the chaff [of the sum]mer *threshing-floor;*[16] [and the wind carried them away, so that no trace of them could be found. But the stone that stru]ck the sta[tue bec]ame a great mountain [and filled the whole earth].

36 "[This was the dream; now we will tell its interpretation in the king's presence. 37 You, O king], are the king of kings, [to] whom [the God of heaven has given the kingdom, the power, the might, and the glory; 38 into whose hand he has given, wherever they dwell, hu]man beings, the wild animals, [and the birds of the air, and whom he has made ruler over them all—you are the head of gold. 39 After you shall a]rise [anot]her king[dom inferior to yours, and then a third kingdom of bronze, which shall rule over the entire earth. 40 Then there shall be a fourth kingdom, strong as ir]on; [just as iron crushes and shatters everything, it shall crush and sma]sh all th[ese, like iron which cr]ushes, *all the earth.*[17] 41 Just as [you sa]w [the feet and toes partly of potter's clay] and partly of iron, it shall be [a divided king]dom; but some of the hardness o[f] ir[on shall be in it, as you saw] the [iron] mixed with [common] clay. 42 [Just as the toe]s of the feet were partly ir[on and partly clay, so the kingdom sha]ll be partly strong [and partly brit]tle. 43 *And*[18] just as you saw the iron [mixed with clay, so will they intermingle with one another *in mar*]*riage,*[19] but they will not ho[ld] together, just as ir[on does not mix with clay].

44 "[And in the da]ys of [those] kings the G[od] of heaven [will set] up a kingdom which [shall nev]er [be destroyed], nor shall [its sovereignty be delive]red [to another people. It shall crush] a[ll th]ese kin[gdoms and put an end to them, and it shall stand forever; 45 just as] you saw that [a stone was hewn] from [the mountain by no human hand, and that it crushed the iron, the bronze, the clay, the silver,] and the gold. A great God [has revealed to the king what shall be in the future. The dream is certain, and its interpretation is reliable]."

---

14. 4QDan[a] LXX. *its brilliance* MT.

15. 4QDan[a]. *partly of* MT.

16. 4QDan[a] LXX. *threshing-floors* MT.

17. 4QDan[a] (cf. LXX). Not in MT.

18. 4QDan[a] MT[qere,mss] LXX. Not in MT.

19. Literally, *in human seed.*

46 *Then*[20] Kin[g Nebuchadnezzar fell upon his face, worshiped Daniel, and ordered that a cereal offering and incense be offered to him. 47 The king said to Daniel, "Truly, your God is God of gods and Lord of kings and a revealer of mysteries, that is why you have been able to] reveal [this mys]tery." 48 [Then the king promoted Daniel], gave him [many gen]erous presen[ts, and [made him ruler over the entire province of Babylon and chief pref]ect over all the wise men of Babylon. 49 Daniel made a re[quest of the king, and he appointed] Shadrach, Meshach, and Abednego [as administrator over] the province of Babylon. [But Daniel himself remained at the king's court].

3 1 [King Nebuchadnezzar made a golden statue] whose height was ninety feet and whose width was ni[ne] feet [and set it up on the plain of Dura] in the province of Babylon. 2 Then *Mechandnezzar*[21] sent for the satraps, [the prefects and the governors, the counselors, the treasurers, the jud]ges, the magistra[tes, and all the officials of the provinces to assemble and attend the dedication of the statue which he had set up.]▲

8 [At that point certain Chaldeans came forward to incri]minate the Jews. 9 [They said to King Nebuchadnezzar, "O king], live [forever]! 10 You, O king, issued a decr[ee, that everyone who hears the sound of the horn, pipe, lyre, trigon, harp, drum, and all kinds of musical instruments shall fall down and worship the golden statue, 11 and whoever does not fall down and worship shall be thrown into a furnace of blazing fire]."▲

19 [Then Nebuchadnezzar was so filled with rage against Shadrach, Meshach, and Abednego that his face became livid. He ordered the furnace heated seven times more than its usual heat 20 and ordered some of his strongest army guards to bind Shadrach, Meshach, and Abednego and to throw them into the furnace of blazing fire. 21 So the men were bound with their coats, their trousers, their hats, and their other garments still on, and were thrown into the furnace of blazing fire. 22 Since the king's command was insistent that the furnace be so overheated, the raging fl]ames [killed the men who led Shadrach, Meshach, and Abednego. 23 But the other three men, Shadrach], Meshach, and Abednego, fell into [the furnace of blazing fire] still bound.

24 Soon King Nebuchadnezzar was astonished and rose up in ha[ste. He said to his counselors], "Did we not throw three men, bound, into the fire?" They answered the king, "True, O king." 25 *Nebuchadnezz[ar]*[22] replied [and said] *to his officials,*[23] "But I see four men loo[se, walking in the midst of the fire, and they are

---

20. 4QDan[a]. MT prefixes b[e] to this word (*b[e.]dyn*), but the meaning is the same.

Chapter 3. 4QDan[a]: 3:1–2; 4QDan[d]: 3:8–10(?), 12–14(?), 23–25; 1QDan[b]: 3:22–30.

21. 4QDan[a] (error?). *King Nebuchadnezzar* MT LXX.

22. 4QDan[d]. *He replied* MT.

23. 4QDan[d]. Not in MT.

unharmed; and the appearance] of [the fo]urth is lik[e] a son of the god[s." 26 Then Nebuchadnezzar approached the opening of the furnace of blazing fire] and said, "Shad[r]ach, Mesha[ch, and Abednego, servants of the Most High God, come forth, come here]!" So Shadra[ch, Meshach, and Abednego] came out [from the fire. 27 When the satraps, the prefects], the governors, and the [ki]ng's counselors [gathered together, they saw that the fire had not had any effect on the bodies of those men; the hair of their heads] had not been singed, [their co]ats [had not been harmed, and not even the smell of fire had touched them].

28 [Nebuchadnezzar exclaimed, "Blessed be the God of Shadrach], *and*[24] Meshach, and Abed[nego, who sent his angel] and delivered [his serva]nts [who trusted in him]. They disobeyed [the royal command] and yielded up [their bo]dies [rather than serve] or [worship any god except their own God. 29 So I am ma]king a decree: Any people, nati[on, or language that speaks anything against the God of Shadrach, Meshach, and Abedne]go shall be cut to pieces, and [their] houses [destroyed; for there is no other god who can] rescue in this way." 30 Th[en the king promoted Shadrach, Meshach, and Abednego in the province of Babylon].

4 [4 I, Nebuchadnezzar, was relaxed in my home and prospering in my palace. 5 I saw a dream which frightened me; my fantasies in bed and the visions of my head terrified me. 6 So I issued a decree that all the wise men of Babylon should be brought before me to let me know the interpretation of the dream. 7 Then the magicians, the enchanters, the Chaldeans, and the diviners came in, and I related to them the dream, but they could not tell me its interpretation. 8 Finally Daniel came in before me—the one named Bel]tesha[zzar after the name of my god, and who is endowed with a holy, divine spirit—and I to]ld [him the dream]:

9 "O Belteshazza[r, chief of the magicians, I know that you are endowed with a holy, divine spirit and that n]o mys[tery *for you is too difficult.*[25] [Here is the dream which I saw; now] tell me [its interpretation. 10 Upon my bed I was seeing things, and there, a tree in the center of the world, and its height was great. 11 The] tree grew large [and strong, its top touched the heavens, and it was visible to the ends of the whole earth. 12 Its leaves] were beautiful, [its] fruit [abundant, and it provided food for all. The wild animals found shade under it, the birds of the air dwelt in its branches, and from it were fed all living beings].

[13 "I continued looking, in the visions of my head while in bed, and there

---

24. 1QDan[b]. Not in MT LXX.

Chapter 4. 4QDan[d]: 4:8–12, 15–19 [Aram 4:5–9, 12–16]; 4QDan[a]: 4:32–33 [Aram 4:29–30].

25. 4QDan[d]. *is too difficult for you* MT (word order). Only one letter of this word remains in 4QDan[d]; meaning uncertain.

was a watcher, a holy one, coming down from heaven. 14 He cried out loudly and said:

"'Hew down the tree and cut off its branches; strip off its foliage and scatter its fruit. Let the animals flee from beneath it and the birds from its branches. 15 But] its stump and roots leave in [the gr]ound, with a band of iron and bronze, [in the grass of] the [field]. With the dew of heaven let him be wet, and with the animals be his lot, in the grass of the earth. 16 Let [his mi]nd be changed [from that of a human], and let the mind of *the beast*[26] be given to him. And let sev[en ti]mes p[ass] over him.

17 "'[By decree of] watchers is the sentence, and *a word*[27] of the holy ones [the de]cision, [so that the living may know that] the Most Hig[h] has sovereignty over the ki[ngdom of mortals, and gives it to whom he will, and sets over it the lowli-est of human beings].'

18 "[This is the dream I, King Nebuchadnezzar, saw; now you, O Belteshaz-zar], declare the interpreta[tion]. Although [all the wise men of my kingdom are unable to tell me the interpretation, you are ab]le, for a spirit of the ho[ly] gods is [in you]."

19 [Then Daniel, called Belte]shazzar, was [severely] perplexed [for a while; his thoughts terrified him. The king said, "Belteshazzar, let not the dream or the interpretation alarm you." Belteshazzar answered, "My lord, may the dream be for those who hate you and its interpretation for your enemies]!▲

[31 While the words were still on the king's lips, a voice from heaven came down: "O King Nebuchadnezzar, to you it is declared: The kingdom has de-parted from you! 32 You shall be driven away from human company, and your dwelling shall be with the wild animals. You shall be made to eat grass like cattle, and seven seasons shall pass over you, until you have learned that the Most High has sovereignty over the realm of huma]ns and [gives it] to whom [he wishes." 33 At once the sentence was fulfilled against Nebuchadnezzar. He was driven from human company, ate] grass [like cattle, and his body was wet with the dew of heaven, until his hair grew like eagles' feathers and his nails became like birds' claws].▲

5 [1 King Belshazzar made a great feast for a thousand of his lords and was drinking wine in the company of the thousand. 2 Under the influence of the wine, Belshazzar ordered them to bring in the vessels of gold and silver which his father Nebuchadnezzar had taken from the temple in Jerusalem, so that the king and his nobles, his wives and his concubines could drink from them. 3 Then they brought in the vessels of gold and silver which had been taken from the temple,

---

26. 4QDan[d]. *the beast* MT.

27. 4QDan[d] MT. *and by word* MT[mss].

Chapter 5. 4QDan[d]: 5:3(?); 4QDan[a]: 5:5–7, 12–14, 16–19; 4QDan[b]: 5:10–12, 14–16, 19–22.

the house of] God in Jerusa[lem, and the king and his nobles, his wives and his concubines drank from them. 4 They drank wine and praised the gods of gold and silver, bronze, iron, wood, and stone].

5 [Suddenly the fingers of a hu]man [hand appea]red and began wri[ting on the plaster of the] king's [palace wall, opposite to the lampstand. When the king saw] the back of the hand a[s it was writing, 6 the king's face turned pale] and his thoughts [ter]rified him. His *lim[bs]*[28] gave way, [and his knees knocked together]. 7 The [king cried] aloud for the enchanters, *the magicians,*[29] the Chal[deans, and the diviners to be brought in, and the king said to the wise men of Baby]lon, "[Who]ever reads this writing and te[lls me] its interpretation [shall be clothed in purple, wear a golden chain around his neck, and rule as third in the kingdom]." ▲

10 [The queen, because of the words of the king and his lords, came into the banqueting hall. The queen said, "O king, live forever! Do] not [let your thoughts terrify you or let your face be pa]le. 11 There is a man [in your kingd]om [endowed with a holy, divine spirit. In the day]s of your father [he was seen to have enlighten]ment, [understanding, and wisdom like the wisdom of the gods. So your father], Ki[ng Nebuchadnezzar, appointed him chief of the magicians, enchanters, Chaldeans, and diviners, 12 because an extraordinary spirit], knowledge, *understanding*[30] to in[terpret dreams, explain riddles, and solve problems were fo]und in this Daniel, whom [the king named Belteshazzar. So now let Daniel be call]ed, *and he will read the writing*[31] [and will give the interpretation]."

13 [Then Dan]iel was brou[ght into] the presence of [the] king. [The king asked Daniel, "Are you Danie]l, one of the exi[les of Judah whom my father the king brought from Judah? 14 I have heard of y]ou [that a divine spirit was in you], and that enligh[tenment, understanding, and extraordinary wisdom were found in you. 15 Now the wise men, the enchanters, have been brought in before me to read this writing and tell me its interpretation, but they could not give the interpretation of the matter. 16 But I have he]ard about you, [that you can give interpretations and solve difficulties. Now if you are] able to read the wri[ting] and tell [me] its interpretation, you shall be clothed in purp[le], wear a golden ch[ain] aro[und your ne]ck, [and] rule [as third] in the kingdom."

17 Then Da[n]iel [ans]wered before the king, "[Let your pre]sents [be for yourself], or give *your reward*[32] to someone else! But [I will re]ad [the] writing for

---

28. Literally, *the joints of his loins.* For *loins,* 4QDan[a] has the Hebrew form, and MT has the Aramaic form.

29. 4QDan[a] LXX. Not in MT.

30. 4QDan[a]. *and understanding* MT.

31. 4QDan[a], 4QDan[b]. Not in MT.

32. 4QDan[a]. *your rewards* MT. *the reward of your house* LXX.

the king and let [him] know the interpretation. 18 [You, O king]—the Most Hi[gh] God [gave your father Nebuchadnezzar] kingsh[ip, grandeur], glory and majes[ty. 19 And because of the] grandeur [that he gave him, all peoples, nations and] lan[guages trembled and were afraid before him]. Whomever he wis[hed he slew, and whomever he wished he kept alive; whomever he wished] he raised [up, and whomever he wished he brought low. 20 But when his heart became proud and his spirit har]dened so that [he acted proudly, he was put down from his royal throne, and his glory was removed from him. 21 He was driven from human company, and his mind was made like that of a beast. His dwelling was with the wild asses, he was fed grass like cattle, and his body was wet with the dew of heaven, until he came to know that] the Most High God [has sovereignty] over the kingdom of [humans and appoints over it whom he wishes].

22 "[And you his son, Be]l[shazzar, have n]ot [humbled your heart, even though you knew all this! 23 You have exalted yourself against the Lord of heaven]!"▲

6 [6 So the supervisors and satraps came thronging in to the king and said to him, "O King Darius, live forever! 7 All the supervisors of the kingdom, the prefects and the satraps, the counselors and the governors agree that the king should establish an ordinance and enforce a prohibition, that] who[ever ad]dresses [a petition to any god or human for thirty days, except to you], O king, [shall be thrown into the den of lions. 8 Now, O king, establish the prohibition] and sign [the document, so that it cannot be revoked, according to the law of the Medes and the Persians which cannot be revo]ked." 9 Therefore [King Darius signed the document and prohibition].

10 [Even after Daniel kn]ew that [the document had been signed, he continued going to his house with windows in] the upper chamber [open toward Jerusalem, getting down upon] his [knees three times a day], and praying [and giving thanks *before*[33] his God, just as he had done pre]viously. 11 Th[en the men rushed in and found Daniel pray]ing and pleading [before his God. 12 So they approached the king and said] concerning the prohibition, "[O king! Did you not sign *the prohibition*,[34] that *all people who p*]*ray*[35] to any g[od or human within thirty days except to you, O king, shall be thrown into the den of lions?" The king answered, "The decree stands firm, according to the la]w of the Med[es and Persians which cannot be revoked]."

Chapter 6. 4QDan[b]: 6:7–21, 26–28 [Aram 6:8–22, 27–29].

33. The forms of this word in the Aramaic are slightly different in 4QDan[b] *(qd]m)* and MT *(qdmt),* but identical in meaning.

34. 4QDan[b]. *a prohibition* MT. Not in LXX.

35. 4QDan[b]. *anyone who prays* MT.

13 [Then they responded in the king's] presence [and] said, "[Daniel, one of the exiles from Ju]dah, pays no [attention to you, O king, n]or to [the prohibi]tion [that] you have issued, but [offers] his [prayers] three times a day." 14 Wh[en] the king heard the charge, he was very dis[turbed]. He made up his mind [to] save [D]aniel and [worked] until the sun went do[wn to res]cue him. 15 But [the]se men rushed in to the king [and said to him, "Keep in] mind, O king, that it is a law of the Med[es and Persians th]at n[o prohibition or decree which the king issues] can be changed."

16 [Then the king issued the order, and] Danie[l was brought *and into*] *the den of lions they th[rew him.*[36] The king said to Daniel, "May your God] whom you constantly serve [save you!" 17 A rock was brought] and placed *in*[37] the mouth of the den, and the king *sealed (it)*[38] [with his own ring and with the rings of his nobles, so that] nothing might be changed in Daniel's case. 18 Then the king returned to *the palace*[39] and sp[ent the night fasting]; no [diversio]ns were brought to hi[m], and sleep fled from him.

19 Then [at the first lig]ht of dawn, [the ki]ng *went*[40] hurried[ly] to the den of lions. 20 When [he dr]ew near the den where Daniel was, he cried out in a sorrowful tone and said to [Daniel, "Daniel, servant of the liv]ing [God], has your God whom you [constantly ser]ve [been able to rescue you from the li]ons?"

21 [Then Daniel s]*aid*,[41] "O king, live forever! 22 My God sent his angel and closed the lions' mouths so they would not harm me, since I was found innocent before him; and also before you, O king, I have done no wrong]." ▲

[25 Then King Darius wrote to all the peoples and nations of every language that dwell in the whole world: "May your welfare be abundant! 26 I issue a decree, that throughout my royal domain people must tremble in fear before the God of Daniel. For he is] *a living God,*[42] who endures forev[er. His kingdom shall never be destroyed, and] his dominion shall be without end. 27 [He saves and rescues, he works signs and wonders in heaven and] on [earth, he who saved Dani]el from the pow[er of the lio]ns."

28 [So this Daniel fared well during the reign of Dariu]s [and] the reign of Cyrus [the Persian].

---

36. 4QDan[b]. *and they threw him into the den of lions* MT.

37. 4QDan[b]. *upon* MT LXX.

38. 4QDan[b] LXX (object understood). *sealed it* MT.

39. 4QDan[b]. *his palace* MT LXX.

40. 4QDan[b]. *arose and went* MT LXX.

41. 4QDan[b] (shorter reading). *said to the king* MT.

42. 4QDan[b] LXX. *the living God* MT.

7 1 [In the first year of King Belshazzar of Babylon, Dan]iel had a dream [and visions of his head as he lay in his bed. Then] he *wrote down the [dream]*:[43]

■ *In the Masoretic Text, and thus our traditional biblical text, the ending of Dan 7:1 is very awkward:* Then he wrote down the dream, he related the sum of the words. *Even before the discovery of the scrolls (or at least their availability), scholars suspected that* he related the sum of the words *may be a later addition to the original text of Daniel. 4QDan[b] is the only scroll to contain 7:1; although it preserves only a few words of the verse, enough remains to show that it contained the shorter reading, not the longer one.*

2 [I, Daniel,[44] saw in] my vision b[y night the four winds of heaven stir]ring up [the great sea, 3 and] fo[ur great animals emerged from the sea, each dif]ferent from one ano[ther]. 4 The first [was like a lion but] with [eagles' wings]. I kept [wat]ching until [its wings were plucked off, and it was lifted up] from the ground and [made to stand up]on [two feet like a human; and it was given a human mind. 5 Another beast appeared, a second one that looked like] a bear, [but raised up] on [one si]de, [and with three ribs in its mouth between its teeth. It was told: "Arise, devour] much flesh!" 6 [After this, as I] looked, [another animal appeared, like a leopard. The animal had] four [wings] of [a bird on] its back and fou[r] h[eads; and dominion was given to it. 7 After this I was watching in the visi]ons by n[ight, and a fourth beast appeared, terrifying and dreadful and very powerful. It had great iron teeth that devoured, crushed, and trampled residue with its feet. It was different from all the beasts that preceded it, and it had ten horns].▲

11 [I looked on. Then because of the sound of the big words which] the horn [was speaking, the animal was killed as I looked on; and its body destroyed and co]nsigned [to be burned with fire].▲

15 [As for me, Daniel], my spirit was dis[turbed because of this, and the visions of my head terrified me. 16 I approa]ched one of those present [to ask him the truth concerning all this. So] he replied [that he would make known] to me the interpretation of [the matter: 17 "As for these great beasts], which number four, f[our kings shall spring up out of the earth. 18 But] the holy ones of the Most Hi[gh shall receive] the kingdom, [and possess the kingdom forever, forever and e]ver."

19 But [I wished to ascertain the truth about the fourth beast], which was so different from all the re[st, very terrifying, with its teeth of iron and cla]ws of

---

Chapter 7. 4QDan[b]: 7:1–6, 11(?), 26–28; 4QDan[a]: 7:5–7, 25–28; 4QDan[d]: 7:15–19, 21–23(?).

43. 4QDan[b] and (probably) LXX. *the dream, he related the sum of the words* MT LXX [mss].

44. Reconstructed from the Greek version by Theodotion. MT reads *Daniel answered and said, I* (see NRSV).

b[ronze, and which devoured and crushed, and trampled the residue with its feet;
20 and about the ten horns that were on its head, and the other horn that sprang
up and before which three of them fell, the horn which had eyes and a mouth
that spoke arro]gant th[ings, and which appeared greater than its fellows. 21 As I
watched, this horn made] war against [the holy ones, and was victorious over
them, 22 until the Ancient of Days arrived; then judgme]nt was pronounced [for
the holy ones of the Most High, and the time came when] the holy ones [took
possession of the kingdom].

23 [Thus he said: "As for the fourth beast, there shall be a fourth kingdom] on
earth, [which shall be different from all the other kingdoms, and it shall devour
the entire earth, and trample it down, and crush it. 24 As for the ten horns, out of
this kingdom ten kings shall spring up and another shall spring up after them.
This one shall be different from those before him, and shall lay low three kings.
25 He shall speak words against the Most High, shall oppress the holy ones of the
Most High, and shall think of changing the times and the law; and they shall be
handed over to him for a tim]e, *two time[s]*,[45] and half a time. 26 But [the cou]rt
shall s[it in judgment, and his dominion shall be taken away, to be consumed and
destroy]ed to the en[d]. 27 Then kingshi[p and do]minion [and the greatness of
the kingdoms under the entire he]aven shall be given to the people of the ho[ly
ones of] the Most High; [their kingdom shall be an everlasting kingdom, and all
domin]ions shall serve and obey [them]."

28 Her[e] is the [e]nd of [the account. As for me, Daniel, my thoughts greatly]
terrified me, and my face grew pale; [but I kept the matter in my mind].

8 1 [In the third year of the reign of] Ki[ng Belshazzar] *a word was revealed*[46] to
me, Daniel, aft[er the one which had been shown to me earlier]. 2 In the vision I was watching, and I saw myself in Susa the capital, [in the province of
Elam; and I watched] in the vision, and I was at the river Ulai. 3 I looked up [and
saw a *la]rge*[47] [ram] standing on the bank of the river; it had *two horns.*[48] [Both
horns were high, but on]e was higher than the other, and the higher one came up
second. 4 [I saw the ram butting we]stward *and eastward,*[49] *northward*[50] and southward. All *the animals*[51] [were power]less [to withstand him, and no one could rescue from] his power; he did as [he p]leased and become powerful.

---

45. 4QDanᵃ: *and two times* MT LXX.

Chapter 8. 4QDanᵃ: 8:1–5; 4QDanᵇ: 8:1–8, 13–16; pap6QDan: 8:16–17(?), 8:20–21(?).

46. 4QDanᵃ*. *a vision was shown* 4QDanᵃ(ᶜᵒʳʳ) MT LXX.

47. 4QDanᵃ 4QDanᵇ LXX. not in MT.

48. Literally, *horns, horns* 4QDanᵃ 4QDanᵇ. *two horns* (dual) MT. *horns* LXX.

49. 4QDanᵃ LXX. Not in MT.

50. 4QDanᵃ. *and northward* MT LXX.

51. 4QDanᵃ LXX. *animals* 4QDanᵇ MT.

5 As I [looked on, a he-goat] appeared from the west, coming to[52] the face of the whole earth without touching the ground. [The goat had a horn between his eyes. 6 He approached the] ram with the two horns [which I had seen standing on the bank of the river, and he rushed toward him with] his [savage] force. 7 I saw him reach[ing the ram; he raged against him and struck the ram, breaking] both his horns. [The ram did not have the force to withstand him; he threw him down to the ground and tram]pled upon him, and [there was] no [one able to rescue the ram from his power. 8 Then the he-goat be]came ve[ry] powerful; [but at the height of his power, the great horn was broken, and in its place there sprang up four horns facing the four winds of heaven]. ▲

13 [Then I heard a holy one speaking, and another holy one said] to the one that sp[o]ke, ["For how lo]ng [is this vision concerning the regular offering, the transgression that desolates, and the surrender of] the sanctuary and host to be trampled?" 14 [And he answered him, "For two thousand and three hundred evenings and mornings]; then the sanctuary shall be purified."

15 [A]nd [while] I, Danie[l, had seen the vision, and trying to understand it, someone appeared standing before me], who looked like a man, 16 and I hea[rd a human voice between the banks of the Ulai, crying, "Gabriel, make] t[h]is man understand the vision." 17 [So he came near where I stood, and as he came I was frightened and fell prostrate. But he said to me], "Underst[and, O mortal one, for the vision is for the end of time." 18 As he was speaking to me, I fell into a trance, prostrate on the ground, but he touched me and made me stand up.]

[19 He said, "Pay attention, and I will inform you of what shall happen after the period of wrath; for it pertains to the appointed time of the end. 20 As for the ram which you] saw [with the two horns, these are the kings of Media and Persia. 21 The he-goat is] the king of Greece, [and the great horn between his eyes is the first ki]n[g. 22 As for (the horn) that was broken, in place of which four more arose, four kingdoms shall arise from his nation, but not with his strength]." ▲

9[11 "Because all Israel has transgressed your law and recorded, refusing to obey your voice, the curse and the oath which are written in the Torah of Moses the servant of God has been poured out over us, because we have sinned against him. 12 He has carried out his which he made against us and against our governing leaders, by bringing upon us a calamity so gre]at that [never under] the en[tire] heave[n has anything been done such as what has been done against Jerusale]m. 13 Just as [it was written] in the Torah of [Moses, this whole calamity] has com[e upon us. We did not seek the f]avor of [our God,[53] turning from our

---

52. 4QDanᵃ. *upon* MT LXX.

Chapter 9. 4QDanᵉ: 9:12–14, 15–16(?), 17(?).

53. 4QDanᵉ (reconstructed). *the Lᴏʀᴅ our God* MT LXX.

iniquities and recognizing] your fidelity, [O LORD.[54] 14 Therefore the LORD, who had been keeping watch over this calamity], brought it [upon us. Indeed, the LORD our God is just in al]l [that he has done, for we did not listen to his voice].

[15 "And now, O Lord our God, who led your people out of the land of Egypt with a strong hand and made for yourself] a name [even to this day, we have sinned, we have acted wickedly. 16 O Lord, in view of all your righteous acts, please] let [your anger and wrath] turn away from your city Jerusalem, your holy mountain. Because of our sins and the iniquities of our ancestors, Jerusalem and your people have become a reproach among all those around us]. 17 So now [listen, O God, to the prayer of your servant and to his] supplicatio[ns, and for your own sake, Lord, let your face shine upon your desolate sanctuary]." ▲

10[4 On the twenty-fourth day of the first month, I was standing on the bank of the great river, that is, the Tigris. 5 As I lifted up my eyes, I looked, and behold], a [ma]n dressed [in linen], whose [loi]ns *was girded*[55] with g[old of Uphaz]. 6 His bo[dy] was like beryl, his fa[c]e like the appearance of lightning, [his] eyes like flaming torches, his arms and legs like the [gl]eam of burnished bronze, and the sound of his *word*[56] was like the noise of a multitude. 7 And I alone, Dan[i]el, saw the vision, for the men who were with me did not see the vision, but great fe[ar] fell upon them, and they fled and hid themselves. 8 As for me, I was l[ef]t alone and saw *this great vision,*[57] and no strength was left in me; my radiant appearance was fearfully changed, and [I retained n]o [strength. 9 Then I] he[ard] the sound of [his words; and when I heard the sound of] his words, I [fell on my face in a deep sleep with my face to the ground].

[10 And behold, a hand touch]ed me *to make me tremble*[58] o[n my hands and knees. 11 And] he said to me, ["O Daniel, man gre]atly beloved, give heed to the wor[ds that] I speak to you, [and stand u]pright, for [now I have been sent to you." While] he was spea[king t]his [word] to me, I stood up trem[bling. 12 Then he] sai[d] to [me], "Do no[t be af]raid, Daniel, for fr[om] the first [da]y that you set your mind to understand and humbled yourself before your God, your words have been heard, and I have come *for your [sa]ke.*[59] 13 *The princes*[60] of the kingdom of Persia with[s]tood me for twenty-o[ne days; but Michael, one of] the chi[ef

---

54. 4QDan[e] (reconstructed) LXX. Not in MT.

Chapter 10. 4QDan[c]: 10:5–9, 11–16, 21; pap6QDan: 10:8–16; 4QDan[a]: 10:16–20.

55. 4QDan[c] (error?); cf. LXX. *were girded* MT.

56. 4QDan[c] LXX. *words* MT.

57. Masculine 4QDan[c]. Feminine MT.

58. pap6QDan. *and set me trembling* MT. *and around me* LXX.

59. 4QDan[c]. *because of your words* MT. *about your word* LXX.

60. 4QDan[c]. *The prince* MT LXX.

pr]inces, [came to help me, so I remained there with the *ki]ngdom*[61] of Persia, 14 and [came] to make you understand [what is to befall your people in the lat]ter days. For the vision is for day[s] yet to come."

> *During Daniel's vision described in Chapter 10, the traditional Masoretic Text tells us in verse 16 that one in the likeness of the sons of men (i.e., one in human form) touched Daniel's lips. The Septuagint, however, says that something in the likeness of a human hand touched his lips. This verse is partially preserved in three scrolls (4QDan^a, 4QDan^c, pap6QDan), but in a very fragmentary form, with the words between* likeness *and* touched *not preserved in any scroll. In pap6QDan, however, the verb* touched *is feminine, while in the Masoretic Text it is masculine; the subject in pap6QDan is most likely* hand *(with LXX), whereas in the Masoretic Text it is the one in human form.*

15 When [he] had spok[en to me according to t]hese [words], I turned *my face*[62] toward the ground [and was dumb. 16 And behold], *something in the likeness of [a human hand*[63] *tou]*ched [my lips; then I] opened my mouth and [spoke. I said] to [him who stood before m]e, "O [my l]ord, [by reason of the vi]sion [pains have] come up[on me, and I retain no strength. 17 How can my lord's servant speak with my lord? As for m]e, now no [strength remai]ns [in me], and no breath is [left in me]."

[18 Again one having the appearance of a man touched me and st]rengthened me. 19 And he said, "O man greatly beloved, fe[a]r not, peace be with you; [be strong and of good courage." And when he spoke to me, I was strengthened and said], *"Speak, my lord,*[64] for you have strengthened me." 20 Then he asked, "Do you know [why I have come to you? But now I must go back to fight against the prince of Persia; and when I leave, the prince of Greece will come. 21 But I will tell you what is inscribed in the book of truth: there is none who contends by my side against these except Michael, your prince].

11 [1 And as for me], in the first year of Darius the Mede, *I took my stand*[65] to confirm and strengthen him. 2 "And now I will show you the truth. Behold, three more kings shall arise in Persia; and a fourth shall be far wealthier than all of them; and [when] he has become powerful through his riches, [he] shall stir everyone up against the kingdom of [Greece]. ▲

---

61. pap6QDan. *kings* MT. *king* MT.

62. Literally, *my nose* pap6QDan. *my face* MT LXX.

63. pap6QDan (reconstructed reading) LXX. *one in the likeness of the sons of men* MT.

64. 4QDan^a. *Let my Lord speak* MT LXX.

Chapter 11. 4QDan^c: 11:1–2, 13–17, 25–29; 4QDan^a: 11:13–16; pap6QDan: 11:33–36, 38.

65. Perfect 4QDan^c. Infinitive construct MT.

[11 "Then the king of the south, moved with anger, shall come out and fight against the king of the north; and he shall raise a great multitude, but it shall be given into his hand. 12 And when the multitude is taken, his heart shall be exalted, and he shall cast down tens of thousands, but he shall not triumph. 13 For the king of the north shall again raise] an army, [gre]ater th[an the former one; and after some years he shall come on with] a great [army] and [abundant] suppl[ies].

14 ["In] those [times] many shall resist [the king of the south; and the men of violence among your own people] shall assert themselves in order to fulfill [the visi]on; [but they shall fail. 15 Then] the king of the north arrives and throws up siegeworks, and captures a well-fortified city. [And the fo]rces of the s[o]uth sh[all] not stand, or even his elite troops, for there shall be no strength to stand. 16 But the one *who comes*[66] against [him] shall do according to his own will, and no[n]e shall [st]and before him; and he shall sta[nd] in the glorious land, and all of it shall be *in his power.*[67] 17 He shall set *his understanding*[68] to come with the strength of his entire kingdom, and he shall bring terms of peace; *he will*[69] perform them. He shall give him the daugh[ter of] *men*[70] in order to destroy *it;*[71] but it shall not stand and [will] not be to his advantage. ▲

[25 "And he shall stir up his power and his courage against the king of the south with a great army; and the king of the south shall wage war with an exceedingly great and mighty army; but he shall not stand, for pl]ots [shall be devised against him]. 26 Even [those who eat his rich food shall be his undoing; his army] shall be swept away, [and] many fa[ll] down slain. 27 [And as for the two kings, their minds] shall be bent on mischief; [they shall speak] lies at the same table, [but to no avail; for the end is yet to be] at the [time] app[oin]ted. 28 [And he shall return to his land with great substance, but his heart shall be set] agai[nst] the holy covenant. And he shall take action, [and return to his own land].

[29 "At the appointed time he shall come again] into the south; but it sh[all] not [be this time as it was before. 30 For ships of Kittim shall come against him, and he shall loose heart and retreat, and shall turn back and be enraged and take action against the holy covenant. He shall turn back and concentrate on those who forsake the holy covenant. 31 Forces from him shall appear and profane the temple and fortress, and shall do away with the continual burnt offering; and they

---

66. MT LXX. The reading of 4QDan^c, *hm*, is uncertain in meaning.

67. 4QDan^c. Literally, *in his hand* MT LXX.

68. Meaning unclear 4QDan^c. *his face* MT LXX.

69. 4QDan^c LXX. *and he will* MT.

70. 4QDan^c LXX. *men* MT.

71. Masculine 4QDan^c. Feminine (= the kingdom) MT.

shall set up the abomination that makes desolate. 32 He shall seduce with flattery those who violate the covenant; but the people who know their God shall stand firm and take action].

[33 "And those among the people who are wise shall make many understand though they shall fall by sword and] flame, and[72] [by captivity and plunder, for some days. 34 When they fall, they shall receive a little help. And] ma[ny shall join themselves to] them [with flattery; 35 and some of those who are wise shall fall, in order to refine and to cleanse them and to make them white], until the time of [the end, for there is yet an interval until the appointed time].

[36 "And the king shall do according to his will; he shall exalt himself and magnify himself] above every [god, and shall speak astonishing things against the God of gods. He shall prosper till the period of wrath is accomplished; for what is determined must take place. 37 He shall have no regard for the gods of his ancestors, or to the one beloved by women; he shall not have regard for any other god, for he shall magnify himself above all]. 38 He shall honor [the god of fortresses instead of these; a god whom his ancestors never knew he shall honor with gold and silver, with precio]us [stones] and with co[stly gifts. 39 He shall deal with the strongest fortresses by the help of an alien god; those who acknowledge him he shall magnify with honor. He shall make them rulers over many and shall divide the land for a price]." ▲

---

72. pap6QDan MT[ms] LXX. Not in MT.

OTHER BOOKS

PSALMS

"**H**appy are those who do not follow the advice of the wicked, . . . but their delight is in the law of the Lord." Thus begins the book of Psalms, a collection of hymns and prayers composed over the course of much of Israel's history. Our English title comes from a Greek word meaning "song," but the Hebrew title, *Tehillim*, means "Songs of Praise." Among all the books of the Bible, the Psalms are most numerous in the Dead Sea Scrolls, which indicates their immense popularity at Qumran. But the form of the Psalter in these most ancient manuscripts is diverse and fascinating. Up to Psalm 89 or so, the scrolls contain material very much in the order used by Jews and Christians today, although there are a few variations. But from Psalm 91 onward, many of the Psalms scrolls differ radically from the Psalter as we know it. The variations involved are of two main types: variations in *arrangement* (that is, a different order of Psalms) and variations in *content* (that is, the inclusion of compositions not found in the traditional book of Psalms. Some of these were previously known, and others completely unknown, before the discovery of the Dead Sea Scrolls).

Description and Contents of the Psalms Scrolls

There are no less than forty Psalms scrolls or manuscripts that incorporate Psalms, ranging in date from the mid–second century BCE[a] to about 50–68 CE.[b] Thirty-seven were found at Qumran: three in Cave 1, one each in the minor Caves 2, 3, 5, 6, and 8, twenty-three in Cave 4, and six in Cave 11. Three more scrolls were discovered farther south along the Dead Sea: two at Masada and

---

a. 4QPs[a].   **b.** E.g., 4QPs[c] and 11QPsAp[a].

one at Naḥal Ḥever. Although none is complete, several of these manuscripts are very substantial—notably, the *Great Psalms Scroll* (11QPsᵃ), followed by 4QPsᵃ, 5/6HevPs, 4QPsᵇ, 4QPsᶜ, and 4QPsᵉ.

Of the 150 Psalms found in the Masoretic Psalter, 126 are preserved in the forty Psalms scrolls and a few other relevant manuscripts such as the *pesharim*. The remaining twenty-four Psalms were most likely included but have since been lost due to deterioration and damage. Of Psalms 1 through 89, nineteen no longer survive,[c] but of Psalms 90 to 150 only five are not represented,[d] since the beginnings of scrolls are usually on the outside and are thus more prone to deterioration. In addition to these Psalms that are found in modern Bibles, at least fifteen "apocryphal" Psalms or similar compositions are also distributed among four manuscripts.[e] Six of these compositions were previously familiar to scholars,[f] but the other nine were completely unknown prior to the discovery of the Dead Sea Scrolls.[g] The presence of these other Psalms or compositions in some of the Psalms scrolls alerts us to the fact that the "Book of Psalms" at Qumran should not automatically be equated with the Psalter that appears in our Bibles.

Different Psalters in the Scrolls and in This Translation

What form or forms of the Psalter are found in these forty manuscripts? Before answering this question, it would be helpful to describe the forms of this book that were known prior to the discovery of the scrolls. The Psalter used by Jews and that used by most Christians today are very much the same, although Hebrew and English Bibles contain minor differences in verse numbering. More significantly, the Greek Bible (Septuagint) used by the early Church—the text that still serves as the Old Testament of the Greek Orthodox Church—contains a Psalter that differs in two respects from the one found in the Masoretic Text. The

---

c. Pss 3–4, 20–21, 32, 41, 46, 55, 58, 61, 64–65, 70, 72–75, 80, and 87.   d. Pss 90, 108(?), 110, 111, and 117.   e. Pss 11QPsᵃ, 4QPsᶠ, 11QPsᵇ, and 11QPsApᵃ.   f. 151A, 151B, 154, 155, David's Last Words (= 2 Sam 23:1–7), and Sirach 51:13–30.   g. The Apostrophe to Judah, the Apostrophe to Zion, David's Compositions, the Eschatological Hymn, the Hymn to the Creator, the Plea for Deliverance, and three of the Songs Against Demons.

first type of variation is in *arrangement*,[h] and the second is in *content*.[i] The existence of Psalters with different arrangements or contents is highly significant for our understanding of the book of Psalms, since many scholars today are focusing on the "shape" of the Psalter and the implications of the order of the Psalms as well as their contents.

As already mentioned, for Psalms 1 through 89 or so, the Psalms scrolls contain material that for the most part reflects the sequence familiar to Jews and Christians today. However, there are two important differences: in two scrolls[j] Psalm 31 is followed directly by 33—we cannot be sure that Psalm 32 was ever part of these scrolls—and in one scroll[k] Psalm 38 is followed directly by 71. Except for these two important variations, our translation of Psalms 1 through 89 is presented in the order of the Masoretic Text.

But for Psalms 91 onward—90 is not preserved—both the arrangement and contents of many Psalms scrolls are very different from what we had known previously. These variations are so numerous and radical that it is necessary to provide a table at the end of this introduction to the Psalms in order to assist readers in locating specific Psalms (see Table 2). The alternative would have been to translate Psalms 91 onward in the order of the Masoretic Psalter. While this course might be more convenient to the reader, it would also be misleading, since virtually none of the Psalms scrolls contains that arrangement. For this later part of the Psalter, five different arrangements are evident in the Psalms scrolls.

- The most prominent arrangement—that found in 11QPs[a] (the largest Psalms scroll), 4QPs[e], and 11QPs[b]—can be termed the "11QPs[a]-Psalter." It should be emphasized here that this term denotes Psalms 1 through 89 plus the arrangement found in 11QPs[a], not only that of 11QPs[a]. As far as possible, our English translation follows this order for the second part of this Psalter, which starts with Psalm 101 and ends with Psalm 151 (see Table 1). While the Septuagint Psalter also ends with this Psalm, it must be pointed out that the overall structure of the 11QPs[a]-Psalter differs substantially from the Greek one.

---

h. E.g., Pss 9 and 10 form a single Psalm.   **i.** The Greek (LXX) Psalter ends with Psalm 151.
j. 4QPs[a] and 4QPs[q].   **k.** 4QPs[a].

- The second arrangement—the Psalter used by Jews and most Christians today—is conveniently termed the "MT-150 Psalter," since the form of the Psalter found in the Masoretic Text contains 150 Psalms. It is most surprising to find that none of the Psalms scrolls from Qumran *unambiguously* confirms the arrangement of this Psalter; for such a sequence, we have to turn to a scroll from Masada (MasPs[b], which ends with Psalm 150).
- The other three arrangements are much smaller (see Table 1). One involves the Four Psalms Against Demons in 11QPsAp[a], which are placed immediately after Psalm 89 in our translation. Another arrangement is found in 4QPs[b], which preserves material from Psalms 91 through 118—but with Psalm 103 followed directly by 112 (thus not including Psalms 92 to 111). The final arrangement is in 4QPs[f], which contains Psalms 22, 107, and 109, followed by three apocryphal Psalms.[1] Since Psalms 22 and 109 and the Apostrophe to Zion occur in other scrolls in combination with other compositions, the translation does not present them in the order found in 4QPs[f]. However, the remaining three pieces (Psalm 107, the Eschatological Hymn, and the Apostrophe to Judah) are not found in any other Psalms scrolls, so these are grouped together after Psalm 151B under the heading "An Unusual Collection from Cave 4."

New Readings and the Status of the Psalter at Qumran

Several interesting readings are also to be found in the Psalms scrolls. One of these is in Psalm 145, which is missing a verse in the Masoretic Text. This is an acrostic Psalm—in other words, one with every verse beginning with a successive letter of the Hebrew alphabet. Although there are twenty-two letters in this alphabet, the Psalm contains only twenty-one verses: a verse beginning with the Hebrew letter *nun* should come between verse 13 (the *mem* verse) and verse 14 (the *samek* verse). 11QPs[a] is the only scroll that preserves Psalm 145; for verse 13

---

1. The Apostrophe to Zion, the Eschatological Hymn, and the Apostrophe to Judah.

it contains not only the *mem* verse but the missing *nun* verse as well! This is an important example of how the Dead Sea Scrolls sometimes preserve material that has fallen out of the Masoretic Text during the process of transmission. This reading is so compelling that the *nun* verse has been included in many modern English Bibles, including the New Revised Standard Version, the New American Bible, the New International Version, and the Good News Bible.

What was the status of the Book of Psalms at Qumran? A text that was written at Qumran, 4QMMT, suggests that the Psalms form the most prominent component in the third part of the Jewish "canon," which was actually still in the process of formation: "[And] we have wr[itten] to you that you should examine the book of Moses, and the words of the Prophets, and Davi[d] . . ."[m] A very similar statement is to be found in Luke 24:44, where Jesus says, "Everything must be fulfilled that is written about me in the Law of Moses, the Prophets, and the Psalms." Another pertinent text is the *War Scroll* (4Q491), which specifically refers to the "book of Psalms."[n] The scriptural status of the Psalter is also supported by the three *pesharim* on the Psalms;[o] by quoting verses from the Psalms and expounding on them, these ancient commentaries clearly affirm that their writers viewed the book of Psalms as Scripture.

It thus seems clear that the "book of Psalms" was viewed as Scripture at Qumran; but it is not easy to determine which specific form(s) of the Psalter were regarded as such. A passage from one of the compositions found in the 11QPs^a-Psalter ("David's Compositions"), is relevant in this regard: "And David, the son of Jesse, was wise, and a light like the light of the sun, and literate, . . . And the total (of his psalms and songs) was four thousand and fifty. All these he composed through prophecy which was given him from before the Most High." Such language indicates that the Psalms of David, particularly those found in the 11QPs^a-Psalter, were viewed as inspired Scripture among those who compiled and used this ancient collection of Psalms.

---

m. 4QMMT C, lines 9–10.   **n.** 4Q491, fragment 17, line 4.   **o.** 1QpPs, 4QpPs^a, and 4QpPs^b.

Table 1: Order of Psalms in this Translation

Psalms 1 to 89

Psalms 1–31   Psalms 39–69
(Psalm 32 absent)   (Psalm 70 absent)
Psalms 33–38   Psalms 72–89
Psalm 71

Four Psalms Against Demons

Exorcism Psalm I   Exorcism Psalm III
Exorcism Psalm II   Psalm 91

Psalms Mainly from 4QPs^b

Psalm 92   Psalms 94–100

The Great Psalms Scroll (Original Contents)

Psalms 101–103   Sirach 51
Psalm 112   Apostrophe to Zion
Psalms 109–110   Psalm 93
Psalms 113–118   Psalm 141
Psalm 104   Psalm 133
Psalm 147   Psalm 144
Psalm 105   Psalm 155
Psalm 146   Psalms 142–143
Psalm 148   Psalms 149–150
Psalms 120–132   Hymn to the Creator
Psalm 119   David's Last Words
Psalms 135–136 (with Catena) David's Compositions
Psalm 145 (with Postscript) Psalm 140
Psalm 154   Psalm 134
Plea for Deliverance   Psalm 151A
Psalm 139   Psalm 151B
Psalms 137–138

An Unusual Collection from Cave 4

Psalm 107   Apostrophe to Judah
Eschatological Hymn

Table 2: How to Locate Psalms in Traditional Order

PSALMS 1 THROUGH 89

■ *For Psalms 1 through 89 the scrolls almost always follow the order of the traditional Psalter, although not every composition is preserved. There are two important exceptions to this arrangement: Psalm 31 is followed directly by Psalm 33 in 4QPs^a and 4QPs^q, and Psalm 38 is followed directly by Psalm 71 in 4QPs^a. The fact that our translation begins with Psalm 2 does not mean that the first psalm was not known at Qumran, since Psalm 1:1 is quoted in the* Florilegium *from Cave 4 (4Q174).*

2 1 [Why do the nations conspire and the peoples plot in v]ain? 2 [The kings of the earth take their st]and [and the rulers take counsel together, against the LORD and against his anointed, saying], 3 "Let us te[ar *their bo*]nds[1] asunder, [and cast their cords from us!" 4 He who sits in the heavens laughs]; *the Lord*[2] holds them in derision. 5 Then he [will sp]eak to th[em in his wrath, and frighten them in his fury, as follows: 6 "But I have installed my king upon Z]ion, my holy mountain." 7 I will indeed make known [the LORD's decree: H]e said to me, "[You are] my [son; today I have begotten you. 8 As]k [of m]e, [and I will surely m]ake [the nations your inheritance, and the very ends of the earth your possession]." ▲

5 7 [But as for me, in the abundance of your steadfast love I will come into your house; I will bow down toward your holy temple in reverence for] you. 8 O LORD, [lead me in your righteousness because of my enemies; make straight] your way [before me]. 9 *There is nothing*[3] reli[able] in their mouths; [their hearts are destruction. Their throats are open graves; they f]latter [with their tongues]. 10 *Punish him,*[4] O Go[d]; let them fall by [their own sche]mes. [Because of their many transgressions cast them out, for they have rebelled against you. 11 But] let all those who take refuge in you [rejoice]; let them forever shout [for joy. Spread your protection over them, so that those who love your name may rejoice in you. 12 For yo]u bless the righteous, O LORD; you surround [them] with favor as *with a shield.*[5]

6 0 [For the Di]rector: on stringed instruments, [set to "Sheminith." A Psalm of David. 1 O LORD, do not rebu]ke me [in your anger], and do not pu[nish me]

Psalm 2. 11QPs^c: 2:1–8; 3QPs: 2:6–7.

   1. MT LXX. 11QPs^c seems to have an incorrect form of the Hebrew word.

   2. 11QPs^c MT. *the LORD* MT^mss.

Psalm 5. 4QPs^s: 5:7–12 [MT 5:8–13]; 4QPs^a: 5:8–12 [MT 5:9–13].

   3. 4QPs^a has about 10 more letters. *For there is no* MT LXX.

   4. Singular 4QPs^a. *Punish them* (plural) MT LXX.

   5. 4QPs^a. *like a shield* MT LXX.

Psalm 6. 4QPs^s: 6:0 [MT 6:1]; 4QPs^a: 6:1, 3 [MT 6:2, 4].

in your wrath. 2 [Have mercy upon me, O LORD; for I am faint; heal me, O LORD, for my bones are stressed. 3 My soul, too], is very frightened; [but as for you, Lord—how long]? ▲

7 12 [If one does not repent, God will sharpen his sword; he has bent his bow, and has made it ready. 13 He] has also prepared his deadly weapons, making his arrows burning shafts. 14 See how they labor with iniquity; they are pregnant with mischief, and bring forth [lies. 15 They make a pit and dig it out—but they fall into the hole that they have made. 16 Their mischief] returns upon their own heads, and their violence descends upon the crowns (of their heads). 17 I will [give thanks to the LO]RD because of his righteousness, and sing praise to the name of [the LORD Most High].

8 0 For the Director: [set to "The Gittith." A Psalm of David]. . . . 3 When I survey your heavens, the work of your fingers, the moon and the stars that you have established, 4 [what are human beings, that you take notice of them—mere mortals that you care about] them? 5 Yet you have made them only slightly lower than God himself, and you crown them with glory and honor! 6 You give them dominion over the works of your hands; you have put everything under their feet: 7 [all flocks and herds, and also the wild animals, 8 the birds of the sky, and the fish of the se]a, whatever travels along the paths of the seas. 9 O LORD, our Lord—how ma[jestic is your name in all] the earth!

9 26 [Let me be glad and rejoice in you; let me sing praise to your name], O Mo[st High].

3 When [my] enemies [turn back, they stumble and perish before you. 4 For you have up]held my rights and my case, *and you have sat*[7] on your throne; *you have passed*[8] [right]eous judgment. 5 [You have rebuked the nations, you have destroyed the wicked; you have blotted out their name] forever and ever. 6 [Desolation] has finish[ed off] the enemy for[ever. You have uprooted their cities—even the memory of them has perished! 7 But the LORD sits enthroned fore]ver, [he has established his throne for judgment]. . . . 11 Sing praises to the LORD who dwells in Zion; proclaim his deeds among the peoples. 12 For the one who avenges blood is mindful of them; he does not forget the cry of the afflicted.

13 Have mercy [upon me, O LORD! Consider what I suffer from those who hate me—you who lifts me up from the gates of death— 14 so that I may recount

---

Psalm 7. 5/6HevPs: 7:13–18 [MT 7:14–19].

Psalm 8. 5/6HevPs: 8:1, 4–10 [MT 8:2, 5–11].

Psalm 9. 11QPs^d: 9:3–6 [MT 9:4–7]; 11QPs^c: 9: 3–7 [MT 9:4–8]; 5/6HevPs: 9:12–21 [MT 9:13–22].

   6. Hebrew vs 3.

   7. 11QPs^c. *you have sat* MT LXX.

   8. 11QPs^c. *passing* MT LXX.

all your praises and, in the ga]tes of daughter Zion, rejoice in your deliverance. 15 The nations have sunk down in the pit that they dug; in the net that they hid their own feet are caught. 16 The LORD has made himself known, (for) he has executed judgment. The wicked are snared in the work of their own hands. Higgaion. Selah.

17 The wicked [will return to Sheol, yes all the nations] that forget God. 18 For the needy will not always be forgotten, nor will the hope of the poor perish forever. 19 Arise, [O LORD, do not let mortals triumph; let the nations] be judged before you. 20 Strike [them with fear, O LORD; let the nations know that they are only human]. Selah.

10 6 He thinks [in his heart, "I will not be moved; throughout all generations I will not experience mis]fortune." [7 His mouth is filled with cursing and lies and violence; under his tongue is trouble and iniquity]. 8 He lies in ambush near the villages; in hiding-places he murders the innocent. His eyes stealthily watch for his unfortunate victims. 9 He lurks in secret like a lion in its den; he lurks to catch the poor, then he catches the poor, when he draws them into his net. ▲

[17 O LORD, you will hear the desire of the humble; you will strengthen their heart, you will incline your ear 18 to do justice for the orphan and the oppressed], so that [people] of the earth may strike te[rror no more].·

11 0[9] For the Director: of David. 1 [In the LORD I take refuge. How can you then say to me: "Flee like a bird to your mountain; 2 for look, the wic]ked are bending their bows, *and they have aimed*[10] *arrows*[11] on the strings, to shoot in the dark at the upright in heart. 3 When the foundations are being destroyed, what can the righteous do?" 4 [The LORD—he is in his holy temple! The LORD— his throne is in heaven. His e]yes observe, *his gaze*[12] examines humankind. ▲

12 [3 May the LORD cut off all flattering lips, the tongue that makes great boasts, 4 those who say, "With] our ton[gues] we will triumph! Our lips [belong to us—who then is our master?" 5 "Because of the oppression of the poor, because of the groaning of the needy—now I will rise] up," says the LORD, "[*for the right*]*eous;*[13] I will pla[ce (them) in the safety for which they yearn." 6 The

---

Psalm 10. 5/6HevPs: 10:6, 8–9, 18.

Psalm 11. 5/6HevPs: 11:1–4. 4QCatenaA: 11:2 (quoted).

   9. Hebrew vs 1.

   10. 4QCatenaA. *they have fitted* MT LXX.

   11. 4QCatenaA LXX. *their arrow* MT.

   12. Literally, *his eyelids.*

Psalm 12. 11QPs^c: 12:4–8 [MT 12:5–9]; 5/6HevPs: 12:5–8 [MT 12:6–9].

   13. 11QPs^c. Not in MT LXX.

LORD's promises are pure pro]mises, like silver refined [*in a fur*]nace[14] on the ground, purif[ied seven times. 7 You, O LORD, will protect them; you will pre-serve] us from this generation [forev]er. 8 [On every s]ide wic[ked people strut about, when depravity is honored by society].

13 0 [For the Director: a Psalm of David. 1 How long, O LORD? Will you forget me forever? How lo]ng will you hide [your face from me? 2 How long must I wrestle with my thoughts, and have sorrow in my heart all day long? How] long must [my enemy] triumph [over me? 3 Consider and answer me, O LORD my God! Give light to my eyes, or I will sleep in death, 4 and my] enemy will say, "[I have overcome him," and my foes will rejoice when I stumble. 5 But I trust in your unfailing love; my heart rejoices in] your sal[vation. 6 So I will sing to the LORD, for he has been good to me].

14 0[15] [For the Director: of David. 1 The fool says in his heart, "There is no God." They are corrupt, they com]mit vile *wickedness;*[16] [there is no one who does good. 2 The LORD looks down from heaven upon humankind to see if there] are any who are [wi]se, [any who seek after God. 3 They have all gone astray, they are all alike corrupt; there is no one who does good—no, not even] one. 4 [Do they never learn, all these evildoers who devour my people as humans eat bread, and who do not] call [upon the LORD]? 5 *Toward this place*[17] [they will be in mighty dread, for God is with the company of the righteous. 6 You (evil-doers) frustrate the plans of the poor, but] the LORD is [their ref]uge. ▲

15 0[18] A Psalm of David. 1 O LORD, who [may dwell in your sanctuary? Who may live] on your holy hill? 2 The one who walks blamelessly, and who does what is right, and who speaks the truth [from his he]art; 3 *who*[19] does his friends no wrong, and casts no slur on his neighbor; 4 in whose eyes vile people are contemptible, but who honors those who fear the LORD; who keeps his oath without wavering, even to his own detriment; 5 who does not [lend his money at interest, and does not] accept a bribe against the innocent. The person who does these things [will never stum]ble.

---

14. Meaning unclear 11QPs^c. *in a furnace* 5/6HevPs MT. *tested* LXX.

Psalm 13. 5/6HevPs: 13:0–2 [MT 13:1–3]; 11QPs^c: 13:0–1, 3–4 [MT 13:1–2, 4–5].

Psalm 14. 11QPs^c: 14: 1–6; 5/6HevPs: 14:3(?).

   15. Hebrew vs 1.

   16. 11QPs^c. *deed(s)* MT LXX.

   17. Literally, *to there* 11QPs^c. *There* MT LXX.

Psalm 15. 5/6HevPs: 15:1–5.

   18. Hebrew vs 1.

   19. 5/6HevPs. *who does not slander with his tongue, who . . .* MT LXX.

16 0 A Miktam of David. 1 Keep me safe, O God, for I take refuge in you. . . . 7 I will bl[ess the LORD who gives me counsel; even at night my heart instru]cts me. 8 [I ke]ep [the LORD always before me; because he is at my right hand], I will not stumble. 9 There[fore my heart is glad, and my soul rejoices]; my [body also] rests without [a care. 10 Because you will not abandon me to the grave, nor will you let] your hol[y one see decay]. ▲

17 0²⁰ A prayer of [David. 1 Hear a righteous claim, O LORD, listen to my cry! Lend] ear *to* [*my prayer,*²¹ which is not from deceitful lips]. . . . 5 My [st]eps have held fast to [your p]at[hs, my feet have not slipped].

6 I am cal[ling] upon [you, for you will answer me, O God; incline your ear to me, hear] my prayer. 7 Favor (us) with [your stead]fast love, [O savior of those who take refuge] from their ad[versaries at] your ri[ght hand. 8 Guard me as *the ap]ple*²² of your eye; [hide me] under [the shadow of your wings], 9 from the wicked who *inter*[*rogate me,*²³ from my mortal e]nemies [who surround me. 10 They close their callous hearts], and they speak arrogantly [with their mouths]. 11 *They have expelled me,*²⁴ now they surro[und me; their eyes are focused to cast me on the ground. 12 They are like a lion ea]ger to tear his prey, like a young lion lurking in [ambush].

13 [Rise up, O LORD; confront them and bring them down! *Re*]*scue*²⁵ my life from the wi[cked with] your [sw]ord, 14 from such *plagu*[*es*]²⁶ *from* [*your*] *hand,*²⁷ [O LORD—from men of this world], whose only [por]tion is *in th*[*eir*] *life.*²⁸ May you fill their bellies with what you have [stor]ed up; [may their children have more than enough, and may they leave their fortune to] their [little ones]. 15 But as for me, I will lo[ok] at your face in righteousness; when I awa[ke], I will be fully content with your appearance.

18 0 [For the Director: of Davi]d [the servant of the LORD], who addressed to the LORD t[he] words of [this] song [on the day when the LORD delivered

---

Psalm 16. 5/6HevPs: 16:1; 4QPsᶜ: 16:7–9.

Psalm 17. 4QPsᶜ: 17:1; 4QCatenaA: 17:1; 8QPs: 17:5–9, 14; 11QPsᶜ: 17:9–15.

20. Hebrew vs 1.

21. 4QCatenaA. *my prayer* (with *to* implied) MT LXX.

22. Literally, *the pupil.*

23. 11QPsᶜ. *ravage me* MT LXX.

24. 11QPsᶜ LXX. (*In*) *our steps* MT. *They have directed me* MTᵐˢ.

25. 11QPsᶜ. *Now rescue* (jussive) MT.

26. 11QPsᶜ. *men* MT. *enemies* LXX.

27. 11QPsᶜ. *(by) your hand* MT LXX.

28. 11QPsᶜ LXX. *in (this) life* MT.

Psalm 18. 11QPsᶜ: 18:0–11 [MT 18:1–12]; 4QPsᶜ: 18:2–13, 15–16, 31–35, 38–40 [MT 18:

him from the ha]nd of all his enemies and from the hand of Sa[ul. He s]aid, 1 *"I tenderly care [for you,*[29] O LORD, my strength. 2 The LORD is] my [rock], my for[tr]ess, and my deliverer, my God, my rock [in whom] I take refu[ge, my shield and the horn of] my [sa]lvation, my stronghold."

3 *Let me call upon*[30] the LORD, who is wor[thy to be praised], and I am sa[ved] from my enemies. 4 [The cords of death entangled me, the torrents of perdition] struck me with fear. 5 The cords of Sheol coiled around me; the snares of death [confronted me. 6 In my distress I cal]led upon the LORD; I cried to my God for help. [He heard my voice from his temple, and my cry before him] reached his ears.

7 Then [the earth] reeled and quaked, [and the foundations of the mountains] shook [and trembled] because he was angry. 8 Smoke went [up from] his nos[trils, and consuming fire from his mouth; burning coals blazed forth from him. 9 Then he bo]wed the heavens and came down; thick dark[ness was un]der his feet. 10 [He rode upon a cherub and flew; he soared] on the wings of the wind. 11 [He made darkness his covering around him], his canopy thick clouds [in]*tensely dark*[31] with water. 12 [Out of the brightness before him] his thick clouds broke through, [with hailstones and bolts of lightning]. 13 The LORD [also thundered in the he]avens, [and the Most High uttered his voice, (with) hail-stones and bol]ts of lightning. [14 And he sent out his arrows, and scattered them; he flashed forth lightnings, and routed them. 15 Then the channels of waters ap-peared], and *the foundatio[ns*[32] of the world] were laid bare [at your rebuke, O LORD], at the blast of brea[th from your nostrils].

16 [He reached from on high] *and he took me;*[33] he drew me out [of mighty waters. 17 He delivered me from my strong enemy], and from [those who hated me; for they were too strong for me]. 18 They confronted me in the day of my disaster, but the LORD was my support. 19 He brought me out into a spacious place; he rescued me because he delighted in me.

20 The LORD has dealt with me according to my righteousness; according to the cleanness of my hands he has rewarded me. 21 For I have kept the ways of the LORD, and have not done evil (by turning away) from my God. 22 For all his ordi-nances were before me, and I did not turn away his statutes from me. 23 I have

---

3–14, 16–17, 32–36, 39–41]; 5/6HevPs: 18:5–11, 17–35, 37–42 [MT 18: 6–12, 18–36, 38–43]; 8QPs: 18:5–12 [MT 18:6–13]; 11QPs^d: 18:25–28, 38–41 [MT 26–29, 39–42]; MasPs^a: 18:25–28 [MT 18:26–29].

29. Probable reading 11QPs^c. *I love you* MT LXX.

30. 11QPs^c. *I call upon* MT.

31. Or, *darknesses* 11QPs^c. *dark* MT LXX.

32. Masculine noun 11QPs^c. Feminine noun 4QPs^c MT.

33. 11QPs^c. *he took me* MT LXX.

been blameless before him, and have kept myself from sin. 24 Therefore the LORD has recompensed me according to my righteousness, according to the cleanness of my hands in his sight.

25 With the faithful you show yourself faithful; with the blameless you show yourself blameless; 26 with the pure you show yourself pure; and with the crooked you show yourself crafty. 27 For you save a humble people, but will bring low those whose eyes are haughty. 28 For it is you who lights my lamp, O LORD; my God lights up my darkness. 29 For with you I can advance against a troop, and with my God I can scale a wall.

30 This God—his way is perfect; the promise of the LORD proves true; he is a shield for all who take refuge in him. 31 For who is God besides the LORD? And who is a rock except our God? 32 This God—who has armed me with strength and has made my way perfect. 33 He has made my feet like the feet of a deer, and has placed me on the heights. 34 He trains my hands for battle, so that my arms can bend a bow of bronze. 35 And you have given me the shield of your salvation, and your right hand has supported me; your *generous help*[34] has made me great. [36 You gave me a wide place for my steps under me, and my ankles did not buckle.]

37 I pursued my enemies and overtook them, and did not turn back till they were destroyed. 38 I struck them down so that they were not able to rise; they fell beneath my feet. 39 For you armed me with strength for the battle; you made my assailants sink under me. 40 And you made my enemies turn their backs to me, and I destroyed those who hated me. 41 They cried for help, but there was no one to save them—to the LORD, but he did not answer them. 42 I beat them fine, like dust before the wind; I poured them out like mud in the streets. ▲

19 3 [There is no speech nor are there words; their voice is not] he[ard, 4 yet their line goes out through all the earth, and their words to the end of the world. *In them*][35] he has pitched a te[nt for the sun, 5 which is like a bridegroom coming from his wedding canopy, like a strong man happy to run his course. 6 Its rising is from] the one end of the hea[vens, and its circuit to their other end, and nothing is hidden from its heat. 7 *The la]ws*[36] of the Lo[RD are perfect, reviving the soul; the testimony of the LORD is sure, making wise the simple]. ▲

22

■ *Psalm 22 is a favorite among Christians since it is often linked in the New Testament with the suffering and death of Jesus. A well-known and controversial reading is found*

---

34. Literally, *humility* or *condescension*.

Psalm 19. 11QPs^c: 19:3–7 [MT 19:4–8].

35. I.e., the heavens.

36. 11QPs^c. *The law* MT LXX.

Psalm 22. 5/6HevPs: 22:3–8, 14–20 [MT 22:4–9, 15–21]; 4QPs^f: 22:14–17 [MT 15–18].

*in verse 16, where the Masoretic Text reads "Like a lion are my hands and feet,"
whereas the Septuagint has "They have pierced my hands and feet." Among the
scrolls the reading in question is found only in the Psalms scroll found at Nahal Hever
(abbreviated 5/6HevPs), which reads* "They have pierced *my hands and my feet*"!

3 But you are the [holy one], who inhabits the praises of Israel. 4 Our ancestors put their trust in you; they trusted; *you delivered them.*[37] 5 They cried to you,
and were saved; they trusted in you, and were not put to shame. 6 But [as for me],
I am a worm, and not human, scorned by others and despised by the people. 7 All
who see me [ridicule me; they make faces at me] and shake their heads: 8 "Commit yourself to the LORD! Let him deliver—let him rescue him, since he delights
in him!" ▲

14 [I have] been poured out [like water, and all] my bon[es are out of joint.
My heart has turned to wax; it has mel]ted away in my breast. 15 [My strength is
dried up like a potsherd], and my tongue *melts in* [*my mouth.*[38] *They*] *have placed*
[*me*][39] *as the dust of death.*[40] 16 [For] dogs are [all around me]; a gang of evil[doers]
encircles me. *They have pierced*[41] my hands and my feet. 17 [I can count all of my
bones; people stare and gloat over me. 18 They divide my garments among
themselves, and they cast lots for my] clothes.

19 But as for you, [O LORD, do not be far away! O you my strength, come
quickly to my aid. 20 Deliver my soul from the sword, my precious life from the
power of the dogs!] ▲

23 [1 The LORD is my shepherd, I shall not want. 2 He makes me lie down [in
green pas]tures; he leads me beside quiet waters; 3 he restores my soul. He
guides me in the right paths for his name's sake. 4 Even when I walk through the
[valley of deepest gloom, I will fear no harm], because you are with me; your rod
and your staff—they comfort me. 5 You prepare [a table before me in the very
pre]sence of my enemies; *you anoint my head with oil;*[42] my cup overflows.
6 [Surely goodness and stead]fast love will run after me all the days of my life, and
I shall dwell in the house of the LORD forever.

24 1 The earth is the LORD's, and everything in it, the world, and [those who
live in it. 2 For he foun]ded it upon the seas, and established it [on the
riv]ers. ▲

---

37. 5/6HevPs. *and you delivered them* MT LXX.

38. Probable meaning 4QPs[f]. *sticks to the roof of my mouth* MT LXX similar.

39. Probable meaning 4QPs[f]. *and you have laid me* MT LXX.

40. 4QPs[f]. *in the dust of death* MT LXX.

41. 5/6HevPs MT[mss] LXX. *Like a lion are* MT.

Psalm 23. 5/6HevPs: 23:2–6.

42. I.e., you welcome me as an honored guest.

Psalm 24. 5/6HevPs: 24:1–2.

25 [0 Of David. 1 To you, O LORD, I lift up my soul. 2 O my God, in you I trust]. Do not let me be put to shame; [do not let my enemies gloat over me. 3 Moreover, no one who waits for you will be put to shame]; those who are inex[cusably] treacherous [will be put to shame].

[4 Show me your ways, O LORD, teach me your paths. 5 Guide me] in your truth; tea[ch me,[43] for you are the God of my salvation. I wait for you all day long. 6 Remember, O Lo]RD, your great mercy [and your steadfast love, for they have been from time immemorial. 7 Do not] remem[ber the sins of my youth or my transgressions; according to your steadfast love remember me, for the sake of your own goodness, O LORD]! . . . 15 My eyes are constantly [toward the LORD, for he will release my feet from the snare].

26 [6 I wash my hands in innocence, and go around your altar, O LORD, 7 proclaiming al]oud a song of th[anksgiving, and tell of all your wonderful deeds. 8 O LORD, I love] the house whe[re you live, and the place where your glory dwells. 9 Do not sweep away] my soul wi[th sin]ners, no[r my life] with [bloodthirsty people, 10 in whose hands are wick]ed schemes, and whose right hands are [fu]ll of bribes. 11 [But as for me, I will live a blameless life; redeem me], *and preserve my life.*[44] 12 My feet stand [on level grou]nd; [in the great assembly I will bless the LORD].

27 [0 Of David.] 1 The LORD is [my li]ght [and my salvation—whom shall I fear? The LORD is my life's stronghold—of whom shall I be afraid? . . . 12 Do not turn me over to the will of my foes, for] false [witnesses have risen up against me], and they brea[the out violence. 13 I am still confident that I will see] the LORD's [goodness] in the lan[d of the living. 14 Wait for the LORD: be strong *and*] *take heart*[45]—[wait for the LORD]!

28 [0 Of David. 1 To you I call, O LORD]; my rock, do not [tu]rn a deaf ear to [me. For if you remain silent to me], I will become like those who go do[wn to the Pit. 2 Hear the sound of my pleas], as I cry to you for help, [as I lift up my hands] toward [your most ho]ly sanctuary.

3 [Do not drag me away with the wicked, with those who car]ry [out evil—who speak amicably with their neighbors while malice is in their hearts. 4 Repay] them [in accordance with their deeds and the evil of their actions! Repay them] for what [their han]ds have done, [and bring back upon them their just deserts! 5

Psalm 25. 11QPs^c: 25:2–7; 5/6HevPs: 25:4–6; 4QPs^a: 25:15.

43. 11QPs^c. *and teach me* MT LXX.

Psalm 26. 4QPs^r: 26:7–12.

44. 4QPs^r. *and be merciful to me* MT LXX.

Psalm 27. 4QPs^r: 37:1; 4QPs^c: 37:12–14.

45. Literally, *and let your heart take courage.*

Psalm 28. 4QPs^c: 28:1–5.

Since they show] no [regard for the works of the LORD and for the work of his hands, he will tear them down and (never) build them up again]. ▲

29 0 A Psalm of Da[vid]. 1 Ascribe to the LORD, O heavenly beings, ascribe to the LORD glory and strength! 2 Ascribe to the LORD the glory due his name; wor[ship the LORD] in holy splendor! ▲

30 8 [I cried to you, O LORD, and to *the Lo*]RD[46] [I made supplication: 9 "What profit is there in my death, in my going down] *to the Pit?*[47] [Can the dust] prai[se you? Can it proclaim your faithfulness]? 10 *The LORD [heard] and was mer[ciful*[48] to me! O LORD, be my helper!" 11 You turned] my mourning [into dancing; you removed my sackcloth, and clothed me with joy], 12 so that [my being] may sing pr[aise to you and not be silent. O LORD my God, I will give you thanks] forever.

31 [0 For the Director: a Psalm of David. 1 In you, O LORD, I take refuge; let me never be put to shame; in your righteousness deliver me. 2 Incline your ear to] me; come quickly to my rescue. Be a rock of refuge for me, a strong fortress to save me. 3 Because you are my rock and my fortress, for your name's sake lead me and guide me. 4 Free [me from the trap that has been secretly laid for me, for you are my refuge. 5 Into your hands I commit my sp]irit; you have re-deemed me, O LORD, God of truth.

6 I hate those who ho[nor worthless idols—as for me, I trust in the LORD. 7 I will be glad and rejoice in your steadfast love, for you have seen my afflic]tion and have understood the anguish of my soul. 8 You have not abandoned me to the power of the enemy, but have set my feet in a spacious place. 9 Have mercy upon me, O LORD, for I am in distress; my eyes grow weak with grief, as do my soul and body. 10 For my life is consumed with sorrow and my years with sighing; my strength fails because of my suffering, and my bones waste away. 11 Because of [all my ene]mies I have become a reproach, especially to my neighbors, an object of dread to my acquaintances—people who see me in the street [run away from] me. 12 I have passed out of mind like one who is dead; I have become like broken pottery. 13 For I hear the slander of many—there is terror all around!—as they conspire against me and plot to take my life.

14 But [for my part] I trust in you, O LORD; I say, "You are [my God]." 15 My times are in your hands; deliver me from the power of my enemies and my

---

Psalm 29. 5/6HevPs: 29:1–2.

Psalm 30. 4QPs[r]: 30:8–12 [MT 30:9–13].

46. 4QPs[r] MT[mss]. *the Lord* MT. *my God* LXX.

47. 4QPs[r]. *into the Pit* MT (different preposition).

48. 4QPs[r] LXX. *Hear, O LORD, and be merciful to me!* MT.

Psalm 31. 5/6HevPs: 31:2–21 [MT 31:3–22]; 4QPs[a]: 31:22–23 [MT 31:23–24]; 4QPs[q]: 31:23–34 [MT 31:24–25].

persecutors. 16 Let your face shine upon your servant; save me in your unfailing love. 17 LORD, [do not let me] be put to shame, for I have called out to you; but let the wicked be put to shame, and let them lie silent in Sheol. 18 Let the lying lips be dumb—those which speak arrogantly against the righteous, with pride and contempt.

19 How vast is your goodness, which you have stored up for those who fear you, which you bestow on those who take refuge in you in full sight of everyone! 20 In the secret place of your presence you hide them from human plots; under your shelter you keep them safe from accusing tongues.

21 May the LORD be blessed, for he has wonderfully shown his steadfast love to me when I was in a besieged city. 22 [But as for me, I said in my alarm, "I am cut off from your si]ght." [Yet you heard my supplications when I cried out to you for help. 23 Love the LORD, all] his s[aints! The LORD pre]serves the faithf[ul, but pays back in full the one w]ho acts haugh[tily. 24 Be str]ong [and let] your hea[rt take courage], all those who wait for the LORD.

> ■ *Psalm 31 is followed by Psalm 32 in the Masoretic Text and the Septuagint—but this is not the case in the Dead Sea Scrolls, where it is followed by Psalm 33 in both 4QPsᵃ and 4QPsᵩ. The fact that Psalm 32, which is a song of thanksgiving, is not found elsewhere in any scroll raises the questions of whether it was originally included but is now lost, or whether it was unknown at Qumran.*

33 ⁴⁹0 *Of David.*⁵⁰ *A Song, a Psalm.*⁵¹ 1 [Give a ringing cry to the LORD, O you righteous ones]; praise is fitti[ng for the upright]. 2 Give than[ks] to the L[OR]D with a lyre; make music to him on a ten-stringed harp. 3 Sing to [*the LORD*⁵² a new song; play skillfully on the strings] with a shout of joy. 4 For [the word of the LO]RD [is upright], and all his work takes place in faithfulness. 5 He loves righteousness [and justice; the earth is full of the LORD's steadfast love]. 6 By the word of the LO[RD the heavens were ma]de, and by the breath of his mouth all their starry host. 7 He gathered the waters [from the sea] like a heap; [he put the deeps into storehouses]. *He made the waters, [they stood firm like] a wineskin.*⁵³ 8 Let all the earth fear the LORD; [let all the inhabitants of the world] stand in awe of

---

Psalm 33. 4QPsᵩ: 33:1–7, X, 8–14, 16–18; 4QPsᵃ: 33:2, 4–6, 8, 10, 12.

49. Preceded by Psalm 31 4QPsᵃ 4QPsᵩ. Preceded by Psalm 32 MT LXX. Joined directly with Psalm 32 in some MTᵐˢˢ.

50. 4QPsᵩ. not in MT; *for David* LXX.

51. 4QPsᵩ. Not in MT. *for David* LXX.

52. Not preserved in the scrolls, but spacing suggests this reading as in some MTᵐˢˢ. *to him* MT LXX.

53. Longer text, precise meaning not clear 4QPsᵩ (cf. Ps 78:13; Exod 15:8). Not in MT LXX.

him. 9 [For he spoke] *and it comes into being;*[54] h[e gave the command and it stood fi]rm. 10 The LORD foils the plans of the nations; he thwarts the schemes [of the peoples. 11 The counsel of the LORD will stand forever, the pla]ns of his heart [from generation to generation].

12 Blessed is the nation whose God is the LORD, the people whom he chose [for his inheritance. 13 The LORD looks from heaven, he sees all hu]mankind. 14 From his dwelling where he sits he watches all [the inhabitants of *the wor*]*ld*[55]— 15 [he who for]ms [the hearts of them all, and considers all their actions. 16 No ki]ng is saved by the might of his army; [no war]rior [is delivered by his great strength. 17 The war-horse is a false basis for victory; despite its great strength it cannot sav]e anyone. 18 But the eye of the LORD is on [those who fear him, on those who place their hope in his unfailing love]. ▲

34 20 [He keeps all his bones, not one of them is brok]en. 21 [Evil] will sl[ay the wicked; and those who hate the righteous will be held guilty]. ▲

35 [0 Of David. 1 Contend, O LORD, with those who contend with me; fight against those who fight against me]. 2 Take hold of a buck[ler and large shield, and rise up to help me! 3 Draw the spear and javelin against my pursuers; say to my soul, "I am your salvation." 4 May those who seek my life be disgraced and put to shame; may those who plot harm against me be diverted] and thwarted. [5 Let them be like chaff before the wind, with the angel of the LORD driving them on. 6 Let their way be dark and slippery], with the angel of the L[ORD pursuing them. 7 For without cause they hid their net for me; without cause they dug a pit for my life].

8 [Let ruin overtake them by surprise. And may the net that they hid] entangle them; [may they fall in it, to their ru]in. [9 Then my soul will rejoice in the LORD and delight in his deliverance. 10 *My entire being*[56] will exclaim, "O LORD, who] is like you? You rescue [the poor from those too strong for them, the poor and the needy from those who rob them." 11 Malicious witnesses come forward; they question me on things of which I know nothing. 12 They repay me] evil for go[od, to the bereavement of my soul. 13 But as for me, when they were sick, my clothing was sackcloth; I humbled mys]elf [with] fasting; [and my prayer turned back upon my bosom. 14 I we]nt about (in mourning) as for my friend and as for my brother; [as one who laments a mother] I bowed down with gloom. 15 But at my stumbling they rejoiced, *they gathered together;*[57] they gathered together

---

54. Probable meaning 4QPs^q. *and it came into being* MT LXX.

55. 4QPs^q LXX. *the earth* MT.

Psalm 34. 4QPs^a: 34:20–21 [MT 34:21–22].

Psalm 35. 4QPs^a: 35:2, 13–18, 20, 26–27; 4QPs^q: 35:4, 6, 8, 10, 12, 14–15, 17, 19–20; 4QPs^c: 35:27–28.

56. Literally, *all my bones.*

57. 4QPs^a. *and they gathered together* MT LXX.

against me; smitten ones whom [I did n]ot [know slandered me without ceasing. 16 Like godless jesters] at a feast *they gnashed*[58] *their teeth*[59] at me. 17 O LORD, for how long will you look on? Rescue [my l]ife [from their ravages, my only life from the lions. 18 I will give you thanks] in the great congregation; in the mighty throng I [will praise y]ou.

19 [Do not] let those who are [wrong]fully my enemies gloat over me, [neither let those who hate me for no reason wink their eyes at me. 20 For they do not spe]ak [peace], but *toward*[60] tho[se who are qui]et in the land, they devise [words] of deceit. ▲

26 Let those who rejoice at [my] distress [be ashamed and confused together. Let those who exalt themselves against me be clothed with shame and dishonor. 27 Let those who delight in my vindication shout for joy and rejoice. And let them say continually, "May the LORD be magnified]; *you who delight in*[61] the welfare of [his servant." 28 And my tongue will declare your righteousness and your praise all the day long].

36 0 [For] the Director: of David, the servant of the LORD. [1 Transgression speaks to the wicked deep in my heart. There is no fear of God before their eyes. 2 For they flatter] themselves in their own eyes, concerning the discovery of their iniquity and [hatred of it. 3 The words of their mouth are wickedness and deceit; they have ceased to act prudently and do good. 4 They plan wickedness] upon their beds; *they conspire on every path*[62] that is n[ot good; they do not reject evil].

5 [Your] lovingkindness, O LORD, is *from the heavens;*[63] [your faithfulness is to the clouds. 6 Your righteousness is like the mountains of God; your justice is like the great deep]; *by it*[64] you deliver [both humans and animals alike, O LORD. 7 How precious is your steadfast love, O God! All people take refuge in the shadow of your wings. 8 They drink of the abundance of your house], and [you give them drink] from the river [of your delights]. . . . 12 [There the evildoers lie fallen—cast down, and unable to ri]se!

---

58. 4QPs[a] LXX. *gnashing* MT.

59. 4QPs[a]. *their teeth* MT LXX.

60. 4QPs[a]. *against* MT LXX.

61. With people as subject 4QPs[a] LXX. *who delights in* (with God as subject) MT.

Psalm 36. 4QPs[a]: 36:0, 2, 4–6, 8 [MT 36:1, 3, 5–7, 9]; 11QPs[d]: 36:12 [MT 36:13].

62. Literally, *he conspires on every path* 4QPs[a]. *they station themselves on a path* MT. *he stations himself on every path* LXX.

63. 4QPs[a]. *in the heavens* MT. *in heaven* MT[mss]. *(in) the heaven* LXX.

64. Probably denoting *your righteousness* 4QPs[a]. Not in MT LXX.

37 0 Of David. 1 Do n[ot fret because of evildoers; do n]ot be envious of [wrongd]oers. 2 [For like the grass they will soon wither; like green pl]ants they will fade away. 3 Tru[st in the LORD, and do good; live in the land and enj]oy security. 4 So ta[ke delight in the LORD, and he will give you the] lon[gings of your heart]. ▲

18 The LORD acknowledges [the days of the blameless, and their inheritance will endure forever]. 19 They will not be disappointed in [bad ti]mes, [and in days of famine they will enjoy plenty]. ▲

38 0 [A Psalm of David. For the memorial offering. 1 O LORD, Do not rebuke me in your wrath, and in] your [bur]ning rage do not ch[asten me. 2 For your arrows have sunk into me, and your hand has pressed down upon me. 3 There is no health in my body be]cause of your indignation; [there is no sound]ness in my bones be[cause of my sin. 4 For my iniquities have gone over my head; like a burden they weigh too heavy for me].

5 My w[oun]ds [grow foul] *and fester*[65] because of [my] folly. [6 I am bent over and greatly bowed down; all the day I go about mourning. 7 For my loins are filled with burning and there is no] health in my body. 8 I am *xxxx*[66] [and greatly crushed; I groan because of the agitation of my heart. 9 O Lord, all my desire is known to you and *my sighing] is not hidden*[67] from you. 10 [My heart throbs, my strength fails me and as for the light of my eyes, even these are not with me. 11 *I have become a plague bef]ore my friends and compani[ons,*[68] and my neighbors stay far away].▲

15 [For you, O LORD, I wait]. O Lord, *you will answer me,*[69] *for (you are) my God.*[70] 16 [I said, "May they not rejoice over me], *those who boast*[71] [against me when my foot slips]." 17 For I am re[ady to fall] and my pain is continually before me. 18 *Thus*[72] [I confess] *my iniquities;*[73] I am anxious because of *my sins.*[74] 19 But

---

Psalm 37. 11QPs[d]: 37:1–4; 4QPs[c]: 37:18–19.

Psalm 38. 4QPs[a]: 38:2, 4, 6, 8–10, 12, 16–23 [MT 38:3, 5, 7, 9–11, 13, 17–24].

65. 4QPs[a] LXX. *fester* MT.

66. Meaning unclear (*npg"*) 4QPs[a]. *I am benumbed* MT. *I was afflicted* LXX.

67. Subject *(my sighing)* treated as masculine 4QPs[a]. Subject treated as feminine MT.

68. 4QPs[a] (cf. Ps 88:19; Job 19:13–14). *My friends and companions stand aloof from my affliction* MT. *My friends and my neighbors drew near before me and stood still* LXX.

69. 4QPs[a]. *you will answer, O Lord* MT LXX.

70. 4QPs[a] (ending vs 15). *my God. 17 For . . .* (beginning vs 16) MT LXX.

71. 4QPs[a]. *they magnify themselves* MT LXX.

72. 4QPs[a]. *For* MT LXX.

73. 4QPs[a]. *my iniquity* MT LXX.

74. 4QPs[a]. *my sin* MT LXX.

those who are *my enemies without cause*[75] are numerous, and ma[ny are those who hate me] *by deceiving me.*[76] 20 *Those who perform*[77] evil instead of good *plunder me*[78] *instead of a good thing.*[79] 21 Do not forsake me, [*my*] *God;* [*O LORD,*[80] do not be fro]m me. 22 Make haste *for me*[81] to help me, O Lord, my salvation.

> ■ *In 4QPsᵃ, Psalm 38 is followed by Psalm 71, not by Psalm 39 as in the Masoretic Text and the Septuagint. At first glance this seems strange, but there is in fact a good explanation. Further study shows that there are only two Psalms—38 and 70— whose titles designate them "for the memorial offering." It appears that Psalm 71 was meant to follow a Psalm for the memorial offering; in the Masoretic Text this Psalm is 70, while in 4QPsᵃ it is 38. Both combinations are thus equally logical and valid.*

71[82] 1 In you, O LORD, I have taken refuge; let me ne[ver] be ashamed. 2 [With your righteousness] *deliver me;*[83] *rescue me,*[84] incline your ear to me, *deliver me.*[85] 3 Be to me a rock of habitation; *my heart/a lion xxxx;*[86] for you are my rock and my fortress. 4 O my God, rescue me from the hand of the wicked, from the grasp of the unjust and *the ruthless.*[87]

5 For y[ou, O Lord, are my hope], my trust, O [L]ORD, from my youth. 6 Upon you I have leaned from [birth]; you are *my protector*[88] from my mother's womb. [My praise is continually of you]. 7 I have become as a wonder to many, but you are my strong refuge. 8 My mouth is filled with your praise and with [your glo]ry all the day. 9 Do not cast me off in the time of old age; do not fors[ake me] when my strength is spent. 10 For my enemies speak against [me; those who lie in wait for my life conspire] together, 11 saying, "God has forsaken

---

75. 4QPsᵃ. *my vigorous enemies* MT LXX.
76. 4QPsᵃ. *wrongfully* MT LXX.
77. 4QPsᵃ. *those who repay* LXX. *and those who repay* MT.
78. Meaning unclear 4QPsᵃ. *they oppose me* MT LXX.
79. 4QPsᵃ. *because I follow good* MT.
80. 4QPsᵃ. *O LORD; my God* MT LXX.
81. 4QPsᵃ. Not in MT LXX.

Psalm 71. 4QPsᵃ: 71:1–14.

82. Preceded directly by Psalm 38 4QPsᵃ. Preceded by Psalm 70 MT LXX.
83. Imperative 4QPsᵃ LXX. *deliver me* (imperfect with imperative force) MT.
84. 4QPsᵃ. *and rescue me* MT LXX. Not in LXXᵐˢ (cf. 31:2).
85. 4QPsᵃ (cf. 31:3). *and save me* MT LXX.
86. *my heart/a lion* (meaning unclear, some further text is missing) 4QPsᵃ. *to come continually you have commanded* MT. *a strong fortress* LXX (cf. 31:3).
87. 4QPsᵃ (cf. Isa 1:17). *the (one who is) ruthless* (participle) MT LXX.
88. 4QPsᵃ LXX. *the one who delivers me* MT.

him; pursue him, *sei[ze him,*[89] for there is no one to deliver (him)." 12 O Go]d, [do not be far from me; O my God], come quickly [to] my a[id]. 13 May [my accusers] be put to shame *and let them be consumed;*[90] [may those who seek my injury be covered with reproach and disgrace].

[14 But as for me, I] will ho[pe continually], and will pr[aise you] all the more. 15 [My mouth will tell of your righteousness, (and) of your salvation all the day long, although I cannot know their magnitude]. ▲

39 12 [Hear my prayer, O LORD, and] lis[ten to my cry; do not be deaf to my tears. For I am your visitor], a foreigner [like all my forebears. 13 Look away from me, so my face may light up before I pass away] and am no mo[re].

40 0 For the Direct[or: a Psalm of David]. ▲

42 4 [I remember] these things, [as I pour out my soul within me: I used to go with the multitude, leading them to the house of God, with shouts] of joy and thanks[giving]—a festive throng moving in proces[sion]! ▲

43 1 [Vindicate me, O God, and plead my cause against an ungodly nation]; rescue me [from deceitful and un]just people. 2 For [you are *the God who protects me;*[91] why have you rejected me? Why must I] go about [mourning] because of [my enemy's persecu]tion? 3 [Send out your light and your truth; let them guide me, and bring me t]o [your holy mountain and to the places where you live]. ▲

44 2 [You drove out the nations with your own hand, but you planted our ancestors; you crushed the peo]ples, but you spre[ad] them far. 3 [For it was not by the sword that they won the land, nor did their own arm bri]ng them victory—but [it was your right hand, and] your [arm], and the lig[ht of your presence, for you took pleasure in them].

4 [You] are [my K]ing, [O God; command victories for Jacob! 5 Through you we push back our enemies; through your name we trample our assailants. 6 For I do] no[t trust in] my bo[w, nor can my sword save me. 7 But you have deliv]ered us from [our enemies; *you*[92] have put to shame those who hate us]. 8 In Go[d we make our boast continually, and we will praise your name forever]. Se[lah]. ▲

---

89. 4QPs^a. *and seize him* MT LXX.

90. 4QPs^a MT^mss LXX. *let them be consumed* MT.

Psalm 39. 11QPs^d: 39:12–13 [MT 39:13–14].

Psalm 40. 11QPs^d: 40:1 [MT 40:2].

Psalm 42. 4QPs^c: 42:4 [MT 42:4]; 4QPs^u: 42:4 [MT 42:5].

Psalm 43. 11QPs^d: 43:1–3.

91. Literally, *the God of my protection*.

Psalm 44. 1QPs^c: 44:3–5, 7, 9, 23–25; 4QPs^c: 44:8–9(?).

92. 4QPs^a. *and you* MT LXX.

22 [Yet for your sake we are being killed all day long, and are considered] as sheep [to be slaughtered. 23 Wake up, LORD, why are you sleeping? G]et up, do no[t reject us] forever. 24 [Why do you h]ide [your face? Why do] you [ignore our misery and our oppression]? ▲

45 5 [Your arrows are sharp in the heart of] the king's ene[mies; let the peoples fall under you]. *A thousand* . . . [93] 6 [Your throne, O God, will last forever and ever. Your royal scepter is a sc]epter of justice. 7 You lo[ve righteousness and hate wickedness. Therefore] G[od, your God, has anointed you] with the oil of joy beyond [your companions. 8 All your garments are fragrant with myrrh, aloes, and cassia]. From ivory palaces stringed instruments ma[ke you glad. 9 Daughters of kings are among your ladies of honor]; at your right hand stands the queen in gol[d of Ophir. 10 Listen, O daughter, pay attention] and give ear; forget about [your peo]ple [and your father's house]. ▲

47 0 [For the Director: of the Korahites. A Psalm. 1 Clap your hands, all you nations; shout to Go]d with cries [of joy]. ▲

48 0 A Song. A Psa[lm of the sons of Korah. 1 Great is the LORD, and highly to be praised in the city of] our God. [His holy mountain, 2 beautiful in its loftiness, is the joy of the whole earth—Mount Zion, like the utmost heights of Zaphon], the cit[y of the great Ki]ng. 3 [God is in its citadels; he has shown himself to be a sure defense].

4 [For] when kin[gs[94] joined forces, they advanced together. 5 When they saw it, they were amazed; they panicked and took to flight]. 6 Trembling se[ized them there—pains like those of a woman in labor, 7 as when you shatter the ships of Tarshish with an east wind].

8 As [we have heard, so we have witnessed in the city of the LORD of hosts, in the city of our God. God will make it secure forever. Selah]. ▲

49 [0 For the Director]: of the sons of Korah. A Psa[lm. 1 Hear this, all you peoples; give ear, all you who live in this wo]rld, 2 both [low and high, rich and p]oor [alike]. 3 My mouth will speak wis[dom; the meditation of my heart will be insight. 4 I will turn] my ear to a proverb; I will [uncover my riddle on the harp].

5 [Why should I be] afraid in tim[es of] trouble, when the wic[kedness of my

---

Psalm 45. 4QPs^c: 45:7–10 [MT 45:8–11]; 11QPs^d: 45:5–7 [MT 45:6–8].

93. Here 11QPs^d contains a longer text than MT and LXX, but only one Hebrew word is preserved.

Psalm 47. 4QPs^a: 47:1 [MT 47:2].

Psalm 48. 4QPs^j: 48:0–2, 4, 6, 8 [MT 48:1–3, 5, 7, 9].

94. 4QPs^j. *the kings* MT LXX.

Psalm 49. 4QPs^c: 49:0–16 [MT 49:1–17]; 4QPs^j: 49:5(?), 8–11, 14, 16(?) [MT 49:6?, 9–12, 15, 17?].

persecutors surrounds] me— 6 [those who trust in] their we[alth] and boast of their [great riches? 7 Truly, no one can redeem another person's life], or give to God a ransom for him, 8 [for the ran]som for their life is [costly]—*he will be ill*[95] forever, 9 so that he should live on forever *and*[96] never [see decay]. 10 But he will see that even wise people die; fools and senseless people perish [together] and leave their wealth to others. 11 [Their minds are on] their houses forever, and their dwelling-places for all generations, [although they had named] lands after [them]selves.

12 But humans with their riches *cannot understand;*[97] [they are like the anim]als that perish. 13 Such is the fate of the overconfident, [and of their followers who approve of their sayings]. Selah. 14 Like sheep [they are destined] for Sheol; [death will feed on them]. The upright [will rule] over them in the morning; [their form will be for Sheol to] consume, [so that] they will have [no home]. 15 But God will redeem [my life from the power of Sheol], for he will receive me. Selah.

16 [Do not be afraid when] some [grow rich], when the wealth of their house [increases], ▲

50 [3 Our God comes and does not stay silent: before him a fire] d[evours], and around him a mighty tempest. 4 He summons the heavens above and the earth, so that he may judge his people: 5 "Gather to me my faithful ones, who ma[de a] co[ve]nant with me by sacrifi[ce." 6 The heavens declare his righteousness, for God himself is judge. Selah]!

7 ["Hear, O my people, and I will speak, O I]srael, [and I will testify against you. I am God, your God]."▲

14 "[Offer to God a sacrifice of thanksgiving, and ful]fill [your vo]ws to the Most High. 15 [Then call upon me in the day of trouble]; I will deli[ver you, and you will glorify me]."

16 [But to the wicked God says], "What right do you have to recite [my statutes, or to take my covenant on your lips]? 17 For you hate (my) instruc[tion, and you cast my words behind you]. 18 When you see *thieves,*[98] you connive with them, and you throw in [your lot] with adulterers. 19 You let loose your mouth for evil, and your tongue devises deceit. 20 You sit and speak against your neighbor, and even slan[der] your own mother's child. 21 These are the things you have done, and I kept quiet—you thought I was just like you. But now I rebu[ke you], and line up the evidence before you.

---

95. Meaning unclear 4QPs[j]. *he should cease trying* 4QPs[j] MT LXX(?).

96. 4QPs[c] MT[mss]. Not in MT LXX[mss]. *because* LXX.

97. 4QPs[c] LXX. *cannot endure* MT.

Psalm 50. 11QPs[e]: 50: 3–7; 4QPs[c]: 50:14–23.

98. Literally, *a thief.*

22 "So think about this, [you who] forget God, or [I will te]ar you to pieces—with no one to rescue you. 23 Those who offer thanksgiving as a sacrifice honor me, and I will show the salvation of God to those who put their ways in order."

51 0 For the Director: a Psalm of David, when the prophet Nathan came to him, after he had committed adultery [with] Bathsheba. 1 Have mercy upon me, O God, according to your steadfast love. According to your abundant compassion blot out my transgressions. 2 Wash me thoroughly from my iniquity, and clean[se] me from my sin. 3 For I acknowledge my transgressions, [and my] si[n is always in fr]ont of me. 4 [Against you and you alone have I sinned, and] do[ne what is evil in your sight], so [that] you are proved right [in your sentence and without fault when you pass judgment]. ▲

52 3 [You love evil rather than good, falseho]od [rather than speaking what is right. Selah. 4 You love all words that devour, you de]ceitful [tongue]. 5 But God will also break you down forever—[he will snatch you up], drive you away from your tent, and uproot you from the land of *the living.*[99] Selah. 6 The righteous will [s]ee this and be afraid; *they will laugh*[100] at (the evildoer), saying, 7 "Look, here is the person who would not make God his refuge, but trusted instead in his abundant wealth and grew strong by destroying others."

8 But as for me, I am like a green olive tree in God's house; I will trust in [G]od's steadfast love forever and ever. 9 *Then*[101] I will give you thanks forever, because of what you have done; and in the presence of *your faithful one*[102] I will [ho]pe in your name, for it [is good].

53 0 For the Director: set to "Mahalath." A Maskil of Da[vid. 1 Fools say in their hearts, "There is no God." They are corrupt and commit loathsome acts; there is no one] who do[es good].

[2 God looks down from heaven on humankind to see if there are any who are wise, who seek after God]. 3 *All*[103] have fallen away; togeth[er they have become morally corrupt; there is no one who does good—not even one. 4 Will these evildoers never learn—those who devour my people like they eat] br[ead], *and who do not call*[104] upon God? [5 There they will be in great terror where there was

---

Psalm 51. 4QPs^c: 51:0–3 [MT 51:1–5]; 4QPs^j: 51:0–4 [MT 51:2–6].

Psalm 52. 4QPs^c: 52:3–9 [MT 52:5–11].

   99. 4QPs^c. *living* (no article) MT LXX.

   100. 4QPs^c LXX^mss. *and they will laugh* MT LXX.

   101. 4QPs^c. Not in MT LXX.

   102. Singular 4QPs^c MT^mss. *your faithful ones* (plural) MT LXX.

Psalm 53. 4QPs^c: 53:0 [MT 53:1]; 4QPs^a: 53:3–4, 6 [MT 53:4–5, 7].

   103. 4QPs^a LXX (cf. 14:3). *All of them* MT.

   104. Literally, *and who does not call* (singular) 4QPs^a. *and they do not call* (plural) MT LXX.

nothing to dread; for God will scatter the bones of those who attack you. You have already put them to shame, for God has rejected them].

[6 O that he may gr]ant [the deliverance of Israel] *on the day of Zion!*[105] [When God restores the fortunes of his people, let Jacob rejoice, let Israel be glad].

54 0 [For the Director: on stringed instruments. A Maskil of David, when the Ziphites came and told Saul, "Is not David] hiding among us?" 1 O God, [save me by your name, and vindicate me by your might. 2 O God, hear my prayer! Listen to the words of my mouth. 3 For] alien people have risen up against me, [and ruthless people seek my life; they have no regard for God. Selah. 4 But surely God is my helper; the Lo]rd is with those who sust[ain my life]. ▲

56 3 *And the day*[106] when I am afraid [I will put my trust in you]. ▲

59 4 [Although I have done no wrong] they run and ma[ke ready; arise to help me, and see my plight! 5 You, O LORD God of hosts], are the God of Isr[ael—arouse yourself to punish all the nations. Show no mercy to any of these] wicked [traitors]. Selah. 6 [Each evening they return, snarling like dogs, and prowl about the city. 7 See what they spew] from their mouths, [with sharp swords on their lips, for they say, "Who will hear us]?" ▲

62 [11 Once God has spoken; twice I have heard this: that power belongs to God, 12 and steadfast love belongs to you, O Lord. For you will repay each person according to] what he [has done].

63 0 [A Psalm of David, when he was in the Wilderness of Judah. 1 O God, you are my God, I will seek you earnestly], my [so]ul [thirsts for you; my body longs for you in a dry and wea]ry [land] without wat[er. 2 Thus I have beheld you in your sanctuary, to look on your power and your glory. 3 Because your lovingkindness is better than life], my [li]ps will praise [you]. ▲

66 16 [Com]e *and hear,*[107] all you who fear God, [and I will tell what he has done for me. 17 I cried to him with my mouth, and he was exalted on my tongue]. 18 If [I] had che[rished wick]edness [in my heart], the Lord [would not have heard me]. 19 Surely [God has listened; he has listened to the sound of my

105. 4QPs^a. *from Zion* MT LXX.

Psalm 54. 4QPs^a: 54:0–1, 3–4 [MT 54:2–3, 5–6].

Psalm 56. 4QPs^a: 56:3 [MT 56:4].

106. 4QPs^a. *The day* MT LXX (cf. *in the day,* vs 10).

Psalm 59. 11QPs^d: 59:4–5, 7 [MT 59:5–6, 8].

Psalm 62. 4QPs^a: 62:12 [MT 62:13].

Psalm 63. 4QPs^a: 63:1, 3 [MT 63:2, 4].

Psalm 66. 4QPs^a: 66:16, 18–20.

107. 4QPs^a. *hear* MT LXX.

prayer. 20 May God be blessed, w]ho has not [rejected] my [pra]yer or withheld [his] lovingkindness from me.

67 0 For the Director: [on stringed instruments. A Psalm, a song. 1 May God be gracious to us and bless] us and make his face shine u[pon us—Selah— 2 so that your way may be known on the earth, your salvation among all nations. 3 Let the peoples praise you], O God; let [all the peoples] praise you. 4 [Let the na]tions [be glad and sing for joy, for you will judge the peoples with uprightness and gui]de [the nations upon the earth]. Selah. 5 *So let [the peoples] praise you,*[108] [O God; let all the peoples praise you. 6 The earth yields its produce; God], our [God, has blessed us]. 7 *May they bless you,*[109] O God; [let all the ends of the earth fear you].

68 [0 For the Director: of David. A Psa]lm. A so[ng. 1 May God rise up, may his enemies be scattered, and may those who hate him flee before him]. 2 Just as [smoke] is blown away, [so drive them away. Just as wax melts before the fire, so may the wicked perish in God's] presence. 3 [But may the righteous be glad, and rejoice in God's presence—may they rejoice] with gladness. 4 [Sing to God, sing praises to his name. Raise a highway for the one who rides through the deserts]—his na[me is the LORD]—and rejo[ice before him]. ▲

13 [Even while you sleep among the sheepfolds, the wings of my dove are covered with silver, its pinions with shin]ing [gold. 14 When the Almighty scattered the kings *in the land,*[110] snow fell on Mount Zalmon]. 15 O mighty [mountain, th]*is*[111] mountain of Bashan; O many-peaked mountain, mountain of Bashan! 16 [Why do you look on in envy], you many-peak[ed mountains], at the [mountain which God has chosen for his dwelling? Yes, the LORD will live there fore]ver. 17 The chariots of G[od are tens of thousands and thousands upon thousands; the Lord has come (from) Sinai into his sanctuary]. ▲

69 0 [For the Director]: set to "Lilies." Of David. 1 Sav[e me, O God! For the waters have come u]p to (my) neck. 2 I have sunk *between the abyss,*[112] *there is no*[113] fo[othold; I have come] into deep waters, *a flowing stream*[114] en[gulfs me. 3 I am weary with crying]; my [throat is parched]. *My teeth are consumed*[115] *in an-*

Psalm 67. 4QPs[a]: 67:0–1, 3–7 [MT 67:1–2, 4–8].

108. 4QPs[a]. *Let the peoples praise you* MT LXX.

109. 4QPs[a]. *May (God) bless us* MT LXX.

Psalm 68. 11QPs[d]: 68:0–4, 13–17 [MT 68:1–5, 14–18].

110. Literally, *there.*

111. 11QPs[d]. Not in MT LXX.

Psalm 69. 4QPs[a]: 69:0–18 [MT 69:1–19].

112. 4QPs[a]. *in (the) deep mire* MT LXX.

113. 4QPs[a]. *and there is no* MT LXX.

114. 4QPs[a]. *and a flowing stream* MT LXX.

115. Meaning unclear 4QPs[a]. *My eyes grow dim* MT LXX.

guish[116] *for the God of Isr*[ael].[117] 4 Ma]ny more than *the hairs*[118] of my head are those who hate me without cause; [many are those who would annihilate me, who are wrongfully my enemies. That which] I did not steal, [should I now restore]?

5 [O God], *you do not know my crown*[119] and [my] wrongs [are not hidden from you. 6 Do not let] those who hope in you *be disgraced,*[120] O L[ord G]OD [of hosts; do not let th]ose who seek you *be dishonored,*[121] O God of Israel. 7 Be[cause it is for] your sake that [I have] bo[rne scorn], that disgrace [has cover]ed my face. 8 *O that [I] would become a stranger* [to my brothers], *an alien*[122] to my mother's children. 9 For it is zea[l for your house] that has consumed me, and the insul[ts of those who insult you] have fallen upon me. 10 *But I struck my soul with fasting,*[123] and it beca[me] a reproach to me. 11 When I made sackcloth [my clo]thing, *then I be-came*[124] [a byword] to them. 12 [*Th*]*ose who sit at the gate gossip about me;*[125] *and the* [*dru*]*nkards play songs about me.*[126]

13 But as for me, *what is my prayer,*[127] [O Lo]RD? *Now it is acceptable;*[128] O Go[d, in] the greatness of your lovingkindness answer me with your faithful help. 14 *Deliver me from the mire, and do not let me sin*[k], *and do not let the one who seizes me conquer me.*[129] [*Del*]*iver me*[130] from those who hate me, *from the depths of the waters.*[131] 15 Do not let the floodwaters en[gulf me], or the depths *sink me,*[132] or the pit [close] *my mouth*[133] [on] me.

16 *Answer me*[134] *according to the goodness of your steadfast love;*[135] according to

---

116. 4QPs[a]. *with waiting* MT LXX.

117. 4QPs[a] (cf. vs 7: *the God of my salvation* Mic 7:7). *for my God* MT LXX.

118. 4QPs[a] (masculine). *hairs* (feminine) MT.

119. Meaning unclear 4QPs[a]. *you know my folly* MT LXX.

120. 4QPs[a]. *be disgraced through me* MT LXX.

121. 4QPs[a]. *I have become estranged* MT LXX.

122. 4QPs[a]. *and an alien* MT LXX.

123. 4QPs[a]. *But I wept in my soul with fasting* MT. *but I bowed down my soul with fasting* LXX.

124. Literally, *and it* [i.e., my soul] *became* (cf. vs 11) 4QPs[a]. *and I became* MT LXX.

125. 4QPs[a]. *They gossip about me, those who sit at the gate* (different word order) MT LXX.

126. 4QPs[a]. *and the drunkards (make) songs* MT. *and the drunkards sang against me* LXX.

127. 4QPs[a]. *my prayer is to you* MT. *in my prayer to you* LXX.

128. 4QPs[a]. *Now is an acceptable time* MT LXX.

129. 4QPs[a]. *and do not let me sink* MT. *so that I do not stick (in it)* LXX.

130. 4QPs[a]. *Let me be delivered* MT LXX.

131. 4QPs[a]. *and from the depths of the waters* MT (cf. Ps 130:1) LXX (*and from the depth of the waters*).

132. 4QPs[a]. *swallow me up* MT LXX.

133. 4QPs[a]. *its mouth* MT LXX.

134. 4QPs[a]. *Answer me, O* LORD MT LXX.

135. 4QPs[a]. *for your lovingkindness is good* MT LXX.

[your] abun[dant mercy] turn to me. 17 *Do not*[136] hide your face from your servant; for [I am in trouble—be] quick to answer me. 18 Come near *onto*[137] me; [set me free] be[cause of my enemies].

76 [8 From the heavens you uttered judgment; the earth feared and was quiet, 9 when God rose up to give judgment, to] save [all the oppressed in the land. Selah. 10 But even human anger will praise you, when you clothe yourself with the la]st bit of your anger. 11 [Make vows to the LORD your God and fulfill them; may all who are a]round him bring gifts [to the one who is to be feared, 12 who cuts off the spirit of princes, who inspires fear among the kings of the earth.]

77 0 [For the Director: for Jeduthun]. Of Asa[ph. A Psalm]. ▲
17 [The clouds poured down water and the skies resounded with thunder, and your arrows fl]ashed [back and forth]. 18 The crash of your thunder was in the whirlwind, and your lightning fla[shes] lit up [the world; the earth trembled and quaked. 19 Your path led through the sea, and] your wa[y] through the [migh]ty waters, [although your footprints were imperceptible. 20 You led your people like a flock by the ha]nd of Moses and Aa[ron].

78 0 [A Maskil of Asaph. 1 Listen, my people, to my teaching]; turn *your ears*[138] to the wo[rds of my mouth]. ▲
5 [For he established a decree in Jacob and appointed a law in Israel, which he commanded our ancestors to teach] their [children, 6 so that the n]ext [generation—the children yet to be born—would know these and rise up and t]ell them to [their ch]ildren. 7 [Then they would put] their trust [in God, and not forget] God's [d]eeds but [keep his comma]nds. 8 [Then they would not be like their ancestors—a stubborn and re]bellious generation, [a generation whose heart] was not steadfast, [whose spirit was not faithful to God]. 9 The Ephraim[ites], although armed [with bows, turned back on the day of battle. 10 They did not] keep God's covenant [and refused to live] by [his l]aw. 11 [They forgot what he had done] and the miracles [he had shown them. 12 In the sight of their ancestors he did marvels in the lan]d of Egypt, in the re[gion of Zoan]. ▲
31 [God's anger rose up against them and he killed] *the sturdiest*[139] amo[ng them, and laid low Israel's finest young men. 32 In spite of all this, they kept on sinning] and would not be[lieve in his wonders. 33 So he ended their days in fu-

---

136. 4QPs^a MT^{mss} LXX. *and do not* MT LXX^{ms}.

137. 4QPs^a. *to* MT. Dative case LXX.

Psalm 76. 4QPs^e: 76:9–11 [MT 76:10–12].

Psalm 77. 4QPs^e: 77:0 [MT 77:1]; 11QPs^b: 77:17–20 [MT 77:18–21].

Psalm 78. 11QPs^b: 78:1; 11QPs^d: 78:5–12; 4QPs^e: 78:6–7, 31–33; pap6QPs(?): 78:36–37.

138. 11QPs^d MT^{mss}. *your ear* MT LXX.

139. 4QPs^e. *some of the sturdiest* MT LXX.

tility and their years in terror. 34 Whenever he killed them, they would seek him—(then) they would repent and seek God in earnest. 35 They would remember that God was their rock, the Most High God their redeemer. 36 But then they would flatter him with their mouths, lying to him] with [their] tongues; 37 [for their hearts were not loyal to him, and they were not tr]ue to [his cove]nant. ▲

81

[0 For the Director: set to "The Gittith." Of Asaph]. 1 [Si]ng aloud [to God our strength; shout with joy to the God of] Jacob! 2 [Start the music, strike] the tambourine, [the melodious lyre] with the harp. 3 [Sound the trumpet at the new moon, and at the full moon, on] our festal [d]ay. 4 [For this is a decree for Israel, an ordinance of the G]od of Jacob. 5 [He established it as a statute *among Joseph,*[140] when he went out against the la]nd of Egypt. [I can hear] a language that I did no[t understand]:

6 "[I relieved] the burden from their should[ers]; *their hand*[141] [was set free] from [(carrying) baskets. 7 In your dis]tress you c[r]ied out and I [re]scued you; I [answered you in the secret place of thunder; I tes]ted you at the waters of Meribah. Selah. 8 Lis[ten, my people, while I warn you—O Is]rael, if only you would listen to me! 9 [Let there be no foreign god among you; you shall not] worship any alien god. 10 [I am the LORD your God, who brou]ght you up from the land of Egypt. [Open wide your mouth and I will fill it]."

11 "[But] my people would [not] listen to me—[Israel would not submit to me. 12 So I gave] them up to their stubborn hearts, [to follow their own devices. 13 If only] my people would listen to me, [if only Israel would follow my ways! 14 Then how quickly] would I subdue their enemies, [and turn my hand against their foes! 15 Th]ose who [hate] the LORD would cower before him, [and their doom would last] forever. 16 But I would feed you with the choicest of the wheat, [and] I would satisfy you with ho[ney from the rock]."

82

0 A Psal[m] of Asaph. 1 God takes his stand in the divine council; he holds judgment among the gods. 2 "How long will you defend the unjust and show partiality to the wicked? Selah. 3 Defend the poor and orphan; up[hold] the rights of the oppressed and destitute. 4 Rescue the weak and the needy; deliver them from the power of the wicked." 5 They know nothing, they understand nothing, they walk around in darkness; all the foundations of the earth are shaken. 6 I say, "You are gods; you are all children of the Most High. 7 Yet you

---

Psalm 81. 4QPs^e: 81:1–2 [MT 81:2–3]; 11QPs^d: 81:4–10 [MT 81:5–11]; MasPs^a: 81:1–16 [MT 81:2–17].

140. Here Joseph is collective, representing his generation and thus the descendants of Jacob (cf. Ps 77:15 and 80:1).

141. 11QPs^d. *their hands* MT LXX.

Psalm 82. MasPs^a: 82:1–8.

will die like mere mortals, [and] you will fall like any prince." 8 Rise up, O God, judge the earth! For all the nations belong to you.

83 0 A Song. A Psalm of Asaph. 1 O God, do not keep silent; do not be quiet or be still, O God! 2 For [s]ee how your enemies [make a commotion], how those who hate you rear their heads. 3 They lay craf[ty pla]ns against your people, and plot together against those you cherish. 4 "Come," they say, "let us wi[pe] them out from being a nation, so that the name of Israel will never be remembered again." 5 For with o[ne] mind they plot together; they form an alliance against you— 6 *the gods of Edom*[142] and the Ishmaelites, of Moab and the Hagrites, 7 of Gebal, *Ammon*[143] and Amalek, of Philistia with the inhabitants of Tyre. 8 Even Assyria has joined them to lend strength to the children of Lot. Selah.

9 Deal with them as you did with Midian, as you did with Sisera and Jabin at the Wadi Kishon, 10 who were destroyed at Endor and became dung for the ground. 11 Make their nobles like Oreb and Zeeb, [a]ll their [pr]inces like Zebah and Zalmunna, 12 who said, "Let us take God's pasturelands for our own possession." 13 Make them like the whirling dust, *O God,*[144] like chaff before the wind. 14 Just as fire consumes the forest or as a flame sets the mountains ablaze, 15 so pursue them with your tempest and terrify them with your storm. 16 Fill their faces with shame [so that they may seek your name, O LORD].

17 [May they always be ashamed and frightened; may they perish in dis]grace. 18 [Let them acknowledge that you, whose name is the LORD—that you alone are] the Most Hi[gh over all the earth].

84 0 For the Director: [set to "The Gittith." Of the Korahites. A Psalm]. 1 How lovely is [your dwelling pl]ace, [O LORD of hosts! 2 My soul] yearns, even fa[ints, for the courts of the LORD]; my heart and my body sho[ut for joy to the living God]. 3 Even the sparrow find[s a home, and the swallow a nest for herself], where she may have [her yo]ung—[near your altars], O LORD of hosts, [my King and my God. 4 Blessed are those who live in your house]; they are always singing your praise. Se[lah].

5 [Blessed is the person whose strength is in you], in whose heart are the highways (for pilgrimage). 6 [As they pass through the Baka valley] they make it a place of springs; [the *autumn rains*[145] also cover it with pools]. 7 They go from strength to stren[gth; the God of gods will be seen in Zion]. 8 [Hear my prayer],

---

Psalm 83. MasPs^a: 83:0–18 [MT 83:1–19].

    142. MasPs^a (possibly metathesis, but see 2 Chron 25:20). *the tents of Edom* MT LXX.

    143. MasPs^a. *and Ammon* MT LXX.

    144. MasPs^a. *O my God* MT LXX.

Psalm 84. MasPs^a: 84:0–12 [MT 84:1–13].

    145. Literally, *early rain.*

O LORD God of ho[sts; listen to me], O God of Ja[cob! Selah. 9 Look at our shield, O God]; have reg[ard for the face of your anointed one].

10 [For one day in your courts is better than a thousand elsewhere. I would rather be a doorkeeper in the house of my God] than live in the ten[ts of wickedness. 11 For the LORD God is a sun and shield]; the Lo[RD] bestows favor and honor. [No good thing does he withhold from those who live uprightly]. 12 O LORD of hosts, [blessed is the person who trusts in you].

85 0 For the Director: of the Korahites. A Psa[lm]. 1 O LORD, you showed favor to your land; [you restored the fortunes of Jacob]. 2 You forgave the iniquity of your people [and forgave all their sin. Selah]. 3 You withdrew all your wrath [and turned from your fierce anger]. 4 Restore us again, O God of our salvation, [and cancel your vexation with us]. 5 Will you remain angry with us forever? [Will you prolong your anger to all generations]? ▲

86 4 [Gladden the soul of your servant—for to you, O Lord, I lift up my soul. 5 For you are] good and forgiving, O Lo[rd, abounding in steadfast love to all who call on you. 6 Hear] my prayer, [O LORD]; list[en to my cry of supplication. 7 In the day of my trouble I call on you, for you will answer me].

8 There is none [like you among the gods, O Lord, and there are no deeds like yours. 9 All the nations you have made will come and worship before you, O Lord, and will glorify your name. 10 For you are great, and perform wondrous deeds—you] alone are G[od].

11 [Teach me your way, O LORD, so I may walk] in your tru[th; give me an undivided heart] to re[vere your name. 12 I will give thanks to you, O Lord] my God, with [all my heart, and I will glorify your name forever. 13 For] great to[ward me is your steadfast love;[146] you have delivered me from the depths of Sheol]. 14 O God, [insolent people are attacking me; a gang of ruthless men seeks my life— men who have no regard for you]. ▲

88 0 [A Song. A Psalm of the Korahites. To the Chief Musician: set to "Mahalath Leannoth." A Maskil] of Heman the Ezra[hite]. 1 [O LORD, God of my salvation, day and nig]ht [I cry out] before you. 2 Let [my prayer] come [before you; turn your ear to my cry. 3 For my soul is fu]ll of troubles, [and my life is drawing near to Sheol. 4 I am counted among those who go do]wn [to the Pit; I am li]ke [a person without strength]. ▲

14 [O LORD, why do you reject me and hide] your face from me? 15 [From my youth I have been wret]ched [and close to death; I suffer your terrors], I am frustrated.[147] 16 [Your wrath has sw]ept over [me; your terrors destroy me]. ▲

Psalm 85. MasPs[a]: 85:0–5 [MT 85:1–6].

Psalm 86. 1QPs[a]: 86:5–6, 8; 4QPs[e]: 86:10–11; 11QPs[d]: 86:11–14.

146. 11QPs[d]. your steadfast love toward me is great (different word order) MT LXX.

Psalm 88. 4QPs[e]: 88:0–1, 3–4 [MT 88:1–2, 4–5]; 4QPs[t]: 88:14–16 [MT 88:15–17].

147. Probable meaning 4QPs[t] (see LXX). I am helpless MT.

89 19 [Then you spoke in a vision *to*] *your chosen ones;*[148] *you said,*[149] "I have lent sup[port to] a war[rior; I have exalted one cho]sen from the people. 20 I have found [my servant David]; *from*[150] my holy oil [I have anointed him]. 21 My hand will always remain *with you;*[151] [my arm will surely strengthen you]. 25[152] I will set (my) *hand*[153] over the sea, [my right hand] over the rivers.

22[154] "The enemy [*will not oppress*],[155] and *the wicked*[156] will not violate him. 26[157] [He will call out to me], *'You are my [Fa]ther!'*[158] 27 I *also*[159] will make him my firstborn, [the most exalted of the kings of] the earth. 30[160] If [his children] forsake [my law and do not walk according to my ordinances], . . ." ▲

43 [Moreover, you have turned back the edge of his sword and have not supported] him *for battle.*[161] 44 [You have] put [an end to his splendor and have hurled his throne to the ground]. 45 You have cu[t short] the days of [his y]outh; [you have covered him with shame. Selah].

46 [How long, O LORD? Will you hi]de yourself forever? [How long will your wrath burn like fire? 47 As for me, remember how fleeting is my time—for what futi]lity [have you created all mortals? 48 What person can live and never see death? Who can save himself from the power of Sheol? Selah].

49 Lo[rd, where is your former steadfast love, which in your faithfulness you swore to David? 50 Remem]ber, O Lord, how [your servants] have been mocked, [how I bear in my heart the insults of all the mighty nations], 51 (the insults) with which [your enemies] have mocked, [O LORD, with which they have mocked *every step*][162] of your [an]ointed one.

52 Blessed [be the LORD forever! Amen and Amen].

Psalm 89. 4QPs^x: 89:19–21, 25, 22, 26–27, 30 [MT 89:20–22, 26, 23, 27–28, 31]; 4QPs^e: 89:43–47, 49–52 [MT 89:44–48, 50–53].

148. 4QPs^x. *to your faithful ones* MT LXX.

149. 4QPs^x. *and you said* MT LXX.

150. 4QPs^x. *with* MT LXX.

151. Plural 4QPs^x. *with him* MT LXX.

152. Preceded by vs 21 4QPs^x. Preceded by vs 24 MT LXX.

153. 4QPs^x. *his hand* MT LXX.

154. Preceded by vs 25 4QPs^x. Preceded by vs 21 MT LXX.

155. 4QPs^x. *will not oppress him* MT LXX.

156. Literally, *the son of wickedness.*

157. Preceded by vs 22 4QPs^x. Preceded by vs 25 MT LXX.

158. 4QPs^x. MT LXX add *my God, and the rock of my salvation.*

159. 4QPs^x. Not in MT LXX.

160. Preceded by vs 27 4QPs^x. Preceded by vs 29 MT LXX.

161. 4QPs^e. *in battle* MT LXX.

162. Literally, *the footsteps.*

FOUR PSALMS AGAINST DEMONS

■ *One of the most interesting Psalms scrolls was found in Cave 11 at Qumran. Known as 11QApocryphal Psalms (or 11QPsAp^a or 11QApPs), this manuscript is dated about 50–70 CE and contains four Psalms for use in exorcisms against demons. Many scholars believe these to be the Four Songs for Playing over the Stricken that are mentioned in David's Compositions, which is part of the large Psalms scroll from Cave 11 (11QPs^a col. 16:9–10). The first three of these Psalms were unknown until the discovery of the Dead Sea Scrolls, but the fourth is found in modern Bibles as Psalm 91.*

The First Exorcism Psalm: On Expelling Demons

Col. 1: 1 [. . . 2 . . .] and the one who weeps for him 3 [. . .] the curse 4 [. . .] by the LORD 5 [. . .] dragon 6 [. . .] the ear[th . . . 7 . . .] exor[cis]ing [. . . 8 . . .] to [. . . 9 . . .] this [. . . 10 . . .] to the demon [. . . 11 . . .] he will dwe[ll. . . .]

The Second Exorcism Psalm: Trusting in the LORD for Protection

■ *This Psalm, which is apparently attributed to Solomon, invokes the God of creation for protection against evil powers. In column 3 God's power is highlighted from Scripture, and in column 4 the Psalmist calls on angelic powers to combat demonic forces. A conclusion to this Psalm appears in the first three lines of column 5.*

Col. 2: 1–2 [. . . of] Solomon. He will invo[ke . . . 3 . . . the spi]rits and the demons [. . . 4 . . .] These are [the de]mons. And the p[rince of enmi]ty [. . . 5 . . . I]srael [. . .] the a[byss . . . 6 . . .] the gre[at . . . 7 . . .] his people [. . .] healing 8 [. . .] leans [upon] your name, and calls [. . . 9 . . . He says to Is]rael, "Hold fast 10 [to the LORD, . . . who made] the heavens [11 and the earth, and all that is in them, w]ho separated [12 light from darkness . . .]"

Col. 3: 1 [. . .] the depth[s] 2 the earth and [. . .] the earth. Who m[ade these signs] 3 and won[ders on the] earth? The LORD, it is he [who] 4 made the[se through] his [power], who summons all [his] an[gels] 5 [and] all the [holy]

The First Exorcism Psalm. 11QPsAp^a, col. 1:1–11.
The Second Exorcism Psalm. 11QPsAp^a, cols. 2:1–5:3.

offspri[ng] to st[a]nd before [him, . . . 6 all the hea]vens and [all] the earth [. . .] who committe[d] sin against 7 [all humani]ty, and [evil] against all pe[ople. But] they know 8 his [wonder]ful [. . .] which they do not [. . .]. If they do not 9 [desist] out of fear of the LORD from [. . . and] from killing the soul of 10 [. . .] the LORD, and [th]ey will fear tha[t] great [spell]. 11 "One of you [puts to flight] a thou[sand."163 . . .] servants of the LOR[D . . . 12 . . . g]reat and [. . .]

Col. 4: 1 [. . . and] great is [. . .] adjuring [you . . .] 2 and the great [. . .] the mighty and [. . .] 3 all the earth [. . .] the heavens and [. . .] 4 May the LORD smite you with a [migh]ty bl[ow] in order to destroy you [. . .], 5 and in his fierce wrath [may he send] against you a powerful angel [to carry out] 6 his [entire com]mand, who [will show no] mercy to you, wh[o . . . 7 . . .] against all these who [will send] you [down] into the great abyss 8 [and to] deepest [Sheol], and who [. . . , and there] you shall lie, and darkness 9 [. . .] very much [. . .]. [No lon]ger on the earth 10 [. . .] forever and [. . .] by the curse of *des[truction164 . . . 11 . . .] the fierce anger of the L[ORD . . . in] darkness for a[ll 12 . . .] affliction [. . .] your gift [. . .]

Col. 5: 1 [. . .] 2 which [. . .] and those possessed by [demons . . .] 3 those crushed [by . . . . Ra]phael has healed [them. Amen, Amen, Selah].

The Third Exorcism Psalm:
The LORD Has Power to Strike Down Demons

■ *This Psalm, which is attributed to David, is uttered against a demon. The reference to this demon's horns in line 7 is particularly interesting in view of popular depictions of the devil as having horns.*

Col. 5: 4 A Psalm of David. Again[st . . . An incanta]tion in the name of the LOR[D. To be invoked at an]y time 5 to the heav[ens. For] he will come to you at nig[ht], and you will [say] to him: 6 "Who are you? [Withdraw from] humanity and from the offspring of the ho[ly one]s! For your appearance is one of 7 [vani]ty, and your horns are horns of illu[si]on. You are darkness, not light, 8 [wicked]ness, not righteousness [. . .] the commander of the army, the LORD, [will bring] you [down 9 into] deepest [Sheo]l, [. . . the] two bronze [ga]tes th[rough which n]o 10 light [can enter], and [the] sun [will] not [shine for you] tha[t rises 11 upon the] righteous to [. . ." And] then you will say,

---

163. Joshua 23:10.

164. Or, *Abaddon.*

The Third Exorcism Psalm. 11QPsApᵃ, cols. 5:4–6:2.

["... 12 ... the right]eous, to come [...] for a de[mon to] harm him, [... 13 ... of tr]uth from [... because] he has [righ]teousness [... 14 ...] and ..."

The Fourth Exorcism Psalm: Psalm 91

■ *Psalm 91 has brought comfort and hope to Jews and Christians over the centuries. Not only does it evoke God's help and protection against physical and human dangers, this Psalm has been connected with exorcisms of demonic forces in both rabbinic and Christian traditions.*

[165]0 [*Of David.*[166] 1 The one who dwells] in the shelter [of the Most High will rest in the shadow of] the Almighty; 2 *who says*[167] [of the LORD, "My refuge] and [my] fortress, [my God] *is the constant one*[168] in whom [I can trust." 3 For h]e will deliver you from [the fow]ler's [snare] and from the dea[dly] pestilence. 4 He will cover [you with] his feathers, and under his w[ings] *you will rest;*[169] [*his*] *faithfulness* [*upo*]*n you*[170] is a shield and his truth a buckler. *Selah.*[171] 5 You will not fear the terror of night, nor the arrow that flies by day; 6 *nor the plague that destroys at* [*no*]*on, nor the pestilence that stalks* [*in dark*]*ness.*[172]

7 A thousand may fa[ll] at your side, ten th[ousand at] your right [hand]— but it *will n*[*ot*] *strike* [*you*].[173] 8 [You will] merely [*look on*] *with your eyes*[174] [*and se*]*e*[175] *the recompense*[176] of the wick[ed. 9 *For you have invo*]*ked* [*your*] *shel*[*ter* ...]

The Fourth Exorcism Psalm: Psalm 91. 11QPsApᵃ: 91:1–14, 16; 4QPsᵇ: 91:5–8, 12–15.

165. Preceded by Apocryphal Psalms 11QPsApᵃ. Preceded by Psalm 90 MT LXX.

166. 11QPsApᵃ (reconstructed). *A Psalm of David* LXX. Not in MT.

167. 11QPsApᵃ LXXᵐˢˢ. *I will say* MT. *he will say* LXX.

168. 11QPsApᵃ. Not in MT LXX.

169. 11QPsApᵃ. *you will find refuge* MT LXX.

170. 11QPsApᵃ. Not in MT LXX.

171. 11QPsApᵃ (see also vs 16b and the final word in this Psalm). Not in MT LXX.

172. 11QPsApᵃ. *nor the pestilence that stalks in darkness, nor the plague that destroys at noon* (different word order) 4QPsᵇ MT LXX.

173. 11QPsApᵃ. *but it will not get close to you* 4QPsᵇ MT LXX.

174. 11QPsApᵃ. *with your eyes look on* (different word order) 4QPsᵇ MT LXX.

175. The Hebrew verb comes before *recompense* 11QPsApᵃ. Verb comes after *the wicked* MT LXX.

176. 11QPsApᵃ and MT use two different but related Hebrew words; the meaning is very similar.

his delight.[177] 10 You will se[e no harm,[178] and] no [disaster] will strike[179] in your t[en]ts.[180]

11 Fo[r] he will give orders to his angels concerning you, to gu[ard you in all] your [ways]. 12 In their hands [they will lift] you [up], so that [you do] not [strike your] foot [against a st]one. 13 [You will tr]ead [on] the cobra [and the viper];[181] you will trample underfo[ot the strong young lion] and the serpent. 14 [Because you de]light [in the LORD he wi]ll [rescue you] and [make you secure 16b and he will sh]ow you [his vic]tory.[182] Selah.[183] Then they will answer "Amen, Amen."[184] Selah.[185]

> ■ In the 11QApocryphal Psalms scroll, Psalm 91 is followed by a fair amount of blank leather, which is very helpful for assessing collections of Psalms such as this one. The blank leather indicates that the collection in this manuscript actually ended with Psalm 91, which is also confirmed by the unusual ending to the Psalm. For the end of another important collection indicated by blank leather, see the comment after Psalm 151 toward the end of our Psalms translation.

PSALMS MAINLY FROM 4QPSᵇ

92

> ■ Until Psalm 101, which marks the beginning of 11QPsᵃ (the largest of all the Psalms scrolls), the translation relies especially on 4QPsᵇ. This manuscript, dating to the second half of the first century CE, preserves a great deal of material from Psalms 91 through 118.

---

177. Meaning unclear 11QPsApᵃ. *For you have made the LORD—who is my refuge—yes the Most High, your dwelling-place* MT LXX.

178. 11QPsApᵃ. *No harm will befall you* MT LXX.

179. 11QPsApᵃ. *no disaster will come near* MT LXX.

180. 11QPsApᵃ. *your tent* MT LXX.

181. 11QPsApᵃ (one Hebrew word reconstructed) LXX. *the lion and the cobra* 4QPsᵇ MT.

182. 11QPsApᵃ. For vss 14–16, MT and LXX include some of this material but have a longer text: 14 *Because he loves me, I will rescue him; I will make him secure, for he has acknowledged my name.* 15 *When he calls upon me, I will answer him; I will be with him in trouble, I will rescue him and honor him.* 16 *With long life I will satisfy him, and I will show him my victory.*

183. 11QPsApᵃ (see vs 4 and the final word in this Psalm). Not in MT LXX.

184. 11QPsApᵃ (see Neh 8:6). Not in MT LXX.

185. 11QPsApᵃ (see vs 4 and the longer text in vs 16b). Not in MT LXX.

Psalm 92. 4QPsᵇ: 92:3–9, 12–14 [MT 92:4–8, 13–15]; 1QPsᵃ: 92:11–13 [MT 92:12–14].

[1 It is good to give thanks to the LORD, to sing praises to your name, O Most High, ... 3 to the music of the lu[te and the lyre], (and) to the melody of the harp. 4 For you, O LORD, have made me glad [by *your deeds*];[186] *people sing for joy*[187] [*at the w*]*ork*[188] of your hands. 5 How great are your deeds, O Lo[RD]! [Your] thoughts are [ver]y profound. 6 *The person who is senseless and knows nothing,*[189] [and] fools cannot understand this: 7 that [although] the wicked spring up like grass, [and although all evildoers flourish, they are doomed to destruction forever]. ▲

11 [My eyes have seen the defeat of my enemies; *my ear*] *has heard*[190] [the rout of my ev]il [assailants. 12 The righteous will flourish like a palm tree, (and) will grow] like a cedar in Lebanon. 13 [They are] pl[anted in the] house of the L[o]RD; they will flourish in the courts of our God. 14 They will still bear fruit *in ripe old age,*[191] *and they will stay*[192] [healthy] and green. ▲

■ *Psalm 93, which is a hymn of praise, follows Psalm 92 in 4QPs*[b]*, the Masoretic Text, and the Septuagint. In the 11QPs*[a]*-Psalter, however, it occurs in a completely different position, following the Apostrophe to Zion. This order is also followed in our translation; see Tables 1 and 2 in the introduction to the Psalms.*

94 1 O LORD, [you God of vengeance, you God of vengeance]—shine forth! 2 [Rise up, O judge] of the earth; [pay back t]o the proud [what they deserve]! 3 [How long will the wick]ed, O LORD, [how long will the wick]ed exu[lt]? 4 [They pour out arro]gant [words; all the evildoers keep boasting]. ▲

8 [Pay attention, you dullest] among the people; [and you fools—when will you ha]ve any sense? 9 [Does the one who implanted the ear no]t hear? [Does the one who formed the eye no]t see? 10 The one who dis[ciplines nations], who teach[es knowledge to humans, does he not punish]? 11 The LORD understands human thoughts, that they are futile. 12 Blessed is the one whom you discipline, O LORD, and whom you teach from your law, 13 granting him respite from the days of trouble, until a pit is [du]g for the wicked. 14 For [the LORD] will not [aban]don his people; [he will not forsake his heritage, 15 for justice will return to righteousness, and all the upright in heart will follow it. 16 W]ho will rise up [for me against the ev]ildoe[rs? W]ho will stand up [for me against the wo]rkers

---

186. Literally, *by your work.*

187. Literally, *it is sung for joy* 4QPs[b]. *I sing for joy* MT LXX.

188. *at the work* 4QPs[b]. *at the works* MT LXX.

189. 4QPs[b]. *The senseless person cannot know* MT LXX.

190. 1QPs[a]. *my ear will hear* MT LXX.

191. 4QPs[b] (cf. Gen 15:15). *in old age* MT LXX.

192. 4QPs[b]. *they will stay* MT LXX.

Psalm 94. 4QPs[b]: 94:1–4, 8–14, 17–18, 21–22; 1QPs[a]: 94:16.

of ini[qui]ty? 17 If the LORD had not been [my] help, [my s]oul would soon have lived in the land of death. 18 When I said, "[My] foot is slipping," your steadfast love, O L[o]RD, supported [me]. ▲

21 They fa[ll upon the righteous], and con[demn the innocent to death]. 22 But [the LORD has be]come [my fortress, and my God the rock of my refuge]. ▲

95 3 [For the LORD is a great God, and a great King above all go]ds. 4 [In] his [hand are the depths of the earth, and the mountain peaks belong to him]. 5 The sea is h[is], for he [made it, and his hands formed] *the dry land.*¹⁹³ 6 [O come, let us worship and bow do]wn, let us kneel bef[ore the LOR]D our Maker. 7 Fo[r he is our God, and we are the people of his pasture and the flock under his care. Today, if] you [hear] his voice, [8 do not harden your hearts, as at Meribah, ... 11 Therefore in my anger I swore an oath, "They will never enter] my rest."

96 1 [Sing to the LOR]D a new song; [sing to the LORD, all the earth. 2 Sing to the LORD, bless his name; proclaim his salvation from da]y to da[y]. ▲

97 6 [The heavens proclaim his righteousness, and] all the peo[ples s]ee [his glory. 7 Let all who worship images be put to] shame, [those who make their boast in id]ols—[worship him, all you gods! 8 Zion hea]rs and rejoices, [and the villages of Judah] are glad, [because of your judgments], O LORD. 9 [For you], O LORD, [are the Most High over all the earth; you are exalted far above all gods]. ▲

98 4 Shou[t for joy] to the LORD, [all the earth; burst into jubilant s]ong and celebrate with music. 5 [Make] music to the LORD with the harp; with the harp [and the sound of melody. 6 With trumpets and bla]st of the ram's horn shout [for joy before the King, the LORD. 7 Let] the sea [roar], and everything in it; [the world, and those who live in it. 8 Let the rivers clap] their hands; [let the hills sing together for joy]. ▲

99 ¹⁹⁴ 0 *Of Davi[d. A Psalm.*¹⁹⁵ 1 The LORD] is king; let [the nations] tremble! [He sits enthroned (above) the cherubim; let the earth quake! 2 The LORD is great in Zion, and he is exalted over all] the nations. . . . 5 Exalt the Lo[R]D our

---

Psalm 95. 4QPsᵐ: 95:3–7; 1QPsᵃ: 95:11.

193. 4QPsᵐ and MT have two different forms of the Hebrew word, but the meaning is the same.

Psalm 96. 1QPsᵃ: 96:1–2; 4QPsᵇ: 96:2.

Psalm 97. 4QPsᵐ: 97:6–9.

Psalm 98. 4QPsᵐ: 98:4–8; 4QPsᵇ: 98:4–5.

Psalm 99. 4QPsᵏ: 99:1–2, 5; 4QPsᵛ: 99:1; 4QPsᵇ: 99:5–6.

194. Preceded by Psalm 135 and other Psalm(s) 4QPsᵏ. Preceded by Psalm 98 4QPsᵇ MT LXX.

195. 4QPsᵏ and LXXᵐˢˢ. *A Psalm of David* LXX. Not in MT.

God, [and worsh]ip at his footstool. He is h[oly! 6 Moses and Aa]ron were among his priests, [and Samuel was among those who called on his name. They called on the LORD, and he answered them]. ▲

100 0 [A Psalm. For giving thanks. 1 Sho]ut joy[fully to the LORD, all the earth]. 2 Worsh[ip the LORD with gladness]; come [into his presence with happy singing]. ▲

THE GREAT PSALMS SCROLL (ORIGINAL CONTENTS)

■ *The largest and most important of the Psalms scrolls is 11QPsᵃ, which was copied about 30–50 CE. Although the beginning of this manuscript is fragmentary, it almost certainly began with Psalm 101. The Psalter found in this scroll—parts of which are also preserved in 4QPsᵉ and 11QPsᵇ—is termed the "11QPsᵃ-Psalter" (as opposed to the "MT-150 Psalter," which is found in modern Jewish and Christian Bibles). The 11QPsᵃ-Psalter contains virtually all of Psalms 1 through 89 in that order, followed by an arrangement that differs greatly from Psalms 90 through 150 as found in our Bibles. As noted in the introduction to the Psalms, this variation is both in arrangement (that is, order of Psalms) and in contents (the 11QPsᵃ-Psalter containing ten compositions not found in the MT-150 Psalter). For Psalm 101 through Psalm 151, this section of The Dead Sea Scrolls Bible presents the Psalms not in the traditional order but in the order of the 11QPsᵃ-Psalter, since that Psalter is the main and most prominent edition of the book of Psalms among the scrolls. (See Table 1 in the introduction).*

101 0 [Of David]. 1 I will sing of [steadfast love and jus]tice; to you, [O Lo]RD, will I sing praise. 2 [I will pay attention to the way that is blameless. Wh]en will you come *for me?*[196] I will wal[k in my house] with integrity of heart. 3 [I will set before my] eyes anything that is [base. I hate the work of those who fall away; it shall not cling to m]e. 4 [A perverse] heart [shall be far from me; I will know nothing of evil. 5 Whoever secretly slanders his neighbor, I will destroy; whoever has a haughty look] and an arrogant he[art, I will not tolerate. 6 I will look with favor on the fai]thful [in the land, so that they may d]well with me; whoever [walks in the way that is blameless shall mi]nister to me. 7 [No

Psalm 100. 4QPsᵇ: 100:1–2.

Psalm 101. 11QPsᵃ: 101:1–8.

196. 11QPsᵃ. *to me* MT.

one who practices deceit shall dwell] in my house; no [one who utters falsehood shall continue in] my presence. 8 Morning by morning I will [destroy all the wicked in the land, cutting] off all [evil]do[ers from the city] of the LORD.

102[0 A Prayer] of one afflicted, when he is fai[nt and pours out his complaint before the LORD]. 1 Hear my pray[er, O LORD, and let my cry come to you]. . . . 4 My heart is [blighted and withe]red [like grass, for I even forget *my food to e]at.*[197] ▲

9 For I eat ashes as my food, and mingle my drink with tears 10 [because of your indignation] and anger; [for you have lifted] me [up], and have cast me aside. 11 [My days are like an ev]ening [shadow, and I] wither away [like grass].

12 [But you, O LORD], sit enthroned forever, and your renown endures through all gene[rations]. 13 You will rise up and have com[pas]sion on Zion, fo[r it is now ti]me to show favor to her—yes, the appointed time has come. 14 For your ser[vants] hold dear [her sto]nes, and have pity on her very dust. 15 *The nations*[198] will fear the name of the LORD, and all the kings *of earth*[199] *his glory.*[200] 16 [For] the LORD will rebuild Zion; he will appear *in glory.*[201] 17 He will regard *the worm*[202] of the destitute, and will not despise their prayer. 18 Let this be recorded for a future generation, so that a people yet to be born may praise the LORD, 19 that he looked down from his ho[ly] *dwelling.*[203] From heaven the LORD looked *at the earth,*[204] 20 to hear the groans of [the prisoners], to set free those who were doomed to die; 21 so that people may declare in Zi[on the name of the LORD, and his] pra[ise in Jerusa]lem, 22 when the peoples [and the kingdoms] gather together [to wor]ship the LORD.

23 For[205] he has weakened *my strength*[206] in midcourse. *"He shortened my days,"* I *say,* 24 *"O my God.*[207] Do not take me away in the midst of my days—you whose years endure throughout all generations!" 25 Long ago *the earth was founded,*[208]

Psalm 102. 11QPs[a]: 102:0–1, 17–28 [MT 102:1–2, 17–29]; 4QPs[b]: 102:4, 9–28 [MT 102:5, 10–29].

   197. 4QPs[b]. *to eat my food* MT LXX.

   198. 4QPs[b]. *And the nations* MT LXX.

   199. 4QPs[b]*. *of the earth* 4QPs[b(corr)] MT LXX.

   200. 4QPs[b]. *your glory* MT LXX.

   201. 4QPs[b]. *in his glory* MT LXX.

   202. 11QPs[a]. *the prayer* 4QPs[b] MT LXX.

   203. 4QPs[b]. *height* MT LXX.

   204. 11QPs[a]. *to the earth* 4QPs[b]. *on the earth* LXX. *at earth* MT.

   205. 4QPs[b] LXX. Not in 4QPs[b] MT LXX.

   206. 4QPs[b] MT[qere, mss]. *his strength* MT.

   207. 4QPs[b] LXX. *"He shortened my days."* 24 *I say, "O my God,"* MT.

   208. 11QPs[a]. *you laid the foundation of the earth* 4QPs[b] MT LXX.

and the heavens are *the works*[209] of your hands. 26 They will perish, but you will endure, and they will all wear out like a garment. *And*[210] like clothing you change them, and they pass away; 27 but you remain the same, and your years will never end. 28 The children [of your servants will dwell secure], and [their offspr]ing [will be established before you, *from generation*] *to generation.*"[211]

103 [0 Of David]. 1 Bless the LORD, O my soul, [and all that is within] me, bless his holy name. 2 [Bless] the LORD, [O my soul, and do not] forget all his benefits— 3 who forgives all your iniquity, *and heals*[212] all your diseases, 4 who redeems your life from the Pit, who crowns you with steadfast love and mercy, 5 who satisfies your years with good things, so that your youth is renewed [like the eag]le's.

6 The LORD works vindication and justice for all who are oppressed. [7 He made known his ways to Moses, his acts to the people of Israel. 8 The LORD is merciful and gracious, slow to an]ger and abounding in steadfast love. 9 [He will n]ot [always accuse, n]or [will he harbor his anger] for[ever]. 10 He does not treat us according to our sins, nor [repay] us [according to] our ini[quities]. 11 For as hi[gh as the heavens are above the earth], so great is [his steadfast love toward those who fear him]; 12 as far as the east is from the west, so far he removes our transgressions from us. 13 Just as a father has compassion for his children, so the LORD has compassion for those who fear him. 14 For [he knows] how we [were for]med; [he remembers that we are but dust]. ▲

20 Bless the LORD, you his angels, you mighty ones who do *his bidding,*[213] in obedience to *his words.*[214] 21 Bless the LORD, all you his heavenly hosts, [you his servants who do his will].

■ *Psalm 103, a hymn of praise, is found in three scrolls, but in each case is followed by a different Psalm. In 4QPs^b it is followed directly by Psalm 112, in 11QPs^a very likely by Psalm 109, and in 2QPs probably by Psalm 104. Because these arrangements are not compatible with each other, in this translation Psalm 103 will be followed by 112 and then 109.*

112 1 [*Blessed*[215] is the person who fears the LORD], who gre[atly] delights in his commandments! [2 His descendants will be mighty on earth; the

---

209. Plural 11QPs^a 4QPs^b MT^mss LXX. Singular MT.

210. 11QPs^a LXX. Not in 4QPs^b MT.

211. 11QPs^a; cf. LXX. Not in MT. *forever* LXX.

Psalm 103. 11QPs^a: 103:1; 4QPs^b: 103:1–6, 9–14, 20–21; 2QPs: 103:2, 4–6, 8–11.

212. 4QPs^b. *who heals* MT LXX.

213. Literally, *his words* 4QPs^b. Literally, *his word* MT LXX.

214. 4QPs^b LXX. *his word* MT LXX^mss.

Psalm 112. 4QPs^w: 112:1, 3, 5, 7, 9; 4QPs^b: 112:4–5.

215. 4QPs^w (by reconstruction). *Praise the LORD! Blessed* MT LXX.

generation of the upright will be blessed. 3 Wealth and riches are in his house], and his righteousness endures [forever]. 4 Light rises in the darkness for the upright; (such a person) is gracious, compassionate, and righteo[us]. 5 Good will come to the per[son who is generous and lends freely; he will co]nduct his affairs [with justice. 6 For the righteous person will never be moved; he will be remembered forever. 7 He will have no f]ear of [bad news]; his heart is steadfast, trusting [in the LORD. 8 His heart is secure, he will have no fear, until he looks in triumph on his enemies. 9 He has distributed freely, he has given to the poor]; his righteousness endur[es forever; his horn will be lifted high in honor. 10 The wicked person sees it and becomes angry; he gnashes his teeth and melts away. The desires of wicked people mount to nothing]!

109

■ *In the 11QPs^a-Psalter, Psalm 109, which is an individual lament, most likely followed Psalm 103. In this translation it necessarily follows Psalm 112; see the note at the end of Psalm 103. Psalm 109 is also found with apocryphal pieces in 4QPs^f; see the introduction to the Psalms.*

²¹⁶0 [For the Director]: a Psal[m] of Dav[id]. 1 [Do not remain silent, O God of my praise. 2 For wicked and deceitful people have opened their mouths against me, and have spoken against me with lying tongues. 3 They surround me with words of hatred, and attack me without cause. 4 In return for my friendship] *they accuse me.*²¹⁷ 5 So they re[ward me evil for goo]d, and hatred for [my friendship].

[6 Appoint] an evil man [against him]; let *one who accus[es*²¹⁸ stand at his right hand. 7 When he is tried, let him be found] guilty; [let his prayer be counted as punishment. 8 May his days be few; may someone else] seize [his position]. ▲

13 [May] his des[cendants] be cut off; [may their name be blotted out in the next generation]. . . . 21 [But as for you, O LORD my Lord, act on my behalf for] your name's sake; because [your steadfast love] is good, [deliver me! 22 For I am poor and needy, and my heart] is wounded within me. [23 I vanish away, like a shadow at evening; I am shaken off like a locust]. 24 My kn[ees] are weak through fasting; [and] my [body has become ga]unt. 25 [I am] an object of scorn to my accusers; when they see me, [they wag] *their heads.*²¹⁹ 26 Help [me, O

Psalm 109. 4QPs^e: 109:1(?), 8(?), 13; 11QPs^b: 109:3–4(?); 4QPs^f: 109:4–6, 24–28; 11QPs^a: 109:21–22, 24–31.

216. In 11QPs^a this Psalm follows Psalm 103, but in MT and LXX it follows Psalm 108.

217. 4QPs^f. *they accuse me, although I am a prayer* MT LXX.

218. 4QPs^f (participle). *an accuser* MT LXX.

219. The form of this word in 4QPs^f can mean *their poison,* but it is more likely an alternative spelling for *their heads* (= MT LXX).

Lo]RD [*my God*]! [220] 27 Let them know that th[is] is your *hand*.[221] 28 They may cu[rse], but yo[u will bless; when they attack, they will be put to] shame; *your servant*[222] will rejoice. 29 [May my accusers be clothed with disgrace; may they be wrapped in] their [own shame as in a cloak]! 30 I will give great thanks [to the LORD with my mouth; I will praise him in the midst of the throng]. 31 For *he has stood*[223] [at the right hand of the needy, to save him from those who condemn him to death]. ▲

> ■ *In 11QPsª Psalm 109 was possibly followed by Psalm 110 (which is now lost), and then by Psalms 113 through 118, which form a very ancient grouping known as the "Passover Hallel." In Jewish tradition, part of the Hallel (Psalms 113 through 114) is sung before and part (115 through 118) is sung after the Passover meal. These six Psalms of praise were most likely found together in 4QPsᵇ, 4QPsᵉ, and 11QPsª, and possibly in 4QPsᵒ, although none of the four manuscripts still preserves all of them.*

113
1 Pra[ise] the LORD. [Give praise, you servants of the LORD, praise the name of the LORD].

114
5 [What is it with you, O sea, that] you flee? [And with you, O Jordan, that you turn back? 6 And with you, O mountains, that you skip like rams, and with you, O hills, (that you skip) like lambs? 7 Tremble, O ear]th, [at the presence of the Lord], *and at the presence*[224] of the God of Jaco[b]!

115
1 [Not] to us, O LORD, *and not*[225] [to us, but to your name give glory, because of your steadfast love and your faithfulness. 2 Why] should the nat[ions] say, "*Where is*[226] their God?" 3 Our God is in the heavens; he do[es] whate[ver] he pleases. 4 Their i[dols are silver and gold, the work of human hands]. ▲

15 [May you be blessed by the LORD], who made heaven [and earth. 16 The heavens are the LORD's heavens, but he has given the earth to hu]mans. 17 *Dead people*[227] do not pra[ise the LORD, nor any who go down into silence. 18 But it is

---

220. 4QPsᶠ. 11QPsª MT LXX add *Save me according to your steadfast love!*

221. 4QPsᶠ. *hand—O* LORD, *you have done it* 11QPsª. *hand—you, O* LORD, *have done it* MT. *hand—and you, O* LORD, *have done it* MTᵐˢˢ LXX.

222. 4QPsᶠ. *and your servant* 11QPsª MT LXX.

223. 11QPsª LXX. *he stands* MT.

Psalm 113. 4QPsᵇ: 113:1.

Psalm 114. 4QPsᵉ: 114:5(?); 4QPsᵒ: 114:7.

224. 4QPsᵒ. *at the presence* MT LXX.

Psalm 115. 4QPsᵒ: 115:1–2, 4; 4QPsᵇ: 115:2–3; 4QPsᵉ: 115:15–18.

225. 4QPsᵒ. *not* MT LXX.

226. 4QPsᵇ. *Where is now* MT LXX.

227. 4QPsᵉ LXXᵐˢˢ. *The dead* MT LXX.

we who will bless the LORD from] this time on and forevermore. Prai[se the LORD]!

116 1 [I love the LORD, for he heard my voice], my cry for mercy; 2 for he turned [his e]ar [to me, so I will call on him as long as I live. 3 The cords of death entangled me, the anguish of She]ol came upon me; [I suffered] distress and an[guish. 4 Then I called on the name of the LORD: "O LORD, please save my life!" 5 The LORD is gracious and righteous], and our God is full of co[mpassion. 6 The LORD protects the simple; when I was in a sorry state, he rescued me. 7 Be at rest once more, O my soul], for the LORD has been good [to you. 8 For you have delivered my soul from death, my eyes] from *tears.*[228] 9 I will wa[lk before the LORD in the land of the living]. 10 I kep[t my faith, even when I said, "I am sorely afflicted]." ▲

17 [I will offer to you] a thanksgiving sac[rifice, and] will call [on the name of the LOR]D. 18 I will fulfill [my vows to the LORD, in the presence of a]ll his people, 19 [in the cour]ts of the LORD's house—[in] your [midst], O Jerusalem. [Praise the LORD]!

118 1 [O give thanks to the LOR]D, for he is good; for his steadfast love endures forever. 2 [Let Is]rael [now say], "His steadfast love endures forever." 3 [Let the house of Aaron now say, "His steadfast love] endures [fore]ver." ▲

6 [The L]ORD is with me; [I will] not [be afraid. Wh]at can mortals do to me? 7 The LORD is on my side among those who help me; *I*[229] will look in triumph on those who hate me. 8 It is better *to trust*[230] in the LORD than to put confidence in hu[mans]. 9 It is better to take refuge in the LORD than to put confidence in [princes]. 10 *All nations surrounded me; in the name of the Lo[RD I cut them off].*[231] 12 They surrounded me like bees, (but) they burned out like a fire of thorns; for in the na[me of the LORD] I cut them off! ▲

[16 "The right hand of the LORD *is lifted high."*[232] 17. I will not die, but live, and I will recount the deeds of the LORD]. 18 The LORD has punished me severely, but he has [not] given me over to death. 19 Open for me the gates of

---

Psalm 116. 11QPs^d: 116:1; 4QPs^b: 116:1–3; 4QPs^o: 116:3, 5, 7–10; 4QPs^b: 116:17–19.

228. 4QPs^o. *tears, (and) my feet from stumbling* MT LXX.

Psalm 118. 4QPs^b: 118:1–3, 6–12, 18–20, 23–26, 29; 4QPs^e: 118:29(?); 11QPs^a: 118:25–29.

229. 4QPs^b. *and I* MT LXX.

230. 4QPs^b LXX. *to take refuge* MT.

231. 4QPs^b. MT LXX add vs 11: *They surrounded me, yes, surrounded me on every side; but in the name of the LORD I cut them off!*

232. 4QPs^b (reconstructed) MT^mss LXX^mss. MT LXX add *the right hand of the LORD does valiantly.*

righteousness, *that I may enter them*[233] and give thanks to the Lord. 20 [This is the gate] of [the Lord, through which the righteous will enter]. ▲

23 [This i]s the [L]ord's doing; [it is marvelous in our eyes]. 24 This is [the day that] the [L]ord [has made]; let us rejoice [and be glad in it. 25 Please] save (us) now, [O Lord]! O Lord, please give us now success! [26 Bl]essed is the one who comes in the name of the Lord. We bless you *by (your) name*[234] from the house of the Lord. 27 The Lord is God, and he has given us light. *The cords of the festal procession are with branches*[235] [up to the hor]ns of the altar. 28 You are my God, and I will give thanks to you; you are my God, I will exalt you. [29 O give thanks] to the Lord, for he is good; for his steadfast love endures forever!

104

■ *Psalm 104 is a great hymn of praise to God the creator. None of the Dead Sea Scrolls presents this Psalm in the order known from the Masoretic Text and the Septuagint, where it follows Psalm 103. In 4QPsᵉ and 11QPsᵃ it comes after Psalm 118, and in 4QPsᵈ after Psalm 147.*

0 *Of David.*[236] 1 Bless the Lord, O my soul! *O Lord our God,*[237] you are very great; *you clothe yourself*[238] with honor and majesty, 2 who wraps yourself in light as with a garment, *who stretches out the heavens like a tent,*[239] 3 *laying*[240] the beams of *his chamber*[241] on the wate[rs], who makes the clouds his chariot, *riding upon*[242] the wings of the wind, 4 who makes the winds *his messenger,*[243] *flaming*[244] fire *his*

---

233. 4QPsᵇ. *that I may enter through them* MT LXX.

234. 11QPsᵃ*. Not in 11QPsᵃ(corr) 4QPsᵇ MT LXX.

235. 11QPsᵃ. *Bind the festival procession with branches* (cf. Judg 16:11; 15:13; Ezek 3:25) MT LXX.

Psalm 104. 11QPsᵃ: 104:X, 1–6, 21–35; 4QPsᵈ: 104:1–5, 8–11, 14–15, 22–25, 33–35; 4QPsᵉ: 104:1–3, 20–22; 4QPsˡ: 104:3–5, 11–12; 2QPs: 104:6, 8–9, 11.

236. 11QPsᵃ 4QPsᵉ(?) LXX. Not in 4QPsᵈ MT.

237. 11QPsᵃ. *O Lord God* 4QPsᵈ. *O Lord my God* MT LXX. *My God* MTᵐˢˢ.

238. 4QPsᵈ. *you have clothed yourself* MT LXX.

239. 4QPsᵈ(corr) 4QPsᵉ 11QPsᵃ MT LXX. Originally omitted by 4QPsᵈ (in error?).

240. 4QPsᵈ LXXᵐˢˢ. *who lays* MT LXX.

241. 4QPsᵈ. *his chambers* MT LXX.

242. 4QPsᵈ. *who rides upon* 4QPsˡ 11QPsᵃ MT LXX.

243. 4QPsˡ. *his messengers* 4QPsᵈ MT LXX.

244. The Hebrew form of this word in 11QPsᵃ differs from that in 4QPsᵈ, 4QPsˡ, and MT, but the meaning is most likely the same.

minister,[245] 5 *setting*[246] the earth on its foundations, that it should *forev*[er] *not*[247] be shaken. 6 [You have covered it] with the deep [as with a garment; the waters stood ab]ove the mountains. [7 At your rebuke they fled; at the sound of your thunder they took to flight]. 8 They rose up to the mountains; they ran down to the valleys *and to ever*[y *pl*]*ace*[248] [that] you assig[ned] for them. 9 You set [a boun]dary they [cannot] cross, so that nev[er again] will they cover the ear[th], 10 *making*[249] springs gush forth into the ravines; they flow between *the mountains.*[250] 11 *The wild animals drink the xxxx,*[251] the wild donkeys *indulge*[252] their thirst. 12 *By the stre*[*ams*[253] the birds of the air nest; they sing] amo[ng the branches. 13 From your lofty chambers you water the mountains; the earth is satisfied by the fruit of your work. 14 You cause the grass to grow for the cattle, and plants for people to cultivate], so as to bring fo[rth food from the earth], 15 wine [to gladden the] human [heart, o]il to m[ake the face shine, and bread to st]rengthen [the human heart]. ▲

20 [You make darkness, and it is nig]ht, when all the anima[ls of the forest] go on the prowl. 21 [The young lions roar for their pre]y, and seek [their] food from G[od]. 22 When the sun [rises], *then they disappear*[254] and lie down in their dens. 23 People [g]o out to their work and to their labor until the evening. 24 O Lor[D], how numerous are your works! In wisdom *all of them have been made;*[255] the earth is full of your creatures. 25 *The sea*[256] is [va]st and wide, *to which*[257] are *many*[258] moving things *beyond numbering*[259]—living things both sm[all] and large. 26 There the ships go to and fro, and leviathan which you formed to frolic in it.

---

245. 4QPs[l]. *his ministers* 4QPs[d] 11QPs[a] MT LXX.

246. 4QPs[d] LXX[mss]. *who has set* 4QPs[l](?) MT LXX.

247. 4QPs[l] MT[mss] LXX. *never* MT (with no preposition).

248. 2QPs. *and to the place* MT LXX.

249. I.e., *(you) making* 4QPs[d]. *who makes* MT LXX.

250. 4QPs[d] LXX. *mountains* MT.

251. 4QPs[d] (object uncertain). *They* [i.e., the springs] *give drink to all the wild animals* MT LXX.

252. Literally, *intoxicate* 4QPs[d]. *quench* 2QPs MT LXX.

253. Literally, *by them.*

254. 4QPs[d] 11QPs[a] LXX. *they disappear* MT.

255. 4QPs[d]. *you have made them all* 11QPs[a] MT LXX.

256. 11QPs[a]. *There is the sea* [or, *This sea*] MT LXX.

257. Literally, *to there* 11QPs[a]. *where* MT.

258. 11QPs[a]. Not in 4QPs[d] MT LXX.

259. This seems to be the meaning of 11QPs[a]. *beyond number* 4QPs[d] MT LXX.

27 All of these look to you, to give *them*[260] their food at the proper time. 28 You give it to them, *and they gather it up;*[261] when you open your hand, they are satisfied with good things. 29 *When*[262] you take away *your breath,*[263] *then they die,*[264] and return to their dust. 30 When you send forth your Spirit, *then they are created;*[265] and you renew the face of the earth. 31 *So may*[266] the glory of the LORD endure forever; may the LORD rejoice in his works— 32 [who looks] *to*[267] the earth and it trembles, who touches the mountains and they smoke! 33 I will sing [to the L]ORD all my life; I will sing praise to my God as long as I am here. 34 May my meditation be pleasing *to him.*[268] 35 *Just as*[269] *sinful people*[270] will vanish from the earth, [so let the] wick[ed be no more. Bl]ess the LORD, O my soul! Praise the LORD!

147

◾ *The arrangement followed here is that of 11QPs[a] (and most likely 4QPs[e]), where Psalm 147, which is a hymn of praise, follows Psalm 104. The two Psalms also occur together in 4QPs[d], but in the opposite order (104 after 147). It seems that the few letters preserved before Psalm 147 in 4QPs[d] are from Psalm 106.*

1 [Praise] the LORD! How good it is to sing praises to our God. [*Praise to*] *our G[o]d is fit[ting];*[271] *and a song of praise is fitting and pleasant.*[272] 2 The LORD builds up Jerusalem; he gathers together the outcasts of Israel. 3 [He heals the broken]hearted and binds up their wou[nds. 4 He determines the number of the stars, and calls ea]ch [of them by name]. ▲

---

260. 11QPs[a] LXX. Not in MT.

261. 11QPs[a]. *they gather it up* MT LXX.

262. 11QPs[a] 4QPs[d]. *When you hide your face, they are terrified. When* MT LXX.

263. 11QPs[a]. *their breath* MT LXX.

264. 11QPs[a] LXX. *they die* MT.

265. 11QPs[a] LXX. *they are created* MT.

266. 11QPs[a]. *May* MT LXX.

267. 11QPs[a]. *at* MT. (The meanings of the two different Hebrew prepositions are very close in this context.)

268. 4QPs[d]. MT LXX add *since I rejoice in the LORD* 11QPs[a].

269. 11QPs[a]. *For* 4QPs[d]. Not in MT LXX.

270. 11QPs[a] (participle). *sinners* (noun) MT LXX.

Psalm 147. 4QPs[d]: 147:1–4, 13–17, 20; 11QPs[a]: 147:1–2, 18–20; MasPs[b]: 147:18–19.

271. 4QPs[d]. Not in 11QPs[a] MT LXX.

272. 4QPs[d]. *for a song of praise is pleasant and fitting* 11QPs[a] MT LXX.

13 [For he strengthens the bars of your] gat[es; he bles]ses your children within you. 14 He grants peace within [your bor]ders, *and*[273] he satisfies you with the finest of whe[at]. 15 He sends out his command to the earth; [his wo]rd ru[ns swift]ly. 16 He spreads snow [like wool; he scatters the frost like ashes]. 17 He hurls do[wn his hail like pebbles—who can withstand his *icy downpour?*][274] 18 He sends forth his word, [and melts them; he makes] his wi[nd blow, and the waters flow. 19 He declares his word to Jacob], his statutes and his ordinances to [Israel. 20 He has not dealt in this way with] any other nation; *he*[275] *has not revealed (any) ordinances to them.*[276] [Praise the LORD!]

106

■ *There is very little evidence among the scrolls for Psalm 106,*[277] *a hymn of praise and confession. Although Psalm 106 seems to precede Psalm 147 in 4QPs^d, our translation here corresponds with the order of the 11QPs^a-Psalter, where 104 precedes 147. Psalm 106 is thus placed after 147, but it should be noted that 106 is not found in 11QPs^a.*

48 [Blessed be the LORD, the God of Israel, from everlasting to everlasting. And let all the people say, "Am]en"! [Pra]ise the LORD!

105

■ *After Psalm 147 11QPs^a (and most likely 4QPs^e) continues with 105, which is a hymn of praise. These are the only two Psalms scrolls to preserve parts of this Psalm.*

1 O *give thanks to the* LORD, *for he is good; for* [*his steadfast love endures forever!*[278] O give thanks to the LORD, call] on his name; make known [his de]eds among the peoples! 2 [Sing to him, sing praises to] him; [tell] of all his wonderful acts! 3 Glory in [his ho]ly name; [*let the*] heart [*of the one who seeks*] *his favor*[279] rejoice! 4 Look to the LORD and his strength; seek [his presence continually! 5 Remember] his wonders that he has done, his miracles, and the judgmen[ts he pro-

---

273. 4QPs^d LXX. Not in MT.

274. Literally, *cold*.

275. 11QPs^a. *and he* 4QPs^d MT LXX.

276. 11QPs^a LXX. *and as for his ordinances, they have not known them* MT.

Psalm 106. 4QPs^d: 106:48(?).

277. The identification of this Psalm is not certain.

Psalm 105. 11QPs^a: 105:X, 1–11, 25–26, 28–29(?), 30–31, 33–35, 37–39, 41–42, 44–45; 4QPs^e: 105:1–3, 23–25, 36–45.

278. 11QPs^a (cf. Ps 118 and 136). Not in MT. *Hallelujah* LXX.

279. 11QPs^a (= 1 Chron 16:10b LXX). *let the hearts of those who seek the* LORD MT LXX.

nounced, 6 O descendants of Abraham], *you his servants,*[280] you children of Jacob, *his chosen one.*[281] 7 *For*[282] he is [the LORD our God]; his judgments are [in all the earth]. 8 He has remembered his covenant forever, the word that he commanded, for a thousand [generations, 9 the covenant that he made] *with*[283] Abraham, *his*[284] sworn promise to Isaac, 10 and which he confirmed [to Jacob as a statute], to Israel as an everlasting covenant, 11 as follows: *"To you*[285] I will give th[e land of Canaan, as the portion you will inhe]rit." ▲

23 [Then Israel came to] Egypt; *Ja*[*cob*[286] lived as an alien in the land of Ham. 24 And the LORD made his people very fruitful, and made them stronger than] their enemies. 25 He then tu[rned] their hearts to hate [his people, to deal deceitfully with his servants. 26 He sent Moses his servant, and Aa]ron whom he had chosen. [27 They performed his wondrous acts among them, and his miracles in the land of Ham. 28 He se]nt darkness, [and made the land dark, for had they not rebelled against *their pro*]*mise?*[287] 29 *He made*[288] [their waters into blood, and caused their fish to die]. 30 *Their land swarmed*[289] [with frogs, even in the chambers of their rulers. 31 He spoke, and there came swarms of flies, and gn]ats throughout [their country. 32 He turned their rain into hail, with lightning flashing through their land. 33 He] struck their vines [and fig trees, and devastated the trees of their country. 34 He spoke, and the locusts arrived], and grasshoppers without [number; 35 they devoured all the vegetation in their land, and gobbled up the produce] of their soil. 36 [He struck down all the firstborn in their land, the finest of a]ll their strength. 37 Then *he led forth his people*[290] [with silver and gold, and there was not] one among [his] tribes who faltered. 38 [*The Egy*]*ptians were glad*[291] when they departed, because dread of [*Israel*][292] had descended [upon them. 39 He spread] out a cloud as a covering, and fire to provide light by night. 40 They asked, and he br[ought quails, and fu]lly satisfied them [with the food

---

280. 11QPs^a(corr) LXX. *(Abraham) his servant* MT LXX^mss.

281. 11QPs^a MT^mss. *his chosen ones* MT LXX.

282. 11QPs^a. Not in MT LXX.

283. 11QPs^a and MT use different Hebrew prepositions, but the meaning is the same.

284. 11QPs^a. *and his* MT LXX.

285. Plural 11QPs^a. Singular MT LXX.

286. 4QPs^e. *and Jacob.*

287. A likely reading 11QPs^a. *his word* MT. *his words* MT^mss LXX.

288. 11QPs^a. *he turned* MT LXX.

289. Feminine *(land)* 11QPs^a. Masculine MT.

290. 4QPs^e 11QPs^a. *he led them forth* MT LXX.

291. 4QPs^e. *Egypt was glad* MT LXX.

292. Literally, *them.*

of] he[aven. 41 He opened the ro]ck, and water gushed out; [it flowed through the desert like a ri]ver. 42 For [he remembered his ho]ly promise, as well as Abraham [his servant].

43 [So he led forth] his peo[ple] with rej[oicing, his cho]sen ones [with shouts of joy]. 44 Then he gave [them the la]nds of the na[tions, and they took possession of what the peoples had toiled for— 45 so] that they might keep [his statutes and ob]serve [his laws. Praise the LORD]!

◼ *Psalms 146 and 148, both of which are hymns of praise, are found only in 11QPs^a and 4QPs^e. Their order and position early in the 11QPs^a-Psalter is in marked contrast to their placement near the end of the MT-150 Psalter.*

146 1 Praise the LORD! [Praise the LORD, O my soul! . . . 9 The LORD watches over foreign strangers, and] sustains the orphan and the widow; but [he subverts] the way [of the wicked. . . . *Let*] *all the earth* [*fear*] *the* LORD, [*let all the inhabitants of the earth revere*] *hi*[*m! . . .*] *in his being known though all his works (which) he created* [*. . .*] *his mighty works.*[293] 10 The LORD will reign forever, your God, O Zion, for all generations. Praise the LORD!

148 [294] 1 *Praise the* LORD[295] from the heavens; pra[ise him in the heights above! 2 Praise him], all his angels; praise him, all his heav[enly host! 3 Praise him, sun and moon]; praise him, all you shining stars! 4 Praise [him, you highest heavens, and you waters] above the skies!

5 *Praise*[296] [the name of the LORD—for he] gave the command, and they were created. 6 And he set them in place forev[er and ever; he fixed their bounds which cannot] be crossed.

7 Praise the LORD fro[m the earth, you sea monsters, and all] ocean depths, 8 you fire and hail, snow and fr[ost, stormy wind] fulfilling his command! 9 You mountains and all [hills, fruit trees and all] cedars! 10 You wild animals and all cattle, [small creatures and flying birds! 11 You kings] of the ea[rth] and all nations, you princes and [all rulers of the earth! 12 Young men and mai]dens alike, old people and chil[dren] together!

◼ *In the Masoretic Text Psalms 120 through 134 form an ancient grouping known as the fifteen "Psalms of Ascent." Most of these Psalms were found together in 4QPs^e and 11QPs^a, but only up through Psalm 132, which means that the 11QPs^a-Psalter has only thirteen Ascent Psalms in this grouping. The remaining two Psalms occur later in the 11QPs^a-Psalter.*

Psalm 146. 4QPs^e: 146:1; 11QPs^a: 146:9, X, 10.

   293. 11QPs^a. Not in MT LXX.

Psalm 148. 11QPs^a: 148:1–12.

   294. Preceded by Psalm 146 11QPs^a. Preceded by Psalm 147 MT LXX.

   295. 11QPs^a. *Praise the* LORD! *Give praise* MT LXX.

   296. 11QPs^a. *Let them praise* MT LXX.

120
[297] 6 [For too l]ong I have *lived*[298] *bef*[*ore*][299] those who hate peace. 7 I am for peace—but when I speak, they are] for [war]. ▲

121
0 A Song *of Ascents.*[300] 1 I lift up my eyes to the mountains—(but) where does [my help] come from? 2 My help comes from the LORD, who made heaven and earth. 3 He will not let your fo[ot slip], *and*[301] he who watches over you will not slumber. 4 Indeed, he who watch[es over Is]rael will neither slumber nor sleep.

5 *By night*[302] the LORD is your keeper, *your shade*[303] at your right hand. 6 [The s]un will not harm you by da[y], nor the moon by night. 7 The LORD will protect you from al[l harm]; he will wat[ch over] your life. 8 *He*[304] will watch over your going out and your coming in, from this time on and fore[vermore].

122
[305] 0 A Song of Ascents. Of David. 1 I re[joiced with those who said to me], "Let us go to the house of the LORD." 2 *My feet*[306] have been standing within your gates, [O Jeru]salem!

3 Jerusalem—built as a city *that is bound*[307] *firmly,*[308] 4 *to which*[309] *the congregation of Israel*[310] [goes up] to give thanks to the name of the LORD. 5 For *th*[*ere*][311] thrones] were set up [for] judgment, *the throne*[312] of the house of David. 6 Pray for the peace of Jeru[salem: "May they prosper who lo]ve you! 7 May peace be within your walls, *peace*[313] within your towers!" 8 [For the sake of my relatives

---

Psalm 120. 4QPs[e]: 120:6–7.

   297. Psalm originally preceded by Psalm 148 11QPs[a]. Preceded by Psalm 119 MT LXX.

   298. 4QPs[e]. *it lived for itself* (i.e., *my soul*) MT. *lived* LXX.

   299. 4QPs[e]. *among* MT. Not in LXX.

Psalm 121. 11QPs[a]: 121:1–8.

   300. 11QPs[a]. *of Ascents* or *for Ascents* MT (with a preposition).

   301. 11QPs[a] MT[mss] LXX. Not in MT.

   302. 11QPs[a]. Not in MT LXX.

   303. 11QPs[a]. *the LORD is your shade* MT LXX.

   304. 11QPs[a]. *The LORD* MT LXX.

Psalm 122. 11QPs[a]: 122:1–9; 4Q522: 122:1–9.

   305. Preceded by an apocryphal composition 4Q522. Preceded by Psalm 121 11QPs[a] MT LXX.

   306. 11QPs[a]. *Our feet* MT LXX.

   307. Masculine (*Jerusalem* as subject) 11QPs[a] (cf. 125:2). Feminine MT.

   308. 11QPs[a]. *firmly together* MT LXX.

   309. 11QPs[a]. *which is where* MT LXX.

   310. 11QPs[a]. *as was decreed for Israel* 4Q522 MT LXX.

   311. 4Q522. *to there* MT LXX.

   312. 11QPs[a]. *the throne* MT LXX.

   313. 4Q522. *security* MT. *and security* 11QPs[a] MT[mss] LXX.

and] friends, *let me say,*[314] "Peace be within you! 9 For the sake of the house of the LORD our G[od, I will seek] *your peace.*"[315]

123 0 [*A Song of*] *David. Of Ascents.*[316] 1 To you I lift up my eyes, O you who sits enthroned in hea[ven! 2 See, just as the eyes] of servants look to [the hand of] their master, as the eyes [of a maid look to the hand of her mistress, so our eyes look to the LORD our God, until he shows us mercy]. ▲

124 7 [We have escaped like a bird from the fowlers' snare; the snare has been broken, and we] have escaped. 8 *Our helper*[317] is in the name of the LORD, who made [heaven and earth].

125 [0 A Song of Ascents]. 1 Those who trust in the LORD are like Mount Zion, *which cannot*[318] [be shaken, but en]dures [forever]. 2 Just as the mountains surround *Jerusalem,*[319] *the LORD*[320] surrounds his peo[ple],[321] from this time on and forevermore. 3 For the scepter of wickedness will not remain over the land allotted to the righteous, and so the righteous will not stretch out *their hand*[322] to do wrong. 4 Do good, O LORD, to those that are good, and to those who are upright *in heart.*[323] 5 (*In*) *tortuous ways*[324] the LORD will lead away *all*[325] *evildoers.*[326] Peace be upon Israel!

126 1[327] When the LORD brought back the *captives*[328] [to Zion], we were *like ones restored.*[329] 2 Then our mouth was filled with laughter, and our

---

314. 11QPs[a]. *let me now say* MT LXX.

315. 4Q522. *your prosperity* (literally, *good*) 11QPs[a] MT LXX.

Psalm 123. 11QPs[a]: 123:1–2.

316. 11QPs[a] (cf. 121:1 MT). *A Song of Ascents* MT LXX.

Psalm 124. 11QPs[a]: 7–8.

317. Meaning unclear 11QPs[a]. *Our help* MT LXX.

Psalm 125. 11QPs[a]: 1–5; 4QPs[e]: 2–5.

318. 11QPs[a]. *it cannot* MT LXX.

319. Masculine (*Jerusalem* as subject) 11QPs[a] (cf. 122:3). Feminine MT.

320. 11QPs[a]. *so the LORD* MT LXX.

321. Literally, *his people surrounds* 4QPs[e]. *surrounds his people* MT LXX.

322. 4QPs[e*]. *hands* 4QPs[e(corr)]. *their hands* MT LXX.

323. 4QPs[e] 11QPs[a] LXX. *in their hearts* MT.

324. 4QPs[e*] 11QPs[a]. *But those who turn aside to their own crooked ways* MT. (*. . . to crooked ways*) LXX.

325. 11QPs[a]. *with* 4QPs[e] MT LXX.

326. Literally, *doers of evil* 11QPs[a] MT[mss]. literally, *doers of the evil* MT LXX.

Psalm 126. 11QPs[a]: 126:1–6; 4QPs[e]: 126:1–5; 1QPs[b]: 126:6.

327. 4QPs[e*]. *A Song of Ascents* 4QPs[e(corr)] 11QPs[a] MT LXX.

328. 4QPs[e] MT[mss] LXX. *return* MT. (The words are similar in Hebrew but come from different roots.)

329. Most likely meaning 11QPs[a] LXX. *like dreamers* 4QPs[e] MT.

tongue with shouts of joy; [then] it was said among the nations: *"He*[330] has done great things for them." 3 The LORD has done great things for us—we are happy. 4 Restore our fortunes, O LORD, like the streams in the Negev. 5 May those who sow in tears reap [with shouts of j]oy! 6 *Those who go forth and weep,*[331] *carrying*[332] the seed for sowing, [will return again with shouts of] joy, *carrying*[333] his sheaves with him.

127 0 [A Song of Ascents]. Of Solomon. 1 Un[less the LOR]D builds the house, [its builders la]bor in vain. [Unless the LORD guards the city], the guard [keeps watch] in vain. 2 It is vain for you [to rise up early and go late to rest, eating the bread of anxi]ous toil—[for] he grants [sleep] to [those he loves. 3 Sons are indeed a heritage of the LOR]D; the fruit [of the womb a re]ward. 4 [Like arrows in the hands of a warrior are the sons (born in) on]e's youth. 5 [Happy is the] man who [has his quiver full of them]. They will not be put [to shame] when [they encounter their enemies at the city gate].

128 3 [Your wife will be] *like the*[334] fruit[ful] vine [within your house; your children will be like olive shoots] around [your table. 4 See, this is how the m]an who fears the LORD [will be blessed]. 5 May *the Lord*[335] bless you [from Zion, and may you see the prosperity of Jerusa]lem all the days of your life. 6 And may you see your children's [children. Peace be upon Israel]!

129 0 A S[ong of Ascents. 1 *"Many times*[336] have they at]tacked me from my youth"—let Israel now say— 2 *"Many times*[337] [have they attacked me from my youth, yet they have no]t gained victory over me." 3 *Wicked people*[338] plowed over my back; [they made their furrows long. 4 The] *Lord*[339] is righteous; he has cut the cords of the wicked. 5 May [all who ha]te Zion be disgraced [and turned back]! 6 May they be like grass on the rooftops, which withers before it can grow, 7 [with which reapers cannot fill their hands], nor sheaf-binders fill

---

330. 4QPs^{e*}. *The LORD* 4QPs^{e(corr)} 11QPs^a MT LXX.

331. 11QPs^{a*} LXX. *The one who goes forth weeping* 11QPs^{a(corr)} MT.

332. Plural 11QPs^a LXX. Singular MT.

333. Plural 1QPs^b 11QPs^a LXX. Singular MT.

Psalm 127. 1QPs^b: 127:1–5; 11QPs^a: 127:1.

Psalm 128. 11QPs^a: 128:3–6; 1QPs^b: 128:3.

334. 1QPs^b. *like a* MT LXX(?).

335. 1QPs^b. *the LORD* MT. Ambiguous LXX.

Psalm 129. 11QPs^a: 129:1–8; 4QPs^e: 129:8.

336. 11QPs^a (for this translation, see 11QPs^a at the beginning of vs 2). *Greatly* MT.

337. 11QPs^a MT^{mss}. *greatly* MT (The two Hebrew words are similar in form and meaning.)

338. 11QPs^a LXX. *the wicked people* MT.

339. 11QPs^a. *the LORD* MT. Ambiguous LXX.

their *arms*.[340] 8 *While those*[341] who pass by do not say, "[May the blessing of the LORD] *your God*[342] be upon you! We bless you in the name of the LORD!"

130 1[343] *Lord,*[344] out of the depths [I cry to you, O LORD. 2 Lord, hea]r my voice! *Let your ear now be attentive*[345] *to me,*[346] [to the sound of my pleas! 3 If you], O LORD, kee[p a record of sins], Lord, who could stand? 4 But with you there is forgiveness, [so that you are revered. 5 I am waiting for the LOR]D, my soul is waiting; *in his word*[347] I put my hope. 6 *Wait,* [O *my soul,*[348] for the Lord] *like wa[tchmen*[349] wait for] the morning, yes, like watchmen for the morning. 7 O Israel, put your hope [in the LORD! For with the LORD] there is steadfast love, and with him is *abundant redemption.*[350] 8 *He*[351] will redeem [Israel from all] their [iniquities].

131 0 [A Song of Ascents. Of David. 1 O Lo]RD, [my] he[art is not proud, my eyes are not haughty; I do not occupy myself with things too great or too wonderful for me]. ▲

132 8 [Rise up, O LORD, and go] to your resting place, you, and the a[rk of] your might. 9 May your priests be clothed with righteousness, and may your faithful ones shout for joy. 10 For the sake of David your servant do not turn away the face of your anointed one. 11 The LORD swore to David [a sure oath] from which he will n[ot] turn back: *"Surely*[352] *one of your physical descendants*[353] I will place upon your throne. 12 [If] your sons keep my covenant and my

---

340. Literally, *bosom.*

341. Literally, *which those* 11QPs^a. *and those* MT.

342. 11QPs^a. Not in MT LXX.

Psalm 130. 11QPs^a: 130:1–8; 4QPs^e: 130:1–3, 6.

343. 4QPs^e*. *A Song of Ascents* 4QPs^e(corr) 11QPs^a MT LXX.

344. 11QPs^a. Not in 4QPs^e MT LXX.

345. 11QPs^a. *Let your ears be attentive* MT LXX.

346. 11QPs^a. Not in MT LXX.

347. 11QPs^a MT^mss LXX^mss. *and in his word* MT. *and in your word* MT^mss. *in your word* LXX.

348. 11QPs^a (cf. Pss 42:6, 12; 43:5). *My soul is waiting* MT LXX.

349. 4QPs^e. *more than watchmen* MT. *more than a watchman* LXX.

350. Apparent meaning in 11QPs^a, although the Hebrew is difficult and somewhat different from that of MT.

351. 11QPs^a. *And he* MT LXX.

Psalm 131. 11QPs^a: 131:1.

Psalm 132. 11QPs^a: 132:8–18.

352. 11QPs^a. Not in MT LXX.

353. Literally, *from the offspring of your body.*

decrees that I teach them, then [th]eir sons also *will accede to*[354] your throne forevermore."

13 For the LORD has chosen Zion; he has de[sired] it for his dwelling-place: 14 "This is my resting-place forever; here I will dwell, for I have desired [it]. 15 I will abundantly bless her (with) [provisions]; I will satisfy her poor with food. 16 I will also [clothe] her priests with salvation; and her faithful ones *will shout for joy.*[355] 17 There I will make a horn sprout up for David; I have s[et up] a lamp for my anointed one. 18 I will clothe his enemies with disgrace, but upon him his crown will be resplendent."

119

■ *Psalm 119 is a Wisdom composition and by far the longest of all the Psalms. It is found between Psalms 132 and 135 in 11QPs[a], where it occupies almost nine columns. This is in marked contrast to its position between Psalms 118 and 120 in the Masoretic Text and the Septuagint.*

1 Blessed are those [whose ways are blame]less, who walk in the law of the LORD! 2 Blessed are [those who observe his decrees], who seek *it*[356] [at all] *times,*[357] 3 who also [do nothing wrong]; (but) walk in his [ways]. 4 You [have laid down your precepts, that are to be] fully [obey]ed. 5 O that [my ways were consistent in observing] *your [tr]uth!*[358] 6 Then [I would not be put to shame, being focused on al]l your commandments. ▲

10 [With] my [whole heart] I seek you; [do not let me stray from your commandments]. 11 I treasure [your w]ord in my h[ea]rt, [so that I may not sin against you]. 12 Blessed are you, O LORD; te[ach me your statutes]. 13 With my lips I declare all the or[dinances (that come from) your mouth. 14 I rejoi]ce in the path of your decrees [as much as in all riches]. 15 *Let me meditate*[359] on your precepts, and focus on your ways. 16 I will find my delight in your *statutes;*[360] I will

---

354. 11QPs[a]. *will sit upon* MT LXX.

355. 11QPs[a]. *will shout indeed for joy* MT LXX.

Psalm 119. 11QPs[a]: 119:1–6, 15–28, 37–49, 59–73, 82–96, 105–120, 128–142, 150–164, 171–176; 4QPs[h]: 119:10–21; 1QPs[a]: 119:31–34, 43–48, 77–80; 4QPs[g]: 119:37–46, 49–50, 73–74, 81–83, 89–92; 5QPs: 99–101, 104, 113–120, 138–142; 11QPs[b]: 119:163–165.

356. 11QPs[a] (apparently *her*). *him* MT LXX.

357. 11QPs[a] MT[mss]. *with their whole heart* MT LXX (cf. 119:20).

358. Most likely reading 11QPs[a]. *your statutes* MT LXX.

359. 4QPs[h] (cohortative form). *I will meditate* 11QPs[a] MT LXX.

360. 11QPs[a] (masculine form, as in vs 12). *statutes* (feminine form) 4QPs[h] MT.

not neglect *your words*.[361] 17 *Fulfill your purpose for*[362] your servant, *and I will live*[363] and obey *your words*.[364] 18 Open my eyes, *that I may see*[365] wonderful things from *your laws*.[366] 19 I am a sojourner on earth: do not hide your commandments from me! 20 My soul is consumed with longing for your laws at all times. 21 You rebuked the arrogant, who are cursed and who stray from your commandments. 22 *Roll away*[367] from me their scorn and contempt, for I have kept your decrees. 23 Even though rulers sit plotting against me, your servant will meditate on your statutes. 24 Your decrees also are my delight—they are my counselors. 25 [My so]ul clings to the dust; [restore me according to your word]. 26 When I recounted my ways, you [answered me; teach me your statut]es. 27 [Make me understand] the way of *your precept;*[368] [then I will meditate on] your marvel[ous works]. 28 My soul is fading away from [grief; strengthen me according to] your [word]. ▲

31 [I cling to] your decr[ees, O Lord; do not put me to shame]. 32 I run [the course of] *your commandme*[*nt,*[369] for you set my heart free. 33 Teach me, O Lo]rd, the w[a]y of your statutes, and I will [observe it to the end. 34 Give me understanding, so that I may keep] your law and ob[serve it with all my heart]. . . . 37 Turn my eyes from looking at worthless things; *be gracious to me*[370] *according to your word*.[371] 38 Fulfill to your servant your promise, which produces reverence for you. 39 Turn away my disgrace that I dread; for your ordinances are good. 40 See how I long for your precepts; in your righteousness *be gracious to me.*[372] 41 *And may the Lord bring me*[373] your *steadfast love,*[374] your salvation according to your promise. 42 *Then he will have an answer*[375] for anyone who taunts me,

---

361. 11QPs[a] MT[mss] LXX. *your word* MT.

362. 4QPs[h] 11QPs[a] MT[mss]. *deal bountifully with* MT LXX (cf. Psalms 57:3 [Heb 36:3] and 138:8 [Heb 137:8]).

363. 4QPs[h] 11QPs[a] MT[mss]. *that I may live* MT LXX.

364. 11QPs[a] MT[mss] LXX. *your word* MT.

365. 4QPs[h]. *and I will see* 11QPs[a] MT LXX.

366. 11QPs[a] MT[mss]. *from your law* MT LXX.

367. 11QPs[a] (cf. LXX). *Take away* MT.

368. 11QPs[a]* MT[mss]. *your precepts* 11QPs[a(corr)] MT LXX.

369. 1QPs[a]. *your commandments* MT LXX.

370. 11QPs[a]. *give me life* 4QPs[g] MT LXX.

371. 11QPs[a]. *in your way* 4QPs[g] MT LXX. *in your ways* MT[mss]. *in your word* MT[mss].

372. 11QPs[a]. *give me life* 4QPs[g] MT LXX.

373. 4QPs[g]. *And may . . . come to me, O Lord* 11QPs[a] MT (LXX similar).

374. 4QPs[g] MT LXX. *steadfast love* 11QPs[a].

375. 11QPs[a]*. *Then I shall have an answer* 11QPs[a(corr)] 4QPs[g] MT LXX.

for I observe your precepts.[376] 43 Do not take the word *of your truth*[377] completely from my mouth, for my hope is *in your words.*[378] 44 I will keep your law continually *and always;*[379] 45 I shall walk about *in its broad streets,*[380] for I have sought out your precepts. 46 I will also speak of your decrees before kings, and shall not be put to shame; 47 for I find delight in your [commandments], which I love. 48 I revere [your] commandments, [whi]ch I love, and *I will rejoice in*[381] your statutes. 49 Remember *your words*[382] t[o your servant, upon whi]ch you have made me hope. 50 This is my comfort in my distress: that your promise gives me life. ▲

59 When I consider my ways, I turn my feet to your decrees. 60 I hasten and do not delay to keep your commandments. 61 Though the cords of the wicked ensnare me round, I will not forget your law. 62 At midnight I will rise to give you thanks, because of your righteous laws. 63 I am a friend to all those that fear you, and to those who keep your precepts. 64 The earth, O LORD, is full of your steadfast love; teach me *your statute.*[383] 65 You have dealt well with your servant, O LORD, according to your word. 66 Teach me good judgment and knowledge, for I believe in your commandments. 67 Before I was afflicted I went astray, but now I obey your word. 68 You are good, O LORD,[384] and do good; teach me your decrees. 69 The arrogant besmear me with lies, but I keep your precepts with all my heart. 70 Their hearts are callous and gross, but *your law is my de[li]ght.*[385] 71 It is good for me that *you afflicted me,*[386] so that I might lea[rn] your [statut]es. 72 The law from your mouth is better to me *than a thousand*[387] [gold and silver pieces. 73 Your hands have made me and formed me]; give me understanding that I may lear[n] your [commandments. 74 Those who fear you will see me and be glad], because [I have hoped] in [your wo]rd. ▲

77 [Let your compassion come to me, that I may li]ve; for [your la]w is my delight. 78 [May the arrogant be put to shame, because *he has sub]verted me*[388] [by

---

376. 4QPsg. *for I trust in your word* 11QPsa MT LXX.

377. 4QPsg. *of truth* 11QPsa MT LXX.

378. 11QPsa. *in your ordinance* 4QPsg MT. *in your ordinances* MTmss LXX.

379. 11QPsa. *forever and ever* MT LXX.

380. 11QPsa. *in freedom* 4QPsg MT LXX.

381. 11QPsa. *I will meditate on* MT LXX.

382. 11QPsa LXXmss. *(the) word* MT. *your word* LXX.

383. 11QPsa. *your statutes* MT LXX.

384. 11QPsa LXX. Not in MT.

385. 11QPsa MTmss. *I delight in your law* MT LXX.

386. 11QPsa MTmss LXX. *I was afflicted* MT.

387. 11QPsa. *than thousands of* MT LXX.

388. 1QPsa (cf. Job 19:6). *they have subverted me* MT LXX.

deceit]; as for me, [I will] meditate on your precepts. 79 [May those who fear you turn to me, so that they may understand] your decrees. 80 [May my heart be blameless in your statutes, so] th[at I may not be put to shame. 81 My soul pi]nes for [your sal]vation; [I hope in your word]. 82 *My eye fails,*[389] watching for your promise; I ask, "When will you comfort me?" 83 For *you have made me*[390] like a wineskin in the smoke, yet I have not forgotten *your steadfast love.*[391] 84 How long must your servant endure? When will you punish those who persecute me? 85 The arrogant have dug *a pit*[392] for me, people who do not live according to your law. 86 All your commandments are trustworthy; but they persecute me without cause—please help me! 87 They have almost wiped me *from the earth,*[393] but I have not forsaken your precepts. 88 According to your steadfast love *be gracious to me,*[394] so that I may obey *the decree*[395] of your mouth. 89 Forever, O LORD, your word is firmly fixed in heaven. 90 Your faithfulness endures to all generations; you have established the earth, and it endures. 91 By your ordinances they stand today; for all things are your servants. 92 If your law had not been my delight, I would have perished *in my iniquity.*[396] 93 I will never forget your precepts, for by them you have given me life. 94 I am yours; save me, for I have sought out your precepts. 95 The wicked are waiting to destroy me, but I pay attention to your decrees. 96 I have seen a limit to all perfection, but your commandment is exceedingly broad. ▲

99 [I have more insight than all my teachers, for your decrees are m]y [meditation. 100 I have more understanding than the elders, for] I [observe your precepts. 101 I hold back my feet from every evil path, so that I may keep] your word. . . . 104 [Through your precepts I get understanding; therefore I hate every] false pa[th]. 105 *Your words are*[397] a lamp to my feet, *a light*[398] to *my paths.*[399] 106 I have taken an oath, and have confirmed it, *to carry out*[400] your righteous ordi-

---

389. 11QPs^a. *My eyes fail* 4QPs^g MT LXX.

390. 11QPs^a. *I have become* 4QPs^g MT LXX.

391. 11QPs^a. *your statutes* MT LXX.

392. 11QPs^a MT^{mss}. *pits* MT. *complaints* LXX.

393. 11QPs^a. *on the earth* MT LXX.

394. 11QPs^a. *give me life* MT LXX.

395. 11QPs^a LXX. *the decrees* LXX.

396. 11QPs^a MT^{mss}. *in my misery* 4QPs^g MT LXX.

397. 11QPs^a MT^{mss}. *Your word is* MT LXX.

398. 11QPs^a. *and a light* MT LXX.

399. 11QPs^a. *to my path* MT LXX.

400. 11QPs^a. *to observe* MT LXX.

nance.[401] 107 I am severely *distraught;*[402] *be gracious to me,*[403] O LORD, according to *your promise.*[404] 108 *Accept*[405] the praise offerings of my mouth, O LORD; teach me *some of your ordinances.*[406] 109 Though I constantly take my life in my hands, *I*[407] do not forget your law. 110 The wicked have laid a snare for me; *as for me, I*[408] have not gone astray *(from) your precepts.*[409] 111 Your decrees are my heritage forever; *they are*[410] the rejoicing of my heart. 112 I have set my heart to perform your statutes forever, to the very end. 113 I hate double-minded people; *I love*[411] your law. 114 You are my refuge and my shield; I have put my hope *in your words.*[412] 115 Depart from me, you evildoers, that I may keep *the commandment*[413] of my God. 116 Sustain me according to your promise, that I may live, and let me not be put to shame *because of my breaking wave.*[414] 117 Hold me up, that I may be safe, *and I will lift up*[415] your statutes continually. 118 You reject all who go astray from your statutes; for their deceitfulness is in vain. 119 All the wicked of the earth *I discount*[416] as dross, *for which reason*[417] I love *all*[418] your decrees. 120 My body trembles in fear [of you], and I am afraid of your judgments. ▲

128 Truly I approve of *(your) complete precepts;*[419] I hate every false way. 129 Your decrees are *streams of honey;*[420] therefore my soul observes them.

---

401. 11QPs^a(corr) MT^mss. *ordinances* 11QPs^a* MT LXX.

402. 11QPs^a. *afflicted* MT LXX.

403. 11QPs^a LXX^mss. *give me life* MT LXX.

404. 11QPs^a LXX^mss. *your word* MT LXX.

405. 11QPs^a MT^mss LXX^mss. *Accept now* MT LXX.

406. 11QPs^a. *and your ordinances* MT LXX.

407. 11QPs^a. *and I* MT LXX.

408. 11QPs^a. *I* MT LXX.

409. 11QPs^a. *and from your precepts* MT LXX.

410. 11QPs^a(corr). *for they are* 11QPs^a* MT LXX.

411. 11QPs^a. *but I love* MT LXX.

412. 11QPs^a MT^mss LXX^mss. *in your word* MT LXX.

413. 11QPs^a. *the commandments* MT LXX.

414. 11QPs^a (error?). *because of my hope* MT LXX.

415. 11QPs^a. *and I will have regard for* MT LXX.

416. 11QPs^a LXX. *you reject* MT. *you discount* MT^mss.

417. 11QPs^a. *therefore* MT.

418. 11QPs^a. Not in 5QPs MT LXX^mss. *continually* LXX.

419. 11QPs^a MT^mss. *all the precepts of everything* MT. *all of your precepts* LXX.

420. 11QPs^a. *wonderful* MT LXX.

130 *Unfold your words, and enlighten the one who*[421] imparts understanding to the simple. 131 I open my mouth and I pant; *because*[422] *I long for*[423] your commandments. 132 Turn to me, and have mercy upon me, as is your custom toward those who love your name. 133 Direct my footsteps *toward*[424] your promise, and do not let any iniquity rule over me. 134 Redeem me from human oppression, that I may observe your precepts. 135 Make your face shine upon your servant, and teach me your statutes. 136 My eyes shed streams of tears *because*[425] people do not keep your law. 137 You are righteous, O LORD, and your judgments are *right.*[426] 138 You have laid down your decrees in righteousness and in all trustworthiness. 139 My zeal wears me out, because my enemies ignore your words. 140 Your promise is thoroughly tested; *your*[427] servant loves it. 141 Though I am lowly and despised, I do not forget your precepts. 142 *[Righteous deed]s are [ri]ghteous deeds*[428] *always,*[429] and your law is truth. ▲

150 Those who pursue wicked schemes draw near; they are far from your law. 151 Yet you are near, O LORD, and all your commandments are true. 152 Long ago I learned from *knowledge of you*[430] that you have established *me*[431] forever. 153 Look on my misery and deliver me; *I*[432] do not forget your law. 154 Defend my cause and redeem me; give me life according to your promise! 155 Salvation is far from the wicked, for they do not seek out your statutes. 156 Great is your compassion, O LORD; *be gracious to me*[433] according to your laws. 157 Many are my persecutors and my adversaries, but I have not swerved from your decrees. 158 I look on the faithless with disgust, because they do not keep your word. 159 Consider how I love your precepts, O LORD! *Be gracious to me*[434] according to your

---

421. 11QPs[a]. *The unfolding of your words gives light* MT LXX.

422. 11QPs[a]. Not in MT LXX.

423. 11QPs[a]. *I desire* MT LXX. (11QPs[a] and MT use different Hebrew words with a similar meaning.)

424. 11QPs[a]. *in* MT. *according to* MT[mss] LXX.

425. 11QPs[a] MT[mss]. *since* MT LXX. (11QPs[a] has two Hebrew words where MT has one; the meaning is similar.)

426. Plural 11QPs[a]. Singular MT LXX.

427. 11QPs[a(corr)]. *and your servant* 5QPs MT LXX. *your cloud* 11QPs[a*] (error).

428. Likely reading 11QPs[a]. *Your righteousness is an everlasting righteousness* MT LXX.

429. 11QPs[a]. *forever* 5QPs MT LXX.

430. 11QPs[a]. *from your decrees* MT LXX.

431. 11QPs[a]. *them* MT LXX.

432. 11QPs[a]. *for I* MT LXX.

433. 11QPs[a]. *give me life* MT LXX.

434. 11QPs[a]. *give me life* MT LXX.

promise.[435] 160 The s[um] of *your words*[436] is truth, and *every righteous ordinance*[437] lasts forever. 161 Princes persecute me without cause, but my heart stands in awe of your words. 162 I rejoice at your word *more than*[438] one who finds great spoil. 163 I [hate] and abhor false[hood], *but*[439] I love your law. 164 [Seven times a day I pr]aise you for [your righteous or]dinances. 165 [Great peace have those who love yo]ur la[w; nothing can make them stumble]. ▲

171 My lips will pour forth praise *to you,*[440] for you teach me your statutes. 172 May my tongue sing of your word, for all your commandments are right. 173 Let your hand be ready to help me, for I have chosen your precepts. 174 I longed for your salvation, O LORD; *your law*[441] is my delight. 175 Let me live, that I may praise you, and let *your ordinances*[442] help me. 176 I have gone astray like a lost sheep; seek out your servant, for I have not forgotten *your decrees.*[443]

135

■ *Psalm 135, a hymn of praise to God, directly follows Psalm 134 in the Masoretic Text and the Septuagint, but in 11QPs^a it follows Psalm 119. Psalm 135 also occurs in two other arrangements, both of which vary from the Masoretic Psalter. In 4QPs^k it is followed by a Psalm that is no longer preserved and then by Psalm 99, and in 4QPs^n Psalm 135:12 is directly followed by Psalm 136:23.*

1 *Give praise, O servants of the* LORD, *praise the name of the* LORD; *praise the* LORD![444] 2 *And exalt the* LORD,[445] you who stand in the house of the LORD, in the courts of the house of our God, *and in your midst, O Jerusalem!*[446] 3 Praise the

---

435. 11QPs^a. *according to your steadfast love* MT. *in your steadfast love* LXX.

436. 11QPs^a MT^mss LXX. *your word* MT.

437. 11QPs^a. *every one of your righteous ordinances* MT LXX.

438. 11QPs^a. *like* MT LXX.

439. 11QPs^a MT^mss LXX. Not in MT.

440. 11QPs^a. Not in MT LXX.

441. 11QPs^a. *and your law* MT LXX.

442. 11QPs^a* MT^mss LXX. *your judgments* 11QPs^a(corr). *your ordinance* MT.

443. 11QPs^a. *your commandments* MT LXX.

Psalm 135. 11QPs^a: 135:1–6, X, 7, 9, 17–21; 4QPs^k: 135:6–8, 10–13, 15–16; 4QPs^n: 135:6–8, 11–12.

444. 11QPs^a MT^mss. *Praise the* LORD, *praise the name of the Lord, give praise, O servants of the* LORD! MT LXX. Compare Ps 113:1: *Praise the* LORD, *give praise, O servants of the* LORD, *praise the name of the Lord!*

445. 11QPs^a (cf. Ps 99:5, 9). Not in MT LXX.

446. 11QPs^a (cf. Ps 116:19). Not in MT LXX.

LORD, for *he*[447] is good; sing *his name,*[448] for that is pleasant. 4 For *he*[449] has chosen Jacob for himself, *and Israel*[450] *as a possession for himself.*[451]

5 *I*[452] know that the LORD is great, and that *our God*[453] is above all gods. 6 The LORD does *what*[454] pleases him, in heaven and on earth, *to do as he does; there is none like the LORD, there is none like the LORD, and there is none who acts like the King of gods,*[455] in the seas *and in all (their) depths.*[456] 7 It is he who makes clouds rise [at the] end of *the earth,*[457] who brings out the wind from his storehouses.

8 It was he who struck down the firstborn of Egypt, [both of humans and animals. 9 He] se[nt signs and wonders into your m]id[st, O Egypt, against Pharaoh and all his servants. 10 He struck down] many [nat]ions, *mighty kings*[458]— 11 Sihon king of the [Amorit]es, [Og king of Bashan, and all the kingdoms of Canaan— 12 and he gave their land as a heritage *to us,*[459] a heri]ta[ge] to [I]srael his people, 136:22 [*as a heritage*] to his people Israel, fo[r his steadfast love endures forever. 23 It is he who remembered*] us [*in our depressed state*], for [*his steadfast love*] endures fore[*ver*].[460]

13 Your name, O LORD, endures forever; [your renown, O LORD, through all generations. 14 For the LORD will vindicate his people, and have compassion on his servants. 15 The idols of the nations are silver and gol]d, *the products*[461] of human hands. 16 [They have] mouths, [but they cannot speak; they have eyes but cannot see]. 17 They have [ears] but cannot hear, *and there is*[462] no breath in their mouths. 18 Those who make them shall become like them—*and everyone*[463] who trusts in them!

---

447. 11QPs[a]. *the* LORD MT LXX.

448. 11QPs[a]. *to his name* MT LXX.

449. 11QPs[a]. *the* LORD MT LXX.

450. 11QPs[a]. *Israel* MT LXX.

451. 11QPs[a] LXX[mss]. *as his possession* MT LXX.

452. 11QPs[a]. *For I* MT LXX.

453. 11QPs[a]. *our Lord* MT LXX.

454. 11QPs[a]. *all that* MT LXX.

455. 11QPs[a], probably also 4QPs[n]. Not in MT LXX.

456. 11QPs[a] MT[mss] LXX. *and all (their) depths* MT. *and (their) depths* LXX[mss].

457. 4QPs[n]. *the earth, who makes lightnings for the rain* 11QPs[a] MT LXX.

458. 4QPs[k]. *and killed mighty kings* MT LXX.

459. 4QPs[n]. Not in MT LXX.

460. 4QPs[n] (but note that MT and LXX read *his servant Israel* in 136:22). In MT, LXX, and (it seems) 11QPs[a], Ps 135:12 is followed by vs 13. Since so little text from 4QPs[n] is preserved, both the readings from Ps 136 and 135:13 onward are included in the translation.

461. 4QPs[k] MT[mss] LXX. *the product* MT.

462. 11QPs[a] MT[mss]. *and there is also* MT LXX.

463. 11QPs[a] MT[mss] LXX. *everyone* MT LXX[mss].

19 O house of Israel, bless the LORD! O house of Aaron, bless the LORD! 20 O house of Levi, bless the LORD! You who fear the LORD, bless the LORD! 21 *May the LORD bless you*[464] from Zion, he who dwells in Jerusalem. Praise the LORD!

136 1 O give thanks to the LORD, for he is good, for his steadfast love endures forever. 2 O give thanks to the God of gods, for his steadfast love endures forever. 3 O give thanks to *the Lord*[465] of lords, for his steadfast love endures forever; 4 to him who alone performs *wonders,*[466] for his steadfast love endures forever; 5 to him who made the heavens by understanding, for his steadfast love endures forever; 6 to him who spread out the earth upon the waters, for his steadfast love endures forever; 7 to him who made the great *luminaries,*[467] for his steadfast love endures forever; *the sun and the moon, for his steadfast love endures forever;*[468] 8 the sun *as rulers*[469] *of the day,*[470] for his steadfast love endures forever; 9 *moon*[471] and stars to rule over night, for his steadfast love endures forever.

10 To him who struck Egypt through their firstborn, for his steadfast love endures forever; 11 and brought Israel out from among them, for his steadfast love endures forever; 12 with a strong hand and with an outstretched arm, for his steadfast love endures forever; 13 to him who divided the Red Sea in two, for his steadfast love endures forever; 14 and made Israel pass through the midst of it, for his steadfast love endures forever; 15 (*who*) *overthrew*[472] Pharaoh and his army in the Red [Sea, for his steadfast love endures] for[ever]; 16 to him who led his people through the [wilder]ness, for [his steadfast love endures] forev[er] ▲

135:12b [. . . *as a heritage to his people Israel,*[473] for his steadfast love endures forever. 136:23[474] It is he who remembered] us [in our depressed state], for [his steadfast love] endures fore[ver]. . . . 26 [O give thanks to the God of heaven], for his steadfast love endures forever.

■ *Both 11QPs^a (col. 16) and 11QPs^b have a longer ending following Psalm 136:26. Since this ending contains material also found in Psalm 118 (vss 1, 15, 16, 8, 9,*

---

464. 11QPs^a LXX^mss (cf. Ps 134:3). *Blessed be the LORD* MT LXX.

Psalm 136. 11QPs^a: 136:1–7, X, 8–16, 26; 4QPs^n: 136:22–24.

465. 11QPs^a uses the singular and MT the plural, but with no difference in meaning.

466. 11QPs^a LXX^mss. *great wonders* MT LXX.

467. 11QPs^a. *lights* MT.

468. 11QPs^a. Not in MT LXX.

469. 11QPs^a MT^mss (apparently with the *sun and moon* of vs 7 as subjects). *as a ruler* MT; cf. *for authority* LXX.

470. 11QPs^a LXX. *over the day* MT.

471. 11QPs^a. *the moon* MT LXX.

472. 11QPs^a LXX^mss. *and overthrew* MT LXX.

473. Note that 136:22 is very similar, but reads *his servant* instead of *his people*.

474. Following Ps 135:12 4QPs^n. Following Ps 136:22 MT LXX and (it seems) 11QPs^a.

X,[475] and 29); scholars originally termed it the "Catena" (meaning a connected series of verses). This cannot be a different form of Psalm 118 since this Psalm is found earlier in 11QPs[a]. Some scholars have suggested that the Catena is in fact a separate composition altogether, but it is more likely a longer ending to Psalm 136 since it follows 136:26 with virtually no break in 11QPs[a] (which typically has spaces between successive compositions or starts them on the next line).

The Catena

1 O give thanks to the LORD, for he is good, for his steadfast love endures forever! 15 Listen to the shouts of joy and victory in the tents of the righteous: "The right hand of the LORD does valiantly, 16 the right hand of the LORD is lifted high, the right hand of the LORD has wrought strength!" 8 It is better to trust in the LORD than to put confidence in humans. 9 It is better to take refuge in the LORD than to put confidence in princes. X It is better to trust in the LORD than to put confidence in a thousand people. 29 O give thanks to the LORD, for he is good, for his steadfast love endures forever! Praise the LORD!

145

■ *Among the Dead Sea Scrolls, Psalm 145 is found only in 11QPs[a], in a form that is most unusual when compared to the Masoretic Text. First, there is a recurring refrain ("Blessed be the Lord and blessed be his name forever and ever"), which clearly shows that this Psalm was meant by those who compiled the 11QPs[a]-Psalter to be recited or sung. Second, 11QPs[a] preserves a verse of this Psalm that is missing in virtually all manuscripts of the Masoretic Text, although it is found in the Septuagint (see the introduction to the Psalms and the footnote on v 13: "God is faithful . . ."). This verse is so necessary and certain that almost all modern English-language Bibles now include it. Third, the ending to the Psalm ("This is for a memorial") is of interest because it is a subscript not found in the Masoretic Text (compare Ps 72:20: "The prayers of David, son of Jesse, are concluded").*

[476]0 *A Prayer.*[477] Of David. 1 I will extol you, O LORD,[478] my God the King, and I will bless your name forever and ever. *Blessed be the LORD and blessed be his*

---

475. The symbol X denotes an unknown verse.

Catena. 11QPs[a]: Catena 1, 15, 16, 8, 9, X, 29; 11QPs[b]: Catena 1, 15, 16.

Psalm 145. 11QPs[a]: 145:1–7, 13, X, 14–21, X.

476. Preceded by Psalm 136 and Catena 11QPs[a]. Preceded by Psalm 144 MT LXX.

477. 11QPs[a]. *A Song of Praise* MT LXX.

478. 11QPs[a]*. Not in 11QPs[a(corr)] MT LXX.

name forever and ever.[479] 2 *Blessed is the day*[480] I will bless you, and I will praise your name forever and ever. *Blessed be the* LORD, *his name*[481] *forever and ever.* 3 Great is the LORD, and greatly to be praised; *his greatness*[482] is unfathomable. *Blessed be the* LORD *and blessed be his name forever and ever.* 4 One generation *will commend*[483] your works to another, and they will tell of your mighty acts. *Blessed be the* LORD *and blessed be his name for ever and ever.* 5 Of the glorious splendor of your majesty *they will speak,*[484] *and*[485] of your wondrous works *I will meditate.*[486] *Blessed be the* LORD *and blessed be his name forever and ever.* 6 And people will speak of the might of your awesome deeds, and *I will recount*[487] your mighty acts.[488] *Blessed be the* LORD [*and blessed be*] *his na*[me] *forever and ever.* 7 They will [pour forth] the fame of your abundant goodness, [and will sing aloud of your righteousness]. ▲

12 [. . . *Blessed be the* LORD] *and blessed be his name forever and ever.* 13 Your kingdom is an everlasting kingdom, and your dominion endures throughout all generations. *Blessed be the* LORD *and blessed be his name forever and ever. God*[489] *is faithful in his words, and gracious in all his deeds.*[490] *Blessed be the* LORD *and blessed be his name forever and ever.* 14 The LORD upholds all who are falling, and raises up all who are bowed down. *Blessed be the* LORD *and blessed be his name forever and ever.* 15 The eyes of all look to you, and *you have given*[491] them their food at the proper time. *Blessed be the* LORD *and blessed be his name forever and ever.* 16 *You yourself*[492] open your hand, and satisfy the desire of every living thing. *Blessed be the* LORD *and blessed be his name forever and ever.* 17 The LORD is just in all his ways, and kind in all his deeds. *Blessed be the* LORD *and blessed be his name forever and ever.* 18 The LORD *is near*[493] and *blessed be his name forever and ever; they*[494] call upon him *in*

---

479. A constant refrain at the end of each vs 11QPs^a. Not in MT LXX.

480. 11QPs^a. *Every day* MT LXX.

481. 11QPs^a*. *and blessed be his name* 11QPs^a(corr) MT LXX.

482. 11QPs^a. *and his greatness* MT LXX.

483. Plural 11QPs^a. Singular MT LXX.

484. 11QPs^a LXX. *and the words of* MT.

485. 11QPs^a. Not in MT LXX.

486. 11QPs^a. *let me meditate* MT LXX.

487. 11QPs^a. *I will recount it* MT LXX^mss. *they will recount* LXX.

488. 11QPs^a MT. *your mighty act* MT^mss LXX.

489. 11QPs^a. *The* LORD LXX. Not in MT.

490. *God . . . deeds* 11QPs^a MT^mss LXX. Not in MT.

491. 11QPs^a*. *you give* 11QPs^a(corr) MT. *having given* LXX.

492. 11QPs^a. *You* MT LXX.

493. 11QPs^a. *is near to all who call upon him* MT LXX.

494. 11QPs^a. *to all who* MT LXX.

faithfulness.[495] *Blessed be the* LORD *and blessed be his name forever and ever.* 19 He fulfills the desire of those *who fear him;*[496] he also hears their cry, and saves them. *Blessed be the* LORD *and blessed be his name forever and ever.* 20 The LORD preserves all those *who fear him,* but he will destroy all the wicked. *Blessed be the* LORD *and blessed be his name forever and ever.* 21 My mouth will speak the praise of the LORD, and let every creature bless his holy name. *Blessed be the* LORD *and blessed be his name forever and ever.*[497] *This is for a memorial*[498] . . .

154

> ▨ *Psalm 154 proclaims the greatness and deliverance of God. While not found in the Masoretic Text and the Septuagint, Psalms 154 and 155 (which occurs later in the 11QPsª-Psalter) are preserved in some manuscripts of the Syriac Psalter. This is significant, since it shows that some traditions known at Qumran were preserved in the writings of Eastern Orthodox Christianity. In the translation below, the missing verses at the beginning and the end of this Psalm have been supplied from the Syriac.*

[1 With a loud voice glorify God; in the congregation of the many proclaim his splendor. In the multitude of the just glorify his name, and with the faithful celebrate his majesty. 3 Unite] your souls with the good ones and with the perfect ones to glorify the Most High. 4 Form a community to make known his salvation, and do not hesitate in making known his might and his majesty to all the simple ones. 5 For it is to make known the glory of the LORD that Wisdom has been given, 6 and it is for recounting his many deeds she has been revealed to humanity: 7 to make known to the simple ones his power, to explain his greatness to those lacking sense, 8 those who are far from her gates, those who stray from her portals.

9 For the Most High is the Lord of Jacob, and his majesty is upon all his works. 10 And the person who glorifies the Most High is accepted like one who brings a meal offering, 11 like one who offers rams and calves, like as one who fattens the altar with many burnt offerings, as a sweet-smelling fragrance from the hand of the righteous ones. 12 From the gates of the righteous her voice is heard, and her song from the assembly of the pious. 13 When they eat until they are full she is mentioned, and when they drink in community together, 14 their meditation is

---

495. 11QPsª. *in truth* MT LXX.

496. 11QPsª. *who love him* MT LXX.

497. *Blessed . . . and ever* (constant refrain) 11QPsª. *forever and ever* (short final refrain) MT LXX.

498. 11QPsª (most likely a subscript; cf. Ps 72:20: *The prayers of David, son of Jesse, are concluded*). Not in MT LXX.

Psalm 154. 11QPsª: 154:3–19.

on the law of the Most High, their words on making known his power. 15 How distant from the wicked is her word, from all arrogant people is it to know her.

16 Behold the eyes of the LORD have pity upon the good, 17 and he increases his mercy upon those who glorify him; from the time of danger he will deliver [their] soul. 18 [Bless] the LORD who redeems the humble from the hand of for-eigne[rs and deliv]ers the pure from the hand of the wicked, 19 [who establishes a horn out of Ja]cob and a judge of the peoples out of Israel. 20 [He will spread out his tent in Zion, and will live forever in Jerusalem].

Plea for Deliverance

This fascinating Psalm affirms God's kindness and faithfulness and appeals for his forgiveness and protection. It is one of several "new" Psalms that were unknown to scholars before the discovery of the Dead Sea Scrolls.

1 For a maggot cannot praise you, nor a worm recount your mercy. 2 But the living can praise you, all those who stumble can praise you, 3 when you reveal your mercy to them, and when you teach them your justice. 4 For in your hand is the soul of every living being; the breath of all flesh you have given. 5 Deal with us, O LORD, according to your goodness, according to your great compassions, and according to your many righteous acts. 6 The LORD has heard the voice of those who love his name and has not deprived them of his mercy. 7 Blessed be the LORD, who performs righteous deeds, crowning his pious ones with mercy and compassions.

8 My soul cries out to praise your name, to give thanks with shouts for your merciful deeds, 9 to proclaim your faithfulness—of praise of you there is no end! 10 I was near death for my sins, and my iniquities had sold me to Sheol; 11 but you saved me, O LORD, according to your great compassion, and according to your many righteous acts. 12 Indeed I have loved your name, and in your shelter I have found refuge. 13 When I remember your power my heart is brave, and I lean upon your mercies.

14 Forgive my sin, O LORD, and cleanse me from my iniquity. 15 Bestow on me a spirit of faith and knowledge, and let me not be dishonored in ruin. 16 Let not Satan rule over me, nor an unclean spirit; 17 neither let pain nor the evil in-clination take possession of my bones. 18 For you, O LORD, are my praise, and in you I hope all the day long. 19 Let my brothers rejoice with me and my father's house, who are puzzled by your graciousness. [. . . Fore]ver I shall rejoice in you.

Plea for Deliverance. 11QPs^a: Plea 1–18.

139

■ *This Psalm continues the personal note found in the Plea for Deliverance by inviting God to examine the Psalmist's heart, to see his devotion, and to do away with his enemies. It is preceded by Psalms 137 and 138 in the MT-150 Psalter and the Septuagint, but followed by the same two Psalms in the 11QPs^a-Psalter.*

[7 Where can I go from your Spirit? Or where can I flee from your presence?] 8 [If I ascend up into heaven, you are there; if I make my bed] in Sheol, there you are! 9 If I take the wings of the dawn, and settle on the farthest limits of the sea, 10 *there*[499] your hand will lead me, and your right hand will hold me fast. 11 *And let me say,*[500] "Surely darkness covers me, *and night has girded me about.*"[501] 12 Even the darkness is not dark to you; the night is as bright as the day, for darkness is as light to you.

13 For you who formed my inmost being, you knitted me together in my mother's womb. 14 I praise you, *for you are fearful; wondrous,*[502] wonderful are your works, as my soul knows very well. 15 *My pain*[503] is not hidden from you, by whom I was made in secret, intricately woven together in the depths of the earth. 16 Your eyes saw my unformed body; in *your books*[504] each of them was written, the number of days *for its formation even for it with its corresponding member from them all.*[505] 17 And how precious are your thoughts to me, O God! *Why is the sum of them so vast?*[506] 18 If I try to count them, they outnumber the sand. *When I come to the end,*[507] *I will still*[508] be with you.

19 If only you would slay the wicked, O God, *so that*[509] bloodthirsty men *would depart*[510] from me, 20 people who speak of you maliciously, your enemies

---

Psalm 139. 11QPs^a: 139:8–24.

499. 11QPs^a. *even there* MT LXX.

500. 11QPs^a. *And I said* MT LXX.

501. 11QPs^a. *and the night around me will become light* MT LXX.

502. 11QPs^a. *for I have been fearfully and wonderfully made* MT LXX.

503. 11QPs^a. *My frame* MT LXX.

504. 11QPs^a. *your book* MT LXX.

505. 11QPs^a (The text is troubled here, but seems to describe the formation of the body). *the days that were formed when not one among them existed* MT LXX (also a troubled text).

506. 11QPs^a. *How vast is the sum of them!* MT LXX.

507. Or, *When I awake.*

508. 11QPs^a. *I will still* MT LXX.

509. 11QPs^a LXX. *even so that* MT.

510. 11QPs^a and MT use different forms of the same verb, with no change in meaning.

who lift themselves up for evil. 21 Do I not hate those, O LORD, who hate you? And do I not *cut myself off from*[511] *those who rise up against you?*[512] 22 I hate them with utter contempt; I regard them as my enemies. 23 Search me, O God, and know my heart! Test me, and know my thoughts! 24 And see if there is any offensive way in me, and lead me in the way everlasting.

137

■ *Psalm 137 is a lament over the destruction of Jerusalem and a plea to God to punish Judah's enemies. In the MT-150 Psalter and the Septuagint this Psalm follows 138, but our translation corresponds with the 11QPs[a]-Psalter by placing it after Psalm 139.*

1 By the rivers *in Babylon,*[513] there *they sat down,*[514] yes we wept, when we remembered Zion. . . . 9 [Happy will be the one who seizes] your little ones and dashes them against the rock!

138 0 Of David. 1 I give you thanks, O LORD,[515] with my whole heart; before *the LORD God*[516] I sing praise to you. 2 I bow down toward your holy temple, and give thanks to your name for your steadfast love and for your faithfulness; for you have exalted your word above every name of yours. 3 On the day I called you answered me; you increased the strength in my soul.

4 All the kings of the earth will praise you, O LORD, for they have heard the words of your mouth. 5 Then they will sing of the ways of the LORD, for the glory of the LORD is great. 6 For though the LORD is exalted, he has regard for the lowly; but he notes the proud from a distance.

7 Though I walk *in the middle*[517] of trouble, you preserve my life against the anger of my enemies; you stretch forth *your hand,*[518] and your right hand rescues me. 8 The LORD will fulfill his purpose for me; your steadfast love, O LORD, endures forever. Do not abandon the works of your own hands.

---

511. 11QPs[a]. *despise those* MT.

512. 11QPs[a] MT[mss]. *your adversaries* MT LXX (probably).

Psalm 137. 11QPs[a]: 137:1, 9.

513. 11QPs[a]. *of Babylon* MT LXX.

514. 11QPs[a]* (in error?). *we sat down* 11QPs[a(corr)] MT LXX.

Psalm 138. 11QPs[a]: 138:1–8.

515. 11QPs[a] MT[mss] LXX. Not in MT.

516. 11QPs[a]* MT[mss]. *the gods* 11QPs[a(corr)] MT LXX.

517. 11QPs[a]. *in the midst* MT.

518. 11QPs[a] MT LXX. *your hands* MT[mss] LXX[mss].

Ben Sira 51

■ *This poem was previously familiar to us as the second canticle following the epilogue of Ben Sira (a book also known as Ecclesasticus or Sirach). The book is not found in the Hebrew Bible, but it is included in the Old Testament of Roman Catholic and Orthodox Bibles and among the Apocrypha of Protestant Bibles. The form of this poem in 11QPs^a is very erotic in places (see, for example, vs 22, where hand can mean penis). Not surprisingly, the Greek version seems to have revised the canticle by substituting pious ideas for such erotic images—but the scrolls now give us access to the original, uncensored poem. Our English translation of the book of Sirach among the Dead Sea Scrolls is found after Proverbs.*

13 While I was a young man, before I had gone astray, I looked for her. 14 She came to me in her beauty, and eventually I sought her out. 15 Even as the blossom drops in the ripening of grapes, making the heart happy, 16 so my foot trod in uprightness; for since my youth I have known her. 17 I inclined my ear but a little, and great was the captivation I found. 18 So she became a wet-nurse for me; to my teacher I give my sceptre. 19 I decided to make sport: I was eager for pleasure, without stopping. 20 I kindled my passion for her, I could not turn away my face. 21 I bestirred my desire for her, and on her heights I could not relax. 22 [I] spread my "hand" [. . .] and perceived her nakedness. 23 I cleansed my "hand" [. . . 30 . . .] your reward in its time.

The Apostrophe to Zion

■ *Like several other Psalms (for example, 46, 48, 76, and 87), the Apostrophe to Zion focuses on Jerusalem, in this case invoking blessing on her, affirming the defeat of her enemies, and looking forward to her salvation and everlasting righteousness. This Psalm, which was unknown before the discovery of the Dead Sea Scrolls, is found in two collections: the 11QPs^a-Psalter (col. 22 of 11QPs^a, frg. 6 of 11QPs^b) and the 4QPs^f-Psalter (cols. 7–8).*

1 I remember you for blessing, O Zion; with all my strength I have loved you. May your memory be blessed forever! 2 Great is your hope, O Zion, that peace and your expected salvation will come. 3 Generation after generation will dwell

---

Sirach 51. 11QPs^a: 51:13–23, 30 [Heb 1–11, 18].

The Apostrophe to Zion. 11QPs^a: Apostrophe 1–18; 4QPs^f: Apostrophe 1 –2, 11–18; 11QPs^b: Apostrophe 4–5.

in you and generations of pious ones will be your splendor: 4 those who yearn for the day of your salvation that they may rejoice in the greatness of your glory. 5 At your glorious abundance they will suckle, and in your magnificent squares they will scamper. 6 You will remember your prophets' acts of devotion, and you will glory in the deeds of your pious ones. 7 Let violence be purged from your midst; let falsehood and deceit be cut off from you. 8 Your children will rejoice in your midst and your precious ones will be united with you. 9 How they have hoped for your salvation, how your perfect ones have mourned for you. 10 Your hope does not perish, O Zion, nor is your longing forgotten.

11 Who is the one to have ever perished (in) righteousness, or who is the one to have ever survived in his iniquity? 12 A person is tested according to his path; everyone is awarded according to his deeds. 13 All around your enemies are cut off, O Zion, and all your foes have been scattered. 14 Your praise is a pleasant odor, O Zion, ascending throughout all the world. 15 Many times I remember you for blessing; with all my heart I bless you. 16 May you attain to everlasting righteousness, and may you accept the blessings of the glorious ones. 17 Accept a vision described for you, and dreams of prophets sought for you. 18 Be exalted and spread out, O Zion! Praise the Most High, your savior: let my soul rejoice in your glory!

93

■ *This hymn of praise follows Psalm 92 in 4QPs^b, the Masoretic Text, and the Septuagint, but in the 11QPs^a-Psalter it occurs in a completely different position: between the Apostrophe to Zion and Psalm 141. This is the order followed in our translation.*

1 *Praise the* LORD*!*[519] The LORD reigns; he is robed in majesty; the LORD is robed, *and he is girded*[520] with strength. Indeed, *you establish the world;*[521] it cannot be moved. 2 Your throne was established from long ago; [you are] from [eter]nity. 3 The floods have lifted up, [O LORD, the floods have lifted up their voice; the floods lift up their surging waves. 4 More majestic than the thun]ders of mi[ghty] waters, [more majestic than the breakers of the sea, majestic is the LORD on high]. 5 Your decrees are [very su]re; holi[ness] *is the beauty of*[522] your house, O LORD, forever[more]. ▲

Psalm 93. 11QPs^a: 93:1–3; 4QPs^m: 93:3–5; 4QPs^b: 93:5.

519. 11QPs^a. Not in MT LXX.

520. 11QPs^a LXX. *he is girded* MT.

521. 11QPs^a (cf. Ps 75:4). *he established the world* LXX. *the world is established* MT (cf. Ps 96:10).

522. Literally, *is lovely for* 4QPs^b (cf. Jer 6:2). *befits* MT LXX.

141

■ *Psalm 141 contains an individual's prayer for help against being corrupted by wicked people. Among the scrolls it is found only in the 11QPsᵃ-Psalter (11QPsᵃ and 11QPsᵇ). Instead of following Psalm 140 as in the Masoretic Text and the Septuagint, in this arrangement Psalm 141 occurs between 93 and 133. Perhaps this prayer for deliverance was placed after Psalm 93's hymn to God's invincible kingship and unchanging decrees in order to give the Psalmist confidence as he sought help.*

5 [Let the righteous strike me—it is a kindness]; and let them correct me—it is oil upon my head. My head will not refuse it, for *my prayer*[523] is continually against their wicked deeds. 6 When they are given over to those who will condemn them, then they shall hear how pleasant my words are. 7 Like a rock that one breaks apart and shatters on the ground, so will *my bones*[524] be scattered at the mouth of Sheol.

8 But my eyes are directed toward you, O LORD my God; in you I take refuge—do not leave me defenseless! 9 Keep me from the trap which they have laid for me, and from the snares of evildoers. 10 Let the wicked fall into their own nets, while I alone escape!

133

■ *As noted earlier, in the Masoretic Text Psalms 120 through 134 form an ancient grouping known as the "Songs of Ascent," but in the 11QPsᵃ-Psalter only Psalms 120 through 132 are grouped together. The fourteenth Song of Ascent is found here, between Psalms 141 and 144.*

0 A Song of Ascents. Of David. 1 See how good and how pleasant it is when brothers live together in unity! 2 It is like the precious oil on the head, running down upon the beard, down on Aaron's beard, running down over the collar of his *robes*.[525] 3 It is like the dew of Hermon, which falls down upon *the mountain*[526] of Zion! For *to this place*[527] the LORD has bestowed *the blessing*[528] forevermore. *Peace be upon Israel!*[529]

Psalm 141. 11QPsᵃ: 141:5–10; 11QPsᵇ: 141:10.

   523. The Hebrew word has been wrongly spelled in 11QPsᵃ (= MT LXX).

   524. 11QPsᵃ. *our bones* MT LXX. *their bones* LXXᵐˢˢ.

Psalm 133. 11QPsᵃ: 133:1–3, X; 11QPsᵇ: 133:1–3, X.

   525. Masculine noun 11QPsᵃ 11QPsᵇ. Feminine noun MT. *robe* LXX.

   526. 11QPsᵃ MTᵐˢˢ. *the mountains* MT LXX.

   527. 11QPsᵃ. *there* MT LXX.

   528. 11QPsᵃ. *the blessing, life* 11QPsᵇ MT LXX.

   529. 11QPsᵃ 11QPsᵇ (cf. 125:5 and 128:6). Not in MT LXX.

144

■ *This prayer for victory is preserved only in 11QPs^a and 11QPs^b, both of which represent the 11QPs^a-Psalter. Whereas it follows Psalm 143 in the Masoretic Text and the Septuagint, in this arrangement 144 occurs between Psalms 133 and 155.*

[530] 1 *Blessed*[531] be the LORD my rock, who trains my hands for war, *and*[532] my fingers for battle. 2 My steadfast love and my fortress, my stronghold and *a deliverer*[533] for me, my shield, and (the one) in whom I take refuge, who subdues *peoples*[534] under me. 3 O God,[535] what are humans that you care about them, or mortals that you think of them? 4 People are like a breath, *and*[536] their days are like a fleeting shadow.

5 Part your heavens, O God,[537] and *come down!*[538] Touch the mountains so that they smoke! 6 Make your lightning flash and scatter them; shoot [your arrows and rout them! 7 Stretch out] your [hand] from above; rescue me and deliver [me from the mighty waters, from the hands of foreigners]. . . .

15 Happy are the people for whom this is so! Happy are the people *whose*[539] God is the LORD!

155

■ *Following the preceding prayer for victory (Ps 144), Psalm 155 includes a plea for deliverance and offers a prayer of thanksgiving for God's granting of salvation. While not found in the Masoretic Text and the Septuagint, Psalms 154 (also in the 11QPs^a-Psalter) and 155 are preserved in some manuscripts of the Syriac Psalter. For the significance of their presence in the 11QPs^a-Psalter, see the note at the beginning of Psalm 154.*

1 O LORD, I have called to you, listen to me. 2 I spread forth my palms to your holy dwelling; 3 incline your ear and grant me my petition, 4 and do not

---

Psalm 144. 11QPs^a: 144:1–7, 15; 11QPs^b: 144:1–2.

    530. Preceded by Psalm 133 11QPs^a 11QPs^b. Preceded by Psalm 143 MT LXX.

    531. 11QPs^a 11QPs^b (reconstructed) MT^mss. *Of David. Blessed* MT LXX.

    532. 11QPs^a MT^mss. Not in MT LXX.

    533. 11QPs^a. *my deliverer* MT LXX.

    534. 11QPs^a MT^mss (cf. Ps 18:48 and 2 Sam 22:48). *my people* MT LXX.

    535. 11QPs^a. *O LORD* MT LXX.

    536. 11QPs^a. Not in MT LXX.

    537. 11QPs^a. *O LORD* MT LXX.

    538. Imperative form 11QPs^a LXX. Imperfect form MT.

    539. 11QPs^a and MT use different Hebrew forms but the meaning is the same.

Psalm 155. 11QPs^a: 155:1–19.

withhold my request from me. 5 Build up my soul and do not cast it down; 6 and do not abandon it in the presence of the wicked. 7 May the Judge of Truth turn back from me the rewards of evil.

8 O LORD, judge me not according to my sin; for no living person is righteous in your presence. 9 Give me discernment, O LORD, in your law and teach me your precepts, 10 so that many may hear of your works and nations may honor your glory. 11 Remember me and do not forget me, and lead me not into what is too difficult for me. 12 Cast far from me the sin of my youth, and may my transgressions not be remembered against me. 13 Purify me, O LORD, from the evil plague, and let it not again turn back on me. 14 Dry up its roots from me, and let its le[av]es not flourish within me.

15 You are (my) glory, O LORD, therefore my request is fulfilled in your presence. 16 To whom can I cry and he would grant my request? And as for mere humans—what more can [their] streng[th] do? 17 My trust, O LORD, is befo[re] you. I cried "O LORD," and he answered me, [and he healed] my broken heart. 18 I slumbered [and sl]ept, I dreamed; indeed [I awoke. 19 You supported me, O LORD, and I invoked the Lo]RD [my deliverer. 20 Now I will behold their shame; I have trusted in you and will not be ashamed. Render glory forever and ever. 21 Save Israel, O LORD, your faithful one, and the house of Jacob, your chosen one].

142

■ *This prayer for deliverance from enemies is preserved only in 11QPsᵃ. Whereas it follows Psalm 141 in the Masoretic Text and the Septuagint, in this arrangement Psalm 142 occurs after 155, perhaps because of the common theme of calling on God for deliverance.*

3 [When my spirit grows faint within me, it is you who knows my way. In the path where I walk they have hidden a trap] for me. 4 *I look*[540] to my right and *I watch*[541]—but there is no one who is concerned for me. I have no refuge left; no one cares about me.

5 I cry to you, O LORD; I say, "You are my refuge, my portion in the land of the living." 6 Listen to my cry; for I am desperately wretched; save me from my persecutors, for they are too strong for me. 7 Set me free from prison, that I may give thanks to your name. Then the righteous *will gather round*[542] me, since you will deal bountifully with me.

Psalm 142. 11QPsᵃ: 142:3–8 [MT 142:4–9].

   540. 11QPsᵃ LXX. *Look!* MT.

   541. 11QPsᵃ LXX. *watch!* MT.

   542. 11QPsᵃ*. *will encircle* 11QPsᵃ(corr) MT.

143

0 A Psalm of David. 1 Hear my prayer, O LORD; give ear to my suppli-cations in your faithfulness; answer me in your righteousness! 2 And do not enter into judgment with your servant, for no one living is righteous before you. 3 For the enemy *persecutes*[543] me. He *has dashed*[544] my life to the ground; he has made me sit in darkness like those long dead. 4 Therefore my spirit faints within me, *and*[545] my heart within me is dismayed.

5 I remember the days of old; I meditate on all your deeds; I contemplate *the works*[546] of your hands. 6 I stretch out my hands t[o yo]u; my soul thirsts for you *in*[547] a parched land. Selah.

7 Answer me quickly, O LORD; my spirit is failing. Do not hide your face from me, or I shall become like those who go down to the Pit. 8 [Let me h]ear of your steadfast love in the morning, [for I have placed my trust in you. Show me the way I should go, for] I lift up [my soul] to you.

149

▨ *This prayer for deliverance from enemies is preserved only in 11QPs[a], although recon-struction indicates that it was also in the second Psalms scroll from Masada (MasPs[b]). In the Masada fragment Psalm 149 originally followed 148, as in the Masoretic Text, the Septuagint, and our Bibles. But in the 11QPs[a]-Psalter, which is followed in this translation, it comes after Psalm 143.*

7 To execute vengeance on the nations (and) punishments upon the peoples, 8 to bind their kings with chains, and their nobles with shackles of iron, 9 to carry out the sentence written against them! This is glory for all his faithful ones, *for the children of Israel, his holy people.*[548] Praise the LORD!

150

▨ *Psalm 150 is preserved in only two scrolls—MasPs[b] and 11QPs[a]—each of which represents a different edition of the book of Psalms. In the Masada fragment Psalm*

Psalm 143. 11QPs[a]: 143:1–8; 4QPs[p]: 143:2–4, 6–8.

    543. 11QPs[a]. *has persecuted* MT LXX.

    544. 11QPs[a]* (cf. Ps 44:20; 51:10). *has crushed* 11QPs[a(corr)] MT LXX (cf. Isa 3:15).

    545. 11QPs[a]. Not in MT LXX.

    546. 11QPs[a] MT[mss] LXX. *the work* MT.

    547. 11QPs[a]. *like* MT LXX.

Psalm 149. 11QPs[a]: 149:7–9, X.

    548. 11QPs[a] MT[ms] (. . . *his personal people);* cf. Ps 148:14. Not in MT LXX.

Psalm 150. 11QPs[a]: 150:1–6; MasPs[b]: 150:1–6.

150 is followed by a blank column denoting the end of the scroll (and the MT-150 Psalter[549] which MasPs[b] represents). In the 11QPs[a]-Psalter, however, Psalm 150 is followed by seven more compositions. It is interesting to note that none of the Psalms scrolls from Qumran clearly supports the MT-150 arrangement. For this we must turn to Masada, where MasPs[b] represents the only unambiguous edition of the MT-150 Psalter. In contrast, the 11QPs[a]-Psalter is found in at least three manuscripts (see the introduction to the Psalms).

1 *Praise God*[550] in his sanctuary; praise him in his mighty firmament! 2 Praise him for his mighty acts; praise him according to his surpassing greatness! 3 Praise him *with the trumpet sounding;*[551] praise him with the harp and lyre! 4 Praise him with tambourines and dancing; praise him with the strings and flute! 5 Praise him with resounding cymbals: Praise him with loud clashing cymbals! 6 Let *all things that breathe*[552] praise the LORD! Praise the LORD![553]

The Hymn to the Creator

▨ *Preserved only in 11QPs[a], this piece can be classified as a Wisdom Psalm that praises God as creator. It has clear affinities with Psalm 104, since both Psalms draw on themes from Genesis 1. The hymn was unknown prior to the discovery of the Dead Sea Scrolls.*

1 Great and holy is the LORD, the holiest of the Holy Ones from generation to generation. 2 Glory precedes him and following him is the rush of many waters. 3 Grace and truth surround his presence; truth and justice and righteousness are the foundation of his throne. 4 Separating light from deep darkness, he established the dawn by the knowledge of his heart. 5 When all his angels had saw this they sang aloud; for he showed them what they had not known: 6 he crowns the hills with fruit, perfect food for every living being.

7 Blessed be he who has made the earth by his power, who has established the

---

549. As noted in the introductory text, "MT-150 Psalter" denotes the form of the Psalter found in the Masoretic Text, with its 150 Psalms.

550. 11QPs[a] MT[mss] LXX[mss]. *Praise the LORD! Praise God* MasPs[b] (reconstructed) MT LXX.

551. 11QPs[a]. *with the sound of the trumpet* MasPs[b] MT.

552. Plural 11QPs[a]. *everything that breathes* (singular) MT LXX.

553. While this Psalm concludes the Psalter in MasPs[b] MT, LXX has one more (Psalm 151) and 11QPs[a] seven more (ending with Psalm 151B).

The Hymn to the Creator. 11QPs[a]: Hymn 1–9.

world in his wisdom. 8 In his understanding he spread out the heavens, and brought forth [the wind] from [his] st[orehouses]. 9 He made [lightning bolts for the rai]n, and caused mist[s] to rise [from] the end [of the earth]. ▲

David's Last Words

■ *Only a few words from this fascinating passage (also found in 2 Sam 23:1–7) are still preserved in 11QPs^a. Not actually a Psalm, these verses were apparently included in order to emphasize the Davidic character of the 11QPs^a-Psalter. Three other compositions that were included for the same reason are David's Compositions, Psalm 151A, and Psalm 151B.*

7 [But the one who touches them uses an iron bar] or the shaft of *battle-axes*,[554] and they are entirely consumed with fire on the spot.

David's Compositions

■ *This piece clearly asserts Davidic authorship of the 11QPs^a-Psalter, thus also asserting that its arrangement and compositions were inspired by God himself. Note especially line 11: "All these he composed through prophecy. . . ."[555] Three other compositions that are included in the 11QPs^a-Psalter for the same reason are David's Last Words, Psalm 151A, and Psalm 151B.*

2 And David, son of Jesse, was wise, and a light like the light of the sun, and a scribe, 3 and discerning and perfect in all his ways before God and men. And the LORD gave 4 him a discerning and enlightened spirit. And he wrote 5 three thousand six hundred psalms; and songs to sing before the altar over the whole-burnt 6 perpetual offering for every day, for all the days of the year: three hundred and sixty-four; 7 and for the sabbath offerings, fifty-two songs; and for the offering of the New 8 Moons and for all the days of the festivals, and for the Day of Atonement: thirty songs. 9 And all the songs that he uttered were four hundred and

---

David's Last Words (= 2 Sam 23:1–7). 11QPs^a: vs 7.

554. Hebrew uncertain 11QPs^a. Not in Psalter MT LXX. *a spear* (2 Sam 23:7) MT LXX.

David's Compositions. 11QPs^a: 27, lines 2–11.

555. David's Compositions is not found in MT LXX and was unknown before the discovery of the Dead Sea Scrolls.

forty-six, and songs 10 for making music over the possessed: four. And the total was four thousand and fifty. 11 All these he uttered through prophecy which had been given him from before the Most High.

140

■ *The position of Psalm 140, which is a prayer for deliverance from enemies, is somewhat puzzling. It appears in the 11QPs^a-Psalter after two compositions that function to assert Davidic authorship of the collection (David's Last Words and David's Compositions). Perhaps the placement of this piece at this point is also explained by its strong Davidic character (note the superscription: "A Psalm of David").*

556 0 For the Director of Music: a Psalm of David. 1 Deliver me, O LORD, from evildoers; protect me from violent [peo]ple, 2 who devise evil plans in their hearts and *stir up*557 [wa]rs *all the day long.*558 3 They make their tongues sharp as a serpent's, and *a spider's*559 poison is beneath [their lips. Selah]. 4 Guard me, O LORD, from the hands of the wicked; [protect me] from [violent] people [who have planned to trip up my footsteps].

134

■ *Of the fifteen Psalms of Ascent, only 120 through 132 are grouped together in the 11QPs^a-Psalter (see the note before Psalm 120). The final Psalm of Ascent is found here, between Psalms 140 and 151A. Since the surrounding two pieces apparently serve to reinforce Davidic authorship, the position of Psalm 134 is difficult to explain. Perhaps, with its reference to Zion in verse 3, this Psalm was also meant to emphasize the Davidic connection; or perhaps it serves as a final liturgy of praise preceding the two autobiographical Psalms that end the 11QPs^a-Psalter.*

0 [A Song of Ascents. 1 Now bless the LORD, all you servants of] the LORD, who stand by night in the house of the LORD! 2 Lift up your hands in the sanctuary, and bless *the name of*560 the LORD. 3 May the LORD, who made heaven and earth, bless you from Zion!

Psalm 140. 11QPs^a: 140:0–4 [Heb 140:1–5].

   556. Preceded by David's Compositions 11QPs^a. Preceded by Psalm 139 MT LXX.

   557. 11QPs^a. *gather together* MT LXX.

   558. 11QPs^a MT^mss LXX. *all day long* MT.

   559. 11QPs^a. *a viper's* MT LXX.

Psalm 134. 11QPs^a: 134:1–3.

   560. 11QPs^a. Not in MT LXX.

151A

■ *Of all the Psalms found in the Dead Sea Scrolls, the Masoretic Text, and the Septuagint, Psalms 151A and 151B (preserved only in 11QPsᵃ) are the only truly Davidic ones in terms of their autobiographical content. Of course, the superscriptions
of many other Psalms ascribe them to David, but close examination of their contents
does not unambiguously link any of them to actual events in his life. Psalm 151A,
however, refers to David's role as shepherd, his musical gift, his anointing by Samuel,
God's choice of him over his brothers, and his kingship. Psalm 151B is very fragmentary, but it contains a clear reference to David's encounter with Goliath.*

[561] 0 A Hallelujah of David, Son of Jesse. 1 I was smaller than my brothers and
the youngest of the sons of my father, when he made me shepherd of his flock
and ruler over his kid goats. 2 My hands made an instrument and my fingers a
lyre, and so I offered glory to the LORD. I said in my mind:

3 "The mountains do not witness to him, nor do the hills proclaim; the trees
have cherished my words and the flock my deeds. 4 For who can announce and
who can speak and who can recount my deeds? The Lord of all saw, the God of
all—he heard and he listened. 5 He sent his prophet, Samuel, to anoint me, to
make me great. My brothers went out to meet him, handsome of figure and appearance. 6 Although they were tall of stature and handsome by their hair, the
LORD God did not choose them. 7 But he sent and fetched me from behind the
flock and anointed me with holy oil, and he made me leader of his people and
ruler over the children of his covenant."

151B

■ *In the Septuagint, the book of Psalms ends with Psalm 151 as a single Psalm. In
11QPsᵃ, however, the 11QPsᵃ-Psalter ends with two distinct Psalms containing
much of the material found in the Greek. (Psalm 151B is clearly a new Psalm because of its superscription.) Because of several differences between the two versions of
Psalm 151, the Greek version cannot simply be a translation of the Qumran version.
The text found in 11QPsᵃ represents the original Hebrew with two originally separate Psalms, which the Greek translator has reworked and synthesized into a single
Psalm.*

Psalm 151A. 11QPsᵃ: 151A:1–7.

561. Psalm 151 is not found in the MT, but it is in the LXX. There are several differences
between individual verses and readings in 11QPsᵃ and the LXX.

Psalm 151B. 11QPsᵃ: 151B:1–2.

[562] 1 At the beginning of [Da]vid's po[w]er after the prophet of God had anointed him. 2 Then I [s]aw a Philistine uttering insults from the r[anks of the enemy]. I [. . .] the [. . .]. [563]

■ *In 11QPs^a the column containing Psalms 151A and 151B is followed by a blank column. The blank leather clearly shows that the collection found in 11QPs^a actually ended with Psalm 151B, a version of which also ends the book of Psalms in the Septuagint. For the end of two more important collections indicated by blank leather, see the comments after Psalms 91 and 150, respectively.*

AN UNUSUAL COLLECTION FROM CAVE 4

■ *4QPs^f is a significant and interesting Psalms scroll, since it preserves one Psalm (22) from the early part of the Psalter, two more (Pss 107, 109) from the later part, and three previously unknown non-Masoretic pieces (the Apostrophe to Zion, the Eschatological Hymn, and the Apostrophe to Judah). The complete manuscript, which dates from about 50 BCE, must have contained additional compositions, probably including Psalm 108 between 107 and 109. Because Psalms 22 and 109 and the Apostrophe to Zion were presented earlier in this English translation, only Psalm 107 and the other two non-Masoretic pieces will be translated at this point.*

107 [1 Give thanks to the LORD, for he is good; for his steadfast love endures forever. 2 Let the re]deemed [of the LORD say this—those] whom he redee[med] from the enemy's power, 3 those whom he gathered in [from the lan]ds, [from east and we]st, [from north and south].

4 Some wandered in dese[rt wa]stelands, find[ing no ro]ad to an [inha]bited town; 5 [they were hungry a]nd [thirsty, and their lives ebbed away within them. 6 Then they cried to the LORD in their trouble, and he delivered them from their distress; 7 he led them on a straight road, until they reached an inhabited town. 8 Let them give thanks to the LORD for his steadfast love, for his wonderful deeds to human]kind. 9 [For he satisfies *the hung*]*ry*,[564] and fil[ls *the thirs*]*ty*[565] [with good things].

---

562. While the LXX contains Psalm 151 as a single composition, 11QPs^a contains two separate compositions. Material found in Psalm 151B begins at 151:6 in the LXX.

563. While the Psalter concludes with Psalm 151 in 11QPs^a LXX, in MasPs^b MT it closes with Psalm 150.

Psalm 107. 4QPs^f: 107:2–5, 8–16, 18–19, 22–30, 35–42.

564. 4QPs^f. *the thirsty* MT LXX.

565. 4QPs^f. *the hungry* MT LXX.

10 [Some s]at in dark[ness and deep gloom], prisone[rs in misery and chains, 11 for th]ey [had rebelled against the words of God, and despised the counsel of the Most High. 12 Their hearts were subjected to bitter labor]; they stumbled, [with no one to help. 13 Then they cri]ed out to the Lo[RD] in the[ir] trouble, and he saved them from their dis[tre]ss; 14 *and he brought them out*[566] of darkness and deep gloom, and broke [apart] their cha[ins]. 15 *Give th[anks]*[567] to the LORD for his steadfast love, for [his won]derful deeds [to humankind]. 16 For he shat[ters the doors of bron]ze, [and cuts through the bars of iron. 17 Some became sick through their rebellious ways, and suffered affliction because of their iniquities; 18 th]ey [loathed any kind of food, and drew near to the gates] of death. 19 Then they cried out to the Lo[RD] in [their] trouble, [and he saved them from] their dist[ress; 20 *he sent out his word and healed them, and delivered them from their destruction.*[568] 22 And let them offer sacrifices of] thanksgiv[ing, and tell of his works] with songs of joy.

23 [Some went out to sea] in ships, [doing busi]ness on the [mighty] wa[ters; 24 they saw the deeds of the LORD]; *let them give thanks for his wonderful deeds*[569] [in the deep ocean. 25 For he gave the word and rai]sed up a [stormy] wind, [which lifted high] *the waves (of the sea).*[570] 26 They mounted up to the heavens [and des]cended to the depths, *and their courage*[571] [mel]ted away *inside th[em].*[572] 27 They reeled and stag[gered like] drunkards, and were entirely at their wits' [end]. 28 Then they cried out to the LORD in the[ir trou]ble, *and he saved them*[573] from their distress; 29 he caused the storm to be cal[m], and *the waves of the sea*[574] were hushed. 30 [*Then he brought them to*] their desired haven, [*and they were glad because things were now quiet.*[575] 31 Let them give thanks to the LORD for his steadfast love, for his wonderful deeds to humankind. 32 Let them exalt him in the assembly of the people, and praise him in the session of the elders].

---

566. 4QPs[f] LXX. *he brought them out* MT.

567. 4QPs[f]. *Let them give thanks* MT LXX.

568. 4QPs[f] (spacing shows that one verse was not included in the original scroll, most likely vs 21). *destruction. 21 Let them give thanks to the LORD for his steadfast love, for his wonderful deeds to humankind* MT LXX.

569. 4QPs[f]. *and his wonderful deeds* MT LXX.

570. 4QPs[f]. *its waves* MT LXX.

571. 4QPs[f]. *their courage* MT LXX.

572. 4QPs[f] (cf. vs 5). *in their peril* MT LXX.

573. 4QPs[f]. *he brought them out* MT LXX.

574. 4QPs[f]. *their waves* MT LXX.

575. 4QPs[f]. *Then they were glad because things were now quiet, and he brought them to their desired haven* MT LXX.

33 [He transforms rivers into a desert, springs of water into thirsty ground, 34 fruitful land into a salty waste, because of the wickedness of those who live there. 35 He turns a desert into pools of water], *parched ground*[576] into *fountains*[577] of water. 36 And there he brings *a mighty people*[578] to live, and they [estab]lish *towns*[579] [where they can live]; 37 they so[w fiel]ds, and pla[nt] vineyards, [and gather a fruitful har]vest. 38 [He blesses them and they multiply greatly], and [he does not let their he]rds [diminish].

39 *When*[580] [their numbers de]crease [and they are brought low through oppression, calamity], and sor[row, 40 the one who pours contempt on princes makes them wan]der in [trackless w]astes; 41 [but then he lifts up] the needy *in their affliction,*[581] [and] *on his account*[582] [makes their families] like flo[cks. 42 The upright] see (all this) [and are glad; *and as for all*] *wickedness, he keeps* [*its*] *mouth shut.*[583]

[43 Let those who are wise pay attention to these things, and consider the steadfast love of the LORD].

■ *The Eschatological Hymn and the Apostrophe to Judah were unknown to scholars prior to the discovery of the Dead Sea Scrolls but are now available to us in 4QPs*. *The first of these compositions offers praise to God, but with an eschatological emphasis (that is, with a view to the end times). The second piece seems also to be eschatological, with a clear focus on Judah. The Apostrophe is also highly anthological, since it contains many words and phrases known from other parts of the Hebrew Bible.*

The Eschatological Hymn

4 many [. . .] and let them praise 5 the name of the LORD. [F]or he comes to judge 6 every ac[ti]on, to remove the wicked 7 from the earth, [so that the chil-

---

576. 4QPs*f*. *and parched ground* MT LXX.

577. 4QPs*f*. *springs* MT LXX. (The two Hebrew words are similar in meaning.)

578. 4QPs*f*. *the hungry* MT LXX.

579. 4QPs*f* LXX*mss*. *a town* MT LXX.

580. 4QPs*f*. *And when* MT LXX.

581. 4QPs*f* LXX*mss*. *in their affliction* MT LXX.

582. 4QPs*f*. Not in MT LXX.

583. 4QPs*f*. This seems to be the meaning here (with God as subject), since the verb *keeps shut* is masculine whereas *wickedness* is feminine. *and all wickedness keeps its mouth shut* MT LXX.

The Eschatological Hymn. 4QPs*f*: col. 9, lines 1–15.

dren of] iniquity will not 8 be found. [And] the hea[v]ens [will give] their dew, 9 and there will be no searing dro[ught within] their [b]orders. And the earth 10 will yield its fruit in its season, and will not 11 cheat of its [pro]duce. The 12 fruit trees [will . . .] their vines, and [. . .] will not cheat of its [. . .]. The 14 oppressed will eat, and those who fear the LORD will be satisfied] . . .

The Apostrophe to Judah

5 [. . .] Then let the heavens and earth give praise together; 6 then let all the stars of twilight give praise! 7 Rejoice, O Judah, in your joy; 8 be happy in your happiness, and dance in your dance. 9 Celebrate your pilgrim feasts, fulfill your vows, for no longer 10 is Belial in your midst. May your hand be lifted up! 11 May your right hand prevail! See, enemies will 12 perish, and all evildoers will be scattered. But you, LORD, are forev[er]; 14 your glory will be forev[er and ev]er! 15 [Pra]ise the Lord!

The Apostrophe to Judah. 4QPsᶠ: col. 10, lines 4–15.

JOB

The Hebrew text of the book of Job is the most problematic found in the Bible. This is due not only to its subject matter, but also to the fact that it is poetry, that it is high dramatic art of lyric quality, and that it may be based on an earlier drama not Israelite in origin.

Remnants of only four manuscripts were unearthed at Qumran, and only one of those (4QJob^a) has more than six small fragments preserved. 2QJob, in fact, has only one fragment with a single complete word and letters from four others. Interestingly, one of the manuscripts of Job of very early date (ca. 225–150 BCE) was inscribed in the archaic paleo-Hebrew script, common before the Babylonian exile (587–539 BCE). All the other identified manuscripts written in this script are among the Books of Moses (that is, Genesis through Deuteronomy), though there is another that deals with the figure of Joshua. Rabbinic tradition attributes the book of Job to Moses. Thus the ancient script was presumably retained for some copies of these books as an attestation of their great antiquity. In addition, there were two copies of an Aramaic translation of the book found.

Unfortunately, the small amount of Job preserved at Qumran does not help much with the difficult Hebrew of the traditional Masoretic Text. Occasionally when the Qumran manuscripts differ from the traditional version, there is not enough text preserved to establish a context firmly. This is problematic, since even the Masoretic Text itself is sometimes obscure, and translators must make educated guesses. Most of the variants are quite minor: singular for plural, transposition of word order, presence or lack of a small word that adds no meaning or is implicit. Once 4QJob^a uses a more familiar form of the word "God" (Job 33:26). In another instance 4QJob^a has a *negative* that is not in the traditional text (Job 37:1), but the full context cannot be confidently established.

8 15 [The wicked lean against their house, but it does not stand.] They clutch onto it, but it does no[t stay. 16 Fresh they may remain while exposed to the sun,] and [their shoots may gro]w [across their ga]rden; [17 . . .].

9 27 [If I say, "I will] forget my complaint, [I will abandon my frown, and smile," 28 . . .].▲

13 4 [Ye]t you are whitewashing [lies; you are all quacks].▲
[19 Who is the one to challenge me? For then I would be silent] and expire. 20 [Only spare me two things, so] I need not hi[de from your face: 21 . . .].▲

[24 Why do you hide your face and consider me] your enemy? 25 [Is it that you want to make a driven leaf tremble? Or would] you [chase dr]y [chaff? 26 For you prescribe bitter things against me and make] me [fall heir to] the iniquities of my youth. 27 [You put my feet in shackles, you watch all] my paths, [and you set boundaries for the soles of my feet].▲

14 4 Who can bring [a clean thing out of an unclean? No one. 5 Since their days are determined, you know] the number of [their] month[s, and you have fixed the limit they cannot overstep. 6 Look away f]r[om them, so that they may rest and, as a hireling, enjoy their days].▲

13 [I wish that you would hide me] in [Sheol, that you would conceal me until your wrath abates, that you would fix me] an appointment and r[emember me! 14 If] mort[als d]ie, [will they live again? All the days of my warfare would I wai]t, until [my release] would co[me. 15 You would call, and I would answer you]. You would l[ong for the wor]k of your hands. 16 [*Th*]en[1] you would number my steps; [you would not watch over my sin. 17 My] transgression [would be sealed in] a bag, [and you would cover over my iniquity].▲

31 14 [What then shall I do when God rises up?] When he demands an account, wh[at shall I answer him]? 15 Did not the one who *made me in the womb*[2] also make him? Did not [the same one] fashion us in the [w]omb? 16 If I have withheld the poor from their [desi]re, or let the eyes of the wi[dow languish], 17 or eaten my morsel alone, while [an orphan] did not eat [any]— 18 indeed, from my yout[h the orphan] grew up with me [as his father, and from my

---

Chapter 8. 4QJob[b]: 8:15–16.

Chapter 9. 4QJob[b]: 9:27.

Chapter 13. 4QJob[b]: 13:4; 4QpaleoJob[c]: 13:19–20, 24–27.

Chapter 14. 4QJob[b]: 14:4–6; 4QpaleoJob[c]: 14:13–17.

1. 4QpaleoJob[c]. *For then* MT.

Chapter 31. 4QJob[a]: 31:14–19; 4QJob[b]: 31:20–21.

2. 4QJob[a]. *in the womb made me* MT.

mother's womb I guided the widow—] 19 if I have look[ed on while anyone perished for lack of clothing or the poor were unclothed, 20 whose loins did not bless me as they were] warm[ed by the fleece of my sheep; 21 if I have raised my hand against the orphan, because I saw my] supporters in the gate, [22 . . .].▲

32 3 [Also against Job's three friends was he angry, bec]ause they had found no reply but [had just pronounced Job guilty]. 4 Elihu had waited to [speak to Job,] because they were older than [he].▲

33 10 [Look, he fin]ds [occasions for hostility against me and] thinks [of me as his enemy. 11 He puts my feet in shackles and] watch[es everywhere I walk].▲

25 [Let] their flesh [be xxxx]³ than a chil[d's; let them return to the days of their youth. 26 They pray] to *God,*⁴ and he is favo[rable to them, so that they see his face with joy, and he repays] to [mortals their righteousness].▲

28 [He has redeemed me from g]o[ing into the Pit, so my life will look upon the light]. 29 See, all the[se things Go]d [does,] two [or three] times [for mortals], 30 to bri[ng them back from the Pit, that the] light [of life may shine on them].▲

35 16 [Job opens his mouth with no substance and multipli]es words without knowledge.▲

36 7 [He does not take his eyes off the righteous, but en]thrones [and exalts them with kings forever. 8 If they be bound in chains and caught] in oppressive bonds, 9 [he tells the]m their misdeeds and their trans[gressions], that [they have acted arrog]ant[ly. 10 He opens] their [ear] to correction [and demands] that they turn from e[vil. 11 If they listen and serve him,] they will spend thei[r] days [in prosperity and] their [years] in contentment. [12 But if they do not listen, they will die by the sword and perish by lack of knowledge. 13 But the godless at heart be]come [an]gry [and do not cry for help when he binds them]. 14 They [die young,] after liv[ing as cult prostitutes. 15 He delivers the afflicted through their affliction and ope]ns [their ear] through ad[versity. 16 He has dra]wn you [also] out of distress into a spacious [and open place . . .]⁵ and the repose of your table opule[ntly] full. 17 [You are ob]se[ssed with the case of the wicked, but justice and judgment will be upheld. 18 Be]ware that [his wealth or a

---

Chapter 32. 4QJobᵃ: 32:3–4.

Chapter 33. 2QJob: 33:28–30; 4QJobᵃ: 33:10–11, 25–26, 28–30.

3. Both 4QJobᵃ and MT *(be healthier?)* are uncertain, but the preserved letters of 4QJobᵃ cannot form the word found in MT.

4. *El* 4QJobᵃ. *Eloah* MT (both forms = *God*).

Chapter 35. 4QJobᵃ: 35:16.

Chapter 36. 4QJobᵃ: 36:7–27, 32–33.

5. 4QJobᵃ and MT have different arrangements, with neither text certain.

large bribe] not seduce you. 19 *Let it not turn you.* (19) *Will . . . arrange . . . ,*[6] or all the forces of strength? 20 Do not long for the night, wh[en peoples disappear in] their [place. 21 Make su]re you do not turn [to evil, for] this have you chosen [rather than affliction. 22 Look, God is exalted in his power]; what teacher is there like him? 23 Who has enjoined upon him [his] way? Or who can say, "You have done wrong?" 24 Remember that *gre[at] is his [wor]k,*[7] of which [mortals] sing. 25 [All humankind] has [looked] upon it; mort[als behold it from afar. 26 Look, Go]d is great, beyond what we [can know; the number of his years is unsearchable. 27 He draws up the drops of wat]er, *and they refine*[8] [rain for his mist].▲

32 [. . .] *if*[9] [. . .] 33 It tells [. . .].[10]

37 1 Also at this [. . .] *does not tremble*[11] [. . .] moved [. . .]. 2 *Listen, listen*[12] to the thunder of his voice and *to*[13] the rumbling [that comes forth from his mouth]. 3 Everywhere [und]er heaven he se[nds it, and] his lightning to the ends of the earth. 4 [Then his voice roars; he thunders] with his majestic voice, and one cannot t[race the lightning by the time] his thunder [is hea]rd. 5 God thunders [marvelously] with [his voice; he does great things which] we cannot compre[hend].▲

14 [Listen to this, Job: st]op; *con[sider*[14] God's wonders. 15 Do you] know [how God c]omm[ands them, and makes his clouds flash lightning]?▲

---

6. 4QJob[a] and MT have different arrangements, with neither text certain.

7. 4QJob[a]. *you proclaim his work great* MT.

8. 4QJob[a] and MT use different forms.

9. 4QJob[a]. *Upon his hands* MT.

10. 4QJob[a] and MT differ slightly, with neither text clear.

Chapter 37. 4QJob[a]: 37:1–5, 14–15.

11. 4QJob[a]. *my heart trembles and* MT.

12. Singular 4QJob[a]. Plural MT.

13. 4QJob[a]. Not in MT.

14. 4QJob[a]. *and consider* MT.

PROVERBS

Proverbs was an important book in Israel for training in wisdom, prudence, and moral character, and Qumran made use of it. Only scraps from two scrolls of Proverbs were found there, and one of those has only two fragments. There are major differences between the Hebrew and the Greek versions of Proverbs, due to intentionally different editions of the book, and the Qumran fragments appear to agree with the traditional Hebrew edition. There are only a few variants, each presumably inadvertent, involving only a single look-alike letter but yielding noticeable differences in meaning.

One verse of Proverbs is cited explicitly by one of the principal books of the Qumran community, the *Damascus Document*. The command is given not to send an "offering to the altar through anyone impure . . . ; for it is written, 'The sacrifice of the wicked is disgusting; but the prayer of the righteous is like a proper offering.' "[a] The formula "for it is written" is sometimes used to introduce authoritative Scripture for deciding a course of conduct, but sometimes, as here, it is used simply to buttress a commonsense practice. In addition, Proverbs 1:1–6 is echoed in 4Q525 fragment 1: "[to kno]w wisdom and disc[ipline,] to understand [. . .]." Proverbs 7:12 is possibly quoted in 4Q184 fragment 1 11–12, where Lady Folly "lies secretly in wait [. . .] in the city streets"; the same motif plays in 4Q415 fragment 9, reminiscent of Proverbs 8:22–31.

1 27 [When your terror arrives like a storm, and your calamity comes on like a whirlwind, when] distress and anguish come [upo]n y[ou], 28 then [they will call on me, but I will not answer]; they will sea[r]ch for me [but] will not find me. 29 Because they despised knowledge and did not choose the fear of the L[o]RD, 30 did not desire [my] cou[nsel] but despised a[ll] my discipline, 31 now they will

---

a. CD 11:19–21, quoting Prov 15:8, though with variants from MT.
Chapter 1. 4QProv^a: 1:27–33.

eat [the fruit of their ways] and be filled with their own devices. 32 *The narrow-mindedness of*[1] [simpletons will kill them, and] the complacency of fools will destroy them. 33 But the one who listens to me will dwell in security and pea[ce without fear of evil].

2 1 My child, if you receive my words and [harbor my] com[mandments within you], [2 . . .].▲

13 6 [Righteousness guards the one whose path is perfect, but *wi*]*ckedness* [*ruins the sinner.*[2] 7 One pretends to be rich, yet has nothing; another pre]tends to be poor, yet has great wealth. 8 [The ransom of one's life is one's riches, but the poor] never hear [a threat. 9 The light of the righteous glows brightly, but the lamp of the wick]ed will [be extinguished].▲

14 7 [Leave the presence of] a foo[l, or you will not perceive words of knowledge. 8 The wisdom of the prudent is to understand one's way], but the folly of foo[ls is deceit. 9 . . .] 10 The heart knows [its own bitterness, and a stranger does not share in its joy. 11 . . . 12 There is a road which seems right to a person], but [it] end[s in the streets of death. 13 Even in laughter the heart aches, and the end of joy is] grief.▲

31 [Those who oppress the poor reproa]ch [their] Maker, [but] those who are gra[cious] to the needy honor him. 32 The wick[ed are] thrown down [by their own wrongdoing, but] *in their death*[3] [the right]eous [have refug]e. 33 Wisdom rests [in the heart of one with understanding], but what is [in] the midst of fools [becomes known. 34 Righteousness] exalts a nation, but [sin *di*]*minishes*[4] peoples. 35 [The kin]g [favors] a servant who acts prudently, but he ra[g]es against [the one who acts shamefully].

15 1 [A soft answer] turns [away wrath], but a harsh word stir[s] up anger. 2 [The tongue of the wi]se ut[ter]s [knowledge] we[ll, but the mouth of foo]ls pours ou[t folly. 3 The eyes of the LORD are] everywhe[re, watching] the evil [and the good. 4 A healing] to[ngue is a tree of] life, [but perversity in it breaks the spirit. 5 Fools despise their] pa[rents'] discipline, [but those who observe correction become prudent. 6 In the house of the righteous there is much tre]asu[re, but in the profit of the wicked there is trouble. 7 The lips of the wi]se

---

1. 4QProv[a]. *The turning aside of* MT.

Chapter 2. 4QProv[a]: 2:1.

Chapter 13. 4QProv[b]: 13:6–9.

2. 4QProv[b] MT. *sin ruins the wicked* MT[ms] LXX.

Chapter 14. 4QProv[b]: 14:7–8, 10, 12–13, 31–35.

3. 4QProv[b] MT (*bmwtw*). *in their piety* (*btwmw*) LXX.

4. 4QProv[b] LXX. *is the loyalty of* MT.

Chapter 15. 4QProv[b]: 15:1–8, 19–31.

d[isperse knowledge, not so the heart of fools. 8 The sacrifice of the wick]ed [is] an abomi[nation to the LORD, but the prayer of the upright is his delight]. ▲

19 [The way of the lazy is hedged with thorns, but the path of the just is] a highway. 20 Wise children make a fa[ther] glad; [only fools despise] their mother. 21 Ignorance is joy to one who la[cks sense, but a person with] understanding moves straight along. 22 [P]lan[s without counsel are] frustrated, but with sufficient advisors you succeed. 23 [A person is] happy [for a proper resp]onse, and [how] good is a word at the [right] mom[ent]! 24 The p[ath of life] goes upward for [the w]is[e, s]o [they] can avoid She[ol below. 25 The Lo]RD [will tear down the house of the proud] but will establish the boundary [for the widow]. 26 Evil [pla]ns [are an abomination to the LORD], but [pleasant words are] pur[e]. 27 Those who acquire unjust gain [bring] tr[ouble to their house], but those who hate br[ibes will live. 28 The heart of] the righteous *considers*[5] how to answer, but the mouth of the wicked b[labbers evil]. 29 The LORD is [fa]r from the wicked, but [hears] the prayer of the ri[ghteous. 30 The ligh]t of the eyes makes the heart glad, [and good] ne[ws puts fat on the bones. 31 The ear that listen]s to the discipli[ne of life will live among the wise]. ▲

---

5. Implicit in 4QProv[b]. Explicit in MT.

BEN SIRA (SIRACH)

Jesus ben Sira was a Jewish teacher who compiled a book of wise sayings and instructions in Hebrew in about 190 BCE. The author's grandson later translated this work into Greek and added a preface of his own. The book has several names, which can be somewhat confusing. It is known as "Sirach" or "Ecclesiasticus" among Catholic and Orthodox Christians, who include it in the Old Testament, and also among Protestants and some Jews, who group it among the Apocrypha. This traditional form of the book is based on the Greek translation made by Ben Sira's grandson, which is found in the Septuagint. Although the Hebrew text was known and read for several centuries into the common era—being discussed in some rabbinic writings—it fell into disuse in most Jewish circles. The Hebrew version is known as the Wisdom of Jesus Ben Sira, or simply Ben Sira, a name increasingly preferred by Jews and by scholars working with the Hebrew text.

Early in the twentieth century substantial Hebrew texts of Ben Sira, copied in the eleventh and twelfth centuries CE, were discovered in the Cairo *genizah*. This term denotes a storeroom attached to a synagogue, in this case in Cairo, that was used for old and damaged manuscripts, since in Jewish tradition these cannot simply be discarded or burned. None of the Cairo copies is complete; when combined, however, these copies provide the Hebrew text for approximately two-thirds of the book.

Three copies of Ben Sira (or, rather, two copies and a poem also included in Ben Sira) were found among the Dead Sea Scrolls. The most substantial manuscript was discovered at Masada, the fortress where over nine hundred Jewish defenders took their own lives in 73 or 74 CE. Abbreviated MasSir, this scroll preserves portions of chapters 39 to 44 of the book's fifty-one chapters. The only

Ben Sira scroll found at Qumran was in Cave 2;[a] it preserves parts of chapters 1 and 6. One manuscript from Cave 11, the *Great Psalms Scroll*,[b] preserves about two-thirds of a poem found in chapter 51: the second canticle (Sir 51:13–30) that follows the epilogue written by Ben Sira. With respect to dates, the earliest of the three scrolls containing material from Ben Sira was copied in the first half of the first century BCE,[c] and the latest about 30 to 50 CE.[d]

In view of Ben Sira's size, it is surprising that so little of the book was found among the Dead Sea Scrolls: just parts of three chapters at Qumran, and portions of six more at Masada. The Masada scroll is significant since it was copied not much more than a hundred years after the original. Moreover, the form of the Masada text confirms that the medieval manuscripts of Ben Sira from the Cairo *genizah* basically represent the original Hebrew version, although with numerous corruptions and later changes.

The Qumran evidence is particularly interesting since it is of two different types. The Cave 2 scroll preserves very little text but may come from a manuscript that contained some or all of Ben Sira. However, the fact that the Cave 11 poem is found in a manuscript of the book of Psalms suggests that it was originally an independent composition. This assessment is confirmed in that the canticle seems to be tacked on at the end of Ben Sira in the later, more complete versions of the book. Comparison of the Hebrew and Greek texts reveals substantial differences in the poem; this is largely because the Greek translator substituted pious ideas for the many erotic images in the original Hebrew found in 11QPs[a]. For example, the following excerpt from 11QPs[a] is highly erotic, with its sexual imagery (note that *hand* can also mean *penis*):

> 21 I bestirred my desire for her, and on her heights I could not relax. 22 [I] spread my "hand" [. . .] and perceived her nakedness.

But the Greek translator has clearly downplayed the erotic imagery by substituting pious language, with the purpose of pursuing wisdom in a more spiritual or philosophical sense:

> I directed my soul toward her, and in my deeds I was exact. I stretched my hands on high, and perceived her secrets.

---

a. 2QSir (2Q18).   **b.** 11QPs[a] (11Q5).   **c.** MasSir.   **d.** 11QPs[a].

Eventually, this Wisdom book fell out of favor in Jewish circles and was excluded by the Rabbis from their list of scriptural books. As mentioned earlier, it survived in Greek (and other) translations as Sirach or Ecclesiasticus and is included in Catholic and Orthodox Bibles. Our oldest copies of Ben Sira, written in the original Hebrew, are among the Dead Sea Scrolls and form the basis of the translation that follows. (The later *genizah* manuscripts are not included in *The Dead Sea Scrolls Bible* for lack of space.) Perhaps the recovery of these ancient texts will foster renewed interest in this fascinating and controversial Wisdom book.

1

■ *Because so little text remains in this small fragment, it is uncertain whether this passage is Ben Sira 1:19–20 or 6:14–15, so both passages are presented here. In these verses Wisdom is personified as she and her, and is to be held onto by righteous people.*

[18 The fear of the LORD is the crown of wisdom, making peace and restoring health to flourish. 19 She pours forth knowledge and discernment, and she elevates the glory of those who h]old [her fast. 20 To fear the LORD is the root of wisdom, and] her [branches are] *long* [*life*].[1]▲

6

■ *The verses presented below deal with the immense value of a faithful friend, and offer further thoughts on wisdom and discipline.*

14 [A faithful friend is a sturdy] sh[elter; whoever finds one has found riches. 15 For a faith]ful [friend] there is no [price; no amount can balance his excellence].▲

20 [She seems very harsh to the foolish; anyone lacking understand]ing [cannot remain with her. 21 She will be like a heavy stone upon him, and he will not hesitate to cast her aside. 22 For discipline is just like her name, and she is not straightfor]ward [to many. . . . 25 Bend your shoulders and carry her, and do not be offended under her shrewd guidance. 26 Draw near to her with all your soul, and observe] her [ways with all your strength. 27 Search out and explore, investigate and discover, and when you take hold of her, do not let] her go. 28 [For at

---

Chapter 1. 2QSir: 1:19–20 (?).
  1. Literally, *length of days.*
Chapter 6. 2QSir: 6:14–15(?), 19–31.

last you will find *the rest she brings,*[2] and she will be changed into pl]easure [for you. 29 Then her fetters will become for you a strong protection, and her collar] a golden robe. 30 [Her yoke is a golden ornament, and her bonds are a cord of pur]ple. 31 You will wear her like a golden robe, [and] carry her like a splendid c[rown]. ▲

39

■ *Most of these verses are part of a long hymn praising the works of the* LORD *(Sir 39:16–31). The final verse contains the beginning of a statement by Ben Sira giving his reasons for compiling this book. His comment that he has "thought this out" and has "set it down in writing" is particularly interesting, since it highlights the role of the scribe as a creative author as well as a collector of material.*

27 [All these prove good for good people, but for evil people] they are t[ur]ned into loathing.

28 [There are winds created for vengeance, and in their fury] they dislo[dge mounta]ins; [at the time of destruction they will pour out their strength and] will appease [the *passion*[3] of] their [Maker. 29 Fire and hail, misfortune and pestilence, these, too, have] been crea[ted for vengeance. 30 Beasts of prey, scorpions and vipers, and an avenging sword for destroying the ung]odly; [all these also are created for their functions, and are in his storehouse at the time] they [are appointed. 31 They delight when he gives them his command, and do not disobey] his bi[dding in their prescribed tasks].

32 [So from the beginning I have been convinced, and having thought this out] I [have set it down in writing: . . .] ▲

40

■ *This chapter contains four themes, with part of each preserved in the fragments of the Masada scroll (MasSir). Verses 1–11 present a disturbing picture of human wretchedness, while verses 12–17 make it clear that injustice will not last or prosper. The third section, verses 18–27, gives a happy description of the joys and blessings of life, while verses 28–30 warn that begging is a disgrace.*

10 [Evil is created for the wicked, and because of them] destruction has[tens]. 11 All that is from [the earth returns to earth, and what is from above returns above].

---

2. Literally, *her rest.*

Chapter 39. MasSir: 39:27–32.

3. Or, *spirit.*

Chapter 40. MasSir: 40:10–19, 26–30.

12 All that is of fa[lsehood and injustice will be wiped out, but what is true will last forever]. 13 The wealth that is from iniquity is [like a mighty river, and like a powerful watercourse in a thundersto]rm. 14 With its deluge rock[s are rolled away; even so, it is suddenly go]ne [forever.] 15 A branch that comes from violence will not ta[ke root; for a blighted root] is on [sheer] rock, 16 like reeds by the banks of a river, which are dried up [before any] grass. 17 (But) kindness, like eternity, will never be cut off, and faithfulness will be established forever.

18 A life of wealth and wages is pleasant, but better than both of these is the one who finds [a treasure]. 19 Children and [founding a city est]ablish one's name, but better than both of these is the one who finds [wisdom. Cattle and farming make] a kinsman [prosperous, but better than both of these is a beloved wife].▲

26 [Riches and strength gladden the heart, but better than] both of these [is the fear of God. There is no want in the fear of the Lord, and] with it there is no need to seek for h[e]lp. 27 [The fear of God is like an Eden of blessing], and its canopy is over all that is glo[rious].

28 [My child, do not lead a beggar's life]; it is better to be a [de]ad man than to be importunate. 29 [When one looks to a stranger's table, one's existence cannot] be considered a life. The tid-[bits that are presented are a pollution of his soul; to a m]an of understand[ing] they are inward torture. 30 In the mouth of a bold person [begging] is s[weet, but] it burns like a fire [inside] him.

41–42:1a

■ *This part of Ben Sira, which is well preserved in MasSir, contains several serious themes that make for heavy reading. Verses 1–4 of chapter 41 remind us of the inevitability of death, while verses 5–14 give a sober warning of the fate of the wicked. The final section, which begins with verse 15 and ends in 42:1a, presents an important list of things that are shameful and should be avoided. Note that the very order of verses in MasSir is not always identical to that of the LXX (for example, vss 14b–15–14a–16b where LXX has vss 14ab–15–16).*

1 O [*death,*[4] how bitter is the th]ought of you to the person living at peace in his home, [to the one] who has no stress and is prosperous in everything, and is still vigorous enough to enjoy pleasure! 2 Hail to death, how welcome is [your] sen[tence to] the one who has no might and is failing in strength, the one who stumbles and trips at [everything], devoid of sight and having lost hope. 3 Do not fear death, decreed for you; remember that those who went before and those who come after (share it) with you. 4 This is the end for every [lving creature

---

Chapter 41. MasSir: 41:1–22.

4. Literally, *O to* [*death*] MasSir.

from Go]d; [so why should you reject the decree of] the Most H[igh]? Whether life is for ten, a hundred, or a thousand years, [there are no punishments for life in Sheol].

5 The ch[ild]ren of sinners are an abominable offspring, [and a godless progeny is in the dwellings of the wic]ked. 6 [From the children of sin]ners domi[n]ion will be lost, [and with their offspring] there will be perpetu[al] contempt. 7 Children will blame [an ungodly father, for] they will suffer disgrace [on] his account. 8 [Woe to you], ungod[ly] people, you who have forsaken the law of the Most High! 9 [If you are fruitful, it is] b[y] means of [calamity]; and when you beget them, it is only for sighing. [When yo]u [stumble], it is for lasting joy; and when you die, it is for a curse. 10 [Whatever comes from] nothing returns to nothing; so it is with the ungodly: from emptiness to emptiness. 11 [People are] futile [in th]eir [bodies, but] a virtuous name will never be cut off. 12 Be concern[ed] about your name, since it will remain with you longer than thousands of precious [treasures]. 13 [The go]od things of life last for a number of days, but the goodness of [a name] has days without number. 14b Hidden [wi]sdom and unseen treasure—of what use is either?

15 Better is the person who hid[es] his folly than the one who hides his wisdom. 14a Hear, my children, instruction concerning shame, [and be asha]med according to my judgment. 16b For not every kind of shame becomes shamefulness, nor is every kind of reproach to be preferred. 17 Be ashamed of sexual immorality before your father or mother, and be ashamed of lies before a prince or a ruler; 18 of intrigue before a master or mistr[ess], and [o]f [trans]gression before the assembly and the people; of treachery before your partner or your friend, 19 and o[f] theft in the place where you live. Be ashamed of breaking an oath or agreement, and *of stretching out your elbow at meals;*[5] of refusi[ng] to grant a request, 21a and of *rejecting the appeal*[6] of your relative; 21b of preventing the dividing of someone's portion, 20 and of keeping quiet before those who greet you; 21c of gazing up[on a woman who has a husband], 20b and of noticing a prostitute; 22a of interfering wi[th] your serva[nt-girl], 22b and of violating her bed; 22c of abusive words before a friend, 22c and of being insulting after making a gift. 42:1a Be ashamed of repeating a rumor you have heard, and of betraying any secrets. Then you wi[ll] show true shame, and will find favor in everyone's sight.

42

■ *The first part (vss 1b–14) follows what preceded by spelling out things of which one should not be ashamed. Much of this advice is very down to earth and practical, rang-*

---

5. I.e., of bad manners when eating.

6. Literally, *turning away the face.*

Chapter 42. MasSir: 42:1–25.

*ing from business practices, household affairs, disciplining of children, and relations be-
tween husband and wife. Of special concern to this author was a father's care and re-
sponsibility for his daughter (vss 9–14). The second section (vss 15–25) celebrates the
works of the Lord in nature. All this material is relatively well preserved in MasSir.*

1b [B]ut do not be ashamed of the following things, and do not show partiality
to people and commit sin: 2 of the law of the Most High and his statute, and of
rendering judgment to acquit the wicked; 3 of keeping accounts with a partner
or with a traveling companion, and of dividing an inheritance and property; 4a of
precision with scales and weights, *and of polishing measures and weights;*[7] 4b
of buying much or lit[tle, 5a and of] profit in trading with merchants; 5b [of
freque]nt [disciplining of children] and 5c a bad servant who goes around limp-
ing; 6 [on an unworthy wife—put]ting a seal, and where there are many hands—
a key; 7 upon the pl[ace] of deposit—a number, and let all [trans]actions be in
writing. 8 Do not be ashamed of (correcting) the re[bellion of the] stupid or
foolish, or of the tottering old gray-[beard] who is occupied with sexual immorality. Then you will be truly well-instructed, [and a person who is mode]st
before everyone alive.

9 [A daughter] is a decep[tive] treasure to her father, [and worry over her ro]bs
him of sleep; when she is young in case she is unwanted, or in her heyday in case
she is [reject]ed; 10 during her virginity in case she is violated, and when with
her husband [in case] she proves unfaithful; in her father's house in case she falls
pregnant, and at her husband's house [in case she proves ba]rr[en. 11 My son],
keep strict watch over a daughter, [in c]ase she [makes you a bad name], a byword
in the city and the assembly of the people, [and puts you to shame in the assembly
at the city g]ate. See that there is no [window] where she stays, [no spot that overlooks the approaches aro]und the house. 12 Do not let her parade her beauty to
any man, [or converse in the house of married women]; 13 for from a garment
comes the moth, [and from a woma]n comes [wo]man's wickedness. 14 Better is
the wickedness of a man than the goodness of a woman, and a daughter who fears
any disgrace.

15 I will now make mention of the works of God, and will declare what I have
seen. By the word of the Lord are his works, and an act of his grace is his doctrine. 16 The shining sun is revealed over everything, [and the gl]ory of the Lord
fills his works. 17 God's holy ones do not have the power to recount all his marvelous works; the Lord has strengthened his hosts to stand firm before his glory.
18 He searches out the abyss and the heart; he understands their secrets. For the
Most High possesses know[ledge, and] sees what is to come for eternity. 19 He
declares what has been [and what will be, and] reveals the mystery of hidden
things. 20 No knowledge escapes him, and n[o]thing is lo[s]t to him. 21 The

---

7. MasSir. Not in LXX.

might of [his] wisdom [is steadfast], h[e is] one and the same [from et]ernity. Nothing can be added [or taken away], and he [needs no o]ne to give him counsel. 22 Are not all his works desirab[le], down to a spark and a fleeting vision? 23 All of them live and rem[ain] forever, [and] each one is preserved for every need. 24 All of them [come in pairs], one opposite the other, and he has made none of them [in vain]. 25 Each one surpasses the good of the other, [so] who could ever have enough of seeing their splendor?

43

■ *This chapter continues with the theme of God's works that was introduced in chapter 42. The works of the Lord are arranged in a list that begins with the sun as the highest created being (vss 1–5), followed by the moon (vss 6–8), the stars (vss 9–10), and earthly phenomena such as the rainbow, lightning, clouds, winds, etc. (vss 11–26). Such arrangements are known as* onomastica *(that is, lists of natural phenomena); a similar arrangement is found in Job 38:1–38. The final section (vss 27–33, with only a few verses preserved in the MasSir) turns the focus away from nature to the Lord and his power. Note the differing arrangement of vv 17a-16b-17b in comparison to LXX (16–17).*

1 The beauty of the higher realms and the pure vault of the sky, the firm heavens m[anifest] its gl[ory]. 2 The sun, when it appears, shines to the full; what a marvelous instrument it is, the work of the [Mo]st High. 3 At noon it makes the world [bo]il, and who can wi[th]stand its scorching heat? 4 Like a [gl]owing [fu]rnace made of cast-iron the [su]n's bo[lt sets the mountain ablaze]; a tongue of fire con[su]mes the world, [and with its flames eyes are scorched]. 5 For great is the Lord who made it, and [his] wor[ds *surpass his strong men*].[8]

6 Moreover, the [mo]on prescribes the changing seasons, ru[ler of a period and for an everlasting sign]. 7 To it belongs the appo[inted] season and from it comes festal days; [and now it delights in its circuit]. 8 The new moon, as its name suggests, ren[ews itself; how marvelous it is in its changing]! A vessel of the host of clouds on high, it [pa]ves [the vault of the heavens with its shining].

9 The beauty of the heavens and the glory of the stars is a witness and glitters in the hei[ghts of God]. 10 At the command of the Lord it stands in its appointed place, and it never relaxes in their watch. 11 Look at the rainbow, and praise its Maker, for [it is] exceedingly majestic [in its glory]. 12 It encircles the sky with its glory, [and] the hands of God have stretched it out in mi[ght].

13 His command [mar]ks the hailstones and makes brilliant the lightnings of

---

Chapter 43. MasSir: 43:1–25, 29–30.

8. Suggested reconstruction MasSir.

judgment. 14 On his account he has opened the storehouses, and makes the clouds fly out like birds. 15 His majesty gives the clouds their strength, and breaks the hailstones in pieces. 17a The sound of his thunder makes his earth tremble, and by his strength he shakes mountains. 16b At his will the south wind blows, 17b as do the whirlwind, hurricane, and storm. He scatters the snow like flocks of birds, and its descent is like settling locusts. 18 The beauty of its whiteness dazzles the eyes, and the mind is amazed as it rains down. 19 He [also] pours out frost like salt, and produces thornlike blossoms. 20 He makes blow [the icy blast of the no]rth wind, and he congeals the source like a clod. . . . 22 The distil[lation of the cloud of m]ist is a healing for all such things, [hurrying to bring refreshment from the heat].

23 [His] word enters the mi[ghty] deep; [he has stretched out] islands [in the ocean. 24 Those who go down to the se]a tel[l of its] extent; we marvel at what our ears hear. 25 [In it are marvelous creatures, the most astonishing of all his works], and [all kinds of living things, and] the might of Rahab.▲

29 [The Lord is exceedingly awesome, and] his [pow]er [is marvelous. 30 You who glorify the Lord: lift up your voices as much as you can, for] God [i]s!▲

44

■ *This chapter opens with a famous hymn in honor of the nation's ancestors (vss 1–15), but the first verse of the Masada scroll reveals an emphasis very different from the one known in the Septuagint. Instead of the well-known phrase "Let us now praise famous men," here we read "Let me now sing the praises of pious men." The emphasis on piety, or godliness, in the Hebrew text contrasts with the fame or renown found in the Greek. The second part (vss 16–23) recounts the piety of ancestors such as Noah and Abraham, but only one verse (17) is preserved in MasSir. For the apparent omission of verse 16 and its mention of Enoch, see the footnote to verse 17.*

1 [Let me now sing the praises of] pious me[n, our] ancestors [in their generations]. 2 The Most High apportioned them great glory, and his greatness from the d[ays of old. 3 Those who ruled over the earth in their royalty, and men of renown by their valor]; counselors because of their discernment, and all-seeing in [their] prophe[cy; 4 leaders of the nation in their statesmanship, and high officials in [their de]crees; skilled of speech in their instruction, and speakers of wise sayings at [their festi]vals; 5 composers of psalms in poetic lines, and authors of prov[erbs in books]; 6 rich men endowed with power, living at eas[e in their homes].

7 All these were honored in their generation, [and in their days had distinction]. 8 Some of them have left behind a name, so that [others might declare it in

---

Chapter 44. MasSir: 44:1–15, 17.

their inheritance]. 9 But of others there is no memory, [so that there was an end of them when they perished]; they lived as though they had never been born, they and [their children after them]. 10 Nevertheless, these were godly men, and [their] good[ness will not be cut off]. 11 Their fortune will remain with their descendants, and [their] inheri[tance with their children's children]. 12 In their covenant their descendants stand, and their descendants also, [for their sake]. 13 Their offspring will continue forever, and their glory will never be eras[ed]. 14 Their bod[ies] are buried in peace, but their name lives on to all generations. 15 The assembly [declar]es [their wisdom], and the congregation proclaims their praise.

[9] 17 Noah the righteous man was found blameless; in the [time of destruction he became the *continuer*].[10] For [his sake there was a remnant, and because of the covenant with him the flood ceased]. ▲

51

■ *This poem was previously familiar to us as the second canticle following the epilogue of Ben Sira. For comments on this composition as part of the large Psalms scroll from Cave 11, on its erotic nature, and on differences between the Hebrew text and the later Greek translation, see the introduction to Ben Sira.*

13 I was a young man, before I had gone astray, I looked for her. 14 She came to me in her beauty, and eventually I sought her out. 15 Even when the blossom drops in the ripening of grapes, making the heart happy, 16 so my foot trod in uprightness; for since my youth I have known her. 17 I inclined my ear but a little, and great was the captivation I found. 18 So she became a wet-nurse for me; to my teacher I give my scepter. 19 I decided to make sport: I was eager for pleasure, without stopping. 20 I kindled my passion for her, I could not turn away my face. 21 I bestirred my desire for her, and on her heights I could not relax. 22 [I] spread my "hand" [. . .] and perceived her nakedness. 23 I cleansed my "hand" [. . . 30 . . .] your reward in its time.

---

9. Later versions of chapter 44 contain vs 16: *Enoch pleased the Lord and was taken up, an example of repentance to all generations.* MasSir omits this verse but contains a blank line between vss 15 and 17.

10. I.e., continuer of the human race.

Chapter 51: 11QPs[a]: 51:13–23, 30. This composition is not found in MT but is in LXX.

RUTH

This charming story about the foreigner Ruth and her devotion to her Israelite mother-in-law survives on fragments from four separate manuscripts, two from Cave 2 and two from Cave 4 at Qumran. Two of the scrolls date from the middle of the first century BCE, one from the late first century BCE or early first century CE, and one from the middle of the first century CE. Since the story is rather straightforward, and since there are few issues that would incite ideological change, all four texts plus the one recorded in the traditional Masoretic Text exhibit the same language with only minor, unimportant variants. Most involve either a single letter mistaken for a similar one, an interchangeably synonymous word, or an insertion of an explicit word for what was already implicit.

1 1 During the period in which the judges ruled, there was a famine in the land. So a man of [Bethlehem] in Judah with his wife and his two sons went to sojourn in the fields of Moab. 2 *The*[1] ma[n]'s name was [Elimelech], his wife's name Naomi, and his two sons' Mahlon and Chilion, Ephrathites of Bethle[hem in Ju]dah. They came to the fields of Moab and *lived*[2] there. 3 Elimelech, [Naomi's husband], died, [and she was left with] her two sons. 4 They married Moabite women, [one] named [Orpah, the other Ruth, and] they lived there about ten years. 5 Then Mahlon [and Chilion] bo[th] died as well, [and the wo]man [was bereaved] of her two children and her husband.

6 Then she prep[ared with her daughters-in-law to return from the fields of Moab, because she had heard] in Moab that the Lor[d] had visited [his people, giving them food. 7 She left the place in which she had been staying, along] with [her t]wo daughters-in-law, [and they set out on the journey back to the land of Judah. 8 But Naomi said to her two daughters-in-law], "Go on, return ea[ch of you to her mother's house. May the Lord deal kindly with you, as you have dealt

---

Chapter 1. 4QRuthª: 1:1–12; 4QRuthᵇ: 1:1–6, 12–15.

   1. 4QRuthᵇ. *And the* 4QRuthª MT LXX.

   2. 4QRuthª Syriac. *were* MT LXX.

with the d]ead and with [me. 9 May the LORD grant that you find rest, each of you in the house of her husband." Then she kissed them]. But they sobbed and [wept 10 and said to her, "We will return with you, to your people." 11 But Naomi said, "Go back], my daughters. Why [would you go with me? Do I still have sons in my womb to be your husbands? 12 Go back, my daughters, go on]; for [I am too] ol[d to have a husband. If I should say I have hope, if I should even have a husband tonight and even b]ear [sons] aga[in,³ 13 would you, on that account, wait until they were grown]? Would yo[u], on that account, keep [from marrying some man? No, my daughters. It is far more bitter for me than for you], for the hand of the LORD has come out against me." 14 [Then they sobbed and wept again]. Orpah [kissed] her mother-in-law [good-bye], but [Ruth clung to her.]

15 [So she said, "Look], your sister-in-law [has gone back] to⁴ [her people] and to⁵ [her] g[od. Follow your sister-in-law]." ▲

2 13 [Then she said, "I have found favor in your sight, my lord, for you have comforted me and have spoken kindly to your maidservant, though I am not so much as one of] your [maidser]vants."

14 [At mealtime Boaz said to her, "Come here. Eat] some [bread and dip your morsel in the vinegar." So she sat beside the] reapers, and he gave her roasted grain, and she a[te and was satis]fied and had some lef[t over. 15 When she ro]se to glea[n], Boaz gave [these] orders to [his] young men: "Let her glean even [among the sheaves], and do not reproach her. 16 [Furthermore] pull sta[lks out of the bundles for her], and leave them for [her] to glean, [and do] not [rebuke her]."

17 [She gleaned] in the field until evening. Then she [beat out what she had gleaned, and it cam]e to about an ephah of barley. 18 She carried it back to [the city, and] her mother-in-law [saw] what she had gleaned. Then she brought out and ga[ve her w]hat was left over *after she had eaten her fill.*⁶ 19 So [her] moth[er-in-law] sai[d] to her, "[Where] did you glean today? Wh[ere] did you work? [Blessed be the one who took notice of you!" She told her mother-in-law with] whom she had worked, [saying,] "The name [of the man] with [whom I] wor[ked] to[day is Boaz]." 20 Naomi [said] to her dau[ghter]-in-law, "May he be blessed by [the LORD, who has not withdrawn] his kindness from the living or the

---

3. 4QRuthᵇ. Not in MT.

4. 4QRuthᵇ. MT uses a different word.

5. 4QRuthᵇ. MT uses a different word.

Chapter 2. 2QRuthᵃ: 2:13–23.

6. 2QRuthᵃ. *from eating her fill* MT LXX.

[dead!" Then Naomi said to her,] "The m[a]n is closely related to us; [he is one of our redeemer kinsmen." 21 Then Ruth the Moabi]te [said], "He even sai[d] *to me*,[7] ['You stay] near [my] young men, [until my] whole ha[rvest] is finished.'" 22 [Naomi said t]o Ruth, [her daughter-in-law, "It is good, my daughter, for you to go out with] his [yo]u[ng] women so that you [will] n[ot be troubled] in [some other] f[ield." 23 So she stayed nea]r Boaz's young women and glea[n]ed until the en[d of the barle]y [harvest], then of the wheat harv[est, while she lived with her mother-in-law].

3 1 Naomi her mother-in-law said to her, "[My daughter, should I not seek] a home for you, where it will go [well for you? 2 Now is not B]oaz, whose [young women] you were wi[th], our rela[tive? [Listen], he [will be winnowing] barley [tonight at the threshing-fl]oor. 3 [So bathe, anoint yourself, put] on your [best cl]othes, [and go down to the threshing-floor. Do not let yourself be recognized by the man until he finishes eating and drinking]. 4 When he lies down, [note the place where he is lying]. Then [go i]n, uncover [his] f[eet, and lie down. Then he will tell you what] you should do." 5 She [said to her, "Everything that you have said I will do]."

6 [So she went down to] the threshing-floor [and did everything her mother-in-law had told her. 7 After Boaz had eaten] and drunk, in [hi]g[h spirits he went to lie down at the edge of the mound of grain]. Then she came softly, uncovered his f[e]et, and lay down. 8 [In the middle of the night], the man [was startled], turn[ed], and look, a wom[an lay at] his [fe]et. ▲

13 "[Stay for the night. In the morning, if he redeems you, good; let him redeem you. But if he does not want to redee]m you, then, [as the LORD lives, I myself will] re[deem you. Lie down until morning]."

14 [So she lay] at his [fee]t until m[orning. Then she arose before one could recognize other people, for he had said] it should [not] be known that *she*[8] had come to the threshing-floor. 15 [And he] s[aid, "Come, hold out the mantle you are wearing." She held] it [out, and] he measured *into it*[9] six measures of barl[ey and laid it on her. Then he went into the city. 16 When she returned to her mother-in-law], she sai[d], *"How*[10] are you, my daughter?" So she [told her all that the man had done for her, 17 and said], "He gav[e me] thes[e] six measures [of] barley; [for he said, 'Do not return empty-handed to your mother-in-law.'"

---

7. 2QRuth[a]. MT uses a different word.
Chapter 3. 2QRuth[a]: 3:1–8; 2QRuth[b]: 3:13–18.
   8. 2QRuth[a]. *the woman* MT. *a woman* LXX.
   9. 2QRuth[b]. Not in MT LXX.
   10. 2QRuth[b] LXX[ms]. *who* MT LXX[mss].

18 Then she said, "Sit quietly, my daughter, unt]il you kno[w how the matter turns out; for the man will not rest until he has it settled today]." ▲

4 3 [He said to the redeemer, "Naomi, who has returned from the fields of Moab, has] to se[ll the parcel of land which belonged to our brother Elim-elech]." ▲

Chapter 4. 2QRuthª: 4:3.

THE SONG OF SONGS (CANTICLES)

The Song of Songs is one of the most controversial books in the Bible, although it contains only eight chapters. A careful reading of this book (whose title means "The Greatest of All Songs") shows it to be a collection of love poems, several of which are very erotic and romantic. The precise sexual details are not always apparent, since they are frequently couched in imagery—much of it sensitive, beautiful, and Middle Eastern—that is not easily understood by modern readers.

Because of its frankness and unabashed celebration of sexual love, some of the early Rabbis and early church fathers were disturbed by this delightful little book, interpreting it in a variety of ways that played down its sexuality. Some early Jewish and Christian sages found the contents plainly unacceptable and attempted to block its acceptance into the canon of the Hebrew Bible. Certain Rabbis, however, recognized the Song of Songs as Scripture but sought to interpret its contents in terms of the relationship between God (the *lover* or *bridegroom*) and Israel (the *beloved* or *bride*). Many church fathers who also accepted this book as Scripture interpreted it as depicting the relationship between Christ and his church. But in more recent times both Jews and Christians have increasingly come to recognize the sexual and romantic nature of the Song of Songs. This trend is to be welcomed by our various faith communities, since it affirms that the God who created us is concerned with our sexuality and romantic dimensions, that these are significant aspects of marriage, and that religious people can enjoy them without shame.

Four scrolls of the Song of Songs (or Canticles) were found at Qumran, three in Cave 4[a] and the fourth in Cave 6.[b] All were copied in the Herodian period (between 30 BCE and 68 or 70 CE),[c] the latest being 6QCant (about 50 CE). Two of these scrolls—4Cant[a] and 4Cant[b]—deserve special mention, both because they are the best preserved and because each has a number of interesting features. Although 4Cant[a] preserves quite a substantial amount of material,[d] the text between Canticles 4:7 and Canticles 6:11 is completely missing. Since in the Masoretic Text Canticles 4:7 forms the end of a content unit and Canticles 6:11 starts the beginning of another unit, it seems that the absence of chapters 4:8 through 6:10 was no mere accident; this material was either deliberately omitted, was not part of the text being copied by the scribe, or occurred elsewhere in the scroll. When compared with the size of the book as a whole, the section missing in this scroll is very large (about 30 percent). One explanation is the sensual language and erotic imagery that is found in much of the missing portion; the Song of Songs was evidently a controversial book before the time of Jesus.

The second noteworthy scroll is 4Cant[b], which also preserves a goodly amount of text[e] but omits two large segments (3:6–8 and 4:4–7) and possibly ended at 5:1, thus containing only the first half of the book found in modern Bibles. It is interesting that 4QCant[a] and 4QCant[b] lack a section at exactly the same point (Cant 4:7). But while 4QCant[a] omits a large piece of text *starting* after 4:7, 4QCant[b] omits the three verses *preceding* the end of 4:7. 4QCant[b] also features several scribal errors and, although written in Hebrew, contains several Aramaic word forms that reveal Aramaic influence on the scribe. Moreover, 4Cant[b] contains several unusual scribal markings that seem to represent letters in either the paleo-Hebrew script, the Cryptic A script (which was used in some Qumran sectarian writings), or a combination of several scripts including Greek. These letters in 4QCant[b] may indicate a sectarian scribal background or a special function of this manuscript among the Qumran community. The actual purpose of the unusual letters is not clear. Since they appear in lines that were slightly or much shorter than the surrounding ones, they may have served as line-fillers written in the spaces at the end of the lines to prevent such lines from being mistaken as "open sections."

---

a. 4Cant[a], 4Cant[b], and 4Cant[c].   **b.** 6QCant.   **c.** 4Cant[c] contains too little text on which to reach a firm conclusion.   **d.** Chapters 3:4–5, 7–11; 4:1–7; 6:11(?)–12; 7:1–7.   **e.** Chapters 2:9–17; 3:1–2, 5, 9–10; 4:1–3, 8–11, 14–16; 5:1.

In the translation that follows, quotation marks are used to indicate the various speakers (for example, the lover and the bride). But since identifying when one speaker closes and another begins is often difficult or ambiguous, it must be pointed out that the speech units and paragraph divisions below are not set in stone. As a comparison between several English Bibles indicates, what is part of one person's speech in one translation can be seen as part of the next speech in another translation.

1 1 [*The Song of S*]*ongs,*[1] whi[ch is by Solom]on.

2 "Let him kiss me with the kisses of [his mouth! For] your love is b[etter than wine; 3 the fragran]ce *of oils*[2] is pleasing, your name is *like a mix*[*ture of rubbed perfumes*].[3] This is w[hy the maide]ns love you. 4 Draw me [after you—let us hur]ry! The k[ing] has brought [me] into his chambers."

"We will *delight* [*and rejoice*[4] in you; we will extol] your love [more than wine]. How right are *your beloved ones!*"[5]

5 "[I am black and be]autiful, O *daughters of*[6] Jerusalem—[like the tents of Kedar, like the curtains of Solo]mon. 6 Do not stare at me because I am da[rk], for [the sun has burned me. My mother's sons were angry] with me; they made me careta[ker of the vineyards—but] I have not taken care of [my own vineyard]! 7 T[ell me, you whom my soul loves, where you pasture your flock (and) where] you [make it lie down at noon. For why should I be] like one who v[eils herself beside the flocks of your companions]?" ▲

2 [8 "Listen! My lover! Look—here he comes, leaping upon the mountains, leaping over the hills. 9 My lover is like a gazelle or a young stag. Look—there he stands] be[hind our wall], g[az]ing in at the windows, peering through the lattice."

10 "[My lover speaks and says] to me: 'Arise, my love, my fair one, and come away. 11 [For see, the winter is pas]t, the rains are over and gone. 12 *Look,*[7]

Chapter 1. 6QCant: 1:1–7.

1. This Hebrew expression means "The Greatest of All Songs."

2. 6QCant. *of your oils* MT LXX.

3. 6QCant; LXX similar. *like perfume poured out* MT.

4. 6QCant. *rejoice and delight* MT LXX.

5. 6QCant. *those who love you* MT LXX.

6. 6QCant has a different, apparently more ancient, form of this word.

Chapter 2. 4QCant[b]: 2:9–17.

7. 4QCant[b] (with *the season of* written first, as in vs 13, then crossed out). Not in MT LXX.

[flowers appear on the] earth, the season of singing has come, and the cooing of [doves is heard in] our land. 13 *Look,*[8] *the fig tree*[9] puts forth [its figs, and the vines in bl]ossom give forth their fragrance. Arise, my love, [my fair one, and come away. 14 O My dove in the clefts of the] rock, in the secret nooks on *the place of leaping,*[10] let me see [your face and let me hear] *your sound;*[11] for your voice is sweet [and your face is lovely. 15 Catch for us the f]*oxes*[12] that ruin [the vineyards—for our vineyards are in full bloom].'

16 "My [lover] is mine and I am his; he grazes [among the lilies. 17 Until the da]y [breathes] and *the shadows*[13] flee, my lover, turn around [and be *like a gazelle*][14] on *the mountains*[15] with many ravines."

3 1 "[Upon my bed *at ni*]*ght, every night,*[16] *I looked for*[17] [the one my heart loves; I sought] him but could not find him. 2 (So I said:) '*I will get up*[18] now [and go about the city, through its streets and squares; I will search for the one my heart loves.' So I looked for him, but could not find him].

[3 "When the watchmen found me as they made their rounds in the city, I asked them: 'Have you seen the one my heart loves?' 4 Scarcely had I passed them by when I found the one my heart loves!' I held on to him and would n]ot let him go until [I brought him into my mother's house, into the room of the one who conceived me]. 5 Daughters of [Jerusalem, I charge y]ou [by the gazelles and by the wild does: do not stir] up [or awaken love until it is ready]!'"[19]

■ *The omission of 3:6–8 in 4QCant*[b] *reflects a shorter text that eliminates the description of King Solomon's dramatic arrival. The longer text found in the Masoretic Text and the Septuagint also appears in 4QCant*[a] *and 4QCant*[c]:

---

8. 4QCant[b]. Not in MT LXX.

9. Apparent meaning 4QCant[b], which spells this word differently (incorrectly?) than does MT.

10. Possible meaning 4QCant[b]. *on the steep pathway* MT LXX.

11. 4QCant[b]. *your voice* MT LXX.

12. 4QCant[b] MT[mss] LXX. *the foxes, the little foxes* MT.

13. The form of this word in 4QCant[b] differs from that in MT because it has been influenced by the Aramaic equivalent.

14. Most likely reading 4QCant[b] (which had a shorter text). *like a gazelle or like a young stag* MT LXX.

15. 4QCant[b] and MT spell this word differently.

Chapter 3. 4QCant[b]: 3:1–2, 5, 9–11; 4QCant[a]: 3:4–5, 7–11; 4QCant[c]: 3:7–8.

16. 4QCant[b]. *at night* MT LXX.

17. 4QCant[b] spells this word differently than MT, possibly in error.

18. 4QCant[b]. *Let me get up* MT.

19. Verses 6–8 4QCant[a] MT LXX. Not in 4QCant[b].

6 "[Who is this coming up from the desert like columns of smoke, perfumed with myrrh and incense made from *all the fragrant spices of the merchant?*[20] 7 Look! It is Solo]mon's [traveling-couch, surrounded by] six[ty of] *Israel's most mighty men.*[21] 8 [All of them] are equipped with [swords and ex]perienced [in battle, each with] his sw[ord] at his side in case of terrors by night.

9 "King [Solomon m]ade for himself [a pa]lanquin from the woo[d of Lebanon]. 10 He ma[de] its posts of silver, [its base of go]ld, its seat of purple—[and its inte]rior was inlaid with [love] by the daughters of Jerusalem. 11 [Come out, you *daugh*]*ters of Jerusalem,*[22] [and gaze] on King Solomon wearing the crown [with which his mother crowned him on] his wed[ding day], *on the day*[23] of his heart's happiness."

4 1 "[How beautiful you are], my lo[ve]. O ho[w beauti]ful! Your eyes are like doves behind your veil; *like a flock of go*[*ats is your hair,*[24] descend]ing from Mount Gilead. 2 *Like a flock of newly shorn ewes are your teeth*[25] *that have come up*[26] from the [washing], all of which bear twins, and not one among them has lost its young. 3 Your lips are like a scarlet ribbon and your mouth is lovely. *Your chin is like a piece of pomegranate*[27] *and is behind*[28] your veil.

> ■ *4QCant*[b] *completely omits verses 4–7 of chapter 4. One possible reason is the parallels between descriptions of the female body in this chapter and those in chapter 6; note that in 6:7 the description of the body ends at exactly the same point where it stops in 4:3. Another explanation is that the mention of breasts in verse 5 could have triggered the omission of the section as a whole. The longer reading was known from the Masoretic Text and the Septuagint, and also appears in 4QCant*[a]*.

4 "[Your neck is like the tower of David, *built in ripples*];[29] *on it*[30] hang a thousand bucklers, all the shields of the mighty men. 5 [Your twin breasts are like two

---

20. I.e., "fragrant spices that have been imported."

21. Literally, *sixty mighty men of Israel's mighty men.*

22. 4QCant[a] (see also vs 10). *daughters of Zion* MT. Not in LXX.

23. 4QCant[a]. *and on the day* MT LXX.

Chapter 4. 4QCant[a]: 4:1–7; 4QCant[b]: 4:1–3, 8–11, 14–16.

24. Probable reading 4QCant[a] (with some reconstruction). *your hair is like a flock of goats* 4QCant[b] MT LXX.

25. 4QCant[a]. *Your teeth are like a flock of newly shorn ewes* 4QCant[b] MT LXX.

26. 4QCant[a]. *that have come up* MT LXX.

27. Most likely meaning 4QCant[a]. *Your cheeks are like pomegranate-halves* 4QCant[b] MT LXX.

28. 4QCant[b]. *behind* 4QCant[a] MT LXX.

29. Or, *built in rows of stones.*

30. Or, *in it* 4QCant[a]. *upon it* MT LXX.

fawns, like the twins of a gazelle] *(which) feed*[31] among the lilies. 6 Until [the day] breathes [and the shadows flee, I will make my way to the mountain of myr]rh, *to the hill*[32] of incense. 7 [You] are altogether [beautiful, my love; there is no flaw in you]!

■ *For this part of the Song of Songs, 4QCant*[a] *contains a much shorter text than the Masoretic Text and the Septuagint, since the text between chapters 4:7 and 6:11 is not included where we would expect it. Unless the missing passage occurred elsewhere in the now lost portion of 4QCant*[a]*, we may assume that it was never part of the Song of Songs in this manuscript. As pointed out in the introduction to the Song of Songs, this omission may have been due to the sensual language and erotic imagery found in much of 4:8 to 6:10. In contrast, however, 4QCant*[b] *contained all or most of this additional material.*

8 "As for you,[33] (come) from Lebanon, my bride; *as for you,*[34] (come) from Lebanon. *Let me depart*[35] from the peak of *Omnon,*[36] *from*[37] the dens of lions and the mountain-haunts of leopards. 9 You have stolen my heart, my sister, *my bride;*[38] you have stolen my heart with a single glance of your eyes, with a single [jewel of] your neck[lace]. 10 How sweet is your love, my sister, my bride! How much bet[ter] is your love than wine, and the frag[rance of] *your oil*[39] than all kinds of spices! 11 Your lips, *my sister, my bride,*[40] drip like a honeycomb; honey [and milk are under your tongue, and the fragrance of your garments is like the fragrance of Lebanon. 12 (You are) a locked garden, my sister, my bride; you are a locked rock garden, a sealed fountain. 13 Your *channels*[41] are an orchard of pome-granates with the choicest fruits, with henna and nard plants, 14 nard and saffron, calamus and cinna]m[on, with all trees of frankincense, myrrh and aloes, along with all] the finest spi[ces. 15 You are a garden fountain, a well of living wat]er, and streams flowing fr[om Lebanon]."

16 "[Awake, O north wind, and come, O south wind]! Make my garden

---

31. 4QCant[a]. *which feed* MT LXX.

32. 4QCant[a] MT[mss]. *and to the hill* MT LXX.

33. 4QCant[b] (Aramaic influence?). *(come) with me* MT. *to here* LXX.

34. 4QCant[b] (Aramaic influence?). *(come) with me* MT. *to here* LXX.

35. Probable meaning 4QCant[b]. *Depart* MT LXX.

36. 4QCant[b]. *Amanah* MT LXX. These are different names for the same mountain.

37. 4QCant[b] (the additional places found in MT LXX probably having been omitted acci-dentally). *from the peaks of Senir and Hermon, from* MT LXX.

38. Thus MT LXX. 4QCant[b] has a different word here, but too little remains for it to be identified.

39. 4QCant[b]. *your oils* MT. *your garments* LXX (cf. vs 11).

40. 4QCant[b] (cf. vss 9, 10, 12; 5:1). *my bride* MT LXX.

41. Or, *shoots.*

breathe out; let [its spices] be wa[fted abroad. Let my beloved come into] his garden, and eat from [his good] fo[rtune]."⁴²

5 1 "[I have entered my garden, my sister, my bride]. I have gathered my myrrh with [my sp]ice, [*I have drunk my wine and my milk*]; *I have eaten my honeycomb and my honey.*"⁴³

"[Eat, friends, and drink! Yes—drink your fill, you lo]vers!"▲

■ *As noted in the introduction to the Song of Songs, 4Cantᵇ possibly ended at 5:1, thus containing only the first half of the book found in modern Bibles. Three separate pieces of evidence support this proposal. First, the final preserved letter in the last line of column 4 is much larger than those in the preceding lines, which may indicate the end of a literary unit or even of the entire scroll. Second, the left edge of the fragment seems to contain the Greek letter gamma or a sign similar in shape to a diple obelismene (which was used in the Greek scribal tradition for separating sections in tragedies and comedies). The presence of this letter before the end of the line strengthens the case that it is the final line of the scroll. Finally, in this part of the scroll, 5:1 marks the end of a separate literary unit; if 4QCantᵇ in fact ended here, it would be appropriate for this to happen at the end of such a unit.*

6 11 "[I went down to the orchard of nut trees to look at the new growth in the valley, to see *whether*⁴⁴ the vines] had budded [and if the pomegranates were in bloom. 12 Before I realized it, my fancy placed me] among the cha[riots of my noble people]."

13 "[Come back, come back, O *Shulammite,*⁴⁵ so that we may gaze at you]."

"Why would you ga[ze at the Shulammite, as one gazes at the dance of two armies]?"▲

7 1 "[How beautiful are your feet] in san[d]als, [O prince's daughter! The curves of your thighs are like jewels], the wo[rk of an artist's hands. 2 Your navel is a rounded bowl that never lacks] mixed wine. [Your *wai*]st⁴⁶ [is a mound of wheat encircled with lilies]. 3 Your [twin] breasts are like two [fawns, like the

---

42. 4QCantᵇ. *his choicest fruit* MT. *the first of his fruit-trees* LXX.

Chapter 5. 4QCantᵇ: 5:1.

43. 4QCantᵇ (with a chiastic pattern of hemistichs, *a-b-b-a*) for the verse. *I have eaten my honeycomb and my honey; I have drunk my wine and my milk* MT LXX (with a parallel pattern of hemistichs, *a-b-a-b*).

Chapter 6. 4QCantᵃ: 6:11(?)–12.

44. 4QCantᵃ (separate word, reconstructed). *whether* MT (with interrogative *he* joined to the following noun).

45. 4QCantᵃ (with one of the two pairs of *come back* most likely omitted, since the reconstructed line would be too long with two). *O Shulammite! Come back, come back* MT LXX.

Chapter 7. 4QCantᵃ: 7:1–7 [Heb 7:2–8].

46. Or, *belly.*

twins of a gazelle. 4 Your neck is like an ivory tower], your eyes are the pools of Hesh[bon by the gate of Bath-rabbim. Your nose is like the tower of] Lebanon looking toward Damas[cus. 5 Your head crowns you like (Mount) Carmel, and] your [*flowing locks*][47] are like purple garments; a [k]ing is held cap[tive by your tresses]."

6 "[*And how*[48] fair and] how delightful you are, my lo[ve, with all your charms! 7 You are stately as a palm tree, and your breasts are like its clusters of fruit. 8 I said: "I will climb the palm tree and take hold of its date-clusters." Oh, may your breasts be like clusters of the vine, and the scent of your breath like apples; 9 may your kisses be like the best wine that goes down smoothly, flowing through lips *and teeth*]."[49]

---

47. Literally, *the hair of your head.*

48. 4QCant[a]. *How* MT LXX.

49. Reconstructed from LXX. *of those who sleep* MT.

QOHELET
(ECCLESIASTES)

Qohelet—perhaps meaning "the assembler"—is concerned with the purpose of life and in particular the inability of material things to provide meaning. As appropriate as this message might have been for the ascetic community reflected in the Dead Sea Scrolls, only two manuscripts of the book were found at Qumran. The Wisdom books apparently were not yet considered of quite the same importance as the Law and the Prophets. The older manuscript, 4QQoh^a, is housed at the Amman Museum rather than with 4QQoh^b and most of the other scrolls in the Rockefeller Museum in Jerusalem.

4QQoh^a is among the oldest manuscripts at Qumran, dating from about 175–150 BCE. Its writing is spacious and penned with flair. There are portions of three contiguous columns preserved, containing text from chapters 5 through 7. The 4QQoh^a scribe made several copying mistakes—for example, once skipping from one occurrence of a word to a repeated occurrence (though he did notice the error and write the missing text supralinearly).

4QQoh^b has only two small fragments from chapter 1 and probably dates from the middle or latter half of the first century BCE.

All the witnesses—the scrolls, the Masoretic Text, and the Septuagint—generally exhibit a similar text, though each is dotted with minor variants. Most of the variants are small particles, late versus classical forms, minor scribal errors, look-alike words, or changes of word order. A few letters are extant at the edges of the 4QQoh^a fragments for 6:8 and 6:12–7:1, but, while they are insufficient to establish any meaning, they do not agree with the words in the Masoretic Text. Some minor features in Hebrew and Greek cannot be mirrored in the opposite language, but when minor differences between the Hebrew texts can be reflected in the Greek, the Septuagint usually agrees with the Masoretic Text, though sometimes it follows the scroll.

1 10 [There are things of which they say, "Look at this! This is new!"] It existed [lo]ng ago, in ages [which have passed before us. 11 No one remembers what happened long ago;] no[r] will [things] in the fut[ure be [remembered by those who come after them. 12 I the Tea]cher was k[ing over Israel in Jerusalem. 13 I applied] myself to study [and investigate with wisdom all that is done under heaven: it is] miserable work [God] has set [humanity to toil over. 14 I have seen everything] *that*[1] is done und[er the sun; and just look, it is all futile, chasing after wind]. 15 [. . .] *gb*[2] [. . .].▲

5 14 [Then those riches are lost in a bad venture, and though they have chil]dren, they have noth]ing [in their possession]. 15 *Indeed,*[3] [they came out of their mother's womb naked, so will they depart], just as they came, [and they will take nothing for their labor to carry away wi]th them. 16 *This*[4] too [is a grievous evil. Just as they came, so will they go]. What gain is there [in striving after wind? 17 All their days they eat in darkness, with much] trouble [and sickness and anger. 18 Here is what I myse]lf [have seen to be] good: [it is pleasant to eat and to drink and to see goo]d [come] from all our labor [under the sun, as many days of life] as [God has gi]v[en] us: [for this is our lot].▲

6 1 [There is an evil I have seen under the sun, and i]t i[s heavy] on [humanity].▲

3 [A man may have a hundred children and live many years, but no matter how many years he has, if his life is not filled with good things, or if he has no burial], I think that *a stillborn child is better off than he.*[5] 4 Although into futility it *comes,*[6] and into darkness it goes, and with darkness its name[7] is covered; 5 still, though it has

---

Chapter 1. 4QQoh[b]: 1:10–14(15?).

1. 4QQoh[b]. MT has a later, equivalent word for *that* (see the opposite in 7:19, 20).

2. Before it breaks off, 4QQoh[b] has two letters that show a text different from that of MT.

Chapter 5. 4QQoh[a]: 5:14–18 [MT 5:13–17].

3. 4QQoh[a]. *As* MT LXX.

4. 4QQoh[a]. *And this* MT LXX.

Chapter 6. 4QQoh[a]: 6:1, 3–8.

5. 4QQoh[a]. *better off than he is a stillborn child* MT LXX.

6. 4QQoh[a] misspells.

7. The 4QQoh[a] scribe first wrote "into darkness its name," having skipped from the first occurence of "darkness" to the second; he then erased "its name" and wrote supralinearly "it goes, and with darkness its name."

not seen [or] known the sun, yet it finds rest, more so than he, 6 *even if he should*[8] live twice a thousand years but without enjoyment. Do they not both go to the same place? 7 All human labor is for the mouth, and still our appetite does not [get] its fi[ll]. 8 *How much*[9] advantage do the wise have ov[er fools? . . .]¹⁰▲

7 1 A [good] name is better [than fine perfume, and the day of death than the day of one's bi]r[th]. 2 It is better to go to the house [of mourning than to go to the house of *j*]*oy*,[11] [since th]at is *all the end* [*of humankind,*[12] and the living ought to take it] to heart. 3 Sorrow is better than laughter; [though it is bad for the face, it is] good for the heart. 4 The wise consider the house of mourning, [but fools] the house of joy. 5 It is better to hear the *rebukes*[13] [of the wise than] *to hear*[14] the song of fools. 6 As the crackling [of thorns und]er the pot, so is the fool's laughter. *This*[15] also is [*wo*]*rthless*.[16]

7 [Extortion makes] the wise [foolish], and [a bribe] *perverts*[17] [the heart. 8 The end of a matter is better] than its beginning. [Patience is better than pride. 9 Do not be quick] in [your] spirit [to anger, since it is foolish to harbor an angry grudge].▲

19 [Wisdom] *helps*[18] [the wise more than ten rulers] *who*[19] [are] in a city. 20 [There is no righteous person on earth] *who*[20] [continually d]oes what is good [and never sins].

---

8. 4QQohᵃ. *though he* MT.

9. 4QQohᵃ. *For what* MT LXX.

10. 4QQohᵃ has several letters both late in this verse and again in verse 12 that do not match the text in MT.

Chapter 7. 4QQohᵃ: 7:1–9, 19–20.

11. 4QQohᵃ (with *smhh* = *joy*) (see verse 4). *feasting* (= *msth*) MT LXX.

12. 4QQohᵃ. *the end of all humankind* MT LXX.

13. 4QQohᵃ. *rebuke* MT LXX.

14. 4QQohᵃ. *one hearing* MT LXX. The 4QQohᵃ scribe skipped the first letter of "hear" but then wrote it above the word. He also apparently wrote the wrong word next, erased it, and continued with "the song."

15. 4QQohᵃ. *And this* MT LXX.

16. In 4QQohᵃ the word "worthless" is written apparently in the bottom margin, as the end of this paragraph. The fragment is broken and there may or may not have been another word or two before it. The words in the top line of the next column were erased, again perhaps explaining the placement of "worthless" in the bottom margin.

17. 4QQohᵃ. *destroys* MT LXX.

18. 4QQohᵃ LXX. *strengthens* MT.

19. 4QQohᵃ has a later, equivalent word for "who," while MT has the classical form (see the opposite in 1:14).

20. 4QQohᵃ has a later, equivalent word for "who," while MT has the classical form.

LAMENTATIONS

The destruction of Jerusalem and the Temple in 586 BCE gave rise to the question, Why did this happen? This cry of lament is recorded as the first word in three of the five poems that make up the collection known as Lamentations (1:1, 2:1, and 4:1) and is the Hebrew title for the book. For the Qumranites—a community that still considered itself in exile (the present Temple being in the hands of impostors and therefore ritually unclean)—these poems must have been of heightened significance.

Four manuscripts—together witnessing to all five chapters of Lamentations—were found in the caves at Qumran. Cave 3, famous for the idiosyncratic *Copper Scroll,* preserved one manuscript (3QLam). A somewhat variant version of the book was unearthed in Cave 4 (4QLam). Finally, the relatively meager cache of twenty-five fragmentary manuscripts found in Cave 5 produced remnants of two scrolls of Lamentations (5QLamᵃ and 5QLamᵇ).

Chapters 1 through 4 of Lamentations were written in a poetic form known as *acrostic.* In an acrostic poem, each line, or group of lines, begins with a letter of the alphabet in its respective order. The versification of our modern Bibles evidences this characteristic, because each chapter is a multiple of twenty-two, the number of letters in the Hebrew alphabet. (Chapter 5, though not acrostic, follows this numerical pattern as well.) The acrostic form is also captured in our modern Bibles by the common practice of printing poetry in *cola* (poetic units that are divisions of the strophe or stanza). To our eye, this is what differentiates poetry from prose. It is noteworthy that while the scribe of 3QLam did copy Lamentations in such a fashion, those of 4QLam, 5QLamᵃ, and 5QLamᵇ did not. Perhaps the ancient concern was much the same as publishing concerns in our time: the need to save space!

Lamentations is quoted at least once in the nonbiblical scrolls. *A Lament for Zion* (4Q179 2 4), a literary piece that appears to be patterned after Lamentations, cites Lamentations 1:1. *A Prayer for Deliverance* (4Q501) capitalizes on the genre of lament, although in this case the enemy is not the Babylonians, the Romans, or any other foreign people, but rather unbelieving Jews. The writer pleads with God to exclude them from the "sons of the covenant" because of their lack of faithfulness. One of the few as yet unpublished manuscripts (4Q241) is also reported to contain a passage from Lamentations.

1

▓ *The most extensive manuscript of Lamentations—4QLam—is a late–first century* BCE *copy unearthed in Cave 4. The first preserved column of the scroll begins in the midst of line 1, with the upper margin clearly visible. Although, given the fragmentary nature of the text, the right margin is not visible (remember, Hebrew reads right to left!), it is clear from the calculated line length that the first half of verse 1 necessarily began at the bottom of the previous column. Thus almost certainly Lamentations was not the first book in this scroll. So, we might ask, what was the book that preceded it? Jews would likely answer that it was preceded by Ruth—according to the order of books represented by the Hebrew canon—whereas Christians would suggest Jeremiah, as is the case in the Christian Bible. The Jewish historian Josephus, writing near the end of the first century* CE, *gives the earliest evidence for an answer to this question. He discusses a twenty-two book Bible (Contra Apionem 1:8), whereas the modern Jewish Bible numbers twenty-four. Josephus's number would suggest that Ruth was included with Judges, and Lamentations with Jeremiah. Unfortunately, the worms that feasted on the Cave 4 manuscript have eliminated any further clues to this mystery. Perhaps future* DNA *testing will reveal whether 4QJerᵉ or one of the two Cave 4 copies of Ruth (4QRuthᵃ or 4QRuthᵇ) was written on skin from the same (or a related) animal.*

[1 How the city sits solitary that was full of people! She has become as a widow,] she that was great among the nations! [She that was a princess among the provinces is become vassal! 2 She] weeps [bitterly] in the night, [and her tears are on her cheeks;] among all her lovers [she has none to comfort her: all her friends have dealt treacherously with her; they have become her] enemies. 3 [Judah] is gone into captivity [because of affliction, and because of great servitude; sh]e d[wel]ls among the nat[ions, she finds no rest; all her persecutors overtook her] in [distress. 4 The roads of Zion mourn, because no one comes t]o the as[sembly; all her gates are desolate, her priests do si]gh; [her virgins are afflicted, and she herself is in bitterness.] 5 Her [adversarie]s [have become] the masters, [her enemies

---

Chapter 1. 4QLam: 1:1–18; 3QLam: 1:10–12.

prosper; for the LORD has afflicted her for the multit]ude of [her] transgression[s. Her young children are gone into captivity before the adversary.]

■ *Ancient scribes were not as accurate as the present-day printing press or copy machine. In verse 6 the copyist of 4QLam appears to have fallen asleep at his task, repeating the negative "not" and then dividing the following word improperly to produce, "he did not find and pasture," from "they did not find pasture." Other variants in this chapter are more difficult to explain and may evidence some confusion in both the traditional Masoretic Text and its Qumran relative.*

[6 And] from the daughter [of Zion all her majesty has depa]rted; her princes [have beco]me like stags that do *not not*[1] *find*[2] *and*[3] pasture, [and] they have fled *without*[4] strength before the pursuer. 7 *Remember, O LORD,*[5] all *our pains*[6] that were from the days of old; when her [people] fell into the hand of the adversary, and none did *help; her adversaries*[7] mocked at [al]l *her calamities.*[8] 8 Jerusalem has sinned grievously; there[fore] she has become *one who shows grief;*[9] all that honored her *despise,*[10] because they have seen her [nak]edness. [She] also [sighs and turns] away. 9 Her uncleanness was in [her] sk[irts; she did not consider her end; therefore she has come down *ap*]*pallingly;*[11] *and*[12] [she] has no [comforter. O LORD, see my affliction; for the enemy] has magnified himself. [10 The adversary has spread out his hand upon all her preciou]s [things; for she has seen that the nations have entered into her sanctuary; concerning] whom you commanded that they should not *bring* 11 *her*[13] precious things as food to refresh *her*[14] soul. O LORD, look and see; for I have become *abject.*[15] 12 *Is all of this nothing to you, you*[16] that pass [by?

---

1. Scribal repetition. 4QLam.

2. Singular 4QLam. Plural MT LXX.

3. 4QLam. Not in MT LXX.

4. 4QLam. *with no* MT.

5. 4QLam. *In the days of her affliction and of miseries Jerusalem remembers* MT LXX.

6. 4QLam. *her pleasant things* MT LXX.

7. 4QLam. *help her; the adversaries saw her, they* MT LXX.

8. 4QLam. *her desolations* MT LXX.

9. 4QLam. *an unclean thing* MT LXX.

10. 4QLam. *despise her* MT LXX.

11. Feminine 4QLam. Masculine MT.

12. 4QLam. Not in MT LXX.

13. 4QLam. *enter into your assembly. 11 All her people sigh, they seek bread; they have given their* 3QLam MT LXX.

14. 4QLam. Not in MT LXX.

15. Masculine 4QLam. Feminine MT LXX.

16. 4QLam. *Is it nothing to you, all you* MT LXX.

Look and se]e if there be any sorrow like my sorrow which *they*[17] brought upon me; with which the L[ORD] has *frightened*[18] me [in the da]y [of] his [ang]er.[19] 13 From on high has he sent fi[re] into my bones, and *he has brought it down;*[20] he has spread a net for my feet; he has turned me [bac]k; he has made me *desolate*[21] *all the day and faint.*[22] 14 *It was bound about my transgressions*[23] by his hand; *his yoke is secured*[24] upon [my] n[eck;] he has made my strength fail. The LORD[25] has *delivered me into the hand of him against whom*[26] I am not able to stand. 15 The Lord has rejected all my *perished ones*[27] in my midst; he has called an asse[mbly] against me to crush my young men. The LORD[28] has trodden as in a winepress the virgin daughter of Judah. 16[29] 17 Zion spreads forth [her] h[ands; there is none] to comfort her *among all her lovers; you, O LORD, are righteous;*[30] the *Lord has kept watch*[31] concerning Jacob, that they that are round about him should be his adversaries. *Zion*[32] has *been banished*[33] among them. 16 For these things *my eyes weep, my tears flow down,*[34] because [the comforter that should refresh *the*] *soul*[35] is far [from me.] My children are desolate, [because] the enemy has prevailed. 18 The L[ord][36] is righteous; [for I have rebelled against his commandment; hear, I pray you, all you peoples, and behold my sorrow: My virgins and my young men have gone into captivity.]▲

---

17. 4QLam. *is* MT LXX.

18. 4QLam. *afflicted* 3QLam MT LXX.

19. 4QLam. *fierce anger* MT LXX.

20. 4QLam LXX. *it prevails against them* MT.

21. Masculine 4QLam. Feminine MT LXX.

22. 4QLam. *ill all the day* MT LXX.

23. 4QLam. *The yoke of my transgressions is bound* (dubious) MT. *He keeps watch over my transgressions* LXX.

24. 4QLam. *they are knit together, they have come up* MT LXX.

25. 4QLam. *Lord* MT.

26. 4QLam. *delivered me into the hands of those against whom* MT. *placed sorrows in my hand,* LXX.

27. 4QLam. *mighty men* MT LXX.

28. 4QLam. *Lord* MT.

29. 4QLam records vs 16 following vs 17.

30. 4QLam. Not in MT LXX.

31. 4QLam. LORD *has commanded* MT LXX.

32. 4QLam. *Jerusalem* MT LXX.

33. 4QLam LXX. *become an unclean thing* MT.

34. 4QLam. *I weep; my eyes, my eyes flow with water* MT LXX.

35. 4QLam. *my soul* MT LXX.

36. 4QLam. LORD MT.

2[5 The LORD has become an enemy; he has swallowed up Israel;] he has swallowed up all her palaces; [he has destroyed his strongholds; and he has multiplied mourning and lamentation in the daughter of Judah.]▲

3 53 They have brought an end [to my life] in [the pit, and have cast a stone upon me. 54 Waters flowed over my head; I said, I am cut off. 55 I called upon your name, O LORD, out of the lowest pit. 56 You] heard my voice; [do not hide your ear to my cry, regarding my relief. 57 You drew near in the day I called upon you; you said, "Fear not." 58 O LORD, you have pleaded the causes of my soul; you have redeemed my life. 59 O LORD, you] have seen [my wrong; judge my cause. 60 You have seen all their vengeance and all their plots against me. 61 You have heard their reproach, O LORD, and all their plots against me. 62 The] l[i]p[s of my assailants and their whispering are against me all day long.]▲

4[5 They that ate] delicacies are de[solate in the stre]ets; [they that were brought up in scarlet em]brace dunghills. 6 For the iniquity [of the daughter of my people] is great[er than the sin of Sodom, which was overt]hrown as in a moment, and no [hands were laid upon her. 7 Her rulers were purer than snow, they were whiter than mi]lk; their bodies were more [rud]dy than cora[l, their polishing was as of sapphire. 8 Their appearance is blacker] than coal; they are not k[nown in the streets. Their skin has shriveled on their bones; it is withered, it has become like wood.]▲

[11 The LORD has accomplished his wrath; he has poured out his fierce anger; and he has kindled a fire in Zion, which has devoured its foundatio]ns. [12 The kings of the earth did not believe, neither did all the inhabitants of the] wor[ld,] that the adversary and the en[emy would] e[nter into the gates of Jerusalem. 13 It is because of the sins of] her prophets, and the iniquities of her pries[t]s, who [have shed the blood of the jus]t in her midst. 14 They wander [as blind me]n in the streets; [they] are p[olluted] with blood, so that *no one*[37] is able to *tou*[*ch*][38] their garments. [15 "Depar]t," they cried to them, *"They are unclean!*[39] Depart, de[par]t, do not [touc]h!" When they fled [and wandered, men said among the nations, "They shall no longer] dwell [here."] 16 The LORD himself [has scattered them; he will no longer regard them.] They [did not ho]nor [the priests; they did not favor the elders. 17 Ye]t [our eyes have failed, watching vainly for our help. In our watching we have watched for a nation that could not save.] 18 They hunt [our] st[eps, so that we cannot go in our streets. Our end is near, our days are fin-

---

Chapter 2. 4QLam: 2:5.

Chapter 3. 3QLam: 3:53–62.

Chapter 4. 5QLam^a: 4:5–8, 11–22; 5QLam^b: 4:17–20.

   37. 5QLam^a. *none* MT LXX.

   38. Unreadable variant text 5QMLam^a. *touch* MT LXX.

   39. 5QLam^a. *Unclean!* MT LXX(?).

ished; for our end has come. 19 Our pursuers] *are*[40] swift[er than the eagles of the he]avens. [They chased us on the mountains;] they laid wait for us [in the wilder]ness. 20 The brea[th] of our nostrils, the [an]ointed of the LORD, [was captured in] their [pits; of whom we said, "Under his shadow we shall live among the nation]s." 21 Rejoice [and be glad,] O daughter of Ed[om, that dwell in the land of Uz, the cu]p shall pa[ss] to you [also;] you will become d[runk, and make yourself naked. 22 The punishment of your iniquity is accomplished, O daugh]ter of Zion; he will no longer e[xile you; he will] p[unish] your iniquity, [O daughter of] Edom; he will uncover [your] si[ns.]

5 1 Re[member, O LORD,] what [has come] upon us. *Look,*[41] [and see our] *re- proaches.*[42] [2 Our inheritance has been turned over to stranger]s, our houses to aliens. [3 We are] orphans [and] father[less;] our mothers *have no daughters or are widows.*[43] [4 We drink our water for a p]rice; [our wood is sold to us. 5 Our pursuers are on our necks; we are weary, and there is no rest] for us. [6 We have covenanted with] E[gypt and] Assyria to be s[atisfied with bread. 7 Our fathers sinned, and are no more; and w]e have b[or]ne their iniquities. 8 Serv[ants rule over us; there is no one to deliv]er [us out] of their hand. 9 We get [our] bread at the peril of our lives, [because o]f the sword in [the] wilderness. [10 Ou]r skin is black like an oven, b[ec]ause of the burning heat of famine. 11 They [ra]ped the women in Zion, virgins in the citie[s of Ju]dah. 12 Princes were hanged up by their hands. [The elders were no]t honored. 13 The young me[n] worked the mill; [and the children] stumbled [under loads of wood.]▲

[16 The crown is fallen from our head:] Woe [to us! for we have sinned. 17 For this our heart is faint; because of these things our eyes are dim;] 18 because of the [mountain of Zion which is desolate; the foxes walk upon it.]▲

---

40. 5QLam[a]. *were* MT LXX.

Chapter 5. 5QLam[a]: 5:1–13, 16–17.

41. Variant grammatical form 5QLam[a].

42. 5QLam[a]. *reproach* MT LXX.

43. 5QLam[a]. *are like widows* MT LXX.

THE EPISTLE OF
JEREMIAH

The Epistle (or Letter) of Jeremiah fails to live up to its billing. Not by form a letter, nor written by the prophet Jeremiah, the document is instead a pointed exhortation concerning the futility of idol worship written in the spirit of Jeremiah 10.

The Epistle of Jeremiah is one of three deuterocanonical books—that is, books from the so-called second canon, or Apocrypha—that were found in the Qumran caves. The other two are Sirach (also known as Ben Sira or Ecclesiasticus) and Tobit. These three books, accepted as fully canonical by the Roman Catholic Church, are not recognized by Protestant or Jewish communities; they are instead labeled "apocryphal," or outside the canon. The Epistle of Jeremiah could also be classified as a "pseudegraph," a document written in the name of a famous personage in order to speak with authority—a reverse plagiarism of sorts. The Epistle of Jeremiah is normally printed in modern translations as the sixth chapter of another apocryphal work, the book of Baruch.

Although the Epistle of Jeremiah was likely composed in Hebrew, the one copy—actually, only a fragment the size of a postage stamp—found in the caves (7QpapEpJer gr) is written in Greek and does not vary substantially from the text known from the Septuagint. Cave 7, the source of the so-called *Jesus Scroll* (7Q5; see the Introduction), is unique among the Qumran caves in that each of the nineteen manuscripts that it preserved was written in Greek.

6 [43 And when one of them is drawn away by one of the passersby and is lain with, she reviles the woman next to her, because she was not as attractive as herself nor was her cord] br[oken. 44 Everything which is don]e [for] th[em is false.] So, [h]ow [can anyone] su[ppose that] they [are] g[ods, or claim th]e[m as gods?][1]

Chapter 6. 7QpapEpJer gr: 6:43–44.

  1. 7QpapEpJer gr. *suppose or claim that they are gods* LXX.

ESTHER

Of the thirty-nine books of the Hebrew Bible—or twenty-four if the Minor Prophets, Ezra-Nehemiah, 1 and 2 Samuel, 1 and 2 Kings, and 1 and 2 Chronicles are each counted as one—only the book of Esther is missing from the collection of manuscripts unearthed in the caves above the banks of the Dead Sea. The absence of Esther from the twenty or so scrolls found among the ruins of Masada and the hideouts used by the rebels of the Bar Kokhba revolt does not raise much of a question, but the absence of Esther from more than 200 biblical scrolls from the caves at Qumran is a bit more curious. To be sure, the books of Nehemiah and 1 Chronicles have not been found either, but they are generally assumed to have been present on the basis of the few crumbs of the scrolls of Ezra and 2 Chronicles respectively.

That Esther has turned up missing might be attributed to nothing more than chance coupled with the relatively small size of the book. In addition, as noted above, it is true that other books composed in the period following the Babylonian exile are either missing (Nehemiah and 1 Chronicles) or nearly so (Ezra and 2 Chronicles). However, some evidence that has come to light just recently reveals that the absence of Esther was purposeful rather than accidental. The Qumran calendar texts—not generally known before 1991—chart festivals and holy days on the community's 364-day year. The feast of Purim, which has its beginnings in the story of Esther, is missing. As a result, the real question now becomes: Why was Esther rejected?

Several answers might be suggested. First, the fact that the festival of Purim was a later addition, not mentioned in the Books of Moses, might have caused the Dead Sea Scrolls community to reject the book. Second, the mere fact that the story concerns the marriage of Esther—a Jew—to a Persian king was likely repugnant to the group's conservative sensibilities. Third, the book itself makes no mention of God whatsoever. Finally, the emphasis on retaliation evident in the final chapters of Esther (chapters 7–9) is contrary to the teachings of the Dead Sea Scrolls: "To no man shall I return evil for evil; I shall pursue a man only for good; for with God resides the judgment of all the living, and he shall pay each man his recompense" (1QS 10:17–18). Any one of these factors would have provided good reason to reject the book of Esther.

CHRONICLES

Only a single small fragment, dated about 50–25 BCE, remains out of the sixty-five chapters of 1 and 2 Chronicles. In contrast, four manuscripts of 1 and 2 Samuel and three of 1 and 2 Kings were preserved, one quite extensively. The relative scarcity of Chronicles at Qumran could be a matter of either chance or design, since Chronicles has a strong focus on Jerusalem and the Temple, from which the Qumran community had removed itself.

This single fragment of Chronicles, however, proves interesting. The text translated here is close to the traditional text, with three small variants—two meaningless, and the third a minor error in the spelling of the name of the Queen Mother. The Queen Mother, of course, is important in dynastic kingship (when the king might have several wives) for determining which branch of the family inherits the royal prerogatives.

Preceding the recognizable text from 2 Chronicles 28:27–29:3, however, are the remains of a few letters in the previous column. They yield no connected text, but neither do they match any of the traditional text of Chronicles within a chapter or two before the recognizable text translated here. So there appear to be two possibilities: either (1) this fragment is not really from a manuscript of the book of Chronicles itself but is from another work that quotes Chronicles, or (2) it is a text of Chronicles that simply has some text that varies from the traditional text. This latter is probably the case. The extensive Samuel manuscript, 4QSam^a, frequently varies from the traditional text in large and significant ways, and half the time its text is to be preferred to the Masoretic Text. More important, 4QSam^a often agrees with Chronicles, the Septuagint, and the narrative of the historian Flavius Josephus, against the isolated Masoretic narrative. At any rate, this small fragment proves either that the book of Chronicles itself was in the Qumran library or, perhaps more significantly, that it was known and considered worth quoting.

28 ²⁷ [Ahaz slept with his ancestors, and they buried him in Jerusalem, in the city, for they did not bring him into the tombs of the kings of Israel. Hezekiah] *son of Ahaz*[1] [succeeded him].

29 ¹ [Hezekiah began to reign when he was twenty-f]ive years old, and [he reigned twen]ty-nine years [in Jerusalem. His mother's name was] *Aybah*[2] [daugh]ter of Zechari[ah]. 2 He did what was right [in the eyes of the LORD, just as David his] father had done. 3 *And he,*[3] in the [first] yea[r of his reign, in the first month], opened the door[s of the house of the LORD and repaired them].

Chapter 28. 4QChr: 2 Chron 28:27.

    1. 4QChr. *his son* MT LXX.

Chapter 29. 4QChr: 2 Chron 29:1–3.

    2. 4QChr. *Abyah* MT.

    3. 4QChr. *He* MT.

EZRA-NEHEMIAH

4QEzra, a manuscript that was copied around the middle of the first century BCE, survives in only three small fragments. It is the only manuscript of Ezra (and there are none of Nehemiah) that was found in the Judean Desert. For the small amount of extant text, it displays almost exactly the same wording recorded in the Masoretic Text. There are only four minor variants. 4QEzra once shows the singular form of the verb in contrast to the Masoretic Text's plural, while in another case the manuscripts show the exact opposite. Twice the Masoretic Text errs in spelling the definite article *-ah,* while 4QEzra has the correct form *-a'.*

This text provides one of the biblical terms that the Qumran community appropriated for identifying itself: *yaḥad* = "the community" (Ezra 4:3), though the word itself is not preserved on the fragment.[1] In fact, the designation forms the title of one of its foundational documents, *Serek HaYaḥad* = the *Community Rule.*

42 [They approached Zerubbabel and the chiefs of the clans and said to them, "Let us build with you; for we seek your] Go[d, as you do, and we have been sacrificing to him since the days of King Esarhaddon of Assyria who brought us here." 3 But] Ze[rubbabel, Joshua, and the rest of the chiefs of Israel's clans said] to them, ["You will have nothing to do with us in building a house for our God]. Rather w[e, the community, will build to the LORD the God of Israel, as King Cyrus of Persia commanded us." 4 Then the people of the] land [intimidated the people of Judah and made them afraid to build. 5 They bribed counselors against them to] frustrate [their] plans, [all the days of King Cyrus of Persia until the reign of King Darius of Persia].

6 [In the reign of Ahasuerus, in the begin]ning of [his] reig[n, they wrote an accusation against the inhabitants of Judah and Jerusalem]. ▲

---

1. See S. Talmon, *The World of Qumran from Within* (Jerusalem: Magnes and Hebrew University Press; Leiden: Brill, 1989), 55–56.

Chapter 4. 4QEzra: 4:2–6, 9–11.

9 [Then wrote Rehum the chancellor, Shimshai the scribe, and the rest of th]eir [associates, the judges, the envoys, the officials, the people of Persia, Erech, Babylonia, Susa, that is, the Ela]mites, 10 and the rest of the nati[ons which the great and noble Osnappar deported and settled in the city of Samaria] and in the rest of the province Beyond *the River,*[2] and no[w 11 this is the copy of the letter that they sent to him: "To Artaxerxes the ki]n[g from your servants,] the people of the province Beyond [the River . . .]." ▲

5 17 [So now, if it seems good to the king, let a search be made in the king's archives in Babylon, whether a decree was made by King Cyrus to rebuild] this [hou]se of God [at Jerusalem; and let the king send us his decision on this matter].

6 1 [Then King Darius made a decr]ee, and *he*[3] searched the arch[ive records, where the documents were stored in Babylon. 2 At Ecbatana, in the palace in *the provi]nce*[4] [of Media], a scroll [was found in which] this was wr[itten: "A record. 3 In his first year, King Cyrus made a decree]: Concerning the house of God at Jerusalem, [let the] hou[se be rebuilt, the place where they offer sacrifices, and let its foundations be securely laid, its height] sixty cub[it]s, its width sixty cubits, 4 [with three cour]ses of [large stones and a course of new timber. Let] the [expenses] be paid by the royal palace. 5 In addition [let the gold and silver] vessels of the hou[se of God, which Nebuchadnezzar took fr]om the temple in Jerusalem and *they*[5] brought to Ba[bylon, be restored and returned to the temple in Jerusalem, each to its place]. You shall put them [in] the house of God." ▲

---

2. 4QEzra. MT has a minor spelling mistake.

Chapter 5. 4QEzra: 5:17.

Chapter 6. 4QEzra: 6:1–5.

3. 4QEzra. *they* MT.

4. 4QEzra. MT has a minor spelling mistake.

5. 4QEzra. *he* MT.

TOBIT

"I, Tobit, have walked in the ways of truth and righteousness all the days of my life" (Tob 1:3). So begins the fascinating tale of Tobit, a Jew of the late eighth century BCE, who lived in exile in Nineveh, the capital of ancient Assyria. The story—which has held up well for its years—chronicles the reverses of Tobit, which culminate in blindness. His son Tobiah, with the help of Azariah—the angel Raphael in disguise—sets out on an adventure that secures a cure for his father's blindness, rescues a damsel in distress from demons (she becomes his wife), and establishes his fortune. Along the way the reader learns that feeding the hungry, clothing the poor, and honoring one's father and mother are the keys to godliness.

Before the discovery of copies of the book of Tobit among the Dead Sea Scrolls, scholars debated whether the tale was originally written in Greek or perhaps a Semitic language (Hebrew or Aramaic). As is often the case with new discoveries, the Dead Sea Scrolls answered the original question but raised another. Of the five scrolls uncovered in Cave 4, four are written in Aramaic while one is in Hebrew. The debate has already begun as to which represents the *original* tongue. Another important discussion concerns the date of the writing. Those experts who argued before the Qumran findings for the first to third centuries CE have now been silenced, because the oldest manuscript—4QTobit^d—dates to 100 BCE (though the tale was probably composed as early at the late third century BCE).

Tobit is one of three deuterocanonical books (that is, from the second canon, or Apocrypha) that were found in the Qumran caves. The other two are Ben Sira (also known as Sirach or Ecclesiasticus) and the Epistle of Jeremiah. These three books, although not recognized as authoritative by Protestant or Jewish communities, are recognized as canonical (sacred Scripture) by the Roman Catholic Church.

The manuscript evidence for Tobit is so complex—three ancient and variant Greek editions are known—that the notes in this chapter have been restricted to only those differences between the five Dead Sea Scrolls manuscripts.

1 [17 I would give my bread to the hungry and my garments to the naked; and if I saw any of my people dead and thrown outside] the wall of Nineveh, [I would bury him.]▲

[19 But one o]f the Ninevites [went] and told [the] king [about me, tha]t I was bur[ying them, and] I hid myself; and when I discovered [that the king] knew about me [and that I was being sought in order to be put to deat]h, I became afraid and fled. [20 And al]l t[hat] I had [was taken away by force,] and there was nothi[ng] left to me [which was not taken to the royal treasury] ex[cept for] my wife [Ann]a and my son Tobiah.

21 And f[orty] days had not [passed before two of] his [sons killed him,] and they fled to the mountains of Ararat. And [his son Esarhaddo]n reigned [in his place; and he] appointed Ahikar, my brother Hanael's son, over all [the] a[ccount]s [of his kingdom and he had co]ntrol over [al]l the accounts of the king. 22 And Ahikar interceded for me, [and I returned to Nineveh. Now Ahi]kar, my brother, was the cupbearer, keeper of the signet, trustee, [and] over- seer of the accounts before Sannacherib, King of Assyria; and Esarhaddon ap- pointed him second to himself. He was my nephew, from the house of my father and from my family.

2 1 And in the days of Esarhaddon, the [kin]g, when I came home again, my wife Anna and my son Tobiah were restored to me; on the day of the feast of wee[ks there was] a fine dinner for [me,] and I reclined to [ea]t. 2 And they brought the ta[b]le before me and I saw that the food which they placed on it was abundant, and [I] said to Tobiah my son, "Go, my son, and get [whom]ever of [our] kinsm[en you] might find; of [our] brethren, [who testifies with a whole heart.] My son, go and get him and let him be brought and he shall dine [to- gether] with me. I will [wait for you until you return." 3 And Tobiah went to seek some poor person of our kinsmen, and when he returned he said, "Father!" And I said to him, "Here I am, my son." And he said in answer, "Father, one of our people has been murdered and has been thrown out in the marketplace, and now he lies there] strangl[ed]."▲

[10 And I did not know that there were sparrows on the wall above me, and their fresh droppings fell into my eyes and produced white films. So I went to the physicians to be healed, but the more they treated me the more my eyes were

---

Chapter 1. 4Q196: 1:17, 19–22.

Chapter 2. 4Q196: 2:1–3, 10–11.

blinded with the white films until I was totally blind. And I was unable to see for four years, and all my brethren were sorry for me, and Ahikar fed me for two years until he went to Ely]mais.

11 And at [that] ti[me, my wife Anna earned a living doing women's work.] ▲

3 [3 And now, O Lord, remember me, and look favorably on me; do not] judge [me for my sins and my ignorances, and the sins of my fathers which they sinned against you, 4 for they disobeyed your commandments;] and you gave us over as spoil, [and captivity, and death, and as a proverb, a byword, a reproach among all the nations among whom you have scattered us. 5 And now your many judgments are true so that you should] deal with me [according to my sins, because we did not keep your commandments and we did not walk in truth before you. 6 And now deal with me as is pleasing to you and command my life to be taken from me, that I may be released from the face of the earth and become] dust; [for it is more profitable for me to die tha]n to live, because [I have heard false] condemnations, [and there is] much [sorrow] in me. Command that [I might now be] released [from this distress; release me to go to the ever]l[asting place,] turn [not your face away from me, O Lord. For it is better for me to die than to see great distress in my life and to hear insults.]

[7 That same day Sarah the daughter of Raguel in Ecbatana of Media was also condemned by her father's maidservants. 8 For she had been given to seven husbands, and Asmodeus the evil spirit slew them before they had been with her as is appointed to wives. And the maid said to her, "You are the one who kills her husbands. You have already had seven husbands, and you have not taken the name of any one of them. 9 Why do you beat us? Because your husbands are dead? Go, follow] after them! Let us ne[ver] see [either] your son [or your daughter]."

[10 On that day her spirit was distressed and she wept. And when] sh[e had gone up] to the upper room of [her father's] house, [she planned to hang herself. But she reconsidered and said,] "They shall [never] condemn [my father by saying to him,] 'You had only one [beloved] daughter [and she hanged herself because of her afflictions.' And I shall bring down the old age of my father to Sheol with grief.] For it is not right for me to ha[ng myself, but to pray to the Lord that I might die and] no longer [have] to hear [cond]emnations and [my father] might not hear [them either." 11 At that same time with hands outstretched] to[wa]rd [the wi]ndow she prayed [and said, "Blessed are you, O merciful God, and blessed is] your holy and honored name fore[ver. Let all your works] bless [you forever. 12 And now I have turned] my face and [my] eyes [t]o you, and have [li]fted up [my] eyes. 13 Command that I be released from [the earth, and that I no more hear condemnation. 14 You, O Master, k]now th[at] I myself am pure f[rom al]l sin [with man, 15 and that I never poll]uted [my] na[me, or the name of m]y [fa-

---

Chapter 3. 4Q196: 3:5, 9–15, 17; 4Q197: 3:6–8; 4Q200: 3:3–4, 6, 10–11.

ther,] in all the land of my captivity. I am [the onl]y [daughter of my father. And he] has [no] other child that shall be [his] heir, nor brother near him, no[r] a near relative, [that I should keep my]self, or a son th[at I mig]ht be a wife for him. Seve[n husbands] of mine are d[ead] already; [why should I still live? And if it is not pleasing to you to slay me, O Lord, then hear me in my condemnation."]▲

[17 Raphael also was sent to heal them both, to h]eal [the] wh[ite films from Tobit's eyes that he might see ligh]t of he[aven with his eyes, and to give Sarah the daughter of Raguel as a wife to Tobiah the son of Tobit; and to release Asmodeus the evil spirit from her. For Tobiah was entitled to her before all of those who desired to have her. At the same time Tobit returned from the courtyard to his house, Sarah the daughter of Raguel came down from her upper room.]

4 [2 And he said in his heart, "I have asked for deat]h; why [do I] not [call my son Tobiah, that I may tell him] about [this] money [before I die?" 3 And he called Tobiah his son, and when he came to him he said to him, "Bury me properly and honor your mother; and do not abandon her all the days of her life, and do that which is] pleasing [to her, and] do not [grieve her in anything. 4 Remember her, my son, for she has seen many dangers for you,] when she bore you in [her] womb. [When she is dead, bury her by me in the same grave.]

5 "My son, be [mi]ndful of God all your days, [and let not your will be set to] sin and to transgress his commandments. [Be] honest [a]ll the days of [your] l[ife, and do not follow the way]s of deception. 6 For [those who] do the [truth shall prosper in their deeds and God shal]l be with you [and to all who do righteousness.] 7 G[ive][1] alms of your substance, my son; [and when you give alms, do not let your eye be envious;] do not hi[de your face from any po]or [man,] and [the face of Go]d shall not be h[idden] from you. 8 As your substance is, my son, [giv]e al[m]s from it [according to your abundance;] if you have little, [do not be afraid to giv]e alms according to that little. 9 Lay up a good [treasure for yourself against the day of necessity.]▲

[21 "And do not fear, my son, because we have beco]me poor. [You will be a rich man if you fear God and flee from all sin and do that which is pleasing before the Lord your G]od."

5 [1 And Tobiah answered and said to his father Tobit,] "All [that you have commande]d me, I will do, [Father. 2 But how shall I be able to receive the money from him,] if he does not [know me and I do not know him? What proof should I give him so that he might know me] and trust [me and give me the money? And I do not know the roads to Media] so as to go [there]."▲

Chapter 4. 4Q196: 4:2, 5, 7, 21; 4Q197: 4:21; 4Q200: 4:3–9.

   1. 4Q196. *be* [*giving*] 4Q200.

Chapter 5. 4Q196: 5:1, 9; 4Q197: 5:1, 12–14, 19–21; 4Q200: 5:2.

[9 And Tobiah entered to tell his father Tobit and said to him, "I have found a man from our kindred of the children of Israel." He replied to him,] "Call [the man to me, so that I might learn about his family and what tribe he belongs to and whether he is] fait[hful enough to go with you, my son]."▲

[12 And he said, "Why do] you [n]eed [to know my tribe?" And he said to him, "I want] to know [the truth, brother; who do you belong to and what is your name?" 13 And he said to him,] "I am Azar[iah, the son of Ananiah the great, of your kindred."] 14 And he said to him, "[Welcome, and God save you, brother. Do not be angry with me, brother, because I sought] to know in t[ruth about your ancestry. And it so happens that you are a brother, of an honest and good lineage, for I knew Ananiah and Nathan, the two sons of Shemaiah the great. And they went together with me to Jerusalem and worshiped with me there and were not deceived. Your kindred are good people; you are of a good family. Warm welcome!"]▲

19 "Let not my son cling [to mon]ey, but [let it be] as r[ubbish compared to our child. 20 As the Lord has given us to live, so it is sufficient for us." 21 And] he said to her, "Do not worry; my son shall leave in good health [and shall return to us in good health. And your eyes will see him on the day which he comes to you in good h]ealth. Do not worry; do not fear concerning him, my sister. [22 For a good angel will go with him and shall prosper his] journ[ey and he shall return in good health] again." And she stopped weeping.

6 [1 The young man went out and the ang]el [went] with him. 2 A[nd the dog cam]e with him [and went along with them. And they journeyed] as one, and [when night] came upon them [they arrived a]t the Tigris River. 3 The young m[an] went down [to wash his feet in the Tigris River. And] a large [fis]h [leaped up] from [the water to swal]low the young man's foot, [and he cried out. 4 And the angel said to the young man, "T]ake hold of [the] f[ish!" So] the young man [gra]bbed [the fish and brough]t it up onto the land. 5 And [the angel] s[aid to him, "Cu]t it [open] and take out [its gall,] its [heart, and its liver. Keep them with] you, but throw away i[ts] entrails. [Its gall,] its [heart,] and its liver [are useful as medicine]." 6 So [he cut it open and took out its gall,] its [he]art, and [its liver. Then he cooked] and ate [some of the fi]sh, and then sa[lted the remaind]er for the journey. The two of them continued together [until] they [were] n[ear] Media.

[7 Then] the young man [as]ked the an[gel and s]aid to him, "Azariah, my brother, *tel[l me,]*[2] what medicine is there in the fish's heart and in its liver, [and in its gall?" 8 He answered] him, "[I]f [you] burn them before a man or woman afflicted by a demon or [evil] spirit, [then every affliction will depart and] their encounters will [never] occur again. 9 And the gall is to be used to anoint [a

---

Chapter 6. 4Q196: 6:6–8, 13–18; 4Q197: 6:1–16, 18.

2. 4Q196. Not in 4Q197.

person's] ey[es on which white scales have appeared; blow on them, on] the white scales, and they will be healed."

10 And w[he]n they entered Media and he was already [approaching Ecbatana, 11 Raphael said to the youn]g man, "T[o]biah, my brother." And he said to him, "Here am I." And he said to him, "[We must lodge] in the ho[use of Raguel, for] the [m]an is from the house of our father and he has a beautiful daughter [named Sarah. 12 He has no male heir,] he has [no on]e except Sarah; and you, her r[ela-tiv]e, [have, more than any other, a claim on her and all that belongs to her father. Take her] as your [wif]e, [for] it is [your] right. [. . . This girl is wise, strong,] and very beautiful, and her father loves [her, and all that is his, he gives to her. 13 And for] you [the inheritance of] her father [is determined.] A just decision has been made for you that you might t[ake her. Now listen to me, my brother;] you must speak concerning this gi[r]l tonight so as to betroth her and take her as [your] wif[e. And] when we re[turn from Rages we will make] a wedding feast [for her.] For I know that Raguel will not be able to keep her from you because he knows [that you have a better claim to betroth] and to take his daughter than any other ma[n. For h]e kno[ws] that if he would give her to [another] man [he would incur a penalty in accordance with the book of] Moses. So now, [let us speak about] this [gir]l tonight, and we shall betroth her [to you and when we return from Rages we will take her and bring her back with us to your house]."

[14 Then Tobiah answered and said to Rapha]el, "Azariah, my brother, I have heard [that she has already been married to seven husbands and they died wh]en they went into her. [I have heard that] a demon killed them. [15 Now,] I am afraid [o]f this demon who l[ove]s her. [I am the only son of my father and I am afraid that I may die and bring the lif]e of my father and my mother [to their grave, grieving for me. . . . they have] no [o]ther [son] who will bury [them]."

[16 But Raphael said to him, "Do you not remember the com]mands of your father who commanded you [to take a wife from the house of your father? No]w listen to me, my brother; [speak] no [more about] this [de]mon. Now, take her, [I know that] this [nig]ht [she will be given to you in marriage. 17 When you enter the bridal chamber, tak]e some of the heart [and liver of the fish, and put them on the ashes of the incense. An odor will be given off;] 18 the demon [will smel]l [it] and f[lee, and will never appear around her again. And when you are about] to [be wi]th her, [both of you must first] sta[nd up and pray, asking the Lord of heaven that mercy and salvation might be granted to you.] Do [n]ot be afraid, [for] she was set apart [for y]ou and for you [the decision was made to take her. . . .] You will save [her, and she will go with you.] I suppose that you [will have children by her, and t]hey will be [like the brothers you never had." When] Tobiah [h]eard the words of Rapha[el and learned that she was h]is sister, and of [his father's lin-eage,] he loved her very much, and his heart *clung*[3] to her exceedingly.

---

3. The scribe left out the verb 4Q197.

7 1 And when they entered Ecb[atana,] Tobiah [said] to him, "Azariah, [my] brother, [le]ad me straight to the house of Raguel our brother." So he led him, and [they] went [to the house of] Raguel and found Raguel sitting before the door of his dwelling. They greeted him first, and he said to them, "You have come in peace. Enter in peace, my brothers," and he brought them into his house. 2 And he said to Edna, his wife, "How much this young man resembles Tobit, the son of my uncle." 3 Edna questioned them and said to them, "Where are you from, my brothers?" They said to her, "We are of the Naphtalites, [who] were captives in Nineveh." 4 And she said to them, "Do you know Tobit, ou[r] brother?" They said to her, "We know him." "Is he well?" 5 They said to her, "He is wel[l." And To]biah [sai]d, "He is my father." 6 Then Raguel jumped up, kissed him, and we[pt. 7 And he answered and said to him,] "Blessings upon [you, my son; you are] the s[on of] a good [and noble] man. [It is a wretched injustice that such a righteous and generous man has become blind." He fell upon] the neck of Tobiah, [the son of his brother, and wept. 8 And his wife Edna and their daughter Sarah also wept. 9 Then] he slau[ghtered] a ram of the flock [and received them willingly.]

[And after they had bathed and washed and reclined] to eat and to drink, [Tobiah said to Raphael, "Azariah, my brother, tell Raguel that he should give me Sarah] my sister." 10 And [Raguel] heard [the word and said to the young man, "Eat and drink and be happy tonight, for there is no man who has the right to take Sarah except you, my brother]." ▲

[11 And To]biah said, "I will not eat here no[r drink until you make a binding agreement with me]." ▲

[13 Then he called his wife Edna, and took a scroll and wrote out a contract;] and he closed [it] with a seal. ▲

8 [17 "Blessed are you, because you have had mercy on two that were the only begotten children of their parents. Show them mercy, O Lord, bring their lives to fulfillment with merc]y and with joy."

[18 Then he commanded his servants t]o fill up [the grave.]

[19 And he kept the wedding feast for them fourteen days. 20 And before the days of the wedding feast were finished, Raguel swore unto him, "You should not depart until the fourteen days of the wedding feast are finished; 21 and you should take the half of your goods, and car]ry [them] with you to the house of [your] f[ather; and the rest," said he, "will be yours when I and my wife die. Do not fear,] my son. I am your father and Edna is [your] m[other, and we belong to you as well as to your wife now and forever. Do not] fear, my son."

Chapter 7. 4Q196: 7:1–6, 13; 4Q197: 7:1–10; 4Q199: 7:11.

Chapter 8. 4Q197: 8:17–21.

9 [1 And Tobiah called Raphael, and said to h]im, 2 "Azariah, my brother, take with you f[our servants, and two camels, and go to Rages of Media. And yo]u shall come to the house of Gab[ae]l. Give him the bond, and r[eceive the money, and bring him to the wedding feast. 4 For you know that my father] shall b[e counting the da]ys. And if [I wait for long, he will be very unhappy. 3 You have observed the] oath [Raguel has sworn, and I cannot disobey his oath."]▲

10 [7 Now when] the fourteen days of [the wedding feast] were completed that Raguel had sworn to observe for Sarah, his daughter, To[b]iah came [to him] and said to him, "Send me back. I already know that [my father does not believe] and even my mother does not believe that she will see m[e] again. Now [I] beg [of y]ou, my father, let me go so that I may go to my own father. I have already explained to you h[o]w I left them." 8 But Raguel said to Tobiah, "My son, stay with me and I will send messengers to Tobit, [you]r father, and t[hey will tell him about you." 9 But he said, "No! I beg you to send me back to my father."]▲

11 [10 Then Tobit got up and went to] meet his son at [the courtyard door. Tobiah walked up to him, 11 with the ga]ll of the fish in his hand, and he blew [it in his eyes, and said] to him, "Do not fear, my father." [And he put the medicine . . . o]n his eyes, 12 and it stung. [13 Next, with both his hands he peeled off the white films from the corner]s of his eyes. Then he saw [his son and threw his arms around him, 14 and he wept and said to him, "I see you,] my son, [the light of my eyes!"]

[Then he said, "Blessed be God, and blessed be his great name, and blessed be all his holy angels."]▲

12 [1 And Tobit called his son Tobiah, and said unto him, "Make sure, my son, that the man that went with yo]u [has his wages,] and we shall give him a bonus."▲

[18 "And I, when I w]as with you, [I did not come as a favor, but by the will of God. Bless him each and every day; praise him. 19 And although you observed me, I did not actually eat o]r drink [anything; but you were seeing a vision. 20 And now bless the Lord upon the earth, and acknowledge God. See, I a]m ascending [to him who sent me. Write down everything that] has happened." And he ascended. [21 Then they stood up and could not see] him. 22 And they were blessing a[nd praising God, acknowledging him for] his great [wo]rks, and marveling how [the an]gel of the • • • [• 4 had appeared [to them.]

Chapter 9. 4Q197: 9:1–4.

Chapter 10. 4Q200: 10:7–9.

Chapter 11. 4Q200: 11:10–14.

Chapter 12. 4Q196: 12:1, 18–22; 4Q200: 12:20–22.

4. In 4Q196 four dots are used to stand for the unspeakable name of God: Yahweh. See also Tob 14:2 and 2 Sam 14:11.

13 1 Then Tobit spoke up and wrote down a prayer of praise, and s[aid, "Blessed is the] living [God] whose kingdom is for all time. 2 For he [afflicts, and h]e shows mercy; he brings down to the lowest Sheol, and he brings up from the [g]rea[t] aby[ss. A]nd who can snatch from his hand? 3 Acknowledge him, O children of Isr[ael, before the nations,] for you are scattered among them. 4 And tell there [of his greatness. Exalt him before al]l the living, because he is your Lord, and he is [your] God. [He is your Father and he is God for al]l [ages. 5 And he will afflict you for] your [si]ns, [and will show mercy to all of you from all the nations where you have been scattered. 6 If you turn t]o him with all your heart [and with all] your [so]ul to [do righteousness, then he will] turn to you, and will never a[gain hide] his [face] from you. [Now see what he has done for you, and acknowledge] him with your whole mouth, and ble[ss the Lord of] righteousness, and ex[alt him. I, in the land of] captivity, give him thanks, and s[how] his [st]rength and majes[ty to a sin]ful [people.] According to your heart, [do] ri[ghteousness] before hi[m; who] kn[ows if you will be p]ardoned? [7 I exalt my God, and] my [so]ul [exalts the] K[ing of heaven, and I shall rejoice] all the day[s of my life . . . and let al]l [. . . prai]se his greatness. 8 Let them speak in psalm[s, and let them give him thanks in Jerusalem. 9 O Jerusalem,] the holy city, he will [afflic]t you [for the works of your sons and will again have mercy on the sons of the righteous. 10 Give thanks to the Lord with right]eousness; acknowl[edge the everlasting King that his tabernacle may be buil]t for yo[u again with joy, and that he may make glad in you those that are captives, and love in you those that are miserable for everlasting generations. 11 A bright light will shine to all the ends of the earth. Many nations will come to you from afar, the inhabitants of all the ends of the earth to your holy name, bearing their gifts in their hands for the King of heaven. Ge]neration after generation will give [joyful praise] in you, [and the] great name [of the Lord will endure for] everlasting [gener]ations. 12 Curs[ed are al]l [that] despise and all that are against [you. And] cursed are a[ll those who hate] you and all [who spea]k [again]st you. Cursed [are those who pull down] your [walls] and all those who overthro[w your towers and those who set fire to your houses. But blessed shall be all who fear you forever.] 13 So rejoice and exult over the chil[dren of the righteous, for they will all be gathered together] and bless the [Lord forever. 14 Blessed are] all who love you, and blesse[d are all who rejoice in yo]ur [welfare. Blessed are all people who grieve with you beca]use of [al]l your afflictions; fo[r they will rejoice with you and see all your glory forever. 15 My soul blesses the Lord,] the great King. 16 Fo[r Jerusalem, his house, will be built as an eternal city. How happy I will be if a remna]nt of my descendants should [see your glory and acknowledge the King of heaven. The gates of Jerusalem] will be built [with beryl and] sapphire, [and all your walls

---

Chapter 13. 4Q196: 13:3–18; 4Q200: 13:1–4, 13–14, 17–18.

with precious stones. The towers of Jerusalem] will be built [with g]old, and woo[d. . . . 17 The streets of Jerusalem will be paved with ruby] and with the stone of [Ophir. 18 The gates of] Jerusalem [will sing] hymn[s of rejoicing, and all her houses] will s[a]y, 'Hal[lelujah, blessed is] the God wh[o has exalted you, forever and] ever,' for in you they will bless [his h]oly n[ame] f[orever and ever]."

14 1 Thus end[ed To]bi[t's words of praise.] And he died in peace at [one hundred twelve years old, and was buried with honor in Nineveh. 2 He w]as fifty-eight years [old when he became blind, and after receiving back the si]ght [of] his [e]yes [*he lived fifty-*]fo[*ur years,*]⁵ and in all [he gave] alms and continued *to bless the* • • •⁶ and to acknowledge [his] maj[esty.]

[3 When he was about to die, he called his son Tobiah and] his [seve]n sons and commanded and said to [him, "My son, take your children 4 and go off to Media, for I believe the word of] God that [Nahum] spo[ke about Nineveh, that all these things will come about and fall upon Assyria and] Nin[eveh. And a]l[l that the prophets of Israel, whom God sent, will occur. None of all their words will be diminished but] all will come to pass at [their] appoin[ted times. So it will be safer in Media than in Assyria and Babylon. For I know and believe] everything that God has said; [al]l will be accomplish[ed and will come to pass; and not a single word of the prophecies will be in vain.] All of [our kinfolk who] live in the land of Israel [will be scattered and will go into captivity from the good land; and all the land of I]srael [will be] a desert; both Sam[aria and Jerusalem will be desolate. And the house of God in grief will remained burned until the] time 5 that God will again have [mercy on them. And he will bring them back to the land of Israel; and they will again build the house, but] not like the form[er one, until] the time [that the appointed fulfillments shall come. After these things they all will return from their captivity and will rebuild] Jerusalem in h[onor. And the house of God will be built in it just as the pro]phe[ts of Israel] have said [concerning it. 6 Then all nations in the whole world will return and fear God] in truth. They will all cast off all [their] idols, [which have led them deceitfully into error; 7 and they will praise the eternal God in righteousness. All the children of Israel who are saved in those days and truly remember God will be gathered together and go to Jerusalem and live securely forever in the land of Abraha]m, [and it will be given over to them. Those who] love [God in truth will rejoice, but those who perpetrate sin and injustice will cease from all the earth.]▲

[10 "On whatever day you bury your mother with me, do not stay that day within the city's boundaries. For I see that there is much injustice in it, and that much deceit is done in it; and they are] not [ashamed. Note, my son,] the deeds

---

Chapter 14. 4Q196: 14:1–3, 7; 4Q198: 14:2–6, 10; 4Q199: 14:10; 4Q200: 14:1–2.

5. 4Q200. *he lived well* 4Q196.

6. 4Q196. *to fear God* 4Q200. See also Tob 12:22 and 2 Sam 14:11.

of Nadin [against Ahikar who raised him. While he was alive, was he not brought down into the earth? For God repaid his dishonor] to [his] face. [And Ahikar came out into the light, but Nadin went into the eternal darkness, because he sought to kill Ahikar. Because he gave alms, Ahikar escaped from the snare of death that Nadin had laid for him. But Nadin himself] fell into the snare [of death and it destroyed him]." ▲

BIBLIOGRAPHY

The translations in this book are based mainly on the critical editions found in the series "Discoveries in the Judaean Desert" and in the other sources listed below. For certain passages photographs of the relevant scrolls have also been consulted, and for a few unpublished scrolls the official editors have kindly supplied the authors with transcriptions or other details.

Editions in the Series "Discoveries in the Judaean Desert"

Alexander, P., et al., in consultation with J. VanderKam. *Miscellaneous Texts from Qumran and Other Sites* (DJD 36; Oxford: Clarendon Press [forthcoming]).

Allegro, J. M. *Qumrân Cave 4. I (4Q158–4Q186)* (DJD 5; Oxford: Clarendon Press, 1968).

Attridge, H. et al., in consultation with J. VanderKam. *Qumran Cave 4. VIII: Parabiblical Texts, Part 1* (DJD 13; Oxford: Clarendon Press, 1994).

Baillet, M. *Qumrân Grotte 4. III (4Q482–4Q520)* (DJD 7; Oxford: Clarendon Press, 1982).

Baillet, M., J. T. Milik and R. de Vaux. *Les 'Petites Grottes' de Qumran* (DJD 3; Oxford: Clarendon Press, 1962) 1. Texts 2. Plates.

Barthélemy, D. and J. T. Milik. *Qumran Cave 1* (DJD 1; Oxford: Clarendon Press, 1955).

Benoit, P., J. T. Milik and R. de Vaux. *Les grottes de Murabba'ât* (DJD 2; Oxford: Clarendon Press, 1961).

Brooke, G. et al., in consultation with J. VanderKam. *Qumran Cave 4. XVII: Parabiblical Texts, Part 3* (DJD 22; Oxford: Clarendon Press, 1998).

Broshi, M., et al., in consultation with J. VanderKam. *Qumran Cave 4. XIV: Parabiblical Texts, Part 2* (DJD 19; Oxford: Clarendon Press, 1995).

Cross, F. M. with D. Parry; E. Ulrich. *Qumran Cave 4. XII: Samuel* (DJD 17; Oxford: Clarendon Press [forthcoming]).

García Martínez, F., E. J. C. Tigchelaar and A. S. van der Woude. *Qumran Cave 11. II: 11Q2–18, 11Q20–31* (DJD 23; Oxford: Clarendon Press, 1998).

Puech, É. *Qumrân Grotte 4. XVIII: Textes Hébreux (4Q521–4Q528, 4Q576–4Q579)* (DJD 25; Oxford: Clarendon Press, 1998).

Sanders, J. A. *The Psalms Scroll of Qumrân Cave 11 (11QPsᵃ)* (DJD 4; Oxford: Clarendon Press, 1965).

Skehan, P. W., E. Ulrich and J. E. Sanderson. *Qumran Cave 4. IV: Palaeo-Hebrew and Greek Biblical Manuscripts* (DJD 9; Oxford: Clarendon Press, 1992).

Tov, E., with R. A. Kraft. *The Greek Minor Prophets Scroll from Naḥal Ḥever (8ḤevXIIgr) (The Seiyâl Collection I)* (DJD 8; Oxford: Clarendon Press, 1990).

Ulrich, E. et al. *Qumran Cave 4. X: The Prophets* (DJD 15; Oxford: Clarendon Press, 1997).

Ulrich, E. et al. *Qumran Cave 4. XI: Psalms to Chronicles* (DJD 16; Oxford: Clarendon Press [forthcoming]).

Ulrich, E., F. M. Cross et al. *Qumran Cave 4. IX: Deuteronomy, Joshua, Judges, Kings* (DJD 14; Oxford: Clarendon Press, 1995).

Ulrich, E., F. M. Cross et al. *Qumran Cave 4. VII: Genesis to Numbers* (DJD 12; Oxford: Clarendon Press, 1994).

Ulrich, E., P. Flint and M. Abegg. *Qumran Cave 1: The Isaiah Texts* (DJD 32; Oxford: Clarendon Press [forthcoming]).

Other Editions

Brownlee, W. H. "The Scroll of Ezekiel from the Eleventh Qumran Cave," *RevQ* 4 (1963) 11–28.

Burrows, M., with J. C. Trever and W. H. Brownlee. *The Dead Sea Scrolls of St. Mark's Monastery*, Vol. 1: *The Isaiah Manuscript and the Habakkuk Commentary* (New Haven, CT: American Schools of Oriental Research, 1950).

Cross, F. M. "The Ammonite Oppression of the Tribes of Gad and Reuben: Missing Verses from 1 Samuel 11 Found in 4QSamᵃ," *The Hebrew and Greek Texts of Samuel: 1980 Proceedings IOSCS—Vienna* (ed. E. Tov; Jerusalem: Academon, 1980) 105–19.

——. "A New Qumran Biblical Fragment Related to the Original Hebrew Underlying the Septuagint," *BASOR* 132 (1953) 15–26.

——. "The Oldest Manuscripts from Qumran," *JBL* 74 (1955) 147–72.

Cross, F. M., D. N. Freedman and J. A. Sanders. *Scrolls from Qumran Cave 1: The Great Isaiah Scroll, the Order of the Community, the Pesher to Habakkuk, from Photographs by J. C. Trever* (Jerusalem: Albright Institute of Archaeological Research and Shrine of the Book, 1972).

Cross, F. M. and D. W. Parry "A Preliminary Edition of a Fragment of 4QSamᵇ (4Q52)," *BASOR* 306 (1997) 63–74.

Freedman, D. N. and K. A. Matthews. *The Paleo-Hebrew Leviticus Scroll* (Winona Lake: Eisenbrauns, 1985).

Herbert, Edward D. *Reconstructing Biblical Dead Sea Scrolls: A New Method Applied to the Reconstruction of 4QSam^a* (Leiden: Brill, 1997).

Nebe, G. Wilhelm. "Die Masada-Psalmen-Handschrift M1039–160 nach einem jüngst veröffentlichen Photo mit Text von *Psalm* 81, 2–85, 6," *RevQ* 53 (1989) 89–97.

Parry, D. W. and E. Qimron. *The Great Isaiah Scroll (1QIsa^a): A New Edition* (Studies on the Texts of the Desert of Judah 32; Leiden: Brill, 1999).

Pfann, Stephen J. "4QDaniel^d (4Q115): A Preliminary Edition with Critical Notes," *RevQ* 17 (1996) 37–71.

Sukenik, E. L. *The Dead Sea Scrolls of the Hebrew University* (Jerusalem: Hebrew University and Magnes Press, 1955).

Talmon, S. "Fragments of Writings Written in Hebrew from Masada" [Hebrew], *Eretz Israel* 20 (Yadin Memorial, 1989) 286–87.

——. "Fragments of Two Scrolls of the Book of Leviticus from Masada" [Hebrew], *Eretz Israel* 23 (1993) 99–110.

——. "Fragments of a Psalms Scroll from Masada, MPs^b (Masada 1103–1742)," in M. Brettler and M. Fishbane (eds.), *Minḥah le-Naḥum: Biblical and Other Studies Presented to Nahum M. Sarna in Honour of His 70th Birthday* (JSOTSup 154; Sheffield: JSOT Press, 1993) 318–27.

——. "Fragments of Hebrew Writings Without Identifying Sigla of Provenance from the Literary Legacy of Yigael Yadin," *Dead Sea Discoveries* 5 (1998) 149–57.

——. *Masada* VI (Jerusalem: Israel Exploration Society and the Hebrew University of Jerusalem, 1999).

Ulrich, E. *The Qumran Text of Samuel and Josephus* (Missoula, MT: Scholars Press, 1978).

Verf, O. "Excavations in Jordan, 1951–1952," *Annual of the Department of Antiquities of Jordan* 2 (1953) 82–88 (+ pl. XII).

Yadin, Y. *The Ben Sira Scroll from Masada. With Introduction, Emendations and Commentary* (Jerusalem: Israel Exploration Society and the Hebrew University of Jerusalem, 1965).

Yadin, Y., S. Talmon et al. *Masada, The Yigael Yadin Excavations 1963–1965. Final Reports* (Jerusalem: Israel Exploration Society and the Hebrew University of Jerusalem, 1989–).